INFORMATION TECHNOLOGY LAW

Information Technology Law

The Law and Society

Third edition

Andrew Murray

Professor of Law, London School of Economics and Political Science

OXFORD
UNIVERSITY PRESS

Great Clarendon Street, Oxford, OX2 6DP
United Kingdom

Oxford University Press is a department of the University of Oxford.
It furthers the University's objective of excellence in research, scholarship,
and education by publishing worldwide. Oxford is a registered trade mark of
Oxford University Press in the UK and in certain other countries

First edition 2010
Second edition 2013

Impression: 2

Published in the United States of America by Oxford University Press
198 Madison Avenue, New York, NY 10016, United States of America

British Library Cataloguing in Publication Data

Data available

Library of Congress Control Number: 2016943971

ISBN 978–0–19–873246–4

Printed in Great Britain by
Bell & Bain Ltd., Glasgow

To those who have made this possible:
My parents Andrew and Sarah Murray
You got me here
My wife Rachel
You have been with me every step of the way
Fifteen years together

PREFACE

It is impossible for me to imagine that it is time for a third edition. Passing editions of this text are now for me a mark of the passage of time. As I noted when writing the preface to the second edition this is a subject which demands substantial rewriting from edition to edition; not just updates to reflect a few new developments in case law or statue. The world this book deals with changes from edition to edition. Again, many chapters have been substantially rewritten to reflect changes in the law, technology, society, and developments in case law. I have had to carve two chapters out of the old single chapter on branding and trademarks in the information society. We now have two chapters on branding, trademarks, and domain names and brand identities, search engines, and secondary markets. This is to reflect the shift in focus of trademark law in the online environment from domain names to search engines and secondary markets. To make space, the chapter on the digital public sphere has become an online-only bonus offering. The focus of the privacy chapters has substantially altered also, with the data protection chapter completely reviewed to reflect the text of the General Data Protection Regulation, and the personal privacy chapter essentially replaced with a state surveillance and data retention chapter to reflect the developments that have taken place in that sphere.

All other chapters have been substantially reviewed and updated to reflect emerging issues in law and technology. The key changes are:

- The law is updated to 31 December 2015.
- The whole text has been reviewed and updated.
- The old chapter 16 on branding and trademarks in the information society has become two chapters; chapter 16 on branding, trademarks, and domain names, and chapter 17 on brand identities, search engines, and secondary markets.
- A new chapter 21 on state surveillance and data retention has replaced the old chapter 20 on data and personal privacy.
- The data protection chapter has been completely rewritten to reflect the adoption of the General Data Protection Regulation, the right to be forgotten, and the *Google Spain (Costeja)* case, as well as the *Schrems* decision.
- There has been significant rewriting of chapter 2 (to reflect developments in net neutrality); chapter 6 (to reflect the role of Blogs in the 2015 UK General Election); chapter 7 (to reflect the Criado Perez incident and others); chapter 8 (to account for the Defamation Act 2013 as well as the *McAlpine v Bercow* and the *Sloutsker v Romanova* cases); chapter 11 (to account for the linking cases, including *PRCA v NLA* and *Nils Svensson & Ors v Retriever Sverige AB* as well as developments in blocking and speculative invoicing); chapter 12 (to account for the *Football Dataco Ltd v Sportradar GmbH* and *Innoweb BV v Wegener ICT Media* cases); chapter 13 (to discuss s. 3ZA of the Computer Misuse Act); chapter 14 (to discuss the Criminal Justice and Courts Act 2015 (revenge porn and rape porn) and other updates); chapter 16 (The Consumer Rights Act 2015, the e-IDAS Regulation 2014, and the Consumer Contracts (Information, Cancellation and Additional

Charges) Regulations 2013); chapter 19 (the development of cryptocurrencies); and chapter 22 (to reflect technological developments).

- Test questions and readings have been reviewed and updated.
- There are two further 'online only' chapters; chapter 23 on the digital public sphere and chapter 24 on virtual environments. These chapters can only be accessed via the Online Resource Centre.

Again I must thank my students, both undergraduate and postgraduate, for the great discussions we have in class. Thanks to all students of LL.210: Information Technology Law; LL4S1: Cyberlaw; LL4S2: Ecommerce Law; LL4S4: Digital Rights, Privacy and Security; and LL4S5 Piracy, Content, and Ownership in the Information Society. Particular thanks are due to Mark Leiser who is finalizing his excellent PhD thesis at Strathclyde University and who has been a constant source of insight and critique over the past three years. I look forward to reading the book, Mark. Thanks also to Bernard Keenan who has been LL.210 class teacher this year and an excellent source of information and discussion, and to Eric King who knows more about interception of communications than anyone else outside GCHQ and who provided a lot of background to chapter 21. Thanks, too, to my no longer new colleague Dr Orla Lynskey who has been inspirational and has got me truly interested in Data Protection Law. Thanks as well to all these people who listen to me talk and tell me when I'm wrong. You all know who you are but I pick out Professor Chris Reed, Professor Arno Lodder, Dr Mathias Klang, Dr Emily Laidlaw, Dr Paul Bernal, Dr Daithi Mac Sithigh, Mr Tijman Wiseman, and Professor Nick Couldry. And of course, as ever, thanks to everyone at OUP who do all the heavy lifting that turns this from manuscript to book, in particular my editor Tom Randall.

Finally, thank you to all my supporters at home. First, to my parents Andrew and Sarah Murray who put me on this path years ago when I went off to Edinburgh University as an undergraduate and who continue to support my work. To Mervyn and Rosemary Miles who have more recently offered the same support and to Dorothy Urquhart who first got me interested in academic pursuits at an early age with well-chosen birthday gifts. Most importantly though, as with the first and second editions, one person read this edition in a number of drafts giving tireless feedback as well as proof-reading the entire text: my wife Rachel. She again has to be singled out once more for her patience, attention to detail, and encouragement throughout the writing process. Again, I hope she is pleased with the end product, as I hope are all readers of this edition.

Andrew Murray, London, 8 January 2016

CONTENTS

GUIDE TO THE BOOK

Information Technology Law: The Law and Society contains a range of useful features, which have been designed to enhance your understanding of the subject.

Highlight Khan's four ground rules for interne

1. Each distinct network would have to stand on its own and n required to any such network to connect it to the internet.
2. Communications would be on a best-effort basis. If a packet d tination, it would shortly be retransmitted from the source.
3. Black boxes would be used to connect the networks (these wo and routers). There would be no information retained by the

Highlights

Featuring definitions of crucial concepts, ideas and principles, the highlight boxes give you an insight into the debates that surround the relationship between law and the information society. They may be a quotation from a leading figure, an outline of a legal term or procedure, or an extract from a case. In every instance they will help you to focus on an understand the key elements of the topic under discussion.

Example Sending TCP/IP communications

Alistair wants to send a message to Barbara. In the real world he piece of paper and then place it inside an envelope before sealing it. He then places the envelope in the care of the Royal Mail who ca She then opens the envelope and reads the message.

TCP/IP works in a similar fashion, except in place of a single e into many 'packets' before being sent. If we were to use TCP/IP te message 'Meet me at 2pm' from Alistair to Barbara, the following

Examples

How do the legal rules developed to meet the challenges of the information society operate in practice? The example boxes use short fictional examples to demonstrate the application of the law clearly and concisely.

Case study *Napster*

Everyone knows at least part of the story of Napster. In June 1999 Boston's Northeastern University, released his 'Napster' protocol.

Fanning created Napster out of frustration: he, like many college fan who was strapped for cash. He was frustrated for several reaso for digital music files but the only option available at the time was which would search the entirety of a library with no specific ability ond, he wanted to swap interesting pieces of music with like-minde

Case studies

From Napster to the economics behind recent US Presidential elections, the case study boxes illustrate the real-life examples that have shaped the developments of information technology law.

FURTHER READING

Books

T Berners-Lee, *Weaving the Web: The Original Design and Ulti Web by Its Inventor* (2000)

K Hafner and M Lyon, *Where Wizards Stay Up Late: The Origin*

C Marsden, *Net Neutrality: Towards a Co-regulatory Solution* (2

Further reading

Select and seek out titles from the further reading sources at the end of each chapter in order to broaden your knowledge of the individual topics covered.

GUIDE TO THE ONLINE RESOURCE CENTRE

This book is accompanied by an **Online Resource Centre**—a website providing free and easy-to-use resources which complement and support the textbook.

http://www.oxfordtextbooks.co.uk/orc/murray3e/

Audio updates

Regular audio updates from the author cover the latest developments in IT law which have occurred since publication of the book.

Web links

A list of useful websites enables you to click straight through to reliable sources of online information, and efficiently direct your online study.

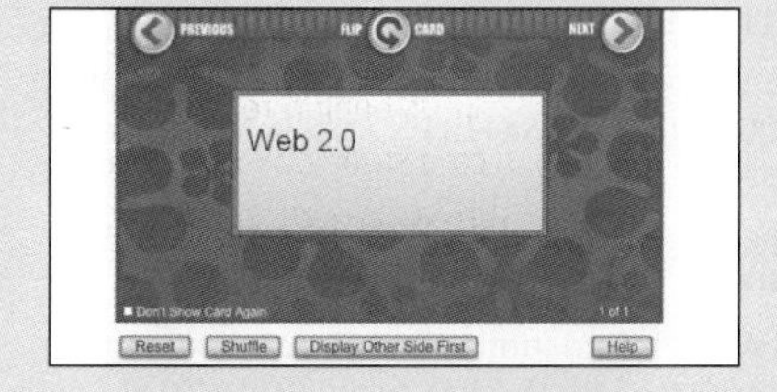

Flashcard glossary of key terms

Test your knowledge and understanding of the specialized terminology used in information technology law, using this useful revision tool which can be downloaded to iPods and other portable devices.

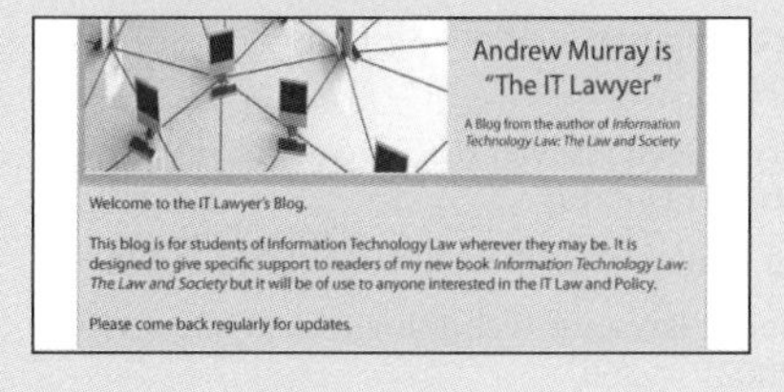

Andrew Murray is "The IT Lawyer"
A Blog from the author of Information Technology Law: The Law and Society
Welcome to the IT Lawyer's Blog.
This blog is for students of Information Technology Law wherever they may be. It is designed to give specific support to readers of my new book Information Technology Law: The Law and Society but it will be of use to anyone interested in the IT Law and Policy.
Please come back regularly for updates.

A link to an IT law blog

Keep up to date with the latest developments in the subject by following an information technology law blog, which is written by Andrew Murray.

Online chapter
An additional chapter, *Virtual Environments* is available to read and download, covering issues such as online micro communities, virtual worlds, and virtual property.

Additional chapter

An additional chapter, Virtual environments, is available to read and download, covering issues such as online micro communities, virtual worlds, and virtual property.

TABLE OF CASES

gents v
36, 16
ETMR
CDR
Civ
González
Benson
VSC
Civ
nbH v
falen
nreported,
460
eljob,
ecember
HC 2808
R
ary
47 USPQ
h Dist
592, 593
antile
5 . . . 244,
65, 266
td v Time
ades
FSR
ades
202/12)

TABLE OF STATUTES

UK statutes

PART I

Information and society

How the world around us has changed as information has become the key to economic success.

1

The world of bits

In reading this book you will be asked to think about the world around you slightly differently. While the question at the heart of most legal textbooks is: 'how does the rule of law affect individuals within the environment over which this law is effective?', the question at the heart of this book is: 'how does the environment over which the law seeks to be effective affect the rule of law?' The reason for this unique approach is the distinctive subject which this book examines. This is the first book to look in detail at the relationship between established legal settlements and the rise of the information society.[1] While you may consider digital information, the internet, and applications such as YouTube or social networking tools, like Instagram, Twitter, or Facebook, to be simply part of the fabric of everyday life,[2] British legal systems, which can trace their roots through at least 700 years of common law tradition,[3] find these developments extremely disruptive. These disruptive effects, once the preserve of the interested academic commentator,[4] have become of critical importance to politicians, economists, lawyers, and, in turn, to us all, as developed economies move from the traditional economic question of 'what can we produce?' to 'what can we control?'

This change in economic language reflects a wider change in modern developed economies. The traditional measure of an economic superpower was their output. Economies were measured by their ability to support communities. Agrarian economies measured how efficiently the land could be managed and farmed to support the

[1] While many books such as Ian Lloyd's *Information Technology Law* (7th edn, OUP 2014), Chris Reed's *Computer Law* (7th edn, OUP 2011), and Diane Rowland, Uta Kohl, and Andrew Charlesworth's *Information Technology Law* (5th edn, Routledge 2015) examine the effect of 'computerization' on the law, they take a technology-centred approach and focus on the narrow application of the law to computer systems, computer programs, and technology-related legal issues such as data protection. This book will take a wider approach looking at the interaction of the law and the information society.

[2] This may be determined by your age. If you are under 25, you were born after the release of the World Wide Web and have never known a world without it. You were probably active on social networking sites before you were a teenager and find a mobile telephone more useful as an IM/SMS device than as a telephone. Older readers though may remember the excitement of their first internet connection and signing their first mobile phone contract.

[3] For a discussion of the Common Law tradition of the English Legal System see SFC Milsom, *Historical Foundations of the Common Law* (2nd edn, Lexis Law 1981). For a discussion of the different legal tradition of Scotland see H MacQueen and AKR Kiralfy (eds.), *New Perspectives in Scottish Legal History* (Frank Cass 1984).

[4] See L Lessig, *Code and Other Laws of Cyberspace* (Basic Books 1999); N Negroponte, *Being Digital* (Hodder & Stoughton 1995); M Castells, *The Internet Galaxy* (OUP 2001); F Webster, *Theories of the Information Society* (Routledge 2000); R Mansell, *Inside the Communication Revolution: Evolving Patterns of Social and Technical Interaction* (OUP 2002).

surrounding community; freeing members of that community from the soil to allow them to carry out more specialized roles such as fletcher, blacksmith, or cooper. Such economies were though conspicuously inefficient, as demonstrated by Adam Smith in *The Wealth of Nations*.[5] In this, Smith demonstrated how specialization could improve individual output, a process which led eventually to the development of the factory, the production line, and, with the introduction of steam power to the equation, the Industrial Revolution.[6]

The industrial economic model became the dominant economic model of the nineteenth and early twentieth centuries. The industrial economy was driven by economies of scale and by mechanization. No longer was economic success measured at a local level; it was now measured by output at a national level.[7] It led industrialized nations, such as the UK, to extend empires across the globe to secure the raw materials which could be turned into textiles, iron, or later aluminium or steel. Industrial economies made money by making things: ships, weapons, clothing, railway tracks, and later aircraft. Industrialists grew wealthy but the workers did not: a few grew exceedingly wealthy while exploiting the human capital of the many.[8] Following the economic downturn of the 1920s, the effects of worker revolt such as the General Strike and the terrible impact of two world wars on the industrial capital of European states, a new economic model began to appear in post-war Europe. This new model of 'post-industrial economics' gives us our first insight into the importance and value of this subject, and therefore this book.

Post-industrial economics emerged in the UK immediately after World War II. With the cost of production of traditional industrial products such as shipbuilding and steel production being cheaper offshore, the UK's industrial capital began to move to places such as India, Malaysia, and Hong Kong. The UK economy started the painful transition from industrial values of 'what can we produce?' to the newly developing service sector and the question 'what can we provide?' With a massive growth in professional services such as banking, insurance, legal services, education, and media, the UK became the archetypal post-industrial, or service, economy. We no longer made money from making things; we made money from providing services. In the 1980s the last vestiges of our old industrial economy were swept aside. We closed car plants, coal mines, shipyards, and steelworks. The UK was going to be the world's leading service economy, but then something happened and it is that something which is at the core of this book. The post-industrial, or service, economy was itself overtaken only 40 years or so after it was first developed. The new economic model is known as the 'information economy' while its correspondent theory in social sciences is the 'information society'. While the UK had invested in banking, insurance, and financial support services, the US, or at least parts of it, had developed an economy built upon the systems that allowed information to be collected, stored, and processed. In so doing they created a new generation of super-rich industrialists who far surpassed the wealth of the nineteenth-century industrialists. These were people like Steve Jobs, Larry Ellison, and most famously Bill Gates who recognized that the value wasn't in the information itself; it was in what you could

[5] A Smith, *An Inquiry into the Nature and Causes of the Wealth of Nations* (1776; new edn, 1982).
[6] Ibid., Book 1, ch. 1.
[7] Gross Domestic Product became the touchstone of economic success.
[8] This of course had been explored by Karl Marx in his famous text *Das Kapital* (1867).

enable people to do with it. They started to ask the question which is at the heart of this book: 'what can we control?'[9] This question is the thesis that underpins both the information society and the knowledge economy. It represents a shift from ownership or control of things to ownership of or control over information.[10] It represents the maturity of information technology and most importantly signals a change in economic value from owning things, or in physical terms *atoms*, to owning information which in the digital environment means *bits*. This transition from the world which saw economic value in atoms to a world which values information in bits will form the focus of the remainder of this chapter.

1.1 An introduction to bits

The move from economic value being sited within physical goods, to economic value being sited within information, is referred to by Nicholas Negroponte, formerly Director of the Media Laboratory at MIT, as the move from atoms to bits.[11] Negroponte, and others,[12] believe that in time this move from atomic value to value in bits may prove to be as important to social scientists and economists as the discovery of quantum physics was to physical scientists.[13] Before we embark on the deeper impact of the move from atoms to bits we need to answer the basic question, 'what is a "bit"'? We all know what atoms are, or at least I assume we do. If you do need to have a basic seminar on atoms and their role in the physical world I suggest you read chapter 9 of Bill Bryson's excellent book *A Short History of Nearly Everything*.[14] On the assumption we know the role and position of atoms in the physical world, what then is a bit, and what is its role in the information society?

Highlight What is a bit?

At its simplest 'bit' is a truncation of the term 'binary digit'. To expand, a binary digit is simply either a 0 or a 1.

The answer to what is a bit therefore doesn't get us any closer to the questions at the heart of this book, 'why are bits economically valuable?', 'how do bits effect social interaction?', and, most importantly for a legal textbook, 'why does the law have to take account of the effect of bits?' To answer these questions we must look, not narrowly at what a bit is, but more widely at what a bit does.

[9] To gain an insight into the thought process of Bill Gates during the early stages of what he calls the 'information age' read B Gates, *The Road Ahead* (Penguin 1995) ch. 2.

[10] The post-industrial economic model may be seen as a step along this road being about ownership of or control over knowledge.

[11] Negroponte (n. 4).

[12] See Y Benkler, *The Wealth of Networks* (Yale University Press 2007); M Castells, *The Rise of the Network Society: Information Age: Economy, Society, and Culture* (2nd edn, Wiley-Blackwell 2009); H Jenkins, *Convergence Culture: Where Old and New Media Collide* (NYU Press 2006).

[13] For more on this read A Murray, *The Regulation of Cyberspace: Control in the Online Environment* (Routledge 2007) ch. 9.

[14] B Bryson, *A Short History of Nearly Everything* (Doubleday 2003).

At the most basic level, therefore, a bit is simply a 0 or a 1, but like atoms, which on their own are not very impressive either, it is how bits can be used to construct larger, more complex systems that give them their economic value and social importance. In the world of computer systems a bit represents a single instruction to the computer. This instruction is either to do (1) or not to do (0) a particular function. The brain of the computer, the microprocessor or central processing unit (CPU), reads the instruction.[15] The CPU may be thought of as a superfast calculator which works in binary. Bits of information are fed to the CPU from the computer memory, the CPU does a calculation and based upon the result the personal computer (or PC) carries out a predetermined function. The process that is followed is called von Neumann architecture after mathematician and computer pioneer Jon von Neumann.[16]

Von Neumann architecture is a four-step system that turns bits into computer operations or data. The first step is *fetch*, which involves the CPU retrieving an instruction (represented by bits) from program memory. These are instructions preloaded into the memory of the computer by a piece of software such as Microsoft Windows or Word. The second step is *decode*. In this step the single instruction is broken up by the CPU in separate instructions which require the CPU to do different operations. Thus a single instruction will usually contain an operational instruction telling the CPU what to do and a series of informational instructions giving the CPU the data it needs to fulfil the operational instruction. Step three is the *execute* step. In this step the CPU will carry out the operational instruction contained in the fetched data. This may be a purely internal process such as an autosave function managed completely by the software instructions fetched from the program memory or it may involve a user input where the actions of the user of the computer cause a particular event to happen (more will be said on this below). The execute step is a series of calculations using binary notation which gives a series of results managed by the CPU and carried out by a series of units on the microprocessor.[17] The final step is *writeback*. Here the CPU 'writes back' the result of its operational process to memory. This may be either the CPU memory (if it is about to carry out a further operation based on this result) or to the main memory if the operational process is complete for now. After writeback the whole process begins again with the cycle being repeated billions of times per second. At its most basic level, therefore, a computer CPU is simply a rather unimpressive calculator. It can add and subtract or multiply and divide but only in binary. It can do this billions of times per second and therefore is very powerful but as we are only dealing in 1s and 0s how does the manipulation of bits affect the established legal order? The answer is in the flexibility of the bit.

1.1.1 **The process of digitization**

Much as atoms can be used in the physical world to construct everything from the human liver to an Airbus A380, bits are the basic building blocks of the information society. In

[15] This is the computer part that is advertised as 'Intel Core' or 'AMD Jaguar' or similar in promotional material.

[16] For more on von Neumann see N Macrae, *John Von Neumann: The Scientific Genius Who Pioneered the Modern Computer, Game Theory, Nuclear Deterrence, and Much More* (American Mathematical Society 2000).

[17] For more on this see Gates (n. 9) which gives an exceedingly lucid description of this complex subject.

his book *The Road Ahead* Microsoft co-founder Bill Gates explains the difference between the analogue world of atoms and the digital world of bits through a simple example.[18] He asks his readers to imagine a 250-watt light bulb attached to a dimmer switch. Using the dimmer the user may select graduated illumination from complete darkness (0) to full illumination (250). By turning the switch halfway you will get something around 125 watts of light and at one-quarter distance about 63 watts. But, as Gates points out, exact replication of the level of illumination achieved in such an analogue set-up is difficult. If I find one night that about one quarter turn is the perfect level of illumination to have a romantic dinner I could make a mark on the dimmer switch and use this as a level for future reference, but if I want to tell my friend in Seattle this I need to try to communicate to him exactly where on the switch I made my mark (usually descriptively by telephone). If he then passes this information on to his friend in Calgary he repeats the process, but, as anyone who has played the childhood game of Chinese Whispers, or Telephone, knows, the message will over time change and deteriorate: this is known as analogue drop-off and affects all analogue transmissions as anyone who has made a copy of a copy of a friend's mix tape knows.[19] If, though, we replace the one 250-watt bulb with eight bulbs of differing output, each double the output of the previous, we create an analogy for a digital system. We now have eight switches, one for each bulb as seen below in Figure 1.1.

Figure 1.1 A 'digital lighting' system

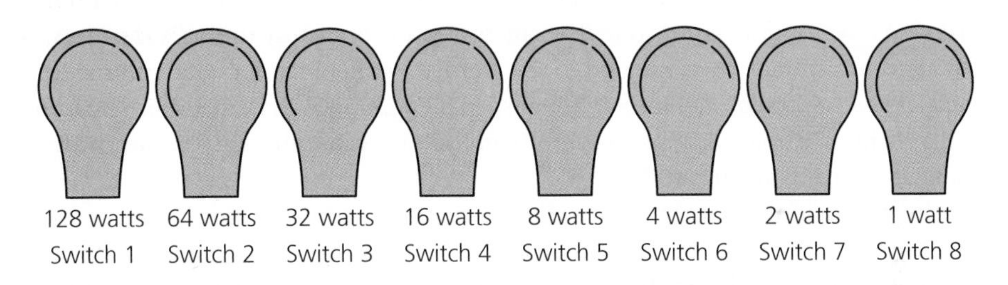

We can still control the level of lighting in the room from darkness (by switching all lights off) to full illumination (by switching them all on). But now instead of representing this as an analogue value between 0 and 250 we represent it using binary notation from 00000000 to 11111111 where 0 is 'off' and 1 is 'on'. Now, if I find that the perfect level of lighting for a romantic meal is in fact 93 watts, I can set my switches as 'off' 'on' 'off' 'on' 'on' 'on' 'off' 'on' or in binary notation 01011101. Now, if I want my friend in Seattle to be able to replicate the *exact* level of lighting I had, I simply send him this code. He may then send this code to his friend in Calgary who can exactly replicate what I did without ever speaking to me. Thus digital transmissions are less likely to suffer drop-off as the message sent is short and precise, unlike analogue transmissions.

If we can represent levels of lighting in digital notation, what else can it be used to represent? The answer is almost anything. Gates gives the traditional example of ASCII or the American Standard Code for Information Interchange.[20] ASCII is the common system used by all computers to encode all the letters and punctuation of the English

[18] What follows is based upon Gates' example contained at 26–8 of Gates (n. 9).

[19] If you are too young to know what a mix tape is, ask your parents.

[20] For more on ASCII visit <http://www.ascii-code.com/> where you can find the digital notation of all characters used on the keyboard.

Language. ASCII gives each character a value between 0 and 255, 255 being the maximum number which can be created by an eight-character byte of bits.[21] Capitals A–Z are given values 65–90 while lower case a–z are given values 97–122, while a space is valued at 32. Thus in ASCII the message 'Long live the Queen' is given as:

01001100 01101111 01101110 01100111 00100000 01101100
01101001 01110110 01100101 00100000 01110100 01101000
01100101 00100000 01010001 01110101 01100101 01100101
01101110

Of course it is not just text that may be represented in this way. As Negroponte points out, we have been able over the years to represent more and more information in binary digits. Music has been distributed digitally since the early 1980s. It is digitally encoded by taking constant samples of the audio waveform (sound pressure measured as voltage): this is a numerical value which may then be encoded as bits. In digital photography each colour and shade is allocated a numerical value which allows for perfect replication and display of the encoded data on an output such as a computer monitor or smartphone screen. Digital video may be seen as a meshing of these two techniques. Here a constant stream of data replicating moving imagery is encoded on a carrier media. Indeed, the applications of bits are seemingly endless, with some physicists even believing that bits may eventually lead to the creation of a Star Trek-style matter transporter.[22] As Negroponte points out: 'the emergence of continuity in [individual bits] is analogous to a similar phenomenon in the familiar world of matter. Matter is made of atoms. If you could look at a smoothly polished metal surface at a subatomic scale, you would see mostly holes. It appears smooth and solid because the discrete pieces are so small. Likewise digital output.'[23]

In the information society we see a shift from encoding information in atoms (such as writing it on the page) to encoding it in bits (such as word processing it). But this move is not limited to the written word: it may be sounds, images, or electrical outputs. Almost anything which may be recorded may be digitized. As digital information is cheaper to store, cheaper to distribute, and cheaper to encode, there has been a widely publicized migration from cue technologies to digital technologies and with it a shift in economic values of information.

1.2 **Moving from atoms to bits**

The economic driver of the move from atoms to bits is clear from the final paragraph of the preceding section. During the 1980s the computer moved out of the research laboratory and the workplace into the home environment. The home computer of the 1980s, devices such as the Sinclair Spectrum and the Commodore C64, were the

[21] In case you wondered what the difference between a bit and a byte was, this is it. A bit is a single binary digit; a byte is a collection of eight bits used to create a single instruction to a CPU. Despite my earlier description of how a CPU works, information is always sent in bytes not bits to the CPU. I left this out of the description at the earlier stage to avoid confusion.

[22] See D Darling, *Teleportation: The Impossible Leap* (Wiley 2005).

[23] Negroponte (n. 4) 15.

trailblazers for the home PC or personal computer.[24] As the PC became a fixture of homes across North America, Europe, Australasia, and the Pacific Rim, computerization of media became the cutting-edge technology. The first entertainment media to be digitized were children's games (although they were often played by adults). The games console was the breakthrough technology of the 1970s. Although the first home games console, the Magnavox Odyssey released in 1972, was a failure, in 1977 games company Atari released the now legendary Atari 2600 games system which sold over 30 million units in its lifetime making it the iPod/iPad of the home video games industry, an industry which remains at the cutting edge of home electronics through products such as the Nintendo Wii U, the Xbox One, and the PS4.[25]

Most people though became aware of the digital revolution in the 1980s. Music was the first traditional mainstream media industry to go digital. With the advent of the Compact Disc digital distribution became the norm. Why did the music industry move over? It was because of perceived benefits in music production, where digitization allowed for greater control over post-production clean-up and mixing and because the traditional analogue distribution systems for music (Compact Audio Tape and Vinyl Disc) were perceived to be of low quality. The CD was more durable, offered better sound quality, and, most importantly, gave greater flexibility in post-production. I wonder since if the music industry has ever regretted being in the vanguard of digitization. The story of the digitization of the music industry is the most turbulent of all. While the first process of digitization in the 1980s was evolutionary rather than revolutionary, the second process, which took place in the 1990s, was set to cause a revolution in the music industry.

The introduction of the CD (as with its sister product the DVD some 15 years later) was not to cause a digital revolution. The industry was in control of this evolution from the outset and the only discernible change to the consumer was a change in carrier media and in media player. Music was still carried on a disc, although now small and shiny rather than large and black, and was still played on some form of turntable device, although now read with a laser beam. Most importantly, both the CD and DVD retained the traditional distribution models of their predecessors, the tape/vinyl disc and the videocassette. You still visited your local HMV, Virgin, or Woolworths to purchase them. They were still carried by road haulage and they were still 'pressed' and packaged in a far-off production line. This is why both CDs and DVDs are evolutionary: they are simply a better way to replicate what was already being done. But, as Negroponte points out, one of the key values of digitization is that it allows us to discard much of the baggage of the atomic world.[26]

[24] Now homes have several PC devices, such as laptops, tablets, games systems, smart TVs, and desktops, which share a wireless network creating a local area network or LAN which allows music, video, or other files to be streamed wirelessly between them.

[25] At this point I feel I should take a line or two of text to defend my decision to begin the story of digitization of the entertainment market with a short discussion of the early success of Atari. Too often academic commentators dismiss the home video games market as unimportant, yet gamers spent $91.5bn on home video games in 2015 globally. That is more than six times the value of the global recorded-music sales in 2014, similar in size to the global magazine business which reported sales of $97bn in 2014 and about 70 per cent of the size of the film industry, including home video sales as well as box-office receipts. See Newzoo Games Market Research, *2015 Global Games Market Report*.

[26] See Negroponte (n. 4) 35–6.

1.2.1 Music goes digital

This occurred with respect to the music industry in 1994 when the release of the MP3 sound compression technique allowed us to reduce the size of music files down to between 6 and 8 megabytes on average.[27] MP3, like all compression techniques, allows us to remove information not required for reproduction of the recorded data. With MP3 much of what is removed is information which refers to sounds recorded but outside normal levels of human hearing. There is a drop-off in quality compared with high bitrate recordings such as full CD quality, but for the purposes of most consumers the MP3 quality is 'good enough'. The smaller file size allowed by MP3 allowed for distribution of music in a completely revolutionary way. Instead of pressing discs and distributing them via traditional routes such as high street stores with all the accompanying overheads these carry, some enterprising individuals demonstrated that music could be carried directly from computer to computer cutting out all the middlemen.

One such service was offered by MP3.com an internet start-up who offered consumers the opportunity to 'space shift' their music collection.[28] The concept was simple. You demonstrated you owned a particular album or single by placing your copy of the CD in your computer's CD drive. Once the MP3.com software confirmed the authenticity of the CD it allowed the music content of the CD to be added to your online library. Then wherever you were in the world, as long as you had internet access, you could access your entire music library via the MP3.com website. There were obvious problems with this system. First, MP3.com never established ownership of the CD placed in the computer: there was nothing to stop you borrowing your neighbour's CD collection and adding it to your library. Second, MP3.com never had the permission of the rights holder to allow you remote access in this fashion.

As a result, a copyright infringement case followed, the outcome of which we'll see in chapter 11. Also there we'll discuss the case which changed the music industry forever: *A&M Records Inc. v Napster Inc.*[29] This is a vitally important legal decision and its legal impact will be discussed in depth in chapter 11, but that is not the aspect of the *Napster* litigation I am interested in here. Napster was also of significant socio-economic impact. People not only learned the 'bad' lesson that they could get music for free, they also learned the 'good' lesson that music could be streamed directly to their computer: no leaving the house, no middlemen, no wasted costs on packaging, transport, etc. This lesson was the revolutionary application of MP3 technology that has permanently altered the music distribution model. Following the success of Napster,[30] industry players such as Apple and Spotify have perfected the online music delivery model to the point now where devices such as smartphones, music systems such as Sonos, and tablets no longer need a separate computer to download music. They are capable of downloading/streaming and playing music directly through their WiFi connectivity.

1.2.2 Digital goods and society

The success of the iPod and its later family of products including the iPhone and iPad heralded the digital future. Music was once again at the vanguard, but not far

[27] Allowing up to 100 tracks to be put on a single CD.
[28] The concept of space-shifting is discussed in greater depth in ch. 11.
[29] 114 F. Supp. 2d 896 (ND Cal 2000).
[30] Before legal action forced it to shut down it had in excess of 26 million customers.

behind was a similar model for digital video. BitTorrent technology may be seen as the TV and film industry's Napster moment. Teenagers today are more likely (if at all) to consume mainstream television programmes such as *Pretty Little Liars* or *Game of Thrones* via video sharing or streaming sites such as YouTube, Vimeo, Hulu, or Popcorn Time[31] rather than through the traditional broadcast model. Equally, book publishers have recently discovered they are not exempt from such developments. The success of the Amazon Kindle family, the Nook, and the iPad Mini has seen the sales of e-books outstrip their physical counterparts.[32] Thus anything we consume which is in nature information carried on a carrier media has gone, or is going through a revolution similar to the one experienced by the music industry in the 1990s.

The experience of the music industry answers to some extent the questions 'why are bits economically valuable?' and 'how do bits effect social interaction?' Although there is much more to explore in relation to both these questions we can open by saying bits are economically valuable because they represent new and revolutionary models to market and deliver those products or services, which are by nature informational products and which are traditionally embedded in or attached to a separate carrier media. The music industry has already been through the full process of disintermediation; other industries are now going through the process including film and television production and broadcasting, telephone service providers, mail service providers, educational providers, publishing, advertising, print media, and even the legal profession.[33] Further, bits effect social interaction as they provide new avenues for communication, exchange of ideas, and for challenge to traditional orthodoxy. The reason the music industry was forced to change was because of Napster. Although there is no doubt the vast majority of Napster users were driven by economic desire to free-ride (for which read get free music), once Napster was gone people realized they also valued the convenience of Napster and for some the feeling of belonging to the 'Napster community'. Although legal download sites such as iTunes replaced the convenience, these corporate sites do not have the same community spirit. This led indirectly to the development of social networking sites, and in particular MySpace which was heavily influenced by popular culture and music culture. MySpace in return influenced popular music through the promotion of bands and singers such as the Arctic Monkeys and Lily Allen, an influence still apparent today via YouTube, which in 2012 turned little-known South Korean pop star PSY into a global superstar. Whereas in the 1970s and 1980s groups of teenagers would meet in their local record shop to discuss music, now they do it on Facebook, Spotify, Instagram, WhatsApp, and YouTube. These sites succeeded mostly because the traditional iTunes model did not support social networking (a rare missed trick from Apple now corrected in Apple Music). What remains though is the most important question for a legal textbook, 'why does the law have to take account of the effect of bits?'

[31] It should be noted that Popcorn Time is subject to a CDPA s. 97A injunction. See *Twentieth Century Fox Film Corporation & Ors v Sky UK Ltd & Ors* [2015] EWHC 1082 (Ch). S. 97A orders are discussed in more depth in ch. 11.

[32] See S Malik, 'Kindle eBook Sales Have Overtaken Amazon Print Sales' *The Guardian* (London, 6 August 2012) <www.guardian.co.uk/books/2012/aug/06/amazon-kindle-ebook-sales-overtake-print>.

[33] For a discussion of some of the challenges the legal profession may face see R Susskind, *Tomorrow's Lawyers: An Introduction to Your Future* (OUP 2013).

1.3 Rivalrous and nonrivalrous goods

Rivalrous and nonrivalrous are terms of economic art. Rivalrous goods are goods whose consumption by one consumer prevents simultaneous consumption by other consumers. This is generally true of any 'atomic' good, for, notwithstanding some recent developments in quantum mechanics, it is generally accepted that no two atoms may occupy the same space simultaneously. Thus, should I borrow my wife's umbrella because it is raining, she cannot use it during the period it is in my possession: my possession is rivalrous to her possession. Atomic goods may be either durable or non-durable, but in general both are rivalrous goods. The umbrella example is an example of a durable rivalrous good. My use of the umbrella presents a barrier to others who desire to use that umbrella at the same time. However, my use of the umbrella does not 'use up' the umbrella, meaning that it, as with other durable rivalrous goods, can still be shared through time. By contrast, non-durable rivalrous goods are destroyed by their use (consumption) and cannot be shared. A concert ticket is a non-durable rivalrous good: if I 'borrow' my wife's ticket to see a concert by her favourite band, the fact that I can return the ticket to her afterwards does not disguise the fact that I have 'consumed' the economic value of that ticket leaving her with a worthless piece of paper. Thus non-durable rivalrous goods cannot be shared through time. By contrast, nonrivalrous goods may be consumed by several consumers simultaneously. Nonrivalrous goods are usually intangible. The most famous example is probably that of an idea as presented by the eighteenth/nineteenth-century scientist, philosopher, and politician Thomas Jefferson.

Highlight Thomas Jefferson's letter to Isaac McPherson

If nature has made any one thing less susceptible than all other of exclusive property, it is the action of the thinking power called an idea, which an individual may exclusively possess as long as he keeps it to himself; but the moment it is divulged, it forces itself into the possession of every one, and the receiver cannot dispossess himself of it. Its peculiar character, too, is that no one possesses the less, because every other possesses the whole of it. He who receives an idea from me, receives instruction himself without lessening mine; as he who lights his taper at mine, receives light without darkening mine.

Here Jefferson captures the key elements of nonrivalrous goods. By taking from the original owner you do not deny them of their possession and enjoyment of the goods, nor do you deny anyone else the opportunity to consume, simultaneously, the same good. In the modern world, technology has enabled us to increase the number of nonrivalrous goods available to us. Television broadcasts are an example of a nonrivalrous good: if I turn on my TV set to watch a broadcast of *The Walking Dead* this does not prevent my next-door neighbour, or anyone else, from watching the same show. Goods that are nonrivalrous are therefore goods that can be enjoyed simultaneously by an unlimited number of consumers.

If we list nonrivalrous goods we find an interesting commonality between them. Nonrivalrous goods include ideas, radio-communications broadcasts (TV and Radio), visual light (think of a beautiful view or a sunset), digital media (you can 'give away' MP3 music while retaining the original), and sound (a speaker at Speaker's Corner may be heard by one person or one thousand without affecting the enjoyment of others). The commonality is that they are all 'informational goods'. All are about transmitting information from one source to another. To return to the earlier language of Negroponte, they are all susceptible to be encoded as binary digital information (bits) to be stored or shared: thus ideas may be written on a document file (as I am currently doing), radio-communications broadcasts are being replaced by digital broadcasts, digital photography and video is capturing that beautiful view, and, as we have seen, MP3s encode sound. Thus the move from the world of atoms to the world of bits, or the move from the industrial to informational society, can be similarly defined as a move from rivalrousness to nonrivalrousness.

1.4 The legal challenge of the information society

What does this all mean to lawyers and to lawmakers? Well, we have now identified three effects of the move from the industrial to the informational society:

1. It represents a shift from ownership or control of things to ownership of or control over information.
2. It represents a new and revolutionary model to market and deliver products or services.
3. It represents a move from rivalrousness to nonrivalrousness.

All three of these pose serious challenges to traditional legal values and traditional legal rules. All traditional legal systems, including the common law systems found in the UK and the civilian tradition found on Continental Europe, have a basic distinction between tangible and intangible goods. Tangible goods represent goods of economic value and are protected. Thus s. 1 of the Theft Act 1968 expects tangibility: 'A person is guilty of theft if they dishonestly appropriate property belonging to another with the intention to permanently deprive the other of it.' The key phrase is 'intention to permanently deprive' as this makes clear that to commit the offence of theft you must take something which is physical and rivalrous. Thus 'copying' an MP3 without the permission of the owner is not theft. Neither is intercepting a transmission without permission.[34] Both of these things are regulated elsewhere,[35] but neither is theft in the true sense of the word. This may not seem important: you may believe this is simply a matter of language, or you may believe it is simply a choice by lawmakers to distinguish between theft proper (the taking of a 'thing') and misappropriation of information. But this simple example reveals a greater tension between traditional legal values and the new economic values of the information society.

[34] Think here of erecting a satellite dish and installing an illegal decoder thus taking the economic benefit of the broadcast from the broadcaster without making payment.

[35] The copying without permission by the Copyright, Designs and Patents Act 1988, the broadcast example would be regulated by the Communications Act 2003 and/or the Regulation of Investigatory Powers Act 2000.

Traditional property theory examines how scarce resources ought to be put to use but in the world of bits scarcity loses its immediate impact. Although there are still limits which apply over storage space and bandwidth, the average user sees bits as almost limitless as they are infinitely scalable: want the new Ed Sheeran album but can't afford it? Someone will make it available for free, not by giving you access to their copy but by creating a brand-new copy for you. Bits never run out, and because bits never run out we can keep creating; the only limit is on how many bits we can store.

The traditional law of atomic property, and with it atomic values of wealth through owning and retaining things, is fundamentally altered by the scalability of bits, meaning those things which appear to be of economic value (information) seem perversely to be of no value because anyone can replicate it at any time at almost no outlay.[36]

Highlight The informational paradox

Information is valuable. It is also (almost) infinitely scalable, nonrivalrous, and intangible.

Our traditional legal values are predicated on an environment where valuable goods are either physical, tangible, and rivalrous or where intangible goods (as protected by intellectual property laws) are fixed to some form of tangible carrier: books, vinyl or compact discs, compact music cassettes, videocassettes, patent specifications, or attached as 'badges' to products. But as John Perry Barlow demonstrated in his famous polemic: 'The Economy of Ideas: A Framework for Patents and Copyrights in the Digital Age': 'with the advent of digitization, it is now possible to replace all previous information storage forms with complex and highly liquid patterns of ones and zeros'.[37] In Barlow's parlance the valuable content (the nonrivalrous good) is being separated from the traditional carrier (which was rivalrous). Not only is the move from atoms to bits affecting traditional property values, it also undermines our traditional models for enforcing intangible, intellectual property rights.

The question of how we protect the value of information in an age where it is instantly replicable, transmissible, and is almost infinitely scalable is the challenge lawyers face today. It is also the core value of this book and it represents the thread that draws together the chapters which follow on disparate subjects such as cyber-speech and defamation, databases, copyright in the information age, and computer crime. The common theme which will emerge is that attempts to broker a piecemeal settlement—here a Database Directive, there a Convention on Cybercrime—are wrong-headed and will eventually lead to a fragmented approach which will fracture not just along jurisdictional lines but also along lines of technology and types of information. This would be the informational age equivalent of fragmented responses to different types of physical things in traditional legal settlements: thus instead of a law of property and chattels we

[36] This was recognized early on by Bill Gates who records in *The Road Ahead*, 'It seemed to me that too many people were accepting, at face value, uncritically the idea that information was becoming the most valuable commodity. Information was at the library. Anybody could check it out for nothing. Didn't that accessibility undermine its value?' (n. 9) 22.

[37] 'The Economy of Ideas: A Framework for Patents and Copyrights in the Digital Age' *Wired 2.03* (March 1994). This paper is discussed further in ch. 3.

have a law of the steam engine, a law of the gramophone, and a law of the pocket watch. This is exactly what we are doing now in the world of bits by producing specific regulations to deal with copyright infringement, indecency, computer crime such as hacking, and informational products such as databases. This book will, in the traditional style, examine the extant and proposed legal-regulatory framework of each of these (and many others), but it will also encourage you, the reader, to question whether it is time to take a more comprehensive approach to the legal regulation of digital information rather than attempting to fit the square peg of the world of bits into the round hole of a legal system designed for a world of atoms.

TEST QUESTIONS

Question 1

John Perry Barlow argues that the valuable content that the law always protected is being separated from the traditional carrier, where the law gave protection. This move from atoms to bits is affecting traditional property values, and undermines our traditional legal enforcement models.

Write a reply to Barlow explaining why you think he is right or wrong.

Question 2

If bits have no economic value, should lawyers be part of the battle to give bits monetary value through the application of legal structures?

FURTHER READING

Books

B Gates, *The Road Ahead* (1995)

N Negroponte, *Being Digital* (1995)

J Palfrey and U Gasser, *Born Digital* (2010)

D Tapscott and A Williams, *Wikinomics* (2008)

Chapters and articles

D Hunter, 'Cyberspace as Place and the Tragedy of the Digital Anticommons' 91 *California Law Review* 442 (2003)

M Lemley, 'Place and Cyberspace' 91 *California Law Review* 521 (2003)

M O'Rourke, 'Property Rights and Competition on the Internet: In Search of an Appropriate Analogy' 16 *Berkeley Technology Law Journal* 561 (2001)

2

The network of networks

People use the term 'internet' every day without thinking what it actually means. It is in fact a compound word made up of 'inter' + 'net'. Inter is from the Latin root meaning between or among, while net is short for network.[1] In short the internet is not a single computer network as you may have previously imagined; it is a system that connects together many individual computer networks, allowing for the transfer of digital data, or bits, across networks. The internet is basically a telecommunications system for computer networks: this is why it is sometimes called the network of networks.

The idea for the first computer network was put forward by a group of computer visionaries in the 1960s. The original idea can probably be traced to the eminent experimental psychologist JCR Licklider. Licklider was a professor at the Massachusetts Institute of Technology (MIT). There he worked on the SAGE project as an expert on the interaction between humans and technology,[2] work which helped convince him of the great potential for human/computer interfaces. This led Licklider to write one of the most important papers in computer science, the 1960 paper, 'Man-Computer Symbiosis'[3] in which he stated:

> It seems reasonable to envision, for a time 10 or 15 years hence, a 'thinking center' that will incorporate the functions of present-day libraries together with anticipated advances in information storage and retrieval . . . *The picture readily enlarges itself into a network of such centers, connected to one another by wide-band communication lines and to individual users by leased-wire services.* In such a system, the speed of the computers would be balanced, and the cost of the gigantic memories and the sophisticated programs would be divided by the number of users.[4]

Licklider was particularly interested in the idea of using wires to tie expensive mainframe computers together. He went on to develop this idea with a colleague, Wes Clark, who at that time worked at MIT's Lincoln Lab and who had several years earlier taught Licklider how to program the TX-2 mainframe computer. Together they wrote

[1] All definitions in this section are drawn from the *Oxford English Dictionary*.

[2] The Semi-Automatic Ground Environment (SAGE) system was the first major real-time, computer-based command-and-control system. It was designed as a new air defence system to protect the US from long-range bombers and other weapons. The SAGE system sent information from geographically dispersed radars over telephone lines and gathered it at a central location for processing by a newly designed, large-scale digital computer. For more information about SAGE see KC Redmond, *From Whirlwind to MITRE: The R&D Story of the SAGE Air Defense Computer* (MIT Press 2000).

[3] JCR Licklider, 'Man-Computer Symbiosis', *IRE Transactions on Human Factors in Electronics* (March 1960) vol. HFE-14. A digital reprint of the paper may be accessed at: <http://memex.org/licklider.pdf>.

[4] Ibid. 11 (emphasis added).

another ground-breaking paper, 'On-Line Man Computer Communication', published in August 1962. In this they described a 'Galactic Network' which 'encompasses distributed social interactions through computer networks'.[5]

These papers and the visionary ideas contained therein may, like many other great ideas, have been destined to remain only an untested thought experiment, but fate was about to intervene. On 4 October 1957 the Soviet Union had launched the first man-made object into space, the satellite Sputnik I. Analysts in the West had not predicted this and it caused immense shock and surprise to the US military and scientific establishment. President Eisenhower determined that the US would never again be taken by surprise on a technological frontier. In response he created a new research agency tied directly to the Office of the President and funded from the Department of Defense budget. This new agency would oversee cutting-edge research of value to both the civilian and military establishments. It was to be called the Advanced Research Projects Agency or ARPA.[6]

As fortune would have it, one of the first problems for ARPA was how to deal with the inefficient use of expensive scientific equipment. One particular problem was that computers were expensive pieces of equipment which were underutilized. They used batch processing techniques which meant that hours or days could be spent inputting data on punch cards before the program could be run, and then the slightest error in data entry would invalidate all this work. Between time, computers often lay idle. By the early 1960s every computer scientist wanted his own computer but the cost of providing this was prohibitive. The answer was clear: the users had to share the resources available more efficiently. This meant two things: first, the development of time-sharing mainframe resources, an idea first put forward by researchers at MIT's Lincoln Lab in the 1950s,[7] and, second, a network of machines which would allow researchers in different parts of the country to share results and resources easily. ARPA decided to appoint Licklider to deal with these problems and in October 1962, only two months after the publication of 'On-Line Man Computer Communication', Licklider found himself appointed as the first Project Director of ARPA's Information Processing Techniques Office or IPTO. Once in post he surrounded himself with a group of like-minded men. This group included his co-author of 'On-Line Man Computer Communication', Wes Clark, Bob Taylor of NASA, and Larry Roberts and Leonard Kleinrock, both outstanding PhD students at the Lincoln Lab. Together these men set out to build a communications system for computers: it would be called the Advanced Research Projects Agency Network or ARPANET.

2.1 **Introducing the internet (history)**

The number of histories of the internet which have been published, both online and offline are too great to list. I do not intend to examine the history of the internet in

[5] The paper was originally published as an ARPA memo, one of a series by Licklider on this subject in 1962. Reprinted in *Proceedings of the IEEE*, Special Issue on Packet Communications Networks (November 1978) 66(11).

[6] ARPA came into existence on 7 February 1958: <http://www.darpa.mil/about-us/darpa-history-and-timeline>.

[7] K Hafner and M Lyon, *Where Wizards Stay Up Late: The Origins of the Internet* (Simon & Schuster 1996) 25.

detail. Those who wish to learn in detail about the development of this fascinating place should either read the excellent *Where Wizards Stay Up Late* by Katie Hafner and Matthew Lyon[8] or the Internet Society's *A Brief History of the Internet*[9] which is without doubt the best online history of cyberspace. Much of the following is drawn from these two sources.

2.1.1 **Building the ARPANET**

Immediately following his appointment, Licklider and his team set to work in developing a network technology which would give effect to his vision. Led by Bob Taylor, they started work on making a shared computer network a reality. One of the key players in this was Leonard Kleinrock, who in 1961 had published one of the first papers on packet-switching theory.[10] Packet switching was a radical new system being developed by Paul Baran of the RAND Corporation for military voice communications. In packet switching, a message or communication is broken into smaller packets which are then addressed and sent individually. Each packet can follow a different route to its destination, and can re-route itself if the connection is broken or damaged. Once all the packets forming a message arrive at the destination, they are recompiled to form the original message. Packet switching is generally seen as more efficient, as there is no 'silent time' between sections of the message as there is with circuit switching, and more robust, as if part of the network is damaged the packets may be 'routed around' the damage.

Baran was working on packet switching as a method to ensure military voice communications could withstand a nuclear first strike,[11] Kleinrock was looking for a way to connect computers without tying up expensive leased lines. Kleinrock convinced Taylor that the best way to connect computers on a network was by using packet switching rather than conventional circuit switching.[12] The packet-switching model was adopted by ARPA and they began work on the network. One of the first problems faced by the fledgling ARPANET was how to make all computers on the network compatible with one another. In the 1960s there was no standard operating system such as Windows: each computer used a different programming language and operating system. Just to get the individual machines to interface, or 'talk', with each other was going to consume vast amounts of the ARPANET project's time and resources. At a meeting for Principal Investigators for the project at Ann Arbor, Michigan, in April 1967, Wes Clark offered a solution. Instead of connecting each machine directly to the network they could install a minicomputer called an 'interface message processor' or IMP at each site. The IMP would handle the interface between the host computer and the ARPANET network. This meant each site would only have to write one interface: that between that host and

[8] Ibid.

[9] <http://www.isoc.org/internet/history/brief.shtml>.

[10] L Kleinrock, 'Information Flow in Large Communication Nets' (July 1961) *RLE Quarterly Progress Report*.

[11] For an explanation as to how this would work see P Baran, *On Distributed Communications* (1964) <http://rand.org/about/history/baran.list.html>.

[12] Circuit switching occurs when a dedicated channel (or circuit) is established for the duration of a transmission. All information is transmitted along this one dedicated link. The most ubiquitous circuit-switching network is the telephone system, which links together wire segments to create a single unbroken line for each telephone call.

the IMP and, as all the IMPs used the same programming language, the network of IMPs would handle the rest.[13] With all the principles of the ARPANET network now in place: it would be a 'layered' design with the IMPs supporting the host computers and it would use packet switching in place of traditional circuit switching, Larry Roberts and the project's engineering partners Bolt, Beranek & Newman, a small computer company in Cambridge, Massachusetts, started building the network. Finally on 29 October 1969, the ARPANET vision became reality when Charley Kline, an undergraduate at UCLA, successfully logged in to the SDS 940 host at the Stanford Research Institute through the Sigma 7 host at UCLA.[14] Further hosts were added at the University of California at Santa Barbara and at the University of Utah, and by December 1969 the original four-node network was in place.

ARPANET may have been the first successful computer network, and it may also have been the forerunner of the modern internet, but it was quite dissimilar to the internet as we know it today. Modern definitions of the internet describe it as 'a computer network comprising or connecting a number of smaller networks, such as two or more local area networks connected by a shared communications protocol'.[15] ARPANET was a single network. Furthermore, ARPANET was what today would be described as a 'closed network': you could only gain access to the ARPANET network if you had a correctly configured IMP which had to be supplied by Bolt, Beranek & Newman. Thus the foundations of the modern internet architecture are not to be found in this part of the network's history. What happened next though was something quite special.

2.1.2 **Building the internet**

The ARPANET success was an exciting moment for network engineers. The design team had demonstrated that functioning computer networks could be constructed. As a result, the early 1970s was a time of intense experimentation with computer networking and other applications of packet switching. One of the first experiments was in the carrier medium. ARPANET used the existing AT&T telecoms system to carry its messages but this was less efficient in areas where there was a lack of good telecoms coverage: areas such as inter-island communications in Hawaii. In 1969 the IPTO awarded funding to Professor Norm Abramson at the University of Hawaii to develop a wireless network. Abramson used this money to construct a simple network of seven computers across the islands, using radios similar to those used by taxis to transmit and receive data. This network, called ALOHANET, used a different transmission system to ARPANET. In ARPANET the IMPs would manage data transmission and reception, ensuring data was properly sent and received without interference. In ALOHANET the terminals were allowed to transmit whenever they wanted to; if the transmission was impeded by other traffic the recipient computer would ask for it to be resent, the sending computer would keep sending the message at random intervals until it got an 'ok' message

[13] This is recorded by Hafner and Lyon (n. 7) 73.

[14] Commentators, including Leonard Kleinrock, recall that the first attempt by Kline to log in failed when the network crashed halfway through the procedure. A later attempt was successful. The record of that day including the log entries may be seen at L Kleinrock, *The Day the Infant Internet Uttered its First Words* <http://www.lk.cs.ucla.edu/internet_first_words.html>.

[15] This definition is taken from the *Oxford English Dictionary*, but it reflects the generally accepted view stated elsewhere.

from the recipient. ALOHANET received a lot of attention, not least from the military who recognized the advantages of a wireless network. The problem was though that the range of the network was limited and to build larger transmitters would centralize the network leaving it open to attack. An alternative was to use satellites. Although slower than ARPANET due to transmission lag a satellite network would allow for international transmissions.[16] To this end the US, the UK, and Norway collaborated on the development of a satellite network: SATNET. Concurrently, local fixed-line networks were being developed in the UK and in France.[17]

With the development of several independent networks, interest in linking these resources grew. Bob Kahn, who had helped design the IMPs at Bolt, Beranek & Newman, was working on a packet-radio project at the time.[18] He wanted to connect his network to the ARPANET computer network but at the time this was impossible as they were radically different networks. Kahn and others sought to end their frustration. What they wanted was a network of networks: an inter-network. They formed a group called the International Network Working Group and appointed Vint Cerf to be its chair.[19] That same year, 1972, Kahn was invited by Larry Roberts to join the IPTO to work on a net project: the Internetting Project. Kahn accepted and immediately started developing designs to connect together all the independent networks which had sprung up since 1969. Kahn realized the solution to the problem was in open architecture networking. Open architecture allows for each individual network to retain its unique network architecture, while connections between networks take place at a higher 'Internetworking Architecture Layer' as seen in Figure 2.1.[20] In an open architecture network, the individual networks may be separately designed and developed and each may have its own unique interface which it may offer to users and/or other providers. Each network can be designed in accordance with the specific environment and user requirements of that network. There are generally no constraints on the types of network that can be included or on their geographic scope.

Figure 2.1 Simplified open architecture network

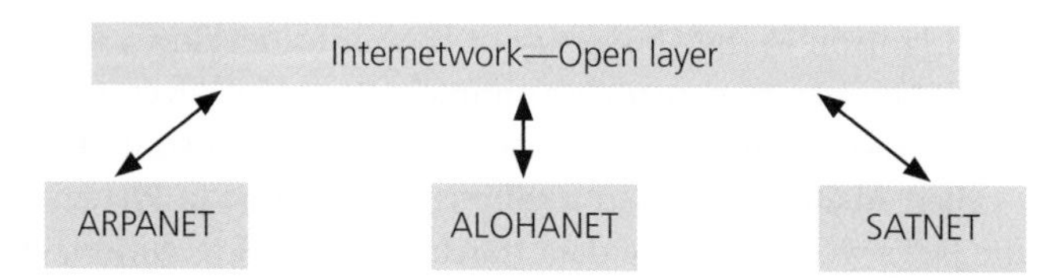

[16] At the time the fixed-line, or undersea, network, which was constructed of copper wire, lacked the necessary capacity between the US and Europe to allow for effective network transmission between the two. This was remedied soon after when the telecoms companies laid high-speed fibre-optic cable in its place.

[17] All this is discussed in Hafner and Lyon (n. 7) ch. 8.

[18] Kahn was a Professor of Electrical Engineering at MIT who joined Bolt, Beranek & Newman to help them overcome communications errors in data transmission.

[19] Vinton 'Vint' Cerf is the man most commonly called 'the father of the internet'. In 1972 he was an assistant professor at Stanford University.

[20] Set out more fully in *A Brief History of the Internet* (n. 9).

Designing this network was similar to designing the ARPANET. Like ARPANET the problem was that since each host (in this case host network) used its own language, what was needed was a version of the IMP which bridged this gap on the ARPANET. Unfortunately the IMPs were also one of Kahn's major obstacles. The language of ARPANET, the Network Control Protocol (NCP), did not have the ability to interface with networks or machines further downstream than a destination IMP on the ARPANET.[21] Thus Kahn would need to rewrite the NCP protocol.

Kahn set about designing a new, open architecture, protocol. In doing so he set out four ground rules for his new Internetwork Protocol:

Highlight Khan's four ground rules for internet protocols

1. Each distinct network would have to stand on its own and no internal changes could be required to any such network to connect it to the internet.
2. Communications would be on a best-effort basis. If a packet didn't make it to the final destination, it would shortly be retransmitted from the source.
3. Black boxes would be used to connect the networks (these would later be called gateways and routers). There would be no information retained by the black boxes about the individual flows of packets passing through them, thereby keeping them simple and avoiding complicated adaptation and recovery from various failure modes.
4. There would be no global control at the operations level.

Kahn began working on his new protocol with Vint Cerf who joined in his role as Chair of the International Network Working Group. According to Cerf, Kahn introduced the problem to him by saying: 'Look, my problem is how I get a computer that's on a satellite net and a computer on a radio net and a computer on the ARPANET to communicate uniformly with each other without realizing what's going on in between.'[22] Cerf was fascinated by the problem and along with Kahn he worked on developing the new protocol which would allow transmission across networks. Each of these networks had its own set of rules though. They used different interfaces, different transmission rates and each allowed for differently sized packets of information to be carried. How could they write a protocol which could be used uniformly across networks? Throughout 1973 Cerf and Kahn continued to work on these problems. Finally in September 1973 Cerf presented his and Kahn's ideas at the International Network Working Group meeting at the University of Sussex. Their idea, later refined and published as the seminal paper, 'A Protocol for Packet Network Intercommunication',[23] was deceptively simple. Cerf realized that carriers of goods often carried packets without ever knowing what was in them. A

[21] The reason for this short-sightedness was that in designing NCP, control over packets of data, and therefore network reliability, was given to the IMPs. This is because this was simpler and cheaper and at the time ARPANET was the only network envisaged by the designers.

[22] Hafner and Lyon (n. 7), 223.

[23] V Cerf and R Kahn, 'A Protocol for Packet Network Interconnection', *IEEE Trans on Comms* (May 1974) vol. Com-22 No. 5 637.

transport container has a standard size and shape, yet it may be carrying anything from televisions to chocolate bars. Due to the common size of the container it can be carried by road, sea, or rail and neither the ship's captain nor the truck or train driver need know what he is carrying. The only people who need to know are the shipper and the recipient. Cerf applied this to digital data. He designed a new protocol: Transmission Control Protocol, or TCP, which would 'box up' the information and address it. Each message fragment, known as a datagram, would be the same size and could be handled by any of the networks. Once sent into the network, packets could take any route to their destination; they were not all destined to follow each other across busy networks. This design would work, and allowed for transmission of data across networks, but by removing the IMPs from the process, there remained the problem of missing or damaged datagrams.

In ARPANET the IMPs were responsible for sending and reassembling all message packets. They worked to ensure message integrity by checking the message at every stage of its journey, so called hop-by-hop transmission. Cerf and Kahn changed all this in designing TCP. They returned to Norm Abramson's work on ALOHANET: to overcome the problem of interference or data corruption he placed the responsibility for data integrity on the sending and receiving computers, so-called end-to-end reliability. In Cerf and Kahn's TCP design when packets of information were sent they carried with them a request for acknowledgement. If safely received the recipient host would signal the transmission host of success. If the packet failed to arrive or was corrupted in transmission the recipient would not signal. If no acknowledgement was received the transmission host would retransmit the packet at random intervals until a successful acknowledgement was received. By placing all these responsibilities with the hosts, the network itself could be significantly simplified. Like the container transports of the real world, only the sender and recipient need know the details of the contents, all the network needed to know was where to send them.

TCP was not quite an instant success. Although it did lead to the development of the first internet, a network which between 1973 and 1975 grew at a rate of about one new network node per month, the protocol itself was redrafted and redeveloped continually over the next few years. The most important of these occurred in January 1978 when Vint Cerf and Jon Postel posted 'TCP Version 3 Specification', which suggested the splitting of TCP into a dual protocol Transmission Control Protocol/Internet Protocol or TCP/IP. TCP had always been a multifunctional protocol but by splitting it into the dual layer TCP/IP these functions could now be clearly seen. The release of the TCP/IP protocol is now seen by most network historians as the day the modern internet came into being and is therefore the logical place to end our short excurses into the history of the network.

2.2 How the modern internet functions

The modern internet still uses the TCP/IP protocol. The TCP element of the protocol breaks the data into packets ready for transmission and recombines them on the receiving end. The IP element handles the addressing and routing of the data and makes sure it gets sent to the proper destination. The easiest way to imagine this working is to think in terms of traditional postal communications.

Example Sending TCP/IP communications

Alistair wants to send a message to Barbara. In the real world he may write his message on a piece of paper and then place it inside an envelope before sealing the envelope and addressing it. He then places the envelope in the care of the Royal Mail who carries the envelope to Barbara. She then opens the envelope and reads the message.

TCP/IP works in a similar fashion, except in place of a single envelope the message is split into many 'packets' before being sent. If we were to use TCP/IP technology to send the simple message 'Meet me at 2pm' from Alistair to Barbara, the following operations would take place:

1. TCP would split the message into packets and number each packet $[\text{Meet}]_1$ $[\text{me at}]_2$ $[\text{2pm}]_3$.
2. Each packet is placed into a digital envelope before passing these envelopes on to the IP protocol.
3. IP would then address the envelopes with Barbara's IP address before sending them out across the network.
4. The network acts like the Royal Mail and carries these envelopes to their destination.
5. Upon arrival TCP opens the envelopes, checks all packets have been delivered safely and reassembles the message.

Let us take as an example the delivery of a file from one computer to another. This is a common internet operation and may occur where your operating system undertakes an automatic update, or it may be a requested download such as a music file from iTunes. We begin operations with two computers the Host (that is the computer on which the file is held) and the Recipient. The first thing to be aware of is that every digital device connected to the internet must have a unique identification or address. Like all communications networks, the internet relies upon the ability to deliver content to another party. The telephone network functions because each telephone connected to the network has a unique identifier, or telephone number. In internet terms a similar system is managed by the IP protocol; currently this may be a version known as IPv4 or IPv6. As internet communications are communications between computers the need for a linguistic addressing tool seemed minimal when the addressing protocol for the internet was developed. The primary addressing tool is therefore a numerical identifier called an IP address. As with a telephone number this number must be unique to allow for the smooth flow of information within the network. IP addresses are used when browsing the web to enable the transmission of communications between the user's web browser and the server hosting the website. They are also used in the header of email messages and, in fact, are required for all programs that use the TCP/IP protocol.

Version 4 of the Internet Protocol (IPv4), which is still in use, uses an IP address consisting of 32 bits, usually shown as a 'dotted quad': four octets of binary numbers represented in decimal form in the range 0–255. For example, the IP address of the computer I am currently using is 151.224.85.103 but as computers do not work in decimal notation this will be converted by the network servers and routers into binary notation and be read by them as 10010111.11100000.01010101.01100111. As it is easier for humans to remember decimals than it is to remember binary numbers we use decimal notation to represent IP addresses when describing them. The address space of the IPv4 protocol (the number of available unique identifiers allowed) is 2^{32} or 4,294,967,296 unique host interface addresses. At the time it was adopted this seemed to be an almost limitless supply of addresses, but as the network has developed the strain on this resource has become quite heavy. For this reason a new version of the protocol, IPv6, has been adopted. In IPv6, addresses are 128 bits rather than 32 bits. This will allow 2^{128}, or about 3.403×10^{38}, unique host interface addresses: a mind-boggling availability of unique identifiers. An IPv6 address is written as eight four-digit hexadecimal numbers separated by colons. Thus to the human eye it looks something like: 21DA:00D3:0000:2F3B:02AA:00FF:FE28:9C5A. Computers, including hosts and routers, will continue to read this as binary notation, but space prevents me from reproducing the binary equivalent of a hexadecimal IPv6 address. Both IPv4 and IPv6 addresses are descending unique identifiers like telephone numbers. You read them from left to right with the first two sets of quads being used to identify the network location of your computer. For example, all computers on the London School of Economics network are allocated an IPv4 address which begins 158.143, while King's College, London operates from the 137.73 address space, while University of Oxford IP addresses begin 163.1, 129.67, or 192.76.[24] This information is of course double-edged. Not only is it essential for the functioning of the network it also allows data transmissions to be tracked to an end user. The privacy implications of this will be discussed in chapter 21.

With both computers in our transaction allocated an IP address the transaction between them can now take place. The host will have the file to be transferred and the IP address of the recipient. The TCP protocol now takes the file and breaks it up into smaller packets and prepares to send them. It places each packet into its electronic envelope and then attaches a header to that file. The header is basically all the information that is needed to deliver the packet and to reassemble the file. Thus it will contain the IP address of the recipient and basic information about the information contained in the packet to ensure that if it becomes damaged (corrupted) en route, the recipient is aware of this and can ask for the data to be resent if necessary.[25] These packets are all then sent into the physical infrastructure of the network which is made up of the wired network of telephone cables (both copper and fibre optic), wireless carriers such as Wireless Local Area Networks such as those provided in your local coffee shop, or Wireless Wide Area Networks such as those operated by mobile telecommunications providers.

How this physical layer carries this information from the host to the recipient is a result of all these early technology designs such as packet switching and network layering. If the host is a major website like iTunes it will have a permanent network connection through a leased data line. If it is a casual user, like your brother sending you a file by email, the connection will be created by their home broadband router to connect their computer to their Internet Service Provider (ISP). Whichever form the initial connection is made, the ISP will transfer the packets to the internet backbone. This is made up of several large telecommunications networks which interconnect with each other.[26]

[24] For more on the operation of IP addresses, including who regulates and assigns them, see A Murray, *The Regulation of Cyberspace: Control in the Online Environment* (Routledge 2007) ch. 4.

[25] For a more technically detailed description of the TCP Protocol see Information Sciences Institute, *Transmission Control Protocol: DARPA Internet Program Protocol Specification* (RFC 793, 1981) <http://www.netfor2.com/rfc793.txt>.

[26] The main carriers of internet backbone traffic are the so-called tier-1 providers: AT&T, CenturyLink, Level 3 Communications, Sprint, TeliaSonera International, Verizon, and Vodafone.

These backbone providers connect to each other to exchange packet traffic through a series of internet exchanges known as Network Access Points. These allow data packets to flow freely across the internet backbone. The management of the data flow across the backbone and through Network Access Points is controlled by a specialist piece of computer hardware known as a router. Routers are specially designed to manage the informational flow of the internet. When a data packet arrives at a router, the router examines the IP address put there by the IP protocol layer on the host. The router checks its records to see if it knows where the recipient is based. If the network containing the IP address is found, the packet is sent to that network. If the network containing the IP address is not found, then the router sends the packet on a default route, usually up the backbone hierarchy to the next router. Hopefully the next router will know where to send the packet. If it does not, again the packet is routed upwards until it reaches one of the routers actually on the backbone. These routers hold the largest records and here the packet will be routed to the correct backbone, where it will begin its journey downward through smaller and smaller networks until it finds its destination.[27]

There are some key operative parameters of the internet which may be gleaned from this short explanation of how TCP/IP works. Among these are that TCP works on a best-effort basis.[28] Routers do not usually attempt to repair damaged packets. If the IP address cannot be found, or if there is a network failure which makes it impossible for packets to be forwarded they will be discarded. The recipient computer may request missing or damaged packets to be resent, the router will not. Second, the route taken by discrete packets may differ from that taken by other packets. Thus there is no reason to assume that if a file is transmitted from a computer in Glasgow to one in London that all will follow the same route, or even that they will take the most direct route. Routers will send packets by the most efficient route in terms of network capacity, not in terms of network geography. Thus if the network between Glasgow and London is extremely congested one packet may go via Stockholm, another via Amsterdam, and another via Detroit. As the fibre-optic cables which make up the backbone all carry data at the speed of light it should be completely unnoticeable to the end user that one packet of data has travelled 1,000 miles while another has travelled 12,000 miles.[29] Third, traditionally the network treated all data packets equally. Because the routers did not know what they were carrying they could not distinguish high-value data (perhaps a streaming video or a VoIP call) from low-value data (such as a spam email). This is the effect of two early network initiatives which are in many ways the opposite sides of the same coin: network neutrality and end-to-end architecture.

End-to-end architecture is a unique feature of distributed computing, as most famously employed in the current incarnation of the TCP protocol. The idea of end-to-end communications was first promulgated by Jerome Saltzer, David Reed, and David D Clark in 1984 in their paper 'End-to-end Arguments in System Design'.[30] The authors examined the developing internet, which at that time was beginning to play host to a variety

[27] For a technical discussion of how internet routers function see S Halabi, *Internet Routing Architectures* (2nd edn, Cisco Press 2000). For a more general discussion of internet architecture see B van Schewick, *Internet Architecture and Innovation* (MIT Press 2012).

[28] This is the second of Khan's four 'ground rules' for TCP.

[29] At the speed of light it takes approx 0.06 seconds to travel 11,000 miles.

[30] (1984) 2(4) *ACM Transactions on Computer Systems* 277.

of different end-user systems such as email, file transfers, online booking systems, and others, and concluded that: 'The function in question can completely and correctly be implemented only with the knowledge and help of the application standing at the end points of the communication system. Therefore, providing that questioned function as a feature of the communication system itself is not possible.'[31] In other words only the host who originated the file and the recipient of the file knew enough about the file to manage its transmission. The intelligence of the network was therefore in its applications held at each end of the communication rather than in the network architecture itself. This made the internet almost unique among communications media. Traditional media were centrally managed: think of the telephone exchange or the television broadcast facility, with dumb terminals at the ends. In fact the only other media of communication which used end-to-end principles was the mail delivery system. But as our discussion of the process of digitization in chapter 1 has demonstrated, the internet offered many more and more exciting opportunities than traditional mail carriers. The network would be developed to carry a variety of digital products from simple text-based emails to MP3 files, to flash games, to streaming MP4 and MPEG videos and on to VoIP telephone calls. The development of these new technologies, especially VoIP and streaming video which are both bandwidth intense and which require for low latency, are challenging the continuing applicability of the end-to-end principle and its allied concept of network neutrality.[32]

2.2.1 **Net neutrality**

Network neutrality, or more commonly net neutrality, is highly prized by many internet pioneers including Professor Sir Tim Berners-Lee creator of the World Wide Web.[33]

Highlight Net neutrality defined

Net neutrality is the principle that data packets on the internet should be moved impartially, without regard to content, destination, or source. It is sometimes referred to as 'The First Amendment of the Internet'.

This previously widely accepted concept has been subject to intense debate and review over the past ten years and remains at the heart of some of the most intense battles over internet regulation.[34]

[31] Ibid. 278.

[32] Latency is the time delay between the moment something is initiated, and the moment one of its effects begins or becomes detectable. In streaming video and voice communications high latency render the system ineffective due to lag.

[33] T Berners-Lee, 'Net Neutrality is Critical for Europe's Future', *Blog of the Vice-President for the Digital Single Market* (2 February 2015) <https://ec.europa.eu/commission/2014–2019/ansip/blog/guest-blog-sir-tim-berners-lee-founding-director-world-wide-web-foundation_en>; 'Tim Berners-Lee: Net neutrality "regulation needed", (*BBC News*, 12 July 2013) <http://www.bbc.co.uk/news/technology-23205244>; T Berners-Lee, 'A Magna Carta for the Web', TED, (March 2014) <http://www.ted.com/talks/tim_berners_lee_a_magna_carta_for_the_web?language = en>.

[34] See e.g. Berners-Lee, ibid.; AA Gilroy, *Access to Broadband Networks: The Net Neutrality Debate* Congressional Research Service R40616 (16 April 2015) <http://www.fas.org/sgp/crs/misc/R40616.pdf>; *United States Telecoms Association et al. v FCC et al.* DC CA No.15–1063.

Modern routers allow network carriers to prioritize certain traffic over others. Network providers argue this is a positive development as it allows them to prioritize traffic with a low latency threshold such as VoIP and streaming media over traffic with a higher latency threshold such as web browsing or a music download.[35] Network providers argue that in this way they can make a more efficient use of the limited resources available to them with everyone receiving the best service possible.[36] Critics argue that it also allows them to discriminate against certain applications or data types.[37] There are concerns that service providers may seek to deteriorate the quality of service of applications which compete with their products. Thus there are concerns that ISPs such as BT, Sky, or Virgin Media which provide integrated services (telephone, video on demand, and internet access) may degrade the quality of service of a competitor product such as Skype, YouTube, or Netflix.[38] In addition, they may place a restrictively low upload speed on your service making it difficult to use file or video sharing services such as YouTube or BitTorrent, or as was discovered by Professor Tim Wu when he surveyed ISPs service contracts, you may simply be contractually barred from certain activities by your ISP.[39]

Against this backdrop the US Federal government and the European Union have both spent considerable time examining whether there is a need to enshrine the principle of net neutrality, that all data should be treated equally, into Federal or European law. The debate in the US began with high-profile backers including Professor Lawrence Lessig, Professor Sir Tim Berners-Lee, Professor Tim Wu, and Craigslist founder Craig Newmark supporting a federally mandated net neutrality law. They met some degree of success when, in 2006, Senators Byron Dorgan and Olympia Snowe introduced the Internet Freedom Preservation Bill (or Dorgan-Snowe Bill)[40] which sought to enshrine the principle of net neutrality. The Bill though quickly became bogged down amid claims from the telecommunications industry that Dorgan-Snowe was disproportionate as there was no evidence that industry self-regulation was failing, that its effect would be to protect internet giants like Microsoft, Google, Yahoo!, and eBay rather than their customers and that it would deter investment by telecoms companies in high-speed data networks as they would not be able to recover their costs. The original bill fizzled out

[35] High Tech Broadband Coalition, *Appropriate Framework for Broadband Access to the Internet over Wireline Facilities* (CC Docket No. 96–45 (2002)); High Tech Broadband Coalition, *Appropriate Regulatory Treatment for Broadband Access to the Internet over Cable Facilities* (CC Docket No. 96–45 (2002)). For an excellent discussion of the issues see C Marsden, *Net Neutrality: Towards a Co-regulatory Solution* (Bloomsbury 2010).

[36] In May 2015 Real Time Entertainment (audio/video streaming sites) accounted for 69 per cent of all fixed-line data (and 40 per cent of mobile data) downloaded at peak times to North American homes. Of that, two services Netflix (36.4 per cent) and YouTube (15.5 per cent) accounted for over 50 per cent of all fixed-line downloaded content—see Sandvine, *Global Internet Phenomena: Latin America & North America* (May 2015) <http://www.sandvine.com/downloads/general/global-internet-phenomena/2015/global-internet-phenomena-report-latin-america-and-north-america.pdf> (registration required).

[37] A Cooper & I Brown, 'Net Neutrality: Discrimination, Competition, and Innovation in the UK and US' (2015) 15 *ACM Transactions on Internet Technology* 2; T Wu, 'Network Neutrality, Broadband Discrimination' (2003) 2 *Journal of Telecommunications and High Technology Law* 141.

[38] See the discussion in L Lessig, *The Future of Ideas* (Random House 2001) ch. 10.

[39] Wu (n. 37), found that among the activities restricted were: any commercial or business use of facilities; operating a server; overusing bandwidth; and in some cases even setting up a home network or wireless network (160–6).

[40] S. 215.

in summer 2006 when it failed to clear a congressional vote, a fate which also befell the Internet Freedom Preservation Bill of 2008,[41] but, undeterred, the campaigners for regulated net neutrality continued to press for action.

In 2007 it became apparent that one of the giant US cable companies, Comcast, was interfering with the ability of their cable modem customers to access BitTorrent services by resetting services that used BitTorrent packets. They were doing this as a traffic management tool to prevent BitTorrent from using up all available bandwidth to the detriment of other customers. They were referred to the Federal Communications Commission (FCC) by two public advocacy groups, Free Press and Public Knowledge. The complaint stated that Comcast's actions violated the FCC Internet Policy Statement, particularly violating the statement's principle that 'consumers are entitled to access the lawful Internet content of their choice . . . [and] to run applications and use services of their choice'. Comcast defended its interference as necessary to manage scarce network capacity. In August 2008 the FCC issued the results of its investigation. They found that Comcast's bandwidth management methods contravened federal policy by 'significantly impeding consumers' ability to access the content and use the applications of their choice'.[42] By the time the order was issued though, Comcast had adopted new management methods and, as a result, the order effectively only required Comcast to disclose the details of those new methods and their implementation. Comcast agreed to comply with the order but also filed for review in the District of Columbia Circuit of the US Court of Appeals, claiming (among other things) that the FCC did not have jurisdiction over its network management methods.

Perhaps buoyed by their initial success in regulating Comcast in October 2009, the FCC decided to seek public input on a new set of draft rules that would codify and supplement existing principles to safeguard internet openness. After holding a series of reviews and public meetings the FCC adopted the *Open Internet Report and Order* in December 2010; this established three basic open internet rules designed to preserve the free and open internet. These took effect on 20 November 2011.

Highlight FCC three basic open internet rules

1. Transparency—broadband providers must disclose information regarding their network management practices, performance, and the commercial terms of their broadband services.
2. No blocking—fixed broadband providers (such as DSL, cable modem, or fixed wireless providers) may not block lawful content, applications, services, or non-harmful devices. Mobile broadband providers may not block lawful websites, or applications that compete with their voice or video telephony services.
3. No unreasonable discrimination—fixed broadband providers may not unreasonably discriminate in transmitting lawful network traffic over a consumer's broadband Internet access service. Unreasonable discrimination of network traffic could take the form of particular services or websites appearing slower or degraded in quality.

[41] HR 3458.

[42] *In re Formal Complaint of Free Press & Public Knowledge Against Comcast Corporation for Secretly Degrading Peer-to-Peer Applications* 23 FCCR 13,028 at 13,054 (2008).

In the interim the appeal in *Comcast* had been heard. In April 2010 the court vacated the FCC's order, holding that the FCC had no authority over Comcast's internet service because 'the Commission had failed to tie its assertion of ancillary authority over Comcast's Internet service to any "statutorily mandated responsibility"'.[43] In essence the FCC had been found to have acted *ultra vires* as they had no mandate or authority to interfere into network management capability as such interference was not ancillary to their primary statutory role. This decision suggests that any attempt actually to enforce the *Open Internet Report and Order* would be fruitless as applying *Comcast*, the FCC have no authority to intervene in network and traffic management. If this were true, the *Open Internet Report and Order* becomes merely a guideline not an order. However, things are not so clear-cut. It has been noted by one commentator that 'the impact of this decision on the FCC's ability to regulate broadband services and implement its broadband policy goals remains unclear',[44] while the then FCC Chairman Julius Genachowski commented in April 2010: 'The court decision earlier this week does not change our broadband policy goals, or the ultimate authority of the FCC to act to achieve those goals. The court did not question the FCC's goals; it merely invalidated one technical, legal mechanism for broadband policy chosen by prior Commissions.'[45] The Chairman made this statement while announcing the next stage of the FCC's broadband, including net neutrality, policy which included the adoption of the Open Internet Order. As may therefore have been expected, the efficacy of the *Open Internet Report and Order* was immediately challenged by a number of telecommunications companies including Verizon and MetroPCS.[46] All these challenges were eventually consolidated into a single review before the US Court of Appeals for the Circuit of the District of Columbia.[47] In the consolidated action the telecommunications companies argued that the *Comcast* decision rendered the FCC Open Internet Order *ultra vires* and in the alternative that it interfered with their First Amendment rights.

The court issued its ruling in January 2014.[48] The court began by framing its terms of reference: 'our task as a reviewing court is not to assess the wisdom of the Open Internet Order regulations, but rather to determine whether the Commission has demonstrated that the regulations fall within the scope of its statutory grant of authority.'[49] The court then broke the Order up into its constituent parts and either vacated or upheld each part. Applying *Comcast* (among other authorities) the court found that an earlier decision of the FCC to classify broadband providers as 'information services' and not 'telecommunication services' meant that broadband service providers were not subject to so-called common carrier regulation under Title II of the Communications Act 1934.[50] The effect of this was to render invalid the provisions of the Open Internet Order on anti-discrimination and anti-blocking as 'the Commission has failed to establish that

[43] *Comcast Corp. v FCC*, 600 F. 3d 642, 661 (2010).

[44] Gilroy (n. 34) 4.

[45] FCC, *FCC Announces Broadband Action Agenda* (8 April 2010): <http://hraunfoss.fcc.gov/edocs_public/attachmatch/DOC-297402A1.pdf>.

[46] *Verizon v FCC*, Case No. 11–1014 (D.C. Cir. January 20, 2011); *MetroPCS Communications et al. v FCC*, Case No. 11–1016 (D.C. Cir. January 24, 2011).

[47] *Verizon Communications Inc. v FCC* 740 F.3d 623 (D.C. Cir. 2014).

[48] Ibid, available from <http://www.cadc.uscourts.gov/internet/opinions.nsf/3AF8B4D938CDEEA685257C6000532062/$file/11-1355-1474943.pdf>.

[49] Ibid. 17.

[50] Ibid. 9.

the anti-discrimination and anti-blocking rules do not impose per se common carrier obligations'.[51] The decision to vacate the key anti-blocking and anti-discrimination provisions gutted the Open Internet Order of its capacity to enshrine and protect net neutrality, leaving only the provision on transparency, but brought about quite unexpected consequences and the next round of attempts to enshrine net neutrality through regulation in the United States.

While the telecommunications companies reacted positively to the outcome of the case by making announcements that they would not seek to interfere with the customer internet experience provided by an open internet,[52] pressure was quickly brought to bear on the US Federal government by free internet advocates. A petition was launched on the White House petitions site. The petition called upon the Obama administration to 'Restore Net Neutrality By Directing the FCC to Classify Internet Providers as "Common Carriers"' and it quickly received over 105,000 signatures.[53] In response the White House replied that 'preserving an open Internet is vital not just to the free flow of information, but also to promoting innovation and economic productivity', but cautioned that 'the FCC is an independent agency' and therefore the President was not able to mandate the FCC to take any action.[54]

While the petition was open for signatures the new FCC Chairman Tom Wheeler issued a statement responding to the *Verizon* decision. In this he stated that the FCC would not appeal the decision, but instead would establish new rules for transparency, non-discrimination, and anti-blocking, based on the decision.[55] With the petition quickly gathering signatories the White House became fully engaged in November 2014. Despite the fact that the President had no power to mandate the FCC, he leveraged political pressure when he made a statement calling upon the FCC to 'implement the strongest possible rules to protect net neutrality' and setting out four bright line rules which he suggested 'reflect the Internet you and I use every day, and that some ISPs already observe': no blocking, no throttling, increased transparency, and no paid prioritization.[56] Finally on 26 February 2015 the FCC issued a new 2015 Open Internet Rules and Order.[57] The order first deals with the *Verizon* decision by reclassifying broadband internet access service as a telecommunications service under Title II of the Communications Act of 1934.[58] The Commission justifies this, not only as a response to *Verizon* but because 'our reclassification of the broadband Internet access service means that we can regulate, consistent with the Communications Act, broadband providers to the extent they are "engaged" in providing the broadband Internet access service'.[59] In essence, the argument made by the Commission is that in the modern world consumers see broadband providers as

[51] Ibid. Tatel CJ at 4.

[52] J Lowensohn, 'Comcast, Verizon, and others promise net neutrality ruling won't hurt customers' (*The Verge*, 14 January 2014) <http://www.theverge.com/2014/1/14/5309268/comcast-verizon-and-others-promise-net-neutrality-ruling-wont-hurt>.

[53] <https://petitions.whitehouse.gov/petition/restore-net-neutrality-directing-fcc-classify-internet-providers-common-carriers>.

[54] Ibid.

[55] FCC, *Statement by FCC Chairman Tom Wheeler on the FCC's Open Internet Rules* (19 February 2014) <http://www.fcc.gov/document/statement-fcc-chairman-tom-wheeler-fccs-open-internet-rules>.

[56] White House, *Net Neutrality: President Obama's Plan for a Free and Open Internet* (10 November 2014) <http://www.whitehouse.gov/net-neutrality>.

[57] FCC15–24 <https://apps.fcc.gov/edocs_public/attachmatch/FCC-15–24A1.pdf>.

[58] Ibid. [59].

[59] Ibid. [339].

being similar to telecommunications providers of old; common carriers who are responsible for carrying and delivering our internet content from point to point. While this may not be technically true (the moment our email leaves our ISP servers anyone can be carrying it by any route) it is how broadband providers advertise themselves by promoting download (and to a lesser extent upload) speeds and network security. Thus, as far as the consumer is concerned, their broadband provider is the party responsible for delivering their email and making sure they can get access to Netflix. As the Commission notes: 'the representation to retail customers that they will be able to reach "all or substantially all Internet endpoints" necessarily includes the promise to make the interconnection arrangements necessary to allow that access. As a telecommunications service, broadband Internet access service implicitly includes an assertion that the broadband provider will make just and reasonable efforts to transmit and deliver its customers' traffic to and from "all or substantially all Internet endpoints" under sections 201 and 202 of the Act... Thus, disputes involving a provider of broadband Internet access service regarding Internet traffic exchange arrangements that interfere with the delivery of a broadband Internet access service end user's traffic are subject to our authority under Title II of the Act.'[60] Having secured a reason to regulate broadband providers under Title II, the Order sets out a new 2015 series of bright line rules, based upon President Obama's statement.

Highlight FCC four basic open internet rules (2015 version)

1. No blocking—A person engaged in the provision of broadband Internet access service, insofar as such person is so engaged, shall not block lawful content, applications, services, or non-harmful devices, subject to reasonable network management
2. No throttling—A person engaged in the provision of broadband Internet access service, insofar as such person is so engaged, shall not impair or degrade lawful Internet traffic on the basis of Internet content, application, or service, or use of a non-harmful device, subject to reasonable network management
3. No paid prioritization—A person engaged in the provision of broadband Internet access service, insofar as such person is so engaged, shall not engage in paid prioritization
4. No unreasonable interference or unreasonable disadvantage standard for Internet conduct—Any person engaged in the provision of broadband Internet access service, insofar as such person is so engaged, shall not unreasonably interfere with or unreasonably disadvantage (i) end users' ability to select, access, and use broadband Internet access service or the lawful Internet content, applications, services, or devices of their choice, or (ii) edge providers' ability to make lawful content, applications, services, or devices available to end users. Reasonable network management shall not be considered a violation of this rule.

In addition to the four basic open internet rules found in the 2015 rules, it should be remembered that the transparency provision of the 2010 rules remains in effect giving us five basic open internet rules in total. The rules took effect on 12 June 2015 but, as may be expected, before they took effect they were challenged by broadband providers.

[60] Ibid. [204].

As soon as the new rules were promulgated the latest round of challenges began with a petition filed by the United States Telecom Association (USTA) claiming that: 'Broadband Internet access fits squarely within the 1996 [Telecommunications] Act's definition of "information service[s]," 47 USC § 153(24), that may not be regulated as common carriage under Title II. And Congress explicitly stated that the term "information service" "includ[es] specifically a service . . . that provides access to the Internet." § 230(f)(2)' and that the FCC has tried 'to evade [the] Court's holding in Verizon'.[61] The claim goes on to suggest that the whole action of the FCC is illegal as well as substantively invalid: 'the Order is independently unlawful because the FCC—in its headlong rush to implement this regulatory sea change at the President's urging—committed a string of glow-in-the-dark [Administrative Procedure Act] violations, any one of which would suffice to invalidate the Order. The FCC's original proposal to adopt a handful of prophylactic rules gave no notice that the FCC intended to craft out of whole cloth a "Title II tailored for the 21st Century", to rewrite its rules concerning mobile services, to redefine fundamentally the broadband service that it reclassified, or to adopt an amorphous "Standard for Internet Conduct", which gives the agency unfettered discretion to regulate new and innovative offerings. And the FCC abandoned its own long-standing classification decisions without grappling with either its prior legal conclusions and factual findings or the billions of dollars invested in reliance on prior policy.'[62] Although the court declined to grant a motion preventing the 2015 rules from coming into effect on 12 June,[63] they did grant a motion for an expedited hearing. It seems in all likelihood that the petitioners will be successful in this action, for as James Tuthill an adjunct professor at Berkeley Law School points out 'simply calling a rose by another name will not change what it is, and the courts won't buy it. It's a certainty that any new rules will be challenged in court, and more than likely they will be overturned, too, given the *Verizon* decision. And it will take another four or five years to reach that point. This is futility.'[64] If Tuthill is right, and it seems quite a reasonable assumption given the strength of the claim made by the USTA, the whole process will be forced to begin anew sometime in the near future.

Of course the issue of net neutrality is not only an American one. The issue is equally economically important, although until recently arguably less politicized, in Europe. One of the reasons the issue was less political was a more competitive European market for internet access. In the US, fixed-line broadband access was and is most commonly achieved via a cable provider. This means that for many subscribers they have a limited choice of perhaps only two or three (or even one) internet access providers. In the EU most people got, and still get, their fixed-line access over digital subscriber lines or DSL (more commonly known as telephone lines). This means that the average European consumer has a choice of several access providers. In the UK for example OFCOM lists

[61] *United States Telecom Association v FCC & Ors* CA D.C. Filed13/5/2015 <http://www.publicknowledge.org/assets/uploads/blog/15.05.13_Motion_for_Stay.pdf> 2.

[62] Ibid. 3.

[63] J Kasperkevic, 'Net neutrality rules to go into effect after court rejects bid to block them' *The Guardian* (London, 11 June 2015) <https://www.theguardian.com/technology/2015/jun/11/net-neutrality-lawsuit-federal-court>.

[64] JP Tuthill, 'FCC throws in the towel, but public has right to know why' (February 2014) *SF Gate* 25 <htpp://www.sfgate.com/opinion/openforum/article/FCC-throws-in-the-towel-but-public-has-right-to-5267613.php>; see also A Hurst, 'Neutering Net Neutrality: What *Verizon v FCC* Means for the Future of the Internet' (2015) 7 *Hastings Science and Technology Law Journal* 43.

over fifty competing fixed-line service providers,[65] although admittedly most home users get their home broadband access from the 'big five' providers: BT/PlusNet, Sky Broadband, Virgin Media, TalkTalk, and EE. The end user can change their ISP simply by requesting their new provider to change the service over to them.[66] Until recently the prevailing theory within Europe was that with greater competition in the internet access market, and with the regulatory authority ready to intervene should one of the behemoths of the internet access market decide to interfere with the quality of service of its customers, there was no need for proscriptive regulatory intervention.

More recently, however, Europe's reliance on market regulation has seemed less secure. As we moved from traditional DSL lines to fibre-optic access the market narrowed. As a result, European nations have taken steps to secure net neutrality. On 29 September 2010 a ministerial declaration from the Council of Europe stated that 'Users should have the greatest possible access to Internet-based content, applications and services of their choice, whether or not they are offered free of charge, using suitable devices of their choice. Such a general principle, commonly referred to as network neutrality, should apply irrespective of the infrastructure or the network used for Internet connectivity.'[67] It then went on to acknowledge that although 'operators of electronic communication networks may have to manage Internet traffic [and] this management may relate to quality of service, the development of new services, network stability and resilience or combating cybercrime[68] . . . exceptions to this principle should be considered with great circumspection and need to be justified by overriding public interests'.[69] As well as the Council of Europe declaration there were developments at the EU level. Two communications from the Commission opened up debate and consultation on EU policy for net neutrality. In April 2011 a communication from the Commission to Parliament and the Council entitled *The Open Internet and Net Neutrality in Europe*,[70] noted that despite Art. 8(4)(g) of the Framework Directive[71] requiring national regulatory authorities to promote the interests of the citizens of the European Union by promoting the ability of end users to access and distribute information or run applications and services of their choice, concerns had been raised about throttling of peer-to-peer (P2P) file-sharing or video streaming by certain providers in France, Greece, Hungary, Lithuania, Poland, and the United Kingdom and blocking or charging extra for the provision of voice over internet protocol (VoIP) services in mobile networks by certain mobile operators in Austria, Germany, Italy, the Netherlands, Portugal, and Romania.[72] The Commission noted that the EU remained committed to 'preserving the open and neutral character of the internet, taking full account of the will of the co-legislators now to enshrine net neutrality as a policy objective and regulatory principle to be promoted

[65] <http://stakeholders.ofcom.org.uk/telecoms/codes-of-practice/broadband-speeds-cop/list-of-isps/>.

[66] <http://consumers.ofcom.org.uk/internet/broadband-switching/switching-broadband-provider/>.

[67] Council of Europe, Declaration of the Committee of Ministers on network neutrality (29 September 2010) para 4 <https://wcd.coe.int/ViewDoc.jsp?id = 1678287>.

[68] Ibid. [5].

[69] Ibid. [6].

[70] COM(2011) 222 final.

[71] Dir. 2002/21/EC.

[72] See (n. 70) [4.1].

by national regulatory authorities'.[73] The Commission also noted though that amendments made in the 2009 Telecoms Reform Package were still being implemented by member states and so recommended no immediate action be taken, rather they would monitor the situation.

The monitoring period ended in summer 2012. A study by the Body of European Regulators of European Communications (BEREC) found that 20 per cent of all internet users, and potentially up to half of EU mobile broadband users, had contracts that allowed their ISP to restrict services like VoIP or P2P. They further found that those fixed and mobile operators with contractual restrictions on P2P, 96 per cent of fixed-line providers, and 88 per cent of mobile providers, enforced them technically.[74] As a result the Commission launched a public consultation into transparency, switching, and internet traffic management with an aim to preserve net neutrality. The public consultation stage closed on 15 October 2012 after which the Commission put together a series of packages on net neutrality and mobile roaming which led on 11 September 2013 to the publication of the Connected Continent legislation package.[75] Key among this was the proposal for a Regulation laying down measures concerning the European single market for electronic communications and to achieve a Connected Continent (the Telecoms Regulation).[76] Although the proposed Regulation covered a lot of ground, including coordination of the Radio Spectrum market and mobile roaming agreements, it also provided for net neutrality through a number of provisions but primarily through chapter IV (Arts. 21–29). As was noted in the explanatory notes to the draft, 'the obligation on providers to provide unhindered connection to all content, applications, or services being accessed by end users—also referred to as Net Neutrality—while regulating the use of traffic management measures by operators in respect of general internet access. At the same time, the legal framework for specialised services with enhanced quality is clarified.'[77] Unfortunately in a series of tripartite negotiations between the Commission, the Council, and the Parliament these strong net neutrality provisions were sacrificed in order to gain agreement on other aspects of the Regulation. After receiving a strong endorsement by the Parliament at first reading in April 2014 an agreement was reached with the Parliament on 9 July 2014. It was sent to the Council for agreement, and there it hit a hurdle. It was reported in March 2015 that the Council proposed an alternative set of net neutrality rules which 'would establish a principle of "net neutrality" but still allow telecoms groups to manage the flow of internet traffic to ensure the network worked efficiently. They will also be able to agree deals with corporate and individual customers to provide faster internet services—although the proposals make clear that these would not be allowed to impair the wider working of the internet in any "material manner"'; in essence a two-speed internet.[78]

[73] EU telecoms reform package [2009] OJ L337.

[74] BEREC, *A View of Traffic Management and other Practices Resulting in Restrictions to the Open Internet in Europe* (29 May 2012) <http://ec.europa.eu/digital-agenda/sites/digital-agenda/files/Traffic per cent20Management per cent20Investigation per cent20BEREC_2.pdf>.

[75] <http://ec.europa.eu/digital-agenda/en/node/67489/#open internet>.

[76] COM(2013) 627 final <https://ec.europa.eu/digital-agenda/news-redirect/11950>.

[77] Ibid. 12.

[78] D Thomas, D Crow, and D Robinson, 'Proposals on European net neutrality open "two-speed" internet' *Financial Times* (London, 3 March 2015) <http://www.ft.com/cms/s/0/5688747c-c192–11e4-bd24–00144feab7de.html>.

The final version of the Regulation as passed on 25 November 2015[79] gives support for only one aspect of net neutrality as explained by the second Recital: 'The measures provided for in this Regulation respect the principle of technological neutrality, that is to say they neither impose nor discriminate in favour of the use of a particular type of technology.' The net neutrality provisions have been removed in favour of provision of technological neutrality, transparency, and market regulation. The key provisions are now found in Arts. 3–5 and allied regulations. By Art. 3 open internet access safeguards ensure technological neutrality: 'End-users shall have the right to access and distribute information and content, use and provide applications and services, and use terminal equipment of their choice, irrespective of the end-user's or provider's location or the location, origin or destination of the information, content, application or service, via their internet access service.' Note there is no quality of service requirement, although it may be argued that Art. 1(3) does appear to provide some form of net neutrality protection: 'Providers of internet access services shall treat all traffic equally, when providing internet access services, without discrimination, restriction or interference, and irrespective of the sender and receiver, the content accessed or distributed, the applications or services used or provided, or the terminal equipment used.' This though is undermined by both Arts. 1(2), 'Agreements between providers of internet access services and end-users on commercial and technical conditions and the characteristics of internet access services such as price, data volumes or speed, and any commercial practices conducted by providers of internet access services, shall not limit the exercise of the rights of end-users laid down in paragraph 1', and the second part of 1(3) 'the first subparagraph shall not prevent providers of internet access services from implementing reasonable traffic management measures. In order to be deemed to be reasonable, such measures shall be transparent, non-discriminatory and proportionate, and shall not be based on commercial considerations but on objectively different technical quality of service requirements of specific categories of traffic. Such measures shall not monitor the specific content and shall not be maintained for longer than necessary.' To ensure these provisions are not abused, there are the transparency requirements of Art. 4 including that 'providers of internet access services shall ensure that any contract which includes internet access services specifies at least the following: (a) information on how traffic management measures applied by that provider could impact on the quality of the internet access services, on the privacy of end-users and on the protection of their personal data and (b) a clear and comprehensible explanation as to how any volume limitation, speed and other quality of service parameters may in practice have an impact on internet access services, and in particular on the use of content, applications and services.' Again the idea here is that the market and consumer choice will play a major role in ensuring no abuse occurs. Both Arts. 3 and 4 are backed up by the requirement that national regulatory authorities monitor service providers for compliance with the Regulation and the requirement of an annual report to BEREC.[80] The final regulation has been the subject of extensive

[79] Reg. 2015/2120.
[80] Art. 5(1).

criticism[81] and there are early indicators that some service providers are seeing this as a green light to introduce tiered services.[82]

This leaves two questions, why did the Council insist on those changes to the Regulation and where will this leave net neutrality in Europe? The answer to the first is unclear. The Council likes to talk of the concept of remote medical care and even remote surgery where a surgeon in Frankfurt could carry out surgery remotely via the internet in Bad Kissengen. This they suggest will only be possible if the surgeon can be assured of a high quality differentiated network connection. It is more likely though that pressure from major network operators, and concerns about how net neutrality may effect filtering and blocking operations carried out extra legally by network operators such as the operation of the Internet Watch Foundation blocking list in the UK, is what is really behind the position of the Council.[83] Where will this leave net neutrality in Europe? The short answer is exactly where it was before. A failure to enshrine net neutrality does not mean it goes away it simply means it is not enshrined by law. In the short term nothing will change but over time network operators may, emboldened by the stops taken in Council, apply more traffic controls and access controls, perhaps leading to a two-speed internet. The timing of the Council intervention could not be worse given the moves of the FCC to ensure net neutrality in the United States. Though as we have seen, they too are likely to come under threat via the action of the petition of the USTA. In short it is likely that, when it comes time to consider a fourth edition of this textbook, the issue of enshrined and protected net neutrality in both Europe and the United States might be no clearer than it is today.

2.3 **Higher-level protocols**

In Figure 2.1, I outlined how TCP/IP created an open layer built over or on top of the closed networks of the ARPANET, the ALOHANET, and the SATNET. In this last section of this chapter I will introduce and explain the third network layer, the applications layer where higher-level protocols such as Hypertext Transfer Protocol allow us to carry out operations such as web surfing. To explain how the modern internet lays higher-level functionality such as web surfing or video streaming on top of the basic networking functionality of TCP/IP, we start by looking at the environmental layering of the modern network.

[81] A Hern, 'EU net neutrality laws fatally undermined by loopholes, critics say' *The Guardian* (London, 27 October 2015) <http://www.theguardian.com/technology/2015/oct/27/eu-net-neutrality-laws-fatally-undermined-by-loopholes-critics-say>; G. Smith, 'This is what the E.U. thinks is "net neutrality"' *Fortune* (New York, 27 October 2015) <http://fortune.com/2015/10/27/this-is-what-the-e-u-thinks-is-net-neutrality/>.

[82] T. Höttges, 'Net neutrality: Finding consensus in the minefield' *Deutsche Telekom Blog* (Bonn, 28 October 2015) <http://www.telekom.com/media/management-to-the-point/291728>.

[83] Indeed a misreporting of the agreed text of the Regulation in UK tabloid newspapers on 28 October 2015 caused the Prime Minister to state in response to a question at Prime Minister's Questions that: 'Like my hon. Friend, I think that it is vital that we enable parents to have that protection for their children from this material on the internet. Probably like her, I spluttered over my cornflakes when I read the Daily Mail this morning, because we have worked so hard to put in place those filters. I can reassure her on this matter, because we secured an opt-out yesterday so that we can keep our family-friendly filters to protect children. I can tell the House that we will legislate to put our agreement with internet companies on this issue into the law of the land so that our children will be protected.' HC Deb 28 October 2015, vol. 601, col. 344.

Stratification or layering may be identified in any informational environment. Both network engineers and communications theorists recognize the vital function played by environmental layers in communications networks. In his book *Weaving the Web*,[84] the architect of the World Wide Web, Tim Berners-Lee, identifies four layers within the architecture of the internet: the transmission layer, the computer layer, the software layer, and the content layer.[85] This may be seen as a simplified version of the seven-layer Open Systems Interconnection Reference Model (OSI model) used by network engineers. This model divides the functions of a protocol into a series of layers. Each layer has the property that it only uses the functions of the layer below, and only exports functionality to the layer above. Typically, the lower layers are implemented in hardware, with the higher layers being implemented in software.[86] Although both the OSI model and the Berners-Lee model are network architecture models, designed to describe the purely functional aspects of the network, they can easily be adapted to illustrate the challenges faced by regulators. For lawyers and regulators this has been most successfully done by Yochai Benkler in his eloquent paper 'From Consumers to Users'[87] and it is that model which will be employed here.

Benkler describes a three-layer network which is similar to Berners-Lee's four-layer environment. Benkler labels his layers (1) the physical infrastructure layer, (2) the logical infrastructure layer, and (3) the content layer. What Benkler does is to reduce the OSI/Berners-Lee model to the three key environmental layers found on the internet. The foundational layer is the physical infrastructure layer. This is the link between the physical world and cyberspace and is made up of wires, cables, spectrum, and hardware such as computers and routers. The second layer is the logical infrastructure layer. This encompasses the necessary software components to carry, store, and deliver content, software such as the TCP/IP protocol, operating systems, and browsers. Finally, the content layer encompasses all materials stored, transmitted, and accessed using the software tools of the logical infrastructure layer. Benkler's model was adapted by Lawrence Lessig in his book *The Future of Ideas*.[88] Lessig rebranded the layers the physical layer, the code layer, and the content layer. This allowed him to discuss the particular effectiveness in using the code layer to regulate the content layer, a subject he had previously raised in *Code and Other Laws of Cyberspace*,[89] and to which he would return in his third book, *Free Culture*.[90] Thus the role of TCP/IP is to act as the 'glue' which connects the physical infrastructure of the communications networks to the higher-level protocols which we use daily to read blogs, post Facebook updates, and send and receive emails. Among the everyday higher-level protocols you may use are SMTP—Simple Mail Transfer Protocol, used to send and receive emails; VoIP—Voice over IP, used for internet telephony such as Skype; and RTP—Real-time Transport Protocol, which streams audio and video

[84] T Berners-Lee, *Weaving the Web: The Original Design and Ultimate Destiny of the World Wide Web by Its Inventor* (Harper Business 2000).

[85] Ibid. 129–30.

[86] The seven OSI layers are: (1) physical layer; (2) data link layer; (3) network layer; (4) transport layer; (5) session layer; (6) presentation layer; and (7) application layer. See D Comer, *Internetworking with TCP/IP: Principles, Protocols and Architecture*, (Pearson 2013) vol. 1.

[87] Y Benkler 'From Consumers to Users: Shifting the Deeper Structures of Regulation toward Sustainable Commons and User Access' (2000) 52 *Federal Communications Law Journal* 561.

[88] See (n. 38).

[89] L Lessig, *Code and Other Laws of Cyberspace* (Basic Books 1999).

[90] L Lessig, *Free Culture: The Nature and Future of Creativity* (Penguin 2005).

content such as YouTube. One protocol suite stands out: it is HTTP—Hypertext Transfer Protocol and its allied programming language HTML—Hypertext Markup Language. Between them these protocols form the foundation of the World Wide Web and are by far the most important higher-level network to operate using TCP/IP.

The World Wide Web, or simply 'the web', is not synonymous with the internet. As we have seen, the internet is the network of computer networks which function using TCP/IP. The web is a higher-level network which uses the internet as its carrier medium. The invention of the web is usually credited to Sir Tim Berners-Lee. Berners-Lee is a physicist who graduated from the University of Oxford in 1976. Upon leaving university he began working with Plessey Telecommunications as a software engineer, where he worked for two years on distributed systems, message relays, and bar-coding. He then joined DG Nash, a small software company, where he developed a multi-tasking operating system and typesetting software for intelligent printers. During this time he also developed a hypertexting system called Enquire.[91] Hypertext was not new, the term had been coined by filmmaker and computer programmer Ted Nelson in 1963 and the concept of hyperlinking was at the core of Project Xanadu, his hypertext project which ran from 1960 and which he discussed at length in his 1981 book, *Literary Machines*.[92] While Nelson was experimenting with hypertext, the first functioning hypertext system, Douglas Englebert's NLS, or oN-Line System, was developed. Englebert developed his system independently of Nelson's work and did not use the term hypertext to describe his system, but there is no doubt it was the first hypertext network. Englebert had been hugely influenced by Vannevar Bush's 1945 paper 'As We May Think',[93] which described a mechanized library system, or memex, with embedded links between documents. In his attempts to build Bush's memex Englebert turned to the potential of digital computers. In 1962 he started work on Augment, a project to develop computer tools to augment human capabilities.[94] This was possibly the most important computer project of the time (arguably even more important than ARPANET) and it produced the first computer mouse, graphical user interface, and hypertext program. All these developments were demonstrated by Englebert at the Fall Joint Computer Conference in San Francisco in December 1968. Englebert received a standing ovation in tribute to his work on his NLS system; as a result the SDS 940 computer he used for these applications was selected as the second ARPANET node. It took another 20 years though for Englebert's invention to find a popular use, and that was in Tim Berners-Lee's web design.

After developing his Enquire system, Berners-Lee joined the European Particle Physics Laboratory (CERN)[95] as a consultant. During his time there he secured funding to develop a digital hypertext library of CERN research which could be accessed from

[91] Hypertext is the now familiar user interface used on the web. It is designed to overcome some of the limitations of fixed written text. Rather than remaining static like traditional text, hypertext makes possible a dynamic organization of information through links and connections (called hyperlinks). Hypertext can be designed to perform various tasks; for instance when a user clicks on the link it will usually cause his browser to load a related web page of information or if he allows his mouse to hover over it, a bubble with a description of the linked file may appear.

[92] T Nelson, *Literary Machines* (Mindful Press 1981).

[93] V Bush, 'As We May Think' (July 1945) *The Atlantic Monthly* 101.

[94] The Augmentation Research Center at Stanford Research Institute in Menlo Park, CA, was the precursor to the internationally famous Xerox PARC facility.

[95] CERN is the contraction of the Laboratory's French name: Conseil Européen pour la Recherche Nucléaire.

any facility on the CERN network. By March 1989 Berners-Lee had completed his project design to allow researchers in the High Energy Physics Department to communicate information online. His design had two key features: (1) like TCP/IP his new protocol was to have an open architecture to allow researchers to connect any computer no matter what operating system it was using, and (2) information was to be distributed using the network itself. Berners-Lee was joined in his project by Robert Cailliau, a computer engineer from Belgium. Throughout 1990 Berners-Lee, assisted by Cailliau, developed the first web server, 'httpd', and the first client, 'WorldWideWeb' a hypertext browser/editor. This work was started in October 1990 and by Christmas Day 1990 Berners-Lee and Cailliau were conversing across the world's first web server at info.cern.ch. In August 1991, Berners-Lee posted a notice to the alt.hypertext newsgroup informing users where his web server and browser software could be downloaded. At this stage the web was still in its infancy; there was no certainty it would develop in the way we experienced in the 1990s, but on 30 April 1993 the future of the web was secured when CERN gave notification that they were not intending to take control of the technology developed by Berners-Lee and Cailliau. On that date CERN announced and certified that the WWW technology developed at CERN was to be put into the public domain 'to further compatibility, common practices, and standards in networking and computer supported collaboration'.[96] This allowed any interested party to use and improve the CERN software, assuring the future of the web.

With its freedom assured the web became the 'killer application' of the internet.[97] The number of internet users quickly increased[98] and today it is estimated that there are almost 3.4 billion people online.[99] Thus while it is important to bear in mind that the internet and the web are two different things, the importance of the web to the development and penetration of the internet cannot be underestimated. Throughout this book we will look at the challenges of both the internet and the web to governments, lawmakers, lawyers, and to regulators and users more generally. Much of the focus of this will be on the regulation of the web: issues such as the distribution of pornographic content across borders via the web, or the distribution of movies and music in breach of copyright via the web, but sometimes it is other aspects of the internet's unique communications media that are at the core of the problem, such as with BitTorrent, a communications protocol which allows users to share large files between computers. BitTorrent is not a web protocol. Like HTTP it runs across TCP/IP and is therefore properly a question of internet governance. Thus this book will look at the regulation and

[96] Original certificate at: <http://cds.cern.ch/record/1164399>.

[97] The term killer application refers to any computer program or application that is so necessary or desirable that it affords the core value of some larger technology, such as an operating system, or a piece of computer hardware. Simply put, a killer application is so compelling that someone will buy the hardware or software components necessary to run it.

[98] Figures for 1993 are not reliable but estimates suggest there were about 1.3 million internet users in January 1993 mostly based in the US (Internet Society, *Global Internet Report 2014* <http://www.internetsociety.org/sites/default/files/Global_Internet_Report_2014_0.pdf>). Accurate figures are available from 1995 when IDC Research began their user survey. From this we know there were 16 million internet users in December 1995, 36 million in December 1996, 76 million in November 1997, 147 million in September 1998, 195 million in August 1999, and 369 million in August 2000. See G Gromov, *History of Internet and WWW: The Roads and Crossroads* <http://www.netvalley.com/intvalstat.html>.

[99] See *World Internet Users and Population Stats* <http://www.internetworldstats.com/stats.htm>.

governance of digital content wherever found. You need to be aware of the distinction between the internet and the web to allow you to distinguish whether we are talking about regulation of the logical infrastructure layer (internet regulation) or regulation at the content layer (usually regulation of web content). Where possible I will make this clear but on some occasions you will need to apply the distinction yourself.

TEST QUESTIONS

Question 1

At present, it is argued, the existence of market failures require government regulation to ensure net neutrality. Is this true? In particular is it true in the United States? And is it true in the United Kingdom?

Question 2

The existence of an IP address, as part of the TCP/IP protocol, means that every device connected to the internet can be identified and tracked at any time. This means one's correspondence can always be tracked and therefore the internet is incapable of complying with Art. 8 ECHR.

Discuss.

FURTHER READING

Books

T Berners-Lee, *Weaving the Web: The Original Design and Ultimate Destiny of the World Wide Web by Its Inventor* (2000)

K Hafner and M Lyon, *Where Wizards Stay Up Late: The Origins of the Internet* (1996)

C Marsden, *Net Neutrality: Towards a Co-regulatory Solution* (2010)

Chapters and articles

Y Benkler, 'From Consumers to Users: Shifting the Deeper Structures of Regulation Toward Sustainable Commons and User Access', 52 *Federal Communications Law Journal* 561 (2000)

M Lemley and L Lessig, 'The End of End-to-End: Preserving the Architecture of the Internet in the Broadband Era', *Berkeley Law & Economics Working Papers* No. 8 (2000)

B Owen, 'The Net Neutrality Debate: Twenty Five Years after US v. AT&T and 120 Years after the Act to Regulate Commerce', 2 (11) *Perspectives from FSF Scholars* (2007)

3

Digitization and society

As we saw in chapter 1 the move from atoms to bits represents a challenge to the traditional economics of bricks and mortar industries as well as to established legal models. Both law and economics have traditionally assumed that value and control may be achieved through rivalrousness and exclusivity, both of which are side effects of the atomic model. As also outlined in that chapter, the information society did not emerge fully formed in the 1980s; it had been slowly developing as the post-industrial society which grew at the end of the World War II slowly moved the bulk of the GDP of post-industrial states, such as the UK, from primary industries, such as mining and quarrying, and secondary industries, such as shipbuilding and car manufacture, into the tertiary sector of banking and insurance, and later to the quaternary sector of information broking.

Given this slow economic and social development of the information society it is amazing that traditional economic and legal models have found it so difficult to adapt to the challenges of digitization. Commentators will cite the speed of growth of information technologies from the 1960s to the present day as one of the reasons we have been caught out,[1] but in truth it is simpler than that: it is simply the disruptive effect of the process of digitization. As we touched upon in chapter 1 a bit can be used as the building block of all types of digital information. It is the informational equal of the atom and can be used to represent, send, and store text, images, or sound. The bit is the natural way to store textual data such as books or academic papers, music, images such as holiday snaps, or even movies. What has driven the adoption of digital technologies over recent years is threefold. First, the cost of storing bits has fallen dramatically over the last 60 years;[2] second, the cost and speed of transmitting bits across computer networks has equally fallen;[3] and, third, consumers have fuelled a demand for the incorporation of greater storage capacity and multi-platform support in all digital devices

[1] See e.g. N Negroponte, *Being Digital* (Hodder & Stoughton 1995) 5–6; F Webster, *Theories of the Information Society* (2nd edn, Routledge 2002) 9–11.

[2] In 1956 it cost $50,000 to buy the world's first hard drive which stored 5MB of data. This is $10,000 per MB of storage. By 1980 a 26MB HDD was down to $5,000 (or $193 per MB). In 1987 a 40MB Iomega HDD was $1,799 (or $45 per MB). By 1995 the price had dropped all the way to 85¢ per MB with the release of the 2.9GB, $2,899 dollar Seagate HDD. Remarkably, the price per MB of HDD storage currently stands at 0.000028¢ per MB (you can buy a 3TB HD for $84.99). Historical data supplied from *Historical Notes about the Cost of Hard Drive Storage Space* <http://ns1758.ca/winch/winchest.html>.

[3] In the late 1990s a connection speed of 28.8K (or 28 KBs) would cost about £30 per month (in addition to the cost of the modem). By the turn of the millennium 56.6K dial-up cost about £25 per month. Now 16MB broadband is available for as little as £4.50 per month or 38MB broadband is £10.

by continually demanding more from device manufacturers.[4] These three effects have brought about a massive change in the way we use, store, and transmit information. It has freed information from the restrictions of atomic carrier media such as CDs, DVDs, and bound texts and has at the same time made information more valuable and more malleable. These developments will form the focus of this chapter.

3.1 The digitization of information

Before the widespread adoption of digital information management information was held in discrete and often poorly catalogued packets.[5] If we take as our example your NHS medical records we see the difference digitization makes to the value and accessibility of informational products. Traditionally NHS medical records were held on a variety of manual filing systems. Your GP and each specialist medical provider you visited would each keep their own discrete set of patient records. Thus if you regularly attended three different hospitals for different treatments you would have at least four sets of medical records, one at each hospital and one held by your GP, meaning no one set was complete or definitive. In addition, as all the data on these records was manually recorded and indexed, searching your file was a time-consuming exercise, and as indexing was a skilled job, and therefore expensive, only key information would be indexed in any event. The development of information technology[6] allows for a single record which can be accessed by all carers contemporaneously and which may, instantly, be searched by any keyword.[7] This example, and the example of the digital music player given in footnote 5, illustrates the power of digital informational management and retrieval. This is developed by Professor Fred Cate, in his book *Privacy in the Information Age*.[8]

[4] Look in your pocket, bag, whatever. Do you have a mobile phone? Does it play music? What about movies? Does it take pictures? What about videos? Can you access the internet on it? What about your email? Can you edit documents? Finally, can you use it to call people? If you answered yes to most of these, think what you would have been able to do with your mobile phone in 1999.

[5] Think for a moment about the difference between a CD collection and a digital music player. A CD collection was made up of hundreds of individual plastic discs which were held discretely and which you would manually search. A digital music player can hold tens of thousands of tracks and can be searched using titles, artists, or genre. You can 'shuffle' your iPod to play music in an unexpected order which can throw up unusual combinations such as Jean-Michel Jarre followed by Iron Maiden in a way not possible when music was held on discrete packets or discs.

[6] The key aspect of IT or information technology is in its ability to harness the power of information. Too often commentators focus on what the technology can do, not what the information allows. This is a critique levelled by Richard Susskind in his book, *Transforming the Law: Essays on Technology, Justice and the Legal Marketplace* (OUP 2000).

[7] This is the theory. In the interests of transparency it should be admitted that the NHS computer system described above is yet to deliver this level of service. The original NHS Connecting for Health scheme was scrapped in 2013. Elements of the scheme now coming on stream such as e-referrals and NHS Care Data have been heavily criticized. See C Jee, 'NHS admits 33 "known issues" with e-Referral service launched today' (*Computerworld UK*, 15 June 2015) <http://www.computerworlduk.com/news/applications/nhs-warns-of-33-known-issues-with-e-referral-service-launched-today-3615745/>; P Bernal, 'Care.data and the community . . . ' (23 February 2014) <https://paulbernal.wordpress.com/2014/02/23/care-data-and-the-community/>.

[8] FH Cate, *Privacy in the Information Age* (Brookings Institution Press 1997) 14–15.

Highlight Cate's four reasons for data growth

1. Information is easier to generate, manipulate, transmit, and store.
2. The cost of collecting, manipulating, storing, and transmitting data is lowered.
3. Electronic information has developed an intrinsic value not found in analogue information due to its very nature.
4. The operating parameters of computer systems and networks generate additional digital information through back-up copies and cache copies.

Professor Cate describes four generic reasons for the growth of digital information and digital information management. The first, which may be clearly seen from the example above, is that it is easier to generate, manipulate, transmit, and store information. Individuals with simple database programs such as MS Access can manage and manipulate more data on a simple home PC than a medium-sized organization such as a school or small business could do in the analogue era. Second, the cost of collecting, manipulating, storing, and transmitting data is lowered. Cheap storage media such as external hard-disk drives and flash media, the advent of cheap internet access and the development of cloud storage systems, such as Dropbox or Google Drive, mean that for a few pence thousands of pages of data may be uploaded, downloaded, or stored. Third, electronic information has developed an intrinsic value not found in analogue information due to its very nature. As digital information is cheaply processed and stored it attracts a premium in the marketplace. This market advantage encourages gatherers of information to favour the collection of digital information over analogue information, leading to vast increases in the volume of digital information available. Finally, Cate notes that the operating parameters of computer systems and networks generate additional digital information through back-up copies and cache copies. Due to these four factors Cate records that 'we are witnessing an explosion in digital data'.[9] The effects of such an explosion are more apparent in 2016 than they were when Professor Cate made that observation in 1997. The economies of scale that digital information offers are now significantly enhanced with both the previously observed collapse in the cost of digital storage media and with increased processing capability including keyword cataloguing and the promise in the near future of a semantic (or intelligent) network.[10]

3.1.1 **Information collection, aggregation, and exploitation**

As we observed in chapter 1, the modern economies of leading industrialized nations are now built upon the processing, storage, and transmission of data. A massive data processing industry has grown up, with Google the prime example of how to turn information into profit. We all know Google and we all use Google. Google is reportedly the world's second most valuable brand, worth almost $174bn.[11] As a company Google

[9] Ibid. 16.

[10] The semantic web is discussed in detail in ch. 22.

[11] Brandz Top 100, 2015 <http://www.millwardbrown.com/BrandZ/2015/Global/2015_BrandZ_Top100_Report.pdf>.

is under twenty years old, so how did Google achieve this so quickly? It has done so by the aggregation of vast amounts of data, including search data, data held in Gmail accounts, and data held in vast personal archives such as Google Drive. Also, as most people leave their Google account signed in (to allow quick access to Google services such as Gmail and YouTube), Google gathers data as you surf the web. This data is then stored and searched for keywords which are then used to make targeted advertisements to the user using the Google Adwords, Adsense, and DoubleClick programs.[12] This type of advertising is much more efficient than television or radio broadcasting which most of the time reaches the wrong audience: it is an advertising cruise missile compared to the old-fashioned technique of pattern bombing.

This is the rub of the business model which makes profits from informational processing. To make money either you have to charge for your service, which means you will be undercut by free services, or you have to offer advertisers a better return on their investment than your competitors; this means gathering data about your customers, a process which may generate bad publicity and cause customers to install privacy protection software or ad blocking software (or both). There is nothing new with this approach; offline supermarkets have done it for years through loyalty cards, as have airlines and hotels. Loyalty cards bring two returns: the obvious one that the customer is more likely to use your service if he gets something in return, but also, less obviously, they aggregate and then sell on the data collected via your loyalty account to third parties, as well as using it themselves.[13] The problem with these schemes, if there is a problem, is the informational asymmetry involved. We as customers are willing to give away vast amounts of personal data to get a Gmail or Yahoo! Mail account or in return for a 1 per cent discount on our weekly shop. We are not aware of the potential value of this data on the secondary market and as a result, arguably, data protection laws have not yet caught up with the benefits that modern information processing brings. We will examine in detail much of these effects in Part VI—Privacy in the Information Society.

3.1.2 **Information disintermediation**

While Professor Cate has caused us to stop and consider the possible downside of the digitization of information as it affects individual privacy, there is, as far as the individual end user is concerned, a very clear upside also. Freed from the restrictions of atomic carrier media, informational products have forged a new distribution system through the internet. While the supply of informational products were traditionally tied to the standard distribution chain of manufacturer-carrier-shop (think of a CD which would be pressed, distributed, and then sold on the high street), the modern distribution system for informational products, such as music, movies, newspapers,

[12] These income streams are now under threat from new technologies, such as ad blockers. It is reported that Google lost $6.6bn revenues to ad blockers in 2014 and with the new Apple mobile operating system iOS9 offering ad blocking capability this threat is likely to grow, along with competition from Facebook.

[13] To read about Tesco's Crucible database, operated by its marketing subsidiary 'Dunnhumby' see H Tomlinson and R Evans, 'Tesco Stocks Up on Inside Knowledge of Shoppers' Lives' *The Guardian* (London, 20 September 2005) <http://www.guardian.co.uk/business/2005/sep/20/freedomofinformation.supermarkets>.

and magazines, is by direct delivery from the producer of the product to the consumer by digital download. This is part of a process known as disintermediation where the middlemen in a supply chain are cut out and the financial benefits are split between the supplier and the purchaser. Now instead of buying your music at Virgin or HMV on a CD you are more likely to download it from iTunes or stream it on Spotify or Apple Music. You may even take it one stage further and get your music direct from the band via SoundCloud or YouTube, thus also disintermediating the record producer. Similarly, whereas you once bought your copy of *The Guardian* at your local newsagent, now you can read the paper online in full, and should you want to read the paper exactly as typeset you can subscribe to the digital edition of the paper. Again you have the option of bypassing the editors and publishers of the newspaper and going straight to the source of many news stories through the advent of so-called citizen journalism where individuals play an active role in the process of collecting, reporting, analysing, and disseminating news and information, usually through the blogosphere.[14] In both of these examples disintermediation of the distribution network may be imprecisely called Web 1.0 distribution. This is the traditional model of digital distribution in which content producers developed websites and download tools which were strictly one-way 'push' media. The second examples, which use social networking tools such as Facebook, SoundHound, or YouTube, and blogging tools such as WordPress, are Web 2.0 systems where digital networks are harnessed to facilitate creativity, sharing of information, and collaboration among users.[15] The challenge online collaborative endeavours bring to traditional informational products is already well known among producers of such products.

In 1994 respected cyber-commentator John Perry Barlow wrote a prophetic paper about the effects of disintermediation and the economic impact it would come to have. This paper, entitled 'The Economy of Ideas: A Framework for Patents and Copyrights in the Digital Age',[16] is widely available online[17] and outlined many of the challenges disintermediation would bring to traditional informational entertainment industries, such as the music industry. He defines the challenge thus:

> [as] digital technology is detaching information from the physical plane, where property law of all sorts has always found definition . . . [this] property can be infinitely reproduced and instantaneously distributed all over the planet without cost, without our knowledge, without its even leaving our possession, how can we protect it? How are we going to get paid for the work we do with our minds? And, if we can't get paid, what will assure the continued creation and distribution of such work?

Barlow, who has some experience of the creative industries having worked as a lyricist for the Grateful Dead, reminds us it is not the ideas that are protected by intellectual property laws, but rather the expression of the ideas.[18] Taken a step further, Barlow

[14] S Forde, *Challenging the News: The Journalism of Alternative and Community Media* (Palgrave Macmillan 2011).

[15] T O'Reilly, 'What is Web 2.0: Design Patterns and Business Models for the Next Generation of Software' (2007) 1 *Communications & Strategies* 17.

[16] *Wired 2.03* (March 1994).

[17] At many sources including: <http://homes.eff.org/~barlow/EconomyOfIdeas.html> and <http://www.selenasol.com/selena/extropia/idea_economy_article.html>.

[18] C Waelde et al., *Contemporary Intellectual Property: Law and Policy* (3rd edn, OUP 2013) ch. 2.

reminds us it is how the expression of the ideas is recorded that is protected: thus patents are specified,[19] trademarks are registered,[20] and copyright material is fixed.[21] In Barlow's terms:

> throughout the history of copyrights and patents, the proprietary assertions of thinkers have been focused not on their ideas but on the expression of those ideas. The ideas themselves, as well as facts about the phenomena of the world, were considered to be the collective property of humanity. One could claim franchise, in the case of copyright, on the precise turn of phrase used to convey a particular idea or the order in which facts were presented. The point at which this franchise was imposed was that moment when the 'word became flesh' by departing the mind of its originator and entering some physical object, whether book or widget. The subsequent arrival of other commercial media besides books didn't alter the legal importance of this moment. Law protected expression and, with few (and recent) exceptions, to express was to make physical . . . For all practical purposes, the value was in the conveyance and not the thought conveyed.

Barlow developed a useful shorthand for this process: 'the bottle was protected, not the wine'. Of course the ability to send information as bits across the telecommunications network changes this. The wine can now be carried without the bottle and as such, Barlow argues that traditional models of property law, in particular traditional intellectual property laws, will be required to evolve if they are to remain useful.

Case study *Napster*

Everyone knows at least part of the story of Napster. In June 1999 Shawn Fanning, a student at Boston's Northeastern University, released his 'Napster' protocol.

Fanning created Napster out of frustration: he, like many college students, was an avid music fan who was strapped for cash. He was frustrated for several reasons. First, he wanted to search for digital music files but the only option available at the time was to use crude search engines which would search the entirety of a library with no specific ability to search for music files. Second, he wanted to swap interesting pieces of music with like-minded individuals but didn't have the tools to do so, and third, he was frustrated by the quality of music available and the cost of replacing older collections on vinyl with newer collections on CD.

Fanning designed his Napster protocol to meet these needs. It was, in his mind at least, primarily a tool designed to create a community where people could meet and talk about music. He initially envisaged that any trading of music files would take place outside the Napster community by email or Internet Relay Chat but late in the development of Napster he added a revolutionary option: the ability to interface directly with the computer of another Napster user and to download from his or her PC music files in MP3 format.

Napster was an instant success. It rapidly gathered members from around the globe and Napster fundamentally altered the market structure for online music distribution with, at the peak of Napster's popularity, almost 3 billion music files being traded among members each month.

[19] Patents Act 1977 (PA), s. 14(2)(b).
[20] Trade Marks Act 1994 (TMA), s. 32(2)(d).
[21] Copyright, Designs and Patents Act 1988 (CDPA), s. 3(2).

In design Napster was much like eBay: a consumer-to-consumer (C2C) trading community, but Napster was designed specifically around a single product: digital music files. This difference drove the early success of Napster, but was ultimately to lead to its downfall. As Barlow had pointed out five years earlier, creative goods are quite distinct from physical goods and, whereas eBay is a valuable C2C reselling community which allows individuals to sell on items at the value the market attaches to them, members of the Napster community were engaged in something quite different. Napster was a C2C trading community, that much is true, but with Napster the trading was in copies of music files meaning the 'seller' never relinquished their original file: this in turn meant that there was no need to charge for files and so all music in the Napster community was available at no cost. The result was a market which was built on a clearly illegal activity and which fundamentally undermined the market model for paid-for digital music downloads: why pay Apple 99¢ per track when you could download it for free from Napster? The Napster market model was about to undermine the entire exercise of designing paid-for music download models: from the point of view of the media distribution industries it had to be closed down, and quickly.[22]

The response from the music industry was exactly as has been predicted by Barlow; information had to be 'propertized' again. The music industry made a two-pronged attack. First, they set out to close down the immediate threat of Napster. As the vast majority of music available on Napster was protected by copyright, a group of leading music studios, including A&M Records, Geffen Records, MCA, Motown, and Capitol Records raised a suit against Napster claiming contributory and vicarious copyright infringement.[23] Following a trial hearing, the district court found that the complainants had successfully established a prima facie case of direct copyright infringement on the part of Napster's users. According to the court, 'virtually all Napster users engage in the unauthorized downloading or uploading of copyrighted music'[24] and 'Napster users get for free something they would ordinarily have to buy [which] suggests that they reap economic advantages from Napster use.'[25] Further the court held that the effect of the use upon the value of the work and potential markets for the work weighed against finding that use of Napster constituted fair use. As a result it rejected Napster's fair use defence and distinguished the Supreme Court's decision in *Sony Corp of America v Universal City Studios*.[26] In particular, the trial judge noted that unlike VCRs, in which users were initially invited to view the television broadcast for free, Napster users obtained permanent copies of songs that they would otherwise have had to purchase. Further, the majority of VCR users merely enjoyed the tapes at home; in contrast, 'a Napster user who downloads a copy of a song to her hard drive may make that song available to millions of other individuals . . . facilitating unauthorized distribution at an exponential rate'.[27] The district court, in short, concluded that the conduct of Napster users could not be considered fair use because it threatened the incentives

[22] Napster will be discussed in depth in ch. 11 but a short discussion of the *Napster* case here is useful.

[23] *A&M Records Inc. v Napster Inc.*, 114 F. Supp. 2d 896 (N. D. Cal. 2000), affd in part and rev'd in part, 239 F. 3d 1004 (9th Cir. 2001).

[24] Ibid. 911.

[25] Ibid.

[26] 464 US 417 (1984).

[27] *A&M Records v Napster* (n. 23) 913.

created by copyright. With this finding, the music industry obtained judgments against Napster for both contributory infringement[28] and vicarious infringement.[29] An appeal by Napster to the 9th Circuit proved to be unsuccessful[30] and in February 2001 Napster was closed down.

3.1.3 **Information management**

The music industry knew that litigation on its own was not going to deal with the problem of illegal trading in MP3 files. What was needed was to replace the 'bottle' which had been lost: the re-propertization of digital content. The music industry had since the mid-1990s been developing cryptography tools such as Digital Rights Management (DRM) and Digital Watermarking. Again this had been predicted by Barlow. He had defined cryptography as 'the "material" from which the walls, boundaries—and bottles—of Cyberspace will be fashioned'.[31] DRMs offer the media distribution industries the most tantalizing opportunity: distribution of their products in a carrier medium which cannot be copied. Since DRMs use an encryption key to control access to the media file, they not only prevent illegal access but also copying—they are a bit like having a book printed on uncopyable paper where the text only becomes visible when the authorized owner of that book is reading it.[32]

The problem with DRM encryption is that any digital technology which can be engineered can also be reverse engineered, in other words, months or years spent designing your encryption protocol may be undone in minutes by a cracker.[33] To prevent widespread cracking of DRMs the entertainment industries sought to give legal support to

[28] Contributory infringement requires both knowledge of the infringing activity and a material contribution (actual assistance or inducement) to the alleged primary infringement. The court interpreted the knowledge requirement as not merely that the Napster system allowed an infringing use, but that Napster had actual notice of the infringement and then failed to remove the offending material. The court concluded that Napster knew or had reason to know of its users' infringement of plaintiffs' copyrights, that Napster failed to remove the material, and that Napster materially contributed to the infringing activity by providing the site and facilities for direct infringement.

[29] Vicarious infringement results when there has been a direct infringement and the vicarious infringer is in a position to control the direct infringer, fails to do so, and benefits financially from the infringement. The court held that Napster was vicariously liable as they failed to exercise their right and ability to prevent the exchange of copyrighted material. Further, Napster had a direct financial interest in the downloading activities since their revenue was dependent on user increase which was driven by the infringing activities of users.

[30] In fact Napster's appeal was partly successful. The Court of Appeal noted that: 'contributory liability may potentially be imposed only to the extent that Napster: (1) receives reasonable knowledge of specific infringing files with copyrighted musical compositions and sound recordings; (2) knows or should know that such files are available on the Napster system; and (3) fails to act to prevent viral distribution of the works. The mere existence of the Napster system, absent actual notice and Napster's demonstrated failure to remove the offending material, is insufficient to impose contributory liability' (1014). This meant the plaintiffs had to give Napster written notice of all infringing files.

[31] Barlow (n. 16).

[32] It should be noted that DRMs do not on the whole prevent the digital media file from being replicated, but what is replicated is the *encrypted* file not the plaintext file, meaning that simply copying the file is worthless unless you have a licence from the copyright owner to access it.

[33] Software cracking is the modification of software to remove encoded copy prevention. Those who carry out this activity are crackers, not hackers. The resultant decrypted files are known as Warez and are widely distributed.

DRM technology by propertizing DRMs. This was achieved through Arts. 11 and 12 of the World Intellectual Property Organisation (WIPO) Copyright Treaty adopted in Geneva in December 1996.[34] Article 11 requires all WIPO states to 'provide adequate legal protection and effective legal remedies against the circumvention of effective technological measures that are used by authors in connection with the exercise of their rights', while Art. 12 requires WIPO states to criminalize attempts to 'remove or alter any electronic rights management information without authority'; or to 'distribute, import for distribution, broadcast or communicate to the public, without authority, works or copies of works knowing that electronic rights management information has been removed or altered without authority'.

In Europe the 2001 Directive on Copyright and Related Rights in the Information Society[35] gives effect to these provisions. This restricts all acts of circumvention[36] and bans the importation, sale, rental, or possession for commercial purposes of all tools designed to allow circumvention of encryption systems,[37] and the distribution of content from which a rights management system has been removed.[38] This would appear to be the end of this tale. Bottles have been recreated through the use of cryptography. Any attempt to tamper with, remove, or damage such bottles is criminalized. The status quo, which was unbalanced by the disintermediation of content and carrier, is digitally restored. But, I am pleased to say that while the content industry may be thinking small: we, their customers are thinking big. Fed up with the iTunes/iPod technical symbiotic relationship,[39] customers continued to lobby for DRM free files from iTunes and finally, on 5 January 2009 Apple announced all iTunes content would be DRM free.[40] Since this announcement nearly all digital music has been made available DRM free, including that sold via iTunes' main competitors operated by Amazon and Google. The crypto-bottle appears to be shattered which is good news as we seek to carry our digital content on ever more intelligent devices that can multitask.

3.2 Digital convergence

I have a smartphone: it is a truly remarkable device. On it you can (among other things): listen to music, phone people, text people, play games, watch videos, send and receive email, surf the web, manage your calendar, take pictures, store pictures, write text, check your stocks, and plan journeys (receiving turn-by-turn directions). Think back 20 years (if you are old enough). To do all these things I would have needed to carry a Discman, a mobile phone, a Gameboy, a laptop computer, a journal or diary, a camera, and a road atlas. Now I have a hand-held device that weighs 112g. This change has

[34] <http://www.wipo.int/treaties/en/ip/wct/trtdocs_wo033.html>.

[35] Dir. 2001/29/EC.

[36] Art. 6(1).

[37] Art. 6(2).

[38] Art. 7(1).

[39] Apple encrypted AAC files as downloaded from iTunes will only play on Apple approved products such as iPods and some mobile phones.

[40] Originally DRM free content, called iTunes plus, was more expensive than DRM encoded content, but from 1 April 2009 all content supplied from iTunes is DRM free.

been brought about by the fifth generic reason for the growth of digital information and digital information management which we can add to Cate's original four: digital convergence.[41]

Convergence can be seen as another side effect of the freeing of content from the carrier. Whereas previously all content had a different carrier medium (photographs used photographic film or paper, music used magnetic tape, optical discs (CD), or vinyl discs, movies use magnetic tape or optical discs (DVD), while text used paper), now freed from these restrictions all content is carried equally, as 0s and 1s. The concept of convergence came to media and communications theory from the mathematical disciplines where it was used to refer to the coming together of physical things such as beams of light or non-parallel lines. Media and communications commentators began to apply the term to the coming together of media platforms in the late 1970s or early 1980s, it being extremely difficult to determine exactly when, and by whom, the term was first used in this context. What is clear though is that communications theorist Ithiel de Sola Pool adopted this contextual use of the term and popularized it among media and communications theorists. In his landmark 1983 book, *The Technologies of Freedom*,[42] Pool wrote of the 'convergence between historically separated modes of communication' and argued that 'electronic technology is bringing all modes of communications into one grand system'.[43]

Despite writing in 1983 it took close to 25 years for Pool's vision to become reality—why did it take so long? One obvious reason was the delay in developing a fully digital informational distribution chain. For complete digital convergence to become a reality we required technological innovations in every stage of the information infrastructure. Information needed to be gathered digitally. This is now commonplace with reporters filing stories by email and the use of digital cameras to record news events and television broadcasts. Then information needed to be stored and delivered in digital form. All media outlets now store information in digital form and deliver it digitally, whether as digital television, digital radio, or as an online newspaper. Second, it required a new generation of portable devices that would allow for delivery of a variety of text and audio-visual media. The arrival of smartphones and tablet devices finally signalled, 25 years after Pool predicted it, the opening of the golden age of media convergence.

What legal challenges does convergence bring? As we have seen, digitization challenged both privacy and property laws. As information and content became cheaper to gather, cheaper to process, and cheaper to distribute, the intellectual connection between information or data and concepts such as personhood, privacy, autonomy, and respect for private property were initially swept aside in a rush to experiment with new technologies and to profit from new data mining and data-gathering techniques. In comparison with digitization, digital platform convergence is still in its infancy and it is still too early to predict with certainty all of the issues that platform convergence will raise but some are already apparent.

[41] Digital Convergence or digital platform convergence or sometimes technological convergence should not be confused with the related but different phenomenon of media convergence. Media convergence is an economic strategy in which communications companies seek financial benefit by making the various media properties they own work together. For a discussion of media convergence see G Meikle and S Young, *Media Convergence: Networked Digital Media in Everyday Life* (Palgrave Macmillan 2011).

[42] I de Sola Pool, *The Technologies of Freedom* (Belknap Press 1983).

[43] Ibid. 28.

One such issue is multiple file copies. When a music publisher sold a CD, he sold and therefore took a royalty for the composer, on the basis that this was one copy of the music sold. Modern digital music systems make multiple copies as a norm. Thus if you use Apple iTunes you may have authorized copies of your iTunes libraries on up to ten devices, including five computers, at any time. Music not purchased from iTunes may be played on any number of devices. Until very recently, though, the law stated that to make a copy of a copyright music file, such as if I were to take a CD and 'rip' it to my iTunes library, this was an infringement of copyright.[44] There was in the UK no right to back up a music file;[45] thus all UK music lovers, myself included, who transferred their CD collection to their MP3 player did so illegally. This was reviewed by the Gowers *Review of Intellectual Property*,[46] where it was recommended that the government 'introduce a limited private copying exception by 2008 for format shifting for works published after the date that the law comes into effect. There should be no accompanying levies for consumers.'[47] This was then taken forward in the Triesman consultation,[48] where it was recommended that 'a new exception to copyright to allow consumers to make a copy of a work they legally own, so that they can make the work accessible in another format for playback on a device in their lawful possession' be created.[49] In 2011 Professor Ian Hargreaves carried out a further review into intellectual property rights. In his report *Digital Opportunity: A Review of Intellectual Property and Growth*[50] he found that producers of copyright material already assume limited private copying occurs and build the cost of this into their products. On this basis he again called on government to introduce an exception which would 'allow individuals to make copies for their own and immediate family's use on different media'.

The Hargreaves' recommendation was investigated by the Intellectual Property Office who supported his finding that producers already charge consumers on the assumption that limited home copying will take place. They found that a limited exemption such as the one proposed by Hargreaves would have no impact on UK copyright industries.[51] Finally, in October 2014 it seemed that what we had all been doing for years, and which had been recommended to be formally made legal in a series of reports from 2006, was to be made legal with the coming into force of the Copyright and Rights in Performances (Personal Copies for Private Use) Regulations.[52] This introduced s. 28B into the Copyright, Designs and Patents Act 1988, which allowed the owner of a copy of a work (this would include e-books, films, and TV programmes legally owned, as well

[44] CDPA 1988, s. 17(2). Note Apple (and other digital music distributers) routinely give end users licences which allow for multiple copies to be installed. Thus it is Apple which gives me the right to make ten copies of any music downloaded from the iTunes store, not the law.

[45] Although s. 50A allows for back-up copies to be made of computer software, this is not permissible for other media.

[46] A Gowers, *Review of Intellectual Property* (2006) <http://www.hm-treasury.gov.uk/media/6/E/pbr06_gowers_report_755.pdf>.

[47] Recommendation 8.

[48] D Triesman, 'Taking Forward the Gowers Review of Intellectual Property Proposed Changes to Copyright Exceptions' (2008).

[49] Ibid. [85].

[50] <http://www.ipo.gov.uk/ipreview-finalreport.pdf>.

[51] UK Intellectual Property Office, *Impact Assessment Copyright Exception for Private Copying* BIS1055 <http://www.ipo.gov.uk/consult-ia-bis1055.pdf>.

[52] Reg. 2014/2361.

as music)[53] to make a copy of the work, provided that the copy was a copy of your copy of the work (and not a third party's), was made for private use, and was made for strictly non-commercial purposes.

As soon as s. 28B came into effect though it was challenged. A number of representatives of the music industry; the British Academy of Songwriters, Composers and Authors, the Musicians' Union, and UK Music challenged the provision by way of judicial review.[54] They claimed that the new provision failed to comply with Art. 5(2)(b) of the Copyright and Related Rights in the Information Society Directive which provides that 'Member States may provide for exceptions or limitations to the reproduction right . . . in respect of reproductions on any medium made by a natural person for private use and for ends that are neither directly nor indirectly commercial, on condition that the rightholders receive fair compensation.'[55] The claimants argued that the UK government could not rationally rely upon Professor Hargreaves' finding that producers of copyright material already assume limited private copying occurs and build the cost of this into their products in implementing the Regulations. They made three essential claims: (1) that the pricing-in economic principle is irrational, illogical, and inapplicable. Pricing-in cannot properly exist in the absence of an ability to price discriminate which ability does not exist in the affected music, publishing, and film sectors, (2) the decision was flawed because the evidence relied upon to justify the conclusion about harm was inadequate/manifestly inadequate, and (3) the Secretary of State was so firmly committed to introducing an exception without a compensation scheme that his 'predisposition' in truth was a 'predetermination' which, in law, was unlawful.[56] In essence the claim made was that the UK scheme in the Regulations was incompatible with Art. 5(2)(b) as the Directive requires 'fair compensation' be given while the Regulations had concluded no compensation was required due to the practice of pricing-in. However, there was insufficient evidence to suggest pricing-in took place, or could take place in the marketplace, and the Secretary of State had allowed himself to be biased in favour of finding pricing-in as he wished to introduce a scheme without compensation. The UK government responded that this had all been reviewed by Hargreaves who found 'there was a strong view expressed that levy systems were bureaucratic and not necessarily conducive to efficiency or even innovation. This was of course a controversial view and one that (as many commentators recognised) tended to split along predictable and partisan lines with content creators disagreeing and content acquirers and copying device sellers agreeing.'[57] They added there were two premises which the government had applied in passing the Regulations: (1) the only relevant 'harm' that would, in principle, need to be compensated for was the risk to rightholders of lost, duplicate sales. The Secretary of State concluded that while consumers considered that they should

[53] Note though s. 28B does not cover computer software, as we have seen there is a pre-existing exception for software under s. 50A.

[54] *R v Secretary of State for Business, Innovation and Skills ex parte British Academy of Songwriters, Composers and Authors & Ors* [2015] EWHC 1723 (Admin).

[55] Dir. 2001/29/EC of the European Parliament and of the Council of 22 May 2001 on the harmonization of certain aspects of copyright and related rights in the information society, Art. 5(2)(b).

[56] *R v Secretary of State for Business, Innovation and Skills ex parte British Academy of Songwriters, Composers and Authors & Ors* (n. 54) 18.

[57] Ibid. [7].

be entitled to copy content they had acquired they were not, to any material degree, prepared to go out and purchase duplicate copies in order to be able to achieve multiple use. In other words, there was no automatic correlation between the desire to copy and lost sales. (2) Either fully, or very substantially, sellers of content had already priced-in to the initial sale price the fact that consumers treated content that they purchased as fair game when it came to copying for personal use.[58]

The case was heard by Mr Justice Green who issued a lengthy judgment on the issues in June 2015. He found that 'the conclusions and inferences which have been drawn from the evidence the Secretary of State has relied upon are simply not warranted or justified by that evidence'.[59] Green J admitted this left the provision in something of a limbo:

> In my judgment it is sufficient therefore to result in the decision being rendered unlawful. However, this has potentially complex implications for section 28B. It does not necessarily result in that section being struck down. It is, in theory, possible for the Secretary of State to re-investigate the issue in order to address the evidential gap which now prevails. If he does this then one possible outcome would be that the gap that I have identified is plugged and the present decision becomes justified. Another outcome might be that following further investigation the gap in the evidence remains un-plugged in which case the Secretary of State could either repeal section 28B or introduce a compensation scheme. A third possibility is that the Secretary of State simply decides to introduce a compensation scheme without more.[60]

On this basis he decided not to issue a final disposal of the case in June, instead he gave the parties more time to consider the implications 'I will hear submissions as to what flows from this conclusion and from the judgment generally. In particular I will hear submissions as to whether any issue of law that I have decided should be referred to the Court of Justice and if so as to the question(s) that should be asked. I will also hear submissions as to the appropriate relief that I should grant given (i) the nature of my conclusion as to why the Defendant's decision to introduce section 28B was unlawful; and (ii) any decision that I might make as to reference.'[61] The parties made their submissions and on 17 July 2015 Green J made his final disposal of the case. Here he made three important decisions: (1) should the Regulations (and thereby s. 28B) be quashed? (2) If so, should this be retrospective or prospective? And (3) should a reference be made to the CJEU? The first decision was made easy by the submission of the Secretary of State that 'he (the Secretary) will now take the opportunity to reflect further and in due course take a view as to whether, and in what form, any further factual enquiries should be carried out and whether a new private copying exception should be introduced. The Secretary of State has not decided on any specific course at this stage and wishes to take time to reflect before making any further decisions. He would not wish to create any uncertainty in the law by submitting that the Regulations remain in force while further policy decisions are made.'[62] The Regulations were thus quashed.[63] The second decision

[58] Ibid. [12]–[13].

[59] Ibid. [20].

[60] Ibid. [21].

[61] Ibid. [317]–[318]. The reference to the Court of Justice, if made, would be on the compatibility of the UK Regulation with Art. 5(2)(b).

[62] *R v Secretary of State for Business, Innovation and Skills ex parte British Academy of Songwriters, Composers and Authors & Ors* [2015] EWHC 2041 (Admin) [5].

[63] Ibid. [11].

was more difficult but on balance Green J thought that this was a complex issue where people would have been acting in reliance on the Regulations. He was happy to rule the Regulations prospectively unlawful but refused to take a position on retrospective effect.[64] Finally, he chose not to refer the issue to the CJEU as this seemed to be more of an issue of UK law not EU law. In essence, the Secretary of State had not carried out a proper consultation before introducing the home copying exception without a compensation scheme. Green J acknowledged that in future if a similar exception without compensation was set up with proper consultation, then the issue may become live again and a reference could be made then.[65]

We now find ourselves in the position that any private copies made between 16 October 2014 and 17 July 2015 are legal while all others are not (absent a license right). The government must now consider its next move. It seems that the introduction of a home copying exemption without a compensation scheme will be difficult and costly in light of this decision. Equally, the setting up of a compensation scheme will be bureaucratic and costly. Commentators are suggesting the whole thing may be quietly forgotten and things may go on as they were before 16 October 2014.[66] Currently that looks the most likely outcome.

This is just one of the challenges of platform convergence. Others include a re-evaluation of the expectation one has to privacy in a world where every movement is likely to be recorded via a smartphone and then uploaded to Twitter, Facebook, or YouTube[67] and the overwhelming production of obscene and indecent material which digital convergence has allowed, including the alarming rise of obscenity and even child-abuse images, through sexting and social networks.[68] The latter is aided by the final palpable effect digitization has had on society: the failure of laws to cross borders adequately.

3.3 **The cross-border challenge of information law**

The cross-border effects of digital information transfers were first identified by Professors David Post and David Johnson in their ground-breaking paper 'Law and Borders: The Rise of Law in Cyberspace'.[69] Here they laid for the first time a legal interpretation, known as classical cyberlibertarianism, which contends that regulation founded upon traditional state sovereignty, based as it is upon notions of physical borders, cannot function effectively in cyberspace as individuals may move seamlessly between zones governed by differing regulatory regimes in accordance with their personal preferences.[70] Simply put, they claimed the internet was unregulable as laws were confined to the jurisdiction in which they were promulgated while content hosted and carried on the internet, including obscene content, flowed seamlessly over these borders.

[64] Ibid. [20]–[21].
[65] Ibid. [25]–[30].
[66] See <http://the1709blog.blogspot.co.uk/2015/07/private-copying-exception-is-no-more.html>.
[67] Discussed in chs. 20 and 21.
[68] Discussed in ch. 14.
[69] (1996) 48 *Stanford Law Review* 1367.
[70] The cyberlibertarian school will be discussed in depth in ch. 4.

The overwhelming problem that lawmakers face in dealing with online pornography is which standard to apply. In the UK we use the Obscene Publication Act 1959 to determine whether an item is obscene (and therefore illegal) or merely indecent. This states: 'For the purposes of this Act an article shall be deemed to be obscene if its effect or (where the article comprises two or more distinct items) the effect of any one of its items is, if taken as a whole, such as to tend to deprave and corrupt persons who are likely, having regard to all relevant circumstances, to read, see or hear the matter contained or embodied in it.'[71] This standard is specifically designed to be flexible and to change over time as community standards change and over the near 60 years it has been in force the UK standard of obscenity has changed quite dramatically.[72]

Internationally, individual states are continually altering their obscenity standard to meet contemporary community standards. What is considered sexually explicit but not obscene in the UK may well be considered to be obscene in the Republic of Ireland, and almost certainly material considered obscene in the Islamic Republic of Iran or in the Kingdom of Saudi Arabia would not be felt to be noteworthy in the UK. Similarly, material which would be considered to be obscene in the UK would probably not be censored in Germany, Spain, or Sweden where a more tolerant approach to erotica and pornographic material is taken. What we are seeing in these differences is a spectrum of community standards which range from extremely conservative to extremely liberal. In general, this system has functioned quite effectively in the real world due to the existence of physical borders and border controls. The easiest way for a state to apply its legal standard of obscenity within its borders is to prevent the importation of materials which offend the standard of that state, while simultaneously criminalizing the production of such materials within the state. In the UK, for example, it is an offence to import indecent or obscene prints, paintings, photographs, books, cards, lithographic or other engravings, or any other indecent or obscene articles under s. 42 of the Customs Consolidation Act 1876, while s. 2 of the Obscene Publications Act 1959 criminalizes the publication, or possession with intent to publish, of an obscene article.

The Customs Consolidation Act allows the UK to apply effective border controls. It allows HM Revenue & Customs to seize obscene items, and where necessary to prosecute those involved in their importation. This control provision continues to apply despite the UK's membership of the European Union, with it being held on several occasions that this power subsists in relation to material deemed obscene under the Obscene Publications Act despite Art. 26 TFEU.[73] But these traditional measures are predicated upon the assumption that the items in question will be fixed in a physical medium, and that they will require physical carriage to enter the state. With the advent of the digital age both these assumptions have been rendered null. The development of a global informational network has dismantled these traditional borders. The result of this is all too apparent, especially to parents trying to control what their children are exposed to. HM Revenue & Customs, along with the police, have given up all attempts to apply the provisions of the Customs Consolidation Act or the Obscene Publications

[71] Obscene Publications Act 1959, s. 1(1).

[72] For a discussion on the evolution of the obscenity standard see ch. 14. Also see A Murray, *The Regulation of Cyberspace: Control in the Online Environment* (Routledge 2007) 205–9.

[73] *Conegate Ltd v HM Customs & Excise* [1987] QB 254 (ECJ); *R v Forbes* [2002] 2 AC 512 (HL).

Acts to content found on the internet. Instead they have decided to focus their limited resources on narrow areas which produce a sound return on their investment. Thus despite surveys which show that 15 per cent of UK adults regularly visit pornographic websites and 41 per cent occasionally do so,[74] and that 14 per cent of 9- to 16-year-olds have in the past 12 months seen images online that are 'obviously sexual',[75] there have been no prosecutions in England and Wales under either the Customs Consolidation Act or the Obscene Publications Act 1959 for privately viewing obscene material using an internet connection.

Instead the authorities have focused their attention on the storing and distribution of child-abuse images,[76] non-photographic pornographic images of children under the Coroners and Justice Act 2009,[77] and extremely pornographic images under the Criminal Justice and Immigration Act 2008 (as amended by the Criminal Justice and Courts Act 2015),[78] and prosecuting those who run pornographic websites from overseas servers but who are resident in the UK and profit from this activity.[79] With the removal of the physical border between the UK and the rest of the world, internet users were afforded the opportunity to access and view pornography held overseas in the blink of an eye and with little opportunity for the authorities to intercept the content en route. This caused a huge upsurge in consumption and left the authorities with a difficult decision to make. They could either invest large sums to attempt to enforce the law in the digital environment,[80] or they could *de facto* deregulate adult obscenity and focus their attentions on more pressing problems such as child-abuse images. The UK authorities, recognizing the limits of the law in relation to this subject, chose to focus their resources on only the most harmful content.

This case study, which will be developed further in chapter 14, demonstrates the difficulty lawmakers find in applying geographically based legal rules in an environment which effectively floats over borders. That is not to say that law is ineffective in dealing with these issues. Throughout this book we will see the courts take effective jurisdiction over online defamation, pornography and child-abuse images, computer hacking, computer fraud and data theft, copyright infringement, and a variety of other issues. The law is effective in cyberspace. The difficulty is in identifying which court has effective jurisdiction and in identifying who is the relevant person to pursue.[81]

[74] J Mann, 'British sex survey 2014: "the nation has lost some of its sexual swagger"' *The Observer* (London, 28 September 2014) <http://www.theguardian.com/lifeandstyle/2014/sep/28/british-sex-survey-2014-nation-lost-sexual-swagger>.

[75] S Livingstone et al., *Risks and Safety on the Internet* (LSE 2011) <http://www.lse.ac.uk/media%40lse/research/EUKidsOnline/EU%20Kids%20II%20(2009-11)/EUKidsOnlineIIReports/D4FullFindings.pdf>.

[76] *R v Barry Philip Halloren* [2004] 2 Cr App R (S) 57; *R v Snelleman* [2001] EWCA Crim 1530; and *R v James* [2000] 2 Cr App R (S) 258.

[77] *R v Palmer* [2011] EWCA Crim 1286; *R v Milsom* [2011] EWCA Crim 2325.

[78] *R v Cheung* [2009] EWCA Crim 2965; *R v Burns* [2012] EWCA Crim 192; *R v PW* [2012] EWCA Crim 1653.

[79] See *R v Ross Andrew McKinnon* [2004] 2 Cr App R (S) 46 and *R v Stephane Laurent Perrin* [2002] EWCA Crim 747.

[80] This could either be achieved by the investment of these funds into additional law enforcement personnel or by using the funds to design a technological solution to the problem, such as a national firewall or filtering system which would in effect rebuild the natural border in cyberspace. See R Deibert et al., *Access Controlled* (MIT Press 2010).

[81] This is discussed more fully in ch. 15.

3.4 Digitization and law

This chapter has outlined several of the challenges digitization brings to lawmakers. By replacing old-fashioned analogue data, which was expensive to gather, store, and search, and which was subject to decay in quality over time and would decay each time it was copied,[82] with digital data, which is cheap to gather, store, and search and which is perfectly replicated every time, we have unleashed a wave of data gathering and data mining which threatens to unbalance our expectation to privacy. In addition, we have allowed an expectation to grow that one may share content and may obtain content for free or at little cost because we convince ourselves that no one is harmed by this.

Digital convergence and multipurpose 'smart' devices are leading us to expect media distinctions to become blurred and are allowing us to consume content from one media device to another without expecting to pay again for the privilege. Also as media devices become more portable and multifunctional we will find once again that barriers between the private and public space are broken down as 'citizen journalists' record events and post them to the web. Finally, the internet has forced lawmakers and lawyers to accept that we are part of an international community and we can no longer expect that we can close our border to things we do not like. The response of the UK legal establishment to the problem of online obscenity is instructive in this. The law enforcement authorities faced the fact that the community had accepted that most 'mainstream' pornography was not damaging to society and chose not to prosecute those who viewed such material, while focusing on the more obscene material people found most offensive. These challenges are just a few of the challenges of the process of digitization and a move to the world of bits. The remainder of this book, starting with the next chapter, will outline how the law and lawmakers have responded to these challenges.

TEST QUESTIONS

Question 1

The law on home copying in the digital age is an ass. Section 28B of the Copyright, Designs and Patents Act 1988 by only allowing for home copies 'made for the individual's private use' is so out of touch with society (and even the terms and conditions of digital content suppliers) that it demonstrates why lawmakers should not be allowed to make law in this particular area as they simply do not understand it.

Discuss the above with use of appropriate examples.

Question 2

Discuss the challenge posed by technological convergence. Is this a challenge of policy, technology, or law? What role in particular should lawyers play in the convergence debate?

[82] This is analogue drop-off, discussed in ch. 1.

FURTHER READING

Books

FH Cate, *Privacy in the Information Age* (1997)

H Jenkins, *Convergence Culture: Where Old and New Media Collide* (2008)

I de Sola Pool, *The Technologies of Freedom* (1983)

Chapters and articles

JP Barlow, 'The Economy of Ideas: A Framework for Patents and Copyrights in the Digital Age', *Wired 2.03*, March 1994

R Deibert and R Rohozinski, 'Beyond Denial: Introducing Next Generation Information Access Controls', in R Deibert et al., *Access Controlled* (2010)

J Smith and R Montagnon, 'The Hargreaves Review: A "Digital Opportunity"', 33 *European Intellectual Property Review* 596 (2011)

PART II

Governance in the information society

How can lawyers, lawmakers, and judges control the actions of individuals in the online and virtual environments? Can traditional laws such as property law and defamation survive in the digital environment?

4

Regulating the digital environment

As discussed in chapter 3, the process of digitization is proving to be a logistical challenge for lawmakers. In the real world we design laws to protect physical goods and to control the actions of corporeal individuals. Thus, as was discussed in chapter 1, s. 1 of the Theft Act 1968 expects that stolen goods are tangible. Similarly, and as discussed in chapter 3, copyright law, although a law designed to deal with intangible goods, makes use of the physical environment to assist in the regulation of copyright infringement, while personal data privacy was, prior to digitization, protected in part by the environmental factors which made storage of, access to, and cross-referencing of information held in physical files expensive and time-consuming. The societal move from value in atoms to value in bits therefore offers a major challenge to lawmakers as it suggests traditional legal rules require to be re-evaluated when we consider extending them into the digital environment. For example, should the provisions of real-world laws such as the Theft Act 1968 apply to online games where virtual property is acquired and sometimes stolen?[1] Similarly should the legal provision designed to prevent abuse of children in the production of child-abuse images, found in s. 1 of the Protection of Children Act 1978, be extended to prevent the production and possession of pseudo-images: images which appear to portray the abuse of a child but which have been computer-generated?[2] These challenges of digitization, allied to the ability of internet communications to cross borders without being subjected to border controls, led some lawyers and academics to suggest that traditional legal rules, predicated on the dual foundations of physicality of goods and persons and jurisdictional boundaries, could not be extended to cyberspace. They believed that the incorporeal and borderless nature of the digital environment would render traditional lawmakers powerless, and would empower the community within cyberspace to elect its own lawmakers and to design its own laws tailored to that environment. Others disagreed, and for a period of time the argument was not about which laws should be applied in the digital environment: it was more simply could we regulate the actions of individuals in the digital environment at all?

[1] In January 2012 the Dutch Supreme Court (Hoge Raad) ruled that theft of a virtual amulet and mask in the online game *Runescape* could be regarded as 'goods' in Dutch law and are susceptible to theft. LJN: BQ9251, Hoge Raad, 10/00101 J.

[2] This question will be discussed in depth in ch. 14.

4.1 **Can we regulate the digital environment?**

4.1.1 **Cyberlibertarianism**

On 8 February 1996 John Perry Barlow published his declaration that cyberspace was a separate sovereign space where real-world laws and real-world governments were of little or no effect.[3] His 'Declaration of the Independence of Cyberspace' was a powerful challenge to lawmakers and law enforcement bodies.

Highlight Barlow's 'Declaration of the Independence of Cyberspace'

Weary giants of flesh and steel you are not welcome among us and have no sovereignty where we gather . . . You have no moral right to rule us nor do you possess any methods of enforcement we have true reason to fear.

The final part of this sentence sets out one of the key supports utilized by the school of thought that was soon to become known as cyberlibertarianism. They believed that as states may only enforce their laws within the confines of their jurisdiction, subject of course to a few specialized examples of extraterritorial effect,[4] when a citizen of a real-world jurisdiction, such as England and Wales, enters cyberspace they cross a virtual border to a new sovereign state where the laws of the old state they left are no longer legitimate or valid. Further, because this person is in a virtual (digital) environment, they have no corporeal body to imprison and any digital goods they own are in limitless supply, meaning that the sequestration of goods is an impractical method of punishment. This led to the belief, as expressed by Barlow, that traditional lawmakers could not enforce their laws against citizens of cyberspace.

There is an obvious weakness in this argument. When one visits cyberspace one does not travel to that place. Unlike the imaginary worlds of childhood fantasy, such as Narnia or Alice's Wonderland, cyberspace is not somewhere to which we are physically transported. This means that if an individual were to engage in illegal or antisocial behaviour online, their corporeal body (and all the assets owned by that individual) remains at all times subject to the direct regulation of the state in which they are resident at that time.[5] Thus a UK citizen who visits online paedophilic communities to engage in the trading and viewing of child-abuse images remains at risk of apprehension and prosecution in the UK as their corporeal body is at all times subject to the actions of UK law enforcement authorities.[6] This belies Barlow's claim that traditional lawmaking and

[3] JP Barlow, 'A Declaration of the Independence of Cyberspace' <http://homes.eff.org/~barlow/Declaration-Final.html>.

[4] For example s. 72 of the Criminal Justice and Immigration Act 2008 gives courts in the UK jurisdiction to prosecute UK nationals and residents who commit sex offences against children abroad. This law applies even where the person in question was not a UK national or resident at the time of the offence but has subsequently become one.

[5] Or the state in which the assets are to be found.

[6] As has been demonstrated on many occasions: see e.g. *R v Fellows & Arnold* [1997] 2 All ER 548; *R v Bowden* [2001] QB 88; *Atkins v Director of Public Prosecutions* [2000] 1 WLR 1427; or *R v Smith & Jayson* [2002] EWCA Crim 683.

enforcement bodies 'do not possess any methods of enforcement we have true reason to fear' and led to a number of responses indicating that there is nothing about the nature of the digital environment which naturally protects individuals from the controls of real-world lawmakers and law enforcement authorities. Professor Chris Reed calls this cyberlibertarian environmental argument 'the Cyberspace fallacy',[7] pointing out that:

> [this] states that the Internet is a new jurisdiction, in which none of the existing rules and regulations apply. This jurisdiction has no physical existence; it is a virtual space which expands and contracts as the different networks and computers, which collectively make up the Internet, connect to and disconnect from each other . . . A moment's thought reveals the fallacy. All the actors involved in an Internet transaction have a real-world existence, and are located in one or more legal jurisdictions . . . It is inconceivable that a real-world jurisdiction would deny that its laws potentially applied to the transaction.[8]

As Reed goes on to demonstrate, wherever traditional law enforcement bodies have faced the challenge of cross-border trade or harm, the ordinary rules of private international law, jurisdiction, and choice of law have proven effective in identifying the correct forum and legal rules to apply.

The lack of physicality found in the digital environment forms only part of the cyberlibertarian school of thought. The other key support, alluded to in Professor Reed's response, is that real-world law enforcement bodies lack legitimacy to interfere in the operations of 'Sovereign Cyberspace'. This is predicated upon the twin beliefs that there is a border between real space and cyberspace, a border not dissimilar to that which we find between jurisdictions in real space, and that once one crosses this border into cyberspace, one may move freely about in 'Sovereign Cyberspace' without barrier or challenge. In other words the cyberlibertarian school believed that cyberspace was a separate state, although not physically.

This concept is most fully explored in the ground-breaking work of two US law professors, David Johnson and David Post, who in May 1996 published their highly influential paper 'Law and Borders: The Rise of Law in Cyberspace'.[9] In this paper they set out fully, and for the first time, a legal interpretation of the cyberlibertarian contention that regulation founded upon traditional state sovereignty cannot function effectively in cyberspace. They argued that, as individuals in cyberspace may move seamlessly between zones governed by differing regulatory regimes in accordance with their personal preferences, it was impossible to regulate the activities of these individuals effectively.

Example Obscenity

Leo is a UK resident who wishes to access and download pornographic images which are in breach of the Obscene Publications Acts. Although illegal in the UK, these images may be legal in the US. Leo therefore may access material hosted in the US and view it on his computer in the UK.

[7] C Reed, *Internet Law: Text and Materials* (2nd edn, CUP 2004).

[8] Ibid. 174–5.

[9] (1996) 48 *Stanford Law Review* 1367.

Example Contempt of court

In 2007 two men attempted to blackmail a member of the UK Royal Family. An s.11 order was granted under the Contempt of Court Act 1981, meaning it was illegal to publish the name of the person involved (it still is). Despite this, it is extremely easy for a UK resident to find the name of the person involved with a quick Google search as the name has been published online by several overseas news organizations and gossip sites which are all accessible in the UK. It would even be possible for a UK resident to publish this person's name, in breach of the Contempt of Court Act, overseas but if identified they may face prosecution.

This meant that citizens of cyberspace could engage in a practice known as regulatory arbitrage. This occurs when an individual or group may potentially be regulated by a number of alternative regulatory bodies and is offered the opportunity to choose by which one to be regulated. The individual then arbitrages (or plays off) these regulators against each other to seek the best regulatory settlement for the individual.[10] In our obscene publications example our UK resident in the real world is directly regulated by the UK border and police forces. There is no opportunity to arbitrage their regulation (in enforcing the Obscene Publications Acts) against anyone else without leaving the jurisdiction of the UK courts. But in cyberspace he or she may seek the shelter of the US regulatory authorities by sourcing their pornographic content from US-based web servers. Technically the UK resident remains in breach of s. 42 of the Customs Consolidation Act 1876 which makes it an offence to import indecent or obscene prints, paintings, photographs, books, cards, lithographic or other engravings, or any other indecent or obscene articles. But with surveys reporting that 15 per cent of UK adults regularly visit pornographic websites, and 41 per cent occasionally do so,[11] it is clear the authorities simply do not have the resources to prosecute such a mass programme of disobedience. This is demonstrated by the fact that to date there have been no prosecutions in England and Wales under either the Customs Consolidation Act or the Obscene Publications Act 1959 for privately viewing obscene material using an internet connection. Thus the UK resident can safely arbitrage the UK regulatory framework of the Obscene Publications Acts and the Customs Consolidation Act for the US regulatory framework which has protection from the US First Amendment.[12] This allows, at least in cyberlibertarian theory, the citizen of cyberspace to choose a different regulatory regime from that which regulates his or her activities in real space, undermining the effectiveness of traditional law-making processes and law enforcement institutions. Accordingly, the only effective 'Law of Cyberspace' would largely be determined by a free market in regulation in which network users would be able to choose those rule sets they found most congenial. Johnson and Post maintained that the various dimensions of inter-networking could be governed by 'decentralised, emergent law' wherein

[10] See AM Froomkin, 'The Internet as a Source of Regulatory Arbitrage' in B Kahin and C Nesson (eds.) *Borders in Cyberspace* (MIT Press 1997).

[11] J Mann, 'British sex survey 2014: "the nation has lost some of its sexual swagger"' *The Observer* (London, 28 September 2014) <http://www.theguardian.com/lifeandstyle/2014/sep/28/british-sex-survey-2014-nation-lost-sexual-swagger>.

[12] *Reno v ACLU*, 521 US 844 (1997).

customary and privately produced laws, or rules, would be produced by decentralized collective action leading to the emergence of common standards for mutual coordination.[13] In other words, they believed that the decentralized and incorporeal nature of cyberspace meant that the only possible regulatory system was one which developed organically with the consent of the majority of the citizens of cyberspace.[14]

Cyberlibertarianism is clearly attractive for internet users. It suggests the development of new internet-only laws designed to reflect the values of the community of internet users and separate from the old world values of state-based lawmakers. Thus we could imagine copyright evolving to allow a private-use copying right which would allow individuals to make and share in a domestic setting multiple copies of files on several devices, rather than the narrower provision of s. 25B of the Copyright, Designs and Patents Act 1988 or, as appears to be the de facto position, a relaxation of indecency laws to allow for far greater distribution of adult content. There are though clearly problems with such an approach. The first is who makes up the community of internet users, and who is authorized to speak for them?

The problem that the cyberlibertarians had to address was that there is no homogenous community of internet users; instead in cyberspace there are a series of heterogeneous communities with few shared values. This problem was highlighted by Professor Cass Sunstein in his book *Republic.com* where he suggested that the nature of the internet was to isolate individuals behind filters and screens rather than to provide for community building and democratic discourse.[15] Sunstein suggested that while a well-functioning system of deliberative democracy requires a certain degree of information so that citizens can engage in monitoring and deliberative tasks,[16] the ability to filter information offered by digital technologies interferes with the flow of this information in two ways. The first is that the user may simply choose not to receive some of this information by using filters to ensure they only receive information of interest to them. As such, there is no homogeneity of information across the macro community of users of the internet, making truly deliberative democratic discourse impossible. Further, Sunstein recognized that with the advent of internet communications it becomes easier to locate like-minded individuals whatever one's shared interests may be. This creates in Sunstein's words 'fringe communities that have a common ideology but are dispersed geographically'.[17] In turn, this leads to community fragmentation. There is little in the way of common experience and knowledge among the larger macro community of internet users. As Sunstein quickly demonstrated, there can be no cyberlibertarian ideal of a 'decentralised, emergent law' as decentralized collective action is highly unlikely to lead to the emergence of common standards for mutual coordination in the highly decentred and filtered environment of cyberspace.

[13] This notion parallels the concept of polycentric or non-statist law. See T Bell, 'Polycentric Law' (1991/2) 7(1) *Humane Studies Review* 4; T Bell, 'Polycentric Law in the New Millennium' paper presented at the Mont Pelerin Society, 1998 Golden Anniversary Meeting, at Alexandria Virginia <http://www.tomwbell.com/writings/FAH.html>.

[14] Johnson and Post (n. 9). See also D Johnson and D Post, 'The New "Civic Virtue" of the Internet: A Complex Systems Model for the Governance of Cyberspace' in CM Firestone (ed.) *The Emerging Internet* (ARIIS 1998).

[15] C Sunstein, *Republic.com 2.0* (Princeton UP 2007). See also on this theme E Pariser, *The Filter Bubble: What the Internet Is Hiding from You* (Penguin 2011); S Turkle, *Alone Together* (Basic Books 2011).

[16] Sunstein (n. 15) 196.

[17] Ibid. 53.

If Sunstein was correct this meant that cyberspace lacked the necessary homogeneity to achieve the necessary levels of internal democratic discourse needed for the creation of cyberspace law and as a result the internet could not be effectively regulated from within. But, as Post and Johnson had demonstrated, attempts to impose external regulatory settlements in cyberspace would be equally ineffectual due to the effects of regulatory arbitrage and a lack of physical borders. This suggested an impasse. There had to be a legal framework which could be utilized in the online environment for it to flourish as a place to do business; further, there had to be a way to regulate and eliminate antisocial and anti-market activities such as the trade in pornography and copyright-infringing digital media files.[18] Fortunately Professor Sunstein was not the only theorist who had taken issue with the cyberlibertarian approach.

4.1.2 **Cyberpaternalism**

A new school of thought was developing; one which did not believe cyberspace was immune from regulatory intervention by real-world regulators. One of the strongest early critics of the cyberlibertarian position was Joel Reidenberg of Fordham Law School. Despite sympathizing with the cyberlibertarian view that the internet leads to the disintegration of territorial borders as the foundation for regulatory governance, Reidenberg argued that new models and sources of rules were being created in their place. He identified two new regulatory borders arising from new rule-making processes involving states, the private sector, technical interests, and citizens. He believed the first set of these was made up of the contractual agreements among various Internet Service Providers. The second was to be found in the network architecture. The key to Reidenberg's analysis was this second border; the new geography of the internet which, unlike the geography of the natural world, was man-made and in our control.

Reidenberg claimed that technical standards could function like geographical borders as they establish default boundary rules that impose order in network environments. Using the network architecture as a proxy for regulatory architecture Reidenberg suggested a new way of looking at control and regulation in the online environment, a conceptualization he called '*Lex Informatica*'.[19] This draws upon the principle of *Lex Mercatoria* and refers to the 'laws' imposed on network users by technological capabilities and system design choices. Reidenberg asserted that, whereas political governance processes usually establish the substantive laws of nation states, in *Lex Informatica* the primary sources of default rule-making are the technology developer(s) and the social processes through which customary uses of the technology evolve.[20] To this end, he

[18] Note: I have not forgotten Professor Reed's point that the corpus of the individual user of online services remains subject to the direct control of the state where the individual is resident. Directly harmful activities such as the trade in child pornography will be directly regulated in this fashion. What is in issue here is more generally harmful or antisocial behaviour which is being engaged upon by a large number of users of online services and for whom direct legal regulation through the courts would be impracticable due to the large numbers of persons involved.

[19] J Reidenberg, 'Governing Networks and Rule-Making in Cyberspace' (1996) 45 *Emory Law Journal* 911; J Reidenberg, 'Lex Informatica: The Formation of Information Policy Rules through Technology' (1998) 76 *Texas Law Review* 553.

[20] On the role of software designers in default rule making see P Quintas, 'Software by Design' in R Mansell and R Silverstone (eds.) *Communication by Design: The Politics of Information and Communication Technologies* (OUP 1998).

argued that, rather than being inherently unregulable due to its design or architecture, the internet is in fact closely regulated by its architecture.

Reidenberg contended that in the light of *Lex Informatica's* dependence on design choices, the attributes of public oversight associated with regulatory regimes could be maintained by shifting the focus of government actions away from direct regulation of cyberspace, towards influencing changes to its architecture. Reidenberg's concept of regulatory control being implemented through the control mechanisms already in place in the network architecture led to development of the new cyberpaternalist school. This new school viewed legal controls as merely part of the network of effective regulatory controls in the online environment and suggested that lawmakers seeking to control the online activities of their citizens would seek to control these activities indirectly by mandating changes to the network architecture, or by supporting self-regulatory activities of network designers. This idea was most fully developed and explained by Professor Lawrence Lessig in his classic text *Code and Other Laws of Cyberspace.*[21] Lessig contends that there are four 'Modalities of Regulation' which may be used individually or collectively, either directly or indirectly, by regulators to control the actions of individuals offline or online.[22] Further, Lessig suggests that Johnson and Post were wrong to suggest that regulatory arbitrage must undermine any attempt to regulate the activities of individuals online as regulators draw their legitimacy from the community they represent (and regulate) and as individuals we are therefore tied to the regulator in a way which Johnson and Post fail to recognize. As Lessig says:

> Even if we could construct cyberspace on the model of the market there are strong reasons not to. As life moves online, and more and more citizens from states X, Y and Z come to interact in cyberspaces A, B and C, these cyberspaces may well need to develop the kind of responsibility and attention that develops (ideally) within a democracy. Or, put differently, if cyberspace wants to be considered its own legitimate sovereign, and thus deserving of some measure of independence and respect, it must become more clearly a citizen sovereignty.[23]

Thus Johnson and Post's position that regulatory arbitrage, coupled with a physical border between real space and cyberspace, must lead to the development of a distinct and separate body of law for cyberspace is, in Lessig's view, tautologous. By attempting to reject real-world regulation, citizens within cyberspace undermine the possibility of competing with real-world regulators, recognizing the independence of cyberspace as a sovereign space, meaning that attempts to develop a separate set of principles for cyberspace will fail. For Lessig the key to regulating all activity, whether it happens to be in the online or the offline environment is to be found in his four modalities of regulation: (1) laws, (2) markets, (3) architecture, and (4) norms. Lessig believes that regulators may, by using carefully selected hybrids of the four, achieve whatever regulatory outcome they desire. If Lessig is correct, there is no doubt that we can regulate the digital environment and the cyberlibertarians were mistaken in their claims to the contrary.

[21] L Lessig, *Code and Other Laws of Cyberspace* (Basic Books 1999).
[22] Ibid. 88ff.
[23] L Lessig, *Code Version 2.0* (Basic Books 2006) 290.

4.2 Lawrence Lessig's modalities of regulation

Lawrence Lessig asked us to reconsider how one is regulated on a day-to-day basis. Although the law may say it is illegal to steal, it is not usually the legal imperative that prevents most of us from stealing; rather, the majority of people do not steal because they do not want to steal in the first place. We do not steal, not because we fear imprisonment but because we have been morally conditioned to accept that theft is a morally reprehensible act. Lessig concluded that four factors, or modalities, control the activities of individuals and each of these modalities functions by acting as a constraint on the choices of actions that individuals have. Thus law constrains through the threat of punishment; social norms constrain through the application of societal sanctions, such as criticism or ostracism; the market constrains through price and price-related signals; and architecture physically constrains (examples include the locked door and the concrete parking bollard). To demonstrate how these four modalities function collectively on the choice of actions for an individual, Lessig had us imagine a 'pathetic dot' which represents the individual and then graphically represented the four modalities as external forces which act upon that dot in control of its actions. This is seen in Figure 4.1.

Figure 4.1 Lessig's modalities in action

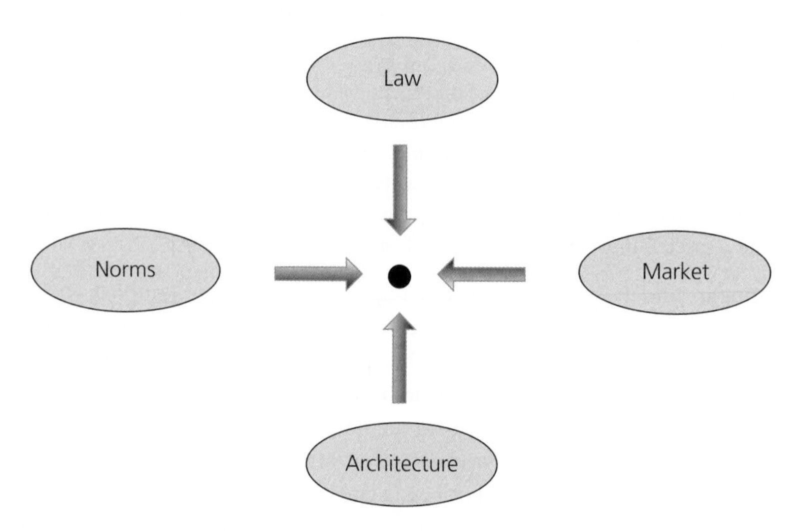

Source: Lawrence Lessig CC: BY: SA

Lessig demonstrated how these modalities function by using examples such as the regulation of smoking,[24] the supply of illegal drugs,[25] or the right of a woman to choose to have an abortion.[26] A further contemporary example, perfect for a discussion of digital property rights, may be found in regulating the illegal secondary market for copyright-infringing MP3 music files. It is clear that in the UK anyone who makes a copy of a copyright protected MP3 music file without the consent of the copyright holder commits an

[24] Ibid. 122–3.
[25] Ibid. 131.
[26] Ibid. 132.

infringement of that copyright.[27] Further anyone who makes a copy of an MP3 file with the intent to sell or hire that copy or distribute it in the course of business commits a criminal offence.[28] Thus the legal controls on copyright infringement are clear. The law states that one cannot make and/or distribute a copy of a protected work in the UK without facing civil, or possibly even criminal, sanctions. To use the language of Lawrence Lessig, the modality of law has been employed to prevent this activity. Yet it appears that the application of the law in this area is of little impact as individuals continue to download and share music using illegal sources. This failure of the law to control individuals is the failure that was predicted by the cyberlibertarian movement. Individuals use the network to evade legal controls and do so by using tools such as BitTorrent.[29] But this does not mean that the MP3 market is not subject to control. For while the direct effects of the law may be failing, the other modalities provide an alternative means of regulation.

The second of Lessig's modalities is markets and here the first successful regulatory intervention may be seen. With the success of technologies such as the iPod and its sister product iTunes, Apple pioneered the technology for online MP3 sales. This market has now massively expanded with a variety of services offering the opportunity to buy or stream an MP3 track or album legally. As the costs of these competing services have fallen we see the market for legal music services appears to be growing faster than for illegal services in the UK.[30] Where the legal control failed to have impact we find that a market solution seems to be having effect. This is exactly as Lessig predicted. In the digital environment, while the effect of direct legal controls is often diluted by a remoteness from the law enforcement authority and by a lack of border controls, other modalities are strengthened, including market modalities which benefit from greater transparency and speed of information.

The MP3 music market also demonstrates something else about the way Lessig's modalities function in the digital environment. It might be assumed that the most effective way to prevent illegal file-sharing is to adjust the architecture of the digital files which carry the music to make illegal sharing of them impossible. This is the industry solution predicted by Lessig. Like Reidenberg, he saw our ability to manipulate the network architecture as the most obvious development in cyber-regulation. Where laws failed to have effect he believed industry would turn more to architectural or design-based modalities: 'We can build, or architect, or code cyberspace to protect values that we believe are fundamental. Or we can build, or architect, or code cyberspace to allow those values to disappear. There is no middle ground. There is no choice that does not include some kind of building.'[31]

[27] CDPA 1998, s. 17.

[28] CDPA 1998, s. 107.

[29] While historically the copyright industries have had some success in litigating against file-sharing technologies such as Napster (*A&M Records Inc. v Napster*, 239 F. 3d 1004 (9th Cir. 2001)) and Grokster/Kazaa (*MGM Studios Inc. v Grokster Ltd*, 545 US 913 (2005)), the completely decentralized nature of BitTorrent has proved a challenging proposition for real-world laws. Despite the recent success of the copyright industry cases such as *Sweden v Neij & Ors* (the Pirate Bay case), Svea Hovrätt, No. B 4041–09, 26 November 2011 and *Twentieth Century Fox & Ors v Sky & Ors* [2015] EWHC 1082 (Ch) (Popcorn Time), both the Pirate Bay and Popcorn Time remain in operation and may still be accessed from within the UK.

[30] The 2014 BPI report shows that streamed and digitally downloaded music now contributes 51.25 per cent of all music sales in the UK while sales held up overall with only a 1.6 per cent fall to £1.03bn. See S Dredge, 'UK music streams doubled in 2014 as digital revenues overtook physical sales' (*Music Ally*, 1 January 2015) <http://musically.com/2015/01/01/uk-music-streams-2014-digital>.

[31] Lessig (n. 23) 6.

In the case of MP3s the music industry did just as Lessig predicted. They began to design a suite of Digital Rights Management software (DRM) and began to place it on their digital music released on CD. Some of the more famous include Cactus Data Shield used by BMG and Universal Music, Sony Extended Copy Protection, and, most famous of all, Apple's FairPlay used on iTunes products. These systems were reinforced by strong legal provisions promulgated by the World Intellectual Property Organization[32] and which once implemented in leading markets made it illegal to remove or reverse engineer the DRM protection in the US[33] and in the European Union.[34] What has happened to all these DRM systems? Cactus Data Shield (CDS) became embroiled in controversy as discs containing the CDS software would not play on non-Windows operating systems, nor on game systems such as the Xbox or the Playstation 2 or on older CD players which played protected discs with audible errors. As a result, discs released with CDS often had to be reissued in a non-protected format rendering the DRM protection valueless. CDS was quietly withdrawn in 2006 and no new discs or downloads have been issued with CDS since. The story of Sony's Extended Copy Protection (XCP) system is even more telling. In 2005 Sony released 52 titles with XCP protection. It quickly became apparent that the XCP system installed a rootkit—a piece of software installed without permission on the user's computer which can take control of hardware settings—and that due to a design flaw in this the software created security holes which could be exploited by malicious software such as worms or viruses. Within 15 days of the flaw being discovered Sony announced that it was backing out of its copy-protection software, recalling unsold CDs from all stores, and offering consumers the chance to exchange their CDs for versions lacking the software. Finally, Apple FairPlay—it is by far the most enduring and successful DRM. It was designed originally to ensure people did not swap purchased music across Apple music devices. FairPlay encrypted audio tracks could be copied to any number of Apple portable music players; however, each player could only have tracks from a maximum of five different iTunes accounts, and in addition the track could only be played on up to five authorized computers simultaneously.[35] Although it seems at first glance that the main beneficiary of FairPlay is Apple itself (it protects the iTunes market and makes the iPod/iTunes partnership irresistible) it appears Apple were forced into FairPlay by the music industry. Following a plea from Steve Jobs, then CEO of Apple Inc., to the music industry,[36] it was announced on 6 April

[32] Arts. 11 & 18 of the WIPO Copyright Treaty of 1996.

[33] §103 of the Digital Millennium Copyright Act 1998 (17 USC §1201(a)(1)).

[34] Art. 6 of the Directive on Harmonisation of Certain Aspects of Copyright and Related Rights in the Information Society (Dir. 2001/29/EC). In the UK this has been given effect in the Copyright and Related Rights Regulations 2003 (SI 2003/2498).

[35] Careful readers may have noticed I refer to FairPlay in both the past and current tenses. This is because while DRM protection has been removed from all music sold via the iTunes store it remains in use on movies, TV programmes, and books.

[36] On 6 February 2007, Steve Jobs published an open letter entitled *Thoughts on Music* calling on the big four music companies to sell their music without DRM. According to Jobs, Apple did not want to use DRM but was forced by the four major music labels with whom Apple negotiates contracts for iTunes. Jobs's main points were: (1) DRM has never and will never be perfect. Hackers will always find a method to break DRM; (2) DRM restrictions only hurt people using music legally. Illegal users aren't affected by DRM; (3) the restrictions of DRM encourage users to obtain unrestricted music which is usually only possible via illegal methods; and (4) the vast majority of music is sold without DRM via CDs, which has proven successful (see Steve Jobs, *Thoughts on Music* 6 February 2007 <http://www.apple.com/uk/hotnews/thoughtsonmusic/>).

2007 that Apple had reached agreement with EMI to make its music available DRM free, while on 6 January 2009 a further announcement made at the Macworld Conference and Expo revealed that from that date all music (but not other content) on iTunes would be DRM free.

All attempts to use design modalities to engineer music files which could not be copied have failed. Nearly all music available today, whether it is in MP3 format or encoded onto a CD, comes free of DRM technology. The provisions of the WIPO treaties, the Digital Millennium Copyright Act, and the Copyright and Related Rights in the Information Society Directive, look dated and irrelevant in the modern digital age, but why? Why, if DRMs are the most effective and efficient way to protect against illegal file-sharing, have they failed to take effect? Surely if Lessig is right and we have to choose to 'build, or architect, or code cyberspace to protect values that we believe are fundamental . . . [or to] build, or architect, or code cyberspace to allow those values to disappear' we cannot end up with the scenario where all the built or architected changes are removed (or, to stick to the building metaphor, are demolished and the environment returned to open plain). Surely if we are all just pathetic dots the industry would have forced its DRM technology on us; after all, as Lessig says, 'Thus, four constraints regulate this pathetic dot—the law, social norms, the market, and architecture—and the "regulation" of this dot is the sum of these four constraints.'[37]

4.3 **Network communitarianism**

The reason for the failure of DRM systems in commercial music releases is explained by a new school of thought which has developed in the last few years. While cyberlibertarians believed the architecture of the network protected individuals from the attentions of real-world regulators, and cyberpaternalists believed rather the opposite, this new school of thought sees the relationship between the digital environment and the real world as a rather more fluid affair. This new school of thought is the network communitarian school.

Unlike cyberlibertarianism and cyberpaternalism this developed in Europe with much of the early work taking place in the UK. I am the main proponent of network communitarianism and in my book *The Regulation of Cyberspace* I set out a model of network communitarian thought.[38] I believe that the cyberpaternalist model fails to account for the complexities of information flows found in a modern telecommunications/media system such as the internet. The main influences on network communitarianism are two European schools of thought which have yet to translate fully to the US, and which have therefore not influenced either cyberlibertarianism or cyberpaternalism. These are Actor Network Theory (ANT), developed in Paris in the 1980s by Michel Callon and Bruno Latour, and Social Systems Theory (SST), developed in Germany by Niklaus Luhmann and Gunther Teubner.

ANT is a theory of social transactions which accepts a role for non-human actors in any social situation. Thus, in a transaction between two individuals in a restaurant, their transaction is also affected by the restaurant itself: one would expect a different

[37] Lessig (n. 23) 123.
[38] A Murray, *The Regulation of Cyberspace: Control in the Online Environment* (Routledge 2007).

transaction in a luxury Michelin-starred restaurant than in a local café bar. The difference is not so much the surroundings themselves but the semiotic, or concepts, which the human actors have communicated to them through memory, experience, and surroundings.[39] A key concept of ANT is that social communications are made up of parallel transactions between the material (things) and semiotic (concepts) which together form a single network. This has the potential to be particularly powerful when applied to the internet. The internet is the largest person-to-person communication network yet designed. It allows individuals to move social transactions in space and time and it allows transactions between people with shared experiences who are geographically remote and between people with no common history who are geographically close.[40] The potential for new networks to form, dissolve, and reform on the internet is massive, leading one to reconceptualize the internet not merely as a communications/media tool but as a cultural/social tool.[41]

SST shares some roots with ANT but is quite distinct. SST attempts to explain and study the flow of information within increasingly complex systems of social communication. Luhmann attempts to explain how communications affect social transactions by defining social systems as systems of communication, and society as the most encompassing social system. A system is defined by a boundary between itself and its surrounding environment, dividing it from the infinitely complex, or chaotic, exterior.[42] The interior of the system is thus a zone of reduced complexity: communication within a system operates by selecting only a limited amount of all information available outside. This process is also called reduction of complexity. The criterion according to which information is selected and processed is meaning.[43] Like ANT, SST is an attempt to map and study the complex process of social interactions in the increasingly complex and connected environment of modern society. Whereas ANT is about the evolution and formation of networks, SST is about the filtering of information flows in the decision-making process and the communication of ideas and concepts between systems.

Although these theories are quite distinct when taken together they can illuminate much of our understanding of communications and social interaction in a networked environment such as the internet with a variety of actors, both human and non-human.[44]

[39] This is a woefully inadequate description of ANT which is extremely complex, rich, and valuable. Students interested in embarking on a study of ANT should start with B Latour, *Reassembling the Social: An Introduction to Actor-network-theory* (OUP 2007).

[40] And obviously between people geographically remote and also with no common history.

[41] This is actually well-worn ground in the field of communications and media studies although it seems quite alien to many lawyers and regulators. See e.g. M Castells, *The Internet Galaxy* (OUP 2001) or R Mansell, *Imagining the Internet: Communication, Innovation, and Governance* (OUP 2012).

[42] Thus a system may be the legal system where lawyers practise their trade and give advice against the background of the corpus of law. Lawyers may be asked 'is it legal to use offshore tax systems to process the profits of a particular transaction?' they will not be asked 'is it moral?' or is it 'socially harmful?' These are questions for, respectively, theologians (or philosophers) and politicians. Thus in the internal language of the legal profession the question is binary legal or illegal, rather than multifaceted in the wider system of society at large.

[43] As with ANT, this is a woefully inadequate description of SST which is extremely complex, rich, and valuable. Students interested in embarking on a study of SST should start with H Moeller, *Luhmann Explained* (Open Court 2006). Law students may then be interested in N Luhmann, *Law as a Social System* (OUP 2008).

[44] For a fascinating attempt to fuse the two together read G Teubner, 'Rights of Non-humans? Electronic Agents and Animals as New Actors in Politics and Law' (2006) 33 *Journal of Law and Society* 497.

This is what is attempted in *The Regulation of Cyberspace*. I re-examined the classical cyberpaternalist model discussed earlier in which a pathetic dot is found to reside among four regulatory modalities which act as a constraint on the choice of actions of that 'dot' and found that in applying the principles of ANT and SST we can consider the 'dot' rather differently. The dot is in ANT terms a material node in the network, while in SST terms is part of a system. In either term the dot is not isolated; it forms part of a matrix of dots or, to put it another way, the dot, which is designed to represent the individual, must always be considered to be part of the wider community and it is here that traditional cyberpaternalism runs into difficulty, for when one examines the modalities of regulation proposed by Lessig we find that of the four, three of them—laws, norms, and markets—are in fact a proxy for community-based control. Laws are passed by lawmakers elected by the community;[45] markets are merely a reflection of value, demand, supply, and scarcity as reflected by the community in monetary terms; and norms are merely the codification of community values. I recognized that these 'socially mediated modalities'[46] reflected an active role for the 'dot' in the regulatory process; far from being a 'pathetic dot' which was the subject of external regulatory forces, the dot was in fact an 'active dot' taking part in the regulatory process.[47] I believe there are two key distinctions between the classic cyberpaternalist model and the new network communitarian model. The first is to replace the isolated pathetic dot with a networked community (or matrix) of dots which share ideas, beliefs, ideals, and opinions (see Figure 4.2).

Figure 4.2 From the pathetic dot to the active dot matrix

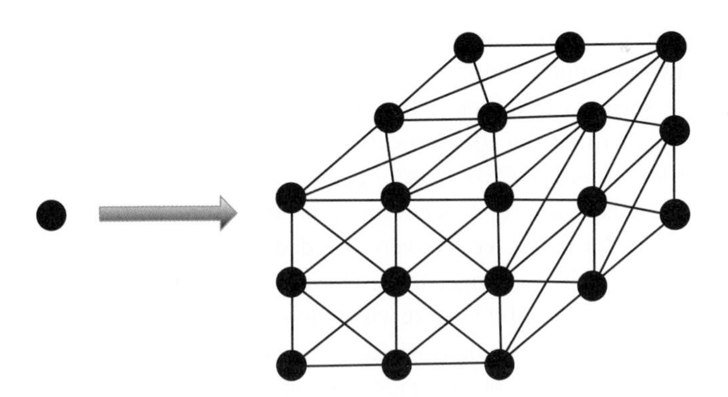

The second is to recognize that the regulatory modalities draw their legitimacy from, and are accountable to, the community (or matrix of dots), meaning the regulatory process is in nature a dialogue not an externally imposed set of constraints, as illustrated in Figure 4.3.

[45] At least in democratic representative politics as found in the UK. In the UK we may view the rights of MPs (our representatives) to make laws as being power drawn from the community at large as part of our social contract between the state and citizen. See J Rousseau, *The Social Contract* (1762, tr. M Cranston, 2004).

[46] Murray (n. 38) 37.

[47] Ibid. ch. 8.

Figure 4.3 The regulatory discourse

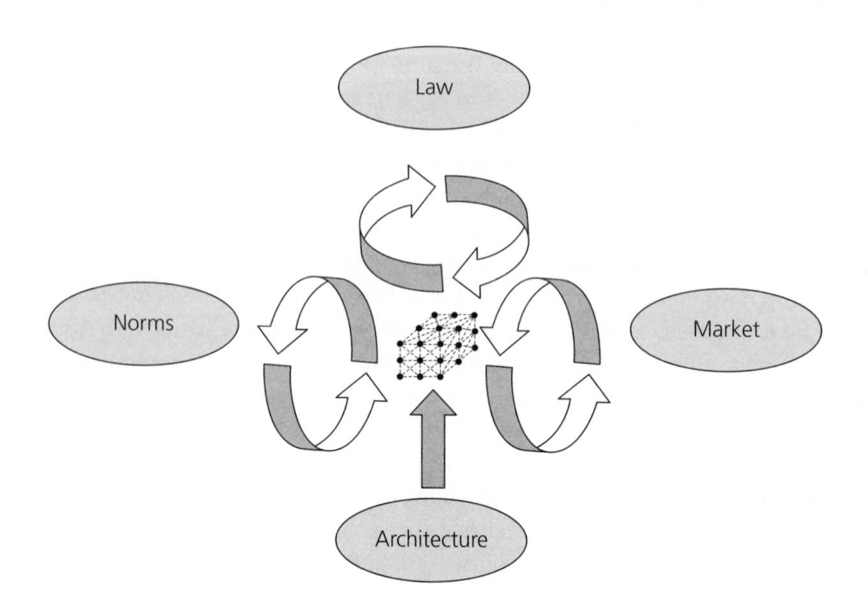

What does this mean for our understanding of internet regulation? First, it suggests that regulation in the online environment is little different to regulation in the real world. Regulation is a process of discourse and dialogue between the individual and society. Sometimes society, either directly through the application of norms, or indirectly by distilling its opinions, norms, or standards down to laws, wishes to force a change in behaviour of the individual.[48] But, sometimes it is the regulatory settlement itself which is challenged by society when there is no longer any support for it. This is most clearly illustrated by the fact that the UK enforcement authorities have declined to prosecute individuals under either the Customs Consolidation Act or the Obscene Publications Act 1959 for privately viewing obscene material using an internet connection. We, the community of dots, have collectively decided that the viewing of pornography by internet connection is no longer to be viewed as morally objectionable and have communicated this decision by both driving the market for material of this type and by communicating to our lawmakers where a line is to be drawn. We wish to sanction and criminalize those who possess or trade in images of child abuse (including pseudo-images) and those who possess or trade in images of sexual violence, harm, bestiality, and necrophilia and to prevent the spread of so-called 'revenge porn'.[49] Thus the regulatory settlement is not imposed upon us—if it were, we would all avoid the viewing of

[48] A good current example of such a change is s. 63 of the Criminal Justice and Immigration Act 2008 (as amended) which makes it an offence to possess 'extreme pornographic images'. These are images of sexual violence (including rape), bestiality, and necrophilia. This is society in the UK setting a limit on the free availability of pornographic images in the online environment. We cannot prevent pornography from entering the UK but we can criminalize the most offensive varieties of pornography to stifle demand, thus also allowing the market to make the production of such material less commercially attractive.

[49] Revenge porn is criminalized by s. 33 of the Criminal Justice and Courts Act 2015.

obscene material for fear of prosecution under the Obscene Publications Acts—but is rather part of a dialogue in which the regulatory settlement evolves to reflect changes in society. This also explains why Digital Rights Management systems failed to have the desired effect. DRMs were viewed by the majority of music consumers to be an unreasonable, and sometimes damaging, restriction on their freedom to enjoy something they viewed, having paid to purchase it, as their property. When Cactus Data Shield prevented them from playing their new CD on their old CD player, or when Apple FairPlay restricted them to having five authorized computers (a potential problem in an extended family) or, worst of all, when Sony Extended Copy Protection was shown to leave their PCs vulnerable to attack, consumers reacted in the way one would expect: they collectively used their market power to respond. The industry could not force its DRM technology on us because we can withhold our market support for them. In network communitarian theory the power to determine the regulatory environment does not rest with the regulator alone.[50]

It may be suggested that network communitarianism is close to anarchy or mob rule, that the community/mob decides what is or is not acceptable and then mobilizes their social and economic power to bring about the changes desired. Such a suggestion would though ignore the subtlety of the network communitarian school. The mob is not in charge, it is not regulation by group power; rather it is regulation by consent and democracy. This is because of the nature of cyberspace itself. As demonstrated by Cass Sunstein[51] the nature of the internet is to isolate individuals behind filters and screens rather than to provide for community building and democratic discourse. There is no such thing as an 'internet community' or even a community of those who use the internet in a geographical location such as the UK. I am less likely to have something in common with my geographical next-door neighbour as with a professor of internet law in New Zealand. The key is that online we form micro-communities; small or even large groups of like-minded people, rather than macro-communities; large communities formed by geo-political connections. These micro-communities are isolated from each other by barriers which impede the flow of communication between them. The true power online is not within the community; it is at the points where communities overlap, the gates through which information flows from one community to another, as illustrated in Figure 4.4.

The points at which online networks meet or overlap are the key points where information flows from one micro-community to another. These include search engines which index community information, social network sites such as Facebook or Twitter where people exchange information in an open environment, and telecommunications networks which carry the information. These key gatekeepers have greater influence on regulatory settlements than individuals, given their unique role.[52] It therefore becomes

[50] In this final analysis network communitarianism in the internet regulation context shares core values with decentred regulation in mainstream regulatory theory. See J Black, 'Decentring Regulation: Understanding the Role of Regulation and Self-Regulation in a "Post-Regulatory" World' (2001) 54 *Current Legal Problems* 103; C Scott, 'Regulation in the Age of Governance: The Rise of the Post Regulatory State', in J Jordana and D Levi-Faur (eds.) *The Politics of Regulation: Institutions and Regulatory Reforms for the Age of Governance* (Edward Elgar 2004).

[51] See n. 15.

[52] A Murray, 'Nodes and Gravity in Virtual Space' (2011) 5 *Legisprudence* 195; E Laidlaw, 'A Framework for Identifying Internet Information Gatekeepers' (2010) 24 *International Review of Law, Computers and Technology* 263.

clear that mobs do not simply form or dissipate online; for the community to be activated it requires a considerable sense of injustice, over-regulation, or market advantage or disadvantage. For those who support network communitarianism it reflects a more realistic dynamic of the way people come together and act in the online world.

Figure 4.4 Overlapping networks

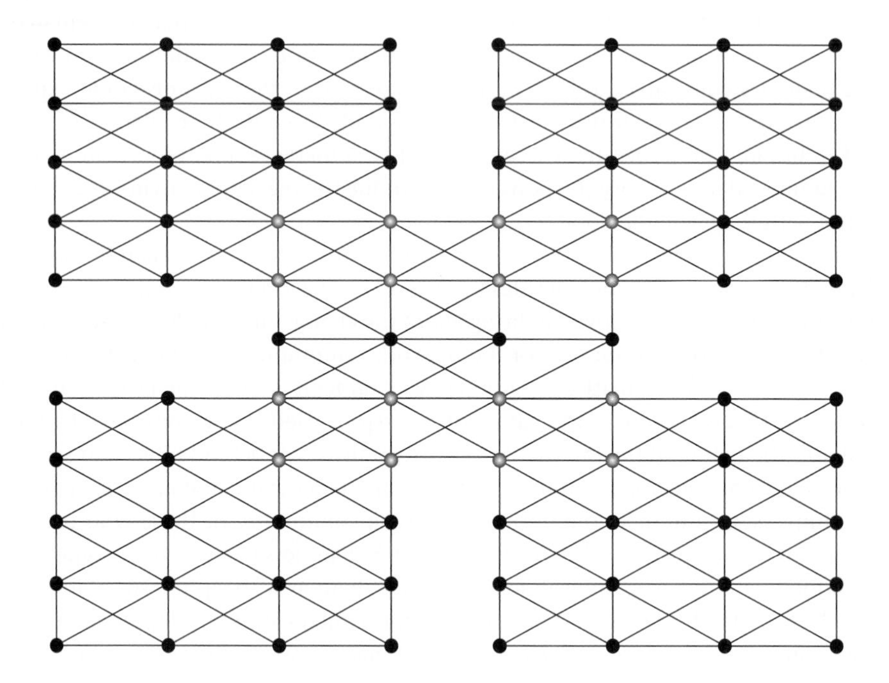

Whichever of the current schools of cyber-regulatory theory you subscribe to—cyberpaternalism or network communitarianism—one thing is clear. There is one key issue that both agree upon: that in the man-made environment of the digital sphere our ability to change the design of that place with a few well-placed keystrokes means that the use of architecture as a modality of control (that is employed by one of the other modalities as a means of enforcing their values) is increasingly in evidence and is increasingly effective. For this reason the remainder of this chapter will look at who some of the key regulators in this environment are. Who are the people with the opportunity to amend the software code of the digital environment and on which basis do they exercise their power?

4.4 **Regulators in cyberspace: private regulators**

There are a number of private regulators at work in the digital environment with the ability to regulate certain activities directly by making design changes to the environment. The first line of private regulation most internet users encounter in the UK is their internet service provider (ISP) since it is impossible for individuals to gain access to the internet without employing the services of an ISP, and as such ISPs act as gatekeepers. As a result of their role as internet information gatekeeper, ISPs have been tasked with ever-increasing regulatory roles in the UK. The most high-profile role for ISPs is their collective role in preventing access to child-abuse images and other illegal content.[53]

In an attempt to control the trade in illegal content the UK government requires ISPs to block access to sites known to contain images of child abuse but which are domiciled beyond the UK, and which are therefore out of the direct control of UK laws. This is affected by a partnership between ISPs and an industry regulatory body known as the Internet Watch Foundation (IWF). The IWF operates the UK internet 'hotline' for the public to report potentially illegal online content (that is, content portraying child abuse,[54] criminally obscene content,[55] including extreme pornography,[56] hosted in the UK, and non-photographic child sexual abuse images hosted in the UK).[57] The IWF is a private industry body which is funded by industry partners and a European Union grant. It regulates content within its remit by creating a blacklist of sites which contain illegal content. This blacklist is then distributed to all UK ISPs who are expected to block access to all sites contained on the list. The blocking of access is therefore effected by private corporations (the ISPs) at the requirement of another private corporation (the IWF), but, it is a requirement of the UK government that this private regulatory system be enforced.[58]

This was illustrated in a parliamentary written answer in 2006 when Home Office Minister Vernon Croaker noted that 'we are setting a target that by the end of 2007 all ISPs offering internet connectivity to the UK general public put in place technical measures that prevent their customers accessing websites containing illegal images of child abuse identified by the IWF'.[59] Failure to implement a private regulatory system would have led to legislation compelling ISPs to filter access. This requirement has subsequently been implemented, without the need for legislation, by all major UK commercial ISPs

[53] Laidlaw (n. 52).

[54] By s. 160 of the Criminal Justice Act 1988, as amended by the Criminal Justice and Public Order Act 1994, it is an offence for a person to have any indecent photograph or pseudo-photograph of a child in his possession. A pseudo-photograph is defined in s. 7(7) of the Protection of Children Act 1978 as 'an image, whether made by computer-graphics or otherwise howsoever, which appears to be a photograph'.

[55] By s. 2 of the Obscene Publications Act 1959 it is an offence to publish an obscene article in the UK. The definition of an obscene article is found in s. 1 and defines it as: '[where] its effect or (where the article comprises two or more distinct items) the effect of any one of its items is, if taken as a whole, such as to tend to deprave and corrupt persons who are likely, having regard to all relevant circumstances, to read, see or hear the matter contained or embodied in it'.

[56] By s. 63 of the Criminal Justice and Immigration Act 2008 it is an offence to possess an 'extreme pornographic image'. An extreme pornographic image is one which (1) is of such a nature that it must reasonably be assumed to have been produced solely or principally for the purpose of sexual arousal, (2) is grossly offensive, disgusting, or otherwise of an obscene character, and (3) portrays, in an explicit and realistic way, any of the following: (a) an act which threatens a person's life, (b) an act which results, or is likely to result, in serious injury to a person's anus, breasts, or genitals, (c) an act which involves sexual interference with a human corpse, (d) a person performing an act of intercourse or oral sex with an animal (whether dead or alive), or (e) an act which involves the non-consensual penetration of a person's vagina, anus, or mouth by another with the other person's penis or an act which involves the non-consensual sexual penetration of a person's vagina or anus by another with a part of the other person's body or anything else where a reasonable person looking at the image would think that the persons were real.

[57] By s. 62 of the Coroners and Justice Act 2009 it is an offence to possess an image of a child which is pornographic, grossly offensive, and which is not a photograph or pseudo-photograph, which either focuses solely or principally on a child's genitals or anal region or portrays any of the prohibited acts found in s. 62(7).

[58] E Laidlaw, 'The Responsibilities of Free Speech Regulators: An Analysis of the Internet Watch Foundation' (2012) 20 *International Journal of Law and Information Technology* 312.

[59] HC Deb 15 May 2006, vol. 446, col. 716W.

under a variety of names or systems. The best known of these is Cleanfeed (officially the BT anti-child-abuse initiative) developed by British Telecom and used by BT and most other major UK ISPs under licence. Cleanfeed works by filtering all user requests through an internet router which compares requests for pages against the IWF blacklist. If the requested page is blacklisted the Cleanfeed system will reroute this request to a BT proxy server which issues an error message to the customer. In theory Cleanfeed is extremely efficient. Unlike older forms of content blocking, Cleanfeed does not block entire sites, only blacklisted pages. Thus if one page on Facebook contained an indecent image Cleanfeed should only block access to that page, not the entire Facebook platform. The problem with the Cleanfeed system prior to 2013 was that internet users who attempted to access a blocked page did not receive an explanation of why that page had been blocked, they simply received an error message such as '404—page not found' or '403—forbidden'. There was no way for the consumer to differentiate between a page that you could not see because the server was overloaded or had been relocated and one that had been blocked by the IWF. This all changed in June 2013 when the UK's four leading ISPs: BT, Sky, TalkTalk, and Virgin Media, signed up to a new agreement with the IWF in the fallout from the Tia Sharp and April Jones murder cases; two tragedies in which it became apparent afterwards that the perpetrators had searched for and gained possession of a large quantity of child-abuse images. A new 'splash page' was agreed which would be displayed if customers landed on a blocked page explaining exactly why the page has been blocked.

Highlight The IWF Splash Page

Access has been denied by your internet access provider because this page may contain indecent images of children as identified by the Internet Watch Foundation.

Deliberate attempts to access this or related material may result in you committing a criminal offence.

The consequences of accessing such material are likely to be serious. People arrested risk losing their family and friends, access to children (including their own) and their jobs.

Stop it Now! can provide confidential and anonymous help to address concerning internet behaviour. They have helped thousands of people in this situation.

0808 1000 900 | help@stopitnow.org.uk | <http://www.stopitnow.org.uk>

If you think this page has been blocked in error please contact <your service provider> or visit our Content Assessment Appeal Process page.

For those wishing to address inadvertent access there is the option to add:

'If you did not intend to view this content, please close your browsers now. You can also anonymously report any potentially illegal content to the Internet Watch Foundation here.'

However, public awareness of the IWF remains low. In their 2013 annual report the IWF noted: 'ComRes, a polling and research consultancy and IWF Donor, conducted a poll of British adults in August 2013 about awareness of the IWF. It found that 19 per cent of British people said that they had heard of IWF, compared to 8 per cent who said the same in October 2012.'[60] This sounds positive but several caveats should be noted. The

[60] Internet Watch Foundation, *Annual & Charity Report 2013*, 21.

first is that the 2014 annual report does not give us an update on this figure, the second is that, as was noted in the 2013 report, this change in the public's awareness of the IWF immediately followed extensive media coverage of the Tia Sharp and April Jones murder trials, and the third is that in July 2008 the IWF had reported that 'only recently, following investment in awareness-raising campaigns, do we believe public awareness of IWF has increased to around 19 per cent'.[61] Thus after five years, extensive investment in annual public awareness days and high-profile media coverage of the IWF in both the 2013 murder trials and the 2008 Wikipedia incident (below), public awareness of the IWF and its work has not changed. More importantly 81 per cent of UK adults appear to remain blissfully unaware of the IWF, which may explain both the statement of Tim Loughton, MP for East Worthing and Shoreham, in a debate on protecting children online in June 2013, at the height of the media debate on this issue, that '[a]pparently, last year 1.5 million adults came across abusive content on the internet, but only 40,000 reports were made to IWF, which has the powers to do something about it. There needs to be much greater publicity on how to report to ensure that action can take place',[62] and the public response to the *Virgin Killer* incident of December 2008.

Case study *Virgin Killer*

In 1976, German band Scorpions released an album called *Virgin Killer*. The album has always been highly controversial as the cover art featured a naked prepubescent girl with a star of broken glass obscuring her genitals. The image has been widely circulated both offline and online for 40 years, but sometime prior to 5 December 2008 it was reported to the IWF who determined that the image was illegal as being potentially in breach of the Protection of Children Act 1978. As a result, on 5 December 2008, the IWF system started blacklisting a Wikipedia article and related image on the album. All major UK ISPs blocked access to the image and Wikipedia page.

This may have gone unnoticed as, although popular, Scorpions remain a relatively obscure band in the UK, but for the peculiarities of the Wikipedia architecture. Wikipedia has a blacklist of its own which it uses to block individuals who have vandalized entries. As traffic to sites that are on IWF's blacklist is all channelled through Cleanfeed proxy servers it appeared to Wikipedia, once the page was blocked, that all the visitors from the UK were coming from the same addresses. This block prevented UK users from editing Wikipedia pages, triggering an investigation by users and leading eventually to the discovery that IWF/Cleanfeed had blocked this page. This immediately brought the IWF to public attention.

After Wikipedia instigated an appeal, the IWF saw sense and on 9 December 2008 they removed the Wikipedia page and image from their blacklist stating that although 'the image in question is potentially in breach of the Protection of Children Act 1978 . . . the IWF Board has today (9 December 2008) considered these findings and the contextual issues involved in this specific case and, in light of the length of time the image has existed and its wide availability, the decision has been taken to remove this webpage from our list'.

[61] Internet Watch Foundation, *Memorandum submitted by the Internet Watch Foundation to the Culture, Media and Sport Committee Inquiry into harmful content on the internet and in video games* (July 2008) 25 <http://www.iwf.org.uk/accountability/consultations/culture-media-and-sport-committee>.

[62] HC Deb 12 June 2013, vol. 564, col. 379.

The Wikipedia controversy did little to change the day-to-day workings of the IWF or the functioning of Cleanfeed. Until 2013 end users were still not aware as to why access to a website had been blocked and, as the media fire surrounding the Wikipedia affair died down, the IWF went back to its day-to-day role. In fact, following the April Jones and Tia Sharp cases the IWF has had its powers strengthened,[63] again with the veiled threat of government regulation in the background.[64]

More controversially, of late the technology behind Cleanfeed has been reappointed to a new rule; policing peer-to-peer file-sharing networks. While the role that the IWF and ISPs play in blocking access to illegal materials is controversial at the least, there is no doubt that their intervention may be justified on the basis that the material in question is illegal to possess. Thus, blocking access to the material is arguably justifiable and not an unreasonable intervention with civil liberties. However, the more recent role ISPs have been asked to play with regard to P2P networks is quite different. In a series of cases which began with *Twentieth Century Fox Film Corporation & Anor v Newzbin Ltd*[65] and culminated (so far) in *Twentieth Century Fox & Orsv Sky & Ors*,[66] the High Court has awarded a series of injunctions under s. 97A of the Copyright, Designs and Patents Act 1988 which require ISPs to take measures to block or at least impede access by their customers to P2P sites using Cleanfeed and related technologies.[67] This is controversial as the blocking of P2P sites prevents not only clearly illegal activity but also may prevent individuals from engaging in lawful activity. As was pointed out by the Pirate Party UK in relation to one such case, *Dramatico Entertainment & Ors v BSkyB & Ors* (The Pirate Bay),[68] 'the Pirate Bay has substantial non-infringing uses; from the promotion of independent musicians, the distribution of independent VODO films to the distribution of free and open source software'.[69] Some have suggested that s. 97A orders are a breach of both the Art. 10 right of freedom of expression as they are restrictions not 'prescribed by law' and are contrary to Art. 15(1) of the Electronic Commerce Directive which provides that 'Member States shall not impose a general obligation on providers . . . to monitor the information which they transmit or store, nor a general obligation actively to seek facts or circumstances indicating illegal activity'.[70] Indeed there is jurisprudence from the European Court of Justice (ECJ) to suggest the latter at the very least. In the decision of the ECJ in *Scarlet Extended SA v SABAM*[71] the court found that Art. 15(1) prohibits national authorities from adopting measures which would require an ISP to carry out general monitoring of the information that it transmits on its network and

[63] T Ross, 'Internet Watch Foundation given powers to police child porn' *The Telegraph* (London, 18 June 2013) <http://www.telegraph.co.uk/news/politics/10127862/Internet-Watch-Foundation-given-powers-to-police-child-porn.html>; 'Internet Watch Foundation Given New Powers to seek Out Images of Child Abuse Online' (Carter Brown, 8 April 2014) <http://www.carterbrownexperts.co.uk/internet-watch-foundation-seek-out-images-of-abuse/>.

[64] R Cellan-Jones, 'Government demands action on web safety' (*BBC News*, 6 June 2013) <http://www.bbc.co.uk/news/technology-22794498>.

[65] [2010] EWHC 608 (Ch).

[66] [2015] EWHC 1082 (Ch).

[67] The case law will be discussed in much greater detail in ch. 11. The discussion here is a sketch of developments.

[68] [2012] EWHC 268 (Ch).

[69] Pirate Party UK, *The Pirate Party UK's Proxy for the Pirate Bay* (10 May 2012) <http://www.pirateparty.org.uk/press/releases/2012/may/10/pirate-party-uks-proxy-pirate-bay/>.

[70] Dir. 2000/31/EC.

[71] (C-70/10) [2012] ECDR 4.

struck down an order of the Belgian courts which would have Scarlet Extended (an ISP) install a filtering system for P2P communications. Both these arguments were considered by Arnold J in *Twentieth Century Fox Film Corp & Ors v British Telecommunications plc (Newzbin II)*[72] where he rejected such concerns. He found that the specific orders made by the English High Court in both *Newzbin* cases, and later confirmed in *Dramatico*,[73] did not breach Art. 15(1) as Recital 47 states clearly that 'Member States are prevented from imposing a monitoring obligation on service providers only with respect to obligations of a general nature; this does not concern monitoring obligations in a specific case and, in particular, does not affect orders by national authorities in accordance with national legislation.' Arnold J felt there was a clear distinction between *Scarlet Extended* where the court was ordering the ISP to install general filtering software and both *Newzbin II*[74] and *Dramatico*[75] where he was making a much narrower order simply to block (or impede access to) a single website. He also analysed carefully the Art. 10 argument. Again *Scarlet Extended* was at the heart of his analysis and he again felt the English cases were clearly distinguishable. He noted that the court had already engaged in a rights balancing operation; balancing the copyright holders' rights under Art. 1 of the First Protocol, noting these are 'rights of others' within Art. 10(2), with the right to free expression under Art. 10(1). He set out that he had followed the approach laid down by Lord Steyn in *Re S*[76] where a balance falls to be struck between Art. 1 of the First Protocol and Art. 10.[77] Confident that he had carried out the balancing necessary to protect Art. 10(1) rights he then considered whether *Scarlet Extended* had changed the balancing provision set out in *Re S*. He concluded it had not:

> Even if it is assumed that the Court of Justice will entirely endorse the Opinion of the Advocate General in *Scarlet v SABAM*, I consider that the present case is clearly distinguishable from that case. Quite simply, the Studios are not seeking an order that BT 'introduce, for all its customers, *in abstracto* and as a preventive measure, exclusively at the cost of that ISP and for an unlimited period, a system for filtering all electronic communications, both incoming and outgoing, passing via its services, in particular those involving the use of peer-to-peer software, in order to identify on its network the sharing of electronic files containing a musical, cinematographic or audio-visual work in respect of which the applicant claims to hold rights, and subsequently to block the transfer of such files, either at the point at which they are requested or at which they are sent'. On the contrary, the order sought by the Studios is clear and precise; it merely requires BT to implement an existing technical solution which BT already employs for a different purpose; implementing that solution is accepted by BT to be technically feasible; the cost is not suggested by BT to be excessive; and provision has been made to enable the order to be varied or discharged in the event of a future change in circumstances.[78]

Following this line of cases it has now become commonplace for copyright holders to seek blocking injunctions under s. 97A. The efficacy of such orders remains open to question. The *Dramatico* case involved well-known Torrent tracker the Pirate Bay. The day after the order was implemented it was reported that visitors to the Pirate Bay from

[72] [2011] EWHC 1981 (Ch) at [163].

[73] *Dramatico Entertainment Ltd and Ors v British Sky Broadcasting Ltd & Ors* [2012] EWHC 1152 (Ch) at [8].

[74] n. 72 at [162].

[75] n. 73 at [8].

[76] [2004] UKHL 47 at [17].

[77] n. 72 at [164].

[78] See n. 72 at [177].

the UK hit record levels as users intrigued by media coverage of the order sought to access the site and found several ways around the block. Similarly *Twentieth Century Fox & Ors v Sky & Ors*,[79] involved another popular BitTorrent file-sharing system, Popcorn Time, which continued in the short term unaffected by simply moving some of its APIs (Application Program Interfaces) to unblocked addresses and carrying on. In theory every time the copyright holders get a s. 97A order blocking any host of Popcorn Time APIs it could simply re-route and allow users to download an update.[80]

Nevertheless, s. 97A orders are now part of the regulatory landscape and the role of the ISP as gatekeeper is part of the armoury of copyright holders. Such is the effectiveness of s. 97A of the CDPA that the UK government abandoned plans to implement s. 17 of the Digital Economy Act 2010, which would have allowed the Secretary of State with the consent of the Lord Chancellor, and both Houses of Parliament, and a court of law, to block access to a location on the internet 'from which a substantial amount of material has been, is being or is likely to be made available in infringement of copyright' or a location which 'facilitates' such behaviour. The success of the s. 97A applications demonstrated a quicker and more traditional approach that would be equally effective, or perhaps ineffective.

4.5 **Regulators in cyberspace: states and supranational regulation**

Of course it is not only private regulators who can utilize the architecture of the network to regulate end users. As Lawrence Lessig demonstrated, states may use architecture-based modalities to control their citizens also. Most states use some form of filtering and/or content blocking. New Zealand, for example, filters out child-abuse images and images of bestiality in a manner similar to Cleanfeed in the UK,[81] while several other states use mandatory filtering or the operation of a state firewall to control access to content online. Probably the most famous example of this is the Chinese State firewall, colloquially known as 'The Great Firewall of China'. According to the Open Net Initiative 'China maintains one of the most pervasive and sophisticated regimes of internet filtering and information control in the world.'[82] The Great Firewall is kept constantly up to date and censors all types of comment with a particular focus on political and dissident speech. Major news organizations such as the BBC and Voice of America are blocked, along, not surprisingly, with the website of the *Epoch Times*.[83] The Ministry of Industry and Information Technology, through the state regulator, the Cyberspace Administration of China, ensures the firewall remains secure by licensing all ISPs who must hold an ICP (internet content provider) licence, as must all website operators who must display their ICP licence number at

[79] n. 66.

[80] It is to be noted that for unrelated reasons the most popular versions of Popcorn Time have closed down.

[81] New Zealand, Department of Internal Affairs, Digital Child Exploitation Filtering System: IRG briefing Document (May 2015) <https://www.dia.govt.nz/vwluResources/DCEFS_IRG-Briefing-Document-May-2015-pdf/$file/DCEFS_IRG-Briefing-Document-May-2015.pdf>.

[82] <http://opennet.net/research/profiles/china>.

[83] Ibid.

the bottom of their web page. Any Chinese web page not displaying an ICP number after a grace period must be blocked by ISPs. To continue to be licensed to operate, ISPs must ensure they comply with ministry regulations, including strict guidelines on pornography and social media[84] and cybersecurity.[85] Because of the highly restrictive nature of state-based censorship in China much has been written about it[86] and systems and tools have been developed to subvert it.[87]

Despite this focus on China it is not the only state which uses filtering and blocking tools to control citizen access to the internet. Saudi Arabia, for instance, closely controls access. The authorities use a commercially available filtering tool allied to local government employees and reporting from ordinary citizens to aid the local implementation of the filtering regime. Saudi Arabia publically acknowledges censoring morally inappropriate and religiously sensitive material.[88] Pornographic content is directly filtered by the State Internet Services Unit, while other sites are blocked upon request from government security bodies. Internet users can also request that certain sites be blocked or unblocked. In 2001 the Council of Ministers issued a resolution outlining content that internet users are prohibited from accessing and publishing. Among other things, it forbids content 'breaching public decency', material 'infringing the sanctity of Islam', and 'anything contrary to the state or its system'. The resolution also includes approval requirements for publishing on the internet and mechanical guidelines for service providers on recording and monitoring users' activities.[89] A new law, approved by the Saudi Shoura (Advisory) Council in October 2006, criminalizes the use of the internet to defame or harm individuals and the development of websites that violate Saudi laws or Islamic values or that serve terrorist organizations.[90] State-based controls such as these are not unusual. The Open Net Initiative lists substantial filtering in a number of countries ranging from Armenia to Yemen.[91]

[84] J Chin, 'China Internet Regulators Announce More Explicit Rules on Web Censorship' *The Wall Street Journal* (New York, 28 April 2015) <http://www.wsj.com/articles/chinas-internet-regulators-put-explicit-new-censorship-rules-in-place-1430233546>.

[85] P Mozur, 'New Rules in China Upset Western Tech Companies' *The New York Times* (New York, 28 January 2015) <http://www.nytimes.com/2015/01/29/technology/in-china-new-cybersecurity-rules-perturb-western-tech-companies.html>.

[86] See e.g. J Lee and C Liu, 'Forbidden City Enclosed by the Great Firewall: The Law and Power of Internet Filtering in China' (2012) 13 *Minnesota Journal of Law, Science, and Technology* 125; R Ensafi et al., 'Analyzing the Great Firewall of China Over Space and Time' (2015) *Proceedings on Privacy Enhancing Technologies* 61; U Orji, 'An Analysis of China's Regulatory Response to Cybersecurity' (2012) 18 *Computer and Telecommunications Law Review* 212.

[87] Q Yang and Y Liu, 'What's on the Other Side of the Great Firewall? Chinese Web Users' Motivations for Bypassing the Internet Censorship' (2014) 37 *Computers in Human Behavior* 249; H Lewis, 'Taking on the "Great Firewall of China"' *New Statesman* (London, 18 October 2012) <http://www.newstatesman.com/staggers/2012/10/taking-great-firewall-china>.

[88] <http://www.isu.net.sa/saudi-internet/contenet-filtring/filtring.htm>.

[89] Council of Ministers Resolution, Saudi Internet Rules (12 February, 2001) <http://www.al-bab.com/media/docs/saudi.htm>.

[90] R Quisti, 'Shoura Approves Law to Combat e-Crimes' (*Arab News*, 10 October 2006) <http://arabnews.com/node/290286>.

[91] In terms of political expression, pervasive filtering is reported for China, Ethiopia, Iran, Syria, Turkmenistan, Uzbekistan, and Vietnam. Substantial filtering is reported for Saudi Arabia and Yemen. No data is reported for Cuba and North Korea, though both are suspected of having extensive filtering practices.

4.5.1 WSIS, the IGF, and the ITU

With such a plurality of approaches and views on internet regulation and content regulation being displayed at national (state) level it is perhaps no surprise that until recently attempts to shape supra-national agreement on internet regulation were unsuccessful. Then in 1998 the International Telecommunications Union (ITU) recognized there was a need for supra-national cooperation on internet regulation. At their Plenipotentiary Conference in Minneapolis that year, they passed Resolution 73, which noted that telecommunications were playing an increasingly decisive and driving role at the political, economic, social, and cultural levels and called upon the United Nations: 'to ask the Secretary-General to coordinate with other international organisations and with the various partners concerned (Member States, Sector Members, etc.), with a view to holding a world summit on the information society'.[92] This request was heard at the ninetieth plenary meeting of the General Assembly of the United Nations in December 2001, where the General Assembly accepted and endorsed a proposal from the ITU that a World Summit on the Information Society (WSIS) be convened, and instructed the Secretary-General of the UN to 'inform all heads of State and Government of the adoption of the present resolution'.[93] The WSIS was to take place in two phases; the first phase taking place in Geneva on 10–12 December 2003 and the second phase taking place in Tunis on 16–18 November 2005. The objective of the Geneva phase was to develop and foster a clear statement of political will and take concrete steps to establish the foundations for an Information Society for all, reflecting all the different interests at stake. The objective of the second phase was to put the Geneva 'Plan of Action' into effect; find solutions and reach agreements in the fields of internet governance and financing mechanisms; and follow-up and implementation of the Geneva and Tunis documents. WSIS invited heads of state/government, international NGOs, and civil society representatives[94] to contribute to a series of preparatory meetings (PrepComms) and to the Geneva and Tunis rounds on a series of issues ranging from the digital divide[95] to freedom of expression, network security, unsolicited commercial communications (spam), and protection of children.[96] Central to the WSIS programme, though, was the issue of internet governance.

WSIS envisaged a 'people-centred, inclusive and development-oriented Information Society where everyone can create, access, utilise and share information and knowledge, enabling individuals, communities and peoples to achieve their full potential

[92] Resolution 73 <http://www.itu.int/wsis/docs/background/resolutions/73.html>. In effect, what they were asking for was a UN Summit. Summits are designed to put long-term, complex problems like poverty and environmental degradation at the top of the global agenda. They are designed to provide leadership and to mould international opinion and to persuade world leaders to provide political support.

[93] Resolution adopted by the General Assembly [on the report of the Second Committee (A/56/558/Add.3)] 56/183, World Summit on the Information Society, 21 December 2001.

[94] In UN parlance, civil society encompasses all those who are not part of government, private enterprise, or intergovernmental organizations—in other words, private individuals.

[95] The 'digital divide' reflects the technology gap which has opened up between technology-rich Western states and technology-poor African and Asian states, and on the growing divide within states between the professional classes with stable and fast internet access and the working class, in particular immigrant communities, where access may be unstable, slow, and difficult to obtain. See P Norris, *Digital Divide: Civic Engagement, Information Poverty and the Internet Worldwide* (CUP 2001); M Warschauer, *Technology and Social Inclusion: Rethinking the Digital Divide* (MIT Press 2004).

[96] For a discussion of WSIS see M Raboy and N Landry, *Civil Society, Communication and Global Governance: Issues from the World Summit on the Information Society* (Peter Lang 2004).

in promoting their sustainable development and improving their quality of life'.[97] Discussion as to how this was to be achieved began in the PrepComms. In these meetings numerous views were expressed about what was and was not 'internet governance', and the public policy involved. Some developing nations noted that they were unable to participate in many of the decision-making processes central to management of the internet, such as management of the domain name system which was primarily in the hands of two American-based private regulators, the Internet Corporation for Assigned Names and Numbers (ICANN) and the Internet Assigned Numbers Authority (IANA).[98] Others, predominantly the US, called for the principle of private sector involvement and investment to be enshrined. In the final PrepComm briefing on 3 December 2003 US Ambassador David Gross outlined what he called the 'three pillars' of the US position.

Highlight The US 'three pillars' for ICT regulation

1. As nations attempt to build a sustainable ICT sector, commitment to the private sector and rule of law must be emphasized so that countries can attract the necessary private investment to create the infrastructure.
2. There is a need for content creation and intellectual property rights protection in order to inspire ongoing content development.
3. Nations must ensure security on the internet, in electronic communications and in electronic commerce.

Due to this divergence of views, when the Geneva Summit got under way the PrepComms had failed to produce agreement on the future development of internet governance. Although committed to a principle of multi-stakeholder agreement, many developing nations, including China, Brazil, and most Arab States, saw the US commitment to private sector initiatives as a barrier to progress while the US, and others including the EU, Japan, and Canada, feared that some governments wished to have a greater say in internet governance purely as a vehicle for censorship or content management. As a result, agreement in Geneva proved impossible. Instead it was noted that:

> governance issues related to the internet are a complex challenge which needs a complex answer and which has to include all stakeholders—civil society, private industry and governments. No single body and no single stakeholder group alone is able to manage these challenges. This multi-stakeholder approach should be the guiding principle both for the technical coordination of the internet, as well as for broader public policy issues related to Cyberspace in general.[99]

To give effect to this recommendation, WSIS put together a Working Group on Internet Governance (WGIG) to report to the Tunis conference with recommendations. The group, chaired by Nitin Desai, Special Adviser to the Secretary-General for the WSIS, met four times between Geneva and Tunis, and published their final report on 18 July 2005.[100]

[97] WSIS, Declaration of Principles, Geneva 12 December 2003, Principle 1.

[98] Further discussion of the domain name system and the role in particular of ICANN takes place in ch. 16.

[99] World Summit on the Information Society, *Visions in Process: Geneva 2003—Tunis 2005* 41 <http://www.worldsummit2003.de/download_de/Vision_in_process.pdf>.

[100] Full details of WGIG may be found at <http://www.wgig.org/>.

The group was asked to carry out their work under three broad heads: (1) to develop a working definition of internet governance; (2) to identify the public policy issues that are relevant to internet governance; and (3) to develop a common understanding of the respective roles and responsibilities of governments, existing international organizations, and other forums, as well as the private sector and civil society in both developing and developed countries.[101] In dealing with the first, the group suggested the following working definition: 'Internet governance is the development and application by Governments, the private sector and civil society, in their respective roles, of shared principles, norms, rules, decision-making procedures, and programmes that shape the evolution and use of the internet.'[102] From this base the group then moved on to its second head of study and listed 13 public policy issues 'of the highest priority'.[103] Having achieved this, the group then made its critical recommendations on the respective roles and responsibilities of governments, existing international organizations, and other forums. It recommended that governments were to drive public policy-making and coordination and implementation, as appropriate, at the national level, and policy development and coordination at the regional and international levels.[104] This was to include development of best practices, capacity building and promoting research and development. The private sector meanwhile was called upon to develop policy proposals, guidelines, and tools for policy-makers and other stakeholders; this included industry self-regulation and arbitration and dispute resolution.[105] To manage the relationship between the public and private sectors (and other stakeholders), WGIG recommended the creation of a new Internet Governance Forum (IGF) which would provide the opportunity for the free exchange of ideas between stakeholders and which would provide public policy guidance.[106] The mandate for the new forum is set out in paragraph 72 of the Tunis Agenda for the Information Society,[107] which states:

Highlight IGF mandate

The Forum is to:

a. Discuss public policy issues related to key elements of Internet governance in order to foster the sustainability, robustness, security, stability and development of the Internet.
b. Facilitate discourse between bodies dealing with different cross-cutting international public policies regarding the Internet and discuss issues that do not fall within the scope of any existing body.

→

[101] Taken from WGIG, *Report of the Working Group on Internet Governance* Château de Bossey, 18 June 2005, [5].

[102] Ibid. [10].

[103] These were: (1) administration of the root zone files and system; (2) interconnection costs; (3) internet stability, security, and cybercrime; (4) spam; (5) meaningful participation in global policy development; (6) capacity-building; (7) allocation of domain names; (8) IP addressing; (9) intellectual property rights; (10) freedom of expression; (11) data protection and privacy rights; (12) consumer rights; and (13) multilingualism. Full discussion of these may be found at WGIG, (n. 101) [15]–[27].

[104] Ibid. [30].

[105] Ibid. [31].

[106] Ibid. [35]–[51].

[107] WSIS, *Tunis Agenda for the Information Society* 18 November 2005 <http://www.itu.int/wsis/docs2/tunis/off/6rev1.html>.

→

c. Interface with appropriate intergovernmental organizations and other institutions on matters under their purview.
d. Facilitate the exchange of information and best practices, and in this regard make full use of the expertise of the academic, scientific and technical communities.
e. Advise all stakeholders in proposing ways and means to accelerate the availability and affordability of the Internet in the developing world.
f. Strengthen and enhance the engagement of stakeholders in existing and/or future Internet governance mechanisms, particularly those from developing countries.
g. Identify emerging issues, bring them to the attention of the relevant bodies and the general public, and, where appropriate, make recommendations.
h. Contribute to capacity building for Internet governance in developing countries, drawing fully on local sources of knowledge and expertise.
i. Promote and assess, on an ongoing basis, the embodiment of WSIS principles in Internet governance processes.
j. Discuss, inter alia, issues relating to critical Internet resources.
k. Help to find solutions to the issues arising from the use and misuse of the Internet, of particular concern to everyday users.
l. Publish its proceedings.

The IGF has met now on ten occasions but has made little progress in the way of hard policy. The main business of the forum takes place at the annual meeting and is formed around themes including openness, critical resources, security, access, and diversity. At the most recent meeting in João Pessoa, Brazil, in November 2015 the forum discussed a number of vital issues of internet governance including 'enhancing multistakeholder cooperation', 'critical internet resources', 'cybersecurity and trust', and 'the internet and human rights'. The transcripts, though, make for depressing reading. Although the IGF attracts politicians, technologists, and civil society representatives from the highest echelons of their profession the outcomes are a series of transcripts in which much rhetoric brings about little in the way of conclusion or active proposal. Unfortunately the IGF has become an annual high-level conference on internet governance issues, and although the value of having so many opinion formers in one room should not be underestimated its mandate does not allow it to take concrete action or make concrete proposals. This chimes with earlier findings in the official publication reviewing the first two IGF meetings,[108] where Markus Kummer, eEnvoy of the Swiss government, notes that: 'governments remain the decision makers'.[109]

The formation of the IGF is a step in the direction of cooperative supranational internet regulation, but the nature of the IGF as a forum to 'discuss public policy issues related to key elements of Internet governance' means it falls far short, currently, of

[108] A Doria and W Kleinwächter, *Internet Governance Forum (IGF) The First Two Years* <http://www.intgovforum.org/cms/hydera/IGFBook_the_first_two_years.pdf>.
[109] Ibid. 16.

playing a meaningful role in the regulation of the internet and digital content. The IGF is unlikely to develop beyond discussion and rhetoric. The PrepComms provided an insight into why international cooperation at an operational level is unlikely to follow from discussion at IGF meetings. There is a digital divide between most developed and developing nations which means that there are different economic interests in play. Further, there appears to be a societal divide between the key states members of the IGF. The US in particular seems quite unshiftable on its twin positions of private sector investment and allowing the market to regulate. This is not acceptable to many nations, including China. Without agreement between these two digital superpowers the IGF will remain locked down and will prove to be merely a forum for discussion. This is not to belittle the potential contribution of the IGF which discusses open access, network standards, protection for freedom, and network stability and security; merely to say that the existence of the IGF does not change, and is unlikely to change, the established primacy of the nation state in internet governance.

The shortcomings of the IGF were thrown into stark relief in December 2012 when the International Telecommunications Union (ITU), a separate UN body responsible for international telecommunications networks standards and technologies, attempted to take management of the infrastructure of the internet. The ITU has always been responsible for the physical infrastructure layer of the network through the operation of the 1988 International Telecommunication Regulation,[110] but the proposals of the World Conference on International Telecommunications went beyond the usual technical remit of the ITU. They drafted a proposal to update the 1998 regulation that went far beyond its original role and included attempts to regulate Internet Protocol, regulate spam messages, and, most controversially, a provision ostensibly on network security which in effect, and, as interpreted by North American and Western European nations, would allow for state regulation of the network space.[111] As the meeting in Dubai, which ran for 11 days, continued and intense negotiation saw a rift develop between Western European and North American states, on the one hand, and Asian and African nations, on the other, a new version of the regulation was finally drafted; one without the Internet Protocol clause but retaining watered-down versions of the spam and network security provisions. Even though the most controversial provision, the network security provision, had been substantially diluted, many governments felt they could not sign up to the final text and of the 193 members present only 89 signed the treaty. Interestingly, it now splits the world into countries that operate open networks and those that do not. Non-signatories include all EU states, the Unites States, Canada, Australia, and Japan. Signatories include China, Russia, Brazil, Turkey, Saudi Arabia, and, rather unusually, South Korea.

The failure of either the IGF or the ITU thus far successfully to reach a common accord on internet regulation does not mean it is impossible and further attempts will be brought forward in the near future by both the ITU and the General Assembly. There is clearly a fracture though between blocs of nations and this may prove difficult to

[110] Available from <http://www.itu.int/pub/T-REG-ACT-1988>.

[111] The draft is available from <http://www.itu.int/en/wcit-12/Documents/draft-future-itrs-public.pdf>. The Articles in question which attempt the amendments outlined in the text are Arts. 4.7, 5B, and 5A.

bridge. Until this is resolved we must assume that the most effective form of online regulation remains that designed and implemented by private actors rather than state or supranational actors.

4.6 **Conclusions**

What does all this mean for the study of cyber-regulation? The cyberpaternalists may argue that the effectiveness of filtering tools in countries such as China, Saudi Arabia, and Burma prove that by using legal controls to mandate changes the network architecture, either by filtering content or by restricting the ability of users to get online control, may be effected in the digital environment. They may further point to the fact that when the IWF blacklisted the Wikipedia entry of *Virgin Killer* reports of the effectiveness of the Cleanfeed system ranged between 85 and 95 per cent effective, this demonstrated that even in democratic nations effective controls may be implemented at network architecture level. Cyberlibertarians may respond by citing that tools such as Peacefire.org's *Circumventor* software allow a large proportion of end users in even the most regulated of states to circumvent state-based controls.[112] The problem faced by cyberlibertarians is that it is impossible to deny that in each case the state *is* effectively controlling the online actions of their citizens, and that these controls may only be circumvented using specialist tools or with expert knowledge of computer networks. This is far removed from John Perry Barlow's claim that real-world regulators 'do [not] possess any methods of enforcement we have true reason to fear'. The experience of the real world and the development of the cyberpaternalist school seem to have consigned cyberlibertarianism to the pages of the history books. What of network communitarianism? Surely these real-life examples of control implemented either at the network gatekeeper level or at state level undermine the network communitarian claim that 'regulation is a process of discourse and dialogue between the individual and society'? The network communitarian response would be that each of these real-world examples can be perfectly rationalized with network communitarian thought. The UK *Virgin Killer* example is a perfect example of network communitarian regulation in action. Once the action of the IWF was brought into the public domain an extensive discourse took place and it only took four days for the block to be removed, this despite the assertion from the IWF that 'the image in question is potentially in breach of the Protection of Children Act 1978'. In other words, the IWF still believe the image may be illegal to download and possess in the UK, but rather than fulfil their remit to 'minimise the availability of this (abusive) content' they chose to listen to the overwhelming view of British internet users that content of this type should not be blocked without consultation. This is network communitarianism in action. What about effectiveness of state-level filtering though? Well, if one looks at the lists of states which effectively filter at a state level we find that overwhelmingly they fall into one of two categories. The first are states where political discourse is routinely suppressed; states such as China, Burma, and Pakistan. The second are Islamic states where religious teachings forbid certain types of content, in particular anti-Islamic content or pornographic content. In each

[112] S Olsen, 'Maxthon: China's Hip Browser' (*cnet News*, 22 June 2006) <http://news.cnet.com/2100-1032_3-6086632.html>.

of these examples because political discourse is suppressed naturally in the real world we see a similar suppression of discourse in the online environment. Thus it appears one may choose to see the regulation in the digital environment in a similar fashion as regulation in the physical environment. It may either be centred, command-and-control regulation or it may be decentred and part of the democratic process. What is clear is that there is nothing particularly special about designing effective regulation in the digital environment.

TEST QUESTIONS

Question 1

If code is law who are the regulators?

Question 2

Is network communitarianism a better regulatory model than cyberpaternalism? Explain why or why not.

FURTHER READING

Books

L Bygrave and J. Bing, *Internet Governance: Infrastructure and Institutions* (2009)

L Lessig, *Code Version 2.0* (2006)

A Murray, *The Regulation of Cyberspace: Control in the Online Environment* (2007)

E Morozov, *The Net Delusion: How Not to Liberate the World* (2012)

J Zittrain, *The Future of the Internet and How to Stop It* (2008)

Chapters and articles

P de Hert, S Gutwirth, and L de Sutter, 'The Trouble with Technology Regulation from a Legal Perspective: Why Lessig's "Optimal Mix" Will Not Work', in R Brownsword and K Yeung (eds.), *Regulating Technologies: Legal Futures, Regulatory Frames and Technological Fixes* (2009)

D Johnson and D Post, 'Law and Borders: The Rise of Law in Cyberspace', 48 *Stanford Law Review* 1367 (1996)

V Mayer-Schönberger, 'Demystifying Lessig', *Wisconsin Law Review* 714 (2008)

A Murray, 'Nodes and Gravity in Virtual Space', 5 *Legisprudence* 195 (2011)

J Reidenberg, 'Lex Informatica: The Formation of Information Policy Rules through Technology', 76 *Texas Law Review* 553 (1998)

5

Digital ownership

The law of property forms one of the central tenets of modern legal systems. The functioning of modern society, based upon principles of free markets and the ability to trade, requires that the legal system recognizes rights in things as well as obligations between persons. Attempting to define property law, and property rights, is difficult in the physical world, but as we shall see it is even more challenging in the digital environment where traditional values, such as possession and rivalrousness, are rendered ineffective by the limitless nature of bits.[1]

The starting point for any discussion of digital ownership is to examine how property law functions in the real world. Definitions of property differ but they all appear to have some elements in common. The first is that property defines a relationship between a person and a thing. Unlike obligations which normalize relations between persons, one tangent of the axis in a property relationship must be a thing. This is because property, and property law, regulates one's right to own, buy and sell, dispose, or destroy. These rights may only be exercised over things: it has been illegal to take rights such as these over persons in the UK for almost 200 years.[2] The second common theme of property law is that it is exclusive. The rights that property law confers upon the owner, or other rights holder such as a lessee, are of the nature of rights *in rem* as opposed to rights *ad personam*. This means that the property rights holder has a right which may be exercised against any individual who attempts to interfere with his or her property right without the need for a prior relationship with that person. This may be contrasted with obligations which arise out of a prior relationship such as a contractual relationship or a relationship which establishes a duty of care in tort.[3] As James Penner explains in his book *The Idea of Property in Law*, the essential element of these rights is the right to exclude others from exercising competing rights over your property.[4]

We tend not to notice the monopolistic nature of property rights when we are dealing with everyday items such as cars, computers, or shoes as the monopoly one person exercises over *their car, their computer,* or *their shoes* cannot effect the wider market for shoes, cars, or computers, but when we are dealing with rare or unique items this becomes more apparent as with rare artworks such as LS Lowry's *A Fairground* which was kept in

[1] Rivalrous and nonrivalrous goods are discussed in ch. 1, while at least some of the effects of digitization and the limitless supply of bits are discussed in ch. 3.

[2] Slavery Abolition Act 1833.

[3] See *Donoghue v Stevenson* [1932] AC 562.

[4] J Penner, *The Idea of Property in Law* (Clarendon 1997) ch. 4.

a private collection and never exhibited for over 50 years,[5] or with intellectual property rights such as copyright where the property right may be used to prevent distribution or exhibition of the work.[6]

Example Physical products

Eleanor has bought a new car. She may use her property rights in it to prevent anyone else from possessing the car or from dispossessing her of, or economically exploiting, the car.

In addition, exclusive property rights create a natural monopoly over property. Although Eleanor's car may not be unique, she holds a monopoly over the use of that car: in other words she monopolizes the rights in relation to that particular car. She may choose to sell or rent the car, she may choose to destroy it, or she may choose merely to enjoy it herself.

The final element of property law which is generally agreed upon by commentators on the subject is that property law, as opposed to property, represents a bundle of rights distinct from the thing itself. Thus by owning a car I have the most basic property right: ownership, but I also possess the right to take economic fruits from it by renting it to someone else, to destroy it (subject to environmental laws), and to securitize it (that is, to use it as security for a loan), among other rights. Thus although we tend to think of property rights as ownership—'this is my car'—there are a bundle of additional rights the property owner also possesses.

5.1 **Digital property**

As discussed in chapter 1, the nature of digital goods is quite unlike physical goods and as a result the application of property law to digital goods is not clear-cut. The problem is that traditional property values and principles assume that goods are rivalrous. Rivalrousness lends itself to the principle of exclusion. Among the many reasons I may have as to why I may wish to exclude others from economically exploiting my property is that in so doing they are likely to affect my enjoyment of my property. We can see this assumption of rivalrousness if we look to s. 1 of the Theft Act 1968 which states, 'A person is guilty of theft if they dishonestly appropriate property belonging to another with the intention to permanently deprive the other of it.' Rivalrousness in physical property means that traditional property laws are as much about the enjoyment of property as they are about exclusion of competing interests. Once we move into intangible properties this aspect of property is removed. In dealing with informational products a different rationale must apply.

[5] See M Kennedy, 'Little-known Lowry Painting Up for Auction' *The Guardian* (London, 23 August 2007).

[6] As with Stanley Kubrick's film version of *A Clockwork Orange* which Kubrick refused to allow to be exhibited in the UK from 1973 to his death in 1999. See A Mullins and J Robins, 'Kubrick Considered "Clockwork Orange" Re-release' *The Independent* (London, 3 December 1999).

Example Informational products

If I make and sell copies of Ernest Cline's novel *Ready Player One* this does not directly affect Mr Cline's enjoyment of his copyright; he may continue to produce copies or adaptations of the work or he may license a film adaptation or a translation. Thus my production of a competing version of his copyright material allows me to enjoy all the fruits of property ownership including the taking of economic rents without directly dispossessing Mr Cline of his prior and better right.

There are two points which have to be made about this example. The first is that you may assume I have made a false assumption here: that the correct comparison is not between properties of a genus, but between property of a type. That is, when I talk about not infringing Mr Cline's rights in his text I'm making the mistake of equating copies of *Ready Player One* generally with specifically *his* copy of *Ready Player One*. Thus if someone produces exact copies of my car and sells them on the open market my interests in *my* car are unaffected: the same may be said here of Mr Cline and *his* book. This though is not the case as copyright protects not the book itself but the intangible expression of an idea as recorded in the pages of a book. To make and sell copies of *Ready Player One* is directly to interfere with, or in copyright terms infringe, Mr Cline's property right. Second, although Mr Cline has not been dispossessed of his property right in the copyright of *Ready Player One*, it is clear my actions will have adversely affected his property interest as the available amount of property rents he may receive for his copyright has been reduced by my action. This, at least in part, explains why we protect certain intangible properties even though they are of a nonrivalrous nature.

5.1.1 **Information as property**

Traditionally property law does not define information as a good unless it is of a particular character. In the case of *International News Service v Associated Press*,[7] the US Supreme Court did recognize a proprietary nature in news information. Following unfavourable reporting on British losses by William Randolph Hearst's INS, they were barred from using Allied telegraph lines to report news from the front. To remedy this they took information printed by Associated Press (AP) on the US east coast and wired it to their west coast newspapers. This was then rewritten by journalists on these papers and published. As the information was rewritten there was no breach of copyright. AP claimed a quasi-proprietary right in their information and surprisingly the Supreme Court upheld their claim in unfair competition based upon this principle.

Recognizing a proprietary interest in raw information is, though, potentially very damaging for competition as it creates an exclusionary effect of preventing third parties from using the information.[8] Because of this Justice Brandeis dissented vigorously in the case and subsequent attempts to apply the principle of quasi-ownership in

[7] (1918) 248 US 215.

[8] See R Smith, *Property Law* (8th edn, Pearson 2014) 5.

information have fallen foul of a narrow interpretation of the case. Thus in *Cheney Brothers v Doris Silk Corporation*[9] Judge Learned Hand confided to the other members of the panel that:

> the Associated Press Case is somewhat of a stumbling block . . . I do not believe that the five justices who united in Pitney, J's opinion meant to lay down a general rule that a man is entitled to 'property' in the form of whatever he makes with his labor and money, so as to prevent others from copying it. To do so would be to short-circuit the Patent Office and throw upon courts the winnowing out of all such designs that might be presented. While I agree that on principle it is hard to distinguish, and that the language applies, I cannot suppose that any principle of such far-reaching consequence was intended. It will make patent cases an exception; it will give to State courts jurisdiction over inventions; it will overthrow the practice of centuries.[10]

To circumvent this problem Hand concluded that *INS* had to be understood as a case that dealt with the narrow and peculiar problems of a news service. Thus the case could be restricted to its facts despite being a decision of the Supreme Court. This approach was confirmed in the later case of *RCA Manufacturing Co. v Whiteman*,[11] where Judge Clark settled that *INS* was to be so restricted, and noted off the record to Judge Hand that 'In principle, this case is entirely indistinguishable from INS, and we might as well admit it. But we have conquered the News case before; it can be done again'[12] before going on to hold that using licences to expand copyright was unconstitutional. With courts in the US striving to restrict *INS* to its facts it is not surprising that UK courts have conspicuously failed to find any type of property right in information of a general nature.[13]

5.1.2 **Statutory intellectual property rights**

This is not to say that ownership in information is impossible in the UK. The most obvious examples are the statutory intellectual property rights created over certain categories of information, perhaps the best-known example of which is to be found in the law of patents. A patent is a statutory property right awarded following a process of application and review to an idea or process which is capable of industrial application.[14] The owner of a patent has, for a limited time,[15] the right to prevent others from developing competing products or services based upon the idea or process outlined in the patent. In other words, a patent protects the use of the idea or process for the lifetime of the patent.

Patents, although valuable, were historically of little direct impact in digital property as the patent must be for a process or idea capable of industrial application, and further cannot be 'a scheme, rule or method for performing a mental act, playing a game

[9] 35 F. 2d 279 (2d Cir. 1929).

[10] Reported in D Baird, 'Property, Natural Monopoly, and the Uneasy Legacy of INS v APU' *Chicago Law & Economics, Olin Working Paper No. 246* <http://ssrn.com/abstract=730024>.

[11] 114 F. 2d 86 (2d Cir. 1940).

[12] Again this is reported in Baird (n. 10) 30.

[13] UK courts have tended to follow the principle of 'no ownership in raw information' as espoused in the Australian case of *Victoria Park Racing & Recreation Grounds Co. Ltd v Taylor* (1937) 58 CLR 479.

[14] Patents Act 1977 (PA), s. 1.

[15] Up to 20 years: PA, s. 25.

or doing business, or a program for a computer'.[16] With digital goods being a series of ones and zeros, operated on by a CPU, it is extremely difficult for them to gain protection given this qualification. Some attempts have been made to protect computer software, despite the Act excluding protection for 'a program for a computer',[17] and also attempts have been made to protect methods of applying software to final products, most famously in the so-called smartphone wars which began in 2009 between a number of smartphone manufacturers including Apple, Google, Samsung, Microsoft, Nokia, Motorola, and HTC.

The outbreak of hostilities began in 2009 when Nokia sued Apple for infringement of ten patents that Nokia held regarding wireless communications standards. They claimed Apple's new iPhone infringed patents on software processes which managed GSM (Global System for Mobile Communications—so-called 2G), UMTS (Universal Mobile Telecommunications System—so-called 3G), and wireless LAN (WLAN) settings. Apple immediately counter-sued claiming Nokia infringed 13 of its patents including a patent that allowed software to manage and update the phone when connected to a computer and one designed to improve the wireless communication quality of phones.[18] This initial case spent 20 months in litigation before Apple agreed to pay an undisclosed sum under a settlement agreement and royalties for the use of parts of Nokia's patents.

This though was a relatively low-key beginning for some of the most costly litigation ever fought globally. The so-called Android v iOS patent wars involved a number of leading hardware and software developers but none more so than Apple and Samsung who litigated against each other in a number of cases globally, claiming damages of billions of dollars. The disputes began in April 2011 when Apple sued Samsung for infringement of seven utility patents, three design patents, three registered trade dresses, and six trademarks in the United States. The claims related to the Samsung Galaxy Smartphone and the related Galaxy Tablet. In the utility patent claim Apple argued Samsung had among others infringed its 381 software patent, this is the so-called 'bounce back' patent which sees a page or screen bounce back to the centre of the screen when it reaches the limits of its scroll—i.e. when you get to the top or bottom of a page on iOS, it will pull down (or up) and then bounce back into place—and the 134 software patent for arranging and displaying instant messages in a spaced timeline. Samsung struck back by suing Apple in South Korea, Germany, and Japan as well as counter-suing in the United States for infringement of a number of Samsung software patents including patents covering HSPA (High Speed Packet Access) telecommunications technology, used for transmission optimization and reduction of power usage during data transmission, and technology for tethering a mobile phone to a PC to enable the PC to utilize the phone's wireless data connection. Since then, these two corporate behemoths have pursued each other in courts across the globe.

Both have experienced success and failure and it is beyond the scope of this book to analyse the litigation in full. Books will be written about just these cases, and indeed the first already has been.[19] Suffice to record that Apple obtained a great but perhaps

[16] PA, s. 1(2)(c).

[17] Patent protection for computer software is analysed in ch. 10.

[18] The case is *Nokia Corp. v Apple Inc.*, Case No. CA-09–791-GMS (Del.).

[19] MC Speth, *Apple vs. Samsung: The Balance between Patent Rights and the Free Market* (Exec Sense 2012).

Pyrrhic victory in August 2012 when a jury in California awarded Apple damages of $1.049bn dollars in relation to the original claims and Samsung's counterclaims were all rejected.[20] Following this victory Apple suffered a number of setbacks. Their important 381 'bounce back' patent was revoked by the US Patent and Trade Mark Office on the basis that it lacked novelty;[21] Apple's claim in London, first raised in June 2011 claiming a breach by Samsung of their registered design right awarded for the design of the iPad tablet computer rather than a patent, was rejected by the Court of Appeal.[22] Apple then suffered the indignity of being dragged back before the court to be censured for failing to follow instructions correctly on how to publicize the judgment on their website.[23] Back in the United States, Apple sought an injunction against several Samsung products (something they successfully achieved for a while in Germany and Australia), which was denied (Apple is appealing). Meanwhile the judge in the Californian case invalidated $450 million of Apple damages[24] before a retrial finally set the level of damages at $929 million, a figure still under appeal by Samsung and which following a 2015 ruling on trade dress looks likely to be reduced to $548 million.[25]

It is clear that patents are playing an increasing role in digital products and nowadays any digital consumer device such as a smartphone, tablet, or satnav will be covered by a myriad of overlapping software, technical, and hardware patents. The growing importance of these in relation to digital products will be considered in further detail in chapter 10 but for the moment it is important to understand that patents are just part of the digital property framework.

Like a patent, a copyright is a statutory informational property right, this time awarded by the Copyright, Designs and Patents Act 1988. Unlike a patent, a copyright arises automatically and is awarded to original literary, dramatic, musical, or artistic works, sound recordings, films, broadcasts, cable programmes, and the typographical arrangement of published editions.[26] Copyright is a natural monopoly right which allows the author or creator of the work to control the distribution of their original work by restricting to them the right to make copies of the original. Copyright is quite unlike traditional property rights as the exclusive rights are to control the making and distribution of copies of the work, or the display or public performance of the work:[27] you cannot directly use your copyright to prevent an individual from reading or viewing your work provided they do not have to make or obtain an illegal copy, or attend an unlawful public performance, to do so. Because the mere use of a copyright work without permission does not interfere with the copyright holder's ability to enjoy his work,[28] traditionally there has not been a concept in copyright which is akin to trespass

[20] *Apple Inc. v Samsung Electronics Ltd Inc.*, Case C 11–1846 (N.D. Calif.). Documents available from <http://cand.uscourts.gov/applevsamsung/casedocs>.

[21] The communication from the USPTO can be seen at <http://www.scribd.com/doc/133538099/13-04-01-Samsung-Statement-Re-381-Rubber-banding-Final-Office-Action>.

[22] *Samsung Electronics (UK) Ltd v Apple Inc.* [2012] EWCA Civ 1339.

[23] *Samsung Electronics (UK) Ltd v Apple Inc.* [2012] EWCA Civ 1430.

[24] <http://www.scribd.com/doc/128003420/13-03-01-Apple-v-Samsung-Final-Order-on-Damages>.

[25] *Apple Inc. v Samsung Electronics Ltd Inc.*, No. 5:11-cv-01846, Fed. Cir., 18 May 2015 <http://www.scotusblog.com/wp-content/uploads/2016/01/Apple-v-Samsung.pdf>

[26] Copyright, Designs and Patents Act 1988 (CDPA), s. 1.

[27] CDPA, ss. 16–27.

[28] As copyright works are nonrivalrous properties. See ch. 1.

in physical property. I cannot 'trespass' on the copyright of Ernest Cline simply by reading *Ready Player One* whereas I could trespass on his property rights by pitching a tent in his front garden or by moving in to his car.[29] Unlike a patent holder, it has always been assumed that a copyright holder cannot therefore prevent passive enjoyment of his copyright protected material. Recently though this assumption has come under sustained challenge in the case of *Public Relations Consultants Association Ltd v Newspaper Licensing Agency Ltd*[30] which will be discussed in chapter 11.

5.1.3 **Confidential information**

There is another potential body of law which may be used to protect digital goods distinct from the application of the statutory property rights. This is by the application of the law of confidential information. In truth, protecting informational products by the application of confidentiality is not an application of property law principles; rather, its roots are in the law of obligations. To qualify for protection the information must first be 'confidential': this has been defined by Lord Greene MR as to mean that the information is not public property and public knowledge.[31] The information does not have to be secret as such, just not readily available to the public. Second, the information must have been disclosed in circumstances which give rise to an obligation of confidence. This generally means that in disclosing the information to the recipient the owner of the information did so for a limited and defined purpose. In *Saltman Engineering v Campbell* the claimants gave the defendants confidential designs for tools which the defendants were to manufacture solely for the claimants. The defendants went on to manufacture and market the tools themselves leading to a claim of breach of confidentiality. The court held the designs had been handed over for a limited purpose only and the defendants were not entitled to use them except for that purpose.[32] The final quality of confidential information is that there must be an actual or anticipated unauthorized disclosure of the information.[33] As is clear from these requirements the status of confidentiality is usually conferred upon information as a result of a pre-existing contractual relationship between the parties.

Confidentiality is a form of protection offered by obligations, not property principles. This has several effects. First, the right to enforce the obligation of confidentiality is a right *ad personam* not a right *in rem*. That is, the rights and reciprocal duties attach to the parties, not the information itself. This can be seen in the case of *Fraser v Evans*.[34] Here the claimant wrote a confidential report for the Greek government. His contract stated that he was to keep confidential any information he gathered in compiling the report. There was though no reciprocal obligation on the Greek government to keep confidential any information Mr Fraser supplied to them. The report was later leaked by an unknown source in the Greek government to a newspaper. Mr Fraser sought

[29] Technically the second example, moving in to his car, is not trespass as trespass relates to real property (land). The second example would almost certainly be prosecuted as theft under the Theft Act 1968.

[30] [2013] UKSC 18 (Sup Ct); [2014] AC 1438 (CJEU).

[31] Lord Greene MR in *Saltman Engineering v Campbell* (1948) 65 RPC 203.

[32] Lord Greene MR (n. 31).

[33] *Coco v AN Clarke (Engineers) Ltd* [1969] RPC 41, per Megarry J.

[34] [1969] 1 QB 349.

to restrain publication of an article based on the document on grounds of breach of confidence. The court held that Mr Fraser was not due an obligation of confidentiality despite the information being described in his contract as confidential. Thus it is clear that information is not confidential itself; it is rather the expectation placed upon the party which creates the circumstance of confidentiality.

What does this mean for the use of confidentiality as a proxy for property protection when dealing with digital information? There is clearly a restricted role for confidentiality where parties are in some form of relationship with each other. Examples would include using confidentiality to protect valuable software code shared between software developers or using confidentiality to protect private areas on websites which are password protected and to which access may only be achieved once one agrees to treat information contained therein as confidential. The problem with utilizing confidentiality as a tool to protect digital property in the wider sense is the first nature of confidential information; that is, that it is not public property and/or public knowledge. The very nature of most property is that it is to be seen in and accessed through the public domain. To draw a property law analogy with the use of confidentiality as a proxy for digital property instead of using the law of property to prevent anyone from stealing, occupying, or damaging my car, I instead lock my car in a garage and keep only a few keys for myself, my wife, and my immediate family to enter. I forbid them from taking the car out and I forbid them from telling anyone about the car. It is clear when you discuss confidential information in this way that it cannot fulfil the roles of property law. Property law is about excluding others from access to your property by enshrining protection for its boundaries in a series of legal principles. Confidentiality is about excluding others from access to your property by removing it from public knowledge. Thus I can never drive my car in public if I rely upon the protection of confidentiality. Equally, returning to the sphere of digital goods we cannot use confidentiality to protect digital goods which are open to the public, observable in public, or which are accessible from a public place. This rules this out as a methodology of protecting software in which the source code is accessible, web pages and their allied content and digital media such as images, sounds, and video accessible from any open network source.

5.2 **Digital trespass**

With the inability of traditional intangible property rights such as patents, copyright, and confidentiality to protect the vast majority of digital goods the owners and developers of digital property have turned to more inventive ways to protect their investment in digital properties.[35] One such approach has been to attempt to use traditional property principles such as trespass in the digital, incorporeal environment. This idea, unsurprisingly, originates in the US and much of the case law on the concept of digital trespass is to be found there, particularly in the state of California.

[35] It should be noted that we should treat computer software as a unique form of digital property as there is a separate and well-established order of protecting software by both copyright law and patents. This will be discussed in full in ch. 10.

5.2.1 **Trespass to servers**

The first case to examine the applicability of trespass to chattels to digital goods was a Californian case from 1996. In *Thrifty-Tel, Inc. v Bezenek*[36] two young hackers tried to gain access to free long-distance calls by means of sending digital signals from their computer to the telephone exchange server. In attempting to gain access to the Thrifty-Tel carrier network, Ryan Bezenek (one of the defendants) overburdened the Thrifty-Tel system, denying some subscribers access to phones lines. At this point Thrifty-Tel took action claiming attempted fraud and misappropriation. To determine whether harm was likely the court looked at whether the actions of the Bezenek brothers amounted to trespass to chattels. The Court of Appeal of California found that the boys' action of the sending of electronic signals to the computers were sufficiently tangible to support a cause of action in trespass. This decision was highly controversial.[37] One commentary notes that *Thrifty-Tel* 'opened the floodgates to judicial adoption of cyberproperty' and that 'courts seized on *Thrifty-Tel* to punish such activity without even considering whether plaintiffs alleged damage to the chattel'.[38]

The reason for the flood of cases referred to was that *Thrifty-Tel* offered a tantalizing opportunity to network providers (such as telecoms companies and ISPs) to use principles of property law, and in particular trespass to chattels, to deal with 'spammers'—individuals who send vast amounts of unsolicited commercial communications across the email system—in a time when there was no legislative framework to protect them from their activities.[39] If, as the court had said in *Thrifty-Tel*, the sending of data down a telephone cable could amount to trespass to chattels then spammers who sent vast amounts of emails simultaneously could equally be found to be digitally trespassing. This was first tested in two cases against a spam organization called Cyber Promotions.[40] The more controversial of the two Cyber Promotions cases was *CompuServe Inc. v Cyber Promotions Inc.*,[41] for in that case the District Court for the Southern District of Ohio found that trespass to chattels could be established without harm to the computer network in question. The court found that there was sufficient tangibility to establish trespass to chattels in 'the electronic signals sent by computer',[42] and found that there was actual trespass (or harm) without damage because, as 'spam email demands the disk space and drains the processing power of computer equipment', it prevents these

[36] 54 Cal Rptr 2d 468 (Ct App 1996).

[37] Critical commentaries include: L Quilter, 'Cyberlaw: The Continuing Expansion of Cyberspace Trespass to Chattels' (2002) 17 *Berkeley Technology Law Journal* 421; C Merrell, 'Trespass to Chattels in the Age of the Internet' (2002) 80 *Washington University Law Quarterly* 675; M Bendotoff and E Gosse, '"Stay Off My Cyberproperty!": Trespass to Chattels on the Internet' (2001) 6 *Intellectual Property Law Bulletin* 12; E Lee, 'Rules and Standards for Cyberspace' (2002) 77 *Notre Dame Law Review* 1275.

[38] M Carrier and G Lastowska, 'Against Cyberproperty' (2007) 22 *Berkeley Technology Law Journal* 1483, 1489.

[39] There is now a legislative framework to deal with spam in both the US (The Controlling the Assault of Non-Solicited Pornography and Marketing Act 2003 (CAN-SPAM Act), 15 USC 7701) and in Europe (Dir. 2002/58/EC of the European Parliament and of the Council of 12 July 2002 Concerning the Processing of Personal Data and the Protection of Privacy in the Electronic Communications Sector (ePrivacy Directive)), Art. 13. Spam regulation will be discussed in ch. 6.

[40] *Cyber Promotions Inc. v America Online Inc.*, 948 F. Supp. 436 (1996); *CompuServe Inc. v Cyber Promotions Inc.*, 962 F. Supp. 1015 (1997).

[41] Ibid.

[42] Ibid. 1021.

resources from being available for paying customers.[43] The court concluded that even though the CompuServe network and its servers were not physically harmed by the defendants' actions, the value of the equipment to CompuServe was diminished and found in their favour. The decision in CompuServe signalled a change in approach in digital trespass. Courts would no longer look for evidence of actual harm, as they had in *Thrifty-Tel*; they would now look for evidence of economic harm. A flurry of cases followed, mostly focused on spam email,[44] but a few cases developed around a different practice which appears to be more closely aligned with the traditional practice of trespass in the real world.

5.2.2 **Copyright and trespass: indexing and scraping**

These cases surrounded the practices of indexing and scraping. These are the practices of accessing websites either for the purpose of gathering data from that website to place in an index (such as a search engine) or to gather data such as prices or availability of goods or services for a price comparison site or similar. The first case on scraping is the well-known case of *eBay Inc. v Bidder's Edge Inc.*,[45] in which the defendants operated an 'auction aggregator' which captured eBay's auction data and supplied it to the public as a form of price comparison. eBay claimed trespass to chattels even though admitting that the actions of Bidder's Edge did not significantly affect the ability of its web servers to function normally. Instead eBay, following a more traditional property law rationale, claimed that as they had not authorized Bidder's Edge to access this information they were in fact trespassing. The District Court for the Northern District of California agreed and issued an injunction prohibiting Bidder's Edge from accessing eBay's web pages.[46] It seems the court was particularly concerned with potential rather than actual harm, for although eBay had conceded the actions of Bidder's Edge were not currently impairing the eBay network, the court was concerned that other companies may begin to aggregate eBay's auction data should eBay's claim fail, at which point actual harm may occur. Thus the decision in eBay may be characterized as being one of potential rather than actual harm.[47]

The US courts were still willing though to push the envelope of digital trespass a little further. In the following case, *Oyster Software Inc. v Forms Processing Inc.*,[48] the District Court for the Northern District of California found trespass to chattels not only where there was no actual damage, but where there was no likelihood of future damage either. In this case the defendant copied the plaintiff's meta tags from his website and placed these copies on his website with the intent of redirecting potential customers from the plaintiff's website to the defendant's. The plaintiff sued for trademark infringement and copyright infringement, but also claimed trespass to chattels by the defendant. The

[43] Ibid. 1022.

[44] Cases such as *Hotmail Corp. v Van$ Money Pie Inc.*, 47 USPQ 2d 1020 (1998); *America Online Inc. v IMS*, 24 F. Supp. 2d 548 (1998); *America Online Inc. v LCGM*, 46 F. Supp. 2d 444 (1998); and *America Online Inc. v National Health Care Discount Inc.*, 121 F. Supp. 2d 1255 (2000).

[45] 100 F. Supp. 2d 1058 (2000).

[46] *eBay v Bidder's Edge* (n. 45) 1073.

[47] Ibid. 1066.

[48] 2001 WL 1736,382.

court took the view that the *eBay* decision had dispensed with the requirement of injury at Californian law and found that the action of making entry to the plaintiff's computers without permission was a trespass to chattels.

Several cases followed, all American, which seemed to establish a general principle that unauthorized access to a computer connected to a public network was a trespass to chattels.[49] Over time, however, decisions emerged which departed from this orthodoxy. In *Ticketmaster v Tickets.com*,[50] the plaintiff sought to press a claim of trespass to chattels against a competitor who was using a spider to list on their website tickets for events sold on the Ticketmaster site.[51] If Tickets.com had no tickets available for an event they would use the information gathered by the spider to offer their customers a link to the relevant page on the Ticketmaster site. In this way they could continue to offer their customers a way to obtain tickets to an event they had no tickets available for and Ticketmaster would obtain a sale. It may sound like both parties won, but Ticketmaster saw things differently. If Tickets.com could offer tickets via Ticketmaster when their allocation of tickets ran out then customers would continue to use Tickets.com and would not transfer to Ticketmaster. Also it created in the customer a link or association between the two companies which was not in place. Ticketmaster claimed that the information Tickets.com obtained by the use of the spider was valuable, and that it spent time and money attempting to frustrate the spider. But the court found that neither of these claims showed damage to their computers or their operation. Distinguishing the *eBay* decision, they found that:

> one must keep in mind that we are talking about the common law tort of trespass, not damage from breach of contract or copyright infringement. The tort claim may not succeed without proof of tort-type damage. Plaintiff Ticketmaster has the burden to show such damage. None is shown here. The motion for summary judgment is granted to eliminate the claim for trespass to chattels. This approach to the tort of trespass to chattels should hurt no one's policy feelings; after all, what is being attempted is to apply a medieval common law concept in an entirely new situation which should be disposed of by modern law designed to protect intellectual property interests.[52]

Ticketmaster at once offered a new approach from the Californian courts. This was a clear indication from the bench that cases such as *eBay* and *Oyster* had gone too far in finding trespass where there was no harm. As the decision in *Ticketmaster* said, no harm, no tort, and as trespass is a tortious claim (in the US) a claim for trespass should not be entertained without evidence of harm.

5.2.3 ***Intel v Hamidi***

This approach was confirmed later that year by the California Supreme Court in the case of *Intel Corp. v Hamidi*.[53] Ken Hamidi was a former employee of Intel who co-founded

[49] See e.g. *Register.com Inc. v Verio Inc.*, 126 F. Supp. 2d 238 (2000); *American Airlines Inc. v Farechase Inc.*, Case No. 067–194,022–02 (DC Tx) 8 March 2003 <http://www.eff.org/files/filenode/AA_v_Farechase/20030310_prelim_inj.pdf>.

[50] 2003 US Dist LEXIS 6483.

[51] A spider (or web crawler) is a computer program that browses the Web in a methodical, automated manner gathering data. They are used extensively by search engines to catalogue the content of websites.

[52] 2003 US Dist LEXIS 6483.

[53] 30 Cal 4th 1342 (2003).

an organization called FACE-Intel ('Former and Current Employees of Intel'), which was critical of the company's employment practices. Between 1996 and 1998, Hamidi, on behalf of the FACE-Intel, sent six separate emails critical of the company to more than 30,000 Intel employees. Intel sued Hamidi, claiming that, even though its chattels were not damaged, it had suffered harm from lost employee productivity and the time it had spent trying to block his messages.[54] The District Court, in an action affirmed by the Court of Appeal, issued a permanent injunction that prohibited Mr Hamidi from 'sending unsolicited e-mail to addresses on Intel's computer systems', but the California Supreme Court reversed these orders finding by a four to three majority that actual damage or impairment to the chattel was a requirement for a trespass to chattels claim.[55] The majority were of the opinion that what Mr Hamidi was doing in sending these mass emails via the Intel mail server was using the server for what it had been designed: the receipt and sending of email. Further, they suggested, Intel, by allowing external access to the mail server through an external internet connection, must expect that external users will use that mail server to send email to Intel employees. The court, however, refused to overrule the *Thrifty-Tel/CompuServe* line of cases, explaining that the spamming activities in those cases 'overburdened the ISP's own computers and made the entire computer system harder to use for recipients'.[56] Thus the final fall-out from a series of cases, mostly heard in California between 1996 and 2003, seemed to be that there was a recognized tort of trespass to chattels on digital communication networks in California, and probably by extension—through cases such as *CompuServe*,[57] *American Airlines*,[58] and *Register.com*[59]—the US as a whole, if the plaintiff could establish damage, or the likelihood of damage, to the network. If there is no harm or no likelihood of harm then, applying *Ticketmaster* and *Hamidi*, the tort is not made out.

5.2.4 *Associated Press v Meltwater US Holdings, Inc.*

Little happened to disturb this settlement until the rise of news aggregation services caught the attention of news publishing services and wire services such as Associated Press (AP). In February 2012 AP filed a copyright infringement suit (note this is not an old-fashioned trespass to chattels case) claiming that Meltwater's 'Global Media Monitoring' product infringed their copyright in news stories shared via the AP news wire service.[60] Meltwater, much as Tickets.com and Bidder's Edge had done were scraping data from the website of another, in this case AP. The difference in this case, which made it a copyright case rather than a simple trespass to chattels case, was that extracted content was then copied and made available to Meltwater customers, allowing a copyright claim rather than a trespass claim. Meltwater offered a news monitoring service to customers. It would scan over 160,000 news websites daily, indexing and archiving their content. It then offered subscribers the opportunity to search this archive, or to set notification keywords which would trigger news alerts to them. The search return

[54] Ibid. 1348.
[55] Ibid. 1347.
[56] Ibid. 1347.
[57] *CompuServe Inc. v Cyber Promotions Inc.* (n. 40): decided in the Southern District of Ohio.
[58] *American Airlines Inc. v Farechase Inc.* (n. 49): decided in Texas.
[59] *Register.com Inc. v Verio Inc.* (n. 49): decided in the Southern District of New York.
[60] 2013 WL 1153,979 (SDNY 21 March 2013).

or notification would include a level of detail for the customer including the headline of the news report and the lede (or opening section). AP established in evidence that the material replicated to Meltwater customers was between 4.5 per cent and 61 per cent of the articles in question. Meltwater argued their service was transformative, that they were an internet search engine like Google and their service changed the nature of the content from editorial to a location tool. This, they argued was protected by fair use. AP, however, showed in evidence that Google news alerts do not systematically include an article's lede and are on average half the length of Meltwater's excerpts. They also showed that while Google News's click-through rate is at least 56 per cent, Meltwater's was 0.08 per cent. This, AP suggested, was due to the nature of the Meltwater service, it was not in fact a search service but rather a subscription news service. Users of Meltwater's service were not using it to locate then access news stories; it was in itself a news service which was a substitute for the AP service. This was possible as Meltwater extracted enough of the salient news of the AP reports to allow customers to understand the whole story without clicking though to the source material. The court agreed and also found that as a result Meltwater's use of AP's copyright material was not transformative. It ruled that Meltwater used AP's copyright works for commercial use and its use of the articles lowered the value of AP's work. Further, Meltwater copied a qualitatively significant part of the AP articles by copying the title, lede, and materials surrounding the targeted keyword. As a result, the District Court held that Meltwater violated AP's copyrights by excerpting articles without a licence and redistributing them to its own subscribers.[61]

5.3 **Virtual property**

In recent years a new form of digital property and ownership has developed. This surrounds disputes over 'property' in virtual gaming environments such as *World of Warcraft*, *Second Life*, or *Eve Online*. These online gaming experiences known as MMORPGs (Massively Multiplayer Online Role Playing Games) attract millions of gamers every year.[62] There has always been an issue of ownership and property with materials and goods gathered in these MMORPG games, with sites allowing players to buy and sell player accounts, valuable items such as swords or potions, or just to trade 'gold', the online currency of most games for cash. These issues have been magnified of late with the development of 'real-world currency' in MMORPGs such as *Entropia Universe* and *Second Life*. In both these games the in-game currency, the Project Entropia Dollar (PED) and the Linden Dollar (L$), have a currency exchange system that allows for the exchange of in-game currency with real-world US$ allowing you seamlessly to transfer money between the real world and the virtual.[63] With these developments speculation in virtual property has risen in recent years and with speculation comes property disputes and questions over property rights for virtual land and goods.

[61] Readers are recommended at this point to read the discussion of *Public Relations Consultants Association Ltd v Newspaper Licensing Agency Ltd* at 11.1.3.

[62] *World of Warcraft* is reported to have 5.5 million subscribers in Q3 2015, down from a high of 12 million in 2010. *Second Life* is reported to have 42 million residents although fewer than 40,000 are usually online at any time, down from several million active users at its peak in 2007/08. *Eve Online* has around 350,000 subscribers who play regularly.

[63] The PED has a fixed exchange rate with the US dollar, where 10 PED = 1US$; the L$ has a floating exchange rate set on the in-game LindX exchange.

5.3.1 **Virtual theft**

Fantasy/Sci-Fi MMORPGs such as *World of Warcraft* and *Eve Online* have proven to be particularly popular in China and the Pacific Rim. Some Chinese gamers in particular see games such as these as a way to make money and will play for hours at a time gathering items and gold to be sold on the open market in a process known as 'gold farming'. It is therefore no surprise that the earliest reported incidents of virtual property misappropriation were generated in China. Original case reports tend to be in Mandarin and are hard to find, so to piece together the story of virtual property in China relies somewhat on media reports. The first of these to come to widespread attention was in 2003. Reuters reported that a Chinese court ordered an online video game company to return virtual property, including a stockpile of biochemical weapons, to a player whose game account was looted by a hacker.[64] It was reported that Li Hongchen had spent two years, and 10,000 yuan playing *Hongyue* (Red Moon) before a hacker stole weapons he had accumulated in February 2003. Mr Li asked the company behind the game, Beijing Arctic Ice Technology, to identify the player who stole his virtual property, but it declined, saying it could not give out a player's private details. The police said they could not help so Mr Li took his case to court. The company argued that the value of the virtual property only existed in the game and was 'just piles of data to our operating companies', but the Beijing's Chaoyang District People's Court ruled that the firm should restore Mr Li's lost items, finding the company liable because of loopholes in the server programs that made it easy for hackers to break in. Following this case there have been many reports of virtual property disputes in China.

In a further case in 2005 an online gamer in Chengdu found his 'currency' and 'equipment' in the online computer game *The Legend of Mir* abruptly disappeared. The gamer, Mr Zhao, appeared to be a gold farmer as it was reported that 'he hired a person to test the game around the clock for three months and paid him 1,500 yuan each month'.[65] It is reported that Mr Zhao complained to the Consumers' Association of Sichuan Province. According to Law of the People's Republic of China on Protection of Consumer Rights and Interests, Art. 44:

> Article 44: A business operator that causes damage to the property of a consumer in providing a commodity or a service must assume civil liability by means of repair, redoing, replacement, return of goods, making up the quantity of a commodity, refund of payment for the commodity and the service fee or compensation for losses, at the request of the consumer. Where the consumer and business operator have a separate agreement, such agreement shall be implemented.

The Consumers' Association judged that Mr Zhao's rights should be so protected and the operators of the game should compensate him. It is not known though how much compensation was paid to Mr Zhao.[66]

However, the most dramatic case to come out of China is that of Qiu Chengwei. It was widely reported in 2005 that Mr Qiu stabbed a fellow gamer, Zhu Caoyuan, in the chest, killing him when he found out he had sold a virtual sword he had loaned to

[64] See 'Online Gamer in China Wins Virtual Theft Suit' (*CNN*, 20 December 2003) <http://www.cnn.com/2003/TECH/fun.games/12/19/china.gamer.reut/>.

[65] S Xuan, 'Virtual Property in Greater China' <http://www.hg.org/article.asp?id=5538>.

[66] Ibid.

Mr Zhu. Mr Qiu was eventually sentenced to a suspended death sentence (life imprisonment) for the murder.[67] Following these cases the Chinese media have called for closer state regulation of virtual property,[68] and proposals were brought forward to put virtual property on a sound legal footing.[69]

China is not the only country to face the issue of virtual theft. The Netherlands has twice had to deal with issues of virtual misappropriation. In 2007 it was reported that five teenagers had been arrested by police in Amsterdam for stealing virtual property known as 'furni' from the online social network site *Habbo*.[70] They had fraudulently obtained log-in details and passwords from other users and then had 'moved' nearly £3,000 worth of furni from the accounts of other users into their accounts. At the time a spokesperson for the Amsterdam Police stated that 'We are trying to bring charges of theft. It is a little difficult and new. There has not yet been a judgment in a case like this . . . The furniture may not be physical objects but because it represents a certain value we think theft is involved.'[71] It is unclear whether charges were ever brought as further reports of the case are not available, but what is clear is that, in a separate case in Leeuwarden, charges were brought against a 15-year-old and a 14-year-old who forced a 13-year-old to transfer a mask, an amulet, and some credits (virtual cash) to their account in the game *RuneScape*. On 6 September 2007 the two older boys attacked the victim kicking him and threatening him with a knife until he transferred the virtual goods and the credit. The attackers were convicted of 'violent theft' and sentenced to 200 hours' community service (for the 15-year-old) and 160 hours' community service (for the 14-year-old).[72] What is interesting is that they were found guilty not of assault but aggravated theft, a decision recently upheld by the Dutch Supreme Court (Hoge Raad). The court announced that a 'virtual amulet and mask in the online game RuneScape can be classified as "goods" in the sense of Art. 310 [of the Dutch Penal Code] and are prone to theft'.[73] The court noted that the goods were acquired by 'effort and time investment' and that as a result it may be 'reasonably interpreted that such virtual objects shall be considered as goods'.[74] They were also influenced in making a finding of theft by the fact that the rules of *RuneScape* did not allow for the transfer of the goods in the manner perpetrated by the defendants. The theft and transfer were 'committed outside the context of the game. It is therefore not virtual actions inside a virtual world, but to actual operations and a virtual world is affected.'[75] The attack on the victim was clearly a common assault; it is the way the Dutch courts have dealt with the transfer of the virtual property which makes this a watershed decision. This is the

[67] 'Chinese Gamer Sentenced to Life' (*BBC News*, 8 June 2005) <http://news.bbc.co.uk/1/hi/technology/4072704.stm>.

[68] See e.g. China View, 'Virtual Sword Theft Is Real Theft' 28 August 2007 <http://news.xinhuanet.com/english/2007–08/28/content_6614685.htm>.

[69] MM Chew, 'Virtual Property in China: The Emergence of Gamer Rights Awareness and the Reaction of Game Corporations' (2011) 13 *New Media & Society* 722.

[70] B Waterfield, 'World's First Arrests for "Virtual Theft"' *The Telegraph* (London, 15 November 2007).

[71] Ibid.

[72] Supreme Court of the Netherlands Ruling: BQ9251, Hoge Raad, J 10/00101, <http://uitspraken.rechtspraak.nl/inziendocument?id=ECLI:NL:HR:2012:BQ9251> (translations via Google translate).

[73] Ibid.

[74] Ibid.

[75] Ibid.

first time a superior court in Europe has dealt with virtual property in this manner, and to date remains the only such case. As the economies in which virtual goods may be found shrink, as online MMORPGs from real-life simulators such as *Second Life* to RPGs such as *World of Warcraft,* are replaced in our affections by casual games, it is likely the Dutch *RuneScape* case may be the only European ruling on such issues for some time.

5.3.2 **Misappropriation of virtual goods**

As with virtual trespass the US leads the development of virtual property law in the Western legal world. Although there have been no cases such as the Dutch *RuneScape* case where criminal charges have been brought for the 'theft' of virtual goods there have been several civil cases in the US for misappropriation of virtual goods. The first, and best known, of these is *Bragg v Linden and Rosedale.*[76] The plaintiff Marc Bragg is a Pennsylvania attorney and was a *Second Life* land developer known as Marc Woebegone. The defendants were Linden Labs, creator and operator of *Second Life* and Philip Rosedale, CEO of Linden Labs. It was alleged that due to a bug in Linden's system Bragg gained an unfair advantage by accessing land auction pages for parcels of land that were not yet released for auction, enabling him to acquire land in *Second Life* below Linden's cost for that land. In particular it was alleged he paid only $300 for an entire region known as 'Taessot'. Linden Labs suspended Bragg's account for investigation, and then closed the account for violation of the Terms of Service—dissolving his virtual assets. Bragg declared that this process caused him actual losses of between $4,000 and $6,000, and filed a civil suit against Linden Labs for breach of contract and unfair trade practices.[77] Linden Labs attempted to have the case struck out claiming that the court lacked personal jurisdiction over Mr Rosedale and argued that because of an arbitration clause in their player agreement, Mr Bragg was compelled to go to arbitration. The court refused all of Linden's motions. It found that a lack of mutuality meant that the arbitration cause should be struck out[78] and that it had jurisdiction over both Linden Labs and Mr Rosedale.[79] The court appeared to be swayed by the evidence laid before it by Mr Bragg that the defendants had promoted *Second Life*'s unique properties of land ownership and preservation of property rights.[80] Having failed to have the case struck out Linden Labs then sought a settlement with Marc Bragg and on 4 October 2007 it was announced that a settlement had been reached. Although the terms of the settlement remain confidential it is worth noting that in Linden's press release they conceded that Mr Bragg's 'Marc Woebegone' account, privileges, and responsibilities to the *Second Life* community had been restored. This suggests the 'winner' in the settlement was Mr Bragg.

This case is extremely interesting in that it is the first time a common law court sat in judgment on a civil virtual property dispute. A note of caution though must be sounded. Despite being a case *about* virtual property it is not a case which *examines*

[76] 487 F. Supp. 2d 593 (E.D. Penn. 2007).

[77] The motion was initially lodged with the Court of Common Pleas of Chester County, Pennsylvania on 3 October 2006. This was moved to the Federal District Court for the Eastern District of Pennsylvania at the motion of the defendants.

[78] See n. 76 600.

[79] Ibid. 596.

[80] Ibid. 593–4.

virtual property. Instead this is a contractual case with elements of jurisdiction thrown in. Even the most cursory read-through of the decision makes it clear that the two legal issues which preoccupy the judge are personal jurisdiction and mutuality; not the issue of ownership of bits. Thus, although textbooks (including this one) will discuss this case, and although students will continue to study it, it is not a true case of digital property or digital ownership.

Neither, unfortunately, are the other American cases which are often cited alongside *Bragg*. These are the sister cases of *Eros LLC v Simon and Ors*[81] and *Eros LLC v Leatherwood & Ors*.[82] In both cases Eros LLC sued for copyright and trademark infringement. Eros were the producers of a *Second Life* sex aid, known as the SexGen Bed, a digital bed with built-in sex position animations which allowed avatars to have virtual sex in *Second Life*. Their products were extremely popular and were widely pirated. They identified Mr Simon and Mr Leatherwood as two of the pirates copying their goods and filed the lawsuits in New York and Florida respectively. In both cases a quick settlement followed with Mr Simon agreeing to pay $525 in damages to Eros and their co-complainants (that being the sum his illicit activities had earned him) and to agree to be enjoined from further unauthorized copying or advertising of goods in *Second Life*. In the case of Mr Leatherwood it appears no financial settlement was sought, instead he was merely enjoined from copying or displaying any of Eros's merchandise without permission. Again, though like the *Bragg* case these are cases *about* virtual property; they do not *examine* virtual property. In both cases it was traditional intellectual property rights, copyright, and trademarks which were in issue. Also the cases quickly and easily reached settlement because the defendants were clearly involved in infringing activity. If anything is to be learned from the *Eros* cases it is not about virtual property; rather it is confirmation, if it were needed, that traditional intellectual property rights apply in virtual environments and infringements which occur there may be pursued in real-world courts.

Where does this leave the law in the UK? We still cannot say for certain whether a judge in the UK would find a property right in virtual property. There is no case law and no legislation on the issue. The international case law is also far from instructive. The American cases of *Bragg* and *Eros* are not cases which examine or establish any precedent as to the propertization of virtual goods and land: they are merely cases in which virtual property is the underlying subject matter of the dispute, not the legal principle in issue. The Chinese and Dutch cases more directly address the issue of property in virtual goods, but again a close examination of the Chinese cases show they are more directly cases of consumer protection law rather than out-and-out property cases. To date it appears the only country which has directly grappled with the concept of propertization of virtual goods is the Netherlands. In both cases they have clearly treated the virtual goods in question as property, but a major note of caution must be sounded in that both are criminal cases of theft rather than civil cases of ownership and appropriation.

[81] Case 1:07-cv-04447-SLT-JMA (DC ED NY), 3 December 2007 <http://www.citmedialaw.org/sites/citmedialaw.org/files/2008–01–03-Judgment%20by%20Consent%20as%20to%20Simon.pdf>.

[82] Case 8:2007-cv-01158 (DC MD Fla.), 19 March 2008 <http://www.dmlp.org/sites/citmedialaw.org/files/2008–03–20-Order%20for%20Judgment%20by%20Consent.pdf>.

What is clear is that people treat virtual goods like property. They accumulate virtual goods and trade in them. They attach value to them, sometimes massive values such as the US$330,000 that Buzz 'Erik' Lightyear paid in 2009 for the Crystal Palace Space Station in *Entropia Universe*,[83] and they develop and sell/rent virtual goods and land. With financial investment in virtual goods and land there is a need to protect investor confidence. Currently that is being maintained by the developers of these online environments: companies like Mindark (*Entropia Universe*), Linden Labs (*Second Life*), Blizzard Entertainment (*World of Warcraft*), and Sulake (*Habbo*). Through their player agreements they contractually manage the relationships between inhabitants of their worlds. They act as a benevolent dictator, setting the 'rules of the game' prior to the participants taking part. But, as the trickle of cases thus far is showing, when players in the game believe they have been treated unfairly, or have been defrauded, duped, or the victim of a crime they may refer to the traditional courts. This is quite usual: we see the same in traditional games such as football where the Football Association (FA) is allowed by tradition, agreement, and law to arbitrate in most disputes which occur on the pitch. But when a player feels they have lost out and the FA is inadequate to offer the resolution they require they often revert to traditional courts of justice.[84]

5.4 **Conclusions**

The shift in economic value from atomic goods to bits has already raised a number of legal questions, including: is virtual space a form of property? Is virtual property to be equated to physical property and how should virtual property and virtual space be legally protected? The US has heard a number of such cases, while cases on virtual property are being heard in such diverse jurisdictions as the People's Republic of China and the Netherlands. The value of bits is greater than that in just informational and entertainment products such as news reports, music, movies, and television shows. These cases from overseas show there is a demand for the propertization of bits, not just for the application of traditional copyright principles.

In the UK the focus of the case law has been on traditional copyright infringement: linking and scraping. While *Shetland Times v Wills*[85] represented an early and laudable attempt to fix copyright law drafted in the 1980s to the digital environment, the more recent case of *Public Relations Consultants Association Ltd v Newspaper Licensing Agency Ltd*[86] has allowed the UK to take a lead in Europe by setting permissions for web users and resetting the interpretation of Art. 5 of the InfoSoc Directive to ensure those merely browsing the web need never seek licence or permission to do so. Copyright owners may of course still require people to pay commercially for content by placing it behind a paywall, but we can now all assume that freely accessible content may be browsed without restrictions. Although it may not seem it, this is a valuable and exciting development in the area of information law.

[83] B Parr, 'Man Pays Record $330,000 for a Virtual Space Station' (*Mashable*, 31 December 2009) <http://mashable.com/2009/12/31/crystal-palace-space-station-sale/>.

[84] See e.g. *Collett v Smith & Anor* [2008] EWHC 1962 (QB) (11 August 2008) in which former footballer Ben Collet sued Gary Smith and Middlesbrough Football Club over a tackle and injury which ended his career.

[85] 1997 SC 316.

[86] [2013] UKSC 18 (Sup Ct); [2014] AC 1438 (CJEU).

TEST QUESTIONS

Question 1

The idea of 'owning' digital property is nonsensical. Ownership implies rivalrousness and digital property (being just ones and zeros) is always nonrivalrous in nature. This is why *Bragg v Linden and Rosedale* is both wrong-headed and a dangerous precedent.

Discuss.

Question 2

Can it really be trespass to chattels when a web spider or scraper visits your server?

FURTHER READING

Books

R Dannenberg et al., *Computer* Games *and Virtual Worlds: A New Frontier in Intellectual Property Law* (2011)

G Lastowska, *Virtual Justice: The New Laws of Online Worlds* (2010)

J Penner, *The Idea of Property Law* (1997)

Chapters and articles

M Carrier and G Lastowska, 'Against Cyberproperty', 22 *Berkeley Technology Law Journal* 1483 (2007)

J Fairfield, 'Virtual Property', 85 *Boston University Law Review* 1047 (2005)

L Quilter, 'Cyberlaw: The Continuing Expansion of Cyberspace Trespass to Chattels', 17 *Berkeley Technology Law Journal* 421 (2002)

B Tarsa, 'Licensing of Virtual Goods: Misconceptions of Ownership', 12(2) *Gnovis* (online journal)

Cyber-speech

6.1 Introduction

One of the most powerful developments of the digital society has been individual empowerment. By converging the functions of broadcast media and telecommunications systems the digital environment has subtly shifted the balance of power in modern society—empowering the individual, perhaps at a cost to society as a whole.

Historically power over information and its mass distribution rested with a few media organizations. When an event happened, be it mundane, such as the passing of planning permission for a new school, or world-shattering, such as the death of a major political or social figure, information about this occurrence could only be distributed via two discrete informational channels. First, individuals who had possession of the information could pass the information on to others who were within their circle of communications. They could do this by face-to-face meeting where they would directly pass on the information to other parties, or they could use one of the telecommunications (communication at a distance) methods developed more recently such as a personal letter or a telephone call. These methods have become more efficient as technology has developed: the fax machine combines the two systems allowing for a letter to be sent instantaneously while mobile and satellite phones have made person-to-person voice calling more efficient and immediate. All these pre-digital personal communications systems, though, share the characteristic of narrowcasting: they may only be used to pass on information to one person or a small group of people at a time.[1]

To address a large group in the pre-digital era one had to have access to a form of broadcast or mass media. Broadcast and mass media are informational media that allow the transfer of information from one to many through a designated central broadcast point. Mass and broadcast media thus centralized the point of information control allowing for control of the information flow by an individual or a small group. Mass media tends to be the term applied to media with a mass reach with a centralized point of production but no centralized distribution point. This is newspapers and similar news media, including magazines, films, newsreels, books, and periodicals. Broadcast media

[1] The largest group an ordinary individual would hope to address without some form of access to media would be a small public meeting in a town hall or at a designated venue such as Speaker's Corner in Hyde Park. A larger group would require considerable organization and the obtaining of permits from the authorities. With the help of technology systems such as Citizen Band, radio would allow a group to be addressed at a distance but only with the aid of costly and bulky equipment and specialist knowledge.

describes mass media which is distributed via a broadcast centre; this is predominantly radio and television. The fact that mass media/broadcast media were in centralized control made these media forms easy to regulate[2] and led many to assume conspiracies of silence would be struck between media providers and states.[3] Digitization has interrupted the settled environment, both socially and legally with digital mass communications technology changing both the way people interact and the way regulators seek to control content. Nowhere is this more clearly demonstrated than in the development of Web 2.0, a term coined to describe this process of media/communications convergence which allows for enhanced creativity, communications, information sharing, collaboration, and functionality of the web.

This chapter will examine several aspects of this shift in power, and with it the responsibility to act with consideration to fellow citizens. It begins with a background discussion of the technologies involved: from web 1.0 systems such as web pages and internet forums to web 2.0 staples such as blogs, media-sharing sites, syndication and ranking sites and social networking sites. In so doing it will look at the social implications of the shift in power from centralized media organizations to decentralized 'citizen journalism'. We will explore what responsibilities citizens owe to each other in this exciting new environment and ask how regulators may ensure social responsibility is met. We also ask and address the vital question: whose values predominate when regulating a global media tool which does not recognize traditional borders. From here we will examine three particular case studies: (1) political speech, (2) hate speech, and (3) commercial speech. These three are proving to be the most difficult issues currently as there are highly divergent regulatory values in play between, in particular, the US, which applies a First Amendment principle, and the European Union which applies a slightly more restrictive 'tolerances' approach. By the end of the chapter the reader should be familiar with the key values, tensions, and current legal settlements in these areas.

6.2 From web 1.0 to web 2.0

Understanding how digital communications upset the established order of media and communications is essential to this chapter and our analysis of cyber-speech. As we saw in chapter 2, the internet has a longer history than most casual users are aware of. Dating from 1969 it is more than 40 years old, but much of its life has been spent hidden away in universities and research labs. The internet only really came of age in the early 1990s when Berners-Lee and Cailliau's hypertext-based World Wide Web application was released to the general public through the NCSA Mosaic web browser. This development, which we may call web 1.0, gave consumers their first experience of

[2] In the UK the BBC was regulated by the BBC Board of Governors and the Broadcasting Standards Commission (BSC); independent television was regulated by the Independent Television Commission (ITC); newspapers were regulated by the Press Complaints Commission; while commercial radio was regulated by the Radio Authority (RA). Three of these, the BSC, the ITC, and the RA became part of the merged super-regulator Ofcom on 1 January 2004, while the Press Complaints Commission was disbanded in 2014 following the Leveson Inquiry. The Independent Press Standards Organisation (IPSO) has (mostly) taken up its duties.

[3] So-called conspiracy theories number in the thousands. Among the more famous are the Kennedy assassination; the death of Diana, Princess of Wales; and the Roswell cover-up.

a converged media/communications tool. Now the average person could address large groups, as large as any media mogul could through their mass media outlet, and in addition they could address groups or individuals globally, not only locally. This is something that previously only a few media barons such as Rupert Murdoch could imagine.

6.2.1 **Web 1.0: internet forums**

For most web 1.0 consumers their first experience of this newly liberated power came through their first experience of internet forums. An internet forum, or message board, is an online media exchange system which allows members to post messages which may be read at a later date by other forum users and to exchange information on a series of related (or even unrelated) issues. Well-known UK internet forums at the time included The Leaky Cauldron,[4] Outpost Gallifrey,[5] and The Student Room.[6]

Internet forums allowed an individual to address groups which could theoretically number in the millions, although which more likely would be measured in the tens of thousands. Nevertheless, with nothing more specialist, or expensive, than a PC with an internet connection the individual for the first time could engage in a form of broadcasting. A posting on an internet forum could transcend space (and even time) and address audiences of a size previously only available to broadcasters. This empowered the individual internet user: it was a technology which magnified speech as previously only commercial print works and broadcast towers could.

Internet forums proved to be extremely powerful tools with Harry Potter fan forum The Leaky Cauldron credited with breaking the story in 2007 that Albus Dumbledore, a leading character in the Harry Potter book series, was gay.[7] Internet forums also allowed special interest groups to form; groups that due to physical remoteness or simply a lack of social acceptance may never have formed in the real world. Among the more unusual internet forums were The Marmite Forum, which brought together fans of a particular yeast extract; Worms Direct, a forum on worm farming; and Looner Fetish, a forum for individuals with a sexual fetish about balloons. The existence of these niche-interest forums, alongside the mass-audience sites such as The Student Room, were suggested to be evidence that predictions made by Nicholas Negroponte in the mid 1990s have come to pass.

Negroponte predicted individualization in delivery of informational content: that narrower common interests may support a community in the digital environment rather than in the physical environment.[8] If you have a very narrow or specialized interest such as worm farming you will find it extremely difficult to find others who share your interests in the physical world. This is because there are few people who share this interest and they are likely to be physically remote from you. The likelihood of finding people who share a socially marginalizing interest such as a sexual fetish about balloons is even less likely, due to social pressures to conform. The introduction of internet

[4] A Harry Potter themed internet forum.

[5] A Dr Who themed internet forum.

[6] A forum for students and young people.

[7] See <https://www.the-leaky-cauldron.org/2007/10/20/j-k-rowling-at-carnegie-hall-reveals-dumbledore-is-gay-neville-marries-hannah-abbott-and-scores-more>.

[8] Discussed in N Negroponte, *Being Digital* (Hodder & Stoughton 1995) 164–71.

forums changed all this. Negroponte cited two primary reasons for this: the first is that internet forums are 'places without space'—that is, they are places in which physical remoteness is unimportant. If an individual with a narrow interest such as worm farming is in a physically remote area, such as the Scottish Highlands then through an internet forum he may form a community with worm farmers in Boise, Idaho, or Kendujhar, India. Thus digital communications shrink distances between people who share an interest. The second effect Negroponte cited was 'being asynchronous'. This allows people to share a two-way conversation across different time zones with each able to leave a message for the other to collect at a later time. However, Negroponte also predicted that new media outlets such as internet forums would lead to a weakening of the social glue that holds society together. This was the negative effect of a multiplication of media and communication resources that he called the *Daily Me*, a personalized news service which only carries news of interest to the reader.[9] The danger of such a development is that internet users may become insular in their views even if they are seeking to normalize dangerous activities such as child abuse.

6.2.2 **Web 1.0: personal websites**

Around about the same time as internet forums began to flourish, individuals also began to offer personal websites. Personal websites were quite different from forums in that they were not designed to offer an interactive function. Instead, they functioned more like a traditional newspaper in that they allowed individuals to 'publish' their views on any subject and to address them to the world at large. Unlike traditional newspapers of course there were almost no start-up costs and no costs of production. Publication was instantaneous and, unlike newspapers, could stand as a (semi-)permanent record without the need to archive. Also, publication on the web was global. A personal web page, like an internet forum, could reach a potential audience that all but the most powerful media mogul could only dream of. They could even make the news as well as react to it. Probably the most famous example of a personal website reaching global acclaim was in January 1998 when Matt Drudge's *Drudge Report* published the story that President Bill Clinton was having an affair with Monica Lewinski, a White House intern.[10]

6.2.3 **Web 1.0: law and society**

Most discussions of internet forums and personal websites focused on the positive aspects of the technologies. As we have seen, they shrank distances, allowed individuals to address large audiences, and provided positive reinforcement. In addition they also allowed individuals to develop new business models (through e-commerce), allowed the sharing of personal content such as images, and allowed people who have lost touch to find each other again. But there were also negative sides to these technological developments and, as is often the case, it was the dark side of the web which first attracted the interest of lawmakers. First, these technologies could be used to service illegal as well as antisocial activities. Internet forums could positively reinforce the actions of child

[9] Ibid. 152–4.

[10] The original *Drudge Report* is archived at <http://www.drudgereportarchives.com/data/2002/01/17/20020117_175502_ml.htm>.

abusers and could be used to facilitate the trading of pornographic images of children;[11] in addition, internet forums and websites could be used for criminal activity such as the distribution of pornographic images, money laundering, or the support of terrorist activity.[12] A further issue with both forums and websites was defamation, which will be examined fully in chapter 8. During the 1990s several defamation actions were raised both in the UK and the US surrounding issues such as falsely accusing an individual of selling items of clothing praising the Oklahoma City bomber[13] and false claims that an individual had made 'squalid and obscene' comments about Thailand.[14] The reason for the explosion in antisocial and illegal activity seen in the 1990s was that the web empowered individuals to address large groups internationally without the need for an intermediary. The same reason that gave rise to all the positive benefits also causes the negative effects as individuals feel they may act independently of state-based regulation in a way that mass and broadcast media never would. Some do this for profit,[15] and may be seen as the negative side of e-commerce. Others do it because they see it as their right to speak freely without state censor or licence—often these individuals quote Art. 10 of the European Convention on Human Rights (ECHR) or, if based in the US, the First Amendment to the US Constitution.

6.2.4 **Web 2.0: social media platforms**

The web has moved on from the pre-millennial explosion which led to, among other things, the dotcom bubble and the creation of the first internet celebrities such as Matt Drudge. Today's internet user would not recognize the structure of web 1.0. Static web pages and internet forums have been replaced by a dynamic, interactive, and socially connected web experience. The kings of the new web, sometimes called web 2.0, are the social media platforms: content aggregators and suppliers who connect people through social groupings. There are a number of these services such as Reddit, Tumblr, Spotify, Pinterest, Diply, and Instagram—each designed to provide a personalized, Negroponte-style, service to news and business reports, ideas, photographs, music, video, or any other media. Unlike Negroponte's *Daily Me*, however, the content the users receive is selected by their social peers or friends rather than by the users themselves. Within this new space, some sites are more successful than others. The lords of this new space are Blogger, Tumblr, WordPress, and Twitter, for blogs and microblogs; Instagram and Pinterest for photo sharing; WhatsApp and Snapchat for instant communications; Reddit for aggregation; YouTube for video content and; above all, Facebook for, well, just about everything.

[11] See M Eneman, 'The New Face of Child Pornography' in M Klang and A Murray (eds.) *Human Rights in the Digital Age* (Routledge-Cavendish 2005).

[12] In April 1997 the US Department of Justice noted that: 'Bombmaking information is literally at the fingertips of anyone with access to a home computer equipped with a modem. To demonstrate such availability, a member of the DOJ Committee accessed a single website on the World Wide Web and obtained the titles to over 110 different bomb-making texts, including "Calcium Carbide Bomb", "Jug Bomb", "How To Make a CO2 Bomb", "Cherry Bomb", "Mail Grenade" and "Chemical Fire Bottle".' Source: US Department of Justice, *1997 Report on the Availability of Bombmaking Information* <http://cryptome.org/abi.htm>.

[13] *Zeran v America Online, Inc.*, 129 F. 3d 327 (1997).

[14] *Godfrey v Demon Internet Service* [1999] 4 All ER 342.

[15] Such as those supplying internet pornography.

Highlight The digital generation

Number of Facebook photo uploads per day (Dec., 2015): 300,000,000.

Number of tweets per day (Dec., 2015): 500,000,000.

Number of Facebook items shared daily (Dec., 2015): 4,750,000,000.

Number of Instagram photo uploads per day (Nov., 2015): 80,000,000.

Number of Facebook 'likes' per day (Dec., 2015): 4,500,000,000.

Interactivity is at the heart of web 2.0. Whereas much of web 1.0 was unidirectional—content was held on central servers and directed to users—web 2.0 is about interactivity. Web 1.0 may be seen to be an extension of traditional broadcast media with content being radiated out from a central source. Sites such as BBC News, university websites like lse.ac.uk, and traditional e-commerce sites such as Amazon simply transported a traditional media/communications model to cyberspace. Web 2.0 sites are different. They have harnessed the network effects to create user interactivity on a previously unparalleled scale.

The evolution from web 1.0 to web 2.0 like the original development of web 1.0 in the 1990s brings both opportunities and challenges. While as a society the development of social networking sites such as Facebook may be seen to be a positive development, they carry risks. Some of these risks include social network stalking, as well as identity theft[16] and bullying.[17] Video networking site YouTube, while promoting the distribution of user-generated content, was the subject of a $1bn copyright infringement lawsuit[18] that went on for seven years before an undisclosed settlement was reached in 2014,[19] while a flurry of pornographic imitators has sprung up. This expresses the web 2.0 challenge from a regulatory perspective. New media has always empowered a challenge to the traditional regulatory settlement but even web 1.0, with its traditional centralized distribution model, was subject to effective regulation (to an extent). Web 2.0, though, functions decentrally: there is no moderator or gatekeeper (on most) web 2.0 sites partly due to the prohibitive costs involved. Web 2.0 sites, if they are moderated, are usually moderated reactively not proactively. They give unprecedented media distribution ability to those least able to manage it: children and young people. The costs of the printing press and the broadcast tower, originally replaced in the 1990s by the cost of the PC and internet connection, have now been replaced by a free mobile phone with video capability: in other words the cost of broadcasting is negligible.

[16] A 2012 *Which?* survey showed that 61 per cent of Facebook users are concerned about strangers accessing information they've posted on Facebook and 59 per cent say they can't keep up with the number of changes Facebook has made to its data security settings. <http://www.which.co.uk/news/2012/05/facebook-privacy-confusion-rife-as-id-theft-soars-286587/>.

[17] Cyberbullying is a major problem surrounding social media. This is discussed along with stalking in greater detail in ch. 7.

[18] *Viacom International, Inc. & Ors v YouTube, Inc. & Ors* 2010 WL 2532404 (SDNY 2010).

[19] S Rabil, 'Google, Viacom settle YouTube copyright suit, terms not disclosed' [2014] 28 WIPR 23. C Nemeth, '"Oh my God, they killed Kenny!" – copyright infringement on YouTube settled' *PA eBulletin* May 2014 6 <http://www.piperalderman.com.au/__files/f/6098/PB007%200514.pdf>.

These developments are the classic double-edged sword. Although there are a great number of positive effects to be felt from web 2.0, primarily in social networking, ease of access, and empowering individuals to distribute content, there are also some potentially harmful negative effects. The remainder of this chapter will discuss these potentially harmful effects against the backdrop of free expression that web 2.0 technologies power. It will ask where the line should be drawn between freedom of expression and protection for the individual and society, given that speech may be psychologically harmful (as in bullying and hate speech), socially harmful (as in pornography), personally harmful (as in defamatory speech), and economically harmful (as in copyright infringement).

6.3 Freedom of expression and social responsibility

6.3.1 Freedom of expression: the 'First Amendment' approach

The 'right' of free expression is jealously guarded in Western democratic culture. Many First Amendment scholars in the US argue that freedom of expression is vital for the functioning of a modern deliberative democracy: in a school of thought which mirrors the foundations of the adversarial system practised at common law they argue that a 'free trade in ideas' advances the search for truth.[20]

Highlight The First Amendment to the US Constitution

Congress shall make no law respecting an establishment of religion, or prohibiting the free exercise thereof; or abridging the freedom of speech, or of the press; or the right of the people peaceably to assemble, and to petition the Government for a redress of grievances.

As explained by Douglas Vick, this school of thought believes that 'When false ideas are expressed by some citizens, the best response is not sanction by the state but vigorous rebuttal by other citizens. Reliance on state regulation makes for an "inert people", the "greatest menace to freedom", but unimpeded public discussion allows the "power of reason" to triumph in the end.'[21] It is the belief of this 'marketplace of ideas' school that censorship or restriction of free speech is harmful as suppression of harmful speech may inadvertently boost its appeal. On the other hand, by allowing the unfettered expression of opinions despicable to the majority of citizens, the fundamental liberal value of tolerance should be promoted.[22]

The other primary school of thought in the US emphasizes the need for free and unrestricted speech in the exercise of personal autonomy, arguing that free speech is a necessary precondition for individual autonomy, self-realization, and self-fulfilment.[23]

[20] See F Schauer, *Free Speech* (CUP 1982) 15–34; W Marshall, 'In Defense of the Search for Truth as a First Amendment Justification' (1995) 30 *Georgia Law Review* 1.

[21] D Vick, 'Regulating Hatred' in M Klang and A Murray (eds.) *Human Rights in the Digital Age* (Routledge-Cavendish 2005) 47.

[22] L Bollinger, *The Tolerant Society* (OUP 1986).

[23] See C Wells, 'Reinvigorating Autonomy: Freedom and Responsibility in the Supreme Court's First Amendment Jurisprudence' (1997) 32 *Harvard Civil Rights-Civil Liberties Law Review* 159.

This school believes that individuals not only have the right to receive information uncensored by the state, 'they have the right to form their own beliefs and express them to others . . . state suppression of speech therefore violates the "sanctity of individual choice" and is an affront to the dignity of the individual'.[24]

6.3.2 **Freedom of expression: the European approach**

The European approach is slightly different. Although the philosophical foundations of free expression share certain common characteristics with the US, in particular John Stuart Mill's assertion that if we tolerate restrictions placed on speech this may restrict the ascertainment and publication of facts and valuable opinion,[25] we have different tolerances than those found in the US.

European values, perhaps shaped by our experiences of the first half of the twentieth century, particularly the powerful effect of the Nazi rhetoric which cost so many lives during the Reich and World War II, provide greater weighting to dignity when striking a balance between the interest of free expression and the (sometimes) conflicting value of respect for human dignity. Thus in Germany and France there are laws which restrict expression designed to deny the holocaust or offend the memory of the country.[26] The experience of the harm speech can do, as demonstrated in Nazi Germany, caused European legislatures to restrict a variety of forms of speech. Seeing how Hitler turned public opinion against disenfranchised groups such as communists, Jews, and homosexuals we have taken steps to protect groups within society who could otherwise feel stigmatized by their distinction from the mainstream, causing them to withdraw rather than to participate in public discourse. For instance in the UK, racial unrest in the 1960s led to the banning of 'threatening, abusive, or insulting' public statements made with the intent to incite racial hatred.[27] In addition it is a criminal offence to possess with the intent to publish material or recordings which are likely to stir up racial hatred.[28]

It may be expected that laws such as those contained in the Public Order Act 1986 (as amended) which restrict speech on grounds of racial or religious hatred or found at the common law of blasphemy, which restricts speech harmful to Christianity,[29] would not survive the modern legal order where Art. 10 ECHR is given effect in the UK through the Human Rights Act. But when one reads Art. 10 in full it becomes clear that such restrictions on speech are justified. It states:

1. Everyone has the right to freedom of expression. This right shall include freedom to hold opinions and to receive and impart information and ideas without interference by public authority and regardless of frontiers. This Article shall not prevent States from requiring the licensing of broadcasting, television or cinema enterprises.

[24] Vick (n. 21). See also Schauer (n. 20) 62, 68.

[25] Discussed in E Barendt, *Freedom of Speech* (2nd edn, OUP 2005) 7–13.

[26] For discussions of German law, see D Kommers, *The Constitutional Jurisprudence of the Federal Republic of Germany* (2nd edn, Duke UP 1997). A discussion of the French position follows.

[27] Race Relations Act 1965, s. 6(1). The law, now found in the Public Order Act 1986, defines 'racial hatred' as hatred against a group based on their 'colour, race, nationality (including citizenship) or ethnic or national origins', s. 17.

[28] Public Order Act 1986, s. 23.

[29] A discussion of the common law of blasphemy may be found in Barendt (n. 25) 186–8.

2. The exercise of these freedoms, since it carries with it duties and responsibilities, may be subject to such formalities, conditions, restrictions or penalties as are prescribed by law and *are necessary in a democratic society, in the interests of national security, territorial integrity or public safety, for the prevention of disorder or crime, for the protection of health or morals, for the protection of the reputation or rights of others, for preventing the disclosure of information received in confidence, or for maintaining the authority and impartiality of the judiciary* [emphasis added].

6.3.3 Freedom of expression: the approaches compared

The key distinction between the US First Amendment approach and the European approach is in the exceptions. The right given in Art. 10 is not absolute: in fact the exceptions found in Art. 10(2) are extensive. This may be compared with the First Amendment to the US Constitution which states: 'Congress shall make no law respecting an establishment of religion, or prohibiting the free exercise thereof; or abridging the freedom of speech, or of the press; or the right of the people peaceably to assemble, and to petition the Government for a redress of grievances.' The First Amendment is noticeable for its lack of exceptions. This does not mean there are no exceptions to it: obscene speech is still illegal,[30] as are words designed to incite imminent violence (so-called 'fighting words').[31]

Despite these limitations the First Amendment is little restricted whereas European restrictions on Art. 10 are varied and extensive and include the aforementioned restrictions on racial and religious hatred and Nazi/Holocaust denial speech as well as restrictions on obscenity, libel, slander, and reporting of matters *sub judicae*, as well as allowing advertising restrictions on products such as tobacco, all of which are much more restrictive than their US counterparts.

This distinction in approaches between the US and the EU/UK has in the past been of little import. Media outlets tended to be focused on a particular state and would comply with the laws and practices of that state: individuals lacking the ability to be heard outside their home jurisdiction need only comply with the legal standard of that place. But as we have seen, the development of web 1.0 and later web 2.0 have both changed the focal point for media organizations who may now address an international audience as easily as a domestic one, and for individuals who are empowered to reach a global mass audience. It was only a matter of time until the inherent tensions between the European approach to free expression and the US approach came to light. It was eventually, and starkly, highlighted in a series of hearings in Paris and in San José and San Francisco, California. In total across six years a series of six judgments were required in the related cases of *LICRA et UEJF v Yahoo! Inc. and Yahoo! France*,[32]

[30] *Miller v California*, 413 US 15 (1973).

[31] *Chaplinsky v New Hampshire*, 315 US 568 (1941).

[32] Tribunal de Grande Instance de Paris (Superior Court of Paris). There are three separate orders in this case. To make sense of the case you should read all three. Order of 22 May 2000 <http://www.lapres.net/yahen.html>; Order of 11 August 2000 <http://www.lapres.net/yahen8.html>; Order of 20 November 2000 <http://www.lapres.net/yahen11.html>.

and *Yahoo! Inc. v LICRA*,[33] an action described by one US commentator as 'a backlash response to the cultural and technological hegemony of the United States in the online world'.[34]

6.3.4 *LICRA et UEJF v Yahoo! Inc. and Yahoo! France*

The cases began in Paris in May 2000 when the International League Against Racism and Anti-Semitism (LICRA) and the Union of French Jewish Students (UEJF) raised an action against Yahoo! Inc. and Yahoo! France alleging that Yahoo! Inc. (the American parent company) hosted an auction site which offered for sale many items of Nazi memorabilia and paraphernalia including copies of the book *Mein Kampf* by Adolf Hitler, and that Yahoo! France provided links and access to this material via the Yahoo.com website.

On 22 May 2000 the Tribunal de Grande Instance de Paris held that access by French internet users to the auction site was an offence under French law.[35] They ordered Yahoo! Inc. to 'take such measures as may be necessary to prevent the exhibition or sale on its Yahoo.com site of Nazi objects throughout the territory of France'. In addition Yahoo! France was ordered to warn all internet users of the risk of viewing sites which contravene French law.

Yahoo! Inc. argued that the Tribunal de Grande Instance de Paris was not competent to make a ruling in this case as the services offered (the auction website and the Yahoo.com site) and Yahoo! Inc. itself were all offered in, or domiciled in, the US. The tribunal replied that as 'the harm is suffered in France; our jurisdiction is therefore competent over this matter pursuant to Article 46 of the New Code of Civil Procedure'. Yahoo! Inc. further argued that there were no technical means capable of allowing them to satisfy the order, and that even if such means were to exist their implementation would be at an undue cost to Yahoo! and would compromise the internet's character as a space of liberty and freedom. This they said was reflected in the application of the US Constitution which guaranteed freedom of opinion and expression to every US citizen, which had been recognized as applying to internet speech in *Reno v ACLU*,[36] and further that, as its services are directed primarily at internet users in the US and its servers are based in the US, the order of 22 May was 'a coercive measure [which] could have no application in the United States'.[37]

[33] There were three hearings in California. A hearing before the District Court in which a decision was filed on 7 November 2001—*Yahoo Inc. v LICRA*, 145 F. Supp. 2d 1168 (N.D. Cal. 2001) an appeal to the 9th Circuit in which a ruling was filed on 23 August 2004—*Yahoo Inc. v LICRA*, 379 F. 3d 1120 (9th Cir. 2004) and an *en banc* rehearing before the 9th Circuit in which a ruling was filed on 12 January 2006—*Yahoo Inc. v LICRA*, 433 F. 3d 1199 (9th Cir. 2006).

[34] M Fagin, 'Regulating Speech across Borders: Technology vs Values' (2003) 9 *Michigan Telecommunications and Technology Law Review* 395, 421 <http://repository.law.umich.edu/mttlr/vol9/iss2/4/>.

[35] It is an offence under Art. R.645–1 of the Penal Code to display or offer for sale any material which offends the collective memory of the country. Such materials include any uniforms, insignia, or emblems resembling those worn by the Nazis. See the Order of 22 May 2000 <http://www.lapres.net/yahen.html>.

[36] 521 US 844 (1997).

[37] For a discussion of this see D Vick, 'The Internet and the First Amendment' (1998) 61 *MLR* 414.

To answer the technical challenges that Yahoo! Inc. had raised, a panel of experts was convened and in August the court ordered that the panel be appointed to review Yahoo!'s technical claims. The panel was formed of one French expert (François Wallon),[38] one American expert (Vinton Cerf),[39] and one independent European expert (Ben Laurie).[40] The experts reported to the tribunal on 6 November 2000. They estimated that 'almost 70 per cent of the IP addresses attributed to French internauts may be associated with certainty to a French domiciliation of the access provider and be filtered'.[41] In fact it was pointed out by the expert panel that 'Yahoo! carries out a posting of advertising banners targeting internauts which the company thinks are French and that it has available the technical means enabling it to identify them'.[42] Two of the consultants (Wallon and Laurie) suggested that in those cases where nationality was not clear from IP address identification, Yahoo! Inc. could ask visitors to Yahoo! sites to make a declaration of nationality. By a combination of these two techniques it was estimated by M. Wallon and Mr Laurie that Yahoo! would achieve a filtering success rate approaching 90 per cent. Vinton Cerf disagreed with points of the technical report. He was concerned about privacy issues if this approach went ahead:

> Some users consider such questions to be an invasion of privacy. While I am not completely acquainted with privacy provisions in the Europe Union, it might be considered a violation of the rights of privacy of European users, including French users to request this information. Of course if this information is required solely because of the French Court Order, one might wonder on what grounds all other users all over the world are required to comply.[43]

Despite these concerns Cerf approved the report of the two other experts.

On the basis of this report the tribunal ordered that 'the combination of technical means available and of the initiatives which it can implement if only for the sake of elementary public morals therefore make it possible to satisfy the injunctions contained in the order of May 22, 2000: that is through filtering of access to the site auctioning Nazi [paraphernalia] and of any other site or service which contains an apology of Nazism' and that '[following] a period of three months which will be allowed for compliance with this order . . . it [Yahoo! Inc.] shall be liable to pay Fr100,000 per day of delay until execution shall have been fully accomplished'.[44]

6.3.5 **Cross-border speech**

Following the order of the court of 22 May Yahoo! France had made steps to ensure compliance with the part of the order directed at them. This was 'to warn all internet users of the risk of viewing sites which contravene French law'. To comply with this order, Yahoo! France modified its terms and conditions which could be accessed

[38] A lawyer with considerable computer law experience.

[39] Vinton (Vint) Cerf is known as the father of the internet and helped design the TCP/IP protocol. He is discussed in ch. 2.

[40] A software designer who among other things wrote Apache-SSL which is used for secure data transmission on the internet.

[41] Order of 20 November 2000 <http://www.lapres.net/yahen11.html>.

[42] Ibid.

[43] Ibid.

[44] Ibid. At current values this is just over €15,244 per day.

through the 'Find out about Yahoo!' link on the bottom of all Yahoo! web pages.[45] In addition Yahoo! France placed a warning when the user chose to search Yahoo.com from Yahoo.fr.[46] In the 20 November order the court noted that 'Yahoo! France has for the most part fulfilled the letter and the spirit of the decision of May 22, 2000 which contains an injunction applicable to Yahoo! France'. As a result of this Yahoo! France were exempted from further enforcement actions.[47] Yahoo! Inc. claimed the order was incompetent but the court reinforced it.

Rather than continue to pursue the action in France, Yahoo! Inc. retreated to the US. There Yahoo! raised a claim in the Federal District Court for the Northern District of California in San José. They sought a declaration that the French decisions were unenforceable in the US as they were in violation of the First Amendment.

Applying the precedents of earlier cases including *Telnikoff v Matusevitch*[48] and *Bachchan v India Abroad Publications Inc.*,[49] the District Court found that the French judgments had violated basic precepts of US law, noting: 'Although France has the sovereign right to regulate what speech is permissible in France, this court may not enforce a foreign order that . . . chills protected speech [occurring] simultaneously within our borders.'[50] In effect the District Court was stating publicly what had always been the issue in this series of hearings: the speech in question was, due to the borderless nature of internet communications, being broadcast simultaneously in both the US and in France (and in fact in every other state worldwide which had internet access). This is the pressure point where the freedom to express oneself and the duty to exercise that freedom responsibly meets: the very application of Shaw's principle.

Highlight Shaw's principle

Liberty means responsibility. That is why most men dread it.[51]

With traditional broadcast and mass media we could entrust the publishers or broadcasters to act to protect wider social values. It did not matter if they agreed with those values or not, as they had made considerable financial investments in their distribution networks they were susceptible to state-based regulation. Further, as the

[45] The new text read 'If in the context of a search conducted on www.yahoo.fr from a tree structure or keywords, the result of the search is to point to sites, pages or forums whose title and/or content contravenes French law, considering notably that Yahoo! France has no control over the content of those sites and external sources (including content referenced on other Yahoo! sites and services worldwide) you must desist from viewing the site concerned or you may be subject to the penalties provided in French law or legal action may be brought against you': ibid.

[46] This warning stated: 'If you continue this search on Yahoo! US, you could be invited to view revisionist sites of which the content contravenes French law and the viewing of which could lead to prosecution': ibid.

[47] Ibid.

[48] 702 A 2d 230 (Md 1997). In which case it was held that an attempt to enforce a libel judgment entered in England was contrary to the public policy of the State of Maryland as well as the First Amendment.

[49] 585 NYS 2d 661 (NY 1992). A similar case in which an attempt to enforce a libel judgment entered in England was contrary to the public policy of the State of New York as well as the First Amendment.

[50] *Yahoo Inc. v LICRA*, 145 F. Supp. 2d 1168 (N.D. Cal. 2001), 1192.

[51] Source: *Oxford Dictionary of Quotations* (7th edn, OUP 2009).

geographical reach of their media outlets was limited by the natural geography of the physical environment it was often the case that a single state regulator could effectively police the speech of a single broadcast outlet. Television capable of reception in the UK was generally broadcast from the UK and was regulated by the Broadcasting Standards Council and the Independent Television Commission.[52] Even the arrival of satellite television changes little. Most viewers in the UK get satellite television signals from two satellite providers, Astra and Eutelsat. These satellites site in a geostationary orbit close enough to each other to be picked up by the same fixed satellite dish. To get a signal from other satellites requires an expensive motorized dish. These satellites carry many hundreds of TV and Radio channels, not all of which are licensed to broadcast to the UK but a second layer of regulation ensures that in most cases only channels licensed to be broadcast within the UK are received here and that is in the satellite decoder. A satellite dish alone does not allow you to watch satellite television; you also need a decoder, and often a 'smartcard' as satellite transmissions are broadcast in an encrypted format. This allows states-based regulators to control satellite signals within their borders. You may not be able to prevent the signal itself from being broadcast across your borders but you can control the possibility of citizens decoding and viewing that signal.

This is the approach taken by successive UK governments. Under s. 177 of the Broadcasting Act 1990 the Independent Television Commission (now Ofcom) can recommend to the Secretary of State for Culture, Media and Sport that a foreign channel is made the subject of a proscription order if it is satisfied the channel repeatedly 'offends against good taste and decency'. A proscription order makes it a criminal offence in the UK to sell smartcards and decoders or subscriptions, to publish programme information, or to advertise designated services. In recent years a number of channels broadcasting hardcore pornography have been proscribed including most famously 'Red Hot Dutch'.[53] No proscription orders have been issued since 2000. This may be due to their doubtful legality at EU Law,[54] or more simply it may reflect the fact that the market is effectively self-regulating with no need for regulator intervention.

What the *Yahoo!* case demonstrated at a stroke was that the internet was different. There is no need of specialist equipment to receive it: it was the first truly global media. Yahoo!'s sites were available both in the US and in France simultaneously. The pages were not simply published in the US, where the First Amendment applied, but were also published in France where Art. R.645-1 of the Penal Code applied. There were two competing regulators, each equally valid in their claim. In addition to this it should be remembered that this case was a web 1.0 case. The defendant was a major multinational company; a traditional media company if you will. In future cases regulators may be trying to control the actions of individuals who use a number of web 2.0 outlets making it extremely difficult to control harmful speech.

[52] The one exception to this was that near to the border viewers in Northern Ireland could pick up television broadcasts from the Republic of Ireland.

[53] For a discussion of these actions see A Harcourt 'Institution-driven Competition: The Regulation of Cross-border Broadcasting in the EU' (2007) 27 *Journal of Public Policy* 293.

[54] See *Danish Satellite TV (DSTV) A/S (Eurotica Rendez-vous Television) v Commission of the European Communities* [2000] EUECJ T-69/99.

6.3.6 *Yahoo! Inc. v LICRA*

The *Yahoo!* case went on to have two appeals in California. In the first appeal,[55] LICRA and EUJF argued that the District Court erred in finding it had jurisdiction to hear the case. They argued that the District Court lacked personal jurisdiction, that the case was not ripe (because they have not yet sought to enforce the French judgment in the US), and that the abstention doctrine applied.[56] The majority (Judges Ferguson and Tashima) found that the District Court had erred in finding personal jurisdiction and reversed the decision.[57] Judge Brunetti wrote a strong dissenting judgment. He argued first that 'the case law in our circuit makes clear that, although wrongful conduct will satisfy the Supreme Court's constitutional standard for the exercise of in personam jurisdiction, it is not necessarily required in all cases; indeed, I believe that the Supreme Court's "express aiming" test may be met by a defendant's intentional targeting of his actions at the plaintiff in the forum state'.[58] Further, he argued that:

> the record provides ample indication that LICRA and UEJF targeted Yahoo! in California by successfully moving the French court to issue an order requiring Yahoo!'s American website to comply with French law, serving Yahoo! with such order in the US, and thereby subjecting Yahoo! to significant and daily accruing fines if Yahoo! refuses to so comply; it is immaterial to the analysis that LICRA and UEJF have yet to enforce the monetary implications of Yahoo!'s refusal to acquiesce in the French court order.[59]

With such a strong dissenting judgment it is no surprise that Yahoo! continued to press their case. They convinced the Court of Appeal to rehear the case and a rehearing *en banc* by a panel of 11 judges was approved. The judgment of the court was given on 12 January 2006 with a narrow majority of 6:5 electing to refuse the appeal and dismiss the case, but this fact does not convey the complexity of this decision.[60] Of the 11 members of the panel 8 found that the court did hold personal jurisdiction over the respondents and could hear the case. Thus on personal jurisdiction the majority verdict would have been 8:3 in favour of allowing the appeal. But, the question of ripeness (argued by UEJF and LICRA in the first appeal) remained. On this ground there were five votes for ripeness, three votes against ripeness, and three members of the court who did not reach the question (the three who had dismissed the appeal on the personal jurisdiction claim). This strange set of affairs led to a very unusual and complex result: the court held that because a three-judge plurality concluded that the suit was not ripe, '[w]hen the votes of the three judges who conclude that the suit is unripe are combined with the votes of the three dissenting judges who conclude that there is no personal jurisdiction over LICRA and UEJF, there are six votes to dismiss Yahoo!'s suit'.[61]

[55] *Yahoo! Inc. v LICRA*, 379 F. 3d 1120 (9th Cir. 2004).

[56] The abstention doctrine states that a court of law should (or in some cases must) refuse to hear a case, when hearing the case would potentially intrude upon the powers of another court (in this case the Tribunal de Grande Instance de Paris).

[57] They did not rule on the two other issues.

[58] *Yahoo!* (n. 55) 1127.

[59] Ibid.

[60] *Yahoo! Inc. v LICRA* 433 F. 3d 1199 (9th Cir. 2006).

[61] Ibid. 1248.

This is a highly unusual decision caused by a large *en banc* panel. Technically there never was a majority to dismiss the appeal on either of the grounds of appeal. Three judges rejected the first ground (personal jurisdiction) and three (different) judges rejected the second ground (ripeness) but because three of the panel never examined that ground we will never know what their decision may have been. It is possible that eight judges may have found in favour of each of Yahoo!'s grounds of appeal but they could still have lost on the narrow 6:5 decision. It is not surprising that following this decision that Yahoo! applied to the Supreme Court to hear the case. Unfortunately *certiorari* was denied in May 2006, effectively ending the case unless LICRA decides to enforce the judgment against Yahoo! in the future which seems highly unlikely as Yahoo! Inc announced in January 2001 that it would no longer allow Nazi or Ku Klux Klan memorabilia to be displayed on its websites and that a new proactive filtering and monitoring system would be installed.[62] This means that since January 2001 Yahoo! Inc. has probably been in compliance with the orders of 22 May and 20 November. The cases in California were in fact mostly moot, which is probably why the Supreme Court denied *certiorari*.

6.3.7 **Free expression online**

This series of cases is in itself fascinating for the insight it provides into the difficulties national laws and state-based regulators are having, and will continue to have in enforcing national legal standards in the digital environment. As predicted by David Post and David Johnson national laws conflict with each other in the borderless environment of the internet.[63] Indeed a case which reflected the *Yahoo! France* case emerged in 2012 as another case was brought by the Union of French Jewish Students. In October 2012 a rather unsavoury hashtag appeared on Twitter: #unbonjuif (a good Jew). The tweets tagged as such were anti-Semitic in nature. In November 2012, UEJF filed a summons requiring Twitter to reveal the identity of account holders who posted material in breach of Art. R.645-1 of the French Penal Code using this hashtag. Taking a lead from Yahoo! Twitter had already voluntarily removed the offending tweets and had taken steps to prevent their republication. However, UEJF felt this did not go far enough. In January 2013 the Tribunal de Grande Instance agreed and issued an order requiring Twitter to identify a number of account holders or face a fine of €1,000 per day. Twitter responded by saying it was reviewing legal options, but earlier in the same month had asserted that it would need an order from a US court before it would, or could, disclose such personal details. The case was settled in July 2013 when Twitter handed over to the prosecutor of the Paris Tribunal de Grande Instance, the data needed to enable him to identify users that he believed had violated French law.[64] The settlement was prompted it seems by a decision of the Cour d'Appel to uphold the

[62] M Ward, 'Yahoo! Looks for Hate' (*BBC News*, 3 January 2001) <http://www.news.bbc.co.uk/1/hi/sci/tech/1098761.stm>; D Usborne, 'Yahoo! to Ban Trade in Racist Material on Website' *The Independent* (London, 4 January 2001) <http://www.independent.co.uk/news/business/news/yahoo-to-ban-trade-in-racist-material-on-website-705370.html>.

[63] D Johnson and D Post, 'Law and Borders: The Rise of Law in Cyberspace' (1996) 48 *Stanford Law Review* 1367.

[64] H Carnegy and T Bradshaw, 'Twitter hands over data to French prosecutors' *Financial Times* (London, 13 July 2013).

decision of the Tribunal de Grande Instance. This is in keeping with Twitter's policy that they may 'disclose your information if we believe that it is reasonably necessary to comply with a law, regulation, legal process, or governmental request'.[65] In fact there are many examples of such requests being met published in the Twitter transparency report. The report for the first six months of 2015 shows that Twitter received 4,363 requests for data (including 299 from the UK) of which at least some data was produced in 58 per cent of cases (51 per cent in the UK) affecting 12,711 accounts (1,041 in the UK).[66]

The issues demonstrated in these cases, and in the Twitter transparency report, are likely to be substantially magnified in the future. The web 2.0 environment invites greater individual speech, facilitated by a platform. Whereas corporations have to fulfil standards of corporate social responsibility and must be sensitive to community values of all their customers wherever they are,[67] individuals have no such responsibility or sensitivities.[68] Furthermore individuals need not necessarily even be aware of different community or legal standards elsewhere. A real concern of web 2.0 is that it becomes a cacophony of speech rather than a marketplace for speech. Everyone feels they can say whatever they want, whenever they want, and they feel it is their right not to be censored and to address the world in breach of Shaw's principle.

Highlight Shaw's principle restated

Liberty means Responsibility: to be allowed to speak in a public forum one must respect other members of that forum. The right to free expression should not be allowed to trump another individual's rights such as their privacy or their right to security or to a fair trial.

The problem with the information society in general and web 2.0 in particular is that it will be very difficult to protect the rights of others as there seems to be an assumption that speech must be protected to protect the 'core values' of internet civil society and further, with the backbone of web 2.0 systems provided from the US, the primacy of free expression is again to the fore.

6.4 **Political speech**

When most commentators discuss the archetypal example of free expression they usually give political speech, or rather political debate and discourse, as the paradigm. The principle of free, that is unrestricted, speech in the political sphere is an extension of

[65] Twitter Inc., *Privacy Policy* <https://twitter.com/privacy?lang=en>.

[66] For up-to-date data see <https://transparency.twitter.com/>.

[67] This may explain why Yahoo! voluntarily removed offensive material from its sites and why Twitter removed the offending tweets.

[68] The numbers of examples to demonstrate this are legion. There is the example of the Twitter users who defamed Conservative peer Lord McAlpine; the unmasking of privacy injunction holders like Ryan Giggs, again on Twitter; or the attempts made to organize violence and looting via Facebook in the 2011 English riots. See ch. 7 for more on this.

democracy itself. This is most clearly enunciated in the judgment of Justice Brandeis in the US Supreme Court case of *Whitney v California* in which he said:

> Those who won our independence believed that the final end of the State was to make men free to develop their faculties, and that, in its government, the deliberative forces should prevail over the arbitrary. They valued liberty both as an end, and as a means. They believed liberty to be the secret of happiness, and courage to be the secret of liberty. They believed that freedom to think as you will and to speak as you think are means indispensable to the discovery and spread of political truth; that, without free speech and assembly, discussion would be futile; that, with them, discussion affords ordinarily adequate protection against the dissemination of noxious doctrine; that the greatest menace to freedom is an inert people; that public discussion is a political duty, and that this should be a fundamental principle of the American government.[69]

In the latter half of the twentieth century the greatest proponent of this principle of 'democratic speech' was the American scholar Alexander Meiklejohn who suggested that the primary purpose of the First Amendment is to protect the right of all citizens to understand political issues and through this to participate in democracy.[70] Although Eric Barendt, writing from the UK point of view, is suspicious of the Meiklejohn position he recognizes that political speech is treated as a special case by courts.[71] He notes that two decisions in particular demonstrate that English courts are willing to give strong protection to political speech and perhaps even raise it above other forms of speech. In *Derbyshire County Council v Times Newspapers* the House of Lords held that it was contrary to public interest to allow any government authority to make a claim for libel as that would fetter free political discourse, with Lord Keith commenting that: 'it is vital that a democratically elected governmental body, or indeed any governmental body, should be open to uninhibited public criticism'.[72] Then in the later case of *R (on the application of ProLife Alliance) v BBC*,[73] the Court of Appeal gave explicit protection to 'freedom of political debate' in holding that the refusal of the BBC to transmit a party election broadcast of the ProLife Alliance on the grounds that it offended good taste and decency was unlawful. Although the House of Lords later upheld an appeal from the BBC, as Barendt notes, it did not in so doing question the value of political speech: its decision was solely based on the view that the BBC should not have to transmit any material which offended taste and decency.[74]

6.4.1 **Political speech: economics and media**

It is though another aspect of the democratic nature of free speech which draws the attention of lawyers in the information environment. If one accepts that political speech is a key component of democratic discourse one must face the challenge that potentially those individuals who have greatest access to media and other mass discourse tools have the potential to dominate political discourse, perhaps to the detriment of democracy.

[69] *Whitney v California*, 274 US 357 (1927), 375–8.

[70] See A Meiklejohn, *Political Freedom: The Constitutional Powers of the People* (Harper & Brothers 1960); A Meiklejohn, 'The First Amendment is an Absolute' (1961) *Supreme Court Review* 245.

[71] Barendt (n. 25) 18–21, 154–5.

[72] [1993] AC 534, 547.

[73] [2002] 2 All ER 756.

[74] *R (on the application of ProLife Alliance) v BBC* [2004] 1 AC 185.

The US famously does not restrict political advertising and promotional spend in election campaigns. This means there is an open avenue of criticism that money, not ideology, buys the White House.

This pattern is not uncommon in US politics where it is quite usual for the candidate who spends most on campaigning to win the presidency. In his paper *Campaign Spending and Presidential Election Results*, David Nice notes that:

> Of the thirty-one presidential elections held from 1860 through 1980, the winner outspent the loser 22 out of 31 times. If we focus just on open races, those with no incumbent running, the winner outspent the loser in 11 out of 12 races. By contrast, when an incumbent was running, a challenger who spent 41 percent or more of the two-party expenditure had a 50 percent chance of victory. All challengers who spent less than 41 percent of the two-party expenditure lost.[75]

This suggests one is to be suspicious of unfettered free political speech at a time of election as the democratic process may be subverted by the candidate best able to get across his or her campaign rhetoric to the electorate.

To prevent the risk of subversion of the electorate in the UK we have strict campaign regulations. In the period immediately prior to a General Election campaign a prospective candidate may only spend £30,700 plus 6p for every registered voter (in a borough constituency) or 9p for every registered voter (in a county constituency).[76] Once selected for election, candidates may only spend £8,700 plus 6p for every registered voter (in a borough constituency) or 9p for every registered voter (in a county constituency).[77] The reason for the distinction between the two types of constituency is to reflect the fact that electioneering in a rural constituency costs more than in an urban one. As the average constituency size for parliamentary elections is approximately 66,250 registered voters this limits local spending by candidates during General Elections to around £12,500. This does not, though, limit national spending by political parties which used to be unlimited. This money could only though be spent on newspaper or billboard advertising with the exception of party political and party election broadcasts, which are strictly regulated;[78] it is illegal to place political advertising on radio and television in the UK.[79]

Following the report of the Neill Committee into Standards in Public Life in 1999 even this provision was changed with new limits placed on national expenditure. By Schedule 9 of the Political Parties, Elections and Referendums Act 2000, in a General Election a political party may only spend £30,000 multiplied by the number of constituencies contested by the party in that part of Great Britain or Northern Ireland; or if higher (a) in relation to England, £810,000; (b) in relation to Scotland, £120,000; and (c) in relation to Wales, £60,000. This means a party which campaigned in all 650 constituencies in the UK would have a maximum national campaign expenditure of £19,500,000.[80]

[75] 19 *Polity* 464 (1987) 468.

[76] Representation of the People Act 1983, s. 76ZA.

[77] Representation of the People Act 1983, s. 76(2)(a).

[78] See Communications Act 2003, s. 333; Broadcasting Act 1990, ss. 36 and 107.

[79] Communications Act 2003, s. 319(2)(g).

[80] In the 2010 General Election the Labour Party spent £8,009,483; the Conservatives spent £16,682,874; and the Liberal Democrats £4,787,595 <http://www.electoralcommission.org.uk/i-am-a/journalist/electoral-commission-media-centre/news-releases-donations/parties-spend-31-million-at-uk-general-election>.

With political advertising strictly regulated, political parties often seek media coverage of speeches and events. To combat an imbalance of coverage between mainstream and minor parties the Representation of the People Act 1983 requires broadcasters to draw up codes of good practice, which are required to be reviewed by the Electoral Commission, to ensure fair and impartial coverage of political speech during elections.[81]

6.4.2 **Online political speech**

The question is how does online speech affect these provisions? These laws are predicated upon the idea that communication between political parties and candidates and the general public will be transmitted through traditional media routes. Whereas the Communications Act and the Broadcasting Act regulate electoral media transmissions through radio and television channels they are silent as to new media channels such as SMS messaging, blogs, websites, and YouTube channels.[82] Any expenditure by political parties on new media messaging will, of course, have to be accounted for in their election returns and will count towards maximum expenditure limits discussed above. In this sense new media advertising may be seen to be akin to traditional billboard or newspaper advertising.

This was the view of the Electoral Commission in their 2003 report *Online Election Campaigns*.[83] Following an extensive review of the use of campaign websites, SMS messaging, and email campaigning (the report predates YouTube and most social networking sites such as Facebook) the Electoral Commission concluded that they: 'value the level playing field and platform for free speech which the internet and other online communication technologies can provide'. As a result they reported that 'while we do not accept that online campaign activities should be entirely free from regulatory restrictions, any regulatory action should be limited to the minimum necessary to protect a fair campaign environment'.[84] As a result they made no proposals to specifically regulate online activities of political parties, except to recommend that s. 146 of the Political Parties, Elections and Referendums Act 2000, which requires the name and address of the promoter of political communications to appear on the communication, be extended to digital communications.

It may be suggested though that the Electoral Commission underestimated the potential impact of digital communications in the field of political speech. At the time of the report it may have seemed, with web 1.0 technologies dominant, that digital communications could be seen to be an incremental development of traditional mass media outlets such as newspapers or billboards. Even the use of SMS messaging suggested a 'broadcast' model with the information originating from a single source. It is therefore understandable that they focused on online campaigning rather than online political discourse more generally. However, with the advent of web 2.0 systems there were a number of new outlets for electioneering beyond the control (and direct funding) of the political parties themselves. These outlets are therefore not subject to expenditure

[81] Representation of the People Act 1983, s. 93.

[82] All the major political parties in the UK have YouTube channels which are used extensively during electioneering. All main parties also use SMS messaging in campaigns.

[83] Electoral Commission, *Online Election Campaigns: Report and Recommendations* April 2003.

[84] Ibid. 4.

limits and, as they are not traditional media outlets, are not subject to the impartiality requirements of radio or television channels. These outlets include political YouTube channels and multimedia bloggers such as Guido Fawkes (Paul Staines), Iain Dale, and Mike Ferguson who operate blogs, Twitter feeds, and Facebook accounts. This issue came to a head ahead of the 2015 General Election campaign when the Electoral Commission wrote to a number of high-profile political bloggers and commentators to inform them that they may need to register as a non-party campaigner and be made subject to Electoral Commission Regulation.[85]

Case study Guido Fawkes (Paul Staines)

Letter from the Electoral Commission 8 January 2015

Dear Mr Staines,

I am writing to draw your attention to new rules on non-party campaigning in the Political Parties, Elections and Referendums Act 2000 ('PPERA') which were recently amended by the Transparency of Lobbying, Non-Party Campaigning and Trade Union Administration Act 2014.

As it is possible the new rules could be relevant to your activities, particularly in relation to your website, I am writing to give a brief overview so that you can consider whether or not you may need to register with the Electoral Commission as a non-party campaigner ahead of the upcoming UK Parliamentary General Election.

Non-party campaigners are individuals or organisations that campaign in the run-up to elections, but are not standing as political parties or candidates. The rules cover spending on certain activities that can reasonably be seen as intended to influence voters to vote for or against political parties or categories of candidates, including political parties or candidates who support or do not support particular policies or issues (we call this the 'purpose test').

....

We are keen to ensure that we support everyone that we regulate, including those who are considering whether they need to register, by providing advice on the rules in relation to planned campaign activities. You may need to register with us now in which case we would be pleased to hear from you. Also, do let us know if you reach the view that you do not currently need to register with us. You may need to register in the future and we would advise you keep your activities under regular review.

The change in the law that the letter refers to is found in ss. 94A and 94B of the Political Parties, Elections and Referendums Act 2000. These require third parties to notify the Electoral Commission if the expenditure by that third party exceeds £20,000 in England, or £10,000 in Scotland, Wales, or Northern Ireland,[86] or within a single constituency 0.05 per cent of the total of the maximum campaign expenditure limits in England,

[85] The letter in full may be seen at <https://orderorder.files.wordpress.com/2015/01/guido-fawkes-non-party-campaigner-letter.pdf>.

[86] Political Parties, Elections and Referendums Act 2000, s. 94(5).

Scotland, Wales, and Northern Ireland[87] which currently is £9,750, if that third party spends that money for reasons which can 'reasonably be regarded as intended to promote or procure electoral success at any relevant election' for:

(i) one or more particular registered parties,

(ii) one or more registered parties who advocate (or do not advocate) particular policies or who otherwise fall within a particular category of such parties, or

(iii) candidates who hold (or do not hold) particular opinions or who advocate (or do not advocate) particular policies or who otherwise fall within a particular category of candidates.[88]

The reason for the amendments made by the Transparency of Lobbying, Non-party Campaigning and Trade Union Administration Act 2014 were not to do with blogging or other online activities. The change in the law was driven by a number of scandals in the 2010–2015 Parliament. Prime among this was a view, held by the coalition Conservative/Liberal Democrat government that trade unions exerted too much power and financial support in some Labour Party selection and election campaigns. There was a particular controversy in Falkirk in 2013 surrounding the influence of the UNITE union in candidate selection,[89] along with the more widespread view that lobbyists had too much influence. The Act was highly controversial and was seen as a party political act by Conservative-led Government to use public outcry around lobbying scandals to regulate and control trade union funding of Labour Party candidates.[90] The Bill passed though and became law and one of the impacts of the Act, which was not entirely intended, was that bloggers such as Guido Fawkes who operates a clearly partisan right-wing blog and Labour List which operates a left-wing blog were written to by the Electoral Commission. It seems that blogs, which were not clearly partisan, such as the Spectator Blog, did not receive such guidance.

By registering, the blogs would have become regulated non-party campaigners, bringing a number of controls into financial management and reporting controls into play. The blogs in question felt that by being singled out they were being treated unfairly. *Conservative Home* editor Paul Goodman reported that he felt the site had no alternative, given the terms of the Lobbying Act, but to 'run some pieces by senior Labour MPs during the election campaign' to get around the issue of being a non-party campaign site.[91]

[87] Ibid. s. 94(5ZA).

[88] Ibid. s. 85(2)(b).

[89] J Cook, 'Labour's Falkirk row becomes national issue for Labour' (*BBC News*, 5 July 2013) <http://www.bbc.co.uk/news/uk-scotland-tayside-central-23193741>.

[90] N Morris, 'David Cameron is accused of using lobbying scandal to curb Labour's trade union support' *The Independent* (London, 3 June 2013) <http://www.independent.co.uk/news/uk/politics/david-cameron-is-accused-of-using-lobbying-scandal-to-curb-labours-trade-union-support-8642757.html>.

[91] <http://order-order.com/2015/01/09/electoral-commission-trying-to-regulate-blogsnotifies-guido-conservativehome-labourlist-libdemvoice/#_@/sYpgvAyueC9AFQ>.

Highlight Registered non-party campaign restrictions

Registered non-party campaigners[92] must

- have a system in place for authorising spending on regulated campaign activity,
- keep invoices and receipts for payments over £200 made as part of their spending on regulated campaign activity,
- report to the Electoral Commission after the election their spending on regulated campaign activity if they have spent more than £20,000 in England or more than £10,000 in any of Scotland, Wales or Northern Ireland,
- check that any donations received may be accepted, and record any donations over £500, and
- comply with the reporting requirements for donations received for spending on regulated campaign activity.

In addition, during a UK Parliamentary general election regulated period:

- they must report certain donations before and after the election,
- they must provide the Electoral Commission with a list of constituencies in which their regulated campaign spending was more than £7,800,
- they may need to provide the Electoral Commission with a statement of accounts after the election.

Mark Ferguson who operates the *Labour List* blog reported that 'It seems particularly bizarre (and that's being generous) that there's one law for "newspapers and periodicals" and another for "websites". Perhaps the government are finding this new-fangled internet thing very confusing. We're still working through what the most appropriate response is to this dreadful law—more worthy of a banana-Republic than a democracy—that clamps down on campaigning and free speech at a time when it's needed most, election time. Whatever response we decide on though, we will not be submitting ourselves to any form of regulation that stops us from writing, reporting and commenting on the election campaign as we see fit.'[93]

It appears in the end than none of the blogs registered with the Electoral Commission and that no sanctions were imposed. In their *Report on the administration of the 7 May 2015 elections, including the UK Parliamentary general election*[94] the Commission note that 'following the growth in online media since PPERA was passed in 2000, we consider that the exemption for editorial content should apply to online newspapers and periodicals, whether or not they have a print edition, in the same way it does for printed newspapers or periodicals. With print media, it is relatively straightforward to determine the difference between a genuine newspaper and a political leaflet in the form of

[92] See Electoral Commission, *Registering as a Non-party Campaigner* <http://www.electoralcommission.org.uk/__data/assets/pdf_file/0011/165962/sp-registering-npc.pdf>.

[93] Ibid.

[94] <http://www.electoralcommission.org.uk/__data/assets/pdf_file/0006/190959/UKPGE-report-May-2015-1.pdf>.

a newspaper; it is however, sometimes harder to clearly differentiate between materials on the internet. This raises questions about internet content such as political material in blogs and whether it should fall under the exclusion for periodicals or be regarded as a piece of election campaign material.'[95] As a result the Commission notes and requests 'we think that the way in which political blogs are treated in relation to the exemption on newspapers and periodicals should be clarified in legislation. In the meantime, we will continue to consider this exemption carefully at future elections and referendums.'[96]

The next big challenge for the regulation of online campaigning is likely to be the EU Referendum. It is clear though that the challenge of fair and balanced online speech is one that the government and the Electoral Commission are still struggling with and are likely to continue to struggle with for the foreseeable future.

6.5 **Hate speech**

While we seek to protect political speech we seek to restrict hate speech. Sometimes there is a fine line between political speech and hate speech. For example should the YouTube channel for the British National Party be protected as political speech or banned as hate speech? We have already touched upon these issues in our discussion of the distinctive approaches to be found in the US and Europe to potentially harmful speech, and in the analysis of the *LICRA et UEJF v Yahoo! Inc.* litigation in France and the US. The entire issue is one which is swathed in social responsibility. Every society suffers from bigotry and ignorance and in every society it is easy for the socially disenfranchised to blame another social, racial, or religious group. In a civilized society though these views are marginalized, and mainstream public and media opinion is ranged against those who hold such socially harmful opinions. The internet, though, empowers those marginalized by mainstream society and it is not always to the benefit of society as a whole.

6.5.1 **Hate speech and society**

Digital media, and in particular web 2.0 technologies, are allowing extremist viewpoints from all ends of the spectrum to proliferate. White supremacists find themselves online alongside Islamic fundamentalists, while homophobes find themselves alongside radical homosexual groups that fight for the removal of all restrictions on homosexual activity including the liberalization of laws which prevent sexual relations between adult and minor males.[97] Those operating these sites do so without regard to their social responsibility: they view their right to represent their views and opinions as paramount. The problem is that in so doing they may cause harm to others. This is why the UK has taken steps to restrict such speech. Racially offensive speech is prohibited by the Public Order Act 1986,[98] as is the possession of with intent to publish material

[95] Ibid. [3.161].
[96] Ibid. [3.162].
[97] The author has visited sites representing all these views. It is not the role of an academic text to publicize these views by listing the websites which promote them. In accordance with good research practice a record of the sites visited is kept by the author and may be supplied on request.
[98] Public Order Act 1986, s. 17.

which is racially offensive.[99] Also prohibited by the Public Order Act is speech which is religiously offensive. The new Part 3A of the Act, introduced by the Racial and Religious Hatred Act 2006, extends the protections previously only available to racially abusive material to prohibit the use of words or actions designed to stir up religious hatred[100] and the publication of material designed to stir up religious hatred.[101] In turn, these provisions were further extended by Sch. 16 of the Criminal Justice and Immigration Act 2008 to cover hatred on grounds of sexual orientation.[102]

The question of compatibility of such laws with Art. 10 of the ECHR is unsurprisingly common. In two key cases though the European Court of Human Rights has found provisions such as those found in the Public Order Act to be in compliance with the Convention. In *Jersild v Denmark*[103] the court found that a Danish conviction of a journalist for aiding the distribution of race hate speech infringed Art. 10. However, this was on the narrow decision that in so doing they prevented a journalist from discharging his duty to aid discussion of matters in the public interest. As for the Danish law itself they found that the state was within the exceptions found in Art. 10(2) in passing a law which prohibited remarks which were insulting to members of targeted groups. In fact the court noted such a law was required by Denmark's obligations under the 1965 International Convention on the Elimination of all Forms of Racial Discrimination. More recently in the case of *Lehideux and Isorni v France*[104] the court found that Art. R.645-1 of the French Penal Code (Restriction on Holocaust Denial Speech) is compatible with Art. 10.

6.5.2 **Inter-state speech**

With European lawmakers extending ever further the protections afforded to marginalized sections of society, in the UK the progression has been from racial hate speech to religious hate speech and most recently to sexual orientation hate speech; gender hate speech may be next and, with the constitutional principles of the US protecting all but the most immediately harmful speech, a rise in conflicts between US-based content and European-based consumers becomes more likely in the web 2.0 environment. We have already visited at length the best-known example of this ideological conflict, *LICRA et UEJF v Yahoo! Inc. and Yahoo! France*. This lengthy litigation produced a most unsatisfactory outcome which demonstrates that attempts to reach international consensus on this issue are unlikely to succeed. A further example closer to home highlights the difficulty of regulating the speech itself rather than the speaker. Some time prior to 2005 two individuals, Simon Sheppard and Stephen Whittle, began operating a website called heretical.com. The site is a standard white-supremacist, neo-Nazi site, common in the US but illegal to operate in the UK under the Public Order Act. The site,

[99] Ibid. s. 23.

[100] Ibid. s. 29B.

[101] Ibid. s. 29C.

[102] Although it should be noted that a strong Christian lobby secured an exemption in Parliament. The new s. 29JA of the Public Order Act states: 'In this Part, for the avoidance of doubt, the discussion or criticism of sexual conduct or practices or the urging of persons to refrain from or modify such conduct or practices shall not be taken of itself to be threatening or intended to stir up hatred.'

[103] (1995) 19 EHRR 1.

[104] (2000) 30 EHRR 365.

and a number of others operated by Sheppard, is hosted in Torrance, California, while Sheppard and Whittle live in the UK. On this site they placed a file called 'Tales of the Holohoax', a holocaust-denial comic strip. Sheppard and Whittle were questioned by police and charged under s. 19 of the Public Order Act 1986. While standing trial the two fled to the United States and claimed asylum which was refused. Eventually after being convicted in their absence they were returned to the UK and on 10 July 2009 Sheppard was sentenced to a total of four years and ten months' imprisonment and Whittle to a total of two years and four months' imprisonment.[105] Both later successfully appealed to have their sentences reduced but the interesting aspect of their story relates to jurisdiction and effective jurisdiction.

Sheppard and Whittle argued that the courts of England and Wales did not have jurisdiction to hear their case as the material was published in California and protected by the First Amendment. This was dismissed by the trial court where the judge applied *R v Smith (Wallace Duncan)*[106] to find that the court had jurisdiction to try them for their conduct because a substantial measure of the activities constituting the crime took place in England,[107] a position upheld on appeal.[108] Thus while the courts of England and Wales successfully established *de lege* jurisdiction, and de facto jurisdiction over Sheppard and Whittle, a problem remained, for while both Mr Sheppard and Mr Whittle could be remanded in prison for their breach of s. 19, there was nothing the English courts could do about the content itself which remained on the servers of the hosting company in Torrance, protected by the First Amendment. In essence the offence continued to be committed. Until early 2011 it was possible to visit heretical.com from the United Kingdom and download the material in question. The courts had successfully prosecuted the perpetrators of the crime, but the crime itself continued to be perpetrated. Eventually the will of the courts of England and Wales prevailed. With Mr Sheppard seeking to obtain parole from prison in early 2011 he voluntarily removed the offending content as a condition of his release. There was a period though—between conviction and application for parole, from July 2009 to early 2011—where the will of the courts of England and Wales was defeated by the off-shoring of the content in question.

This is a problem for any content hosted in the United States. With the US Supreme Court ruling in *Reno v ACLU*[109] that the First Amendment applies to internet communications, the US government finds that it cannot enter into any international treaty or agreement which would conflict with its duty to uphold the US Constitution.[110] This was demonstrated in the negotiations of the Council of Europe Convention on Cybercrime.[111] The Convention which aims to provide a framework for the development of a common policy against all aspects of cybercrime including internet pornography, computer hacking, and distribution of malicious code was signed by the Council of Europe states and several invited non-member states including the US. It was the intent of the drafters that that Convention would have an article dealing with hate speech but the US delegation stated that due to the effect of *Reno v ACLU*, they would be unable

[105] All taken from *R v Sheppard & Anor* [2010] EWCA Crim 65 [1]–[8].
[106] (No. 4) [2004] EWCA Crim 631.
[107] *R v Sheppard & Anor* (n. 105) [20].
[108] Ibid. [20]–[33].
[109] 521 US 844 (1997).
[110] See Vick (n. 37).
[111] CETS No. 185, Budapest, 23.XI.2001.

to sign a convention which restricted free expression. Because of this, and because the framers of the Convention wanted the US to sign, all references to hate and xenophobic speech were removed from the main Convention and were placed into a separate Additional Protocol to the Convention on Cybercrime Concerning the Criminalisation of Acts of a Racist and Xenophobic Nature Committed through Computer Systems.[112] This additional protocol was not signed by the US.[113]

We may never find common ground between the US and other leading democratic states including EU states on this issue, but as Douglas Vick points out 'it is far from certain that sexism, racism, homophobia or religious intolerance are greater problems in the US than in countries with well-developed anti-hate legislation'.[114] When the Programme in Comparative Media Law and Policy concluded its three-year research project into industry self-regulation and content,[115] it concluded that data havens were not unusual in digital communications, with Europe and in particular the UK, acting as a similar 'offshore centre' for online gambling for citizens of the US. Thus, short of blocking access to US-based websites which breach the Public Order Act, it appears UK regulators and UK citizens may have to accept that while as noted by District Judge Fogel in *Yahoo Inc. v LICRA* 'the Internet in effect allows one to speak in more than one place at the same time'[116] individuals will in most cases be subject only to the effective jurisdiction of the place where they are domiciled or ordinarily resident. This means we may find a more US-style marketplace of speech occurs online as US citizens debate sensitive subjects from behind the shield of the First Amendment.

6.6 **Commercial speech**

One area in which the US First Amendment is less strongly applied is in the field of commercial speech. Commercial speech, sometimes known as promotional or advertising speech, is speech expressed on behalf of a company or individual for the intent of making a profit. It is economic in nature and usually has the intent of convincing the audience to follow a particular course of action, often purchasing a specific product.

6.6.1 **Commercial speech and the First Amendment**

The concept of commercial speech, in First Amendment Jurisprudence, was introduced in the case of *Valentine v Chrestensen*.[117] The respondent had purchased a former US Navy submarine which he toured around the US for exhibition. He had brought the submarine to New York and had moored it at a state pier in the East River. To promote his exhibit he prepared and printed a handbill advertising the boat and soliciting visitors for a stated admission fee. On attempting to distribute the bill in the city streets, he

[112] CETS No. 189, Strasbourg, 28.I.2003.
[113] It should be noted that the UK also have not signed the Protocol.
[114] Vick (n. 21) 51.
[115] Programme in Comparative Media Law and Policy, *Self-Regulation of Digital Media Converging on the Internet: Industry Codes of Conduct in Sectoral Analysis* (2004) <http://pcmlp.socleg.ox.ac.uk/sites/pcmlp.socleg.ox.ac.uk/files/IAPCODEfinal.pdf>.
[116] 145 F. Supp. 2d 1168 (N.D. Cal. 2001), 1192.
[117] 316 US 52 (1942).

was advised by the petitioner, the Police Commissioner, that this activity would violate §318 of the New York Sanitary Code which forbade distribution in the streets of commercial and business advertising matter. Mr Chrestensen argued the city ordinance was in breach of the First Amendment but the Supreme Court ruled that the Constitution does not protect commercial speech.

Although the Chrestensen principle has been questioned over the years, and has been somewhat diluted, the Supreme Court continues to recognize that commercial speech does not receive the same level of Constitutional protection as other forms of speech.[118] This must come as somewhat of a relief to anyone who operates an email account, discussion board, blog, or other interactive service.

6.6.2 Commercial speech and the information society

The digital environment is awash with unsolicited commercial communications, colloquially known as spam.[119] Accurate statistics on spam are difficult to source. The internet appears equally awash with a variety of spam statistics making reliable data almost impossible to source.

Highlight Spam data

Reports from Symantec and Cisco suggest the high-water mark of spam was in July 2010 when approximately 230 billion spam messages were in circulation each day, accounting for in excess of 90 per cent of all email traffic. Since then there has been a steady decline in spam messages. Statistics for November 2015 record that spam messages accounted for 54.1 per cent of all email traffic.[120]

Spam messages clearly remain a problem despite huge reductions in spam traffic, much of which can be credited to Google introducing a new machine intelligence-driven Spam filter into its Gmail system.[121]

Somewhat surprisingly there have been few surveys of consumer responses to spam, but in 2002 a Harris Poll revealed that 80 per cent of those surveyed said that they found spamming very annoying and 74 per cent favoured making spam illegal.[122] Why

[118] See *Ohralik v Ohio State Bar Association*, 436 US 447 (1978); cf. *44 Liquormart Inc. v Rhode Island*, 517 US 484 (1996).

[119] Unsolicited Commercial Communications are colloquially known as spam because of the Monty Python sketch in which a couple go into a restaurant and the wife tries to get something other than spam. In the background are a bunch of Vikings who sing the praises of spam. Pretty soon the only thing you can hear in the sketch is the word 'spam'. That same idea would happen to the internet if large-scale inappropriate postings were allowed. You couldn't pick the real postings out from the spam.

[120] Symantec Intelligence Report November 2015 <https://www.symantec.com/content/en/us/enterprise/other_resources/intelligence-report-11-2015-en-us.pdf>.

[121] J Vijayan, 'Google Taps Neural Network Tech to Bolster Anti-Spam Efforts' (*eWeek*, 11 July 2015) <http://www.eweek.com/security/google-taps-neural-network-tech-to-bolster-anti-spam-efforts.html>.

[122] Harris Interactive, 'Large Majority of Those Online Wants Spamming Banned' 3 January 2003.

then do spammers continue? There are two predominant reasons for this. The first is that unlike traditional unsolicited commercial communications, digital commercial communications benefit from all the advantages discussed in Part I. It is infinitely replicable, easy to store, and, the key for spammers, almost costless to send. As any internet user knows you only pay for your access cost. Once you are connected to the network the costs of carrying data across the network are borne by the telecommunications providers, not the customer. Excepting issues of bandwidth availability it costs no more to send 1 million emails than to send one. The same is not true of traditional media: 1 million telephone calls will cost around 1 million times the cost of a single telephone call and 1 million letters will cost (bulk discounts aside) 1 million times the cost of a single letter. Thus it seems email is almost designed for spam messages. For the spammer there are almost no overheads and massive reach. But if everyone just filters and deletes their spam why do spammers keep doing it? Well surprisingly spam brings about relatively high response levels. A 2008 paper by a group of researchers at Berkeley and UCSD demonstrated that one in every 12.5 million emails sent elicited a positive response. Although this may sound like a tiny response rate it meant that for a small-scale spam operation, such as the one they mimicked, it could generate revenues of around $140 per day. Large-scale operations though are of a different order. An operation such as the Storm network could drive revenues of around $9,500 per day. This is a massive return, equivalent to nearly $3.5m per year, in return for a relatively small outlay.[123]

6.6.3 Regulating spam in Europe

Despite the obvious appeal of spam to a number of people, the question of how to regulate spam is clearly a major issue. Steps have been taken in both the European Union and the US to control spam. The EU began consultation on spam regulation in the summer of 2000 when they began to consider the Commission proposal for a directive on privacy and electronic communications. In their explanatory memorandum the Commission noted that:

> Four Member States already have bans on unsolicited commercial e-mail and another is about to adopt one. In most of the other Member States opt-out systems exist. From an internal market perspective, this is not satisfactory. Direct marketers in opt-in countries may not target e-mail addresses within their own country but they can still continue to send unsolicited commercial e-mail to countries with an opt-out system. Moreover, since e-mail addresses very often give no indication of the country of residence of the recipients, a system of divergent regimes within the internal market is unworkable in practice. A harmonised opt in approach solves this problem.

On the basis of this the Commission proposed that the draft Privacy in Electronic Communications Directive use an opt-in approach where only those persons who had given prior consent to the receipt of unsolicited messages could lawfully receive them. This approach is highly controversial, not least with the business community and during the parliamentary hearings on the draft Directive this was replaced with an opt-out

[123] Chris Kanich et al., 'Spamalytics: An Empirical Analysis of Spam Marketing Conversion', *Proceedings of the 15th ACM Conference on Computer and Communications Security* 3 (2008) <http://www.icsi.berkeley.edu/pubs/networking/2008-ccs-spamalytics.pdf>.

approach instead. However, at the last stage of the co-decision procedure the Council reinstated the opt-in proposal and the final wording as passed in the Directive on Privacy and Electronic Communications[124] states:

Highlight Article 13(1) of the Directive on Privacy and Electronic Communications

Electronic mail for the purposes of direct marketing may only be allowed in respect of subscribers who have given their prior consent.

Recital 40 makes clear that 'prior *explicit* consent of the recipients is obtained before such communications are addressed to them', the use of the term explicit making clear that an opt-out system is incompatible with the Directive. There remains though one important exception to Art. 13(1). Under Art. 13(2) if there has been a prior commercial relationship between the sender of the communication and the recipient thereof the communication may be sent without prior explicit consent 'provided that customers clearly and distinctly are given the opportunity to object, free of charge and in an easy manner, to such use of electronic contact details when they are collected and on the occasion of each message in case the customer has not initially refused such use'. In effect what Art. 13(2) says is that if you have a prior commercial relationship the opt-in requirement is reversed and it becomes an opt-out requirement.

The Directive was given effect in the UK in December 2003 when the Privacy and Electronic Communications (EC Directive) Regulations 2003 came into force. By reg. 22(2) it became a harm to: 'transmit, or instigate the transmission of, unsolicited communications for the purposes of direct marketing by means of electronic mail unless the recipient of the electronic mail has previously notified the sender that he consents for the time being to such communications being sent by, or at the instigation of, the sender'. The Art. 13(2) exception is given effect in reg. 22(3).

Rather disappointingly for many anti-spam campaigners it is not an offence to send spam; rather reg. 30(1) states that: 'a person who suffers damage by reason of any contravention of any of the requirements of these Regulations by any other person shall be entitled to bring proceedings for compensation from that other person for that damage'. The trouble with this is that it effectively makes it a tort claim and in most cases where individuals receive spam messages the harm or damage suffered is either unquantifiable or of such low value as to be *de minimis*. That is not to say the Regulations are unenforceable.

6.6.4 *Mansfield v John Lewis*

Until recently there had been few cases enforcing the Regulations. In December 2005 Nigel Roberts, a businessman from Alderney, lodged a claim under the regulations in Colchester County Court against Logistics UK, a Stirlingshire-based company. Logistics UK did not defend the action and agreed to pay Mr Roberts £270 in damages and £30

[124] Dir. 2002/58/EC, Official Journal L201, 31/07/2002 P. 0037–0047.

in costs. Then in March 2007 it was reported that Gordon Dick, an electronic marketing specialist from Edinburgh, won £750 in damages and costs of £616.66 when he pursued Henley-on-Thames-based Transcom under the regulations. More recently, in June 2013 Steve Higgins, a businessman form Northampton, won £750 in damages and £60 costs against Jean Patrique cookware.

In 2014 though the County Court in the unreported case of *Mansfield v John Lewis Partnership* may have made a key contribution to the effectiveness of the Regulations. The value and importance of this decision should not be overstated; it is merely a County Court Small Claims decision and therefore is of no binding authority yet it is probably the fullest discussion of the Regulations to date. According to reports Mr Mansfield had been browsing the website of Waitrose supermarket, which is owned by John Lewis, to check the price of a home delivery. The Waitrose website requires all potential customers to supply an email address before it allows access to the home delivery finder; this he did but he then left the Waitrose website without buying anything. Mr Mansfield then began receiving marketing emails from the John Lewis Partnership. After writing an objection to the receipt of these emails using a standard form available online,[125] he raised a small claims action. John Lewis argued that because he had not opted out of receiving their emails, he had opted in; this is called soft opt-in and is used on many websites. However Mr Mansfield argued that an opportunity to opt out that is not taken is simply that, it does not convert to automatic consent under the law. In the alternative, John Lewis's lawyers argued that because he had browsed the website he had negotiated with them for a sale and a business relationship existed between them, this would have permitted John Lewis to email Mr Mansfield under reg. 22(3)(a).

Mr Mansfield relied sensibly on the Information Commissioner's Office guidance on direct marketing.[126] At para. 68 this states that 'Best practice is to provide an unticked opt-in box, and invite the person to confirm their agreement by ticking. This is the safest way of demonstrating consent, as it requires a positive choice by the individual to give clear and explicit consent.' Further, in para. 71 which deals with soft opt-in (or opt-out if one prefers) it states: 'An opt-out box is a box that the user must tick to object or opt out of receiving marketing messages. However, the fact that someone has failed to object or opt out only means that they have not objected. It does not automatically mean that they have consented. For example, they may not even have seen the box if they were using a smartphone or other small screen device. For this reason, we would always advise the use of opt-in boxes instead.' Mr Mansfield laid all of this before the judge who agreed with him that he had not consented to the receipt of marketing emails from John Lewis in terms permissible by reg. 22. As a result Mr Mansfield was paid undisclosed damages.

This is an important case as it was the first time, to this author's knowledge, that a soft opt-in (or opt-out) has been explicitly rejected by a UK judge. It suggests the Information Commissioner's warning that they are not advised should perhaps be upgraded to not-normally used. Of course this case has no authority; there is not even a written judgment so it is impossible to read too much into it. However, it emphasizes the value of reg. 30(1) and the small claims procedure.

[125] <http://www.scotchspam.org.uk/resources.html>.

[126] <https://ico.org.uk/media/for-organisations/documents/1555/direct-marketing-guidance.pdf>.

Interestingly though the largest award made in the UK against an individual sending spam messages was not made under the Regulations. In September 2006 it was reported that Microsoft had reached an out-of-court settlement with Paul Fox, a UK-based spammer who used spam to promote his pornographic websites, under which Mr Fox would pay £45,000 by way of damages and as a contribution to Microsoft's legal costs. Rather than attempt to pursue Mr Fox under the regulations though, Microsoft chose to file a complaint that he had breached the terms and conditions of their Hotmail service, which state: 'You may not use any Microsoft Services to send Spam. You also may not deliver Spam or cause Spam to be delivered to any of Microsoft's Services or customers.' It is also abundantly clear several years on from the enactment of the Regulations that they are having little, if any, effect on the volume of spam sent and received in the UK or the EU, the reductions in spam received reported recently are almost entirely down to technical breakthroughs. The reason for this is clear when you look at where most spam originates: as of 7 January 2016, online spam tracking project Spamhaus reports that eight of the top ten spam-producing nations are outside the EU.[127]

6.7 **Conclusions: cyber-speech and free expression**

The internet is the best communications medium yet designed. For the first time an individual can address large groups and can do so without regard for traditional borders or nation states. Although we must view this as being on the whole positive, the breaking down of borders has affected the ability of nation states to protect their community values in the online environment. This legal-regulatory failure was first predicted in 1996 by David Johnson and David Post,[128] but it is only now we are seeing the effects of this. Speech in cyberspace is speech which crosses borders like the flow of a river, and just as the government of France can do little to stop the waters of the River Rhône crossing the border from Switzerland into France there is little they can do about content hosted on US-based servers being available to the citizens of France. The effect of this is that governments are being asked to reconsider if and how they wish to regulate expression.

The major challenges are in the three key areas outlined in this chapter: (1) political speech, (2) extremist/hate speech, and (3) spam. It is likely that the first will, in the UK at least, remain subject to light-touch regulation for as long as traditional media outlets—TV, radio, and press—remain the primary focus of electioneering for UK political parties. But we must learn from the experiences of the 2015 general election; the first time that the Electoral Commission and online bloggers have been at loggerheads.

The regulation of spam is probably another area which will continue to see light-touch legal controls. Major revisions to the Privacy and Electronic Communications (EC Directive) Regulations 2003 are unlikely in the foreseeable future. This is because, as we have seen, despite the odd success such as Mr Mansfield, legal controls are largely ineffective in dealing with spam: much more effective are technical controls such as filtering and blocking.

[127] <http://www.spamhaus.org/statistics/countries/>. The ten were: United States, China, Russia, Ukraine, Japan, United Kingdom, India, Germany, Brazil, and Hong Kong.

[128] Johnson and Post (n. 63) and accompanying text.

The area of major tension in the next few years is likely to remain extremist and hate speech. The *#unbonjuif* case is the latest in a long line of cases involving speech and social media platforms. Collectively they demonstrate the futility of localized legal enforcement proceedings unless the defendant is domiciled in or has assets domiciled in the jurisdiction in question. These challenges will continue to grow in the web 2.0 environment, where individuals rather than corporations play a greater role in media content production, and will be discussed fully in the next chapter.

Whatever the future holds in all these areas we should remember that the positive effects that digital communications have had on free expression and the free, full, and frank exchange of views and ideas between individuals far outweigh the negative; but it is to be hoped that those engaged in online expression remember their social responsibilities as well as their rights.

TEST QUESTIONS

Question 1

Critically analyse the complete *LICRA et UEJF v Yahoo! Inc.* litigation set. In particular, analyse whether the apparently divergent outcomes of the Tribunal de Grande Instance de Paris and the United States Court of Appeal for the 9th Circuit support Johnson and Post's thesis that in cyberspace traditional laws fail to be effective due to a lack of borders.

Question 2

Discuss critically the statement that 'the divergent approaches of the United States and European states in relation to the regulation of online expression, in particular the distinction between the "marketplace of speech" concept and the "human dignity" concept have left such international uncertainty in regulation of this area that the effect has been to effectively deregulate all forms of online speech'.

FURTHER READING

Books

E Barendt, *Freedom of Speech* (2nd edn, 2005)

F Schauer, *Free Speech* (1982)

C Sunstein, *Republic.com 2.0* (2007)

B Winston, *Messages: Free Expression, Media and the West from Gutenberg to Google* (2005)

Chapters and articles

M Fagin, 'Regulating Speech across Borders: Technology vs Values', 9 *Michigan Telecommunications and Technology Law Review* 395 (2003)

DW Vick, 'The Internet and the First Amendment', 61 *Modern Law Review* 414 (1998)

DW Vick, 'Regulating Hatred', in Mathias Klang and Andrew Murray (eds.), *Human Rights in the Digital Age* (2005)

7

Social networking and antisocial conduct

7.1 Introduction

Speech, as we have seen in chapter 6 is not always harmless or positive. The internet spreads antisocial comment as quickly and efficiently as it circulates news reports, political speech, and educational speech. In recent years the explosion in social networking has magnified this to the point where the internet now feels like a global hubbub of personalized views, expressions, and opinions. It is through sites like Facebook and Twitter that the closest approximation of Negroponte's *Daily Me* is developing.[1] It is only like the *Daily Me* from one side of the coin though: for the consumer it approximates Negroponte's vision of a personalized delivery of detail or information. As a user of Facebook or Twitter I can choose with whom to be friends or whom to follow; thus my daily diet of Facebook updates and stories or tweets is tailored to my specifications. What Negroponte did not capture, not unreasonably in 1995, was the other side of the *Daily Me* story: who is producing this content? Negroponte imagined a web 1.0-style *Daily Me* where my local newspaper, local wine shop, or national organization such as the National Trust would send me updates and news stories, tailored to my preferences.

Highlight Negroponte's *Daily Me*

Unique information about me determines news services that I might want to receive about a small obscure town, a not so famous person, and (for today) the anticipated weather conditions in Virginia . . . a machine could call your attention to a sale on a particular Chardonnay or beer that it knows the guests you have coming to dinner tomorrow night liked last time.[2]

Much more interesting today, for lawyers at least, is who is producing this content for us? It is not, as Negroponte imagined, corporations, local businesses, and public bodies; the explosion of social media platforms (SMPs) means that I get my daily news and updates via those I follow on Twitter, such as David Allen Green, who writes the Jack of Kent blog; Paul Bernal, a law lecturer at UEA; and the enigmatic and slightly obsessive Ern Malley, whose (surprising) identity I know but I cannot share. On Facebook a similar selection process means I get news and updates from among others Mathias

[1] N Negroponte, *Being Digital* (Hodder & Stoughton 1995) 164–71.
[2] Ibid. 164–5.

Klang, an Associate Professor at the University of Massachusetts, Boston; Daniel Paré, an Associate Professor in the Department of Communication at the University of Ottawa; and Matthew Richardson, a barrister at Henderson Chambers and originator of the Blaney Blarney Order.[3] It is not just the consumption of news and information that has been personalized; it is also its production. The internet, through SMPs, has become the world's most complex, most connected, most global, coffee shop. People treat SMPs like private conversations and do all the things they normally would in a private discussion with friends: they gossip,[4] they share (and break) confidences, they bully, and they act antisocially. The problem is that SMPs are not comparable to private conversations in pubs or coffee shops. Whereas conversations in pubs and cafes are ephemeral—there one second and gone the next, and localized: only available to those in very close proximity—conversations via SMPs are permanent, or at least semi-permanent and potentially global. In your cafe or pub conversation, you may address five or ten people who will quickly forget what you have said. Via Twitter a single tweet (before re-tweets) can reach over 80 million followers, more than the population of the UK;[5] re-tweets can send messages stratospheric in terms of readers. The most re-tweeted message (correct at December 2015) is a photo message taken by Oscars' host Ellen DeGeneres: 'If only Bradley's arm was longer. Best photo ever. #oscars' sent at 3:06 a.m. on 3 March 2014. It has been re-tweeted over 3.3 million times and, given that Ellen DeGeneres has over 45.5million followers herself, must have been read by in the region of 100 million Twitter users.[6] These figures pale into insignificance when one considers the most popular videos on YouTube. The most watched YouTube video (again as of December 2015) is Gangnam Style by PSY which has garnered 2.49 billion views, with the most popular viral video probably being Charlie Bit My Finger—Again! with 833 million views.

The reach of individuals, powered by SMPs, is therefore quite staggering. Unfortunately by treating SMPs like pub or cafe conversations the level of discourse can be depressingly mundane. On Wednesday 6 January 2016 the trending topics for Twitter worldwide in English were '#Twitter10k' (a proposal to allow 10,000 character tweets); '#DrummondPuddleWatch' (a six-hour live Periscope broadcast of people trying to avoid a large puddle in Newcastle, England); 'Pierre Boulez' (reports of the death of the composer and conductor); 'Alex Gordon' (a discussion of a baseball transfer); and 'Prince George' (who was beginning his first day at nursery school). None of these address important issues, most are quite humdrum, but at least none are harmful. In the past Twitter trends have actively ignored court orders, defamed individuals, and promoted criminal messages. Below trending activity we find individuals being bullied and harassed by both Facebook and Twitter; breaches of personal confidences; and, via YouTube, a video which caused riots throughout the Islamic world and which led to at least 54 deaths as a result.[7]

[3] 'Court Order Served over Twitter' (*BBC News*, 1 October 2009) <http://news.bbc.co.uk/1/hi/technology/8285954.stm>.

[4] Gossip is discussed more in ch. 8. It is worth noting that it is reported by the Social Issues Research Centre at the University of Oxford that gossip accounts for 55 per cent of male conversation time and 67 per cent of female time. See K Fox, 'Evolution, Alienation and Gossip: The Role of Mobile Telecommunications in the 21st Century' SIRC <http://www.sirc.org/publik/gossip.shtml>.

[5] The most followed individual on Twitter is Katy Perry with just over 80,300,000 followers (correct at 6 January 2016).

[6] The tweet may be found at <https://twitter.com/theellenshow/status/440322224407314432>.

[7] 'The "Innocence of Muslims" Riots' *New York Times* (New York, 26 November 2012) <http://topics.nytimes.com/top/reference/timestopics/subjects/i/innocence_of_muslims_riots/index.html>.

7.2 Social networking, gossip, and privacy

For several years SMPs like Facebook and Twitter have found themselves at the heart of a variety of antisocial activities including a number of cases of defamation which will be discussed in the following chapter. For many in the mainstream, however, the first time they became aware of the legal implications of postings on SMPs was in relation to the Ryan Giggs privacy case in 2011.

Late 2009 to early 2011 brought a rash of applications to the English courts for privacy injunctions and super-injunctions.[8] For a period it seemed as if everyone, from the media itself, to celebrities and businesses and politicians and individuals, was obsessed by who had injunctions and why they had them. A privacy injunction is usually applied for by an individual, or occasionally a business, under Art. 8 ECHR. The usual basis for such an injunction is that the reporting of the facts surrounding the application will unduly affect the children or spouse of an applicant, or that the information in the possession of the press was obtained illegally by invading the private sphere of the individual in question. Privacy injunctions are still quite a novel intervention of the English courts as, prior to the passing of the Human Rights Act 1998, it had been held that there was no common law right to privacy in English law. This was most clearly stated by Glidewell LJ in *Kaye v Robertson*.[9]

Highlight Glidewell LJ in *Kaye v Robertson*

It is well known that in English law there is no right to privacy, and accordingly there is no right of action for breach of a person's privacy. The facts of the present case are a graphic illustration of the desirability of Parliament considering whether and in what circumstances statutory provision can be made to protect the privacy of individuals.[10]

The eventual passage of the Human Rights Act remedied this deficiency of English law. Section 1 ensured that Convention rights were woven into the fabric of English law, while s. 2 ensured English courts were required not only to take account of Convention rights but also the large body of jurisprudence which interpreted them. This meant a body of European privacy law now became part of English law. This included cases such as *Von Hannover v Germany*.[11] This case was brought by Caroline von Hannover, better known as Princess Caroline of Monaco. She was followed on a daily basis at home in France by paparazzi photographers who took pictures of her doing everyday things such as picking up her children from school, doing the shopping, or playing sport. These pictures were then published in German magazines. Under German law, Princess Caroline is deemed to be a 'public figure par excellence', and as such the public

[8] Technically a super-injunction is an injunction with reporting restrictions which mean that the existence of the injunction, and the facts relating to it, cannot be reported by anyone to whom it is known.

[9] [1991] FSR 62.

[10] Ibid. 66.

[11] (2005) 40 EHRR 1.

is deemed to have a legitimate interest in knowing how she generally behaves in public, even when not performing any kind of official function. Princess Caroline challenged this, first in the German courts, then at the European Court of Human Rights (ECtHR). The majority of the judges said that the question of the correct balance between Art. 8 and Art. 10 centred on 'the contribution that the published photos and articles make to a debate of general interest'.[12] In the case of Princess Caroline, the photographs made no such contribution as she exercised no official function and the photographs related solely to her private life.[13] The case was widely interpreted to create a positive obligation on states to ensure that the privacy of individuals can be protected from interference by other private individuals, including the media. It should be noted though that before we move on to the domestic law in this area in the more recent case of *Von Hannover v Germany (No. 2)*,[14] the court has retreated somewhat from this position. This action was brought by Caroline von Hannover because German courts had refused her injunctions preventing the publication of images which she claimed were obtained in breach of her Art. 8 rights. This time the ECtHR held that, in balancing Art. 8 and Art. 10 rights, 'An initial essential criterion is the contribution made by photos or articles in the press to a debate of general interest'.[15] In measuring this courts are told that there are four relevant factors: (1) a distinction has to be made between private individuals and persons acting in a public context, as political figures or public figures; (2) the conduct of the person concerned prior to publication of the report or the fact; (3) the way in which the photo or report are published and the manner in which the person concerned is represented in the photo or report; and (4) the context and circumstances in which the published photos were taken.[16] In the *Von Hannover (No. 2)* case the court found that 'the national courts [had] carefully balanced the right of the publishing companies to freedom of expression against the right of the applicants to respect for their private life' and that 'accordingly, there has not been a violation of [Art. 8]'.[17] This recent decision should be borne in mind as we consider the English law.

Around the same time that the *Von Hannover* case was being heard by the ECtHR the House of Lords was considering privacy at English law. The case was *Campbell v MGN*.[18] Again this is a non-internet case but it forms the foundations of the privacy injunction cases that were to follow. The claimant in this case was the model Naomi Campbell. She was photographed leaving a Narcotics Anonymous meeting in London and then arriving for a further meeting at the same location. The photographs were then printed with a related story in the *Daily Mirror* newspaper. Ms Campbell admitted, perhaps predicting a *Von Hannover No. 2*-style decision, that there was a public interest justifying publication of the fact that she was a drug addict and was having therapy, but claimed damages for breach of confidentiality and compensation under s. 13 Data Protection Act 1998 for the publication of further details. Campbell won in the House of Lords. By a narrow 3:2 majority it was held that the additional information relayed in the photographs and story was confidential as its publication would have caused substantial offence to a

[12] Ibid. [60].
[13] Ibid. [72].
[14] (2012) 55 EHRR 15.
[15] Ibid. [109].
[16] Ibid. [109]–[113].
[17] Ibid. [124]–[126].
[18] [2004] UKHL 22.

person of ordinary sensibilities in her position,[19] and that her Art. 8 rights outweighed MGNs Art. 10 rights, so that publication of the additional information was an infringement of her Art. 8 rights.[20]

Thus by the end of the summer of 2004 a strong set of privacy rights had been established in English law thanks to the Human Rights Act, *Von Hannover*, and *Campbell*. This was later strongly confirmed by Eady J who responded to criticism in the media that judges had gone too far to protect privacy in his judgment in *Mosley v News Group*.[21] Here he stated that:

> the law now affords protection to information in respect of which there is a reasonable expectation of privacy, even in circumstances where there is no pre-existing relationship giving rise of itself to an enforceable duty of confidence. That is because the law is concerned to prevent the violation of a citizen's autonomy, dignity and self-esteem. It is not simply a matter of 'unaccountable' judges running amok. Parliament enacted the 1998 statute which requires these values to be acknowledged and enforced by the courts. In any event, the courts had been increasingly taking them into account because of the need to interpret domestic law consistently with the United Kingdom's international obligations. It will be recalled that the United Kingdom government signed up to the Convention more than 50 years ago.[22]

Emboldened by the decisions of *Campbell* and *Mosley* a number of businesses and individuals sought to use Art. 8 as a tool to obtain a pre-publication privacy injunction. This often had the desired effect of preventing publication in the mainstream media of the content in question but the information, much like a dammed river, simply rerouted to find weaknesses elsewhere and overwhelmingly this was SMPs.

The wider public first became aware of the large number of privacy injunctions and super-injunctions the High Court was awarding in late 2009. The Dutch commodity trading company Trafigura has courted controversy for most of the 20 years it has traded. It was named as being part of the Oil for Food scandal of the late 1990s and early 2000s,[23] and was forced to pay the Côte d'Ivoire government €152m in compensation in 2007 following an incident which saw illegal toxic waste dumped in Abidjan in 2006.[24] On 12 October 2009 Labour MP Paul Farrelly asked a parliamentary written question:

Highlight Paul Farrelly's written question

To ask the Secretary of State for Justice, what assessment he has made of the effectiveness of legislation to protect: (a) whistleblowers and (b) press freedom following the injunctions obtained in the High Court by (i) Barclays and Freshfields solicitors on 19 March 2009 on the publication of internal Barclays reports documenting alleged tax avoidance schemes and (ii) Trafigura and Carter-Ruck solicitors on 11 September 2009 on the publication of the Minton report on the alleged dumping of toxic waste in the Ivory Coast, commissioned by Trafigura.

[19] Ibid. [92].

[20] Ibid. [124].

[21] [2008] EWHC 1777 (QB).

[22] Ibid. [7].

[23] For details on the scandal see 'The UN's Oil-for-Food Scandal: Rolling Up the Culprits' *The Economist* (London, 13 March 2008) <http://www.economist.com/node/10853611>.

[24] See 'Two Jailed over Ivorian Pollution' (*BBC News*, 23 October 2008) <http://news.bbc.co.uk/1/hi/world/africa/7685561.stm>.

The second injunction he was referring to had been obtained by Trafigura on 11 September 2009. It barred *The Guardian* from reporting details from an expert report commissioned by Trafigura in the months following the Côte d'Ivoire scandal.[25] The only thing *The Guardian* was allowed to state was that the injunction had been obtained by Carter-Ruck. On 12 October Mr Farrelly asked his question. In the ordinary course of things newspapers can report the proceedings of Parliament but this time it was confirmed the injunction remained in effect. *The Guardian* went on the offensive by saying as much as it could while remaining within the injunction. In a story on *The Guardian* website the paper's investigations executive editor, David Leigh, wrote:

> Today's published Commons order papers contain a question to be answered by a minister later this week. The Guardian is prevented from identifying the MP who has asked the question, what the question is, which minister might answer it, or where the question is to be found. The Guardian is also forbidden from telling its readers why the paper is prevented—for the first time in memory—from reporting Parliament. Legal obstacles, which cannot be identified, involve proceedings, which cannot be mentioned, on behalf of a client who must remain secret.[26]

This did enough to tip off the wider world to what was going on. Very quickly a report on the Guido Fawkes blog suggested it was the Minton report and Paul Farrelly's question,[27] as did the Spectator blog.[28] Things really took off, however, once the story broke on Twitter. A number of leading Twitter users, including Stephen Fry, sent out tweets naming Trafigura. Following the lead of Guido Fawkes he tweeted: 'Outrageous gagging order. It's in reference to the Trafigura oil dumping scandal. Grotesque and squalid.' This made him, along with Guido Fawkes and *The Spectator*, potentially a high-profile target for any future legal action. Throughout the day of 13 October *The Guardian* editor Alan Rusbridger kept his followers updated on the moves to overturn the ban, while campaigners began to dig up and post links to all sorts of articles that the oil firm would surely have rather remained hidden. By midday on 13 October the trending topics on Twitter UK included 'Trafigura', 'Carter Ruck', 'Farrellys', 'dumping', 'gagging', 'toxic', and 'injunction'. This was all done in contempt of court. The order which Maddison J made on 11 September extended to 'persons unknown', meaning that this was a *contra mundum* order and could be enforced against anyone.[29] By 12.45 p.m. Trafigura had given up the fight. David Leigh tweeted 'It appears that carter-ruck have suddenly decided to abandon the fight. No court after all.'

Two lessons may be learned from the Trafigura tale. The first is that the internet, and particularly SMPs, view attempts to restrict freedom of expression as damage and route around it. This is the positive message that the internet in general, and SMPs in particular, will ensure that attempts to control or restrict free expression and comment will not succeed, even if draconian instruments such as super-injunctions are used. The second lesson is that individuals who use SMPs do not respect the rule of

[25] *RJW & SJW v Guardian News and Media Ltd & Persons Unknown* [2009] EWHC 2540 (QB).

[26] D Leigh 'Guardian Gagged from Reporting Parliament' (*Guardian Online*, 12 October 2009) <http://www.guardian.co.uk/media/2009/oct/12/guardian-gagged-from-reporting-parliament>.

[27] <http://order-order.com/2009/10/12/guardian-gagged-from-reporting-parliament/>.

[28] A Massie, 'British Press Banned from Reporting Parliament. Seriously' *The Spectator* (London, 13 October 2009).

[29] *RJW & SJW v Guardian News and Media Ltd and Persons Unknown* (n. 25), [29].

law. Whether it was right or not, there was a valid order of the court in place, an order that prohibited not only *The Guardian* but also persons unknown from reporting the question asked in Parliament, the details of the Minton report, or details of the company which had obtained the order. Following *The Guardian*'s hints on 12 October a number of individuals, some high profile such as Paul Staines (Guido Fawkes), Alan Massie, and Stephen Fry and many more just ordinary citizens, had wilfully ignored and broken this order. In the instant case you may argue the end justifies the means, but when citizens ignore the rule of law so fundamentally it is only a matter of time until problems arise.

7.2.1 The spring of 2011 and the Ryan Giggs affair

Matters finally came to a head in the spring of 2011. Throughout 2010 the existence of privacy injunctions had become widely acknowledged both in the mainstream media and online. A number of them involved famous celebrities and—the catnip of the tabloid media—the hint of a sex scandal or affair. In January 2010 Tugendhat J refused to grant a full injunction to England football captain John Terry, after granting initially an emergency injunction, to prevent publication of details of an affair he had had with Vanessa Perroncel, the girlfriend of then teammate Wayne Bridge.[30] In November 2010 the Court of Appeal lifted a super-injunction awarded by Eady J in April to Take That member Howard Donald. The injunction had prevented his ex-girlfriend Ms Ntuli from revealing details of their relationship, as well as preventing publication of details of his identity or the existence of the injunction;[31] the court lifted the anonymity order and the reporting restrictions but left the remainder of the injunction in place.

It seemed privacy and super-injunctions were suddenly everywhere. A number of orders were put in place in the spring of 2011. In January 2011 the Court of Appeal awarded a privacy and anonymity injunction, thereby overturning the earlier decision of Tugendhat J, to a well-known sportsman, who (in the words of the court):

> has, for some time, been in an apparently long-term and conventional relationship with another person, to whom I shall refer as 'XX'. Since his relationship with XX had started, but before August 2010, a story had been published, without JIH having received any prior notice, suggesting that he had had a sexual liaison with another person, whom I shall call 'YY'. The story whose publication JIH is seeking to prevent concerns an alleged sexual encounter he had with a different person, to whom I shall refer as 'ZZ' last year.[32]

In a separate case in April 2011 an order was made in favour of an individual who, in the words of Eady J, was being subjected to 'a straightforward and blatant blackmail case'.[33] The defendant had intimate photographs of the claimant which they initially were negotiating to sell to Associated Newspapers Ltd (the publishers of the *Daily Mail*) but which they then offered to pass on to the claimant for a sum of money. In a further case in April 2011 the Court of Appeal overturned an earlier decision of Collins J, and awarded an injunction to 'a married man, [who] works in the entertainment industry,

[30] *Terry v Persons Unknown (Rev 1)* [2010] EWHC 119 (QB).
[31] *Ntuli v Donald* [2010] EWCA Civ 1276.
[32] *JIH v News Group Newspapers Ltd (Rev 1)* [2011] EWCA Civ 42 [7]–[8].
[33] *OPQ v BJM & Anor* [2011] EWHC 1059 (QB) [1].

[and who] had an affair with a colleague',[34] and the same month the High Court granted anonymity to both a 'leading actor' (originally reported as 'a world-famous celebrity') and a prostitute, later named as Helen Wood, relating to sexual encounters that the actor, who is married with children, had with Ms Wood.[35]

Since there appeared to be a new privacy and anonymity injunction granted almost daily there was bound to be a point where the system would break under the pressure. The case which the media turned into a test case, and which SMPs broke, was *CTB v News Group Newspapers Ltd*.[36] This was an application brought by a footballer to prevent publication of an extramarital affair he had entered into with former *Big Brother* contestant Imogen Thomas. An emergency injunction was awarded by Eady J on 14 April 2011 and then made permanent on 21 April. In this he granted the injunction partly on the basis that 'tawdry allegations about an individual's private life do not attract the robust protection under Article 10 afforded to more serious journalism'.[37] On 14 April *The Sun* newspaper ran a story revealing as much as they could while remaining within the confines of the injunction. They stated that a footballer had had an affair with Ms Thomas and that they had been made the subject of an injunction.[38] This began speculation as to who the footballer was, and in late April speculation became rife on Twitter as to the identity not only of CTB but also a number of others who had similar injunctions such as ETK, NEJ, JIH, and others. It was at this point that the worst excesses of SMPs became apparent. A mob mentality emerged with little regard for the rule of law, or indeed accuracy of reporting. Everyone began to speculate widely as to the identity of the people who had privacy and anonymity injunctions and why they had them. Few people were in possession of all the facts and indeed no one seemed to care that in each case a judge, or a panel of judges, had determined that, applying the balancing test, an injunction was in order. Fewer again concerned themselves that they may be committing an offence under the Contempt of Court Act 1981. A number of innocent parties (and some less innocent) found themselves dragged into the debate. Twitter users erroneously stated that TV presenter and journalist Jeremy Clarkson was having an affair with Jemima Khan and that she had intimate photographs of the two. This was not true: as has widely been reported since Jeremy Clarkson did have an injunction but it was to prevent publication of details of an affair he was having with his ex-wife, Alex Hall.[39] Jemima Khan was badly shaken by the vitriol shown towards her on Twitter. She originally tried to make light of the issue, tweeting 'Got a nice text from Francie Clarkson and also one from Jeremy, "it's odd I'm sure I would remember if any photos of us existed".' At the same time she sent tweets saying 'the proof that I haven't got a super-injunction is that the papers have printed my name (and no one else's for fear of being sued)' and 'I've woken up trapped in a bloody nightmare'. As time went by and the messages she received became more vitriolic she tweeted 'I hope the people who made this story up realise that my sons will be bullied at school because of it.' This last comment was particularly ironic as one of the key reasons the privacy injunction in

[34] *ETK v News Group Newspapers Ltd* [2011] EWCA Civ 439.

[35] *NEJ v Wood & Anor* [2011] EWHC 1972 (QB).

[36] [2011] EWHC 1232 (QB).

[37] Ibid. [33].

[38] The story may be seen at <http://www.thesun.co.uk/sol/homepage/news/3526696/Footie-stars-affair-with-Big-Brothers-Imogen-Thomas.html>.

[39] *Jeremy Clarkson v Alexandra Hall (formerly known as AMM v HXW)* [2010] EWHC 2457.

the *ETK* case had been awarded was 'to preserve the stability of the family while the appellant and his wife pursue a reconciliation and to save the children the ordeal of *playground ridicule* when that would inevitably follow publicity'.[40] Thus while the courts were awarding injunctions to prevent children from being ridiculed or bullied in the playground, the actions of Twitter users were causing innocent children to be so bullied and ridiculed. The absence of speech caused by the injunction had caused Twitter users to fill the vacuum with incorrect gossip and speculation.

Jemima Khan was not the only innocent victim of the mob mentality of Twitter users at this time. Speculation was rife as to the identity of the world-famous celebrity who was referred to in court as NEJ. Quickly Twitter users determined, quite erroneously, that it was Ewan McGregor. This led to the almost satirical outcome that an entirely innocent man was pilloried by Twitter and Facebook users for having an affair he did not have to protect another man who had an injunction. This of course affected not only Mr McGregor himself; like Jemima Khan it affected his wife and children also. What was becoming clear was that all privacy injunctions were doing was creating an information vacuum which users of SMPs would quickly fill without care for accuracy or the well-being of the people they were naming.

The focus on CTB became fiercer. A number of footballers' names were mentioned and journalist Giles Coren was threatened with a contempt of court action in relation to tweets he had made which (arguably) identified a different footballer (identified in court papers as TSE).[41] On 8 May a Twitter account, which still cannot be identified publicly in the UK as it also relates details of extant injunctions, posted the claim that CTB had been involved in a seven-month extramarital relationship with model Imogen Thomas and naming CTB as Ryan Giggs. The same day a large number of Twitter users in breach of the order of 21 April started naming Giggs as CTB. On 16 May Eady J upheld the injunction. The dam finally broke on 20 May when lawyers for CTB indicated that they were likely to seek a Norwich Pharmacal Order in California requiring Twitter Inc. to hand over customer data relating to a number of accounts which were naming Giggs as CTB. Within less than two hours the name of Ryan Giggs became the no. 1 trending item on Twitter worldwide (see Figure 7.1). By threatening Twitter users, Giggs's legal team had inadvertently triggered Twitter's autoimmune response known as #IamSpartacus. This occurs when members of the Twitter community feel that Twitter is under attack. The offending message or material is re-tweeted as often as possible, often with the hashtag #IamSpartacus attached. The idea is, as in the classic movie *Spartacus*, to form a single group meaning that an attack on one is an attack on all. There is no way lawyers can sue all Twitter users so by banding together the group defends the users under threat.

Faced with #IamSpartacus Giggs's lawyers dropped their plans to identify Twitter users. Immediately thereafter, on 22 May, the Scottish newspaper *The Sunday Herald*, which was not covered by the English court order, identified Giggs in Scotland and on 23 May John Hemming MP used parliamentary privilege to name Ryan Giggs as CTB. This meant that newspapers could now name Giggs using the defence of reporting parliamentary proceedings. Interestingly that wasn't quite the end of the CTB case. Attempts by News Group to have the order of 21 April varied failed,[42] but newspapers

[40] *ETK v News Group Newspapers Ltd* [2011] EWCA Civ 439 [17] (emphasis added).
[41] *TSE & Anor v News Group Newspapers Ltd* [2011] EWHC 1308 (QB).
[42] *CTB v News Group Newspapers Ltd & Anor* [2011] EWHC 1326 (QB).

Figure 7.1 Mentions of the name Ryan Giggs on Twitter on 20 May 2011

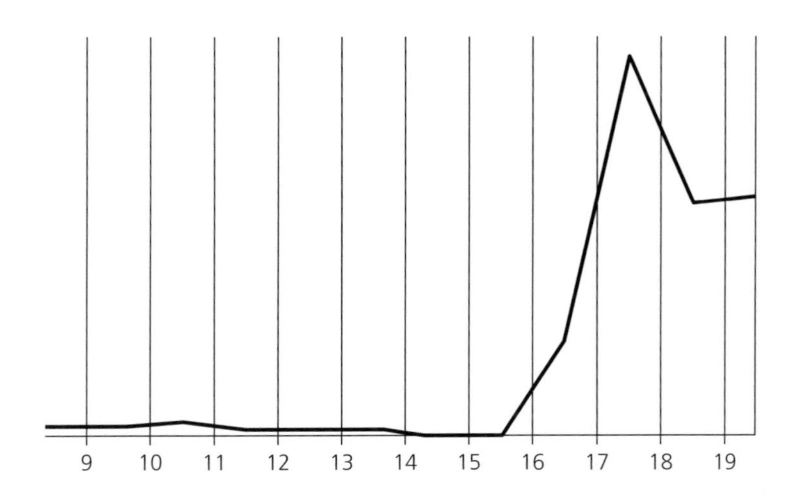

identified Giggs anyway. Eventually in March 2012 the case was finally disposed of with Tugendhat J finding that News Group had not breached the original injunction and that Giggs was not entitled to damages.[43] The most telling part of Tugendhat J's judgment is at paragraph 12 where he notes:

> NGN can hardly say that it has won this action. The fact that Mr Giggs was named as the subject of the Article was not something achieved by NGN in this action. *It was a consequence of the acts of third parties out of court.* There is no suggestion that NGN was behind the widespread publication of Mr Giggs's identity, so this is not a case where it could be said that his identity came into the public domain as a result of a breach by NGN of the injunction. And the effect of the undertaking given by Ms Thomas and NGN's own statement is that it is no more free to publish a story about Mr Giggs today than it was immediately after Eady J had granted the injunction on 14 April.

You can almost hear the disappointment in Tugendhat J's voice. Many claim the outcome of the CTB case to be victory for the power of SMPs and for free speech. For the judges involved in the maelstrom of spring 2011 it is quite the opposite. The will of the courts, the rule of law itself, was undermined by the actions of Twitter and Facebook users. Maybe if you are a free speech activist the end justifies the means. Attempts to gag the press in genuinely important cases such as Trafigura must be resisted but if one looks across the landscape of cases which became the focus of national attention in spring 2011 most of them are of the nature of sexual indiscretion. They are titillating stories—few are genuinely of national importance. We now know the identities of many involved but not always the full tale as injunctions remain in place. So we know that Ryan Giggs had an affair not only with Imogen Thomas but also with his sister-in-law Natasha Giggs. We know Jeremy Clarkson had an affair with his ex-wife Alex Hall; and that journalist Andrew Marr had an affair and thought he had fathered a love child; that banker Fred Goodwin had an affair with a colleague;[44] and that Zac Goldsmith, his ex-wife Sheherazade Goldsmith, and his sister Jemima Khan (there was a reason she

[43] *Giggs (previously known as CTB) v News Group Newspapers Ltd & Anor* [2012] EWHC 431 (QB).
[44] *Goodwin v News Group Newspapers Ltd (Rev 1)* [2011] EWHC 1341 (QB).

was falsely linked to Jeremy Clarkson) have an injunction covering hacked emails taken from the accounts of Mrs Khan and Mrs Goldsmith.[45] Interesting though this is I am not sure any of these pass the balancing test, and I am not sure we are any better informed for thousands of people having ignored the rule of law and the Contempt of Court Act. It is no surprise that the establishment felt something had to be done.

7.2.2 The Neuberger report, the joint committee on privacy and injunctions and the Right to be Forgotten

There was already an ongoing enquiry in the light of growing public concerns about the use and effect of super-injunctions and the impact they were having on open justice. The Neuberger committee had been set up in April 2010 and by the time of the spring of discontent in 2011 they were near to reporting. As a result, the final Neuberger report said little about SMPs. Instead, as per its remit, it focused upon the effects of anonymity and super-injunctions on open justice and the operation of the courts. As a result the final report, *Report of the Committee on Super-Injunctions: Super-Injunctions, Anonymised Injunctions and Open Justice*,[46] mentions the internet only twice. The first is in relation to the changing nature of the technological landscape: 'that anonymisation was a rare occurrence historically, and is less so now, may be due not only to the development of the law after the Human Rights Act but also, amongst other things, to changes in the nature of society and social attitudes, and to technological changes, such as the growth of the internet'.[47] The second relates to notification procedures for hearings:

> where a respondent, or non-party, is a media organisation only rarely will there be compelling reasons why advance notification is or was not possible on grounds of either urgency or secrecy. It will only be in truly exceptional circumstances that failure to give a media organisation advance notice will be justifiable on the ground that it would defeat the purpose of an interim non-disclosure order. Different considerations may however arise where a respondent or non-party is an internet-based organisation, tweeter or blogger, or where, for instance, there are allegations of blackmail.[48]

Thus it may be argued the report does little to solve the problems of *CTB*, *NEJ*, or *ETK*, the problem of speculation and gossip. But looking a little further into the report we find it does much indirectly to deal with the problem. The report makes a number of recommendations in relation to balancing the Art. 8 rights of individuals with the Art. 10 rights of media organizations, and in ensuring super-injunctions are not used to defeat the ends of open justice, as arguably appeared to be the case in *Trafigura*. It recorded that anonymity injunctions cannot be awarded at the agreement of the parties: 'interim non-disclosure orders which contain derogations from the principle of open justice cannot be granted by consent of the parties. Such orders affect the Article 10 Convention rights of the public at large. Parties cannot waive or give up the rights of the public.'[49] It also reiterated that 'derogations from open justice can only properly

[45] *Goldsmith & Anor v BCD* [2011] EWHC 674 (QB).

[46] <https://www.judiciary.gov.uk/wp-content/uploads/JCO/Documents/Reports/super-injunction-report-20052011.pdf>.

[47] Ibid. 1.14.

[48] Ibid. Annex A: Draft Practice Guidance for Interim Non-Disclosure Orders [22].

[49] Ibid. [16].

be made where, and to the extent that, they are strictly necessary in order to secure the proper administration of justice'.[50] The report went on to make a number of recommendations to ensure that the balancing principle was properly applied, that injunctions were only granted where strictly necessary and that injunctions be kept under review at regular intervals by the court.

It may be argued that, by tightening up the procedures for obtaining and retaining an anonymity or super-injunction, the need for the sort of speculation endured in spring 2011 in SMPs is removed. The actions of social network users in general and Twitter users in particular in spring 2011 were driven, arguably, by a sense of injustice: who were these people to decide what could and could not be reported about their private lives when it may be in the public interest? It was perhaps as much a sense of righteous indignation as much as idle speculation and gossip which drove on Twitter users: or rather, to be more accurate, there was a small core of indignant individuals who set up Twitter accounts with the specific aim of 'outing' the individuals who had obtained these injunctions and they fed or supported a much larger community of speculators and gossips. Another major factor in the spring 2011 events was that SMP users were driven by mainstream media. Throughout the CTB/Giggs affair mainstream media had been reporting the story almost every day, especially *The Sun* which often kept the story, which it had a pecuniary interest in, having paid Ms Thomas for her side of the story, on its front page. The mainstream media were at the centre of events in April/May 2011. They sensed that judges were giving weight to Art. 8 rights over Art. 10 and wanted to break that trend to ensure they could continue to report kiss'n'tell stories which are the staple of most UK tabloids. With the rebalancing exercise of the Neuberger report the drive of mainstream media to recruit and encourage SMP users was removed and since that eventful two months they have stopped stoking the fires. An extensive number of anonymity and super-injunctions remain in place—perhaps not quite as many as in the spring of 2011 but extensive all the less—so why is there no longer the same debate and gossip in SMPs? It is because the newspapers are no longer stoking the story.

A second enquiry was quickly set up. The Parliamentary Joint Committee on Privacy and Injunctions was, as it name suggests, a joint committee of the Commons and Lords. It was set up in summer 2011 and was to look specifically at the events of spring 2011 and to report to Parliament what, if any, changes to the law were required to prevent similar events from happening again. The Committee took evidence from expert witnesses throughout autumn/winter 2011 and then reported on 27 March 2012.[51] For most, the key recommendations of the Committee were in relation to whether the UK needed a new privacy statute designed to remove the problems seen in spring 2011: 'We conclude that a privacy statute would not clarify the law. The concepts of privacy and the public interest are not set in stone, and evolve over time. We conclude that the current approach, where judges balance the evidence and make a judgment on a case-by-case basis, provides the best mechanism for balancing article 8 and article 10 rights.'[52]

[50] Ibid. [1.36].

[51] Joint Committee on Privacy and Injunctions, *Privacy and Injunctions* (2010–12, HL 273, HC 1443) <http://www.publications.parliament.uk/pa/jt201012/jtselect/jtprivinj/273/273.pdf>.

[52] Ibid.

For us, though, the most interesting outcomes are how they believed the law should deal with SMPs. The report concluded that:

> Where an individual has obtained a clear court order that certain material infringes their privacy and so should not be published we do not find it acceptable that he or she should have to return to court repeatedly in order to remove the same material from internet searches. Google acknowledged that it was possible to develop the technology proactively to monitor websites for such material in order that the material does not appear in the results of searches. We find their objections in principle to developing such technology totally unconvincing. Google and other search engines should take steps to ensure that their websites are not used as vehicles to breach the law and should actively develop and use such technology. We recommend that if legislation is necessary to require them to do so it should be introduced.[53]

This was a highly controversial move, but one which in a separate set of circumstances has come to pass, in some way. In essence, the committee was attempting to force online information intermediaries to police content by actively filtering search results. It is arguable whether this is legal in EU law, following a series of CJEU decisions which say that the Art. 14 safe harbour provision of the Electronic Commerce Directive[54] is applicable to information gateways such as Google[55] and that those intermediaries cannot be compelled to design and implement filtering and blocking systems as to do so would be a breach of Art. 15(1) of the Electronic Commerce Directive.[56]

Although active monitoring would not be compatible with EU law, passive removal of links and sites upon request is possible and two developments have seen a version of the Joint Committee's recommendation come to pass. Specifically with reference to defamation claims s. 13 of the Defamation Act 2013 allows a court to make an order against 'any person who was not the author, editor or publisher of the defamatory statement to stop distributing, selling or exhibiting material containing the statement'. This is of course a reactive rather than proactive action and requires the court to make the order first. This is perfectly compliant with Arts. 14 and 15 but much narrower than suggested by the Joint Committee. The other development is the so-called Right to be Forgotten introduced by the case of *Google Spain v AEPD and Mario Costeja González*.[57] This case will be discussed in much more depth in chapter 20, but for the moment it is important to recognize that it created a right for EU citizens to apply to data processors, which includes web search services such as Google, to have data about them removed if that data is 'inaccurate, inadequate, irrelevant or excessive for the purposes of the data processing' (in Google's case providing a search facility).[58] Following the decision in *Google Spain*, Google have set up a system which allows EU citizens to make a simple request, using an online form, to have data regarding them removed from Google search returns. This in theory can be used by persons seeking to restrict information about themselves, but as it is restricted to data which is

[53] Ibid. [114]–[115].

[54] Dir. 2000/31/EC.

[55] *Google v Louis Vuitton Malletier* [2010] ETMR 30.

[56] *Scarlet Extended SA v Société Belge des Auteurs, Compositeurs et Editeurs SCRL* (SABAM) [2012] ECDR 4.

[57] Case C-131/12 [2014] <http://curia.europa.eu/juris/document/document.jsf?text=&docid=152065&pageIndex=0&doclang=en&mode=lst&dir=&occ=first&part=1&cid=720760>.

[58] Ibid. [93].

'inaccurate, inadequate, irrelevant or excessive' the applicant would have to establish their interest to privacy outweighed the interests of the public to be aware of the issues. Of course the ability to display a relevant court order would no doubt be of assistance in this.

One person who has made extensive use of the Right to be Forgotten is ex-FIA chief Max Mosley. Since 2008 he has fought to have reports of a visit he made to a brothel suppressed. He famously fought a UK privacy case which went all the way to the ECtHR, with little success,[59] but more recently has had success arguing that the Right to be Forgotten should apply to his case. In 2013, before the *Google Spain* case, a French court ordered Google to 'remove and cease, for a period of five years beginning two months after this decision, the appearance of nine images identified by Max Mosley in the Google Images search engine results'.[60] Post the decision in *Google Spain*, Mr Mosley has bought a further action in the UK to have the same images removed under the Right to be Forgotten.[61] Applying under s.10 of the Data Protection Act to have links to the images removed from the Google Image search facility, Google applied to have the case struck out. They relied on Arts. 13 and 15 of the Electronic Commerce Directive and argued they could rely upon the mere conduit defence and the no obligation to monitor defence.[62] Counsel for Mr Mosley argued that Google could not rely upon Art. 13 as they made thumbnail copies of the image which was beyond caching or carrying the images. This was rejected by Mitting J 'I have no doubt that on the evidence Google does not modify images when it reduces them to "thumbnails". All that it does is to reduce their size and definition. The image conveys precisely the same information and impression to the viewer as does the original. In my judgment, for an image to be modified the information and impression given to a viewer must be altered by, for example, the alteration of the image itself or the addition of something, including text, to it.'[63] The other claim made by Mr Mosley was that only the Data Protection Directive regulated data protection issues and that the Electronic Commerce Directive was not relevant to the case. The reason for this is that Recital 14 of the Electronic Commerce Directive says 'The protection of individuals with regard to the processing of personal data is solely governed by Directive 95/46/EC of the European Parliament and of the Council of 24th October 1995 on the protection of individuals with regard to the processing of personal data and on the free movement of such data . . . and therefore it is not necessary to cover this issue in this Directive in order to ensure the smooth functioning of the internal market, in particular the free movement of personal data between Member States.'[64] This question of the interaction between the Data Retention Directive and the Electronic Commerce Directive was not fully discussed in *Google Spain*. In his analysis Mitting J concluded that 'the two Directives must be read in harmony and

[59] *Mosley v News Group Newspapers Ltd* [2008] EWHC 1777 (QB); *Mosley v United Kingdom* [2012] EMLR 1.

[60] A Sage, 'Google ordered to remove Max Mosley sex party images' (*Reuters*, 6 November 2013) <http://www.reuters.com/article/2013/11/06/france-google-idUSL5N0IR3SL20131106>.

[61] *Mosley v Google Inc.* [2015] EWHC 59 (QB).

[62] Ibid. [32]–[34].

[63] Ibid. [39].

[64] This is given effect by Art. 1(5)(b) which states 'This Directive shall not apply to questions relating to information society services covered by Directives 95/46/EC'.

both, where possible, must be given full effect to.'[65] This though did not dispose of the case for as Mitting J observed there remained the question of whether Google was being asked to monitor its users in breach of Art. 15. Noting that Google already have the ability to monitor for child sexual abuse images, he felt it was not clearly disproportionate to order Google to remove the images in question. On this basis he rejected Google's application to strike out the claim and ordered a full trial to go ahead.

The fact that Google are fighting this case may seem a little odd given that they have a service set up which according to reports dealt with 218,320 requests to remove links between 29 May 2014 and 23 March 2015.[66] The problem for Google is that removing links to static web pages is quite easy. If they find in favour of the applicant they simply blacklist that URL for any search term which includes their name. With images it is more complicated. The image may be hosted on any site and then connected with the name by either content or meta tag. Simply blocking one URL is unlikely to make the image disappear permanently. To chase images is more costly and time-consuming, hence the defence against the Mosley action.

The Right to be Forgotten is therefore being repurposed into an important privacy tool. It is far too soon to say another spring like 2011 is unlikely to be seen, and Twitter and Facebook remain awash with gossip. However, stricter policing by Twitter and Facebook and the application of the Right to be Forgotten will help those who possess privacy injunctions. The real test of the new system though will be when a celebrity goes head to head with an established media outlet, as occurred between *The Sun* and Ryan Giggs in 2011, for at the end of the day it seems unlikely Twitter users would have been discussing the identity of CTB were they not encouraged to do so by the tabloid press.

7.3 **Making criminal threats and organizing criminal activity**

7.3.1 **The Paul Chambers case**

If gossip and speculation were the most antisocial form of activity occurring on SMPs we would have little to worry about. However, SMPs are used for a variety of more antisocial activities including criminal activity. Probably the best-known case of this variety is *Chambers v DPP*.[67] Paul Chambers has become something of a cause célèbre of the Twitter community but some may not know the story of his prosecution. Paul Chambers, known on Twitter as @PaulJChambers, had begun a romantic exchange with another Twitter user, Sarah Tonner known as @Crazycolours. He had arranged to travel to Belfast to meet her on 15 January 2010. He and Sarah were exchanging messages via Twitter about his trip the week before on 6 January 2010 when they heard the

[65] *Mosley v Google Inc.* (n. 61) [43]–[44].

[66] S Tippman and J Powles, 'Google accidentally reveals data on "right to be forgotten" requests' *The Guardian* (London, 14 July 2015) <http://www.theguardian.com/technology/2015/jul/14/google-accidentally-reveals-right-to-be-forgotten-requests>.

[67] [2012] EWHC 2157.

news that the airport he was to fly from, Robin Hood Airport near Doncaster, might close due to snow conditions. They swapped tweets joking about how he might get to Belfast the following week if the airport closed. Two messages sent by Chambers were: '@Crazycolours: I was thinking that if it does then I had decided to resort to terrorism' and '@Crazycolours: That's the plan! I am sure the pilots will be expecting me to demand a more exotic location than NI.'[68] Chambers then heard the news that Robin Hood Airport had closed. He tweeted his fateful message.

Highlight Paul Chambers' tweet

Crap! Robin Hood Airport is closed. You've got a week and a bit to get your shit together otherwise I am blowing the airport sky high!!

It should be noted there is one essential difference between this final message and the ones before. Whereas the previous messages were in the form of replies to @Crazycolours this was a general tweet. This meant this tweet went to all his followers rather than just to @Crazycolours and into his timeline. There was no evidence that anyone found his tweet to be threatening or menacing and initially nothing more was said or thought of the tweet. Then, on 11 January 2010, five days after it was sent, the duty manager responsible for security at Robin Hood Airport, while off duty at home, found the tweet. The court records:

> Mr Duffield did not see this 'tweet' on the appellant's time line, and it was never sent to him or to the airport. Rather he was at home searching generally for any 'tweets' which referred to Robin Hood Airport. In cross-examination he said that he did not know whether the 'tweet' was a joke or not, but as even a joke could cause major disruption it had to be investigated. Accordingly he referred the 'tweet' to his manager, Mr Armson. Mr Armson was responsible for deciding whether any perceived threat to the airport should be graded as 'credible' or 'non-credible'. If 'credible', it was to be referred immediately to the Ministry of Defence, but if 'non-credible', as a matter of standard practice it was to be reported to the airport police. Mr Armson examined the appellant's 'tweet'. He regarded it as 'non-credible', not least because it featured the appellant's name and, as he noted, the appellant was due to fly from the airport in the near future. Nevertheless in accordance with airport procedure he passed this 'tweet' to the airport police. The airport police themselves took no action, presumably for exactly the same reason, but they decided to refer the matter on to the South Yorkshire police.[69]

On 13 January Chambers was arrested on suspicion of involvement in a bomb hoax and was eventually charged following advice from the Crown Prosecution Service (CPS) with sending by a public electronic communication network a message of a 'menacing character' contrary to s. 127(1)(a) of the Communications Act 2003.

[68] Ibid. [12].
[69] Ibid. [13].

Highlight Section 127 (1) of the Communications Act 2003

A person is guilty of an offence if he:

(a) sends by means of a public electronic communications network a message or other matter that is grossly offensive or of an indecent, obscene or menacing character; or

(b) causes any such message or matter to be so sent.

On 10 May 2010 Chambers was found guilty by District Judge Jonathan Bennett at Doncaster Magistrates' Court. That decision was recorded in full by legal blogger David Allen Green (Jack of Kent).[70] Alarmingly for all users of SMPs, the CPS had argued that s. 127(1)(a) was a strict liability offence without the need to establish *mens rea*. Thankfully Judge Bennett rejected this assertion and relying on *DPP v Collins*,[71] found that 'the prosecution must show some *mens rea* to satisfy me, to the requisite standard of proof, for me to find this case is proved'.[72] Judge Bennett was particularly convinced that Chambers had some form of *mens rea* because he posted the message to his timeline rather than in a reply to @Crazycolours as he had done previously. He recorded:

> I do not have to accept what the defendant tells me about his state of mind at face value. I also note the defendant is an experienced, and clearly very heavy user, of 'Twitter'. Furthermore he has travelled by air, although he had not used Robin Hood airport previously. I found strange his evidence in relation to airport threats not seeming to relate to him and appearing to be in another world. Of particular significance is the fact that this 'tweet' was posted to the public timeline, unlike most of his 'tweets' in the time frame around this particular posting. This message would have been of particular significance to the lady known as 'crazy colours' in Northern Ireland to whom the defendant was going to see on his air journey. He chose to post it in the public domain where in theory it was open for anyone to see, as indeed did Mr Duffield. I am therefore satisfied that the defendant sent the message via 'Twitter' and it was of a menacing nature in the context of the times in which we live. Furthermore I am satisfied the defendant was, at the very least, aware that this was of a menacing nature and I find him guilty of the offence.[73]

Chambers appealed and in November 2010 his appeal was lost. Her Honour Judge Davies, sitting with two magistrates found that Chambers' tweet contained menace and that he must have known that it might be taken seriously. Judge Davies told the court that Chambers had been an unimpressive witness and said: 'Anyone in this country in the present climate of terrorist threats, especially at airports, could not be unaware of the possible consequences.'[74] An appeal by stated case was allowed and was stated on 3 March 2011. An initial hearing by the Divisional Court failed to produce a verdict after

[70] <http://jackofkent.blogspot.co.uk/2010/05/paul-chambers-disgraceful-and-illiberal.html>.
[71] [2006] UKHL 40.
[72] <http://jackofkent.blogspot.co.uk/2010/05/paul-chambers-disgraceful-and-illiberal.html>.
[73] Ibid.
[74] M Wainwright, 'Twitter Joke Trial: Paul Chambers Loses Appeal against Conviction' *The Guardian* (London, 11 November 2010) <http://www.guardian.co.uk/uk/2010/nov/11/twitter-joke-trial-appeal-verdict>.

a highly unusual split between the two judges,[75] so a further hearing before three judges rather than the usual two was arranged. Finally, on 27 July 2012, Chambers saw his conviction quashed by a Divisional Court chaired by the Lord Chief Justice, Lord Judge.[76]

The court was quite scathing of the earlier decisions. After quickly disposing of a claim that a tweet was not a message sent by a public electronic communications network but was rather content created and published on a social media platform,[77] the court set about the key issue of Chambers' intent and actions. In considering the *actus reus* of the message Lord Judge made a strong policy statement. He noted that:

> The 2003 Act did not create some newly minted interference with the first of President Roosevelt's essential freedoms—freedom of speech and expression. Satirical, or iconoclastic, or rude comment, the expression of unpopular or unfashionable opinion about serious or trivial matters, banter or humour, even if distasteful to some or painful to those subjected to it should and no doubt will continue at their customary level, quite undiminished by this legislation. Given the submissions by Mr Cooper, we should perhaps add that for those who have the inclination to use 'Twitter' for the purpose, Shakespeare can be quoted unbowdlerised, and with Edgar, at the end of King Lear, they are free to speak not what they ought to say, but what they feel.[78]

Applying this policy, and taking account of the fact that none of Chambers' 600 + followers, nor the employees of the Airport, nor the Airport Police had treated this as a credible threat, the message was not to be read as a 'menacing' message and as such could not make out the offence under s. 127(1).[79] Although this would have disposed of the appeal the court continued to examine the *mens rea* element. Lord Judge usefully set out further guidance:

> The mental element of the offence is satisfied if the offender is proved to have intended that the message should be of a menacing character (the most serious form of the offence) or alternatively, if he is proved to have been aware of or to have recognised the risk at the time of sending the message that it may create fear or apprehension in any reasonable member of the public who reads or sees it. We would merely emphasise that even expressed in these terms, the mental element of the offence is directed exclusively to the state of the mind of the offender, and that if he may have intended the message as a joke, even if a poor joke in bad taste, it is unlikely that the *mens rea* required before conviction for the offence of sending a message of a menacing character will be established.[80]

This was a victory on every level, not only for Chambers and his legal team but also for all users of SMPs throughout England and Wales. It represented a significant rap on the knuckles for the CPS for bringing and continuing to press the case, and to the lower courts for not being sufficiently flexible in analysing both the *actus reus* and *mens rea* elements of the offence. Most important though, Lord Judge and the Divisional Court returned to SMP users everywhere the right to be offensive and rude without the fear of being criminalized. Though we may not agree with some of the more offensive content

[75] D Allen Green, 'The High Court is Unable to Agree on Twitter Joke Trial Appeal' *New Statesman* (London, 28 May 2012) <http://www.newstatesman.com/blogs/david-allen-green/2012/05/twitter-joke-trial-appeal-no-decision>.

[76] [2012] EWHC 2157.

[77] 'Whether one reads the "tweet" at a time when it was read as "content" rather than "message", at the time when it was posted it was indeed "a message" sent by an electronic communications service for the purposes of s. 127(1). Accordingly "Twitter" falls within its ambit': ibid. [25].

[78] Ibid. [28].

[79] Ibid. [31]–[34].

[80] Ibid. [38].

contained on Twitter and Facebook, such as jokes tweeted by comedian Frankie Boyle, which are often distasteful, it would be entirely incorrect to criminalize his actions because others found them to be 'grossly offensive' or to criminalize Paul Chambers because someone else deemed his message to be of a 'menacing character'. There has been a great deal of fall-out from the *Chambers* decision—not least the publication of interim guidance on social media prosecutions by the Director of Public Prosecutions and the concurrent launch of a public consultation.[81] The new guidance states that prosecutors are to carry out an initial assessment and place messages into four categories:

1. Communications which may constitute credible threats of violence to the person or damage to property.
2. Communications which specifically target an individual or individuals and which may constitute harassment or stalking within the meaning of the Protection from Harassment Act 1997 or which may constitute other offences, such as blackmail.
3. Communications which may amount to a breach of a court order. This can include offences under the Contempt of Court Act 1981 or section 5 of the Sexual Offences (Amendment) Act 1992.
4. Communications which do not fall into any of the categories above and fall to be considered separately . . . : i.e. those which may be considered grossly offensive, indecent, obscene or false.

The guidance notes that 'as a general approach, cases falling within (1), (2) or (3) should be prosecuted robustly where they satisfy the test set out in the Code for Crown Prosecutors. Whereas cases which fall within (4) will be subject to a high threshold, and in many cases a prosecution is unlikely to be in the public interest.'[82] The DPP upon unveiling the guidelines, stated that 'the guidelines make it clear to prosecutors that the decision of whether to prosecute under section 127 of the Communications Act or section 1 of the Malicious Communications Act must be consistent with the fundamental right to freedom of speech. If we are to protect this essential right, then the threshold for prosecution must be high.'[83] With the publication of this guidance it was to be hoped that we would never see another *Chambers*-style prosecution. However, finding the line between acceptable speech and unacceptable speech on SMPs remains fraught with difficulty.

7.3.2 The Facebook riot cases

In the summer of 2011 civil unrest broke out in England. After a spring spent discussing the identity of CTB and NEJ, we spent the summer watching riots and looting break out in Tottenham, spreading quickly to several other London boroughs including Croyden and Enfield, and then over the next few nights to other parts of the country including the West Midlands and Manchester. The government initially found it difficult to control the spread of civil unrest with the riots beginning in Tottenham on Saturday 6 August and then spreading on successive nights to other London boroughs and other

[81] <http://www.cps.gov.uk/consultations/social_media_consultation_index.html>.
[82] <http://www.cps.gov.uk/consultations/social_media_consultation.html>.
[83] K Starmer, 'Social Media Prosecutions: Why I Have Published Guidelines Today' (*Huffington Post*, 19 December 2012) <http://www.huffingtonpost.co.uk/keir-starmer-qc/twitter-laws-social-media-prosecutions_b_2328248.html>.

parts of England. The final night of unrest was Wednesday 10 August when a combination of bad weather and a full deployment of police following the cancellation of all leave saw an end to the unrest. One innovation of the unrest was the way it was organized. The overwhelming majority of those involved were under 30 and as a result they used SMPs and other media platforms to organize activities. In the media the unrest was dubbed 'the Blackberry riots' due to the extensive use made of the BBM network by participants.[84] The problem became so bad that David Lammy, the MP for Tottenham, and Chuka Umunna, the MP for Streatham, called for BBM to be suspended, a call that for a while at least seemed to be under serious consideration by the government.[85]

In the aftermath of the unrest, courts worked overtime to prosecute all the offenders. A large number of individuals were charged with public order offences as well as theft and burglary. A smaller number were charged with incitement offences relating to messages placed on Facebook in particular. Among these were Jordan Blackshaw and Perry Sutcliffe. Their cases became linked and formed part of the same appeal against sentence, *R v Blackshaw (Rev 1)*.[86] Jordan Blackshaw set up a Facebook page entitled 'Smash down in Northwick Town'. He set the page up at 10.30 a.m. on 8 August 2011, saying the action would start behind the McDonalds in Northwich at 1 p.m. the next day. As the court notes:

> The riots were in full flow. The appellant knew perfectly well that they were. The purpose of his website was to wreak 'criminal damage and rioting in the centre of Northwich', and the event called for participants to meet in a restaurant in Northwich at lunchtime on 9th August. The website was aimed at his close associates, who he referred to as the 'Mob Hill Massive', and his friends, but he also opened it to public view and included in the website references to ongoing rioting in London, Birmingham and Liverpool. He posted a message of encouragement on the website that read 'we'll need to get on this, kicking off all over'.[87]

Instead of actually starting a riot in Northwich, all Blackshaw achieved was to draw attention to himself. Locals saw the event and reported him to the police. The police posted a warning to anyone thinking of taking part and nine people who said they would attend did not in fact turn up. There was no unrest in Northwich. The court records what happened next:

> Following his arrest at 11.00 on 9th August, the appellant admitted that he had watched media coverage of the riots on the television and that he set up the website. He agreed that the event would be carried out, and that he would have attended himself if he had had enough alcohol. He said that it was not something that he would have done sober, and claimed that he had set the site up for a 'laugh and to meet people to drink with', but in later discussions he agreed that what he had done was stupid and that the effect of his actions was to encourage rioting and looting. He accepted responsibility for his actions. As we have indicated, his later guilty plea made clear that he had not set up the website as a joke. He believed that the offences he was inciting would happen.[88]

[84] 'The BlackBerry Riots', *The Economist* (London, 13 August 2011) <http://www.economist.com/node/21525976>.

[85] 'Govt to Discuss Blocking Social Media during Unrest' (*Information Age*, 11 August 2011) <http://www.information-age.com/channels/comms-and-networking/news/1647483/govt-to-discuss-blocking-social-media-during-unrest.thtml>.

[86] [2011] EWCA Crim 2312.

[87] *R v Blackshaw (Rev 1)* (n. 86) [55].

[88] Ibid. [57].

Perry Sutcliffe's story is similar. In the early hours of 9 August he set up a Facebook page called 'The Warrington Riots'. The page contained a photograph of police officers in riot equipment in a stand-off with a group of rioters and a photograph of himself and others in a pose the police described as 'gangster-like'. He then sent invitations to 400 Facebook friends inviting them to meet at a carvery in Warrington at 7.00 p.m. on 10 August. Like Blackshaw, he also made the page viewable to the general public. In Sutcliffe's case 47 people said they would attend but in the end, like Blackshaw, no one actually turned up and no unrest occurred after police closed the site down. Sutcliffe was arrested on the morning of 9 August. Like Blackshaw, Sutcliffe pleaded guilty. The court records that:

> After he entered his plea it was said on his behalf that he went back to the Facebook site and cancelled the event. It was further said that he woke up at around 10.00 and received a telephone call from a friend who had seen the entry on Facebook and, asked him about it. This had prompted the appellant to go to the Facebook site and cancel the event, posting a remark to the effect that it was a joke ... A forensic analysis of the appellant's computer equipment establishes that the posting on Facebook which cancelled the event and said it was 'only jokin f... hell' was created at 10.54am, literally a few minutes before the police arrived. Although we approach the decision in the appeal on the basis that the appellant decided to retract the Facebook entry, as his advocate suggested, the inference seems clear that this decision followed an intimation that the police were searching for him.[89]

The court therefore seems satisfied that Sutcliffe did cancel the event but believes this is only so because he had been tipped off that the police were searching for him.

As is clear already, neither contested the charges, both pleading guilty: Blackshaw to an offence contrary to s. 46 of the Serious Crime Act 2007 (encouraging or assisting offences believing one or more will be committed); Sutcliffe to an offence contrary to s. 44 of the same Act (intentionally encouraging or assisting an offence). Both were initially sentenced to four years' imprisonment, as in the judge's words 'a deterrent effect'. Both appealed their sentence and both were dismissed. The Court of Appeal noted that, although they were conscious of the fact that no unrest actually occurred as a consequence of their actions, 'the fact that no rioting occurred in the streets of Northwich or Warrington owed nothing to either appellant. The reality was that armed with information from members of the public who were disturbed at the prospect, the police were able to interfere and bring the possibility of riot to an end.'[90] The sentences though seem out of proportion with the harm caused despite this.

Highlight Average prison sentences for the 2011 riots

As of 10 August 2012, there had been 2,138 persons found guilty and sentenced for their part in the disorder. Of those sentenced, 1,405 (66 per cent) were sentenced to immediate custody with an average custodial sentence length (ACSL) of 17.1 months.[91]

[89] Ibid. [61]–[63].

[90] Ibid. [72].

[91] Ministry of Justice, *Statistical Bulletin on the Public Disorder of 6th to 9th August 2011–September 2012 Update* <http://www.gov.uk/government/uploads/system/uploads/attachment_data/file/219665/august-public-disorder-stats-bulletin-130912.pdf>.

Thus the average sentence for taking part in the unrest including sentences for burglary, theft, and violent disorder, is 17.1 months while both Blackshaw and Sutcliffe were given four years, nearly three times the average, for something that did not happen. Why? The answer unfortunately appears to be a fear of technology on the part of the court, linked to a desire to send out a message to others who may consider using BBM or Facebook to organize disorder.

Highlight The court sends a message

We are unimpressed with the suggestion that in each case the appellant did no more than make the appropriate entry in his Facebook. Neither went from door to door looking for friends or like minded people to join up with him in the riot. All that is true. But modern technology has done away with the need for such direct personal communication. It can all be done through Facebook or other social media. In other words, the abuse of modern technology for criminal purposes extends to and includes incitement of very many people by a single step. *Indeed it is a sinister feature of these cases that modern technology almost certainly assisted rioters in other places to organise the rapid movement and congregation of disorderly groups in new and unpoliced areas* [emphasis added].[92]

Clearly the message is being sent not just to Blackshaw and Sutcliffe, but to anyone else who may use SMPs to organize disorder: the courts will come down on you particularly hard. A group of individuals have found this out the hard way. They include Anthony Gristock who was sentenced to three years and eight months in prison after setting up a Facebook page entitled 'Bring the riots to Cardiff'. The online newspaper *Wales Online* records that 'Gristock posted messages on Facebook suggesting targets for rioting'. He wrote: 'Rolex, Post Office, Boss, the land of opportunity.' In another message he told website users to target 'the real banks' and named The Sony Centre and the Apple Store in Cardiff city centre as possible sites for disturbance.[93] Also given long sentences were Shawn Divin and Jordan McGinley. They both set up a Facebook page called 'Riot in the toon', an attempt to incite members of the public to take part in a riot within the City of Dundee. Again no actual damage occurred and Divin was sentenced to three years and three months and McGinley to three years. On appeal their sentences were slightly reduced to two years five months and two years three months, less than their English and Welsh counterparts but in part this was due to their ages of 16 and 18.[94] In summing up, Lord Mackay demonstrated that the Scottish courts take this as seriously as their English counterparts: 'an appropriate starting point for sentencing the appellants on the offence to which they pled guilty is one of three years. A sentence of that length not only reinforces the view that the imposition of a custodial sentence is necessary. It reflects the gravity of the offence to which the appellants pled guilty. The appellants

[92] [2011] EWCA Crim 2312 [73].

[93] S Morgan, 'London Riots: Jail for Facebook User who Wanted Riots in Cardiff' (*Wales Online*, 10 October 2012) <http://www.walesonline.co.uk/news/wales-news/london-riots-jail-facebook-user-2020720>.

[94] *Divin and McGinlay v Her Majesty's Advocate* [2012] HCJAC 81.

may have thought they were engaged in some form of prank. They were not. The agreed narrative and the transcript of the Facebook pages make that clear.'[95]

It appears therefore that the sentences approved in *R v Blackshaw (Rev 1)* will continue to set the tone for anyone who uses SMPs or other media outlets to organize criminal activity or unrest. The courts have set a hard line and it appears they intend to follow it.

7.4 **Cyberbullying, trolling, and harassment**

One of the most troubling forms of antisocial behaviour is bullying. The media abound with tragic tales of teenagers pushed beyond breaking point by the actions of others through various media, but in particular through SMPs, leading to their eventual suicide. Perhaps the most haunting tale is that of 15-year-old Amanda Todd. Todd committed suicide on 10 October 2012 at her home in Port Coquitlam, British Columbia, Canada. Prior to her death, she had posted a video on YouTube, entitled 'My Story: Struggling, bullying, suicide and self harm', which showed her using a series of flashcards to tell of her experiences of being bullied. The video went viral after her death, resulting in international media attention. Todd had been bullied and stalked for years by a man who had obtained a topless picture of her via webcam while posing as a boy her age. According to Todd's mother 'The Internet stalker she flashed kept stalking her. Every time she moved schools he would go undercover and become a Facebook friend.'[96] Todd's story is unfortunately not at all unusual. Similar tales may be told by the families of 13-year-old Megan Meier of Dardenne Praire, Missouri;[97] and closer to home 13-year-old Erin Gallagher from County Donegal[98] and 15-year-old Thomas Mullaney, from Bournville, in Birmingham.[99]

There is clearly a line between bullying and harassment. Bullying is an unfortunate fact of life for many youngsters and it is important that we do not create criminal records where one is not required. Equally, though, cyberbullying is a social problem that at times needs a legal response. Whereas in the past the bullied teenager could find space free from the actions of their tormentors such as the privacy of their own bedroom, the problem with WhatsApp, Snapchat, Facebook, Twitter, and Instagram is that it brings the bully into their private space: they find there is nowhere to escape, often driving them to extreme actions. The law then needs to get involved when the bully goes beyond simple bullying and moves towards harassment. Harassment is behaviour intended to disturb or upset and which is usually found threatening or disturbing; it is regulated by the Protection from Harassment Act 1997. This provides that a person 'must not pursue a course of conduct (a) which amounts to harassment of another,

[95] Ibid. [30].

[96] G Shaw, 'Amanda Todd's Mother Speaks Out about her Daughter, Bullying' *The Vancouver Sun* (Vancouver, 14 October 2012) <http://www.vancouversun.com/news/Amanda + Todd + speaks + about + daughter + death/7384521/story.html>.

[97] <http://www.meganmeierfoundation.org/megansStory.php>.

[98] G Harkin, 'Family Devastated after Tragic Erin Takes Own Life after Vicious Online Bullying' *Irish Independent* (Dublin, 29 October 2012) <http://www.independent.ie/irish-news/family-devastated-after-tragic-erin-13-takes-own-life-after-vicious-online-bullying-28824852.html>.

[99] 'Facebook Bullying Suicide Boy's Parents in Law Change Call' (*BBC News*, 12 July 2011) <http://www.bbc.co.uk/news/uk-england-birmingham-14121631>.

and (b) which he knows or ought to know amounts to harassment of the other'.[100] This raises the question of how one ought to know that their course of action amounts to harassment. However, this is covered by s. 1(2) which provides that 'the person whose course of conduct is in question ought to know that it amounts to harassment of another if a reasonable person in possession of the same information would think the course of conduct amounted to harassment of the other'. If found guilty of harassment the offender may both be charged under s. 2, which can lead to a maximum six months' imprisonment, and may be issued with a restraining order under s. 5, which if breached may lead to up to five years' imprisonment.[101] If the harassment is of such a nature as to put the victim in fear of violence on at least two occasions (this is what the media often colloquially refer to as stalking) then under s. 4 of the Act the offender may be charged with the aggravated offence of 'putting people in fear of violence'; this, like breaching a restraining order under s. 5, can lead to imprisonment of up to five years.

In addition to the provisions of the Protection from Harassment Act, cyberbullying may also lead to prosecutions under the Malicious Communications Act 1988, the Communications Act 2003, or the Crime and Disorder Act 1998. By s. 1 of the Malicious Communications Act 1988 it is an offence to send an indecent, offensive, or threatening letter, electronic communication, or other article to another person. This is a summary offence—and as such may lead to a maximum sentence of imprisonment of only six months—as is the already discussed offence of improper use of the public electronic communications system under s. 127 of the Communications Act 2003. Since both of these offences are summary in nature, the court cannot issue a restraining order. An alternative, which allows for a restraining order to be granted, is to apply for an Antisocial Behaviour Order (ASBO) under s. 1 of the Crime and Disorder Act 1998.

A mixture of all these strategies has been tried, both in relation to cyberbullying, namely where an individual is bullied by someone they know or by someone who has formed an abusive relationship to them, and with the more widespread problem of trolling, namely where someone leaves abusive, insulting, or threatening messages to produce a response from the person being trolled. In 2009 Keeley Houghton, an 18-year-old from Malvern, Worcestershire, became probably the first person in the UK to be sentenced to a custodial sentence for Facebook harassment. She pleaded guilty to harassment and was sentenced to three months in a young offenders' institution after she posted a message on Facebook saying that she would kill another girl.[102] More recently, notorious troll Sean Duffy from Reading was sentenced to 18 weeks in prison having admitted two counts of sending offensive communications under s. 1 of the Malicious Communications Act 1988. He was also given a five-year Antisocial Behaviour Order which prevents him from signing up to, or uploading any content to, any social networking site or from purchasing any device with internet access without notifying the police. Duffy had posted a string of insulting comments on a Facebook page in memory of teenager Natasha MacBryde, who threw herself under a train in Bromsgrove after being bullied, as well as leaving similar comments on the memorial

[100] Protection from Harassment Act 1997, s. 1(1).

[101] Protection from Harassment Act 1997, s. 5(6).

[102] H Carter, 'Teenage Girl Is First to Be Jailed for Bullying on Facebook' *The Guardian* (London, 21 August 2009) <http://www.guardian.co.uk/uk/2009/aug/21/facebook-bullying-sentence-teenage-girl>.

pages of Laura Drew, Hayley Bates, and Jordan Cooper.[103] Another troll, Colm Coss from Manchester, was also jailed for 18 weeks after admitting offences under s. 127 of the Communications Act 2003 in relation to Facebook comments,[104] while Liam Stacey was sentenced to 56 days in prison after admitting an offence under s. 4A of the Public Order Act 1986 for sending racially abusive tweets to footballer Fabrice Muamba.[105]

Some actions against bullies and trolls have been more controversial. During the 2012 Olympic Games, Twitter troll Reece Messer, a 17-year-old from Weymouth, was arrested at 2.45 a.m. by Dorset police and given a harassment warning under s. 1 of the Malicious Communications Act 1988. There is no doubt that Messer is an unapologetic troll but on this occasion the response seems like an overreaction. Why did they feel the need to formally arrest him at 2.45 a.m.? Could they not have waited until the morning? One of the tweets was probably in breach of the Act but in general the exchange between Messer and diver Tom Daley that began the police action was no different to many seen on Twitter. Messer began by tweeting after Daley had performed poorly in his first event, 'you let your dad down I hope you know that'. This was particularly upsetting to Daley who had recently lost his father after a battle with cancer. Daley retweeted the message to his followers with an addition stating 'After giving it my all . . . you get idiot's sending me this.' Two tweets followed from Messer 'hope your crying now you should be why can't you even produce for your country your just a diver anyway a over hyped [expletive deleted]' and 'haha Tom Daley just tweeted me now I know he's feeling bad'. Quickly Daley's followers began a campaign to have Messer banned from Twitter and set up a twitition for this purpose. Before he could grasp the situation Messer realized he was trending not only in the UK but also worldwide: 'how am I trending worldwide?' Realizing the situation had got out of control he apologized to Daley: 'please I don't want to be hated I'm just sorry you didn't win I was rooting for you pal to do britain all proud just so upset'. He then realized he was on Sky News: 'what the hell I'm on sky news?' There is nothing in these tweets to suggest s. 1 of the Malicious Communications Act should be applied. Messer later stated he didn't know Daley had lost his father who famously was his coach for many years; this may or may not be true, but certainly none of these tweets merit a 2.45 a.m. arrest under the Act. It is the case that later on that day Messer did appear to send a tweet which clearly falls under the ambit of s. 1, 'i'm going to find you and i'm going to drown you in the pool you cocky [expletive deleted] you're a nobody people like you make me sick'. This is clearly a threat and qualifies under s. 1 of the Act; the question is why did Messer send this when he appeared to be repentant? The answer is that the Twitter mob had lit their torches and were battering at his door in a search for justice. A 17-year-old boy responded in the only way he knew how, by issuing threats. Although a record of threats issued to

[103] S Morris, 'Internet Troll Jailed after Mocking Deaths of Teenagers' *The Guardian* (London, 13 September 2011) <http://www.guardian.co.uk/uk/2011/sep/13/internet-troll-jailed-mocking-teenagers>.

[104] 'Jade Goody Website "Troll" from Manchester Jailed' (*BBC News*, 29 October 2010) <http://www.bbc.co.uk/news/uk-england-manchester-11650593>.

[105] The details of his offence are found in the note of appeal against sentence. For some inexplicable reason the note suggests he pleaded guilty to an offence under s. 31(1)(b) of the Public Order Act. This is impossible as this section was repealed in 2000. The author understands it was s. 4A under which he was charged and pleaded guilty: <http://www.judiciary.gov.uk/Resources/JCO/Documents/Judgments/appeal-judgment-r-v-stacey.pdf>.

Messer has now been lost (unlike his tweets which were preserved) it seems at least one Twitter user expressed a desire that he burn to death while another recorded they would physically like to assault him. A hashtag was set up #ThingsBetterThanRiley69 in response to which the mob consensus appears to be 'being the middle person in The Human Centipede'. They wished him ill, harm, and trauma. Many of these tweets may also have been in breach of s. 1 or s. 127 of the Communications Act. In a real sense it can be argued that until he was incited to make such responses Messer did not break the law. The Twitter community led to his arrest.

Another controversial case with a whiff of mob justice is the Matthew Woods case. Woods, after a drunken night out, decided to post a number of sick and offensive jokes about April Jones, a five-year-old from Wales who disappeared in October 2012, to his Facebook page. There is no doubt the jokes were offensive and in poor taste, but what happened next is an alarming example of mob justice. Police arrested Woods after a furious mob of 50 people turned up at his home the following night. Initially they said that this was for his own safety but then they charged him under s. 127(1) of the Communications Act. Woods pleaded guilty at a hearing the following day and was sentenced to 12 weeks in a young offenders' institution. It is unlikely that he would be prosecuted under the new CPS guidelines, which would be a step in the right direction as his 'jokes', although designed to be offensive, were not to the author's mind 'grossly offensive or of an indecent, obscene or menacing character'. Yet in a move which mirrored the statements of Judges Bennett and Davies in *Chambers*, magistrates said he (Woods) had committed a 'disgusting and despicable' crime.[106] But why was this? Well, as explained by the chairman of the Bench at Chorley Magistrates Court, Bill Hudson: 'The reason for the sentence is the seriousness of the offence, the public outrage that has been caused.'[107] In other words the statement of Woods was grossly offensive as the public were grossly offended. This would create a crazy situation where the perception of the audience would determine the criminality of SMP messages; the mob would rule. Thankfully the judgment of the court in *Chambers* overrules this: 'the mental element of the offence is satisfied if the *offender* is proved to have intended that the message should be of a menacing character'.[108] The same must surely be true of offensive content as well as menacing content.

The *Chambers* position was tested in summer 2013 with the Caroline Criado-Perez case. Ms Criado-Perez is a journalist and feminist campaigner. She has campaigned to increase the representation of women in the media and in 2013 was active in the campaign to feature a woman on the new £10 note when Winston Churchill was to replace Elizabeth Fry (currently the only female featured on the reverse of a Bank of England banknote) on the £5 note. This campaign was successful but immediately upon the announcement of the Bank's decision Criado-Perez began to receive harassment via Twitter. It was reported that the threats were of a number of 50 per hour and many were of the nature of rape and death threats. Also caught up in the Twitterstorm was MP Stella

[106] 'Fury over Chorley Man's Sick April Facebook Comments' *Lancashire Telegraph* (Blackburn, 9 October 2012) <http://www.lancashiretelegraph.co.uk/news/9974086.Fury_over_Chorley_man_s_sick_April_Facebook_comments/>.

[107] C Skelton, 'Matthew Woods Deserves Support as Much as Airport Tweeter Paul Chambers' *The Guardian* (London, 12 October 2012) <http://www.guardian.co.uk/commentisfree/2012/oct/12/matthew-woods-support-paul-chambers>.

[108] *Chambers v DPP* [2012] EWHC 2157 [38].

Creasy who also received threats. Following extensive investigations only three people were charged and subsequently found guilty; Isabella Sorley[109] who sent the graphic series of tweets 'Fuck off and die . . . you should have jumped in front of horses, go die; I will find you and you don't want to know what I will do when I do . . . kill yourself before I do; rape is the last of your worries; I've just got out of prison and would happily do more time to see you berried; seriously go kill yourself! I will get less time for that; rape?! I'd do a lot worse things than rape you', John Nimmo who tweeted equally graphically 'Ya not that gd looking to rape u be fine; I will find you; come to geordieland bitch; just think it could be somebody that knows you personally; the police will do nothing; rape her nice ass; could I help with that lol; the things I cud do to u; dumb blond bitch', and Peter Nunn who sent a series of messages to Stella Creasy including one too graphic to record here and another saying 'If you can't threaten to rape a celebrity, what is the point in having them?' Many people felt this was an inappropriate response to the barrage of hateful messages sent. Had *Chambers* swung the pendulum too far the other way? Perhaps, certainly it started a strong campaign for Twitter to do more itself. This is the problem of SMPs such as Twitter; they are firehoses of speech which simply overwhelm common sense. Bullies and trolls appear on both sides: sometimes they are the mob demanding something be done about someone like Reece Messer or Matthew Woods, sometimes it is a mob objecting to a woman campaigning, quite reasonably, to have a woman represented on a banknote. The police are being caught in the middle of this. Free speech advocates argue they are far too involved with a public sphere. In their 2015 report 'Careless Whispers: How speech is policed by outdated communications legislation'[110] campaign group Big Brother Watch note that in the three years November 2010 to November 2013, 6,329 people were charged or cautioned under s. 127 of the Communications Act 2003 or under the Malicious Communications Act 1988 (at least 4,259 people were charged and at least 2,070 people were cautioned). Although social media-only actions could not accurately be recorded as most police forces did not keep those records it was clear there was a significant increase in cases and charges. This led Big Brother Watch to find 'It is arguable that the outdated nature of the law is why we are seeing an increase in legal cases involving comments made on social media', and to recommend 'that there needs to be serious reform in this area, to ensure that the laws are brought up to date'. Meanwhile both the Criado-Perez case and the more recent #gamergate case have led many women to campaign for greater protection. This has been met to some extent by new actions from Twitter including a new 'report abusive' function[111] and a new filtering system which is supposed to prevent newly created accounts from sending abusive messages to recipients.[112] What is clear is that this will remain a tightrope for SMPs, the police, and the prosecution service. If they are overzealous free speech campaigners and libertarians will criticize them. If they are too timid they will fail victims.

[109] In an interview given after her release from prison Ms Sorley blames her actions on alcohol while Mr Nimmo says he was 'bored and leaped on a bandwagon'. See P Smith, 'This Is What It's Like To Go To Prison For Trolling' (*Buzzfeed News*, 2 March 2015) <http://www.buzzfeed.com/patricksmith/isabella-sorley-john-nimmo-interview>.

[110] <http://www.bigbrotherwatch.org.uk/wp-content/uploads/2015/02/Careless-Whisper.pdf>.

[111] <https://support.twitter.com/articles/20169998-reporting-abusive-behavior>.

[112] A Hern, 'Twitter announces crackdown on abuse with new filter and tighter rules' *The Guardian* (London, 21 April 2015) <http://www.theguardian.com/technology/2015/apr/21/twitter-filter-notifications-for-all-accounts-abuse>.

7.5 YouTube and 'Innocence of Muslims'

Of course the problem of determining what is offensive, or even grossly offensive, to individuals is magnified by the global audience for SMP content. This has already been seen in the related cases of *LICRA et UEJF v Yahoo! Inc. and Yahoo! France*,[113] and *Yahoo! Inc. v LICRA*[114] which were discussed extensively in chapter 6. There was a clear distinction between attitudes in France and in the United States in relation to the Nazi memorabilia which had been listed on Yahoo! auctions. This distinction was seen again in *R v Sheppard & Anor*,[115] also discussed in chapter 6, where the website host in California continued to host 'Tales of the Holohoax' despite Sheppard and Whittle being prosecuted and found guilty in the UK of an offence under the Public Order Act 1986.

That the internet fails to respect borders and with it distinctive national, cultural, and religious values was thrown into sharp relief in the autumn of 2012. A trailer and later full 74-minute movie appeared on YouTube, entitled 'Innocence of Muslims'. Both are designed to inflame controversy—they apparently show Christians being attacked and a medical clinic trashed by a Muslim mob in Egypt while the police stand idly by. Then it moves to a very poorly scripted and acted retelling of the life of the prophet Muhammad. There is little doubt that the film was designed to provoke outrage and so it proved. It was allegedly written and produced by a Coptic Christian, Nakoula Basseley Nakoula, who was born in Egypt but who lives in the United States. He claims he was driven to produce the movie because of the increasing persecution of Copts and poor human rights standards in Egypt, with a rise in church-burnings, growing religious intolerance, and sectarian violence that has been seen against the 10 per cent population of Egypt that are Copts, and complaints that authorities have failed to protect this population.[116] The movie provoked outcry in the Islamic world. Violent demonstrations took place in a number of countries including Egypt, Yemen, Pakistan, and Sudan. More peaceful demonstrations took place in over 20 other countries including the UK. A number of calls were made for YouTube to remove the videos but YouTube cited the First Amendment and refused to take them down. The White House itself requested YouTube to take down the video, a request that was turned down.[117] Instead YouTube and its parent company Google stated that they would block access to the movie locally where the content was illegal. On this basis they blocked local access from India and Indonesia, as well as in Libya and Egypt.[118] Google/YouTube were extremely bullish in

[113] Tribunal de Grande Instance de Paris (Superior Court of Paris). There are three separate orders in this case. To make sense of the case you should read all three. Order of 22 May 2000 <http://www.lapres.net/yahen.html>; Order of 11 August 2000 <http://www.lapres.net/yahen8.html>; Order of 20 November 2000 <http://www.lapres.net/yahen11.html>.

[114] There were three hearings in California. A hearing before the District Court in which a decision was filed on 7 November 2001: *Yahoo Inc. v LICRA*, 145 F. Supp. 2d 1168 (N.D. Cal. 2001); an appeal to the 9th Circuit in which a ruling was filed on 23 August 2004: *Yahoo Inc. v LICRA*, 379 F. 3d 1120 (9th Cir. 2004); and an *en banc* rehearing before the 9th Circuit in which a ruling was filed on 12 January 2006: *Yahoo Inc. v LICRA*, 433 F. 3d 1199 (9th Cir. 2006).

[115] [2010] EWCA Crim 65.

[116] R Ibrahim, 'The Collective Punishment of Egypt's Christian Copts' (*Middle East Forum*, 6 September 2012) <http://www.meforum.org/3338/egypt-christian-copts-collective-punishment>.

[117] Reuters, 'White House "Innocence Of Muslims" Request Denied: Google Will Not Remove Film From YouTube' (*Huffington Post*, 14 September 2012) <http://www.huffingtonpost.com/2012/09/14/white-house-innocence-of-_n_1885684.html>.

[118] Ibid.

their response. White House officials asked Google to reconsider whether the video had violated YouTube's terms of service. Google said that the video was within its guidelines, and added they would only 'further restrict the clip to comply with local law rather than as a response to political pressure'.[119]

In response to Google's bullish approach courts around the world have dealt with the problems the movie has caused. A Brazilian court has ordered that YouTube remove the movies or face daily fines of $5,000.[120] In Egypt meanwhile YouTube itself was blocked by an order of the Egyptian courts until YouTube in Egypt blocked the video.[121] Meanwhile back home (in YouTube terms) in California an action brought by one of the actresses seen in the movie, who claimed she was misled as to the nature of the movie, failed to see her gain the temporary restraining order she sought preventing YouTube from distributing the movie or trailer.[122] In rejecting her initial application Judge Fitzgerald of the District Court for the Central District of California noted that it was not clear the application had been properly served on all parties.[123] She then applied for a preliminary injunction on copyright infringement, an order also rejected by the court on the basis that 'Garcia [has not] established a likelihood of success on the merits. Even assuming both that Garcia's individual performance in the Film is copyrightable and that she has not released this copyright interest, the nature of this copyright interest is not clear. Nor is it clear that Defendants would be liable for infringement.'[124] Upon appeal the Court of Appeals for the Ninth Circuit found that Garcia was entitled to a preliminary injunction because she was likely to succeed on the merits of her copyright claim. The court determined that Garcia likely owned an independent, copyrightable interest in her own performance in the film.[125] A recent *en banc* decision of the ninth circuit though reversed that position.[126] The court expressed its sympathy for Garcia but could not find in her favour 'at this stage of the proceedings, we have no reason to question Garcia's claims that she was duped by an unscrupulous filmmaker and has suffered greatly from her disastrous association with the Innocence of Muslims film. Nonetheless, the district court did not abuse its discretion when it denied Garcia's motion for a preliminary injunction under the copyright laws.'[127] Thus the

[119] Ibid.

[120] J Langlois, '"Innocence of Muslims" Ordered Removed from YouTube by Brazilian Court' (*Global Post*, 26 September 2012) <http://www.globalpost.com/dispatch/news/regions/americas/brazil/120926/innocence-muslims-ordered-removed-youtube-brazilian-court>. It seems that this request has not been acceded to.

[121] P Kingsley, 'Egypt Court Bans YouTube over Innocence of Muslims Trailer: Month-Long Suspension of Website over Anti-Muslim Film a "Backwards Step" for Free Speech, Says Human Rights Group' *The Guardian* (London, 10 February 2013) <http://www.guardian.co.uk/world/2013/feb/10/egypt-court-bans-youtube-muslims>.

[122] *Garcia v Google Inc.* 743 F.3d 1258 (2014).

[123] *Garcia v Nakoula & Ors*, Case 2:12-cv-08315-MWF-VBK (CD Calif). Minute Order available at <http://www.citmedialaw.org/sites/citmedialaw.org/files/2012–10–18-Minutepercent20Order percent20onpercent20TRO.pdf>.

[124] *Garcia v Nakoula & Ors*, Case 2:12-cv-08315-MWF-VBK (CD Calif). Minute Order available at <http://www.citmedialaw.org/sites/citmedialaw.org/files/2012–11–30-Orderpercent20onpercent 20Preliminarypercent20Injjunction.pdf>.

[125] *Garcia v Google Inc.* (n. 122).

[126] *Garcia v Google Inc.* DC No. 2:12-cv-08315-MWF-VBK, 18 May 2015 <http://cdn.ca9.uscourts.gov/datastore/general/2015/05/18/12–57302 percent20EBpercent20opinion.pdf>.

[127] Ibid. 30.

route of using a copyright takedown notice to have the video removed from YouTube now seems closed.

Innocence of Muslims is a case very similar to the *Yahoo! France* cases: different cultural values and even legal values in different jurisdictions unable to agree a common approach. It is also very different to *Yahoo! France*. The ubiquitousness and open availability of SMPs turns everyone into a global publisher and SMPs are going to have to ask themselves more clearly for which of their users' actions they ought to be responsible.

7.6 **Conclusions**

This chapter has covered a lot of ground: a number of unrelated legal concepts, privacy, the right to be offensive, blasphemy, and incitement to violence. In common they share a utility of social media platforms or SMPs. The modern internet experience has become focused on SMPs. A quick review of the most visited sites on the web shows that search engines and SMPs dominate. Google dominates as the most visited website but Facebook is no. 2, YouTube no. 3, Twitter no. 10, Weibo no. 15,[128] LinkedIn no. 19, VK no. 20,[129] and Instagram no. 25. With the exception of Amazon, Taobao, eBay, and Wikipedia, all other sites in the top 25 are forms of search engines. With the exceptions of search and shopping SMPs have come to define the modern user experience of the internet, yet strangely it is among the least regulated parts of the network. Most SMPs will allow anyone to post anything which does not offend against their decency and copyright policies. Thus you are much more likely to have a YouTube video removed because in the background a ten-second snippet of 'Empire State of Mind' can be heard playing on the radio than because your video offends a substantial number of people who belong to a faith with around 1.6 billion followers. This seems an odd way to promote freedom of speech: commercial speech seems to be given a higher order of protection than religious interests or other interests such as privacy and in the case of *CTB* and cases like it a certified order of the court which is being willingly breached. I should state for the avoidance of doubt that I am not in favour of censorship of SMPs, but perhaps the balance of interests and responsibilities of both users and SMPs themselves needs to be revisited. When a video or message is more likely to be removed because of incidental copyright inclusion rather than in accordance with a legal court order or because of potential offence to 1.6 billion people, the balance seems off. Maybe Facebook, Twitter, and YouTube/Google should reconsider Shaw's principle that 'Liberty means responsibility. That is why most men dread it.'[130]

[128] Weibo is a Chinese language microblogging site.
[129] VK is a Russian language social networking site.
[130] Source: *Oxford Dictionary of Quotations* (7th edn, OUP 2009).

TEST QUESTIONS

Question 1

People cannot say what they like on Twitter. It is a public space not a private one and all Twitter speech must be regulated accordingly. If you break the terms of an injunction you should expect to be prosecuted for contempt of court; trolls should expect prosecution under relevant criminal provisions while anyone who tweets 'You've got a week and a bit to get your shit together otherwise I'm blowing the airport sky high!' should expect to be treated as making a criminal threat or communication.

Discuss.

Question 2

Is there a right not to be offended in one's religious beliefs? Should YouTube take down copies of the movie 'Innocence of Muslims'? If not, should they selectively block access to it on a country-by-country basis?

FURTHER READING

Books

R Cohen-Almagor, *Speech, Media and Ethics: The Limits of Free Expression* (2008)

M Mandiberg (ed.), *The Social Media Reader* (2012)

D Stewart (ed.), *Social Media and the Law* (2013)

Chapters and articles

J Balkin, 'Digital Speech and Democratic Culture: A Theory of Freedom of Expression for the Information Society', 79 *New York University Law Review* 1 (2004)

G Letsas: 'Is There a Right Not to Be Offended in One's Religious Beliefs?', in Lorenzo Zucca (ed.), *Law, State and Religion in the new Europe: Debates and Dilemmas* (2011)

J Rowbottom, 'To Rant, Vent and Converse: Protecting Low Level Digital Speech', 71 *Cambridge Law Journal* 355 (2012)

A Zuckerman, 'Common Law Repelling Super Injunctions, Limiting Anonymity and Banning Trial by Stealth', 30 *Civil Justice Quarterly* 223 (2011)

Defamation

Although the UK recognizes and seeks to protect the individual rights found in Art. 10 of the European Convention on Human Rights and Art. 19 of the Universal Declaration of Human Rights, one form of speech which has continually found itself subject to strict regulation in the UK is defamatory speech: that is speech harmful to the reputation of others. Defamation occurs when one publishes, or makes public, a statement which damages a person's reputation and tends to lower him in the estimation of right-thinking members of society. Defamatory statements are commonplace. Co-workers tend to defame other co-workers, students often defame lecturers, and individuals in pubs and bars defame a variety of public figures from footballers to actors to politicians. As an experiment, think back to the last time you said something about someone that you either knew or suspected not to be true, or about which you were recklessly unaware of its veracity, and which was likely to lower the reputation of that person among those present.

It is a fact of life that we like to 'gossip' about other people,[1] and the best gossip as we all know is salacious and shocking gossip. This causes people to exaggerate, or even to make up stories about others to attain or secure social status. This was not an issue where the nature of discourse was just gossip. When gossip was passed over pints of beer or glasses of wine in the local pub or exchanged over coffees in Starbucks it was short-lived: in the air for a second and then gone again. Actionable defamation, that is the type of defamatory statement which causes an action to end up before a judge, was a world away from gossip. It tended to be statements published in the press or broadcast on television or radio. This is partly due to the extensive audience such statements could reach and partly due to the fact that a publisher or broadcaster indicated deep pockets which could be called upon to fulfil a damages award. As is the common theme of this book the nature of digital communication and the information society has changed all this. As was discussed at length in chapters 6 and 7 the nature of digital communications is that individuals now possess the broadcast abilities of the traditional mass media/broadcast sector. Further, as discussion forums, blogs, video and photo streams, and social network updates provide a semi-permanent record of statements, they lose the character of ephemera that gossip has. Finally, entries on blogs,

[1] It is reported by the Social Issues Research Centre at the University of Oxford that gossip accounts for 55 per cent of male conversation time and 67 per cent of female time. See K Fox, *Evolution, Alienation and Gossip: The role of mobile telecommunications in the 21st century* SIRC <http://www.sirc.org/publik/gossip.shtml>.

social network sites, and video-and photo-sharing sites require the assistance of commercial internet service providers and content hosts which assure the availability of deep pockets. It is therefore unsurprising that a number of defamation cases arising both from traditional media sites and from user-generated media entries have been brought in the UK and further afield.

8.1 **The tort of defamation**

The tort occurs when one individual makes a defamatory statement about another in which the defamed party may be identified.[2] The defamatory statement must be 'published' that is, it must be communicated to at least one other person. You may defame a natural person, either a living person[3] or a corporation;[4] although in English law it is against the public interest for local authorities, government-owned corporations, and political parties to bring defamation actions,[5] while trade unions[6] lack personality to raise actions. English law makes a distinction between libel: that is a written or recorded defamatory statement, including a statement made in a broadcast, and slander: a spoken or otherwise transient defamatory statement. In general libel is treated more strictly by the courts than slander, at least in part on the basis that a recorded statement is more likely to be damaging than a transitory one.

Modern telecommunications and mass communication technologies have tended to blur this line somewhat. A statement made on a live television broadcast could reach a far greater audience than a statement written in a local newspaper or in an academic textbook and thus modern telecommunications caused an imbalance in the respective potential effects of libel and slander. Because of this s. 1 of the Defamation Act 1952 stated that: 'For the purposes of the law of libel and slander, the broadcasting of words by means of wireless telegraphy shall be treated as publication in permanent form.' Although s. 1 has since been repealed, the current version of this provision may be found in s. 166(1) of the Broadcasting Act 1990 which states: 'For the purposes of the law of libel and slander (including the law of criminal libel so far as it relates to the publication of defamatory matter) the publication of words in the course of any programme included in a programme service shall be treated as publication in permanent form.' Digital communications have, of course, caused further imbalances in traditional defamation principles. As almost all content in the digital environment is recorded, there can be little doubt that any defamatory statement contained therein would be subject to an action in libel rather than slander. Even in the unlikely event

[2] It is irrelevant whether or not you intended to identify the defamed party. If they *can* be identified, they may then claim for defamation.

[3] Famously in *Rex v Ensor* (1887) 3 TLR 366 Stephen J stated: 'The dead have no rights and can suffer no wrongs. The living alone can be the subject of legal protection, and the law of libel is intended to protect them.' For a critique of this see F Cameron, 'Defamation Survivability and the Demise of the Antiquated "Actio Personalis" Doctrine' (1985) 85 *Columbia Law Review* 1833.

[4] *Jameel v Wall Street Journal* [2007] 1 AC 359.

[5] *Derbyshire v Times Newspapers Ltd* [1993] AC 534; *Goldsmith v Boyrul* [1997] 4 All ER 268. However, it should be noted that individuals working within such organizations whose reputation is impaired can still commence proceedings. See *Reynolds v Times Newspapers Ltd* [1999] 4 All ER 609.

[6] *EETPU v Times Newspapers Ltd* [1980] 1 All ER 1097.

that the material was broadcast only as a live webcast which was not recorded it would be treated as libel not slander, for s. 201(1)(c) of the Broadcasting Act 1990 makes clear that a programme service includes 'any other service which consists in the sending, by means of a telecommunication system, of sounds or visual images or both'. Such a definition clearly includes all internet-based programme services from YouTube to Livestream.

8.1.1 **Statements and publication**

When a defamatory statement is made several issues arise. There are questions of who may be liable in damages, questions of when and where the statement was made, issues surrounding defences, and the role and potential liability for distributors of the defamatory statement. Although the law of defamation is well established and we have the assistance of the Defamation Acts 1996 and 2013 in interpreting the various roles and potential liabilities involved in an action for defamation we find these issues have become extremely complex when dealing with a media that is capable of crossing borders, which keeps a constant record of all 'discussions' and which allows individuals access to a mass communication channel.

The first issue to address is who is responsible and potentially liable for an online defamatory statement? Primary liability for any defamatory statement rests with the author of the statement: that is the person who made the utterance or who wrote the defamatory text. Liability does not only rest with the author. Liability also arises for editors, publishers, and distributors of a defamatory statement. Distributors and publishers of defamatory statements have always proven to be popular defendants, or co-defendants, as they possess deep pockets, a character often not true of the author or even of the editor of the original libel. As distributors are in a particularly perilous position, distributors are rarely aware of all the content of the material they distribute, and even if they were they have little opportunity of knowing the veracity of statements made in material they distribute; they are offered a particular defence in s. 1 of the Defamation Act 1996, known somewhat unimaginatively as the distributor defence. This states that a distributor of a defamatory statement has a defence if he shows that he took reasonable care in relation to its publication, and he did not know, and had no reason to believe, that what he did caused or contributed to the publication of a defamatory statement. This defence, as we shall see below, is important for ISPs and hosting services who cannot possibly be aware of all the content they host, and/or, supply. In fact the particular challenges faced by internet hosting services and ISPs, who deal with vastly more material than usual distributors of newspapers and magazines imagined in s. 1 of the 1996 Act have led to the promulgation of a specific defence for operators of websites in s. 5 of the Defamation Act 2013 which will be discussed in more detail below.

The next issue is where the harm occurs; although there are special considerations which arise with internet publication, which will be discussed in detail below, the general rule on jurisdiction and harm is complex enough as was demonstrated in the case of *Berezovsky v Forbes, Inc. (No.1)*.[7]

[7] [2000] 1 WLR 1004; 2000 WL 544123.

Case study *Berezovsky v Forbes, Inc. (No.1)*

Mr Berezovsky is a Russian businessman who, although now resident in Britain, was at the time of the alleged defamation living and working in Russia. In 1996 *Forbes Magazine* published an article claiming that Mr Berezovsky was involved in criminal activity and labelling him as a Russian mafia godfather and insinuating that he was involved in the murder of television producer Vladislav Listiev.

Mr Berezovsky decided to litigate claiming the article to be defamatory; surprisingly he chose to litigate in England. This seems a remarkable decision. Mr Berezovsky was living and working, at this time, in Russia. He was in fact a member of the Russian government holding the office of Deputy Secretary of the Security Council of the Russian Federation, while the magazine was published in the US. England therefore seemed an unusual forum for this dispute, but of course English libel laws are famously accommodating of plaintiffs, leading to complaints about so-called libel tourism.[8] Unsurprisingly the defendant challenged the jurisdiction of the English courts. Evidence was laid before the court showing that of the 788,346 copies of the issue in question only 1,915 (0.25 per cent) were sold in England and Wales with over 98.9 per cent of the issues being sold in the US and Canada. *Forbes* claimed that as Mr Berezovsky was not resident in England and Wales and as the magazine was published in and marketed towards and overwhelmingly sold in the North American market the correct forum for this dispute was either Russia or the US. Mr Berezovsky countered that he had a considerable reputation to protect in England and Wales. He explained in an affidavit that 'Over the past several years I have had extensive contacts with England, in business, in government service and personally. During the years in which I pursued my career in international business and finance, I worked frequently in London and with persons and companies based in London. This is entirely understandable, given London's status as the international business and financial capital of Europe, where all of my business interests have been based, and of which Russia is an increasingly important part.'

In the High Court Popplewell J placed a stay on proceedings on the basis that Russia was the better forum for the claim as Mr Berezovsky's links to England and Wales were not strong. The case went to the Court of Appeal. Hirst LJ found that Mr Berezovsky amply met the criteria for a hearing in England and Wales and with the agreement of May LJ and Sir John Knox, reversed the decision of Popplewell J. The case eventually ended up before the House of Lords. There *Forbes's* appeal was dismissed. In the leading judgment Lord Steyn noted that: 'In 1994/5 he [Berezovsky] visited London on 22 occasions and in 1996/7 on 9 occasions, the reduced rate being due to his involvement in government. He kept an apartment in London. His wife from whom he has separated lives in London with their two children. He also had two daughters from a previous marriage at Cambridge University. As Hirst LJ observed it was surprising on this evidence that the judge found that Mr Berezovsky's connections with England were

[8] The Defamation Act 2013, s. 9 has taken steps to reduce the availability of libel tourism in England and Wales. It will be discussed in greater detail below.

tenuous. The new material admitted in the Court of Appeal included concrete evidence from three independent sources as to the effect of the Forbes article on Mr Berezovsky's business reputation. The three deponents were a commercial solicitor, the managing director of a Swiss company, and the managing director of a Russian oil company. It is not necessary to set out their evidence in detail. It is sufficient to say that the Forbes article was known to executives of financial institutions and deterred them from entering or continuing London-based negotiations with Mr Berezovsky.'[9] On this basis Lord Steyn found the necessary connection with the jurisdiction of the court was made.

Lord Steyn then dealt with three challenges to the assumption that the courts of England and Wales were the correct forum for the case, all of which are of key importance when dealing with issues of online jurisdiction as we shall see later when we discuss cases such as *Dow Jones v Gutnick*[10] and *Jameel v Dow Jones Inc.*[11] The first of these was whether Russia was a better forum for the case to be heard. Lord Steyn rejected this claim on the basis that 'only 19 copies [of the relevant issue of *Forbes Magazine*] were distributed in Russia . . . and most importantly . . . it is clear that a judgment in favour of the plaintiffs in Russia will not be seen to redress the damage to the reputations of the plaintiffs in England'.[12] Next, on the claim that the US was the better jurisdiction Lord Steyn noted that: 'the connections of both plaintiffs with the United States are minimal. They cannot realistically claim to have reputations which need protection in the United States. It is therefore not an appropriate forum.'[13] Finally, and most importantly, Lord Steyn addressed a claim raised by counsel for the appellant that 'the correct approach is to treat multi-jurisdiction cases like the present as giving rise to a single cause of action and then to ascertain where the global cause of action arose'.[14] Lord Steyn rejected this. He found that such an argument 'runs counter to well established principles of libel law. It does not fit into the principles so carefully enunciated in Spiliada.[15] The present case is a relatively simple one. It is not a multi-party case: it is, however, a multi-jurisdictional case. It is also a case in which all the constituent elements of the torts occurred in England. The distribution in England of the defamatory material was significant. And the plaintiffs have reputations in England to protect. In such cases it is not unfair that the foreign publisher should be sued here.'[16] This last point is particularly important when dealing with online publication. Lord Steyn is directly rejecting a claim that when publication is of a global nature it is the role of the court to identify a single cause of action and raise a single claim where that cause arose; in the Berezovsky case this would probably be the US. Instead he reaffirms the principle of *lex loci delicti*: that is wherever harm has occurred those who are victims of that harm may raise an action. Thus a web page which is accessible worldwide may lead to an action in any jurisdiction in which the claimant's reputation has suffered.[17] This is an application of the multiple publication rule (to which we will return below). It states that whenever a new publication or republication of a defamatory statement

[9] *Berezovsky v Forbes, Inc. (No.1)* (n. 7) 1010–1011.
[10] [2002] HCA 56.
[11] [2005] EWCA Civ 75.
[12] *Berezovsky v Forbes, Inc. (No.1)* (n. 7) 1014–1015.
[13] Ibid. 1015.
[14] Ibid. 1011.
[15] *Spiliada Maritime Corp v Cansulex Ltd (The Spiliada)* [1987] AC 460.
[16] *Berezovsky v Forbes, Inc. (No.1)* (n. 7) 1012–1013.
[17] This will be discussed in depth below.

takes place, a fresh cause of action arises wherever and whenever that occurs. This rule made sense in the real world when to republish a statement usually meant taking some form of affirmative action such as paying for redistribution or reprinting of the statement. In the digital environment though it has taken on a new dimension as material hosted on a single web server anywhere in the world may be continually republished in a variety of jurisdictions by the simple act of a new reader visiting the web page and downloading the defamatory statement to his computer screen. As we shall see below this has caused great difficulty for authors and publishers online.

8.1.2 Taking jurisdiction in claims against non-EU respondents

Such is the extent of the perceived injustice to online publishers caused by the outcome of the *Berezovsky* case (and subsequent cases) that the law has been reformed in this area as part of the package of reforms brought forward in the Defamation Act 2013. The new law is found in s. 9 of the Act and sets out a series of new standards for judges to apply in claims raised against respondents from outside the European Union, Iceland, Norway, and Switzerland.[18]

Highlight Actions against a person not domiciled in the UK or EU

Defamation Bill: cl. 8(3)

Defamation Act 2013: s. 9

(1) This section applies to an action for defamation against a person who is not domiciled—

(a) in the United Kingdom;

(b) in another Member State; or

(c) in a state which is for the time being a contracting party to the Lugano Convention.

(2) A court does not have jurisdiction to hear and determine an action to which this section applies unless the court is satisfied that, of all the places in which the statement complained of has been published, England and Wales is clearly the most appropriate place in which to bring an action in respect of the statement.

The intent of this provision is statutorily to overrule the *Berezovsky* assumption that wherever harm has occurred, those who are victims of that harm may raise an action. This is the specific response from Parliament to the challenge of the global digital network which sees communications replicated instantly and globally. As shall be discussed the *Berezovsky* principle was to cause great difficulty with challenges founded upon minimal connections of the parties to the action with the jurisdiction of England and Wales but where the material could be accessed within the jurisdiction.[19] In essence the effect of s. 9 is to give statutory weight to the later decision of the Court of Appeal in

[18] Iceland, Norway, and Switzerland being the only non-EU Lugano Convention nations.

[19] See *King v Lewis* [2004] EWCA Civ 1329 and *Jameel v Dow Jones* [2005] EWCA Civ 75 (discussed respectively at 8.2.3 and 8.2.4).

Jameel v Dow Jones, Inc.[20] over the House of Lords decision in *Berezovsky,* a decision that would naturally be inferior in terms of judicial authority and precedence. The new standard does not, of course, prevent actions being brought against non-European respondents; it merely asks the judge in considering whether England and Wales is the most appropriate location for the hearing to balance the interests of justice in hearing the action in England and Wales with those of alternative jurisdictions.[21] The explanatory notes to the Act give guidance to Judges and Masters in deciding this: 'subsection (2) provides that a court does not have jurisdiction to hear and determine an action to which the section applies unless it is satisfied that, of all the places in which the statement complained of has been published, England and Wales is clearly the most appropriate place in which to bring an action in respect of the statement.' This means that in cases where a statement has been published in this jurisdiction and also abroad the court will be required to consider the overall global picture to determine where it would be most appropriate for a claim to be heard. It is intended that this will overcome the problem of courts readily accepting jurisdiction simply because a claimant frames their claim so as to focus on damage which has occurred in this jurisdiction only. This would mean that, for example, if a statement was published 100,000 times in Australia and only 5,000 times in England that would be a good basis on which to conclude that the most appropriate jurisdiction in which to bring an action in respect of the statement was Australia rather than England. There will, however, be a range of factors which the court may wish to take into account including, for example, the amount of damage to the claimant's reputation in this jurisdiction compared to elsewhere, the extent to which the publication was targeted at a readership in this jurisdiction compared to elsewhere, and whether there is reason to think that the claimant would not receive a fair hearing elsewhere.[22]

It must be said though that it is unlikely s. 9(2) would have changed the outcome in *Berezovsky* if it had been in effect at the time, given the strong wording of Lord Steyn's judgment. Further, as we shall see, the courts had already taken steps to close the window of jurisdictional choice in cases such as *King v Lewis* and *Jameel v Dow Jones.*

8.1.3 **Defences**

The final general issue is to examine when defences may be raised to a claim in defamation. There are several defences; the most complete defence is truth.[23] This new statutory defence replaces the old common law justification defence that can be traced back to at least the case of *McPherson v Daniels* in 1829.[24] The new defence is arguably marginally wider than the old justification defence although it does follow the previous formulation quite closely. It states that 'it is a defence to an action for defamation for the defendant to show that the imputation conveyed by the statement complained of is substantially true.' The interesting word there is substantially; there is no need for the defendant to be able to demonstrate that all aspects of the statement are true. This

[20] Ibid. Discussed at 8.2.4.

[21] As shall be seen in the discussion of *Sloutsker v Romanova* [2015] EWHC 2053 (QB), discussed at 8.2.6.

[22] Explanatory note to s. 9 of the Defamation Act 2013. Available at: <http://www.legislation.gov.uk/ukpga/2013/26/notes/division/5/9>. See also *Sloutsker v Romanova* [2015] EWHC 2053 (QB), discussed at 8.2.6.

[23] Defamation Act 2013, s. 2.

[24] (1829) 10 B & C 263.

is the statutory version of the justification defence established in *Chase v News Group Newspapers Ltd*,[25] where the Court of Appeal indicated that in order for the defence of justification to be available 'the defendant does not have to prove that every word he or she published was true. He or she has to establish the "essential" or "substantial" truth of the sting of the libel.'[26] In short, were an individual to make a defamatory accusation about an individual; such as they are a paedophile who abused children at a hospital in Manchester, it would not matter to their defence if it turned out they could prove the truth of the charge of paedophilia but in fact, following further investigation, it was established that the abuse had taken place at a hospital in Oldham.

An alternative is 'honest opinion' which replaces the old 'fair comment' defence.[27] This defence may be available if the statement is expressed to be a personal opinion on a matter. To claim the defence, three factors need to be established: (1) the statement complained of must be a statement of opinion; (2) the statement should, in general or specific terms, give the basis of the opinion; and (3) it must be possible than an honest person could have held the opinion based upon the facts or available privileged statements at the time the opinion was given. It should be particularly noted though that the defence fails if it is established by the claimant that the respondent did not hold the opinion stated.[28] Thus if I genuinely hold the opinion that the banking crisis and financial crash of 2008 were caused by the actions of one banker and I write a news story or blog entry stating this opinion and giving my reasons I cannot be successfully sued by that banker in defamation because of the honest opinion defence, even if I am wrong in my assumptions. If, though, the banker could show that I only wrote the story because of a long-standing enmity between us, then any honest opinion defence would be swept aside.

The final generic defence open to the author of a defamatory statement is the public interest defence. In recent years the public interest defence has become known as 'the Reynolds defence' after the case that established the principles under which it may be raised. The case was *Reynolds v Times Newspapers Ltd & Ors*,[29] and the principle established was that the public interest defence could be raised when a newspaper or other media organization published a defamatory statement if they could prove it was in the public interest to publish it and that it was the product of responsible journalism.[30] As with the other defences the Public Interest defence has been placed

[25] [2002] EWCA Civ 1772.

[26] Ibid. [34].

[27] Defamation Act 2013, s. 3.

[28] Defamation Act 2013, s. 3(5).

[29] [1999] UKHL 45; [1999] 4 All ER 609; [1999] 3 WLR 1010.

[30] Lord Nicholls set out ten factors which should be taken account of in determining whether responsible journalism was practised. They are: (1) The seriousness of the allegation. The more serious the charge, the more the public is misinformed and the individual harmed, if the allegation is not true. (2) The nature of the information, and the extent to which the subject matter is a matter of public concern. (3) The source of the information. Some informants have no direct knowledge of the events. Some have their own axes to grind, or are being paid for their stories. (4) The steps taken to verify the information. (5) The status of the information. The allegation may have already been the subject of an investigation which commands respect. (6) The urgency of the matter. News is often a perishable commodity. (7) Whether comment was sought from the claimant. He may have information others do not possess or have not disclosed. An approach to the plaintiff will not always be necessary. (8) Whether the article contained the gist of the claimant's side of the story. (9) The tone of the article. A newspaper can raise queries or call for an investigation. It need not adopt allegations as statements of fact. (10) The circumstances of the publication, including the timing.

on a statutory footing by the Defamation Act 2013. The defence is found in s. 4 which states, 'It is a defence to an action for defamation for the defendant to show that (a) the statement complained of was, or formed part of, a statement on a matter of public interest; and (b) the defendant reasonably believed that publishing the statement complained of was in the public interest.' This defence seems simple to understand but is actually loaded with complexity. By replacing the old Reynolds defence with this new statutory defence, the old Reynolds test which contained clear guidance from Lord Nicholls as to the types of consideration which should be undertaken before deciding whether or not to publish a story is consigned to history. In the explanatory notes to the Act it is indicated it is the intent of the drafters to retain the Reynolds principles so it may be that the guidance given by Lord Nicholls remains applicable in the new framework but this also brings problems. As Jacob Rowbottom has pointed out while the defence remains ostensibly the same the environment is different.[31] So while in *Reynolds*, and the later Privy Council case of *Seaga v Harper*,[32] the requirements of 'responsible journalism' formed the foundation of the privilege to publish, whether one were a professional journalist or an individual these requirements were 'devised in the late 1990s, before the full extent of the freedom to publish on the digital media had been realised. The standards of responsible journalism were therefore formulated with the practices associated with traditional investigative journalism in mind.' As Rowbottom notes, these standards are difficult to meet even if you are a 'smaller title within the traditional mass media'; they are almost impossible to meet if you are an individual blogger. The concern for digital media outputs is that they are overwhelmingly quick responses from individuals, they do not meet media standards of editorial control, and thus it is unlikely that s. 4 will be very useful to individuals or even small to medium-sized digital media outlets. This is best captured by the response of Lord McNally, Minister of State for Justice, who when asked about the defence in Grand Committee responded:

> The noble Viscount, Lord Colville, and the noble Baroness, Lady Bakewell, explained to us what the responsible journalist does in these matters. The noble Lord, Lord Triesman, rightly reminded us of the question of what to do when the intention of the publisher or owner is to destroy a reputation. Do we give impunity to that? That is why, when our friends in the Libel Reform Campaign come close to asking for a blank cheque, I have to say that we cannot give it to them. We also have a responsibility, as well as a recognition that there is irresponsible publication. We are moving on to new media . . . I would say to Twitterers the Twittering equivalent of 'caveat emptor': 'Twitterer beware'. Twittering is not beyond the law. We somehow got the idea that new media is a law-free area. People are going to find that it is not.[33]

It is clear therefore that the public interest defence is one to be approached with some degree of caution unless one is a professional journalist.

There are three further narrower and more specialized defences laid out in the 2013 Act. By s. 7 there is the defence of privilege. This allows the reporting of a number of official reports, documents, and records without fear of a subsequent action in defamation. There are absolute privileges for fair and accurate statements made in judicial

[31] J Rowbottom, 'In the Shadow of Big Media: Freedom of Expression Participation and the Production of Knowledge Online' (2014) *Public Law* 491.

[32] [2008] UKPC 9.

[33] HL Deb 19 December 2012, vol. 741, col. GC558.

proceedings[34] and contemporaneous reports of such proceedings,[35] and for statements made in either House of Parliament.[36] Qualified privilege is awarded for fair reports of judicial proceedings, parliamentary proceedings (internationally not only the UK Parliament), public meetings and notices, press conferences at which matters of public interest are discussed, and reports of proceedings of scientific or academic conferences held anywhere in the world.[37] The reason for these privileges is to allow journalists, including citizen journalists, to report proceedings of judicial, legislative, and public meetings accurately without the risk of an action in defamation. By s. 6 there is a new extension of the privilege principle to peer-reviewed publications. This privileges publications in academic or scientific journals (whether paper published or electronic journals) as long as the publication is an academic or scientific publication and provided it has been peer-reviewed by the editor of the journal and at least one further peer-reviewer. The same privilege extends to the reviewer's report.[38] This privilege was brought forward after extended lobbying from the academic and scientific community following the case of *BCA v Singh*.[39]

The final defence is one of particular importance to this text; it is the s. 5 defence available to operators of websites. This is a specialist defence open only to internet intermediaries. Although flagged up here it will be discussed in full at 8.3.3.

8.2 Digital defamation: publication and republication

It is clear that publication in an online forum, social network site, or via SMS or MMS would qualify as publication for the law of defamation. It is equally clear that in all cases the publication would be of the nature to raise an action in libel rather than slander. The first major issue raised by digital distribution of defamatory material is the method of distribution and what this means for publication and republication.

As we have already seen in Lord Steyn's judgment in *Berezovsky v Forbes*, the standard usually employed by a court in taking jurisdiction over a defamation action is that of *lex loci delicti*. This means that wherever a claimant suffers a loss or harm to his reputation an action may be raised. Traditional media outlets could take steps to limit their exposure to overseas actions. As we saw in chapter 6, traditional media outlets could have defined or specific markets where they would broadcast or distribute their content. By targeting their publications or broadcasts to specific jurisdictions they could avoid extraterritorial actions as they would be in a position to establish that as publication took place only within a specific jurisdiction harm could not have occurred outside that jurisdiction. This principle would defend publishers and broadcasters even if a few copies of the defamatory material crossed borders in the bags or suitcases of travellers between states. Obviously, and as illustrated by *Berezovsky v Forbes*, once the publisher or broadcaster actively distributes his product in other states he runs the risk of facing a libel action in any state in which he markets his product. In *Berezovsky*, a key piece

[34] *Watson v McEwan* [1905] AC 480.
[35] Defamation Act 1996, s. 14.
[36] Bill of Rights 1689. Although this may be waived under s. 13 of the Defamation Act 1996.
[37] Defamation Act 1996, Sch. 1 (as amended by s. 7 of the Defamation Act 2013).
[38] Defamation Act 2013, s. 6(4).
[39] [2009] EWHC 1101 (QB); [2010] EWCA Civ 350.

of evidence throughout was that *Forbes Magazine* had 566 subscribers in England and Wales and the issue in question sold a further 1,349 copies at newsstands. Thus traditional media publishers could balance the risks of being pursued in an overseas jurisdiction against the commercial benefits of trading in the jurisdiction.

The online distribution model is very different. A static or dynamic digital space (web page, social media platform, or broadcast site) is stored and updated via a server. That server may then be accessed anywhere in the world, and at any time unless access to the server is blocked. At the risk of sounding repetitive it is the same central issue which has driven the discussion in chapters 4, 6, and 7: digital communications cross borders without challenge and may be stored and recovered at any time. The effect of this, when faced with the challenges raised by the law of defamation, is though potentially paralysing. Previously publishers or broadcasters could choose to extend the audience for their publication or broadcast by entering a new market, or jurisdiction depending on whether you view this as a commercial or legal development. However, the suggested implication of digital publishing is that any publisher, no matter how small or localized their intended audience may be, could potentially be seen to publish simultaneously in every country worldwide where their content could be read. Even more potentially damaging, applying the principle in *Berezovsky*, every time their content was accessed by any user worldwide would count for defamation law purposes as a republication of that content in the place where the user accessed it. Could defamation law really be that strict? If so would anyone publish anything which was remotely at risk of a defamation suit online given that they could potentially have to defend themselves in any court in any jurisdiction worldwide?

8.2.1 *Dow Jones v Gutnick*

The answer to some of these questions came in the winter of 2002 when the High Court of Australia handed down the long-anticipated judgment in *Dow Jones & Co. Inc. v Gutnick*.[40] This case has many factual similarities to the *Berezovsky* case but was the first defamation case to answer the question 'does internet publication qualify as publication within a jurisdiction?'

Case study *Dow Jones & Co. v Gutnick*

On 30 October 2000 *Barron's* magazine published an article entitled 'Unholy Gains' and placed a copy on the *Barron's Online* website.

The article raised a number of allegations about Mr Gutnick, a well-known Melbourne entrepreneur. It claimed that he was involved in the manipulation of stock prices, warning readers to avoid investment products with which the plaintiff was associated and calling for an investigation into the plaintiff's conduct by US securities regulators. It also questioned Mr Gutnick's connection with a convicted money-launderer and tax evader called Nachum Goldberg and suggested that Mr Goldberg assisted Mr Gutnick in a tax evasion scheme by laundering money through religious charities.

[40] [2002] HCA 56; 210 CLR 575.

Mr Gutnick raised a statement of claim in the Supreme Court of Victoria. In this he claimed he had been defamed within the State of Victoria both in print and online. Unlike *Berezovsky*, it seems a very small (though unspecified) number of physical copies of the magazine were distributed in Victoria.[41] Instead Mr Gutnick's claim focused upon the *Barron's Online* site. He produced evidence that there were 550,000 subscribers to the *Barron's Online* website worldwide at the relevant time: when questioned the defendant conceded that of that number 1,700 subscribers had paid by credit card from Australia, including several hundred subscribers in Victoria.

As with the *Berezovsky* case the defendant applied to have the proceedings stayed on the basis of the doctrine of *forum non conveniens*. The defendant claimed that the article was published in the US, specifically New Jersey, and that that was the correct forum for this claim. In particular Howard Gold, the editor of *Barron's Online*, in an affidavit to the court stated that: 'stories which were written and edited in New York are transmitted by a dedicated computer to [our] corporate campus in New Jersey. There the data is transferred from Barron's' two computers in New Jersey on to six further servers which hold the stories or articles. All six servers are physically located in New Jersey.'[42] At trial Hedigan J dismissed the defendant's claims citing with approval Lord Steyn's judgment in *Berezovsky*. Dow Jones sought leave to appeal to the Victoria Court of Appeal, but this was refused. Almost three months later, Gleeson CJ and Hayne J granted special leave to appeal to the High Court of Australia.

The key issues in dispute in *Dow Jones* are exactly the same as in *Berezovsky*, but with the focus being on digital publishing rather than print publication. First, the court had to decide whether the article had been 'published' in Australia generally and Victoria in particular. The court examined both sides of the argument: the single publication argument put forward by Dow Jones which claimed that publication was a single event which took place in New Jersey and the multiple publication argument put forward by Mr Gutnick which argued that publication occurred wherever the consumer read the material and concluded that: '[b]ecause publication is an act or event to which there are at least two parties, the publisher and a person to whom material is published, publication to numerous persons may have as many territorial connections as there are those to whom particular words are published'.[43] Having established the multiple publication rule should apply equally to online publications as to other types of publications they then turned their attention to the question of when an article was published in a given territory if it is made available via a web server in another jurisdiction.

Highlight Gutnick before the High Court of Australia

Defamation is to be located at the place where the damage to reputation occurs. Ordinarily that will be where the material which is alleged to be defamatory is available in comprehensible form assuming, of course, that the person defamed has in that place a reputation which is thereby damaged. It is only when the material is in comprehensible form that the damage to reputation is done and it is damage to reputation which is the principal focus of defamation, not any quality of the defendant's conduct.

→

[41] *Gutnick v Dow Jones & Co. Inc.* [2001] VSC 305.

[42] Ibid. 309.

[43] *Dow Jones & Co. Inc. v Gutnick* [2002] HCA 56, 63.

→

In the case of material on the World Wide Web, it is not available in comprehensible form until downloaded on to the computer of a person who has used a web browser to pull the material from the web server. It is where that person downloads the material that the damage to reputation may be done. Ordinarily then, that will be the place where the tort of defamation is committed.

The above is the key passage from the decision. It was the key passage both on a micro and a macro level. On the micro level it established that in this case the Supreme Court of Victoria was right to find jurisdiction, a finding that led eventually to Dow Jones settling the case for A$180,000 in damages and A$400,000 costs.[44] The effects on the macro level were much greater. The High Court of Australia had said explicitly what everyone had suspected following the *Berezovsky* decision: digital content hosted on a web server would be deemed to be 'published' at the point of access not at the point of storage. Thus a web server hosted in the US could publish material in any country which allowed access to that server. In other words an online publication could lead to litigation for defamation in potentially any jurisdiction worldwide.

Some commentators suggested the potential chilling effects of *Dow Jones* on internet speech would be calamitous. The *New York Times* famously editorialized: 'To subject distant providers of on-line content to sanctions intent on curbing free speech—or even to 190 libel laws—is to undermine the internet's viability.'[45] Others though were more measured, pointing out that all the High Court of Australia had done was apply a well-established principle of libel laws that had been seen in a series of previous cases culminating in the *Berezovsky* case.[46] As these commentators pointed out, international communications and media had not proven to be hamstrung by the multiple publication rule in the past and there was no reason to suggest that things would be any different with online publications. Although the scale of international publication was undoubtedly magnified by online publishing, publishers had little to fear of being dragged before a succession of courts across the globe. As Professor Jonathan Zittrain pointed out there still needs to be a reason for the court to take jurisdiction:

> The Australian court was unpersuaded by the 'pile on' argument that Gutnick could next sue the company in Zimbabwe, or Great Britain, or China. It pointed out that Gutnick himself lived in Australia, and Dow Jones quite explicitly sold subscriptions to the online Barron's to Australians. These facts helped Australia escape the dilemma of justifying almost any country's intervention if it was to justify its own. Without its special if not unique relationship to one party in the case, Australia may well have declined to intervene in the dispute.[47]

[44] ABC News, *Dow Jones settles Gutnick action*, 12 November 2004.

[45] Editorial, 'A Blow to Online Freedom' *New York Times* (New York, 11 December 2002) <http://query.nytimes.com/gst/fullpage.html?res=9D05E7DE143AF932A25751C1A9649C8B63>.

[46] D Rolph, 'The Message, Not the Medium: Defamation, Publication and the Internet in *Dow Jones & Co Inc v Gutnick*' (2002) 24 *Sydney Law Review* 263; M Richardson and R Garnett, 'Perils of Publishing on the Internet: Broader Implications of *Dow Jones v Gutnick*' (2004) 31 *Griffith Law Review* 4.

[47] J Zittrain, 'Be Careful What You Ask For: Reconciling a Global Internet and Local Law' in Adam Thierer (ed.) *Who Rules the Net?: Internet Governance and Jurisdiction* (Cato Institute 2003).

There is therefore little risk of a greater chilling effect with online speech as with any other form of speech. In fact it can be argued that as we saw in ch. 6, with the ease of access and widespread audience offered through digital publication, online publishing finds itself protected from the chilling effects of defamation law to a greater extent than other forms of publishing. Additionally, as we saw in ch. 6 in our discussion of the *LICRA et UEJF v Yahoo! Inc. and Yahoo! France*,[48] an order of an extraterritorial court can only be enforced against the author of a statement found to be defamatory if either (a) the author is resident in or has assets domiciled within the jurisdiction in question, or (b) the local courts where the author is resident recognize the order of the foreign jurisdiction, something which a US court is unlikely to do when faced with libel orders from overseas.[49]

8.2.2 *Loutchansky v Times Newspapers*: republication and limitation

The fall-out from the *Gutnick* decision was predictable. Those states perceived to be plaintiff-friendly in defamation actions found cases were quickly raised following online publication of allegedly defamatory material. At the forefront of this were the courts of England and Wales.

The first of a series of cases which have helped establish the level of connection required for the English courts to take jurisdiction over an international defamation action was *Loutchansky v Times Newspapers Ltd*.[50] The *Loutchansky* case is very similar to the *Berezovsky* case. Dr Loutchansky, a Russian national, claimed that two news stories published in *The Times* newspaper on 8 September 1999 and 14 October 1999 were defamatory. The stories claimed that Dr Loutchansky was the boss of a major Russian criminal organization and that he was involved in, among other things, money-laundering. The defendants accepted that the articles were defamatory of Dr Loutchansky, but argued qualified privilege, and also argued that Dr Loutchansky's action was time barred.

This claim was based on s. 4A of the Limitation Act 1980 which states that in actions of libel or slander 'no such action shall be brought after the expiration of one year from the date on which the cause of action accrued'. Dr Loutchansky had failed to raise the case in time, but he argued that, in relation to material *The Times* placed on its web servers, each time that the material was accessed by a reader was a fresh publication of the stories, thus allowing him to comply with the Limitation Act. This is another application of the debate between a single publication rule and the multiple publication rule already discussed extensively in *Berezovsky* and *Gutnick*: in this case it is not the place of publication which is in issue it is the time of the publication.

As we have already seen, common law courts tend to apply the multiple publication rule when approaching this issue. In this case counsel for the newspaper argued that this approach had been rendered incompatible with the Limitation Act through the application of internet technology. Lord Lester of Herne Hill QC, acting for the respondents, argued that the Court of Appeal should adopt a single publication rule on the basis that the emergence of the internet and the extensive period for which material was archived

[48] Tribunal de Grande Instance de Paris (Superior Court of Paris) 2000.

[49] See *Telnikoff v Matusevitch* 702 A 2d 230 (Md 1997); *Bachchan v India Abroad Publications Inc.*, 585 NYS 2d 661 (NY 1992).

[50] [2002] 2 WLR 640; [2002] QB 783.

and accessible through online services meant that should the multiple publication rule be endorsed there would be ongoing liability of an open-ended nature for material placed online. This he argued was incompatible with the intent of the Limitation Act which was to provide for a limited period following publication for an action to be brought.[51] Lord Lester went on to claim that the existence of internet-based libraries of newspaper stories provided an important public service and it was the law that was out of step with this service. If the law did not change he warned that: 'if a newspaper defendant which maintained a website of back numbers was to be indefinitely vulnerable to claims in defamation for years and even decades after the initial hard copy and internet publication, such a rule was bound to have an effect on the preparedness of the media to maintain such websites, and thus to limit freedom of expression'.[52]

The court considered all Lord Lester's arguments, but ultimately dismissed them. They did not accept that the effect of the multiple publication rule in the information society was to undermine the intent of the Limitation Act. In the opinion of the court, given by Lord Phillips MR, it was pointed out that an action based on internet publication was subsidiary to the action based on print publication. In other words each publication was a separate action with separate twelve-month limitation periods, and essentially with separate quanta of damages attached thereto: as Lord Phillips says, 'the scale of such publication and any resulting damage is likely to be modest compared with that of the original publication'.[53] On this basis the court dismissed the claim that the multiple publication rule interfered with the working and intent of the Limitation Act.

This only left the claim that the multiple publication rule was out of step with the new order of internet publication and record keeping. The court quickly rejected this claim as well. Lord Phillips stated that although the court accepted 'that the maintenance of archives, whether in hard copy or on the Internet, has a social utility . . . [we] consider that the maintenance of archives is a comparatively insignificant aspect of freedom of expression. Archive material is stale news and its publication cannot rank in importance with the dissemination of contemporary material. Nor do we believe that the law of defamation need inhibit the responsible maintenance of archives. Where it is known that archive material is or may be defamatory, the attachment of an appropriate notice warning against treating it as the truth will normally remove any sting from the material.'[54] In other words, once the publisher of the material becomes aware of the fact that it may be defamatory, they may take simple steps to limit their exposure by simply adding an addendum to the archive material informing readers of this. This would work in much the same way as a retraction in print.

Of course the passing of the Defamation Act has seen *Loutchansky* at least partially overruled. The new provisions contained in s. 8 have introduced a single publication rule for the purposes of s. 4A of the Limitation Act. The rule though 'does not apply in relation to the subsequent publication if the manner of that publication is materially different from the manner of the first publication'.[55] The Act gives some definition to this in s. 8(5) noting that 'in determining whether the manner of a subsequent

[51] [2002] QB 783, 814.
[52] Ibid. 817.
[53] Ibid. 818.
[54] Ibid. 817–18.
[55] s. 8(4).

publication is materially different from the manner of the first publication, the matters to which the court may have regard include (amongst other matters): (a) the level of prominence that a statement is given; and (b) the extent of the subsequent publication'. This suggests that any attempt to use s. 8 unreasonably to avoid a defamation claim by first publishing the information in a hidden section of a website or blog before moving it to greater prominence once the limitation period has expired will fail. In relation to the *Loutchansky* case as the material was not moved or altered, just continually downloaded s. 8 would likely have been effective to bar Dr Loutchanky's claim. This is the key mischief s. 8 seeks to remedy. As every access is a republication, s. 4A of the Limitation Act is in effect rendered pointless, absent the point made by Lord Phillips on quantum of damages. Section 8 ensures the effectiveness of s. 4A is reinvigorated.

8.2.3 *King v Lewis*

The next case to develop this principle was the case of *King v Lewis*.[56] This involved an action brought by Mr Don King, a famous boxing promoter and US resident, against three defendants: Mr Lennox Lewis, a UK citizen, but at the time a US resident, Mr Judd Burstein, a New York-based lawyer and US citizen, and Lion Promotions LLC, a Nevada-based promotion company. Mr Lewis and Lion Promotions were suing Mr King and a co-defendant, Mike Tyson, in New York claiming interference with an agreement between Mr Lewis and Mr Tyson in connection with a proposed rematch of their world heavyweight title contest, claiming $35 million in compensatory damages and $350 million in punitive damages. The New York litigation received a great deal of publicity, at least in part due to Mr Burstein putting the complaint on the boxing website boxingtalk.com. The proceedings in London followed the publication of two online articles surrounding the New York litigation. The first appeared on the site fightnews.com on 5 July 2003, was written by Mr Burstein and was entitled 'My Response to Don King.' In this Mr Burstein claimed that Mr King had made anti-Semitic remarks about him and accused him of bigotry.[57] The second appeared on boxingtalk.com on 8 July 2003 and was an interview with Mr Burstein carried out by a Mr Leon. It repeated all the claims made by Mr Burstein in the earlier article.[58] Although it may seem that the Courts of New York were the most appropriate forum for a dispute between three US-based individuals and a US-based corporation involving claims made on US-based websites, Mr King chose to raise his action in England. This is a not uncommon action for individuals with reputations to protect, as we have seen in the *Berezovsky* case, and may be explained in the instant case because to raise an action in the US he would need to overcome the standard in *New York Times v Sullivan*.[59] This states that where a public figure attempts to bring an action for defamation, they must prove that the statement was made with 'actual malice'. This means that the person making the statement must know the statement to be false, or must have issued the statement with reckless disregard as to its truth. In England Mr King did not have to meet the *Sullivan* standard but he did need to show *lex loci delicti*.

[56] [2004] EWCA Civ 1329.
[57] Ibid. [8].
[58] Ibid. [9].
[59] 376 US 254 (1964).

In dismissing an appeal from Mr Justice Eady's decision to allow Mr King to serve the claim form out of the jurisdiction, the Court of Appeal examined Mr King's claim to have the case heard in England and Wales. The court seemed to be convinced that Mr King had a reputation to protect in England,[60] and appeared to be particularly swayed by the fact that Mr King 'would wish to adduce evidence from a number of witnesses based in the UK, on such matters as his reputation and connection with this country and, in particular, his links with Jewish charity work in London'.[61] What is less satisfactory is that the court never sought, or was given, any actual evidence of publication occurring in England and Wales. Instead they were content to state that: 'The libels alleged consist in two texts stored on websites based in California. In the ordinary way they can be, and have been, downloaded here. It is common ground that by the law of England the tort of libel is committed where publication takes place, and each publication generates a separate cause of action. The parties also accept that a text on the Internet is published at the place where it is downloaded. Accordingly there is no contest but that subject to any defences on the merits the respondent has been libelled in this jurisdiction.'[62] The court never investigated the degree of publication in England and Wales. Were the stories downloaded on one occasion or one hundred? We may never know for this dispute was merely about the procedural issue of whether the courts of England and Wales could issue a claim against the defendants. The court was not interested in discussing the merits of the case at this time; this would be a matter for later trial.[63] It is unfortunate though that the court did not consider this issue since on the wording of the decision of the Court of Appeal in *King* a single download within the jurisdiction of England and Wales would be sufficient to enable a libel action to be raised within this jurisdiction if the plaintiff had a reputation to protect in the jurisdiction. This seems close to the tenuous connection or 'pile on' argument which some had predicted would lead to a massive rise in libel tourism and multijurisdictional claims and which had been rejected by Jonathan Zittrain.[64] The next case was to have a significant impact on this.

8.2.4 *Jameel v Dow Jones*

King v Lewis may be seen as the archetypal case of forum shopping and the reason why we need s. 9 of the Defamation Act. Earlier I argued that s. 9 in fact makes little difference to the day-to-day operation of the courts in online defamation cases. This is because of the decision of the Court of Appeal in *Jameel v Dow Jones Inc*.[65] This is another in the long line of cases starting with *Berezovsky* and including *Gutnick* in which an international businessman has challenged stories in US-based business-oriented publications which accuse him of links to organized crime. In this case a Saudi businessman Yousef Jameel and his brother Mohammed Jameel were accused in an article in the *Wall Street Journal* of providing financial support for al Qaeda. The story arose

[60] [2004] EWCA Civ 1329 [13].
[61] Ibid. [38].
[62] Ibid. [2].
[63] There appears to have been no later trial on the merits of the claim. It may be suspected this was a negotiating lever designed to reach a settlement of the dispute in New York.
[64] See (n. 47).
[65] [2005] EWCA Civ 75.

when the US obtained secret al Qaeda documents relating to the formation of the al Qaeda movement in 1988. Among these documents was one called 'the Golden Chain' which purported to list 20 Saudi financial backers of Osama Bin Laden: on this list was Mr Jameel.[66] The *Wall Street Journal* published a news story based upon this discovery entitled 'War on Terror' by Glenn Simpson on 18 March 2003 and placed it on the wsj.com website. Via the website one could link to the list of names on the Golden Chain.

On 15 April 2003 Mr Jameel's solicitors wrote to Dow Jones asking them to remove the Golden Chain document from their website and warning their client would take action to 'protect his reputation in England'.[67] When Dow Jones refused to do so a claim was raised in the High Court. Mr Justice Eady found in favour of the plaintiff but Dow Jones immediately appealed to the Court of Appeal and it was in the judgment of the court, handed down by Lord Phillips MR, that we see a new approach to internet defamation cases in England and Wales develop.

The question which was to become the focus of much of the court's time was whether Mr Jameel had suffered any actual harm in England and Wales. While Mr Jameel managed to force an admission from Dow Jones that there were approximately six thousand subscribers to wsj.com in England and Wales,[68] Dow Jones countered that only five subscribers had actually followed the hyperlink from the story to read the Golden Chain document, and that of these five one was Mr Jameel's solicitor, one was a consultant to the claimant's businesses, and another was a director of a business associated with Mr Jameel. In the words of Lord Phillips, '[t]hey are members of the claimant's camp'.[69] With only two subscribers having apparently read the defamatory document who were not connected to the litigation the questions for the court were whether a substantial tort had taken place and/or whether an abuse of process would occur should the claim be allowed to proceed. On the former issue Lord Philips concluded that '[i]f the claimant succeeds in this action and is awarded a small amount of damages, it can perhaps be said that he will have achieved vindication for the damage done to his reputation in this country, but both the damage and the vindication will be minimal. The cost of the exercise will have been out of all proportion to what has been achieved. The game will not merely not have been worth the candle, it will not have been worth the wick.'[70] On the latter he concluded:[71]

Highlight Defamation and abuse of process

It would be an abuse of process to continue to commit the resources of the English court, including substantial judge and possibly jury time, to an action where so little is now seen to be at stake. Normally where a small claim is brought, it will be dealt with by a proportionate small claims procedure. Such a course is not available in an action for defamation where, although the claim is small, the issues are complex and subject to special procedure under the Civil Procedure Rules.

[66] [2005] EWCA Civ 75 [8].
[67] Ibid. [14].
[68] Ibid. [16].
[69] Ibid. [17].
[70] Ibid. [69].
[71] Ibid. [70].

It can now clearly be seen that s. 9 and *Jameel* follow similar reasoning, although arguably s. 9 goes further than *Jameel* in that it allows the court to dismiss applications where there may be a sufficient connection with the jurisdiction of England and Wales, i.e. the *Jameel* standard, but where there is an identifiable jurisdiction in which it would be 'more appropriate' to bring the action. It is only these few cases though where the court may be convinced that the English courts are inappropriate, though sufficiently connected with the case that s. 9 will be of impact.

8.2.5 **Online defamation post *Jameel***

In several cases subsequent to the *Jameel* decision, but before the passing of s. 8, the courts have had recourse to the *de minimis* provision set out therein and on both occasions they have upheld and applied the *Jameel* principle.

The first of these cases was *Al Amoudi v Brisard & Anor*.[72] This case involved an Ethiopian-born businessman, Mohammed Hussein Al Amoudi, who was normally resident in Saudi Arabia but who spent about two and a half months a year living in England, and Jean Charles Brisard a French national resident in Switzerland, an author and international expert and investigator on terrorism financing. It was alleged by Mr Al Amoudi that he was defamed by M. Brisard in two entries he made on his website in which he claimed Mr Al Amoudi was '(i) a knowing participant in the economic, financial and/or terrorist networks of the terrorist Osama Bin Laden and/or is likely to have knowingly facilitated ties with the said network; and/or (ii) that, being himself a part of the vast financing system that is the trade mark of Osama Bin Laden's terrorist operations, he has knowingly financed and/or facilitated the financing of Osama Bin Laden's terrorism'.[73] M. Brisard argued that 'in the relevant period the reports containing the words complained of were not downloaded within this jurisdiction' or in the alternative 'if and in so far as the claimant can prove that the reports were downloaded within this jurisdiction within the relevant period, they were downloaded by lawyers acting for the claimant or for others named in the reports or by persons or friends or business associates of the claimant'.[74] In either case M. Brisard argued the claim was an abuse of process applying the *Jameel* principle. The claim was heard by Gray J who concluded that it is for the claimant to prove that the material in question was accessed and downloaded within the jurisdiction of the courts of England and Wales.[75] As the plaintiff had been unable to demonstrate this he refused the plaintiff's application for summary judgment and remanded the case to be heard at a full hearing where the evidence could be fully tested.[76]

Subsequently it was applied in *Brady v Norman*.[77] This case is rather different from the previous cases as there is no international element to this case. Both plaintiff and defendant are UK-based, with the plaintiff, Mr Brady, being the former general secretary

[72] [2006] EWHC 1062 (QB); [2007] 1 WLR 113.
[73] [2007] 1 WLR 113, 115.
[74] Ibid. 116.
[75] 'I am unable to accept that under English law a claimant in a libel action on an Internet publication is entitled to rely on a presumption of law that there has been substantial publication'. Ibid. 123.
[76] It appears the case never went to trial.
[77] [2008] EWHC 2481 (QB).

of the rail union ASLEF, and the defendant Mr Norman, the current general secretary. Mr Brady's claim arose out of an article published in the July 2006 edition of *Loco Journal*, the monthly magazine of ASLEF. In the article entitled 'The Brady Era is Over' it was stated that 'the Certification Officer had ruled the previous week that Mr Brady had legitimately been excluded from ASLEF membership for bringing the union into disrepute'.[78] The offending issue of the magazine, as well as being distributed to ASLEF members was placed on the ASLEF website. Mr Brady conceded that ASLEF members, as well as ex-members, officers and their widows, and the union's professional advisers had a legitimate interest in receiving information about what took place at the union conference,[79] but argued that by placing the *Loco Journal* report on the ASLEF website the union and its officers had made it available to non-privileged individuals who had no interest in the union's activities. Mr Brady's legal team estimated this may have led to 202 further publications which were the publications in dispute.[80] Deputy Judge Richard Parkes QC rejected Mr Brady's claims. He ruled that the court could not infer that just because the material was available to be read online it would be read by members of the public who had no direct interest in the operations of the union. Like Mr Al Amoudi, Mr Brady was asking the court to assume online publication had occurred. The distinction between the *Brady* case and the *Al Amoudi* case was that Mr Brady could establish the article had been accessed online, in this case on 202 occasions, what he could not establish though was that those accessing the online publication were not covered by the same legitimate interest as those receiving the original published version of the magazine. As Richard Parkes QC concludes: 'Without some evidence to justify the inference (for instance, evidence that the ASLEF site and the information contained in it provide an attractive resource for transport enthusiasts generally, rather than simply for members and staff) it seems to me to be no more than pure speculation to infer that an "outsider" would have read the words complained of. An inference is a conclusion reached on the basis of evidence and reasoning: it is not a matter of guesswork. It would not have been right to ask the jury to take a guess. I therefore held that there was no sufficient evidence of website publication to individuals in non-privileged circumstances to leave to the jury.'[81]

More recently it has been applied in the related cases of *Kaschke v Osler*[82] and *Kaschke v Gray and Hilton*.[83] Both cases involved comments left on political blog sites. In Osler, the site in question was a blogging site operated by the defendant, http://www.davidosler.com; while in the *Gray and Hilton* case it was two blogs, John's Labour Blog (operated by Gray) and Labour Home (operated by Hilton). Each claim involved a similar set of facts. In Osler it was alleged that Mr Osler had made an entry into his blog suggesting links between Ms Kaschke, a German citizen now living in London, and the Baader-Meinhof gang. The article also attracted a number of comments which were also claimed to be defamatory. *Gray and Hilton* related to similar facts. Mr Gray also made an entry on his blog recounting Mr Osler's story and adding his own views, again clearly insinuating Ms Kaschke was linked to the Baader-Meinhof gang. Mr Gray posted a copy of his blog

[78] Ibid. [5].
[79] Ibid. [10].
[80] Ibid.
[81] Ibid. [26].
[82] [2010] EWHC 1075 (QB).
[83] [2010] EWHC 1907 (QB).

entry into Mr Hilton's blog. Ms Kaschke raised actions against all three claiming defamation. In *Osler*, Eady J examined Ms Kaschke's claims and dismissed her claim applying *Jameel*: 'It is necessary to try and assess what a jury would make of the alleged injury to Ms Kaschke's reputation. If the jury came to the conclusion that none of the defences raised could succeed, I cannot imagine that the damages would be other than very modest. I would take the view that any such award would be out of all proportion to the time and money spent on this litigation and, in particular, to the cost of a two-week jury trial.'[84] In the subsequent case of *Gray and Hilton*, Stadlen J followed Eady J's line of inquiry and came to the same conclusion: 'the reason for that is that there is in my judgment sufficient other material emanating from Ms Kaschke to which my attention has been drawn to lead to the conclusion that there is no realistic prospect of an award of more than very modest damages in this action and that for similar reasons to those identified by Eady J it would be an abuse of process for this action to proceed to trial'.[85]

8.2.6 *Sloutsker v Romanova*

As we await the first cases to be decided under the Defamation Act 2013 we get one final major decision made under the old legal settlement.[86] The factual framework of *Sloutsker v Romanova* will be familiar to anyone who has read *Berezovsky, Loutchansky,* or *Jameel*. Mr Sloutsker is a Russian citizen and businessman. He was from 2002 to 2010 a Senator of the Russian Senate. In 2011 he emigrated to Israel where he still lives. Ms Romanova is a journalist who writes for the *Novaya Gazeta* newspaper and other outlets. Her husband was an ex-employee of one of Mr Sloutsker's companies. He was prosecuted and imprisoned in Russia for stealing assets from Mr Sloutsker's company. During 2011 and 2012 it was alleged that Ms Romanova wrote a number of libellous stories about Mr Sloutsker. Four publications were complained of in the claim: '(1) A blog post written by the defendant on the website of the Moscow-based radio station Echo Moscow; (2) & (3) two articles quoting the defendant published on the Russian website gazeta.ru; and (4) a programme broadcast on Radio Liberty.'[87] These variously contained a number of defamatory claims including 'that the Claimant had put a contract out for the murder of Alexei Kozlov, which was to be carried out whilst Mr Kozlov was being transferred to prison' (in the blogpost) and 'that the Claimant had ordered the fabrication of evidence in the criminal prosecution of Alexei Kozlov and had put a contract out for the murder of Mr Kozlov, which was to be carried out whilst Mr Kozlov was being transferred to prison' (the second article).[88] Mr Sloutsker raised a claim in the High Court of England and Wales in January 2013 but given the slow process of serving documents in Russia it was July 2014 before the documents reached Ms Romanova. In September 2014 the defendant applied to set aside service. She submitted that the court should decline jurisdiction and/or that she had not been validly served.[89] In January 2015 she dismissed her

[84] [2010] EWHC 1075 (QB) at [25].

[85] [2010] EWHC 1907 (QB) at [21].

[86] Although the Defamation Act 2013 came into effect on 1 January 2014 given the time delay in complex defamation actions most cases currently still being heard commenced before that date and are governed by the previous law. See e.g. *Bewry v Reed Elsevier (UK) Ltd* [2014] EWCA Civ 1411 as well as *Sloutsker v Romanova*.

[87] *Sloutsker v Romanova* [2015] EWHC 2053 (QB) [7].

[88] Ibid. [9].

[89] Ibid. [10].

solicitors and began to act for herself. The judge, Warby J, notes that thereafter 'between 13 January and 19 June 2015 there had been no response at all from the defendant, who had not engaged with the proceedings in any way'.[90] Following these extensive delays Warby J found that service of proceedings had been validly made for both the Civil Procedure Rules and under Russian Law.[91]

The key question for this textbook is the jurisdictional question. Could Mr Sloutsker, an Israeli-resident Russian citizen find sufficient connection to the jurisdiction of England and Wales to successfully raise a defamation claim against a Russian-resident Russian citizen? The analysis of this is spread across two judgments, the March 2015 judgment[92] and the July 2015 judgment.[93] In the March judgment Warby J reviewed the legal position. He recognized that the law was subject to change once s. 9 of the Defamation Act came into effect but that this did not apply to the case before him.[94] Instead he applied the common law test from *Berezovsky* and *Jameel*, that there must be a 'real and substantial tort' within the jurisdiction of the court.[95] He gave considerable weight to Lord Woolf MR's words in *King v Lewis* 'The more tenuous a claimant's connection with this jurisdiction and the more substantial any publication abroad, the weaker the presumption in favour of England and Wales being the natural forum for the claim . . . the same principles apply to internet publication as apply to hard copy publication, except that the court's discretion in an internet context "will tend to be more open-textured than otherwise". It is clear from the context in which Lord Woolf made that remark that he intended it to be taken as an indication that the court should not be shy of allowing foreigners who publish via the internet to be sued in this jurisdiction, given that such publishers will have chosen to disseminate their information via a global medium.'[96] He also noted that 'in *King* the Court of Appeal rejected "out of hand" a submission that the court should take into account whether or not the defendant had "targeted" this jurisdiction, concluding that this was too subjective and nebulous a criterion, liable to manipulation and "much more likely to diminish than enhance the interests of justice".'[97] On this basis Warby J found that significant publication had taken place in the UK: 'Even on the defendant's figures, however, and allowing for the qualifications she puts forward, the sting of the allegations made on each of the Blogpost, the Second Article and the Third Article could easily have reached as many as 60,000 readers in this jurisdiction.'[98] This, along with the fact that the claimant is 'very well known' among the Russian and Jewish communities in the UK and has business interests in the UK[99] was enough to convince Warby J that the High Court could take jurisdiction over the case.[100]

In the July 2015 judgment Warby J revisits and develops much of this. He records that the claimant has provided 'further evidence of his links with this jurisdiction, referring

[90] Ibid. [11].
[91] Ibid. [12].
[92] [2015] EWHC 545 (QB).
[93] [2015] EWHC 2053 (QB).
[94] [2015] EWHC 545 (QB) [39].
[95] Ibid. [41].
[96] Ibid. [42]–[43].
[97] Ibid. [44].
[98] Ibid. [69].
[99] Ibid. [59].
[100] Ibid. [79].

to several visits to London over the past few months. I established that these were not all in connection with this case, but included business visits relating to real estate investment. He also explained his intention to relocate to London with his family over the next 2 years. Family means his 16-year-old son and 11-year-old daughter and his parents, both in their 80s but in good health. These are matters of obvious relevance to the extent of any need for vindication.'[101] Finding in favour of the claimant Warby J concludes: 'These were serious libels. The allegation of conspiracy to murder is the most serious, but the addition of imputations of corruption makes the matter worse. The allegations were published to a relatively substantial audience in this jurisdiction, where the claimant has a substantial and valuable reputation. My assessment of him as a witness is that he is a robust character, and that whilst his evidence of distress is genuine he has not suffered lasting emotional injury. He is however entitled to a sum that will vindicate him in the eyes of interested third parties who are unlikely to read this judgment. Adopting the approach I have indicated above, and taking account of all the factual matters I have identified, I have reached the conclusion that the appropriate global award of damages to compensate for the injury to reputation, and to feelings, and to ensure adequate vindication in respect of these serious allegations is £110,000.'[102]

There is much about this judgment that is surprising. It is surprising that Warby J placed more emphasis on the judgements in *King* and *Berezovsky* than he did on *Jameel* given that most cases post-*Jameel* have followed that more closely than certainly *Berezovsky*. It is also surprising that having acknowledged in his judgment s. 9 of the Defamation Act he applied more closely the apparently outdated jurisprudence of *Berezovsky* and *King* rather than the fresher approach found in *Jameel*. Admittedly s. 9 was of no relevance to the case with the claim having begun before it came into effect. However, it is suggested *Jameel* could have been applied more robustly. While admittedly the finding that 'the Blogpost, the Second Article and the Third Article could easily have reached as many as 60,000 readers in this jurisdiction' lifts it far from *Jameel* territory and more towards *King* in terms of volume we should bear in mind Gray J's words from *Al Amoudi*, 'I am unable to accept that under English law a claimant in a libel action on an Internet publication is entitled to rely on a presumption of law that there has been substantial publication.'[103] In *Sloutsker* Warby J seemed to make such an assumption. All the figures which lead him to conclude 'the Blogpost, the Second Article and the Third Article could easily have reached as many as 60,000 readers in this jurisdiction' are extrapolated from general visitor numbers. For example, on the republication of the blogpost: 'Mr Dawkins estimates that newsru.com has 29,494 visitors per day from the UK. He arrives at this by using figures from Statshow.com for the total readership and Alexa.com for the percentage visiting from the UK. Using the same technique he arrives at not less than 24 per day for og.ru, and 49,148 per day for nR2.ru, from the UK. The website kommersant.ru provided the claimant's solicitors with monthly data for page views and estimates for unique page views of the site from the UK in April and May 2012. The page views in May 2012 were 238,000. The unique page views per month from the UK are estimated to be between 21,441 and 59,500 (the estimate is that 20–25 per cent of page views are unique page views). The defendant has no data to offer for og.ru or nR2.ru.

[101] [2015] EWHC 2053 (QB) [90].
[102] Ibid. [92].
[103] See (n. 75).

For the other two sites, the defendant's solicitors' estimates, using data obtained in June 2014 from alexa.com and trafficestimate.com, are of 63,371 monthly visits from the UK to newsru.com and 38,075 to kommersant.ru. The former is much lower than Mr Dawkins' figure, but the latter is within the bracket he provides.'[104] This signals a return to the jurisprudence of *Berezovsky* and *King*: it equates availability with consumption and assumes that harm follows. Beyond this there are issues surrounding the level of damages awarded. To award £110,000 on that basis that 'He [the claimant] is however entitled to a sum that will vindicate him in the eyes of interested third parties who are unlikely to read this judgment' is barely credible. Damages may only be awarded as compensation for harm, unless punitive or exemplary damages are awarded, which was not the case here.[105] To suggest compensatory damages be set at a level to send a message to those 'unlikely to read this judgment' is baffling. As the claim was essentially unchallenged, the defendant having effectively broken off all communication with the court, we are not likely to see an appeal. The matter will no doubt now pass to Russia where the claimant will seek to enforce his claim, or more likely having vindicated his reputation by winning in the High Court the claimant will take no further action.

It seems likely that *Sloutsker* will be little more than a footnote in the history of defamation actions. Anyone who has begun an action since 1 January 2014 has to meet the more stringent test of s. 9 of the Defamation Act. This is not to say that *Sloutsker* could not have met this standard had it been applied, it is simply to record that *Sloutsker* is unlikely to reset the steady jurisprudence the High Court and Court of Appeal have developed post-*Jameel*.

8.3 **Intermediary liability**

Finding a court willing to take jurisdiction over your claim is only the first stage in establishing a successful libel claim. Next you have to correctly identify the author, publisher, or distributor of the defamatory statement and have them brought before the court. In traditional publishing this is usually quite simple. The author often attaches his or her name to the article, byline, or book in question. The publisher is always identifiable by the addition of publishers' details in nearly all commercially produced material and the distributor will usually include the person who sold you the material in the first place. As with almost everything in the information society the addition of the digital elements of distribution confuses the usual principle. When the author of a defamatory statement signs him- or herself as noxious2256, and when the site itself is published by an offshore anonymous corporation apparently domiciled in Panama or Russia it can prove difficult, if not impossible, to identify those primarily liable for the defamatory statement.[106] If you have been defamed online it seems all too often that the only party which can be identified as being liable is the ISP or local host who has carried the defamatory statement, or who has allowed access to it. Thus it is not surprising that an extensive body of litigation has grown up around the liability of ISPs and local hosts for hosting and carrying defamatory content.

[104] [2015] EWHC 545 (QB) [63].

[105] [2015] EWHC 2053 (QB) [74].

[106] One way around this is the so-called Blaney Blarney order. See D Cran and G Warren, 'Service by Twitter—The UK Courts Embrace Technology' (2010) 21 *Entertainment Law Review* 81.

8.3.1 *Godfrey v Demon Internet*

The first examination of ISP liability in the UK is to be found in the case of *Godfrey v Demon Internet Service.*[107]

Case study *Godfrey v Demon Internet Service*

Dr Laurence Godfrey was a lecturer in physics, mathematics, and computer science based in London. On 13 January 1997, a posting, apparently originating in the US, was made to an internet newsgroup *soc.culture.thai* which, although we are not told the exact nature of it, is referred to by Moreland J as 'squalid, obscene and defamatory of the Plaintiff'.

Demon Internet carried the *soc.culture.thai* forum and stored postings for about a fortnight during which time the posting was available to be read by its customers.

On 17 January 1997, Dr Godfrey sent a fax to Demon Internet informing them that the posting was a forgery and that he was not responsible for its posting and requesting them to remove the posting from their Usenet news server as it was defamatory of him.

The defamatory posting was not removed as requested but remained available on the Demon Usenet server until its expiry on 27 January 1997. As a result of this Dr Godfrey raised a defamation action against Demon Internet.

There were two primary questions in issue. The first was, in applying the multiple publication rule were Demon Internet the publishers of the statement on each of the occasions a Demon customer accessed it via the Demon Server? The second was, could Demon avail itself of the defences contained in s. 1 of the Defamation Act 1996? On the first issue Moreland J was clear: 'In my judgment the Defendants were clearly not the publisher of the posting defamatory of the Plaintiff within the meaning of Section 1(2) and 1(3) and incontrovertibly can avail themselves of Section 1(1)(a).'[108] He was, unfortunately for Demon Internet, equally as unequivocal on the second question: 'However the difficulty facing the Defendants is Section 1(1)(b) and 1(1)(c). After the 17th January 1997 after receipt of the Plaintiff's fax the Defendants knew of the defamatory posting but chose not to remove it from their Usenet news servers. In my judgment this places the Defendants in an insuperable difficulty so that they cannot avail themselves of the defence provided by Section 1.'[109]

In effect the decision of *Godfrey* is to treat information society service providers as akin to distributors, or republishers, that is, they are immune from suit, under s. 1 of the Defamation Act 1996, until such time as they are made aware of the nature of the defamatory material. At this point then under s. 1(1)(c), their immunity is stripped and by s. 1(1)(b) they are required to 'take reasonable care in relation to its publication': in practice they must decide whether the statement is likely to be defamatory and if they believe it may be they must take steps to prevent further distribution or republication of the statement or face liability. This provides a balanced approach where information society providers are not expected to actively monitor content they carry and/or host

[107] [1999] 4 All ER 342; [1999] EWHC QB 244.
[108] Ibid. [19].
[109] Ibid. [20].

but where, unlike the position in the US following the promulgation of §230 of the Communication Decency Act, liability may arise from a failure to act once they have been made aware of the defamatory nature of the content in question.

8.3.2 Intermediary defences: the E-Commerce Directive and Regulations

Soon after the *Godfrey* decision a change was made to the UK law in this area. The European Commission had for some time been looking to harmonize European Law in this area and in the Electronic Commerce Directive[110] a number of provisions were brought forward to harmonize the liability of ISPs for: (a) carrying, (b) caching, and (c) hosting material including obscene material and defamatory material.

Highlight Electronic Commerce Directive, Arts. 12–14

Article 12: Where an information society service is provided that consists of the transmission in a communication network of information provided by a recipient of the service, or the provision of access to a communication network, Member States shall ensure that the service provider is not liable for the information transmitted.

Article 13: Where an information society service is provided that consists of the transmission in a communication network of information provided by a recipient of the service, Member States shall ensure that the service provider is not liable for the automatic, intermediate and temporary storage of that information, performed for the sole purpose of making more efficient the information's onward transmission to other recipients of the service upon their request.

Article 14: Where an information society service . . . consists of the storage of information provided by a recipient of the service, Member States shall ensure that the service provider is not liable for the information stored at the request of a recipient of the service, on condition that: (a) the provider does not have actual knowledge of illegal activity or information and, as regards claims for damages, is not aware of facts or circumstances from which the illegal activity or information is apparent; or (b) the provider, upon obtaining such knowledge or awareness, acts expeditiously to remove or to disable access to the information.

Article 12 creates a 'mere conduit' defence similar to that given to telecommunications companies and which protects them from slander claims 'published' by the telephone network. This defence will not apply if the ISP originated or modifies the content of the message. Article 13 extends a caching defence. Again there are requirements that the ISP does not originate or modify the content of the message, but with this defence comes a further requirement that 'the provider acts expeditiously to remove or to disable access to the information it has stored upon obtaining actual knowledge of the fact that the information at the initial source of the transmission has been removed from the network, or access to it has been disabled, or that a court or an administrative authority has ordered such removal or disablement'.[111] This requires ISPs who retain cache copies of

[110] Dir. 2000/31/EC of the European Parliament and of the Council of 8 June 2000, OJ L178, 17 July 2000.

[111] Art. 13(1)(e).

web pages or other content to remove such copies from their system once they become aware that the original has been removed for whatever reason. Failure to do so may expose such ISPs to liability for the content they cache. Article 14 provides that ISPs who host material have a form of distributor defence not dissimilar to that seen in *Godfrey*. In harmonizing the rules for liability of information society service providers the E-Commerce Directive does remarkably little to change the previous UK law, with perhaps the only major change being the introduction of the takedown requirement for cache copies found in Art. 13(1)(e).

The UK gave effect to the E-Commerce Directive in the E-Commerce (EC Directive) Regulations 2002.[112] Regulations 17, 18, and 19 repeat the wording of the Arts. 12, 13, and 14 almost verbatim. A significant addition to the Directive's provisions though is to be found in reg. 22. Reflecting criticisms made of the Directive in an earlier DTI consultation, reg. 22 attempts to address the issue of what constitutes 'actual knowledge' for the purpose of regs. 18 and 19. This provides an illustrative list of factors which a court may consider in determining whether a service provider has received notice through any means of contact that the service provider has made available, as required by reg. 6(1)(c).[113] To date, the Regulations appear to have functioned extremely smoothly. Despite some initial concerns that the Regulations may be abused by individuals and organizations who sought to use the notification procedure to take down critical comment, this appears not to have been the case.

Several cases have examined the intermediary defences. The first was *Bunt v Tilley & Ors*.[114] Mr Bunt claimed that Mr Tilley and two other individuals had made defamatory statements about him using online services. He wished also to bring proceedings against three information service providers on the basis that the individual defendants published the offending words 'via the services provided' by their ISPs, although as Eady J pointed out he did not plead that any of the three corporate defendants had at any stage hosted any website relevant to the claims.[115] The foundation of Mr Bunt's claims against the ISPs seemed to be that they had enabled the individuals in question to publish the allegedly defamatory statements by providing them with a connection to the internet. This claim raised substantial points of significance as to the basis upon which a provider of such services could, if at all, be liable in respect of material which is simply communicated via the services which they provide. Should Eady J side with Mr Bunt's interpretation of the Regulations, ISPs could be liable for any material they carried across their network, even if they themselves did not host said material should they become aware of the nature of the material their customer was publishing and fail to take steps to block their customer from continuing to use their service. Fortunately for the information service industry Eady J dismissed Mr Bunt's claims. He held that ISPs fell within the definition of 'information society service' provider by applying the definition of an information society service given in reg. 2(1) of the E-Commerce

[112] SI 2002/2013.

[113] Reg. 6(1) obliges an ISP to make certain information available to the end user 'in a form . . . which is easily, directly and permanently accessible'. Reg. 6(1)(c) refers to the service provider's contact details, including email addresses, which facilitate rapid and direct communication with the ISP.

[114] [2006] EWHC 407 (QB); [2006] 3 All ER 336.

[115] Ibid. [5].

(EC Directive) Regulations.[116] They were therefore able to rely upon defences within regs. 17–19 and the claims against the ISPs were accordingly struck out. In a sense *Bunt* merely confirms what we thought we already knew; that the Regulations prevent the attribution of liability to telephone companies or other passive telecommunications providers (such as ISPs) for the distribution of defamatory material over their communication networks.

Metropolitan International Schools Ltd v Designtechnica Corp. looked specifically at the liability of internet search providers.[117] Here, the claimant claimed that the first defendant hosted several web forums in which threads were hosted which accused the claimant (a distance learning operator) of a number of faults including providing poor value for money, exploiting students, and being 'little more than a scam'. The third defendant in the action was the search engine giant Google. The claimant claimed they were jointly liable as they: 'published or caused to be published at www.google.co.uk and/or www.google.com a search return for the Train2Game thread which . . . set out the following words defamatory of the Claimant as the third and fourth highest search result: "Train2Game new SCAM for Scheidegger"'.[118] Mr Justice Eady was asked by Google to deny a request to serve the order out of jurisdiction on Google. The case therefore became the first UK case to examine the liability of search engine providers for defamation committed on a catalogued website.

At the heart of the claim were Google's previews. Each search return displays not only a link to the page but also one or two lines of text which preview the page. It was these previews which contained the defamatory material referred to above. Eady J began by distinguishing the decision in *Godfrey*. He found that Google was not the 'publisher' of the snippet, noting that: 'A search engine is a different kind of Internet intermediary. It is not possible to draw a complete analogy with a website host. One cannot merely press a button to ensure that the offending words will never reappear on a Google search snippet: there is no control over the search terms typed in by future users. If the words are thrown up in response to a future search, it would by no means follow that the Third Defendant has authorised or acquiesced in that process . . . [and on this basis] I believe it is unrealistic to attribute responsibility for publication to the Third Defendant, whether on the basis of authorship or acquiescence.'[119]

Eady J went on to consider whether the search engine giant could be liable as an intermediary carrier, and vitally whether the provisions of the E-Commerce (EC Directive) Regulations would apply to them. In the instant case he found no liability for Google on the basis of his previous analysis but found that 'the United Kingdom government has so far taken the view that it is unnecessary or inappropriate to extend protection expressly to search engines. It would not be appropriate, therefore, for me to proceed as though there were a comparable statute in effect in this jurisdiction. I think that, for the Third Defendant to be classified as or deemed a "host", statutory intervention would be needed.'[120] As a first instance decision this case is of influential authority only, although a dearth of alternative authorities suggests that it will be highly influential

[116] Ibid. [41].
[117] [2009] EWHC 1765 (QB).
[118] Ibid. [15] (Scheidegger was the former trading name of the claimant).
[119] Ibid. [55], [64].
[120] Ibid. [112].

should similar facts arise. On this basis it is somewhat of a mixed victory for Google, for although Eady J found they were not liable as publishers, and vitally were found to have no duty to 'take down' material under the *Godfrey* principle as they were 'not hosting a website and do not have anything from which to "take down" the offending words';[121] they have been denied entry to the safe harbour provisions found in the Regulations. No doubt Google would argue that it is better to be found not liable in the first place than to have to seek shelter in the safe harbour, and that is undoubtedly true, but to draw a distinction between ISPs and hosts on the one hand and search engine providers on the other may yet have unforeseen consequences.

The liability of search providers has been revisited more recently in the case of *Hegglin v Persons Unknown*.[122] Here the court was asked to consider whether Google Inc. (registered in Delaware and located in California) could be served proceedings to appear in a hearing relating to the defamation of Mr Hegglin by persons unknown. On a series of internet websites a number of malicious, harmful, and defamatory comments had been made about Mr Hegglin, including that he was a paedophile, a murderer, a sympathizer of the Ku Klux Klan, a corrupt businessman, and a money launderer for the mafia. Mr Hegglin had been unable to identify who was so defaming him but he sought to bring Google into the action by applying ss. 10 and 14 of the Data Protection Act 1998 (the prevention of data processing likely to cause damage or distress and the rectification, erasure, or destruction of inaccurate data). Mr. Justice Bean found at an interim hearing that Google Inc., although they had been cooperative with Mr Hegglin in seeking to block access to sites containing the defamatory material, could be served, on the basis that: 'there is at least a good arguable case that Google is under an obligation, enforceable in this jurisdiction, to comply with the requirements of the 1998 Act when processing the claimant's personal data, both when hosting a website on which such data appears or . . . when operating a search engine such as google.co.uk on which his data is processed.'[123] Following this decision the case was settled, the terms of the settlement were not revealed but it appears Google agreed to increase its efforts to block access to the defamatory materials in question.[124] This case may be seen as an extended application of the Right to be Forgotten set out in the case of *Google Spain SL v AEPD*.[125] Indeed one commentator suggested that Google had settled to avoid the 'opening of a floodgate of [defamatory material] claims in much the same way as the so-called "right to be forgotten" ruling has done'.[126] The same commentator though goes on to note that Google would likely face further cases in the future raised under the same basis: 'Google has deferred [this claim] to another day.'[127]

[121] Ibid. [78].
[122] [2014] EWHC 2808 (QB).
[123] Ibid. [20].
[124] O Bowcott and S Gibbs, 'Google settles online abuse court case' *The Guardian* (London, 24 November 2014) <http://www.theguardian.com/technology/2014/nov/24/google-settles-online-abuse-court-case-daniel-hegglin>.
[125] Case C-131/12, 13 May 2014 <http://curia.europa.eu/juris/liste.jsf?num=C-131/12>. This case will be discussed in greater depth in ch. 20.
[126] David Cook, cybercrime specialist at Slater & Gordon cited in K Hall, 'Google dodges "costly" legal precedent, settles Daniel Hegglin case' (*The Register*, 24 November 2014) <http://www.theregister.co.uk/2014/11/24/google_dodges_costly_precedent_daniel_hegglin_online_abuse_case/>.
[127] Ibid.

More commonly of late there has been a focus on the role of intermediaries who host social network sites and blogs. In two recent cases it is the operation by Google of the popular blog hosting service Blogger that came under scrutiny. First, in *Davison v Habeeb*[128] Ms Davison claimed a number of bloggers had defamed her, including some hosted by the Blogger service. She claimed that Google were not only publishers of the comments but were also promoters of the comments also as 'a Google search against "Peter Eyre", which brings up "Peter Eyre's Space" (one of the blogs complained of) as the second snippet and a reference to his articles in the *Palestine Telegraph* as the fourth snippet'.[129] Although HH Judge Parkes QC gave short shrift to the Google search facility forming part of the claim, 'The answer to that submission, of course, is to be found in the analysis in *Metropolitan International Schools v Designtechnica*: the operation of the Google search engine is entirely automatic',[130] he finds the operation of Blogger to be entirely different: 'Mr White submits that although there is no precise analogy between a service like Blogger.com and a search engine, it is clear from Eady J's reasoning in Metropolitan International Schools that Blogger.com is not a publisher, but simply a facilitator. It is true that there can be no intervention by Google Inc. in the process of posting material on Blogger.com. But then it is unclear that there could have been any intervention by Demon Internet in the process of posting on the newsgroup which it hosted in Godfrey. I accept that it is unrealistic to suppose that, absent notification, Blogger.com adopts as its own any of the content which it facilitates. But this is a summary application. In my view it must be at least arguable that the fifth defendant should properly be seen as a publisher responding to requests for downloads like Demon Internet, rather than a mere facilitator, playing a passive instrumental role.'[131] Thus for HH Judge Parkes QC, Blogger clearly is a publisher at English law. He then revisited *Godfrey* and asked when Google could be responsible for material hosted on the Blogger service at English law: 'it is arguable that [Google] is a publisher at common law, following notification it would be unable (or at least arguably unable) to establish that it was ignorant of the existence of the defamatory material on Blogger.com, or to rely on the defence at s. 1, Defamation Act 1996, exactly as the defendant was unable to rely on that defence in *Godfrey v Demon Internet*'.[132] This leaves one final question: do reg. 19 of the E-Commerce (EC Directive) Regulations and Art. 14 of the E-commerce Directive protect Google from the claim? HH Judge Parkes QC embarked on a lengthy analysis of reg. 19 and Google's level of actual knowledge of the defamatory content. He concluded that the 'Blogger.com service provides an information society service'[133] meaning it qualified for reg. 19 protection and then found that it was impossible for Google to know with any degree of certainty whether the information was defamatory as they were faced with conflicting claims as to the defamatory nature of the content between the claimant and the operator of the blog: on this basis Google 'was in no position to adjudicate'.[134] Ultimately therefore Google was held to be a publisher in English law, but protected by reg. 19.

[128] [2011] EWHC 3031 (QB).
[129] Ibid. [40].
[130] Ibid.
[131] Ibid. [41].
[132] Ibid. [46].
[133] Ibid. [56].
[134] Ibid. [68].

This position was reviewed in the following case of *Tamiz v Google Inc.*[135] Mr Tamiz raised a claim in relation to eight comments that were posted on a blog bearing the name 'London Muslim' in late April 2011. The blog was moderated by an individual who was unaware of Mr Tamiz's complaints until Google, with Mr Tamiz's permission, passed his complaint on to the blog moderator. The offending comments were then immediately removed by the blog moderator. Despite this Mr Tamiz decided to take legal action. Instead of suing the individuals who made the comments or even the blog moderator, Mr Tamiz attempted to pursue a claim against Google Inc. and Google UK Ltd. Google claimed that they were not the authors of the comments under English law and in any event even if they were they were protected by reg. 19 of the E-Commerce (EC Directive) Regulations and Art.14 of the E-Commerce Directive. In the High Court Eady J examined the line of cases that began with *Godfrey* and extended through *Designtechnica* and *Davison*. He highlighted the need for judges to be consistent in dealing with new technologies and that there was a need to remain proportionate in their decisions, in terms of Art. 10 ECHR. He departed from HH Judge Parkes QC:

> It seems to me to be a significant factor in the evidence before me that Google Inc is not required to take any positive step, technically, in the process of continuing the accessibility of the offending material, whether it has been notified of a complainant's objection or not. In those circumstances, I would be prepared to hold that it should not be regarded as a publisher, or even as one who authorises publication, under the established principles of the common law . . . its role, as a platform provider, is a purely passive one.[136]

He was then asked whether s. 1 of the Defamation Act 1996 made any difference to his finding. The confusion had arisen in *Designtechnica*, another decision of Eady J where he seemed to suggest a publisher at common law and a commercial publisher under s. 1 may be different. He replied quite unequivocally:

> In this brief and passing comment, I was contemplating the somewhat counter-intuitive hypothesis that Google Inc should be considered as a 'publisher', contrary to my primary finding. I was obviously finding it difficult to envisage how it could on that hypothesis, in any meaningful sense, not be 'a person whose business is issuing material to the public, or a section of the public, who issues material containing the statement in the course of that business'. All I was suggesting, in the passage at [80], was that if Google Inc was to be regarded as a publisher of the search 'snippets', it was difficult to see how it would not fall within the definition of a commercial publisher.[137]

Although perhaps not the clearest clarification in the world, here Eady J was telling us he does not see a commercial publisher as a separate classification from a publisher; he was in essence musing when a platform provider would not be a commercial publisher. For the avoidance of doubt he added that 'whereas Google Inc in the course of its business makes facilities available, including by way of a platform for bloggers who use Blogger.com, it cannot be said to fall within the definition of a "commercial publisher"'.[138] Although he had already found that Google was not a publisher of the content, he took the time to review the application of reg. 19. He noted that in guidance issued by the CJEU in *L'Oréal*

[135] [2012] EWHC 449 (QB).
[136] Ibid. [39].
[137] Ibid. [46].
[138] Ibid. [42].

SA v eBay International AG,[139] the intermediary must be 'aware of facts or circumstances from which the illegal activity or information is apparent'[140] before the protection of Art. 14/reg. 19 is lost. In addition the CJEU noted that notifications made to intermediaries cannot be 'insufficiently precise or inadequately substantiated'.[141] Applying this guidance he found that 'it may be thought by Mr Tamiz to be implicit in his complaints that he was denying, outright, any allegation of theft or drug dealing, but it cannot be right that any provider is required, in the light of the strict terms of Regulation 19, to take all such protestations at face value. Clearly more is required for a provider to acquire a sufficient state of knowledge to be deprived of the statutory protection.'[142]

Mr Tamiz appealed this decision and on Valentine's Day 2013 the Court of Appeal issued their judgment.[143] In general the court supported the findings of Eady J but with, for Google, one major distinction. Counsel for Mr Tamiz tried to argue that Google was a publisher, acting not just through its employees but also through the bloggers who user the Blogger platform. He argued:

> it has control over the blogger, who in turn has control over the comments posted on the blog. Google Inc is therefore to be regarded as a primary publisher, potentially liable for defamatory material on the blogs, irrespective of knowledge or fault and irrespective of whether it has been notified of any complaint, subject however to any statutory defences. Alternatively it is a secondary publisher, facilitating publication in a manner analogous to a distributor, subject to the common law defence of innocent dissemination as well as to statutory defences, though it will be difficult to establish the defence of innocent dissemination if it has the power to prevent continuing publication and chooses not to exercise that power.[144]

This was rejected by Richards LJ:

> By the provision of that service [Blogger] Google Inc plainly facilitates publication of the blogs (including the comments posted on them). Its involvement is not such, however, as to make it a primary publisher of the blogs. It does not create the blogs or have any prior knowledge of, or effective control over, their content. It is not in a position comparable to that of the author or editor of a defamatory article. Nor is it in a position comparable to that of the corporate proprietor of a newspaper in which a defamatory article is printed. Such a corporation may be liable as a primary publisher by reason of the involvement of its employees or agents in the publication. But there is no relationship of employment or agency between Google Inc and the bloggers or those posting comments on the blogs: such people are plainly independent of Google Inc and do not act in any sense on its behalf or in its name. I am also very doubtful about the argument that Google Inc's role is that of a secondary publisher, facilitating publication in a manner analogous to a distributor.[145]

In one important manner though he departed from Eady J's judgment:

> In relation to the position after notification of the complaint, however, additional considerations arise, and it is in relation to this period that I take a different view from that of Eady J on the issue of publication . . . If Google Inc. allows defamatory material to remain on a Blogger blog after it has been notified of the presence of that material, it might be inferred to have associated itself with, or to have made itself responsible for, the continued presence of that material on the

[139] [2011] ETMR 52. This case will be discussed in greater detail in ch. 17.
[140] *L'Oréal* at [120]; Tamiz at [58].
[141] *L'Oréal* at [122]; Tamiz at [58].
[142] Tamiz at [60].
[143] *Tamiz v Google Inc.* [2013] EWCA Civ 68.
[144] Ibid. [22].
[145] Ibid. [25]–[26].

> blog and thereby to have become a publisher of the material. In relation to comments A and B a period of over five weeks elapsed between notification and removal. In the context of the defence under section 1 of the 1996 Act, Eady J described Google Inc's response as somewhat dilatory but not outside the bounds of a reasonable response. Whilst I accept the judge's assessment in the context of the statutory defence, it is in my view open to argument that the time taken was sufficiently long to leave room for an inference adverse to Google Inc. The period during which Google Inc might fall to be treated on that basis as a publisher of the defamatory comments would be a very short one, but it means that the claim cannot in my view be dismissed on the ground that Google Inc was clearly not a publisher of the comments at all.[146]

Thus a clear warning has been sent from the Court of Appeal to platform providers such as Google, but also to Facebook, Twitter, and others. You are not a primary publisher for the purposes of the Defamation Act but like Demon Internet, you may find yourself responsible as a distributor of the material if you are made aware of it and you fail to act to remove it in a reasonable time. In the instant case the court found Google were not liable, but not because they were shielded from liability but because applying the *Jameel* principle:

> the earliest point at which Google Inc could have become liable in respect of the comments would be some time after notification of the complaint in respect of them. But it is highly improbable that any significant number of readers will have accessed the comments after that time and prior to removal of the entire blog. It follows, as the judge clearly had in mind, that any damage to the appellant's reputation arising out of continued publication of the comments during that period will have been trivial; and in those circumstances the judge was right to consider that 'the game would not be worth the candle'.[147]

This was a very nervous 'win' for Google and one which no doubt was of concern to their counsel as well as to advisers to other platform providers. The court in finding Google not liable did not consider reg. 19 but it is hard to imagine it would have saved Google once it was aware of the offending content.

Finally, we have the recent decision of the European Court of Human Rights in *Delfi AS v Estonia*.[148] At first glance this case appears to make major changes to the liability of internet intermediaries for defamatory content but upon reflection its impact is likely to be less than it may initially seem. An individual identified as 'L' who was the sole or major shareholder and a member of the supervisory board of SLK (or AS Saaremaa Laevakompanii (Saaremaa Shipping Company)) brought the claim. On 24 January 2006 Delfi, an internet news portal, published a story entitled 'SLK Destroyed Planned Ice Road'. This story suggested that SLK (who operated a ferry between islands) had intervened to prevent a winter 'ice road' from being constructed between some Estonian islands and the mainland. After all, stories on the Delfi site was the standard comments box. Here readers could publish unmoderated comments and read comments left by others. According to the report of the case 'the articles received about 10,000 readers' comments daily, the majority posted under pseudonyms. Nevertheless, there was a system of notice-and-takedown in place: any reader could mark a comment as leim (an Estonian word for an insulting or mocking

146 Ibid. [27], [34]–[36].
147 Ibid. [50].
148 Application no. 64569/09. Grand Chamber, 16 June 2015 <http://hudoc.echr.coe.int/eng?i=001-155105>.

message or a message inciting hatred on the Internet) and the comment was removed expeditiously. Furthermore, there was a system of automatic deletion of comments that included certain stems of obscene words. In addition, a victim of a defamatory comment could directly notify the applicant company, in which case the comment was removed immediately.'[149] The complainant complained about twenty comments which had been left below the news story including: 'If there was an iceroad, [one] could easily save 500 for a full car, fckng [L.] pay for that economy, why does it take 3 [hours] for your ferries if they are such good icebreakers, go and break ice in Pärnu port . . . instead, fcking monkey, I will cross [the strait] anyway and if I drown, it's your fault', 'they bathe in money anyway thanks to that monopoly and State subsidies and have now started to fear that cars may drive to the islands for a couple of days without anything filling their purses. burn in your own ship, sick Jew!' and 'The people will chatter for a couple of days on the Internet, but the crooks (and also those who are backed and whom we ourselves have elected to represent us) pocket the money and pay no attention to this flaming—no one gives a shit about this.' It appears all the comments in question were published on 24/25 January 2006. L, through his lawyers, complained to Delfi about these comments on 9 March 2006 and Delfi took them down on the same day. In their claim L's lawyers had sought 500,000 Kroons (circa €32,000) in non-pecuniary compensation; this was rejected by Delfi on the basis that they had taken the comments down immediately upon their notification of them.

L raised a civil claim against Delfi for damages. At a District Court hearing in Estonia in May 2007 his claim was dismissed as the Estonian Information Society Services Act, which implemented the safe harbour principles found in Arts. 12–14 of the E-commerce Directive, protected Delfi. In October 2007, however, the Court of Appeal remitted the case back to the District Court finding that it had erred in finding Delfi were protected by the Act and a second hearing in the District Court in June 2008 found that Delfi had held themselves out in such a way as be seen to be a publisher rather than merely a host or distributor of content found in the comments section of the website. As a result it could not disclaim liability and merely following notice and takedown was not enough to remove liability. The District Court awarded though only 5,000 Kroons (€320) damages. The Court of Appeal upheld this decision, emphasizing that 'Delfi had not been required to exercise prior control over comments. However, having chosen not to do so, it should have created some other effective system which would have ensured rapid removal of unlawful comments from the portal. The Court of Appeal considered that the measures taken by the applicant company were insufficient and that it was contrary to the principle of good faith to place the burden of monitoring the comments on their potential victims. The Court of Appeal also rejected Delfi's argument that its liability was excluded under the Information Society Services Act. It noted that Delfi was not a technical intermediary in respect of the comments, and that its activity was not of a merely technical, automatic and passive nature; instead, it invited users to add comments. Thus, they were a provider of content services rather than of technical services.'[150] This decision was then upheld by the Estonian Supreme Court, who agreed with

[149] Ibid. [12]–[13].
[150] Ibid. [28]–[29].

the Court of Appeal that Delfi did not qualify for the protection of the Information Society Services Act on the basis that:

> a user of the defendant's service cannot change or delete a comment he or she has posted. He or she can only report an inappropriate comment. Thus, the defendant can determine which of the comments added will be published and which will not be published. The fact that the defendant does not make use of this possibility does not prompt the conclusion that the publishing of comments is not under the defendant's control. The defendant, which governs the information stored in the comment environment, provides a content service, for which reason the circumstances precluding liability, as specified in section 10 of the ISSA, do not apply in the present case.[151]

In one respect though the Supreme Court vacated the decision of the Court of Appeal. They found, vitally, that the removal of content could interfere with the personality rights and the freedom of expression rights of the writers of comments. As a result of this, and as a result of the costly new moderating process which Delfi had to set up to comply with the decision of the Supreme Court, Delfi applied to the European Court of Human Rights claiming that this interfered with their right to free expression under Art. 10 and was in breach of the 2003 Council of Europe Declaration on Freedom of Communication on the Internet.[152]

The ECtHR initially ruled on the case in October 2013 when it found that there had been no violation of Art. 10 on the basis that the interference by the state had been proportionate and was for the legitimate aim of protecting the reputation and rights of others.[153] The case was then remitted to the Grand Chamber. In June 2015 the much-delayed decision of the Grand Chamber was published. It is (for the ECtHR) a lengthy 88 pages and unusually contains two concurring and one dissenting opinion. It is a decision which has been much commented upon but which we can hopefully reduce to a few key facts and issues. First, it should be noted that the Grand Chamber effectively bypassed the question of supremacy of EU law in the case by going straight to the ECHR principles. Once there the court reiterated the standard three stages normally applied to claims of an interference with Art. 10(1): that the restriction be lawful, achieve a legitimate aim, and be necessary in a democratic society. The court found that the Estonian Law was lawful in the sense that it was sufficiently clear and the impact of the law was foreseeable.[154] The court found that 'as a professional publisher, the applicant company should have been familiar with the legislation and case-law, and could also have sought legal advice'.[155] As a result the actions were lawful. As the parties had already agreed that the restriction had pursued the legitimate aim of protecting the reputation and rights of others, the court then examined the question of whether the restrictions were necessary. The court reiterated that the internet could be harmful as well as beneficial[156] and emphasized that the comments could be seen as hate speech and incitements to violence which on their face value were unlawful.[157] On this basis the court had little difficulty in finding the actions of

[151] Ibid. [31].
[152] <https://wcd.coe.int/ViewDoc.jsp?id=37031>.
[153] *Delfi* (n. 148) [63].
[154] Ibid. [121].
[155] Ibid. [129].
[156] Ibid. [133].
[157] Ibid. [153].

moderators did not amount to private censorship and noted that a large news organization was better placed to police content on its website than a private citizen.[158] Finally, the court found that a notice and takedown approach was insufficient to deal with hate speech of the nature of the comments in question:

> in cases such as the present one, where third-party user comments are in the form of hate speech and direct threats to the physical integrity of individuals, as understood in the Court's case-law, the Court considers, that the rights and interests of others and of society as a whole may entitle Contracting States to impose liability on Internet news portals, without contravening Article 10 of the Convention, if they fail to take measures to remove clearly unlawful comments without delay, *even without notice from the alleged victim or from third parties*.[159] On this basis the action was necessary. It should also be noted that the court seemed to be influenced also by the low level of damages awarded.[160]

As already observed there has been a great degree of comment on this case[161] but the impact of it may be less than internet lawyers and free speech activists may fear. The primary reason for this is the relationship between EU Law and the ECtHR. By referring the case to Strasbourg and not Luxembourg the impact of the decision is limited. The ECtHR has a supervisory role and is not intended to interpret either domestic or EU law. The extent of its ruling was to hold that the Supreme Court's reasoning and decision to order Delfi to pay damages amounting to €320 was within Estonia's margin of appreciation and not in breach of Art. 10 of the Convention. As a result there was no ruling on the safe harbour provisions of the E-Commerce Directive. This suggests that intermediary websites may continue to operate as they did prior to the *Delfi* decision if they can fit themselves into the categories of protected internet intermediary service providers. There is considerable jurisprudence from the CJEU on when intermediaries may avail themselves of these protections, including *SABAM v Netlog*[162] in which a social networking site which received a request from the Belgian copyright society (SABAM) to implement a general filtering system to prevent the unlawful use of copyright protected work by its users was found to be protected by the Art. 15 prohibition on general monitoring, and *Google France v Louis Vuitton Malletier* (and joined cases)[163] in which the court held that the test for whether a service provider could benefit from Art. 14 protection was whether its service was 'neutral, in the sense that its conduct is merely technical, automatic and passive, pointing to a lack of knowledge or control of the data which it stores'.[164] As Woods observes 'one could argue that, insofar as a site invites comment on a

[158] Ibid. [158]–[159].

[159] Ibid. [159] (emphasis added).

[160] Ibid. [160].

[161] See e.g. L Woods, '*Delfi v Estonia*: Curtailing online freedom of expression?' (*EU Law Analysis*, 18 June 2016) <http://eulawanalysis.blogspot.co.uk/2015/06/delfi-v-estonia-curtailing-online.html>; D Voorhoof, '*Delfi AS v. Estonia*: Grand Chamber confirms liability of online news portal for offensive comments posted by its readers' (*Strasbourg Observers*, 18 June 2015) <http://strasbourgobservers.com/2015/06/18/delfi-as-v-estonia-grand-chamber-confirms-liability-of-online-news-portal-for-offensive-comments-posted-by-its-readers/>.

[162] [2012] 2 CMLR 18 (C360/10).

[163] [2011] All ER (EC) 411 (C236/08, C237/08, C238/08).

[164] Ibid. [114].

particular topic, it is not neutral though one might question how overt that invitation might be.'[165] In *L'Oréal v eBay*:[166]

> the Court held that the Article 14 exemption should not apply where the host plays an 'active role' in the presentation and promotion of offers for sale posted by its users so as to give it knowledge of, or control over, related data. Further, if a host has knowledge of facts that would alert a 'diligent economic operator' to illegal activity, it must remove the offending data to benefit from the Article 14 exemption.[167]

The question of the compatibility of the Luxembourg and Strasbourg positions is open. Woods suggests the CJEU may have come to a similar decision:

> The Strasbourg court's reasoning put Delfi in a position of effectively having to monitor user content. Had Delfi been found to be an intermediary in the sense of Articles 12–14, this would have been contrary to Article 15 of the eCommerce Directive, as implemented in domestic law. Given that Delfi was found not to be such an intermediary, then Article 15 does not come into play. It also seems that this finding is not unlikely under EU law. There is then no automatic conflict between this ruling and the position under EU law.[168]

In a separate commentary a different view emerges:

> Hopefully, at least within the EU, Member States will realise that, even if they are permitted to demand monitoring under the ECHR, EU law prohibits it: the judgments of the CJEU in *Google France* and *L'Oréal v eBay* have made this clear for a while now. As a result, more than anything else, the Estonian courts have created a problem for themselves by misapplying EU law and refusing to submit a preliminary question to the CJEU. The resulting problem of how to bring their law into line with the EU requirements should now also be limited to them, not the rest of EU. What the effect will be for European countries outside of the EU is a more troubling consideration.[169]

There is something to be said for either interpretation and we cannot be sure of the impact of *Delfi* on EU Law, and in particular the impact of the safe harbour provisions, until a reference is taken to the CJEU, thus we can say the impact of *Delfi* is limited until such time as that reference is made. Additionally the impact of *Delfi* is limited by the relatively narrow decision of the ECtHR. As one commentator suggested

> the extent of its ruling was holding that the Supreme Court's reasoning and decision to order Delfi to pay €320 was within Estonia's margin of appreciation and not in breach of Article 10 of the Convention.[170]

This may slightly oversimplify the judgment but as the Grand Chamber makes clear, the comments in question mainly constituted violence and hate. As a result the establishment of their unlawful nature did not require any linguistic or legal analysis by Delfi, since they were on the face of it manifestly unlawful. In addition, such speech does not qualify for Art. 10 protection and their removal was not private censorship. It is unlikely we could extend *Delfi* to more nuanced speech which requires a value judgement, in particular defamatory speech which turns on accusations unknowable to the

[165] Woods (n. 161).
[166] [2012] All ER (EC) 501 (C324/09).
[167] Woods (n. 161).
[168] Ibid.
[169] C Angelopoulos, '*Delfi v Estonia*: ISPs and the freedom to impart information' (*The IP Kat*, 24 June 2015) <http://ipkitten.blogspot.co.uk/2015/06/delfi-v-estonia-isps-and-freedom-to.html>.
[170] Taylor Wessing, 'Delfi v Estonia—what is the real impact?' (*Lexology*, 28 July 2015) <http://www.lexology.com/library/detail.aspx?g=1aead6a4–4c67–46ad-a183-b84bf9f02ef2>.

hosting site. As a result *Delfi* may be understood to be a balanced decision: one which creates a positive obligation on news sites and other such content sites[171] to police violent or hate speech without being over-restrictive.

8.3.3 The operators of websites' defence

Some solace for counsel for intermediaries may be found in the introduction of s. 5 of the Defamation Act 2013. Although s. 5 does not affect the outcome of decisions such as *Tamiz* it bolsters the defences available to some internet intermediaries, in particular those who operate a website. In essence s. 5 gives intermediary defences similar to those found in the E-Commerce Directive to ordinary operators of websites such as bloggers but it would also appear to extend to anyone who operates a website on which third party comments may be hosted, including Google's Blogger platform and social media platforms such as Facebook and Twitter. Under s. 5(2) it is a defence for the operator to show that they did not post the statement complained of on the website. Thus in the *Tamiz* case it is possible that both the operator of the London Muslim blog, and indeed Google, would be able to rely on a s. 5(2) defence. However, like the safe harbour provisions found in the E-Commerce Directive, and indeed s. 1 of the Defamation Act 1996 as applied in *Godfrey v Demon*, the defence comes with limits. By s. 5(3) the defence is defeated if the complainant could not identify the originator of the putatively defamatory statement and if a notice of complaint has been served on the website operator and they have failed to act accordingly. What does it mean to 'act accordingly'? Well, unlike the previous provisions found in the 1996 Defamation Act, or even the safe harbour provisions of the E-Commerce Directive, there is no requirement that the content be taken down by the website operator. This is not just another notify and takedown provision (at least not initially). Instead when a complaint is made to a website operator under s. 5(3)(b) this triggers the application of the Schedule of the Defamation (Operators of Websites) Regulations 2013.[172] This sets out an extremely complex procedure for the website operator to follow which has led to many criticizing the provision as being unduly administratively onerous on website operators who wish to rely upon the defence.[173] The first stage is that except in cases where the website operator does not know how to contact the poster of the statement complained of, or the complainant has successfully complained to the website operator at least twice before about the same or a related statement from the same poster, the website operator will pass the complaint on to the poster of the statement within

[171] *Delfi* does not apply to social media platforms. This is made clear in the judgment: 'the case does not concern other fora on the Internet where third-party comments can be disseminated, for example, an Internet discussion forum or a bulletin board where users can freely set out their ideas on any topics without the discussion being channelled by any input from the forum's manager; or a social media platform where the platform provider does not offer any content and where the content provider may be a private person running the website or a blog as a hobby' *Delfi* (n. 148) [116].

[172] SI 2013/3028.

[173] See e.g. A Hurst, 'Defamation Act 2013: Section 5, it's decision time for website operators' (6 January 2014) <http://inforrm.wordpress.com/2014/01/06/defamation-act-2013-section-5-its-decision-time-for-website-operators-ashley-hurst/> and Charles Russell 'UK Defamation Act 2013, Update: Website Operators' September 2013 <http://www.charlesrussell.co.uk/UserFiles/file/pdf/Reputation percent20Management/Defamation_Act_Website.pdf>.

48 hours, along with a notification that the statement may be removed. If the poster of the statement fails to respond to this notification within the time set out in the notification (which is 5 days after notification), or if they respond in part but fail to provide all necessary information as is required by the Schedule, then the post or message must be removed within 48 hours for the defence to remain in effect. Similarly, if the poster of the statement indicates they do not object to the statement being removed, the operator of the website must remove it within 48 hours. If the poster of the original content replies in full stating that they do not wish to have the statement removed, then the operator of the site should reply to the complainant within 48 hours noting that the statement will not be removed and if permitted to do so by the poster of the statement giving their contact details; if not permitted, they must inform the complainant that they are not permitted to pass over these details. Thus an operator of a website may continue to host a statement which has been claimed to be defamatory in nature without fear of being held liable for statements they did not make. The idea behind this is to ameliorate the chilling effects of the notice and takedown approach used previously. The complainant may of course if they feel they have been genuinely defamed then make a Norwich Pharmacal application to have the website operator compelled to give up the identification details of the poster of the message or content allowing them to pursue an action directly.

8.4 **Digital defamation and UGC**

In the web 2.0 environment user-generated content (UGC) is king. In everything from consumer reviews in sites such as TripAdvisor to user-generated videos on YouTube, the web 2.0 economy is built on UGC. The problem with UGC though is its completely unfiltered nature which increases greatly the risks of defamation occurring. An increasing number of cases are being brought against individuals and services which host UGC. Many cases are minor in nature but demonstrate a propensity for an increase in this type of defamation action. For example, a 15-year-old schoolboy in Finland was found guilty of criminal libel for a video he posted on YouTube showing his teacher singing at the school party with English subtitles under the headline 'Karaoke of the mental hospital'.[174] Meanwhile in the US a number of cases have been raised including an action against TripAdvisor brought by the owner/operator of a hotel and convention centre listed as 'the dirtiest hotel in America' in a 2011 list of TripAdvisor's dirtiest hotels;[175] and an action by an eBay seller over negative feedback left by a buyer.[176]

The best advice to give to individuals in the UK is to be cautious in any statement they publish, republish, or otherwise distribute. The reason for recommending

[174] 'Teen fined for YouTube karaoke video' (*Reuters*, 24 August 2007) <http://www.reuters.com/article/internetNews/idUSL2478621120070824>.

[175] The action was dismissed. *Kenneth M Seaton, d/b/a Grand Resort Hotel and Convention Ctr. v TripAdvisor* No. 3:11-cv-549 (ED Tenn) <http://digitalcommons.law.scu.edu/cgi/viewcontent.cgi?article=1125&context=historical>.

[176] See J Campbell, 'Miami Lawyer Sues Man Over eBay Feedback' (*NBC Miami*, 11 April 2010) <http://www.nbcmiami.com/news/business/Miami-Lawyer-Sues-Man-Over-eBay-Feedback-90572279.html>.

caution is clear from the UK case law dealing with individual liability for statements made in the online environment. The first reported case was *Keith-Smith v Williams*.[177] This involved a series of claims made on a Yahoo! discussion group called 'In the Hole' by Tracey Williams about Michael Keith-Smith, a UK Independence Party candidate in the 2005 general election. Among other claims Ms Williams suggested that Mr Keith-Smith was a racist, a Nazi, a sex offender, and a sexual deviant. Ms Williams may have thought she was safe from litigation as she did all this hiding behind a pseudonym. Mr Keith-Smith obtained a court order requiring Yahoo! to identify Ms Williams and in an undefended action in the High Court in March 2006 he secured a total award of £10,000 in damages, being £5,000 in compensatory damages and £5,000 in aggravated damages. Although the judge notes with some regret that 'the defendant possibly, or indeed probably, does not have the means to pay an award of damages or costs',[178] he felt it important to make the award to clear Mr Keith-Smith's reputation.

This case has been followed by a flurry of other cases examining personal liability for postings in internet discussion forums and on Twitter. In *Sheffield Wednesday Football Club & Ors v Hargreaves*,[179] the court was asked to make a so-called 'Norwich Pharmacal Order', that is an order that a person who assists another in committing a tort must reveal the identity of the wrongdoer to allow the party who has suffered harm to take action. Mr Hargreaves was the operator of a site called owlstalk.co.uk, a specialist site for fans of Sheffield Wednesday football club to discuss matters relating to the club. Although Mr Hargreaves himself never posted any inflammatory or defamatory statements several of his users did, including some statements questioning the financial probity of several of the directors of the club. Mr Hargreaves refused to name the individuals without a court order. In discussing whether or not to make the order to identify 11 users of the owlstalk board, Judge Richard Parkes QC noted a balance had to be struck between the rights of those allegedly defamed and the rights of the posters to privacy. Applying this balance he ruled that the identity of seven of the 11 individuals should be protected, stating: 'I do not think it would be right to make an order for the disclosure of the identities of users who have posted messages which are barely defamatory or little more than abusive or likely to be understood as jokes. That, it seems to me, would be disproportionate and unjustifiably intrusive.'[180] The remaining four though had posted statements which Judge Parkes thought 'may reasonably be understood to allege greed, selfishness, untrustworthiness and dishonest behaviour on the part of the Claimants'. He concluded 'in the case of those postings, the Claimants' entitlement to take action to protect their right to reputation outweighs, in my judgment, the right of the authors to maintain their anonymity and their right to express themselves freely'.[181] Thus four users of the owlstalk board were identified, although reports in the media suggest no further action was taken.[182]

[177] [2006] EWHC 860 (QB).
[178] Ibid. [15].
[179] [2007] EWHC 2375 (QB).
[180] Ibid. [17].
[181] Ibid. [18].
[182] P Gray, 'UK Libel Law v Freedom of Expression' *Liverpool Daily Post* (Liverpool, 14 October 2008).

8.4.1 **Facebook and Twitter libel**

A number of cases have now come through the courts looking specifically at libels committed on Facebook and Twitter. The first was *Applause Store Productions Ltd & Anor v Raphael*.[183] On 19 June 2007, a false Facebook profile for Matthew Firsht was set up, containing private information including reference to his date of birth, relationship status, purported sexual preferences, and his political and religious views. The following day a Facebook group was set up, with a link to the profile, called 'Has Matthew Firsht lied to you?' This contained material which was defamatory of him and his company Applause Store, indicating he owed substantial sums which he avoided paying with lies and implausible excuses.[184]

Mr Firsht discovered the false profile and group page on 4 July 2007 and requested it be removed. It was removed on 6 July 2007 and on 1 August 2007 his solicitors obtained a Norwich Pharmacal Order order against Facebook for disclosure of the registration data provided by the creator of the offending material. That evidence indicated that the defendant created both the profile and the group page. The defendant was known to Mr Firsht, being a former close friend. This suggested he had indeed set up the profile page as whoever created the profile knew that Mr Firsht had a twin brother, was from Brighton, practised a variety of Judaism, and was familiar with his company and work as well as the unusual spelling of his name.[185]

Mr Raphael denied setting up either the profile or the group page: he suggested he had an alibi but this was rejected by Judge Richard Parkes QC. With this established the judge looked at the harm caused by the placing of the false statements on Facebook. The first problem Mr Firsht faced was overcoming the *Jameel* principle as Facebook does not store data showing how many users view a profile or group. Therefore he could not produce evidence of publication which extended beyond a small group of six who actually saw the material, all of whom were connected to him in some way.[186] However, Judge Parkes accepted that Facebook was a medium in which users regularly searched for the names of others whom they know, and anyone who had done so against Mr Firsht's name in the time between the publication of the false entries and their removal would have found the offending material without difficulty. He judged that it was likely 'a not insubstantial number of people [would] have done so. By that I have in mind a substantial two-figure, rather than a three-figure, number.'[187]

With the *Jameel* hurdle cleared it was necessary to show harm had occurred to Mr Firsht and his company. Judge Parkes commented that although the libel was 'not at the top end of the scale, it is serious enough to say of a successful businessman that (as I have found the words to mean) he owes substantial sums of money which he has repeatedly avoided paying by lying and making implausible excuses, so that he is not to be trusted in the financial conduct of his business and represents a serious credit risk'.[188] On this basis he awarded libel damages of £15,000 to Mr Firsht, including aggravated damages to reflect the fact that Mr Raphael denied making the remarks and £5,000 to Applause Store Productions.

183 [2008] EWHC 1781 (QB).
184 Ibid. [3]–[4].
185 Ibid. [48].
186 Ibid. [70].
187 Ibid. [78].
188 Ibid. [79].

Subsequently in *Bryce v Barber*,[189] a university student was awarded £10,000 in damages for remarks made by another on his Facebook account. The defendant, Jeremiah Barber, posted indecent images of children on Raymond Bryce's Facebook profile along with the comment 'Ray, you like kids and you are gay so I bet you love this picture, Ha ha.' Mr Bryce claimed that the material would be seen by more than 800 people (his Facebook friends and others within the network), defame his character, and even subject him to violence. The defendant also attached the names of 11 other individuals to the images which meant that they may well have been seen by thousands. Tugendhart J agreed and awarded him damages for stress endured and any ensuing anxiety brought by knowing that those close to him would have seen the offensive image, stating that 'This was not only defamatory but a defamation which goes to a central aspect of Mr Bryce's . . . public reputation.'[190]

Similarly Twitter has been the cause of several defamation actions. One high-profile early case was *Cairns v Modi*.[191] The case was brought by former New Zealand international cricketer, Chris Cairns against the Commissioner of the Indian Premier League, Lalit Modi. On 5 January 2010 Modi had sent the tweet 'Chris Cairns removed from the IPL auction list due to his past record in match fixing. This was done by the Governing Council today.'[192] He then sent a further tweet in reply to an inquiry from a journalist. 'We have removed him from the list for alleged allegations [*sic*] as we have zero tolerance of this kind of stuff. The Governing Council has decided against keeping him on the list.'[193] Modi removed the offending tweets within a few hours and as a result at an interim hearing Mr Modi argued that no real or substantial tort had occurred in the United Kingdom. He argued that he had at the time about 90 followers on Twitter and of these, a proportion would not read the tweet once it had been sent out. He suggested that in the jurisdiction in proceedings only about 35 people would have actually seen the remarks.[194] Tugendhat J took advice from two experts who both sided with the suggestion of the defendant on actual publication numbers but neither went further as to how many might have seen the remarks through other means, such as searching for the defendant.[195] Tugendhat J decided that given the sensationalist nature of the remarks and the fact that the remarks could have been searched and republished, and not just by the defendant's followers, that the actual number of direct followers that Mr Modi had was irrelevant.[196] He continued that the court was entitled to infer that publication in the United Kingdom had been far greater than the estimated figures for those who had received direct tweets from the defendant and that even if the publication in the particular jurisdiction could only be described as insignificant, there remains the possibility and real risk of wider publication[197] and in this instance, despite the fact that the remarks had been removed quickly the claimant could bring proceedings. At a later

[189] Unreported July 26, 2010 (HC).
[190] See generally: <http://www.telegraph.co.uk/technology/facebook/7912731/Law-student-wins-10000-after-being-branded-a-paedophile-on-Facebook.html>.
[191] [2010] EWHC 2859 (QB).
[192] [2012] EWHC 756 (QB) [6].
[193] Ibid. [7].
[194] [2010] EWHC 2859 [20].
[195] Ibid. [19]–[20].
[196] Ibid. [30].
[197] Ibid. [41].

full hearing on the facts Bean J found that Mr Cairns had been defamed and awarded him damages of £90,000.[198]

Subsequent to this in *Cruddas v Adams*,[199] Mr Cruddas, founder and Executive Chairman of CMC Markets and former treasurer of the Conservative Party, raised an action against Mr Adams following a prolonged series of stories and messages via Mr Adams' blogs and Twitter following the 'cash for access scandal'.[200] Mr Cruddas brought the action in regard to 9 blog entries and 12 tweets. Eady J found that Mr Cruddas had been defamed both by the blog entries and by Twitter and awarded damages of £45,000.

The most interesting, and high-profile, Twitter defamation case to date though is *McAlpine v Bercow*.[201] This was a case brought by another former Conservative Party treasurer Lord Robert McAlpine. After retiring from politics Lord McAlpine had settled outside the public eye, but on 4 November 2012 he was incorrectly identified by a large number of Twitter users as being implicated in a child abuse scandal in Wales following a botched *Newsnight* investigation broadcast on the BBC leading the BBC to later pay damages of £185,000 plus costs. It is estimated that over 10,000 Twitter users in the UK tweeted or retweeted messages which were defamatory of the peer. Obviously he could not sue all of them so he took a rather pragmatic approach. He offered to settle with all users who had fewer than 500 followers in return for an apology and a donation to BBC Children in Need.[202] He then chose to pursue actions against a few high-profile individuals. Initially it was reported that 20 high-profile individuals would be sued, including comedian Alan Davies, journalist George Monbiot, and Sally Bercow, the then wife of the Speaker of the House of Commons. Monbiot and Davies apologized and made reparation. Davies agreed to pay £15,000 in damages[203] and Monbiot reaching an interesting settlement where he agreed to do work for three charities over three years to the value of £25,000.[204] Sally Bercow, however, refused to apologize or settle and was the recipient of a writ. Lord McAlpine alleged that her tweet 'Why is Lord McAlpine trending? *innocent face*' was defamatory as 'in their natural and ordinary meaning, and/or in the alternative, by the way of innuendo the Tweet meant that he was a paedophile who was guilty of sexually abusing boys living in care'.[205] In her defence Bercow claimed that her tweet was simply a question—the enquiry as to why Lord McAlpine was trending was 'entirely neutral, and there is nothing else to be inferred from the question. [The] question does not suggest any reason why [Lord McAlpine] was, or might have been, trending. [The] question was as neutral as the statement on the Twitter screen itself which listed

[198] [2012] EWHC 756 (QB) [138].

[199] [2013] EWHC 145 (QB).

[200] 'Tory Peter Cruddas sold access to PM, Sunday Times alleges' (*BBC News*, 25 March 2012) <http://www.bbc.co.uk/news/uk-politics-17501618>.

[201] [2013] EWHC 1342 (QB).

[202] R Greenslade, 'Twitter users should learn lessons from Sally Bercow's libellous tweet' *The Guardian* (London, 24 May 2013) <http://www.theguardian.com/media/greenslade/2013/may/24/twitter-medialaw>.

[203] M Sweney, 'Lord McAlpine settles libel action with Alan Davies over Twitter comment' *The Guardian* (London, 24 October 2013) <http://www.theguardian.com/media/2013/oct/24/lord-mcalpine-libel-alan-davies>.

[204] G Monbiot, 'My Agreement with Lord McAlpine' (*Monbiot*, 12 March 2013) <http://www.monbiot.com/2013/03/12/my-agreement-with-lord-mcalpine/>.

[205] *McAlpine v Bercow* [2013] EWHC 1342 (QB) [33].

the Claimant under the heading "Trends".'[206] The problem Ms Bercow faced was not the question itself it was the addition of the statement *innocent face*, as Counsel for Lord McAlpine pointed out, 'it is not neutral, even to a reader who knew none of the events of the preceding two days. The question is followed by the words "innocent face".'[207] The trial turned on the interpretation of this short phrase. Counsel for Lord McAlpine argued that 'the words "innocent face" are to be read as irony, that is, as meaning the opposite of their literal meaning. People sometimes ask a question to which they already know the answer. They may do that as an indirect way of bringing out into the open something they already know, or believe to be, a fact. They sometimes seek to conceal what they are up to (or pretend to conceal what they are up to) by putting on an expression which suggests that they do not already know the answer to the question. Sir Edward submits that the reasonable explanation for the Defendant inserting the words "innocent face" in the Tweet is to negate a neutral interpretation, and to hint, or nudge readers into understanding that the Claimant has been doing wrong.'[208] Counsel for Ms Bercow though claimed the meaning was quite different: 'the words "innocent face" are to be read literally: that the expression which the reader is being invited to imagine on the Defendant's face in asking the question is "deadpan". It is an expression to convey that she is asking it in a neutral and straightforward manner. She has noticed that the Claimant is trending and all she is asking is that someone should tell her why.'[209] In weighing up the evidence Tugendhat J was not convinced by Ms Bercow's version of events: 'in my judgment the reasonable reader would understand the words "innocent face" as being insincere and ironical. There is no sensible reason for including those words in the Tweet if they are to be taken as meaning that the Defendant simply wants to know the answer to a factual question.'[210] He went on to note, 'the Defendant is telling her followers that she does not know why he is trending, and there is no alternative explanation for why this particular peer was being named in the tweets which produce the Trend, then it is reasonable to infer that he is trending because he fits the description of the unnamed abuser. I find the reader would infer that. The reader would reasonably infer that the Defendant had provided the last piece in the jigsaw.'[211]

With this finding Ms Bercow's defence was pierced and rather than continue to fight the case she agreed to pay damages of an undisclosed amount, reported in some newspapers as being £15,000 and to make an apology in open court. The apology was made on 21 October 2013 and on 22 October 2013 in compliance with the terms of the settlement Ms Bercow communicated this via Twitter. Although the level of damages paid to Lord McAlpine under the settlement was not large Ms Bercow was also liable for his costs as well as her own with many estimates of costs being in the region of £100,000. This case illustrates just how easily a simple throwaway tweet can end up being extremely expensive in the longer term.

[206] Ibid. [34].
[207] Ibid. [67].
[208] Ibid. [68].
[209] Ibid. [75].
[210] Ibid. [84].
[211] Ibid. [85].

8.5 **Conclusions**

As a communications media the internet is an obvious breeding ground for comment which is harmful. In addition several unique characteristics of cyberspace make the publication of defamatory content more likely online than in any other mass media forums. The impression of anonymity that the internet gives affords people the sense of security that encourages the making of reckless statements, some of which may be defamatory. The cross-border nature of the network allows individuals to defame from overseas and to seek the protection of provisions such as the First Amendment to the US Constitution. The internet archives material for later access in a more efficient way than other mass media allowing defamatory statements to be found easily and accessed long after they were originally made. And finally, the encouragement to participate and create found in web 2.0 is turning everyone into a social networker or citizen journalist.

While there is no doubt that overall the freedom of expression afforded to individuals via the internet is a force for good in society, we cannot allow individual reputations to be sullied because of the thoughtless actions of a few. This is the challenge of online defamation. As we have seen throughout this chapter, issues such as the multiple publication rule, international and cross-border publications, and the liability of intermediaries and carriers have all been to the fore. The application of the multiple publication rule in cases such as *Loutchansky* have challenged the usual rules on both the time and place of publication, arguably rendering the limitation period valueless and leading directly to amendments to the law contained in the Defamation Bill. Although later cases such as *Jameel* and *Al Amoudi* have taken steps to rebalance the rights of the competing parties it is clear that internet republication has forced a substantial rethink of what it means to publish a statement.

Further, as often online defamation occurs in anonymity, or may be caused by the actions of an individual domiciled overseas where enforcement may prove difficult, we are likely to see a continuation of the line of cases on intermediary liability which began in the UK with the *Godfrey* case and which most recently may be seen in the *Tamiz* and *Davison* cases. The UK/EU Law arguably strikes a sensible balance here through the safe harbour provisions found in the European law, and until the CJEU looks at this balance we should not assume *Delfi* makes a distinctive change to this position.

Finally, we come to the very topical and growing issue of UGC defamation. The explosion of interest surrounding social networking sites such as Facebook and Twitter have changed the nature of social interaction. Individuals no longer communicate in small groups in pubs, restaurants, or clubs; they now socialize online in large groups. While offline statements tended to stay in the ether for a few seconds before disappearing they are now retained in a publicly accessible forum. The growth of social network defamation is likely to be one of the defining points of information technology law in the next ten years. The *McAlpine* litigation case is unlikely to be the last word on this. This is not necessarily a bad thing. Anything which causes people to show respect and consideration for their fellow users can only be positive.

TEST QUESTIONS

Question 1

In their commentary on the Defamation Bill, the Ministry of Justice noted:

'We do not believe that the current position where each communication of defamatory matter is a separate publication giving rise to a separate cause of action is suitable for the modern internet age.'

Prepare a short response, outlining whether or not you agree with the Ministry and why (or why not).

Question 2

Twitter is a conversation not a publication. You shouldn't be suing people for saying: 'Why is [name] [*innocent face*] trending?' You should be engaging them in conversation to point out what they have said is wrong and why. Only then will your reputation be properly protected while speech is protected and free.

Discuss critically.

FURTHER READING

Books

M Collins, *The Law of Defamation and the Internet* (3rd edn, 2011)

S Levmore and M Nussbaum, *Offensive Internet: Speech, Privacy, and Reputation* (2012)

DJ Solove, *The Future of Reputation: Gossip, Rumor, and Privacy on the Internet* (2008)

Chapters and articles

B Jordan: 'Existing Defamation Law Needs to be Updated so That it is Fit for the Modern Age' *Entertainment Law Review* 41(2010)

D Mangan, 'Regulating for Responsibility: Reputation and Social Media' IRLCT 16 [2015]

J Rowbottom, 'In the Shadow of Big Media: Freedom of Expression, Participation and the Production of Knowledge Online' Public Law 491 [2014]

J Zittrain, 'Be Careful What You Ask For: Reconciling a Global Internet and Local Law' in A Thierer (ed.), *Who Rules the Net?: Internet Governance and Jurisdiction* (2003)

Digital content and intellectual property rights

Intellectual property law as applied to digital goods and services. How laws designed for 'creations of the mind' have been adapted and applied in the digital environment. The challenge of free content vs reward.

11 Copyright in the digital environment

11.1 Linking, caching, and aggregating

11.2 Peer-to-peer networks

11.3 Information and the public domain: the Creative Commons

11.4 Conclusions

12 Databases

12.1 Copyright and the database right

12.2 The database right

12.3 Databases and the information society

12.4 Conclusions

9

Intellectual property rights and the information society

Intellectual property is a subject with a complex and varied history. It can trace its roots back to the late medieval period, but for a long time little interest was shown by the legal profession in this marginal and esoteric subject. It was never taught in the undergraduate LLB syllabus and was rarely seen even at LLM level. Textbooks on intellectual property law were scarce with William Cornish's 1980 text *Intellectual Property* probably the first such book published in the UK. All this was about to change though. With the move from the post-industrial society to the information society, interest in intellectual property and intellectual property rights (or IPRs) exploded. The information society and, more importantly, the information economy, placed value in information rather than in physical goods, industrial processes, or even services. The only body of law which had a relationship with information in its pure form was the long-neglected intellectual property rights and so lawyers and law schools had to reacquaint themselves quickly with this marginalized subject.

It soon became apparent that intellectual property and the information society shared a common root: both dealt with protecting the economic value of intangibles. Nothing in the digital environment can be touched, held, or physically possessed. In nature this makes virtual goods similar in form to intellectual property. The parallels with, in particular, the law of copyright are clear. Copyright is awarded to the expression of an idea, rather than to a thing. But the expression must be recorded in some form for the copyright to take effect. Thus when we think of copyright goods we think of physical items, most commonly books manufactured from paper and binding or music CDs or video DVDs. Of course the physical element of the copyright product is not the part of the product protected by copyright: the book, CD, or DVD is merely a physical carrier for the informational product.[1] The same is true of digital goods in the information society. As we saw in chapter 5, digital goods have no weight or form, and to be possessed we need a carrier media for them, usually in the form of a hard drive or an internet server or else in the form of a flash memory card or old-fashioned CD or DVD. There is therefore a natural synergy between traditional intellectual goods and modern information goods. The character traits they share mean that as the information society was going through its formative phase, intellectual property rights, or IPRs, became the natural interface between the traditional legal world and the developing

[1] See JP Barlow, 'The Economy of Ideas: A Framework for Patents and Copyrights in the Digital Age', *Wired 2.03*, March 1994.

informational society. This interface still plays an important role today with copyright forming the backbone of our system for the protection and exploitation of software as well as forming a focal point for the ongoing debate between the rights of artists and creators to be rewarded in the information society and for individuals to share and distribute content of all types. The law of trademarks still drives domain name disputes and search engine keyword disputes, while new forms of IPRs such as the database right have developed to meet some of the unique challenges of the digital society. This section will examine some of the key relationships between IPRs and the information society, beginning here with a short introduction to IPRs, including a short discussion of their role and history.

9.1 **An introduction to IPRs**

Intellectual property rights (IPRs) are the collective name given to a suite of legal protections, mostly statutory, but some at common law, which seek to protect the creator, author, or inventor of an intangible creation. There are many theories as to the development and role of IPRs in modern society[2] although the most common theme is the protection of the incentive-innovation-reward cycle.[3] This states that innovations or creations which benefit society as a whole should be encouraged and the creator should be rewarded for their creation. As intellectual property is intangible it would be easy for a free-rider to replicate the valuable creation of the original author or inventor without rewarding him or her for their creativity. Thus the author of a book could find unauthorized copies of their book being printed and circulated with no reward to them for their creativity,[4] or the inventor of a new industrial process could find competitors using their invention to compete against them in the marketplace. As intellectual property can be so easily misappropriated without some form of legal protection for these 'fruits of the mind' there would no incentive to create.

IPRs, by protecting the creator/inventor/author, build a cycle of incentive-innovation-reward which benefits society as a whole. The cycle begins by incentivizing creative individuals to spend time indulging their creativity, secure in the knowledge that, should they produce something valuable, they will eventually be rewarded for this. By allowing creative individuals the time to create, they produce something innovative, whether that be an innovation capable of industrial application (an invention) or an innovative cultural product (such as a book, film, or music). Knowing that they are protected by IPRs, that person then publishes or otherwise exploits their innovative output at which point they are rewarded through means such as royalty payments. The financial security this offers allows them to begin the whole process anew at the incentive stage.

[2] See W Cornish, *Intellectual Property: Omnipresent, Distracting, Irrelevant?* (OUP 2004); W Landes and R Posner, *The Economic Structure of Intellectual Property Law* (Belknap 2003); R Blair and T Cotter, *Intellectual Property: Economic and Legal Dimensions of Rights and Remedies* (CUP 2005); R Spinello and H Tavani, *Intellectual Property Rights in a Networked World: Theory and Practice* (Information Science Publishing 2004).

[3] C Waelde et al., *Contemporary Intellectual Property: Law and Policy* (3rd edn, OUP 2013) 9.

[4] This often occurred in nineteenth-century USA which failed to recognize the copyright of other states. This policy was attacked by Charles Dickens in his lecture tour of the US in 1842.

IPRs are an essential part of modern society: they underpin a great number of creative industries including the music and film industries, the computer software and games industries, publishing, dance, theatre and drama, pharmaceuticals, and the computer industry. There are a large variety of IPRs ranging from the three central IPRs (copyright for the original expression of ideas, patents for inventions capable of industrial application, and trademarks for badges or signs capable of distinguishing the operation or product of one business from another) to the newer or less common IPRs including the database right for organized bodies of information, registered and unregistered design rights for industrial and architectural designs, semiconductor topography rights for designs of microchips, and plant variety rights for newly engineered plant varieties. In this text we will focus only on those which have the greatest interaction with informational goods and services: copyright, patents (only in relation to computer software), trademarks, and the database right. In order to provide the backdrop to the chapters which follow there will now follow a short introduction to these four rights.

9.1.1 **Copyright**

Copyright developed in the sixteenth and seventeenth centuries as a response to the rapid growth of movable-type printing presses which facilitated the production and distribution of printed text. We can think of copyright as the first legal response to a challenge of new technology and the development of copyright may be seen to be analogous to the development of legal rules and principles for the information society. Prior to the development of movable-type printing press technology by Johannes Gutenberg in what is now modern-day Germany in the 1440s, the concept of having rights in creative works had never been considered. Creative works were nonrivalrous, meaning that the fruits of the labour of the mind could be shared between many.[5]

The nature of creative works meant that when the concept of exclusive property in land and goods was developed, there was no parallel for works of the mind. Throughout the intellectual highs of the ancient Greek and Roman worlds and the intellectual dark ages which followed, there was no exclusive property in the written or spoken word. During this period creative works were often distributed by travelling storytellers, usually wandering minstrels, who would travel from town to town and engage in singing, acting, storytelling, and comedy. With most citizens unable to read, the minstrel was often the only way for individuals to learn the stories from the scriptures, or to hear news of recent events such as famous victories in battle. The concept of anyone 'owning' such knowledge would have been quite impossible for the average medieval European to imagine.

The printing press changed all this. It industrialized the process of distribution, replacing the scribe or the minstrel with the press and the bookseller. This meant an industry grew up around publishing, a profitable industry in which often the profits went to the publisher and the bookseller, not the author, poet, or playwright.[6] For around 100 years

[5] As famously recounted by Thomas Jefferson in his *Letter to Isaac McPherson*, 13 August 1813, where he notes: 'He who receives an idea from me, receives instruction himself without lessening mine; as he who lights his taper at mine, receives light without darkening me.' Full text at <http://odur.let.rug.nl/~usa/P/tj3/writings/brf/jefl220.htm>.

[6] It is often recorded that William Shakespeare made his fortune through lands he purchased in Stratford-upon-Avon and from performances of his plays. He made little if any money from productions of Folios of his plays.

the publishing industry and the authors who supplied it with its raw materials were in dispute over who had the right to issue copies of works to the general public.[7] This dispute was ended in 1710 when the world's first Copyright Act, the Statute of Anne, came into force. This gave to authors of books, including play texts and poems, a monopoly right to control the publication of copies of their work for a period of 21 years (if the work was already published when the Act came into force) or 14 years (for new works).

The Statute of Anne is the foundation of modern copyright law, which for the UK is to be found in Part I of the Copyright, Designs and Patents Act (CDPA) 1988. Today copyright protects a wide variety of expression. It still protects the written word but now also protects music, dance, theatrical performances, works of art, photographs, sound recordings, films (and video recordings), television and radio broadcasts, and cable programmes. Copyright reaches into almost every aspect of our lives. The most common interactions that people have with copyright on a day-to-day basis are in their use of modern entertainment products. Music is nearly always sold subject to copyright terms. If you buy a CD or download a track from iTunes, you do not own that music. Instead you are awarded a non-exclusive licence to make use of that music. This does not extend to making copies of the music, playing or performing it in public, or selling or distributing further copies. You are given a basic right to listen to the music for your own consumption and usually, in the modern digital distribution model, to make a limited number of copies on MP3 players or similar devices. The same is true of movies or television programmes. You are entitled to watch a television programme or to make a single recording for the purpose of 'time shifting' the broadcast;[8] however, you are not entitled to sell, rebroadcast, or distribute any copy you may make.[9] The other primary point of interaction between the general public and copyright law is in relation to computer software. You are unlikely to own any software on your computer. Again like music and movies, computer software is licensed to the end user. When you first install any new software on your computer you will be asked to agree to an 'end-user licence agreement'. This lists all the terms and conditions of your agreement with the software developer who owns the copyright. Most people never read these agreements, simply clicking on the 'I accept' button. This is not good practice as these contracts are legally enforceable and usually contain a number of clauses which limit the software developer's liability for damage or harm and require the customer to accept and install software updates. Occasionally end-user licence agreements can even be used to justify the installation of spyware or similar potentially harmful software on to your computer.

Today copyright arises automatically and persists for an extensive period. For literary, dramatic, musical, and artistic works, including computer software, this period is the lifetime of the author and for 70 years after his or her death. It is clear this period, designed for traditional literary and artistic works, rather overprotects modern copyright works such as computer software and games, which are unlikely to have a commercial lifespan of more than five years, and with hardware upgrades being constantly

[7] This dispute which mostly gave the 'copy-right' to publishers during the seventeenth century is discussed in detail in A Murray, *The Regulation of Cyberspace: Control in the Online Environment* (Routledge 2007) 169–75. See also R Deazley, *On the Origin of the Right to Copy: Charting the Movement of Copyright Law in Eighteenth Century Britain (1695–1775)* (Hart 2004).

[8] CDPA 1988, s. 70(1).

[9] CDPA 1988, s. 70(2).

developed very few digital devices will survive long enough for original software and games to enter the public domain in a meaningful fashion. Also thanks to international cooperation, a copyright valid in one Berne Convention state will be recognized and enforced in other Berne Convention states,[10] meaning that copyright protection is extensive, almost global. It allows the copyright holder a series of exclusive rights to: (1) copy the work; (2) issue copies of the work to the public; (3) to rent or lend the work to the public; (4) to perform, show, or play the work in public; (5) to communicate the work to the public; and (6) to make an adaptation of the work or do any of the above in relation to an adaptation.[11] Anyone who commits any of these acts without the copyright holder's permission infringes copyright allowing the copyright holder to enforce their copyright and to seek an award of damages. Copyright is therefore a diverse and long-lasting right. Although not seen as a particularly powerful form of protection, its wide range of protection and lack of a record of pre-existing copyrights and copyright holders causes a high degree of tension in the information society, which is a short-term society with emphasis on immediacy and which has a tendency to 'cut and paste' information.

9.1.2 **Patents**

Patents are quite different to copyright in terms of aim, scope, and history. Patents originated as Letters Patent, a letter from a monarch or similar overlord issued to a tradesman offering him a monopoly over a process for a period of time in return for services to the state.

Highlight John of Utynam's patent

The first recorded Letter Patent in England was issued by King Henry VI to John of Utynam in 1449. John was a glazer with a new methodology for producing coloured glass. The King gave John an exclusive grant of use of his methodology in England for a period of 20 years. In payment the King required John to create stained-glass windows for the King's new educational institutions: Eton College and King's College, Cambridge. Under the terms of the letter John had to tutor his assistants in the skills of making coloured glass ensuring that his techniques would become part of the public domain in England once his patent expired.

The idea of Letters Patent was widespread throughout Europe but it is probably Venice which invented the modern patent system when in 1474 it passed a decree that tradesmen who disclosed a new technology would be granted a ten-year monopoly over the use of that technology.[12]

The first formal recognition of a patents system in England, as opposed to individual Letters from the Crown, came in the form of the Statute of Monopolies in 1624. This

[10] The 'Berne Convention' is the Berne Convention for the Protection of Literary and Artistic Works of 1886.

[11] CDPA 1988, s. 16(1).

[12] Waelde et al. (n. 3) 364.

provided that patents would only be available to 'the true and first inventor' of processes and for a period of not more than 14 years.[13] This is the foundation of the modern patent system but it left the award of Letters Patent to the discretion of the Crown; it was only in the nineteenth century that the modern system of patent law and procedure developed when in 1852 the Patent Office was established and with it a process for the examination of patent applications and the issuing of a UK patent.

The history of patents is therefore longer and more chequered than the history of copyright. Although Letters Patent predate Copy Rights, the modern system of copyright became established in the eighteenth century, whereas modern patent law owes much to nineteenth-century developments. This probably owes much to the technological drivers behind the two systems. Copyright became industrialized with the development of the movable-type printing press in the 1440s whereas patents had to await the industrial revolution driven by the invention of the Boulton and Watt Steam Engine in the 1770s to become industrialized. This emphasizes the close historical relationship between IPRs and technology.

Modern UK Patent Law is to be found mostly in the Patents Acts 1977 and 2004, with the 1977 Act containing the bulk of the rules on patentability and enforcement. Strangely, the Act does not define an invention, merely defining the scope of protection offered to an invention.[14] Instead, the Act characterizes how an invention may be recognized by setting out a test for patentability.[15]

Highlight Test for patentability

An invention must:

(a) be new (usually referred to as novel)

(b) involve an inventive step

(c) be capable of industrial application

(d) not be found within the list of excluded matter.

The list of excluded matter is extremely important as within this list we find 'a scheme, rule or method for performing a mental act, playing a game or doing business, or a program for a computer'.[16] This represents a long-standing principle that one should not be able to gain a monopoly over an intellectual or business process. The addition of computer software to this category suggests that a computer program is viewed primarily as a method of conducting business or perhaps as a substitute for a mental process and as a result steps are taken to exclude software from patentability.[17] In addition, it

[13] Statute of Monopolies 1624, s. 6.

[14] Patents Act 1977, s. 125(1).

[15] Patents Act 1977, s. 1(1). For further discussion on the nature of patentability see Waelde et al. (n. 3) 404–64.

[16] Patents Act 1977, s. 1(2)(c).

[17] It should be noted that the framers of the Patents Act 1977 were bound to implement this exclusion as there was a similar exclusion in the European Patent Convention of 1973 to which the UK was a signatory.

should be noted that material which is capable of protection by copyright is generally excluded from patentability[18] and, as we have already seen, the Copyright, Designs and Patents Act 1988 treats software as a literary work.[19] Thus on two principles, one a direct exclusionary principle, the other an indirect exclusionary principle, software is not to be treated as a patentable invention. As we shall see in chapter 10 the application of this principle is not as simple as one might expect.

Should your invention clear all these hurdles you will be granted a patent after a lengthy examination of your patent application, including publication of the application to allow for public scrutiny of it. A patent is awarded for a maximum period of 20 years, although you will need to pay a renewal fee annually after the first 5 years of the patent's life. Unlike copyright, patents do not arise automatically; they must be registered, and unlike copyright patents are not automatically of international effect. A patent application is only valid in the state in which it is made, and claims often seen on consumer items that a 'worldwide patent [is] applied for' are inaccurate. A multinational patent application may be made under the Patent Cooperation Treaty which allows a single application to be made in a PCT signatory state and undergo a single examination before being passed to other PCT patent offices for local registration. Multinational patent applications are very lengthy, complex, and expensive and thus in many ways we can see patents as the antitheses of copyright: they are a strong and effective monopoly right, but are limited both temporally and geographically, with multinational patents usually only preferred for inventions of a high degree of economic potential.

9.1.3 **Trademarks**

Trademarks are a more contemporary creation.[20] Like the modern patents system they may be seen to be the fruit of the Industrial Revolution. Trademarks have their roots in the common law of 'passing off', a claim in tort which first appeared in the early nineteenth century.[21] Passing off allowed, and indeed allows, a business enterprise to protect the goodwill it has established in its trading name or brand identity to raise an action in tort against anyone who damages that goodwill by causing the public to confuse their brand, product, or service with that of the claimant.[22] The three essential elements of a passing off claim were, and remain: (1) the establishment that the claimant has goodwill in the name, brand, or identity in question; (2) that there has been a misrepresentation (by the defendant); and (3) that misrepresentation has caused damage to the claimant's goodwill.[23]

The problem with relying on the tortious claim was that the claimant always had to first establish goodwill. It would be much easier if the claimant could instead rely upon some form of presumption. This, along with the growing internationalization of trade

[18] Patents Act 1977, s. 1(2)(b).

[19] CDPA 1988, s. 3(1)(b).

[20] Although we are discussing trademarks here as a form of IPR, the major analysis of trademarks and the information society takes place herein in Part V, E-commerce, at chs. 16–17.

[21] See C Wadlow, *The Law of Passing Off* (4th rev edn, Sweet and Maxwell 2011); H Carty, *An Analysis of the Economic Torts* (2nd edn, OUP 2010).

[22] See *Perry v Truefitt* (1842) 6 Beav 66.

[23] See *Erven Warnink BV v J Townend & Sons* [1979] AC 731; *Reckitt & Coleman Products v Borden, Inc.* [1990] 1 All ER 873.

in the late nineteenth century,[24] led to the Trade Marks Registration Act 1875. This created a domestic register of trademarks allowing businesses to protect their brand or identity without the need to establish goodwill during a passing-off claim. Unlike patents, or even copyright, trademarks are protected for a potentially unlimited term. Provided the mark remains in use and the trademark holder renews their registration periodically the mark may be retained in perpetuity.[25]

The modern law of trademarks is to be found in the Trade Marks Act 1994. This provides that 'any sign capable of being represented graphically which is capable of distinguishing goods or services of one undertaking from those of other undertakings' may be registered as a trademark.[26] Once registered, the mark must be renewed every ten years.[27] The Act protects the trademark holder against a variety of threats, including piracy (the use in the course of trade of a mark or sign which is *identical* to the trademark and is used in relation to goods or services similar to those for which the trademark is registered); unfair competition (the use of a sign which is similar to the trademark and used in relation to goods or services identical with or *similar* to those for which the trademark is registered and there is a likelihood of confusion); and misappropriation (the use of a 'famous mark', being a trademark which has a 'reputation' in the UK in a manner which without due cause takes unfair advantage of, or is detrimental to, the distinctive character or the repute of the trademark).[28]

Internationally, trademark protection functions similarly to patent protection. There is no global or even international trademark.[29] Trademarks, like patents, are awarded by domestic trademark registries and are limited in effectiveness to the jurisdictional reach of the office which registered the mark. Like patents, there is a procedure to seek a basket of international trademarks through a cooperation procedure. This procedure is the Madrid system, which was created under the Madrid Agreement Concerning the International Registration of Marks of 1891. Under the Madrid system a trademark owner can apply to have their trademark protected in several countries simultaneously by filing a single application with their domestic trademark office and electing to have this application forwarded to any number of Madrid protocol nations.[30] A trademark so registered is equivalent to an application, or a registration of the same mark, effected directly in each of the countries designated by the applicant. If the trademark office of a designated country does not refuse protection within one year, the protection of the mark is the same as if it had been originally registered with that office. The Madrid

[24] Waelde et al. (n. 3) 546–8.

[25] It should be noted that UK Trade Mark No. 1 registered on 1 January 1876 (the first day of operation of the new register) by Bass Breweries is still in operation and use. It may be viewed at: <http://www.ipo.gov.uk/tmcase/Results/1/UK00000000001>.

[26] TMA 1994, ss. 1(1), 40(1).

[27] TMA 1994, ss. 42, 43.

[28] TMA 1994, s. 10.

[29] There is though a community trademark which has effect throughout EU member states and is managed by the Office for Harmonization in the Internal Market (Trade Marks and Designs) (OHIM), which is located in Alicante, Spain. This is similar to the European Patent which is administered by the European Patent Office in Munich, the main distinction between the two being that the European Patent Office is not an EU body but a treaty body created by the European Patent Convention of 1973.

[30] On 7 December 2015 there were 97 Madrid protocol signatories including the EU, the UK, and the US. A full list may be accessed at <http://www.wipo.int/export/sites/www/treaties/en/documents/pdf/madrid_marks.pdf>.

system and the PCT system are very similar and, as with the PCT system, Madrid applications are lengthier, more complex, and more expensive than a domestic application and tend to be preferred for trademarks with a high degree of economic potential.

9.1.4 **The database right**

Compared to these three traditional IPRs, the database right is a modern development. The database right came into effect following the promulgation of the Database Directive of 1996.[31] The database right, more properly known as the *sui generis* database right to distinguish it from copyright protection of databases, was brought in to meet the challenge of protecting increasingly valuable databases of information which may not qualify for copyright protection.

The information economy places considerable value in databases: everything from customer contact databases to direct marketing databases, to databases of customer shopping habits. Although commercially valuable it was not clear that the contents of a database were protected. If a company were to obtain a copy of a competitor's database and were to make use of it for their own commercial gain it was not clear if there would be an action open to the original owner of the database. In some EU states, most notably the UK, there was a suggestion that the contents of a database would be protected by copyright law. This is because the UK has a famously low standard of originality requirement for copyright protection of compilations of data.[32] In other states, notably France and Germany, the law of copyright clearly would not protect databases. This divide started to affect the market for database industries with most EU-based database industries deciding to base themselves in the UK. To harmonize the law, and to allow for a free market in the database industry, the Directive was passed.

The Directive provides for two different forms of database protection. Copyright protection is available where in creating the database the designer of the database displays a high level of skill or originality. This standard is found in the Copyright, Designs and Patents Act which states that copyright protection for databases is available when 'by reason of the selection or arrangement of the contents of the database the database constitutes the author's own intellectual creation'.[33] A database which fails to meet this higher standard will be protected by the *sui generis* database right. This protects the contents of a database for a period of 15 years from the end of the calendar year in which the making of the database was completed.[34] The protection of the database right is afforded to the maker of the database: that is, the person 'who takes the initiative in obtaining, verifying or presenting the contents of a database and assumes the risk of investing in that obtaining, verification or presentation'.[35] One peculiarity of the database right is that by reg. 17(3):

> Any substantial change to the contents of a database, including a substantial change resulting from the accumulation of successive additions, deletions or alterations, which would result in

[31] Dir. 96/9/EC.

[32] See *Ladbroke (Football) Ltd v William Hill (Football) Ltd* [1964] 1 WLR 273 (HL); *Independent Television Publications Ltd v Time Out Ltd* [1984] FSR 64.

[33] CDPA, s. 3A(2), giving effect to Art. 3(1) of the Database Directive.

[34] The Copyright and Rights in Databases Regulations 1997 (SI 1997/3032), reg. 17(1).

[35] Reg. 14(1).

the database being considered to be a substantial new investment shall qualify the database resulting from that investment for its own term of protection.[36]

This means that a continually updated database may qualify for permanent protection as at some point during the 15 years of its original protection the accumulation of changes and amendments made to the database will cause it to qualify for a new, and further, period of protection. The *sui generis* database right protects the maker of the database from unauthorized extraction or re-utilization of all or a substantial part of the contents of the database.[37] This suggests a level of protection somewhat less than that available at copyright law meaning the *sui generis* database right is rather weak. One advantage offered by the database right is that, like copyright, it requires no registration or recording by a public office to be of effect. Like copyright law it arises automatically and will be recognized by all states which recognize the database right, in effect all 28 EU states.

9.2 **IPRs and digitization**

As with all other areas of the law, the way we think about and deploy IPRs is being challenged by the information society and the process of digitization. However, the interaction between IPRs and the developing discipline of cyberlaw is rather different to most other areas of law. At this point in this book we have examined the difficulties that traditional (physical) property law as well as principles of free expression and defamation have had in adapting to the information society. Further on we will look at how criminal law and commercial law are similarly finding the information society to be a challenge but IPRs, founded in the fires of technological developments past, and characterized as the focal point between legal controls and intangible (informational) products and services, are flourishing in the information society. The story of this part of the book is less about the need for the traditional legal rules to develop and evolve to meet the challenges of the information society, but more questioning as to whether the widespread adoption of traditional intangible property principles, as found in IPRs, are beneficial to the development of the information society.

It has become common to think of information technology law, or cyberlaw, as applied intellectual property law. Courses in information technology law at both undergraduate and postgraduate level in UK universities tend to devote a large proportion of their time to dealing with the IP/IT interface, looking at copyright in software; patents for software and business methods; trademarks for domain names and search terms; and the database right and copyright in cyberspace, including hypertext linking, deep linking, framing, and misappropriation of copyright material. Governments and intergovernmental organizations have also spent a considerable amount of time looking at these issues and the rump of decided cases in cyberlaw subjects are concerned with the application of IPRs in the digital environment. To observe all these is not to criticize. It is to be expected that when something becomes economically valuable there will be a move to 'enclose' it using property rights. With digital properties, as we saw in

[36] Reg. 17(3).
[37] Reg. 16(1).

chapter 5, it was difficult to extend traditional property models and so all parties with an interest turned to the models at hand to protect intangible property which were IPRs. But as cyberlaw continues to evolve and develop as a cognate discipline, critics are now challenging what many perceive as an over-reliance on models developed for another age and for different challenges in dealing with the information economy and the information society.

Chief among these critics is Professor Lawrence Lessig who has campaigned tirelessly against what he sees as the misapplication of copyright law to create what he calls a 'second enclosure movement' in cyberspace.[38] Professor Lessig believes so passionately in this cause that he, along with like-minded individuals, founded the Creative Commons movement in 2001 to allow individuals the option of permitting certain uses of their creative works including music, video, and photographs, rather than the 'all rights reserved' approach found in copyright law. This system, which Lessig branded 'some rights reserved' has proven to be extremely successful with in excess of 400 million works making use of Creative Commons licences.[39] It is not only copyright law which has attracted criticism in the digital environment. All of our four key IPRs have been the subject of criticism for overprotecting content or systems in the information society. Many commentators have critiqued the US Patent and Trademark Office for awarding patents for software and for business methods which have overprotected the patentee and have chilled innovation,[40] while the heavy-handed approach taken by trademark owners when dealing with individuals who register domain names which are similar to their pre-existing trademark or which use their trademark in a domain name as a means of operating a legitimate complaint site (so called 'sucks' sites)[41] have also been critiqued.[42]

What is clear is that there is a tension between what citizens of the information society want and expect: liberty, free use of content, and unfettered free expression; and what the intellectual property industry is seeking: protection, control over use and abuse, and reward. This tension is not unlike that seen in chapter 6 between those individuals who argue speech should be free and those who argue that in the interests of society it is necessary to place limits on free expression. It is clear that, if the information society is to function, a balance must be struck between the interests of IPR holders and the interests of the rest of us to 'rip, mix, and burn' digital content.

TEST QUESTIONS

Question 1

Describe which forms of intellectual property right are applied in the information society and how and to what they are applied.

[38] L Lessig, *Free Culture: How Big Media Uses Technology and the Law to Lock Down Culture and Control Creativity* (Penguin 2004).

[39] Creative Commons stopped updating their data in 2010 at which point there were 400 million works. Based on exponential growth this is likely to be in excess of 1 billion works today but we have no up-to-date data.

[40] K Blind, J Edler, and M Friedwald, *Software Patents: Economic Impacts and Policy Implications* (Edward Elgar 2005).

[41] e.g. <http://www.ryanairsucks.com> or <http://www.bmwsucks.com>.

[42] M Mueller, *Ruling the Root: Internet Governance and the Taming of Cyberspace* (MIT Press 2002).

Question 2

Do intellectual property rights need to adapt to the information society?

FURTHER READING

Books

W Cornish, *Intellectual Property: Omnipresent, Distracting, Irrelevant?* (2004)

S Stokes, *Digital Copyright: Law and Practice* (2014)

C Waelde, G Laurie, A Brown, S Kheria, and J Cornwell, *Contemporary Intellectual Property: Law and Policy* (3rd edn, 2013)

Chapters and articles

JP Barlow, 'The Economy of Ideas: Selling Wine Without Bottles on the Global Net', *Wired 2.03*, March 1994

L Lessig, 'Intellectual Property and Code', 11 *St John's Journal of Legal Commentary* 635 (1996)

L Lessig, 'The International Information Society', 24 *Loyola of Los Angeles Entertainment Law Review* 33 (2004)

10 Software

10.1 **Protecting software: history**

The information society is founded upon the symbiotic relationship between hardware devices and the software which operates these devices. Digital hardware cannot function without software, while software, without hardware to implement its commands, is merely a series of ones and zeros recorded on a storage device. As hardware without software was valueless, computer hardware was originally supplied with software pre-installed and maintained by the hardware manufacturer. Thus if you bought or—more likely, given the prohibitive cost—leased an early IBM mainframe computer such as the IBM 1401, the machine would be supplied complete with software, much in the same way an e-reader is sold today.[1] There was no competitive market for the supply of computer software and as a result no software industry or interest in the ownership of IPRs in software. This changed as the 1960s drew to a close. IBM's success in the computer markets of the 1960s led the US Department of Justice to inquire whether IBM was committing antitrust violations both by leasing rather than selling mainframe computers and by selling hardware and software as a 'bundled' single product. As a response to these investigations and in an attempt to head off an antitrust suit IBM announced on 23 June 1969, that it would unbundle much of its software and would price and license that software separately from its hardware and support services. From this date on, separate markets for computer hardware and computer software existed. Software was now a stand-alone product which would require legal protection in the marketplace lest any unscrupulous individual attempt to free-ride on the investment of another.

Almost immediately the legal profession became interested in the newly developing market in computer software. There were early questions as to how software should be protected. Should it be by the application of patent law or by the law of copyright or should it be a *sui generis* form of protection? Again, as in many areas involving the interface of law and the information society, early jurisprudence on this subject is to be found in the US. In 1972 in the case of *Gottschalk v Benson*,[2] the US Supreme Court ruled that a process which converted binary-coded decimal numbers into true binary

[1] A typical IBM 1401 system would have cost about $370,000 if purchased outright in 1961 (the year of its launch). This is the equivalent of around $2,930,000 at 2015 values. To lease an IBM 1401 cost $2,000 per month or $15,800 per month at 2015 values.

[2] *Gottschalk, Commissioner of Patents v Benson & Ors*, 409 US 63 (1972).

numbers (a process valuable in software development) was not patentable. Justice Douglas in giving the opinion of the court said that this decision should not be seen to deny patentability to all software, and noted that 'It may be that the patent laws should be extended to cover these programs' but that this was 'a policy matter to which we are not competent to speak'.[3] The court revisited this issue only six years later in the case of *Parker v Flook*.[4] Here the court found that the addition of a new software-based system to calculate safety limits in a catalytic conversion process was insufficient to qualify the process as a whole for patent protection, the only novelty being in the software design.

The failure of the fledgling software industry to convince the Supreme Court, or the prior President's Commission on the Patent System,[5] that patents should be extended to software, led to the industry seeking protection elsewhere. Almost as soon as IBM had unbundled its software development arm, Elmer Galbi, a consultant with IBM, had suggested the need for a *sui generis* form of legal protection for computer software based on modification of the patent system.[6] This idea received limited support from the Supreme Court, and led to Congressman Hamilton Fish Jr introducing a Bill which would enshrine *sui generis* software protection in the US Code.[7] The Bill was unfortunately seriously flawed and opponents claimed it was too heavily influenced by proposals emanating from IBM, which risked extending IBM's near-monopoly of the software industry. The Bill was therefore allowed to lapse and while the anti-protectionist movement continued to find success in cases such as *Gottschalk* and *Flook* they saw there was little need to make changes to the law as it stood.

The economic reality though was that, unless some formal system of protection for computer software could be found, the fledgling software industry was under threat. With software patents at this point being rejected by the judiciary and the executive, and with no realistic prospect of an agreed approach to *sui generis* protection, it appeared that copyright offered the only realistic alternative. Copyright expansion was the preferred route of the World Intellectual Property Organization and offered several apparent advantages. First, as copyright law does not require prior registration to be effective the expansion of copyright to software would not increase the administrative burden of patents offices. Second, as copyright is a 'soft' protection, with only a broad requirement of originality required to gain copyright protection and no need to establish inventiveness or a development on the prior art, there was no need to establish a database of prior art for software. Further, as software, when written as source code, looks like written text it seemed apt to extend copyright, as the natural form of protection for literary works, to software.

[3] Ibid. 66.

[4] 437 US 584 (1978).

[5] Report of the President's Commission on the Patent System, *To Promote the Progress of Useful Arts*, S. Doc No. 5, 90th Cong., 1st Sess. (1967).

[6] E Galbi, 'Proposal for New Legislation to Protect Computer Programming' (1970) 17 *Journal of the Copyright Society* 280; E Galbi, 'Software and Patents: A Status Report' (1971) 14 *Communications of the ACM* 274.

[7] See R Stern, *Computer Law: Intellectual Property Rights in Computer-Related Subject Matter Cases and Materials* (George Washington Law School 1997) ch. 13 <http://docs.law.gwu.edu/facweb/claw/ch-13.htm>.

The US introduced a new Copyright Act in 1976 and in this it was made clear that Congress intended to extend copyright protection to software.[8] What was not clear though was how much protection computer programs should be given and whether there should be special exceptions to the exclusive rights of the copyright owners, as with some other types of literary works. Because Congress didn't want to delay the passage of the Act, it appointed the National Commission on New Technological Uses of Copyrighted Works to report back about computer programs and other new technologies and put a placeholder provision in the Act.[9] The Commission reported back in July 1978. Its main recommendation was that a new definition be added to §101 of the Copyright Act to the effect that: 'a computer program is a set of statements or instructions to be used directly or indirectly in a computer in order to bring about a certain result'. This would fully extend copyright protection to software by affording them the status of 'a literary work'. As this required a change in the law Congress had to pass an amendment to the Copyright Act, and so it came to pass on 12 December 1980 that the US became the first country formally to extend copyright law to computer programs.

Meanwhile the UK had also been considering how to protect computer software. There had been discussions similar to those seen across the Atlantic and the prevailing view was that the listing of the source code of a computer program in a printout would protect that code as a literary work.[10] This assumption was tested in a number of interim hearings, such as *Sega Enterprises v Richards*.[11] This case involved the early computer game *Frogger*. Mr Richards was alleged to have copied elements of the *Frogger* source code to produce his own copy of the *Frogger* game system which he then sold in competition to Sega. Mr Richards admitted he copied elements of Sega's code; the only question was whether Sega had copyright protection in their source code. The court examined this question and found that:

> copyright under the provisions relating to literary works in the Copyright Act of 1956 subsists in the assembly code program . . . the machine code program derived from it by the operation of the part of the system of the computer called the assembler is to be regarded . . . as either a reproduction or an adaptation of the assembly code program, and accordingly, for the purposes of deciding this motion . . . copyright does subsist in the program.[12]

This decision, although the result of only an interim hearing, is exactly what commentators had predicted. The 1956 Copyright Act was sufficiently flexible to protect software without the need for expensive amendment as the US had done.

[8] The definition of literary works found in §101 of the 1976 Act states that they are 'works, other than audiovisual works, expressed in words, numbers, or other verbal or numerical symbols or indicia, regardless of the nature of the material objects, such as books, periodicals, manuscripts, phonorecords, film, tapes, disks, or cards, in which they are embodied'.

[9] §117 was the placeholder provision. It stated: 'Notwithstanding the provisions of sections 106 through 116 and 118, this title does not afford the owner of copyright in a work any greater or lesser rights with respect to the use of the work in conjunction with automatic systems capable of storing, processing, retrieving, or transferring information, or in conjunction with any similar device, machine, or process, than those afforded to works under the law, whether title 17 or the common law or statutes of a State, in effect on December 31, 1977, as held applicable and construed by a court in an action brought under this title.'

[10] D Bainbridge, *Information Technology and Intellectual Property Law* (6th rev. edn, Bloomsbury, 2014),71–5.

[11] [1983] FSR 73.

[12] Ibid. 75. Nowadays we would tend to refer to the 'assembly code' as the source code.

Despite the limited success of the now well-established software industry in cases such as *Richards*, the industry remained nervous. None of the early cases in the UK had gone to a full hearing. Usually when the industry won an interim decision the defendant would settle and would move on to a new project. This was the time when computer games and even business software could be written at home as a hobby and if one project fizzled out another was always just around the corner. Then a case in Australia changed things quite dramatically. The case was *Apple Computers, Inc. v Computer Edge Pty Ltd* and the decision of the Federal Court for New South Wales was exactly what the software industry had feared.[13]

Case study *Apple Computers, Inc. v Computer Edge Pty Ltd*

The defendants were importing computers from Taiwan which copied the design of the Apple II minicomputer. They were selling the machines under the name 'Wombat' and claimed the machines had no Apple software installed.

This claim was found to be false when the claimants proved that programs installed on three silicon chips found within the Wombat's hardware contained within them the names of several Apple programmers. The defendants argued that the code contained on the chips was not protected by the Australian Copyright Act 1968.

It fell to Beaumont J to decide the case. He found that none of the programs are literary works within the meaning of the statute, stating: 'in my view, a literary work for this purpose is something which was intended to afford "either information or instruction or pleasure in the form of literary enjoyment" [whereas] the function of a computer programme is to control the sequence of operations carried out by a computer'. He went on to add that should copyright require to be extended to software this was a decision for the legislature not the judiciary.

Although the decision of Beaumont J was quickly overruled by the Appeal Court,[14] the damage was done. The first common law case on software copyright, outside the US, to go to a full hearing had found that copyright law did not automatically cover computer software. In panic, legislatures across the globe moved to place their now economically significant copyright industries on a sound legal footing, as the US had done in 1980. The Federal Australian Government passed the Copyright Amendment Act 1984 and in the UK the Copyright (Computer Software) Amendment Act 1985 finally and formally brought computer software within the protection afforded to a literary work under the Copyright Act 1956.

10.2 **Copyright in computer software**

10.2.1 **Obtaining copyright protection**

The current position UK law holds in relation to copyright for computer software is to be found in the Copyright, Designs and Patents Act 1988 (CDPA), as amended. The key provision is s. 3(1)(b) which states that '"literary work" means any work, other than a

[13] *Apple Computers Inc. v Computer Edge Pty Ltd* [1983] FCA 328.
[14] *Apple Computers Inc. v Computer Edge Pty Ltd* [1984] FSR 481.

dramatic or musical work, which is written, spoken or sung, and accordingly includes a computer program'. This means that all the general principles of copyright law developed with respect to literary works over the centuries now apply equally to software: including the requirements for the subsistence of copyright protection and the protection afforded by copyright. To gain copyright protection software is required to fulfil the subsistence requirements of a literary work: namely, that it is original,[15] it has been 'recorded',[16] and that it qualifies for protection in the UK.[17]

Originality is in UK law quite a low threshold test which essentially requires that the author of the work has not copied (plagiarized) the work or elements of the work from others. The classic test of originality is drawn from the case of *University of London Press Ltd v University Tutorial Press Ltd.*[18] This case involved exam papers written by academics for the University of London. The question was, were exam questions sufficiently original to allow copyright law to protect them as literary works? Peterson J considered that 'The originality which is required relates to the expression of the thought . . . the Act does not require that the expression must be in an original or novel form, but that the work must not be copied from another work—that it should originate from the author.'[19] This extremely low originality threshold is often disparagingly called the 'sweat of the brow' standard: the author need not show literary originality, only that he or she expended effort on the creation of the work and that the work is not plagiarized from another source. UK courts continue to apply the test, properly called skill, labour, and judgement. In the infamous case of *Ladbroke (Football) Ltd v William Hill (Football) Ltd*,[20] the selection of a number of scheduled football matches for inclusion on a football pools coupon was found to qualify as a literary work due to the degree of skill, judgement, and labour necessary to select the correct combination of matches to allow the best selection for the customer and the bookmaker. There is therefore little doubt that computer software which is not copied or plagiarized from another source will be sufficiently original for copyright protection to subsist. This will apply whatever form the software comes in as the Act does not distinguish between software in higher-level source code or machine-readable object code. This is deliberate and designed to prevent a repeat of the *Apple Computers, Inc. v Computer Edge Pty Ltd* decision, and is also designed to 'future-proof' the Act against any developments in software design and engineering.

The UK is unusual in applying a skill, labour, and judgement standard. Most states apply a more stringent standard which requires an intellectual contribution from the author. This can be problematic when dealing with software design, in particular the design of operating systems or business software which are required to follow narrow design protocols to ensure interoperability and stability. This distinction between the UK standard and the higher Continental *droit d'auteur* standard could have fragmented the European software industry, with greater protection being found in the UK than in Continental Europe. The risk of this was highlighted in 1985 when a German court

15 CDPA 1988, s. 1(1).
16 Ibid. s. 3(2).
17 Ibid. s. 1(3).
18 [1916] 2 Ch 601.
19 Ibid. 608–9.
20 [1964] 1 WLR 273.

found that to be protected by copyright, a computer program must result from individual creative achievement exceeding the average skills displayed in the development of computer programs.[21] This meant a program which automated or replicated an existing process with no special design or technique could not be afforded copyright protection. Fortunately the Software Directive harmonized the originality standard.[22] By Art. 1(3) 'a computer program shall be protected if it is original in the sense that it is the author's own intellectual creation. No other criteria shall be applied to determine its eligibility for protection.' Thus, when looking specifically at the originality threshold for software the skill, labour, and judgement standard is exported throughout Continental Europe. The effectiveness of Art. 1(3) was confirmed in the post-Directive German case of *Buchhaltungsprogram*,[23] where the Federal Supreme Court of Germany declined to follow *Sudwestdeutsche Inkasso* and instead applied a lower standard of originality based upon Art. 1(3). There appears little doubt therefore that following the enactment of Art. 1(3) the originality threshold is easily met throughout the EU: to qualify the software must simply be original, in that it was created by the author and was not copied or plagiarized from another source.

The second requirement for copyright protection to arise is that the software must be 'recorded, in writing or otherwise'.[24] To be distributable software must be recorded: thus the very act of making software will usually fulfil this requirement. However, the manner in which software is recorded is unusual. Software will usually be distributed as encoded binary data (a series of zeros and ones) either stored magnetically (on a HDD) or electrical charges held on surface-mounted chips on a circuit board (flash or solid state storage) or even as a series of electrical or optical pulses carried across telecommunications networks (as a download). The obvious question is whether a series of binary representations encoded in this fashion qualifies as being 'recorded, in writing or otherwise'. Section 178 of the CDPA assists slightly by giving a broad definition of 'writing' as 'includ[ing] any form of notation or code, whether by hand or otherwise and regardless of the method by which, or medium in or on which, it is recorded'. Although not definitive, the broad definition of writing given in s. 178 suggests that the courts would have little difficulty in applying this definition to any of the forms of distribution discussed above. In fact there seems little question that even temporary copies of a software file or instruction are sufficient to meet the recording threshold as under s. 17(6) copyright may be infringed by 'the making of copies which are transient'. To state an infringing copy may be transient, is at least strongly indicative that the original may be equally transient.[25]

The final requirement for copyright protection is that the work in question must qualify for protection under the CDPA; this is a requirement of domicile. The copyright holder is required to demonstrate that UK copyright law, as opposed to the copyright law of

[21] *Sudwestdeutsche Inkasso KG v Bappert and Burker Computer Gmb H* (1985) Case 52/83, BGHZ 94, 276.

[22] Dir. 91/250/EEC.

[23] *Buchhaltungsprogram*, unreported BGH, 14 July 1993.

[24] CDPA 1988, s. 3(2).

[25] In truth the requirement of recording is as much a requirement of evidence as copyright law. We require fixing of copyright materials in a recorded form so that, should an infringement claim arise, the court has a fixed record of the original work with which it can compare the allegedly infringing copy. Thus something which was fixed transiently could establish copyright, provided some archive of the event was kept which could be presented to the court.

another state should be applied. There are a number of ways a literary work, including software, can qualify for protection under the CDPA. By s. 153, if the author is a British citizen, a citizen of a British overseas territory, was a domiciled British resident at the time the software was made, or is a UK-registered company, then any work they produce is eligible for UK copyright protection. Alternatively if the author falls into none of these categories then, if the software was first published in the UK, it qualifies for UK protection.

It should be noted though that even software which does not meet these strict criteria can qualify for protection in the UK. By s. 155(3) first publication overseas shall not preclude the author from being able to claim 'simultaneous publication' in the UK where the work is published in the UK within 30 days of the original publication. Despite those extremely generous provisions many reading this may assume that the requirement of a UK connection for the work may rule many software products out of UK copyright protection. If we take a computer game for example, like the well-known *Call of Duty* series, these are 'authored' by a company called Infinity Ward located in Encino, California and published by Activision, a company based in Santa Monica, California. Should Activision choose to release the next *Call of Duty* game in the US on a date more than 30 days prior to its UK publication date, it does not qualify for UK copyright protection as the author does not meet the residency requirement and the work does not meet the publication requirement. This would suggest the game was not protected in the UK and would be open to all manner of infringing acts including the making and distributing of illegal (pirate) copies. This, obviously, is not the case as such a rule would affect not only software but movies, music, and works of literature. The truth is that once the work qualifies for US copyright protection, under the terms of the Berne Convention,[26] the UK agrees to extend copyright protection to that work as if it were a UK copyright work.[27] The Convention provides a truly global copyright protection with 168 signatories each recognizing the copyright of all the others.[28] Thus once you obtain copyright in any one of the Berne signatory states you are automatically protected in all 168. It is therefore almost impossible to imagine that a software work would not be protected in the UK on grounds of qualification.

10.2.2 **The scope of copyright protection**

Once copyright protection has been obtained in an original piece of software, what rights does this confer on the copyright holder?[29] As a literary work software qualifies for the same protection as books, movies, or music. This affords the copyright owner six 'restricted acts', actions that only the copyright holder may legally carry out or may permit others to carry out.

[26] Berne Convention for the Protection of Literary and Artistic Works 1886.

[27] Ibid. Art. 5(1).

[28] A full list of the UK's bilateral obligations under the Convention may be found in the Schedule to the Copyright and Performances (Application to Other Countries) Order 2008, SI 2008/677.

[29] It should be noted that the copyright owner may be a different person from the author. This is particularly important when dealing with computer software which may be created by a collaborative effort of many hundred programmers. Under s. 11(2) where a literary, dramatic, musical, or artistic work is made by an employee in the course of his employment, his employer is the first owner of any copyright in the work subject to any agreement to the contrary. Thus although Microsoft may have had several hundred programmers all acting as co-authors on the Windows 10 project the copyright holder will be Microsoft Corp.

Highlight The six restricted acts

1. to make copies of the work[30]
2. to issue copies of the work to the public[31]
3. to rent or lend the work to the public[32]
4. to perform, show or play the work in public[33]
5. to communicate the work to the public[34]
6. to make an adaptation of the work or do any of the above in relation to an adaptation.[35]

These acts all have specific meaning both within the CDPA, and within the broader scope of copyright law. By s. 17(2), copying is defined as 'reproducing the work in any material form'. This extends beyond making complete (or literal) copies of the work and may include copying the structure or plot of a play or story or the use of characters created by another.[36] This is particularly common with computer software as the value of the software is in the structure of the software and what it does rather than in the source or object code which is never usually seen by the consumer. Thus, a software designer may study the structure of an original piece of software—say, an original computer game such as Team 17's *Worms*—and then by copying the gaming engine and underlying protocols produce a competing game such as *Snails*, a variant on the worms theme produced for mobile phones. As *Snails* will not share any of the original code with *Worms* there can be no question of literal copying. Instead in cases of 'non-literal copying' the question becomes whether the latter piece of software has copied these elements of the original which are afforded protection.[37] As a result, much of the case law discussed in the following section will focus on non-literal infringement.[38]

[30] CDPA 1988, ss. 16(1)(a), 17.

[31] Ibid. ss. 16(1)(b), 18.

[32] Ibid. ss. 16(1)(ba), 18A.

[33] Ibid. ss. 16(1)(c), 19.

[34] Ibid. ss. 16(1)(d), 20.

[35] Ibid. ss. 16(1)(e), 21.

[36] The use of structure and concepts was discussed in depth in *Baigent & Anor v The Random House Group Ltd (The Da Vinci Code)* [2006] EWHC 719 (Ch), aff'd [2007] EWCA Civ 247.

[37] For the avoidance of doubt the author does not suggest the producers of *Snails* committed any form of copyright infringement. It is perfectly acceptable and indeed normal practice to be inspired by a successful game and to produce variants on the game idea. For example, at the moment the First-person Shooter of FPS seems to be the dominant game variety played on home consoles with a number of competing titles all based on the system pioneered by *Wolfenstein 3D* in 1992 and *Doom* in 1993.

[38] This is not to deny the massive effect software piracy has on the software industry. The *Business Software Alliance June 2014 Global Software Piracy Study*, calculated that global software piracy cost the industry $62.7bn in 2013 with 43 per cent of all software installed being illegal copies. Software piracy is a legally clear issue. The production, distribution, and installation of pirated software are all infringements of copyright, with those who produce and distribute pirated software committing a criminal offence under s. 107 of the CDPA. The issue with software piracy is one of enforcement, not one of legal certainty.

An adaptation is specifically defined in relation to software in s. 21(3)(ab) of the CDPA as 'an arrangement or altered version of the program or a translation of it'. Adaptations tend to occur when a piece of software written for one operating system, such as Apple's Yosemite OS, is rewritten to operate on a different operating system such as Microsoft's Windows 10. Adaptations can also occur when an original piece of software is rewritten, usually by an agent employed by the end user of the software, to allow the end user to cancel a contractual arrangement with the software vendor and replace the vendor's software with his own. With commercial software often leased at substantial service costs, which include fees for maintenance and upgrades, it is tempting for end users to seek to replace supplied software with their own version. This is of course perfectly legal provided the software they develop is neither copied from nor is an adaptation of the original software. As with non-literal copying there have been several cases on this issue which will be examined below.

The remaining rights reserved to the copyright holder, the right to issue copies of the work to the public, and the right to communicate the work to the public are less problematic. These rights allow copyright holders to control the distribution of their work, and ensure that the copyright holder is adequately rewarded for their efforts. There is though one unusual aspect of the right to issue copies of the work to the public which should be highlighted; exhaustion of the right. The right conferred on the copyright holder under s. 18 is only the right to first distribute copies of the work in the European Economic Area. Once that has been done the right, with respect to *that copy* of the work, is exhausted allowing the owner of that copy of the work to sell it on. This can be clearly seen with an example.

Example Exhaustion of the first sale right

Ana buys a legitimate copy of a computer program in Portugal. She then imports it into the UK when she moves to London. She later decided to sell her copy of the software on eBay.co.uk. The principle of exhaustion means Ana may legally sell her copy of the software in the UK without the permission of the copyright owner (assuming she removes any installations of the software from her computer).

Bárbara bought her copy of the same software in Brazil. She also moves to London. If Bárbara tries to sell her copy of the software on eBay.co.uk she would technically be in breach of copyright. As Brazil is not an EEA state she may not resell her copy legally within the EEA without the permission of the copyright holder.

Similarly the exhaustion of the copyright holder's right to first distribution only gives Ana the right to resell her copy of the software. It does not allow her to rent or lease her copy, nor does it allow her to make additional copies of the software.

10.3 Copyright infringement and software: literal copying

To carry out any restricted act without the permission of the copyright holder invites an action for copyright infringement. An action for copyright infringement is usually a civil action, although many people imagine it to be a criminal action due to the language used by the copyright industry in campaigns such as the 'copying is theft' campaign operated by the Federation Against Copyright Theft. In truth only a small number of activities involve the criminal law, most of which involve making literal copies available to the public.[39] In fact the divide between the civil enforcement of copyright infringement and the application of the criminal law follows quite closely the divide between literal, or pirated, copies and non-literal copies.

10.3.1 **Offline piracy**

Literal copies, usually known as pirated copies, are precise copies of a work and are usually produced with a view to selling or otherwise distributing them as a substitute for the original. As a complete copy of a work there is no doubt that literal copies infringe. There are a variety of offline ways in which software piracy may occur. The most simple and obvious being the production of illegal copies on DVD or flash memory stick/card in a back-street factory which are then sold on in markets, on the street, or in pubs. Although this type of activity is more common overseas it does still occur infrequently in the UK (online piracy has generally overtaken offline sales). If such a case were to arise either the police or trading standards officers, often with the support of the copyright holder or the Federation Against Software Theft, would deal with it.

It should not be assumed that all piracy has moved online; variants of software piracy still occur in the UK. One variant is the illegal pre-loading of software by hardware suppliers. Here the hardware supplier installs the software onto the hard drive of a PC, tablet, or smartphone and then sells the device with the software pre-installed. There are many reported cases of this practice, including *Microsoft v Electro-Wide Ltd*,[40] in which Laddie J found that 'an original equipment manufacturer who pre-loads software onto a computer for sale to the public needs a relevant licence from the copyright owner each time he loads the software'.[41] Another, more common variant of pre-loading is multiple installations, or end-user piracy. This usually occurs where a small-to-medium-sized business installs more copies of a piece of software than they are licensed to, i.e. where there may be a few dozen or a few hundred PCs but not quite as many licences.[42] This type of infringement is notoriously difficult to track down as it is widespread and usually at a low level, too low in terms of monetary value to pay for a detailed investigation. To combat this problem, commercial software manufacturers have employed a variety of authentication measures. This is usually achieved through a 'product activation key', a unique identifier supplied with the software which the end user must enter when the software is first installed. Today these are registered online with the copyright owner so that they may ensure only the licensed number of copies of the software is currently in use. Unregistered software will not be updated or supported. These systems are, however, open to attack through the use of key generators, small programs which can mimic the operations of the registration system used by the copyright owner to defeat the activation process. To attempt to defeat the use of key generators some software

[39] The bulk of criminal copyright offences may be found in ss. 107–112 of the CDPA 1988.

[40] [1997] FSR 580.

[41] Ibid. 582.

[42] The Business Software Alliance periodically audits and fines companies. In a recent example a company was fined £16,000 for using unlicensed Autodesk software as well as paying £17,500 for new software licences. BSA, 'Engineering design company Project Options Ltd pays out £33,000 for using unlicensed software' 10 June 2014 <http://www.bsa.org/news-and-events/news/2014/june/uk06102014projectoptions>.

companies have developed further anti-piracy systems such as Microsoft's Office 365 program which it uses to protect its Office products. This sees the concept of software as a product replaced with the concept of software as a service. Instead of paying a fee to own your copy of Microsoft Office the user pays an annual subscription fee which sees the licensed user receive updates to the software, technical support, cross-platform licensing, and cloud storage space. By building an ongoing service relationship with the customer Microsoft hope eventually to weed out end-user piracy.[43]

10.3.2 **Online piracy**

More commonly today software piracy in the UK is an online activity. With fast broadband connections and the prevalence of wireless networks, two online piracy methods have increased in importance. The first is client-server piracy. This is similar in effect to pre-loading piracy but with the distinction that only a single copy of the software is installed on a server which may then be accessed and used by any user on the network. This type of software installation is usually legal if you have the right form of licence but in some cases the number of end users exceeds the number of licences the network operator has purchased. In these cases infringement occurs.

More damaging though in terms of both volume and value is the worryingly commonplace occurrence of file-sharing services. The legal regulation of online copyright infringement will be discussed in greater depth in the following chapter, but here it is worth noting that in the UK the practice of swapping discs or buying illegal copies of software in markets or car boot sales has been replaced with trading illegal files on file-sharing technologies such as BitTorrent. The size of the illegal peer-to-peer (P2P) market should not be underestimated. Data supplied by Statista reveals that although P2P traffic is reducing it is still a significant part of internet traffic, with P2P traffic making up 5.5 per cent of all internet traffic in North America in 2015.[44] This is more than Facebook and Amazon Instant Video combined.[45]

10.3.3 **Employee piracy**

The final, less common, but potentially extremely harmful form of literal infringement is employee piracy. This occurs when an employee leaves their employer's employ and takes with them a complete copy, or a copy of a section, of their employer's product,

[43] Modern network enabled software suites like Office 365 are proving to be successful in reducing piracy rates. However, The Business Software Alliance still reports that, despite a 3 per cent drop in illegal installations in 2014, 24 per cent of all installed software in the UK was unlicensed. BSA, 'UK Unlicensed Software Rate Drops to 24 Percent' 24 June 2014 <http://www.bsa.org/news-and-events/news/2014/june/06242014globalsoftwaresurvey>.

[44] This is down from a high of 19.2 per cent in 2010 (Source: <http://www.statista.com/statistics/190826/percentage-of-p2p-filesharing-in-peak-period-traffic-in-north-america/>). The drop in P2P traffic in part reflects the rise of data behemoths such as Netflix, YouTube, and Amazon Video. A separate survey reveals that Netflix alone used 36.5 per cent of all downstream internet bandwidth during peak periods in North America for March 2015 for its HD heavy service while YouTube accounted for 15.6 per cent of downstream internet traffic. See T Spangler, 'Subscription-video leader accounts for more usage than YouTube, Amazon and Hulu combined in North America during primetime' *Variety* (Los Angeles, 28 May 2015) <http://variety.com/2015/digital/news/netflix-bandwidth-usage-internet-traffic-1201507187/>.

[45] See Spangler ibid.

usually with a view to producing a competing product of their own. An example of this type of infringement may be seen in the case of *IBCOS Computers Ltd v Barclays Mercantile Highland Finance Ltd*.[46] This case involved a software developer, Mr Poole, who wrote a suite of programs for his employer, IBCOS, which handled accounts and payrolls for agricultural machinery dealers. This software, called ADS, was owned by the plaintiff. Under the terms of Mr Poole's contract he could not develop any competing products within two years of his termination of his contract of employment. After leaving IBCOS Mr Poole wrote a new software suite similar to ADS called Unicorn which he supplied to Barclays Mercantile for marketing and sale. Mr Poole was careful to ensure that Unicorn was not marketed until after his two-year limitation period had expired.

IBCOS claimed that Mr Poole had used elements of the ADS code in the Unicorn program and raised an infringement action. When the two programs were compared side by side it became clear that Mr Poole had copied elements of the ADS code. There were common errors of punctuation and spelling in the comment lines of the programs[47] and the same programming errors and redundant code were found in the same places.[48] Faced with this evidence Jacob J had little difficulty finding that copying had occurred. The only remaining question was whether the copying had been sufficient to qualify as a 'substantial part' of the original.[49] A key question here was whether Jacob J should consider each work separately and individually or whether he could treat the entire ADS software suite—which comprised of 335 program files, 171 record layout files, and 46 screen layout files—as a single work.[50] Rejecting an earlier suggestion made in an interlocutory hearing in the case of *Total Information Processing Systems Ltd v Daman Ltd*[51] that the mere linking of several programs is not in itself an original literary or artistic work, Jacob J found that ADS was a compilation capable of independent copyright protection which existed in addition to and separately from the individual copyrights in each of the elements.[52] With this decided, Jacob J then considered whether the evidence indicated that substantial copying had occurred of both the individual elements of ADS and of ADS as a whole. He found substantial elements of the individual programs were repeated in Unicorn and, in comparing the overall structure of Unicorn to ADS, found that both programs shared: nine levels of security; a unique ability to create different invoice types; a common internal sales system within the ordinary sales ledger package; month-end sales audits combined with VAT; a 22-character parts description; use of three separate programs for the stock ordering facility; 12 labour rates; five levels of subtotalling; and both had a redundant and unnecessary holiday stamp facility.[53] These common features were in Jacob J's view too many in number and too similar in design to be caused by Mr Poole's programming style and his reuse of common routines. He therefore found in favour of IBCOS, finding infringement of both the individual elements of ADS and of ADS as a whole.

[46] [1994] FSR 275.

[47] Ibid. 297–8.

[48] Ibid. 299.

[49] By s. 16(3)(a) of the CDPA 1988 infringement by copying only occurs where the alleged infringer has copied 'the work as a whole or any substantial part of it'.

[50] Figures from *IBCOS v Barclays Mercantile* (n. 46) 289.

[51] [1992] FSR 171.

[52] *IBCOS v Barclays Mercantile* (n. 46) 292–3.

[53] Ibid. 304–5.

The principles Jacob J set out in *IBCOS* were later to be applied in the similar case of *Cantor Fitzgerald International v Tradition (UK) Ltd.*[54] Cantor Fitzgerald (CF) are inter-dealer brokers in bonds, which means they act as the middlemen in a bond transaction. In September 1991 CF dismissed their Managing Director, Mr Howard, who then approached Tradition with a view to setting up an inter-dealer brokerage for them. To get the Tradition system up and running Mr Howard hired a number of members of staff from CF including Mr Harland, then the head of the Systems Department at CF and almost his entire programming team. CF claimed that in setting up their inter-dealer brokerage Tradition infringed several of CF's copyrights in its brokerage software. They claimed that Tradition had directly infringed by installing copies of the CF brokerage system on their system. This was admitted by Tradition and was easily disposed of. CF further claimed that elements of the CF software had been copied in the design of the new Tradition software. Tradition admitted that they had included some of the CF code in their program but that this accounted for less than 4 per cent of the complete CF code. They therefore argued this was not a 'substantial part' as required by s. 16(3)(a) of the CDPA.

It fell to Pumfrey J to determine whether the elements copied were in fact substantial, and how substantiality should be measured. He first noted that due to the way a computer program operates there is an argument that 'every part of a computer program is essential to its performance, and so every part, however small, is a "substantial part" of the program'.[55] This he rejected as over-broad. Instead he preferred to follow the lead of Jacob J in thinking of computer software as similar to a literary work with the focus of substantiality resting on the quality of what is taken rather than the quantity: 'Substantiality is to be judged in the light of the skill and labour in design and coding which went into the piece of code which is alleged to be copied. It is not determined by whether the system would work without the code; or by the amount of use the system makes of the code.'[56] On this basis Pumfrey J went on to examine the software suites as a whole, and each of their component parts, as Jacob J had done in *IBCOS*. He found that the direct copies of the CF software loaded onto the Tradition system were infringing, but found that, mostly because the Tradition programmers had copied small elements of the CF system with a view to developing a better program suite, little of the new Tradition software infringed CF's copyright, although on a few key elements including one called LIFFE.BAS there had been infringement. The case therefore brought a mixed result for both parties with CF claiming a partial win but more importantly these two cases, *IBCOS* and *Cantor Fitzgerald*, have set the standard test for partial literal copying, an activity that tends only to occur in this type of piracy.

10.4 Copyright infringement and software: non-literal copying

Much less common than literal copying, but much more legally complex is the idea of non-literal copying. Non-literal copying occurs when the structure, design, or characterization of a literary work is copied. Famously in 2006 the High Court had to decide

[54] [2000] RPC 95.
[55] Ibid. 130.
[56] Ibid. 135.

whether Dan Brown's blockbuster novel *The Da Vinci Code* (DVC) had copied elements of a previous non-fiction book *The Holy Blood and the Holy Grail* (HBHG).[57] The claim made by the authors of HBHG was that Mr Brown had copied the central theme (in chronological order) of HBHG, and that without this central theme there is very little structure to be found in either HBHG or DVC. They claimed that this central theme therefore formed a bridge between the two works by which Brown substantially copied HBHG in his own work DVC. This was a complex claim which took up a considerable amount of court time. When Peter Smith J finally produced his lengthy judgment he found against the claimants finding that the shared central theme could not be identified from the evidence and that:

> even if there is a Central Theme as alleged by the Claimants in HBHG it . . . is merely an expression of a number of facts and ideas at a very general level. There is nothing in them in my view that goes beyond that proposition. It follows therefore that the Central Theme as expressed is not such as to justify being protected against copying.[58]

The Da Vinci Code case is a typical literary non-literal infringement case. Debates in such cases usually centre on the dividing line between shared ideas (which are not copyrightable) and shared structures, themes, and concepts (which may be). In cases involving literary works there is never any doubt that the reader is able to distinguish between the two works and will experience both rather differently; this is because with books the reader consumes the actual written word. In *The Da Vinci Code* case the issue was not that the consumer may buy DVC in preference to HBHG as one was a non-fiction book and the other a thriller novel, but rather that the author and publisher of DVC had profited from the expressed ideas of the authors of HBHG. With software the issue is very different. The end user rarely sees the source code and will never usually see the object code. The way we consume and experience software is therefore very different to other literary works. We do not consume the protected element of the work as we do with books, films, music, or with artistic works; instead we experience software through the 'user interface', usually a 'graphical user interface' which uses graphical icons, and visual indicators (icons) to control software operations. Because of this unique way we interface with software it is possible for the consumer experience to be replicated without copying any of the underlying code: this is known as 'look and feel infringement'.

10.4.1 **Look and feel infringement**

Look and feel infringement first came to the attention of the legal establishment in the 1980s but it was not until the 1990s that the UK developed any case law in the field. Initially, look and feel infringement was driven not as an attempt to avoid the impact of copyright law while free-riding on the work of others, but more prosaically because a software program, or suite, written from one operating system (such as Windows) would not run on a different operating system (such as IBM's O/S2). Thus a successful piece of software written for one operating system would need to be translated to work on another operating system. In making the translation every effort would be

[57] *Baigent & Anor v The Random House Group Ltd* (n. 36).
[58] Ibid. [259].

made to ensure the translated program would work in the same way as the original: in other words would have the same 'look and feel'. If such a translation was carried out by the copyright holder there would be no copyright issue, but if a third party decided to translate, or 'port-over', a program without the permission of the copyright holder litigation may follow.

After considerable discussion of look and feel infringement in US courts,[59] the first opportunity for a British judge to examine the application of look and feel principles was Ferris J in *John Richardson Computers Ltd v Flanders (No. 2)*.[60] Mr Richardson was a pharmacist who had written a program which would print labels for dispensed drugs and keep a stock count of prescription drugs in a small dispensing pharmacy. This program was written in BASIC and could be used on Tandy and Video Genie machines. Although his program was successful Mr Richardson realized he was not a professional programmer and his program had some shortfalls. He therefore set up a company, John Richardson Computers (JRC) and employed Mr Flanders, a professional programmer. Mr Flanders rewrote the original program for the new BBC microcomputer with great success.

After leaving JRC's employ in 1986, Mr Flanders began work on a new program called 'Pharm-Assist' for the IBM series of computers. It was this subsequent program which led JRC to take action against Mr Flanders. This was the first major non-literal software copyright case in the UK. The case was allocated to Ferris J who had to decide both on the scope and limits of copyright protection under the CDPA, and how to develop a test for infringement applicable to the UK. Following an analysis of the facts Ferris J concluded that there were six issues which he needed to address:

Highlight Ferris J's six issues

1. Does copyright subsist in a computer program?
2. If it does, is the copyright in the BBC program vested in the claimant?
3. Assuming the above, what ought to be the approach of the Court to the appraisal of an allegation of breach of copyright in a computer program where it is not claimed that the source code itself has been copied?
4. Are there objective similarities between the BBC program and the defendant's program which enable the defendant's program to be regarded in any respect as a copy of the BBC program?
5. Were any such similar features in fact copied from the BBC program?
6. Is any copying which may be found to have occurred the copying of a substantial part of the BBC program?[61]

[59] *Whelan Associates Inc. v Jaslow Dental Laboratory Inc.*, 797 F. 2d 1222 (3d Cir. 1986); *Lotus Development Corp. v Paperback Software*, 740 F. Supp. 37 (D. Mass. 1990); *Computer Associates International Inc. v Altai*, 982 F. 2d 693 (2nd Cir. 1992); and *Lotus Development Corp. v Borland International Inc.*, 49 F. 3d 807 (1st Cir. 1995).

[60] [1993] FSR 497.

[61] Adapted from [1993] FSR 497, 515.

Having established the first two questions were to be answered in favour of the claimant, Ferris J turned his attention to the key question 'what ought to be the approach of the court to the appraisal of an allegation of breach of copyright in a computer program where it is not claimed that the source code itself has been copied?' He reviewed prior English authorities on non-literal copying of literary works, and the US case law on non-literal copyright infringement before establishing a new four-part UK test for non-literal infringement based in part on the US authority *Computer Associates International Inc. v Altai*.[62]

Highlight The John Richardson four-part test

1. Was the plaintiff's work protected by copyright?
2. Were there similarities between the plaintiff's and the defendant's programs?
3. Were these similarities caused by copying or were other explanations possible?
4. In the event that copying is established, did the copied elements constitute a significant part of the original work?

The complication of the test developed by Ferris J was that at its fourth stage, he envisaged the use of a test from *Altai* known as the abstraction-filtration-comparison test. This was an extremely complex test; one which was quickly abandoned in the United States in the following case of *Lotus Development Corp. v Borland International Inc.*[63] Some critics believe Ferris J never fully understood the complexities of the abstraction-filtration-comparison test and in adapting it to fit English law he made a number of errors in its application.[64]

These criticisms crystallized in the later case of *IBCOS*.[65] This case, discussed previously under the literal infringement heading at 10.3.3, found Jacob J highly critical of Ferris J's approach noting that: 'For myself I do not find the route of going via US case law particularly helpful.'[66] In particular, Jacob J was concerned that the abstraction-filtration-comparison approach may be too strict for UK copyright law, noting that:

> United States copyright law is not the same as ours, particularly in the area of copyright works concerned with functionality and of compilations . . . United States case law has, ever since *Baker v Selden*, been extremely careful to keep copyright out of the functional field, either by saying there is no copyright in, or that copyright cannot be infringed by taking, the functional . . . I doubt that would have happened here.[67]

[62] See (n. 59).

[63] *Computer Associates International v Altai* (n. 59).

[64] R Arnold, 'Infringement of Copyright in Computer Software by Non-Textual Copying: First Decision at Trial by an English Court *John Richardson Computers v Flanders*' (1993) *EIPR* 250; D Rowland and E MacDonald, *Information Technology Law* (3rd edn, Routledge 2005) 40; S Lai, *The Copyright Protection of Computer Software in the United Kingdom* (Hart 2000) 33.

[65] *IBCOS v Barclays Mercantile* (n. 46).

[66] Ibid. 302.

[67] Ibid. 292.

With this in mind Jacob J suggests an alternative four-part test:

Highlight The *IBCOS* four-part test

1. What are the work or works in which the claimant claims copyright?
2. Is each such work 'original'?
3. Was there copying from that work?
4. If there was copying, has a substantial part of that work been reproduced?

Unlike Ferris J, Jacob J did not propose the use of the *Altai* test at any point, instead trusting judges to apply their forensic skills in the same way a judge would be asked to in a non-literal literary infringement case. It has been argued that these two decisions are compatible with each other as *IBCOS* was a literal infringement case, while *Richardson* was a case on non-literal infringement.[68] This cannot escape the fact though that in *IBCOS* Jacob J clearly stated that 'going via the complication of the concept of a "core of protectable expression" merely complicates the matter so far as our law is concerned. It is likely to lead to overcitation of US authority based on a statute different from ours.'[69] Clearly, therefore, *Richardson* and *IBCOS* suggest two different tests for non-literal infringement in English law and, as both cases were decided before the High Court, neither had greater authority. For a period therefore there were two equally valid tests at English law. This remained unresolved until Pumfrey J in the later literal infringement case, *Cantor Fitzgerald International v Tradition (UK) Ltd*,[70] elected to follow the approach of Jacob J in *IBCOS*. Although *Cantor Fitzgerald* was again a High Court decision and could not overrule or enshrine either of the tests, Pumfrey J made it clear that in his view the *IBCOS* standard was to be preferred. This case probably signalled the end of the brief flirtation the English courts had with the *Altai* test, but does not signal the end of the development of the law in relation to non-literal infringement of computer software.

10.4.2 Look and feel: *Navitaire v easyJet*

In 2004 came probably the most significant non-literal infringement case in the UK to date: *Navitaire Inc. v easyJet Airline Co. & Anor.*[71] This involved an attempt by a customer to reverse-engineer and replicate a piece of proprietary software. The software in question, called 'OpenRes', was supplied under licence by the claimant to the defendant for use on their website. It allowed them to take bookings online and operate flights without the need to issue a physical ticket. By 1999 it became clear that easyJet wanted to radically overhaul their booking software to offer further routes, greater language support, and easier operability. EasyJet negotiated with Navitaire about this upgrade but no agreement could be reached. Instead easyJet approached the second defendant,

[68] D Bainbridge, *Introduction to Information Technology Law* (6th edn, Longman 2007) 50.
[69] [1994] FSR 275, 302.
[70] *Cantor Fitzgerald International v Tradition* (n. 54).
[71] [2004] EWHC 1725 (Ch) (2004).

BulletProof Technologies, with the request that BulletProof should write a new booking system which would allow easyJet to install these much-needed upgrades but which would operate in all other respects in exactly the same way as OpenRes. This was important for easyJet for two reasons. First, they did not want to have to retrain all their ticketing agents on a new booking interface, and second, they wanted to migrate databases held on the OpenRes system to the new system.

BulletProof worked closely with easyJet's IT department over an extended period to create a new booking system 'eRes'. In designing eRes, BulletProof did not examine or make use of the OpenRes code; instead they worked from an operational copy of OpenRes, copying the structure of the software and emulating the functions of OpenRes. Because none of the code had been directly copied, Navitaire raised a non-literal infringement claim focusing upon eRes's emulation of OpenRes command codes used by operators,[72] as well as emulations of the screen displays used particularly in the report screens, and the underlying business logic of the OpenRes system.

Pumfrey J examined each of these claims in turn and in depth. He rejected Navitaire's claim that their command codes were protectable forms of expression. He found that the use of 'single [command] words in isolation are not to be considered as literary works' and that as a result 'the individual command words and letters do not qualify'.[73] This is based upon a decision in an earlier case *Exxon Corp. v Exxon Insurance Consultants International Ltd*,[74] which had ruled that single words are unlikely to be sufficiently original to qualify for copyright protection unless sufficient skill, labour, and judgement have been expended on the creation of the word. He then examined whether strings of command codes such as; 'A13JUNLTNAMS' could qualify for protection. Again the answer was in the negative. These were not 'recorded' in the program code, rather they were commands entered by the user. In any event, Pumfrey J noted that Recital 13 of the Software Directive[75] appeared to forbid protection of user interfaces meaning that the command codes could not be protected.[76] He then went on to consider whether Navitaire had copyright in the screen displays produced by the OpenRes software. He found that there were two types of screen display: one a simple text-based display which provided an interface for the input of data, and the second more dynamic graphical user-interface screens which made use of icons. The former he held were not protectable, but the latter were protectable and, to the extent that the defendants had substantially copied these, there was an infringement of copyright.

The key claim though was the final one: that in copying the look and feel of the OpenRes system the defendants had infringed the underlying business logic of

[72] 'Command codes' are strings of characters which function as a type of shorthand in the booking system. They are explained by Pumfrey J at [26]: 'For example, in OpenRes, the command A13JUNLTNAMS (where the flight date is 13 June, the originating airport is Luton (LTN) and the destination airport Amsterdam (AMS)) should produce a screen displaying the available flights on that day.'

[73] *Navitaire v easyJet* (n. 71) [80].

[74] [1982] RPC 69.

[75] See (n. 22).

[76] Recital 13 reads 'Whereas, for the avoidance of doubt, it has to be made clear that only the expression of a computer program is protected and that ideas and principles which underlie any element of a program, including those which underlie its interfaces, are not protected by copyright under this Directive.'

the OpenRes system. This was the most important aspect of this case. To the end user OpenRes and eRes were substantively the same. They looked the same, they operated in the same way, and they produced the same results; eRes was a direct emulation of OpenRes. Whether or not this was a breach of copyright was likely to have far-reaching consequences. Pumfrey J described this as a question of 'copying without access to the thing copied, directly or indirectly'.[77] He noted that this claim was moving away from the literary element of software to its functional element:

> The claim depends first upon the contention that the manner in which a machine behaves under the control of a program represents part of the skill and labour that went into the program. This is not an unreasonable observation. On the contrary, it is the whole object of the programmer to get the computer to behave in the required manner.[78]

Despite seeing the merit of the claim Pumfrey J was not willing to extend copyright protection in this manner:

> The questions in the present case are both a lack of substantiality and the nature of the skill and labour to be protected. Navitaire's computer program invites input in a manner excluded from copyright protection, outputs its results in a form excluded from copyright protection and creates a record of a reservation in the name of a particular passenger on a particular flight. What is left when the interface aspects of the case are disregarded is the business function of carrying out the transaction and creating the record, because none of the code was read or copied by the defendants. It is right that those responsible for devising OpenRes envisaged this as the end result for their program: but that is not relevant skill and labour. In my judgement, this claim for non-textual copying should fail. I do not come to this conclusion with any regret. If it is the policy of the Software Directive to exclude both computer languages and the underlying ideas of the interfaces from protection, then it should not be possible to circumvent these exclusions by seeking to identify some overall function or functions that it is the sole purpose of the interface to invoke and relying on those instead. As a matter of policy also, it seems to me that to permit the 'business logic' of a program to attract protection through the literary copyright afforded to the program itself is an unjustifiable extension of copyright protection into a field where I am far from satisfied that it is appropriate.[79]

Pumfrey J closes his analysis with an analogy which is extremely helpful in understanding his logic:

Highlight Pumphrey J's pudding analogy

Take the example of a chef who invents a new pudding. After a lot of work he gets a satisfactory result, and thereafter his puddings are always made using his written recipe, undoubtedly a literary work. Along comes a competitor who likes the pudding and resolves to make it himself. Ultimately, after much culinary labour, he succeeds in emulating the earlier result, and he records his recipe. Is the later recipe an infringement of the earlier, as the end result, the plot and purpose of both (the pudding) is the same? I believe the answer is no.[80]

[77] *Navitaire v easyJet* (n. 71) [113].
[78] Ibid. [114].
[79] Ibid. [129]–[130].
[80] Ibid. [127].

10.4.3 Look and feel: *Nova Productions v Mazooma Games*

The outcome of *Navitaire* was widely predicted[81] and has been widely welcomed.[82] In the years that have followed, the courts have taken the opportunity to reinforce the *Navitaire* test. *Nova Productions Ltd v Mazooma Games Ltd*[83] was the subsequent case to reach the Court of Appeal. Nova Productions designs, manufactures, and sells arcade games. It brought two actions for infringement of copyright in one of its pool-based arcade games, Pocket Money. The first action was against Mazooma in relation to the creation and use of software for a game called Jackpot Pool. The second action was against a company called Bell Fruit in relation to a game called Trick Shot. Both claims alleged infringement in artistic works, being the graphics and the frames generated and displayed to the user of the game, and the computer program as a literary work.

At first instance, Kitchin J found for the defendants. He concluded there was no reproduction of any artistic copyright work, first because the features of similarity relied upon were either implemented quite differently or were different in appearance, and second, because those features represented ideas expressed at a very high level of generality or abstraction with no meaningful connection with the artistic nature of the graphic works relied on.[84] Applying the principles of *Navitaire*[85] he then rejected the software claim on the basis that any similarities derived were cast at such a level of abstraction and were so general that they could not amount to a substantial part of the computer program.[86]

On appeal it agreed that the individual frames stored in the memory of a computer were 'graphic works' within the meaning found in the CDPA.[87] However, save for the fact that they were of a pool table with pockets, balls, and a cue, nothing of the defendants' screens amounted to a substantial reproduction of a corresponding screen in Nova's game.[88] However, Nova argued that there was a further artistic work in the screen graphics, that being:

> something beyond individual freeze-frame graphics . . . there is a series of graphics which show the 'in-time' movement of cue and [power] meter . . . what the defendants had done was to create 'a dynamic re-posing' of the [original]—one in which the detail of the subjects had changed, but an essential artistic element of the original was carried through to the Defendants.[89]

Jacob LJ in giving the leading judgment rejected both claims. He found there was no reproduction of a substantial part of the screen display,[90] and further there was also no

[81] M Simons, 'EasyJet Software Case "a Complete Nonsense"' (*Computer Weekly*, 19 May 2003) <http://www.computerweekly.com/news/2240050844/EasyJet-software-case-a-complete-nonsense>; JC Perez, 'Developer Sues Accenture Subsidiary' (*Infoworld*, 6 May 2003) <http://www.infoworld.com/d/developer-world/developer-sues-accenture-subsidiary-420>.

[82] S Stokes, 'The Development of UK Software Copyright Law: From John Richardson Computers to Navitaire' (2005) 11 *Computer and Telecommunications Law Review* 129; M Heritage and P Jones, 'The End of "Look and Feel" and the Invasion of the Little Green Men? UK Copyright and Patent Protection for Software after 2005' (2006) 12 *Computer and Telecommunications Law Review* 67.

[83] [2007] EWCA Civ 219 (March 14, 2007).

[84] *Nova Productions Ltd v Mazooma Games Ltd and Ors* [2006] EWHC 24 (Ch) (20 January 2006) [245].

[85] Ibid. [248].

[86] Ibid. [253].

[87] See s. 4(1).

[88] *Nova Productions v Mazooma Games* (n. 83) [12].

[89] Ibid. [13].

[90] Ibid. [18].

foundation for Nova's 'in-time' argument.[91] With the artistic copyright claim quickly disposed of the court could turn its attention to the claim that the defendants' programs infringed Nova's copyright in the Pocket Money program itself. Nova tried to persuade the court that notwithstanding the decision in *Navitaire* someone who copies the function of a computer program to write his own program to achieve the same result is clearly appropriating part of the skill and labour expended in designing the program.[92] Jacob LJ rejected this submission. He also saw nothing in the Software Directive to suggest, as Nova contended, that the preparatory design work of a computer program should be protected as such, even if it consisted only of ideas as to what the program should do. It was clear to Jacob LJ from the Directive that for computer programs as a whole, including the preparatory design work, ideas were not to be protected. What was protected by way of preparatory design work was that work as a literary work, the expression of a design which was to go into the ultimate program, not the ideas themselves.[93]

What is most important about the *Nova* decision is not the actual outcome, which could have been confidently predicted prior to the first-instance hearing in the High Court, but the very definite response of the Court of Appeal to a challenge to the principles of *Navitaire*. Nova made an early attempt to have the case referred to the European Court of Justice (ECJ) on the basis that there was a need to interpret the Software Directive's references to 'literary works' and 'preparatory design material for a computer program'. This was robustly rejected by the court.[94] The court then took an equally robust view of attempts to reinterpret *Navitaire* and in so doing they gave *Navitaire* a stamp of authority.

10.4.4 Look and feel: *SAS Institute v World Programming Ltd*

The final case in our trilogy of standard non-literal infringement cases is *SAS Institute v World Programming Ltd*.[95] This is an extremely complicated case involving copyright in the design of a software platform and the programming language used to develop that platform. SAS are a well-known business software supplier. In the 1970s SAS developed an analytical software suite called the 'SAS System' which allowed users to carry out a number of data processing and analysis functions by writing their own in the SAS language used by the SAS system. These additional modules would then interface with pre-existing SAS modules allowing for complete interoperability of the system. The problem for the customer was that they were then locked in to the SAS system as they had to continue using the necessary components of the SAS system in order to be able to run their existing SAS language application programs, as well to create new ones.

[91] At [16] Jacob LJ notes: 'Graphic work is defined as including all the types of thing specified in s. 4(2) which all have this in common, namely that they are static, non-moving. A series of drawings is a series of graphic works, not a single graphic work in itself. No-one would say that the copyright in a single drawing of Felix the Cat is infringed by a drawing of Donald Duck. A series of cartoon frames showing Felix running over a cliff edge into space, looking down and only then falling would not be infringed by a similar set of frames depicting Donald doing the same thing. That is in effect what is alleged here.'

[92] *Nova Productions v Mazooma Games* (n. 83) [48].

[93] Ibid. [50].

[94] Ibid. [35].

[95] [2010] EWHC 1829 (Ch).

The alleged infringer, World Programming Ltd (WPL), identified a possible market for alternative software capable of executing application programs written in SAS language. WPL tried to emulate the functionality of the SAS software in their own program, the 'WPL Program' but crucially did so without access to the SAS source code. Instead they studied the SAS manual and two versions of the SAS software Learning Edition (which is used to train programmers and users of SAS software) and Full Edition. SAS brought proceedings against WPL for copyright infringement. They challenged the decisions in *Navitaire* and *Nova* claiming it was a breach of copyright to study how a computer program functions and then to write a similar program to reproduce the functionality. In addition, SAS alleged that WPL copied the SAS manual to create the WPL program and its accompanying manual, copied vital SAS program components, and breached the terms of a licence agreement. The case raised three interesting questions:

Highlight The SAS questions

1. the extent to which copyright protected ideas, procedures, methods of operation and mathematical concepts as distinct from expressions of those ideas etc.
2. the extent to which copyright protected the functionality and interfaces of computer programs and the programming languages in which they were expressed
3. the test to be applied to determine what amounted to reproduction of a substantial part in cases such as the instant case.

In the High Court, the case came before Arnold J who produced an extremely lengthy and detailed judgment running to 333 paragraphs before referring the case to the ECJ. He found that the UK courts should interpret the 1988 Act so as to protect 'expressions' and not 'ideas, procedures, methods of operation and mathematical concepts as such'. Accordingly, it was necessary to distinguish between 'expressions', on the one hand, and 'ideas, procedures, methods of operation and mathematical concepts as such', on the other. What was protected by copyright in a literary work was the form of expression of the literary work itself. In particular it was the skill, judgement, and labour in devising the form of expression that were protected by copyright, not the structural material behind it which may be equated to ideas.[96] Clearly here Arnold J is following the lead of *Navitaire* and *Nova*. He went on to state that when considering whether a substantial part of a literary work had been reproduced, it was necessary to focus upon what had been reproduced and to consider whether it expressed the author's own intellectual creation.[97] He then examined whether a programming language could be protected as a copyright work. He supported the views of Pumphrey J in *Navitaire* that a programming language was not a work:

[96] Ibid. [206]–[207].
[97] Ibid. [243].

> I do not agree that this demonstrates, as counsel for SAS Institute argued, that an exclusion of programming languages was deliberately not included in the Software Directive. To the contrary, I consider that it indicates that Article 1(2) is to be broadly interpreted. Furthermore, I think that the distinction which Pumfrey J drew between a computer program and the language it is written in is, despite his hesitancy on the point, perfectly consistent with the distinction between expressions and ideas, procedures, methods of operation and mathematical formulae.[98]

Applying this decision he found that on the assumption that Pumphrey J had correctly interpreted Art. 1(2) of the Software Directive, the defendant had not infringed the claimant's copyrights in the SAS components by producing WPS.[99]

His decision was hesitant though, just as Pumphrey J's had been. The key phrase in this decision was 'on the assumption that Pumphrey J had correctly interpreted Art. 1(2) of the Software Directive'. As Arnold J acknowledged, 'I also agree with Pumfrey J, however, that the correct interpretation of Article 1(2) of the Software Directive on this point is not *acte clair* and that a reference to the ECJ is required in order to determine it.'[100] Arnold J therefore sent a number of questions to the ECJ but the key questions for our purpose were:

> [Q.1] Where a computer program (the First Program) is protected by copyright as a literary work, is Article 1(2) of Directive 91/250 to be interpreted as meaning that it is not an infringement of the copyright in the First Program for a competitor of the rightholder without access to the source code of the First Program, either directly or via a process such as decompilation of the object code, to create another program (the Second Program) which replicates the functions of the First Program?
>
> . . .
>
> [Q.3] Where the First Program interprets and executes application programs written by users of the First Program in a programming language devised by the author of the First Program which comprises keywords devised or selected by the author of the First Program and a syntax devised by the author of the First Program, is Article 1(2) of Directive 91/250 to be interpreted as meaning that it is not an infringement of the copyright in the First Program for the Second Program to be written so as to interpret and execute such application programs using the same keywords and the same syntax?[101]

In May 2012 the ECJ gave its answers to these key questions. It found quite unequivocally that 'neither the functionality of a computer program nor the programming language and the format of data files used in a computer program in order to exploit certain of its functions constitute a form of expression of that program for the purposes of art. 1(2) of Directive 91/250'.[102] This is about as clear guidance as it was possible for the ECJ to give. As such it is difficult to think of an occasion where non-literal copying would be upheld now. Although earlier UK cases like *Richardson* and *IBCOS* had suggested a form of non-literal copyright protection *Navitaire, Nova*, and now *SAS* suggest this is no longer correct at English or EU law and that software copyright is mostly restricted to direct infringement. The decision of the ECJ was then given effect by Arnold J who,

[98] Ibid. [217].
[99] Ibid. [332].
[100] Ibid. [218].
[101] The full list is at *SAS Institute Inc. v World Programming Ltd* [2012] 3 CMLR 4 [AG35].
[102] Ibid. [39].

following the ECJ ruling, dismissed all of SAS's claims in relation to their software copyright.[103] In a final twist SAS then appealed Arnold J's decision but the Court of Appeal upheld his decision.[104]

10.5 **Copyright infringement and software: permitted acts**

Not all activities involving the reproduction of elements of computer software infringe the rights of the copyright holder: some acts are permitted by the CDPA. First, there is a wide range of acts classified as 'fair dealing'. These are permitted activities, regulated by the Act, which apply to all literary works, software included.

The list of permitted acts is contained in chapter 3 of the Act and covers an extensive variety of activities. In terms of software the most commonly useful fair dealing defences are likely to include the right to make copies for the purpose of private study[105] and copying in the course of criticism, review, or news reporting.[106] The private study exception allows an individual to make a copy of a literary work 'for the purposes of research for a non-commercial purpose'. This allows individuals to study the work but, crucially, in relation to software does not allow the user to 'convert a computer program expressed in a low level language into a version expressed in a higher level language'[107] or to 'observe, study or test the functioning of a computer program in order to determine the ideas and principles which underlie any element of the program'.[108] The reason for these exceptions is that there are specific fair use provisions for software found elsewhere in the Act which deal with these activities, and which will be discussed below.

The other general fair dealing right which may be implemented in relation to software is the criticism or review right. This allows the reviewer to carry out restricted activities in relation to the work for the purpose of 'criticism or review, of that or another work, or of a performance of a work provided that it is accompanied by a sufficient acknowledgement'.[109] This right may be useful in particular when reviewing features of a piece of software in an online review or similar. Fair dealing rights also extend to a number of specific situations such as the use of copyright material in education and examinations,[110] libraries and archives,[111] and in the administration of justice,[112] but by far the most interesting section of the Act for those who deal with software design and development are the provisions contained in ss. 50A–50C, entitled: 'computer programs: lawful users'.

Sections 50A–50C contain four permitted acts specifically designed to allow for fair use of and development of computer software. These are the backup right, the decompilation right, the study and testing right, and the adaptation right. The simplest of these rights, and the most useful for an end user rather than developer, is the backup right

[103] *SAS Institute Inc. v World Programming Limited* [2013] EWHC 69 (Ch).
[104] *SAS Institute Inc. v World Programming Limited* [2013] EWCA Civ 1482.
[105] CDPA 1988, s. 29.
[106] Ibid. s. 30.
[107] Ibid. s. 29(4)(a).
[108] Ibid. s. 29(4A).
[109] Ibid. s. 30(1).
[110] Ibid. ss. 32–36A.
[111] Ibid. ss. 37–44A.
[112] Ibid. ss. 45–50.

contained in s. 50A. This allows a lawful user of a copy of a computer program to 'make any back up copy of it which it is necessary for him to have for the purposes of his lawful use'. This allows a lawful user[113] to make a copy of their software to be stored in case the software requires to be reinstalled at some point in the future should the original installation become corrupt. When this right was first introduced by the Copyright (Computer Programs) Regulations 1992[114] it was envisaged that the backup copy would be on a removable media such as a floppy disk but today with software usually requiring to be installed on to the HDD of the user before it can be used the 'backup' copy is usually the original installation disc. This raises the interesting, and as yet unanswered question of whether an end user could use s. 50A to allow them to install software on their hard drive.[115]

The remaining three rights are of greater use to software developers than users. The decompilation right contained in s. 50B, allows a lawful user of a copy of a computer program expressed in a low-level language (i.e. in object code) to convert it into a version expressed in a higher-level language, (i.e. source code) or, incidentally in the course of so converting the program, to copy it.[116] This right is subject to quite strict restrictions. One may only decompile for the purposes of the permitted objective 'to obtain the information necessary to create an independent program which can be operated with the program decompiled or with another program'.[117] Decompilation may only therefore be carried out to allow for interoperability of programs. The reason for the introduction of s. 50(B) is to ensure that software developers with a dominant position in either the operating systems market or part of the applications software market cannot use their market dominance to prevent competition. The fear was that dominant market players such as Microsoft would be able to prevent new entrants into the market by not revealing vital information about the APIs[118] used by the dominant software or about digital rights management systems they use to recognize and allow access to content. Imagine, if you will, a company wishes to produce a new word-processing program. When they launch this program they want their customers to be able to access and edit files sent by friends and colleagues using the market-leading Microsoft Word program, also they want files produced on their word processor to be equally accessible to users of Microsoft Word. This is interoperability, the ability of one program to interface with another. Without the ability to access the APIs Microsoft uses, such interoperability would be impossible, or at least substantially compromised. This is remedied by s. 50B, which allows developers, when the designer of the original software withholds such information, to dissect the code of the original program to allow interoperability to take place.

[113] Helpfully defined in the Act as a person who 'has a right to use the program (whether under a licence to do any acts restricted by the copyright in the program or otherwise)', s. 50A(2). In effect this means anyone who has bought or otherwise licensed a legal copy of the software.

[114] SI 1992/3233.

[115] Although as yet unanswered the author is of the view that it is unlikely a judge would view an installed copy of a piece of software as a 'backup' as it would be the primary use piece of software.

[116] CDPA 1988, s. 50B(1).

[117] Ibid. s. 50B(2)(a).

[118] Applications programming interfaces or APIs are an expression of a software component in terms of its operations, inputs, outputs, and underlying types. An API defines functionalities that are independent of their respective implementations, which allows definitions and implementations to vary without compromising the interface.

The third permitted right is the right to 'observe, study or test the functioning of the program in order to determine the ideas and principles which underlie any element of the program if he does so while performing any of the acts of loading, displaying, running, transmitting or storing the program which he is entitled to do'.[119] This section may seem to be rather superfluous. It suggests a lawful user may study a copy of their own software, surely something that sensibly shouldn't worry the courts? However, the reason for s. 50BA is twofold. First, it reinforces and gives some guidance as to the application of the idea/expression dichotomy which courts have had some difficulty with in relation to software. It also allows developers to produce software designs which emulate installed software as in the *Navitaire* case, provided they do not copy the code of the original.

The final permitted right is the right for the lawful user of a piece of software to copy or adapt that software, including for the purpose of error correction.[120] Often the end-user licence supplied with a piece of software precludes the end user from carrying out repairs or corrections to the software. This may be problematic, particularly if the copyright holder elects to end technical support for that piece of software or if the commercial relationship between the software supplier and the end user breaks down. There are some inherent ambiguities in s. 50C, in particular, what is the exact meaning of 'necessary' found in s. 50C(1)(a)[121] and what qualifies as an 'error' for the purpose of s. 50C(2)? Some guidance on the latter point may be gleaned from Jacob J's decision in *Mars UK Ltd v Teknowledge Ltd*.[122]

This was a case involving the upgrade of software on vending machines. Mars provide software on a programmable memory chip that allows vending machine operators to ensure only legal coins are accepted by their machines. This is done via a complex set of measurements including weight, size, and electrical resistance of coins. When coinage changes, as with the introduction of new 5p, 10p, and 50p coins in the 1990s these coin-sorter units must be reprogrammed. When this occurs Mars produce a reprogramming unit and license agents to carry out reprogramming on their behalf. Teknowledge were a private company who in the 1990s reverse-engineered Mars' Cashflow software which managed most modern coin-sorter units. Mars claimed this was a breach of their copyright. Teknowledge claimed that they were permitted to produce a 'spare part' for replacement or repair, a common law defence found in an earlier House of Lords case, *British Leyland v Armstrong*.[123] In evaluating this claim Jacob J had to consider whether this common law defence had survived the passing of ss. 50A–50C of the CDPA. In finding the common law defence no longer applied he also seemed to indicate that the error correction defence was different to a repair or update defence. Thus it seems that 'error correction' is limited to correcting errors in coding which directly interfere with the operability of the software: anything required to be carried out to update or repair software caused by environmental changes (as in *Mars*) is not error correction. Thus if you need to upgrade software because of the

[119] CDPA 1988, s. 50BA(1).

[120] Ibid. ss. 50C(1), (2).

[121] Section 50C(1)(a) states: 'It is not an infringement of copyright for a lawful user of a copy of a computer program to copy or adapt it, provided that the copying or adapting is necessary for his lawful use.'

[122] [1999] EWHC 226 (Pat).

[123] [1986] AC 577.

development of a new virus threat, the development of a new standard protocol, or simply to reflect changes in operating practice, this appears not to be error correction and not permitted by the s. 50C exception.

10.6 **Software licences**

10.6.1 **End-user licence agreements (EULAs)**

One area where software copyright remains impactful is end-user licence agreements (EULAs). For while it may be the case that the decisions in *Navitaire, Nova,* and *SAS* undermine its applicability in non-literal infringement cases, the end user, except in the very few cases where the permitted acts apply, still needs the permission of the software publisher to make local copies of the software in their hard drive and then in the RAM memory of the user device. Software licences are as old as software as a product. It became clear in the early days of software products that technically the end user could not install the software onto their computer as to do so necessitated making a copy of the software which was a restricted act. Software publishers therefore began to include licence agreements routinely with their software; the problem was how to ensure the end user read the licence in cases where the software was not delivered under an existing legal relationship, as was the case with original mainframe computers. The solution, for commercial consumer software, was the EULA: a standardized form of licence that could be included with the software and which the consumer would accept by some form of action or notification. The early version of such licences was the 'shrink-wrap' licence. These would see licence conditions printed on the outside of the box which contained the installation disks for the software and which could be read through the shrink-wrap packaging which surrounded the box. The thesis was once you broke the shrink-wrap you accepted the licence terms. The problem with this is you were limited by what you could print on the outside of the box, and you took up valuable advertising and promotions space with dense legal language. Quickly, therefore, shrink-wrap licences evolved and, instead of printing the conditions on the outside of the box, software publishers would seal the disks inside an envelope inside the box with a copy of the terms and conditions contained inside the box. By opening the envelope you accepted the licence conditions. The problem now was that you could not see the licence conditions until you opened the box, meaning after you had bought the software.

The legality of these licences was questionable and courts on both sides of the Atlantic debated their legality and enforceability. In *Step-Saver Data v Wyse Technology,*[124] Court of Appeals for the 3rd Circuit held that conditions contained in a shrink-wrap licence were additional offer terms to the terms of the sale agreement. The incorporation of the licence terms would materially alter the sale agreement for the software and as such they did not become part of the parties' agreement. This rationale was followed in a number of subsequent US decisions such as *Arizona Retail Systems v Software Link.*[125] However, in the later case of *ProCD v Zeidenberg,*[126] the Court of Appeals for the

[124] 939 F. 2d 91 (3rd Cir. 1991).
[125] 831 F. Supp. 759 (D. Ariz. 1993).
[126] 86 F. 3d 1447 (7th Cir. 1996).

7th Circuit held that Zeidenberg did accept the licence offer by clicking through (this related to a click-wrap contract discussed below). The court noted that he 'had no choice, because the software splashed the license on the screen and would not let him proceed without indicating acceptance'.[127] However, the court stated that Zeidenberg could have rejected the terms of the contract and returned the software. The court looked at a number of contracts where terms and conditions were found to be binding, even though the terms were not made known until after the contract had been concluded. Examples used included theatre tickets and airline tickets, where the purchaser is not aware of the terms of issue (placed on the reverse of the ticket), until after they have booked and paid for the ticket. However, the purchaser can return the ticket if they do not agree to the terms and conditions. A similar right of return existed in the present case; if the defendant did not agree to the licence terms, he could return the disk and receive a refund from the purchaser. Thus, the court considered that the licence would be binding on the defendant.[128] Commentators suggest that it is *ProCD* that is the outlier rather than *Step-Saver* or *Arizona Retail*,[129] yet despite this *ProCD* has been applied in cases such as *Bowers v Baystate Technologies*.[130] This had led US commentators to admit that in the United States the legal status of shrink-wrap contracts is somewhat unclear.

Because of the problems of the legality of shrink-wrap licences, and due to developments in delivery methods, software publishers moved throughout the 1990s to newer methods of delivering licence conditions. *ProCD* was not strictly a shrink-wrap case; it represented the next development in EULAs, the click-wrap agreement. These agreements are the forerunners of today's browse-wrap agreements. Instead of containing the licence conditions on or in the box, a pop-up box opens when you begin to install the software: it asks you to click 'I Accept' and will prevent installation of the software until the user accepts the terms. A browse-wrap licence comes with downloadable software and is today the most common form of licence. This, like a click-wrap agreement, is a pop-up box requiring customer agreement and may appear either before or after the purchase and delivery of the content.

The legality of browse-wrap contracts is equally unclear in the United States. In *Specht v Netscape*,[131] Court of Appeals for the 2nd Circuit held that a browse-wrap contract which did clearly communicate all terms to the user at the time of installation could not have those terms enforced. They noted that an essential ingredient to contract formation is the mutual manifestation of assent,[132] and found that 'a consumer's clicking on a download button does not communicate assent to contractual terms if the offer did not make clear to the consumer that clicking on the download button would signify assent to those terms'.[133] However, in *Hubbert v Dell Corp.*[134] the Court of Appeals for the

[127] Ibid. 1451.

[128] This (arguably) is not dissimilar to the ticket cases in English law. See *Parker v The South Eastern Railway Co.* (1877) 2 CPD 416, but cf. *Olley v Marlborough Court Hotel* [1949] 1 KB 532 and *Thornton v Shoe Lane Parking* [1971] 1 All ER 686.

[129] See e.g. C Pitet, 'The Problem with Money Now, Terms Later: *ProCd, Inc. v Zeidenberg and the Enforceability of Shrinkwrap Software Licenses*' (1997) 31 *Loyola of Los Angeles Law Review* 325.

[130] 320 F. 3d 1317 (2003).

[131] 306 F. 3d 17 (2d Cir. 2002).

[132] Ibid. 35–6.

[133] Ibid. 37.

[134] 835 NE 2d 113 (5th Dist 2005).

Fifth District found that consumers of Dell products, who were repeatedly shown the words 'All sales are subject to Dell's Term[s] and Conditions of Sale', as well as a conspicuous hyperlink, over a series of pages, were bound by these conditions. The court found that this repeated exposure and visual effect would put a reasonable person on notice of the terms and conditions.

There has been little examination of the legality of shrink-wrap, click-wrap, or browse-wrap agreements in UK law. The only case precisely on point is *Beta Computers v Adobe Systems*.[135] This is a decision by the Court of Session and has caused problems for English commentators for, in deciding that shrink-wrap licences were enforceable in Scotland, Lord Penrose utilized a unique property of Scottish contract law, namely *jus quastium tertio*.[136] Strictly there is no equivalent in English law but the Contracts (Rights of Third Parties) Act 1999 creates a close statutory approximation. It may be assumed therefore that the authority of *Beta* suggests 'wrap' licences are legal in all parts of the UK. Whatever the position, it is clear that the licence terms must be reasonable otherwise the Unfair Contract Terms Act 1977 or the Unfair Terms in Consumer Contracts Regulations 1999 may intervene to strike those terms out. In *St Albans City & District Council v International Computers*,[137] the Court of Appeal considered that a limitation of liability clause limiting damages to £100,000 was unreasonable (the actual loss amounting to £1.3m). Therefore, the common term limiting liability to the purchase price of the software is likely to be deemed unreasonable in any event.

10.6.2 **F(L)OSS**

All of this discussion assumes a proprietary EULA—that is, a licence on standard commercial terms distributed by commercial operations like Microsoft, Apple, Oracle, or SAP. There is an alternative though. Supporters of open source software argue that software should be a shared resource which everyone can use and improve rather than a proprietary and closed resource. The main exponents of this movement are the Free Software Foundation, an organization set up by campaigner Richard Stallman. A central plank of their philosophy for Free (Libre) Open Source Software (F(L)OSS) is the GNU General Public Licence (GNU GPL).[138] The current version of the GPL, GPLv3, is highly controversial and is sometimes called a 'copyleft' licence, after a concept developed by Stallman. The distribution rights granted by the GPL for modified versions of a GPL work are not unconditional. When someone distributes a GPL work plus their own modifications, the requirements for distributing the whole work cannot be any greater than the requirements that are in the GPL. This requirement is known as copyleft. The key clause in the licence is s. 5(c) which states:

[135] 1996 SLT 604.

[136] P Johnson, 'All Wrapped Up? A Review of the Enforceability of "Shrink-Wrap" and "Click-Wrap" Licences in the United Kingdom and the United States' (2003) 25 *EIPR* 98.

[137] [1997] FSR 251.

[138] The reason it is Free (Libre) Open Source Software rather than just Free Open Source Software is to differentiate two meanings of free not recorded in English: Gratis and Libre. As Stallman says F(L)OSS software is 'Free as in speech, not free as in beer.'

Highlight The copyleft clause: GPLv3 s. 5(c)

You must license the entire work, as a whole, under this License to anyone who comes into possession of a copy. This License will therefore apply, along with any applicable section 7 additional terms, to the whole of the work, and all its parts, regardless of how they are packaged. This License gives no permission to license the work in any other way, but it does not invalidate such permission if you have separately received it.

This is a 'viral' clause which infects any new work with the GPL conditions. It works because the original GPL work is protected by copyright and the licensee has no right to redistribute it, not even in modified form (barring fair use), except under the terms of the licence. Unsurprisingly the GPL licence is extremely controversial for this reason as it infects works which use as little as one line of GPL code. As a result it makes it very difficult for commercial software operators to produce software which interfaces GPL code. Microsoft's Steve Ballmer has called it 'a cancer that attaches itself in an intellectual property sense to everything it touches',[139] while Linux creator Linus Torvalds refused to use GPLv3 for his releases of the Linux kernel arguing that it did not reflect open source principles.[140]

Some suggested that the viral impact of GPLv3 would drive users away from the GPL licence and anecdotal data suggests this is true, with reports suggesting that the numbers of GPL licences are falling with users instead looking to less aggressive open source licensing solutions[141] and with major distributors such as Microsoft banning GPL software from their Windows marketplace.[142] There is no doubt creators will still want to create and distribute open source software, but as we move to more controlled operating environments such as Windows 10 and the iOS system there will be less opportunity for its distribution.

10.7 **Patent protection for computer software**

Section 1(2)(c) of the Patents Act 1977 is quite clear: 'the following (among other things) are not inventions for the purposes of this Act, that is to say, anything which consists of a scheme, rule or method for performing a mental act, playing a game or doing business, *or a program for a computer*'. Equally clear is Art. 52(2)(c) the European Patent Convention, 'the following in particular shall not be regarded as inventions . . . schemes, rules and methods for performing mental acts, playing games or doing business, *and programs for computers*'. With two such unarguably clear statements of the law at both European and UK level it may be assumed that this final section of this chapter would be necessarily short but unfortunately the law on patent protection for computer

[139] T Greene, 'Ballmer: "Linux is a cancer"' (*The Register*, 2 June 2001) <http://www.theregister.co.uk/2001/06/02/ballmer_linux_is_a_cancer/>.

[140] Linus Torvalds, 'GPLv3 Position Statement' 25 September 2006 <https://lkml.org/lkml/2006/9/25/161>.

[141] SJ Vaughan-Nichols, 'The fall of GPL and the rise of permissive open-source licenses' (*ZDNet*, 16 December 2014) <http://www.zdnet.com/article/the-fall-of-gpl-and-the-rise-of-permissive-open-source-licenses/>; C Metz, 'Open Sourcers Drop Software Religion for Common Sense' *Wired* 15 February 2012 <http://www.wired.com/2012/02/cloudera-and-apache/all/>.

[142] 'Microsoft Bans Open Source from the Marketplace' (*IT* Pro, 17 February 2011) <http://www.itpro portal.com/2011/02/17/microsoft-bans-open-source-marketplace/>.

software is less clear than one might hope. Software developers have long sought patent protection for their output. As previously discussed, as early as 1972 in the case of *Gottschalk v Benson*,[143] the US Supreme Court examined the patentability of computer software, a question they were to return to in 1978 in the case of *Parker v Flook*.[144]

The UK courts had begun looking at the patentability of software processes even earlier. In *Gevers' Application*[145] the court examined whether a data processing operation using punch cards was a 'manner of manufacture' under the Patents Act 1949. Mr Gevers had designed an index of word trademarks using punched cards and a processing system which allowed use of these cards to check for similarity between applications for trademarks and previously registered marks. Graham J allowed Mr Gevers' application, finding that his punched cards shared a similarity to a cam control for a lathe and could be distinguished from a card which contained written or printed information intended to convey information to the human eye or mind.[146] In the later case of *Burrough's Corporation (Perkin's Application)*,[147] the court held that 'computer programs which have the effect of controlling computers to operate in a particular way, where such programs are embodied in physical form, are proper subject matter for letters patent'.[148] Although it may be assumed that the 1977 Patents Act statutorily overruled these early cases[149] software designers have continued to seek patent protection for their output. This is because the level of protection offered by patent law is much greater than that offered by copyright law, with the core idea of the software being protectable by patent and although patents are of a short lifespan, only 20 years as opposed to copyright's 70 years plus, this is more than sufficient when dealing with most software applications which tend to be of a short shelf life. Further, the recent retreat from expansive look and feel protection seen in both the US and the UK has increased demand for software patents.

There is a problem with the wording of the Patents Act. There is a deliberate ambiguity designed to allow a patent to be awarded to an invention which contains a software element, but is not solely software-based. This ambiguity can be seen if you look at s. 1(2)(c).[150]

Highlight Patents Act 1977, s. 1(2)(c)

It is hereby declared that the following (among other things) are not inventions for the purposes of this Act, that is to say, anything which consists of a scheme, rule or method for performing a mental act, playing a game or doing business, or a program for a computer; but the foregoing provision shall prevent anything from being treated as an invention for the purposes of this Act only to the extent that a patent or application for a patent relates to that thing as such.

143 See (n. 2).
144 See (n. 4).
145 [1969] FSR 480.
146 Ibid. 486–7.
147 [1973] FSR 439.
148 Ibid. 450.
149 On which see *Gale's Application* [1991] RPC 305.
150 The wording of the European Patent Convention is again similar. It states, at Art. 52: 'The following in particular shall not be regarded as inventions . . . schemes, rules and methods for performing mental acts, playing games or doing business, and programs for computers . . . only to the extent to which a European patent application or European patent relates to such subject-matter or activities as such.'

This ambiguity requires patent examiners to walk a very fine line. It is designed to ensure that patents may be awarded for inventions which rely upon software as an element of their design, think-engine management systems, or today even the humble washing machine, but to exclude pure software inventions such as hyperlinking or 'cut and paste'. The problem is that courts are required to develop tests which allow through the patentable 'software-related invention' but which prevent the patenting of software. With such high values at stake it is no surprise that this fine distinction has come again and again under attack. The first attempt to define where this line should be drawn was the case of *VICOM/Computer-related Invention*.[151]

10.7.1 **VICOM/Computer-related invention**

This was an application to the European Patent Office (EPO) under the Convention. It related to a new processing system for digital images, the process itself being described as a series of mathematical algorithms.

The Appeal Board of the EPO decided that a claim for a technical process, carried out under the control of a programme cannot be regarded as related to a 'computer program as such'. They reached this decision in applying an approach which became known as the 'technical effect' approach. It asks judges or patent examiners to examine the application as if the excepted element (the software) were not present and then to ask 'does the application without the excepted element meet the standard of patentability?' If the only novel or original element is in the excepted element the answer will be no and the application should be refused. If the software element is merely part of the novelty of the invention the answer will be yes and a patent should be awarded.

In allowing VICOM's appeal the Board noted that: 'the computer program referred to... merely serves to calculate the element values of the small generating kernel and the weighting values. It does not form part of the image processing methods claimed, nor is it embodied in the apparatus claims. Indeed such a program would not be patentable in view of the Board's foregoing considerations.'[152] The Board also gave some helpful pointers as to what would be patentable and what not:

Highlight Technical Board of Appeal guidance

1. A computer of known type set up to operate according to a new program cannot be considered as forming part of the state of the art.
2. A claim directed to a technical process which process is carried out under the control of a program (whether by means of hardware or software), cannot be regarded as relating to a computer program as such.
3. A claim which can be considered as being directed to a computer set up to operate in accordance with a specified program (whether by means of hardware or software) for controlling or carrying out a technical process cannot be regarded as relating to a computer program as such.

[151] [1987] 2 EPOR 74.
[152] Ibid. [18].

The *VICOM* decision was highly influential both before the Board of Appeal of the EPO and before the UK courts. It was applied by the Court of Appeal in *Merrill Lynch's Application*,[153] in which the court rejected Merrill Lynch's application to patent a system for automating market trades. The court found that the inventive step of Merrill Lynch's system was contained in the software which tracked the market and executed trades: as such the 'invention' was not patentable. Repeatedly throughout the late 1980s and 1990s *VICOM* was followed by the UK courts in a series of cases including *Genentech Inc.'s Patent*,[154] *Gale's Application*,[155] *Wang Laboratories Inc.'s Application*,[156] and *Fujitsu Ltd's Application*.[157] It appeared a clear and simple test to determine that the patentability of software-related inventions, as opposed to pure software, had been achieved. Yet even as this stability had established itself, activities were taking place elsewhere which threatened to undermine it.

10.7.2 The effect of *State Street Bank*

In the US the decision in *Borland* had reduced considerably the scope of look and feel protection. Further it had indicated that functional elements of software such as command systems or interfaces were unlikely to be protectable. This led to a new wave of patent applications for software elements.

In *State Street Bank & Trust Co. v Signature Financial Group*,[158] the US Court of Appeals for the Federal Circuit found that a patent application which was, to all intents and purposes, the amalgamation of two excluded subject matters (computer software and a method of doing business) was patentable. The application involved a claimed invention of a 'Data Processing System for Hub and Spoke Financial Services Configuration'. In layman's terms this was a computerized system for moving funds within a series of accounts managed by the applicants. The case therefore shares many similarities with the English case of *Merrill Lynch*. In a departure from the previous case law the court found that systems such as these were patentable if they produced 'a useful, concrete and tangible result'.[159] Almost immediately the US Patent and Trademark Office issued new guidelines to examiners indicating that software which produced such a result may be patentable.[160] With the US Patent and Trademark Office now entertaining patent applications for software inventions pressure grew on other jurisdictions to follow suit. The EPO was well placed to consider an expansion of patent policy.

In February 1999 the Board of Appeal considered the case of *IBM's Application*.[161] This involved an application to patent a data processing system for Windows-based computers such that any information displayed in one window which is obscured by a second

153 [1989] RPC 561.
154 [1989] RPC 147.
155 See (n. 149).
156 [1991] RPC 463.
157 [1997] RPC 608.
158 149 F. 3d 1368 (Fed. Cir. 1998).
159 Ibid. 1374. It should be noted that in the case of *In re Bernard L Bilski and Rand*, 88 USPQ 2d 1385 (2008), the US Court of Appeals for the Federal Circuit overruled parts of the *State Street* test noting that 'those portions of our opinions in State Street and AT&T relying solely on a "useful, concrete and tangible result" analysis should no longer be relied on'.
160 H Rockman, *Intellectual Property Law for Engineers and Scientists* (Wiley 2004) 229–30.
161 [1999] RPC 861.

window is automatically moved to allow the first window to be clearly displayed. In a paradigm-shifting ruling, perhaps influenced by the *State Street* ruling in the US, the Board ruled that a computer program was not excluded from patentability per se. It stated that:

> the exclusion from patentability of programs for computers as such (Article 52(2) and (3) of the EPC) may be construed to mean that such programs are considered to be mere abstract creations, lacking in technical character. The use of the expression 'shall not be regarded as inventions' seems to confirm this interpretation. Programs for computers must be considered as patentable inventions when they have a technical character.[162]

Highlight Decision of the Board of Appeal in *IBM's Application*

A patent may be granted not only in the case of an invention where a piece of software manages, by means of a computer, an industrial process or the working of a piece of machinery, but in every case where a program for a computer is the only means, or one of the necessary means, of obtaining a technical effect, where, for instance, a technical effect of that kind is achieved by the internal functioning of a computer itself under the influence of said program.

In short, the Board found that if the effect of the software was to cause a computer to function in a novel and inventive manner that software may be patentable.

This was to be the first in a long line of cases in which the EPO and the Board of Appeal gave ever narrower interpretations of the meaning of Art. 52(2)(c) of the Convention. In *PBS Partnership/Controlling Pension Benefits Systems*,[163] the Board of Appeal held that a program which calculated pension benefits and life assurance benefits could be patentable, despite the fact that the program itself would usually be excluded subject matter under Art. 52 as well as the operation it was performing. This is an extremely complex decision. The process that the program was performing was a method of doing business which is excluded from patentability by Art. 52(2)(c), and the system or apparatus that was to be protected was software which was similarly excluded. But by a tortuous process of interpretation the Board found that although business practices were not patentable under the Convention and that a non-technical process for carrying out that activity was similarly not protected, 'An apparatus[164] constituting a physical entity or concrete product suitable for performing or supporting an economic activity, is an invention within the meaning of Art. 52(1) EPC.'[165] This is extremely difficult to conceptualize. While both the operation itself and software in the abstract were excluded subject matters, the design of a software-based system to carry out the process could be patentable:[166] as David Bainbridge notes: 'it seemed to diminish the exclusion of computer programs as such from inventions almost to vanishing point'.[167]

[162] Ibid. 870.
[163] [2002] EPOR 52.
[164] Being an organizational structure, including a suitably programmed computer or system of computers.
[165] See (n. 163) [5].
[166] Although in this case it was not as it lacked the necessary inventive step.
[167] Bainbridge (n. 68) 155.

10.7.3 De facto software patents under the European Patent Convention

From this position it was a simple step to allow de facto software patents while the Convention retained the fiction that they were excluded subject matter. In *HITACHI/Auction Method*[168] the Board considered a patent for an online Dutch auction system. The auction would start with a preliminary data exchange between the bidder's computers and the server (auction) computer in order to collect bids from the participants. Each bid would comprise two values, a 'desired price' and a 'maximum price in competitive state'. Once this was complete the auction would run automatically and requires no further bidder interaction. An auction price is set and successively lowered until it reaches the level of the highest bid or bids as determined by the 'desired price'. In the case of several identical bids the price is increased until only the bidder having offered the highest 'maximum price' is left who is then declared successful.[169] The Board found that there are three requirements which must be fulfilled for a claim of this nature to be patented:

Highlight Technical Board of Appeal requirements for patentability

1. It should be an 'invention'. That is, it must be new, inventive and industrially applicable.
2. The term 'invention' is to be construed as 'subject-matter having technical character'.
3. Verification that the claimed subject matter is an invention within the meaning of Art. 52(1) EPC must be done before performing the three other tests, i.e. the novelty, the inventive step and the industrial applicability tests.[170]

The Board then confirmed the fact that a mixture of a technical and non-technical feature may be patentable, finding that 'contrary to the examining division's assessment, the apparatus of claim three is an invention within the meaning of Art. 52(1) EPC since it comprises clearly technical features such as a "server computer", "client computers" and a "network"'.[171] Although the application in the instant case was ultimately rejected as it lacked an inventive step, this is, like the *Pension Benefits Case* before, an incredible decision. It seems to suggest that the clothing of a business method, or perhaps even a mathematical formula or a scheme for carrying out a mental act in a technical apparatus may be patentable.

The Board seems to accept that this approach is controversial, perhaps even counter to the original intent of the drafters of the Convention, in noting that:

> The Board is aware that its comparatively broad interpretation of the term 'invention' in Art. 52(1) EPC will include activities which are so familiar that their technical character tends to be overlooked, such as the act of writing using pen and paper. Needless to say, however, this does not imply that all methods involving the use of technical means are patentable. They still have to be new, represent a non-obvious technical solution to a technical problem, and be susceptible of industrial application.[172]

[168] [2004] EPOR 55.
[169] Adapted from *HITACHI/Auction Method* ibid. [19].
[170] Ibid. [20].
[171] Ibid. [26].
[172] Ibid. [34].

The high-water point in this expansive interpretation of Art. 52 is to be found in the connected cases of *MICROSOFT/Clipboard Formats I*[173] and *MICROSOFT/Clipboard Formats II*.[174] Both cases involved patent applications made by Microsoft to cover aspects of their Windows clipboard system, in particular allowing non-file data to be transferred from one application to another via the clipboard. The Board followed *Hitachi* and found that a method applying technical means was an invention and that a computer system was a technical means. The Board emphasized the difference between a computer system and a computer program:

> The Board would like to emphasise that a method implemented in a computer system represents a sequence of steps actually performed and achieving an effect, and not a sequence of computer-executable instructions (i.e. a computer program) which just have the potential of achieving such an effect when loaded into, and run on, a computer. Thus, the Board holds that the claim category of a computer-implemented method is distinguished from that of a computer program. Even though a method, in particular a method of operating a computer, may be put into practice with the help of a computer program, a claim relating to such a method does not claim a computer program in the category of a computer program.[175]

This is the clearest exposition to date of the distinction between computer programs, which are excluded from patentability and a computer-implemented method, which is not. Although the computer-implemented method may just describe the operation of the software, it is seen as distinct from the software. Again, patent examiners are being asked to walk a very fine line.

10.7.4 *Aerotel Ltd v Telco and Macrossan's Application*

The UK courts have watched all these developments with interest. Although the Board of Appeal has no authority over UK patent law, the relationship between a UK patent and a European patent is such that decisions of the EPO, and its Board of Appeal, are highly influential on UK patent law and policy. This tension between the expansive European approach and the UK approach which was still heavily influenced by *VICOM* came to a head in *Aerotel Ltd v Telco and Macrossan's Application*.[176]

The case concerned two inventions; one a system allowing for pre-paid calls to be made from any telephone (Aerotel), the other an automated method of acquiring the documents necessary to incorporate a company through the use of an online database (Macrossan). In giving the judgment of the court Jacob LJ spent a considerable amount of time examining the prior UK case law, including *Merrill Lynch, Gale*, and *Fujitsu* and the Board of Appeal decisions including *Pensions Benefits, Hitachi*, and *Microsoft*. It was clear from his examination that little common ground now lay between the two jurisdictions and Jacob LJ found it was incumbent upon the court to review and modernize the UK law.

[173] [2006] EPOR 39.
[174] [2006] EPOR 40.
[175] Ibid. [42].
[176] [2006] EWCA Civ 1371; [2007] 1 All ER 225.

Highlight The *Macrossan* test

The new test came in two stages:

1. UK authority should be preferred over the recent EPO line of authority. Jacob LJ was quite forthright in his view on this: 'The fact is that this court is bound by its own precedent: that decided in Merrill Lynch, Gale and Fujitsu—the technical effect approach with the rider.'
2. A clear and simple test which brought the *Merrill Lynch* test up to date should be used. This involved the development of a new four-stage test:
   a. construe the claim
   b. identify the contribution
   c. ask whether the contribution is solely of excluded matter
   d. check whether the contribution is technical.

Macrossan may be seen as either an attempt to entrench the *VICOM* 'technical effect' approach, something to be criticized,[177] or as an attempt to bridge the divide between the UK approach and the European approach by inviting the Board of Appeal to reconsider post-*VICOM* developments in light of the fact that *VICOM* has never been expressly overruled.[178] It is clear the court in *Macrossan* intended the latter. At [29] Jacob LJ invites the Board of Appeal to reconsider their recent jurisprudence:

> We are conscious of the need to place great weight on decisions of the Boards of Appeal, but, given the present state of conflict between the old (*Vicom* etc.) and the new (*Hitachi* etc.) approaches, quite apart from the fact that there are three distinct new approaches each to some extent in conflict with the other two, it would be premature to do so. If and when an Enlarged Board rules on the question, this Court may have to re-consider its approach. If such a ruling were to differ from what this court had previously decided a question would arise as to what should be done: should this court (and first instance courts) follow the previous rulings in our courts, leaving it to the House of Lords (or the future Supreme Court) to decide what to do or should the new ruling of the Enlarged Board be followed? It may be that the better course then would be for a decision of the first instance court to be 'leapfrogged' to the House of Lords or Supreme Court. For the present we do not have to decide this. All we decide now is that we do not follow any of the trio. The fact that the BGH has already declined to follow Pension Benefits reinforces this view—doing so will not lead to European consistency.

Unfortunately this request initially fell on deaf ears. The President of the Board of Appeal refused to acknowledge the differences in approach between the EPO and UK courts[179] and a clear distinction remained. In summer 2007 Professor Pompidou, the President of the Board of Appeal who had refused Lord Justice Jacob's request, was replaced by Alison Brimlow. Ms Brimlow had been the Comptroller General of the UK Patent Office and so was familiar with the perceived divide between the *VICOM*

[177] See e.g. Bainbridge (n. 68) 157.

[178] D Booton, 'The Patentability of Computer-Implemented Inventions in Europe' (2007) *Intellectual Property Quarterly* 92.

[179] Letter from Professor Alain Pompidou President of the EPO Board of Appeal to Lord Justice Robin Jacob (undated).

approach and the *Hitachi* approach. On 22 October 2008 she referred a number of questions to the Enlarged Board of Appeals of the EPO concerning the patentability of computer software.[180] Among the questions asked were: 'Can a claim in the area of computer programs avoid exclusion under art. 52(2)(c) and (3) merely by explicitly mentioning the use of a computer or a computer readable storage medium?' and 'Does the activity of programming a computer necessarily involve technical considerations?' In May 2010 the Enlarged Board of Appeals answered her referral. They noted that the referral was inadmissible and defended the EPO's interpretation of Art. 52(2) and (3) as based on sound and consistent logic, and as having 'created a practicable system for delimiting the innovations for which a patent may be granted'.[181] The divide between the UK courts and the EPO remains therefore as distinct as ever.

The UK courts continue to apply the *Macrossan* test, in cases such as *Re AT&T Knowledge Ventures LP*[182] and *Symbian Ltd v Comptroller General of Patents*.[183] The problem with *Macrossan* is that while it informs how to approach the test for exclusion it does not give guidance as to how to resolve the question; for that one must look to *AT&T Knowledge Ventures LP v Comptroller General of Patents Designs and Trade Marks*.[184] This case involved a patent application for a 'content broker hosting service system', essentially a software system which selected multimedia files for delivery to the customer based upon compatibility with the customer's device, connected to the multimedia supplier. The judge, Lewison J, set out five signposts for indicating whether or not the invention made a technical contribution to the art in terms of the *Macrossan* test:

Highlight The *AT&T* signposts

1. Whether the claimed technical effect has a technical effect on a process which is carried on outside the computer;
2. whether the claimed technical effect operates at the level of the architecture of the computer; that is to say whether the effect is produced irrespective of the data being processed or the applications being run;
3. whether the claimed technical effect results in the computer being made to operate in a new way;
4. whether there is an increase in the speed or reliability of the computer;
5. whether the perceived problem is overcome by the claimed invention as opposed to merely being circumvented.

The first signpost refers to those occasions where a computer is being used to control a real-world apparatus or process such as a manufacturing process or an engine management system. These are generally permissible as they bring about a useful technical

180 *President's Reference/Computer Program Exclusion* [2009] EPOR 9.

181 *President's Reference/Computer Program Exclusion* [2010] EPOR 36 at [10.8.2] and [10.13.2].

182 [2009] EWHC 343 (Pat).

183 [2008] EWCA Civ 1066. For a discussion of the *Symbian* case see C De Mauny, 'Court of Appeal Clarifies Patenting of Computer Programs' (2009) 31 *European Intellectual Property Review* 147.

184 [2009] EWHC 343 (Pat).

effect in the physical world and so go beyond abstract computer programs. The second signpost is rather more complicated. As we have already seen when discussing *MICROSOFT/Clipboard Formats* and *Hitachi*, any program can be said to bring about a change in the operation of a computer. Under the *Macrossan* test such programs are not considered patentable as their contribution is solely within excluded matter: what is required is a further technical effect or contribution. In *Symbian*,[185] the invention related to a dynamic link library (DLL) having a first part and an extended part. Functions in the first part could be linked to by ordinal number while those in the extended part could be linked to via a further library of additional functions. The extended part provided flexibility for third parties to develop new functions for inclusion in the DLL, but meant that those new functions would not be overwritten by updates to the DLL. The invention was ultimately found to be patentable as it solved a problem within the computer. This can be distinguished from inventions that depend solely on the data being processed or the applications being run, such as the invention in *Fujitsu Ltd's Application*.[186] In that case, the invention was a program for modelling crystal lattice structures and displaying the results on screen and the computer itself was held simply to be performing the kind of computational activities for which computers are used.

The third and fourth signposts are intended to give general examples of what might constitute a further technical effect or contribution, such as new functionality for the computer or an increase in speed. The emphasis is on what the computer program has achieved in the computer itself, although the effect may also apply to computer networks. In *HTC Europe v Apple Inc.*[187] the Court of Appeal expanded the fourth signpost to 'whether a program makes a computer a better computer in the sense of running more efficiently and effectively as a computer'.[188] In that decision, Apple's innovation of a touch screen control method called 'The Multi Touch feature' was found to be patentable as it provided a new interface for application programmers to create programs, in which conflicting inputs from the touch screen no longer needed to be resolved at the application level.

The fifth and final signpost is intended to prevent the patenting of programs that only result in a technical effect indirectly, that is by virtue of programming that reflects an organizational or administrative fix external to the program itself, rather than by an improvement to the technology itself.

The application of these signposts demonstrates a distinct approach to that of the EPO which remains much more laissez-faire than the UK courts in this field. It seems currently this divide will remain as both regimes are fixed in their approaches. In fact the issue becomes even more confused when one adds the new unitary patent into the mix. This is an EU harmonization initiative which borrows elements of EPC infrastructure. As we saw earlier, the EPO was formed by the EPC and is thus not an EU body. However, under the Unitary Patent Protection Regulation[189] and the Unitary Patent Co-operation Regulation,[190] a scheme for unitary patent recognition in EU

[185] See (n. 183).
[186] See (n. 157).
[187] [2013] EWCA Civ 451.
[188] Ibid. [51].
[189] Reg. 1257/2012 OJ L361/1.
[190] Known as the Translation Arrangements Regulation: Reg. 1260/2012 OJ L361/89.

member states was formed. The proposed system will see the awards of a single unitary patent granted under the EPC that will be recognized in all EU member states which will be awarded for payment of a single application/renewal fee, subject to control by a single court (the proposed Unified Patent Court) and uniform protection. This means that revocation as well as infringement proceedings are to be decided for the unitary patent as a whole rather than for each country individually. This process has been on hold until recently due to two challenges against the legitimacy of the programme by the Kingdom of Spain.[191] However in May 2015 the CJEU rejected both challenges and found the process to be in compliance with EU law.[192] The unitary patent may now move ahead and while EU member states must request to join only two have yet to make such a request, Spain and Poland, and Spain may now join as its legal challenge is at an end. Thus it is likely within the next two to three years that three patent regimes will be recognized in the UK: the UK patent issued by the UK Intellectual Property Office, the European patent issued by the European Patent Office, and the unitary patent issued by the European Patent Office but with a separate regulatory oversight system in the Unified Patent Court and different recognition rules in EU member states who join the unified patent. The whole issue becomes murkier rather than clearer.

10.8 **Conclusions**

Of all the areas where law and the digital society interface the question of how the law should protect computer software is probably the most complex. This is due to many factors. First, there is the long history: the software industry was the first fully formed digital industry, emerging in the 1970s before digital entertainment media, digital criminal activity, or e-commerce. Second, the product of the software industry is both traditionally the most valuable of any digital industry and the most complex. The software industry emerged before the legal system could adapt, meaning that software has never had a planned legal response in the way that computer crime, electronic contracting, or databases have. Whereas it may be argued that software is a unique product, and would have been suited to a *sui generis* form of protection, it has instead fallen between two stools: copyright protection designed primarily for artistic expression not functional goods, and patents which seek to protect inventions, not systems of performing human acts. In the 1980s any hope of a software patent law was abandoned in favour of expansive look and feel copyright protection. The 1990s and the 2000s have seen a strong move away from copyright protection for all except literal infringement and a shift back towards software patents both explicitly (as in the US) and implicitly (in Europe).

[191] C-146/13 and C-147/13.

[192] *Spain v European Parliament and Council of the EU* C-146/13 <http://curia.europa.eu/juris/documents.jsf?num = C-146/13> and *Spain v Council of the EU* C-147/13 <http://curia.europa.eu/juris/liste.jsf?num = C-147/13>.

Whatever method of protection is followed, copyright law or patent law, the value of the software industry to the GDP of developed nations ensures some form of protection will be afforded to software. It is essential, however, that whatever form the next generation of software protection takes we do not repeat the mistakes of the look and feel cases of the 1980s and 1990s in providing a form of protection that is either under- or over-inclusive. Competition within the industry requires that innovation is not stifled by the application of IPRs, while free-riders must be discouraged. Protecting software products has proven to be one of the most intractable problems of the information society, a problem we have yet to deal with fully.

TEST QUESTIONS

Question 1

Rachel, a UK-based client of yours, comes to see you for advice.

Her company Spinround Games specializes in producing games for children with motor control difficulties. They are highly interactive games which make use of motion sensor technologies (similar to Xbox Kinect), bright sounds and bright colours designed to stimulate attention and movement among children between four and eight.

A considerable amount of time has gone into developing the Spinaround system which uses both a specially designed hardware platform and carefully designed software such as the bestselling 'Xander's Dance World' and their new product 'Flying with Allen'. Spinaround Games were until recently the only developer in this niche but valuable market.

Two months ago a rival developer PlayDay Games launched their own software but not hardware. Their games are designed to be compatible with the Spinaround system although Spinaround have not licensed them to use the Spinaround system and have never discussed with PlayDay any of the design specifications of the Spinaround system. Spinaround suspect PlayDay may have reverse-engineered their games software to ensure that PlayDay's products would work on the Spinaround system.

PlayDay have initially released two games 'PlayDate with Wendy' and 'Dance with Julio'. Dance with Julio looks and plays exactly like Xander's Dance World with similar characters, colours, movements, and goals. Also PlayDay have announced that coming soon will be four more games including 'In the Air with Flair' which, according to prelaunch advertising, looks just like 'Flying with Allen'.

Advise Rachel.

Question 2

Following the decision of the ECJ in *SAS Institute Inc.v World Programming Ltd* [2012] 3 CMLR 4 that the functionality of a computer program is not protected by copyright as it falls on the wrong side of the ideas/expression divide, and that the programming language used is also not protected by copyright as it is a functional element which allows instructions to be given to a computer, discuss what future role you believe copyright law will play in protecting computer software.

FURTHER READING

Books

D Bainbridge, *Software Licensing* (1999)

S Lai, *The Copyright Protection of Computer Software in the United Kingdom* (2000)

P Leith, *Software and Patents in Europe* (2011)

Chapters and articles

D Booton, 'The Patentability of Computer-implemented Inventions in Europe', *Intellectual Property Quarterly* 92 (2007)

P Cole 'Patentability of Computer Software as Such', *Patently O Law Journal* (2008), <http://patentlyo.com/media/docs/2008/10/cole.pdf>

K Moon, 'The Nature of Computer Programs: Tangible? Goods? Personal Property? Intellectual Property?', 31 *European Intellectual Property Review* 396 (2009)

S Stokes, 'The Development of UK Software Copyright Law: From John Richardson Computers to Navitaire', 11 *Computer and Telecommunications Law Review* 129 (2005)

Copyright in the digital environment

The move from physical to digital distribution models and the development of the internet are two of the most disruptive events of the twentieth century. They have changed the way the developed world trades, communicates, and socializes. But as with all disruptive technologies the positive benefits they bring are tinged with negative effects. As well as allowing people to keep in touch over long distances and allowing new models of commerce to develop they have also allowed the internet to become the largest and most efficient copying machine built by man. This development is not accidental it is in the DNA of the internet that it copies and distributes digital information.

The difficulty that the designers of the ARPANET had to overcome was how to supply data from one computer to another in a remote location. This entailed copying the data, splitting it into packets, and delivering these packets to remote locations: in essence the building of a platform for the copying and distribution of digital content. While computers were expensive and network connections slow, this was not a problem. The very idea that someone would pay several thousand dollars for a computer to allow them to download and store copies of music, movies, or games across a network connection which operated at 9,600 bits per second,[1] was frankly laughable. But in the last twenty-five years the cost of computers, storage media, and high-speed downloads have tumbled as the information society has become part of our everyday lives. This coupled with an explosion of digital consumer devices such as tablets and smartphones has created a new marketplace for digital consumer entertainment products, products that are at extreme risk of piracy and given the nature of the internet as a copying and distribution device have been pirated extensively. This increase in piracy is occurring at a time when producers of digital consumer goods are trying to establish new delivery models for their products through direct download delivery sites such as Apple's iTunes, Amazon's Kindle Store, and Netflix Download. When they are asked to compete against free services such as BitTorrent it is hard for them to develop their market: what rational person is going to pay £13.99 to download an HD movie from iTunes if they can get it for free via a BitTorrent client?

This chapter focuses on the battle between producers of content and free riders; between the copyright industries and their own consumers; between taking profit from content and making it free. It is a battle fought on many levels; an economic level, an artistic level, a legal level, and an ideological level. Some people believe passionately

[1] To underline how much download speeds have accelerated in the last twenty-six years a standard 9600 bps modem in use in 1990 would take about 85 minutes to download a 6mb MP3 music file; today a 48MB/s fibre connection would take around 1 second.

that the copyright industries have been profiteering, charging on average £8.99 for a full album download on iTunes which involves no cost of physical production (no need for a CD case, album sleeve, or even a CD), no distribution costs (no need for fleets of vans to deliver CDs to shops), and no overheads for the retailer (iTunes has no shops on which it needs to pay rent, rates, heating, or staff costs). Others believe equally passionately that failure to control peer-to-peer (P2P) file-sharing has had long-term deleterious effects for all copyright industries. Some believe passionately that the internet allows an artistic freedom which was impossible in the old distribution model when artists needed to be signed to a music label before their music could reach the shops; others worry about an explosion of mediocre music, films, and video games. Some believe that the illegal file-sharing of copyright protected media is the single biggest threat the copyright industry has faced. They believe there is a need to review, rewrite, and extend copyright protection to afford additional protection to copyright holders in an attempt to rebalance the interests of copyright holders and users. They argue this is necessary because the level of protection copyright holders had before the advent of the information society has been eroded by the simple, free, and (mostly) anonymous practice of file-sharing. Others believe the copyright industry is seeking to extend copyright protection in a way which may prove harmful to society. Finally, some believe that in the digital environment with its limitless supply of ones and zeros information wants to be and should be free. Others disagree. This will be the story of this chapter but before we get to the heart of the modern debate about file-sharing and free riding copyright content we must begin with an analysis of how the internet has challenged the application and development of copyright law.

11.1 Linking, caching, and aggregating

When ARPANET was designed and built in the 1960s few considerations were given to copyright issues. As the network was designed only to connect research computers the copyright in the material accessible on ARPANET was usually owned by the university or research centre where the mainframe computer could be found. Since all involved in the ARPANET project were entering the project with the express aim of sharing research materials and findings, there was no conceptualization of copyright infringement being pursued for any ARPANET activity.

Copyright became more of an issue as the network deregulated; the advent of private internet service providers saw copyright issues come to the fore. In particular the World Wide Web posed a major challenge to established copyright orthodoxy. It is founded upon hyperlinking: the very nature of its DNA being the ability to join together original content, or to draw original content from one place and place it in another (as is done with embedded images). This, coupled with the widespread geographical reach of the web and its foundations as an easy-to-use and easy-to-access platform, meant that quickly copyright law and web-based applications came into direct competition with each other.

11.1.1 Web-linking

First among common web-copyright issues was the issue of linking. It may seem clear that when one places original material on a website that it is the intent of the copyright holder that, absent a password protection system to control access, the material may be accessed and read (including making a cache copy of the content in the end user's browser cache),[2] but this is only part of the issue. Web pages function by getting referrals from other pages (links), these links are what make the web dynamic, and so one may assume that as well as implying that placing content on a public web page allows for reading and caching of that content it also allows for linking to that content. This is not necessarily the case.

This issue first arose in 1996 in the case of *Shetland Times Ltd v Wills*.[3] The pursuer was an established newspaper publisher producing a local newspaper servicing the Shetland Isles. Some time prior to October 1996 they began publishing an online version of their newspaper on the expectation that once this became popular they would be able to sell advertising space on the front page of the site. Dr Wills operates a web-only news publication, the *Shetland News*. In October 1996 it became clear to the pursuers that the *Shetland News* was embarking upon a programme of so-called deep-linking: this is linking directly to pages in the body of a site, bypassing the front page. Their activities are described by Lord Hamilton:

> Since about 14 October 1996 the defenders have included among the headlines on their front page a number of headlines appearing in recent issues of the *Shetland Times* as reproduced on the pursuers' web site. These headlines are verbatim reproductions of the pursuers' headlines as so reproduced. A caller accessing the defenders' web site may, by clicking on one of those headlines appearing on the defenders' front page, gain access to the relative text as published and reproduced by the pursuers. Access is so gained and subsequent access to other such headlines also gained without the caller requiring at any stage to access the pursuers' front page. Thus, access to the pursuers' items (as published in printed editions and reproduced by them on their web site) can be obtained by bypassing the pursuers' front page and accordingly missing any advertising material which may appear on it.[4]

The final sentence here demonstrates the crux of the case. By deep-linking to *Shetland Times* news stories the *Shetland News* was misappropriating the advertising revenue from these stories. The *Shetland Times* sought an interim interdict (the Scottish equivalent of an injunction) to prevent the *Shetland News* from using any of their headlines on its site or from linking directly to any of their content other than their home page. Lord Hamilton had two decisions to make, (1) whether a newspaper headline qualified as a 'literary work' under s. 17 of the Copyright, Designs and Patents Act, and (2) whether a web page constituted a 'cable programme' under s. 20 of the Copyright, Designs and Patents Act as then worded.[5] He evaluated both claims in an interim hearing. Due to

[2] For those unfamiliar with the operations of web browsers a cache copy is a stored copy of a web page previously visited by the user. These are used to reduce the amount of information that needs to be transmitted across the network during a browsing session as information previously stored in the cache can often be reused by the browser. This reduces bandwidth and processing requirements of the web server, and helps to improve responsiveness for users of the web. Modern browsers employ a built-in cache, but some ISPs also use a caching proxy server, which is a cache that is shared between all users of that network. Thus if a customer of BT broadband visits http://www.bbc.co.uk/news, BT will cache a copy in its server, then when the next customer requires http://www.bbc.co.uk/news instead of calling upon the BBC server to deliver the page BT will supply the copy from its server. The server periodically checks with the BBC server to see if a page update is needed.

[3] 1997 SC 316.

[4] Ibid. 318.

[5] It should be noted s. 20 of the CDPA 1988 has been completely rewritten since this case was heard, with new text being introduced by The Copyright and Related Rights Regulations 2003 (SI 2003/2498).

the nature of the hearing no authority was laid before the court making the opinion of little authority, however, he found that:

> While literary merit is not a necessary element of a literary work, there may be a question whether headlines, which are essentially brief indicators of the subject matter of the items to which they relate, are protected by copyright. However, in light of the concession that a headline could be a literary work and since the headlines at issue (or at least some of them) involve eight or so words designedly put together for the purpose of imparting information, it appeared to me to be arguable that there was an infringement, at least in some instances, of s. 17.[6]

This at the time was of passing interest. The question of replicating headlines or short descriptions of text was no doubt important, especially when one is creating a link to content on another site; the real question though was whether Lord Hamilton felt a website was itself capable of copyright protection. Although the wording of s. 20 has changed since the case, the decision on this final issue was of widespread importance. This may only have been an interim hearing, and the jurisdiction of the court may have been limited, but this was the first time a judge anywhere in the world had been asked to rule on the copyright status of a website. Lord Hamilton found that a web page operated by sending information across a network which fitted with the definition of a cable service as then defined as 'a service which consists wholly or mainly in sending visual images, sounds or other information by means of a telecommunications system, otherwise than by wireless telegraphy'.[7] On this basis, and on the basis that at an interim hearing the pursuer only needs to demonstrate a 'balance of convenience' in their favour, he found that 'the pursuers have, in my opinion, a *prima facie* case that the incorporation by the defenders in their website of the headlines provided at the pursuers' website constitutes an infringement of s. 20 of the Act by the inclusion in a cable programme service of protected cable programmes'.[8]

The *Shetland Times* case was at once unimportant and yet of international influence. As an interim hearing it carried almost no precedence, yet as the first published judicial opinion on copyright protection for web content, this four-page decision which discussed no previous authority was discussed and analysed globally.[9] Lord Hamilton was often, and unfairly given the nature of the hearing, criticized for extending the definition of a cable programme to cover a website. Most critics attacked his interpretation that a website could operate as a cable programme. They pointed out that the definition of a cable programme as one which 'sends visual images, sounds or other information' suggested a push media system; a type of media platform where a broadcaster sends programmes or other content unbidden (such as TV or radio), whereas a website is a pull media system; the customer must select what to receive and ask for it. Whatever the critics thought, Lord Hamilton had decided both that the contents of web pages could be protected by copyright law and that deep-linking without the permission of the

[6] 1997 SC 316, 319.

[7] This was found in s. 7(1) of the CDPA 1988. This section was repealed in whole by The Copyright and Related Rights Regulations 2003.

[8] 1997 SC 316, 319.

[9] Just a few of these papers include: H MacQueen, 'Copyright in Cyberspace' (1998) *JBL* 297; J Adams, 'Trespass in a Digital Environment' (2002) *IPQ* 1; J Connolly and S Cameron, 'Fair Dealing in Webbed Links of Shetland Yarns' (1998) (2) *JILT* <http://www2.warwick.ac.uk/fac/soc/law/elj/jilt/1998_2/connolly/>; and S Pitiyasak, 'Does Thai Law Provide Adequate Protection for Copyright Infringement on the Internet?' (2003) 25 *EIPR* 6.

copyright holder could infringe copyright. In making this decision the door had been opened for further copyright challenges to web-based content and, as may be expected, a number of cases followed, looking at how copyright law should deal with linking and in particular deep-linking.

Across Europe claims were raised against deep-linking. One of the earliest cases was the French case of *Havas Numerique et Cadre On Line v Keljob*.[10] This case involved two online job agencies and the operator of a specialized jobs search engine. The claimants, the job agencies, claimed that in offering direct links from their search results to particular pages within the claimants' sites the defendant was in infringement of their copyright and database rights. At an interim hearing the Tribunal de Commerce de Paris distinguished between simple hyperlinks and the practice of deep-linking. The court observed that linking was implicitly permissible and even encouraged providing only that the link is via the homepage. The court found though that links, which appropriate the referenced site's contents mask the URL of the linked site or fail to inform the user that he or she has transferred to the site of a different content provider, infringes the property rights of the linked website owner. Accordingly, the court found the defendant's deep links to be parasitical and an unlawful appropriation of the claimants' work. On appeal though this decision was reversed.[11] The Grande Instance de Paris found that Keljob merely operated a search engine which provided results to its users and openly redirected them to pages within the claimants' sites. As a result, there was no copying and no distribution in any manner which was unfair.

A similar case was heard in Germany where the Landgericht (District Court) of Cologne heard the case of *Stepstone v Ofir*.[12] This was a case involving two competing online job agencies. The defendant would routinely deep-link to job details held on the claimant's website. The claimant claimed copyright infringement; the defendant argued that by placing information on a publicly accessible web page the claimant had given an implied licence to link to it. The court held that the defendant, in deep-linking to content within the claimant's site, had infringed the claimant's exclusive right of copying, distribution, and representation, in particular the distribution right.[13] Most cases to date, however, have dealt with news aggregation sites which act in a similar fashion to the Shetland News. These sites copy headlines from a variety of news sites and then deep-link to stories within these sites: currently the best-known news aggregator is Google News.

Probably the earliest such case arose in the Netherlands where in the case of *PCM v Kranten.com* the court held that deep-linking was not a reproduction of the copyright work and as a result no copyright infringement occurred.[14] The headlines which were copied in the form of the links were also found not to infringe as there is a specific

[10] Tribunal de Commerce de Paris, 26 December 2000 <http://www.legalis.net/cgi-iddn/french/affiche-jnet.cgi?droite=decisions/dt_auteur/ord_tcomm-paris_261200.htm> (in French only).

[11] *Cadremploi v Keljob*, Tribunal de Grande Instance de Paris, 5 September 2001 <http://www.juriscom.net/txt/jurisfr/da/tgiparis20010905.pdf> (in French only).

[12] Landgericht, Köln, February 28, 2001: 28 O 692/00. Discussed in G Smith, *Internet Law and Regulation* (4th edn, Sweet & Maxwell 2007) 70.

[13] Stepstone also pursued Ofir in France. On this occasion the Nanterre Tribunal of Commerce held that the actions of Ofir did not infringe Stepstone's copyright. See *SARL Stepstone France v SARL Ofir France*, Tribunal de Commerce de Nanterre 8 November 2000 <http://www.legalis.net/breves-article.php3?id_article=83> (in French only).

[14] *Sub nom. Algemeen Dagblad BV v Eureka Internetdiensten* [2002] ECDR 1.

journalistic exception in Dutch copyright law which allows reproduction of copyright work in a press report provided the original source is acknowledged.[15] A contrary position though was taken in Denmark in the case of *Danish Newspaper Publishers Association v Newsbooster.com*.[16] Newsbooster operated a subscription news service. The subscriber would choose a number of keywords, and then Newsbooster would select news stories of interest to him based upon these keywords and would send him links in the form of email messages. The emails would contain a précis of the story and a deep link to the story on the originator's site. The Publishers Association, representing the news originators, demanded that the group negotiate payments with them, or remove links to its sites. In a claim similar to the *Shetland Times* one, the Publishers Association argued that Newsbooster was a direct competitor of the newspapers and by bypassing their front pages, Newsbooster's links deprived them of advertising revenue and violated the newspapers' copyright as well as database rights. The court found that Newsbooster had infringed the newspapers' copyright and issued an injunction, noting that 'Newsbooster repeatedly and systematically reproduces and publishes the newspapers' headlines and articles'.[17]

These cases suggested a split approach was developing. In France and the Netherlands authorities were in place suggesting that deep-linking was not an infringement of copyright,[18] while in Germany and Denmark a contrary position had developed. Of course it is not this simple; each case must be measured on its merits and it is clear for instance that the actions of Keljob in providing a job search engine were very different from those of Newsbooster in providing direct emailed links to news stories.

It seemed as though some form of consensus approach had developed. In Germany the decision in *Stepstone* has been rendered less influential by the decision of the Bundesgerichtshof (Federal Court of Germany, Germany's highest court) in *Paperboy*.[19] Paperboy offered a news aggregation service comprising elements of a mainstream aggregation page, as previously seen in *Kranten*, and a personalized email service, similar to that seen in Newsbooster. The court in a very different decision to the previous German law found that 'Where a hyperlink is made to a page on a third party's website which constitutes a work protected by copyright, the making of that hyperlink does not infringe the right of reproduction of that work'[20] and, further, that:

> a copyright owner who makes available on the internet a work protected under copyright law, without technological protection measures, must be taken to have enabled any use which an on-demand user can make. In general, there is no infringement of copyright where access to a work is facilitated by the setting of hyperlinks, whether in the form of ordinary links or through the use of deep links.[21]

[15] Interestingly for a UK audience a similar 'fair dealing' provision is found in s. 30(2) of the CDPA 1988.

[16] [2003] ECDR 5.

[17] Ibid. [16].

[18] Similar authority had been seen in Austria. See *Meteodata v Bernegger Bau* (unreported, 17 December 2002, Supreme Court of Austria), discussed in Hobinger, 'Austria: Deep Linking: Copyright Note Allows Display of Foreign Contents on Website' (2003) (4) World Internet Law Report 18.

[19] *Sub nom. Verlagsgruppe Handelsblatt GmbH v Paperboy* [2005] ECDR 7.

[20] Ibid. [H7].

[21] Ibid. [H8].

The Danish courts also moved away from the hardline position found in Newsbooster in the case of *Home A/S v Ofir*.[22] Ofir operates an internet portal site linking to such items as job adverts and homes for sale. In 1998, the parent company of Ofir had contacted Home, an online real estate portal similar to the UK site primelocation.com, offering them free advertising in national newspapers to the value of kr250,000, in exchange for the right to get data from their servers to be used in the real estate section of Ofir's portal. Home indicated they were not interested as they felt it would be self-cannibalizing. Ofir later launched their estate agency portal. In operating this portal they used a search robot to update their database daily. This robot obtained thirteen essential items of information on a daily basis from Home's database. The Ofir database was arranged and compiled without favouring any particular broker. The real estate broker's name was given and when the user clicked on the property, he was transferred either to the broker's homepage or directly to the property. Home claimed Ofir's actions were in breach of copyright and raised an action. In contradistinction to the earlier *Newsbooster* case the court found that Ofir's deep-linking to Home's database did not infringe Danish copyright law. In particular the court noted that deep-linking was a generally desirable function of the internet as a medium for searching and exchanging an incredibly extensive and steadily increasing quantity of information, stating that: 'it should be an ordinary practice that search engines make available deep links which allow the user to access the required information in an effective manner. Parties, including providers in the Internet, should thus expect that search services will establish links to these pages which are published.'[23]

11.1.2 *Google Inc. v Copiepresse SCRL*

By 2006 it appeared that a clear consensus had developed in Continental Europe: deep-linking would be allowed, and should be expected, except in those occasions where one party has acted in a manner which may be deemed to compete unfairly with the activities of another. Then the whole debate on linking was reopened by the Belgian case of *Google Inc. v Copiepresse SCRL*.[24]

The case surrounds two aspects of the Google search engine/portal. The first is the Google cache facility which Google offers on all its catalogued entries. You may or may not have noticed the Google cache in your everyday use of Google. It is part of the Google instant preview service: hover over a search result, and then hover over the arrows that appear to the right of the result and the instant preview and cached copy appear. The cache copy is a locally stored facsimile of the original site as it was catalogued by the Google robot. The cache facility was described in some detail to the court in *Copiepresse*; the claimants argued that, in making and then offering to their users access to the Google cache, Google were reproducing and/or communicating to the public works (or parts of works) protected by copyright without having the authorization of the copyright holder.

[22] Unreported, 24 February 2006, Danish Maritime and Commercial Court, discussed in Mercado-Kierkegaard, 'Clearing the Legal Barriers—Danish Court Upholds "Deep Linking" in *Home v. Ofir*' (2006) 22 *Computer Law and Security Report* 326.

[23] Ibid. 332.

[24] [2007] ECDR 5.

Highlight The Google cache facility

When Google crawls the Web it creates a copy of each page examined and stores it in a cache memory, which enables it to consult that copy at any time, and in particular when the original (or Internet) page becomes unavailable. When you click on the link 'cached copy' of a web page, Google displays that page in the form that it was found the last time that it was indexed. Furthermore, the cached material forms the basis for a determination by Google as to whether a page is relevant to your search. When a cached page is displayed, it is preceded by a framed heading which reminds you that this is a cached copy of the page and not the original page and citing the search terms which led to its inclusion in the research results.

Copiepresse at [68]

The second issue was the operation of the 'Google News' service or on the Google.be site 'Google.Actualités'. Google News is available as an option at the top of the Google Search page. Today it operates just as a specific search targeted at news sites and blogs bringing up topical search returns so that users can search for current news stories. This is in part as a result of the *Copiepresse* case. Historically, if you clicked on the Google News link without entering a search term you were given a newspaper-style offering of topical news stories, with acknowledgement of the source of each story and in traditional Google style a clear hyperlink taking you to the original version of the story. Like a traditional internet news site, there were a variety of subheadings a user may select such as 'World News', 'Technology', and 'Sport'. For this reason the claimants argued that Google News was more than a search facility, it was an information portal, not unlike www.bbc.co.uk. The expert appointed by the court agreed. He felt that as 'the user finds articles without any action being necessary on his part and is not obliged to undertake a specific search . . . the Google News site is thus a portal for information drawn from the press'.[25] On this basis the claimants contended as well that the Google News site was also in breach of Belgian copyright law as again, through this facility, Google were reproducing and/or communicating to the public works (or parts of works) protected by copyright without having the authorization of the copyright holder. At an earlier interlocutory hearing the court found that Google had infringed both the copyright and database right of the newspaper publishers, Google appealed that decision and it was this hearing before President of the Court Magerman and Deputy Registrar Wansart which examined the issues in depth.

First the court examined the operation of the Google cache facility. They found that as the cache function operated by allowing a user access to a version of the original website held on the Google server rather than directing the user to the original site (as a hyperlink would do) the cache was 'a physical reproduction of the work and a communication of it to the public within the meaning of Art. 1 of the Law on copyright'.[26] The next question was whether or not Google had made the copy. In their defence Google claimed that as it only copied the HTML code for the page (a code which only contains

[25] Ibid. [92].
[26] Ibid. [71].

the text and no image); they never created a copy of the page. Rather, the internet user creates a copy of the work when she accesses the cache. As such the user is the author of any reproduction or communication to the public, the only act undertaken by Google being the provision of a facility allowing or enabling a communication to be made to the public by internet users.[27] The court quickly dismissed this tortuous interpretation of the manner in which the copy was made, finding that 'Google stores in its memory a copy of webpages. The fact that that copy preserves the HTML code of those pages—i.e. that it is converted into computer language—does not seem particularly relevant.'[28] In summary, the court held that Google's cache operation was both an act of reproduction and a communication to the public.

The court next turned to the Google News site. Google argued that Google News was not an information portal, rather it was:

> [a]search engine . . . specialised in news material, which allows internet users easily to identify the news articles which may be of interest to them among the headlines published on the internet in the last 30 days and to consult them, at source, by going to the sites of the publishers making those articles available with just one mouse click.[29]

The court felt the distinction between an information portal and a search engine was unimportant as the same questions were raised however the Google News site was characterized.[30] The true question was about the nature of the Google News operation. The claimants argued that in producing the Google News service Google had specifically infringed their copyright by reproducing headlines and extracts drawn from their copyright work. This then raised the question of whether headlines could be protected at copyright law; one of the same questions Lord Hamilton had wrestled with over ten years previously. Google argued that headlines used in press articles are not original at all, claiming them to be merely turns of phrase in current use in language, citing by way of example 'The King visits Sweden' or 'Tom Boonen, world champion'. The court rejected this claim finding that: 'while not all the news article headlines can be considered as original—some of them in fact appear to be purely descriptive and do not therefore show the distinctive stamp of their author—nevertheless one cannot assume that a press article headline would never be sufficiently original to benefit from the protection of the Law on Copyright'[31] and went on to note that the short extract, usually the first two lines of the story, which was displayed alongside the link was equally susceptible to copyright protection.[32] The court therefore found that Google News did reproduce and distribute copyright protected works.

[27] Ibid. [72].

[28] Ibid. [74].

[29] Ibid. [86].

[30] 'In relation to the argument that "Google Actualités" or "Google News" service is not a "mere search engine service" but is an "information portal", the court noted that it is settled law that a hyperlink referring to a work protected by copyright is not a reproduction and that if there is a reproduction, it is the work of the internet user. However, this is not the case here as Google News reproduces and communicates to the public, on the homepage of its website, the headlines of press articles and an extract from those articles.' Ibid. [H12].

[31] Ibid. [105].

[32] '[I]n order to infringe the author's exclusive right, a reproduction does not need to be complete and may be merely partial, provided that there is some "borrowing", whether complete or partial, of that which makes the work "original"', ibid. [109].

With the *Copiepresse* case established Google needed to bring forward a defence which would allow them to continue their activities. They laid two main defences: (1) Freedom of Expression under the ECHR, and (2) Fair Dealing. Google first argued that the Google News service was protected by Art. 10 of the European Convention on Human Rights, arguing that freedom of expression protects the various aspects of the communication process, those being the freedom to receive and to communicate information.[33] Google recognized that the freedom to receive and to communicate information can be limited in order to protect the rights of others, including copyright, but argued nevertheless that the restriction of the right of freedom of expression sought by the claimants was disproportionate since Google News was a free tool for access to information and did nothing more than perform a sign posting function to facilitate research for information on the internet.[34] The court rejected this claim. It noted that copyright is based on a balance between, on the one hand, recognition of the legitimate interests of authors and, on the other hand, of the interests, which are also legitimate, of the public and of society in general and that copyright law had already been designed to take account of this balance by allowing fair dealing exceptions. Thus, Google could not claim a blanket Art. 10 exception; they would need to establish that they fell within a fair dealing exception.[35]

This left only one line of defence for Google to run. They offered two alternative Belgian fair dealing defences which mirror UK provisions: (1) quotation for the purpose of critique, argument, review, or teaching,[36] and (2) fair dealing in reporting the news.[37] The court rejected both defences. In response to the critique, argument, or review defence it noted that 'the Google News service is based on the automated indexing of news articles made available to the public on the internet by a robot. The classification of the articles by theme is done automatically, without any human intervention.'[38] Therefore 'Google News does not undertake any analysis, comparison or critique of those articles, which are not the subject of any commentary at all.'[39] In regard to the news defence the court first noted that 'This argument by Google seems to contradict the argument presented previously when describing the Google News service, when Google presented its activity as a specialised search engine service and not as an information portal.'[40] This dry observation by the court preceded their *coup de grâce*:

> One should observe the justification for this exception. As noted by Google in its written arguments, the purpose of this exception is to enable the media to react rapidly to news events, the rapidity with which the information has to be reported not enabling them to seek the prior consent of the author. That is not the situation in which Google finds itself. It would be permissible for Google—which draws up a list of information, from around 500 information sources in French, refreshing that information every 15 minutes—to obtain, in advance, the agreement of the publishers of the website on which that information was collected. Google cannot therefore rely on the exception for news reporting.[41]

[33] Ibid. [53].
[34] Ibid. [54].
[35] Ibid. [56]–[62].
[36] For a similar UK provision see s. 30(1) of the CDPA.
[37] For a similar UK provision see s. 30(2) of the CDPA.
[38] [2007] ECDR 5 [130].
[39] Ibid. [138].
[40] Ibid. [143].
[41] Ibid. [147]–[149].

Google therefore was found to be in breach of copyright in the operations of both its cache operation and its Google News operation. Google appealed the decision but in May 2011 the Court of Appeal of Brussels upheld the decision of the Court of First Instance, reiterated the order and imposed a fine for each day Google failed to comply with the order after ten days from publication.[42] Google then brought to bear its commercial might in the hope of forcing a settlement on the issue. Google removed the offending material from the Google News site and their cache, as required by the judgment, but also the company removed the newspapers represented by Copiepresse from the main Google index, meaning they were no longer visible to users of Google worldwide.[43] This had an obviously deleterious effect on the online business model of the newspapers in question, forcing them to seek a settlement with Google.

The question remained as to how a UK court would receive the continental line of authority. The authority of the *Shetland Times* case had been statutorily overruled: cable programmes have had no separate copyright protection since the Copyright and Related Rights Regulations 2003 came into effect. The question now would be whether the defendant had infringed copyright by communicating the infringing article to the public or (in relation to headlines and cache copies) had reproduced the original works. We now have an answer in the UK's very own news aggregation and scraping case *Public Relations Consultants Association (PRCA) v The Newspaper Licensing Agency (NLA)*.[44]

11.1.3 *Public Relations Consultants Association v The Newspaper Licensing Agency*

The issues in the case are remarkably complex but also hide a central issue which is deceptively simple. The Newspaper Licensing Agency (NLA) acts as a clearance and collecting society for its members who are publishers of newspapers and current affairs magazines. It operates its services in relation to both print and online publications. Meltwater BV is a multifaceted software as a service company which, among its portfolio, offers Meltwater News, a media monitoring service used extensively by public relations companies to monitor news reports in relation to their clients and their services. Part of the service offered by Meltwater News is an interactive analytical service. Meltwater monitors websites, including those operated by NLA members, and uses a spider program to scrape content from their servers. Its software then creates an index which records the position of every word in every article on every indexed website: in essence it is creating a searchable database at this point in the same way Google does. The client can then select any search terms they wish in order to search interactively through a search portal similar to Google search, but in addition they can set keyword alerts: this leads to the creation of a daily or weekly news monitoring report which is emailed to the client.

The Meltwater News report contains three things: (1) a hyperlink to each relevant article, the link consisting of the headline from the article (clicking on the link would

[42] The full order is at <http://cdn.arstechnica.net/CopiepresserulingappealGoogle_5May2011.pdf>.

[43] M Lasar, '*Google v. Belgium* "link war" ends after years of conflict' (*Ars Technica*, 19 July 2011) <http://arstechnica.com/tech-policy/2011/07/google-versus-belgium-who-is-winning-nobody/>.

[44] [2010] EWHC 3099 (Ch) (High Ct); [2011] EWCA Civ 890 (Court of Appeal); [2013] UKSC 18 (Sup Ct); [2014] AC 1438 (CJEU).

take the customer through to the article as it appears on the original publisher's website); (2) the opening words of the article after the headline; and (3) an extract from the article showing the context in which the keyword appears.[45] Again, this is factually similar to the US case but the distinction between the US and UK cases is to be found in the legal structure in dispute. Whereas Meltwater in the United States sought to rely upon a fair use defence without a licence for their actions, the cause of the dispute in the UK was the licensing arrangements which manage the Meltwater News service. Meltwater agreed to pay an annual licence to the NLA to hold a web developer licence (WDL). This allowed the licensee to carry out monitoring services such as those operated by Meltwater News, but according to the licence Meltwater may only supply its services to other licence holders, that is to say to end users also licensed by the NLA, by obtaining a separate web end-user licence (WEUL).[46] In short, according to NLA, both Meltwater and their clients required separate licences: Meltwater in carrying out their practice of scraping news content, indexing it, and then preparing the Meltwater News report required a WDL, while each of their clients required a WEUL to access the news story in full by following the link contained in the Meltwater News report. Thus the NLA not only required Meltwater to have a licence to extract the data, which is usual, but also that the end user should have a separate licence to access the content on the website of the original publisher with intent to read the content found there.

This seems at odds with the usual position that it has always been assumed that a copyright holder cannot therefore prevent passive enjoyment of his copyright protected material. The general principle has always been that copyright law prevents illegal copies being made not the passive enjoyment of them. To analogize with the analogue world for a moment, if I buy (or am given) a 'pirated' book then I commit no copyright infringement if I read the book. Many infringements will have been committed upstream including the production and distribution of the book but as long as I make no copy or attempt to distribute the book I commit no infringement. I need no licence or permission of the author simply to read the content as it does not involve making of a copy. Technology changes all of this. When we consume a digital file, by necessity a copy is made as part of the process of consumption. This is true of all digital content from movies to web-page content; when we access it we make a local copy in the RAM memory of the computer, and another copy as the screen display. It has always been recognized that there is the potential to use this technological development as a means to leverage end-user control in the way seen in *Meltwater* where licences may be used as a method to control access to content in the same way that fences are used to delineate controlled access to physical property. Because this risk existed, steps have been taken to ensure that digital content is not treated differently from analogue content. Article 5 of the InfoSoc Directive[47] was designed to ensure that the temporary acts of reproduction which are automatically carried out by digital systems did not lead to the consumption of digital content being treated differently to analogue content.

[45] The description of the service draws heavily from that of Proudman J at [2010] EWHC 3099 (Ch) [25]–[27].

[46] [2010] EWHC 3099 (Ch) [18].

[47] Dir. 2001/29/EC of the European Parliament and of the Council of 22 May 2001 on the harmonization of certain aspects of copyright and related rights in the information society.

Highlight Article 5 of the InfoSoc Directive

Temporary acts of reproduction, which are transient or incidental [and] an integral and essential part of a technological process and whose sole purpose is to enable:

(a) a transmission in a network between third parties by an intermediary, or

(b) a lawful use of a work or other subject-matter to be made, and which have no independent economic significance, shall be exempted from the reproduction right provided for in Article 2.

The intent of Art. 5 was to ensure that digital consumption and analogue consumption were treated equally. No matter in which format you consumed, you did not need a licence or permission from the copyright holder. The fact that your computer automatically made copies of content as part of the process of consumption was not legally relevant. Copyright infringement (if at all) occurred upstream of the consumer in the same way as had always been the case in the analogue environment.

The problem with Art. 5 has always been in the phrasing. What exactly is meant by 'essential' and what is meant by 'no independent economic significance'? These problems were magnified when the Court of Justice of the European Union (CJEU) considered the case of *Infopaq International v Danske Dagblades Forening* (*Infopaq I*).[48] This was a case not dissimilar to *Meltwater* in factual origin. Infopaq also supply a media monitoring service similar to Meltwater News but with a different set of operating parameters. Rather than using a spider to scrape and gather news stories from websites, Infopaq would scan in material from hard-copy newspapers to produce a final report similar to Meltwater's which would then be sent to the client. There are also many differences between Infopaq and Meltwater. Infopaq did not have a licence; something Meltwater had conceded they would need, but more importantly the process Infopaq used was manual rather than automated. Their process involved five stages and in at least two of these stages a manual intervention was required to delete temporary copies made in the scanning and indexing process. The question was asked whether digital copies of the scanned material made then deleted during the scanning process fell within the temporary copies exception. Perhaps not surprisingly, the court found that the actions of Infopaq were not covered by Art. 5(1) since their actions, which required manual intervention, were not acts of temporary reproduction as these were, according to Recital 33, 'acts enabling "browsing" and "caching", [acts] which have the purpose of facilitating the use of a work or making that use more efficient. Thus, an inherent feature of those acts is to enable the achievement of efficiency gains in the context of such use and, consequently, to lead to increased profits or a reduction in production costs.'[49] Thus the action of Infopaq in making a temporary copy that required manual intervention to delete, and which was economically significant in its own right, were clearly not covered by Art. 5(1). This decision is undoubtedly correct. It is not, and never was, the intent of Art. 5(1) to license manual acts of reproduction which, although temporary in themselves, create a new economic work. The problem of the necessarily narrow interpretation of Art. 5(1) which had been applied in *Infopaq I* became apparent when *Meltwater* came before the High

[48] Case C-5/08 [2010] FSR 20.
[49] At [49].

Court. There Proudman J applied the narrow interpretation of *Infopaq I* and found that for s. 28A of the Copyright, Designs and Patents Act 1988 (which implements Art. 5 of the Infosoc Directive) to apply, *Infopaq*'s five conditions had to be met:

Highlight *Infopaq*'s five conditions

1. The act must be temporary.
2. It must be transient or incidental.
3. It must be an integral and essential part of the technological process.
4. The sole purpose of the process must be to enable a transmission network between third parties by an intermediary or the lawful use of the work or protected subject matter.
5. The act must have no independent economic significance.

This is the position in *Infopaq I* but Proudman J added a twist to her interpretation. She was being asked a subtly different question to the court in *Infopaq I*: whereas they were looking at acts of reproduction designed ultimately to be consumed by third parties, she was being asked whether the end users required a separate licence, i.e. for the act of consumption. To answer the question of whether consumption, in the form of a local computer-generated copy read and then automatically deleted, was covered by Art. 5(1) she referred to an early report from the European Economic and Social Committee, a report which had previously been cited with approval by Kitchen J in the case of *Football Association Premier League Ltd v QC Leisure*.[50] Unfortunately Kitchen J was looking at a different aspect of the report from Proudman J. While he was looking at the meaning of independent economic significance, Proudman J used the report to examine whether the temporary copying exception covered any copy in which end-user intervention was required. Applying the report, she found that it did, as the:

> exception cannot have been intended to legitimise all copies made in the course of browsing or users would be permitted to watch pirated films and listen to pirated music. The kind of circumstance where the defence may be available is where the purpose of the copying is to enable efficient transmission in a network between third parties by an intermediary, typically an internet service provider.[51]

This appears to be an incorrect interpretation. As already noted, it was in fact that the intent of the temporary copying exemption to ensure that an act which had previously been permitted (consumption) remained so permitted. The wording of the Directive seemed to ensure that: at Recital 33 it states that the temporary copying 'exception should include acts which enable browsing as well as acts of caching to take place, including those which enable transmission systems to function efficiently'. Proudman J by contrast seems to suggest that browsing is only permitted where it is an 'essential part of a technological process and carried out for the sole purpose of enabling either efficient transmission in a network between third parties by an intermediary, or a lawful use of a work'.[52]

[50] [2008] EWHC 1411(Ch).
[51] [2010] EWHC 3099 (Ch) [110].
[52] InfoSoc Directive, Recital 33.

In the period following the decisions of both Proudman J and the Court of Appeal, the CJEU has looked twice more at Art. 5. In the reference from the UK in *Football Association Premier League Ltd v QC Leisure*,[53] they essentially reviewed Proudman J's opinion that an unauthorized act of consumption was not permitted by Art. 5 as it remained in essence unlawful. The court found this was not the case, noting that 'a use should be considered lawful where it is authorised by the right holder or where it is not restricted by the applicable legislation'.[54] For the avoidance of doubt the court went on to say that 'mere reception as such of those broadcasts—that is to say, the picking up of the broadcasts and their visual display—in private circles does not reveal an act restricted by European Union legislation or by that of the United Kingdom'.[55] Applying the *FA Premier League* decision, the same would be true of browsing a web page without a licence. In addition the CJEU revisited the original *Infopaq I* decision in *Infopaq International v Danske Dagblades Forening* (*Infopaq II*).[56] The court was asked to clarify some of its earlier findings, in particular in relation to lawful use. It found that:

> in respect of the lawful or unlawful character of the use, it is not disputed that the drafting of a summary of newspaper articles is not, in the present case, authorised by the holders of the copyright over these articles. However, it should be noted that such an activity is not restricted by European Union legislation. Furthermore, it is apparent from the statements of both Infopaq and the DDF that the drafting of that summary is not an activity which is restricted by Danish legislation. In those circumstances, that use cannot be considered to be unlawful. In view of the foregoing, Article 5(1) of Directive 2001/29 must be interpreted as meaning that the acts of temporary reproduction carried out during a data capture process, such as those in issue in the main proceedings, fulfil the condition that those acts must pursue a sole purpose, namely the lawful use of a protected work or a protected subject-matter.[57]

As a result of these decisions, when the case (now renamed *PRCA*) came before the Supreme Court the decision of Proudman J, which had found favour in the Court of Appeal, was reversed. Lord Sumption gave the judgment of the court. He examined the case law which had taken place between the original decision of Proudman J (and the Court of Appeal) and suggested an alternative to *Infopaq*'s five conditions for the application of Art. 5.

Highlight Lord Sumption's six conditions[58]

1. The exception in Article 5(1) applies to copies made as an integral and necessary part of a 'technological process', in particular the digital processing of data. For this purpose, the making of copies is a 'necessary' part of the process if it enables it to function 'correctly and efficiently': *Infopaq II*, at [30], [37].

→

[53] [2012] All ER (EC) 629.
[54] Ibid. [168].
[55] Ibid. [171].
[56] Case C 302/10 <http://eur-lex.europa.eu/LexUriServ/LexUriServ.do?uri=CELEX:62010CO0302:en:html>.
[57] Ibid. [44]–[46].
[58] [2013] UKSC 18 [26].

→

2. These copies must be temporary. This requirement is explained and defined by the words which follow, namely that the making of the copies must be 'transient or incidental and an integral and essential part of a technological process'. It means (i) that the storage and deletion of the copyright material must be the automatic consequence of the user's decision to initiate or terminate the relevant technological process, as opposed to being dependent on some further discretionary human intervention, and (ii) that the duration of the copy should be limited to what is necessary for the completion of the relevant technological process: *Infopaq I*, at [62], [64].
3. The exception is not limited to copies made in order to enable the transmission of material through intermediaries in a network. It also applies to copies made for the sole purpose of enabling other uses, provided that these uses are lawful. These other uses include internet browsing: *Infopaq I*, at [63] and *Infopaq II*, at [49(4)]. The sole purpose of the process must be to enable a transmission network between third parties by an intermediary or the lawful use of the work or protected subject matter.
4. For the purpose of Article 5(1), a use of the material is lawful, whether or not the copyright owner has authorised it, if it is consistent with EU legislation governing the reproduction right, including Article 5(1) itself: *Premier League*, at [168-173], *Infopaq II*, at [42]. The use of the material is not unlawful by reason only of the fact that it lacks the authorisation of the copyright owner.
5. The making of the temporary copy must have no 'independent economic significance'. This does not mean that it must have no commercial value. It may well have. What it means is that it must have no independent commercial value, i.e. no value additional to that which is derived from the mere act of digitally transmitting or viewing the material: *Premier League*, at [175], *Infopaq II*, at [50].
6. If these conditions are satisfied no additional restrictions can be derived from Article 5(5).

This is a stunningly comprehensive and helpful test. Not only has Lord Sumption analysed all the EU case law for us he has given the source of each part of his test and explained it. The key is that Lord Sumption agrees with, and applies, the key findings of *Infopaq II* and *FA Premier League* that (1) Art. 5(1) is not limited to intermediary transmission but extends also to other lawful uses, including internet browsing; (2) that the authorization of the copyright owner is not relevant to Art. 5(1); and (3) that temporary copies may have commercial value, as long as this does not amount to value added over that afforded by viewing or transmitting the material. This may be read as being in direct contradistinction to Proudman J's original position (pre *Infopaq II* and *FA Premier League*) that 'the defence may be available where the purpose of the copying is to enable efficient transmission in a network between third parties by an intermediary, typically an internet service provider'.[59] Lord Sumption is clear throughout not to

[59] See (n. 51).

be critical of Proudman J's decision, nor the Court of Appeal's upholding of it for they did not have the benefit of the later cases that he had, having the benefit of these cases though it is clear that the Proudman analysis no longer stands. From here it seemed an obvious decision for Lord Sumption; he finds in favour of the PRCA and disposes of the case. However, perhaps surprisingly, he chose not to do this. Having very clearly and carefully dissected both the meaning and application of Art. 5, and the decisions of the lower courts in *Meltwater* and the CJEU in both *Infopaq* cases and *FA Premier League* he then refers the case to the CJEU. With the law seemingly clear this may seem unusual but Lord Sumption, as always, has his reason: 'I recognise the issue has a transnational dimension and that the application of copyright law to internet use has important implications for many millions of people across the EU making use of what has become a basic technical facility. These considerations make it desirable that any decision on the point should be referred to the Court of Justice for a preliminary ruling, so that the critical point may be resolved in a manner which will apply uniformly across the European Union.'[60] This could be read as either an invitation or a challenge to the CJEU. Either 'having done all the hard work for you, I invite you to extend my reasoning across the EU providing Art. 5 protection to internet users in all 28 jurisdictions' or 'I challenge you to disagree with my reasoning'. It seems clear that Lord Sumption meant this as an invitation not a challenge: he was keen to see a harmonized application of Art. 5 in such an important matter.

The CJEU ruled in the *PRCA* case in June 2014.[61] The court agreed with all of Lord Sumption's analysis. They started by addressing the question of temporary copies, which had been a difficulty ever since *Infopaq I*. Were screen displays and cache copies made while browsing temporary? The answer on both counts was yes:

> it is apparent from the documents before the court, first, that the on-screen copies are deleted when the Internet user moves away from the website viewed. Secondly, the cached copies are normally automatically replaced by other content after a certain time, which depends on the capacity of the cache and on the extent and frequency of Internet usage by the Internet user concerned. It follows that those copies are temporary in nature.[62]

Next the court revisited the two *Infopaq* decisions to address the question of essentiality, in essence could the internet function without these processes? First, the court rejected the Proudman assertion that the copies were created by an act of the user: 'It is irrelevant, in this regard, that the process in question is activated by the Internet user'.[63] It then went on to find that 'on-screen copies and the cached copies must be regarded as being an integral [and essential] part of the technological process'.[64] On the basis of this analysis they rejected the claim made by the NLA that applying *Infopaq I* the actions of the user in initiating and ending screen displays meant the process was not an incidental and technical process. Finally, to dispose of the case the court found that under Art. 5(5) 'although the copies make it possible, in principle, for Internet users to access works displayed on websites without the authorisation of the copyright holders, the

[60] [2013] UKSC 18 [38].
[61] [2014] AC 1438 (CJEU).
[62] Ibid. [26].
[63] Ibid. [30].
[64] Ibid. [33]-[37].

copies do not unreasonably prejudice the legitimate interests of those rights holders'.[65] Their final ruling was clear and unambiguous and draws a line under all the confusion caused by the special circumstances of *Infopaq I*.

Highlight The *PRCA* ruling

Article 5 of Parliament and Council Directive 2001/29/EC of 22 May 2001 on the harmonisation of certain aspects of copyright and related rights in the information society must be interpreted as meaning that the copies on the user's computer screen and the copies in the Internet 'cache' of that computer's hard disk, made by an end-user in the course of viewing a website, satisfy the conditions that those copies must be temporary, that they must be transient or incidental in nature and that they must constitute an integral and essential part of a technological process, as well as the conditions laid down in article 5(5) of that Directive, and that they may therefore be made without the authorisation of the copyright holders.[66]

This ruling has variously been called the ruling that saved the internet,[67] or potentially a Pirate's Charter.[68] In truth it is neither, it is the simple application of Art. 5 as was intended by the drafters. One thing which has been missed in the hyperbole which surrounded this case was that internet browsing was never under threat; this was a case about the *commercial* exploitation of copyright content not the simple act of browsing. It should be acknowledged, however, that had NLA won and established the principle that Art. 5 did not cover the transient copies made on screen displays and in caches it would have been possible at a later date for another claimant to seek to drive such a wedge home so it is gratifying that the Supreme Court and the CJEU have clearly closed off such a possibility.

11.1.4 Linking and the right to communicate: *Svennson, BestWater, and C More Entertainment*

The *PRCA* case is not the only opportunity the CJEU have had recently to review linking to materials under EU Copyright Law. In the recent reference from Sweden *Nils Svensson & Ors v Retriever Sverige AB*,[69] the court was asked whether a link provided to a story found elsewhere on the web was a 'communication to the public' under Art. 3 of the InfoSoc Directive.

[65] Ibid. [56].

[66] Ibid. [64].

[67] P Sherrell and W Smith, 'CJEU decision in Meltwater—the internet is saved, browsing does not require a licence' (*Bird & Bird*, 5 June 2014) <http://www.twobirds.com/en/news/articles/2014/global/cjeu-decision-in-meltwater-the-internet-is-saved-browsing-does-not-require-a-licence>.

[68] M Hart, 'The Legality of Internet Browsing in the Digital Age' [2014] 36 *EIPR* 630 (arguing the contrary).

[69] Case C-466/12 [2014] 3 CMLR 4.

Highlight Article 3 of the InfoSoc Directive

1. Member States shall provide authors with the exclusive right to authorise or prohibit any communication to the public of their works, by wire or wireless means, including the making available to the public of their works in such a way that members of the public may access them from a place and at a time individually chosen by them.
2. Member States shall provide for the exclusive right to authorise or prohibit the making available to the public, by wire or wireless means, in such a way that members of the public may access them from a place and at a time individually chosen by them:
   (a) for performers, of fixations of their performances;
   (b) for phonogram producers, of their phonograms;
   (c) for the producers of the first fixations of films, of the original and copies of their films;
   (d) for broadcasting organisations, of fixations of their broadcasts, whether these broadcasts are transmitted by wire or over the air, including by cable or satellite.

This was a parallel issue to the temporary reproduction issue discussed in *PRCA*. Prior to *Svennson* the CJEU had not met head on the issue of whether a hyperlink was a communication to the public in the sense of Art. 3, although a number of cases had dealt with communication to the public through other technological means.[70] At issue in *Svennson* were links to news stories on the Göteborgs-Posten website. The claimants, Nils Svensson and other Swedish journalists, had written articles for the *Göteborgs-Posten*, which published them in print as well as making them available on its website. Retriever Sverige AB operates a service not dissimilar to Meltwater. It offers a subscription-based service whereby customers can access newspaper articles through the provision of a hyperlink that links to the original website where the requested content is freely accessible. Svensson sued Retriever for equitable remuneration, arguing that Retriever had made his article available through the search-and-alert functions on its website. This, he maintained, falls within the copyright-relevant acts of either communication to the public or the public performance of a work, neither for which had he given consent. Retriever denied any liability to pay equitable remuneration. They argued that the linking mechanisms did not constitute copyright-relevant acts, and therefore no infringement of copyright law occurred. The Swedish District Court rejected the claimants' application. An appeal against the judgment of the District Court was then brought

[70] For example in *Sociedad General de Autores y Editores de España (SGAE) v Rafael Hoteles SA*, C-306/05 [2006] ECR I-11519 the court found that where a hotel made broadcasting signals available over the hotel's closed network that 'while the mere provision of physical facilities does not as such amount to communication, the distribution of a signal by means of television sets by a hotel to customers staying in its rooms, whatever technique is used to transmit the signal, constitutes communication to the public within the meaning of Article 3(1) of that directive'. More recently in *Società Consortile Fonografici v Marco Del Corso*, C-135/10 [2012] ECR I-0000 the CJEU found that the free-of-charge broadcasting of phonograms in private dental practices does not fall under the definition of communication to the public, as the number of persons was small, the music played was not part of the dental practice, the patients 'enjoyed' the music without having made an active choice, and in any case patients were not receptive to the music under the dental practice's conditions.

before the Swedish Court of Appeal, which referred the case for a preliminary ruling to the CJEU asking for a clarification on the interpretation of Art. 3 of the Information Society Directive. The court had little difficulty in dismissing the claim:

> In order to be covered by the concept of 'communication to the public', within the meaning of Article 3(1) of Directive 2001/29, a communication, such as that at issue in the main proceedings, concerning the same works as those covered by the initial communication and made, as in the case of the initial communication, on the Internet, and therefore by the same technical means, must also be directed at a new public, that is to say, at a public that was not taken into account by the copyright holders when they authorised the initial communication to the public. In the circumstances of this case, it must be observed that making available the works concerned by means of a clickable link, such as that in the main proceedings, does not lead to the works in question being communicated to a new public. The public targeted by the initial communication consisted of all potential visitors to the site concerned, since, given that access to the works on that site was not subject to any restrictive measures, all Internet users could therefore have free access to them. In those circumstances, it must be held that, where all the users of another site to whom the works at issue have been communicated by means of a clickable link could access those works directly on the site on which they were initially communicated, without the involvement of the manager of that other site, the users of the site managed by the latter must be deemed to be potential recipients of the initial communication and, therefore, as being part of the public taken into account by the copyright holders when they authorised the initial communication. Therefore, since there is no new public, the authorisation of the copyright holders is not required for a communication to the public such as that in the main proceedings.[71]

The court on this basis quickly concluded that:

> Article 3(1) of Directive 2001/29/EC of the European Parliament and of the Council of 22 May 2001 on the harmonisation of certain aspects of copyright and related rights in the information society, must be interpreted as meaning that the provision on a website of clickable links to works freely available on another website does not constitute an 'act of communication to the public', as referred to in that provision.[72]

The court has had cause to revisit this issue twice subsequently. In *BestWater International GmbH v Mebes and Potsch*,[73] the court extended the *Svensson* analysis to find that embedding a video containing copyrighted material does not constitute copyright infringement. The respondents act on behalf of a competitor of complainant and both operate websites where they promote the products marketed by their client. They each embedded a video produced by BestWater into their sites. BestWater argued that by so embedding the video into their sites they had communicated it to the public without permission. The court applied *Svensson* and found that the conclusion (from *Svensson*) 'is not called into question by the fact that when users click on the link in question, the copyrighted work appears giving the impression that it is shown from the site where the link is found, when it actually comes from another site'.[74] This can be distinguished from earlier domestic cases such as *Shetland Times*, and the court acknowledged a risk in this approach:

> this technique can be used to make available to the public a work in avoiding the need to copy and so fall into the scope of the provisions relating to the reproduction right, but the fact

[71] See (n. 69) [24]–[28].
[72] Ibid. [42].
[73] C-348/1, 21 October 2014; [2014] ECR I-0000.
[74] Ibid. [17].

> remains that its use does not lead to what the work in question is communicated to a new public. Indeed, whenever and as long as this work is freely available on the site pointed to the Internet link, it must be considered that when the copyright holders have authorized this communication, they have taken into account all Internet users as public.[75]

The court returned to this issue recently in the case of *C More Entertainment AB v Linus Sandberg*.[76] This is another reference from Sweden. C More Entertainment is a pay-TV that transmits ice hockey games on a pay per view basis at 89 kronor (approximately £7) per game. The respondent created links to bypass the paywall, allowing users of Mr Sandberg's site access to the transmissions of two live games before C More Entertainment took technical steps to prevent such access. C More Entertainment filed a lawsuit before the Swedish courts to obtain compensation for copyright infringement. The Högsta domstolen (Swedish Supreme Court) asked the Court of Justice whether broadcasters have the right to prohibit a sports event broadcast live on the internet for payment from being transmitted to the public in this manner. The court found first that the InfoSoc Directive does not apply to live broadcasts:

> As is clear from the explanatory memorandum to the Commission Proposal of 10 December 1997 (COM(97) 628), which led to the adoption of Directive 2001/29, confirmed by recital 25 in the preamble to that directive, 'making available to the public', for the purposes of Article. 3 of the directive, is intended to refer to 'interactive on-demand transmissions' characterised by the fact that members of the public may access them from a place and at a time individually chosen by them. That is not the case of transmissions broadcast live on internet, such as those at issue in the main proceedings.[77]

However the court did acknowledge that member states could make domestic law under the Rental and Lending Rights Directive,[78] to 'grant broadcasting organisations the exclusive right to authorise or prohibit acts of communication to the public of their transmissions provided that such protection does not undermine that of copyright'.[79] This leaves us in a rather unsatisfactory position. It means that the law on on-demand services is clear. Applying *PRCA*, *Svennson*, and *BestWater* links to available online content cannot be either a new communication under Art. 3 or unauthorized reproduction, due to the effects of Art. 5. However, it appears from *C More*, that it is for domestic law to determine how to police live broadcasts carried over IP, meaning there is a potential discrepancy between the regulation of on-demand and live services.

11.2 **Peer-to-peer networks**

Linking, caching, and aggregation are not usually the first things people think about when they are asked for their views on copyright in the digital environment. Although these issues are of vital importance to the future development of network design and functionality most media coverage of online copyright issues focuses on illegal file-sharing and the harm it may cause to copyright industries. This is perhaps not surprising;

[75] Ibid. [18].
[76] Case C-279/13 [2015] ECDR 15.
[77] Ibid. [26]–[27].
[78] Dir. 2006/115.
[79] See (n. 76) [36].

much early high-profile litigation focused on this issue, and indeed still does, such as with the case of *Sweden v Neij et al.* (the *Pirate Bay* case).[80]

The problem is that, as stated at the outset of this chapter, the internet is to date the largest and most efficient copying machine built by man. In addition most users access the internet from home in what they imagine is anonymity. Although in practice they can be traced, for the average user the idea that law enforcement agencies or copyright holders will track their activities while they are safely in their own bedrooms seems remote. It is not surprising therefore that the internet is used extensively to share music, movies, and games without the permission of the copyright holder. The technology behind file-sharing, and the ways file-sharing systems have attempted to get around copyright law have both grown in sophistication as the years have gone by. To date there have been at least four generations of file-sharing technologies, as well as a raft of accompanying litigation.

11.2.1 **Early cases**

Probably the first case to examine file-sharing technologies was *UMG Recordings v MP3.com.*[81] MP3.com offered to digitize all music available on CD in the US with a view to offering a service known as My.Mp3.com. This would allow subscribers to listen to an MP3 version of music they owned from any computer anywhere in the world. It worked by storing MP3 copies of the music on a server which could be accessed by the subscriber across a network connection. To prevent subscribers from illegally accessing music they did not own, MP3.com required their customers to prove ownership of a copy of a particular music track by either inserting their copy of the original CD into their computer, allowing the MP3.com software to confirm the authenticity of the CD, (this was called the 'Beam-it Service') or they could purchase the CD from one of defendant's online retailing partners (the 'Instant Listening Service'). A group of music publishers including UMG, Sony, and Warner raised a claim against MP3.com claiming that both their processes of digitization and distribution were in infringement of copyright. MP3.com claimed their process was protected by Fair Use (the US equivalent of Fair Dealing). They relied in particular on two earlier decisions, *Sony Corporation of America v Universal City Studios, Inc.*[82] and *Recording Industry Association of America v Diamond Multimedia Systems Inc.*[83]

Sony v Universal is the famous 'Sony Betamax' case. It was a claim centred on the legality of the home video cassette recorder (VCR). Universal, alongside a host of other movie studios and the Motion Picture Association of America, argued that the Sony Betamax VCR was a device which could be used to infringe copyright in their content and that Sony by knowing what use their customer would make of the device were secondarily liable for any primary infringement carried out by their customers.[84]

[80] Stockholms Tingsrätt, No. B 13301–06, 17 April 2009 <http://www.ifpi.org/content/library/Pirate-Bay-verdict-English-translation.pdf> and Svea Hovrätt, No. B 4041–09, 26 November 2011 <http://www.scribd.com/doc/44068712/Pirate-Bay-appeal-ruling-Svea-Appeals-Court-Swedish>.

[81] 92 F. Supp. 2d 349 (SDNY 2000).

[82] 464 US 417 (Sup. Ct 1984).

[83] 180 F. 3d 1072 (9th Cir. 1999).

[84] This secondary infringement claim was made under the US copyright principles of vicarious and contributory infringement. These will be discussed extensively when the *Napster* case is discussed below.

This was a long, complex, and ultimately ground-breaking case when after eight years of litigation the US Supreme Court ruled by a narrow 5:4 majority that Sony were protected from liability as their Betamax VCR had a protected fair use, to be used for the purpose of 'time shifting'. This is described by the court as the practice of 'the average member of the public [using] a VCR principally to record a programme he cannot view as it is being televised and then to watch it once at a later time'.[85] The court found that although there was a risk that some time-shifting practices may cause harm to copyright holders:

> the record and findings of the District Court lead us to two conclusions. First, Sony demonstrated a significant likelihood that substantial numbers of copyright holders who license their works for broadcast on free television would not object to having their broadcasts time-shifted by private viewers. And second, respondents failed to demonstrate that time-shifting would cause any likelihood of non-minimal harm to the potential market for, or the value of, their copyrighted works. The Betamax is, therefore, capable of substantial non-infringing uses. Sony's sale of such equipment to the general public does not constitute contributory infringement of respondents' copyrights.[86]

A similar principle was sought by the defendants in the *RIAA v Diamond* case. Diamond produced the Rio Mp3 player, one of the first commercially available portable MP3 players. The Rio was first marketed in 1998 and it allowed the customer to carry with them 32MB of MP3 music (about 10–12 tracks). Although this seems quite unremarkable in the current MP3 market, the Rio was ground-breaking in several ways, including a 12-hour playback time on a single battery and the first music download store 'RioPort' which was the first to license commercial downloads. The RIAA took action against Diamond as the Rio was not compatible with the terms of the Audio Home Recording Act 1992, a piece of protectionist legislation which required digital music device manufacturers to install a system known as Serial Copy Management System.[87] Although ultimately the case was decided on a different point, one of the defences put forward by Diamond was that the Rio was a device to allow users to 'space shift' copies of their music. Building upon the 'time shifting' defence seen in Sony, Diamond argued that the Rio 'merely makes copies in order to render portable, or "space-shift", those files that already reside on a user's hard drive'.[88] The court agreed finding that 'Such copying [space shifting] is paradigmatic noncommercial personal use entirely consistent with the purposes of the Act.'[89]

This 'space shifting' defence was again raised in the *MP3.com* case. The defendant argued that all the My.Mp3.com service offered was the opportunity for the user to listen to their music at any place where they had internet access without the need to carry the original copy of the CD with them. They argued that as the user was required to demonstrate that they owned the original recording through either the 'Beam-it' or 'Instant Listening' service there was little risk of the copyright holder suffering harm.

[85] 464 US 417, 421.

[86] Ibid. 456.

[87] Serial Copy Management System is a copy protection scheme that was created in response to the digital audio tape (DAT) invention. In order to prevent DAT recorders from making second-generation or serial copies, SCMS sets a 'copy bit' in all copies of original recordings. This prevents anyone from making further copies of those copies, or serial copies.

[88] 180 F. 3d 1072, 1079.

[89] Ibid.

On this occasion though the court disagreed with this line of defence. The key distinction between *MP3.com* and the previous *Sony* and *Diamond* cases was where the primary infringement occurred. In both the previous cases the device supplier merely supplied a device which was capable of being used for infringing copyright which could then be used for fair (therefore protected) or unfair (therefore unlawful) purposes; in the case of MP3.com, they were committing the primary infringement (copying) therefore the fair use defence of space shifting, which may be available to their users, did not extend to them. The court summed this up simply: 'Although defendant recites that My.MP3.com provides a transformative "space shift" by which subscribers can enjoy the sound recordings contained on their CDs without lugging around the physical discs themselves, this is simply another way of saying that the unauthorised copies are being retransmitted in another medium—an insufficient basis for any legitimate claim of transformation.'[90] The court found that what MP3.com was doing was transforming the copyright protected music files which were encoded on CDs in CD-DA[91] format into MP3 format in a process known as 'ripping'. They were then retransmitting the 'ripped' MP3 file to their subscribers. As MP3.com was committing the infringement for a commercial purpose they could not be defended by the 'space shifting' exception. The simplicity of this distinction allowed the judge, District Judge Rakoff, to dispose of the case pithily, saying '[t]he complex marvels of cyberspatial communication may create difficult legal issues; but not in this case'.[92]

Judge Rakoff has been proven correct in his prediction. While the *MP3.com* case may have proven to be somewhat of a damp squib, legally speaking, it was merely a precursor to a number of cases involving the transformation and retransmission of a variety of video, audio, and software files both in the US and internationally. This series of cases encompasses some of the most celebrated internet law cases, including *MGM Studios, Inc. v Grokster, Ltd*,[93] *Sweden v Neij et al.*,[94] *Universal Music Australia Pty Ltd v Sharman License Holding Ltd*,[95] *Viacom International, Inc. et al. v YouTube, Inc. et al.*,[96] and possibly most famously of all *A&M Records, Inc. v Napster, Inc.*[97]

11.2.2 *A&M records, Inc. v Napster, Inc.*

Napster was created by Shawn Fanning a 17-year-old freshman (first-year student) at Northeastern University in 1999. The idea that Fanning had was to create a music community site where fans of bands or singers could go, chat, and share music with each other.[98] The file-sharing aspect of Napster did not seem to hold primacy in Fanning's original design, rather his focus was on creating a music community, but as part of his design he included the ability for users to swap MP3 files directly with each other. In so doing, without perhaps realizing the ground-breaking nature of this development

[90] 92 F. Supp. 2d 349, 356.
[91] Compact Disc Digital Audio.
[92] 92 F. Supp. 2d 349, 351.
[93] 545 US 913 (2005).
[94] See (n. 80).
[95] [2005] FCA 1242.
[96] Case no. 1:2007cv02103, Filed: 13 March 2007.
[97] 239 F. 3d 1004 (9th Cir. 2001).
[98] Renee Ambrosek, *Shawn Fanning: The Founder of Napster* (Rosen Publishing Group 2006), 30.

he created the first fully functional P2P protocol, the Napster protocol. To explain the contribution of the Napster protocol we need to examine the distinction between P2P and traditional server-client file systems.

Prior to Fanning's development of the Napster protocol, online file transfers had always followed a web 1.0 model where the file was stored on a web server which could be accessed by anyone with the requisite permission and then downloaded from that server. MP3.com had used a model such as this with their fêted (and fated) My.Mp3.com service. This model remains familiar to us today and is used by services as diverse as Apple's iTunes Store, BBC's iPlayer, YouTube, and streamed music systems such as Last.fm or Spotify. Fanning though introduced the concept of P2P file-sharing to the masses. This operates very differently from traditional server-client file transfers. Instead of operating a central server containing all the files available for download a P2P system stores the files on the hard drives of the network subscribers. Subscribers choose which files they will share and these are placed in a 'shared' folder. The P2P software can access this folder and may transfer data out of this folder to another user by creating a network connection between the users or 'peers'.

Example Shawn Fanning's party analogy

Fanning described the difference between client-server networks and the Napster network by using an analogy of attending a party.

In the client-server party each guest turns up empty-handed to the party and all the food and drink is supplied by the host. To get a drink you must ask the host to supply it and you can only have what the host has supplied. Your host may be efficient but he has to serve everybody and you may have to wait in a queue.

At a Napster party all the guests bring their own food and drink. There is still a host, but all he does is greets you at the door and takes a note of what you have brought. Then anytime anyone wants a drink they can ask the host who has brought a particular product. The host can check his list and put them in touch with the right person and they can then exchange drinks directly with each other.

The Napster party works as long as people are not too greedy and are willing to share.

Peer-to-peer systems seemed to offer a solution to the MP3.com problem. Like Sony and Diamond it is the end user who does the copying of files, not the service provider. This seemed to offer Napster a degree of protection against copyright infringement claims. The first line of defence was that they did not commit primary infringement; any sharing (and therefore copying) of files was done by their customers. Second, their customers would, it was imagined, be deemed to be acting in a non-commercial capacity allowing them to claim fair use defences such as time and space shifting should the copyright holders decide to pursue a claim.

However, there were, though, two problems with the Napster concept and design. The first was one that Shawn Fanning could not have imagined in the spring of 1999: Napster became a global phenomenon. Jupiter Media, the respected media research agency reported that by February 2001 Napster had 26.4 million users,[99] a remarkable reach for a program only released in June 1999. Although this may at first seem a positive outcome for Fanning and his internet start-up Napster, Inc. it meant that the music publishing industry and the Recording Industry Association of America quickly focused their attention on this fledgling company. The second was a design problem which was ultimately to prove to be Napster's downfall. If you recount the party host analogy given by Shawn Fanning he explains that at the Napster party there is a host who keeps track of what each person has brought and who introduces guests to each other. In the Napster environment this function was fulfilled by 'the Napster server'. When a new user first downloaded and installed the Napster software, the software would catalogue the MP3files she held on her computer and would place copies of these (with the user's permission) into a shared music folder. Then when the user first logged on to the Napster exchange site the Napster server would log her IP address (to allow sharing of files later) and the files which were in her shared music folder. The Napster server would then add this information to its searchable database allowing other users to discover what files the user had available for sharing. A keyword search of that database would return a list of users with file names which matched that keyword as well as details of how fast a connection they could offer. Thus a user searching for 'Backstreet Boys' (this was 2000 remember) would have returned a list of available files and users. They would then select one user, or peer, before the Napster server would instigate a digital handshake allowing the transfer to take place between users or peers. The Napster server meant that Napster always knew what files their subscribers were sharing and technically, as the Napster server had to make that digital handshake, could prevent the sharing of files between users of the service.

These two factors led a number of music publishers to file a complaint with the District Court for the Northern District of California on 6 December 1999. The plaintiffs contended that Napster's activities constituted 'contributory and vicarious federal copyright infringement'.[100] On 26 July 2000, the District Court granted the plaintiffs' motion for a preliminary injunction. The injunction was slightly modified by written opinion on 10 August 2000. The District Court preliminarily enjoined Napster 'from engaging in, or facilitating others in copying, downloading, uploading, transmitting, or distributing plaintiffs' copyrighted musical compositions and sound recordings, protected by either federal or state law, without express permission of the rights owner'.[101] Napster appealed to the Federal Court of Appeals for the Ninth Circuit. The case was heard on 2 October 2000 by Chief Judge Schroeder and Circuit Judges Beezer and Paez. On 12 February 2001 Judge Beezer issued the opinion of the court.

The court examined each of the plaintiffs' claims as well as three affirmative defences put forward by Napster. First, Judge Beezer examined the claim that 'Napster users are engaged in the wholesale reproduction and distribution of copyrighted works,

[99] 'Global Napster Usage Plummets, But New File-Sharing Alternatives Gaining Ground, Reports Jupiter Media Metrix' (*The Free Library*, 20 July 2001) <http://www.thefreelibrary.com/GLOBAL+NAPSTER+USAGE+PLUMMETS,+BUT+NEW+FILE-SHARING+ALTERNATIVES...-a076784518>.

[100] Contributory and vicarious copyright infringement are two different forms of secondary infringement actionable under the Federal Copyright Act 1976. Although we have no direct equivalents in the UK ss. 22–26 of the CDPA 1988 cover much of the same ground and many similar concepts are discussed in *CBS Songs Ltd v Amstrad Consumer Electronics Plc* [1988] AC 1013.

[101] *A&M Records, Inc. v Napster, Inc.* 114 F. Supp. 2d 896 (N.D. Cal. 2000), 927.

all constituting direct infringement.'[102] Although the plaintiffs accepted that Napster never actually copied any of the files in issue, the plaintiffs had to establish primary infringement on the part of Napster's users as without a primary infringement there could be no secondary infringement by Napster. Factually it was clear that the activities of Napster users were clearly in breach of the exclusive rights of the copyright holders; users were copying copyright protected music files and they were distributing them. It seemed all the copyright holders had to establish was that they were the rights holders to the music in question to establish primary infringement had occurred, but Napster felt their customers could have an affirmative fair use defence and presented to the court three such defences: (1) sampling, (2) space shifting, and (3) use with permission.

Napster first claimed that its users 'download MP3 files to "sample" the music in order to decide whether to purchase the recording'.[103] Napster further argued that the District Court had erred in refusing a sampling defence as it '(1) erred in concluding that sampling is a commercial use because it conflated a noncommercial use with a personal use; (2) erred in determining that sampling adversely affects the market for plaintiffs' copyrighted music, a requirement if the use is noncommercial; and (3) erroneously concluded that sampling is not a fair use because it determined that samplers may also engage in other infringing activity'.[104] Judge Beezer rejected this claim noting that:

> [e]vidence relied on by the District Court demonstrates that the free downloads provided by the record companies consist of thirty-to-sixty second samples or are full songs programmed to 'time out', that is, exist only for a short time on the downloader's computer. In comparison, Napster users download a full, free and permanent copy of the recording. The determination by the District Court as to the commercial purpose and character of sampling is not clearly erroneous.[105]

Napster then attempted to run a variant of the Diamond space-shifting defence. They argued that 'Space-shifting occurs when a Napster user downloads MP3 music files in order to listen to music he already owns on audio CD.'[106] Again the court was not impressed, with Judge Beezer noting that:

> Both Diamond and Sony are inapposite because the methods of shifting in these cases did not also simultaneously involve distribution of the copyrighted material to the general public; the time or space-shifting of copyrighted material exposed the material only to the original user. In Diamond, for example, the copyrighted music was transferred from the user's computer hard drive to the user's portable MP3 player. So too Sony, where 'the majority of VCR purchasers did not distribute taped television broadcasts, but merely enjoyed them at home'. Conversely, it is obvious that once a user lists a copy of music he already owns on the Napster system in order to access the music from another location, the song becomes available to millions of other individuals, not just the original CD owner.[107]

This only left the defence of use with permission but as Judge Beezer pointed out the 'plaintiffs did not seek to enjoin this and any other noninfringing use of the Napster system',[108] thus this defence was also ruled out. The court therefore established that

[102] 239 F. 3d 1004 [17].
[103] Ibid. [39].
[104] Ibid.
[105] Ibid. [40].
[106] Ibid. [44].
[107] Ibid. [45].
[108] Ibid. [46].

Napster users did not have a fair use defence and that the plaintiffs would likely succeed on a claim for copyright infringement against Napster users. On this basis the court moved on to examine the plaintiffs' claims for secondary infringement against Napster.

The court first examined whether Napster had committed contributory copyright infringement. Contributory infringement is established by the application of a two-part test. The defendant must (1) know, or have reason to know of the direct infringement, and (2) materially contribute to the infringing activity. This is where the Napster server proved to be Napster's downfall. As the Napster server recorded all files available for distribution in real time, and as many of these files contained material that was clearly being offered in breach of copyright, Napster could have knowledge of the infringing activity of its subscribers. The court though was careful to tread a fine line. They did not want to outlaw P2P systems just because they could be used for copyright infringement. Judge Beezer explained that:

> if a computer system operator learns of specific infringing material available on his system and fails to purge such material from the system, the operator knows of and contributes to direct infringement. Conversely, absent any specific information which identifies infringing activity, a computer system operator cannot be liable for contributory infringement merely because the structure of the system allows for the exchange of copyrighted material. To enjoin simply because a computer network allows for infringing use would, in our opinion, violate Sony and potentially restrict activity unrelated to infringing use.[109]

Nevertheless this did not assist Napster as 'We nevertheless conclude that sufficient knowledge exists to impose contributory liability when linked to demonstrated infringing use of the Napster system. The record supports the district court's finding that Napster has actual knowledge that specific infringing material is available using its system, that it could block access to the system by suppliers of the infringing material, and that it failed to remove the material.'[110] As the Napster software and server hardware were essential to the swapping of copyright protected files the court therefore had little difficulty in finding the second arm of the test also proven: Napster were found liable for contributory infringement.

The court then turned to the question of vicarious infringement. Vicarious infringement requires the application of a three-part test: (1) there has been a direct infringement; (2) the vicarious infringer is in a position to control the actions of the direct infringer; and (3) the vicarious infringer benefits financially from the infringement. The first element of the test had already been established so the court focused on the remaining questions. Napster argued they did not benefit financially; they did not charge subscribers for either the software or access to the service, in fact Napster argued they made no money at all through the availability of infringing files on the Napster network. The court disagreed. It felt that without the availability of infringing files Napster would not have grown at the phenomenal rate at which it grew. This, the court felt was a direct financial benefit:

> [f]inancial benefit exists where the availability of infringing material 'acts as a draw for customers'. Ample evidence supports the district court's finding that Napster's future revenue is directly dependent upon 'increases in user-base'. More users register with the Napster system as the 'quality

[109] Ibid. [56].
[110] Ibid. [57].

> and quantity of available music increases'. We conclude that the district court did not err in determining that Napster financially benefits from the availability of protected works on its system.[111]

This left only one final question, had Napster been in a position to control its users? Again the Napster server was the Achilles heel of the Napster operation; the court found that through it Napster had 'the ability to locate infringing material listed on its search indices, and the right to terminate users' access to the system'.[112]

There remained one crumb of solace for Napster. The court recognized that merely indexing file names did not mean that Napster had to have knowledge of what these files contained, as Judge Beezer explained: 'we recognize that the files are user-named and may not match copyrighted material exactly (for example, the artist or song could be spelled wrong)'.[113] However, this was not enough to save Napster. The Appeals Court did vary the terms of the injunction as they felt that the injunction of the District Court that 'Napster ensures that no "copying, downloading, uploading, transmitting, or distributing" of plaintiffs' works occur on the system' was overbroad. Instead the Appeals Court placed the burden of establishing infringement on the plaintiffs who were required to 'provide notice to Napster of copyrighted works and files containing such works available on the Napster system before Napster has the duty to disable access to the offending content'.[114] Since this order seemed to offer Napster the opportunity to continue to operate, Napster remained in operation. A cat-and-mouse game developed between copyright holders and Napster users. The copyright holders gave Napster details of tens of thousands of infringing files which it was required by the injunction to block. Users would then change file names allowing the injunction to be circumvented and the whole process would begin anew. It proved impossible though for Napster to continue to meet the demands of the injunction and in July 2001 the Napster service was closed down.[115] Following protracted discussions to try and save Napster, including a reported deal to sell the company to German music publisher Bertelsmann for $85 million, Napster eventually went into liquidation. Its trademarks and brand name were bought at a bankruptcy auction by Roxio Inc. and they rebranded their press-play music service 'Napster 2.0'. Today Napster is owned by Rhapsody and operates as a leading subscription-funded cloud music service.

11.2.3 **Post-*Napster*: *MGM Studios, Inc. v Grokster, Ltd***

The music industry had claimed a victory, but at what cost? It seemed the Court of Appeals had suggested the P2P technology Napster had used was not in of itself illegal (and in fact was not dissimilar to traditional search engines which also may assist individuals in obtaining illegal materials), but rather the problem was the Napster server

[111] Ibid. [61].
[112] Ibid. [67].
[113] Ibid.
[114] Ibid. [86].
[115] On the last day of service the ten most downloaded tracks were reported to be: (1) Everly Brothers—'Bye Bye Love'; (2) The Clash—'I fought the law (and the law won)'; (3) Jerky Boys—'Fanning my balls' (a play on Shawn Fanning's name); (4) Judge Jules—'Gatecrasher'; (5) Warren Zevon—'Send Lawyers, Guns and Money'; (6) Jimmy Buffet—'A Pirate Looks at 40'; (7) Metallica–'Seek and Destroy'; (8) Dr Dre—'Bang Bang'; (9) Red Hot Chili Peppers—'Give it away'; and (10) Doobie Brothers—'Listen to the Music'.

which allowed Napster a high degree of oversight and control. If a P2P system could be designed which did not use a central index server it seemed its implementation would not infringe US copyright law.

Two such systems were quickly developed. One was to design a decentralized P2P network which operates more like the internet. This does away with the need to have a central server. Instead when one logs in to the network a connection is made to the nearest active user, or node, on the network. As this node already has onward connections any requests may be forwarded throughout the network without the need for a central server. If we return to Shawn Fanning's party analogy, this is a party without a host. The new arrival joins at the fringes of the party and talks to the person nearest to them. If they have a request for a particular food or drink they ask the person they are talking to for it. Assuming this person does not have what the user requests he passes this request on to anyone he is within speaking distance of (in network terms has a network communication with) and the request spreads across the room as it passes from person to person, growing exponentially as it goes. Eventually one person responds saying she has the item requested and the response is relayed back across the same route the request took, allowing the requester and the provider to be introduced. The transfer then takes place in the usual way. Decentralized P2P systems have some advantages but also some strong disadvantages. As they are completely decentralized there can be no claim of a controlling mind and they are (in theory at least) difficult to disrupt. But they can be extremely slow and they carry a large amount of network traffic as requests are sent and replies received.

A better system, technically, is the semi-structured system allowed by the use of so-called 'supernodes'. A semi-structured system combines the advantages of the centralized and decentralized systems. Instead of having a central server, semi-structured P2P systems use a number of users as temporary information hosts, or supernodes. The easiest way to explain is to return to the party analogy one last time. Now when a new guest arrives at the party he is met by a host but this host is one of many hosts and no one host is in control of the party or the venue. Hosts are chosen because of their ability to connect quickly with a group of guests and when a new guest joins the party the nearest host to them meets them and asks them to give them details of what they have brought to the party and what they want to eat or drink. Their (local) host can then tell them immediately if anyone in their immediate circle of guests can supply them with what they want by checking their list of available food and drinks. If no one within the host's immediate circle has what the guest is looking for they ask the hosts nearest to them to check their lists and so the request is transferred on in the same way as it was in the decentralized party but here the communications are only between hosts. These hosts, or supernodes, thus act as local search servers and provide the backbone of the network. Cleverly, though, a supernode can leave at any time and she will be immediately replaced by whichever guest is best placed to fill the gap. The semi-structured network in effect decentralizes the server function as well as the file transfer and search functions.

Several P2P providers began offering either decentralized or semi-structured P2P services. Famous brand names to use one or other of these technologies included Kazaa, eMule, EDonkey, Gnutella, Grokster, and Morpheus. Users quickly migrated to these new P2P systems, many of which had been developed outside the US;[116] it seemed

[116] For instance Kazaa was owned and operated by Dutch Company Consumer Empowerment, while Grokster Ltd, creators of Grokster, was registered in Nevis, West Indies.

that the music industry had won the battle but lost the war. Even worse for copyright holders, while Napster had only allowed the sharing of MP3 audio files these new services allowed sharing of any type of file, meaning Hollywood movie studios, television networks, and software developers were now all affected. The copyright holders began afresh. In spring 2003 a number of entertainment industry plaintiffs[117] raised an action against Grokster and StreamCast suppliers of leading P2P technologies Grokster and Morpheus.[118]

Initially the legal omens looked good for the P2P service providers. At a preliminary hearing before Judge Steven Wilson of the US District Court for the Central District of California a motion by the defendants for summary judgment in their favour was granted.[119] Although Judge Wilson recognized that customers of Grokster and StreamCast were engaging in unlawful activities he could see nothing to suggest either of the defendants had knowledge of their customers' activities or had the ability to control them. He noted that '[although] the Court is not blind to the possibility that Defendants may have intentionally structured their businesses to avoid secondary liability for copyright infringement, while benefiting financially from the illicit draw of their wares . . . the Court need not decide whether steps could be taken to reduce the susceptibility of such software to unlawful use'.[120] He went on to note that although he shared some sympathy with the plight of the plaintiffs 'to justify a judicial remedy, however, [the] Plaintiffs invite this Court to expand existing copyright law beyond its well-drawn boundaries'.[121]

By removing the element of control and knowledge that the Napster central server offered, the second-generation P2P providers had escaped potential contributory or vicarious liability. The copyright holders appealed to the Court of Appeal for the Ninth Circuit. The appeal was heard by Circuit Judges Boochever, Noonan, and Thomas, with Judge Thomas issuing the opinion of the court on 19 August 2004. The court affirmed Judge Wilson's decision finding that 'the defendants are not liable for contributory and vicarious copyright infringement'.[122] As with the earlier opinion of Judge Wilson, Judge Thomas was sympathetic to the plight of the copyright holders but noted that the defendants could not be held liable for either contributory or vicarious copyright infringement without the court expanding the scope of either or both forms of infringement.[123] At appeal the plaintiffs attempted to have the court extend the scope of vicarious liability by arguing that the defendants had 'turned a blind eye to detectable acts of infringement for the sake of profit'.[124] The court though rejected this claim. Judge Thomas was clear that any expansion of the law of copyright should come from Congress, not through judicial activism:

[117] The plaintiffs fell into two camps: (1) the motion picture industry plaintiffs; and (2) the music industry plaintiffs.

[118] *MGM Studios, Inc. v Grokster, Ltd* 259 F. Supp. 2d 1029 (C.D. Cal. 2003); *MGM Studios, Inc. v Grokster, Ltd* 380 F.3d 1154 (9th Cir. 2004); *MGM Studios, Inc. v. Grokster, Ltd* 545 US 913 (2005).

[119] *MGM Studios, Inc. v Grokster, Ltd* 259 F. Supp. 2d 1029 (C.D. Cal. 2003).

[120] 259 F. Supp. 2d 1029, 1046.

[121] Ibid.

[122] *MGM Studios, Inc. v Grokster, Ltd* 380 F.3d 1154 (9th Cir. 2004).

[123] 380 F.3d 1154, 1160–2.

[124] This was a development of part of the Napster decision. See *A&M Records, Inc. v Napster, Inc.*, 239 F.3d 1004, 1023.

Highlight Judge Thomas in *MGM v Grokster*

The introduction of new technology is always disruptive to old markets, and particularly to those copyright owners whose works are sold through well-established distribution mechanisms. Yet, history has shown that time and market forces often provide equilibrium in balancing interests, whether the new technology be a player piano, a copier, a tape recorder, a video recorder, a personal computer, a karaoke machine, or an MP3 player. Thus, it is prudent for courts to exercise caution before restructuring liability theories for the purpose of addressing specific market abuses, despite their apparent present magnitude.

Indeed, the Supreme Court has admonished us to leave such matters to Congress. In *Sony* the Court spoke quite clearly about the role of Congress in applying copyright law to new technologies. As the Supreme Court stated in that case, the direction of Art. I is that Congress shall have the power to promote the progress of science and the useful arts. When, as here, the Constitution is permissive, the sign of how far Congress has chosen to go can come only from Congress.

[380 F.3d 1154, 1167]

The decision of the Court of Appeals for the Ninth Circuit is interesting on several levels. Judge Thomas and his brethren were sending a message to both the plaintiffs and to Congress. At the time of the *Grokster* case Congress was considering a revision to US copyright law, Judge Thomas was suggesting both that the plaintiffs would make better use of their time in lobbying Congress, and that Congress was the proper forum to review, and if necessary amend the Copyright Act. Also he was expressing the need for copyright law to balance the interests of traditional copyright industries, and the need to ensure new technology is allowed space to develop, given the monopolistic nature of copyright law. Finally, he was making a thinly veiled comment that the Supreme Court should not intervene given the current interest of Congress in the matter. Despite Judge Thomas's comments the plaintiffs appealed to the Supreme Court who agreed to hear the case.

The case was argued before the Supreme Court on 29 March 2005, with the decision of the court issued on 27 June 2005. The Justices of the Supreme Court were unanimous that the decision of the Court of Appeals should be overturned. Between the Ninth Circuit hearing and the Supreme Court hearing the plaintiffs had developed their 'turning a blind eye' argument. They presented the justices with the argument that Grokster and StreamCast had 'clearly voiced the objective that recipients use it to download copyrighted works, and each took active steps to encourage infringement'.[125] By making this claim the plaintiffs were inviting the justices to extend a principle from patent law, known as the 'active inducement' principle to copyright law.[126] The court

[125] 545 US 913, 919.

[126] For a discussion of this see P Samuelson, 'Legally Speaking: Did MGM Really Win the Grokster Case?' (October 2005) 48 *Communications of the ACM* 19.

was willing to hear this argument. Justice Souter, who gave the opinion of the court,[127] noted that 'The rule on inducement of infringement as developed in the early [patent] cases is no different today. Evidence of active steps . . . taken to encourage direct infringement.'[128] Justice Souter was encouraged that there was a tradition of borrowing from patent law in cases such as this. He noted that 'Sony took the staple-article doctrine of patent law as a model for its copyright safe harbour rule, the inducement rule, too, is a sensible one for copyright.'[129]

Highlight The active inducement principle

We adopt it here, holding that one who distributes a device with the object of promoting its use to infringe copyright, as shown by clear expression or other affirmative steps taken to foster infringement, is liable for the resulting acts of infringement by third parties.

[Justice Souter, *MGM v Grokster* at 932]

In making this decision the Supreme Court had ignored its previous direction from Sony that courts should not intervene to extend the scope of copyright protection, and the plea from Judge Thomas that new technologies should be allowed to develop. The court did not clearly define when active inducement would be found, instead the court gave guidance as to what may or may not constitute 'active inducement'. Justice Souter noted that 'mere knowledge of infringing potential or of actual infringing uses would not be enough here to subject a distributor to liability. Nor would ordinary acts incident to product distribution, such as offering customers technical support or product updates, support liability in themselves. The inducement rule, instead, premises liability on purposeful, culpable expression and conduct, and thus does nothing to compromise legitimate commerce or discourage innovation having a lawful promise.'[130] What is clear therefore is that there must be some form of clear campaign or inducement which incites infringement to occur. Had the defendants been involved in such a campaign?

Justice Souter examined the evidence: of StreamCast he noted that they 'beamed onto the computer screens of users of Napster-compatible programs ads urging the adoption of its OpenNap program, which was designed, as its name implied, to invite the custom of patrons of Napster, then under attack in the courts for facilitating massive infringement'.[131] Meanwhile Grokster were 'distribut[ing] an electronic newsletter containing links to articles promoting its software's ability to access popular copyrighted

[127] Concurring opinions were also issued by Justice Ginsberg and Justice Breyer. The reason for the concurring opinions is that some Justices were split over whether the case differed substantially from the *Sony* case. Justice Ginsburg, joined by Justice Kennedy and Chief Justice Rehnquist, felt that 'this case differs markedly from Sony' based on insufficient evidence of noninfringing uses. Justice Breyer, joined by Justices Stevens and O'Connor, felt that 'a strong demonstrated need for modifying Sony (or for interpreting Sony's standard more strictly) has not yet been shown'.

[128] 545 US 913, 931.

[129] Ibid. 932.

[130] Ibid. 932–3.

[131] Ibid. 933.

music'.[132] In particular he found three things on the record to be damning of both defendants: (1) 'each company showed itself to be aiming to satisfy a known source of demand for copyright infringement, the market comprising former Napster users;'[133] (2) 'neither company attempted to develop filtering tools or other mechanisms to diminish the infringing activity using their software';[134] and (3) 'StreamCast and Grokster make money by selling advertising space, by directing ads to the screens of computers employing their software. As the record shows, the more the software is used, the more ads are sent out and the greater the advertising revenue becomes. Since the extent of the software's use determines the gain to the distributors, the commercial sense of their enterprise turns on high-volume use, which the record shows is infringing.'[135]

Following the decision of the Supreme Court the defendants followed different paths. Grokster closed its site on 7 November 2005. A note on its home page reads: 'The US Supreme Court unanimously confirmed that using this service to trade copyrighted material is illegal. Copying copyrighted motion picture and music files using unauthorized peer-to-peer services is illegal and is prosecuted by copyright owners. There are legal services for downloading music and movies. This service is not one of them. YOUR IP ADDRESS IS XXXXXX AND HAS BEEN LOGGED. Don't think you can't get caught. You are not anonymous.'[136] StreamCast, however, continued to fight the suit on remand and on 27 September 2006, the US District Court for the Central District of California granted summary judgment in favour of the plaintiffs.[137] StreamCast promised to appeal the decision,[138] but on 22 April 2008, StreamCast Networks filed for Chapter 7 Bankruptcy.[139] Other P2P network providers fearing lawsuits similar to the *Grokster* one began either shutting down their services or taking steps to make them legal. Sam Yagan, president of MetaMachine, announced in a congressional hearing that they were closing their eDonkey and Overnet P2P systems following the *Grokster* decision.[140] The others eventually followed suit with Kazaa migrating to a paid model for a period before closing in 2012 and LimeWire creating a filtering system which allowed copyright holders to blacklist their protected content and instigating a legal download store, before it too closed in October 2010.

11.2.4 *Sweden v Neij et al.* (the *Pirate Bay* case)

The now 'old-fashioned' P2P technologies litigated in the US cases has been supplanted by the more efficient BitTorrent technology. BitTorrent works in a completely different manner to both centralized and decentralized P2P technologies. BitTorrent is an internet protocol, similar in function to File Transfer Protocol. To use the BitTorrent

[132] Ibid.
[133] Ibid. 934.
[134] Ibid. 935.
[135] Ibid.
[136] From <http://www.grokster.com/>.
[137] From: <http://w2.eff.org/IP/P2P/MGM_v_Grokster/motion_summary_judgement.pdf>.
[138] M Hickins, 'StreamCast Up Streaming Creek' (*Internet News*, 28 September 2006) <http://www.internetnews.com/bus-news/article.php/3634866>.
[139] Bitplayer, 'Morpheus throws in the towel' *Los Angeles Times* (Los Angeles, 1 May 2008) <http://opinion.latimes.com/bitplayer/2008/05/morpheus-throws.html>.
[140] US Senate Committee on the Judiciary, Testimony of Sam Yagan, President MetaMachine, Inc. (developer of eDonkey and Overnet), September 28 2005.

protocol you need a BitTorrent client; a specialized program which allows the transfer of files using the BitTorrent system. These BitTorrent clients are well known and include 'Popcorn Time', 'µTorrent', and 'BitLord'. These have a similar relationship to the BitTorrent protocol as web browsers such as Internet Explorer and Chrome have to HTTP. Once installed a BitTorrent client allows for the uploading and downloading of BitTorrent files. To obtain a file via BitTorrent the user first has to obtain a small file called a Torrent file. This contains metadata used by the BitTorrent client to obtain the location of the file. What makes BitTorrent both efficient and attractive is its method of sharing files. Instead of the file transfer taking place between two users (a P2P transfer) it allows for an interaction between several users simultaneously (a multi-peer transfer) by breaking large files down into smaller chunks and having different users transmit each chunk independently. Thus if we return to (and stretch) Shawn Fanning's original party metaphor BitTorrent is an extremely large and unmanaged party. When a new guest arrives they may want a cocktail, perhaps a Cosmopolitan. They look at a 'guest book' at the door which lists those party guests who have the component parts of their drink. They can then search out these individuals who each supply one component (vodka, triple sec, cranberry juice, and lime juice) and once complete they can assemble the cocktail. In truth BitTorrent is much more complex than this as people are simultaneously uploading (seeding) and downloading (leeching) file chunks. For the purposes of our analysis though, the key part of the analogy is the operation of the guest book which is analogous to these small Torrent files which are essential to finding all the parts of your larger music, video, or software files. These tend to be made available through BitTorrent indexes, sites which specialize in tracking and listing available Torrent files. The largest and historically best-known index was the Swedish site The Pirate Bay, which due both to its high profile and popularity as a Torrent index has had several confrontations with law enforcement authorities and copyright holders.

On 31 May 2006 The Pirate Bay was raided by Swedish police officers who removed all of The Pirate Bay's servers and questioned three of The Pirate Bay's 'stewards' Gottfrid Svartholm, Mikael Viborg, and Fredrik Neij on suspicion of operating a business infringing copyright. This, in Sweden, as in the UK, may be a criminal offence.[141] The site was offline for three days and the Motion Picture Association of America claimed victory with MPAA chairman Dan Glickman announcing that 'The actions today taken in Sweden serve as a reminder to pirates all over the world that there are no safe harbors for internet copyright thieves.'[142] Despite this, reports of The Pirate Bay's death were premature. The site was up and running again on 2 June 2006, their logo amended to depict their traditional pirate ship firing cannonballs at the Hollywood sign. The investigation continued throughout 2006 and 2007 and eventually on 31 January 2008 The Pirate Bay's operators Gottfrid Svartholm, Fredrik Neij, Peter Sunde, and Carl Lundström were charged with 'promoting other people's infringements of copyright laws'.[143]

[141] The UK equivalent provision may be found in CDPA, s. 107.

[142] This quote, and all other factual data about The Pirate Bay raid is drawn from: Quinn Norton, 'Secrets of the Pirate Bay' (*Wired*, 16 August 2006) <http://www.wired.com/science/discoveries/news/2006/08/71543>.

[143] L Larsson, 'Charges filed against the Pirate Bay four' Computer Sweden (Stockholm, 31 January 2008) <http://www.idg.se/2.1085/1.143146>.

Two specific charges were levied: (1) 'complicity in the production of copyrighted material' and (2) 'complicity to make copyrighted material available'.[144] The first related to making copies available via The Pirate Bay site, the second to making and indexing Torrent files via the site. The trial began on 16 February 2009 and on day two of the trial the state prosecutor dropped the charge of 'complicity in the production of copyrighted material'; this was reported to be in response to evidence given on day one about the technical operations of The Pirate Bay.[145] The second, lesser charge remained.

The defendants argued that the actions of The Pirate Bay were no different to those of other indexing and search websites such as Google, Yahoo!, or Microsoft's Live search. Those sites provide a search facility for HTML-based content which may or may not be made available in breach of copyright. There is no doubt that a proportion of content available on the web is there without the permission or licence of the copyright holder, but Google and others do not take steps to identify positively which content is in breach of copyright and which is not. This, the defendants argued, also reflected how The Pirate Bay functioned. Torrents may contain material made available with the permission or licence of the copyright holder, or they may contain content made available in breach of copyright, all The Pirate Bay does is index torrents; it does not question their content. The prosecution responded that, unlike Google, The Pirate Bay actively use their technology to assist in the commission of copyright infringement and they directly profit from this. The prosecutor said he was not asking the court to rule on the legality of BitTorrent itself, but rather what the defendants did with the technology. He said that the Swedish Supreme Court had previously ruled that someone running a Bulletin Board which shared copyright material had been found guilty of assisting copyright infringement and that The Pirate Bay should be viewed in this light. He went on to estimate that the site had made between 5m and 10m kroner (£400,000–£800,000), turnover directly attributable to illegal file-sharing.[146] In making his case the prosecutor was clearly drawing on the same principles which had led the US Supreme Court to find that Grokster/StreamCast had actively induced copyright infringement.

On 17 April 2009 the District Court of Stockholm announced its decision.[147] All four accused were found guilty of complicity to make copyright material available, the court having rejected the defendant's 'Google defence'. They were each sentenced to one year in prison and collectively found liable for damages totalling 30m Swedish krona (around £2.4m). The defendants immediately appealed and their appeal was heard by the Svea Court of Appeal. Unfortunately for the four accused it did not reverse the judgment of the District Court.[148] Instead it found that:

> a search by its nature is such that it is primarily a valuable tool in lawful activity and generally socially, this legitimate use dominates, the diffusion or transfer of illegal materials which despite precautions cannot be excluded. The operation of such a service in objective terms may be regarded as permissible under the aforementioned theory. Regarding The Pirate Bay we can

[144] K Fiveash, 'Pirate Bay prosecutor tosses infringement charges overboard' (*The Register*, 17 February 2009) <http://www.theregister.co.uk/2009/02/17/pirate_bay_half_charges_dropped_report>.

[145] Ibid.

[146] Information and data drawn from *The Pirate Bay Trial Day 10: Calls for Jail Time* <http://torrentfreak.com/the-pirate-bay-trial-day-10-calls-for-jail-time-090302/>.

[147] See (n. 80).

[148] Ibid.

conclude that the Court of Appeals investigation shows that the service to the vast majority is used for file-sharing of music, movies and games etc. How large proportion of the works entered in TPB's database of rightholders consent has not been clarified in the case.[149]

The Court of Appeal therefore upheld the District Court decision but varied the terms of the order. Their prison sentences were reduced, Neij to ten months; Mr Sunde to eight months, and Lundström four months. Gottfrid Svartholm was too ill to attend court and so a sentencing decision on him was postponed. The fine though was increased to 46m Swedish krona (around £4.1m). Three of the accused, Neij, Sunde, and Lundström then applied for leave to appeal to the Swedish Supreme Court while Svartholm left the country fleeing to Cambodia. In February 2012 the Swedish Supreme Court ruled it would not hear the case,[150] Peter Sunde and Fredrik Neij applied to the ECtHR to have their sentences overturned but their application was refused while Peter Sunde also applied for a pardon (which was rejected). Sunde then stood for election in the 2014 European elections as a candidate for the Pirate Party of Finland. He was eventually arrested in May 2014 near Malmö and transferred to Västervik Norra prison where he served his sentence. Carl Lundström served his time in prison, partly by electronic tag, and partly in prison in Gothenburg. Gottfrid Svartholm was arrested in Cambodia and was deported to Sweden where he was imprisoned for the full one-year term originally imposed. He was then extradited to Denmark where he had been named as a suspect in a case where millions of personal identification numbers were stolen from a police database. He is currently in prison in Denmark having been found guilty of computer misuse offences. Fredrik Neij was arrested in Thailand in November 2014 and served two-thirds of his 10-month sentence in Skänninge prison in central Sweden. He was released on June 1 2015 bringing to an end the formal criminal process in *the Pirate Bay* case.

Despite the successes of copyright holders in cases such as *Napster*, *Grokster*, *Sharman*, and *The Pirate Bay*, the popularity of P2P file-sharing remains strong with popular Torrent protocol Popcorn Time the current market leader. Even if Swedish prosecutors had been able to close down The Pirate Bay permanently, which seems unlikely given the number of global mirror sites on offer, other Torrent indexes would quickly have filled the void; indeed Popcorn Time integrates the BitTorrent index and client into a single package meaning the experience for the end user is no different to popular commercial sites such as Netflix or Amazon Instant Video. The days of closing down a few P2P site operators being an effective method to control the illegal trade in copyright protected music, video, and software files appear long gone in the completely decentralized world of BitTorrent. New techniques have therefore been developed in an attempt to stem the tide of illegal files.

11.2.5 **Site blocking**

One technique is to seek to block access to sites which offer file-sharing technology or indexes. Many websites which offer access to unlawful and illegal materials are blocked by intermediaries and ISPs. The technology is not new; the UK has been blocking access to sites that are known to contain child-abuse images since 2004 through the

[149] Ibid. 24–5.

[150] M Peckham, 'Pirate Bay Founders Lose Supreme Court Appeal, Going to Jail' *Time* (New York, 1 February 2012) <http://techland.time.com/2012/02/01/pirate-bay-founders-lose-supreme-court-appeal-going-to-jail/>.

application of the 'Cleanfeed' content-blocking tool. It is quite a simple operation to block access to a website; the difficulty, as we shall see is in making that block effective.

As the legal action against The Pirate Bay approached its conclusion it became apparent that simply fining and even jailing The Pirate Bay founders was not going to be enough to close down the site. With a real danger that authorities would seize The Pirate Bay's domain name they relocated from thepiratebay.org to thepiratebay.se while supporters rushed to mirror the site in a number of locations.[151] The physical servers which hosted The Pirate Bay were moved out of Sweden and then dispensed with entirely as The Pirate Bay moved its operation into the cloud. It is currently reported that The Pirate Bay is hosted at cloud hosting companies in two countries where they run several Virtual Machine instances.[152] If these companies are compelled to stop hosting The Pirate Bay, the operators of the site can switch it to another hosting company within minutes. Using two hosts should mean no downtime in any switch. It became clear that The Pirate Bay couldn't be 'killed'. As a result, a number of countries have taken stops to block access to The Pirate Bay and other copyright infringing sites. As referred to above, The Pirate Bay website is subject to legal orders requiring ISPs to block or restrict access to it in at least 14 countries, including the UK. The effectiveness of such blocks though is questionable.

The first initial legal interventions into file-sharing sites in the UK were not actually blocks. The first case in the UK was actually a criminal prosecution brought against Alan Ellis the owner/operator of Oink's Pink Palace. Oink was an invitation-only BitTorrent community which had around 180,000 members. Unlike most open access BitTorrent sites, such as The Pirate Bay, one of Oink's rules was that users could not pay to gain membership to the site, but had an opportunity to donate money to the site. Oink placed an emphasis on the sharing of torrents for high-quality MP3 and lossless audio formats. Members were required to maintain minimum upload-to-download ratios to ensure the site remained vibrant. Following an extensive investigation by authorities the Palace was closed in October 2007. Due to the fact that the site invited donations, which netted Ellis considerable sums, he was charged with conspiracy to defraud but in January 2010 a Jury at Teesside Crown Court cleared him of the charges.[153] The cases which followed all focused instead on the Copyright, Designs and Patents Act 1988 rather than attempting a criminal prosecution.

The first of these was *Twentieth Century Fox & Ors v Newzbin Ltd.*[154] This case was similar to *Oink's Pink Palace* in that it involved a service domiciled within the United Kingdom and therefore easily made subject to the jurisdiction of the High Court. Newzbin was an indexing service for Usenet files. It was a subscription-only service netting a substantial annual profit.[155] It was also clear that a substantial percentage of indexed content was there in breach of copyright conditions. There was a fig leaf of a copyright enforcement system using a reporting and 'delisting' tool but Kitchin J did not believe it was offered as a genuine service to copyright holders: 'I have no doubt that this is another superficial attempt to conceal the purpose and intention of the defendant to make

[151] Listing site Proxy Bay lists 160 Pirate Bay mirrors.

[152] 'Pirate Bay Moves to The Cloud, Becomes Raid-Proof' (*Torrent Freak*, 17 October 2012) <http://torrentfreak.com/pirate-bay-moves-to-the-cloud-becomes-raid-proof-121017/>.

[153] 'Music file-sharer "Oink" cleared of fraud' (*BBC News*, 15 January 2010) <http://news.bbc.co.uk/1/hi/england/tees/8461879.stm>.

[154] [2010] EWHC 608 (Ch).

[155] Ibid. [15].

available binary content of interest to its users, including infringing copies of films. As will be seen, the defendant has done nothing to enforce this restriction.'[156] The claimants sought a wide injunction to prevent Newzbin from supplying links to any material in breach of copyright. Kitchin J felt he could not award such a widely drafted injunction noting that he had only been briefed on the rights of the parties before him and that an injunction could only in his view be awarded to rights holders (many of which were not represented before him). He did though grant a narrower injunction under s. 97A of the CDPA to the claimants. Almost immediately Newzbin Ltd was sold to a third party who resurrected the site with a Seychelles hosting agreement and operating from the same web address under the name Newzbin II. This prevented the claimants from recovering costs and allowed the site to continue to operate outside the jurisdiction of the High Court. The claimants then returned to the court with a new strategy. If Newzbin was now outside the jurisdiction of the court could they block access to it? The claimants returned to the High Court to seek a new and innovative injunction.[157] They were aware of the Cleanfeed system and now sought an order under s. 97A not against the host, which as it was located in the Seychelles was beyond the jurisdiction of the court, but against BT requiring it to add Newzbin to its list of blocked Cleanfeed sites. As most major UK ISPs share the Cleanfeed list for their content-blocking system, this would be effective beyond only BT customers and would in effect for most of the population block access to the Newzbin site in the same way as child-abuse images are blocked from access.

There was, though, a problem that Arnold J had to overcome before he could grant the injunction. A Belgian case on ISP filtering had been referred to the ECJ for judgment. The final decision of the court was still outstanding at the time Arnold J heard the *BT* case but the opinion of the Advocate General had been issued and it was very negative in relation to applying the Belgian equivalent of s. 97A in the manner the court was being asked to do. The case was *Scarlet Extended SA v SABAM*,[158] and it involved an application by SABAM, the Belgian authors collecting society to require Belgian ISPs to install a system for filtering file-sharing content with a view to preventing illegal file-sharing. Scarlet is one of Belgium's larger ISPs and refused to comply with the request. They argued this was 'contrary to Art.15 of the E-Commerce Directive because it would impose on Scarlet, de facto, a general obligation to monitor communications on its network, inasmuch as any system for blocking or filtering P2P traffic would necessarily require general surveillance of all the communications passing through its network'.[159]

Highlight Article 15(1) of the E-Commerce Directive

Member States shall not impose a general obligation on providers, when providing the services covered by Arts. 12, 13 and 14, to monitor the information which they transmit or store, nor a general obligation actively to seek facts or circumstances indicating illegal activity.

[156] Ibid. [45].
[157] *Twentieth Century Fox & Ors v British Telecommunications plc* [2011] EWHC 1981 (Ch).
[158] (C-70/10) [2012] ECDR 4.
[159] Ibid. [H3].

The Advocate General (AG) had recommended that the court find that Art.15(1) prevented the Belgian authorities from making and enforcing the order sought. He was strongly of the opinion that the injunction sought, which was for all communications on the ISP's network and for an unlimited time at the ISP's cost, was unreasonable. He noted that the solution was doubtless intended to be applied on a widespread basis, across all ISPs and to other major players involved in the internet, not merely in Belgium but beyond.[160] When the court decided the case in full in November 2011 they upheld the AG in full and found that:

> the injunction imposed on the ISP concerned requiring it to install the contested filtering system would oblige it to actively monitor all the data relating to each of its customers in order to prevent any future infringement of intellectual-property rights. It follows that that injunction would require the ISP to carry out general monitoring, something which is prohibited by Art. 15(1) of the E-Commerce Directive. Moreover, the injunction to install the contested filtering system is to be regarded as not respecting the requirement that a fair balance be struck between, on the one hand, the protection of the intellectual-property right enjoyed by copyright holders, and, on the other hand, that of the freedom to conduct business enjoyed by operators such as ISPs.[161]

Of course at this point Arnold J did not know this, but surely given the report of the AG he knew it was unlikely the court would depart from the opinion. He therefore had to anticipate whether the application before him would also offend Art. 15(1). Arnold J was extremely bullish in finding this would not be the case:

> I consider that the present case is clearly distinguishable from that case (SABAM). Quite simply, the Studios are not seeking an order that 'BT introduce, for all its customers, *in abstracto* and as a preventive measure, exclusively at the cost of that ISP and for an unlimited period, a system for filtering all electronic communications, both incoming and outgoing, passing via its services, in particular those involving the use of peer-to-peer software, in order to identify on its network the sharing of electronic files containing a musical, cinematographic or audio-visual work in respect of which the applicant claims to hold rights, and subsequently to block the transfer of such files, either at the point at which they are requested or at which they are sent.' On the contrary, the order sought by the Studios is clear and precise; it merely requires BT to implement an existing technical solution which BT already employs for a different purpose; implementing that solution is accepted by BT to be technically feasible; the cost is not suggested by BT to be excessive; and provision has been made to enable the order to be varied or discharged in the event of a future change in circumstances. In my view, the order falls well within the range of orders which was foreseeable by ISPs on the basis of section 97A, and still more Article 8(3) of the Information Society Directive. I therefore conclude that the order is one 'prescribed by law' within Article 10(2) ECHR, and hence is not contrary to Article 10 ECHR.

And with this thorny issue disposed of Arnold J went on to make the order applied for. This was a vital win for the copyright industry. Prior to this case it was not clear that s. 97A could be applied to an ISP in this form as they are unlikely to have 'actual knowledge' of infringement, and in any event it was assumed they would benefit from the defences of Arts.12 and 15(1) of the E-Commerce Directive. The issue was so thorny that

[160] [2011] EWHC 1981 (Ch) [175].
[161] [2012] ECDR 4 [H7].

the government had introduced specific blocking legislation in the form of s. 17 of the Digital Economy Act 2010. This would allow the Secretary of State to pass Regulations permitting a court to make 'a blocking injunction in respect of a location on the internet which the court is satisfied has been, is being or is likely to be used for or in connection with an activity that infringes copyright'.[162] But despite efforts of BT to argue they lacked actual knowledge and benefited from these defences, Arnold J stated that they had been put on notice by the applicants of the infringing nature of the Newzbin II site,[163] and he was equally dismissive of Arts. 12[164] and 15.[165]

With the legal principle established the copyright industry moved to reinforce their position. They quickly brought applications against a number of other ISPs requiring them to block Newzbin II and then moved to bring an action to block access to that significant thorn in their side, The Pirate Bay.[166] *The Pirate Bay* action began when a number of copyright holders made a joint s. 97A application against all of the UK's leading ISPs. It again came before Arnold J and he had little difficulty in following the path he had set out in *Twentieth Century Fox* and again the order sought was awarded. In the aftermath of The Pirate Bay block some people reported that it would be ineffective but data from Neilsen Media reports that between September 2011 and September 2012, traffic to The Pirate Bay from the UK has dropped 75 per cent.[167]

Following this success s. 97A orders have become the default method to block access to illegal file-sharing and streaming sites in the UK. In 2013 they were used to block access to file-sharing sites, Fenopy, H33t, and Kickass Torrents,[168] SolarMovie, and TubePlus[169] as well as the sports streaming website FirstRow Sports.[170] In 2014 file-sharing sites including BTdigg, BTloft, ViTorrent, and LimeTorrents among others were blocked,[171] alongside Viooz, Megashare, zMovie, and Watch32.[172] Controversially s. 97A was also used to block access to a number of sites which traded goods in breach of trademark law with Arnold J holding that the general injunction power of the court found in s. 37(1) of the Senior Courts Act 1981 could substitute for the specific power found in relation to copyright infringements in s. 97A.[173] The most recent case, at the time of writing, is *Twentieth Century Fox Film Corp & Ors v Sky UK Ltd & Ors*,[174] in which an injunction was awarded against nine websites including popcorntime.io.

[162] As an aside the government has decided not to implement s. 17 of the Digital Economy Act following the successful use of s. 97A CDPA to obtain blocking injunctions. 'Government drops website blocking' (*BBC News*, 3 August 2011) <http://www.bbc.co.uk/news/technology-14372698>.

[163] [2011] EWHC 1981 (Ch) [157]–[158].

[164] Ibid. [113].

[165] Ibid. [162].

[166] *Dramatico Entertainment Ltd & Ors v British Sky Broadcasting Ltd & Ors* [2012] EWHC 268 (Ch).

[167] D Lee, 'More piracy sites faced with blocking as BPI contacts UK ISPs' (*BBC News*, 23 October 2012) <http://www.bbc.co.uk/news/technology-20026271>.

[168] *EMI Records Ltd & Ors v British Sky Broadcasting Ltd & Ors* [2013] EWHC 379 (Ch).

[169] *Paramount Home Entertainment & Ors v British Sky Broadcasting Ltd & Ors* [2013] EWHC 3479 (Ch).

[170] *Football Association Premier League & Ors v British Sky Broadcasting & Ors* [2013] EWHC 2058 (Ch).

[171] *1967 Ltd & Ors v British Sky Broadcasting & Ors* [2014] EWHC 3444 (Ch).

[172] *Paramount Home Entertainment International & Ors v British Sky Broadcasting & Ors* [2014] EWHC 937 (Ch).

[173] *Cartier International AG & Ors v British Sky Broadcasting & Ors* [2014] EWHC 3354 (Ch).

[174] [2015] EWHC 1082 (Ch).

11.2.6 **Speculative invoicing**

Speculative invoicing is a highly controversial enforcement system first introduced into the UK by law firm Davenport Lyons (DL), and then taken on for a period by niche firm ACS: Law. It is now more widely practised but due to the public perception of the practice as being little more than a 'legalized shakedown' it remains very much a niche practice.[175]

The practice first came to light in March 2007 when DL sent letters to 500 individuals who, they claimed, had shared a computer game called Pinball Dreams 3D. The letters offered to settle the claim in return for a payment of in the region of £600; failure to settle would lead to DL taking further action.[176] This practice may be seen as a twist on the class action lawsuit where a collection of individuals bands together to pursue a corporation: here the corporation is ameliorating the costs of pursuing hundreds of actions by packaging them together and 'invoicing' each for part of the costs and damages.

The practice was initially attractive to copyright holders. As well as Topware Interactive, DL were retained by Codemasters, Reality Pump, Techland, and Atari to pursue claims relating to games titles such as The Lord of the Rings, the Colin McRae Rally series, and Operation Flashpoint.[177] Then a stream of bad publicity dogged the practice. First it became clear that claims were being made based on IP address data alone. This meant individuals who may not have adequately secured their wireless servers could find themselves receiving demands for the actions of individuals who had illegally piggy-backed on their server.[178] The bad publicity surrounding what many saw as strong-arm tactics reached a head in late 2008 with two separate episodes.

Case study Ken and Gill Murdoch

In October 2008 Davenport Lyons sent a letter on behalf of Atari to Ken and Gill Murdoch of Inverness accusing them of sharing Atari's Race 07 game. Ken (66) and Gill (54) said that they had never played a computer game before and contacted *Which?* The story quickly became a minor cause célèbre with Davenport Lyons dropping the claim but not before their tale was reported by the *Daily Express*, the BBC, and the *Daily Mail*.

[175] M Masnick, 'Court Lets Malibu Media Move Forward With Discovery In Copyright Case, But Blocks "Speculative Invoicing"' (*TechDirt*, 19 August 2015) <http://www.techdirt.com/articles/20150818/17282532001/court-lets-malibu-media-move-forward-with-discovery-copyright-case-blocks-speculative-invoicing.shtml>.

[176] M Ballard, 'Games firm pursues 500 pinball "pirates" through UK courts' (*The Register*, 28 March 2007) <http://www.reghardware.co.uk/2007/03/28/uk_share_hunt>.

[177] A Mostrous and J Richards, 'Computer games industry threat to downloaders: "pay up or we'll sue"' *The Times* (London, 20 August 2008).

[178] It is illegal under s. 125 of the Communications Act 2003 to 'dishonestly obtain an electronic communications service', this includes making use of another's wireless internet connection without permission. See J Leyden, 'UK war driver fined £500' (*The Register*, 25 July 2005) <http://www.theregister.co.uk/2005/07/25/uk_war_driver_fined/>.

Case study Davenport Lyons and Smut

Davenport Lyons decided to represent the copyright holders of several hardcore pornographic titles. A substantial number of claim letters were issued in late 2008 relating to a number of film titles, all of which appear to be material which it would be illegal to trade in, or potentially even possess, in the UK. Quite apart from the question as to whether a Court of Equity would entertain an application from a copyright holder who is seeking to enforce their copyright in obscene material, Davenport Lyons had unfortunately sent several of their claims letters to respectable elderly citizens leading to a further round of bad publicity. This bad publicity led to Atari severing relations with the firm, while the tactics caused *Which?* to report the firm to the Solicitors' Regulatory Authority.

Immediately thereafter, DL suspended their practice in speculative invoicing: the bad publicity surrounding these two events having caused a number of major clients, including Atari, to abandon the strategy and discouraged the firm from continuing the practice. With the withdrawal of DL from the practice it was taken up by a number of others but in particular ACS:Law. For a period between 2008 and 2011 ACS:Law became a beacon for consumer anger as it developed a business model based on speculative invoicing. In essence ACS:Law acted for a small number of clients such as Media CAT Ltd. These are businesses which were given contractual permission of copyright holders to 'inquire claim demand and prosecute through the civil courts where necessary any person or persons identified as having made available for download a film for which [an agreement] has expressly licensed'.[179] These copyright monitoring companies, then capture IP addresses from file-sharing sites in large numbers and pass them on to their legal representatives to allow for a Norwich Pharmacal application to be made. These applications would be made in huge volumes: *Media CAT Ltd v Adams* mentions 10,000 letters being sent out after a Norwich Pharmacal application. Following the Norwich Pharmacal award it would then be served by the lawyers on the ISPs where subscriber identity was obtained. Then the 'invoice' letters before action would be sent out, threatening litigation if the subscriber did not pay up. It took nearly three years to get one of these cases to a full hearing and when it did in *Media CAT Ltd v Adams* HH Judge Birss QC was damning of the process. He found the claims far exceeded any damages likely to have accrued. He noted that the 'sum of £495 is demanded as compensation. This sum is said to include damages as well as "ISP administration costs (and its legal costs where applicable), a contribution to our clients legal costs incurred to date and all additional costs". However no breakdown of the figure is given.'[180] He was critical also of the distribution of money generated:

> I was provided with a copy of the agreement between Sheptonhurst (the copyright holder) and Media CAT which purports to give Media CAT the right to bring proceedings. Mr Tritton pointed out that the agreement shows (or appears to show) that a 65 per cent share of all

[179] *Media Cat Ltd v Adams* [2011] EWPCC 006 [5].
[180] Ibid. [19].

revenues generated from this whole exercise will go to Media CAT's lawyers—ACS:Law. Media CAT receives 15 per cent and Sheptonhurst receive 20 per cent of the revenue. Mr Tritton submitted that the agreement was 'champertous' in that it was an assignment of a bare right to litigate and contrary to public policy.[181]

In the end HH Judge Birss threw the case out. In a damning verdict he recorded the following commentary:

The question in my judgment is whether the effect the notices of discontinuance undoubtedly have of bringing these cases to an end and thereby terminating any scrutiny by the court of the claims is an unwarranted advantage to Media CAT amounting to an abuse of the court's process . . . Media CAT and ACS:Law have a very real interest in avoiding public scrutiny of the cause of action because in parallel to the 26 court cases, a wholesale letter writing campaign is being conducted from which revenues are being generated. This letter writing exercise is founded on the threat of legal proceedings such as the claims before this court. The information annexed to Mr Batstone's letter refers to ACS:Law having 'recovered' £1 Million. Whether that was right and even if so whether it was solely in relation to Media CAT or other file sharing cases I do not know. Simple arithmetic shows that the sums involved in the Media CAT exercise must be considerable. 10,000 letters for Media CAT claiming £495 each would still generate about £1 Million if 80% of the recipients refused to pay and only the 20% remainder did so. Note that ACS:Law's interest is specifically mentioned in the previous paragraph because of course they receive 65% of the revenues from the letter writing exercise. In fact Media CAT's financial interest is actually much less than that of ACS:Law. Whether it was intended to or not, I cannot imagine a system better designed to create disincentives to test the issues in court. Why take cases to court and test the assertions when one can just write more letters and collect payments from a proportion of the recipients? . . . The GCB episode is damning in my judgment. This shows that Media CAT is a party who, while coming to court to discontinue, is at the very same time trying to ram home claims formulated on exactly the same basis away from the gaze of the court. That will not do. I find that these notices of discontinuance are indeed an abuse of the court's process. The advantage of discontinuing as opposed to applying to amend is unwarranted in that it avoids judicial scrutiny of the underlying basis for wider campaign orchestrated by Media CAT and ACS:Law to generate revenue under the various agreements such as the Sheptonhurst agreement.[182]

A short period after the *Media CAT* decision a Solicitors Disciplinary Tribunal suspended Andrew Crossley of ACS:Law for a period of two years and ordered him to pay costs in excess of £76,000.[183] In their report they were extremely critical of the speculative invoicing model, finding that it diminished the trust which the public placed in solicitors and encouraged solicitors' independence to be compromised because of the financial interest they had in the process.

At this point we may all have assumed that the process was dead in the water but recently it has resurfaced. In March 2012 a variation of the speculative invoicing process arrived at the door of the High Court. Instead of using a copyright monitoring company, this time the actions are brought by the copyright holders themselves both directly for their own work and as agents for other copyright holders. The case, *Golden Eye (International) Ltd v Telefónica UK Ltd*,[184] has a number of similarities to *Media CAT*. The applicants were seeking 9,124 personal details under a Norwich Pharmacal order

[181] Ibid. [41].
[182] Ibid. [98]–[102].
[183] *Solicitors Regulation Authority v Andrew John Crossley*, Case No. 10726-2011, 16 January 2012.
[184] [2012] EWHC 723 (Ch).

to be served on Telefónica, operator of the O2 broadband network. They intended to send letters similar to those in *Media CAT* demanding a payment of £700. They were doing so in regard of their own work and under agreement for twelve other claimants who had contractually agreed for Golden Eye to represent them in the case in return for a proportion of any damages received. The claims are in relation to a number of pornographic films produced by Golden Eye and Ben Dover Productions and a number of other porn producers and relate to their sharing by BitTorrent technology. At an initial hearing Arnold J examined closely the relationship between Golden Eye, their legal representatives, and the other claimants. He determined the case was distinguishable from *Media CAT* and awarded the Norwich Pharmacal order to Golden Eye and Ben Dover Productions. However, in regard to the other twelve claimants he was concerned the activity was close to champertous and refused to grant the order in relation to them:

> I have not accepted that the agreements between Golden Eye and the Other Claimants are champertous. Nor have I been persuaded that those agreements mean that the Other Claimants are not genuinely intending to try to seek redress. It does not follow, however, that it is appropriate, when balancing the competing interests, to make an order which endorses an arrangement under which the Other Claimants surrender total control of the litigation to Golden Eye and Golden Eye receives about 75% of the revenues in return. On the contrary, I consider that that would be tantamount to the court sanctioning the sale of the Intended Defendants' privacy and data protection rights to the highest bidder. Accordingly, in my judgment, to make such an order would not proportionately and fairly balance the interests of the Other Claimants with the Intended Defendants' interests. If the Other Claimants want to obtain redress for the wrongs they have suffered, they must obtain it themselves.[185]

Golden Eye appealed this decision and in December 2012 the Court of Appeal reversed this decision.[186] Patten LJ gave the judgment of the court:

> The judge's refusal to grant relief to the Other Claimants was based on his disapproval of the recovery sharing arrangements with Golden Eye which is confirmed by his statement that to make the order would be tantamount to the court sanctioning the sale of the intended defendants' rights to the highest bidder. I have to say that I find those reasons difficult to follow. The court is not sanctioning the sale of anything. Indeed its ability to control the process (as the judge has done in this case) and ultimately to refuse relief was the primary reason why Arnold J rejected the submission that the litigation arrangements made with Golden Eye in this case do not jeopardise or undermine the proper administration of justice. If the arrangements are not therefore unlawful and are not simply a money-making exercise designed to take advantage of the vulnerability of the subscribers rather than a genuine attempt to protect the rights of the Other Claimants, I can see no justification for refusing relief based on a disapproval of those arrangements. Indeed it is difficult to articulate what that disapproval can be based on.[187]

This decision reopened the door of speculative invoicing. While the Court of Appeal trust their ability to manage the process and that of the Chancery Division and the Patents County Court, the problem is that the end effect means individuals still receive letters through their doors demanding large sums of money for a copyright infringement they may or may not have committed, for as we know an IP address leads to a router not a person. Speculative invoicing letters continue to drop onto people's

[185] Ibid. [146].
[186] *Golden Eye (International) Ltd v Telefónica UK Ltd* [2012] EWCA Civ 1740.
[187] Ibid. [28].

doorsteps. In July 2015 letters were sent by a US firm TCYK LLC, apparently set up to exploit the copyright in the 2012 Robert Redford film *The Company You Keep*, demanding payment of an 'appropriate fee' from alleged copyright infringers of their copyright to customers of Sky Broadband. It was reported in at least one reputable media outlet 'the piracy is alleged to have taken place in 2013, but the company making the claims is relying on subscriber data from 2015'.[188] It has also been reported that Golden Eye (and other porn producers) began a second round of speculative invoicing claims against 1,400 Virgin Media customers in autumn 2014 (although only 800 names were disclosed under the Norwich Pharmacal order).[189] This practice continues to tarnish the legal profession in the minds of the public for although the tone of the current letters is less confrontational, these letters, and in particular where they relate to pornographic movies, continue to be portrayed in the media as a legalized form of threat of blackmail or extortion. It should be made clear that the author makes no value judgement on firms providing this service to clients or on those clients, and is at pains to point out the legitimacy of the process in the eyes of the law. The observation is merely the perception of the process in the public sphere where it undoubtedly harms the public perception of the profession.

11.3 Information and the public domain: the Creative Commons

The Creative Commons movement started in 2001 when a group of individuals with the support of the Center for the Study of the Public Domain at Duke University came together with a view to finding a way to free digital content from the constraints of a copyright law designed for the atomic environment. The Creative Commons project is closely linked to US law professor Lawrence Lessig who set out his vision for Creative Commons in a 2004 paper simply entitled 'The Creative Commons'.[190] In this Lessig describes the Creative Commons movement as 'a kind of environmentalism for culture',[191] the idea being 'to build a layer of reasonable copyright law'.[192]

The reason why the Creative Commons movement came about is that Lawrence Lessig and co-founder James Boyle (among others) believed that a rebalancing of copyright interests was necessary in the information society. They had seen in the previous ten years what Lessig described as two extremes: first, 'in the beginning of the Internet the architecture of the Internet disabled any ability to control the distribution of copyright works . . . The architecture meant that copyright was not respected because anybody could copy and perfectly distribute any copyrighted work without control.'[193] However, in 1995 the copyright industry responded to this threat: 'the copyright industry . . . in

[188] D Pegg, 'Sky Broadband customers targeted for allegedly pirating Robert Redford film' *The Guardian* (London, 15 July 2015) <http://www.theguardian.com/business/2015/jul/15/sky-broadband-customers-targeted-allegedly-pirating-robert-redford-film>.

[189] M Jackson, '800 Virgin Media Customers Pursued by Internet Porn Piracy Lawyers' (*ISP Review*, 24 October 2014) <http://www.ispreview.co.uk/index.php/2014/10/800-virgin-media-customers-pursued-internet-porn-piracy-lawyers.html>.

[190] L Lessig, 'The Creative Commons' (2004) 65 *Montana Law Review* 1.

[191] Ibid. 11.

[192] Ibid.

[193] Ibid. 10.

response to the Internet launched a campaign to change the technical and legal infrastructure that defined the Internet from an architecture of no control to an architecture of total control . . . we have thus moved from one extreme to the other'.[194]

Lessig and Boyle believed neither of the extremes represented the interests of most internet users. They felt most people wanted to make use of copyright material without the strict restrictions the copyright industry was seeking to implement for commercially valuable copyright content while ensuring that commercially valuable content was protected, or to put it in Lessig's own words, 'But the world is divided not into two, but into three. There are those who believe in all rights reserved, those who believe in no rights at all, but there are also many who believe that some rights should be controlled but not all.'[195] This third group is represented by Creative Commons, its famous strapline is 'some rights reserved', a reflection of this balance between the extremes. Creative Commons does not seek to overthrow or subvert copyright law,[196] but rather allows copyright holders to embed permissions into their copyright material allowing others to reuse, share, or copy that material without seeking the active permission of the copyright holder. Creative Commons achieves this through the application of six mainstream licences.

Highlight The Creative Commons licenses

1. Attribution (BY): This license lets others distribute, remix, tweak, and build upon the work, even commercially, as long as they credit the author for the original creation.
2. Attribution-Share Alike (BY–SA): This license lets others remix, tweak, and build upon the work even for commercial reasons, as long as they credit the author and license their new creations under the identical terms. All new works based on the original will carry the same license, so any derivatives will also allow commercial use.
3. Attribution-No Derivatives (BY-ND): This license allows for redistribution of the work, commercial and non-commercial, as long as it is passed along unchanged and in whole, with credit to the author.
4. Attribution-Non-Commercial (BY-NC): This license lets others remix, tweak, and build upon the work non-commercially, and although their new works must also acknowledge you and be non-commercial, they don't have to license their derivative works on the same terms.
5. Attribution-Non-Commercial-Share Alike (BY-NC-SA): This license lets others remix, tweak, and build upon the work non-commercially, as long as they credit the author and license their new creations under the identical terms.
6. Attribution-Non-Commercial-No Derivatives (BY-NC-ND): This license is the most restrictive of the six main licenses. This license is often called the 'free advertising' license because it allows others to download the work and share it with others as long as they mention the author and link back to them, but they can't change the work in any way or use it commercially.

[194] Ibid.

[195] Ibid.

[196] An alternate movement 'copyleft' seeks to subvert copyright by forcing release of content into the public domain. Copyleft principles inform the GNU Free Documentation License, details from: <http://www.gnu.org/licenses/licenses.html#FDL>.

To use a Creative Commons licence the author visits the Creative Commons website[197] and answers a series of questions, including which jurisdiction they reside in and what they want others to be able to do with the work. Based on answers to these questions they will be recommended a Creative Commons licence for their work. The Creative Commons licence is actually the three-part document: there is the commons deed (human readable code); the legal code (lawyer readable code); and the metadata (machine readable code).

The commons deed is a summary of the key terms of the actual licence (the legal code). It states simply and clearly, what others can and cannot do with the work.[198] The commons deed itself has no legal value, and its contents do not appear in the actual licence.

The legal code is the actual licence. Until the release of the version 4.0 Creative Commons licences, licences were required to be specifically tailored to each separate jurisdiction to ensure that they complied with local copyright law. At the time of writing there are 59 jurisdictions using 'ported' Creative Commons licences, including England and Wales and Scotland. In each of these jurisdictions a legal project lead has drafted local versions of the main (US) licence to ensure they comply both with local copyright law and the ethos of the Creative Commons movement. The Creative Commons movement has recently abandoned the idea of translating or 'porting' licences into local versions. The current versions of the licences, version 4.0, are designed to be used without porting. They are described as global licences. In the words of Creative Commons 'we've worked closely with our wide international network of affiliates and countless other experts and stakeholders to make 4.0 the most internationally enforceable set of CC licenses to date. The 4.0 licenses are ready-to-use around the world, without porting.'[199] As a result Creative Commons now claim that their licences are in use in over 70 jurisdictions worldwide.[200]

The metadata describes the key licence elements that apply to a piece of content to enable discovery through creative content enabled search engines.[201] Once the licence is attached others may then use the work within the confines of what is permitted by the licence without asking for the permission of the copyright holder. The idea is that content is made available to be shared and reused while allowing the copyright holder to set limits that she is comfortable with. Creative Commons has been remarkably successful.

As has already been stated, Creative Commons licences are available in 59 jurisdictions and to date almost 350 million Flickr images are licensed under a Creative Commons

[197] Some sites such as Flickr offer a licence tool which assists the author in obtaining a CC licence.

[198] For example the CC BY (Version 4.0) Code states: 'You are free to Share—copy and redistribute the material in any medium or format, Adapt—remix, transform, and build upon the material for any purpose, even commercially. The licensor cannot revoke these freedoms as long as you follow the license terms. Under the following terms: Attribution—You must give appropriate credit, provide a link to the license, and indicate if changes were made. You may do so in any reasonable manner, but not in any way that suggests the licensor endorses you or your use.'

[199] Creative Commons, 'What's New in 4.0' <http://creativecommons.org/version4>.

[200] <https://wiki.creativecommons.org/wiki/Jurisdiction_Database>.

[201] Google allows for specialized creative commons searches. A wide variety of search functions may be accessed via <https://search.creativecommons.org/>.

licence,[202] the substantial part of the over 400 million total Creative Commons licensed works of all types.[203] Creative Commons therefore is a flourishing and successful alternative to the 'all rights reserved' copyright model contained in the Copyright, Designs and Patents Act. It is not expected to replace all rights reserved copyright, and the Creative Commons movement acknowledges that for some it will not be the appropriate model of protection: particularly for creators who wish to exploit their works commercially.[204] However, for the vast majority of internet users who wish merely to allow their photographs, music, and videos to be seen, heard, or viewed, or who are happy for their work to be reused, remixed, and reworked Creative Commons provides a real alternative to the statutory copyright scheme.

11.4 **Conclusions**

This chapter has covered substantial ground. At the heart of the information society is a conflict between a culture of free use and access, of 'rip, mix, and burn' and of remixing and mashing and the culture of creative reward, publication, and commercial exploitation. This conflict is driven by the very nature of the information society in general and the internet in particular. The information society is built upon the sharing and exploitation of information, while copyright law is about the protection and control of information. One is about exploitation, the other about reward. The internet is, when one thinks about it in simple terms, just a massive device for the copying and distribution of information: in a very real sense it is designed to infringe copyright massively. For the past 15 years, and no doubt for at the very least the next 15, lawyers, judges, and lawmakers have been trying to establish where the legal balance in interests between these two extremes are to be struck. Some companies have become famously successful by trading in information; prime among these is Google. Some people see the activities of Google in not only cataloguing websites but also caching data, digitizing books, and appropriating newspaper headlines as being in breach of copyright and its values,[205] while others see it as the greatest success story of the information society thus far.[206] This frames the predicament faced by judges, lawyers, and lawmakers: when is the exploitation of other people's data lawful and when, at copyright law, is it unlawful? In essence what makes Google different from The Pirate Bay?[207]

These questions will no doubt continue to challenge lawyers and lawmakers as the information society is still in its formative phase. Eventually we may find YouTube regulated as a TV broadcaster, Google may have to license all content for its Google News service, and we may even succeed in regulating P2P file-sharing sites, but these things will not happen overnight.

[202] For an up-to-date figure see: <http://www.flickr.com/creativecommons/>.

[203] <http://wiki.creativecommons.org/Metrics>.

[204] However, the three non-commercial licences can allow an author or creator to publicize and share their work while retaining the commercial interests in it.

[205] See, e.g. H Porter, 'Google is just an amoral menace' *The Observer* (London, 5 April 2009) <http://www.guardian.co.uk/commentisfree/2009/apr/05/google-internet-piracy>.

[206] See, e.g. D Vise and M Malseed, *The Google Story: Inside the Hottest Business, Media and Technology Success of Our Time* (Delta 2008).

[207] This question was raised by Carl Lundström at the conclusion of *The Pirate Bay* trial.

TEST QUESTIONS

Question 1

Prepare a short note outlining the advice you would give in the following scenario.

Danielle operates a small internet service provider (ISP) based in central London called Access Internet. She specializes in fast access for business and prides herself in providing stable 50Mbps access to a variety of businesses in WC1, WC2, EC1, and EC2. She leases fast fibre-optic cables from Speed Telecommunications which she then in turn leases to clients.

Danielle has recently received a letter before action from Glennister Entertainment. They claim to be a market leader in online interactive movie experiences offering users the ability to effectively act as a movie director by choosing how the story will develop as they watch a movie. Glennister Entertainment say that they have identified that clients of Danielle are allowing their staff to access a site based in Bulgaria, parrot.net which hosts illegal and unauthorized copies of Glennister Entertainment products including 'The Throne King' and 'A Storm of Demons'. Glennister Entertainment demand that Danielle take steps to 'block access to parrot.net and any other site of which she is aware on which Glennister Entertainment products are hosted illegally'.

Advise Danielle.

Question 2

The decision of the Court of Appeal in *The Newspaper Licensing Agency Ltd v Meltwater Holding BV* was not only legally incorrect it was also functionally incorrect in that it had the potential to do irreparable damage to the functions of the web by effectively outlawing the following of hypertext links without the permission of in-linked page owners. The Supreme Court had no decision but to overrule it.

Discuss critically the above comment.

FURTHER READING

Books

C Doctorow, *Information Doesn't Want to Be Free* (2014)

A Johns, *Piracy: The Intellectual Property Wars From Gutenberg To Gates* (2011)

L Lessig, *Free Culture* (2005)

N Netanel, *Copyright's Paradox* (2010)

W Patry, *How to Fix Copyright* (2012)

Chapters and articles

E Baden-Powell, 'Think before You Link: Yesterday's News—Today's Copyright Conundrum' 17 *CTLR* 25 [2011]

M Hart, 'The Legality of Internet Browsing in the Digital Age' 36 *European Intellectual Property Review* 630 [2014]

S Klein, 'Search Engines and Copyright' 39(4) *IIC* 451 (2008)

L Lessig, 'The Creative Commons' 65 *Montana Law Review* 1 (2004)

Databases

One clearly identifiable effect the information society has had on the law is the introduction of a new, *sui generis* form of intellectual property protection in the form of the database right. Databases are structured collections of records or data stored in an indexed filing system usually, although not necessarily, held on a computer system. The structure is achieved by organizing the data according to a database model which allows data to be accessed, cross-referenced, recompiled, and extracted according to data labels. Databases are diverse in design and scope. At the most basic level a telephone directory may be classified as a database: it is ordered using an alphabetical structuring and data may be retrieved by users accessing at the correct page. At the other end of the scale are massive digital databases such as the Lexis/Nexis database which catalogues and cross-references case law, commentaries, newspaper reports, and statutory material from a number of jurisdictions. The Lexis/Nexis database also requires a much more sophisticated approach from the user since instead of merely following an alphabetical listing the user will use keywords and search phrases to find and extract the data they need. Technically, the internet itself, or at very least the web, is a database with search engines such as Google, Yahoo!, and Bing providing the means to locate and extract data: few would think to classify the web as such though.

The database right is designed to protect the investment made in the gathering and indexing of data or files within a database model. It shares some similarities with copyright but is distinctively its own form of protection and has different boundaries to copyright protection. The database right was introduced throughout European Union member states following the promulgation of Directive 96/9/EC of the European Parliament and of the Council of 11 March 1996 on the legal protection of databases.[1] In the UK the Directive was implemented by the Copyright and Rights in Databases Regulations 1997,[2] which made some amendments to the Copyright, Designs and Patents Act (CDPA) 1988 to define the boundaries between copyright and *sui generis* database protection more clearly, and separately introduced the database right into the UK effective from 1 January 1998.

12.1 Copyright and the database right

The roots of the *sui generis* database right are to be found in copyright law. As we have seen throughout chapters 10 and 11 the relationship between informational products

[1] OJ L077, 27/03/1996.
[2] SI 1997/3032.

and copyright law is a fraught one. Although copyright protection has the required flexibility to allow it to be moulded to new types of creative output, such as software or web pages, it also often conflicts with the values or practices seen in the start-up industries which surround such new products. Thus many of the early software cases such as *John Richardson Computers v Flanders*,[3] reflected the conflict between the expansive protection copyright offered and the practice of translating software between operating systems common at the time, while the *Google v Copiepresse* decision suggests a conflict between the 'information wants to be free' ethos of the internet and the values protected by copyright.[4]

A similar conflict of values arose with regard to the protection of databases in the early 1990s. A database as a collection of (usually written) material seemed to fall naturally under copyright protection: a parallel could be drawn with anthologies of poetry or essays for which the publisher obtains copyright protection.[5] Databases became common, and valuable, from the early 1980s as the cost of personal computers fell and major organizations saw the benefits of moving from old-fashioned paper-based records to the modern computer records.[6] With database contents being of potentially great value, both internally as a business asset and on the open market as a commodity, businesses sought legal protection of their databases through the application of copyright law.

Within the UK this seemed perfectly possible, for a database could be categorized as a compilation under s. 3(1)(a) of the CDPA, which meant that if it fulfilled the requirements of originality and connection to the UK it would be protected as a copyright work. In the UK these requirements are not particularly onerous. The connection requirement may simply be achieved as under s. 154(1)(c) of the CDPA: 'A work qualifies for copyright protection if the author was at the material time a qualifying person, that is a body incorporated under the law of a part of the United Kingdom.' Thus any UK incorporated corporation would have the protection of the CDPA extended to their databases in the event they were deemed to be original. This meant the application of the skill, labour, and judgement test discussed in chapter 10, and drawn from *University of London Press Ltd v University Tutorial Press Ltd*[7] in which Peterson J stated that 'the Act does not require that the expression must be in an original or novel form, but that the work must not be copied from another work—that it should originate from the author'.[8]

[3] [1993] FSR 497. Discussed fully at 10.4.1 'Look and feel infringement'.

[4] [2007] ECDR 5. Discussed fully at 11.1.2 '*Google Inc. v Copiepresse SCRL*'.

[5] Anthologies will usually be classified as 'compilations' under CDPA, s. 3(1)(a). The editor or publisher will be awarded copyright protection for the original elements of the compilation (the selection and ordering of the works for instance), although copyright in the works themselves will remain with their original authors.

[6] The benefits of digitization of records are multipart. Three benefits identified by Fred Cate, *Privacy in the Information Age* (Brookings Institution Press 1997) are: (1) it is easier to generate, manipulate, transmit, and store information; (2) the cost of collecting, manipulating, storing, and transmitting data is lowered; and (3) electronic information, due to its very nature, has developed an intrinsic value not found in analogue information, i.e. because digital information is cheaply processed and stored, it attracts a premium in the marketplace. In my contribution to M Klang and A Murray (eds.), *Human Rights in the Digital Age* (Routledge Cavendish 2005) I identify a fourth benefit: convergent media platforms allow digital information to be reutilized across convergent platforms at little extra cost.

[7] [1916] 2 Ch 601. Discussed fully at 10.2.1 'Obtaining copyright protection'.

[8] *University of London Press v University Tutorial Press* (n. 7) 608–9.

This means any original database, that is, one in which the creator of the database has expended skill, labour, and judgement in its creation rather than simply copying it from another source, would be protected by copyright law in the UK.

It is important to be clear about what is actually protected by this copyright. It is the design and structure of the database itself, not the individual contents of the database which may be separately protected by their own copyright as literary, artistic, or musical works. Thus if an individual were to create a database of photographs of cityscapes (a so-called photo-library), they could obtain copyright protection of the database as a whole (its structure, its selection of contents, and its 'model') while the copyright in each image in that database would remain with the original photographer. This means that a competing, and almost identical, database may be built by a competitor provided they put in the work of gathering and cataloguing the images.

12.1.1 **The listings cases**

The application of the CDPA to listings of information in the form of a simple database was confirmed by two cases involving the publisher of a directory of solicitors and barristers in the late 1980s. The first was the case of *Waterlow Publishers Ltd v Rose*.[9] The plaintiff under, contract to the Law Society of England and Wales, compiled and arranged for publication *The Solicitors' and Barristers' Directory and Diary* which contained a geographical listing of solicitors and barristers by region. To enable them to produce this publication the Law Society gave to the plaintiffs a list of all solicitors. The publishers then supplemented and verified this data by sending questionnaires to all firms asking for further data, including areas of practice specialism. Prior to 1984 the defendant owned a printing company which printed copies of the directory; this work was then transferred to another firm. Following this, the defendant resolved to publish his own competing directory entitled *The Lawyers' Diary*. To launch his diary the defendant began by using a copy of the *Solicitors' Diary* to obtain the information he needed, which in his defence he said was necessary as 'it would have been impossible to do otherwise because the 1984 Solicitors' Diary was the only list of solicitors available'.[10] The defendant sent to solicitors copies of their entries in the current edition of the *Solicitors' Diary* and asked them to confirm whether the data was accurate and to make any necessary changes. The plaintiff argued that this action was in breach of their copyright in the *Solicitors' Diary*.

The Court of Appeal had to decide three factors: (1) was the *Solicitors' Diary* protected as a copyright work, (2) was the plaintiff the author of that work, and (3) did the defendant's actions breach copyright in the work. Slade LJ made short work of the first question, finding that 'Section 48(1) of the Copyright Act 1956 (the 1956 Act) defines "literary work" as including "any written table or compilation". The "literary work" in which Waterlow claims copyright by its pleading is thus the "compilation" consisting of section 5 of the Solicitors' Diary 1984.'[11] Was the plaintiff the author of the work

[9] [1995] FSR 207. NB: the case was actually decided on 27 October 1989 and was reported at the time in *The Independent* and *The Times* newspapers. It was not formally reported in the Law Reports though for some time.

[10] Ibid. 212.

[11] Ibid. 214.

though? Here Slade LJ was less sure. He believed that the plaintiff was either the author or co-author of the work, 'I think it clear that if one accepts Laddie's definition of the author of a "compilation", Waterlow, if not the sole author, was at least a co-author of that compilation.'[12] In either event it did not matter as the plaintiff 'had a good cause of action for infringement of the copyright either as author or as co-author or by virtue of the presumption contained in section 20(4)'.[13]

Slade LJ then turned his attention to the final question. Had the defendant infringed the plaintiff's copyright? He noted that the defendant claimed that '[he was] designing his own directory on different lines and with a different layout from that of Waterlow's production, and [in] exercising his own independent skill and judgment in arranging the material, he would not be infringing'.[14] However, this was rejected as:

> these submissions afford no valid defence to the claim of infringement: Mr Rose's suggestion that the database which he was in the process of constructing for his own directory was based solely on the material supplied to him by the solicitors with whom he had communicated is unsustainable. In 20 per cent of the cases where he sent out forms to individuals or firms, the recipients ignored them. The judge rejected his evidence that in such cases he proposed simply to omit them from the directory, and Mr Rose has not sought to challenge this rejection before this court. Furthermore, it has been common ground before this court that in 60 per cent of the cases the forms would be returned unaltered so that the material contained in them would be unchanged.[15]

The court therefore found in favour of the plaintiff and in so doing clearly established the principle that databases were protected as compilations under English law, and that the correct standard of originality was therefore the literary standard of skill, labour, and judgement.

A similar decision was reached in the following case of *Waterlow Directories Ltd v Reed Information Services Ltd*.[16] This High Court case arose from the same publication, the *Solicitors' Diary*. The defendants on this occasion published another competing directory, the *Butterworths Law Directory*. In 1990 in order to update its directory, the defendant compared the *Solicitors' Diary* with their directory and highlighted those names and addresses which appeared in the *Solicitors' Diary* but not *Butterworths Law Directory*. The highlighted names and addresses were copied onto a word processor which was then used to produce letters inviting those solicitors and barristers to appear in the new edition of *Butterworths Law Directory*. Out of 12,620 firms of solicitors in the *Solicitors' Diary* about 1,600 were highlighted in this way.

The plaintiff argued this infringed their copyright in the *Solicitors' Diary*. Aldous J agreed finding that:

> it is accepted that copyright subsists in the plaintiff's directory and that the plaintiff owns that copyright. Further, it is accepted that the defendant, using the plaintiff's directory, copied onto a word processor about 1,600 out of 12,600, names and addresses of solicitors and the names and addresses of organisations onto a computer. Thus it appears to me there has been reproduction and infringement if the amount reproduced constitutes a substantial part of the work. What is

[12] Ibid. 217–18.
[13] Ibid. 218.
[14] Ibid. 222.
[15] Ibid.
[16] [1992] FSR 409.

> a substantial part of a work is a question of degree, depending on the circumstances, and it is settled law that the quality of that which is taken is usually more important than quantity. In the present case, it is a reasonable inference that the parts reproduced by the defendant were important in that they enabled the defendant to carry out a comprehensive mailing . . . That benefit was perceived to be substantial and at this stage of the action I hold that there is a strong case that the part taken by the defendant was a substantial part.[17]

On this basis Aldous J held that:

> it was clear that a person could not copy entries from a directory and use such copies to compile his own directory. Even if it was correct that a person could use the information in a directory to compile another directory provided that reproduction did not take place, that was not the case before the court. The defendant had reproduced the names and addresses from the plaintiff's directory onto a word processor and a computer.[18]

The second *Waterlow* case confirmed that extraction of data for a different application (in this case to turn directory entries into a mailing list) was an infringement of copyright. By the time of this second judgment (October 1990), it was clear that the CDPA provided considerable, perhaps even comprehensive, protection to original databases.

12.1.2 **The Database Directive**

The UK standard was causing difficulties at a European level. As we saw in chapter 10, the UK is unusual in applying the skill, labour, and judgement standard. Most states apply a more stringent standard which requires an intellectual contribution from the author. This distinction between the UK standard and the higher Continental *droit d'auteur* standard was leading to a fragmentation of the European database industry: with greater protection being found in the UK than in Continental Europe.[19] This was in turn affecting the internal market, with companies who deal in databases and their contents being more likely to set operations in the UK than in Continental Europe.[20] To remedy this situation, and to harmonize legal protection of databases throughout the EU, the Commission issued a formal proposal for a directive on the legal protection of databases.[21] Following some amendment the proposal was passed on 11 March 1996 as Directive 96/9/EC, usually known simply as 'the Database Directive'.

The Directive creates a two-tier approach to database protection by first creating a pan-European copyright in some databases, and then supplementing this with the *sui generis* database right where copyright does not apply. Article 1 defines a database (for the purposes of the Directive) as 'a collection of independent works, data or other materials

[17] Ibid. 414.

[18] Ibid. 410.

[19] This is acknowledged in the text of the Directive where at Recital 1 it states 'Whereas databases are at present not sufficiently protected in all Member States by existing legislation; whereas such protection, where it exists, has different attributes.' Dir. 96/9/EC of the European Parliament and of the Council of 11 March 1996 on the legal protection of databases, Recital 1.

[20] This is also acknowledged in the Directive: 'Whereas such differences in the legal protection of databases offered by the legislation of the Member States have direct negative effects on the functioning of the internal market as regards databases and in particular on the freedom of natural and legal persons to provide on-line database goods and services on the basis of harmonized legal arrangements throughout the Community', Dir. 96/9/EC, Recital 2.

[21] Proposal for a Council Directive on the Legal Protection of Databases, 35 OJ C156/4 (1992).

arranged in a systematic or methodical way and individually accessible by electronic or other means'.[22] Article 1 also clarifies that a program used to build, access, or update the contents of the database is to be distinct from the database itself, stating that '[p]rotection under this Directive shall not apply to computer programs used in the making or operation of databases accessible by electronic means'.[23] Thus if a software developer is asked to design a bespoke database management tool that is not part of the database: the database consists only of the data stored in the database. The software will though qualify separately for copyright protection, or perhaps even patent protection, as discussed in chapter 10.

The distinction between copyrightable databases and other databases is to be found in Art. 3(1): 'databases which, by reason of the selection or arrangement of their contents, constitute the author's own intellectual creation shall be protected as such by copyright. No other criteria shall be applied to determine their eligibility for that protection.' The essential characteristic of copyright protected databases therefore is that they must be 'the author's own intellectual creation'. This suggests a standard higher than the traditional UK standard of 'sweat of the brow', but unfortunately the Directive does not develop this further.

The UK government has implemented Art. 3(1) by way of the new s. 3A of the CDPA, introduced by reg. 6 of the Copyright and Rights in Databases Regulations 1997.[24] Section 3A(2) implements Art. 3(1) almost word for word stating that: 'For the purposes of [copyright law] a literary work consisting of a database is original if, and only if, by reason of the selection or arrangement of the contents of the database the database constitutes the author's own intellectual creation.' What does this mean? The UK courts have had some interaction with s. 3A. In *Navitaire Inc. v easyJet Airline Co. & Anor*[25] Pumphrey J touched upon s. 3A in dealing with the extraction of data from an airline booking system. He seemed quite perplexed as to how to interpret s. 3A(2) within the spirit of the Directive finding that:

> I cannot help but feel that section 3A is directed to the contents of the database. The one pointer against this conclusion is to be found in the European Parliament and Council Directive (96/9/EC) of 11 March 1996 on the Legal Protection of Databases ('the Database Directive') which section 3A is intended to implement. Recital 15 says 'Whereas the criteria whether a database should be protected by copyright should be defined to the fact (sic: the French text is "devront se limiter au fait que", which is clearer) that the selection or the arrangement of the contents of the database is the author's own intellectual creation; whereas such protection should cover the structure of the database.' In an electronic database, there is no compelling need to view the programs or scripts creating the database as part of the database, even though they define its 'arrangement' and 'structure'. Anyway, they acquire copyright even if no database is ever generated from them, and my inclination would be to say that they do so by virtue of the fact that they are computer programs.[26]

In the later case of *Pennwell Publishing (UK) Ltd v Ornstien & Ors*[27] Deputy Judge Fenwick QC, disappointingly did not engage fully with s. 3A(2) when invited to do so, but did

[22] Dir. 96/9/EC, Art. 1(2).
[23] Ibid. Art. 1(3).
[24] SI 1997/3032.
[25] [2004] EWHC 1725 (Ch) (2004).
[26] Ibid. [274].
[27] 2007 EWHC 1570 (QB).

comment that: 'it is not necessary, in the light of my other findings, for me to reach a conclusion as to whether the database either in its form on the Outlook system or in the form of the JuniorContacts.xls spreadsheet was an original work within the meaning of the Copyright Designs and Patents Act 1988, but it is right to indicate that I was far from persuaded that the exercise of assembling a list of contacts addresses would be sufficient to qualify'.[28]

A much fuller picture emerged in *Football Dataco Ltd v Yahoo! UK Ltd*,[29] a Court of Justice of the European Union (CJEU) decision which originated in the UK courts as *Football Dataco Ltd v Brittens Pools Ltd*.[30]

Case study *Football Dataco*

Football Dataco is a company owned by the FA Premier League, the Football League, the Scottish Premier League, and the Scottish Football League. It organizes and administers all football fixtures in the English and Scottish Leagues. Each season, through a complicated computer process accounting for a large number of variables, it produces the football fixture lists of that season for each league club. It then builds a database of all fixtures and licenses others to extract data from that database such as football pools companies, betting sites, and news organizations. Football Dataco handle all requests to reprint or extract any part of the database within the UK. Internationally a subsidiary called Fixtures Marketing (whom we will discuss later at 12.2.1, 'The *Fixtures Marketing* cases') handles overseas requests. It is reported that they charge £266 plus VAT to reprint the fixtures of one English club and that to reprint the fixtures of all clubs for one season costs around £3,931 plus VAT for a date-ordered listing. They attracted controversy for charging fanzines and non-profit organizations £1 plus VAT to reprint a single fixture.[31]

In 2004 Football Dataco's international subsidiary Fixtures Marketing lost a number of cases at the CJEU. These cases are discussed in depth below, but the key finding of these cases was that the database of football fixtures created by Football Dataco did not qualify for *sui generis* database protection because the makers of the database had not 'substantially invested qualitatively and/or quantitatively in either the obtaining, verification or presentation of the contents'.[32] Despite this reversal both Football Dataco and its international subsidiary Fixtures Marketing continued to pursue a number of actions in both the UK and overseas claiming that in spite of this finding they remained protected by traditional copyright protection under Art. 3(1) of the Directive and s. 3A(2) of the CDPA. They based this upon the classic decision of *Ladbroke (Football) Ltd v William Hill (Football) Ltd*.[33] In the High Court Floyd J agreed with this line of argument and found that the fixture lists were protected by database copyright, but not by the

[28] Ibid. [107(f)].
[29] [2012] ECDR 10.
[30] [2010] EWHC 841 (Ch); [2010] EWCA Civ 1380.
[31] D Conn, 'Fanzine Fight for the Right to Print Fixtures' *The Guardian* (London, 21 December 2005) <http://www.guardian.co.uk/media/2005/dec/21/newmedia.comment>.
[32] See fully at 12.2.1 'The *Fixtures Marketing* cases'.
[33] [1964] 1 WLR 273.

sui generis database right or any other copyright. This was appealed and at the Court of Appeal Jacob LJ ruled that while the application of Art. 7 was *acte clair* following the decision of the European Court of Justice (ECJ) in the *Fixtures Marketing* cases the same was not true of Art. 3. He therefore, with the support of Hooper LJ and Rimer LJ, referred to the ECJ the questions:

> (1) In Article 3(1) of Directive 96/9/EC on the legal protection of databases what is meant by 'databases which, by reason of the selection or arrangement of their contents, constitute the author's own intellectual creation'? and in particular: (a) should the intellectual effort and skill of creating data be excluded? (b) does 'selection or arrangement' include adding important significance to a pre-existing item of data? (as in fixing the date of a football match); (c) does 'author's own intellectual creation' require more than significant labour and skill from the author, if so what?
>
> (2) Does the Directive preclude national rights in the nature of copyright in databases other than those provided for by the Directive?[34]

The ECJ ruled on 1 March 2012. They rejected all of Football Dataco's claims. In a completely unambiguous judgment they ruled that Art. 3(1) of the Directive must be interpreted as meaning that a database is protected by copyright only when the selection or arrangement of the data which it contains amounts to an original expression of the creative freedom of its author. As a consequence, the intellectual effort and skill of creating that data are not relevant in order to assess the eligibility of that database for protection by that right; it is irrelevant, for that purpose, whether or not the selection or arrangement of that data includes the addition of important significance to that data; and the significant labour and skill required for setting up that database cannot as such justify such a protection if they do not express any originality in the selection or arrangement of the data which that database contains. Further, the Directive must be interpreted as meaning that it precludes national legislation which grants databases copyright protection under conditions which are different from those set out in Art. 3(1).[35]

The law now seems completely unambiguous in this area. It is indeed a higher standard of creativity than the UK standard of skill, labour, and judgement which is required for Art. 3(1) and s. 3A(2). Just as the ECJ had previously ruled in the *Fixtures Marketing* cases in relation to Art. 7, you cannot gain copyright protection for simply ordering something which is created or pre-existing for a different purpose. Article 3 protection is for creative collections, anthologies, and suchlike; not a way to supplement *sui generis* protection where an investment has been made in developing the database. We are now clear. Article 3 protection is a higher-level protection which exists where the author through their selection or arrangement has created something original. Article 7 covers the design and building of databases where there has been significant investment in the design and collection of the data for the database: unfortunately for Football Dataco and Fixtures Marketing, as shall be seen at 12.2.1 'The *Fixtures Marketing* cases', neither of these protections apply to the creation of 'spin-off' databases where the content of the database is created for another purpose and the database is only a subsidiary of that purpose.

[34] [2010] EWCA Civ 1380, [22].
[35] Taken from [2012] ECDR 10, [H6].

12.2 **The database right**

The *sui generis* database right was introduced in Chapter III (Arts. 7–11) of the Database Directive. The right is awarded on creation of the database to the 'maker' of the database; in the Directive this is defined simply as the person who 'takes the initiative and the risk of investing'.[36] The UK regulations give a far greater definition of a maker in reg. 14. The maker of a database is defined there as 'the person who takes the initiative in obtaining, verifying or presenting the contents of a database and assumes the risk of investing in that obtaining, verification or presentation'.[37] This is subject to several exceptions and limitations:

(1) where a database is made by an employee in the course of his employment, his employer shall be regarded as the maker of the database, subject to any agreement to the contrary;[38]

(2) where a database is made by Her Majesty or by an officer or servant of the Crown in the course of his duties, Her Majesty shall be regarded as the maker of the database;[39]

(3) where a database is made by or under the direction or control of the House of Commons or the House of Lords the House by whom, or under whose direction or control, the database is made shall be regarded as the maker of the database, and if the database is made by or under the direction or control of both Houses, the two Houses shall be regarded as the joint makers of the database;[40] and finally,

(4) a database is made jointly if two or more persons acting together in collaboration take the initiative in obtaining, verifying or presenting the contents of the database and assume the risk of investing in that obtaining, verification or presentation.[41]

The UK regulations make clear that the maker of the database will be the first owner of the database right.[42]

Once the maker of the database has been identified, and for simplicity's sake we may assume that this is usually the person who pays for the database to be constructed, what rights does database right afford to the maker? The protection afforded by the *sui generis* right may be found in Arts. 7(1) and 7(5) of the Directive.

Highlight Database Directive: Article 7(1)

Member States shall provide for a right for the maker of a database which shows that there has been qualitatively and/or quantitatively a substantial investment in either the obtaining, verification or presentation of the contents to prevent extraction and/or re-utilization of the whole or of a substantial part, evaluated qualitatively and/or quantitatively, of the contents of that database.

[36] Dir. 96/9/EC, Recital 41.
[37] SI 1997/3032, reg. 14(1).
[38] Ibid. reg. 14(2).
[39] Ibid. reg. 14(3).
[40] Ibid. reg. 14(4).
[41] Ibid. reg. 14(5).
[42] Ibid. reg. 15.

Some of these key terms are further defined: 'extraction' means 'the permanent or temporary transfer of all or a substantial part of the contents of a database to another medium by any means or in any form', while 're-utilization' means 'any form of making available to the public all or a substantial part of the contents of a database by the distribution of copies, by renting, by on-line or other forms of transmission. The first sale of a copy of a database within the Community by the rightholder or with his consent shall exhaust the right to control resale of that copy within the Community.'[43] Article 7(5) supplements the protection found in Art. 7(1).

Highlight Database Directive: Article 7(5)

The repeated and systematic extraction and/or reutilization of insubstantial parts of the contents of the database implying acts which conflict with a normal exploitation of that database or which unreasonably prejudice the legitimate interests of the maker of the database shall not be permitted.

Collectively the effect of Arts. 7(1) and 7(5) are to ring-fence the contents of a database: their aim is to prevent competitors from either substantially recreating a protected database by the extraction of a substantial part of the original, or a series of insubstantial extractions, or from making use of a substantial part of database without the permission of the database maker or owner.

The UK has implemented these provisions by reg. 16. The implementation of Art. 7(1) is found in reg. 16(1) which states: 'Subject to the provisions of this Part, a person infringes database right in a database if, without the consent of the owner of the right, he extracts or re-utilises all or a substantial part of the contents of the database.' Regulation 16(2) implements Art. 7(5): 'for the purposes of this Part, the repeated and systematic extraction or re-utilisation of insubstantial parts of the contents of a database may amount to the extraction or re-utilisation of a substantial part of those contents'. The final part of the implementation jigsaw is found in reg. 12(1) where 'substantial' is defined as 'substantial in terms of quantity or quality or a combination of both'.

The *sui generis* right is therefore rather different to a copyright. It has a different standard of originality, and protects in quite a different way. It is not copying per se which is restricted but rather *substantial* or *repeated* extraction or reutilization of the database contents. Also there are many restrictions contained within the Directive and given effect in the regulations which limit the scope of the *sui generis* right. Article 8(1) provides that: '[t]he maker of a database which is made available to the public in whatever manner may not prevent a lawful user of the database from extracting and/or re-utilizing insubstantial parts of its contents, evaluated qualitatively and/or quantitatively, for any purposes whatsoever',[44] while Art. 9 provides three 'fair dealing' exceptions:

[43] Dir. 96/9/EC, Art. 7(2).
[44] Given effect by reg. 19(1).

> Member States may stipulate that lawful users of a database which is made available to the public in whatever manner may, without the authorization of its maker, extract or re-utilize a substantial part of its contents:
>
> (a) in the case of extraction for private purposes of the contents of a non-electronic database;
>
> (b) in the case of extraction for the purposes of illustration for teaching or scientific research, as long as the source is indicated and to the extent justified by the non-commercial purpose to be achieved;
>
> (c) in the case of extraction and/or re-utilization for the purposes of public security or an administrative or judicial procedure.[45]

The term of protection is also less than with copyright law. By Art. 10(1) the right 'shall expire fifteen years from the first of January of the year following the date of completion', unless the database is subsequently made available to the public during this period in which case 'the term of protection by that right shall expire fifteen years from the first of January of the year following the date when the database was first made available to the public'.[46] However, there is one substantial qualification to these terms. By Art. 10(3), 'Any substantial change, evaluated qualitatively or quantitatively, to the contents of a database, including any substantial change resulting from the accumulation of successive additions, deletions or alterations, which would result in the database being considered to be a substantial new investment, evaluated qualitatively or quantitatively, shall qualify the database resulting from that investment for its own term of protection.' Neither the Directive nor the UK regulations have a full and satisfactory definition of when a change is 'substantial'. One assumes though that this is to be the same definition found as applied in reg. 7(1) for which there is some degree of case law discussed at 12.2.1 'The *Fixtures Marketing* cases' and 12.2.2 *British Horseracing Board v William Hill*, below. In any event given that a database has to be continually updated to remain useful it seems likely that most databases will undergo 'substantial' amendment in the 15 years that protection runs. For example, if you were to update as little as 0.01 per cent of the database on a daily basis you would cumulatively update over 54 per cent of the database over a 15-year period. Thus it seems that for any managed database perpetual protection will be available.

12.2.1 The *Fixtures Marketing* cases

With a completely new form of IP protection it is not surprising that the courts have been busy trying to set the limits of what is permissible and what is not. A series of questions arose in several national courts, almost all of which were eventually referred to the ECJ for interpretation. These questions included: (1) What amounts to a substantial investment for qualification of the right? (2) Does the right accrue where the database is a 'spin-off' from investment in another field—e.g. where broadcasters schedule television programmes the 'spin-off' is a database of scheduled television programmes? (3) What amounts to repeated and systematic extraction? (4) Does the

[45] Given effect variously by SI 1997/3032, Sch. 1 and reg. 20(1).
[46] Dir. 96/9/EC, Art. 10(2).

right cover instances where information is generated/created and cannot be obtained from alternative sources? Many of these questions arose initially in a series of cases arising from the rights to football fixtures lists. These cases, known collectively as the *Fixtures Marketing* cases included *Fixtures Marketing Ltd v Organismos Prognostikon Agonon Podosfairou (OPAP)*,[47] *Fixtures Marketing Ltd v Oy Veikkaus AB*,[48] and *Fixtures Marketing Ltd v Svenska Spel AB*.[49]

All three involved material extracted from a database of football fixtures created by combining the individual fixtures lists of the English Premier League, the English Football League, the Scottish Premier League, and the Scottish Football League. This database was then managed by Fixtures Marketing on behalf of the leagues with a view to commercially exploiting the contents of the database. All three of the respondents had in various ways made use of details from the relevant fixtures lists without the permission of the claimant. OPAP were using fixtures drawn from the database on fixed-odds betting coupons; an online betting site in Greece, Oy Veikkaus, were using fixtures from the database for their football pools coupon in Finland; and Svenska Spel were doing likewise in Sweden. All three cases were heard together before the ECJ.

The questions referred varied from case to case but the key questions were contained in the OPAP reference which simply asked:

> (1) What is the definition of database and what is the scope of Directive 96/9 and in particular Art. 7 thereof which concerns the sui generis right? (2) In the light of the definition of the scope of the directive, do lists of football fixtures enjoy protection as databases over which there is a sui generis right in favour of the maker and under what conditions? and (3) How exactly is the database right infringed and is it protected in the event of rearrangement of the contents of the database?

Although wide in scope these are key questions. The judge of the Athens Court of First Instance was inviting the ECJ to clarify the scope of the Directive and to determine what may amount to 'a substantial investment' under reg. 7(1), whether or not a 'spin-off' database may qualify for protection at all and finally what amounts to 'extraction and/or re-utilization a substantial part'.

The court gave full consideration to all these issues with a very full opinion given by Advocate General Stix-Hackl. As to the initial question, that of what qualifies as a 'database' under Art. 1(2), the court first noted that 'nothing in the directive points to the conclusion that a database must be its maker's own intellectual creation to be classified as such . . . the criterion of originality is only relevant to the assessment whether a database qualifies for the copyright protection'.[50] This confirmed the widely held view that the *droit d'auteur* standard of an *œuvre de l'ésprit* (in English usually referred to as a 'spark of originality') was not applicable to the *sui generis* database right. From here the court went on to answer the question finding that 'classification of a collection as a database requires that the independent materials making up that collection be systematically or methodically arranged and individually accessible in one way or another'.[51]

[47] [2005] 1 CMLR 16. Case originated in The Athens Court of First Instance, Greece.
[48] [2005] ECDR 2. Case originated in The Vantaa District Court, Finland.
[49] [2005] ECDR 4. Case originated in The District Court, Gotland, Sweden.
[50] [2005] 1 CMLR 16, [26].
[51] *Fixtures Marketing Ltd v OPAP* (n. 47) [30].

Highlight Definition of a database (from *Fixtures Marketing*)

Any collection of works, data or other materials, separable from one another without the value of their contents being affected, including a method or system of some sort for the retrieval of each of its constituent materials.

This makes clear that the definition of a database is to be interpreted broadly, certainly broad enough to cover everyday directories such as telephone directories or legal directories such as seen in the *Waterlow* cases. This led on to the second element of the first question: what amounts to 'a substantial investment' under Art. 7(1)?

Highlight Definition of a substantial investment (from *Fixtures Marketing*)

The expression 'investment in . . . the . . . verification . . . of the contents' of a database must be understood to refer to the resources used, with a view to ensuring the reliability of the information contained in that database, to monitor the accuracy of the materials collected when the database was created and during its operation. The expression 'investment in . . . the . . . presentation of the contents' of the database concerns, for its part, the resources used for the purpose of giving the database its function of processing information, that is to say those used for the systematic or methodical arrangement of the materials contained in that database and the organisation of their individual accessibility. Investment in the creation of a database may consist in the deployment of human, financial or technical resources but it must be substantial in quantitative or qualitative terms. The quantitative assessment refers to quantifiable resources and the qualitative assessment to efforts which cannot be quantified, such as intellectual effort or energy.

Thus, to qualify for protection under Art. 7(1), the maker of the database must have invested substantially, either in financial terms, or in terms of effort, skill, and manpower, and that investment *must* be made to ensure the database is accurate and/or functional. The investment cannot be for any other purpose such as commercializing or marketing the database or for some other reason unrelated to the creation of the database itself.

The court then answered the second question. It noted that, given the wide interpretation of Art. 1(2), it had indicated that 'the date and the time of and the identity of the two teams playing in both home and away matches are covered by the concept of independent materials within the meaning of Art. 1(2) of the directive in that they have autonomous informative value . . . [as such] it follows that a fixture list for a football league such as that at issue in the case in the main proceedings constitutes a database within the meaning of Art. 1(2) of the directive'.[52] It also answered the question of whether a 'spin-off' database could ever be protected.

[52] Ibid. [33], [36].

Highlight Protecting 'spin-off' databases (from *Fixtures Marketing*)

The fact that the creation of a database is linked to the exercise of a principal activity in which the person creating the database is also the creator of the materials contained in the database does not, as such, preclude that person from claiming the protection of the sui generis right, provided that he establishes that the obtaining of those materials, their verification or their presentation, in the sense described at above, required substantial investment in quantitative or qualitative terms, which was independent of the resources used to create those materials.

This ultimately proved to be Fixtures Marketing's downfall. The makers of the database were the professional football leagues of England and Scotland. The database was created as part of their primary function, namely the setting of league fixtures for the football season. Further, as they were the originators of the contents of the database, they did not need to verify the accuracy of the database. As the court recorded:

> Finding and collecting the data which make up a football fixture list do not require any particular effort on the part of the professional leagues. Those activities are indivisibly linked to the creation of those data, in which the leagues participate directly as those responsible for the organisation of football league fixtures. Obtaining the contents of a football fixture list thus does not require any investment independent of that required for the creation of the data contained in that list. The professional football leagues do not need to put any particular effort into monitoring the accuracy of the data on league matches when the list is made up because those leagues are directly involved in the creation of those data. The verification of the accuracy of the contents of fixture lists during the season simply involves, according to the observations made by Fixtures, adapting certain data in those lists to take account of any postponement of a match or fixture date decided on by or in collaboration with the leagues. Such verification cannot be regarded as requiring substantial investment. The presentation of a football fixture list is closely linked to the creation as such of the data which make up the list. It cannot therefore be considered to require investment independent of the investment in the creation of its constituent data.

Ultimately therefore the database of football fixtures created by the football leagues and distributed under licence to Fixtures Marketing did not qualify for Art. 7 protection because the makers of the database had not 'substantially invested qualitatively and/or quantitatively in either the obtaining, verification or presentation of the contents'. With this decision made the court, unfortunately, declined to answer the third question.[53]

12.2.2 *British Horseracing Board Ltd v William Hill*

The *Fixtures Marketing* cases are an extremely important series of cases which usually would have been met with a fanfare at their outcome. The court had examined the scope of the Database Directive and had given guidance on the application of Art. 7(1), but they were little commented upon by the profession, academics, or the media for the same day the ECJ had given its opinion an almost identical case, which had been bundled together with the *Fixtures Marketing* cases and which answered the third

[53] Ibid. [54].

question that the court had declined to answer in the *OPAP* case: this was the case of *British Horseracing Board Ltd v William Hill Organisation Ltd*.[54]

The facts of this case are extremely similar to the *Fixtures Marketing* cases, and it is for this reason that *William Hill* was disposed with jointly with the *Fixtures Marketing* cases. William Hill operate a chain of high-street betting shops which among other things allow for betting on horse racing, an operation known as 'off-course bookmaking'. For many years William Hill had been operating their high-street bookmaking shops using information supplied from Weatherbys, a private company who compiled the Jockey Club database which contained advance information about race meetings, runners, and riders. In 1999 the Jockey Club database was merged with the British Horseracing Board (BHB) database, although Weatherbys continued to supply data to William Hill's high-street operation under a licence. The issue though was William Hill's website. They had no licence or permission to use data from the BHB database for online gambling. William Hill began to operate an internet gambling site in May 1999. It offered a variety of daily bets using information that had originated in the BHB database. William Hill argued they did not need a separate licence for this operation as the information they used was not subject to database protection, in particular William Hill argued that the information had been made publicly available via newspapers, teletext, and the specialist betting information service Satellite Information Services Limited ('SIS') which provides a raw data feed of all races taking place that day to all its subscribers, which includes William Hill. BHB argued that the database was a major part of their operation. It was estimated to contain some 800,000 entries and cost some £4m per annum to maintain, over 25 per cent of BHB's entire annual expenditure.[55] BHB argued that by extracting the daily data for races to be run that day William Hill extracted and reutilized a 'substantial part' of the database. Their argument was based on the principle that Art. 7(1) states 'substantial' is to be evaluated 'qualitatively and/or quantitatively'. Although the data extracted each day may be so small in proportion to the overall size of the database so as to be quantitatively insubstantial, it was, argued BHB, qualitatively substantial as the data extracted each day was the only data of commercial value for that day: by extracting that data William Hill effectively were avoiding payment to use the only commercially valuable part of the database for that day. In the alternative, BHB argued that by making daily extractions from the BHB database William Hill were actively involved in systematic extraction and/or reutilization of insubstantial parts of the contents of the database in breach of Art. 7(5).

BHB launched their case in the summer of 2000 and the initial hearings were before Laddie J on 12–14 December 2000. Laddie J's judgment was issued on 9 February 2001.[56] In this he found that:

> Article 7(1) provides that substantiality is to be assessed by looking at the quantity and quality of what is taken but it does not require them to be looked at separately. It contemplates looking at the combination of both . . . Here what the defendant is doing is making use of the most recent and core information in the BHB Database relating to racing. William Hill is relying on and taking advantage of the completeness and accuracy of the information taken from the [Raw Data Feed], in other words the product of BHB's investment in obtaining and verifying that data. *This is a substantial part of the contents*.[57]

[54] [2005] 1 CMLR 15; [2005] RPC 13.
[55] [2005] 1 CMLR 15, [32].
[56] *British Horseracing Board Ltd & Ors v William Hill Organisation Ltd* [2001] EWHC 517 (Patents).
[57] Ibid. [53].

With regard to the subsequent claim under Art. 7(5), Laddie J found that 'William Hill's borrowing from [the database] from day to day comes within Art. 7(5) as repeated and systematic extractions and re-utilizations of parts of its contents.'[58]

Unsurprisingly William Hill appealed this decision. The appeal was heard by the Court of Appeal (Peter Gibson, Clarke, and Kay LLJ) who stayed proceedings on 31 July 2001 to refer the case to the ECJ.[59] The Court of Appeal referred 11 questions to the ECJ, some similar to those raised elsewhere in the *Fixtures Marketing* cases but many were important and were either unique to this reference or had not been answered elsewhere.[60] In a ground-breaking judgment the court substantially disregarded the opinion of Advocate General Stix-Hackl, the same Advocate General who had advised them on the *Fixtures Marketing* cases. The court went through the reference in great detail answering all the questions closely. It began by answering the prior questions:

> (2) What is meant by 'obtaining' in Article 7(1) of the Directive? In particular, are the facts and matters in [issue in the case] capable of amounting to such obtaining? and (3) Is 'verification' in Article 7(1) of the Directive limited to ensuring from time to time that information contained in a database is or remains correct?

The Court applied the reasoning seen in the *Fixtures Marketing* cases in answering these questions. It ruled that 'investment in the selection, for the purpose of organising horse racing, of the horses admitted to run in the race concerned relates to the creation of the data which make up the lists for those races which appear in the BHB database. It does not constitute investment in obtaining the contents of the database. It cannot, therefore, be taken into account in assessing whether the investment in the creation of the database was substantial.'[61]

This is an application of the 'spin-off' principle discussed above. While BHB were creating data for another purpose the database was merely a spin-off from that purpose. Therefore the investment made in creating the data could not count towards a 'substantial investment' in the database: that would require it to come from further investment in gathering or generating external data (i.e. data not required for the purpose of running BHB operations) or verifying the data.

This led to question 3: how high is the verification standard? The court unfortunately did not answer this directly, but they did indicate what did not qualify as verification: 'the process of entering a horse on a list for a race requires a number of prior checks as to the identity of the person making the entry, the characteristics of the horse and the classification of the horse, its owner and the jockey . . . However, such prior checks are made at the stage of creating the list for the race in question. They thus constitute investment in the creation of data and not in the verification of the contents of the database.'[62] At this point the court could have concluded its analysis by finding in a similar fashion to the *Fixtures Marketing* cases that the BHB database was merely a 'spin-off database' and as such did not qualify for protection because the makers of the database had not 'substantially invested qualitatively and/or quantitatively in either the obtaining, verification or presentation of the contents'. Fortunately though the court, perhaps influenced

[58] Ibid. [73].
[59] *British Horseracing Board Ltd & Ors v William Hill Organisation Ltd* [2001] EWCA Civ 1268.
[60] The 11 questions may be found at [2005] 1 CMLR 15, [AG27].
[61] *British Horseracing Board v William Hill* (n. 54) [38].
[62] Ibid. [39], [40].

by the number of references which had been made under the Directive, went on to analyse the remaining questions.

The court next addressed the seventh, eighth, and ninth questions together. These were:

> (7) Is 'extraction' in Article 7 of the directive limited to the transfer of the contents of the database directly from the database to another medium, or does it also include the transfer of works, data or other materials, which are derived indirectly from the database, without having direct access to the database? (8) Is 're-utilisation' in Article 7 of the directive limited to the making available to the public of the contents of the database directly from the database, or does it also include the making available to the public of works, data or other materials which are derived indirectly from the database, without having direct access to the database? and (9) Is 're-utilisation' in Article 7 of the directive limited to the first making available to the public of the contents of the database?

These questions all came about because of William Hill's practice of drawing the information it needed for its online betting sites not from the BHB database directly, but from third party sources such as the SIS Raw Data Feed and newspaper listings such as *The Racing Post*. The court began with a general observation that:

> [t]he use of expressions such as 'by any means or in any form' and 'any form of making available to the public' indicates that the Community legislature intended to give the concepts of extraction and re-utilisation a wide definition . . . those terms must therefore be interpreted as referring to any act of appropriating and making available to the public, without the consent of the maker of the database, the results of his investment, thus depriving him of revenue which should have enabled him to redeem the cost of the investment.[63]

Following this, the court went on to find that '[s]ince acts of unauthorised extraction and/or re-utilisation by a third party from a source other than the database concerned are liable, just as much as such acts carried out directly from that database are, to prejudice the investment of the maker of the database, it must be held that the concepts of extraction and re-utilisation do not imply direct access to the database concerned'.[64] The court therefore found that:

> The terms 'extraction' and 're-utilisation' in Art. 7 of the Directive must be interpreted as referring to any unauthorised act of appropriation and distribution to the public of the whole or a part of the contents of a database. Those terms do not imply direct access to the database concerned. The fact that the contents of a database were made accessible to the public by its maker or with his consent does not affect the right of the maker to prevent acts of extraction and/or re-utilisation of the whole or a substantial part of the contents of a database.[65]

Finally the court turned to the key questions:

> (1) May either of the expressions: 'substantial part of the contents of the database'; or 'insubstantial parts of the contents of the database' in Article 7 of the Directive include works, data or other materials derived from the database but which do not have the same systematic or methodical arrangement of and individual accessibility as those to be found in the database? (4) What is meant in Article 7(1) of the directive, by the expressions: 'a substantial part, evaluated qualitatively . . . of the contents of that database'? and 'a substantial part, evaluated quantitatively . . . of the contents of that database'? (5) What is meant in Article 7(5) of the directive, by

[63] Ibid. [51].
[64] Ibid. [53].
[65] Ibid. [67].

the expression 'insubstantial parts of the database'? (6) In particular, in each case: does 'substantial' mean something more than 'insignificant' and, if so, what? does 'insubstantial' part simply mean that it is not 'substantial'? and (10) In Article 7(5) of the directive what is meant by 'acts which conflict with a normal exploitation of that database or unreasonably prejudice the legitimate interests of the maker of the database'? In particular, are the facts [of this case] capable of amounting to such acts?

While the preliminary issues were valuable, in particular the answer to questions 7, 8, and 9, what the court was about to do in answering these five questions was interpret the key provisions of Arts. 7(1) and 7(5), in particular what amounted to a 'substantial part' for Art. 7(1) and when would repeated extractions under Art. 7(5) infringe the maker's database right?

The court first turned to Art. 7(1) and sought first to clarify what constituted a 'substantial part' of a database.

Highlight A 'substantial part' (from *BHB*)

The expression 'substantial part, evaluated quantitatively', of the contents of a database within the meaning of Art. 7(1) of the Directive refers to the volume of data extracted from the database and/or re-utilised, and must be assessed in relation to the volume of the contents of the whole of that database. If a user extracts and/or re-utilises a quantitatively significant part of the contents of a database whose creation required the deployment of substantial resources, the investment in the extracted or re-utilised part is, proportionately, equally substantial.

The expression 'substantial part, evaluated qualitatively', of the contents of a database refers to the scale of the investment in the obtaining, verification or presentation of the contents of the subject of the act of extraction and/or re-utilisation, regardless of whether that subject represents a quantitatively substantial part of the general contents of the protected database. A quantitatively negligible part of the contents of a database may in fact represent, in terms of obtaining, verification or presentation, significant human, technical or financial investment.

[at 70–1]

This was a surprising outcome. While the definition of a 'substantial part, evaluated quantitatively' was in line with predictions, the definition of a 'substantial part, evaluated qualitatively' was not what had been expected. It had always been imagined that a 'substantial part, evaluated qualitatively' would refer to the commercial value of that part of the database as against the database as a whole. So, for example, in the current case the data for that day's race meetings would qualify as a substantial part of the database as a whole evaluated qualitatively. What the ECJ said though was that it was not the value of the data at extraction which was to be measured; it was the value of the data at its addition to the database. Thus data which was difficult or costly to obtain or verify would be 'qualitatively substantial' whether or not this was subsequently of any greater value commercially than the rest of the database. As BHB had expended no greater effort or money in obtaining the data for the current day's races than for any other data in the database the court held that 'those materials do not represent a substantial part, in [quantitative or] qualitative terms, of the BHB database'.[66]

Finally the question of whether William Hill had infringed Art. 7(5) was addressed.

Highlight Purpose of Article 7(5) (from *BHB*)

The purpose of Article 7(5) is to prevent circumvention of the prohibition in Article 7(1) of the Directive. Its objective is to prevent repeated and systematic extractions and/or re-utilisations of insubstantial parts of the contents of a database, the cumulative effect of which would be to seriously prejudice the investment made by the maker of the database just as the extractions and/or re-utilisations referred to in Article 7(1) of the Directive would.

[at 86]

In other words, the purpose of Art. 7(5) is not to prevent users repeatedly accessing a database to extract or reutilize insubstantial parts of the database, as William Hill was doing; it was to prevent the cumulative construction of a competing database, or the accumulation of data from a database over a period of time which would lead to a cumulative 'substantial part'. Again, this was somewhat surprising and had not been widely predicted. It made the application of Art. 7(5) extremely narrow, so narrow as perhaps to be of little practical application.

The end result of the immediate case was that BHB lost. On nearly every point the ECJ ruled against them. Their database was not sufficiently original to qualify for database protection as there had been no independent significant investment in the obtaining or verification of the data. Even if the database were protected the actions of William Hill were not infringing: they neither extracted nor reutilized a substantial part of the database, nor did they make repeated extractions or reutilizations which 'conflict with a normal exploitation of that database or which unreasonably prejudice the legitimate interests of the maker of the database' under Art. 7(5). The case was remanded back to the Court of Appeal for disposal and on 13 July 2005 the Court of Appeal gave judgment in favour of William Hill but not without reservation.[67] Lord Justice Clark observed that 'I am conscious that in doing so I have agreed to allowing an appeal against a decision which I was inclined to think was correct when the case was last before the Court of Appeal in July 2001. The reason for my change of view is of course the decision and reasoning of the ECJ.'[68]

12.2.3 After *BHB*

The immediate fall-out of the decisions of the ECJ of 9 November 2004, and in particular the *BHB* decision, was a concern that by interpreting Arts. 7(1) and 7(5) so narrowly the court had effectively undermined the protection offered by the *sui generis* database

[66] Ibid. [74], [80].
[67] *British Horseracing Board Ltd & Ors v William Hill Organisation Ltd* [2005] EWCA Civ 863.
[68] *British Horseracing Board v William Hill* (n. 54) [37].

right. In the aftermath of the decision news reports and professional journals reported that the effect of the decision was effectively to narrow the protection afforded to makers of databases.[69] This in time led to a number of similar academic articles.[70] The common view of many of these comments is that the court had been forced to narrow the scope of the Directive for there was a danger that 'this new property right would arise virtually everywhere there was a website'.[71] In time though a clearer view of the decisions of 9 November developed, at least in part formed by the Commission Evaluation of the Database Directive which was carried out immediately after these decisions.[72]

The report set out to evaluate three particular criticisms of the *sui generis* database right: (1) its scope is unclear and it is poorly targeted; (2) the database right 'locks up' data to the detriment of research and the academic community; and (3) the database right is too narrow in scope and fails to protect investors.[73] In evaluating these claims the Commission examined (1) the impact of the 9 November 2004 judgments; (2) whether there was an indication that the academic community and the research community at large were paying unnecessary costs to access data; and (3) the measure of the size of the EU database community.[74]

The outcome was rather surprising, in particular for critics of the *Fixtures Marketing/BHB* decisions. In response to the question 'Has the ECJ's interpretation of the scope of the "sui generis" right devalued the uniform levels of protection achieved for "non-original" databases?', the findings of an online survey found that '43 per cent of the respondents believe that the legal protection of their databases will be the same as before the ECJ rulings (or even reinforced); only 36 per cent believe that the scope of protection will be either weakened or removed'.[75] Although this is not a statistically significant result it was not what may have been expected in the immediate aftermath of the 9 November decisions. Further, it appeared that a majority of respondents actually welcomed the effect of the decisions:

> most respondents to the Commission services' on-line survey believe that the protection of databases is stronger than before adoption of the Directive. However, a majority of respondents feel that, after the ECJ's rulings, fewer databases will be protected by the 'sui generis' right. This allays fears of monopoly abuses which were usually expressed with respect to 'single-source' databases (databases where the database maker and the proprietor of the underlying information are the same person or entity).[76]

[69] See e.g. T Frederikse, 'Database Protection Narrowed: *British Horseracing Board v William Hill*' *Swan Turton e-bulletin*, 10 November 2004; R Kemp, D Meredith, and C Gibbons, 'Database Right and the ECJ Judgment in *BHB v William Hill*: Dark Horse or Non-Starter?' Kemp Little Bulletin; 'William Hill Wins Horseracing Database Appeal' (*Out-Law*, 19 July 2005) <http://www.out-law.com/page-5922>.

[70] See e.g. R Kemp and C Gibbons, 'Database Right After *BHB v William Hill*: Enact and Repent at Leisure' (2006) 22 *Computer Law and Security Report* 493; S Kon and T Heide, 'BHB/William Hill—Europe's Feist' (2006) 28(1) *EIPR* 60; T Aplin, 'The ECJ Elucidates the Database Right' (2005) 2 *IPQ* 204.

[71] Taken from Kemp, Meredith, and Gibbons (n. 69) [48].

[72] Commission of the European Communities, 'First Evaluation of Directive 96/9/EC on the Legal Protection of Databases', 12 December 2005.

[73] Ibid. [1.2].

[74] Ibid. [4.1.4].

[75] Ibid. [1.2].

[76] Ibid. [1.2].

This suggests that many even within the industry were unhappy with the idea of a broad database right which would have protected spin-off—or in the Commission's terms, 'single-source'—databases. There was an obvious concern about market abuse with such databases, a concern allayed by the decisions of 9 November 2004.

In response to the other questions the Commission found the database right to be functioning well. They found that the research and academic communities were still able to access data and that the 9 November decisions had assisted in this[77] and that the database industry in Europe was healthy both before and after the 9 November decisions.[78] Thus the Commission Evaluation suggested that the decisions of the ECJ had actually proved positive for both our understanding and the health of the database right. By narrowing the scope of the right the ECJ had actually restored confidence in the right, and had prevented overprotection of spin-off, or single-source, databases which may have harmed the competitiveness of European data industries as end users would have had to pay for access to single-source data which would have led to potential market abuse from companies in a dominant position. Following the publication of the Evaluation the views of commentators softened with the 9 November decisions, now seen as broadly positive and reinforcing of the *sui generis* right, with most noting that the narrow interpretation promulgated has assisted all sides in the database industry, with the obvious exception of single-source database makers.[79]

12.2.4 **The *Football Dataco* decisions**

Much of this chapter appears to be taken up with the activities of Football Dataco and their subsidiary Fixtures Marketing. After losing the *Fixtures Marketing* cases, and perhaps working on the assumption that eventually they would lose the *Football Dataco* fixtures listing decision, Football Dataco invested heavily in a new product called 'Football Live'. To create Football Live, Football Dataco sends reporters to football matches across the country to record details of the match on a minute-by minute-basis. The reporters, usually ex-professional footballers, record things like goals scored and when they were scored, goalscorers, yellow and red cards and who and when they got them, penalties and when they were awarded, and substitutions (who was substituted, when, and by whom). In addition they also are invited to make value judgements like 'man of the match' and most aggressive player in the last ten minutes. The contents of this database are then licensed to news organizations who can supply minute-by-minute match reports via websites and apps and to betting organizations that use them to allow betting in play on any number of options such as next player to score, next corner kick, or next player to receive a yellow card.

Although most people pay to extract data from the Football Live database a number of organizations, following the principles of the *Fixtures Marketing* cases were extracting data without a licence. Football Dataco brought a joint action against UK-based bookmaker Stan James and a German aggregation service, Sportradar, which operates

[77] Ibid. [4.3].

[78] Ibid. [4.2].

[79] See e.g. M Prinsley, 'An Opportunity to Improve Protection for Databases in Europe?' (2006) 6(3) *World Data Protection Report* 3; C Waelde, 'Databases and Lawful Users: The Chink in the Armour' (2006) 3 *IPQ* 256; A Masson, 'Creation of Database or Creation of Data: Crucial Choices in the Matter of Database Protection' (2006) 28(5) *EIPR* 261.

a database of sports statistics called Betradar. Within Betradar is a section called Live Scores which reports information drawn from a number of live streams including internet streams. Much of what was reported in Betrader came from sources extracting data from the Football Live stream. Like much Football Dataco litigation this has been extensive and time-consuming. The case has seen three reported hearings from the High Court,[80] two of the Court of Appeal,[81] and one from the CJEU.[82] The key rulings are to be found in the CJEU and final Court of Appeal decisions.

The Court of Appeal drew a clear line between the fixtures database and the Football Live database. Sir Robin Jacob (formerly Jacob LJ before retirement) gave the lead judgment. The key question was: did the Football Live database exhibit the qualities required to gain protection under Art. 7? Sir Robin noted that 'this test has been considered by the Court in the quartet of horseracing/football fixture cases'.[83] He noted that the common approach in all four: 'investment in creating data was not the right kind of investment. So that if only that kind of investment is involved in the creation of a database, there is no *sui generis* right in it.'[84] This was the contention of Stan James and Sportradar: the investment was all spent on the reporter who recorded the data and then entered it into the database. The database itself was merely an effect of the reports: 'Mr Silverleaf contended firstly that there can be no Art. 7 right unless there is investment in collecting together materials which have already been recorded. The process of actually recording data is to be regarded as creative in the same way as the process of creating a football fixture list or list of finally approved runners and riders.'[85] Sir Robin felt differently that data is often pre-existing and that databases often reflect an investment in the gathering and verifying of this data. To Sir Robin there was a difference between the sporting fixtures cases where the data could only be created by the organization seeking to exert ownership over it, and who therefore invested in its creation and subsequently sought to profit from this by claiming database protection, and the instant case where the data was independent of the person recording it and the investment was made in the recording of the data:

> The factual data provided by the football analyst to the sports information processor and then recorded by the sports information processor (sometimes after some conversation to verify its accuracy) in Football Dataco's database is pre-existing data. Only a metaphysicist would say a goal is not scored until the football analyst tells the sports information processor that it has been scored. The same metaphysicist might also deny that a temperature exists unless and until it is recorded. But he would feel hot in a Turkish bath even without a thermometer . . . I am entirely confident that a scientist who takes a measurement would be astonished to be told that she was creating data. She would say she is creating a record of pre-existing fact, recording data, not creating it . . . the policy of the Directive is that databases which cost a lot of investment and can readily be copied should be protected. The right is created to protect the investment which

[80] *Football Dataco Ltd v Sportradar GmbH* [2010] EWHC 2911 (Ch); *Football Dataco Ltd v Stan James (Abingdon) Ltd* [2012] EWHC 747 (Ch); and *Football Dataco Ltd v Sportradar GmbH* [2012] EWHC 1185 (Ch).

[81] *Football Dataco Ltd v Sportradar GmbH* [2011] EWCA Civ 330 and *Football Dataco Ltd v Sportradar GmbH* [2013] EWCA Civ 27.

[82] *Football Dataco Ltd v Sportradar GmbH* (C-173/11) [2013] FSR 4.

[83] *Football Dataco Ltd v Sportradar GmbH* [2013] EWCA Civ 27 [31].

[84] Ibid. [32].

[85] Ibid. [35].

> goes into the creation of a database. If a database produced by collecting data ascertained (not created) by the database creator is not protected, there will be no incentive to create databases of that sort.[86]

On this basis Sir Robin had little difficulty in finding the Football Live database to be protectable under Art. 7. The clear distinction between this case and the sports listing cases was that the investment being made by Football Dataco was in the gathering of data for the purpose of creating the Football Live database; this was different from the creation of data for other purposes and then incidentally entering it into a database.[87] With the question of protectability disposed of he then went on to find both Stan James and Sportradar infringed Football Dataco's *sui generis* database right by allowing customers to extract data from the Football Live database without a licence.

12.3 **Databases and the information society**

Before leaving databases we must look at one final issue unique to online databases. With more databases publicly accessible via a web portal there is an increased risk of unauthorized linking to the contents of these databases. This raises issues similar to those discussed in the 'Linking, caching, and aggregating' section of chapter 11.[88] Many of the cases discussed in that section including *Stepstone v Ofir*,[89] *Havas Numerique et Cadre On Line v Keljob*,[90] and *Google Inc. v Copiepresse SCRL*[91] involved claims not only of copyright infringement but also claims of unauthorized extraction and/or reutilization in breach of the Database Directive. Most of these cases though, with the exception of *Google v Copiepresse* and *NVM Estate Agents v ZAH*,[92] were decided prior to the decisions of 9 November 2004. However, the last part of the *Football Dataco* action was on this point. While the Court of Appeal felt capable of answering questions of protectability and unauthorized extraction the one question which was referred to the CJEU was in this area. The CJEU was essentially asked one question in the reference from the Court of Appeal:

> where a party uploads data from a database protected by [the] *sui generis* right onto that party's webserver located in member state A and in response to requests from a user in another member state B the webserver sends such data to the user's computer so that the data is stored in the memory of that computer and displayed on its screen (a) is the act of sending the data an act of 'extraction' or 're-utilisation' by that party? and (b) does any act of extraction and/or re-utilisation by that party occur: (i) in A only; (ii) in B only; or (iii) in both A and B?[93]

The complication in the case was that Football Dataco was uploading data to a server in the UK. Sportradar though were a German/Swiss company who operated via servers in Austria and supplied data to a number of customers in a number of countries including

[86] Ibid. [39], [44].
[87] Ibid. [45]–[69].
[88] See 11.1–11.1.1.
[89] Landgericht, Köln, February 28, 2001: 28 O 692/00. Discussed in full at 11.1.1 'Web-linking'.
[90] Tribunal de Commerce de Paris, 26 December 2000. Discussed in full at 11.1.1 'Web-linking'.
[91] [2007] ECDR 5. Discussed in full at 11.1.2 '*Google Inc. v Copiepresse SCRL*'.
[92] 136002/KG ZA 06–25, LJN AV5236, 16 March 2006.
[93] *Football Dataco Ltd v Sportradar GmbH* (C-173/11) [2013] FSR 4 [AG13].

Gibraltar. Sportradar therefore argued that their activities were not subject to the jurisdiction of the English courts and sought from the Landgericht Gera (Regional Court, Gera, Germany) a formal declaration that its activities did not infringe any intellectual property right held by Football Dataco. The High Court declared that it had jurisdiction to hear the claim in so far as it sought to establish joint liability on the part of Sportradar and those of its customers which use its website in the United Kingdom, but that it did not have jurisdiction to hear the claim in so far as it sought to establish primary liability on the part of Sportradar. Both parties appealed against the High Court's decision to the Court of Appeal, which made for the reference to the CJEU.[94]

The court first examined whether communication of the contacts of a database via a web server constituted extraction or reutilization of that data. They found that:

> the concept of 're-utilisation', must, in the general context of Art. 7, be understood broadly, as extending to any act, not authorised by the maker of the database protected by the *sui generis* right, of distribution to the public of the whole or a part of the contents of the database. The nature and form of the process used are of no relevance in this respect. That concept covers an act, such as those at issue in the main proceedings, in which a person sends, by means of his web server, to another person's computer, at that person's request, data previously extracted from the content of a database protected by the *sui generis* right. By such a sending, that data is made available to a member of the public.[95]

Therefore the court clearly determines that the process of scraping data from the database of another party and delivering it to customers via a web server is capable of infringing the *sui generis* right. The question then became whether the English courts had jurisdiction over Sportradar and for which parts of their operation. The court acknowledged that the Directive does not aim to introduce a uniform law at EU level; rather it aims to remove the differences which existed between national laws in relation to the legal protection of databases, and which adversely affected the functioning of the internal market.[96] Sportradar argued that in that context, 'an act of re-utilisation within the meaning of Art. 7 must in all circumstances be regarded as located exclusively in the territory of the Member State in which the web server from which the data in question is sent is situated'.[97] The court rejected this and found that 'the protection by the *sui generis* right provided for in the legislation of a Member State is limited in principle to the territory of that Member State, so that the person enjoying that protection can rely on it only against unauthorised acts of re-utilisation which take place *in that territory*'.[98] 'The referring court will be entitled to consider that an act of re-utilisation such as those at issue in the main proceedings is located in the territory of the Member State of location of the user to whose computer the data in question is transmitted, at his request, for purposes of storage and display on screen.'[99]

What the court has decided therefore is that Sportradar (or anyone else who scrapes content) is subject not only to the jurisdiction of the court where their servers are based or where the company operates from but also any country where they target customers

[94] Ibid. [AG11], [AG12].
[95] Ibid. [20]–[21].
[96] Ibid. [24]–[25].
[97] Ibid. [44].
[98] Ibid. [27] (emphasis added).
[99] Ibid. [43].

in relation to any data made available to those customers there. Whether or not a company targets users within the jurisdiction is a question for the national court to decide. In the instant case Sportradar admitted targeting English customers and therefore was liable for infringement in England.[100]

In the recent Dutch referral *Innoweb BV v Wegener ICT Media* the CJEU returned to this issue.[101] This case involved a website, http://www.autotrack.nl, operated by Wegener on which a user may browse up to 200,000 second-hand cars for sale. Innoweb operated a meta search engine called http://www.gaspedaal.nl which would index a number of automotive classified sites allowing the user to search multiple sites simultaneously. To allow GasPedaal to index AutoTrack when a GasPedaal customer input a search term it would be 'translated' into the format required by AutoTrack then results displayed on the GasPedaal site. The court was told that:

> GasPedaal carries out approximately 100,000 searches on the AutoTrack website in response to queries. Thus, approximately 80 per cent of the various combinations of makes or models listed in the AutoTrack collection are the object of a search daily. In response to each query, however, GasPedaal displays only a very small part of the contents of that collection. In every case, the contents of those data are determined by the user on the basis of criteria which he keys into GasPedaal.[102]

Nine questions were referred to the CJEU from the Dutch court; the key one being:

> Is Article 7(1) of Parliament and Council Directive [96/9] to be interpreted as meaning that the whole or a qualitatively or quantitatively substantial part of the contents of a database offered on a website (online) is re-utilised (made available) by a third party if that third party makes it possible for the public to search the whole contents of the database or a substantial part thereof in real time with the aid of a dedicated meta search engine provided by that third party, by means of a query entered by a user in 'translated' form into the search engine of the website on which the database is offered?[103]

The court responded robustly to this question:

Highlight Is meta indexing a breach of Article 7(1)?

The act on the part of the operator of making available on the Internet a dedicated meta search engine such as that at issue in the main proceedings, into which it is intended that end users will key in queries for 'translation' into the search engine of a protected database, constitutes 'making available' the contents of that database for the purposes of Art. 7(2)(b) of Parliament and Council Directive 96/9.

That 'making available' is for 'the public', since anyone at all can use a dedicated meta search engine and the number of persons thus targeted is indeterminate, the question of how many persons actually use the dedicated meta engine being a separate issue.

→

[100] *Football Dataco Ltd v Sportradar GmbH* [2013] EWCA Civ 27 [89].
[101] C-202/12 [2014] Bus LR 308.
[102] Ibid. [13].
[103] Ibid. [18]. Note the court only answered the first three questions.

→

Consequently, the operator of a dedicated meta search engine such as that at issue in the main proceedings re-utilizes part of the contents of a database for the purposes of Art. 7(2)(b) of Parliament and Council Directive 96/9.

That re-utilization involves a substantial part of the contents of the database concerned, if not the entire contents, since a dedicated meta search engine such as that at issue in the main proceedings makes it possible to search the entire contents of that database, like a query entered directly in that database's search engine. Accordingly, the number of results actually found and displayed for every query keyed into the dedicated search engine is irrelevant. As the Commission of the European Union observed, the fact that, on the basis of the search criteria specified by the end user, only part of the database is actually consulted and displayed in no way detracts from the fact that the entire database is made available to that end user.[104]

This is an important decision for any meta-indexing site including price comparison sites. It does leave hanging of course the interesting question of what is the position of content not of sufficient originality to qualify for protection under Art. 7, the kind of content at the heart of the *BHB* and *Football Dataco* cases? This was exactly the scenario in the recent case of *Ryanair Ltd v PR Aviation BV*.[105]

This is a very interesting case and should be considered alongside the *PRCA v NLA* decision discussed at 11.1.3.[106] It started out as a standard meta-indexing/scraping case in the Netherlands but became something else along the way. PR Aviation operates a comparison website on which consumers can search through the flight data of low-cost airlines, compare prices and, on payment of commission, book a flight. Like GasPedaal (above), it obtains this information directly from the websites in question, including Ryanair. At a first hearing before the Rechtbank (Local Court) in Utrecht, Ryanair's database claim was thrown out; the court finding the data did not qualify for *sui generis* protection, although a copyright claim was successfully made out. An appeal to the Gerechtshof te Amsterdam (Court of Appeal, Amsterdam) found that PR Aviation had a defence against the copyright claim, and again found the database claim failed as Ryanair had not established the existence of 'substantial investment' in the creation of its data set. An appeal to the Hoge Raad der Nederlanden (Netherlands Supreme Court) saw the case take an unusual turn. The Hoge Raad referred a single question to the CJEU on the database right:

> does the operation of Directive 96/9 also extend to online databases which are not protected by copyright on the basis of Chapter II of that Directive, and also not by a sui generis right on the basis of Chapter III, in the sense that the freedom to use such databases through the (whether or not analogous) application of Articles 6(1) and 8 in conjunction with Art. 15 of Directive 96/9, may not be limited contractually?[107]

[104] Ibid. [50]–[53].
[105] [2015] 2 CMLR 36.
[106] [2014] AC 1438 (CJEU).
[107] [2015] 2 CMLR 36 [28].

What is this question about? It starts to become clear when you examine Ryanair's general terms and conditions, which PR Aviation agreed to in accessing their site. They say:

> this website and the Ryanair call centre are the exclusive distributors of Ryanair services. Ryanair.com is the only website authorised to sell Ryanair flights. Ryanair does not authorise other websites to sell its flights, whether on their own or as part of a package. You are not permitted to use this website other than for the following, private, non-commercial purposes: (i) viewing this website; (ii) making bookings; (iii) reviewing/changing bookings; (iv) checking arrival/departure information; (v) performing online check-in; (vi) transferring to other websites through links provided on this website; and (vii) making use of other facilities that may be provided on the website. The use of automated systems or software to extract data from this website or www.bookryanair.com for commercial purposes, ('screen scraping') is prohibited unless the third party has directly concluded a written licence agreement with Ryanair in which permits it access to Ryanair's price, flight and timetable information for the sole purpose of price comparison.[108]

Ryanair were claiming that in the alternative to a database or copyright infringement that PR Aviation were in breach of these terms and conditions. PR Aviation were relying upon a number of statutory rights found, among other places, in the Database Directive, in particular Art. 6(1), 'the performance by the lawful user of a database or of a copy thereof of any of the acts listed in Article 5 which is necessary for the purposes of access to the contents of the databases and normal use of the contents by the lawful user shall not require the authorization of the author of the database. Where the lawful user is authorized to use only part of the database, this provision shall apply only to that part'; and Arts. 8(1) and (2): 'the maker of a database which is made available to the public in whatever manner may not prevent a lawful user of the database from extracting and/or re-utilizing insubstantial parts of its contents, evaluated qualitatively and/or quantitatively, for any purposes whatsoever. Where the lawful user is authorized to extract and/or re-utilize only part of the database, this paragraph shall apply only to that part. (2) A lawful user of a database which is made available to the public in whatever manner may not perform acts which conflict with normal exploitation of the database or unreasonably prejudice the legitimate interests of the maker of the database.' Importantly, by Art. 15 of the Directive any contractual terms which attempt to interfere with the rights of end users as set out in Arts. 6(1) and 8 are null and void. In this way PR Aviation sought to have Ryanair's contractual terms rendered null. However, the problem for the Hoge Raad was that, although Ryanair had begun the case relying, in part, on having a *sui generis* database right, which had been found inapplicable by the courts, this is why they had referred that complex question to the CJEU. Essentially they wanted to know, if a claim to either a copyright right under Chapter II of the Directive or a *sui generis* right under Chapter III failed, what did this mean for Arts. 6(1) and 8, and vitally for Art. 15? The court was clear:

> the answer to the question referred is that Directive 96/9 must be interpreted as meaning that it is not applicable to a database which is not protected either by copyright or by the *sui generis* right under that Directive, so that Arts. 6(1), 8 and 15 of that Directive do not preclude the author of such a database from laying down contractual limitations on its use by third parties, without prejudice to the applicable national law.[109]

[108] Ibid. [16].
[109] Ibid. [45].

These recent cases give us a strong impression of the future of database rights in the online environment. Those who operate meta indexes and scraping sites will have to ensure they comply contractually with the owner of the data or will have to ensure they meet the defences available under the Database Directive as implemented. The operation of unlawful price comparison or meta-indexing sites are controllable, by database rights, where the content qualifies, or by contractual law where it does not. In the case of the latter though readers are reminded of Art. 5 of the InfoSoc Directive,[110] and the application of that in *PRCA v NLA*.[111] This may allow the narrowest window for a few services to escape through, but only for a few.

12.4 **Conclusions**

Anyone interested in the operation of the Database Directive has much to thank Football Dataco/Fixtures Marketing for. Their series of cases before the CJEU have settled the boundaries of both *sui generis* and copyright protection for databases. We know from the *Fixtures Marketing* cases that *sui generis* protection extends only to cases where there has been significant investment in the gathering and verifying of data and the design of the database itself, not in the creation of the data. We also know from the *Football Dataco v Yahoo!* case that a higher level of creative investment, beyond skill, labour, and judgement, is required to qualify for Art. 3 copyright protection. Just as the ECJ had previously ruled in the *Fixtures Marketing* cases, you cannot gain copyright protection for simply ordering something which is created or pre-existing for a different purpose.

Finally the *Football Dataco v Sportradar* cases complete the jigsaw with two vital pieces of information. First, the excellent analysis of Sir Robin Jacob in the Court of Appeal clearly draws bright lines between the unprotectable at Art. 7 creation of data which leads to spin-off databases and, as seen in the *Fixtures Marketing* cases, the protectable gathering of data by observation. This is an extremely lucid analysis and also has the benefit of providing good policy: we will not protect by Art. 7 that which can only be created by one person or a defined group of persons as that creates a monopoly over not just the database but also the information in it, but we will protect those who invest in gathering data which others may gather equally by a similar investment. Finally the CJEU dealt with the one outstanding issue of jurisdiction, again in a most lucid and sensible way. To have decided other than they did would have risked reintroducing a fractured Europe where informational intermediaries such as Sportradar gravitated towards countries with the weakest database protections as a safe harbour for their activities.

[110] Dir. 2001/29/EC of the European Parliament and of the Council of 22 May 2001 on the harmonization of certain aspects of copyright and related rights in the information society, Official Journal L.167, 22/06/2001.

[111] See (n. 106).

TEST QUESTIONS

Question 1

The *sui generis* database right is an unnecessary addition to the legal landscape. Copyright law was perfectly positioned to regulate the developing database industry. It has taken a number of cases involving sporting fixtures lists to even define what the scope of the right is, and in the end it is just about trying to harmonize the UK 'sweat of the brow' standard with European *droit d'auteur*. In the end though, we still have two standards—Arts. 3 and 7: nothing has changed and the Directive should therefore be repealed.

Discuss.

Question 2

Did the decision of the European Court of Justice in the case of *British Horseracing Board v William Hill* [2005] 1 CMLR 15 undermine the effectiveness and value of the *sui generis* database right?

FURTHER READING

Books

E Derclaye, *The Legal Protection of Databases: A Comparative Analysis* (2008)

Chapters and articles

N Eziefula, 'Database Rights Back on the Sport Radar', *Entertainment Law Review* 242 (2012)

A Masson, 'Creation of Database or Creation of Data: Crucial Choices in the Matter of Database Protection', 28 (5) *EIPR* 261 (2006)

M Schellekens, 'A Database Right in Search Results?—an Intellectual Property Right Reconsidered in Respect of Computer generated Databases' 27 (6) *Computer Law and Security Review* 620 (2011)

C Waelde, 'Databases and Lawful Users: The Chink in the Armour', 3 *IPQ* 256 (2006)

TEST QUESTIONS

Question 1

[illegible]

Question 2

[illegible]

FURTHER READING

Books

[illegible]

Chapters and articles

[illegible]

PART IV

Criminal activity in the information society

The information society offers opportunities for criminals as well as law abiding citizens. How does the law reduce the risks of criminal activity in the information society?

13

Computer misuse

Computer misuse is the collective term for a number of criminal offences committed by means of a computer, often through access to the internet and which are regulated by the Computer Misuse Act (CMA) 1990 (as amended). These include computer hacking (unauthorized access); the creation and distribution of computer viruses and other malware; and denial of service attacks. The need for specific legislation in this area became clear in the winter of 1984 when two computer hackers, Stephen Gold and Robert Schifreen, gained unauthorized access to the BT Prestel computer network and successfully accessed several secure areas of the service.[1]

Their story began in spring 1984 when they obtained a Prestel username and password. There are a variety of tales as to how they did this, and neither has ever confirmed the truth. What does appear to be the case is that they did not obtain these details by watching a Prestel engineer enter his username and password at a trade show, as is widely reported on some internet sites.[2] It would appear the password and username were either obtained through the acquisition of a private phone book belonging to a BT engineer[3] or by the actions of Robert Schifreen attempting a variety of passwords and usernames until one was accepted, a so-called 'brute force attack'.[4] Whatever approach

[1] Prestel was an early commercial computer network service in the UK. Prestel was a 'Videotex' system—that is, a system similar to traditional teletext systems operated by terrestrial TV broadcasters. It could carry text and simple graphics across telephone lines for display on a domestic TV via a Prestel terminal. It was operated by the Post Office (BT) and allowed access to a wide range of Prestel content supplied by the Post Office and by third parties as well as allowing for emailing between Prestel customers. Prestel was for a while an important commercial service used by banks, financial institutions, travel agents, and media organizations to supply and trade data and to carry out transactions. It even led to the first online banking service in the UK; Homelink, a cooperation between the Nottingham Building Society and the Bank of Scotland.

[2] See Wikipedia, *Entry for Computer Misuse Act* <http://en.wikipedia.org/wiki/Computer_Misuse_Act>; 'What is the Computer Misuse Act of 1990?', *Wisegeek*, <http://www.wisegeek.org/what-is-the-computer-misuse-act-of-1990.htm>.

[3] H Cornwall, *The Hacker's Handbook* (rev. sub edition, E Arthur Brown 1986) 209.

[4] P Mungo and B Glough, *Approaching Zero: The Extraordinary Underworld of Hackers, Phreakers, Virus Writers and Keyboard Criminals* (Random House 1992) 34.

was used it appears Prestel did not take security seriously. The Prestel network required that a username was always a ten-character string of letters and/or numbers, and that a password was a four-character string. The username/password combination discovered by Gold and Schifreen was 2222222222/1234. Using this new-found information Gold and Schifreen spent a considerable amount of time on the Prestel network. They identified several weaknesses in Prestel's security and gained system-manager-level access when, in October 1984, in another security breach, a BT engineer left his log-in details on his log-in page.[5] They soon learned how to enter subscription-only areas of Prestel, accessing valuable commercial services providing investment advice for clients of the stockbroker Hoare Govett and commentaries and news reports on international currency markets supplied by the *Financial Times*, as well as accessing the Homelink internet banking system.[6] Their most infamous act though was to begin their downfall. They managed to gain access to subscribers' personal email accounts, including the email account of the Duke of Edinburgh. One hacker (it is not clear which) sent an email, allegedly from the Duke to the Prestel System Manager, saying 'I do so enjoy puzzles and games. Ta ta. Pip! Pip! HRH Hacker.'[7] This act, along with a further act which could only have been carried out by a Prestel engineer with the highest network clearance (or a hacker with similar clearance),[8] caused BT to reset all system manager passwords and then set a trap for the hackers. They were soon identified and were arrested on 10 April 1985.

The problem for the authorities was what were they to be charged with? It was not clear that they had committed a criminal act. There was no theft or damage to property and although there was deception it was not clear they had committed fraud. The authorities could not simply let them go for that would send the signal that hacking was okay. Eventually it was decided that they would be charged under s. 1 of the Forgery and Counterfeiting Act 1981, which states: 'A person is guilty of forgery if he makes a false instrument, with the intention that he or another shall use it to induce somebody to accept it as genuine, and by reason of so accepting it to do or not to do some act to his own or any other person's prejudice.' The argument of the Crown was that the defendants had infringed this provision since, when asked to log in to the Prestel network, they had given false details. In the words of counsel for the Crown '[t]he relevant instrument was the control area of the user segment of the relevant Prestel computer whilst it had recorded and/or stored within it the electronic impulses purporting to be a

[5] Cornwall (n. 3) 209.

[6] Ibid. 210–11. Cornwall notes that they could not transfer money on the Homelink system due to external security measures put in place by the Nottingham Building Society and the Bank of Scotland. It is not clear whether they attempted to do so.

[7] Ibid. 211. In another 'prank' they managed to issue an *FT* newsflash claiming that the pound was worth fifty dollars on international currency exchanges.

[8] The act itself was a minor one. It was the nature of the way it was carried out which forced Prestel to act. It is reported by Mungo and Glough, (see n. 4 at 36), in some detail: 'When subscribers dial into Prestel, they immediately see page one, which indexes all other services. Only the system manager can alter or update listings on this page, but [Schifreen], exploiting his [system manager] status, made a modest change and altered the word Index to read Idnex. Though it was perfectly harmless, the change was enough to signal to Prestel that its security had been breached. The other pranks had been worrisome, but altering the first page was tantamount to telling Prestel that its entire system was insecure.'

customer identification number and customer password'.[9] The problem for the Crown was the definition of 'instrument' found in s. 8 of the Act. This states than an 'instrument' is 'any document, whether of a formal or informal character . . . [including] any disc, tape, soundtrack or other device on or in which information is recorded or stored by mechanical, electronic or other means'.[10] This suggests a degree of permanence is required, but in the Prestel system the username and password were only held for a fraction of a second while the system authenticated them.

At trial the defendants were found guilty and fined.[11] Both immediately appealed and before the Court of Appeal argued, among other things that 'in the context of section 8(l)(d), storage does not include temporary storage in the input buffer because it is immediately passed elsewhere; and (b) the instrument is not *ejusdem generis* with disc, tape and sound track since there was no evidence that the device was in any way physically altered. The impulses always remained separate from the device itself.'[12] The Court of Appeal upheld their claim. In giving the judgment of the court Lord Lane CJ found that:

> the user segment in the instant case does not carry the necessary two types of message to bring it within the ambit of forgery at all. Moreover, neither the report nor the Act, so it seems to us, seeks to deal with information that is held for a moment whilst automatic checking takes place and is then expunged. That process is not one to which the words 'recorded or stored' can properly be applied, suggesting as they do a degree of continuance.[13]

On this basis the court found that 'the language of the Act was not intended to apply to the situation which was shown to exist in this case . . . It is a conclusion which we reach without regret. The Procrustean attempt to force these facts into the language of an Act not designed to fit them produced grave difficulties for both judge and jury which we would not wish to see repeated.'[14]

The Crown appealed to the House of Lords, but were unsuccessful in their attempts to have the decision of the Court of Appeal overturned. Lord Brandon of Oakbrook gave the opinion of the court that:

> section 8(l)(d) contemplates that information may be recorded or stored by electronic means on or in (i) a disc, (ii) a tape, (iii) a sound track (presumably of a film) and (iv) devices other than these three having a similar capacity. The words 'recorded' and 'stored' are words in common use which should be given their ordinary and natural meaning. In my opinion both words in their ordinary and natural meaning connote the preservation of the thing which is the subject matter of them for an appreciable time with the object of subsequent retrieval or recovery. Further, in relation to information recorded or stored on or in a disc, tape or sound track, that is the meaning of the two expressions which appears to me to be clearly intended. For both these reasons I have reached the conclusion that the respondents' case on the first question is right and that the Crown's case on it is wrong.[15]

[9] *R v Gold and Schifreen* [1988] 1 AC 1063, 1064.
[10] Forgery and Counterfeiting Act 1981, s. 8(1)(a), (d).
[11] *R v Gold and Schifreen* [1987] QB 1116, 1117.
[12] Ibid. 1118–19.
[13] Ibid. 1124.
[14] Ibid.
[15] *R v Gold and Schifreen* [1988] 1 AC 1063, 1072–3.

He then went out of his way to criticize the Crown for prosecuting the case in this manner.

Highlight Lord Brandon's rebuke

I share the view of the Court of Appeal (Criminal Division), as expressed by Lord Lane CJ, that there is no reason to regret the failure of what he aptly described as the Procrustean attempt to force the facts of the present case into the language of an Act not designed to fit them.

The Crown had lost the first case on computer hacking in the UK and had done so in a blaze of publicity and with a stinging rebuke from both the Court of Appeal and the House of Lords. There was a great deal of concern both that the UK was unable to deal with the growing threat of computer hacking and that the outcome of this case may encourage others to take up hacking as a hobby.[16] Against this background moves were made to introduce a new Act which would close this loophole in the criminal law. The Law Commission and the Scottish Law Commission produced a joint report recommending that a new offence of unauthorized access to computer data be created,[17] and in the next parliamentary sitting Conservative MP Michael Colvin sponsored a private member's bill which would give effect to the Law Commissions' recommendations: the Bill, supported by the government, became the CMA 1990.

13.1 **Hacking**

The Act in its original form was remarkably concise, comprising only 18 sections with no schedules. This may be due to the origins of the Act as a private member's bill rather than as a government bill. The meat of the Act was in part I (ss. 1–3) entitled 'Computer Misuse Offences'. Here were to be found three new criminal offences: the unauthorized access offence, the aggravated unauthorized access offence, and the unauthorized modification offence. The first two of these were designed to deal with computer hacking.

Section 1, the main hacking provision, is a well-designed criminal law provision. It does not use colloquial terms such as 'hacking',[18] 'phreaking',[19] or 'cracking'[20] and instead simply defines the illegal activity. It states:

[16] It is suggested by Mungo and Glough (n. 4) 39–41, that the outcome of this case encouraged another young hacker, Nick Whitely, to begin a campaign which included wiping data from university networks as well as computer firm ICL, a practice which led to him being dubbed 'the Mad Hacker'.

[17] Law Commission Report No. 186, 'Computer Misuse' (Cm. 819), 1989.

[18] Strictly speaking, a hacker is anyone who displays skilled software development. They are not always malicious and the term is often applied to skilled programmers working in all aspects of software development.

[19] Phreaking is using a computer or other device for tricking telephone systems to obtain free calls. Phreaking used to be common when internet access was obtained on a cost-per-minute dial-up account. It is less common now with ADSL and fibre packages.

[20] A cracker, rather than a hacker, is someone who breaks into someone else's computer system, bypasses passwords or licences in computer programs or in other ways intentionally breaches computer security.

Highlight Computer Misuse Act, s. 1

A person is guilty of an offence if:

(a) he causes a computer to perform any function with intent to secure access to any program or data held in any computer, or to enable any such access to be secured;

(b) the access he intends to secure, or to enable to be secured, is unauthorised; and

(c) he knows at the time when he causes the computer to perform the function that that is the case.

Despite its clarity and brevity several questions remained. The first was what was meant by unauthorized access generally: was this an offence designed to prevent hacking as portrayed in the media—that is, using one computer to gain access to another, or could the unauthorized access be simply the obtaining of access to a single computer by accessing it directly without permission? In other words, to commit the s. 1 offence did one need to hack into a computer or network from an external source? Guidance could be found in s. 17(5) which states that:

> Access of any kind by any person to any program or data held in a computer is unauthorised if—
>
> (a) he is not himself entitled to control access of the kind in question to the program or data; and
>
> (b) he does not have consent to access by him of the kind in question to the program or data from any person who is so entitled.

This seemed clearly to suggest the latter approach was correct and that access could include direct access to a single computer. This, though, was thrown in doubt when the case of *R v Cropp* was heard before Snaresbrook Crown Court.[21] Mr Cropp was charged with unauthorized access to a computer with intent to commit a further offence under s. 2 of the CMA 1990. He had returned to the premises of an ex-employer to purchase goods on behalf of his current employer. When left alone by the salesperson for a few minutes Mr Cropp entered a discount code onto the Point of Sale computer effecting a 70 per cent discount on the goods sold meaning that his new employer was invoiced for only £204.60 (plus VAT) instead of £710.96 (plus VAT). His activity was traced and he was charged but when he came to trial the defence counsel entered a plea of no case to answer. The grounds for this claim were that in order to contravene s. 1(1) (and therefore s. 2(1)) of the Act the prosecution had to establish that the accused had used one computer to gain access to another computer. Somewhat surprisingly the judge upheld the submission, finding that:

> It seems to me, doing the best that I can in elucidating the meaning of s. 1(1)(a), that a second computer must be involved. It seems to me to be straining language to say that only one computer is necessary when one looks at the actual wording of the subsection: 'Causing a computer to perform any function with intent to secure access to any program or data held in any computer.'

[21] *R v Cropp*, Snaresbrook Crown Court, 5 July 1991, unreported, but see case note at (1991) 7 CLSR 168.

This outcome caused consternation for the Crown. It had been assumed that unauthorized access meant any access: this decision threatened to limit the scope of the Act extensively. As a result the Attorney General sought clarification of this issue from the Court of Appeal by way of an Attorney General's reference.[22] The Court of Appeal ruled that the judge in *Cropp* had erred. Lord Taylor CJ gave the opinion of the court:

> The ordinary cannons of construction require this court to look at the words of the section and to give them their plain and natural meaning. Doing that, we look again at the relevant words. They are, 'he causes a computer to perform any function with intent to secure access to any program or data held in any computer'.
>
> Mr Lassman argued successfully before the judge and sought to argue before this court, that the final phrase, 'held in any computer' should really be read as 'held in any other computer' or alternatively should be read 'held in any computer except the computer which has performed the function'.
>
> To read those words in that way, in our judgment, would be to give them a meaning quite different from their plain and natural meaning. It is a trite observation, when considering the construction of statutes, that one does not imply or introduce words that are not there when the plain and natural meaning is clear. In our judgment there are no grounds whatsoever for implying or importing the word 'other' between 'any' and 'computer' or excepting the computer which is actually used by the offender from the phrase 'any computer' at the end of subsection 1(a).[23]

This was a relief for the law enforcement bodies. If the Court of Appeal had confirmed the original outcome of the case the CMA could have been emasculated at its first application.[24] As it was, by confirming that the unauthorized access offences could be committed on a single computer, they opened up a further role for ss. 1 and 2. They had confirmed it could be used not only to prosecute the traditional computer hacker as imagined and portrayed in the media; it could also be applied to employees who accessed data held on their employer's computers without permission.

13.1.1 **Employee hackers**

In the few years following promulgation of the CMA there were a number of cases involving employee misuse of their employer's resources: many centred on abuse of the Police National Computer system (PNC) by serving police officers and civilian support staff.

The first was *R v Bennett*.[25] Superintendent Bennett used the PNC to identify his ex-wife's new partner by using details he had gathered on him by observation. Superintendent Bennett pleaded guilty to a breach of s. 1 and was fined £150. Several subsequent cases followed including *R v Bonnett* in which a special constable was convicted under s. 1 for unlawfully accessing the PNC without authority to find out who owned the car registration number BON1T, because he wanted to buy it,[26] and *R v Begley*, in which a WPC used the PNC to access records in an attempt to track down a woman who had had a

[22] AG's Reference No. 1 of 1991 [1992] 3 WLR 432.

[23] Ibid. 437.

[24] E Dumbill, 'Computer Misuse Act 1990—Recent Developments' (1992) 8 *Computer Law and Practice* 105.

[25] Unreported, Bow Street Magistrates' Court, 10 October 1991.

[26] Unreported, Newcastle-under-Lyme Magistrates' Court, 3 November 1995.

relationship with her boyfriend.[27] These cases, and many similar cases from the private sector,[28] were easily dealt with by the courts. They were simple criminal prosecutions where the only question was whether or not the accused had committed the infringing act. The first major challenge to the application of ss. 1 and 2 to these 'insider hackers' was to come in the case of *DPP v Bignell*.[29]

Bignell was another in the series of cases involving misuse of the PNC. The respondents were two married police officers Paul and Victoria Bignell. They accessed the PNC to extract details of motor vehicles owned by a Mr Howells, the new partner of PC Bignell's ex-wife for purposes not entirely clear from the case report. At trial at Bow Street Magistrates' Court both defendants were found guilty of breaching s. 1 of the CMA and were fined. However, as a conviction would mean that they were both likely to lose their jobs as police officers they appealed this decision. On appeal they challenged the decision of the stipendiary magistrate on the basis that 'their use of the computer, even if it was found to be for private purposes, was not within the definition of "unauthorised access" provided by s. 17(5) of the Act because the access had been with authority even though that authority was used for an unauthorised purpose'.[30]

This extremely complex and convoluted defence became known as the defence of 'authorized access for unauthorized purpose'. Basically the respondents were arguing that despite the fact that they were using the PNC for purposes for which they were not authorized to use it, they did have authority to use the computer system, meaning that broadly their access was authorized and it was only their purpose which was not. As the Act states that the s. 1 offence is committed when 'the access he intends to secure is unauthorised'[31] no offence was committed.

This appeal was upheld at Southwark Crown Court in September 1996 but the Crown appealed to the Divisional Court. Astill J and Pill LJ heard the appeal and on 16 May 1997 they issued their judgment: they would reject the appeal and uphold the decision of the Crown Court. Astill J gave the decision of the court. He examined both the original Law Commission Report and the wording of s. 17 before concluding that the respondents were entitled to access data contained on the PNC as part of their normal duties as police officers; therefore they were entitled to access the data, although their purpose for accessing it may have been unauthorized. Astill J attempted to quell concerns that this left employers with little control over how employees used their computer systems by pointing out that 'The authority of the Commissioner is not undermined because the respondents remain subject to internal disciplines. The use of the computer for an unauthorised purpose involves the use of a false Reason Code and that is a matter subject to disciplinary procedures. In addition the respondents could have been prosecuted under the Data Protection Act 1984.'[32]

[27] Unreported, Coventry Magistrates' Court. This case, and the others discussed in this section are discussed in M Wasik, 'Computer Misuse and Misconduct in Public Office' (2008) 22 *International Review of Law, Computers & Technology* 135.

[28] Private sector cases included *R v Borg* in which a computer officer at a financial services firm was cleared of unlawfully accessing her employer's system with a view to defrauding £1m, and *R v Speilmann* in which an ex-employee of a financial news service was found guilty of a breach of s. 1 in accessing his ex-employer's system to modify and delete emails. Details of these unreported cases, and many others may be found at <http://www.computerevidence.co.uk/Cases/CMA.htm>.

[29] [1997] EWHC Admin 476; [1998] Cr App R 1.

[30] [1997] EWHC Admin 476, [4].

[31] Computer Misuse Act 1990, s. 1(1)(b).

[32] [1997] EWHC Admin 476, [17].

There has been a considerable amount of analysis of the *Bignell* decision.[33] While some acknowledge that the Crown may have erred in not raising a prosecution under the Data Protection Act,[34] most commentators were highly critical of the outcome. The problem was the way Astill J had interpreted s. 17(2) and (5). Section 17(2) states that:

> A person secures access to any program or data held in a computer if by causing a computer to perform any function he—
>
> (a) alters or erases the program or data;
>
> (b) copies or moves it to any storage medium other than that in which it is held or to a different location in the storage medium in which it is held;
>
> (c) uses it; or
>
> (d) has it output from the computer in which it is held (whether by having it displayed or in any other manner).

While s. 17(5) states:

> Access of any kind by any person to any program or data held in a computer is unauthorised if:
>
> (a) he is not himself entitled to control access of the kind in question to the program or data; and
>
> (b) he does not have consent to access by him of the kind in question to the program or data from any person who is so entitled.

Astill J concluded that:

> s. 17(2)(a) to (d) sets out four ways in which a person secures access. S. 17(5)(a) and (b) define unauthorised access by reference to access 'of the kind in question'. That refers to the four kinds of access set out in s. 17(2)(a) to (d) and the respondents did have authority to secure access by reference to s. 17(2)(c) and (d) at least. It therefore follows that 'control access of the kind in question' in s. 17(5)(a) must apply to the respondents because they were authorised to secure access by s. 17(2)(c) and (d).[35]

Thus, for Astill J, s. 17(5) is tied to s. 17(2), but as has been pointed out by several commentators this should not be the case. Clive Gringras notes that:

> The Bignells instructed that a false 'reason code' be typed into the police national computer. Why? They wanted the computer to perform this function to allow them to gain access to data which were 'not necessary for the efficient discharge of genuine police duties'. In other words, they were not authorised to secure access to the data. The offence should have been made out. The reason that the court did not come to this conclusion was because they did not restrict their analysis of the facts with the precise wording of the statute. The Act is drafted in terms of 'causing a computer to perform a function' together with the intention to 'secure unauthorised access to any program or data'. It is therefore an error in law for the court to have provided a judgment littered with references to 'accessing a computer'. The Act does not sanction those who access computers; it sanctions those who use computers to secure access to data and programs. This difference is fundamental and because it was not appreciated by the Divisional Court we, those

[33] See e.g. C Gringras, 'To Be Great Is to Be Misunderstood: The Computer Misuse Act 1990' (1997) 3 *Computer and Telecommunications Law Review* 213; Z Hamin, 'Insider Cyber-threats: Problems and Perspectives' (2000) 14 *International Review of Law, Computers and Technology* 105; Wasik (n. 27).

[34] To be fair to the Crown, an earlier attempt to prosecute a serving police officer under the Data Protection Act 1984 for extracting data from the PNC with a view to passing it on to a friend who worked for a debt collection agency had failed. See *R v Brown* [1996] 1 AC 543.

[35] [1997] EWHC Admin 476, [17].

who rely on the safety of the material stored by computers, are left again waiting for an appeal to set straight the Act.[36]

David Bainbridge was equally forthright, 'As part of their normal duties, the police officers were entitled to access such computer information. *But being entitled to access computer material is not the same as being entitled to control access to such material.* This is an important and crucial distinction which the court failed to make.'[37] What Astill J had failed to do was distinguish between 'access to data', as defined under s. 17(2) which forms the *actus reus* of the offence under s. 1(1)(a) and '*unauthorised* access' as defined by s. 17(5) and which forms the *mens rea* of the offence under s. 1(1)(b). In effect the Divisional Court had fused the two elements together leaving what David Bainbridge called 'an unsatisfactory gap in the Computer Misuse Act 1990'.[38]

The opportunity for the courts to revisit *Bignell* came quickly. Sometime between January 1996 and March 1997 Joan Ojomo, an employee of American Express working in the credit section of the company's office in Florida, gained access to customer accounts and extracted confidential information which she passed on to others, including a Mr Adeniyi Allison who was resident in London. The information she gave to him and others was then used to encode other blank credit cards which could then be used fraudulently to buy goods and to obtain money from ATMs. Miss Ojomo was arrested, and as a result of the subsequent investigation, Mr Allison was arrested and held in London on suspicion of conspiracy to: (1) secure unauthorized access to the American Express computer system with intent to commit theft; (2) secure unauthorized access to the American Express computer system with intent to commit forgery; and (3) cause unauthorized modification to the contents of the American Express computer system. At committal the magistrate declined to commit Mr Allison on the first two charges but did commit him on the third. The US government then sought extradition of Mr Allison, while Mr Allison brought a *habeas corpus* claim on the basis that none of the offences were extradition offences. A series of cross-appeals from both the US government and Mr Allison emerged before, on 13 May 1998, the Divisional Court certified a question of law of general public importance:

> Whether, on a true construction of s. 1 (and thereafter s. 2) of the Computer Misuse Act 1990, a person who has authority to access data of the kind in question none the less has unauthorised access if:
>
> (a) the access to the particular data in question was intentional,
>
> (b) the access in question was unauthorised by a person entitled to authorise access to that particular data,
>
> (c) knowing that the access to that particular data was unauthorised.

The case, *R v Bow Street Magistrates Court and Allison, ex parte Government of the US of America*,[39] was heard on 13 July 1999 with the full judgment issued on 5 August 1999. This was remarkable timing. It had been just over two years since the *Bignell* decision

[36] Gringras (n. 33) 215.

[37] D Bainbridge, *Introduction to Information Technology Law* (6th edn, Longman 2007) 443 (emphasis added).

[38] Ibid. 443.

[39] [2000] 2 AC 216.

and now the House of Lords had been referred a case on exactly the same point of law. Lord Hobhouse gave the decision of the House. He found first of all that offences committed under ss. 2 or 3 were clearly extraditable as s. 15 of the Act clearly stated that they were to be so.[40] The question then remained, had there been an offence under either of these sections? It was clear that in her daily work it was possible for Miss Ojomo to access all customer accounts held on the American Express database but she was only authorized to access those accounts that were assigned to her. However, she had accessed various other accounts and files which had not been assigned to her and which she had not been given specific authority to work on. This meant the court had to revisit the *Bignell* decision and determine whether these activities of Miss Ojomo were in breach of s. 2.

Lord Hobhouse was extremely critical of the approach taken in *Bignell*. He found that:

> [the decision of Astill J] introduces a number of glosses which are not present in the Act. The concept of control is changed from that of being entitled to authorise to authorised to cause the computer to function. The concept of access to a program or data is changed to access to the computer at a particular 'level' [and] he characterised the defendants as persons who had 'control access' (using the word 'control' as a noun) 'of the kind in question'. It was this use of language, departing from the language of the statute and unnecessary to the decision of that case, which misled the magistrate and the Divisional Court in the present case.[41]

The actual interpretation of 'control' and 'access' was in his Lordship's opinion much simpler:

> Section 17 is an interpretation section. Subsection (2) defines what is meant by access and securing access to any programme or data. It lists four ways in which this may occur or be achieved. Its purpose is clearly to give a specific meaning to the phrase 'to secure access'. Subsection (5) is to be read with subsection (2). It deals with the relationship between the widened definition of securing access and the scope of the authority which the relevant person may hold. That is why the subsection refers to 'access of any kind' and 'access of the kind in question'. Authority to view data may not extend to authority to copy or alter that data. The refinement of the concept of access requires a refinement of the concept of authorisation. The authorisation must be authority to secure access of the kind in question. As part of this refinement, the subsection lays down two cumulative requirements of lack of authority. The first is the requirement that the relevant person be not the person entitled to control the relevant kind of access. The word 'control' in this context clearly means authorise and forbid. If the relevant person is so entitled, then it would be unrealistic to treat his access as being unauthorised. The second is that the relevant person does not have the consent to secure the relevant kind of access from a person entitled to control, i.e. authorise, that access.
>
> Subsection (5) therefore has a plain meaning subsidiary to the other provisions of the Act. It simply identifies the two ways in which authority may be acquired—by being oneself the person entitled to authorise and by being a person who has been authorised by a person entitled to authorise. It also makes clear that the authority must relate not simply to the data or programme but also to the actual kind of access secured. Similarly, it is plain that it is not using the word 'control' in a physical sense of the ability to operate or manipulate the computer and that it is not derogating from the requirement that for access to be authorised it must be authorised to the relevant data or relevant programme or part of a programme. It does not introduce any concept that authority to access one piece of data should be treated as authority to access other pieces of

[40] Ibid. 222–3.
[41] Ibid. 225.

data 'of the same kind' notwithstanding that the relevant person did not in fact have authority to access that piece of data. Section 1 refers to the intent to secure unauthorised access to any programme or data. These plain words leave no room for any suggestion that the relevant person may say: 'Yes, I know that I was not authorised to access that data but I was authorised to access other data of the same kind.'[42]

Bignell was overruled and a commonsense approach prevailed. Lord Hobhouse clearly set out the different roles of s. 17(2) and (5). Authority to access data was to the specific data, or for a specific purpose; there was to be no aggregation of data as 'data of a specific kind' as set out in *Bignell*. Because Miss Ojomo had no permission to access the specific data in question her access was unauthorized and therefore in breach of s. 1. Further, because this access was secured with the intent to go on and commit fraud, this was an extraditable offence under s. 2.

Allison remains the leading case on unauthorized employee, or insider, hacking. Employees who access data without authority risk prosecution under the CMA, even if they are authorized to access other data of that type. The *Allison* principle has been applied in several subsequent but unreported cases including *R v Culbert*,[43] in which an ex-employee of Associated Newspapers pleaded guilty to two counts of making an unauthorized modification to a computer system and one of gaining unauthorized access after he offered to damage his employer's computerized print centre in return for £600,000; *R v Carey* in which a computer engineer deleted a number of design drawings over a dispute about payment;[44] and *R v Curzon* in which an employee at Royal Wootton Bassett Academy accessed the school's email system using the log-in and password of another school employee to read private emails from the Head.[45] The risk of insider hacking remains high, as was recorded in reports by the Audit Commission[46] and the Office of the Information Commissioner,[47] but prosecution for more serious breaches continues to discourage this type of attack.

13.1.2 **External hackers**

Of course when the CMA was passed it was external hackers in the mould of Stephen Gold and Robert Schifreen whom most people had in mind. This has recently been the focus of a number of police investigations into the activities of journalists at tabloid newspapers, such as Operation Weeting, but while the media is, of course, focusing on phone hacking and the operations of journalists, cases such as these are usually legally simple. The law has developed instead in a number of lower-profile cases. Following the *Cropp* decision a number of cases followed including *R v Goulden*,[48] in which a software contractor, in dispute with a client over unpaid fees 'locked' the client's computer system by installing a security program and refused to hand over the password until his fees were paid, was fined £1,650; and *R v Pryce*,[49] in which teenage hacker Richard Pryce—aka

[42] Ibid. 223–4.
[43] Unreported, Southwark Crown Court, 13 October 2000.
[44] Unreported, Hove Crown Court, 19 September 2002.
[45] Unreported, Swindon Magistrates' Court, 17 August 2012.
[46] The Audit Commission, *ICT Fraud and Abuse* (June 2005).
[47] Office of the Information Commissioner, *Annual Report 2004* (July 2004) 34–6.
[48] Southwark Crown Court, *The Times*, 10 June 1992.
[49] Unreported, Bow Street Magistrates' Court, 21 March 1997.

the 'Datastream Cowboy'—pleaded guilty to 12 charges of unlawful access after accessing websites operated by among others, Lockheed Martin and the US Air Force.

The most famous early case was probably the 'addicted hacker' case *R v Bedworth*.[50] Paul Bedworth, along with co-accused Karl Strickland and Neil Woods, was charged under ss. 1 and 3 of the CMA. Together they formed a group called Eight Legged Groove Machine (8LGM). They gained access to a number of high-profile networks including JANET (the Joint Academic Network), the National Assessment Agency, BT, the *Financial Times*, and the European Commission. Once in they often left messages signed 8LGM or 'eight little green men'. They did not meet, or even know each other or their real names until they were introduced by the arresting officers; all contact was by bulletin boards. Strickland and Woods entered guilty pleas and both were sentenced to six months in prison.[51] Bedworth, however, pleaded not guilty. For some reason the prosecution had charged him with conspiracy to commit offences under ss. 1 and 3 of the CMA, rather than the direct offences. Why this was done is not clear as he appeared to be equally culpable with his co-accused. In any event, Bedworth claimed he was addicted to computer use and by virtue of that addiction was unable to form the necessary intent. The defence called expert witnesses to impress upon the jury that Bedworth had an addiction described as 'computer tendency syndrome' and the jury duly acquitted, despite the fact that the judge had made it clear to the jury that obsession and dependence were no defence to criminal charges. This outcome was surprising, and was heavily criticized.[52] It appears though to be a unique case. At the time there was a considerable amount of concern that the case would establish a precedent which would be followed by other defendants, but this has not turned out to be the case. Instead it seems that the jury was influenced by the defendant's background: at the time he was 18 and about to start university. If so, he can count himself most fortunate.

Cases of external attacks prosecuted under ss. 1 and 2 continue to be seen with some regularity. Few are reported but the evidence suggests that although incidences of external hacking attacks remain high the law is quite effective in dealing with offenders. In *Ellis v DPP (No. 1)* the appellant appealed against three convictions under s. 1.[53] Mr Ellis was an ex-student and alumnus of the University of Newcastle upon Tyne. On three occasions he had used non-open access computers on campus to browse the internet. Mr Ellis did this knowing he was not permitted to use these computers for this purpose, having previously been advised by an administrative officer at the university that as an alumnus he could only make use of public access computers in the library. On each occasion Mr Ellis did not enter a false password or make any other false declaration to gain access to the computers as they had been left logged in by authorized users who had failed to log out after using them.[54] The question for the court was whether using a logged-in terminal without permission was unauthorized access under s. 1. Judgment was given by Lord Woolf, CJ. He found that s. 1 was 'sufficiently wide to cover the

[50] Unreported, Southwark Crown Court 21 May 1993.

[51] *R v Strickland*, *R v Woods*, unreported, Southwark Crown Court 21 May 1993.

[52] See among others 'The Case of the Artful Dodger' *Computer Weekly* (25 March 1993); C Christian, 'Down and Out in Cyberspace' (1993) 90 *Law Society Gazette* 2; A Charlesworth, 'Addiction and Hacking' (1993) *New Law Journal* 540.

[53] *Ellis v DPP (No. 1)* [2001] EWHC Admin 362.

[54] Mr Ellis in interview drew an analogy between what he did with the computers and picking up someone else's discarded newspaper to read. *Ellis v DPP (No. 1)*, ibid. [8].

use which was made of the computers by the appellant',[55] and that the 'evidence of Mr Hulme, the administrative officer, was perfectly satisfactory evidence on which the magistrates could decide that the appellant was aware that he was unauthorised to use the computers in the way which he did'.[56] As a result the Divisional Court upheld Mr Ellis's convictions.

A further ambiguity was clarified in the later case of *R v Cuthbert*.[57] Mr Cuthbert made a donation through the Disasters Emergency Committee (DEC) website to support the Asian Tsunami Appeal in the aftermath of the natural disaster on 26 December 2004 but became suspicious as to the veracity of the site when he did not receive an immediate acknowledgement of his donation. As he was a freelance information security consultant he decided to test the security of the website by increasing his privileges to see if he could find anything amiss. In so doing he was caught by the site's security measures and reported to the authorities. Given that Mr Cuthbert's actions were in good faith, surprisingly he was prosecuted and at trial he was fined £400 plus costs.[58] In sentencing, District Judge Purdy said that it was 'with some considerable regret' that he passed down a guilty verdict, but the Act made it quite clear that Cuthbert had knowingly performed unauthorized actions against DEC's systems.[59] This case makes clear that intent does not affect the applicability of s. 1. Although Mr Cuthbert was of good intention, strictly he was still guilty of the unauthorized access offence. This has led some commentators to suggest that professionals involved in testing security systems could find themselves liable to prosecution under the CMA, but as Richard Walton points out, 'penetration testing for security purposes is a legitimate and legal activity. The starting point for all such testing is the cooperation and authorisation of the owners of the system under test. No unauthorised activity is involved and so no breach of the CMA can occur. Uninvited security testing is a form of vigilanteism that is not legitimate and clearly breaches the CMA. Professionals avoid this sort of behaviour.'[60]

13.1.3 **Extradition and the *McKinnon* case**

Recently there has been considerable focus on the ability to extradite so-called hackers for breaches of ss. 1 and 2 (and ss. 3, 3A, and 3ZA) of the CMA. The Police and Justice Act 2006 has made several amendments to ss. 1–3 of the CMA.[61] One of the key changes made by the amendments was that penalties for the s. 1 offence were increased with considerable extensions to penalties available for cases prosecuted on indictment. When the CMA was introduced s. 1 was a summary offence only, with the maximum penalty being 'imprisonment for a term not exceeding six months or to a fine not exceeding level 5 on the standard scale or to both'.[62] This was quite different to the s. 2 offence which carried much heavier penalties on indictment 'on conviction on

[55] *Ellis v DPP (No. 1)*, ibid. [16].
[56] Ibid. [17].
[57] Unreported, Horseferry Road Magistrates' Court 6 October 2005.
[58] He also lost his job as a freelance information security consultant at ABN Amro Bank.
[59] Reported in R Walton, 'The Computer Misuse Act' (2006) 11 *Information Security Technical Report* 39, 43.
[60] Ibid. 43–4.
[61] The bulk of the amendments are to s. 3 and the introduction of a new s. 3A. These will be discussed at 13.3 'Denial of service and supply of devices' and 13.3.2 'Section 3A'.
[62] See s. 1(3).

indictment, to imprisonment for a term not exceeding five years or to a fine or to both'.[63] With the enactment of s. 35 of the Police and Justice Act 2006, the s. 1 offence became indictable with a maximum penalty much closer to the s. 2 offence of 'imprisonment for a term not exceeding two years or to a fine or to both'.[64] The reason for this extension is to be found in the All Party Internet Group Report, 'Revision of the Computer Misuse Act'.[65] There they outline that 'Raising the tariff to one year would make the offence extraditable. Making s. 1 indictable would make it possible to prosecute for a criminal attempt at the offence, viz: it would not have to actually succeed.'[66] Thus by making s. 1 an indictable offence with a maximum penalty of two years' imprisonment it achieves this double aim. This has not been uncontroversial, particularly against the highly charged political debate surrounding the CMA and extradition centred on the Gary McKinnon case.

Gary McKinnon became the focus of much debate on the scope and application of anti-hacker legislation. McKinnon was a UK hacker who gained access to a number of US military sites, including the Department of Defense, the US Army, Navy, and NASA. He appears to have been originally motivated by a desire to discover evidence of extra-terrestrial visits and technologies which he, in common with other UFOlogists, believes are held in US military files. Whatever his original motivation McKinnon gained entry to a number of sensitive systems including 53 Army computers, 26 Navy computers, 16 NASA computers, and one at the Department of Defense. It is alleged he gained access to administrative accounts and installed unauthorized remote access and administrative software called 'remotely anywhere' that enabled him to access and alter data upon these computers at any time and without detection by virtue of the program masquerading as a Windows operating system. He appears to have become more political in his intentions as time went by, posting a message on one computer 'US foreign policy is akin to Government-sponsored terrorism these days . . . It was not a mistake that there was a huge security stand down on September 11 last year . . . I am SOLO. I will continue to disrupt at the highest levels.'[67]

McKinnon was tracked down by the UK National Hi-Tech Crime Unit and was arrested in March 2002 for breaches of the CMA.[68] He was bailed to appear before the courts on 9 October 2002 but was informed in September 2002 that he would not need to appear as the US authorities had decided not to proceed with an extradition request.[69] Then in June 2005 he was arrested pursuant to an extradition request from the US government. By then the controversial Extradition Act 2003 had been brought

[63] See s. 2(5)(c). Section 2 could also be charged as a summary offence in which case the maximum penalty is 'imprisonment for a term not exceeding twelve months or to a fine not exceeding the statutory maximum or to both', s. 2(5)(a).

[64] See s. 1(3)(c). It should also be noted that the maximum sentence on summary procedure is now 'imprisonment for a term not exceeding 12 months or to a fine not exceeding the statutory maximum or to both' (s. 1(3)(a)).

[65] All Party Internet Group, 'Revision of the Computer Misuse Act' (June 2004) <http://www.cl.cam.ac.uk/~rnc1/APIG-report-cma.pdf>.

[66] Ibid. [93].

[67] *McKinnon v Government of the USA and Secretary of State for the Home Department* [2007] EWHC 762 (Admin), [8].

[68] I Grant, 'US Took 39 Months to Demand McKinnon's Extradition' *Computer Weekly* (19 January 2009).

[69] Ibid.

into force making it easier for the US authorities to extradite McKinnon. Between June 2005 and summer 2010 McKinnon and his supporters repeatedly challenged the right of the US authorities to extradite him, which if successful could have seen him charged under USA-PATRIOT Act of 2001 which could lead to a maximum prison sentence of 70 years. He unsuccessfully challenged the Home Secretary's decision to issue an extradition certificate before the Divisional Court[70] and the House of Lords.[71]

Following his defeat in the House of Lords McKinnon signed a statement admitting offences under the CMA, including under ss. 2 and 3. He hoped that this might convince the Crown Prosecution Service to prosecute him in the UK under UK law. Following this, his case was referred to the Director of Public Prosecutions, but on 26 February 2009 the CPS issued a statement: 'Having reached our conclusions on these matters, as is our wider duty in accordance with the Attorney General's guidance for handling criminal cases in the USA, we also reconsidered in which jurisdiction the case is best prosecuted—and that remains the US.'[72] McKinnon's legal team raised a judicial review action, arguing that due to his recently diagnosed Asperger's syndrome, the decision to certify his extradition was illegal as the Secretary of State failed to account for this supervening event which affects McKinnon's human rights as he was required to do under s. 6 of the Human Rights Act 1998.[73] This application was lost in July 2009 and it appeared certain McKinnon would be extradited.[74] Then amazingly, following a change of government, the new Home Secretary Theresa May announced she would reconsider McKinnon's case afresh.[75] Another lengthy delay followed until 16 October 2012. Home Secretary Theresa May then announced to the House of Commons that the extradition had been blocked, saying that 'Mr McKinnon's extradition would give rise to such a high risk of him ending his life that a decision to extradite would be incompatible with Mr McKinnon's human rights.' She stated that the Director of Public Prosecutions would determine whether McKinnon should face trial before a British court.[76] On 14 December, the Director of Public Prosecutions announced that McKinnon would not be prosecuted in the United Kingdom because of the difficulties involved in bringing a case against him when the evidence was in the United States.[77]

This case has been highly controversial for many reasons, not least the extended time Mr McKinnon spent under threat of extradition. Most commentaries focus on the long delay between McKinnon's first arrest in 2002 and his subsequent arrest in 2005. This also meant that the 2003 Extradition Act applied to the eventual extradition request,

[70] *McKinnon v Government of the USA and Secretary of State for the Home Department* [2007] EWHC 762 (Admin).

[71] *McKinnon v Government of the US of America &Anor* [2008] UKHL 59.

[72] S Ragan, 'UK Refuses to Charge McKinnon—NASA Hacker One Step Closer to Extradition' (*The Tech Herald*, 26 February 2009) <http://www.thetechherald.com/articles/UK-refuses-to-charge-McKinnon-NASA-hacker-one-step-closer-to-extradition/4550/>.

[73] *McKinnon v Secretary of State for the Home Department* [2009] EWHC 170 (Admin).

[74] *R (on the Application of Gary McKinnon) v Secretary of State for Home Affairs* [2009] EWHC 2021 (Admin).

[75] Home Office, *Latest on Gary McKinnon Case*, 4 November 2010 <http://www.homeoffice.gov.uk/media-centre/news/mckinnon-case>.

[76] 'Gary McKinnon's Mother "Overwhelmed" as Extradition Blocked' (*BBC News*, 17 October 2012) <http://www.bbc.co.uk/news/uk-19968973>.

[77] M Kennedy, 'Gary McKinnon Will Face No Charges in UK' *The Guardian* (London, 14 December 2012) <http://www.guardian.co.uk/world/2012/dec/14/gary-mckinnon-no-uk-charges>.

an Act which itself has been the subject of controversy for the procedure it put in place wherein, at the extradition hearing stage, requests from the USA, Canada, Australia, and New Zealand are no longer required to be supported with evidence of a prima facie case against the accused. The key controversy, though, is why McKinnon was never charged under the CMA. There is no doubt the UK authorities could have charged McKinnon in 2002 or subsequently. For the Act to apply the act must have a connection with the UK. This is defined under s. 5(2) as being *either*:

(a) that the accused was in the home country concerned at the time when he did the act which caused the computer to perform the function; or

(b) that any computer containing any program or data to which the accused secured or intended to secure unauthorised access by doing that act was in the home country concerned at that time.

As McKinnon was in London at the relevant time he is clearly liable to the regulation of the CMA 1990 under s. 5(2)(a), even though the computers he hacked into were in the US. Further, as he purportedly admitted offences under ss. 1–3 there was no need for a long and costly trial. Although the harm may have occurred in the US there is no barrier to simply disposing of the McKinnon case at very little further cost to the public purse by having him tried in the UK where he would admit the charges. It is certainly not unusual for UK hackers to be prosecuted here for harm which they have caused overseas. In *R v Caffrey*,[78] a UK teenager, was charged—and later cleared—of an offence under s. 3 of the CMA for a distributed denial of service attack (DDOS) carried out on the Port of Houston Authority, while in *R v McElroy*[79] another UK teenager who hacked into a US Department of Energy Research Lab was given 200 hours' community service under the CMA. Why the UK authorities refused to charge McKinnon in the UK is a mystery, especially as hundreds of thousands of pounds of costs accumulated as he fought extradition. The final decision of the DPP not to prosecute him in the UK seemed, at last, a sensible application of his discretion.

Gary MacKinnon will not be the last UK citizen to face extradition for CMA offences. In 2013 Pakistani student Usman Ahzaz, lost an appeal against extradition to the United States.[80] He had been operating a botnet of over 100,000 computers, at least 800 of which were in the United States. He was caught in an FBI sting operation. He appealed on the basis that he had committed no offence under s. 1 or s. 3 of the CMA. He had been asked by an FBI agent to install software he thought was malware onto the botnet but it was in fact benign. Counsel for Mr Ahzaz argued at worst he committed an attempt to commit the offences detailed. Gross LJ rejected this. He found that 'by his knowingly unauthorised action in installing the software believed to be malicious onto the computers in question, the conclusion is inescapable that the Appellant was altering the data on those computers, so constituting an offence under s. 1, read with

[78] Unreported, Southwark Crown Court, 17 October 2003. See R Allison, 'Youth Cleared of Crashing American Port's Computer' *The Guardian* (London, 18 October 2003) <http://www.guardian.co.uk/technology/2003/oct/18/uknews.onlinesupplement>.

[79] Unreported, Southwark Crown Court, 3 February 2004. See J Leyden, 'Victory for Commonsense in Nuke Lab Hacking Case' (*The Register*, 4 February 2004) <http://www.theregister.co.uk/2004/02/04/victory_for_commonsense_in_nuke/>.

[80] *Ahzaz v United States* [2013] EWHC 216 (Admin).

s. 17(2)(a) of the 1990 Act.'[81] For good measure Gross LJ also found he had committed an offence under s. 3, 'it is plain that the Appellant's conduct would, if proved, constitute an offence under s. 3. In the present case, the Appellant (on the facts as alleged) had control of the computers in question without the knowledge or authorization of their owners. The Appellant, for reward, agreed to install, surreptitiously, and did install software he believed to be malicious on those computers. There is no dispute that his action in doing so was, to his knowledge, unauthorized. The obvious reason for the Appellant acting as he did was to impair the operation of the computer or the program or data in question, within the meaning of s. 3(2)(a) and/or (c) of the 1990 Act.'[82] On this basis he, along with Gloster J, upheld the extradition order.

We are likely to see many more similar cases as states become ever more concerned with network safety and security. The next major test for the UK courts will be the case of Lauri Love who was arrested following the issue of an extradition warrant in 2013. He now faces a series of extradition hearings to determine whether he should be extradited to the United States in relation to a number of alleged CMA offences which been indicted in the districts of Virginia, New Jersey, and New York between various dates in 2012 and 2013, including an alleged attack on the Federal Reserve Bank of Chicago.[83]

13.2 **Viruses, criminal damage, and mail-bombing**

13.2.1 **Early cases: the Mad Hacker and the Black Baron**

Section 3 is deliberately vague and has been the subject of a great deal of speculation and rewriting over the years. As originally passed in 1990 s. 3 stated:

Highlight Computer Misuse Act, s. 3 (original 1990 wording)

(1) A person is guilty of an offence if:
  (a) he does any act which causes an unauthorised modification of the contents of any computer; and
  (b) at the time when he does the act he has the requisite intent and the requisite knowledge.

(2) For the purposes of subsection (1)(b) above the requisite intent is an intent to cause a modification of the contents of any computer and by so doing—
  (a) to impair the operation of any computer;
  (b) to prevent or hinder access to any program or data held in any computer; or
  (c) to impair the operation of any such program or the reliability of any such data.

[81] Ibid. [22].
[82] Ibid. [21].
[83] W Ashford, 'UK man arrested for hacking into US government computers' *Computer Weekly* (17 July 2015) <http://www.computerweekly.com/news/4500250126/UK-man-arrested-for-hacking-into-US-government-computers>.

This offence, known rather unimaginatively as the 'unauthorized modification' offence was to fulfil three separate roles:

(1) to regulate and control the production and distribution of computer viruses and other malware by making it an offence to distribute software which impaired the performance of any computer;

(2) to formalize the law on 'digital criminal damage'; and

(3) to criminalize the installation of software devices such as Trojans which allow hackers back-door access to computers and computer networks almost at will.

One of the first challenges for s. 3 was to clarify the law with relation to 'digital criminal damage'; this is when someone directly amends or erases data held on a computer without permission. While the pre-CMA case of *Gold and Schifreen* had clearly demonstrated that the pre-existing law could not adequately deal with computer hacking, the pre-existing law on criminal damage was unclear. The Criminal Damage Act 1971 states that 'a person who without lawful excuse destroys or damages any property belonging to another intending to destroy or damage any such property or being reckless as to whether any such property would be destroyed or damaged shall be guilty of an offence'.[84] The definition of property may be found in s. 10 which states it is to be 'property of a tangible nature, whether real or personal, including money'.[85] This would seem to suggest that it would not cover information which by nature is intangible but this was rejected in the case of *Cox v Riley*.[86] Here the accused erased programs from a printed circuit card used to control his employer's computer-controlled saw. He was charged under the Criminal Damage Act 1971 but argued that the programs were not tangible property within the meaning of the Act. Nevertheless, he was found guilty on the basis that the printed circuit card had been damaged and was now useless. This approach was confirmed in the later case of *R v Whitely*.[87]

Case study The Mad Hacker

Nicholas Whitely was a 21-year-old hacker known as the 'Mad Hacker'. He was charged with ten offences of intending or recklessly damaging property by hacking into various university computer networks via the Joint Academic Network (JANET) between March and July 1988. He deleted and added files, made sets of his own users, and then deleted any files which would have recorded his activity. He managed to attain the status of a system operator which enabled him to act at will without identification or authority. As a result of his actions, computers failed, were unable to operate properly, or had to be shut down for periods of time.

He was found guilty at Southwark Crown Court on 24 May 1990 and appealed to the Court of Appeal. By the time his appeal was heard the CMA was in force but, as his charges predated the Act, the question remained: had Mr Whitely breached s. 1 of the

[84] Criminal Damage Act 1971, s. 1(1).
[85] Ibid. s. 10(1).
[86] (1986) 83 Cr App R 54.
[87] *R v Whitely* (1991) 93 Cr App R 25.

Criminal Damage Act? Lord Lane CJ gave the judgment of the court. He dismissed the appeal, stating that 'the Act required that tangible property had been damaged, not that the damage itself should be tangible'.[88] He added that 'there could be no doubt that the magnetic particles upon the metal discs were a part of the discs and if the defendant was proved to have altered the particles in such a way as to cause an impairment of the value and usefulness of the disc to the owner, there would be damage within the meaning of section 1',[89] before citing with approval the judgment of Auld J in *Cox v Riley* that 'the term "damage" for the purpose of this provision, should be widely interpreted so as to include not only permanent or temporary physical harm, but also permanent or temporary impairment of value or usefulness'.[90] Thus despite the Criminal Damage Act appearing to be restricted to tangible property, the courts had interpreted it widely as applying to data stored on disks and servers.

It was the intent of the Law Commission that s. 3 should replace the Criminal Damage Act when dealing with damage to computer data. In its report 'Computer Misuse',[91] the Law Commission came to the conclusion that clarification of the pre-existing law was required. They looked at the definition of property in the 1971 Act and concluded that 'for the commission of a criminal offence to depend on whether it can be proved that data was damaged or destroyed while it was held on identifiable tangible property not only is unduly technical, but also creates an undesirable degree of uncertainty in the operation of the law'.[92] The promulgation of s. 3 had the desired effect for although the Criminal Damage Act remained a possible alternative method to prosecute acts of digital criminal damage subsequent cases have all been decided under the CMA, and an amendment introduced by the Police and Justice Act 2006 seeks to remove any confusion by introducing s. 10(5) into the Criminal Damage Act which reads: 'For the purposes of this Act a modification of the contents of a computer shall not be regarded as damaging any computer or computer storage medium unless its effect on that computer or computer storage medium impairs its physical condition.'

A number of cases have been successfully prosecuted under s. 3 dealing with both criminal damage and the creation and sending of viruses. One of the first was *R v Goulden* which has been previously discussed.[93] As well as being found to have infringed s. 1, Mr Goulden was found to have infringed s. 3 by installing the security program which he used to lock his client's computer. Also found to have infringed s. 3 were Gareth Hardy, a computer engineer who 'time locked' his employer's computers so that one month after his employment was ended all data became encrypted,[94] Jeremy Feltis, a computer operator who worked for Thorn UK, who 'sabotaged' his employer's computers by disconnecting vital connections,[95] and Alfred Whittaker who installed bespoke software on a client machine with a hidden time lock which locked the client's computers when he was not paid on time.[96]

[88] Ibid. 28.
[89] Ibid.
[90] Ibid. 29.
[91] Law Commission Report No. 186 (n. 17).
[92] Ibid. [2.29].
[93] See (n. 48).
[94] *R v Hardy*, unreported, Old Bailey, 1992.
[95] *R v Feltis* [1996] EWCA Crim 776.
[96] *R v Whittaker*, unreported, Scunthorpe Magistrates' Court, 1993.

Without doubt though the first cause célèbre of s. 3 was the case of the 'Black Baron'.[97]

Case study The Black Baron

Christopher Pile was a self-taught computer programmer who became fascinated with the design of computer viruses. He designed several viruses including the infamous SMEG.Pathogen and SMEG.Queeg viruses, named after expressions from the BBC television series 'Red Dwarf'. The reason Pathogen and Queeg were seen to be so dangerous was that they were early examples of polymorphic viruses, viruses which can mutate to take on different forms in an attempt to defeat antivirus software. The SMEG part of the virus referred to an encryption code system which could change the shape and nature of the virus at each infection: this was made available by Pile to other virus writers as part of a toolkit.

Pile was traced and arrested by officers from the Computer Crime Unit (the forerunner of the National Cybercrime Unit). He pleaded guilty to five charges under s. 2 and five of unauthorized modification of data under s. 3 and was sentenced to 18 months' imprisonment. Pile was the first virus writer to be successfully prosecuted under s. 3 and prosecutions for the writing and distribution of viruses remain rare, with the only recent cases being of an individual found guilty of sending a computer virus to a competitor by way of an email attachment[98] and a designer of mass mailing viruses who infected thousands of computers.[99]

13.2.2 Later cases: web defacement and mail-bombing

The value of s. 3's wide definition came to be recognized as new forms of attacks developed. In 1997 the first successful prosecution for web defacement took place. Two defendants, Ian Morris and Richard Airlie, hacked into the website of an estate agency and replaced pictures of homes for sale with pornographic images. They were convicted under ss. 2 and 3 and were fined £1,250 and sentenced to 100 hours' community service.[100] In 2006 another individual was sentenced to eight months' imprisonment, suspended for two years, and given a two-year supervision order for defacing members' profiles on loveandfriends.com dating website.[101]

Section 3 has also been applied to 'mail-bombing' attacks. These occur when the attacker sends huge volumes of email to an address in an attempt to overflow the mailbox or overwhelm the server where the email address is hosted. To mail-bomb one merely sends tens, or even hundreds of thousands, of emails simultaneously to the same email server causing the server to fail, thereby denying the lawful user of the server the ability to use it; thus denial of service.

The first mail-bombing prosecution in the UK took place in 2005 when David Lennon, a 16-year-old from London, was charged under s. 3 for mail-bombing the network

[97] *R v Pile*, unreported, Plymouth Crown Court, 15 November 1995.

[98] *R v Brogden*, unreported, Exeter Crown Court, 19 April 2001 <http://www.sophos.com/pressoffice/news/articles/2001/04/va_comserve.html>.

[99] *R v Vallor*, unreported, Southwark Crown Court, 21 January 2003 <http://news.bbc.co.uk/1/hi/wales/2678773.stm>.

[100] *R v Morris and Airlie*, unreported, Cardiff Crown Court, 1997.

[101] *R v Byrne*, unreported, Southwark Crown Court, 7 November 2006.

of Domestic and General Group plc. Lennon had been employed by D&G for three months but had then been dismissed. He decided to take revenge by mail-bombing the D&G network by using an automated mail sender to send email messages purporting to come from D&G's HR manager to random recipients within the company. By using this methodology he managed to generate in excess of 5 million emails which caused network failures in the D&G network. He was arrested and charged.

Following his arrest he admitted sending the emails but said that his intention was to cause a 'bit of a mess up' in the company; that he did not consider what he was doing was criminal; and it was not his intention to cause the damage to D&G.[102] On 2 November 2005, District Judge Kenneth Grant, sitting as a Youth Court in Wimbledon, ruled that there was no case to answer on the basis that s. 3 was intended to deal with the sending of malicious material such as viruses, worms, and Trojan horses which corrupt or change data, but not the sending of emails.[103] The Director of Public Prosecutions appealed to the Divisional Court where Jack J gave the leading opinion:

> It is not in dispute, that the owner of a computer which is able to receive emails is ordinarily to be taken as consenting to the sending of emails to the computer. His consent is to be implied from his conduct in relation to the computer. Some analogy can be drawn with consent by a householder to members of the public to walk up the path to his door when they have a legitimate reason for doing so, and also with the use of a private letter box. But that implied consent given by a computer owner is not without limit. The point can be illustrated by the same analogies. The householder does not consent to a burglar coming up his path. Nor does he consent to having his letter box choked with rubbish. That second example seems to me to be very much to the point here. I do not think that it is necessary for the decision in this case to try to define the limits of the consent which a computer owner impliedly gives to the sending of emails. It is enough to say that it plainly does not cover emails which are not sent for the purpose of communication with the owner, but are sent for the purpose of interrupting the proper operation and use of his system. That was the plain intent of Mr Lennon in using the Avalanche program. The difference can be demonstrated in this way. If Mr Lennon had telephoned Ms Rhodes and requested consent to send her an email raising a point about the termination of his employment, she would have been puzzled as to why he bothered to ask and said that of course he might. If he had asked if he might send the half million emails he did send, he would have got a quite different answer. In short the purpose of Mr Lennon in sending the half million emails was an unauthorised purpose and the use made of D&G's email facility was an unauthorised use.[104]

Keene LJ agreed stating that:

> The critical issue is that of 'consent' as that word is used in s. 17(8) of the Act. I, for my part, see a clear distinction between the receipt of emails which the recipient merely does not want but which do not overwhelm or otherwise harm the server, and the receipt of bulk emails which do overwhelm it. It may be that the recipient is to be taken to have consented to the receipt of the former if he does not configure the server so as to exclude them. But in my judgment he does not consent to receiving emails sent in a quantity and at a speed which are likely to overwhelm the server. Such consent is not to be implied from the fact that the server has an open as opposed to a restricted configuration.[105]

102 *DPP v Lennon* [2006] EWHC 1201 (Admin).

103 Ibid. [7].

104 Ibid. [9]. It should be noted that although Jack J refers to half a million emails, in fact 5 million were sent.

105 *DPP v Lennon* (n. 102) [14].

With the ruling of the Divisional Court clear the case was remitted back to Wimbledon Youth Court, and on 23 August 2006 Lennon was sentenced to a two-month curfew with electronic tagging.[106]

13.3 Denial of service and supply of devices

Mail-bombing is only one type of denial of service (DoS) attack. More sophisticated attacks can take down complete networks and/or web servers rendering websites unavailable. There are a variety of DoS techniques which all take the form of asking the recipient server to deal with more requests for information than it can deal with, causing it to overload.[107] There are two basic varieties of DoS attack: the standard DoS attack where one individual with considerable resources, or more likely a number of individuals acting in a coordinated fashion, attacks a single server or web server, and DDoS where malicious code such as a Trojan is used to create a network of 'slave' computers under the control of one operator which can all be triggered at one time to carry out the attack.

Under the CMA as passed in 1990 DoS attacks were probably not illegal, while those engaged in DDoS attacks would probably only be liable for the installation of the Trojan software not the actual attack itself, meaning the authorities would need to track down at least one infected 'zombie' computer to introduce as evidence. This is because s. 3 as originally enacted required the accused to carry out an act of 'unauthorised modification of the contents of any computer' but a DoS, or even a DDoS attack, does not modify the contents of any computer; it merely stops it from functioning while the attack is ongoing and once an attack concludes the server is released and returns to service.[108]

This raised several problems both legal and practical. Practically it meant that it would prove to be extremely difficult to prosecute for a DoS, or even a DDoS, in the UK unless either some further offence was committed (such as blackmail or fraud) or unless the prosecuting authorities could establish either a s. 1 or s. 2 offence, or they could find evidence of unauthorized modification of contents. Legally this meant the UK was failing in its duties under the Council of Europe Convention on Cybercrime.[109] Articles 4 and 5 of the Convention, on data interference and system interference, were much more widely drawn than s. 3 of the CMA. In particular, Art. 5 required signatory states to 'adopt such legislative and other measures as may be necessary to establish as criminal offences under its domestic law, when committed intentionally, the serious hindering without right of the functioning of a computer system by inputting, transmitting, damaging, deleting, deteriorating, altering or suppressing computer data'. This is clearly aimed at DoS attacks in any form.

Faced with both a clear failure in the current law, and the demands of the international community, the UK All Party Internet Group (APIG) reviewed the scope of s. 3 as

[106] J Oates, 'Kid Who Crashed e-Mail Server Gets Tagged' (*The Register*, 23 August 2006) <http://www.theregister.co.uk/2006/08/23/email_bomber_guilty/>.

[107] For a quick primer on denial of service attacks see US Computer Emergency Readiness Team, 'Cyber Security Tip ST04-015: Understanding Denial-of-Service Attacks' <http://www.us-cert.gov/cas/tips/ST04-015.html>. For greater detail see R Overill, 'Computer Crime: Denial of Service Attacks: Threats and Methodologies' (1999) 6 *Journal of Financial Crime* 351.

[108] There is a difference with a mail-bombing attack (as Mr Lennon found to his cost) as the emails themselves are stored in the mail server and as such may be an 'unauthorised modification of the contents of any computer'.

[109] CETS No. 185, Budapest, 23.XI.2001.

part of their 2004 revision of the CMA.[110] They reported evidence from the Association of Remote Gambling Operators that criminal DDoS attacks were being made on gambling websites accompanied by monetary demands to make the attacks stop.[111] They reported a split in opinion as to whether s. 3 was adequate as it stood to deal with DoS attacks noting that 'almost every respondent from industry told us that the CMA is not adequate for dealing with DoS and DDoS attacks . . . We understand that this widespread opinion is based on some 2002 advice by the Crown Prosecution Service that s. 3 might not stretch to including all DoS activity. Energis and ISPA told us that they knew of DoS attacks that were not investigated because "no crime could be framed"',[112] while:

> the Government, many academic lawyers and also, we understand, the NHTCU, believe that s. 3 is sufficiently broad to cover DoS attacks. In April 2003 the Internet Crime Forum (ICF) Legal Subgroup pointed out that s. 3 did not require unauthorised access, merely unauthorised 'modification of the contents of any computer'. They expressed the opinion that the test applied would be whether the attack had rendered unreliable the data stored on a computer or impaired its operation.[113]

This inherent uncertainty was enough to convince APIG to recommend that:

> the Home Office rapidly bring forward proposals to add to the Computer Misuse Act an explicit 'denial-of-service' offence of impairing access to data. The tariff should be set the same as the s. 1 'hacking' offence. There should be a further 'aggravated' offence along the lines of the current s. 2 where the denial-of-service is merely one part of a more extensive criminal activity.[114]

These proposals eventually formed part of the review of the CMA found in ss. 35–8 of the Police and Justice Act 2006. Section 3 was substantially rewritten to ensure it criminalizes all forms of DoS/DDoS attacks. The current wording states:

Highlight Computer Misuse Act, s. 3 (new wording)

(1) A person is guilty of an offence if–

(a) he does any unauthorised act in relation to a computer;

(b) at the time when he does the act he knows that it is unauthorised; and

(c) either subsection (2) or subsection (3) below applies.

(2) This subsection applies if the person intends by doing the act–

(a) to impair the operation of any computer;

(b) to prevent or hinder access to any program or data held in any computer;

(c) to impair the operation of any such program or the reliability of any such data; or

(d) to enable any of the things mentioned in paragraphs (a) to (c) above to be done.

(3) This subsection applies if the person is reckless as to whether the act will do any of the things mentioned in paragraphs (a) to (d) of subsection (2) above.

110 All Party Internet Group (n. 65).
111 Ibid. [59].
112 Ibid. [60].
113 Ibid. [61].
114 Ibid. [75].

The 'unauthorized amendment' offence of the original s. 3 has been replaced with an 'unauthorized impairment' offence which clearly covers all forms of DoS/DDoS attack and which came into force on 1 October 2008.[115] It has been highly controversial both in the planning and the execution. In particular a number of critics argue that DoS/DDoS attacks can take the form of a legitimate protest. The Swedish academic Mathias Klang in his essay 'Virtual Sit Ins, Civil Disobedience and Cyberterrorism'[116] wrote that, 'the present legislative trend which criminalises DoS attacks . . . are much too far reaching and seriously hamper the enjoyment of individuals' civil rights'.[117] Klang's argument is that a DoS attack can, and should be allowed to, function as a form of virtual sit-in. When protestors wish to be heard on a variety of issues from equality and civil rights to enfranchisement or to protest the actions of government, one well-known approach is to occupy a public place to make themselves heard and to reach the media.[118] This argument has recently found itself in the mainstream as people draw comparisons between the activities of groups such as Anonymous and mainstream civil rights movements such as Occupy.

In his book *The Net Delusion*, Evegny Morozov writes 'Many cyber-attacks—especially those of the DDoS variety—may simply be construed as acts of civil disobedience, equivalent to demonstrations in the streets. It's not obvious that a campaign to limit the public's ability to practice those would abet the cause of democratization. If society tolerates organizing sit-ins in university offices and temporarily halting their work, there is nothing wrong—at least, in principle—with allowing students to organize DDoS attacks on university websites.'[119] Yochai Benkler meanwhile highlights that DDoS is a nonviolent action, 'it causes disruption, not destruction, and the main technique that Anonymous has used requires participants to join self-consciously and publicly, leaving their Internet addresses traceable. By design, these are sit-ins: Participants illegally occupy the space of their target. And they take personal responsibility for the consequences.'[120] It is arguments such as these which led Anonymous to launch a White House petition in January 2013 to ask the US government to recognize the validity of DDoS attacks as a form of civil disobedience.[121] The petition unfortunately only

[115] Like the changes to s. 1 discussed above this was brought into force by the Police and Justice Act 2006 (Commencement No. 9) Order 2008, SI 2008/2503.

[116] M Klang, 'Virtual Sit Ins, Civil Disobedience and Cyberterrorism' in M Klang and A Murray (eds.), *Human Rights in the Digital Age* (Routledge Cavendish 2005).

[117] Ibid. 145.

[118] Klang notes that: 'While the origins of the sit-in are difficult to locate, a popular point of origin stems from 1960 when four African American college students in Greensboro, North Carolina protested against the whites-only lunch counter by sitting there every day. After the publication of an article in the *New York Times* they were joined by more students and their actions inspired similar protests elsewhere.' Ibid. 138.

[119] E Morozov, *The Net Delusion: The Dark Side of Internet Freedom* (Public Affairs 2011) 228.

[120] Y Benkler, 'Hacks of Valor: Why Anonymous Is Not a Threat to National Security' (*Foreign Affairs*, 4 April 2012) <http://www.foreignaffairs.com/articles/2012-04-04/hacks-valor?page=show> (subscription required).

[121] The petition which may be accessed at <https://petitions.whitehouse.gov/petition/make-distributed-denial-service-ddos-legal-form-protesting> was entitled: *Make, distributed denial-of-service (DDoS), a legal form of protesting*. It stated: 'With the advance in internet technology, comes new grounds for protesting. Distributed denial-of-service (DDoS), is not any form of hacking in any way. It is the equivalent of repeatedly hitting the refresh button on a webpage. It is, in that way, no different than any "occupy" protest. Instead of a group of people standing outside a building to occupy the area, they are having their computer occupy a website to slow (or deny) service of that particular website for a short time.'

received 6,048 signatures, far short of the 25,000 signatures needed for a response at that time, and as a result has been archived.

Despite these arguments these activities are clearly illegal in the UK. The question is, should we be worried about this development? If Klang, Morozov, and Benkler are right, a serious restriction on civil liberties has occurred: as well as criminalizing DDoS attacks which are carried out for criminal purposes such as fraud or blackmail, s. 3 also prevents the use of DoS or DDoS as a peaceful tool of protest. While clearly Klang, Morozov, and Benkler are right to draw our attention to this, it may be argued that the outcome of s. 3 is not as dark as they suggest. Sit-ins are not absolutely protected speech in UK law and a sit-in which occupies private property, or which blocks a public highway, may be broken up with protestors arrested. Further a virtual sit-in is not akin to a real-world sit-in. A real-world sit-in has a highly visible presence where the protestors may be seen and heard: in fact, this it may be argued is the prime import of the sit-in: it is less about appropriation of place and more about communication of a message. A virtual sit-in effected through a DoS attack is very different. There is no visible presence, rather the opposite: the web page or server in question merely lists an error message when sought without explanation of why the error occurs.[122] In a real-world equivalent it is like protestors building some form of barrier around a property which screens it from public view without explanation as to why they have done it. Further, the internet as a whole is a communications media; there are much more effective means for protestors to be heard online than through a DoS/DDoS attack. They may set up a protest site, buy advertising through Google or similar, or make themselves heard through social network sites such as Facebook, Twitter, or YouTube. A DoS/DDoS attack is an extremely damaging form of attack, especially for e-commerce sites; it does not seem unreasonable to criminalize those involved in such an assault.

The actions of Anonymous provide an opportunity to review this. The media has extensively covered a number of Anonymous campaigns such as Operation Avenge Assange. Their actions often take the form of DDoS attacks and, as we have seen, they draw an analogy to the actions of the Occupy movement in real space. A number of individuals have been arrested and charged with Anonymous activity in the US and UK. One of the first members of the collective to come to trial in the UK was James Jeffery. He was charged under ss. 1 and 3 of the CMA after he illegally gained access to the British Pregnancy Advisory Service and downloaded details of 10,000 users of the site which he considered publishing. He also defaced the website with the Anonymous logo and a statement. He attacked the site because he disagreed with termination advice given by the service.[123] A larger-scale case involving a number of Anonymous members saw the first successful prosecutions for DDoS attacks in the UK. Four men were charged with being part of the DDoS attack on a number of attacks on payment sites such as PayPal, Visa, and Mastercard in December 2010 as part of Operation Payback. All four were convicted with two, Christopher Weatherhead and Ashley Rhodes, being given prison sentences for their actions. It is reported that in his sentencing remarks, Judge Testar said:

[122] Although it must be acknowledged that groups such as Anonymous promote a great deal of publicity around their DDos attacks, the counterargument then is that the DDoS is not itself necessary as a means of communication.

[123] *R v Jeffery*, unreported, Southwark Crown Court, 13 April 2012. S Malik, 'BPAS hacker jailed for 32 months' *The Guardian* (London, 13 April 2012) <http://www.theguardian.com/world/2012/apr/13/bpas-hacker-james-jeffery-jailed>.

'The defendants were actually rather arrogant. They thought they were far too clever to be caught and used various methods to try to cloak and preserve their anonymity. It seems to me that the police were a little bit more clever than the conspirators.'[124]

13.3.1 **Section 3ZA**

Section 3ZA is a newly added provision of the Act, added by s. 41 of the Serious Crime Act 2015. It came into effect on May 3 2015 and is in effect an aggravated form of the s. 3 offence.

Highlight Computer Misuse Act, s. 3ZA

Unauthorised acts causing, or creating risk of, serious damage:

(1) A person is guilty of an offence if—

(a) the person does any unauthorised act in relation to a computer;

(b) at the time of doing the act the person knows that it is unauthorised;

(c) the act causes, or creates a significant risk of, serious damage of a material kind; and

(d) the person intends by doing the act to cause serious damage of a material kind or is reckless as to whether such damage is caused.

(2) Damage is of a 'material kind' for the purposes of this section if it is—

(a) damage to human welfare in any place;

(b) damage to the environment of any place;

(c) damage to the economy of any country; or

(d) damage to the national security of any country.

(3) For the purposes of subsection (2)(a) an act causes damage to human welfare only if it causes—

(a) loss to human life;

(b) human illness or injury;

(c) disruption of a supply of money, food, water, energy or fuel;

(d) disruption of a system of communication;

(e) disruption of facilities for transport; or

(f) disruption of services relating to health.

(4) It is immaterial for the purposes of subsection (2) whether or not an act causing damage—

(a) does so directly;

(b) is the only or main cause of the damage.

[124] *R v Weatherhead, Rhodes, Gibson and Burchall*, unreported, Southwark Crown Court, 24 January 2013. See J Halliday, 'Anonymous Hackers Jailed for Cyber Attacks' *The Guardian* (London, 24 January 2013) <http://www.guardian.co.uk/technology/2013/jan/24/anonymous-hackers-jailed-cyber-attacks>.

There is little explanation from government as to why this was felt necessary given that a prosecution on indictment raised under s. 3 carries a maximum tariff of ten years' imprisonment; the same as the tariff for the aggravated offence under s. 2. It seems this may have been driven by fears over cyber-attacks by terrorist groups driven by fears over Islamic terrorism and groups like the Islamic State. Such risks are though blown quite out of proportion and in any event there are already a number of legal redresses available for dealing with such an attack including s. 3 of the CMA, the Terrorism Acts 2000 and 2006, and common law offences such as murder, criminal damage, or actual or grievous bodily harm. The few indicators given by government give little away. In their fact sheet on the Act, the Home Office states simply that 'hitherto the most serious offence under the Act was the section 3 offence of unauthorised access to impair the operation of a computer. The maximum sentence of 10 years' imprisonment which this offence carried did not sufficiently reflect the level of personal and economic harm that a major cyber attack on critical systems could cause.'[125] The explanatory notes to the Serious Crime Bill are equally unclear: 'The Government's UK Cyber Security Strategy included a commitment to "review existing legislation, for example the 1990 Act, to ensure that it remains relevant and effective". Following that review, this Part introduces a new offence in respect of unauthorized acts in relation to computers causing serious damage.'[126]

It seems unlikely s. 3ZA will be used often, if at all. In fact in their impact assessment the Home Office acknowledges that 'we assume there will be one case every other year (high estimate); one case every two or three years (best estimate); or no cases in a ten year period (low estimate)'.[127] What we can say is that the *actus reus* requirement is that the accused undertakes an unauthorized act in relation to a computer and that act causes, or creates a significant risk of causing, serious damage of a material kind. The *mens rea* requirement is that the accused, at the time of committing the act, knows that it is unauthorized and intends the act to cause serious damage of a material kind or is reckless as to whether such damage is caused. The term 'material kind' is as defined in s. 3ZA(2). The new offence is triable by indictment only and the maximum penalty, as set out in s. 3 ZA(6) is fourteen years' imprisonment. However, should the defendant's act cause loss of life, injury or illness, or cause serious damage to national security the maximum penalty under s. 3ZA(7) is life imprisonment.

One intriguing question surrounding s. 3ZA is its application to the security services. Laurence Eastham, the editor of the *Society for* Computers & Law magazine notes that the offence may be committed by causing damage to the economy of any country or damage to the national security of any country.[128] This would presumably include countries such as North Korea, Russia, and Syria. Could the offence cover the activities of GCHQ or the SIS? Interestingly there appears to be no specific exemption for members of the UK Security Services, although they would no doubt be able to rely upon the

[125] Home Office, Serious Crime Act 2015, Fact sheet: Part 2: Computer misuse, March 2015 <http://www.gov.uk/government/uploads/system/uploads/attachment_data/file/415953/Factsheet_-_Computer_Misuse_-_Act.pdf>.

[126] Serious Crime Bill, Explanatory Notes: <http://www.publications.parliament.uk/pa/bills/cbill/2014–2015/0116/en/15116en.htm>.

[127] <http://www.parliament.uk/documents/impact-assessments/IA14–21B.pdf>.

[128] <http://www.scl.org/site.aspx?i=ne37488>.

general saving provisions for law enforcement officers found in s. 10 CMA and the provisions of the Regulation of Investigatory Powers Act 2000 to authorize their activities.

13.3.2 **Section 3A**

Section 3A was introduced by s. 38 of the Police and Justice Act 2006, and recently amended by the Serious Crime Act 2015.

Highlight Computer Misuse Act, s. 3A

(1) A person is guilty of an offence if he makes, adapts, supplies or offers to supply any article intending it to be used to commit, or to assist in the commission of, an offence under section 1, 3 or 3ZA.

(2) A person is guilty of an offence if he supplies or offers to supply any article believing that it is likely to be used to commit, or to assist in the commission of, an offence under section 1, 3 or 3ZA.

(3) A person is guilty of an offence if he obtains any article

(a) intending to use it to commit, or to assist in the commission of, an offence under section 1, 3 or 3ZA, or

(b) with a view to its being supplied for use to commit, or to assist in the commission of, an offence under section 1, 3 or 3ZA.

(4) In this section 'article' includes any program or data held in electronic form.

Section 3A, like the changes to s. 3, was introduced to meet the UK's international commitments under the Cybercrime Convention. Article 6 requires signatory states to criminalize the production and distribution of devices designed to circumvent security protection or to facilitate in attacks on computers and computer systems. The aim of Art. 6, and therefore s. 3A, is to criminalize so-called 'hacking tools'. These are software tools which make it easier to infiltrate computer networks or to design and build viruses, Trojans, and other malware. This seems like a pretty straightforward issue but it has in fact proven to be extremely controversial.

When APIG reviewed the CMA in 2004 they recommended that the UK use an opt-out in Art. 6 not to implement it in full.[129] The reason for this recommendation was that 'such offences would result in significant difficulties because almost all these tools are "dual use" and are widely employed by security professionals and system administrators'.[130] These concerns led the House of Lords Committee on Science and Technology to note that s. 3A left 'security researchers . . . at risk of being criminalised because of the recent amendment to the Computer Misuse Act'.[131] The government replied that

[129] All Party Internet Group (n. 65) [82].

[130] Ibid. [80].

[131] The Government Reply to the Fifth Report from the House of Lords Science and Technology Committee, Session 2006–07 HL Paper 165, 3.

this was not the case as 'those in the legitimate IT security sector, who make, adapt and supply tools as part of their daily work should have confidence that the new offence will be used appropriately and be assured that their practices and procedures fall within the law'.[132] The government stated that the security industry would be protected in CPS guidelines to be issued when the new law came into force. This guidance was duly published on the CPS website.[133] It states that the following factors, among others, should be taken into account by prosecutors when considering a prosecution under s. 3A CMA:

> Section 3A(2) CMA covers the supplying or offering to supply an article 'likely' to be used to commit, or assist in the commission of an offence contrary to section 1 or 3 CMA. 'Likely' is not defined in CMA but, in construing what is 'likely', prosecutors should look at the functionality of the article and at what, if any, thought the suspect gave to who would use it; whether for example the article was circulated to a closed and vetted list of IT security professionals or was posted openly.
>
> In determining the likelihood of an article being used (or misused) to commit a criminal offence, prosecutors should consider the following:
>
> - Has the article been developed primarily, deliberately and for the sole purpose of committing a CMA offence (i.e. unauthorised access to computer material)?
> - Is the article available on a wide scale commercial basis and sold through legitimate channels?
> - Is the article widely used for legitimate purposes?
> - Does it have a substantial installation base?
> - What was the context in which the article was used to commit the offence compared with its original intended purpose?

This guidance appears to do little to protect IT security professionals. One specialist website for such professionals notes that 'sadly the CPS guidance, far from clarifying the matter, at first sight seems likely to increase the confusion. It offers examples where there is little or no ambiguity. But it apparently fails to address the hugely important grey area of security testing tools that by definition can also be exploited maliciously.'[134]

As many experts predicted at the time s. 3A has been little relied upon. It seems there have only been three convictions achieved in the eight years s. 3A has been in effect; these are *R v Paul McLoughlin* (Southwark Crown Court, 13 May 2011);[135] *R v Glenn Mangham* (Southwark Crown Court, 17 February 2012);[136] and *R v Lewys Stephen Martin*.[137] None of the three involved could be mistaken for computer security professionals and all were involved in extended computer misuse activities. It seems that s. 3A will be of limited use and will only be used alongside charges under ss. 1–3.

[132] Ibid. 3.

[133] At <http://www.cps.gov.uk/legal/a_to_c/computer_misuse_act_1990/index.html>.

[134] The H-Security, *UK Crown Prosecution Service Publishes Computer Misuse Act Guidance* <http://www.h-online.com/security/news/item/UK-Crown-Prosecution-Service-publishes-Computer-Misuse-Act-guidance-735749.html>.

[135] <http://www.theregister.co.uk/2011/05/18/gaming_trojan_conviction/>.

[136] <http://www.bbc.co.uk/news/uk-england-york-north-yorkshire-17079853>.

[137] [2013] EWCA Crim 1420.

13.4 Conclusions

There is little doubt of the value and need for the Computer Misuse Act 1990. It is a vital tool in the armoury of the police and the CPS. Without the CMA there would be no simple way of prosecuting those who illegally gain access to computer networks and systems, perhaps with a view to committing further offences or doing harm. However, the utility of the Act has been somewhat undermined by amendments and alterations over the years. While the Act as passed in 1990 has been robust enough to withstand the challenge of dealing with insider (employee) attacks and the *Bignall* defence, malicious attackers such as the Mad Hacker and even the challenge of extradition and the long-running *MacKinnon* case, the need for s. 3A is understandable, and provides compliance with the Convention on Cybercrime. The rather vague wording of the section and the CPS guidelines, however, mean that it is rarely prosecuted and is arguably unnecessary, given that in two of the three cases charged so far under s. 3A the defendant was also charged with offences under s. 1 or s. 3. Its direct utility it seems has been restricted to one case in eight years. It is equally difficult to imagine a raft of cases under s. 3ZA, which seems to be beyond all else a grandstanding move by the government. Even the impact assessment notes a possibility of no cases in ten years being brought under s. 3ZA. If and when cases are brought it seems beyond doubt that s. 3ZA will be part of a portfolio of charges brought against anyone accused. The need to add a new criminal offence onto the statute books to deal with what would appear to be covered elsewhere in the criminal law seems questionable at best.

TEST QUESTIONS

Question 1

The actions of Anonymous are illegal and clearly in breach of s. 3 of the Computer Misuse Act 1990 (and Art. 5 of the Convention on Cybercrime). There is no defence or justification for their actions. They should be arrested and prosecuted as a matter of urgency.

Discuss.

Question 2

Should Gary McKinnon have been tried in the UK under the Computer Misuse Act?

FURTHER READING

Books

O von Busch and K. Palmås, *Abstract Hacktivism* (2006)

H Cornwall, *The Hacker's Handbook* (1995)

J Erickson, *Hacking: the Art of Exploitation* (2003)

S Fafinski, *Computer Misuse: Response Regulation and the Law* (2009)

Chapters and articles

Z Hamin, 'Insider Cyber-threats: Problems and Perspectives', 14 *IRLCT* 105 (2000)

A Karanasiou, 'The Changing Face of Protests in the Digital Age: On Occupying Cyberspace and Distributed-Denial-Of-Service (DDoS) Attacks', 28 *IRLCT* 98 (2014)

M Klang, 'Civil Disobedience Online', 2 *Journal of Information, Communication & Ethics in Society* 2 (2008)

A Nehaluddin, 'Hackers' Criminal Behaviour and Laws Related to Hacking', *Computer and Telecommunications Law Review* 159 (2009)

M Wasik, 'Computer Misuse and Misconduct in Public Office', 22 *IRLCT* 135 (2008)

14

Pornography and obscenity in the information society

The human obsession with pornography and obscenity is as old as society itself.[1] Erotic imagery is common in all cultures and societies including ancient Rome[2] and Greece,[3] to the India,[4] China, and Japan[5] of the Middle Ages and the early modern period up to the present day. In common with this cultural obsession one of the first roles played by any new technology has been to improve and streamline the distribution and production of erotica and pornography. As soon as humans divined how to make cave paintings they produced erotic images. With the process of industrialization, more efficient methods of producing images and text were developed and at every development erotica and pornography seemed to lead the way. Early photography produced the first nude and erotic images,[6] leading to the development and sale of the infamous 'French Postcards' of the latter part of the nineteenth century. Then the moving image began to take over from the still image. Again, erotica and pornography was at the forefront of developments with the introduction of 'stag' films such as *Red Headed Riot* and burlesque films such as *Peeping Tom's Paradise*.

Through the first half of the twentieth century the main outlets for pornography remained these film rolls and still photographs. Then in the 1940s photo magazines began to be produced culminating in the launch of *Playboy* in 1953. Basically, the technology behind pornography remained unchanged until the development of home video cassettes. This allowed people to watch pornographic films in the comfort of their own homes for the first time without needing specialist equipment. In the 1970s it was the porn industry in America that is widely credited with the eventual success

[1] Erotic cave paintings found across Europe which are estimated to be up to 40,000 years old depict highly realistic drawings of sexual activity including recreational (i.e. non-reproductive) sexual activity.

[2] A number of erotic frescoes have been discovered preserved in Herculaneum and Pompeii.

[3] Erotic images are often found on Greek vases, and Greek plays and texts often contain erotic themes.

[4] Most famously recorded in the *Kama Sutra*.

[5] China and Japan shared an erotic art tradition known as Shunga. It can be traced back to fourteenth-century China but has its peak in Japan in the seventeenth to nineteenth centuries.

[6] In *Nude Photography, 1840–1920*, Peter Marshall notes: 'In the prevailing moral climate at the time of the invention of photography, the only officially sanctioned photography of the body was for the production of artist's studies. Many of the surviving examples of daguerreotypes are clearly not in this genre but have a sensuality that clearly implies they were designed as erotic or pornographic images': <http://web.archive.org/web/20070218141330/http://photography.about.com/library/weekly/aa013100a.htm>.

of the VHS video format over rival Betamax,[7] although it should be noted that other factors contributed to VHS's eventual success. The home VCR began a 'golden age of porn' where the industry grew to a massive size.[8] The adult content industry continues to embrace new technologies, making greater use of DVD technology than Hollywood through a series of 'interactive' DVDs[9] and moving to HD at an early stage of its development. It is no surprise therefore that the internet with its unique ability to host and distribute text, video, audio, and image has proven to be an attractive home for modern producers and distributors of pornography. When the accessibility and reach of the internet is paired with the economic benefits of convergence for the producers of pornographic content (HD video cameras are now available on mobile phones for free if the user signs a carrier contract, while high-quality HD-Camcorders are on sale for less than £90) it is no surprise that there has been an explosion of the availability of pornographic and obscene images: the question is how does the law deal with this?

14.1 **Obscenity**

As erotica started to give way to pornography and obscenity the law became involved in the control of pornographic goods. The law intervenes in several ways. First, it draws a line between types of erotica: erotic content (such as erotic art or literature—this is material produced around a sexual theme but not produced wholly or principally for the purpose of sexual arousal); pornographic content (this is material produced solely or principally for the purpose of sexual arousal);[10] obscene material (this is material likely to deprave and corrupt persons);[11] and extreme content (this includes child-abuse images and violent or extremely obscene content). The law then intervenes to determine how each class of erotic, pornographic, or obscene content is to be controlled.

Erotic material may, in general, be sold and distributed freely and usually with few controls.[12] Bookshops often have an erotic literature section and there is no law which prevents a bookseller from selling a 15-year-old a copy of *Fanny Hill* or *Tropic of Cancer* (although many booksellers may voluntarily refuse to sell such titles to minors). By comparison, pornographic content is more closely regulated. It is content which it is legal to sell and distribute but usually within closely restricted channels. For example, material rated as R18 (or restricted 18) by the British Board of Film Classification may only be shown to adults in specially licensed cinemas, and videos/DVDs may only be supplied to adults in licensed sex shops and not by mail order.[13] By comparison, obscene content may not legally be imported, published, or supplied in the UK[14] although it

[7] P Johnson, 'Pornography Drives Technology: Why Not to Censor the Internet' (1996) 49 *Federal Communications Law Journal* 217.

[8] L Glass 'Second Wave: Feminism and Porn's Golden Age' *Radical Society* October 2002.

[9] D Kennedy 'The fantasy of interactive porn becomes a reality' *New York Times* (New York, 17 August 2003) <http://www.nytimes.com/2003/08/17/movies/17KENN.html>.

[10] This definition is taken from s. 63(3) of the Criminal Justice and Immigration Act 2008.

[11] This definition is taken from s. 1(1) of the Obscene Publications Act 1959. It should be noted this is not restricted to sexually obscene material. This definition would also include violent material such as snuff movies and other such content.

[12] Although, as we shall see below, this was not always the case.

[13] Video Recordings Act 1984, s. 12.

[14] Obscene Publications Act 1959, s. 2; Customs Consolidation Act 1876, s. 42.

may be legally possessed provided there is no intent to publish, whereas extreme content may not be imported, supplied, published, or possessed.[15]

14.1.1 The *Hicklin* principle

The way the law has traditionally dealt with pornography and obscenity is illuminating. The UK common law standard is known as the 'Hicklin principle' after the case of *R v Hicklin*.[16] Here Lord Cockburn CJ famously stated that the test was whether there is a tendency 'to deprave and corrupt those whose minds are open to . . . immoral influences, and into whose hands a publication of this sort may fall'.[17] According to *Hicklin* the essence of corruption is the suggestion of impure thoughts. Moreover publications likely to have this effect on young or other vulnerable people are to be ruled obscene regardless of the literary or artistic merits of the work.

The *Hicklin* principle was voraciously applied and led to works such as *Lady Chatterley's Lover*, *The Well of Loneliness*, and *Tropic of Cancer* being banned from publication in the UK. This did not prevent publication of these books in English elsewhere (both *Lady Chatterley* and *Tropic of Cancer* were published in Paris) but to import such editions was in itself an offence under s. 42 of the Customs Consolidation Act 1876. The dual effect of banning the publication of obscene material in the UK and banning the importation of obscene material from outside the UK allowed the state to control quite strictly the availability of obscene content. Prior to 1959 little distinction was drawn between erotic, pornographic, and obscene content with almost all sexually explicit content likely to be classified as obscene under the *Hicklin* standard. But that year the obscenity laws were relaxed slightly. Following recommendations from a House of Commons Select Committee the Obscene Publications Act was passed. Although it retained the spirit of the *Hicklin* principle it changed it in one key aspect; s. 1(1) of the Act states an article is deemed to be obscene if:

> its effect or (where the article comprises two or more distinct items) the effect of any one of its items is, if taken as a whole, such as to tend to deprave and corrupt persons who are likely, having regard to all relevant circumstances, to read, see or hear the matter contained or embodied in it.

The key change in the new test is that it asks the jury to consider the effect of the content on persons who are likely to see the content in question (i.e. adults) rather than 'those whose minds are open to immoral influences' i.e. children or other vulnerable groups. Following the entering into force of the 1959 Act, a number of important cases clarified that the new obscenity standard was indeed distinct from indecency (the usual standard of pornographic material) including most famously *R v Penguin Books Ltd*.[18]

[15] Currently in the UK it is illegal to view or possess images of child abuse under s. 160(1) of the Criminal Justice Act 1988, while by s. 45 of the Sexual Offences Act 2003 a child is defined as anyone under 18 years of age. Moreover, it is illegal to possess 'extreme pornography' under s. 63 of the Criminal Justice and Immigration Act 2008 (as amended) and 'non-photographic pornographic images of children' under s. 62 of the Coroners and Justice Act 2009.

[16] (1868) LR 3, QB 360.

[17] Ibid. 371.

[18] [1961] Crim LR 176.

14.1.2 **The Obscene Publications Acts**

The law on obscenity has remained mostly unchanged since 1959, the only amendments being the addition of a number of extreme obscenity offences which criminalize possession, rather than the importation, sale, or possession with intent to supply materials, and the new offence of publishing so-called 'revenge porn'.[19] To control the supply of pornography, and to restrict the supply of obscene content the UK law enforcement authorities continued to rely on a mixture of border controls and supply controls. By restricting the availability of pornographic content to licensed sex shops the authorities could oversee the type of content that was being made available to ensure it did not breach the Obscene Publications Act; additionally it meant that pornography produced in the UK for the most part met community standards. Further, by strictly enforcing border controls the authorities could restrict the supply of unclassified (and often obscene) materials.[20]

The arrival of the internet changed the nature of the distribution model for all forms of content including pornographic content. Like other entertainment products including music, film, and video games much so-called 'adult entertainment' is now produced and distributed in a disintermediated digital format. Although there remains a market for physical product distribution in the form of DVDs, the demand for purely digital distribution of adult content has, like music and mainstream film and TV, increased exponentially in the last ten years and has particularly increased with the availability of high speed ADSL, LTE (4G) and fibre connections and the development of video streaming technology. This has left our border authority quite impotent for, as predicted by David Post and David Johnson in 1996, the borderless nature of the internet undermines effective border controls.[21]

This loss of ability to police our borders adequately has by turn rendered the Obscene Publications Act impotent. For while the Obscene Publications Act remains enforceable its focus on the supply or possession with intent to supply obscene material within the UK is undermined by the fact that the vast majority of indecent and obscene material to be found online is hosted overseas. This is why it is not surprising to find that, despite surveys which show that 56 per cent of UK adults watch online pornography occasionally or regularly while 34 per cent of children are believed by their parents to have so done,[22] there have been no prosecutions in England and Wales under either the Customs Consolidation Act or the Obscene Publications Act 1959 for privately viewing obscene material using an internet connection. The authorities have instead focused their meagre resources on extremely obscene material and UK distributors of obscene material with, to date, nearly all prosecutions for internet obscenity centring on the

[19] These will be discussed in full below. Further it should be noted that as obscenity is tested on the so-called community standard the classification of obscene materials has weakened over the years. In 2004 for the first time a movie which portrays actual sex between actors was given an '18' certificate. The movie *9 Songs* attracted little public outcry, a considerable change from the controversy surrounding *Women in Love* which in 1969 portrayed male full frontal nudity for the first time or *Last Tango in Paris* which in 1972 had portrayed anal sex on screen.

[20] The courts would tend to apply the provisions of the Obscene Publications Act strictly when dealing with material seized at the border. See, e.g. *R v Uxbridge Justices, ex parte David Webb* [1994] 2 CMLR 288.

[21] 'Law and Borders—The Rise of Law in Cyberspace' (1996) 48 *Stanford Law Review* 1367.

[22] J Mann, 'British Sex Survey 2014' *The Observer* (London, 28 September 2014) <http://www.theguardian.com/lifeandstyle/2014/sep/28/british-sex-survey-2014-nation-lost-sexual-swagger>.

storing and distribution of child-abuse images[23] or extremely pornographic images,[24] the prosecution of those who disclose private sexual photographs (the legal definition of revenge porn),[25] or the prosecution of those who run pornographic websites from overseas servers but who are resident in the UK and profit from this activity.[26]

With the removal of the physical border between the UK and the rest of the world internet users were afforded the opportunity to access and view pornography held overseas in the blink of eye and with little opportunity for the authorities to intercept the content en route. This caused a huge upsurge in consumption and left the authorities with a difficult decision to make. They could either invest large sums to attempt to enforce the law in the digital environment,[27] or they could de facto deregulate adult pornography and focus their attentions on more pressing problems such as child pornography and extreme content. The UK authorities recognizing the limits of the law in relation to this subject chose to focus their resources on only the most harmful content.

14.2 **Pornography**

The dividing line between indecent content and obscene content is a vital one. Although pornographic content may be either indecent or obscene it is only obscene content which may not be published, supplied, or imported: in other words one may legally trade in indecent content, provided all necessary regulations are complied with, but one cannot legally trade in obscene content.

14.2.1 **The UK standard**

As already discussed, the dividing line between indecency and obscenity is defined by a community standard. Since 1959 that standard has been to determine whether the content in question will tend to deprave and corrupt persons who are likely to read, see, or hear the content. This line is not fixed and will vary with changes in society. In 1961 the focus of the test was on literary works such as *Lady Chatterley's Lover* when famously counsel for the prosecution Mervyn Griffith-Jones asked if it were the kind of book 'you would wish your wife or servants to read'. The jury on that occasion found Penguin Books not guilty of a breach of s. 1 of the Obscene Publications Act 1959, but today the very concept that a publisher may be tried for obscenity for publishing a book of the nature of *Lady Chatterley's Lover* seems nonsensical: society has moved on. Even the publication of Bret Easton Ellis's 1991 novel *American Psycho* with its graphic

[23] See *R v Barry Philip Halloren* [2004] 2 Cr App R (S) 57; *R v Snellman* [2001] EWCA Crim 1530 and *R v James* [2000] 2 Cr App R (S) 258.

[24] See *R v Burns (Robert)* [2012] EWCA Crim 192; *R v PW* [2012] EWCA Crim 1653.

[25] Crown Prosecution Service, *Prosecutors continue to tackle revenge porn across the country*, 13 August 2015 <http://www.cps.gov.uk/news/latest_news/prosecutors_continue_to_tackle_revenge_porn_across_the_country/>.

[26] See *R v Ross Andrew McKinnon* [2004] 2 Cr App R (S) 46 and *R v Stephane Laurent Perrin* [2002] EWCA Crim 747.

[27] This could either be achieved by the investment of these funds into additional law enforcement personnel or by using the funds to design a technological solution to the problem such as a national firewall or filtering system which would in effect rebuild the natural border in cyberspace. For an excellent discussion of this subject see R Deibert et al., (eds.), *Access Denied: The Practice and Policy of Global Internet Filtering* (MIT Press 2008).

descriptions of sexual abuse, torture, and murder did not cause the UK authorities to consider a prosecution under the Obscene Publications Act; although the novel was subject to restrictions in other parts of the world.[28]

Similarly standards in mainstream films have moved on considerably. In 1969 a film adaptation of DH Lawrence's *Women in Love* sparked a great deal of controversy when the British Board of Film Censors (later to become the British Board of Film Classification) passed it for cinema display. The film contained the first full frontal male nude scene as Oliver Reed and Alan Bates wrestled naked. A few years later a great deal of controversy (although no prosecutions for obscenity) dogged films like *A Clockwork Orange*, *Straw Dogs*, and *Last Tango in Paris*. Today mainstream movies frequently portray sex and often sex and violence are mixed in so-called 'torture porn' movies such as *Hostel*. Despite some controversy there is little call for these movies to be banned. Also, the way sex is portrayed in mainstream movies shows how community values have changed. It had always been assumed that the portrayal of the erect male member would automatically rule a film unclassifiable as certificate 18 but that changed in 1999 when Catherine Breillat's movie *Romance* became the first movie to display an erect penis to be passed for cinema display. Since then several movies which portray actual sexual intercourse between actors have been passed for display including Mike Winterbottom's *9 Songs* which in 2004 became the first film certified 18 to show full sexual intercourse including ejaculation.

This change in community values also led to the creation of the R18 certificate in 1982 for adult movies which may be supplied through licensed sex shops and displayed in licensed 'adult only' cinemas. The number of R18 titles has increased dramatically since 2000 when Mr Justice Hooper upheld a decision of the Video Appeals Committee of the British Board of Film Classification that R18 certificates should not be withheld to adult entertainment products on the basis that they had the potential to cause harm to children.[29] Hooper J (in a finding not dissimilar in effect to the move from the *Hicklin* standard to the new Obscene Publications Act standard in 1959) held that 'the risk of [the videos in question] being viewed by and causing harm to children or young persons is, on present evidence, insignificant'.[30]

The most dramatic case to date though on developing community attitudes is *R v Peacock*.[31] Michael Peacock is a distributer of hardcore gay pornography. Some of the DVDs he distributed included films which featured extreme sexual acts between men, such as BDSM (including whipping, staged kidnapping, and rape play), fisting, and urolagnia. The jury found Peacock not guilty of an offence under the Obscene Publications Act, deciding that the scenes depicted in the DVDs were unable to deprave or corrupt any viewer watching them. Defence solicitor Nigel Richardson later told the press that the jury had recognized that the pornography found in the DVDs would

[28] In Germany, the book was deemed harmful to minors, and its sales and marketing were severely restricted from 1995 to 2000. In Australia, the book is sold shrink-wrapped and is classified R18. The book may not be sold to those under 18. Along with other Category 1 publications, its sale is theoretically banned in the state of Queensland. In New Zealand, the Government's Office of Film and Literature Classification has rated the book as R18. The book may not be sold or lent in libraries to those under 18.

[29] *R v Video Appeals Committee of British Board of Film Classification, ex parte British Board of Film Classification* [2000] EWHC Admin 341.

[30] Ibid. [47].

[31] Unreported, Southwark Crown Court, 6 January 2012.

only be seen by 'gay men specifically asking for this type of material' and not by the general public.[32]

It is clear that the UK has become a considerably more permissive society in relation to indecency and obscenity in the fifty years that the Obscene Publications Act has been in force. The problem with internet pornography is that the UK legal definition of the community standard is in danger of being overtaken by external community values. This is arguably what happened in *Peacock*. While UK community standards have moved on considerably the law in the UK is still strict in its application of both indecency regulations (such as the R18 standard) and obscenity laws. Despite the *Peacock* decision, which as a jury decision does not set a precedent;[33] so-called 'hardcore' pornography may only legally be supplied by licensed sex shops and only strictly to those over the age of 18 and never by mail order. 'Soft' pornography is more widely available with newsagents permitted to sell so-called 'top shelf' magazines, again though only legally to those over 18. The internet is, however, at least in relation to pornography, a case study in cyberlibertarianism.[34]

As we saw in chapter 4 the cyberlibertarian ethos that traditional lawmakers could not enforce their laws against citizens of cyberspace due to the nature of cyberspace as a unique and separate jurisdiction has been widely debunked by the cyberpaternalist school which demonstrated that control of content and the actions of persons could be effected in cyberspace through code (or design-based) controls. But to effect such controls requires a degree of cooperation among lawmakers. In some areas cooperation has been forthcoming, as with regulation of the domain name system discussed in chapter 16 or in relation to hacking and other computer misuse offences discussed in chapter 13, but with pornography and in particular the dividing line between indecency and obscenity there is a problem.

As we have seen the line between indecency and obscenity is a community standard and the internet plays host to individuals from many social backgrounds in one place. Lawmakers across the globe cannot agree a common standard: what is considered sexually explicit but not obscene in England may well be considered to be obscene in the Republic of Ireland, and almost certainly material considered obscene in the Islamic Republic of Iran or in the Kingdom of Saudi Arabia would not be felt to be noteworthy in England. Similarly material which would be considered to be obscene in England would probably not be censored in Germany, Spain, or Sweden where a more tolerant approach to erotica and pornographic material is taken. What we are seeing in these differences is a spectrum of obscenity which ranges from extremely conservative to extremely liberal, and upon which individual states position themselves. In general, this system has functioned quite effectively in the real world due to the existence of physical borders and border controls. These traditional measures are predicated though upon the assumption that the items in question will be fixed in a physical medium, and that they will require physical carriage to enter the state. With the advent of the digital age both of these assumptions have been rendered null. The development of a global informational network has dismantled traditional borders: a point which was

[32] 'Not guilty verdict in DVD obscenity trial' (*BBC News*, 6 January 2012) <http://www.bbc.co.uk/news/uk-16443697>.

[33] Despite it having no binding legal effect it arguably does show how internet content has dramatically moved community values.

[34] See ch. 4, 'Can we regulate the digital environment?' at 4.1.

so eloquently made by David Post and David Johnson in their seminal paper 'Law and Borders—The Rise of Law in Cyberspace'.[35]

> Cyberspace has no territorially-based boundaries, because the cost and speed of message transmission on the Net is almost entirely independent of physical location: Messages can be transmitted from any physical location to any other location without degradation, decay, or substantial delay, and without any physical cues or barriers that might otherwise keep certain geographically remote places and people separate from one another. The Net enables transactions between people who do not know, and in many cases cannot know, the physical location of the other party. Location remains vitally important, but only location within a *virtual* space consisting of the 'addresses' of the machines between which messages and information are routed.[36]
>
> The Net thus radically subverts a system of rule-making based on borders between physical spaces, at least with respect to the claim that Cyberspace should naturally be governed by territorially defined rules.[37]

Thus the traditional concept of border controls is undermined in the digital environment, making it very difficult for individual states to enforce and protect their community standard in the face of competing community standards found elsewhere. This can be demonstrated with an example.

Example Access

Richard is a UK resident who accesses and downloads pornographic images held on a server based in Germany. The image is in compliance with the German community standard but arguably is in breach of the UK community standard.

To consider a prosecution against Richard the UK prosecuting authorities would first have to identify that the item is obscene by applying the UK community standard, a task now further complicated by *Peacock*.[38] If the image was found to be 'obscene' under the UK community standard they would next have to prove that either Richard imported the item in breach of s. 42 of the Customs Consolidation Act 1876, or that he possessed the item with intent to publish in breach of s. 2 of the Obscene Publications Act 1959. Neither of these claims would necessarily succeed. The second claim would only succeed in relation to members of communities which trade or share images or files: for individuals who merely access and view pornographic websites there would be no intent to publish or distribute further, and therefore no offence under the Obscene Publications Act. The former claim is one mired in extreme complexity. Whereas identification of an importer was relatively straightforward when dealing with physical goods, it becomes much more complex in relation to digital information. The question is: does the consumer import the image into the UK, or is the image imported into the

[35] See (n. 21).

[36] Ibid. 1370–1.

[37] Ibid. 1370.

[38] If they could not establish the item to be in breach of s. 1 of the Obscene Publications Act, then he would be entitled to view the item under Art. 28 of the Treaty on the Functioning of the European Union. See *Conegate Ltd v HM Customs & Excise* [1987] QB 254 (ECJ); *R v Forbes* [2002] 2 AC 512 (HL).

UK by the supplier, or even their ISP, who then makes it available to the consumer? The answer may at first seem straightforward: if Richard downloads an obscene image from a German website then he should be deemed to be the importer. But what if the website appears to be from the UK? Perhaps the supplier is using a UK-based domain name like www.gbporn.co.uk,[39] and seems to be implying they are based in the UK. In such circumstances does Richard exhibit sufficient intent and knowledge to be classed as an importer? As UK border controls are nullified the consumption of pornography is de facto deregulated meaning that the point of control over pornographic content is at its point of supply: as very little online pornographic content is hosted in the UK this means that we are reliant upon the community standards found elsewhere.

14.2.2 **A global standard?**

Pornography is hosted on web servers sited across the globe; there is no one community standard that prevails, but one community has greater impact than any other. Although there are no completely reliable statistics detailing where most pornographic websites are hosted it is clear that the US hosts substantially more sexually explicit web pages than any other state with one survey suggesting it hosts around 60 per cent of all adult web pages. The same survey reveals that only around 7 per cent of global adult content is hosted in the UK.[40] Together these two statistics suggest that in effect much of the pornography available in the UK has met the US community standard rather than the UK standard.[41]

The US is in many ways a unique marketplace for the production and distribution of pornography due to the effects of the First Amendment. Whereas UK citizens are willing to accept that free expression does not mean limitless freedom to say or do whatever one wishes, US citizens strongly support their First Amendment right to enjoy freedom of speech, even where that right strays into the potentially destructive areas of pornography and hate speech. The question of whether it is appropriate to apply the First Amendment to pornographic content has long vexed US scholars and judges. Some scholars have argued that there can never be a true marketplace of speech in relation to pornographic imagery because there is no real freedom of speech for women in a country in which women are relegated to the particular gender roles that society gives them,[42] others, though, argue that pornographic magazines 'consciously attempt to express a view of social and sexual life'.[43] Whatever position one holds on the validity of First Amendment protection for pornographic imagery the law is quite clear: material of a sexual nature will be protected by the First Amendment unless that material is determined by the court to be obscene.[44] The current US standard of obscenity was set

[39] At the time of writing no site or registration existed in relation to this address.

[40] D Holmes, 'Infographic: What Countries Host the Most Porn?' (*Pando*, 13 August 2013) <https://pando.com/2013/08/05/infographic-what-countries-host-the-most-porn/>.

[41] In fact it's the California community standard as the same survey reveals that 66 per cent of US-hosted adult content is hosted in the State of California.

[42] This is known as the MacKinnon/Dworkin debate and is found most clearly in the work of Catherine MacKinnon and Andrea Dworkin. See C MacKinnon, *Feminism Unmodified: Discourses on Life and Law* (Harvard University Press 1987) 127–213; A Dworkin, 'Against the Male Flood: Censorship, Pornography, and Equality' (1985) 8 *Harvard Women's Law Journal* 1.

[43] W Brigman, 'Pornography as Political Expression' (1983) 17 *Journal of Popular Culture* 129. See also A Dershowitz, 'Op-Ed' *New York Times* (New York, 9 February 1979).

[44] *Roth v US*, 354 US 476 (1957).

out in the landmark case of *Miller v California*,[45] wherein the Supreme Court established a three-part test for obscenity.

Highlight The *Miller* standard

To be obscene, a judge and/or a jury must determine:

(1) That the average person, applying contemporary community standards, would find that the work, taken as a whole, appeals to the prurient interest; *and*

(2) That the work depicts or describes in a patently offensive way, as measured by contemporary community standards, sexual conduct specifically defined by the applicable law; *and*

(3) That a reasonable person would find that the work, taken as a whole, lacks serious literary, artistic, political, or scientific value.

Chief Justice Burger went on to make clear that 'Under the holdings announced today, no one will be subject to prosecution for the sale or exposure of obscene materials unless these materials depict or describe patently offensive "hard core" sexual conduct specifically defined by the regulating state law, as written or construed.'[46] Although at the time it was felt that such a widely drawn standard would lead to wide local differences in obscenity laws this did not turn out to be the case. The scope of community standards was narrowed the next year in *Jenkins v Georgia*,[47] when the court found that the film *Carnal Knowledge* could not be found to be patently offensive to the local community. Later, further guidance would come in the case of *Pope v Illinois*,[48] which found that the test for literary, artistic, political, or scientific value, had to be based upon national, not local, standards.

Cyberspace not only removed the barriers between states, it also broke down barriers between communities. The US's approach to policing obscenity, much like the UK's, was predicated on the existence of a product fixed in a physical medium and sold or displayed through a physical outlet. The digitization of pornography rendered the *Miller* concept of 'contemporary community standards' redundant. In cases where pornographic material was posted onto a publicly accessible bulletin board system (BBS) or website it was more difficult to prosecute using local community standards, as in these cases it was not possible to show knowledge or intent to trade within a particular community. This was demonstrated in cases such as *American Libraries Association et al. v Pataki*[49] and *PSINet v Chapman*,[50] where attempts to apply local community standards had to be carefully handled lest they be found to be in violation of the implicit confines on state power imposed under the US Constitution's Commerce Clause.[51] During the 1990s, the quantity of online publicly available pornographic content grew rapidly

[45] 413 US 15 (1973).
[46] Ibid. 27.
[47] 418 US 153 (1974).
[48] 481 US 497 (1987).
[49] 969 F. Supp. 160 (SDNY 1997).
[50] 63 F. 3d 227 (4th Cir. 2004).
[51] Article I, Section 8, Clause 3 of the US Constitution.

through the development of BBS trading communities, free access websites, and fledgling file-sharing systems.[52] With more pornography becoming freely available, US lawmakers were faced with a new problem: children were able to access all content, including adult content, as quickly and easily as adults, for as noted by Lawrence Lessig 'a kid in cyberspace need not disclose that he is a kid'.[53]

14.2.3 **US statutory interventions**

Faced with a growing problem of children being exposed to online adult content, state and federal lawmakers attempted to take legal control of the online environment. In 1996 two such attempts came to public prominence, and provoked controversy. In the State of New York, Governor George Pataki oversaw the introduction of §235.21(3) to the New York State Penal Code (NYSPC). This made it a crime to disseminate information 'harmful to minors' via a computer system. At the same time the Federal Government introduced the Communications Decency Act 1996 (CDA) as Title V of the Telecommunications Act of 1996. Both measures were felt to be in breach of the First Amendment by free speech advocates and were immediately challenged— §235.21(3) of the NYSPC was challenged by an extensive coalition of groups including the American Library Association, Peacefire, and the American Civil Liberties Union.[54] They contended that the change in the NYSPC was unconstitutional as it unduly burdened free speech in violation of the First Amendment and it unduly burdened interstate commerce in violation of the Commerce Clause. At a summary hearing on 20 June 1997, the plaintiffs succeeded in their claim and were awarded summary judgment. District Judge Loretta Presky noted that:

> The State asserted that only a small percentage of Internet communications are 'harmful to minors' and would fall within the proscriptions of the statute . . . I conclude that the range of Internet communications potentially affected by the Act is far broader than the State suggests. I note that in the past, various communities within the United States have found works including *I Know Why the Caged Bird Sings* by Maya Angelou, *Funhouse* by Dean Koontz, *The Adventures of Huckleberry Finn* by Mark Twain, and *The Color Purple* by Alice Walker to be indecent. Even assuming that the Act applies only to pictures, a number of Internet users take advantage of the medium's capabilities to communicate images to one another and, again, I find that the range of images that might subject the communicator to prosecution (or reasonably cause a communicator to fear prosecution) is far broader than defendants assert. For example, many libraries, museums and academic institutions post art on the Internet that some might conclude was 'harmful to minors'. Famous nude works by Botticelli, Manet, Matisse, Cezanne and others can be found on the Internet. In this regard, I point out that a famous painting by Manet which shows a nude woman having lunch with two fully clothed men was the subject of considerable protest when it first was unveiled in Paris, as many observers believed that it was 'scandalous'. Lesser known artists who post work over the Internet may face an even greater risk of prosecution, because the mantle of respectability that has descended on Manet is not associated with their as yet obscure names . . . Individuals who wish to communicate images that might fall within the Act's proscriptions must thus self-censor or risk prosecution, a Hobson's choice that imposes an unreasonable restriction on interstate commerce.[55]

[52] D Thornburgh and H Lin, *Youth, Pornography, and the Internet* (National Academy Press 2002) ch. 3 <http://www.nap.edu/openbook.php?record_id=10261&page=71>.
[53] L Lessig, *Code and Other Laws of Cyberspace Ver.2.0* (Basic Books 2006) 248.
[54] *American Libraries Association et al. v Pataki*, (n. 49).
[55] Ibid. [91].

This is an extremely important passage of an extremely important decision in relation to the legal control of internet content. In this passage Judge Presky sets out the boundaries within which state legislatures must work if they are to produce a set of legal controls which do not offend against the Commerce Clause, and as we can see, she draws these boundaries narrowly. Although state legislatures retain the power to control the supply of obscene material, a power which the Supreme Court recognized in *Miller v California*,[56] attempts to control the supply of sexually explicit, though not obscene, material are unlikely to be effective given the *Pataki* decision. The problem faced by state legislatures was that they could not sufficiently precisely define the terms of the content they were seeking to control, a problem exacerbated by the lack of a common national standard. What may be deemed to be acceptable in California, may be felt to be unacceptable in Tennessee, and with state laws requiring individuals to self-censor it is almost impossible to imagine how such regulations could not offend against the Commerce Clause. What was clearly needed was a federal response.

The Communications Decency Act was introduced to the Senate on 1 February 1995 by Senators James Exon, a Democrat from Nebraska, and Slade Gorton, a Republican from Washington, in response to the previously discussed fears that internet pornography was on the rise. In March 1995, the Senate Commerce Committee unanimously adopted the Exon/Gorton proposal as an amendment to the in progress Telecommunications Reform Bill. In June 1995, the Senate attached the Exon/Gorton amendment to the Bill by 84 votes to 16. On 1 February 1996, the Bill was passed by both Houses, becoming law on 8 February 1996.

The introduction of the CDA explicitly outlawed intentionally communicating 'by computer in or affecting interstate or foreign commerce, to any person the communicator believes has not attained the age of 18 years, any material that, in context, depicts or describes, in terms patently offensive as measured by contemporary community standards, sexual or excretory activities or organs'.[57] Opponents of the Act argued that 'just as a librarian cannot be expected to determine the age and identity of all patrons accessing a particular book in the library's collection, the provider of online information cannot be expected to police the usage of his or her online offerings. To impose such a requirement would result in reducing the content of online material to only that which is suitable for children.'[58]

A campaign against the Bill began on its introduction and by 1 February 1996 over 115,000 signatures had been collected on a petition against the Act. On 2 February 1996, in response to the adoption of the Act by Congress, thousands of websites turned black for 48 hours as part of the Electronic Frontier Foundation's, 'Turn the Web Black' protest. On 8 February 1996 the EFF launched its blue ribbon 'Free Speech Campaign.' This asked those who ran web pages to display a distinctive blue ribbon logo in support of their campaign against the CDA and almost overnight the blue ribbon logo populated the web. Publicity campaigns such as these were though merely a sideshow to the main

[56] See (n. 45). Chief Justice Burger made this clear by stating: 'This Court has recognized that the States have a legitimate interest in prohibiting dissemination or exhibition of obscene material when the mode of dissemination carries with it a significant danger of offending the sensibilities of unwilling recipients or of exposure to juveniles' (at 16).

[57] §502(2).

[58] D Sobel, 'The Constitutionality of the Communications Decency Act: Censorship on the Internet' (1996) 1 *Journal of Technology Law & Policy* 2.

event. As soon as President Clinton signed the CDA on 8 February, the American Civil Liberties Union and 23 other co-plaintiffs, including the Electronic Privacy Information Center, the Electronic Frontier Foundation, and the Planned Parenthood Federation of America, raised a complaint before the Federal District Court in Philadelphia seeking a temporary restraining order against the implementation of the indecency provisions of the CDA on the grounds that 'the Act is unconstitutional on its face and as applied because it criminalizes expression that is protected by the First Amendment; it is also impermissibly overbroad and vague; and it is not the least restrictive means of accomplishing any compelling governmental purpose'.[59] The complaint was heard by District Judge Ronald Buckwalter, who, on 15 February, granted the plaintiffs an order insofar as the CDA referred to indecent, but not obscene content.[60] With the order in place the plaintiffs then extracted from the Federal Government a stipulation that they would not 'initiate any investigations or prosecutions for violations of 47 USC Sec.223(d) for conduct occurring after enactment of this provision until the three-judge Court hears Plaintiffs' Motion for Preliminary Injunction'.[61] With this safeguard in place to ensure that the CDA would not be enforced while a question mark remained over its constitutionality the plaintiffs prepared a case to be heard before the District Court.

Hearings were quickly arranged and held over six days from 21 March to 10 May.[62] The decision was given on 11 June and all three judges agreed that on the face of it the CDA was unconstitutional. Chief Justice Sloviter reflected the views of the court in noting: 'I have no hesitancy in concluding that it is likely that plaintiffs will prevail on the merits of their argument that the challenged provisions of the CDA are facially invalid under both the First and Fifth Amendments.'[63] The Federal Government, as expected, immediately sought to appeal the decision to the US Supreme Court, and on 6 December 1996 the Supreme Court noted probable jurisdiction and agreed to hear the case on 19 March 1997. The government filed its brief on 21 January; the plaintiffs' briefs were filed on 20 February. Oral argument was heard, as scheduled, on 19 March, following which everyone waited for the court's ruling. The court finally issued its decision on 26 June, and by a 7:2 majority it found in favour of the plaintiffs. The first decision the court had to come to was whether the First Amendment applied in cyberspace. Here Justice Stevens, who gave the majority opinion, was clear:

Highlight The First Amendment of cyberspace

The Internet provides relatively unlimited, low-cost capacity for communication of all kinds. The government estimates that 'as many as 40 million people use the Internet today, and that figure is expected to grow to 200 million by 1999'. This dynamic, multifaceted category of communication includes not only traditional print and news services, but also audio, video, and still

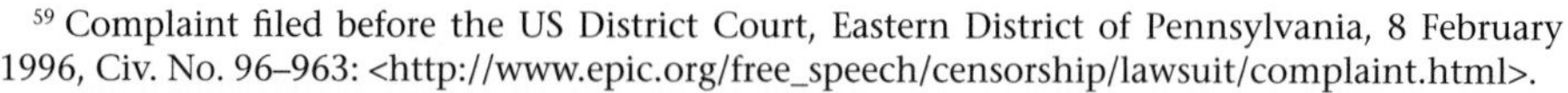

[59] Complaint filed before the US District Court, Eastern District of Pennsylvania, 8 February 1996, Civ. No. 96–963: <http://www.epic.org/free_speech/censorship/lawsuit/complaint.html>.

[60] *ACLU v Reno* 929 F. Supp. 24 (1996).

[61] Stipulation of 23 February 1996: <http://www.epic.org/free_speech/censorship/lawsuit/stipulation.html>.

[62] The plaintiffs' case was heard on 21 and 22 March and 1 April while the government's case was put on 12 and 15 April. Closing arguments were heard on 10 May.

[63] *ACLU v Reno* 929 F. Supp. 824 (1996), 856.

→

images, as well as interactive, real-time dialogue. Through the use of chat rooms, any person with a phone line can become a town crier with a voice that resonates farther than it could from any soapbox. Through the use of Web pages, mail exploders, and newsgroups, the same individual can become a pamphleteer. As the District Court found, 'the content on the Internet is as diverse as human thought'. We agree with its conclusion that our cases provide no basis for qualifying the level of First Amendment scrutiny that should be applied to this medium.

[*Reno v ACLU* 521 US 844 (1997), 862.]

Thus with the prior question of whether First Amendment protection could be applied within cyberspace clearly answered in the affirmative, the court could go on to assess the constitutionality of the CDA. Again, Justice Stevens was clear:

> In order to deny minors access to potentially harmful speech, the CDA effectively suppresses a large amount of speech that adults have a constitutional right to receive and to address to one another. That burden on adult speech is unacceptable if less restrictive alternatives would be at least as effective in achieving the legitimate purpose that the statute was enacted to serve.[64]

The plaintiffs' success was complete. They had won every round and the Supreme Court had, as they hoped, extended First Amendment protection into cyberspace. The effect of this decision cannot be overstated. Not only had the narrow victory ensured that the *Miller/Pope* obscenity standard was to be applied in cyberspace, a much more important victory had been won: the Supreme Court had confirmed that the US Constitution, including the First Amendment protection for indecent but not obscene content, applied to that part of cyberspace over which the US government and courts could exert authority. This meant that two years later when the Clinton administration attempted to resurrect parts of the Communication Decency Act in the Child Online Protection Act 1998 the US Supreme Court again ruled such legislation was unconstitutional.[65]

14.2.4 **The decision heard 'round the world'**

The *Reno* decision had impact not only in the US. As previously established the inability of UK border authorities to prevent the massive influx of digital pornographic content hosted outside the UK means we are reliant on regulation at the point of supply and/or production of pornographic content. As a considerable proportion of that content is produced in and hosted in the US the *Reno* decision had massive impact in the UK. Further, the impact of *Reno* is more far-reaching than may have been initially recognized. On the surface it meant that any producer of pornographic content could use the US as a 'safe haven' for their content as any content hosted on a US-based server

[64] Ibid. 880.

[65] The Child Online Protection Act 1998 attempted a slightly different wording to the CDA by putting more emphasis on knowledge and intent: 'Whoever knowingly and with knowledge of the character of the material, in interstate or foreign commerce by means of the World Wide Web, makes any communication for commercial purposes that is available to any minor and that includes any material that is harmful to minors shall be fined not more than $50,000, imprisoned not more than 6 months, or both.' It was ruled unconstitutional by a 5:4 Supreme Court majority in the case of *Ashcroft v ACLU* 542 US 656 (2004).

would effectively gain First Amendment protection, provided their material was not obscene, applying the *Miller/Pope* standard; a standard which is far more permissive than the UK standard. This suggested if online pornographic content were to be effectively regulated international cooperation would be required as any form of regulation would require the cooperation of enforcement authorities in the US. This though would prove extremely difficult to achieve in the post-*Reno* environment for, as explained by Douglas Vick, 'The *Reno* decision will constrain the international community's efforts to establish a comprehensive body of common rules for regulating Internet content. Under American law, treaties and other international accords are hierarchically inferior to the provisions of the US Constitution. A treaty provision, just like a congressional statute, is unenforceable if it fails to conform with First Amendment law.'[66]

This handicap could clearly be seen in negotiations to draft the Council of Europe, Convention on Cybercrime.[67] The Convention deals with only one 'content-related offence', that being the production or distribution of child-abuse images using a computer system.[68] We know several of the states that took part in the drafting process were keen to include further content-related offences, but that these never made the final text. The reason for this is to be found in the Explanatory Report:[69]

> The committee drafting the Convention discussed the possibility of including other content-related offences, such as the distribution of racist propaganda through computer systems. However, the committee was not in a position to reach consensus on the criminalisation of such conduct. While there was significant support in favour of including this as a criminal offence, some delegations expressed strong concern about including such a provision on freedom of expression grounds.[70]

Although the identity of the delegations in question are not revealed, it is clear that at least one of these would be the US delegation: the US delegation could not, as Douglas Vick had predicted, sign the US government up to any treaty provisions which would conflict with First Amendment protection. With child-abuse images being clearly classed as obscene in US law,[71] Art. 9 could be left in place, but any attempts to extend the Convention into more general content regulation could not be countenanced by the US delegation because of the principle of the First Amendment.

In the twenty years since the *Reno* decision, sexually explicit content on the internet has been effectively deregulated. This has not led, as some predicted, to the internet becoming mired in obscene content and sexually explicit content remains a small proportion of internet content.[72] There remains though the problem of more vulnerable members of society, especially children. One of the reasons R18 videos may only be sold

[66] D Vick, 'The Internet and the First Amendment' (1998) 61 *MLR* 414, 419.

[67] Council of Europe, ETS No. 185, *Convention on Cybercrime*, Budapest, 23 November 2001: <http://conventions.coe.int/Treaty/en/Treaties/Html/185.htm>.

[68] Art. 9.

[69] Council of Europe, ETS No. 185, *Explanatory Report on the Convention on Cybercrime*: <http://conventions.coe.int/Treaty/EN/Reports/Html/185.htm>.

[70] Ibid. [35].

[71] *New York v Ferber* 458 US 747 (1982).

[72] In July 2013 the Ministry of Truth blog attempted to get to the bottom of the question of how much pornographic traffic there was on the internet. Their answer was that '2–3 per cent of global Internet traffic, measured in terms of both individual visits to websites and page views [was pornographic]'. <http://www.ministryoftruth.me.uk/2013/06/24/how-big-is-online-porn/>. For comparison in 2001 *Forbes* estimated that 10 per cent of the US DVD home sales market and 20 per cent of the rental market was adult titles. See D Ackman, 'How Big is Porn?' *Forbes* (New York, 25 May 2001) <http://www.forbes.com/2001/05/25/0524porn.html>.

through licensed sex shops is to prevent children from gaining access to them; but with the internet, hardcore pornographic content may be streamed directly to the laptop, or smartphone, of teenagers or even pre-teens. The focus switches from regulating the supply of pornographic content to the adult population to the protection of minors. There are a variety of techniques used, including parental controls on mobile phones, software tools such as FamilyShield and Windows Live Family Safety, and the use of server side controls such as Sky Broadband Shield and BT Cleanfeed, but the legal system is little involved in these self-regulatory regimes. Instead the law has focused on a small proportion of available online pornographic content: that proportion of content so clearly obscene that in the view of the authorities it must be controlled: this is extreme pornographic material including images of child abuse.

14.3 **Child-abuse images and pseudo-images**

Child-abuse images are the most extreme form of pornographic image and are always obscene no matter which community values apply.[73] There are a number of reasons why child-abuse images are treated differently to adult pornography but prime among them is that to produce a child-abuse image a child must be abused: thus the image is a record (and evidence) of a crime in a way pornographic images are not. This is known as the 'direct harm rationale'. To produce images of child abuse a child must be harmed: as a result, the law must take steps to protect children and to prevent such harm and to do so the production, distribution, and even possession of child-abuse images are criminalized.[74]

Although nearly all countries agree the need for the criminalization of child-abuse images on the direct-harm rationale the enforcement of this agreement is though not as simple as it sounds. First, there is the relatively simple question of how old is a child? This is not an issue when one is dealing with young children; all governments and lawmakers agree that a 5-year-old is a child. What, though, about a 17-year-old? Or even perhaps a 15-year-old? A strict application of the direct-harm rationale assumes that in the production of a child-abuse image a child has been abused: this means the 'child' cannot have legally consented to the production of the image in the way adult performers do. This is true only if the 'child' has not reached the age of consent within their state: once they reach majority they can legally have sex, and equally they can consent to it being recorded without direct harm having occurred to them.

The first problem is that different states have different ages of majority. Until relatively recently the age of consent in Canada was 14,[75] while in the UK it is 16. Throughout the US it varies from 16 to 18 while in some states it is as high as 20 (Tunisia) while in

[73] There is a debate over terminology for images such as these. The Internet Watch Foundation note on their website that: '"child pornography", "child porn" and "kiddie porn" are not acceptable terms. The use of such language acts to legitimise images which are not pornography, rather, they are permanent records of children being sexually abused and as such should be referred to as child sexual abuse images.' I will refer to these images as 'child-abuse images' but may refer to them as being of a pornographic nature.

[74] Under s. 1 of the Protection of Children Act 1978 it is an offence to 'take, or permit to be taken, any indecent photograph of a child' and to 'to distribute or show such indecent photographs'. While by s. 160 of the Criminal Justice Act 1988 it is an offence for a person to have any indecent photograph of a child in his possession.

[75] The Tackling Violent Crime Act 2008 raised the legal age of sexual consent in Canada from 14 to 16, the first time it had been raised since 1892.

others as low as 12 (Angola).[76] With child-abuse images streaming across borders as easily as other forms of pornographic imagery, some form of agreement is needed on this basic issue.

This has been achieved in part though the Convention on Cybercrime.[77] Article 9 seeks to form international agreement and cooperation on 'Offences related to child pornography.' Article 9(3) states: 'For the purpose of [this provision], the term "minor" shall include all persons under 18 years of age. A Party may, however, require a lower age-limit, which shall be not less than 16 years.' Thus although there may be no common agreement on the age of sexual majority between member states there is agreement that when dealing with child-abuse images they will adopt a common age of 18 in most circumstances.[78] As the majority of child-abuse images are consumed in Western Europe, Japan, and North America the Convention on Cybercrime provides a useful point of commonality among law enforcement authorities who can then organize international operations to attempt to break so-called 'child pornography rings'.

A second problem is that it is not always clear how old a 'child' in an image actually is. Again with young children this is not an issue, but a 14-year-old can look 18 and vice versa. Should the law ban the production, distribution, and possession of images of young adults who appear to be younger than they actually are? Equally, should an individual who possesses a pornographic image of a person who appears to be over 18 face prosecution if it is subsequently established that the person in question is in fact a minor? These are questions that have been faced in courts overseas. In Sweden a child is defined as 'a person whose puberty development is incomplete, or when it can be discerned from the image or from the circumstances around it, is less than 18 years old'.[79] In a challenging test case the defendant paid two 16-year-old girls to take part in pornographic films. The girls informed him of their age before filming took place but the films were produced anyway. The Stockholm District Court and the Court of Appeal both interpreted the law to mean that if the age of the girls could not be discerned by the images the man could not be guilty of producing or distributing child pornography despite the fact that he was aware of their age. The courts found that as the girls had passed through puberty and therefore it was not possible to understand from the images that they were under-age these were not images of child pornography as defined in the Criminal Code.[80]

[76] BH Oluka, 'Before you marry or even have sex in Africa, do you know the age of consent? In Angola, it is 12 years', *Mail & Guardian Africa* (Johannesburg, 23 March 2015) <http://mgafrica.com/article/2015-03-23-before-you-marry-or-even-have-sex-in-africa-do-you-know-the-age-of-consent-in-angola-it-is-12-years>.

[77] See (n. 67).

[78] The UK has taken steps to ensure UK law complies with Art. 9. In England and Wales s. 45(2) of the Sexual Offences Act 2003 amends s. 7(6) of the Protection of Children Act 1978 to read '"Child" . . . means a person under the age of 18.' In Scotland the relevant provisions are to be found in the Protection of Children and Prevention of Sexual Offences (Scotland) Act 2005. Interestingly, a side-effect of this would be that a couple in a perfectly legal sexual relationship where one (or both parties) were aged between 16 and 18 would be unable to make a home sex video or take pictures of their partners in sexually suggestive positions. For this reason the Sexual Offences Act 2003 introduced s. 1A into the Protection of Children Act. This provides that it is not an offence to make or possess a photograph of a child over 16 if at the time the offence was charged the defendant and the child were either (a) married or (b) living together as partners in an enduring family relationship.

[79] Swedish Criminal Code Chapter 16, para 10a.

[80] Stockholm District Court Case nr B 7047–01. Discussed in full in M Eneman, 'The New Face of Child Pornography' in M Klang and A Murray (eds.), *Human Rights in the Digital Age* (Routledge Cavendish 2005).

To prevent these issues arising in the US the Child Protection and Obscenity Enforcement Act 1988 requires that producers of pornographic material keep records of all performers engaged by them with proof that they were over 18 at the time the material was produced.[81] The UK strikes a middle ground between these approaches. There is no requirement of record-keeping but we are less laissez-faire than the Swedish position. By s. 160 it is an offence to possess an image of a person under 18, whether or not they look older than they actually are.[82] Therefore in the UK it is not technically illegal to possess an indecent image of a person of 18 or over who looks younger than they are, but it is illegal to possess a computer-manipulated or computer-generated image which is specifically designed to create the impression that a minor is portrayed: these are so-called pseudo-images.

14.3.1 **Policing pseudo-images in the UK**

Pseudo-images are mostly a product of the digital society. The creation of pseudo-images involves powerful computer software such as Photoshop or Paint Shop Pro either to create photorealistic images which portray children being abused or to manipulate pre-existing pornographic images to make adult actors appear prepubescent by digitally removing pubic hair (and other post-pubescent hair such as chest hair or underarm hair) and the resizing of genitals and breasts. These images raise a number of issues. First among them is the simple question of should we criminalize such images at all? As discussed, child-abuse images are criminalized under the direct-harm principle. Pseudo-images are quite different: in the same way that actors are not actually killed in violent action movies or horror movies, no children are harmed in the production of pseudo-images. But there are compelling arguments which suggest we cannot consider pseudo-images so lightly.

There is strong evidence which points to a connection between viewing child-abuse images and the act of abuse itself.[83] In current research there are four main hypotheses on the paedophile's use of child-abuse images: (1) to develop their sexual motivation, (2) to lower their level of sexual impulse control, (3) as a substitute for sexual contact with a child, and (4) to break down the child's resistance while attempting to seduce the child. A study presented in 2003 showed that two-thirds of perpetrators arrested for internet sex crimes against children also possessed stills pictures and film sequences containing child-abuse images.[84] Therefore there is a clear psychological link between the consumption of child-abuse images and the act of child abuse; further as most paedophiles do not differentiate between pseudo-images and genuine images and as genuine images are easier to produce than pseudo-images producers will tend to continue to produce genuine images. All of these factors suggest that although children may not

[81] US Code, Title 18 § 2257.

[82] If the 'child' in an image or video cannot be identified, not uncommon where images may have come from overseas, the question of whether a person in an image is under 18 becomes a question of fact for the jury to decide. See *R v Land* [1998] 1 Cr App R 301 and *R v Charles William Owen* (1988) 86 Cr App R 291.

[83] See, e.g. C Bagley and K King, *Child Sexual Abuse* (Routledge 1989) 219; C Itzen (ed.), *Home Truths About Child Sexual Abuse* (Routledge 2000) ch. 7.

[84] J Wolak, K Mitchell, and D Finkelhor, 'Internet Sex Crimes Against Minors: The Response of Law Enforcement', Crimes against Children Research Center November 2003, University of New Hampshire <http://www.unh.edu/ccrc/pdf/CV70.pdf>.

be directly harmed in the production of pseudo-images such images do cause indirect harm on several levels.

This 'indirect-harm rationale' is applied in Art. 9(2)(c) of the Convention on Cybercrime which states that 'the term "child pornography" shall include pornographic material that visually depicts realistic images representing a minor engaged in sexually explicit conduct'. The UK was an early adopter of legislation to criminalize pseudo-images with the Criminal Justice and Public Order Act 1994 extending the ambit of both the Criminal Justice Act 1988 and the Protection of Children Act 1978 to cover such images.[85] The extended wording of s. 1(1) of the Protection of Children Act reads:

> It is an offence for a person:
>
> (a) to take, or permit to be taken or to make, any indecent photograph or pseudo-photograph of a child; or
>
> (b) to distribute or show such indecent photographs or pseudo-photographs; or
>
> (c) to have in his possession such indecent photographs or pseudo-photographs, with a view to their being distributed or shown by himself or others; or
>
> (d) to publish or cause to be published any advertisement likely to be understood as conveying that the advertiser distributes or shows such indecent photographs or pseudo-photographs, or intends to do so.

Section 160(1) of the Criminal Justice Act now reads:

> It is an offence for a person to have any indecent photograph or pseudo-photograph of a child in his possession.

A pseudo-photograph is defined in s. 7(7) of the Protection of Children Act as 'an image, whether made by computer-graphics or otherwise howsoever, which appears to be a photograph'.

The newly extended scope of s. 160 was examined by the Court of Appeal in *R v Fellows and Arnold*.[86] Mr Fellows was a computer officer at Birmingham University. Without the knowledge of the university he constructed a large database of child-abuse images on the university network and made it available via the internet. Mr Arnold was a 'customer' of Mr Fellows who was granted access to Mr Fellows' database in return for supplying him with further images. Both were prosecuted under the Protection of Children Act and both claimed that the Act did not extend to their activities as 'computer data was not a "photograph" for the purposes of section 1'.[87]

This argument was rejected by Evans LJ. He began by examining the dictionary definition of a photograph as 'a picture or other image obtained by the chemical action of light or other radiation on specially sensitised material such as film or glass': this he said could not apply to an indecent image held on a computer hard drive as 'There is no "picture or other image" on or in the disc; nothing which can be seen.'[88] But, he went on to note that under s. 7(2) a photograph was defined as including 'a copy of an indecent photograph'. Could the images on the hard drive be such a copy? Evans LJ

[85] Section 84 of the Criminal Justice and Public Order Act 1994 made the necessary amendments to s. 160 of the Criminal Justice Act 1988 and ss. 1, 4, 5, and 7 of the Protection of Children Act 1978.

[86] [1997] 2 All ER 548; [1997] 1 Cr App R 244.

[87] [1997] 1 Cr App R 244, 245–6.

[88] Ibid. 253.

believed so: 'There is nothing in the Act which makes it necessary that the copy should itself be a photograph within the dictionary or the statutory definition, and if there was, it would make the inclusion of the reference to a copy unnecessary. So we conclude that there is no restriction on the nature of a copy, and that the data represents the original photograph, in another form.'[89]

He then gave an *obiter* opinion on the scope of the new pseudo-photographs provisions. As the appellants had been charged prior to s. 84 of the Criminal Justice and Public Order Act 1994 coming into effect they could not be charged with possession or distribution of pseudo-photographs but Evans LJ believed he should examine the scope of the new provision in any event. He noted that it was the view of the court that '[these new provisions] seem to us to be concerned with images created by computer processes rather than the storage and transmission by computers of images created originally by photography'.[90] Thus the collective view of the *Fellows* court was that digitized images held on hard drives were not photographs but were copies of photographs originally taken in the traditional manner and that pseudo-images were only images created by computer and could not be images stored on computer.

If the law had been left in this form it could have caused substantial difficulties for the prosecuting authorities. A completely digital picture (taken with a digital camera and then downloaded onto a hard drive) would appear to fall between these two definitions: being neither a photograph, or a copy of a photograph, nor a pseudo-image. In one of those strange twists that often occurs though when new legislation is introduced there remain outstanding appeals on the old legislation. Even as Evans LJ gave the judgment of the court in *Fellows* he knew that it had already been replaced by statutory developments, for his judgment was given on 27 September 1996 while the wording of s. 7(4) of the Protection of Children Act had been changed on 3 February 1995 to read 'references to a photograph include (a) the negative as well as the positive version; and (b) data stored on a computer disc or by other electronic means which is capable of conversion into a photograph'. Therefore while Evans LJ had to follow a complicated line of reasoning to find that data held on a hard drive could be a copy of a photograph, the new wording of s. 7(4), if it had applied in the case before him, would have allowed him simply to find the appellants guilty of distribution of 'indecent photographs'. The UK continues to take a hard line with the possession of both actual and pseudo-images being aggressively prosecuted.

Highlight Prosecuting possession of child-abuse images

Akdeniz reports that between 1988 (when the possession offence was introduced) and 2004 there were 1,831 prosecutions under s. 160 (with 1,267 convictions) and 624 police cautions. Meanwhile between 1980 and 2004 there were 4,771 prosecutions under s. 1 of the Protection of Children Act with 3,789 convictions and 732 police cautions. Subsequent research by McManus and Almond shows that between 2005 and 2013 there were 1,834 convictions under s. 160 and 8,043 convictions under s. 1. Further, McManus and Almond show that the trend

→

[89] Ibid. 254.
[90] Ibid. 255.

for convictions is upward with the greatest number of convictions under s. 160 being 278 in 2011/12 and under s. 1 being 1,247 in 2012/13.

[Y Akdeniz, *Internet Child Pornography and the Law* (Ashgate 2008), 25; and MA McManus and L Almond, 'Trends of Indecent Images of Children and Child Sexual Offences between 2005/2006 and 2012/2013 within the United Kingdom' (2014) 20 *Journal of Sexual Aggression* 142]

It may be that the law enforcement authorities prosecute aggressively because the courts have indicated they take a hard-line stance in enforcing the provisions of both s. 160 and s. 1. Many cases of what would usually be thought of as possession of child-abuse images are being prosecuted under s. 1 of the Protection of Children Act for the more serious offence of making indecent images.

This follows the decision of the Court of Appeal in *R v Bowden*.[91]

Highlight *R v Bowden*

A person who either downloads images on to disc or who prints them off is making them.

The Act is not only concerned with the original creation of images, but also their proliferation. Photographs or pseudo-photographs found on the Internet may have originated from outside the United Kingdom; to download or print within the jurisdiction is to create new material which hitherto may not have existed therein.

The impact of this decision is that anyone who 'saves' an indecent image (even if the copy is merely in their browser's cache) is deemed to have 'made' an image under s. 1: this does seem to stretch the framer's original intent in framing both s. 1 and s. 160 and given that the s. 1 offence carries a maximum term of imprisonment of ten years, as compared to five years under s. 160, seems to suggest this was intended to prevent the more serious offence of original creation of indecent images. But Bowden demonstrates the hard-line approach taken in the UK. We can see this at work again when dealing with pseudo-images. In *Goodland v DPP*, the Divisional Court suggested that the creation of a crude pseudo-photograph by Sellotaping two images together and then photocopying the resultant gestalt image, could trigger the Protection of Children Act.[92]

14.3.2 **Non-photographic pornographic images of children**

Recently the law has moved on from *Goodland*. Although in that case the image crudely produced was found ultimately not to be a pseudo-photograph, the introduction of s. 62 of the Coroners and Justice Act 2009 may have changed that position. *Goodland* was interesting as it examined the potential line between pseudo-images and other forms of content. Simon Brown LJ noted that 'there being several features of this combination of images which give the lie to [the fact that this appears to be a genuine photograph] . . . in my judgment, an image made by an exhibit which obviously consists, as this one does,

[91] [2001] QB 88.
[92] [2000] 1 WLR 1427, 1442, per Simon Brown LJ.

of parts of two different photographs Sellotaped together cannot be said to "appear to be a photograph".'[93] In the same case counsel for the prosecution tried to define the line between pseudo-images and legal-to-possess artistic content: 'The exhibit must appear to be a product of photography rather than, for example, a cartoon, sketch, painting, or other indecent representation of a child.'[94] This distinction is now rendered practically moot as s. 62 of the Coroners and Justice Act puts non-photographic pornographic images of a child (NPPICs) on the same footing as a pseudo-image. The image in question must be pornographic and grossly offensive, disgusting, or otherwise of an obscene character. To be pornographic it must be of such a nature that it must reasonably be assumed to have been produced solely or principally for the purpose of sexual arousal. Finally, the image must fall within s. 62(6) and (7). This requires that it is an image which focuses solely or principally on a child's genitals or anal region and that it portrays a prohibited act.[95]

The definition of a child is given in s. 65. It is that the impression conveyed by the image is that the person shown is a child, or the predominant impression conveyed is that the person shown is a child despite the fact that some of the physical characteristics shown are not those of a child. This is less than precise and has been criticized by Julia Hörnle for requiring juries to make subjective evaluations of the impression conveyed by a purely imagined image.[96] This is a serious offence with a maximum penalty of three years in prison and a fine.[97] It does have a number of defences under s. 64 which are in common with those found under extreme pornography provisions. Interestingly, the Act does not criminalize publication of NPPICs although Julia Hörnle points out that this would be an offence under the Obscene Publications Acts 1959 and 1964.[98] This is perhaps less certain following *Peacock* but is still likely to be true.

At the date of writing s. 62 has been discussed in seven reported cases but little has yet been learned about its scope. In *R v Cutler*,[99] one defendant, Steven Freeman, was charged with a number of child-abuse image offences including some under s. 62. The court noted that 'there was no separate penalty imposed on him' for this.[100] In *R v Richard Palmer*[101] the defendant pleaded guilty to three offences of possessing prohibited images of children contrary to s. 62. He had been contacting a 12-year-old girl via the internet and her parents reported him to the police. When the police investigated they found the images in question. Despite Palmer suffering from Asperger's syndrome the judge HH Judge Curran sentenced Palmer to two years in prison. This seemed extremely severe for such a low level of offending and on appeal it became apparent that 'the

[93] Ibid.

[94] Ibid. 1441.

[95] The prohibited acts are: (a) the performance by a person of an act of intercourse or oral sex with or in the presence of a child; (b) an act of masturbation by, of, involving or in the presence of a child; (c) an act which involves penetration of the vagina or anus of a child with a part of a person's body or with anything else; (d) an act of penetration, in the presence of a child, of the vagina or anus of a person with a part of a person's body or with anything else; (e) the performance by a child of an act of intercourse or oral sex with an animal (whether dead or alive or imaginary); or (f) the performance by a person of an act of intercourse or oral sex with an animal (whether dead or alive or imaginary) in the presence of a child.

[96] J Hörnle, 'Countering the Dangers of Online Pornography—Shrewd Regulation of Lewd Content?' (2011) 2 *European Journal of Law and Technology* 1.

[97] Coroners and Justice Act 2009, s. 66(2)(b).

[98] Hörnle (n. 96).

[99] [2011] EWCA Crim 2781.

[100] Ibid. [2].

[101] [2011] EWCA Crim 1286.

judge had in mind the need to protect the public from the potential risk which he thought the appellant posed to young girls arising out of his internet contact. A Sexual Offences Prevention Order could only be made if there were a sentence of at least two years' imprisonment.'[102] On appeal the sentence was reduced to a 24-month community order with a 12-month supervision order. The third case is *R v Milsom*,[103] which was similar to *Cutler*. Again the appellant had been charged with multiple offences including five charges of possession of prohibited images of a child, contrary to s. 62. More serious though were charges under s. 1 of the Protection of Children Act and s. 14 of the Sexual Offences Act 1956. The one interesting statement made by the court in relation to s. 62 was that 'the court has no power to impose a sentence of imprisonment for public protection for the offences under s. 62'.[104] *R v Streeter*[105] was also an appeal against sentence. Alongside offences under s. 1 of the Protection of Children Act and s. 160 of the Criminal Justice Act the appellant was charged with two offences under s. 62. He was appealing a banning order preventing him from working with children; it was clear the s. 62 offences were minor compared with his other offences and were not considered by the court in upholding the order. In *R v Slater*[106] the appellant was charged with fifteen offences under s. 1 of the Protection of Children Act, four under s. 160 of the Criminal Justice Act and three under s. 62. His appeal only related to the s. 160 offences and therefore s. 62 was not discussed. *R v Honey*[107] was another appeal against sentence. The appellant faced a number of serious charges and among these charges he was charged with making 3,119 images under s. 1 of the Protection of Children Act and 11 images which fell under s. 62. The court did not consider s. 62 in its decision. Finally we have most recently, *R v Nestoros*,[108] which like the other six reported cases is an appeal against sentence. Here the appellant had been found guilty of multiple offences under the Protection of Children Act, the Criminal Justice Act, and the Coroners and Justice Act in relation to an unbelievable 4.2 million images. Again the appeal did not focus on s. 62 so after seven reported appeals against sentence relating to s. 62 there is little more we can say about its application than on the day it came into effect.

There clearly remains much to be determined about the scope and application of s. 62. What is clear though is that prosecutions are successfully being obtained under the Act.

14.3.3 **Policing pseudo-images internationally**

Internationally the regulation of pseudo-photographs has proven more controversial. While the UK has taken a clear view that the risk of indirect harm to children is too great to allow any form of pseudo-photograph, including non-photographic images, to be possessed and/or distributed other states take different views. In the US attempts to regulate pseudo-images have run up against the First Amendment with campaigners claiming that as there is no direct harm to children pseudo-images are to be afforded the same artistic protections as classical paintings which often portray naked infants and cherubs. The claims of artistic and free speech activists and the state came to a head

[102] Ibid. [24].
[103] [2011] EWCA Crim 2325.
[104] Ibid. [14].
[105] [2012] EWCA Crim 2103.
[106] [2013] EWCA Crim 2290.
[107] [2015] EWCA Crim 371.
[108] [2015] EWCA Crim 1424.

in *Ashcroft v Free Speech Coalition*,[109] a challenge to the constitutionality of the Child Pornography Prevention Act (CPPA) 1996.

In 1982 in the case of *New York v Ferber*,[110] the US Supreme Court held that it was not a breach of the First Amendment to restrict the distribution of child-abuse images as the restriction on free expression was reasonable to protect children from the harm inherent in making such images. This principle had later been extended in the case of *Osborne v Ohio*,[111] to further cover the mere possession of child-abuse images. But the Supreme Court had been clear in both decisions that the restriction of the First Amendment was reasonable because of the risk of direct harm to children. The CPPA sought to extend the *Ferber/Osborne* principle significantly. It sought to extend the definition of 'child pornography' to include: 'any visual depiction, including any photograph, film, video, picture, or computer or computer-generated image or picture, whether made or produced by electronic, mechanical, or other means, of sexually explicit conduct, where such visual depiction is, or appears to be, of a minor engaging in sexually explicit conduct'.[112] This would extend the *Ferber/Osborne* principle to cover what in the US is known as 'virtual images', what we call pseudo-images, but as we have seen there is no direct harm in the production of pseudo-images and so the constitutionality of the Act was challenged by the Free Speech Coalition (FSC).

The FSC alleged that by prohibiting images that 'appear to be' children engaged in sexual activity, and prohibiting speech that 'conveys the impression' that the images depict minors engaged in sexual activity, were overbroad, vague, and had a chilling effect on the legitimate work of the adult entertainment industry. The Supreme Court agreed and the Act was struck down. Justice Kennedy gave the leading opinion. He found that despite the fact that 'the sexual abuse of a child is a most serious crime and an act repugnant to the moral instincts of a decent people'[113] there was no evidence of direct harm occurring with relation to virtual images 'While the government asserts that the images can lead to actual instances of child abuse the causal link is contingent and indirect. The harm does not necessarily follow from the speech, but depends upon some unquantified potential for subsequent criminal acts.'[114] In seeking to prevent the production and distribution of virtual images the Act was overbroad, in Justice Kennedy's words 'the CPPA prohibits speech despite its serious literary, artistic, political, or scientific value. The statute proscribes the visual depiction of an idea—that of teenagers engaging in sexual activity—that is a fact of modern society and has been a theme in art and literature throughout the ages.'[115] Thus the CPPA was struck down despite a strong dissenting opinion from Chief Justice Rehnquist who felt that 'Congress has a compelling interest in ensuring the ability to enforce prohibitions of actual child pornography, and we should defer to its findings that rapidly advancing technology soon will make it all but impossible to do so.'[116]

Ashcroft suggested it was impossible for the US government to restrict the supply of virtual child pornography in the same way *Reno* had made it impossible for them to

[109] 535 US 234 (2002).
[110] 458 US 747 (1982).
[111] 495 US 103 (1990).
[112] Child Pornography Prevention Act 1996 § 121(2).
[113] 535 US 234, 244.
[114] Ibid. 250.
[115] Ibid. 246.
[116] Ibid. 258.

control the supply of adult content. A subsequent attempt has been made to restrict the availability of virtual images in the Prosecutorial Remedies and Other Tools to end the Exploitation of Children Today (PROTECT) Act 2003. After a lengthy exposition in §501 as to why the Supreme Court should not strike out the following provisions, §502 goes on to ban the production and distribution of virtual images which are 'indistinguishable' from actual images of a minor. It is the hope of Congress that in so limiting the definition of 'virtual images' and by explicitly stating that 'drawings, cartoons, sculptures, or paintings' are explicitly excluded from its scope that the Act will avoid the same fate as the CPPA. To date this provision has not been challenged but at least one commentator believes despite the efforts of Congress it is still unconstitutional.[117] The current position in the US is therefore that only pseudo-images which are indistinguishable from real images of child abuse are illegal;[118] all other forms of pseudo-images are protected by the First Amendment.

This issue has also been extensively reviewed in Canada in the case of *R v Sharpe*.[119] Although not dealing directly with pseudo-images (Mr Sharpe was charged with possession of pornographic texts and some images), the question before the Canadian Supreme Court was similar to the one in *Ashcroft*: could the Federal Government of Canada restrict the creation, possession, and distribution of material which did not directly harm a child in its production or does such a law infringe the rights of Canadian citizens under the Canadian Charter of Rights and Freedoms? Mr Sharpe argued that the provisions of the Canadian Criminal Code were overbroad as they covered not just child-abuse images but also textual representations of sexual relationships between adults and children, as well as other materials such as pseudo-images which he argued he should be allowed to possess as part of his freedom of thought and expression.

The Supreme Court was faced with a challenging decision: prior to Mr Sharpe's challenge Canada had developed one of the most hard-line approaches to all forms of child pornography including drawings produced by hand and handwritten texts.[120] The issue was that, as Mr Sharpe argued, this came perilously close to a 'thought crime' as it criminalized the recording of one's own thoughts and expressions. The Supreme Court rejected most of Mr Sharpe's claims finding that the restrictions in the Criminal Code were proportional but they did create two narrow exceptions for (1) self-created expressive material (any written material or visual representation created by the accused alone, and held by the accused alone, exclusively for his or her own personal use), and (2) private recordings of lawful sexual activity (any visual recording, created by or depicting the accused, provided it does not depict unlawful sexual activity and is held by the accused exclusively for private use). The second of these is similar to the defence found in s. 1A of the Protection of Children Act; the first has no counterpart in UK law (it would be assumed that the Director of Public Prosecutions would be expected to show discretion in cases such as these).

Pseudo- or virtual images have therefore caused a degree of divergence between major common law jurisdictions. While lawmakers in each jurisdiction appear agreed that

[117] B Slocum, 'Virtual Child Pornography: Does it Mean the End of the Child Pornography Exception to the First Amendment?' (2004) 14 *Albany Law Journal of Science & Technology* 637.

[118] To be indistinguishable the image must be such that 'an ordinary person viewing the depiction would conclude that the depiction is of an actual minor engaged in sexually explicit conduct'. PROTECT Act § 502(c) (codified as 18 USC § 2256(11)).

[119] 2001 SCC 2.

[120] *R v Pointon*, unreported, Manitoba Provincial Court, October 23, 1997. Discussed in *R v Sharpe*.

they should be outlawed on the indirect-harm principle, States with strong protections for freedom of thought and expression may be expected to resist attempts to outlaw all but the most clearly obscene examples of pseudo-pornography. This raises the question, if *Reno* effectively deregulated adult content globally why has *Ashcroft* not had the same effect with pseudo-images? The reason is fourfold. First, Congress could take steps to control certain forms of pseudo-imagery through the PROTECT Act. This is because these forms of image are obscene under the *Miller* standard and are therefore not protected by the First Amendment. Second, in 'consumer states' like the UK, possession of pseudo-images is illegal. This places it on a different footing to obscene content and means the authorities can easily prosecute consumers of such images here. Third, the size of the available market is smaller making it easier for law enforcement authorities to police; and finally, the cost of production of high-quality pseudo-images remains high, meaning that simple economics, rather unfortunately, lead suppliers to produce actual images of child abuse which remain illegal in nearly every state worldwide.

14.4 **Extreme pornography**

Extreme pornography is a relatively new term in UK law. It arrived in summer 2005 when the Home Office and the Scottish Executive launched their joint consultation paper: 'Consultation: on the possession of extreme pornographic material.'[121] The consultation was launched after a campaign from Liz Longhurst to ban possession of violent pornography; images portraying sexual asphyxia, necrophilia, and rape, following the rape and murder of her daughter, Jane, in March 2003 by Graham Coutts, a man seemingly obsessed with violent sexual imagery.[122] The consultation process led eventually to the promulgation of s. 63 of the Criminal Justice and Immigration Act 2008 which came into force on 26 January 2009.[123] Section 63 outlaws the possession of extreme pornographic images: these are pornographic images (defined in s. 63(3) as an image of such a nature that it must reasonably be assumed to have been produced solely or principally for the purpose of sexual arousal) which portray 'in an explicit and realistic way' one of five categories of act or activity.

Highlight Extreme pornography: the categories

(a) an act which threatens a person's life,

(b) an act which results, or is likely to result, in serious injury to a person's anus, breasts or genitals,

(c) an act which involves sexual interference with a human corpse,

→

[121] Home Office/Scottish Executive, Consultation: on the possession of extreme pornographic material, August 2005: <http://www.homeoffice.gov.uk/documents/cons-extreme-porn-3008051/cons-extreme-pornography?view=Binary>.

[122] For discussion of the Longhurst campaign and the events surrounding it see A Murray, 'The Reclassification of Extreme Pornographic Material' (2009) 72 *MLR* 73.

[123] By the Criminal Justice and Immigration Act 2008 (Commencement No. 4 and Saving Provision) Order 2008, SI 2008/2993.

(d) a person performing an act of intercourse or oral sex with an animal (whether dead or alive), or

(e) an act which involves the non-consensual penetration of a person's vagina, anus or mouth by another with the other person's penis, or an act which involves the non-consensual sexual penetration of a person's vagina or anus by another with a part of the other person's body or anything else, and a reasonable person looking at the image would think that the persons were real.

This is a far-reaching addition to the list of banned items. Before January 2009 only child-abuse images (and pseudo-images) were proscribed in this manner. Why has the government extended the law in this fashion? The answer is given in the original consultation paper.[124]

Highlight Banning possession of extreme pornography

The issue arises due to the wide range of extreme pornography available via the internet which cannot, in practice, be controlled by our existing laws. Extreme pornography featuring violent rape, sexual torture, and other abusive non-consensual acts existed in various forms before the internet but the publication and supply could be controlled by the Obscene Publications Acts 1959 and 1964, the Civic Government (Scotland) Act 1982, and by Customs legislation (the Customs Consolidation Act 1876 and Customs and Excise Management Act 1979). Closing down sources of supply and distribution obviated the need for a possession offence. However, the global nature of the internet makes this approach much more difficult.

This demonstrates the problem highlighted originally by Post and Johnson in 1996,[125] that although the community standards applied in obscenity regulations are local, the internet both fails to respect traditional borders, and is largely given the benefit of the US First Amendment following the *Reno* decision.[126] Faced with the inability to control this most extreme of pornographic content the government felt compelled to act in light of Mrs Longhurst's high-profile campaign. The only effective method of control which they could apply was to pass a possession offence: basically bracketing extreme pornography with child-abuse images. The difficulty with this approach is that while we may justify the criminalization of the possession of child-abuse images on the direct-harm rationale (and pseudo-images and even NPPICs on the indirect-harm rationale), it is more difficult to justify a blanket ban on the possession of extreme images.

[124] Home Office/Scottish Executive, Consultation above (n. 121) [1].

[125] See (n. 21).

[126] In fact it is reported that the UK Government approached the US Government asking them to take steps to close down a number of necrophilia websites at the heart of the *Graham Coutts* case including 'Necrobabes' which was frequently visited by Coutts ahead of the murder, but were told the sites were protected by the Constitution. See 'Blunkett meets Ashcroft', *Channel 4 News*, 7 March 2004 <http://www.channel4.com/news/2004/03/week_1/07_terror.html>.

An examination of the proscribed content found in s. 63 reveals that it covers five broad headings: (1) snuff and similarly highly violent content; (2) sadomasochism and 'torture porn'; (3) necrophilia; (4) bestiality; and (5) rape porn. Although all of these acts may themselves be criminal offences if carried out against an unwilling victim, in most cases pornographic content of this nature is produced in much the same way as action movies produce scenes of violence and murder: using actors and careful stage direction. The direct-harm approach cannot therefore be justified in all cases. Although there are no doubt cases where actual criminal activity may be recorded in the making of extreme pornography, the definition given in s. 63(7) and (7A) that the image must 'portray, in an explicit and realistic way' the act in question is too wide to justify the application of the direct-harm principle when in most cases these images will be staged by paid actors.[127]

During consultation the government attempted to make an indirect-harm argument, suggesting that 'it is possible that such material may encourage or reinforce interest in violent and aberrant sexual activity to the detriment of society as a whole'.[128] The difficulty with this argument is, though, that while there is extensive statistical data to prove a link between the consumption of pseudo-child-abuse images and further offending by paedophiles there is little evidence of a link between consumption of extreme pornography and further offending,[129] a fact admitted by the government.[130]

The government therefore took the decision to outlaw the possession of such images on public policy grounds rather than on the harm principle. The policy justification was that 'there is a small category of pornographic material which is so repugnant that, in common with child-abuse images, its possession should not be tolerated'.[131] The danger with a public policy argument though is that you must judge the mood of the public correctly: with s. 63 it is arguable that the government failed to meet the public mood fully. By outlawing possession of BDSM images an extensive backlash occurred, led by members of the BDSM community who were concerned that the provision would be used to strike at their community. A strong campaign from the BDSM community assisted by anti-censorship groups and human rights organizations forced the government to make a number of concessions while s. 63 was being debated in Parliamentary Committee.[132] These concessions were designed to allay the fears of the BDSM community that s. 63 would be used as a proxy to clamp down on their lifestyle and activities but may have led s. 63 to miss, at least initially, one of its targets.

When consultation began on s. 63 it was clear that its scope was meant to include violent pornography, in particular content which pairs sex and violence such as 'rape images'. But due to concessions made in Committee the original wording of s. 63(7) (a) 'an image of an act which threatens or appears to threaten a person's life' became 'an image [which] portrays, in an explicit and realistic way an act which threatens a

[127] The obvious exception is the bestiality provision as animals like children cannot consent.

[128] Home Office/Scottish Executive, Consultation, (n. 121) [27].

[129] See Murray, (n. 122). See also M Popovich, 'Establishing New Breeds of (Sex) Offenders: Science or Political Control?' (2007) 22 *Sexual and Relationship Therapy* 255; A D'Amato, 'Porn Up, Rape Down' Northwestern Public Law Research Paper No. 913013: <http://www.ssrn.com/abstract=913013>.

[130] Home Office/Scottish Executive, Consultation, see (n. 121) [31].

[131] Ibid. [33].

[132] A full discussion of the progress of s. 63 through Committee may be found in Murray, (n. 122).

person's life'. This substantially narrowed the scope of s. 63(7)(a) as violent sexual content, including rape fetish content which does not portray in an explicit and realistic way an act which threatens a person's life, was not within the scope of the offence. The key difference between the original wording and the final version was the removal of the words 'or appears to' which would have allowed authorities to take action against clearly staged violent pornography but which now they could not. To remedy this lacuna in the law the government was forced to pass an amendment by s. 37 of the Criminal Justice and Courts Act 2015. This added a new s. 7A to s. 63 criminalizing the possession of:

> an image [which] portrays, in an explicit and realistic way, either an act which involves the non-consensual penetration of a person's vagina, anus or mouth by another with the other person's penis, or an act which involves the non-consensual sexual penetration of a person's vagina or anus by another with a part of the other person's body or anything else, and a reasonable person looking at the image would think that the persons were real.

This came into effect on 13 April 2015, effectively closing the loophole in the law created during deliberation of the original wording of s. 63. It also brought the law in England and Wales in line with the law in Scotland where possession of such images was already illegal.[133]

Section 63 remains a relatively new provision but it is one that has been extensively prosecuted, with figures released under a Freedom of Information request revealing that 4,068 prosecutions were brought in England and Wales up to August 2013.[134] We can assume that figure is now far higher as prosecutions seem to average around 1,300 per year. Further, as bestiality images make up around 85 per cent of all prosecutions and the government admitted in their impact assessment for s. 37 of the Criminal Justice and Courts Act 2015 that they expected rape porn prosecutions to be of a similar level to bestiality prosecutions this number seems likely to rise considerably. It seems though, despite the high level of prosecutions being brought, it is unlikely that it will have much effect on the large amount of extreme pornographic content available on the internet. As has already been discussed, most of this content is hosted in the US where much of it can gain the protection of the First Amendment: therefore s. 63 is unlikely to close down many pornographic websites. The police do not devote considerable resources to a crime that they see to be of relatively low priority when compared to more serious offences such as possession of images of child abuse, and a large number of prosecutions have come as a result of investigations into other matters or via reports made by members of the public. The first person charged with possession of extreme pornographic images was investigated after an engineer found the images on his computer while carrying out a repair,[135] while the first person to receive a custodial sentence under s. 63 was arrested on drugs offences with the images in question coming to light in the course of the drugs investigation.[136] In the over five years it has been in effect s. 63 has been at the centre of a number of successful prosecutions but in most cases it is one

[133] See s. 42 of the Criminal Justice and Licensing (Scotland) Act 2010.

[134] <http://www.whatdotheyknow.com/request/prosecutions_for_possesion_of_ex>.

[135] 'Man had "grossly offensive and disgusting" porn images on computer' *St Helens Star* (18 June 2009) <http://www.sthelensstar.co.uk/news/4445020.Man_had__grossly_offensive_and_disgusting__porn_images_on_computer/>.

[136] J Ozimek, 'First prison sentence for extreme porn' (*The Register*, 29 September 2009) <http://www.theregister.co.uk/2009/09/29/newcastle_sentencing/>.

of a volume of charges usually alongside other charges[137] with the images often coming to light either during a supervision meeting made under a sexual offences supervision order or during a licence review for ex-prisoners released on licence.

An important consideration is when one is deemed to be 'in possession' of the images in question. This was the subject of one of the first appeals against conviction in the case of *R v Ping Chen Cheung*.[138] The police had stopped the appellant in the street and had asked to search his laptop bag which appeared swollen, bulked out by content. Inside the bag the officers found a large amount of counterfeit DVDs. Although most were mainstream movies a small bundle of eight DVDs was found that formed the charge under s. 63. The appellant claimed he was unaware these DVDs were in the bag which had been given to him by a third party. The question was whether or not the appellant was said to be in possession of the DVDs absent his knowledge of the nature of the DVDs. The court found possession was a simple statutory question like drugs possession: 'The offence created under the 2008 Act is a new offence. However, we have no doubt that the concept of possession in section 63 does carry with it both a physical and a mental element in the same way as possession has been interpreted in offences under the Misuse of Drugs Act 1971.'[139] This position has been upheld and even reinforced in a number of cases since. In *R v Oliver (Philip)*, the Court of Appeal upheld a conviction under s. 63 for an ex-prison governor who had downloaded extreme images before their criminalization in January 2009 and who despite not accessing them following criminalization allowed others to access them through software which allowed for the contents of his hard drive to be shared. The court did not accept his assertion that he had no recollection of the images or how they got on his computer. More recently it has been reported in the media that two men have pleaded guilty to offences under s. 63 when their knowledge of the content is (if the reported facts are true) extremely thin at best.[140] According to reports of the case two men were sent in an unsolicited fashion videos via the messenger service WhatsApp. The first, Mark Kelly, stated he had deleted the videos from his WhatsApp account after watching some of the content and being disturbed by it. He was unaware that they had also been saved to the camera roll of his phone. The second, Gary Ticehurst, said he received the videos from someone he did not know after he got a new phone. He said he did not look at the videos and forgot he had them on his phone. Judge Worsley, found that there was no evidence of the defendants sharing the content or getting sexual gratification from them and gave the men a two-year conditional discharge and ordered them to pay £500 costs each. This demonstrates just how easy it is to get a criminal record through the application of s. 63. An individual found in possession of images or videos will be 'in possession' of them if they are aware they are in their control or if they are unaware of the content of said files. They may though be able to avail themselves of the statutory defence under either s. 65(2)(b) or (c).

[137] See e.g. *R v Smith (Robert)* [2013] EWCA Crim 167; *R v Horn (Stephen)* [2014] EWCA Crim 653; *R v Labonn (Jacque Cecil)* [2014] EWCA Crim 1652.

[138] [2009] EWCA Crim 2965.

[139] Ibid. [14].

[140] J Robinson, '"Respectable" men convicted of possessing extreme pornography after they were sent it via someone they didn't know on WhatsApp' *Daily Mail* (London, 1 August 2014) available from: <http://www.dailymail.co.uk/news/article-2713545/Respectable-men-convicted-possessing-extreme-pornography-sent-didn-t-know-WhatsApp.html>.

14.5 **Revenge porn**

The prevalence of digital photographic devices and the use of images as a form of communication rather than as a repository of memory have caused an explosion in the number and circulation of sexualized images. Most often these take the form of so-called 'sexting' images; the sending of sexually explicit, or sexualized, images from one person to another, usually that person's partner or someone they are sexually interested in. There are a number of social problems linked to the practice of sexting. Prime among these is the prevalence of sexting among children and youths for whom it has become socially normative. In their paper 'Cyber safety for adolescent girls: bullying, harassment, sexting, pornography, and solicitation',[141] Smith, Thompson, and Davidson record that in Europe 15 per cent of 11- to 16-year-olds had received peer-to-peer sexual messages or images while 3 per cent said they had sent or posted such images, while the UK levels were 12 per cent and 4 per cent.[142] They also report much higher levels of sexting in the United States noting that 'the prevalence of adolescent sexting varies widely, from 9.6 per cent to 28 per cent', while also noting that the prevalence of sexting in the UK seemed to be rising, noting that the Child Online and Exploitation Protection Centre (CEOP) identified a marked increase in self-generated indecent images (SGIIs) being uploaded to the internet.[143] Even if we were to assume that the number of children receiving sexually explicit peer messages in the UK was around 12 per cent and the number of those sending messages was around 4 per cent with around 3.7million children in the 11–16 age bracket in the UK, that would equate to 444,000 children receiving such images and, more worryingly, 148,000 children generating such images. Predominantly, the issue of children sharing such images is not a legal problem; the issue is societal not legal. The law already has a regime to deal with the making and distribution of images of children under the age of 18 through the Protection of Children Act and the Criminal Justice Act.[144] The problem with sexting is often the sender and recipient will both be under 18 and it is often not appropriate to apply the full force of the law.[145]

The rise in the prevalence of sexting has though had another unintended side effect. With sexual partners often using sexting to supplement their relationship a large number of young adults now possess images of their partners in sexualized poses. When a break-up occurs it seems a not insignificant number of jilted ex-lovers take to the internet and share these images against the wishes of their ex-partner. This practice is so commonplace that is has been given a specific name: revenge porn. The posting of revenge porn can take a number of variations. There are websites, not hosted in the UK, where one can send images to be hosted and shared. One of the most infamous of these sites was IsAnyoneUp.com. The website operated as a revenge porn site between 2010 and 2012. During that time nude and semi-nude images of thousands of women were

[141] 26 *Current Opinion in Obstetrics and Gynaecology* 360 (2014).
[142] Ibid. 362.
[143] Ibid.
[144] See 14.3.
[145] Although the UK has not followed this pattern, teenagers in British Columbia, North Carolina, and Virginia have been convicted of child pornography offences. A 14-year-old boy from the north of England reportedly had a crime report made against him in September 2015 for sending a naked picture of himself to a teenage girl he was flirting with via Snapchat.

posted with links to their Twitter accounts and Facebook pages. However, an investigation revealed that a large number of images had been hacked rather than posted by ex-partners and eventually the site operator Hunter Moore was charged with computer misuse and identity theft charges. In February 2015 Moore pleaded guilty and was sentenced to two years in prison. Despite this, a large number of revenge porn sites continue to operate.

The alternative approach used is more direct, less permanent, but often more damaging. That is, to directly post images or video to popular social networking sites such as Twitter or Facebook identifying the victim (often images are posted directly to the victim's Facebook page). Clearly this is very harmful to the victim both psychologically and socially, yet until recently there was little the law could do. When the victim in *AMP v Persons Unknown*[146] had intimate photographs removed from her mobile phone, which she had either lost or which had been stolen in 2008 she had to resort to a mixture of copyright law and a rather inventive application of the Protection from Harassment Act developed by her barrister to attempt to gain control over the illegally obtained, and circulated, images. At the time no one who distributed the images committed an offence, at least not until they were formally notified by AMPs orders that such distribution was in breach of the order of the court.

Today *AMP* would find a drastically different legal landscape. Recognizing the harm that revenge pornography causes to victims a number of jurisdictions have passed specific revenge porn laws, beginning in Israel in January 2014 and including Canada, Japan, and recently England and Wales. The law for England and Wales is found in ss. 33–35 of the Criminal Justice and Courts Act 2015. This makes it an offence to 'disclose a private sexual photograph or film if the disclosure is made (a) without the consent of an individual who appears in the photograph or film, and (b) with the intention of causing that individual distress.' The offence has a number of defences for law enforcement purposes, journalism, and the public interest or where the image was previously made available for reward. Consent, according to s. 33(7) could be general consent or specific consent. The key phrase for the offence is 'private sexual' and these components of the offence are defined in s. 35. A photograph or film is 'private' if it shows something that is not of a kind ordinarily seen in public,[147] while it is sexual if 'it shows all or part of an individual's exposed genitals or pubic area, (b) it shows something that a reasonable person would consider to be sexual because of its nature, or (c) its content, taken as a whole, is such that a reasonable person would consider it to be sexual.'[148] The new offence came into effect on 13 April 2015 and was immediately prosecuted by the authorities. The first reported case involved a 21-year-old from Romford who threatened to post intimate pictures of a 20-year-old woman from Reading online, three days after the new laws came into force. He then sent the photographs to her family and shared them on Facebook. He was charged on 15 May and pleaded guilty the next day at Reading Magistrates' Court. Since then a number of cases have been reported in the media, including the first female convicted under the new law in September 2015. In an August 2015 press release the Crown Prosecution Service listed six completed cases

[146] [2011] EWHC 3454 (TCC).
[147] See s. 35(2).
[148] See s. 35(3).

and five ongoing cases charged under s. 33.[149] It should be assumed that many more cases will follow.

14.6 **Private regulation of pornographic imagery**

As the discussion throughout this chapter has demonstrated, the development of web hosting and delivery of pornographic content have undermined the effectiveness of states regulators to control their borders and to police the production, distribution, and consumption of pornographic content in all forms, be it indecent, obscene, or extremely obscene.[150] Pornography and obscenity are the areas where there is arguably the greatest need for alternative regulatory measures, such as those predicted by Lawrence Lessig in *Code and Other Laws of Cyberspace*,[151] which make use of the design features of the internet to allow for effective regulation. Some such measures have been implemented by ISPs, mostly designed to restrict the supply of child-abuse images and pseudo-images. In the UK a hybrid hierarchical/design control system known as Cleanfeed is used.[152] Cleanfeed is a two-part hybrid system: first, suspect images need to be identified and blacklisted; this is carried out by a private regulatory authority known as the Internet Watch Foundation, then the suspect images, pages, or sites are blocked though the Cleanfeed technical protocol.

Central to the functioning of Cleanfeed is the Internet Watch Foundation (IWF). The IWF was formed in 1996 following agreement between the government, police forces, and the ISP industry that something had to be done to tackle the problem of child-abuse images on the Usenet system. The ISPs suggested a self-regulatory body which would operate a 'hotline' to allow members of the public to report potentially illegal images; the experts at the IWF would then establish whether the report had identified an illegal image of child abuse and if they adjudged the image to be illegal they would add it to their blacklist of banned images or sites which ISPs would then block access to, thus protecting them from the risk of being prosecuted for possession of an indecent image of a child under s. 160 of the Criminal Justice Act. Over time, the focus of the IWF's work has moved from Usenet to content hosted on websites and that now forms the bulk of the IWF's day-to-day work. As well as informing ISPs of material that should be blocked, the IWF also passes relevant information to the law enforcement authorities allowing them to take steps to trace the source of the illegal material: material hosted in the UK is reported directly to the relevant local UK police service or the National Crime Agency's CEOP Command, whereas material hosted offshore is reported to the Virtual Global Taskforce for investigation.[153]

[149] Crown Prosecution Service, 'Prosecutors being advised to learn from revenge porn cases across the country to help them tackle this "humiliating" crime', 7 August 2015 <http://www.cps.gov.uk/news/latest_news/prosecutors_being_advised_to_learn_from_revenge_porn_cases/index.html>.

[150] See also 4.4 'Regulators in cyberspace: private regulators'.

[151] See L Lessig, *Code and Other Laws of Cyberspace* (Basic Books 1999); *Code Ver. 2.0* (Basic Books 2006) discussed in depth in ch. 4.

[152] Cleanfeed is actually the internal BT project name for the system; its actual name is the BT Anti-Child-Abuse Initiative. Over time though Cleanfeed has become the common label of the system.

[153] To learn more about the NCA's CEOP Command and the Virtual Global Taskforce visit their websites at <http://ceop.police.uk/About-Us/> and <http://www.virtualglobaltaskforce.com/> respectively.

The IWF is generally well regarded for the work it does and is recognized to have assisted the UK in virtually eradicating child-abuse content hosted within the UK.[154] The work of the IWF is not though without controversy. Many commentators have written on the lack of public accountability of the IWF,[155] and in December 2008 the issue of a private regulator with the ability to 'blacklist' content for an estimated 95 per cent of the UK online population became spectacularly newsworthy when the IWF ordered the blocking of the Wikipedia entry for Scorpions' album 'Virgin Killer'.

Case study The *Virgin Killer* affair

'Virgin Killer' is a 1976 album by the German band Scorpions. It is highly controversial due to the nature of the cover art for the album which portrays a 10-year-old girl posing nude, with a faux glass shatter obscuring her genitalia.

Despite a high degree of controversy the album had been on sale in the UK with the controversial cover and indeed was still available for purchase on Amazon.co.uk at the time. The effect of the IWF block though was much greater than attempted.

When the Cleanfeed system was updated to block access to the Wikipedia page in question ISPs passed all traffic from their customers through a few proxy servers used to manage the Cleanfeed system to ensure the blacklisted page was blocked. This caused problems for users of the site. Wikipedia allows users to edit its entries anonymously but keeps a record of the IP addresses of those who make changes. It may then use this information to selectively block users who vandalize the site or otherwise break its rules. The proxy filtering made it impossible to uniquely distinguish users coming from nearly all UK ISPs.

On discovery of an inordinately high number of requests to edit pages coming from a few IP addresses, and to prevent vandalism, Wikipedia instituted a blanket ban on anonymous edits from the 'big six' ISPs, which account for 95 per cent of British residential internet users.

This had the immediate effect of requiring nearly all registered users in the UK to request the lifting of IP autoblocks on their accounts before they could edit, and the de facto permanent effect of barring any contributions from people without user accounts on the site. This effect was noticed immediately and complaints to ISPs led to the actions of the IWF being uncovered.

For many people this was the first time they had heard of the IWF (another problem with private/industry regulators) and the public outcry was deafening.[156] The IWF quickly backtracked and referred their decision to their appeals procedure, which upheld the original decision, but, faced with rising public anger at their heavy-handed

[154] In 2006, at the tenth anniversary of the IWF it was disclosed that reported child-abuse content hosted in the UK, which was 18 per cent in 1997, had been reduced to 0.2 per cent in 2006. P Robbins, 'Tackling the threat of child abuse online' (*BBC News*, 24 October 2006) <http://news.bbc.co.uk/1/hi/technology/6080364.stm>. The figure since then has remained static with about 0.3 per cent discovery of child-abuse images being hosted in the UK in 2014.

[155] See, e.g. E Laidlaw, 'The Responsibilities of Free Speech Regulators: An Analysis of the Internet Watch Foundation' (2012) 20 *International Journal of Law and Information Technology* 312.

[156] See, e.g. R Cellan-Jones, 'Wikipedia is censored' BBC dot.life, 8 December 2008 <http://www.bbc.co.uk/blogs/technology/2008/12/wikipedia_is_censored.html> (and in particular see the 295 user comments); J Schofield, 'Wikipedia page censored in the UK for "child pornography"' *The Guardian* (London, 8 December 2008) <http://www.guardian.co.uk/technology/blog/2008/dec/08/internet> (again read the 114 user comments).

approach, the IWF decided to reconvene to 'consider the contextual issues involved in this specific case'. They noted that as the 'IWF's overriding objective is to minimise the availability of indecent images of children on the internet, however, on this occasion our efforts had the opposite effect so the Board decided that the webpage should be removed from the URL list.'[157] The whole affair had an extremely negative effect on public opinion of the IWF and they are having to work hard to restore confidence in themselves. It is noted in the 2008 Annual Report that 'we are committed to improving our services so issues raised by this incident will be addressed, in collaboration with our industry partners, in the year ahead'.[158]

Once a site is blacklisted by the IWF it is passed on to its industry partners for blocking. This is usually achieved through the Cleanfeed content blocking system. The system uses the blacklist and a number of proxy servers to block access to the content in question. For example, if there is blacklisted content on the website yourpiccshere.com/nastynasty/porn, then when a user requests access to any content on the yourpiccshere.com server that request will be sent to a Cleanfeed server where the blacklist is held. If the content requested is not on the blacklist (say yourpiccshere.com/holiday/spain) then the proxy will allow access to the content, though if the customer is seeking to obtain access to the blacklisted content they will be blocked from accessing the site.

A major problem with Cleanfeed was that the end user did not know that Cleanfeed had blocked his access. There was no 'blocked by Cleanfeed' message; instead the user simply received a 'not found' error, meaning there was no way the average user could tell if content had been blocked by Cleanfeed or was just unavailable, and as the IWF does not publish its blacklist we had no way of knowing how many sites had been blocked in error, or had been blocked in full when only one page or image held on that site was illegal. This would have been the effect of the Wikipedia block if it had not been for Wikipedia's complex editing safeguards designed to prevent defacement of its pages. This has now changed and the IWF Blocking: Good Practice note[159] 'strongly recommends that all relevant members serve a splash page with an agreed standard text' which states that 'access has been denied by your internet access provider because this page may contain indecent images of children as identified by the Internet Watch Foundation'. This should mean that if sites are blacklisted by the IWF in error, or if overblocking, as occurred with the *Virgin Killer* case were to happen again end users should be aware of it and should be able to take steps under the Content Assessment Appeal Process to have the block removed.[160]

14.7 **Conclusions**

The regulation of pornographic and obscene content is one of the greatest challenges for the information society. As an 'informational product' pornography benefits from the same economies of production and distribution seen in music and video production but with the potential for far greater negative social impact. There are several challenges

[157] Taken from the 2008 Internet Watch Foundation Annual Report at 9. The 'opposite effect' mentioned is that due to the high level of publicity the affair had sparked, people were searching for the image and were accessing it at a number of sites not yet blocked, usually via a search engine like Google or Yahoo!.

[158] Ibid.

[159] <http://www.iwf.org.uk/members/member-policies/url-list/blocking-good-practice>.

[160] <http://www.iwf.org.uk/accountability/complaints/content-assessment-appeal-process>.

which will continue to test communities and lawmakers in the next 10 to 20 years. First among them is how to prevent children from coming into greater contact with pornography than they already do. With children routinely having their own computer, tablet, or smartphone from an early age this is becoming a major problem. Second is the question of how we wrest back local community values in a place where there is no local community. This may prove impossible, but is certainly worth exploring. Third is to determine where obscene content becomes unacceptably obscene: this to date has led to the banning of the possession of images of child abuse, pseudo-images, NPPICs, and 'extreme pornographic images'. Should we add to this list? Or would it be an infringement of our freedom of thought and expression if we continually grow a list of banned items? Finally, we may wish to consider how technology is changing the nature of sexual encounters and question how we wish to deal with online advertising of brothels, and how to deal with new phenomena including sexting (in addition to the regulation of revenge porn), and online grooming. Some of these will be discussed in the next chapter.

TEST QUESTIONS

Question 1

Do you agree with the criminalization of pseudo-photographs? Is pseudo-pornography not just merely another example of human expression? Should such material not be protected by freedom of expression provisions?

Question 2

Should we treat 'extremely pornographic images' and 'non-photographic pornographic images of a child' in the same way as child-abuse images? Are s. 63 of the Criminal Justice and Immigration Act and s. 62 of the Coroners and Justice Act proportionate to the harm?

FURTHER READING

Books

Y Akdeniz, *Internet Child Pornography and the Law: National and International Responses* (2008)

A Gillespie, *Child Pornography: Law and Policy* (2011)

A White, *Virtually Obscene* (2006)

Chapters and articles

J Hörnle, 'Countering the Dangers of Online Pornography—Shrewd Regulation of Lewd Content?' 2 *European Journal of Law and Technology* (2011): <http://ejlt.org//article/view/55/121>

A Murray, 'The Reclassification of Extreme Pornographic Images' 72 *MLR* 73 (2009)

A Nair, 'Real Porn and Pseudo Porn: The Regulatory Road' *International Review of Law, Computers & Technology* 223 [2010]

J Rowbottom, 'Obscenity Laws and the Internet: Targeting the Supply and Demand *Criminal Law Review* 97 (2006)

D Vick, 'The Internet and the First Amendment' 61 *MLR* 414 (1998)

15

Crime and law enforcement in the information society

As most online transactions take place with the identity and location of participants hidden behind the computer screen it offers opportunities for those with criminal intent to reach out globally to commit fraud, theft, and harassment; to offer illegal gambling and pornography, and to commit direct cyberattacks.[1] Although by far the most common form of illegal activity online is simple copyright infringement,[2] there are a growing number of criminal activities being operated through the internet including the unregulated production and distribution of pornography, revenge porn images, and child abuse images,[3] direct cyberattacks such as denial of service attacks and privacy attacks including hacking, phishing, and the installation of Trojans,[4] computer fraud, online harassment, and grooming. Such activities often take place overseas but target UK citizens. The most infamous form of computer fraud is the advance-fee fraud (discussed below), which was for a period so prevalent in Nigeria that it became known internationally simply as the '419 Fraud': 419 referring to the Article of the Nigerian Criminal Code dealing with such fraud.[5] A variation of the 419 Fraud, the 'Russian Scam' targets users of online dating sites and is often perpetrated by criminals based in Russia and Eastern Europe, while 'cheque overpayment fraud' or 'criminal cashback' schemes are common on internet auction sites. This chapter will look at advance-fee fraud as well as a number of other criminal activities common in the information society, including the illegal appropriation of personal data, commonly known as phishing, and offences against the person committed through information and communication technologies, including harassment, cyberstalking, and grooming.

[1] Of course IP addresses offer a route to track criminals, but the average computer user does not know how to trace an IP address and even when law enforcement authorities become involved they often find that the address is either 'spoofed' through a re-router or leads to an internet cafe.

[2] Discussed in ch. 11.

[3] Discussed in ch. 14.

[4] Discussed in ch. 13.

[5] Article 419 forms part of Chapter 38, 'Obtaining Property by false pretences; Cheating.' It (along with the rest of the Nigerian Criminal Code) may be found at: <http://www.nigeria-law.org/Criminal%20Code%20Act-Tables.htm>.

15.1 **Fraud and identity theft**

15.1.1 **Fraud**

The risk of online fraud is extensive. The National Fraud Authority estimates that just one type of online fraud, 'online ticket fraud' cost UK citizens £1.5 billion in 2012,[6] while the overall annual loss to the UK economy in all forms of fraud, offline and online, was estimated to be £52 billion with £9.1 billion of that falling directly on individuals.[7] The £9.1 billion figure represents an average loss per UK adult of £189. Many aspects of fraud are, of course, criminalized with much of the current law of England and Wales to be found in the Fraud Act 2006. The Act was introduced to replace the old deception offences found in the Theft Acts.[8] The problem with the deception offences was that to commit deception it was widely accepted that a human mind had to be deceived. Deception of a computer system which would process an instruction automatically without human intervention was apparently not covered by the Theft Acts.[9]

The Fraud Act 2006 was enacted in response to the growing threat of computer and online fraud, much of which could be operated directly on a computer system. The Act came into force in January 2007: it creates three new forms of fraud and a further offence of obtaining services dishonestly. Section 1 states that a person is guilty of fraud if he commits any of the offences listed in ss. 2–4: these are (1) fraud by making a false representation;[10] (2) fraud by failing to disclose information;[11] and (3) fraud by abuse of position.[12] These new offences, although all still offences of deception, have been extended clearly to cover fraud committed on an automated system. For instance s. 2(5) plainly states that 'a representation may be regarded as made if it (or anything implying it) is submitted in any form to any system or device designed to receive, convey or respond to communications (with or without human intervention)'. Thus it will clearly cover all types of electronic communication including email, SMS, and IRC, as well as instructions sent to an automated system like an online bank or credit card clearing system. If a UK-based fraudster were therefore to make a false representation, in breach of s. 2, such as to give false credit card details to an online bank or ecommerce site with a view to making a gain,[13] he would commit an offence. This would cover most forms of online fraud, including 'card not present fraud' where the fraudster improperly gains credit card details and uses them to buy goods and services online; asset transfer fraud where a fraudster gains access to online banking services or similar and transfers

[6] National Fraud Authority, *Annual Fraud Indicator 2013*: <http://www.gov.uk/government/uploads/system/uploads/attachment_data/file/206552/nfa-annual-fraud-indicator-2013.pdf>.

[7] Ibid.

[8] These were obtaining property by deception (1968 Act, s. 15); obtaining a money transfer by deception (1968 Act, s. 15A); obtaining services by deception (1978 Act, s. 1); and evasion of liability by deception (1978 Act, s. 2).

[9] In *DPP v Ray* [1974] AC 370, Lord Morris stated: 'For a deception to take place there must be some person or persons who will have been deceived.'

[10] Fraud Act 2006, s. 2.

[11] Fraud Act 2006, s. 3.

[12] Fraud Act 2006, s. 4.

[13] Gain is defined in s. 5(2) as '(a) gain in money or other property; (b) include any such gain or loss whether temporary or permanent; and "property" means any property whether real or personal (including things in action and other intangible property)'.

assets to himself; and most forms of advance-fee fraud where the fraudster tricks the victim into advancing them funds in the hope of making a future gain.

The problem is that in the online environment fraud, like pornography, usually originates overseas but has its effects in the UK. As discussed in the introduction to this chapter, the best known is probably the 'Nigerian advance-fee fraud', known colloquially as the '419 Fraud'. There are many variations of the 419 Fraud but they all follow a similar pattern.

Case study The '419' advance-fee fraud

The victim receives an email from someone claiming to represent a company or individual with a large sum of money or similar assets which they require to transfer. They claim to have no ability to transfer the funds or assets directly themselves, usually due to banking regulations or some other legal impediment. They ask the victim for their assistance in making the transfer and in return offer them from 10–40 per cent of the value of the asset or funds (usually worth millions of pounds).

When the victim offers to help, the fraudster begins to ask for funds to be paid to effect the transfer. These may include small amounts to bribe officials or larger amounts required to show the victim is in good financial standing. Once the funds are transferred the fraudster disappears with the funds.

A variant of the 419 Fraud, popular in Eastern Europe, is the 'Russian Scam'.

Case study The 'Russian Scam'

The victim is usually selected from a dating site, or singles site. They are contacted by a young woman who claims to be looking to marry a UK citizen. She will often send pictures of herself and will spend some time communicating with the victim by email, social media, or perhaps even by telephone (although this is unusual as the fraudster is usually a man; when this occurs women are hired by the fraudsters to make such calls).

The fraudster will then make requests for funds. These may involve payments for medical expenses for the young woman's mother, or for assistance with housing costs. She will then indicate that she is willing to travel to the UK to meet the victim and will ask for expenses for visas, travel tickets, and hotel rooms. The fraudster then disappears with the funds.

Although these frauds have names which reflect where they developed, advance-fee frauds can originate anywhere. Many 419 Frauds are now effected from China and former Soviet Bloc countries as well as Nigeria and other sub-Saharan African countries, while Russian Scams often originate in Africa and China as well as in former Soviet Bloc countries. Advance-fee fraud is though only one form of internet-based fraud.

Whereas advance-fee fraud tends to be practised in developing nations, other more sophisticated forms of fraud are practised in Europe and other developed nations. Here the most common form of dishonest representation is 'card not present' fraud. Like the 419 Fraud there are a variety of ways this is practised but the end result is usually the same.

Case study 'Card not present' fraud

The fraudster gets hold of personal credit card details including the name of the account holder, the card number, expiry date, and the CVC or card verification code. This may be acquired in a number of ways: either simply by using discarded credit card receipts, or by 'skimming' a card in a restaurant, bar, or shop, or by 'phishing' for such details online (discussed in greater depth below).

Once these details are known the fraudster may purchase goods or services online. The fraudster may also choose to sell the information on to third parties, this, although not a breach of s. 2 of the Fraud Act, may amount to the common law offence of conspiracy to defraud.

Thus common frauds committed though the application of Information and Communication Technology (ICT) would in most cases be either a breach of s. 2 of the Fraud Act 2006 or one of the subsequent sections, depending upon the nature of the fraud, or may, if involving two or more people amount to conspiracy to defraud at common law. But with so many frauds originating overseas can the international community effectively police this activity?

Some basic standards for international cooperation are found in the Council of Europe Convention on Cybercrime.[14] Article 8 requires that:

> Each Party shall adopt such legislative and other measures as may be necessary to establish as criminal offences under its domestic law, when committed intentionally and without right, the causing of a loss of property to another person by:
>
> (a) any input, alteration, deletion or suppression of computer data, [or]
>
> (b) any interference with the functioning of a computer system, with fraudulent or dishonest intent of procuring, without right, an economic benefit for oneself or for another person.

It is clear though that Art. 8 only covers certain forms of fraud. 'Card not present' fraud is covered by Art. 8 as it requires the inputting of computer data with fraudulent intent. However, advance-fee fraud appears not to be covered unless one takes an extremely expansive view of the term 'input of computer data' to cover the contents of emails or instant messages sent by the fraudsters to their victims.

The reason for the narrow scope of Art. 8 may be because the Convention is focused on 'cybercrime' or as the preamble to the Convention puts it 'the present Convention is necessary to deter action directed against the confidentiality, integrity and availability of computer systems, networks and computer data as well as the misuse of such systems, networks and data by providing for the criminalisation of such conduct'. It is less focused on traditional criminal activity which makes use of ICT as a communications media, and more focused on new forms of criminal activity which makes use of the unique nature of ICT communications.

[14] CETS No. 185, Budapest, 23.XI.2001.

The recent growth in advance-fee frauds is as a result of the 'globalization effect' of the information society. Fraudsters, often based in the poorest parts of the world, can use ICT to contact potential victims in the richest nations at a relatively low cost: there is nothing uniquely technology-driven about this form of fraud: instead it is an old form of fraud being reborn through the global reach the information society offers.[15] By contrast internet-enabled 'card not present' fraud is a new form of an old fraud. 'Card not present' fraud, as it name suggests, is based on giving false credit or debit card details to a vendor or supplier of services when the card is not available for inspection. As such it tended historically to be carried out by post or by telephone. Internet-based 'card not present fraud' is a new way of carrying out this form of fraud not previously available: as such it is unlike advance-fee fraud as it has created a new way of committing this fraud rather than merely a new way of communicating with victims.

As advance-fee fraud is a traditional form of fraud it may be assumed that steps have been taken by states to outlaw the practice: indeed as we have seen it is illegal in the UK under s. 2 of the Fraud Act 2006, and in Nigeria under Art. 419 of the Criminal Code. The issue is not the need for further measures; it is rather for international cooperation in the detection and prosecution of such activity.

In 2007 the first fruits of this international cooperation were reported when a joint operation of UK, US, Dutch, Spanish, Canadian, and Nigerian law enforcement agencies led to the arrest of nearly 70 people and the recovery of thousands of forged documents and cheques with a value of £8m.[16] This operation was led by the UK's Serious Organised Crime Agency using intelligence supplied from partner organizations and was carried out in Nigeria with the help of local investigators. This was the first in a series of operations designed to reduce the threat of advance-fee fraud from Nigeria, one of which in 2009 saw the closure of 800 scam websites and the arrest of a number of fraudsters.[17]

Alongside these common online frauds a number of new frauds have developed, mostly around online auction sites. These include overpayment fraud and escrow fraud.

Case study Overpayment fraud

This begins when a buyer pays for goods (usually bought via an internet auction site) with a cheque drawn for a higher amount than the agreed price.

The buyer/fraudster will then ask the seller/victim to refund the overpayment by wire transfer. The seller/victim pays the cheque into his bank account and after three or four days assumes the cheque has cleared. He will then usually send the goods and refund the difference as requested.

→

[15] The advance-fee fraud was originally known as the 'Spanish prisoner fraud' and can be dated back to the early 1900s.

[16] 'UK police in Nigerian scam haul' (*BBC News*, 4 October 2007) <http://www.news.bbc.co.uk/1/hi/uk/7027088.stm>.

[17] This followed an earlier operation which had seen the arrest of 23 (mostly Nigerian) email scammers in Spain. Details of both operations may be found at: AFP, 'Nigeria's anti graft police shuts 800 scam websites' 22 October 2009 (archived at <http://www.social-engineer.org/wiki/archives/NewsArticles/BreitBart.pdf>).

→

After about 16–20 days the seller/victim's bank will bounce the cheque for being a forgery leaving the seller/victim with no payment but having both shipped the goods *and* paid an amount of cash to the buyer/fraudster. The goods plus cash element of this fraud lead to it being dubbed in some quarters 'criminal cashback'.

Case study Escrow fraud

This occurs when a buyer offers to buy a high value item such as a car, boat, or designer watch. The seller will not wish to send the item without knowing the money for payment is secured; the buyer will not want to release the funds until they receive the item in case the seller is fraudulent. The answer is to escrow the funds: putting them in the hands of a reputable third party to hold until such time as the goods are received and the buyer is satisfied they are as described.

This is commonplace and there are a number of reputable escrow agencies but in the case of escrow fraud a fraudulent agency has been set up. The seller then sends the item believing the funds to be safely escrowed, but both the buyer and the escrow agency then disappear.

These are only a few of the number of current online frauds but by far the commonest form of online fraud currently is identity fraud.

15.1.2 **Identity theft and identity fraud**

Online identity fraud is now a massive industry. We are particularly susceptible to identity fraud in the information society for a number of reasons but prime among these are: (1) the way information is gathered and stored in the information society, and (2) the increased use of identity proxies to prove our identity.

The information society, is as we have seen, both a social and economic market built around the ownership, storage, manipulation, and transfer of data. Much of this data may be used to identify the individual including IP addresses, dates of birth, name, address, telephone number, credit card details, and banking details, among others. There is therefore a large amount of personal data held by companies and organizations with whom we do business. There is always a risk of loss of this data either by the data controller, or in transit between the data subject and the data controller.[18] A loss of data can lead to identity fraud. There is no easy way to prove the identity of an individual when they deal with a website for there are no biometric indicators which we use in real life to establish identity: as Lawrence Lessig says 'In cyberspace . . . you enter without an identity and you identify only what you want—and even that can't be authenticated with any real confidence.'[19] Thus we use customer IDs, passwords, and passkeys to identify ourselves. Often these passwords and passkeys give access to financial data and resources, in particular online bank accounts or credit card accounts or other payment accounts like PayPal, or they allow others to use our accounts fraudulently to buy or sell goods, such as our internet auction accounts.

[18] This will be discussed further in ch. 20.

[19] L Lessig, *Code and Other Laws of Cyberspace Ver. 2.0* (Basic Books 2006) 248.

These proxies for identity are highly prized by the criminal fraternity and have led to the rise of a new form of identity fraud known as 'phishing'.

Case study Phishing

Phishing is usually carried out by email. An email is sent to many tens of thousands of email accounts at random and says something like the user's account has been suspended due to unusual activity, or that security measures are being upgraded and they need to confirm their details. The email will contain a link which will take the user to a 'shell' website made to look like the genuine site but when they enter their details they are retained by the fraudster who then uses them to gain access to their accounts.

This is a false representation and is illegal under s. 2 of the Fraud Act 2006.

Like advance-fee fraud and 'card not present' fraud, phishing represents a real harm to the UK economy with UK banks absorbing losses of £60.4m in online banking fraud in 2014.[20] The tactic for dealing with phishing has largely been the same as with other forms of online fraud: suppression in the UK and cooperation on an international level.

On a domestic level the Court of Appeal reviewed phishing in the case of *R v Wellman*.[21] This was an appeal against sentence. Mr Wellman had, along with others, obtained passwords and user IDs for over five thousand individuals by a mix of phishing and Trojans and had compromised over 1,000 online bank accounts. He pleaded guilty at Leeds Crown Court and was sentenced to two terms of 6 years' imprisonment to run consecutively; a total of 12 years in prison. At appeal this was reduced to one term of 4 years and one of 6 to run consecutively; a total of 10 years. In giving the judgment of the court Mackay J noted that 'it is hard to imagine a more sophisticated and determined course of criminal conduct in this sphere of offending'.[22]

Sentences such as these demonstrate how seriously the UK courts are taking the risk of phishing; a risk recognized internationally and which has led, like advance-fee fraud, to a high level of international cooperation. In 2004 the United Nations organized an expert group on fraud and the criminal misuse and falsification of identity. The group met twice (in March 2005 and January 2007) and recommended that states take steps to update their laws to reflect recent technological developments, that states should ratify, or accede to, the United Nations Crime Conventions and Council of Europe Cybercrime Convention, and that states should review rules on territorial jurisdiction to keep pace with ongoing evolution of fraud and identity-related offences and consider establishing extraterritorial jurisdiction in lieu of extradition.[23]

The expert group recommendations were passed on to the United Nations Office on Drugs and Crime; a body that fosters cooperation in the international fight against drug trafficking and organized crime. They created a further Expert Group on Identity-Related

[20] The UK Cards Association, *2014 Fraud Data*: <http://www.theukcardsassociation.org.uk/wm_documents/2014%20annual%20fraud%20figures%20release%20-%20FINAL.PDF>.

[21] [2007] EWCA Crim 2874.

[22] Ibid. [12].

[23] Taken from <https://www.unodc.org/documents/organized-crime/E_CN_15_2007_8.pdf>.

Crime to examine the issue. The group discussed 'legal approaches to criminalize identity theft',[24] and reported that they had doubts 'as to whether a single unified offence would be viable in most legal systems, but noted that it should be possible to address the problem through a combination of adjustments to existing crimes and the development of a series of new offences to address the novel forms of crime'.[25] They went on to recommend that 'in developing materials with respect to criminalisation and other legislative responses to identity related crime, it was important to adopt a flexible approach'.[26]

The final outcome of the Group's work was the *United Nations Office on Drugs and Crime Handbook on Identity Related Crime*, published in April 2011.[27] The Handbook has taken on board the recommendations of the Expert Group by setting out a range of options to be taken into account when addressing domestic law in relation to identity-related crimes. For lawmakers the most useful part of the guide is probably Part V, the practical guide to international cooperation. It lists all the international instruments that allow for international cooperation, extradition, and extraterritorial actionability of orders. It also sets out a series of case studies in areas such as phishing, card cloning, and auction fraud and suggests strategies that lawmakers and law enforcement bodies may take to regulate the activity. In addition to the Handbook, the Economic and Social Council (ECOSOC) have passed a series of resolutions culminating in resolution 2009/22 on 'International cooperation in the prevention, investigation, prosecution and punishment of economic fraud and identity-related crime'.[28] This encourages member states to undertake a number of activities to reduce the risk and prevalence of identity related crime, including:

(a) to combat economic fraud and identity-related crime by ensuring adequate investigative powers and, where appropriate, by reviewing and updating the relevant laws;

(b) to develop and maintain adequate law enforcement and investigative capacity to keep abreast of and deal with new developments in the exploitation of information, communications and commercial technologies in economic fraud and identity-related crime, including websites and other online forums used to facilitate trafficking in identity information or documents, such as passports, driving licences or national identity cards;

(c) to consider, where appropriate, the establishment of new offences and the updating of existing offences in response to the evolution of economic fraud and identity-related crime, bearing in mind the advantages of common approaches to criminalization, where feasible, in facilitating efficient and effective international cooperation;

[24] See Commission on Crime Prevention and Criminal Justice, Papers for the Eighteenth Session, Vienna, 16–24 April 2009: Thematic discussion: Economic fraud and identity-related crime: <http://www.unodc.org/documents/treaties/organized_crime/ECN152009_CRP12.pdf>.

[25] Ibid. [6].

[26] Ibid. [9].

[27] <http://www.unodc.org/documents/treaties/UNCAC/Publications/Handbook_on_ID_Crime/10-57802_ebooke.pdf>.

[28] <http://www.unodc.org/documents/treaties/organized_crime/ECOSOC_resolution_2009_22.pdf>.

(d) to strengthen international cooperation to prevent and combat economic fraud and identity-related crime, in particular by making full use of the relevant international legal instruments;

(e) to develop an approach for the collection of comparable data on the nature and extent of identity-related crime, including, where feasible, from the victim's perspective, that would allow the sharing of data among appropriate law enforcement entities and provide a central source of data at the national level on the nature and extent of identity-related crime, taking due account of national law.

In 2013 ECOSOC, concerned about levels of identity theft rising, passed a further resolution inviting member states to provide extra-budgetary resources for the purpose of fighting identity theft and the extend the budget of the United Nations Office on Drugs and Crime.[29] Despite these efforts the latest data from the UK Cards Association suggests that the problem continues to grow.[30]

15.2 Grooming, harassment, and cyberstalking

As well as offering an opportunity for fraud, the anonymous and intrusive nature of the information society allows users to stalk, harass, and groom others from a distance. We may classify these as offences against the person enabled and supported by ICT. Each of these offences is slightly different and has produced a slightly different legal response. All are illegal in the UK and in many cases the law has recently been amended or updated to account for changes in technology.

15.2.1 Grooming

Grooming is the act of befriending or establishing an emotional connection with a child, in order to lower the child's inhibitions in preparation for sexual abuse. Grooming is not new; it existed before the advent of the information society and would be carried out through personal interaction with a child, perhaps at a public place such as a park or by a person with a position of trust such as a teacher, religious leader, or group leader (such as a scoutmaster). The information society makes it easier for strangers to groom children due to the nature of the communications media. First, children are comfortable: they are usually sitting at home and using websites familiar to them such as Habbo, Poptropica, or Club Penguin, or, if older, Kik, Facebook, Yik Yak, or Instagram; this causes them to lower their guard. Second, internet social networking sites such as the ones mentioned cause children not to recognize 'stranger danger' as easily as they are accustomed to meeting new people in this environment and so do not equate new people to 'strangers'. Third, the anonymity offered by social networking sites allows adults to pose as children so the victim believes they are talking to someone of their own age; this again causes them to lower their defences.

[29] ECOSOC resolution 2013/39 of 25 July 2013.
[30] See (n. 20) and related text.

Grooming was only formally criminalized in 2003. Prior to the passage of the Sexual Offences Act 2003 law enforcement authorities had to use a hotchpotch of legislation to prosecute many of the acts which the offender may have committed in grooming a child including the Obscene Publications Act 1959 or the Protection of Children Act 1978 (as offenders would often use pornography to convince a child it was okay to engage in sexual conduct); the Malicious Communications Act 1988 (which outlaws the sending of offensive or threatening communications); and the Protection from Harassment Act 1997 (which outlaws activity which the offender knows amounts to harassment).

These were felt to be inadequate to deal with the increased risk of grooming following the development of ICT communications such as email, IRC, and social networking sites. In their famous 2001 report, 'Chat Wise, Street Wise',[31] the Internet Crime Forum reported that a US survey had found that 'just under one in five of 10–17 year olds surveyed claimed to have received some kind of sexual solicitation on the Internet within the previous twelve months',[32] and that the UK Law as it stood did not adequately deal with the issue of 'online enticement of a child'.[33]

The solution was s. 15 of the Sexual Offences Act 2003. This introduces the complicated offence of 'Meeting a child following sexual grooming', a provision which as its name suggests doesn't criminalize the act of grooming itself, but rather the further act of intending to meet a child following grooming. To commit the offence the offender (who must be aged 18 or over) must either have met or communicated with the child (being a person under 16) on at least one previous occasion;[34] the offender must then either meet the child or travel with the intention of meeting the child; and at that time, the offender has the intention of committing a relevant sexual offence (including sexual activity with a child, causing a child to engage in sexual activity, engaging in sexual activity in the presence of a child, or causing a child to watch a sexual act). The reason why the offence is framed in this way is to prevent the risk of criminalizing innocent communications with children, by including the final element that the offender must either meet, or travel with intent to meet the minor for the purpose of some form of sexual encounter it removes any element of uncertainty.[35] The offence has been prosecuted extensively with, among others, a serving police child protection officer and a priest facing charges.[36]

In 2010 the Court of Appeal had an opportunity to review grooming, albeit in relation to offline communications in *R v G*.[37]

[31] Internet Crime Forum, Chat Wise, Street Wise March 2001 <http://www.internetcrimeforum.org.uk/chatwise_streetwise.pdf>.

[32] Ibid. [56].

[33] Ibid. Executive Summary.

[34] The law used to require at least two previous communications but this was amended by s. 36 of the Criminal Justice and Courts Act 2015.

[35] See House of Commons Select Committee on Home Affairs, Fifth Report, 24 June 2003, ch. 5: <http://www.publications.parliament.uk/pa/cm200203/cmselect/cmhaff/639/63908.htm>.

[36] See 'Priest "paid for girl's grooming"' (*BBC News*, 15 May 2007) <http://news.bbc.co.uk/1/hi/england/merseyside/6657715.stm>; 'Child Protection Officer On Grooming Charge' (*Police Oracle*, 29 April 2009) <http://www.policeoracle.com/news/Child-Protection-Officer-On-Grooming-Charge_19061.html>.

[37] [2010] EWCA Crim 1693.

Case study *R v G*

The case involved a man known to the family of the victim. He appeared to be a close family friend and had known the victim and her family for some time. It is reported the victim's family and his family intended to holiday together.

He was accused of assaulting the victim on five occasions and was convicted under s. 15. The appellant appealed this conviction arguing that the previous communication he had had with the child was of a non-sexual nature, all he had done was arrange to meet her, as a family friend, after school. In essence his appeal was based on the claim that the prior communication must have been undertaken with a view to instigate a sexual relationship for the s. 15 offence to be made out and in his case this was not true.

The decision of the court was given by Leveson LJ:

> On the face of it, the fact that the description of the offence in the heading is 'meeting a child following sexual grooming etc' might be taken to suggest that the behaviour antecedent to any arranged meeting must itself be sexual in nature. The phrase 'sexual grooming', however, does not appear in the section and although the origin of the offence might have been a concern that paedophiles could use the internet to contact and groom children, the language of the provision is far wider than 'virtual' sexual contact. Thus, the only requirement prior to the intentional meeting during which A (over 18) intends to do anything to B (under 16) which, if carried out, would involve the commission by A of a relevant offence is meeting or communication 'on at least two occasions'. There is absolutely no requirement that either communication be sexual in nature. As the editor of Smith and Hogan, Criminal Law observes, this reflects the fact that persons in this position will (or, as we add, may) seek to secure the confidence of their target by discussing innocuous issues in earlier conversation. Indeed, at that time, B need not necessarily be a sexual target at all; the word 'etc' clarifies that the heading should not be used to derive the conclusion that the earlier meetings need be sexual. The aim of the statute is to penalise those who use a relationship which they have developed (whether innocently or otherwise) as a platform from which to launch sexual offending.[38]

He also took the opportunity to clarify the *mens rea* element:

> We turn to the all important intended meeting. The statute visualises the commission of an offence whether or not that meeting takes place; it is sufficient if, with the intention of meeting, A travels to B or B travels to A. In each case, however, A must intend to commit a relevant (sexual) offence. Thus, either when A travels to B, waits for B to arrive or at the moment of meeting, A's sexual intention must be proved. It is not enough that, during the course of a meeting, started without any such intention, A then decides to take advantage of the situation and commit an offence: the crime then will be the commission of or the attempt to commit that offence. The offence contained within s. 15 is not engaged.[39]

In the instant case he found that the offence had been made out and that the judge's direction to the jury had been correct and dismissed the appeal.

[38] Ibid. [16].
[39] Ibid. [17].

R v G tells us quite a lot about the scope of the offence. It is now clear that in essence it is about two things: (1) has the accused been in contact with the victim prior to the meeting in question? The nature of that contact is not important, and (2) what was the intent of the accused at the time they travelled to meet the victim?

15.2.2 **Sexual communication with a child**

Of late there have been claims that the grooming offence has been less effective in dealing with online abuse of children. In particular, the advent of HD webcams and instant messaging services now means paedophiles can abuse children virtually at a distance. In their 2013 report 'Threat Assessment of Child Sexual Exploitation and Abuse' the Child Exploitation and Online Protection Centre identified online child sexual exploitation as one of four 'key threats' to children's safety online.[40] Children are becoming sexualized at an earlier age and can easily be fooled into thinking they are trading intimate images with someone close to their age. Paedophiles pose as children and once they receive a sexual image from a child will use this to blackmail the child into sending more, often more explicit, images. As the paedophile never travels, nor intends to travel, to meet the child they do not commit the offence of grooming. As a result the National Society for the Prevention of Cruelty to Children ran a campaign suggesting a new offence was needed to target paedophiles who communicate sexually with a child. The government considered the proposal and, at the WePROTECT summit in December 2014, the Prime Minister announced the intention to create a new offence in response to the campaign.[41]

The new law is to be found in s. 67 of the Serious Crime Act 2015 which creates a new s. 15A of the Sexual Offences Act 2003. This makes it an offence when an adult (being a person over 18) communicates with a child (being under 16) 'for the purpose of obtaining sexual gratification'. To commit the offence the communication must be sexual or is intended to encourage the child to make a communication that is sexual. That is, the communication must be of a sexual nature or be trying to elicit a sexual communication (such as an indecent image) from the child. The provision is intended to criminalize the act of communicating with a child either directly in a sexual manner or with the intent to elicit sexual communications from the child. This was felt to be a necessary addition to the law for although a paedophile who received a sexual image of a child would have committed an offence under the laws which regulate child-abuse images (discussed in ch. 14) the act of soliciting such an image was not an offence. At the time of writing s. 15A has not yet been brought into force, which is rather unusual given that the government was a strong supporter of the provision and nearly all of the remainder of the Act, except that those provisions relating to Scotland *have* been brought into force. It may be that the government has got cold feet on this, but it may be that by the time you read this it is in force.

[40] CEOP, June 2013: <https://www.ceop.police.uk/Documents/ceopdocs/CEOP_TACSEA2013_240613%20FINAL.pdf>.

[41] S Swinford et al., 'New law will prevent paedophiles soliciting pictures from children' *The Telegraph* (London, 10 December 2014) <http://www.telegraph.co.uk/news/uknews/law-and-order/11286683/Paedophiles-have-nowhere-to-hide-as-spies-and-police-target-dark-web.html>.

15.2.3 **Harassment and stalking**

Harassment and stalking are rather different to grooming. Harassment is behaviour intended to disturb or upset, and, which is usually found threatening or disturbing, stalking is an aggravated form of harassment where the victim finds themself followed and continually contacted by the offender. In harassment and stalking cases the victim is usually an adult, although in law it is possible to harass or stalk a minor. In a legal sense there is no distinction between the two: both are classified as harassment and are primarily regulated by the Protection from Harassment Act 1997. This provides that a person 'must not pursue a course of conduct (a) which amounts to harassment of another, and (b) which he knows or ought to know amounts to harassment of the other'.[42] This raises the question: how ought one to know that their course of action amounts to harassment, given that many harassers/stalkers suffer from mental impairment? This is covered, though, by s. 1(2) which provides that 'the person whose course of conduct is in question ought to know that it amounts to harassment of another if a reasonable person in possession of the same information would think the course of conduct amounted to harassment of the other'.

If found guilty of harassment the offender may both be charged under s. 2, which can lead to a maximum six months' imprisonment, and be issued with a restraining order under s. 5, which if breached may lead to up to 5 years' imprisonment.[43] If the harassment is of such a nature as to put the victim in fear of violence on at least two occasions (this is what the media often colloquially refers to as stalking) then under s. 4 of the Act the offender may be charged with the aggravated offence of 'Putting People in Fear of Violence', this, like breaching a restraining order under s. 5, can lead to imprisonment of up to 5 years.

In addition to the provisions of the Protection from Harassment Act, online harassment (or cyberstalking as it is usually known) may also lead to prosecutions under the Malicious Communications Act 1988 or the Communications Act 2003. By s. 1 of the Malicious Communications Act 1988 it is an offence to send an indecent, offensive, or threatening letter, electronic communication, or other article to another person. This is a summary offence and as such may only lead to a maximum sentence of imprisonment of six months, as is the offence of improper use of the public electronic communications system under s. 127 of the Communications Act 2003, which makes it an offence to send, by means of a public electronic communication system, a message or other matter that is grossly offensive or of an indecent, obscene, or menacing character; or which is sent for the purpose of causing annoyance, inconvenience, or needless anxiety to another and which is known to be false. As both these offences are summary in nature, and as the court cannot issue a restraining order unless the prosecution is brought under the Protection from Harassment Act, the authorities will tend to prosecute under the Protection from Harassment Act rather than the Malicious Communications Act or the Communications Act.[44]

[42] Protection from Harassment Act 1997, s. 1(1).

[43] Protection from Harassment Act 1997, s. 5(6).

[44] An extensive discussion of harassment and bullying on social network platforms can be found in ch. 7 at 7.4.

15.3 **Cyberterrorism**

Cyberterrorism is now seen as part of the front line of the 'war on terror'. The concept of 'informational warfare', that is, states fighting campaigns using informational tools and weapons in addition to traditional ordnance, is well established and dates from at least the early 1990s.[45] The concept of cyberterrorism, that is individuals or groups using the network capabilities of the information society to launch unlawful attacks and threats of attack against computers, networks, and the information stored therein to intimidate or coerce a government or its people in furtherance of political or social objectives, is newer, dating from around the turn of the millennium.[46] Although terrorist acts are clearly criminal, it was not clear initially that the types of activities carried out by cyberterrorists would be illegal. Cyberterrorists may carry out denial of service attacks, which as we saw in ch. 13, were not clearly criminalized until 1 October 2008 when ss. 35–38 of the Police and Justice Act 2006 were brought into force; otherwise they may commit offences of unlawful access to data or unlawful modification of data under ss. 1–3 of the Computer Misuse Act 1990, but often they would simply publish materials in support of terrorist organizations or aims, or incite hatred. Prior to the passage of a series of anti-terror measures from 2000 onward this was not illegal unless the materials were in support of an organization proscribed by Sch. 1 of the Prevention of Terrorism (Temporary Provisions) Act 1989, a list which predominantly listed Irish dissident groups in a time when the rising risk was from extremist Islamic organizations such as al Qaeda.

However, the law has changed substantially in the past 16 years. The Terrorism Act 2000 introduced several new offences which could take place online. Prime among these were: possession of items for a terrorist purpose; possession of information or documents of a kind likely to be useful to a person committing or preparing an act of terrorism; and inciting terrorism overseas.

Section 57 provides that it is an offence to possess an article in circumstances which give rise to a reasonable suspicion that possession is for a purpose connected with the commission, preparation, or instigation of an act of terrorism. On conviction on indictment, this may lead to a maximum sentence of imprisonment of 15 years.[47] The wording of the section, and the fact that there was a separate offence of possession of information or documents of a kind likely to be useful to a person committing or preparing an act of terrorism under s. 58, punishable by up to 10 years in prison,[48] may lead one to suspect that by 'article' the framers of s. 57 had in mind items such as weapons, bomb-making equipment, training video, or similar articles. Unfortunately the definition of 'article' found in s. 121 is extremely vague defining it simply as 'includes substance

[45] Information Warfare was first introduced in a formal sense in 1992 in the US Department of Defense Directive TS3600.1. See Kaomea, Hearold, and Page, 'Beyond Security: A Data Quality Perspective on Defensive Information Warfare' MIT Total Data Quality Management Program Working Papers 1994 <http://web.mit.edu/tdqm/papers/other/kaomea.html>.

[46] This definition is taken from one of the early discussions of cyberterrorism before the Special Oversight Panel on Terrorism of the US House of Representatives Committee on Armed Services which took place on 23 May 2000. It is taken from the testimony of Dorothy Denning, then Professor of Computer Science at Georgetown University. Testimony at: <http://www.stealth-iss.com/documents/pdf/CYBERTERRORISM.pdf>.

[47] Terrorism Act 2000, s. 57(4)(a).

[48] Terrorism Act 2000, s. 58(4)(a).

and any other thing'. This has led the authorities to attempt to prosecute possession of information or data under s. 57.

In the first case of this type, *R v M*,[49] the prosecution claimed that possession of data stored electronically on computer hard drives or CDs was capable of being an 'article' under s. 57. The prosecution's case was that the s. 57 articles were electronic storage devices such as hard drives, CDs, and DVDs, a USB storage device, and a video recording, as well as two documents. At the preliminary hearing, the defendants submitted that 'data' was not an article, arguing that the prosecution's interpretation of s. 57 made s. 58(1)(b) completely redundant and made nearly all of s. 58(1)(a) redundant. The defendants argued that the only conduct which would be caught by s. 58 if the prosecution's interpretation was allowed would be collecting information but not writing it down. The Court of Appeal allowed the appeal finding that the issue was whether the items listed were 'articles'. They found that CDs and computer hard drives holding electronic data were capable of being articles within the meaning of s. 57, but that it was clear that Parliament had laid down a different regime for documents and records under s. 58 and 'articles' under s. 57.

This decision which seemed to sensibly delineate the difference between 'articles' and 'data' or 'information', was though unfortunately not followed in the later case of *R v Rowe* in which a five-judge bench found *R v M* to be *per incuriam*.[50] Mr Rowe had been arrested in possession of a notebook which contained mortar instructions and a substitution code which listed components of explosives and places of a type susceptible to terrorist bombing. The prosecution case was that the appellant was shortly to embark on a terrorist venture and that the notebook and the code were held for terrorist purposes. Mr Rowe was charged and found guilty of possession of a terrorist article under s. 57. Following the decision in *R v M* he appealed against conviction. On this occasion the Court of Appeal refused his appeal. The judgment of the court was given by Lord Phillips CJ:

> There is undoubtedly an overlap between section 57 and 58, but it is not correct to suggest that if documents and records constitute articles for the purpose of section 57, section 58 is almost superfluous. Collecting information, which falls within section 58 alone, may well not involve making a record of the information. Equally a person who possesses information likely to be useful to a person committing or preparing an act of terrorism may well not be in possession of it for a purpose connected with the commission, preparation or instigation of an act of terrorism. Sections 57 and 58 are indeed dealing with different aspects of activities relating to terrorism. Section 57 is dealing with possessing articles for the purpose of terrorist acts. Section 58 is dealing with collecting or holding information that is of a kind likely to be useful to those involved in acts of terrorism. Section 57 includes a specific intention, section 58 does not. These differences between the two sections are rational features of a statute whose aims include the prohibition of different types of support for and involvement, both direct and indirect, in terrorism. There is no basis for the conclusion that Parliament intended to have a completely separate regime for documents and records from that which applies to other articles. For these reasons we have concluded that the decision in *R v M* was based on false assumptions and false analysis and that it was wrong.[51]

This suggests that possession of data for publication on a website or some other forum may amount to a s. 57 offence if that data or information is of a nature as to be directly

[49] [2007] EWCA Crim 298.
[50] [2007] QB 975.
[51] Ibid. 985–6.

associated with a specific terrorist purpose. The nature of s. 57, and s. 58, has though arguably been changed by new provisions introduced by Part I of the Terrorism Act 2006 and we shall return to this analysis below.

The other major provision of the Terrorism Act 2000 which may apply to online activities is the s. 59 offence of inciting terrorism overseas. This formed the focus of one of the most high-profile cyberterrorism cases in the UK to date. The case involved a group of young men who operated a network of at least 32 websites and a number of chat forums dedicated to fighting a jihadist cause, in particular in Iraq. According to evidence:

> the sites included assertions that it was the duty of Moslems to fight armed Jihad against Jews, crusaders, apostates and their supporters in all Muslim countries and that it was the duty of every Muslim to fight and kill them wherever they are, civilian or military. There were also films, much of it emanating from Al-Qaeda in Iraq, posted to the websites showing very explicit acts of terrorist murder, including the beheading of civilian hostages, attacks on the police, government officials and on coalition forces in Iraq. In the internet chat forums individuals disposed to join the insurgency were provided with routes by which to travel into Iraq and manuals of weapons and explosives were requested.[52]

Those involved included Younes Tsouli, a Moroccan-born UK resident who called himself Irhabi_007; 'Irhabi' being the Arabic word for terrorist, and '007' a reference to the fictional secret agent James Bond. Tsouli had been among the most wanted supporters of terrorist activity of UK and US Law enforcement agents. All involved were charged under s. 59 for inciting terrorists to commit murder overseas. On 4 July 2007, after two months at trial, Tsouli and his co-defendants Waseem Mughal and Tariq Al-Daour pleaded guilty to 'inciting another person to commit an act of terrorism wholly or partly outside the UK which would, if committed in England and Wales, constitute murder' and admitted to conspiring together and with others to defraud banks, credit card companies, and charge card companies to pay for the hosting of the websites and chat rooms. Tsouli was sentenced to 10 years' imprisonment, Mughal to 7½ years, and Al-Daour to 6½ years.[53]

The Attorney General referred these sentences to the Court of Appeal for being unduly lenient, and on 18 December 2007 the sentences of all three men were increased: Tsouli's sentence was increased to 16 years, Mughal to 12 years, and Al Daour 12 years.[54] In giving the judgment of the court Gage LJ noted that:

> The offenders' conduct involved the preplanning of a sophisticated and intricate misuse of computers. Its execution was funded by the proceeds of fraud and was carried out with no little technological skills . . . their purpose was to facilitate publication of material on the website and in the chat room forums, exhorting in strong terms others to participate in acts of extreme violence on a very large scale. The material which was published leaves no doubt about what was intended. It was also published in the context of the armed conflict in Iraq involving, as it did, British and American soldiers. Their conduct covered a comparatively short period. However, we infer that but for their arrest their conduct would have covered a much longer period.[55]

The use of the Terrorism Act 2000 to prosecute those operating terrorist websites and chat forums has now arguably been superseded by Part I of the Terrorism Act 2006. By

[52] *Attorney General's Reference (Nos. 85, 86, and 87 of 2007)* [2007] EWCA Crim 3300.
[53] Ibid. [4].
[54] Ibid. [41].
[55] Ibid. [40].

s. 1(2) it is an offence to publish a statement or to cause another to publish a statement, which is likely to be understood by some or all of the members of the public to whom it is published as a direct or indirect encouragement or other inducement to them to the commission, preparation, or instigation of acts of terrorism or Convention offences, if at the time it is published it is intended to encourage members of the public to be directly or indirectly encouraged or induced to commit, prepare, or instigate acts of terrorism. This offence is punishable on indictment with a prison sentence of up to 7 years. In addition there is a separate offence under s. 2 of dissemination of terrorist publications. This makes it an offence to distribute, sell, circulate, offer for sale, or transmit electronically material intended to encourage members of the public to be directly or indirectly encouraged or induced to commit, prepare, or instigate acts of terrorism. Like s. 1, the penalty for such an offence may be 7 years' imprisonment if charged on indictment. Section 3 lays out specific provisions to regulate the publication of terrorist materials via the internet.

Due to the risk of a website being hijacked or defaced without the knowledge of the operator of that site, or of comments made in an unmoderated forum being published without the forum operator's knowledge, there is a notification procedure. The procedure requires that a constable gives notice, either in person or by sending it by recorded delivery to the last recorded address of the 'relevant person' (usually the operator of the site),[56] which declares that in the opinion of the constable giving it, the statement or the article or record is unlawfully terrorism-related.[57] The notice requires the relevant person to secure that the statement or the article or record, so far as it is so related, is not available to the public or is modified so as no longer to be so related;[58] warns the relevant person that a failure to comply with the notice within two working days will result in the statement, or the article or record, being regarded as having his endorsement;[59] and explains how he may become liable by virtue of the notice if the statement, or the article or record, becomes available to the public after he has complied with the notice by republication elsewhere.[60] If the recipient of the notice fails to take steps to remove the material or render it inaccessible to the public within two working days, then under s. 3(2) the statement is deemed to be 'endorsed by the relevant person',[61] this allows for criminal prosecution under either or both of ss.1 and 2. Part I came into force on 13 April 2006[62] and has, perhaps unsurprisingly, been the subject of a number of reviews by the appellate courts.

In *R v Rahman and Mohammed* the Court of Appeal reviewed the sentences of two men convicted under s. 2 for separate offences.[63] Mr Rahman had been found in possession of a letter and some video clips held on his computer. He pleaded guilty under s. 2(2)(f) of having terrorist material in his possession which he intended to disseminate. Mr Mohammed was selling Islamic material from stalls at markets in the north of

[56] Terrorism Act 2006, s. 4.
[57] Ibid. s. 3(3)(a).
[58] Ibid. s. 3(3)(b).
[59] Ibid. s. 3(3)(c).
[60] Ibid. s. 3(3)(d).
[61] There are defences under ss. 3(5) and 3(6) when a statement is republished without the knowledge or assistance of the original publisher.
[62] The Terrorism Act 2006 (Commencement No. 1) Order 2006, SI 2006/1013.
[63] [2008] EWCA Crim 1465.

England. Although most of his material was legal some breached the provisions of the Act. He too pleaded guilty under s. 2 when charged. Mr Rahman was sentenced to 6 years in prison (near the maximum sentence under the Act), while Mr Mohammed was given a sentence of 3 years.[64] On appeal these were reduced to 5½ years and 2 years respectively,[65] with Lord Phillips CJ noting: 'offences under section 2 of the 2006 Act are capable of varying very widely in seriousness and this is reflected by the fact that, while the offence carries a maximum sentence of 7 years imprisonment if tried on indictment, it may be tried summarily'.[66] Despite this the court felt a sentence of 5½ years was reasonable in Mr Rahman's case, even though he had not actually disseminated any of the material.

In the case of *R v Zafar* the Court of Appeal considered the interplay between s. 57 of the 2000 Act and Part I of the 2006 Act.[67] Zafar is the conclusion of the *R v M/Rowe* line of analysis discussed earlier. The defendants here were the same ones in *R v M* (that being an earlier interlocutory appeal). All had been charged with the possession of articles for a purpose connected with the commission, preparation, or instigation of an act of terrorism under s. 57; the articles in question being 'documents, compact discs or computer hard drives on which material had been electronically stored. The material included ideological propaganda as well as communications between the defendants and others which the prosecution alleged showed a settled plan under which the defendants would travel to Pakistan to receive training and thereafter commit a terrorist act or acts in Afghanistan.'[68] Following the decision in *Rowe* the Recorder of London gave a further ruling that he would be bound by that decision. That ruling was upheld in a second interlocutory appeal,[69] and at a subsequent trial the accused were found guilty on almost all charges.[70] All appealed against conviction. Their appeal was upheld with Lord Phillips CJ again giving the judgment of the court. A crucial part of the court's deliberation was how Part I of the 2006 Act could be read alongside s. 57 of the 2000 Act. Applying the extremely expansive interpretation of s. 57 found in *Rowe* seemed to suggest Part I of the 2006 Act was unnecessary. Here Lord Phillips noted that 'Parliament, did not envisage that [s. 57] would extend to possessing propaganda for the purpose of incitement to terrorist acts. That belief is strengthened by the fact that Parliament considered it desirable to legislate in relation to possessing propaganda with the intention of inducing acts of terrorism by section 2(2)(f) of the Terrorism Act 2006.'[71]

Where does this leave the interplay between s. 57 of the 2000 Act and Part I of the 2006 Act? It appears that if one possesses documents, including digital data, with the intent to use them to instigate a specific terrorist attack (i.e. what may be defined as preparatory materials), this will cause a prosecution to be brought under s. 57. If though the materials are rather in the form of propaganda materials, then it falls within the scope of Part I of the 2006 Act. However, against this is the further confusion that the authority of *Attorney General's Reference (Nos. 85, 86, and 87 of 2007)* still applies also.

[64] Ibid. [31], [33].

[65] Ibid. [33], [49].

[66] Ibid. [8].

[67] *R v Zafar* [2008] QB 810. It should be noted that Zafar has been subject to a mildly disapproving review from the House of Lords in *R v G* [2009] UKHL 13. The decision was not, however, overruled and the principles discussed in this text are still unmoved by the *R v G* decision.

[68] Ibid. 816–17.

[69] *R v M* (No. 2) [2007] 3 All ER 53.

[70] [2008] QB 810, 818.

[71] Ibid. 822.

This means that if one operates a website which promotes or supports terrorist activity in the widest sense, one would probably be charged under Part I of the 2006 Act. If one offers support or advice, including instruction or maps, via a website or other forum to individuals planning a particular terrorist attack one would probably be charged under s. 57. If, though, as Younes Tsouli and his co-defendants did, one operates a website or forum which provides advice and encouragement to terrorists overseas to commit a terrorist act such as murder or endangerment to life one may be charged under s. 59 which allows for sentences up to a mandatory life sentence.

The more recent case of *R v Brown* dealt with the question of whether the Terrorism Acts 2000 and 2006 were an unreasonable restriction on the fundamental right to free expression.[72] Mr. Brown sought leave to appeal his conviction under both s. 58 of the Terrorism Act 2000 and s. 2 of the Terrorism Act 2006. He had for some time been selling via his website the famous 1971 publication *The Anarchist Cookbook*, a publication which details bomb-making recipes as well as recipes for toxins. He accepted that the publication could be useful to terrorists but argued that his motivation for selling it was commercial rather than ideological, pointing out that the terms and conditions of his website bound buyers to use it only for lawful purposes. After being arrested and sentenced to 3 years' imprisonment Mr. Brown sought to appeal against his conviction and sentence. He argued that ss. 2 and 58 breached his fundamental right to free expression. The decision of the court was given by the Lord Chief Justice who found that neither provision infringed on Mr. Brown's right to free expression. In relation to s. 58 he noted that:

> In relation to the offence created by section 58 of the 2000 Act, a statutory defence is provided: that there was a reasonable excuse for the applicant's action or possession of information likely to be useful to an individual committing or preparing an act of terrorism. In other words, the prohibition in section 58 is not itself absolute, once the offence created by section 58 is not an offence of strict liability. The actions which would otherwise constitute the offence may be excusable. The question whether the excuse is reasonable on the basis of the exercise of the right to freedom of speech or freedom of expression may be left to the jury to be decided as a question of fact in the individual case.[73]

In relation to s. 2, the answer was similar:

> it is difficult to see how a criminal act of distribution or circulation of a terrorist publication with the specific intent, or in the frame of mind expressly required as an essential ingredient of this offence to encourage or assist acts of terrorism, can be saved by reference to the principle of freedom of speech, unless that principle is absolute, which, as we have indicated, it is not.[74]

These are hardly surprising outcomes given Art. 10(2) of the European Convention on Human Rights:

> The exercise of these freedoms, since it carries with it duties and responsibilities, may be subject to such formalities, conditions, restrictions or penalties as are prescribed by law and are necessary in a democratic society, in the interests of national security, territorial integrity or public safety, for the prevention of disorder or crime, for the protection of health or morals, for the protection of the reputation or rights of others, for preventing the disclosure of information received in confidence, or for maintaining the authority and impartiality of the judiciary.

[72] [2011] EWCA Crim 2751.
[73] Ibid. [22].
[74] Ibid. [23].

Finally we have the Supreme Court case of *R v Gul*.[75] This is a case at the very heart of the Terrorism Acts; the definition of terrorism itself. Mr. Gul had uploaded videos to a number of websites, including YouTube, showing attacks by al Qaeda, the Taliban, and other proscribed groups on military targets in Chechnya, and on the Coalition forces in Iraq and in Afghanistan, the use of improvised explosive devices against Coalition forces, excerpts from martyrdom videos, and clips of attacks on civilians, including the 9/11 attack on New York. According to the report of the case 'these videos were accompanied by commentaries praising the bravery, and martyrdom, of those carrying out the attacks, and encouraging others to emulate them.'[76] Mr. Gul was charged under s. 2 of the 2006 Act. He argued that the provision did not apply to these videos as they showed a justified use of force by freedom fighters resisting occupation of their country. He particularly argued three claims:

(1) The first is that the 2000 Act, like the 2006 Act, was intended, at least in part, to give effect to the UK's international treaty obligations, and the concept of terrorism in international law does not extend to military attacks by a non-state armed group against state, or inter-governmental organization, armed forces in the context of a non-international armed conflict, and that this limitation should be implied into the definition in section 1 of the 2000 Act;

(2) it would be wrong to read the 2000 or 2006 Acts as criminalizing in this country an act abroad, unless that act would be regarded as criminal by international law norms; and

(3) as a matter of domestic law and quite apart from international law considerations, some qualifications must be read into the very wide words of section 1 of the 2000 Act.[77]

The court, in the joint judgment of Lords Neuberger and Judge, found against Mr. Gul. In response to his first claim the court noted that 'there is no accepted norm in international law as to what constitutes terrorism'[78] and that while it is true that some other provisions of the 2000 and 2006 Acts give effect to treaties that do not extend to insurgent attacks on military forces in non-international armed conflicts, there was no reason why the United Kingdom could not go further in the 2000 Act than the treaties had. And even if those treaties had intended to limit the definition of terrorism that they applied, that would only affect the particular provisions of the 2000 Act that implemented those treaties.[79] This claim was thus refused. In response to the second claim the court found that this claim was irrelevant as 'the present case does not involve a defendant who has committed acts, which are said to be offences, abroad: the activities said to be offences were committed in the UK—and by a UK citizen.'[80] This only left the final, domestic, claim. Here the court found that:

> unless it is established that the natural meaning of the legislation conflicts with the European Convention on Human Rights (which is not suggested) or any other international obligation

[75] [2013] UKSC 64.
[76] Ibid. [2].
[77] Ibid. [24].
[78] Ibid. [44].
[79] Ibid. [54].
[80] Ibid. [56].

> of the United Kingdom (which were considered and rejected), our function is to interpret the meaning of the definition in its statutory, legal and practical context. We agree with the wide interpretation favoured by the prosecution: it accords with the natural meaning of the words used in section 1(1)(b) of the 2000 Act, and, while it gives the words a concerningly wide meaning, there are good reasons for it.[81]

In all, this is not a terribly surprising outcome. One man's terrorist is another man's freedom fighter and in terms of the rule of law we cannot allow individuals to interpret definitions to suit their ends. The seriousness of Mr Gul's challenge, particularly the international law aspects of it, may be seen in the fact that the case made it to the Supreme Court. This was an extremely important issue and the very wide definition of terrorism given in the Acts may be rightly criticized, but given the high level of sophistication of modern terrorist groups such as the Islamic State, which uses social media and online video to great effect, it is perhaps no surprise that the Supreme Court upheld the wide definition. This issue will continue to press lawmakers and judges in the coming years as recruitment videos for groups like Islamic State continue to be posted online. The problem is that there can sometimes be a very fine line between protected religious speech and unprotected speech which promotes or supports terrorist activity and the courts have to ensure that while restricting and controlling the latter they do not inadvertently and illegally restrict the former.

15.4 **The convention on cybercrime**

A common theme across several of the examples of online criminal activity we have examined in this section (hacking and viruses; indecency, pornography, and obscenity; fraud and identity fraud and also cyberterrorism) is that, with a truly global network, criminals in any part of the world can impact on any other part of the world. Criminal law is the one area where the warnings of the cyberlibertarian school have been proven substantively correct. There are of course solutions to some of these problems, including the installation of filters, such as the IWF/Cleanfeed filter and localizing the offence as the UK has done by outlawing the possession of extreme pornography and NPPICs. But to deal with the underlying problem of child-abuse images being produced in such diverse places as the Ukraine, the US, and Vietnam, or fraud being perpetrated in Nigeria, China, and Russia, we need to harmonize law enforcement provisions and seek measures to reduce jurisdictional disputes. To date though international cooperation has been limited, with only one substantial international convention being agreed, despite some 25 years of discussion.

Only the Council of Europe Convention on Cybercrime[82] attempts to harmonize international cybercrime laws. As of 18 September 2015 the treaty had been signed by 45 Council of Europe states, including the UK, and 4 non-European states.[83] It has been ratified by and has entered into force in 47 states, including the US and the UK.[84] The

[81] Ibid. [38].
[82] See (n. 14).
[83] These are: Canada, Japan, South Africa, and the US.
[84] Beyond the signatories the Convention has entered into force in Australia, the Dominican Republic, Mauritius, Panama, and Sri Lanka by accession.

substantive provisions are all found in Chapter II, Section 1 and fall into five subsections: offences against data and systems;[85] computer-related offences;[86] content-related offences;[87] offences related to infringement of copyright;[88] and ancillary offences.[89] In addition, the Convention provides for procedural systems to support the enforcement of the substantive provisions. Mutual assistance and cooperation provisions found in Arts. 23 and 25 require states parties to cooperate in the investigation and evidence gathering of convention crimes reported to them by other states partners: or to put it another way, as favoured by critics of the convention

> The treaty requires that [domestic] governments help enforce other countries' 'cybercrime' laws—even if the act being prosecuted is not illegal [domestically] . . . That means that countries that have laws limiting free speech on the Net could oblige [local law enforcement] to uncover the identities of anonymous [domestic] critics, or monitor their communications on behalf of foreign governments. [Domestic] ISPs would be obliged to obey other jurisdiction's requests to log their users' behaviour without due process, or compensation.[90]

Although there is some element of truth in these criticisms of the Convention critics have blown the risk out of proportion. Article 25(4) states that 'except as otherwise specifically provided in articles in this chapter, mutual assistance shall be subject to the conditions provided for by the law of the requested Party or by applicable mutual assistance treaties, including the grounds on which the requested Party may refuse co-operation'. This means that the requested state can refuse a mutual assistance request where it exceeds the agreed parameters of the requested state except in specific cases set out, mostly in Art. 27, which itself provides safeguards.[91] Nevertheless, campaigns such as the EFF campaign in the US and the Statewatch campaign in the UK have made the Convention controversial.[92]

From a UK perspective the Convention changes little, except in the area of cooperation. Even before implementation, the UK fulfilled all the substantive requirements of the Convention through domestic provisions that were partly the catalyst for the reforms to the Computer Misuse Act found in the Police and Justice Act 2006. Even the procedural elements of Art. 25 change little in the UK as previously (and

[85] These are: Art. 2: illegal access (hacking); Art. 3 illegal interception of data; Art. 4: data interference (criminal damage and viruses); Art. 5 system interference (denial of service); and Art. 6 production or use of a device for any of the aforementioned purposes.

[86] These are: Art. 7: computer-related forgery, and Art. 8 computer-related fraud.

[87] This is a single offence under Art. 9 of production, distribution, or possession of child pornography.

[88] This is a single Article, Art. 10 which requires signatories to cooperate in the detection and prosecution of criminal copyright infringement under the Paris Act of 1971, the Rome Convention, and the WIPO Copyright and Phonograms and Performances Treaties.

[89] These are: Art. 11 attempts and aiding and abetting; Art. 12 corporate liability; and Art. 13 sanctions and measures.

[90] D O'Brien, 'The World's Worst Internet Laws Sneaking Through the Senate' (Electronic Frontier Foundation, 3 August 2006) <http://www.eff.org/deeplinks/2006/08/worlds-worst-internet-laws-sneaking-through-senate>.

[91] By Art. 27(4) 'The requested Party may, in addition to the grounds for refusal established in Art. 25(4), refuse assistance if: (a) the request concerns an offence which the requested Party considers a political offence or an offence connected with a political offence, or (b) it considers that execution of the request is likely to prejudice its sovereignty, security, ordre public or other essential interests.'

[92] For the Statewatch campaign see: 'CoE "cybercrime" convention: legitimising internet surveillance' Statewatch Bulletin 10.6 <http://database.statewatch.org/article.asp?aid=2945>.

indeed currently) that was/is met by the mutual assistance provisions of the Crime (International Cooperation) Act 2003. As we have seen repeatedly in this section, greater cooperation in these fields can only be positive despite the concerns of the EFF and Statewatch.

15.5 Conclusions

As with all aspects of life the information society offers opportunities for criminal activity to those attracted to that lifestyle. It also offers challenges to law enforcement authorities, courts, and legislators. The challenges are on several levels. The first was that the information society both afforded opportunities for new and unique harms, such as hacking, denial of service, and the writing and distribution of viruses and Trojans. Second, it afforded new ways of committing old harms such as the production and distribution of obscene, harmful, violent, or abusive content, fraud and theft, and harassment and stalking. These were issues which called for the law to be updated and the UK Government has been extremely busy over the last 20 years in implementing the necessary changes to the law found in the Computer Misuse Act 1990, the Protection of Children Act 1978, the Police and Justice Act 2006, the Terrorism Acts 2000 and 2006, the Protection from Harassment Act 1997, and the Criminal Justice and Immigration Act 2008, among others. Our laws are among the most well-developed for dealing with the threats of e-crimes of all varieties: computer misuse crimes, content-related crimes, and computer-enabled crimes. The next challenge was designing effective law enforcement structures to deal with the challenges of cybercrime. Here, too, the UK was an early adapter, setting up the National Hi-Tech Crime Unit in 2001 to investigate computer fraud, hacking, data theft, and network attacks, as well as supporting the work of the Internet Watch Foundation in dealing with content-related crime, in particular images of child abuse. Many of these operations have now been assumed under the umbrella of the National Crime Agency with the National Hi-Tech Crime Unit becoming the NCA's National Cyber Crime Unit, while the Child Exploitation and Online Protection Centre, created in 2006 to work with the IWF and Scotland Yard's Child Abuse Investigation Command, also comes within the NCA framework as CEOP Command. We therefore have a highly integrated investigation and evidence-gathering organization in the NCA. We also give leadership on international cooperation. The UK leads the way in forging international partnerships in dealing with child-abuse images, and the NCA's forerunner SOCA has provided vital leadership in the international campaign to deal with Nigerian e-fraud. We have also finally ratified the Cybercrime Convention meaning that we are now in full partnership with those other countries that countries that have ratified and enacted the Convention.

TEST QUESTIONS

Question 1

Is the UK law on grooming sufficiently robust to adequately protect children online? Are adults adequately protected by the law of harassment?

Question 2

Discuss critically the decision of the Court of Appeal in *Attorney General's Reference (Nos. 85, 86, and 87 of 2007)*. Were the sentences out of proportion to the harm? In particular, are there any grounds for mitigation on principles of freedom of expression?

FURTHER READING

Books

N Anderson, *The Internet Police: How Crime Went Online, and the Cops Followed* (2013)

J Clough, *Principles of Cybercrime* (2010)

G Jacobson, *Cybersecurity, Botnets, and Cyberterrorism* (2009)

D Wall, *Cybercrime: The Transformation of Crime in the Information Age* (2007)

M Yar, *Cybercrime and Society* (2nd edn, 2013)

Chapters and articles

J Chang, 'An Analysis of Advance Fee Fraud on the Internet' *Journal of Financial Crime* 71 [2008]

A Gillespie, 'Cyber-bullying and Harassment of Teenagers: The Legal Response' *Journal of Social Welfare and Family Law* 213 [2006]

A Gillespie, 'Indecent Images, Grooming and the Law' *Criminal Law Review* 412 (2006)

N MacEwan, 'The New Stalking Offences in English Law: Will They Provide Effective Protection from Cyberstalking?' *Criminal Law Review* 767 (2012)

P Romero, 'An Immunological Approach to Counter-terrorism and Infrastructure Defense Law in Electronic Domains' *IJLIT* 101 [2006]

PART V

E-commerce

We all want to do business online but how can we be sure we are protected? How do we contract online? How do we make payments and how do we sign an agreement?

19 Electronic payments

Branding, trademarks, and domain names

As the value of online commerce continues to grow, the importance of protecting one's trading identity online is magnified, leading to an increased use of traditional branding techniques, such as trademarks, in the online environment. In this chapter we will discuss the traditional role of trademarks within the creation of brand portfolios and examine the roles trademarks play in the online environment, both as traditional brands and as internet addresses or domain names. We begin with a short discussion of branding and the role of trademarks.

16.1 Trademarks and branding

The issue of 'branding' is one which lawyers have traditionally remained apart from, instead choosing to focus on the narrow legal question of protection of trademarks. However, one lawyer who does examine branding is Professor Cornish in his 2002 Clarendon Lectures.[1] His view is that branding and trademarks share a common foundation: 'branding is the watchword of marketers; lawyers talk of trademarks and associated get-up. By these terms the two groups mean broadly the same phenomenon; but each inclines to a contemptuous view of what the other contributes to business functioning and general welfare.'[2] A general definition of branding given by Colin Bates of 'BuildingBrands', a UK brand consultancy, is that it is 'a collection of perceptions in the mind of the consumer', which he goes on to develop saying: 'a brand is very different from a product or service: a brand is intangible and exists in the mind of the consumer'.

If this is the definition of branding as found in the marketing and branding industry what is a trademark as defined by the legal services industry? The answer is to be found in s. 1 of the Trade Marks Act (TMA) 1994 which defines a trademark as: 'any sign capable of being represented graphically which is capable of distinguishing goods or services of one undertaking from those of other undertakings'. It appears from this that Professor Cornish is correct: there is little substantive difference between the marketing concept of branding and the legal concept of a trademark. Both are intangible, both are distinctive, and both are capable of definition and recording. Yet, despite these superficial similarities, the two live in very different environments, and an understanding of the conflict between the role of brands and trademarks is essential for the discussion that follows in this chapter, for it is this conflict which has been at the heart of a significant amount of litigation and arbitration.

[1] *Intellectual Property: Omnipresent, Distracting, Irrelevant?* (OUP 2004).
[2] Ibid. 73.

In the modern consumer-driven society brands have developed a purpose much greater than that intended for trademarks. To understand this purpose take a second, look up from this book and look around (and at) yourself. Chances are, you and the surrounding environment are emblazoned with brand identities. Sony, Apple, Dell, and HP proclaim you buy their electronics while Ralph Lauren, Hugo Boss, Abercrombie & Fitch and others proclaim that you choose their clothes. You proudly wear these brands to identify yourself with a brand image: Prada, Louis Vuitton, and Versace (aspirational); Hugo Boss, Zara, and Paul Smith (professional); Marks & Spencer, Next, and Principles (practical); Topshop, French Connection, and H&M (fashionable). You may prefer an Apple laptop to a Dell as Apple portray themselves as creative and 'outside the box'; you probably choose which car you drive as much for the badge on the bonnet as for the practicalities of what it does.

The development of this 'brand society' and its interaction with the legal process was examined by Neil MacCormick in his paper 'On the Very Idea of Intellectual Property: An Essay According to the Institutionalist Theory of Law',[3] where he notes that intellectual property rights (IPRs) when viewed as a legal concept display three properties:[4]

Highlight MacCormick's three legal properties of IPRs

1. They prescribe the circumstances in which the IPR comes into being and vests in a particular person.
2. The law provides what privileges and other rights belong to the holder of the IPR.
3. The law must specify how an IPR is extinguished and how it can be transferred from one person to another.

This is what MacCormick describes as the 'institutional facts' of IPRs. What is abundantly clear, though, is that this is a lawyer seeking to rationalize what intellectual property rights are from a legal perspective. He fails to capture, and indeed does not seek to, the complexity of trademarks as cultural icons. This is a weakness of the legal analysis. The lawyer talks of 'badges of identity', 'trademark registries', and 'infringement and enforcement', whereas the brand consultant talks of 'aspiration values', 'target audiences', and 'lifestyle choices'. The current value of trademarks is not measured in terms of brand recognition, as was the case in the past, but by brand identity. This means that we no longer value brands by their ability to distinguish goods and services as being provided by a particular company or individual but by the lifestyle offered by that brand. This has allowed brands to develop quite astonishing dollar values. In the 2015 annual survey by Millward Brown, 'the Brandz Top 100 Most Valuable Global Brands,' each of the top 20 global brands are valued as being worth in excess of $40bn each, with the global number one brand, Apple, being valued at a staggering $246.9bn.[5]

[3] [2002] *IPQ* 227.

[4] Ibid. 136.

[5] <http://www.millwardbrown.com/BrandZ/2015/Global/2015_BrandZ_Top100_Chart.pdf>. It should be acknowledged that other valuations are lower. Interbrand values Apple at $170.2bn while Brand Finance at only $128.3bn. Each valuation though is indicative of the huge value of brands.

With such vast sums of money involved, and with more business being conducted in the online environment, it is only to be expected that both brand owners and their legal advisers would soon turn their attention to brand protection and development in the online environment. This has clear potential for a clash of cultures and it is this which forms the core of this chapter. The following discussion is split into three sections. First, we will analyse the UK law on trademark protection. From here we move on to a discussion of brand identity in the online environment, before we conclude with an analysis of the legal conflicts which have arisen from these culture clashes and the proposed legal solutions to these conflicts.

16.2 Trademarks in the global business environment

The legal system takes a narrow view of the role of trademarks, viewing a trademark as a tool of brand recognition rather than brand identity. There are two varieties of trademark, the registered trademark (or true trademark) and the common law of passing off (sometimes referred to as unregistered trademarks).[6] The more familiar of these to most people is the registered trademark which is sometimes referred to in literature by the addition of a commonly recognizable symbol ® or ™. The addition of such symbols is not though a prerequisite to a registered trademark and therefore one should never assume that an unadorned name or mark is not a registered trademark.

16.2.1 Registered and unregistered trademarks

In the UK registered trademarks are regulated by the Trade Marks Act 1994, which implemented the First Trade Marks Directive.[7] By s. 63 of the Act, the registrar of trademarks is required to maintain a register, which contains a record of all registered trademarks. To gain registration in the register an applicant must make an application under s. 32. The procedure is governed by a set of rules which require the registrar to examine each application to see whether it complies with the Act and rules. If it does, he publishes it whereupon anyone objecting to the application may oppose it or make observations as to whether or not it should be granted. If no notice of opposition is given or all opposition proceedings are withdrawn or decided in the applicant's favour, the registrar registers the mark unless it appears to him, having regard to matters coming to his notice since accepting the application, that it was accepted in error. If accepted onto the register the mark is registered for a period of ten years from the date of registration in the first instance,[8] which may be renewed for further periods of ten years.[9] Once registered the proprietor of a registered trademark has exclusive rights in the trademark

[6] For more detail on both these see L Bently and B Sherman *Intellectual Property Law* (4th edn, OUP 2014) ch. 31.

[7] Dir. 89/104/EEC of the Council, of 21 December 1988, to approximate the Laws of the Member States relating to Trade Marks and gives effect to the Madrid Protocol for the International Registration of Marks.

[8] TMA, s. 42(1).

[9] Ibid. s. 42(2). The oldest trade mark in the Registry is Trade Mark No. 1 of 1876 (the year the register was created). It is the red triangle logo of the Bass brewery: <http://www.ipo.gov.uk/tmcase/Results/1/UK00000000001>.

that are infringed by its use in the UK without his consent.[10] Those rights have effect from the date of filing of the application for registration.[11] However, no action may be taken before the date on which a trademark is registered and no offence is committed by anything done before publication of the registration.

Infringement of a registered trademark is regulated by s. 10 of the Act. This states that a trademark may be infringed by using in the course of trade a sign:

(a) which is identical to the registered trademark in relation to goods or services which are identical with those for which the mark is registered;[12]

(b) where, because the sign is identical with the registered trademark and is used in relation to goods or services similar to those for which the mark is registered, or, because the sign is similar to the registered mark and is used in relation to goods or services that are identical with or similar to those for which that mark is registered, there exists a likelihood of confusion on the part of the public, which includes the likelihood of association with the registered mark;[13] or

(c) which is identical with or similar to the registered trademark and is used in relation to goods or services which are not necessarily similar to those for which the trademark is registered, where the trademark has a reputation in the UK and the use of the sign, being without due cause, takes unfair advantage of, or is detrimental to, the distinctive character or repute of the trademark.[14]

Use for these purposes includes affixing a sign to goods or their packaging, offering or exposing goods for sale, putting them on the market, stocking them for those purposes under such sign, offering or supplying services under the sign, importing or exporting under the sign or using it on business papers or in advertising.[15] Sections 11 and 12 of the Act provide that a trademark is not infringed, inter alia, by the use: (a) by a person making use of his own name or address;[16] (b) of indications concerning the kind, quality, quantity, intended purpose, value, geographical origin, time of production of goods or rendering of services or other characteristics of goods or services;[17] or (c) of the trademark where it is necessary to indicate the intended purpose of a product or service.[18]

Unregistered trademarks function similarly (without the registration process of course). The correct legal term for the protection of an unregistered trademark is 'the tort of passing off'. Unlike registered trademarks, which are a creature of statute, passing off is a common law invention. The modern law is to be found in a handful of cases of which the most recent are the decisions of the House of Lords in *Reckitt & Colman Products Ltd v Borden Inc.*[19] and *Erven Warnink BV v J Townend & Sons.*[20] In the first of those cases, Lord Oliver set out what is known as the 'Classic Trinity' which lies at the

[10] Ibid. s. 9(1).
[11] Ibid. s. 9(3).
[12] Ibid. s. 10(1).
[13] Ibid. s. 10(2).
[14] Ibid. s. 10(3).
[15] Ibid. s. 10(4).
[16] Ibid. s. 11(2)(a).
[17] Ibid. s. 11(2)(b). This includes terms such as 'Scotch' Whisky or 'Lion Quality' Eggs.
[18] Ibid. s. 11(2)(c). This includes terms such as 'Ford' exhausts or games controllers for 'Sony Playstation4'.
[19] [1990] RPC 341.
[20] [1979] AC 731.

root of the modern English law of passing off. He said that a claim may be brought where:

(a) the claimant's goods or services have acquired a goodwill or reputation in the market and are known by some distinguishing feature; *and*

(b) there is a misrepresentation by the defendant (whether or not intentional) leading or likely to lead the public to believe that goods or services offered by the defendant are goods or services of the claimant; *and*

(c) the claimant has suffered, or is likely to suffer, damage as a result of the erroneous belief engendered by the defendant's misrepresentation.[21]

16.2.2 **Trademark characteristics**

Both registered trademarks and the law of passing off share common characteristics of domesticity and specificity. Domesticity is the provision that a trademark will only be protected within the jurisdiction in which it is registered or used. For registered trademarks domesticity can be established by reference to the TMA: s. 9(1) states, 'The proprietor of a registered trade mark has exclusive rights in the trade mark which are infringed by use of the trade mark *in the United Kingdom* without his consent.' There is no cross-border protection of UK registered trademarks. The concept of domesticity in trademarks is reflected throughout the globe. There is no such thing as an 'international trademark'. Although two international agreements create provisions for the international protection of trademarks—the Paris Convention for the Protection of Industrial Property and the Madrid Agreement/Protocol—neither creates a truly international trademark as both require recognition by national governments and/or the domestic registrar of trademarks.

Unregistered trademarks also display domesticity. The clearest example of such a provision in the UK is the case of *Anheuser-Busch v Budejovicky Budvar*.[22] In this case the Court of Appeal followed the so called 'hard-line' school of passing off in determining that goodwill, a necessary prerequisite for an action of passing off, has a territorial component. There is a separate 'soft-line' school of thought which is recognized in Australia.[23] This school claims to protect the unregistered trademarks of commercial organizations that do not trade within the jurisdiction in question.[24] Does this mean that unregistered trademarks, at least in some corners of the globe, do not demonstrate domesticity? The answer is no. In those cases where the soft-line approach is followed the court will look for evidence of reputation in the trademark within the jurisdiction in question.[25] The soft-line/hard-line dichotomy is not about domesticity, it is rather a question of whether the court is to look for goodwill on the part of the trademark holder or merely reputation. Whichever approach is correct, in both schools of thought unregistered trademarks benefit from domesticity.

[21] [1990] RPC 341, 406.

[22] [1984] FSR 413.

[23] See H Carty, 'Passing Off and the Concept of Goodwill', (1995) *Journal of Business Law* 139; F Martin, 'The Dividing Line between Goodwill and International Reputation', (1995) *Journal of Business Law* 70.

[24] See e.g. the case of *Conagra Inc. v McCain Frozen Foods (Aust) Pty* (1991) 23 IPR 193.

[25] Ibid. 237.

The second characteristic of trademarks is specificity. Put simply, you only gain protection if there is a likelihood of confusion on the part of the consumer. As the consumer is unlikely to be confused by similar trademarks on entirely dissimilar products, such as Penguin chocolate biscuits and Penguin books, protection is limited to those products which share characteristics with the trademark owner's product. In the UK, for registered trademarks, this is assured by categorizing all applications into one of 45 classes of goods or services.[26] The classification of the register in this manner ensures adequate protection for the trademark owner—no one else can use that mark for similar goods/services—while allowing others the right to make use of popular trade names/marks in different sectors of the economy where the public are unlikely to be confused.

Specificity of trademarks has a basis in equity, something which can clearly be seen when one looks at the common law protection offered to unregistered trademarks. Passing off as a common law delict/tort has a basis in equity. The concept of specificity has developed here also under a different title, 'the common field of activity'.[27] The common field of activity ensures that you cannot claim goodwill in your trade name/mark outside the class of goods or services in which you trade. It is designed to ensure one person does not gain a complete monopoly over a name or mark which would unfairly restrict others gaining access to a (different) market. Domesticity and specificity help create the 'one mark many owners' ethos. It has proved to be an extremely efficient method for regulating trademarks, allowing adequate protection but also free access. The internet domain name system, or DNS, though, uses a 'one mark one owner' ethos which is alien to experienced trademark practitioners. This clash of cultures has led many domain name/trademark disputes.

16.3 Domain names as badges of identity

DNS is the system of global navigation used on the internet. Each page of information, each image, and each file is given an address called a uniform resource locator (URL) which, like the address of every home, office, or shop, must be unique if the user is to locate it. This address is made up of several sections, illustrated below.

The key aspect of a domain name is the second-level domain. Second-level domains are available on a first-come, first-served basis, and may be obtained through any one of a number of domain name registries. Registries are private companies who have been accredited by the relevant registrar[28] and may usually offer registration in any one of a number of top-level domains.[29] Registration of a second-level domain is extremely

[26] Full classificatory list at <http://www.gov.uk/government/publications/how-to-classify-trade-marks/trade-mark-classification-list-of-goods-and-services>.

[27] See *Rolls Razor Ltd v Rolls (Lighters) Ltd* (1949) 66 RPC 137; *Fortnum & Mason plc v Fortnum Ltd* [1994] FSR 438.

[28] A registrar, as distinct from a registry, is the regulatory authority tasked with the role of overseeing a particular TLD. The key registrar is the Internet Corporation of Assigned Names and Numbers (ICANN) which manages the generic top-level domains including the new generic top-level domains or New gTLDs. Country code TLDs such as .uk, .jp, and .fr are managed at a national level. The .uk registrar is Nominet UK. We will examine the roles, and rules, of ICANN and Nominet UK below.

[29] Any individual may register in any ICANN-regulated generic TLD. Some country code TLDs are restricted to citizens of that country such as the Greek country code TLD (.gr). Others, such as the UK's .uk, are open to registration by anyone in a similar manner to the generic TLDs.

Highlight Properties of a uniform resource locator (URL)

<http://www.lse.ac.uk/collections/law>

The above is the homepage of the Law Department at the London School of Economics.

The URL may be broken down as follows:

http://—This page uses hypertext transfer protocol.

www.—This page is found on the World Wide Web.

lse.ac.uk—The unique address of the London School of Economics. This is made up of two domain names: a top-level domain and a second-level domain. Internet addresses are read right to left. The top-level domain is the .ac.uk section of the domain. This tells the user the address is used by a UK-registered academic organization. The second-level domain comes to the left of the first period, i.e. lse. This is the identifier of the site operator. As a whole, the domain name must be unique. There can be only one lse.ac.uk address, although variations such as lse.com, or lse.co.uk are possible. Before they can be used, second-level domains require to be registered, of which more below.

collections/law—This is a tertiary or file location domain. Any text which follows the top-level domain is used to identify individual pages of information within the site managed by the owner of the domain name. Such tertiary domains do not require registration and will not be discussed further.

cheap and simple with a .co.uk registration costing as little as £3.49 per annum and a .com registration available for as little as £10.99 per annum. To get a second-level domain all you need to do is fill out an online form and give the registry your credit card details.

Although functionally domain names, once registered, are addresses of pages of information in the online environment, there is an important distinction between these domain names and traditional addresses in that the make-up of a domain name, in particular the exact nature of the second-level domain, is chosen by the registrant. This is quite unlike a traditional address and more like a trademark registration in that the registrant has control over the allocation of the identifier. Thus, while McDonalds may have a restaurant in your town or city, when searching for that restaurant you will navigate in part by an assigned address (such as 36 South Street) and in part by the familiar, and protected, brand identifiers of McDonalds such as the Golden Arches. You would not expect your local McDonalds to have a specific address such as 1 McDonald Road, but due to the way domain names are allocated you do expect McDonalds online presence to be at specific domains including mcdonalds.com and mcdonalds.co.uk.

Due to this dual nature of domain names as both address tools and brand identifiers, some domain names have attracted high values, and many domain names have been litigated over. The most valuable domain names are varied, but tend to show two characteristics: (1) they are located in the .com top-level domain, which is the prime real estate of the domain name world,[30] and (2) the second-level domain is usually a short, generic, English-language term. Thus, according to reports the most expensive internet domain name sold to date, is sex.com which was sold in 2010 for $13m,[31] with other high-value transactions including the domain names fund.com which sold for $9.99m in 2008, porn.com which sold for $9.5m in 2007, and diamond.com sold in 2006 also for $7.5m.

The commercial value of some domain names suggests that it is possible for domain names to have brand values which far exceed their role as mere internet addresses. This reflects their selection rather than allocation. Domain names have much more in common with trademarks than with addresses. They are selected and registered much like a trademark. In addition they are developed to reflect brand identities in a similar way to trademarks. Some of the most famous brand identities of our age are based upon domain names. The 'old-world' identities of Coca-Cola, Mercedes, and Tesco have been joined by Amazon.com, eBay.com, and Google.com. Second, domain names can be treated as traditional property. In *Kremen v Cohen*,[32] the court considered the question whether a domain name was intangible property. The Court of Appeal for the 9th Circuit stated that a domain name is a form of intangible property because

(i) it represents an interest of precise definition,

(ii) it is subject to exclusive possession or control, and

(iii) a registrant has a legitimate claim to exclusivity.[33]

Thus more and more domain names start to look like trademarks. They have value, they are registrable, and they are (legally) intangible property rights. The key difference with domain names is that they are awarded purely on a first-come, first-served basis with no examination of the application as found with trademarks.

This vastly increases the risks of names being registered which are in breach of a trademark of another business or individual or even, given the low cost and simple process of registration, the risk that individuals or companies will deliberately register marks similar to those of famous or well-known brands (such as coca-coladrinks.net, or barclaysbank-online.co.uk), a process known as cybersquatting, or based on misspellings of well-known marks (such as macdonalds.com or eboy.com), a process known as typosquatting. Thus risks surround trademarks in the online environment at every turn.

16.4 **Early trademark/domain name disputes**

This conflict of values quickly led to disputes over rightful ownership of domain names. These issues were first brought to the attention of the wider public by a journalist for *Wired* magazine named Joshua Quittner. Mr Quittner, while preparing a story for *Wired*

[30] In an earlier paper the author referred to the .com top-level domain as 'the electronic equivalent of Rodeo Drive or Bond Street'. See A Murray, 'Internet Domain Names: The Trade Mark Challenge' (1998) *International Journal of Law and Information Technology* 285, 301.

[31] A Shontell and J D'Onfro, 'Million-dollar URLs: The most expensive domain names of all time' (*Business Insider*, 10 July 2015) <http://www.techinsider.io/most-expensive-domain-names-of-all-time-2015-7>.

[32] *Kremen v Cohen*, 337 F. 3d 1024 (9th Cir. 2003).

[33] It should be noted this was not the first decision to set out this position. Domain names had previously been found to be a form of intangible property in the cases of *Caesars World Inc. v Caesars-Palace.com*, 112 F. Supp. 2d 502 (E.D. Va. 2000) and *Online Partners.com Inc. v Atlanticnet Media Corp.*, 2000 US Dist LEXIS 783, 101242 (N.D. Cal. 2000).

on the potential value of commercially recognizable domain names,[34] registered the domain name 'mcdonalds.com' in an attempt to illustrate the risks faced by the owners of famous or well-known names. After a short flurry of communications between Mr Quittner and McDonalds (and their lawyers) Mr Quittner assigned the name to the McDonalds Corporation in return for a donation towards computer equipment for a primary school.[35] While the actions of Mr Quittner may be seen to be harmless the courts were suddenly abuzz with trademark lawyers seeking to reclaim valuable cyberproperty that their clients had failed to secure.

The UK courts first wrestled with this matter in the case of *Pitman Training Ltd v Nominet UK*.[36] The dispute in this case centred around the right to use the domain name pitman.co.uk, and the competing interests of two parties, Pitman Training Ltd and Pearson Professional Ltd.[37] Both the training company and the publishing company had at one time been owned by a single company, but in 1985 they had demerged and Pearson Professional had bought the publishing business. As part of the demerger, Pitman Training Ltd agreed not to use the name Pitman, except in relation to their core business. The problem arose when the two companies, who had coexisted peacefully in the actual world for 11 years, tried to register their presence on the internet.

On 15 February 1996, Pearson registered the domain name pitman.co.uk, but took no action to develop their web presence. Then, on 15 March 1996, Pitman Training Ltd also registered the domain name with Nominet UK.[38] They went on to establish a web presence in July 1996. Pearson had no knowledge of the Pitman Training website until December 1996, but immediately upon discovering it they contacted both Pitman Training and Nominet UK, demanding that the right to use the domain name be reassigned to them. On 4 April 1997 Nominet, following threats of legal action from Pearson's lawyers, agreed to reassign the domain name to Pearson, a transfer affected on 7 April. On 9 April, Pitman issued a writ against Pearson and Nominet requiring the immediate reinstatement of their rights to the domain name.

The problem for the judge was that each party was entitled to make use of the Pitman trade name in their respective fields. Trademarks, registered or unregistered, benefit from specificity. In virtual reality though there is no specificity of domain names: there can be only one pitman.co.uk and there is no method of differentiating between Pitman Training and Pitman Publishing. It was this lack of specificity which led to the dispute before the court. The decision of the court was that the plaintiffs had no viable or reasonably arguable cause of action against the second defendant (Pearson) and the interim injunction was lifted, allowing Nominet to ratify the transfer of registration to Pearson. The impact of this case in UK law is that the High Court was willing to uphold the policy of Nominet that registration of second-level domain names should be allowed on a first-come, first-served basis.

[34] J Quittner, 'Billions Registered' (*Wired 2.10*, October 1994) <http://www.wired.com/wired/archive/2.10/mcdonalds.html>.

[35] For more on the actions of Mr Quittner see the *Daily Telegraph*, 14 January 1997.

[36] [1997] EWHC Ch 367.

[37] Pearson Professional own Pitman Publishing Ltd who produce academic/student texts.

[38] Nominet is the .uk registrar meaning they oversee the allocation of all .uk top-level domain registrations. Such a duplication of registration should not have occurred. In the event of parties who have equal claim to second-level domain names Nominet runs a first-come, first-served policy see: Nominet UK: Rules for the .uk domain and sub-domains.

16.4.1 Cybersquatting before the UK courts

The *Pitman* case was rather unusual. That was two parties with competing rights, a bit like the equal claims to the name 'Budweiser' in *Anheuser-Busch*.[39] More common among the early cases were cybersquatting claims. Probably the first such case was that of *Harrods Ltd v UK Network Services Ltd*.[40] This case involved a well-known UK cybersquatter, Mr Michael Lawrie. Mr Lawrie registered the domain name harrods.com which he then warehoused. The court determined that Mr Lawrie's possession of the domain name, and the potential use he may make of it, constituted trademark infringement and passing off. Unfortunately, Mr Lawrie did not turn up in court; the arguments to support this contention were not outlined and discussed in full. This though was quickly remedied by what is still the key decision on cybersquatting in the UK, *British Telecommunications plc and Ors v One in a Million Ltd & Ors*.[41]

This was an appeal to the Court of Appeal by the defendants against summary judgment given to a number of leading British companies in a series of actions against them. The defendants dealt in domain names. They specialized in registering well-known names and trademarks without the consent of the person or company owning the goodwill in the name or mark and offering those names for sale to the owners of such goodwill. They registered burgerking.co.uk which they offered to Burger King for £25,000 and bt.org which they offered to British Telecommunications for £4,700. The plaintiffs objected to the defendants' registration of, among others marksandspencer.com, britishtelecom.co.uk, ladbrokes.com, virgin.org, cellnet.net, and sainsburys.com. At trial the judge, Jonathan Sumption QC,[42] had granted injunctions to restrain the defendants from such registration and dealings, explaining that:

(a) it was enough for a plaintiff to show that a defendant intended to infringe the plaintiff's rights in future even though the mere registration of a deceptive company name or a domain name did not amount to passing off; and

(b) the use of a trademark in the course of the business of a professional dealer for the purpose of making domain names more valuable and extracting money from the trademark owner amounted to 'use in the course of trade'.

The appellants appealed on the basis that the action was premature. They submitted that if a name could be used for a legitimate purpose, it was not an instrument of fraud and relief should not be granted unless it was established that the defendant either threatened to pass off or was, with another, part of a common design to pass off. They said that in their case they registered domain names with a view to making a profit by selling them to the owners of the goodwill, using the blocking effect of the registration to obtain a reasonable price or, in some cases, selling them to collectors or to other persons who could have a legitimate reason for using them. They submitted that could amount neither to passing off nor a threat to pass off.

In dismissing the appeal, Aldous LJ analysed several strands of authority which had held that in the law of passing off injunctive relief may be granted before the harm

[39] See (n. 22).
[40] Unreported, High Court, Ch D, 9 December 1996.
[41] [1999] 1 WLR 903; [1998] EWCA Civ 1272; [1998] 4 All ER 476.
[42] Now Lord Sumption, Justice of the Supreme Court.

occurs.[43] He discerned from those cases that the court has jurisdiction to grant injunctive relief where a defendant is equipped with or is intending to equip another with an instrument of fraud. He added that the question as to whether a name is an instrument of fraud must depend upon all the circumstances: for instance, a name which by reason of its similarity to another name will inherently lead to passing off is such an instrument but not if it would not inherently lead to passing off. The court should consider the similarity of the names, the intention of the defendant, the type of trade and all the surrounding circumstances. If, after taking all the circumstances into account, the court should conclude that a name was produced to enable passing off, was adapted to be used for passing off and, if so used, was likely to be fraudulently used, an injunction would be appropriate.

He identified three categories of cases in which a court would grant an injunction: 'First, where there is passing-off established or it is threatened; second, where the defendant is a joint tortfeasor with another in passing off either actual or threatened; and third, where the defendant has equipped himself with or intends to equip another with an instrument of fraud.'[44] After reviewing the party to party correspondence and other dealings between the parties, Aldous LJ concluded that 'there was clear evidence of systematic registration by the appellants of well-known trade names as blocking registrations and a threat to sell them to others'.[45] He was also satisfied that threats to infringe the trademarks of the claimants had been established. The defendants sought to sell domain names that were confusingly similar to registered trademarks. Those domain names indicated origin, which was the purpose for which they were registered, and they were to be used in relation to the services provided by the registrant who trades in domain names. The Court of Appeal concluded that the deputy judge's analysis in respect of passing off and trademark infringement had been correct.

BT v One in a Million is still the leading UK case law on both passing off and trademark infringement in the case of cybersquatting and domain name warehousing, but we must analyse a few further decisions before we move on to look at the extrajudicial procedures which have extensively replaced court actions in such circumstances.

The first case is *Phones4u Ltd v Phone4u.co.uk*.[46] Phones4u Ltd was a UK chain of mobile phone retailers. It adopted the name Phones4u for some of its stores and its mail order business in 1995, and changed its corporate name and other shop names in 1997. By 1999 the company enjoyed an annual turnover of nearly £44m and the red, white, and blue Phones4u logo appeared on most of Phones4u's 63 shops countrywide. By 2004 the number of such shops exceeded 350. Phones4u registered the domain name phones4u.co.uk in 1999, and launched its website in October 2000. The second defendant was an individual, Abdul Heykali, who had worked for a small mobile phone retailer in London. Towards the end of 1999, Mr Heykali set up a mobile phone

[43] In *Farina v Silverlock* (1855) 1 K&J 509 the defendant sold materials for an infringing product. An injunction was granted, inter alia, to prevent the defendant from enabling passing off; in *John Walker & Sons Ltd v Henry Ost & Co., Ltd* [1970] RPC 489 an injunction was granted to prevent the supply of bottles and labels to facilitate passing off abroad, and in *Glaxo plc v Glaxowellcome Ltd* [1996] FSR 388 where the defendant had incorporated a company combining the name of two well-known public companies just prior to their merger. These cases collectively are sometimes known as 'instruments of fraud cases'.

[44] [1999] 1 WLR 903, 927.

[45] Ibid. 934.

[46] [2006] EWCA Civ 244.

retail business called Mobile Communication Centre. In August 1999, he registered the domain name phone4u.co.uk. In November 1999, the site read, 'this site will be going mobile soon . . . Up and running by 1st of January 2000.' By September 2000, however, the site's content was merely an image of a phone followed by '4U.co.uk'. The site finally went live in July 2001. At that time, a disclaimer appeared: 'Phone4U.co.uk are solely an Internet based company and do not have the costs associated with running high street shops . . . Phone 4U.co.uk is NOT connected with the high street mobile phone retailer Phones 4U.'

Although some key facts were disputed, the judge accepted that Mr Heykali had chosen phone4u.co.uk at the recommendation of a friend and in ignorance of the claimants' business for use in connection with an internet-based mobile phone company. The court was persuaded that Mr Heykali thought it common practice on the internet to combine descriptive words with the phrase '4U'. However, by February or March 2000 Mr Heykali had become aware of the claimants while searching for a Vodaphone dealership which he obtained from the claimants themselves in March 2000. The claimants by then knew of Mr Heykali's domain name and expressed concern that emails intended for them were being misdirected to Mr Heykali. In response to a cease-and-desist letter from the claimants, Mr Heykali incorporated a company under the name Phone4U Ltd (later changed to Phone4u.co.uk Internet Ltd) and denied any wrongdoing. He also recognized that his domain name was potentially very valuable. The court found that he deliberately exaggerated the number of misdirected emails he had received, and falsely suggested to the claimants that he had already been offered £100,000 for the domain name.

For reasons that were never adequately explained, the claimants took no further steps to stop Mr Heykali's activities until proceedings were issued in February 2004. Following a decision of the High Court in March 2005, in which the court found that the claimants had no goodwill in the mark 'Phones4U' in August 1999 when the domain name was registered and that there had been no deception in the use of the domain name across the five-year period it had been in use, the claimants appealed to the Court of Appeal. The lead judgment was that of Lord Justice Jacob. He found that the test for passing off was that of the *Jif Lemon* decision: '(a) reputation, i.e. goodwill; (b) misrepresentation; and (c) damage or its likelihood'. The court went on to state that there did not have to be evidence of direct diversion of sales caused by misrepresentation in order to prove damage. Jacob LJ adopted the 'more modern' definition of damage: '(a) by diverting trade from the plaintiffs to the defendants; (b) by injuring the trade reputation of the plaintiffs whose [goods are] admittedly superior in quality to that of the defendants; and (c) by the injury which is inherently likely to be suffered by any business when on frequent occasions it is confused by customers or potential customers with a business owned by another proprietor or is wrongly connected with that business'.[47]

The court agreed with the appellants on the four arguments raised in support of their appeal, namely that:

1. The judge applied the wrong test in deciding whether or not the appellants had protectable goodwill. Jacob LJ was convinced that the appellants had sufficient goodwill by the relevant date to found a claim in passing off. Looking at the

[47] Per Slade LJ in *Chelsea Man v Chelsea Girl* [1987] RPC 189 at 202.

evidence he stated that 'To infer from all that, that hardly anyone knew the name, that the name was not "an attractive force which brings in custom" by August 1999 is simply untenable.'[48] The court held that the judge had incorrectly applied the test for distinctiveness required to obtain a trademark registration in holding that the phrase 'Phones4u' was not inherently distinctive and had muddled the test for registration with the test for goodwill sufficient for passing off.

2. At the date of registration of 'phone4u.co.uk' an instrument of fraud had been created.
3. The judge wrongly characterized a large number of instances of deception as 'mere confusion'. The defendants' email evidence showed that customers of the appellant thought they were communicating with those who owned and ran the Phones4u shops. Examining the evidence, Jacob LJ could see 'clear and convincing evidence of damage to goodwill . . . the emails collectively tell a clear story of people trying to contact and deal with or complain to or make inquiries of, Phones4u—the chain of shops they already knew'.[49]
4. The judge erred in placing significance on the parties' coexistence for five years without deception without first considering the extent of the defendants' use of the mark during that time which had been almost non-existent. Turning finally to the trademark infringement claim, the court considered the effect of the colour limitations on the registration. Jacob LJ sought the view of the Registry before formally delivering the judgment. The Registry replied that the registrar has always regarded colour limitations on the face of the register to be a limitation of rights. On this advice, the court held that, despite the original certificate of registration and the original entry being in monochrome, the colour limitation stated on the register was effective to limit the registrations to the colours claimed. Had there not been such a limitation, Jacob LJ stated that the defendants' use of the words 'Phones4u' or a trivial variant would have infringed the appellant's trademark.[50]

Thus the appellants were ultimately victorious in their passing off claim but Jacob LJ criticized the long delay of four years between the original complaint and the commencement of proceedings. He quoted the words of James LJ in 1879: 'the very life of a trademark depends on the promptitude with which it is vindicated'.[51] This decision tells us the courts are still willing to apply both trademark law and the law of passing off to protect businesses from cybersquatters but the evolution of extrajudicial dispute resolution procedures has taken most claims beyond the judicial process.

More recently two decisions of the CJEU have thrown the applicability of *One in a Million* into doubt. In *Céline SARL v Céline SA*[52] the ECJ held:

> the purpose of a company, trade or shop name is not, of itself, to distinguish goods or services but to identify a company, and the purpose of a trade name or a shop name is to designate a

[48] [2006] EWCA Civ 244, [31].
[49] *Phones4u Ltd v Phone4u.co.uk* (n. 46) [37]–[38].
[50] Ibid. [49]–[50].
[51] *Johnston v Orr-Ewing* (1879) 13 Ch D 434, 464.
[52] C-17/06 [2007] ECR I-7041.

> business which is being carried on. Accordingly, where the use of a company name, trade name or shop name is limited to identifying a company or designating a business which is being carried on, such use cannot be considered as being 'in relation to goods or services' within the meaning of Art.5 (1) of the (First Trade Marks) Directive.

Although the court tempered this slightly by finding that 'where the sign is not affixed to goods, there is still use "in relation to goods or services" where a third party uses that sign in such a way that a link is established between the sign which constitutes the company, trade or shop name of the third party and the goods marketed or the services provided by the third party' this does not seem to apply in the case where a domain name is simply registered and warehoused, as in the *One in a Million* scenario. In the later case of *Belgian Electronic Sorting Technology NV v Peelaers*,[53] in a discussion of the Misleading and Comparative Advertising Directive, the court held that 'registration of a domain name was not a form of representation which was made in order to promote the supply of goods or services. It was nothing other than a formal act by which the body designated to manage domain names was asked to enter it into its database and link internet users who type in that domain name only to the internet protocol (IP) address specified by the domain-name holder. That purely formal act did not necessarily imply that potential consumers could become aware of the domain name and was therefore not capable of influencing the choice of those potential consumers. In contrast, the use of the domain name to host a website was clearly intended to promote the supply of the goods or services of the domain-name holder.'

The Intellectual Property and Enterprise Court has considered the impact of the first of these cases, *Céline*, on *One in a Million* in the case of *Vertical Leisure v Poleplus Ltd and Bowley*.[54] This was a case similar to *One in a Million*, an individual, Mr Bowley, registered a number of domain names around the word 'silkii' including silkii.co.uk. The name referred to a particular product of the claimant; a tool allowing the connection of a length of silk to a pole dancing pole allowing for the material to be incorporated into a pole dancing routine. The product had been showcased in the UK in early 2013 but not launched until April 2013. Based upon knowledge of the product at the early showcase events it was claimed the second defendant had registered the domain names. The Judge HH Judge Hacon, was unsure as to whether *Céline* had changed the authority of *One in a Million* in relation to a trademark claim:

> so far as infringement of the trade mark was concerned, the Court of Appeal held that the defendants had no realistic prospect of success against the allegation of infringement under section 10(3) of the 1994 Trademarks Act 1994, in other words, the equivalent to article 5(2) of the trademark directive. I would be wary of concluding, at least beyond any doubt, that the law as set out in BT remains unaltered, bearing in mind in particular Case C-17/06 *Céline SARL v Céline SA* and Case C-407/07 *L'Oréal SA v Bellure NV*; at least I would be wary of reaching that conclusion without further argument on the law for which there was no time today.[55]

The question was moot though for Judge Hacon could dispose of the case under the secondary passing off claim, finding that:

> by registering the domain names Mr Bowley did trade in circumstances by which a misrepresentation would be made to the relevant public who consulted the register, and, secondly, he

[53] C-657/11 [2013] ETMR 45.
[54] [2014] EWHC 2077 (IPEC).
[55] Ibid. [16].

> created an instrument of fraud. Mr Bowley offered, as I have mentioned, the domain names for sale to the claimant because, by implication, he realised the message that they would convey, which was the only reason they had any value for the claimant. He has no realistic prospect of defending the action. Therefore, essentially for the reasons given by Aldous LJ, I conclude the claimant is entitled to summary judgment against Mr Bowley.[56]

The cases mentioned, *Céline* and *L'Oréal* suggest that registration of an identity is not 'use' in terms of Art. 5(2) of the Trade Mark Directive (and thus s. 10(3) of the Trade Marks Act). This suggests that on trademark grounds *One in a Million* is certainly no longer good law. As HH Judge Hacon makes clear though it remains good law in the law of passing off, and as most claims of cybersquatting may be brought under either head, assuming goodwill is present, it is unlikely to affect the course of most claims before UK courts. The question of whether *Belgian Electronic Sorting Technology* is likely to have an impact remains unanswered. It suggests a domain name registration if unused is merely an instruction to a registrar. Is this enough to create an instrument of fraud? The case was not cited in *Vertical Leisure* so either defence counsel thought it was unlikely to affect the current law or it was not picked up. It seems much more likely that the former is the case as with regard to instruments of fraud no communication to the public is required and the decision in *Belgian Electronic* is therefore not applicable. It seems *One in a Million* is still good law in relation to passing off claims, but is less clearly still authoritative in trademark claims.

16.5 **The ICANN UDRP**

The increasing numbers of domain name/trademark disputes that were being taken to the courts internationally led to calls for a cheaper, more efficient, and more streamlined system of dispute resolution to be put in place. The opportunity to review the dispute resolution procedure applicable to the generic top-level domains (including essentially the .com domain) arose in the late 1990s during a wide-ranging review of the management of generic top-level domains.

From 1991, the registrar for generic top-level domains had been a small private contractor called Network Solutions Inc. who had a complete monopoly over registrations in the .com.net, and .org domain name space. By the mid 1990s, this monopoly was being challenged by campaigners who believed it was unsuitable given the developing commercial value of, in particular, .com domains. The campaigners proposed that Network Solutions monopoly be broken up, and that a not-for-profit organization known as the Internet Society take over regulation of the domain name registration process.[57] To give effect to these proposals the Internet Society created a working group to take them forward. The group known as the International Ad Hoc Committee announced they would create seven new top-level domain names which would compete with .com and Network Solutions monopoly.[58] The US federal government then entered the debate by directing that the domain name system should be privatized and that competition

[56] Ibid. [21].

[57] J Postel, *New Registries and the Delegation of International Top Level Domains* (1996) <http://www.watersprings.org/pub/id/draft-postel-iana-itld-admin-01.txt>.

[58] Final Report of the International Ad Hoc Committee: Recommendations for Administration and Management of gTLDs, 4 February 1997 <http://mailman.apnic.net/mailing-lists/apple/archive/1997/02/msg00008.html>.

within the domain name system should be increased.[59] The campaigners for reform started working alongside the US National Telecommunications and Information Administration; the body was given management of the federal domain name project, and between them they drew up the by-laws for a new regulatory authority and set out that the body should have responsibility for, among other things, internet protocol addresses and domain names. On 1 October 1998, the new regulatory and management body for internet addressing was named: it would be known as the Internet Corporation for Assigned Names and Numbers (ICANN). The new regulator would be an American not-for-profit corporation managed by a representative board of directors drawn from around the world. By the terms of its articles of association it was authorized to take responsibility for several key areas of internet stability and governance.

Highlight ICANN's responsibilities

ICANN are to oversee the operational stability of the Internet by:

I. Coordinating the assignment of Internet technical parameters as needed to maintain universal connectivity on the Internet;

II. Performing and overseeing functions related to the coordination of the Internet Protocol (IP) address space;

III. Performing and overseeing functions related to the coordination of the Internet domain name system (DNS), including the development of policies for determining the circumstances under which new top-level domains are added to the DNS root system;

IV. Overseeing operation of the authoritative Internet DNS root server system; and

V. Engaging in any other related lawful activity in furtherance of items (I) through (IV).

One of ICANN's first challenges was the development of policies regulating the management and allocation of domain names to allow for competition in the registry market for the generic top-level domains: .net, .org, and .com. To this end, ICANN set to work on its first active project: creating a register accreditation system that would allow new registries to enter the market. Trademark holders were understandably apprehensive about any changes to be introduced into the market for domain names. They were concerned that by creating competition in the market for the generic top-level domains alternative routes for cybersquatting would open up. In an attempt to meet these concerns the US Department of Commerce placed the trademark holders' concerns at the centre of its proposed reforms, and made trademark dispute resolution a key part of ICANN's mandate. The result was the creation of a new alternative dispute resolution (ADR) system applicable to those cases where the intellectual property right holder can establish that the domain name registration of the current holder is 'abusive'.[60]

[59] The White House, 'A Framework for Global Electronic Commerce' 1 July 1997 <http://clinton4.nara.gov/WH/New/Commerce/>.

[60] WIPO, 'The Management of Internet Names and Addresses: Intellectual Property Issue, Final Report of the WIPO Internet Domain Name Process' 30 April 1999 [152]–[228] <http://www.wipo.int/amc/en/processes/process1/report/finalreport.html>.

Highlight Abusive registration (ICANN Rules)

An abusive registration occurs when the domain name is identical or misleadingly similar to a trade or service mark in which the complainant has rights; and

(i) the holder of the domain name has no rights or legitimate interests in respect of the domain name; and

(ii) the domain name has been registered and is used in bad faith.

The new policy, known as the ICANN Uniform Domain Name Dispute Resolution Policy (UDRP) was formally adopted on 24 October 1999. Although called the ICANN UDRP, the dispute resolution component of the policy is not to be supplied by ICANN itself; rather it uses 'approved dispute-resolution service providers' who supply panellists to hear claims and who manage the administration of complaints.[61] The first UDRP claim was raised on 9 December 1999, the domain name in dispute being worldwrestlingfederation.com; this led to success for the claimant on 14 January 2000.[62]

The UDRP is a 'mandatory administrative procedure' meaning that all registrants who have registered in the generic top-level domains administered by ICANN are required to submit to the UDRP if a challenge is raised to their registration.

Highlight Prerequisites for a UDRP claim

You are required to submit to a mandatory administrative proceeding in the event that a third party (a 'complainant') asserts to the applicable Provider, in compliance with the Rules of Procedure, that:

(i) your domain name is identical or confusingly similar to a trademark or service mark in which the complainant has rights; and

(ii) you have no rights or legitimate interests in respect of the domain name; and

(iii) your domain name has been registered and is being used in bad faith.

[UDRP Policy para. 4(a)]

The key aspect of this requirement is part (iii), the question of whether the registrant is *mala fides*. This is explained further in para. 4(b) of the UDRP Policy where it is stated that a panellist may use as evidence that the registration and use of a domain name is in bad faith:

> (i) circumstances indicating that you have registered or you have acquired the domain name primarily for the purpose of selling, renting, or otherwise transferring the domain

[61] See <http://www.icann.org/en/help/dndr/udrp/providers>.

[62] *World Wrestling Federation Entertainment Inc. v Michael Bosman*, Case No. D99–0001 <http://arbiter.wipo.int/domains/decisions/html/1999/d1999-0001.html>.

name registration to the complainant who is the owner of the trademark or service mark or to a competitor of that complainant, for valuable consideration in excess of your documented out-of-pocket costs directly related to the domain name; or

(ii) you have registered the domain name in order to prevent the owner of the trademark or service mark from reflecting the mark in a corresponding domain name, provided that you have engaged in a pattern of such conduct; or

(iii) you have registered the domain name primarily for the purpose of disrupting the business of a competitor; or

(iv) by using the domain name, you have intentionally attempted to attract, for commercial gain, Internet users to your web site or other on-line location, by creating a likelihood of confusion with the complainant's mark as to the source, sponsorship, affiliation, or endorsement of your web site or location or of a product or service on your web site or location.

When faced with a complaint the registrant (or formally, under the UDRP Policy, the Respondent) has a variety of defences set out in para. 4(c) of the policy. These are:

(i) before any notice to you of the dispute, your use of, or demonstrable preparations to use, the domain name or a name corresponding to the domain name in connection with a bona fide offering of goods or services; or

(ii) you (as an individual, business, or other organization) have been commonly known by the domain name, even if you have acquired no trademark or service mark rights; or

(iii) you are making a legitimate noncommercial or fair use of the domain name, without intent for commercial gain to misleadingly divert consumers or to tarnish the trademark or service mark at issue.

The process itself is quick and simple. The complainant opens the dispute by filing a complaint with the provider of his choice and sending a copy to the respondent at the address shown on the Whois database.[63] At this point, the provider reviews the complaint for compliance with the UDRP rules. If the complaint is in compliance, the proceeding continues; if the complaint is non-compliant, the complainant has five days to remedy the deficiencies or the complaint will be deemed withdrawn. Within 20 calendar days of the complaint, the respondent must respond specifically to the allegations in the complaint and offer any defences which allow for the retention of the domain name (see above). The respondent will be deemed to have defaulted if no response is filed within this 20-day window. Assuming the respondent responds, after the receipt of the response, the provider has five days to appoint a panel to hear the dispute.

The panel is usually made up of one independent panellist, but under certain conditions may consist of a panel of three panellists. The make-up of panels is detailed in para. 6 of the ICANN Rules for Uniform Domain Name Dispute Resolution Policy.[64] Basically this sets out that if neither party seeks the appointment of a three-member panel then a single panellist will be appointed by the dispute resolution provider.[65] However, under para. 6(c) if either the complainant or the respondent elects to have the dispute decided by a three-member panel, then the dispute resolution provider is

[63] See <http://www.whois.net/>.

[64] At <http://www.icann.org/resources/pages/rules-be-2012-02-25-en>.

[65] Rules [6(b)]. Note: furthermore, the cost of appointing the panellist will be met by the complainant. There is no cost to the respondent under this scenario.

required to convene a three-member panel consisting of one member selected from a list compiled by the complainant, one selected from a list compiled by the respondent, and the third being appointed by the dispute resolution provider.[66] Once appointed the panel decides the complaint by electronic communications and is normally required to make a decision within 14 days of appointment, this decision to be notified to the parties within three days of being made. There is no right of appeal under the ICANN UDRP, although recourse may of course be made to the courts.

Since the first ICANN UDRP decision was issued in January 2000, the UDRP has handled more than 56,000 cases.[67] This makes the UDRP by far the most successful and far-reaching aspect of ICANN's functions. However, despite its popularity, the UDRP has been heavily criticized. The most vociferous critic of the UDRP has probably been Professor Milton Mueller of Syracuse University. In his book, *Ruling the Root,* he describes the UDRP as: 'heavily biased in favour of complainants. It allows the trade-mark holder to select the dispute provider, thereby encouraging dispute resolution providers to complete for the allegiance of trademark holders. The resultant forum shopping ensures that no defendant friendly service provider can survive.'[68] This may explain the pre-eminence of the WIPO UDRP service, which is seen to be sympathetic towards trademark holders' interests. Another critic, Professor Michael Froomkin, focuses on the procedure's failure to comply with some of the basic principles of natural justice. He notes that the UDRP:

> would have little chance of surviving ordinary 'arbitrary and capricious' review, because it denies respondents minimal levels of fair procedure that participants would be entitled to expect . . . three aspects of the UDRP are particularly troubling: (1) the incentive for providers to compete to be 'complainant friendly'; (2) its failure to require actual notice combined with the short time period permitted for responses; and (3) the asymmetric consequences of a decision.[69]

Elsewhere, I have focused upon the lack of training or experience of UDRP panellists, noting that 'almost half of all panellists employed by the two major UDRP providers[70] are untrained and inexperienced in adjudication',[71] and the potential bias of panellists noting that:

> the WIPO UDRP panel contains a high proportion of intellectual property practitioners. Of the 193 WIPO panellists currently practicing within the legal profession, 110 (57%) list a specialism

[66] The regulations on the selection and appointment of panellists in such cases are contained in Rules [6(e)]. The fees for a three-member panel shall be paid in their entirety by the complainant, except where the election for a three-member panel was made by the respondent, in which case the fees shall be shared equally between the parties [6(c)].

[67] Accurate data is hard to come by, but data supplied by the two largest dispute resolution service providers, WIPO and the National Arbitration Forum, shows that to October 2015 WIPO had taken 32,523 cases while to the end of 2014 the NAF had taken over 23,000, while smaller providers had also taken thousands of claims. Sources: <http://www.wipo.int/amc/en/domains/statistics/cases.jsp> and <http://www.adrforum.com/news#Item2574>.

[68] M Mueller, *Ruling the Root: Internet Governance and the Taming of Cyberspace* (MIT Press 2002), 193.

[69] M Froomkin, 'Wrong Turn in Cyberspace: Using ICANN to Route around the APA and the Constitution' (2000) 50 *Duke Law Journal* 17, 136.

[70] The two major UDRP providers being WIPO and the National Arbitration Forum.

[71] A Murray, 'Regulation and Rights in Networked Space' (2003) 30 *Journal of Law and Society* 187, 203.

> in intellectual property. In addition, of the 41 academic lawyers listed, 22 (53.7%) are listed as intellectual property professors or lecturers. Although it is to be expected that a high proportion of UDRP panellists would be experienced in intellectual property law given the nature of the disputes in question, and although there is no claim here made of individual bias by panellists in favour of intellectual property rights holders, for those panellists involved in the practice of IP law it may be difficult to maintain neutrality as the major aspect of their full-time vocation is the protection of IP rights from erosion and this might be expected to mean that certain 'habits of thought' are prevalent.[72]

The UDRP may therefore be classified as a policy which has been successful and popular with the community generally, but one which is controversial. But with much of ICANN's public image tied to the UDRP, ICANN has had to do everything possible to support the UDRP and its service providers.

16.6 **The new gTLD process and dispute resolution**

Recently ICANN have had an opportunity to review their dispute resolution procedures with the introduction of the new generic Top Level Domains (gTLDs). The scarcity of available domain name space has meant a push for a greater number of gTLDs to alleviate pressure on the ever-expanding use of the DNS. The creation of 'New gTLDs' formally began in 2008. It reached fruition in 2011 when the ICANN Board agreed to allow applications for new gTLDs from any interested party upon payment of a substantial management fee.[73] By October 2015, 769 new gTLDs had been approved,[74] falling mostly into four categories: trademarks such as .cartier, .toshiba, and .barclays; geographical such as .vegas, .london, and .sydney; vocational such as .pharmacy, .realtor, and .attorney; and speculative such as .beer, .porn, and .poker.[75]

With such an expansion of available domain names there were obviously concerns raised by trademark holders. ICANN has met their concerns in a two-part process, a pre-screening process for the gTLDs themselves then an expedited form of the UDRP for registrations made within the new gTLD space.

The first stage was pre-screening and allowing for challenges to applications to register the new gTLD itself. Once all applications were received by the deadline of 29 March 2012, a period of objection opened up where objections against grant could be lodged on one of four grounds: string confusion (where the applied for name is confusingly similar to an already in use or applied for string, such as .bom or .cam); legal rights objections (where the name is confusingly similar to a legal trademark or right in a name, such as .coach or .merck); community objections (where a challenge may be brought by representatives of a community to whom the name is impliedly or implicitly addressed, such as .amazon or .patagonia); and finally a limited public interest challenge which may be brought where the gTLD string is contrary to generally accepted legal norms of morality and public order that are recognized under principles of international law. Each objection gives rise to an arbitration process with the WIPO Arbitration

[72] Ibid. 216.

[73] ICANN, *Approved Board Resolutions—Singapore*, 20 June 2011 <http://www.icann.org/resources/board-material/resolutions-2011-06-20-en>.

[74] Up-to-date data is at <https://newgtlds.icann.org/en/program-status/statistics>.

[75] The full list is at <http://newgtlds.icann.org/en/program-status/delegated-strings>.

and Mediation Centre dealing with legal rights objections; the International Centre for Dispute Resolution dealing with string confusion objections; and the International Centre of Expertise of the International Chamber of Commerce dealing with both community and public interest challenges. Any concerned trademark holder could therefore lodge an objection with the WIPO Arbitration and Mediation Centre under the legal rights head. This led to 71 claims being lodged with WIPO including objections to .delmonte, .coach, and .moto. Once the objection was lodged the procedure followed was very similar to the UDRP procedure. The only addition was a case manager who had the power to consolidate claims relating to the same domain space for simpler disposal,[76] thereafter a single expert or three-expert panel would dispose of the objection.[77]

WIPO have published data on the process which reveals that of the 71 claims, two were dismissed for non-compliance and six were terminated, in three cases due to the withdrawal of gTLD applications. Expert panels upheld four legal rights objections, with dissenting opinions in three of these cases and rejected 59 legal rights objections. The only successful challenges were .delmonte, .direct, .weibo, and 微博. This process is now complete but with future rounds of new gTLDs planned by ICANN it will be dusted off once round two begins, which is unlikely to be before 2018.

A second protection for trademark holders throughout the gTLD process was the operation of the Trademark Clearinghouse (TMCH). This is an ICANN-mandated centralized repository of data on trademarks that are registered, court-validated, or protected by statute or treaty. It provides authenticated information about trademarks to registries and registrars. Brand owners were invited to submit their trademark data into the database prior to the launch of the new gTLD process (it could also be added afterwards). After the data was verified, trademark owners received a unique authentication key which gave them first priority in the registration of gTLDs which related to their trademarks (the sunrise period). Additionally, if an application was made to register a gTLD that matched a trademark on record, the applicant would be alerted to the registered trademark and would have to acknowledge the trademark before completing registration. Finally, upon completion of registration TMCH would notify the owner on record that the domain had been registered allowing them to raise an objection with the WIPO Arbitration and Mediation Centre.

Now that the first new gTLDs are operating we move on to the second phase of the dispute resolution process. This is dealing with registrations within new gTLDs such as sony.london or microsoft.coding. There are two procedures for dealing with these; the first is the Uniform Rapid Suspension system (URS). Like the UDRP, which also applies to new gTLDs, this is offered by providers; in this case the National Arbitration Forum and the Asian Domain Name Dispute Resolution Centre. It is a fast-track procedure for the clearest trademark infringement cases. It is not intended for use in proceedings with open questions of fact or more involved legal scenarios. While the substantive criteria of the URS are similar to the UDRP criteria, the URS is supposed to carry a higher burden of proof for complainants. The URS also includes a range of additional registrant defenses over an extended time period. The only remedy a URS panel may grant a successful complainant is the temporary suspension of a domain name for the remainder

[76] WIPO, Rules for New gTLD Dispute Resolution for Existing Legal Rights Objections, 20 June 2011 <http://www.wipo.int/export/sites/www/amc/en/docs/wipolrorules.pdf> para.7.

[77] Ibid. para. 8.

of the registration period. The URS Procedure and Rules are very similar to the UDRP except that this is only available to registered trademark or service mark holders,[78] and only available against registrations in new gTLDs,[79] and has a higher standard of proof than the UDRP (being essentially an administrative rather than judicial process) of 'clear and convincing evidence'[80] as against a 'preponderance of evidence' (balance of probabilities) for the UDRP. In return for the higher standard of proof, a simpler, cheaper, and more streamlined process is available for the claimant. Whereas the UDRP costs on average $1,500, can take up to 60 days, and allows for unlimited annexes as well as amendments and supplemental filings, the URS costs $375, allows only three annexes and no amendments or supplemental filings, and vitally decides claims in under 21 days. Unlike the UDRP, and perhaps learning from the Nominet DRS (discussed below), the URS has an appeals process. By para. 12 of the Procedure:

> Either party shall have a right to seek a *de novo* appeal of the Determination based on the existing record within the URS proceeding for a reasonable fee to cover the costs of the appeal. An appellant must identify the specific grounds on which the party is appealing, including why the appellant claims the Examiner's Determination was incorrect.

The Procedure or Rules give little detail as to how appeals are to be run but make it clear that a panel must hear the appeal. The first URS decision was facebok.pw, decided in October 2013. A January 2015 report reveals that to 31 December 2014 there were 234 URS cases with 106 domains suspended by default (undefended) judgment, 72 suspended by final judgment, and 7 suspended by appeal; whereas 18 claims were denied, and 18 cases were withdrawn.[81]

In addition to the URS, there is the Trademark Post-Delegation Dispute Resolution Procedure (Trademark PDDRP). This is a much more complex and judicial procedure intended to be used where a New gTLD Registry is accused of supporting trademark infringement at the top-level or second-level (i.e. where a trademark owner believes a registry is facilitating trademark infringement *mala fides*). This like the Nominet DRS (below) is a multi-part process. First, a complaint must be filed with the relevant service provider, in this case the WIPO Arbitration and Mediation Centre. A complaint is limited to 5,000 words or 20 pages, excluding attachments, unless the WIPO Center determines that additional material is necessary. Assuming the complaint is valid, within five days the complaint will be sent for a threshold review. This is a review by a single panellist to determine whether the complaint satisfies the criteria set out in section 9 of the Trademark PDDRP.[82] Assuming the threshold review is successful, only then will the Registry be invited to file a response. This should be done within 45 days of the threshold review.[83] Thereafter the service provider has 21 days to form either a single-person or three-person review panel along lines similar to the UDRP,[84] and the panel must 'make reasonable efforts to ensure that the Expert Determination is issued within 45 days of the appointment of the Expert Panel and absent good cause, in no event later

[78] URS Procedure para. 1.2.5.
[79] URS Rules para. 3(f).
[80] URS Procedure para. 8.2.
[81] MT Ianiro et al., *AIPLA Trademark Internet Committee Project: Summary of URS Decisions* 7 January 2015.
[82] Available via: <http://newgtlds.icann.org/en/program-status/pddrp>.
[83] Trademark PDDRP, s. 10.
[84] Ibid. s. 13.

than 60 days after the appointment of the Expert Panel.'[85] The Panel have a number of remedies available to them. They may:

(1) order 'remedial measures for the registry to employ to ensure against allowing future infringing registrations, which may be in addition to what is required under the registry agreement, except that the remedial measures shall not:

  (a) Require the Registry Operator to monitor registrations not related to the names at issue in the PDDRP proceeding; or

  (b) Direct actions by the registry operator that are contrary to those required under the Registry Agreement';

(2) 'Suspend the accepting new domain name registrations in the gTLD until such time as the violation identified in the Determination is cured or a set period of time'; or

(3) 'In extraordinary circumstances where the registry operator acted with malice, providing for the termination of a Registry Agreement.'[86]

As with the URS there is an appeal *de novo* permitted under s. 20 and by s. 21 ICANN will suspend all remedies for 20 days to allow for an appeal. This procedure is unlikely to be used frequently and at the date of writing there are no PDDRP decisions or cases pending.

16.7 **The Nominet DRS**

Nominet UK set up their dispute resolution procedure in autumn 2001, with the first published 'Expert' decision coming on 15 November 2001.[87] Although based in part on the ICANN UDRP, there are essential differences between the Nominet DRS and the UDRP, most obviously the opportunity to obtain summary decision where the complaint is undefended, the addition of a mediation procedure in defended complaints, and the opportunity for an appeal against the decision of a Nominet expert.

To raise a complaint the complainant must file a complaint with Nominet, either physically, or via the Nominet website.[88] The rules governing the complaint (and the response if one is forthcoming) are then to be found in the 'Procedure for the conduct of proceedings under the Dispute Resolution Service' (the Procedure).[89] Paragraph 3(c) of the Procedure sets out in full the requirements of the complaint document. There is a strict word limit of 5,000 words (not including annexes and appendices);[90] it must specify how and where the complainant may be contacted;[91] specify (where known) the respondent's contact details;[92] set out the domain name which is the subject of the

[85] Ibid. s. 19.1.
[86] Ibid. ss. 18.3.1–18.3.3.
[87] *Eli Lilly & Co. v Clayton* [2001] DRS 1.
[88] Although it should be noted a physical (signed) copy of the complaint still requires to be lodged with Nominet.
[89] <http://www.nominet.uk/wp-content/uploads/2015/08/30367_DRSProcedure_version3.pdf>.
[90] DRS Procedure [3(c)(i)].
[91] Ibid. [3(c)(ii)].
[92] Ibid. [3(c)(iii)].

dispute and the name or mark which is identical or similar to the domain name and in which the complainant asserts it has rights;[93] and describe in accordance with the dispute resolution policy[94] the grounds on which the complaint is made, including, in particular, what rights the complainant asserts in the name or mark; why the domain name should be considered to be an abusive registration in the hands of the respondent; and discussing any applicable aspects of para. 3 of the policy, as well as any other grounds which support the complainant's assertion.[95] This complaint, if found to be valid, is then sent by Nominet's DRS team to the respondent who has 15 days to respond.[96] If no response is forthcoming the complainant can seek a summary decision.[97] If a response is received the complainant is then given a final five days to submit to them a reply to the respondent's response.[98] At the end of submission of the documents of pleading Nominet will (if both sides are engaged) refer the dispute to informal mediation under para. 7 of the Procedure. The mediation procedure is done by telephone and email and may last for up to ten days.[99] If mediation is unsuccessful, or if there is no reply to the complaint making mediation impossible, then the dispute may be referred to an independent 'Expert', who acts as an arbiter and decides the dispute under the DRS Policy.

To succeed under the DRS policy a complainant must establish two things: (1) that they have rights in respect of a name or mark which is identical or similar to the domain name;[100] and (2) that the domain name, in the hands of the respondent, is an abusive registration.[101] The first limb of this test is relatively easy to establish with the Appeal Panel in *Seiko UK Ltd v Designer Time/Wanderweb* noting that '[t]he requirement to demonstrate "rights" is not a particularly high threshold test'[102] with, among others, personal names[103] and registered company names[104] being sufficient to establish this limb of the test.

The second limb is more testing. To establish an abusive registration the complainant is referred to para. 3 of the policy, which sets out a number of situations in which abusive registration will be deemed to have occurred. In addition, under para. 3(c), Cybersquatters who are engaged in the process of warehousing domain names are caught by a specific provision that 'there shall be a presumption of Abusive Registration if the Complainant proves that Respondent has been found to have made an Abusive Registration in three or more Dispute Resolution Service cases in the two years before the Complaint was filed'.

[93] Ibid. [3(c)(iv)].

[94] <http://www.nominet.uk/wp-content/uploads/2015/08/DRS-Policy.pdf>.

[95] DRS Procedure [3(c)(v)].

[96] Ibid. [5(a)].

[97] Ibid. [5(e)].

[98] Ibid. [6(a)].

[99] Ibid. [7(e)].

[100] Policy, [2(a)(i)]. Note 'Rights' are defined as: 'rights enforceable under English law. However, a Complainant will be unable to rely on rights in a name or term which is wholly descriptive of the Complainant's business' in [1] of the Policy.

[101] Policy [2(a)(ii)]. Note an 'Abusive Registration' is defined as: 'a Domain Name which either: (i) was registered or otherwise acquired in a manner which, at the time when the registration or acquisition took place, took unfair advantage of or was unfairly detrimental to the Complainant's Rights; OR (ii) has been used in a manner which took unfair advantage of or was unfairly detrimental to the Complainant's Rights' in [1] of the Policy.

[102] [2002] DRS 248, [9].

[103] *Stoneygate 48 Ltd v Rooney* [2006] DRS 3844.

[104] *J F Home Improvements Ltd v Giddy* [2005] DRS 3051.

Highlight Abusive registration (Nominet rules)

Abusive registration occurs when there are:

i. Circumstances indicating that the Respondent has registered or otherwise acquired the Domain Name primarily for the purposes of selling, renting, or otherwise transferring the Domain Name to the Complainant or to a competitor of the Complainant, for valuable consideration in excess of the Respondent's documented out-of-pocket costs directly associated with acquiring or using the Domain Name; OR as a blocking registration against a name or mark in which the Complainant has Rights; OR for the purpose of unfairly disrupting the business of the Complainant;

ii. Circumstances indicating that the Respondent is using the Domain Name in a way which has confused people or businesses into believing that the Domain Name is registered to, operated or authorized by, or otherwise connected with the Complainant;

iii. The Complainant can demonstrate that the Respondent is engaged in a pattern of registrations where the Respondent is the registrant of domain names which correspond to well known names or trade marks in which the Respondent has no apparent rights, and the Domain Name is part of that pattern.

Once the complainant has established a prima facie case the burden of proof switches to the respondent. Paragraph 4 of the policy contains a non-exhaustive list of factors which may be evidence that the domain name is not an abusive registration. These are:

> Before being aware of the complainant's cause for complaint, the respondent has used or made demonstrable preparations to use the domain name or a domain name which is similar to the domain name in connection with a genuine offering of goods or services; OR the respondent has been commonly known by the name or legitimately connected with a mark which is identical or similar to the domain name; OR the respondent made legitimate non-commercial or fair use of the domain name; OR the domain name is generic or descriptive and the respondent is making fair use of it.[105]

Perhaps unsurprisingly these defences have been the subject of a great degree of criticism and discourse. Possibly the most controversial decision was that of *Ryanair Ltd v Coulston*.[106] The respondent in that dispute was an individual called Michael Coulston. He once had a bad experience when travelling with Ryanair in which his luggage was temporarily lost and his holiday ruined, since when he devoted some considerable time and energy to publicizing what he perceived as deficiencies in the way in which Ryanair dealt with problems and complaints by its customers. He did this under the campaign name the 'Ryanair Refund Campaign'. As part of his activities he registered the domain name ryanair.org.uk on 20 September 2003 and used it as the address for his campaign by hosting a site critical of Ryanair.

Mr Coulston claimed he made a non-commercial fair use of the name as permitted under para. 4 of the policy. Ryanair claimed that the actions of Mr Coulston were

[105] In relation to fair use para. 4(b) of the policy states: 'Fair use may include sites operated solely in tribute to or in criticism of a person or business.'

[106] [2006] DRS 3655.

designed to confuse Ryanair customers (and potential customers) and as such were for the purpose of unfairly disrupting the business of the complainant in breach of para. 3. In deciding the dispute the expert, Anna Carboni, found that:

> Although I do not have full details of the chronology of statements and information posted to the Respondent's website, it is probable—as he asserts—that his initial purpose in registering the Domain Name was to tell his own story of the lost baggage and to comment on the Complainant's customer complaints policies. Nevertheless, my findings in relation to the inherent likelihood of confusion in adopting an essentially identical Domain Name to the mark Ryanair, lead me to conclude that the Domain Name was from the start registered in a manner which took unfair advantage of and was unfairly detrimental to the Complainant's Rights and, as such, was an Abusive Registration.

Unsurprisingly there has been a great deal of criticism of that decision with many commentators suggesting that somehow it is a restriction on the right to free speech. But if one examines the decision closely it is clear that it turned on some very narrow facts. Mr Coulston lost because the domain name ryanair.org.uk was simply too close in character to the complainant's ryanair.co.uk and customers were being confused. Mr Coulston admitted in his evidence that the emails he received at ryanair.org.uk were predominantly (in descending order of frequency): (1) spam; (2) messages from people who urgently need to change or correct booking details; (3) messages from people who have not received a confirmation of a booking; (4) messages from people with general Ryanair questions (e.g. about baggage allowances); (5) messages from people wanting to criticize Ryanair; and (6) messages from people wanting to praise Ryanair. Thus it is clear people were confusing his site with the official Ryanair site when it came to opening communications with the airline.[107] The decision of the expert was really that Mr Coulston's name selection for his site was deliberately chosen to mirror the name of the 'official' website which directly caused confusion. Mr Coulston was free to choose a more fitting domain name for his site such as ryanaircampaign.org, which he did and which, following a further complaint by the airline to the ICANN UDRP, was ruled not to be in bad faith.[108]

Once an expert decision is made either party then has 15 days to lodge an appeal.[109] If an appeal is made an appeal panel of three experts is convened. The appeal panel considers all the evidence laid before the expert at the original hearing and may additionally consider two further documents: an appeals notice and an appeal notice response, both of which are limited to 1,000 words. The panel has complete discretion to review all evidence from the original hearing and may make decisions by majority. Once the appeal decision is made, the DRS is closed and the only route of further recourse open to the parties is to refer their dispute to the courts.

16.7.1 **Reviewing the Nominet DRS**

The DRS has proven to be extremely robust. It has dealt with in excess of 10,000 disputes, yet very few cases have left the DRS for the courts. The first was an attempt to

[107] Admittedly this may have been out of frustration as Ryanair offer only a limited means of communication, except by premium-rate telephone number.
[108] *Ryanair Ltd v Michael Coulston*, WIPO Case No. D2006–1194 (December 12 2006).
[109] DRS Procedure [18].

bypass the DRS procedure by seeking a judicial review of the initial DRS decision rather than following the appeal procedure set out in the policy. The case involved the domain name itunes.co.uk which had been registered by a company called Cyberbritain Group Ltd. A DRS claim was raised by Apple Computer Inc., owners of the iTunes brand. The itunes.co.uk registration had been made before the UK trademark application was published. However, Apple Computer Inc.'s complaint related only to the later use of the name. In her decision the independent expert, Claire Milne, found that following the launch of Apple's iTunes music download service this use included: (1) direction of traffic on the domain to a website owned by an associate company of Cyberbritain Group Ltd; (2) an offer to sell the domain name to Napster; (3) direction of traffic to Napster under an affiliate scheme (from which profit would be generated); and (4) an offer to sell the domain name for £50,000. On the basis of these findings, the expert found that the registration was abusive and ordered transfer.

Mr Cohen (the owner of Cyberbritain Group Ltd) stated following the decision that he would not use the DRS appeals procedure but instead he intended to apply for judicial review. Cyberbritain Group Ltd duly started judicial review proceedings. Apple Computer, Inc. joined as an interested party and Nominet argued that (a) they were not subject to judicial review and (b) failure to use the appeal stage of the DRS barred Cyberbritain from seeking judicial review. Apple Computer, Inc. also argued that Cyberbritain had waited too long to apply. At an initial hearing the judge rejected the application to review Nominet judicially, citing the failure to use the appeal process and the delay. He avoided the question of whether they were judicially reviewable, as he did not need to decide it. The domain name has since been transferred to Apple Computers, Inc. as decided by the expert.

A second more recent case asked whether the courts could review cases of abuse registration independently of the Nominet DRS.[110] Mr Toth is a well-known 'domainer', the accepted name for someone who speculates in the value of domain names (and who may or may not be a cybersquatter). He had registered the domain name emirates.co.uk and had then been subjected to the full application of the Nominet DRS following a complaint from Emirates Airline. At the initial hearing the expert found for Mr Toth and ejected the Emirates complaint, but on appeal the panel upheld the complaint and decided that the domain name should be transferred. Mr Toth then applied to the court for a declaration that the domain name was not an abusive registration within the meaning of the policy. Emirates argued that the parties had agreed to the Nominet DRS and that Mr Toth's contract with Nominet did not provide for a cause of action independent of that procedure. Mr Toth argued that the policy did not prevent a *de novo* challenge in the courts. Initially before the Patents County Court Mr Toth succeeded but, on appeal to the Chancery Division, Mann J overturned this and found that the court had no jurisdiction to review the decision of the DRS. He examined the contract that Mr Toth had agreed to when he registered the domain name and found 'the court can have no role to play in any determination about abusive registration. The contract creates and completely regulates the dispute in such a way as to leave nothing for the court to bite on.'[111] In reply to a query from Mr Toth as to what therefore was meant by para. 20 of the Procedure which requires Nominet to stay the DRS Procedure

[110] *Toth v Emirates* [2012] EWHC 517 (Ch).

[111] Ibid. [48].

if court proceedings are brought, Mann J suggested this would be in relation to cases within the normal jurisdiction of the court such as a trademark dispute.

These cases have given considerable steel to the Nominet DRS. The independence the courts have granted it mean that it provides a strong regime for the resolution of disputes in the .uk domain name space.

16.8 Conclusions

To suggest that domain names and brand identifiers such as trademarks fulfil the same function is wrong, but to say they have similar functions (and often values) is right. The protection of brand identity, and brand values, online has been at the forefront of much litigation in recent years. The incredible growth of the domain name system caught out those who seek to protect traditional IP portfolios, and those who regulated the domain name system were caught out by the huge potential values of what they had on offer. The early cases of cybersquatting, domain name warehousing, and concurrent use demonstrated a 'clash of cultures' between the two. The arrival of the extrajudicial dispute resolution procedures at the turn of the millennium has done much to solve this problem. Although neither the ICANN UDRP nor the Nominet DRS are perfect, they are bridging the divide between the two cultures and may be put down as one of the few successes of 'internet law'.

TEST QUESTIONS

Question 1

Flutter Inc. (an online gambling site) has always operated from the domains Flutter.com and Flutter.co.uk but they have just become aware of two new websites, Flutterbetting.com and Flutterwager.co.uk. The global board is concerned that the owners of these sites may harm their business by damaging their goodwill with existing and potential customers and want advice on what to do next. An investigation has revealed that Flutterbetting.com has been registered with registry GoMammy.com by an Italian gambling service Giochi Sportivi SpA. An under construction page reveals that they intend to use it to run an online casino gambling service similar to Flutter's. An individual named Peter Flutterwager has registered Flutterwager.co.uk with the UK registry, 2&2.co.uk. The site currently resolves only to a 2&2 holding page saying the site is awaiting development. There is no other information available on Mr. Flutterwager's intentions for Flutterwager.co.uk.

The board have asked for your advice on what actions, if any, they should institute against either or both of these domain name registrations. The board is also considering registering the domain.flutter under the new gTLD process so they could offer sites such as slots.flutter, poker.flutter, blackjack.flutter, and roulette.flutter. They want to know how much this would cost and what procedure they need to follow. Write your advice to the board on all these issues.

Question 2

Do you believe the ICANN/Nominet UDRP procedures provide an equitable system for resolving domain name disputes? How could they be improved?

FURTHER READING

Books

T Bettinger and A Waddell (eds.), *Domain Name Law and Practice: An International Handbook* (2nd edn, 2015)

N Brown and G Levine, *Domain Name Arbitration: A Practical Guide to Asserting and Defending Claims of Cybersquatting Under the Uniform Domain Name Dispute Resolution Policy* (2015)

M Mueller, *Ruling the Root: Internet Governance and the Taming of Cyberspace* (2002)

J Wolfe and A Chasser, *Domain Names Rewired: Strategies for Brand Protection in the Next Generation of the Internet* (2012)

Chapters and articles

L Helfer and G Dinwoodie, 'Designing Non-National Systems: The Case of the Uniform Domain Name Dispute Resolution Policy' 43 *William & Mary Law Review* 141 (2001)

J Lipton, 'Beyond Cybersquatting: Taking Domain Name Disputes Past Trademark Policy' 40 *Wake Forest Law Review* 1361 (2005)

A Murray, 'Internet Domain Names: The Trade Mark Challenge', *IJLIT* 285 (1998)

E Null and D Prahl, 'The New Generic Top-Level Domain Program: A New Era of Risk for Trademark Owners and the Internet', 101 *Trademark Reporter* C 1757 (2011)

Brand identities, search engines, and secondary markets

While the ADR procedures offered by among others ICANN and Nominet, discussed in chapter 16, remain the most commonly employed procedures with respect to online trademark disputes, with on average 220 cases per month raised with WIPO alone in 2015, much recent focus has been on the wider interaction between trademarks and the digital environment. Two key areas of dispute have arisen, the employment of marks by search engines and the use of marks in secondary markets such as eBay. The first is due to a diminution of the role of domain names with the creation of so called omniboxes as replacements for the old-fashioned address bar in web browsers. Users rely on domain names much less following this development. Now a user is much less likely to type 'macdonalds.com' looking for the fast-food restaurant only to find that is an advertising redirect portal; instead, they will type 'macdonalds' into the omnibox and be taken to the Google search page which opens with 'showing results for mcdonalds' and a link to the official McDonalds page. The second is the ruse of the secondary or peer-to-peer market in which anyone may be using a brand name or trademark in a commercial context, sometimes with knowledge it is accurate, sometimes ignorant as to the accuracy of the branding, and sometimes deliberately to mislead with counterfeit goods. With the predominance of the ADR procedures in domain name disputes, recent case law has focused less on domain names and more on search and secondary markets such as eBay.

17.1 Jurisdiction and online trademark disputes

While the modern ADR systems for domain name disputes discussed in the previous chapter can avoid jurisdictional challenges through contractual agreements the question of jurisdiction, as so often seems to be the case, raises its head again in relation to online trademark abuses. Thus, the question of whether my UK trademark is capable of being applied in a dispute I may have with Google about the placement of an advertisement, which is carried on the google.com search page but not on the google.co.uk page, is significant. Is that page somehow located in the United States or given that it may be accessed in the UK is there vitally 'use' of the mark by Google in the UK?

The problem of jurisdiction, on a global scale, is one which arises again and again in the context of online activity, and this harks back to the cyberlibertarian argument of Johnson and Post discussed in chapter 3.[1] While there is no simple global solution to this issue there is helpful local guidance at the EU Level. Here jurisdiction in trademark infringement and passing off claims is governed by the Brussels Regulation,[2] which applies equally to online content and offline content. The rules are quite complex but we begin with the general principle found in Art. 2 'persons domiciled in a Member State shall, whatever their nationality, be sued in the courts of that Member State'. This seems to suggest that corporations not domiciled in a EU member state such as Google or eBay would not be subject to the jurisdiction of that state. However, this is qualified by Art. 5(3) 'in matters relating to tort, delict or quasi-delict, [they may be sued] in the courts for the place where the harmful event occurred or may occur'. Although not abundantly clear this includes actions for trademark infringement and for passing off. The ECJ has reviewed the application of this to online trademark disputes in the recent case of *Wintersteiger AG v Products 4U Sondermaschinenbau GmbH*.[3]

Case study *Wintersteiger AG v Products 4U Sondermaschinenbau*

Wintersteiger is an Austrian company who make and sell ski and snowboard servicing tools, replacement parts, and accessories which they sell internationally. It owns the Austrian trademark 'Wintersteiger'. Products 4U, is a German company. It also develops and sells ski and snowboard servicing tools, as well as accessories for tools made by other manufacturers, in particular Wintersteiger. The sale of those accessories, which Products 4U described as 'Wintersteiger-Zubehör' (Wintersteiger accessories) was not authorized by Wintersteiger. Products 4U sells its goods internationally including in Austria. In December 2008 Products 4U started to use the keyword 'Wintersteiger' in relation to adverts placed using the Google Adwords programme (which among other things placed ads next to Google natural search returns for that term). Vitally that use made by Products 4U of the term was limited to Google's German top-level domain, i.e. the website google.de. The court noted that 'the advertisement on 'google.de' gave no indication that there was any economic link between Wintersteiger and Products 4U. On the other hand, Products 4U had not entered any advertisement linked to the search term 'Wintersteiger' in Google's Austrian top-level domain, this being the website 'google.at'.[4]

Wintersteiger raised an action in the Austrian courts claiming that the Austrian courts had jurisdiction under Art. 5(3) of Brussels Regulation, basing their argument on the fact that google.de could be accessed in Austria, and that the site was configured in German, the language that was also spoken in Austria. Products 4U argued that since google.de was directed exclusively at German users, the advertisement at issue was therefore also intended only for German customers and the Austrian courts had no jurisdiction under Art. 5(3).

[1] See section 3.3.
[2] Reg. 44/2001.
[3] [2012] ETMR 31.
[4] Ibid. [12].

The court took a narrow approach, probably to limit the option of forum shopping where local search pages such as google.de or google.at are accessible throughout the EU. The court began by observing that:

> the rule of special jurisdiction laid down, by way of derogation from the principle of jurisdiction of the courts of the place of domicile of the defendant, in Art. 5(3) of the regulation is based on the existence of a particularly close connecting factor between the dispute and the courts of the place where the harmful event occurred, which justifies the attribution of jurisdiction to those courts for reasons relating to the sound administration of justice and the efficacious conduct of proceedings.[5]

This meant that the mere accessibility of a web page from within a member state did not give that member state jurisdiction to hear claims regarding the alleged infringement of national trademark rights.

The court confirmed that the last phrase of Art. 5(3) means both the place where the damage occurred (i.e. where the event which may give rise to liability resulted in damage); and the place of the event giving rise to the damage.[6] The place where the damage occurred is determined by identifying the 'centre of interests'[7] of the person whose rights have been infringed. In an action 'relating to infringement of a trade mark registered in a Member State through the use, by an advertiser, of a keyword identical to that trade mark on a search engine website operating under a country-specific top-level domain of another Member State may be brought before the courts of the Member State in which the trade mark is registered'.[8] The event giving rise to the damage in a case such as this would be 'the activation by the advertiser of the technical process' aimed at displaying the advertisement. On that basis, the 'place of the event' would be the place of establishment of the advertiser and not of the provider of the referencing service.[9] In the instant case therefore the relevant jurisdiction would be either Austria (as the place of registration of the trademark) or Germany (as the place of establishment of the advertiser), the location of the service provider or its servers was not relevant.[10]

17.2 **Search engines**

The issue behind the *Wintersteiger* case is a reflection of the modern internet: in a very real sense if you are not listed in the first page of Google search returns you do not exist in the online world. Google dominates the online experience with around 3.5 billion searches per day on Google, which represents about 89 per cent of all internet searches. Google determines in a very real sense how we experience the Web. In addition, as people switch from entering URLs to search terms, Google controls more of our web experience.[11] Google is obviously a profit-making enterprise and a large part of Google's profits come from selling advertising on its search pages. This is through the delivery of ads placed at the head and right-hand side of a search return surrounding the natural

[5] Ibid. [18].
[6] Ibid. [19].
[7] Ibid. [21].
[8] Ibid. [29].
[9] Ibid. [37].
[10] Ibid. [36].
[11] The use of search in place of URLs is demonstrated by the list of most searched keywords for 2014. They were: (1) Facebook; (2) YouTube; (3) Google; (4) Hotmail; (5) Gmail; and (6) fb.

search results. Obviously the Google algorithm determines the Google natural search returns and although they may be manipulated slightly it is now difficult to manipulate them extensively. If you want to be seen online, and you are not already a well-known name, it can be very difficult because, until you build up enough links and hits, you will languish in the lower reaches of a Google return.

Example Getting seen on Google

Maria wants to open a new online business selling legal textbooks. She discovers quickly that her business is struggling to register in Google search returns as whenever anyone searches for a textbook like 'Andrew Murray Information Technology Law' the first page is taken up with major suppliers such as Amazon, Waterstones, and WH Smith.

She discovers an easy way around this is to buy an advertisement to be placed on the first page of search returns in the sponsored links section. She simply gives Google details of which search keywords she would like to have her advert displayed against, how much she would like to spend for each 'click through' she receives, and an overall budget for the day, week, or month. Then whenever someone types in a search term—say 'Information Technology Law' her advert will be displayed.

This is okay as long as someone is using a generic term like 'Information Technology Law' or a personal name like Andrew Murray. The problem is what to do when someone like Maria purchases a sponsored link using a trademark like 'Louis Vuitton', 'Chanel', or 'Gucci'.

This example illustrates the trigger point for the first in a series of cases referred to the ECJ between 2008 and 2012 in relation to the Google-sponsored listing function.[12] The first began in France as a series of cases involving a number of trademarks including those owned by Louis Vuitton Malletier (LVM).[13] In early 2003 LVM became aware that when its trademarks were being used as Google search terms some of the adverts delivered provided links to sites offering imitation versions of its products. They discovered this was because Google offered advertisers the possibility of selecting not only keywords which correspond to LVM's trademarks, but also those keywords in combination with expressions indicating imitation, such as imitation and copy. Upon this discovery LVM brought proceedings against Google. The case was first heard in the Tribunal de Grande Instance de Paris which held Google liable for trademark infringement. An appeal to Cour d'appel de Paris upheld this decision and Google appealed to the Cour de Cassation who referred the case to the ECJ for a preliminary ruling.[14] There were three key questions for the court:

(1) is the application of trade marks to the selection of advertisements to be displayed a use in the course of trade;

[12] There were five references in all but we will only discuss three. The five were *Google France, Google Inc. v Louis Vuitton Malletier* [2010] ETMR 30 (France); *Die BergSpechte Outdoor Reisen v Günter Guni* [2010] ETMR 33 (Austria); *Portakabin v Primakabin* [2010] ETMR 52 (Netherlands); *Eis.de GmbH v BBY Vertriebsgesellschaft mbH* (C-91/09) unreported 26 March 2010 (ECJ) (Germany); and *Interflora Inc. v Marks & Spencer plc* [2012] ETMR 1 (UK).

[13] *Google France, Google Inc. v Louis Vuitton Malletier* [2010] ETMR 30.

[14] The case history is reported at [H6].

(2) is the use made by Google in placing sponsored listings likely to dilute the value of the trade mark; and

(3) can Google seek refuge in the safe harbour as an information society service provider by Art. 14 of the Electronic Commerce Directive?

The first question related to Google's use of the trademarks in selling advertising. Was this the kind of use of a trademark that could be prevented by a trademark holder? In essence was it use in the course of trade? The court began by looking at the activity of the advertiser rather than Google: 'use of a sign identical with a trade mark constitutes use in the course of trade where it occurs in the context of commercial activity with a view to economic advantage and not as a private matter'.[15] With regard to the advertiser purchasing the referencing service and choosing as a keyword a sign identical with another's trademark, it must be held that that advertiser is using that sign within the meaning of that case law.[16] What about Google though? The court ultimately decided that Google was not using the signs in the course of trade:

> The referencing service provider operates 'in the course of trade' when it permits advertisers to select, as keywords, signs identical with trade marks, stores those signs and displays its clients' ads on the basis thereof, it does not follow, however, from those factors that that service provider itself 'uses' those signs [in the course of trade] . . . A referencing service provider allows its clients to use signs which are identical with, or similar to, trade marks, without itself using those signs. That conclusion is not called into question by the fact that that service provider is paid by its clients for the use of those signs. The fact of creating the technical conditions necessary for the use of a sign and being paid for that service does not mean that the party offering the service itself uses the sign . . . a referencing service provider is not involved in use in the course of trade.[17]

Therefore, while the advertisers themselves are using the trademark in the course of trade, Google is not. This was a blow to LVM as most of the advertisers in question were not based within the EU and they would need to begin litigation elsewhere. The second question then was whether the use of the trademarks in paid-for advertising was likely to dilute the mark or cause loss to the trademark holder. The court saw a connection between the use of the trademarks on Google and elsewhere, 'With regard to the use by internet advertisers of a sign identical with another person's trademark as a keyword for the purposes of displaying advertising messages, it is clear that that use is liable to have certain repercussions on the advertising use of that mark by its proprietor and on the latter's commercial strategy.'[18] Again, as with the first question, the court found that the actions of the advertisers were likely to infringe:

> in the case of offers of imitations for sale where a third party attempts, through the use of a sign which is identical with, or similar to, a reputable mark, to ride on the coat-tails of that mark in order to benefit from its power of attraction, its reputation and its prestige, and to exploit, without paying any financial compensation and without being required to make efforts of its own in that regard, the marketing effort expended by the proprietor of that mark in order to create and maintain the image of that mark, the advantage resulting from such use must be considered to be an advantage that has been unfairly taken of the distinctive character or the repute of that mark.[19]

[15] Per *Arsenal Football Club plc v Reed* [2003] ETMR 19 at [40].
[16] [2010] ETMR 30 [50]–[51].
[17] *Google v Louis Vuitton* (n. 13). [55]–[58].
[18] Ibid. [93].
[19] Ibid. [103].

But, once again, when the court looked at Google it found it not liable for the actions of its customers, for as it had already ruled Google did not 'use' the trademarks.[20]

This left the remaining question somewhat moot but the court answered it anyway. The court here seemed to suggest that although Art. 14 protection was available to Google it was not clear Google would qualify for safe harbour protection:

> In order to establish whether the liability of a referencing service provider may be limited under Art. 14, it is necessary to examine whether the role played by that service provider is neutral, in the sense that its conduct is merely technical, automatic and passive, pointing to a lack of knowledge or control of the data which it stores . . . the role played by Google in the drafting of the commercial message which accompanies the advertising link or in the establishment or selection of keywords is relevant.[21]

However, this was a question for the referring court to determine.[22] In the event the referring court did not need to determine this as changes to Google's Adwords policy mean they comply with the decision of the court.[23]

Quickly on the heels of the *Louis Vuitton* decision the ECJ had another reference from the Netherlands.[24] The case essentially asked the same questions as *Louis Vuitton* in regard to potential liability for search engines and in essence the same answers were given. The one fresh issue dealt with in this case was a question of exhaustion. That is, once the trademark holder has put their goods into the market they are said to have exhausted their interest and they cannot then oppose the use of that trademark to commercialize the goods in a second-hand market—essentially this gives you the right to resell your old designer clothes on eBay with a full description including the name of the designer. Primakabin sells and leases new and second-hand mobile buildings. Among the second-hand units it leases are those manufactured by Portakabin. Primakabin was using Portakabin's trademark to buy Google advertising. Portakabin objected to this as they believed Primakabin were using their brand to advertise new Primakabin products at a loss to them. Primakabin argued they were advertising the second-hand Portakabin units they leased.

In a very confusing decision the court found that 'A trademark proprietor is not entitled to prohibit an advertiser from advertising, on the basis of a keyword identical with, or similar to, that trademark, which the advertiser has chosen for an internet referencing service without the consent of the proprietor, the resale of second-hand goods originally placed on the market in the EEA under that trademark by the proprietor or with his consent.'[25] But equally it found that:

> a trade mark proprietor is entitled to prohibit an advertiser from advertising, on the basis of a keyword identical with, or similar to, that mark, which that advertiser has selected for an internet referencing service without the consent of the proprietor, in relation to goods or services identical to those in respect of which the mark is registered, where that advertising does not enable average internet users, or enables them only with difficulty, to ascertain whether the goods or services referred to by the ad originate from the proprietor of the trade mark or from an undertaking economically linked to it or, on the contrary, originate from a third party.[26]

[20] Ibid. [104]–[105].
[21] Ibid. [114], [118].
[22] Ibid. [119].
[23] See <http://support.google.com/adwordspolicy/bin/answer.py?hl=en&answer=6118>.
[24] *Portakabin v Primakabin* [2010] ETMR 52.
[25] Ibid. [78].
[26] Ibid. [54].

How then to connect the two? Well, the answer is again that the referring court must do a little work to determine whether or not the use made of the mark was in fact infringing. There is some guidance on how to achieve this. The court says the trademark holder may only oppose advertising in relation to 'exhausted' items when 'there is a legitimate reason which justifies him opposing that advertising, such as use of that sign which gives the impression that the reseller and the trade mark proprietor are economically linked or use which is seriously detrimental to the reputation of the mark'.[27] The court then gives some guidance to the referring court on how to determine this.[28]

This was a case more about the roles of advertisers and their competitors than the search intermediary but it does add one more piece to the jigsaw, one that is finally completed with reference to our last ECJ case in this section, *Interflora Inc. v Marks & Spencer plc.*[29]

Case study *Interflora Inc. v Marks & Spencer plc*

This case originated in the UK and began when Marks & Spencer (M&S), the well-known high street retailer began to advertise their M&S flower delivery service with a Google advertisement that could be triggered by the search terms 'Interflora'. Interflora is a trademark of Interflora Inc., a network of florists which allow customers to place orders for the flower deliveries in person, by telephone, or through their website. Once placed the order is fulfilled by the network member closest to the address to which the flowers are to be delivered. It is a very old and efficient system which allows independent florists to operate a national flower delivery service. Once they became aware of the use of their trademark by M&S in this fashion Interflora raised a trademark infringement action.

The case began before Arnold J in the High Court.[30] He quickly realized the complexity of the case and the need for a reference to the ECJ. He therefore stayed proceedings and referred ten questions to the ECJ for a preliminary ruling. However, following the decision of the court in *Louis Vuitton*, he withdrew six of these questions leaving four fresh questions for the court to consider.[31] The essence of the four remaining questions could be reduced to two key questions:

> (1) whether the proprietor of a trade mark is entitled to prevent a competitor from displaying—on the basis of a keyword which is identical to that trade mark and which has been selected in an internet referencing service by the competitor without the proprietor's consent—an advertisement for goods or services identical to those for which that mark is registered; and
> (2) in those circumstances, is it relevant
>
> (i) that the advertisement concerned is liable to lead some members of the relevant public to believe, incorrectly, that the advertiser is a member of the trade mark proprietor's commercial network; and
>
> (ii) that the provider of the internet referencing service does not permit trade mark proprietors to prevent signs identical to their trade marks being selected as keywords?[32]

[27] Ibid. [89].
[28] Ibid. [93].
[29] [2012] ETMR 1.
[30] [2009] EWHC 1095 (Ch).
[31] [2010] EWHC 925 (Ch).
[32] [2012] ETMR 1 [27]–[28].

The court answered the first question by reference to the decision in the *Portakabin* case:

> a trade mark's function of indicating origin is adversely affected when internet users are shown, on the basis of a keyword identical with the mark, a third party's advertisement, such as that of a competitor of the trade mark proprietor, depends in particular on the manner in which that advertisement is presented. That function is adversely affected if the advertisement does not enable reasonably well-informed and reasonably observant internet users, or enables them only with difficulty, to ascertain whether the goods or services referred to by the advertisement originate from the proprietor of the trade mark or an undertaking economically connected to it or, on the contrary, originate from a third party.[33]

As had been indicated in the *Portakabin* decision, this was for the referring court to decide. As with *Portakabin*, the court gave guidance on how this may be achieved:

> In carrying out its examination of the facts, the referring court may choose to assess, first, whether the reasonably well-informed and reasonably observant internet user is deemed to be aware, on the basis of general knowledge of the market, that M&S's flower-delivery service is not part of the Interflora network but is, on the contrary, in competition with it and, second, should it become apparent that that is not generally known, whether M&S's advertisement enabled that internet user to tell that the service concerned does not belong to the Interflora network. In particular, the referring court may take into account that, in the present case, the commercial network of the trade mark proprietor is composed of a large number of retailers which vary greatly in terms of size and commercial profile. The Court considers that, in such circumstances, it may be particularly difficult for the reasonably well-informed and reasonably observant internet user to determine, in the absence of any indication from the advertiser, whether or not the advertiser—whose advertisement is displayed in response to a search using that trade mark as a search term—is part of that network.[34]

The second question was more complicated and the court separated off the two sub-questions into questions of trademark dilution and unfair advantage. In relation to dilution the court directed that:

> When the use, as a keyword, of a sign corresponding to a trade mark with a reputation triggers the display of an advertisement which enables the reasonably well-informed and reasonably observant internet user to tell that the goods or services offered originate not from the proprietor of the trade mark but, on the contrary, from a competitor of that proprietor, the conclusion will have to be that the trade mark's distinctiveness has not been reduced by that use, the latter having merely served to draw the internet user's attention to the existence of an alternative product or service to that of the proprietor of the trade mark. If, on the other hand, the referring court were to conclude that the advertising triggered by the use of the sign identical to the Interflora trade mark did not enable the reasonably well-informed and reasonably observant internet user to tell that the service promoted by M&S is independent from that of Interflora and if Interflora were to seek moreover from the referring court, in addition to a finding that the mark's function of indicating origin has been adversely affected, a finding that M&S has also caused detriment to the distinctive character of the Interflora trade mark by contributing to turning it into a generic term, it would fall to the referring court to determine, on the basis of all the evidence submitted to it, whether the selection of signs corresponding to the trade mark Interflora as keywords on the internet has had such an impact on the market for flower-delivery services that the word 'Interflora' has come to designate, in the consumer's mind, any flower-delivery service.[35]

[33] Ibid. [44].
[34] Ibid. [51]–[52].
[35] Ibid. [81]–[82].

The final part of the second question was whether M&S had gained an unfair advantage through the availability of the Interflora trademark as an advertising keyword. The court found:

> Where a competitor of the proprietor of a trade mark with a reputation selects that trade mark as a keyword in an internet referencing service, the purpose of that use is to take advantage of the distinctive character and repute of the trade mark. In fact, that selection is liable to create a situation in which the probably large number of consumers using that keyword to carry out an internet search for goods or services covered by the trade mark with a reputation will see that competitor's advertisement displayed on their screens. It is clear from those particular aspects of the selection as internet keywords of signs corresponding to trade marks with a reputation which belong to other persons that such a selection can, in the absence of any 'due cause', be construed as a use whereby the advertiser rides on the coat-tails of a trade mark with a reputation in order to benefit from its power of attraction. If that is the case, the advantage thus obtained by the third party must be considered to be unfair.[36]

This is a very strong finding in favour of the trademark holder. In essence, the question for the domestic court is to determine whether or not a 'reasonably well-informed and reasonably observant internet user' can tell that (or can only tell with difficulty) whether the advertiser and the trademark holder are economically connected.

With the fallout of the *Interflora* case still being felt in the courts of England and Wales, a more recent case has demonstrated the application of the *Google France* decision in England and Wales. In *Cosmetic Warriors Ltd, Lush Ltd v Amazon.co.uk Ltd, Amazon Eu Sarl*,[37] the issue in dispute was the use by Amazon of the 'Lush' trademark to direct consumers to alternative products. Lush, a well-known ethical cosmetic company had taken the deliberate decision not to allow its goods to be sold on Amazon because it took issue with some of Amazon's business practices and did not wish to be associated with Amazon. As a result, no Lush cosmetics were on sale through Amazon. To direct consumers to alternative products, which Amazon did sell, they bid on the keyword 'Lush' as a Google AdWord. When a user searched for Lush on Google, the following sponsored advert would appear headlined 'Lush Soap at Amazon.co.uk' offering 'Low prices on Lush Soap' and 'Free UK Delivery on Amazon Orders'. The court noted that 'if a consumer clicks on the relevant link he is taken to the amazon.co.uk website and presented with the opportunity to browse or purchase equivalent products to Lush Soap. There is no overt message either within the advertisement or on the Amazon site that Lush Soap is not available for purchase from Amazon.'[38] Amazon also used another form of advertisement on Google, subtly different. This one was headlined 'Bomb Bath at Amazon.co.uk' and offered 'Low prices on Bath Bombs' and 'Free UK Delivery on Amazon Orders'. This advert did not mention Lush anywhere.

The court applied both *Google France* and *Interflora* and found that 'It is clear, following Google France, that if the ad appeared as a result of Amazon having bid on Lush as a keyword, Amazon has used the mark in the course of trade in relation to the relevant goods.'[39] However, there was a subtle difference in the two adverts. The first clearly mentioned the name 'Lush', whereas the second did not; did this make a difference?

[36] Ibid. [86], [89].
[37] [2014] EWHC 181 (Ch).
[38] Ibid. [8].
[39] Ibid. [38].

The judge, John Baldwin QC, thought it did. In relation to the first advert, which mentioned 'Lush' explicitly he found that:

> the average consumer seeing [the advert] would expect to find Lush soap available on the Amazon site and would expect to find it at a competitive price. Moreover, I consider that it is likely that if he were looking for Lush soap and did not find it immediately on the Amazon site, then he would persevere somewhat before giving up. My reason is that the consumer is likely to think that Amazon is a reliable supplier of a very wide range of goods and he would not expect Amazon to be advertising Lush soap for purchase if it were not in fact available for purchase.[40]

However, the second advert was different:

> In Interflora Arnold J held there to be infringement although the offending ad made reference only to 'M&S Flowers Online' and not to 'Interflora'. But that was, in part, because Interflora represents a network of flower shops and the court was not satisfied that the average consumer would appreciate that Marks & Spencer were not members of that network. So I think that case is different on the facts from the one before me. [In relation to the advert delivered], there was [also] an ad for a third party as well as one for Amazon. In my judgment the presence of such other ads makes the position even clearer. The average consumer could not reasonably fail to appreciate that the Amazon ad was just another ad from a supplier offering similar products to those requested by the internet searcher. My conclusion on this part of the case does not, however, depend on the presence of this other ad.[41]

On this basis the court found that the use of the Lush mark in the first advert was infringing, because the advert did not pass the test of enabling normally informed and reasonably attentive internet users to ascertain whether the goods or services referred to in the advertisement originated from Lush or from an unconnected third party, whereas in the second advert there was no infringement as the advert did not make use of the Lush mark and the average consumer would realize it was an advert for a competing product. The judge took the view that consumers would expect an advert for Lush products to include at least some reference to the Lush mark or some indication to distinguish it as a Lush advert from other adverts thrown up by a Google search. Although Marks & Spencer's flower delivery advert had been held to infringe Interflora's registered trademark even though the advert did not mention Interflora, that case could be distinguished.

17.3 **Secondary markets**

It is not only search engines that have been subject to this form of trademark litigation. eBay has found itself at the heart of litigation in both the United States and the EU. Litigation began in France, home of many luxury goods brands. In June 2008 a series of early cases established that eBay was liable under French law for allowing the abuse of trademarks on their eBay France site. On 4 June the Tribunal de Grande Instance de Troyes, in *Hermes v eBay*,[42] found eBay to have 'committed acts of counterfeit' and 'prejudice' by failing to monitor the authenticity of goods being sold on its website by

[40] Ibid. [42].
[41] Ibid. [47–48].
[42] Decision available in French from <www.legalis.net/spip.php?page=jurisprudence-decision&id_article=2320>.

a user identified as 'Mrs Cindy F'. As a result they were ordered to pay Hermes damages of €20,000 and to block the user from the eBay site. However, this case was a mere appetizer for the later joined cases of *Louis Vuitton Malletier v eBay, Christian Dior Couture v eBay*, and *SA Parfums Christian Dior v eBay*.[43] In all three cases eBay was found to have operated a site which supported both the trade in counterfeit goods and the illegal sale of genuine goods without a licence of the trademark holder. The cases related to a number of luxury goods brands and items including Dior and Louis Vuitton handbags and clothes as well as Guerlain, Givenchy, and Kenzo perfumes and cosmetics. In total, damages amounting to €38.6m were awarded to the claimants and eBay was banned from selling four perfumes—Christian Dior, Kenzo, Givenchy, and Guerlain in France. eBay appealed to the Cour de Cassation arguing that the French courts did not have jurisdiction to hear the case as eBay is a US/Swiss Corporation. The court rejected this in late 2010.[44] eBay then defended on the basis that they were an information society service host provider under Art. 14 of the Electronic Commerce Directive and as such were entitled to safe harbour protection. In May 2012 the court ruled that eBay was not simply a host but played an active role that gave them the knowledge of or control over the data that they stock, which means they do not benefit from the safe harbour provisions of Art. 14.[45] They added that they considered that eBay plays an active role in its online marketplace, as it uses optimization services to assist sellers, sends unsolicited messages to the buyers to invite them to buy, and sends invitations to the unsuccessful bidders for them to participate in other offers. This decision left eBay liable in France for the actions of its sellers because of its active role which gives it the knowledge of and control over the unlawful items that it lists.

A later landmark decision of the ECJ suggests the reasoning of the Cour de Cassation has been proven right. The case was a reference from the High Court of England and Wales. It was brought by L'Oréal and a number of other beauty product companies in relation to a number of activities on eBay. L'Oréal and the other claimants had brought a number of items to eBay's attention and were dissatisfied with how eBay dealt with their complaints. The items were a mixture of counterfeit goods (in a few cases), unlawful imports from outside the European Economic Area, items not intended for sale (such as testers), and items sold without the packaging in which they were originally marketed. The case was referred to the ECJ by Arnold J who asked ten questions,[46] we will look at the three key questions: (1) was the use of the trademarks a use in the course of trade? (2) could the trademark owner prevent the sale of genuine but unboxed items? and (3) were eBay liable for the actions of the users of the site?

The first question was whether the sale of items on an auction site such as eBay was use in the course of trade. The court first determined that where an individual sells an item through an online marketplace this is not a sale in the course of trade, however, where 'the sales made on such a marketplace go beyond the realms of a private activity, the seller will be acting "in the course of trade"'.[47] In addition, the court confirmed their

[43] Tribunal de Commerce de Paris, 30 June 2008. Decision available in French from <http://www.legalis.net/spip.php?page=jurisprudence-decision&id_article=2353>.

[44] *Louis Vuitton Malletier (Société) v eBay Inc. and eBay International AG* [2011] ILPr 16.

[45] Decision available in French from <www.legalis.net/spip.php?page=jurisprudence-decision&id_article=3398>.

[46] *L'Oréal SA & Ors v eBay International AG & Ors* [2011] ETMR 52 [H11].

[47] Ibid. [55].

earlier finding from *Louis Vuitton* that when eBay bought advertisements on Google they acted in the course of trade.[48] The next question then was: could the trademark holders prevent the sale of unboxed goods which may be genuine? The court said yes and on two separate potential grounds, namely

(1) where the consequence of that removal is that essential information, such as information relating to the identity of the manufacturer or the person responsible for marketing the cosmetic product, is missing; or

(2) where the trademark owner has established that the removal of the packaging has damaged the image of the product and, hence, the reputation of the trademark.[49]

The final and, for our purposes, key question was: was eBay liable for these actions? The court determined that eBay could be infringing the rights of trademark holders in two ways. First, by advertising online using services such as Google sponsored links to advertise the claimants' products,[50] and second, by actively promoting sales on the eBay site via adverts and other promotional services such as mailings and re-offers, eBay could be liable for the infringements committed by their customers.[51] Could then eBay benefit from the Art. 14 safe harbour? Following the line of authority begun with *Louis Vuitton* the court concluded that 'the fact that the service provided by the operator of an online marketplace includes the storage of information transmitted to it by its customer-sellers is not in itself a sufficient ground for concluding that that service falls, in all situations, within the scope of Art. 14(1).'[52] An example of a situation when Art. 14 will not apply is when 'the service provider, instead of confining itself to providing that service neutrally by a merely technical and automatic processing of the data provided by its customers, plays an active role of such a kind as to give it knowledge of, or control over, those data'.[53] The final determination of this question is of course one for the referring court but the ECJ left clear guidance:

> Article 14(1) must be interpreted as applying to the operator of an online marketplace where that operator has not played an active role allowing it to have knowledge or control of the data stored. The operator plays such a role when it provides assistance which entails, in particular, optimising the presentation of the offers for sale in question or promoting them. Where the operator of the online marketplace has not played an active role within the meaning of the preceding paragraph and the service provided falls, as a consequence, within the scope of Article 14(1), the operator none the less cannot, in a case which may result in an order to pay damages, rely on the exemption from liability provided for in that provision if it was aware of facts or circumstances on the basis of which a diligent economic operator should have realised that the offers for sale in question were unlawful and, in the event of it being so aware, failed to act expeditiously in accordance with Article 14(1)(b).[54]

Following the decision of the ECJ the parties agreed a settlement in January 2014. This was unsurprising as eBay, not waiting for the outcome of the case, had made several

[48] Ibid. [87].
[49] Ibid. [83].
[50] Ibid. [84]–[90].
[51] Ibid. [91]–[97].
[52] Ibid. [111].
[53] Ibid. [113].
[54] Ibid. [123]–[124].

changes to their business plan to ensure they would comply with a negative judgment.[55] However, the guidance from the ECJ is clear.

The High Court returned to this issue, and applied the *L'Oréal* guidance, in the previously discussed case of *Cosmetic Warriors Ltd, Lush Ltd v Amazon.co.uk Ltd, Amazon Eu Sarl*.[56] In addition to the challenge to the two adverts placed on Google AdWords by Amazon, Lush also challenged the internal processes of Amazon's site, as explained by Baldwin QC:

> if a consumer searches for the word 'Lush' in the relevant 'department' of Amazon's UK site (e.g. 'Beauty' or 'Health and Personal Care'), the first thing to happen after the letters 'lu' are typed, is that a drop-down menu appears and various options are offered such as 'lush bath bombs' or 'lush cosmetics' or 'lush hair extensions', the consumer being offered the opportunity to click on one of these options whereupon a new page will appear. In the case of a consumer clicking on 'lush bath bombs' or 'lush cosmetics' the new page will offer similar products to those available from Lush without any overt reference to the Lush item not being available. In the case of a consumer clicking on Lush hair extensions, the consumer is presented with a page containing hair extensions from a third party manufacturer called Lush as well as other third party products. Slightly different results may be obtained if the consumer enters the term 'Lush' as a search into 'All Departments' (i.e. all departments of Amazon) but the general picture is the same. There will be a drop-down menu identifying various Lush goods and a display of products which are similar to or equivalent to those sold by Lush, there will be no display of any Lush products of the Claimants and there will be no overt message to the effect that the Claimants' Lush products are not available from the amazon.co.uk website.[57]

This is not too dissimilar to the activities of eBay advertising L'Oréal products on their site. The court found that Amazon not only operated a marketplace but were the designers of the search facility: 'Amazon is both the designer and operator of the search engine and the operations on its site. Although it may be wearing different hats when it designs its search engines and sells its goods, I have no doubt that the design of the search engine is carried out in order to maximize the sale of goods from the site.'[58] From this it was a very short step to find Amazon used the Lush mark in the course of trade through its application to the drop-down menu.

Highlight Trademarks in drop- down menus

The average consumer is unlikely to know how the drop-down menu has the content which it displays, but is likely to believe that it is intended to be helpful to him and is some consequence of other searches that have been carried out. In my judgment it would inform the average consumer that if he were looking for Lush Bath Bombs on Amazon, he would find them by clicking on that menu item. I reject the contention that the average consumer who was typing Lush

→

[55] Stefan Krawczyk, eBay's European government relations director stated afterwards 'A lot of cases will still have to be assessed by the national courts. We've moved on—we fulfill most of these conditions now anyways.' Source: *New York Times*, 12 July 2011 <http://www.nytimes.com/2011/07/13/business/global/ebay-suffers-setback-on-trademark-infringement.html>.

[56] See n 37.

[57] Ibid. [11], [13].

[58] Ibid. [57].

→

into the search box would think that the drop-down menu reference to Lush Bath Bombs was a reference merely to products which were similar to or competitive with the Lush product . . . On the facts of this case, I do not think Amazon can escape from the conclusion that it has used the Lush sign in the course of trade in relation to the relevant goods based on the principles to be found in *Google France* and *L'Oréal v eBay*. It has used the sign as part of a commercial communication that it is selling the goods on its website.[59]

Finally, the question was whether this use had damaged the Lush trademark and again Baldwin QC had little difficulty: 'the use complained of by Lush clearly damages the original function and the advertisement and investment function of the Lush trade mark'.[60]

Ultimately, the use of the Lush trademark in the drop-down menu function was found to be infringing in relation to the menu options 'lush bath bombs' and 'lush cosmetics', but not in relation to 'lush hair extensions', that being the brand of a separate company in relation to the supply of clip-in hair extensions.

17.4 **Conclusions**

The nature of branding online has changed of late. Domain names have lost their focus as branding tools and the few brands which still rely on their domain name identity, such as Amazon.com, are mostly hangovers from that time in the development of the network when domain names were valuable pieces of real estate. With the replacement of the address bar by the multifunctional omnibox much greater value has been attached to listing on search engines. Recently the focus of trademark holders has therefore turned to the invisible use of the brands and marks in search engine listings, particularly advertisements, and to the regulation of secondary markets which arguably support a trade in counterfeit goods. It was only a matter of time until the quasi-deregulated environment of online commerce would come into conflict with brands and trademark values and thus we have had a series of cases at domestic and European level in the last six years. These cases have now established a strong legal framework for the legal regulation of trademarks and brand identities in relation to keyword advertising and use in secondary markets. With the law now more settled in this area we can expect a steady stream of cases in the next few years as trademark holders enforce their rights in this arena.

TEST QUESTIONS

Question 1

A client, Jada, who is based in London, comes to see you for advice on the following scenario. Advise her of any potential claims she may have in trademark law.

[59] Ibid. [60–61].
[60] Ibid. [75].

Her company 'Streetbags' specializes in handbags and travel bags with designs supplied by famous urban artists including Blek Le Rat, D*face, and KAWS. Since their launch in 2014 they have quickly become a highly desirable fashion accessory featured in *Vogue*, *Elle*, and *Glamour*. Limited edition Streetbags can sell for up to £12,000. Collection bags range in price from £750 to £2,500.

Recently your client has noted that a search on Google using the term 'Streetbags' returns not only her company page but also 'Ads' for a number of unrelated sites. One Ad links to the web page of a UK-based dealer 'Cheap Designer Bags UK'. Their site offers Streetbags for sale for between £80–£150. An investigation by Streetbags reveals these are cheap fake bags produced in the Far East, not the genuine Streetbags product only ever produced in the EU. A second link takes the user to the home page of Streetbags competitor 'Urban Style', a start-up company which has recently began to commission its own bags designed by less-well-known artists such as Isaac Cordaal and Lake. Yet to launch, Urban Style have indicated their bags will be priced in the £150 to £350 price range.

It has also come to the attention of Streetbags that auction site eBay hosts a number of Streetbags sales. Some appear to be genuine resales of genuine Streetbags by customers, but a number of listings seem to be suspect, offering new Streetbags for suspiciously low prices. Streetbags believe fake bags imported from the Far East are fulfilling these sales.

Question 2

To be an infringement of a trademark someone must mistakenly believe that good, service, or product is associated with the trademark holder in some way (confusion) unless the mark is an identical mark used for identical goods or services. Where goods are sold as being 'inspired by' or 'related to' or similar on eBay or Amazon Marketplace is this trademark infringement?

FURTHER READING

Chapters and articles

A Blythe, 'Trade Marks as Adwords: An Aid to Competition or a Potential Infringement? An Evaluation of the Law in the Light of Recent Decisions' 37 (4) *EIPR* 225 [2015]

J Davis, 'Revisiting the Average Consumer: An Uncertain Presence in European Trade Mark Law' *IPQ* 15 (2015)

J-S Dupont, 'Uncharted Territories of Trade Mark Use' *IPQ* 139 (2015)

C Morcom, 'Trade Marks and the Internet: Where Are We Now?' 34 (1) *EIPR* 40 [2012]

E Moro, 'Protection of Reputed Trademarks and Keywords: Looking for Ariadne's Thread among Flowers, Perfumes and Bags' 2 *UCL Journal of Law and Jurisprudence* 64 (2013)

Electronic contracts

The ability to trade and to make payment is the foundation of all modern societies and the information society is no different in this respect. The information society has provided a number of commercial opportunities for entrepreneurs. The most well-known, software designers Bill Gates, Steve Ballmer, and Paul Allen became multibillionaires from their Microsoft software packages while competitors Steve Jobs and Stephen Wozniak made billions from both hardware and software development for Apple. Others, such as Michael Dell, focused on producing hardware while the next generation of internet entrepreneurs made money from either selling goods or services in the information society—as demonstrated by Amazon founder Jeff Bezos, eBay founder Pierre Omidyar, or Craigslist founder Craig Newmark—or have simply packaged and sold information as a standalone product, as was done by Facebook founder Mark Zuckerberg, YouTube creators Jawed Karim, Chad Hurley, and Steve Chen, or, most famously, the Google guys Larry Page and Sergey Brin.

The cornerstone of the ability to extract revenue from all these products and services are two legal principles which underpin all commerce: (1) the binding legal agreement, or contract, and (2) the universal recognition of a form or token of payment. Without the legal certainty offered by a contract, and the recognition and acceptance of a token or form of payment in return for goods and services, all forms of commerce lack the necessary foundations of certainty and liquidity: this is why from earliest times the rules on pacts, or contracts, and token or payment have been at the heart of all trading cultures and communities. This remains true of today's information society. Whatever form business takes, be it the trading of data, entertainment products, news and information, or systems for the management and development of software or hardware, these twin requirements of certainty and liquidity remain underpinned by the law of contract and the law relating to payment and payment methods. This chapter and the one which follows will look at how this traditional area of law is reacting to the challenges of digital products and services and virtual payments or payment alternatives.

18.1 **Contracting informally**

Contracting is one of the most commonplace and simple applications of legal principles. Every day people enter into dozens of legally binding contracts without thinking about it. They enter into contracts of carriage with public transport operators, contracts of sale with shops, garages, and supermarkets, and contracts for the supply of services with hairdressers or dentists. These informal contracts are often entered into without a single word being exchanged, yet a contract is formed all the same.

Example Informal contracts

Kiera is travelling from home to university for class. She decides to take the bus. She gets on the bus and pays her fare (or shows a pass) and then takes a seat on the bus. She doesn't say anything to the driver; the driver doesn't say anything to her yet a contract has been formed where the customer agrees to pay the fare for the journey undertaken and to comply with the bus company's general conditions of carriage and the driver (as agent for the bus company) agrees to carry the customer in accordance with the same general conditions of carriage.

An equivalent type of transaction takes place daily in supermarkets where the customer offers to buy goods from the supermarket by taking them to the checkout and the checkout operator, as agent for the supermarket, accepts this offer. The customer agrees to pay the advertised price and in return the supermarket agrees to transfer title in the goods to the customer. The reason these contracts may be formed without the exchange of written, or even oral, terms is because these are informal contracts: contracts that have no legally defined form and which may be formed simply by a *consensus ad idem* or a meeting of the minds.

18.1.1 **Contract formation**

The rules for the formation of informal contracts seem extremely simple; to form a contract all parties to the contract must agree on the terms of the contract, and to be bound by these terms. In English law this is usually assumed to take place when an offer is accepted with consideration,[1] in Scots law the element of consideration is unnecessary.[2] This apparent simplicity though belies the complexity of contract law and in particular the rules of contract formation. Many of these rules affect the time and even place of formation of the contract, and even in informal contracts they prescribe certain conditions for the formation of a concluded contract which are of particular import in dealing with electronic and online contracts.

The basics of any form of contract are that a set of offered terms and conditions must be accepted. The question is how can one recognize an offer and an acceptance? Although this may seem a simple question the intent of parties plays a significant role in determining when, or if, *consensus ad idem* has occurred.

This came to light in a series of shop display cases in the 1950s and 1960s. This series began with *Pharmaceutical Society of Great Britain v Boots Cash Chemists (Southern) Ltd.*[3] Boots, the well-known high-street pharmacy, had begun a trial of self-service shopping in some of its stores. This allowed customers to buy some pharmacy products by putting them in a basket and taking them to a cashier for payment. The Pharmaceutical Society

[1] M Chen-Wishart, *Contract Law* (5th edn, OUP 2015) chs. 2 and 3.

[2] See H MacQueen and J Thompson, *Contract Law in Scotland* (3rd edn, Bloomsbury Professional 2012).

[3] [1953] 1 QB 401.

argued this was in breach of the Pharmacy and Poisons Act 1933 which made it illegal to sell a listed poison without supervision of a registered pharmacist. The question before the Court of Appeal was whether the display of goods on the shelf was a standing offer to sell which was accepted by the customer upon placing the drugs in the basket or whether it was merely an 'invitation to treat' with the offer being made by the customer at the till and the acceptance being affected by the cashier. The court found the latter position was preferred with Birkett LJ noting that 'it would be wrong to say that the shopkeeper is making an offer to sell every article in the shop to any person who might come in and that that person can insist on buying any article by saying "I accept your offer".'[4]

This decision was later affirmed and developed in *Fisher v Bell*,[5] in which a shop window display was described as an invitation to treat, and *Partridge v Crittenden*,[6] in which a classified advert in a periodical was also similarly defined. These cases are very important in discussing electronic contracting, and in particular online contracts. We can draw on these cases to establish that a display on an e-commerce site such as Amazon should clearly be an invitation to treat and not a standing offer to sell.[7] The offer should come from the customer with the acceptance following at a later stage in the sales process. But one question remains, how should the contract formation process be structured when one of the parties is a computer? Traditionally a contract is formed by a meeting of the minds, meaning both parties must agree to the terms and as a computer cannot form the necessary intent to form the agreement, this suggests that a human agent is required.

Computers are not the first non-human actor to be involved in contract formation. We have used vending machines for decades and ticket machines in stations and in car parks have stood in for human operators for some time. The role of automated ticket machines was reviewed by the Court of Appeal in the famous case of *Thornton v Shoe Lane Parking Ltd*.[8] The case, which is no doubt familiar to any student of English contract law, established the principle that a contractual term displayed or communicated to a contractual counterparty after *consensus ad idem* is reached is not incorporated into the contractual terms. What, though, is less often analysed in the many discussions of *Thornton* is the approach the court developed for dealing with contract formation and non-human actors. It is perfectly explained in the words of Lord Denning MR.[9]

Highlight Lord Denning in *Thornton v Shoe Lane Parking Ltd*

The customer pays his money and gets a ticket. He cannot refuse it. He cannot get his money back. He may protest to the machine, even swear at it. But it will remain unmoved. He is committed beyond recall. He was committed at the very moment when he put his money into the machine.

The contract was concluded at that time. It can be translated into offer and acceptance in this way: the offer is made when the proprietor of the machine holds it out as being ready to receive the money. The acceptance takes place when the customer puts his money into the slot.

[4] Ibid. 407.
[5] [1961] 1 QB 394.
[6] [1968] 2 All ER 421.
[7] But see *Carlill v Carbolic Smokeball Company* [1893] 1 QB 256.
[8] [1971] 2 QB 163.
[9] Ibid. 169.

This is an important principle. Because a machine lacks the ability to form the necessary intent to conclude a contract the court has rationalized the display constructed by the machine's operator as a standing offer similar to that found in the much earlier case of *Carlill v Carbolic Smokeball*.[10]

This standing offer reflects the intent of the machine operator and this is then capable of acceptance by the customer who indicates her acceptance of the terms by putting her money in the slot. This principle is assumed to extend to a number of self-service operations including vending machines and self-service petrol pumps.[11] This would suggest that an online e-commerce site such as Amazon would have to operate under this standing offer principle as they use non-human agents to conclude their contracts. This is at odds with our understanding from cases such as *Boots Cash Chemists*, *Fisher v Bell*, and *Partridge v Crittenden*, that shop displays, both interactive displays and passive displays, are merely invitations to treat. So the question is, is an e-commerce website like a shop display or like a vending machine?

18.2 **Regulating offer and acceptance**

With no case law to clarify the issue commentators were left to speculate as to the nature of e-commerce sites. Most agreed that despite the lack of a human actor the interactive nature of websites rendered them more akin to self-service shop displays than to vending machines or ticket machines which issued a restricted choice of products.[12] The lack of clarity though raised the spectre of different approaches developing throughout Europe, with some countries taking the 'standing offer' principle while others followed the 'invitation to treat' principle. Such a lack of harmonization could adversely affect the development of e-commerce in Europe as a significant proportion of both business-to-business (B2B) and business-to-consumer (B2C) transactions were likely to take place across borders.

18.2.1 **Articles 9–11 of the Electronic Commerce Directive**

To alleviate this risk, and to harmonize some rules on contract formalities, the Commission placed e-commerce and electronic contracting at the heart of its fifth framework programme on the information society. The result was the Electronic Commerce Directive,[13] which is a wide-ranging document dealing not only with electronic contracting, but also with SPAM emails and, as we have seen, protection for ISPs and other third-party intermediaries. The key provisions of interest to contract lawyers are to be found in Arts. 9–11.

On reading these, the first thing to become clear is that the Electronic Commerce Directive does not harmonize what is known as the contractual trigger—that is, the

[10] See (n. 7).

[11] Chen-Wishart (n. 1) 57.

[12] See e.g. A Murray, 'Entering into Contracts Electronically: The Real WWW' in L Edwards and C Waelde (eds.), *Law and the Internet: A Framework for Electronic Commerce* (Hart 2000); D Bainbridge, *Introduction to Information Technology Law* (6th edn, Longman 2007) 363.

[13] Dir. 2000/31/EC of the European Parliament and of the Council of 8 June 2000 on certain legal aspects of information society services, in particular electronic commerce, in the internal market.

moment at which *consensus ad idem* is legally deemed to have occurred. In earlier drafts of the Directive it was proposed that this should be done with an original draft version of the Directive, suggesting that 'electronic contracts be concluded when: the recipient of the service has received from the service provider, electronically, an acknowledgement of receipt of the recipient's acceptance, and has confirmed receipt of the acknowledgement of receipt'.[14]

This approach was criticized during the legislative passage of the Directive with critics believing that in effect the Directive was seeking to harmonize rules of contractual formation which lie beyond the general competence of the Commission, and certainly well outside the competence of the information society programme. These critiques of the draft led to attempts to define a common contractual trigger being dropped. In their place we have a set of common principles with the key principles being found in Arts. 10 and 11.

Article 10 requires transparency in the contract-making process. While there is no common rule of contractual formation, there is a set of common principles which all e-commerce sites have to follow, including, essentially, by Art. 10(1)(a) the provision that the customer be informed of the technical steps she must follow to conclude the contract. Article 10 has been given effect in the UK by reg. 9 of the Electronic Commerce (EC Directive) Regulations 2002,[15] which enacts Art. 10 in full and without amendment. The combined effect of Art. 10/reg. 9 may be seen on any UK e-commerce website. If one were to visit a well-known internet bookseller's site and were to examine their conditions of sale, one would find that condition 1 states:

> Your order is an offer to [Name] to buy the product(s) in your order. When you place an order to purchase a product from [Name], we will send you a message confirming receipt of your order and containing the details of your order (the 'Order Confirmation'). If you are using certain [Name] Services (e.g. [Name] mobile applications) the Order Confirmation may be posted on a Message Centre on the website. The Order Confirmation is acknowledgement that we have received your order, and does not confirm acceptance of your offer to buy the product(s) or the services ordered. We only accept your offer, and conclude the contract of sale for a product ordered by you, when we dispatch the product to you and send e-mail or post a message on the Message Centre of the website confirming to you that we've dispatched the product to you (the 'Dispatch Confirmation'). If your order is dispatched in more than one package, you may receive a separate Dispatch Confirmation for each package, and each Dispatch Confirmation and corresponding dispatch will conclude a separate contract of sale between us for the product(s) specified in that Dispatch Confirmation. Your contract is with [Name]. Without affecting your right of cancellation set out in section 2 below, you can cancel your order for a product at no cost any time before we send the Dispatch Confirmation relating to that product.

Thus, clearly the customer is informed, in accordance with reg. 9(1)(a) of the UK regulations, that the web page operated by this retailer is to be treated as an invitation to treat in accordance with the principles of *Boots Cash Chemist*. The order placed by the customer is then to be treated as an offer to buy. An immediate acknowledgement of this order sent out by this retailer is just that—an acknowledgment of the offer, not an acceptance. Either party remains in a position to withdraw from the contract until such

[14] Draft E-Commerce Directive, COM (1998) 586 final 18/11/98, Art. 11(1)(a).
[15] SI 2002/2013.

time as the retailer sends their dispatch confirmation email. This forms acceptance and concludes the contract.

At first glance this may seem to favour the retailer as they can withdraw from the contract at any time up to dispatch of the goods, but looking closely it is clear that the customer is also protected as they may withdraw their offer (cancel their order) at any point up to dispatch. This is the common position taken by almost all e-commerce sites. It allows for a human check to be made in the order process before the offer is accepted and the contract finalized. This prevents contracts from being formed by non-human actors on erroneous terms as demonstrated in the Argos TV case of 2005 when a processing error led to a £350 television set being advertised at only 49p for 31 hours leading to 10,000 orders being placed, including one order for 80 TVs. Even though customers had completed the checkout procedure and had given their credit or debit card details to pay for the televisions ordered, Argos simply referred to their terms and conditions and cancelled all orders, refunding all monies paid.[16]

18.2.2 **Communicating acceptance**

This leaves one final question of contract formation. When, precisely, is acceptance effectively communicated to the offeror? To put it another way, does the delivery rule or the postal rule apply to acceptances which come in the form of a confirmation email? If we return to the example terms and conditions above we see they say that 'acceptance will be complete at the time we send the Dispatch Confirmation E-mail to you'. This though is not the complete picture because for an acceptance to be effective it has to be communicated to the offeror and there are two general principles which are used to determine when this is fulfilled. The first is the more commonplace principle that to be effective an acceptance must be delivered to the offeror. This principle applies in face-to-face oral negotiations but also to a number of 'at distance' communications. Most famously in the case of *Entores Ltd v Miles Far East Corporation*,[17] Lord Denning (as Denning LJ) carried out an extensive examination of the principle of delivery in relation to an acceptance sent by Telex, concluding that 'the rule about instantaneous communications between the parties is different from the rule about the post. The contract is only complete when the acceptance is received by the offeror: and the contract is made at the place where the acceptance is received.'[18]

This conclusion brings about several consequences for electronic contracting. First, it suggests that communications by Royal Mail are a *sui generis* form of communication for the purposes of contract formation rules, and that it is only they which are regulated

[16] These errors are common. In January 2012 Argos also offered a £450 camera for £120. They also cancelled these orders. In March 2012 Tesco refused to honour purchases of a 64GB third-generation iPad offered online for £49.99 instead of £659, while in January 2014 tools and hardware retailer Screwfix had an error which caused all items including sit-on lawnmowers worth £1,600 to be priced at £34.99. It cancelled all orders except those already delivered or collected. Sometimes they are honoured. In 2002 Kodak fulfilled orders for a digital camera sold for £100 instead of its intended price of £329. This was because Kodak's terms and conditions at the time stated the contract would be concluded when they sent the order confirmation email, not the later dispatch confirmation stage. Kodak have since amended their terms and conditions. Also in January 2012 Marks & Spencer honoured sales of a £599 television wrongly priced at £199 following a petition. However, it is believed few orders were made as the error was in the early hours of Sunday morning.

[17] [1955] 2 QB 327.

[18] Ibid. 334.

by the postal rule in place of the delivery rule. This principle was later affirmed in the House of Lords case of *Brinkibon Ltd v Stahag Stahl und Stahlwarenhandels-Gesellschaft.*[19] More recently two Scottish cases, *McIntosh v Alam*[20] and *Carmarthen Developments Ltd v Pennington,*[21] have extended the *Entores/Brinkibon* principle to facsimile communications. Elsewhere, and before the implementation of the Electronic Commerce Directive, I had suggested that email communications may be treated differently to those other forms of telecommunications on the basis that one of the key arguments in support of the postal rule is that the offeror in accepting a posted letter of acceptance accepts the risk of delay or misdirection of a non-instantaneous means of communication.[22] As email displays the characteristics of non-instantaneous communications it must be treated differently to telephone, facsimile, or telex.[23]

The Electronic Commerce Directive, though, suggests this is unlikely. Article 11(1), as given effect by reg. 11(2)(a) of the Electronic Commerce (EC Directive) Regulations, states that 'the order and the acknowledgement of receipt will be deemed to be received when the parties to whom they are addressed are able to access them'. Regulation 11(2)(a) strictly only applies to the offer (termed here the order) and the acknowledgement of receipt of that offer, not to the acceptance, which will usually occur much later when the goods are dispatched. Despite this, it is hard to imagine a court accepting an argument that the delivery rule applies to offers and acknowledgements but not to acceptances. Therefore, it seems likely that should the question arise a UK court would find that the delivery rule applies to acceptances sent by email which conclude an online commercial transaction, such as a dispatch confirmation email.

Before leaving this issue it is important to note that Art. 11(1) first indent and Art. 11(2), and reg. 11(1) of the UK Regulations 'shall not apply to contracts concluded exclusively by exchange of electronic mail or by equivalent individual communications'.[24] This does not affect the preceding analysis on contract formation as the sections excepted are to do with delays and input errors in the contracting process not the provision found (in the UK Regulations in reg. 11(2)(a)) that 'the order and the acknowledgement of receipt will be deemed to be received when the parties to whom they are addressed are able to access them.'

18.3 **Contractual terms**

Having established when a contract is formed the next question is what are the terms of the contract? The terms of any contract, whether it is an electronic contract or a traditional contract, will be those agreed upon by the parties at the time the contract is concluded. This can clearly be seen in the series of cases known as the ticket cases

[19] [1983] 2 AC 34.

[20] 1997 SCLR (Notes) 1171.

[21] [2008] CSOH 139.

[22] See e.g. C Gringras and E Todd, *The Laws of the Internet* (3rd edn, Tottel 2008) 38–40; J Dickie, 'When and Where are Electronic Contracts Concluded?' (1998) 49 *Northern Ireland Legal Quarterly* 332.

[23] Murray (n. 12) 24–5.

[24] The Electronic Commerce (EC Directive) Regulations 2002, reg. 11(3).

concluding in *Thornton v Shoe Lane Parking Ltd.*[25] Here Lord Denning led the Court of Appeal in finding that the issue of the ticket by an automated ticket machine was the point at which the contract was concluded, meaning that the terms of issue printed on the reverse of the ticket did not form part of the contract. This is the latest of a long line of ticket cases where terms printed on tickets or receipts have been held only to be validly incorporated into the contract if the terms have been brought to the other party's attention before the contract is concluded.[26] Thus terms not brought to the attention of the counterparty to the contract before the delivery of the final acceptance will not form part of the contract. How does one incorporate terms into the contract? As any student of contract law knows, contractual terms usually fall into one of three categories: express terms, terms incorporated by reference, and implied terms.[27]

18.3.1 **Express terms**

The incorporation of express terms into electronic contracts poses little difficulty. Such terms will be clearly set out in the transmission of information between parties and as such should be easily identified. There are, though, two problem issues regarding express terms which parties should always bear in mind when negotiating an electronic contract. The first is that parties must take care to identify the document or documents which are intended to constitute the contract. This will be more common with contracts concluded by email which have to be individually drafted and which have the potential for prolonged exchanges between the parties at the negotiation stage, than with online contracts. The second potential problem of express terms is their interpretation by the courts in the event of a dispute. Contracting parties should attempt to limit as far as possible any inconsistencies or ambiguities in their contractual terms. In the event of any disagreement between the parties on the terms of the contract the court will apply the established rules of contractual interpretation.[28]

18.3.2 **Terms incorporated by reference**

The structure of the web, with its use of interconnected, hyperlinked pages, lends itself to incorporation by reference.[29] Consequently, terms incorporated by reference are common in relation to electronic contracts. The terms that the contracting party wishes to incorporate are set out in a separate document and are incorporated into the final contract by a reference to this separate document somewhere in the contractual documentation. Commonly this document is a separate web page hosted on the same server as the online shop or marketplace. This is usually known as the terms and conditions page and is accessible via a hypertext link embedded at several points in the order system usually being expressly referred to during the checkout process.

To be effectively incorporated the terms must not only be clear and unambiguous, they must also clearly have been intended to form part of the contract. This means that the party relying upon these incorporated terms must take all steps to bring them to the attention of the other party before the contract is concluded and in such a manner as

[25] See (n. 8).
[26] See in particular *Parker v South Eastern Railway Co.* (1877) 2 CPD 416.
[27] For detail on these categories see Chen-Wishart (n. 1) ch. 10.
[28] Ibid.
[29] As do email systems which support HTML and allow for embedded hypertext links.

to make it clear these terms are intended to be contractual terms.[30] These terms and conditions must therefore be clearly signposted. A passive link to terms and conditions contained on another page will not necessarily be sufficient to incorporate these terms into the contract. To incorporate any external terms and conditions effectively, the site operator must offer a clearly marked and prominent link to the specific terms and conditions they wish to incorporate into the contract before the customer makes their offer.

Fortunately the site operator can easily ensure the terms and conditions have been incorporated into the contract by requiring the customer to indicate they have knowledge of, and have accepted, these terms and conditions before processing their order. This is done by requiring the customer to check a box during the checkout process acknowledging they have read and accept the terms and conditions or by expressly stating at the submission of the order that the customer agrees to these terms and conditions as a condition of the order being placed. If the customer has acknowledged they are aware of the terms, then the terms and conditions will be incorporated into the contract even if the customer has not actually read them.[31]

18.3.3 **Implied terms**

Finally, as with traditional contracts, there may be occasions where terms will be implied into electronic contracts. As implied terms usually come about apart from the contract formation process the fact that a contract has been concluded in cyberspace will be of no impact to the rules on formation of contract. Implied terms may be implied by fact, such as terms required to give a contract business efficacy,[32] and terms implied on the basis of custom or usage.[33] Additionally, terms may be implied by the common law such as the implied term of seaworthiness implied into contracts for the carriage of goods by sea,[34] and the implied rule of non-derogation from grant.[35] As the introduction of these terms is uniform, no matter how the contract was negotiated and concluded, the use of electronic means to conclude the contract will not affect the established rules and reference should be made to traditional contract texts for further guidance on implied terms.[36]

18.4 **Enforcing terms: consumer protection provisions**

Once the contractual terms are agreed and finalized it cannot be assumed that all are enforceable. In a B2C contract consumer protection provisions may strike out some terms. When dealing with electronic consumer contract terms in the UK there are two

[30] Thus courts have continually held that where 'contractual' terms are found in places where the customer would not expect to find them they do not form part of the contract. See *Chapelton v Barry UDC* [1940] 1 KB 532; *Taylor v Glasgow Corporation*, 1952 SC 440 (both involving tickets/receipts); and *Lightbody's Trustees v Hutchison* (1886) 14 R 4 (advertising leaflet).

[31] Some terms will require a greater degree of highlighting than others. Exclusionary terms for instance will require a significantly greater degree of explicitness. See Denning LJ in *Spurling v Bradshaw* [1956] 2 All ER 121, 125F: 'Some clauses which I have seen would need to be printed in red ink on the face of the document with a red hand pointing to it before the notice could be held to be sufficient.'

[32] *The Moorcock* (1889) 14 PD 64.

[33] *London Founders Association Ltd* and *Palmer v Clarke* (1888) LR 20 QBD 576.

[34] *Steel v State Line Steamship Co.* (1877) LR 3 App Cas 72.

[35] *Lyme Valley Squash Club Ltd v Newcastle-under-Lyme BC* [1985] 2 All ER 405.

[36] Chen-Wishart (n. 1) at 10.4.

primary sources of consumer protection for contracts concluded online or by email. They are the Consumer Contracts (Information, Cancellation and Additional Charges) Regulations 2013, the UK implementation of the Consumer Rights Directive,[37] and the Consumer Rights Act 2015.

18.4.1 The Consumer Rights Act 2015

The Consumer Rights Act focuses on attempts by suppliers of goods and/or services to restrict liability for negligence or harm, or to avoid statutory duties. In addition it provides some basic quality standards provisions for goods or services supplied. By s. 65 a party to a contract cannot exclude liability for death or personal injury caused by negligence,[38] while by ss. 31, 47, and 57 suppliers cannot contract out of liability for legal minimum provisions of quality in relation to order contracts for the sale and supply of goods, contracts for the sale and supply of digital goods, and contracts for the supply of services. These minimum provisions in part replace provisions found previously in the Sale of Goods Act 1979 and the Supply of Goods and Services Act 1982 and in part are new.

Statutory provisions as to the quality of goods are found in ss. 9–18 of the Act. These include that the goods are of satisfactory quality; they are fit for purpose and are as described. An important new provision is that by s. 16 if the goods supplied contain a digital component which does not meet the standard contracted (or the statutory minimal standards including 'satisfactory quality') the goods may be rejected for the failure in the digital component. Similar provisions relating to the quality of services supplied are to be found in ss. 49–53 and require that services be performed with 'reasonable care and skill' and within a reasonable time.

Completely new provisions are to be found in Part 1, Chapter 3, 'Digital Content'. By ss. 34–41 a set of minimum quality provisions, similar to those found in ss. 9–18 are applied to digital content. Digital content is defined in s. 2 as 'data which are produced and supplied in digital form'. This would include software, digital music and video, and e-books and applies however that content is delivered—i.e. there is no difference between a music or movie download or stream than music or movies delivered on CD or DVD. By s. 34 digital content must be of satisfactory quality, while by ss. 35–36 it must be fit for purpose and as described. Section 39(5) is a useful new addition to the consumer's armoury. It provides that the processing facility for digitally supplied contact must be available for a reasonable time. Thus if you pay £15 to access and download an online article and due to network failures you can't download it right away the supplier must give you a reasonable time to make the download. It should be noted that where the consumer agrees to an express term limiting access (such as 24 hours' access) then that term would apply, assuming it is reasonable.

In the event that goods, including digital goods, or services fail to meet the statutory minimum quality threshold then under ss. 19–24, 42–45, and 54–56 consumers are given a variety of enforcement rights including (for goods) a right to reject the goods under s. 20 and a right to repair or replacement under s. 23, (for digital goods) a right

[37] Dir. 2011/83/EC.

[38] Note a similar provision applying to B2B contracts may be found in s. 2 of the Unfair Contract Terms Act 1977.

to a refund under s. 45, and a right to a price reduction under s. 44, and (for services) a right to a repeat performance under s. 55. In general the rights across all three classifications boil down to repudiation (rejection and refund) or repair, reperformance, or reduction in price.

In addition to these specific statutory terms there is also a general prohibition on unfair terms.

Highlight The Consumer Rights Act, s. 62

(1) An unfair term of a consumer contract is not binding on the consumer . . .

(4) A term is unfair if, contrary to the requirement of good faith, it causes a significant imbalance in the parties' rights and obligations under the contract to the detriment of the consumer.

(5) Whether a term is fair is to be determined—

(a) taking into account the nature of the subject matter of the contract, and

(b) by reference to all the circumstances existing when the term was agreed and to all of the other terms of the contract or of any other contract on which it depends.

This means that in any B2C contract if the court finds that term to be biased in favour of the supplier of the goods or services it may be struck out. The Consumer Rights Act is so new that we have as yet no case law on its terms (it only came into effect on 1 October 2015). The House of Lords though did discuss the meaning of an unfair term under the previous law, the Unfair Terms in Consumer Contracts Regulations 1994, in *Director General of Fair Trading v First National Bank Plc* where Lord Bingham described it as:

> causing a significant imbalance in the parties' rights and obligations under the contract to the detriment of the consumer in a manner or to an extent which is contrary to the requirement of good faith. The requirement of significant imbalance is met if a term is so weighted in favour of the supplier as to tilt the parties' rights and obligations under the contract significantly in his favour. This may be by the granting to the supplier of a beneficial option or discretion or power, or by the imposing on the consumer of a disadvantageous burden or risk or duty.[39]

Schedule 2, Part 1 provides an excellent illustrative list of the types of terms which may be found to be unfair. These include terms which 'inappropriately exclude or limit the legal rights of the consumer in relation to the trader or another party in the event of total or partial non-performance or inadequate performance by the trader of any of the contractual obligations' and which 'irrevocably bind the consumer to terms with which he had no real opportunity of becoming acquainted before the conclusion of the contract'.

18.4.2 The Consumer Contracts (Information, Cancellation and Additional Charges) Regulations 2013

These provisions of the Consumer Rights Act are not, of course, unique to electronic contracts and neither are the Consumer Contracts (Information, Cancellation and Additional Charges) Regulations 2013 although they arguably have a greater direct

[39] [2002] 1 AC 481, 494.

impact on electronic contracts through their regulation of 'off-premises' contracts. These include 'contracts concluded on the business premises of the trader or through any means of distance communication immediately after the consumer was personally and individually addressed in a place which is not the business premises of the trader in the simultaneous physical presence of the trader and the consumer',[40] which includes electronic contracts.

The Regulations seek to ensure that consumers are fully informed of all their contractual obligations, as well as their consumer rights and cancellation rights before they enter into a contract. By regs. 13 and 14 and Schs. 2 and 3, a supplier of goods or services must supply a considerable amount of information before a distance contract concluded by electronic means is concluded, including the price of the goods or service including all taxes; any delivery costs; arrangements for payment and delivery; the main characteristics of the goods, services, or digital content; the geographical address at which the trader is established; and, where available, the trader's telephone number, fax number, and email address, to enable the consumer to contact the trader quickly and communicate efficiently, as well as information about any after-sales services and guarantees. Should a trader fail to supply the material required, then by regs. 13(1) and 14(5) the consumer may not be bound by the contract and the trader may not be able to enforce (any of) the terms of the contract against the consumer. This is a considerable disadvantage to the trader and therefore ensures compliance, but with one or two provisions the penalty is greater. Where a trader fails to inform a consumer of their right to cancel, or when the consumer may have to bear reasonable costs of cancellation or returning items, they may commit an offence under reg. 19 which could see them fined at a level up to point 5 on the standard scale (currently £5,000). Finally, with reference particularly to contracts concluded on websites or via apps, the Regulations require clear labelling as to when payment is required; this may be seen as a response in particular to apps which are unclear on in-app purchases. Regulation 14(3) provides that 'the trader must ensure that the consumer, when placing the order, explicitly acknowledges that the order implies an obligation to pay' while reg. 14(4) provides that:

> if placing an order entails activating a button or a similar function, the trader must ensure that the button or similar function is labelled in an easily legible manner only with the words 'order with obligation to pay' or a corresponding unambiguous formulation indicating that placing the order entails an obligation to pay the trader.

A failure to comply with either of these provisions releases the consumer from any obligations under the contract or order under reg. 14(5).

Moreover, as the consumer cannot inspect the goods prior to purchase or evaluate the supplier in the same way they can with an on-site purchase, consumers who enter into off-site or distance contracts (including electronic contracts) are given a cooling-off period, during which time they may reject and return the goods in question. By reg. 29 the consumer is given a right to cancel a distance or off-premises contract at any time in the cancellation period without giving any reason. The normal cancellation period is found in reg. 30. For contracts for the supply of services or for the delivery of digital content supplied without a carrier medium it is 14 days after the day on which the contract is entered into. For the supply of goods it is 14 days after the day on which

[40] Reg. 5.

the goods (or if multiple items are ordered the day upon which the final item) come(s) into the physical possession of the consumer or their agent. There is also an extended cancellation period under reg. 31. This applies when the trader does not provide the consumer with the information on the right to cancel, which as we have seen is also an offence under reg. 19. In such cases the cancellation period does not begin until the trader gives the consumer the requisite information, or if they fail to do so within 12 months the period will be 12 months and 14 days.[41] In addition, it should be noted that by regs. 27 and 28 some contracts cannot be cancelled. By reg. 27(2) there is no right to cancel contracts for the supply of prescription medicines, for products supplied by the NHS or other healthcare provider, or contracts for passenger transport services. By reg. 28 the right to cancellation does not apply to, among others, price-sensitive goods such as gold or shares, personalized goods, perishable goods, the supply of a newspaper, periodical, or magazine, sales concluded at public auction, and the supply of accommodation, transport of goods, vehicle rental services, catering, or services related to leisure activities, if the contract provides for a specific date or period of performance. Furthermore, by reg. 28(3) the consumer may lose their right to reject under certain circumstances. The right to reject will cease to be available when (a) in the case of a contract for the supply of sealed goods which are not suitable for return due to health protection or hygiene reasons, if they become unsealed after delivery; (b) in the case of a contract for the supply of sealed audio or sealed video recordings or sealed computer software, if the goods become unsealed after delivery; or (c) in the case of any sales contract, if the goods become mixed inseparably (according to their nature) with other items after delivery (such as mixing sand with cement to create mortar).

Special rules apply to the supply of services and digital content within the cooling-off period. Both have similar provisions under regs. 36 and 37 but for our purposes the more interesting and important is reg. 37 which applies to digital content. By reg. 37(1) where there is a contract for the supply of digital content not on a tangible medium, the trader must not begin supply of the digital content before the end of the cancellation period. This obviously is quite unworkable, when you ordered an app on an app store or a piece of music on iTunes or Google Play you would have to wait 14 days for it to be delivered to you. Thus there are exceptions: reg. 37(1) will not apply if the consumer has given express consent, and the consumer has acknowledged that the right to cancel the contract under reg. 29(1) will be lost. This is achieved via terms and conditions for the app store or content store, agreed to whenever the store software is installed or updated.[42]

The regulations also make some special provisions with regard to returning items and shipping costs. The consumer must send back the goods or hand them over to the trader without undue delay and in any event not later than 14 days after the day on which the consumer informs the trader that they wished to cancel and return the goods.[43] In addition, by reg. 35(5) the consumer must bear the direct cost of returning goods unless either the trader has agreed to bear those costs, or the trader failed to provide the consumer with the information about the consumer bearing those costs,

[41] Reg. 31(3).

[42] Interestingly while the Google Play store gives a seven-day cancellation period in replacement of the statutory period, Apple give a fourteen-day cancellation period in iTunes and the App Store.

[43] Reg. 35(4).

but by reg. 34(2) and (3) the trader must reimburse the consumer for delivery costs incurred unless the consumer expressly chose a kind of delivery costing more than the least expensive common and generally acceptable kind of delivery offered by the trader, in which case the trader must reimburse any payment for delivery received from the consumer up to the amount the consumer would have paid if the consumer had chosen the least expensive common and generally acceptable kind of delivery offered by the trader. This is for the practical reason that sellers could inflict disproportionately high shipping costs on the buyer which they could then not recover following a rejection of the goods. Thus if a T-shirt was advertised at £4.99 plus £15 postage and packaging, then without this protection upon a rejection of the item the consumer would only be in line for a refund of £4.99, but with this protection is eligible for a refund of the whole amount of £19.99. The buyer is in turn, though normally responsible for return shipping costs. This is because the buyer may control the costs of shipping by choosing the most competitive service; there is therefore less risk of abuse of process.

This particular issue was reviewed by the European Court of Justice when discussing similar provisions found in the now repealed Distance Selling Directive[44] in *Handelsgesellschaft Heinrich Heine GmbH v Verbraucherzentrale Nordrhein-Westfalen*,[45] where the claimant, a mail-order company, stated in its general terms and conditions that the consumer was to pay a flat-rate charge for delivery, which the claimant would not refund in the event of withdrawal from the contract. The court determined that the Distance Selling Directive imposed on the supplier, in the event of the consumer's withdrawal, a general obligation to reimburse which covered all of the sums paid by the consumer under the contract, regardless of the reason for their payment.[46]

To define the enforceable terms of an electronic contract is a complex task. It may be assumed that a well-ordered e-commerce site will have a set of clear and fair terms, but one can never be sure how the courts will interpret contracts and their terms until long after the contract has been concluded. It should be remembered, though, that the vast majority of contracts, especially B2C contracts, pass off without problem. Therefore, for most contracts the terms of the contract are simply what both parties believe them to be.

18.5 **Formal contracts**

Not all contracts are as simply accommodated into the framework of the information society. While the vast majority of everyday contracts are informal in nature, there are a small number of core contractual agreements which are required to be formally concluded, usually in writing and sometimes with the requirement of a signature. These contracts tend to be for higher-value items or of a nature so as to create an ongoing contractual undertaking: they include contracts for the sale or transfer of an interest in land, guarantees, or an assignment of intellectual property rights.

The initial problem with many formal contracts was that for many there was a statutory requirement that they be 'in writing'. Although one could define an electronic

[44] Dir. 97/7/EC.
[45] [2010] 3 CMLR 26.
[46] Ibid. [H5].

document, such as one created on a web page or via email as a written document in the colloquial sense, there was a degree of debate as to whether it met the statutory definition of writing found in the Interpretation Act 1978 as 'includ[ing] typing, printing, lithography, photography and other modes of representing or reproducing words in a visible form'.[47] This rather dated definition of writing as being something in a tangible form suggested that should the rule of *ejusdem generis* be applied it was unlikely that a series of binary digits would qualify.

Some form of updating of the law was required and this became urgent when in 1996 the United Nations Commission on International Trade Law (UNCITRAL) adopted its Model Law on Electronic Commerce.[48] The model law requires all UNCITRAL states (including the UK) to formally recognize electronic contracts. Article 5 states that 'Information shall not be denied legal effect, validity or enforceability solely on the grounds that it is in the form of a data message.' Building upon this principle, the model law goes on to ensure that all supporting principles required to provide for recognition of electronic contracts are in place. First, Art. 6 endows equivalence for electronic documentation by requiring that, 'where the law requires information to be in writing, that requirement is met by a data message if the information contained therein is accessible so as to be usable for subsequent reference'; then, through Art. 7, it requires that states give legal recognition to electronic signatures; finally, and perhaps most importantly, Art. 11 formally provides for the legal recognition of electronic contracts.

As we have seen, UK law could comply with Arts. 5 and 11, at least in relation to informal contracts, but with the Interpretation Act suggesting 'contracts in writing' had to be in a tangible form and with signatures often required to be 'in writing' there was an inability to comply with Arts. 6 and 7. This led the Department of Trade and Industry to undertake a review of the UK legal position; a review which concluded that: 'the position on the requirement for information to be "written" or "in writing" . . . cannot at present be met using electronic means'.[49] The DTI recognized that 'these uncertainties and limitations . . . are important barriers to the development of electronic commerce',[50] and opened consultation on the best approach to removing these barriers.[51]

This led to the promulgation of the Electronic Communications Act 2000. The Act was designed to ensure the UK complied fully with the UNCITRAL model law, and to position the UK to allow for smooth implementation of the Electronic Commerce Directive,[52] which was also under construction at this time as a means to ensure the EU, which is a separate UNCITRAL member, also complied with the model law. The main provision of the Electronic Communications Act was s. 8. It allows for electronic documentation to

[47] Interpretation Act 1978, Sch. 1.

[48] The UNCITRAL Model Law on Electronic Commerce (1996) with additional Art. 5 bis as adopted in 1998 is available at <http://www.jus.uio.no/lm/un.electronic.commerce.model.law.1996/doc.html>.

[49] DTI, 'Building Confidence in E-Commerce: A Consultation Document' 5 March 1999 URN 99/642 at [16]. Available at: <http://www.cyber-rights.org/crypto/consfn1.pdf>.

[50] Ibid. [17].

[51] At [18] the DTI set out two broad approaches and asked for views to be expressed by members of the public. The approaches considered were: (1) to allow for individual Acts and Statutory Instruments on a case-by-case basis, or (2) allow, through enabling legislation, a power for government ministers to adopt changes through statutory instruments where necessary. This is the approach taken and may be found in s. 8 of the Electronic Communications Act.

[52] Dir. 2000/31/EC.

be used in the formation of a contract where some sort of formality is required. It states that Ministers may make subordinate legislation allowing for electronic communications to be used where appropriate to do anything which is 'required to be or may be done or evidenced in writing or otherwise using a document, notice or instrument' or which 'is required to be or may be done by post or other specified means of delivery'.[53]

Immediately it is clear that s. 8 does not give complete equivalence to all 'data messages' in accordance with Art. 6. Instead s. 8 enabled ministers to take a case-by-case approach to equivalence, designing specific rules to allow the integration of electronic data messages into existing statutory schemes with the least disruption. Today, following the promulgation of over sixty regulations and orders in the sixteen years since the Electronic Communications Act was passed, the process of integration is complete. Key provisions, including the Consumer Credit Act 1974 (Electronic Communications) Order 2004,[54] Part 8 of the Land Registration Act 2002, and the Automated Registration of Title to Land (Electronic Communications) (Scotland) Order 2006,[55] now allow everyday transactions such as an application for consumer credit (including a credit card application) and a transfer of an interest in land to be concluded electronically.

The UK approach was originally slow, costly, and cumbersome to design and implement, but parties, and the courts, now have a clear framework to apply in the event of a challenge to the legality or enforceability of any formal contract concluded electronically. It appears now, sixteen years on, that the UK approach was a sound one, but we did have around eight to ten years of uncertainty, and a cost of a considerable amount of legislative time to get us to this point.

18.6 **Electronic signatures**

Allowing electronic forms and delivery to be used for formal contracts is only half of the solution to online formal electronic contracting. Most formal contracts not only have requirements of form, they also usually require adoption of the terms of the contract, usually through the addition of a signature, stamp, or seal. This, obviously, proves extremely difficult for an electronic document which has no physical structure upon which a signature may be added. We have had to be extremely inventive in designing structures to replace traditional signatures as there is no way simply to replicate a manuscript signature, which is by far the most common form of signature, when dealing with intangible, digital documents. To this end, a number of techniques were tried in the 1990s, including digitally encoding a signature made with an 'electronic pen and paper system',[56] or even using other biometric data such as fingerprints or iris scans.[57] However, it soon became clear that systems such as these attempted to replicate physical signatures instead of seeking to fulfil the function of a signature: in other words, systems like these promoted form over function.

[53] Electronic Communications Act 2000, s. 8(2) lists a number of 'purposes' for which a minister may make a s. 8 order.

[54] SI 2004/3236.

[55] SI 2006/491.

[56] B Wright, 'Alternatives for Signing Electronic Documents' (1995) 11 *Computer Law and Security Report* 136.

[57] C Reed, 'What Is a Signature?' (2000) 3 *JILT* <http://www2.warwick.ac.uk/fac/soc/law/elj/jilt/2000_3/reed/>.

This was made clear in an excellent article by Professor Chris Reed called 'What Is a Signature?' In this, Reed distinguishes between the form of a signature—being usually facsimiles of the traditional manuscript signature such as 'the use of initials, marks, seals (for some but not all types of document), the adoption of a printed name and the use of rubber stamps'[58]—and the function of a signature. Reed notes that:

> the approach adopted by the courts . . . was to determine whether the particular form of signature adopted had already been recognised as valid in previous decisions, and if not, to decide whether it was acceptable in the particular circumstances. Often no reasons were given to explain why the signature method in question was legally acceptable; it appears that the judges in each case simply satisfied themselves that the method adopted achieved the same authentication effects as a manuscript signature.[59]

This, as noted by Reed, is not necessarily the best way to approach the adoption of a system to formalize electronic documents given the radically different nature of the intangible, nonrivalrous, and easily replicable digital document when compared with the tangible, rivalrous, and difficult-to-reproduce nature of an original manuscript signature, or its facsimiles. Reed suggests we focus on the function of a signature. He identifies three functions of a signature; one primary and two subsidiary.

Highlight The primary function of a signature

The primary function is authentication. This reflects that a signature is an evidentiary tool used to reduce reliance on post-agreement oral evidence which attempts to deny the apparent accuracy of a document or explain its true meaning.

This primary function consists of three 'sub-functions'. These are that a signature provides evidence of:

1. the identity of the signatory;
2. that the signatory intended the 'signature' to be his signature; and
3. that the signatory approves of and adopts the contents of the document.

In addition to this primary function there are two subsidiary functions of a signature: (1) to validate official action (such as a judge signing an order of court), and (2) for consumer protection reasons.[60] Quite rightly Reed suggests that the function of a signature should take priority over its form. There is no need for the traditions of physical signatures being carried over into the information society. Reed argues that the (at that time) newly adopted Electronic Communications Act 2000 and Electronic Signatures Directive[61] shows that the primary method for promulgating electronic signatures is to be through the use of encryption technology.

[58] Ibid.

[59] Ibid.

[60] Reed is not strongly in favour of recognizing this as a separate function. He notes that 'The consumer's signature merely supplements this method of protection by providing evidence (a) that the other party has supplied the required information, and (b) that the consumer has agreed to the terms. Thus, although signatures have a secondary effect in respect of consumer protection, this effect is achieved through their primary functions as evidence of identity and agreement.'

[61] Dir. 1999/93/EC.

18.6.1 Identity and electronic signatures

Both the Electronic Signatures Directive and s. 7 of the Electronic Communications Act 2000 were promulgated to meet the requirements of Art. 7 of the UNCITRAL Model Law on Electronic Commerce. This required that member states adopt a provision that:

> Where the law requires a signature of a person, that requirement is met in relation to a data message if: (a) a method is used to identify that person and to indicate that person's approval of the information contained in the data message; and (b) that method is as reliable as was appropriate for the purpose for which the data message was generated or communicated, in the light of all the circumstances, including any relevant agreement.

Article 7 may be seen as enunciating Reed's primary function of authentication. As with Reed, there is no discussion of form, merely function.

To implement Art. 7 the EU originally enacted the Electronic Signatures Directive 1999. This has since been repealed and replaced (from 1 July 2016) by Section 4 of the Regulation on electronic identification and trust services for electronic transactions in the internal market (commonly referred as 'e-IDAS' Regulation) 2014.[62] This is the culmination of a lengthy review programme. Despite the legal framework for electronic contracts and electronic signatures dating from the late 1990s, the uptake of electronic signatures has been somewhat disappointing and the number of digital contracts formalized by electronic signatures remains low, due to the complexity and cost of the procedure and the fact the different member states have different interpretations of the Electronic Signatures Directive. In 2006 the Commission issued a report on the uptake of electronic signatures in the EU and proposals as part of the Commissions i2010 project. Viviane Reding, then Commissioner for Information Society and Media, noted that although the framework provided by the Directive provided 'A reliable system of electronic signatures that work across intra-EU borders the Commission was not fully satisfied with the take-up of e-signatures.'[63] This failure has eventually led the Commission to propose a new draft Directive on electronic identification and trust services for electronic transactions in the internal market.[64] This eventually was replaced with the eIDAS Regulation, adopted because a Regulation allows for both repairing the weaknesses of the current legal framework and the creation of a new single market in digital services. As the Commission notes, the Regulation:

> (1) ensures that people and businesses can use their own national electronic identification schemes (eIDs) to access public services in other EU countries where eIDs are available, and
> (2) creates an European internal market for electronic Trust Services—namely electronic signatures, electronic seals, time stamp, electronic delivery service and website authentication—by ensuring that they will work across borders and have the same legal status as traditional paper based processes. Only by providing certainty on the legal validity of all these services, businesses and citizens will use the digital interactions as their natural way of interaction.[65]

The Regulation is wide-ranging and covers a number of eID and Trust services. Chapter II, Arts. 6–12, covers electronic identification. This provides that where member states

[62] Reg. (EU) No 910/2014.

[63] See Europa, 'Electronic Signatures: Legally Recognised but Cross-Border Take-up too Slow' <http://europa.eu/rapid/press-release_IP-06-325_en.htm?locale=no>.

[64] COM(2012) 238/2.

[65] <http://ec.europa.eu/digital-agenda/en/trust-services-and-eid>.

issue electronic identification to citizens of businesses of that state that these identifiers shall receive mutual recognition in other member states if it meets the qualification requirements.[66] Essentially mutual recognition is available when the eID is issued by the notifying member state; under a mandate from the notifying member state; or independently of the notifying member state but recognized by that member state;[67] and that identification can be used to access at least one service which is provided by a public sector body and which requires electronic identification in the notifying member state.[68] eIDs are classified in one of three levels of assurance: low, substantial, and high.[69]

Highlight Low, substantial, and high assurance

Assurance level low shall refer to an electronic identification means in the context of an electronic identification scheme, which provides a limited degree of confidence in the claimed or asserted identity of a person, and is characterised with reference to technical specifications, standards and procedures related thereto, including technical controls, the purpose of which is to decrease the risk of misuse or alteration of the identity;

Assurance level substantial shall refer to an electronic identification means in the context of an electronic identification scheme, which provides a substantial degree of confidence in the claimed or asserted identity of a person, and is characterised with reference to technical specifications, standards and procedures related thereto, including technical controls, the purpose of which is to decrease substantially the risk of misuse or alteration of the identity;

Assurance level high shall refer to an electronic identification means in the context of an electronic identification scheme, which provides a higher degree of confidence in the claimed or asserted identity of a person than electronic identification means with the assurance level substantial, and is characterised with reference to technical specifications, standards and procedures related thereto, including technical controls, the purpose of which is to prevent misuse or alteration of the identity.

When giving recognition to eIDs from other member states there is only a requirement that recognition is given to those which meet or exceed the assurance level required by the recognizing state for the activity in question.

Chapter II does not require member states to create an eID scheme where one is not already in use but it does require them to notify the Commission of any schemes in use and any changes made to those schemes,[70] and to notify both the Commission and other member states who offer mutual recognition, should there be a security breach.[71] In the UK the key eID scheme is GOV.UK Verify, which is currently in public beta testing. When a citizen goes online to carry out a number of beta services on a gov.uk website they are directed to Verify to prove their identity. Four certified identity providers,

[66] Reg. (EU) No 910/2014, Art. 6.
[67] Art. 7(a).
[68] Art. 7(b).
[69] Art. 8(1).
[70] Art. 9.
[71] Art. 10.

Verizon, The Post Office, Digidentity, and Experian, carry out the identification procedure. Like the eID standards of the Regulation there are four levels of assurance. Level 1 is used when a relying party needs to know that it is the same user returning to the service but does not need to know who that user is. This equates to 'low' on the eID scale. Level 2 is used when a relying party needs to know on the balance of probabilities who the user is and that they are a real person. This equates to 'substantial' on the eID scale. Level 3 is used when a relying party needs to know beyond reasonable doubt who the user is and that they are a real person. This equates to 'high' on the eID scale. Level 4, which is currently only planned, is as level of assurance 3, but with a biometric profile captured at the point of registration. This would clearly be 'high' on the eID scale and indeed would go beyond the scale somewhat.

Chapter III of the Regulation goes on to create a legal framework for the recognition and regulation of trust service providers; these are certification companies who carry out the process of identification and who issue eID certificates. These already have a role in EU law in anti-money laundering provisions but the Regulation creates a new regime for a single framework for recognition and regulation, not dissimilar to the data protection regime that we will see in future chapters. Article 17 requires member states to designate a supervisory authority for trust service providers; this can either be a domestic regulator or one shared with another or other member state or states. This body, among other powers and duties, confers, and can withdraw, qualified status on trust service providers.[72] This is important for the purpose of recognizing qualified electronic signatures, which will be discussed below. The Regulation also provides that member states 'lay down the rules on penalties applicable to infringements of this Regulation [and that] the penalties provided for shall be effective, proportionate and dissuasive',[73] and that trust service providers will be liable 'for damage caused intentionally or negligently to any natural or legal person due to a failure to comply with the obligations under this Regulation'.[74]

For our purposes though the key part of the Regulation is Section 4 of Chapter III, Arts. 25–34. This is the new law on electronic signatures and, whereas the old law described two types of electronic signature; a [standard] electronic signature and an advanced electronic signature, we now find three varieties: (1) electronic signature; (2) advanced electronic signature; and (3) qualified electronic signature.

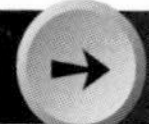

Highlight Forms of electronic signatures

1. An 'electronic signature' is data in electronic form which is attached to or logically associated with other data in electronic form and which is used by the signatory to sign; 'standard' electronic signature is one in which 'data in electronic form are attached to or logically associated with other electronic data and which serve as a method of authentication'.
2. An advanced electronic signature shall meet the following requirements:

   (a) it is uniquely linked to the signatory;

→

[72] Art. 17(4)(g).
[73] Art. 16.
[74] Art. 13(1).

→

(b) it is capable of identifying the signatory;

(c) it is created using electronic signature creation data that the signatory can, with a high level of confidence, use under his sole control; and

(d) it is linked to the data signed therewith in such a way that any subsequent change in the data is detectable.

3. A qualified electronic signature [is] based on a qualified certificate issued in one Member State [and] shall be recognised as a qualified electronic signature in all other Member States. Qualified certificates for electronic signatures shall contain:

(a) an indication, at least in a form suitable for automated processing, that the certificate has been issued as a qualified certificate for electronic signature;

(b) a set of data unambiguously representing the qualified trust service provider issuing the qualified certificates including at least, the Member State in which that provider is established and:

- for a legal person: the name and, where applicable, registration number as stated in the official records;
- for a natural person: the person's name;

(c) at least the name of the signatory, or a pseudonym; if a pseudonym is used, it shall be clearly indicated;

(d) electronic signature validation data that corresponds to the electronic signature creation data;

(e) details of the beginning and end of the certificate's period of validity;

(f) the certificate identity code, which must be unique for the qualified trust service provider;

(g) the advanced electronic signature or advanced electronic seal of the issuing qualified trust service provider;

(h) the location where the certificate supporting the advanced electronic signature or advanced electronic seal referred to in point (g) is available free of charge;

(i) the location of the services that can be used to enquire about the validity status of the qualified certificate;

(j) where the electronic signature creation data related to the electronic signature validation data is located in a qualified electronic signature creation device, an appropriate indication of this, at least in a form suitable for automated processing.

What is immediately clear looking at the distinction between an advanced electronic signature and a qualified electronic signature is that the EU is using qualified here in the common language definition 'possesses a certain quality or qualities' rather than in the usual legal definition 'limited or modified' (as in qualified acceptance). To be qualified a signature is required to meet much stricter standards than merely to be 'advanced'.

What is the difference between the three? An electronic signature is of little legal value whatsoever, only being subject to a non-discrimination provision: 'An electronic signature shall not be denied legal effect and admissibility as evidence in legal proceedings solely on the grounds that it is in an electronic form or that it does not meet the requirements for qualified electronic signatures.'[75] In essence, the evidentiary value of an electronic signature is no greater than any other documentary materials. An advanced electronic signature is afforded a different but no greater evidentiary value. In essence their role is within public services. By Art. 27(1), 'if a Member State requires an advanced electronic signature to use an online service offered by, or on behalf of, a public sector body, that Member State shall recognise advanced electronic signatures, advanced electronic signatures based on a qualified certificate for electronic signatures, and qualified electronic signatures.' Thus the role of an advanced electronic signature is directed towards the provision of public services. It is the qualified electronic signature which in law is the equivalent of a traditional manuscript signature: in fact, Art. 25(2) says as much: 'a qualified electronic signature shall have the equivalent legal effect of a handwritten signature'. The attachment of a qualified electronic signature is therefore probative of the document.

This is why qualified status on trust service providers is so important since to be a qualified electronic signature all certification of the signature must be from a qualified trust service provider. What then in practice is a qualified electronic signature?

18.6.2 Qualified electronic signatures

A qualified electronic signature is a form of electronic signature based in encryption technology with a matching certificate issued by a qualified trust service provider. While there are many ways to demonstrate one has accepted the terms of a document and intend to be bound by them, all are at risk of forgery or fraud, except for one system known as public key encryption or PKE signatures. The attachment of an unencrypted form of identification risks interception and/or reproduction without authorization; even a biometric signature could be replicated or added at a later date by a forger. Further, digital documents, unlike physical documents, may be changed with no apparent trace of the change: words could be deleted or altered; a value of $1 per unit could be changed easily to $2 per unit without any obvious change on the face of the document. And as a digital document may be signed at a distance there is no way for a counterparty to prove identity without there being some form of third party witness to prove the identity of a signatory.[76]

The system, which fulfils all these requirements, is an authenticated digital signature. This is the system adopted by the EU in describing both advanced and qualified signatures. Digital signatures use a particular functionality of encryption technology. Encryption is a well-known and tried system for protecting the content of messages, but

[75] Art. 25(1).

[76] This point may be demonstrated by a short experiment. Should a disgruntled employee of a firm want to take revenge on his employer he may pose as a member of senior management of that firm and enter into an online transaction on unfavourable terms. Assuming the counterparty never meets this person, when he 'signs' the document acting on behalf of the company the counterparty has no reason to suspect anything is amiss. It is only when the contract comes to be fulfilled that the issue will come to light. When dealing at a distance, therefore, you want some system of independent identification of counterparties.

previously it has not been of much use as a methodology of identifying the originator of the message, or demonstrating their intent to be bound to the message. This was because of the nature of traditional or symmetric key encryption.

When using symmetric keys the originator of the message and the recipient of the message would use the same key to encrypt and decrypt the message.

Example Symmetric encryption

Romeo has a message that he must transmit securely to Juliet. To secure the message he uses the Caesar cipher. Caesar cipher is one of the simplest and most widely known encryption techniques. It is a type of substitution cipher in which each letter in the plaintext is replaced by a letter some fixed number of positions down the alphabet. For example, with a shift of +3, A would be replaced by D, B would become E, and so on. Using a +3 shift the message 'attack' becomes 'dwwdfn'. The method is named after Julius Caesar, who used it to communicate with his generals. Romeo chooses his cipher and sends the key to Juliet. He then separately encodes his message and sends that to Juliet as 'ciphertext'.

Note: Romeo and Juliet use the same key to encode and decode the messages.

Thus a basic cipher such as Caesar cipher relied on both the originator and recipient of the message having the same cipher key. This is good for sending secure messages (assuming the key is kept secure) but no good for proving identity as at least two people have copies of the key. Thus a message sent in encrypted form could be sent by any one of two people (or more depending on how many copies of the key there are).

Asymmetric or public key encryption (PKE) works differently. Here two keys are created: one known as the private key, the other the public key. The keys are mathematically linked but vitally you cannot discover one key by examining the other, and the keys only work in pairs—that is, if you encrypt a message with one key it can only be decrypted by the other. This technology was first suggested in the nineteenth century but was not developed until more powerful computers could be used to create the pairs of keys.

PKE is extremely powerful as an encryption tool as one never has to send the decryption key to the message recipient. One weakness of symmetric encryption is that you must at some point communicate to the recipient of your message the key you are using; this is liable to intercept allowing your enemies to decrypt all your messages.[77] With PKE, keys need never be traded in this fashion.

[77] There are two very famous examples of intercepted keys from the history books. It is believed that Sir Francis Walsingham, spy master of Queen Elizabeth I of England, obtained a secret code used by Queen Mary I of Scotland to communicate with a Catholic nobleman named Anthony Babington from Chartley Hall, Staffordshire, where Mary was being held. This allegedly unearthed a plot to overthrow Elizabeth leading to the execution of Mary. In another example in World War II the German 'Enigma' code was broken by scientists at Bletchley Park with the help of a captured Enigma machine recovered from a German U-boat in 1941.

Example Asymmetric PKE encryption

Romeo has another message that he must transmit securely to Juliet. To secure the message he uses PKE. He takes his message and encrypts it using Juliet's public key. As this message can only be decrypted by the paired key (the private key) the public key may be made publicly available anywhere including on the internet at no risk to the security of the message.

Romeo then sends the encoded (ciphertext) message to Juliet, who then decrypts it using her private key. The private key never leaves Juliet's possession making the entire transaction secure.

Note: this time Romeo and Juliet use different keys to encode and decode the messages.

This was the reason for the design of PKE. It allowed British agents in Moscow to send messages back to London with no risk of the key being compromised. In addition PKE encryption is resistant to so-called 'brute force' attacks, making it the preferred choice of encryption today for all secure services and internet sites.[78]

One interesting side-effect of PKE, though, is that it may be used in reverse. An individual who wishes to prove their identity may encrypt a message (or even part of that message) using their private key. They can then send this to someone else and, providing the public key they have previously published can decrypt the encrypted part of the message, there is overwhelming proof that the message must have been encrypted using the private key, and as the private key is within the possession of one person we therefore have a way of proving identity, and the desire to adopt the contents of a digital document: in other words, a signature.

Example Asymmetric PKE signatures

Romeo now wants to 'sign' a contract with Juliet. To achieve this he encrypts all (or more likely part of) the document using his private key. He then sends the document to Juliet. She uses Romeo's public key to decrypt the encrypted part of the document. If she is successful she knows the document part could only have been encrypted using Romeo's private key, and as only Romeo has access to that key it is as unique, in evidentiary terms, as a manuscript signature.

The problem with a PKE signature is that by itself it does not prove identity: only possession of a key pair. To explain; there is nothing to stop me from setting up a fake website passing myself off as the UK operation of an international company who does not yet trade in the UK, someone like China Telecom. I then create a matching key pair and place the public key on my website. Then, if I induce someone to trade with me, I sign all contractual documents using my private key. When my victim checks my signature using my public key it will, of course, demonstrate that the signature is valid, but of course I am not who I say I am. This returns us to the common problem of proving identity when people are in remote locations.

[78] The standard encryption used for secure websites (such as financial transactions and online banking) is either 128 bit or 256 bit Secure Socket Layer (SSL) a form of PKE.

The solution for electronic signatures is to issue a certificate of authenticity; a virtual ID card for key pairs. To create an authenticated signature (in particular a qualified, and therefore probative, signature) the user either creates her own key pair and sends them to a certification agency such as Verizon, Experian, or BT along with proof of identity, or, more usually and commonly, approaches the certification agency and asks them to create a key pair and to issue a certificate at the same time. The certification agency must carry out necessary checks to establish the identity of the individual or business before issuing the certificate, and may be held liable for damages should someone rely upon that certificate to their loss through any fault of the certification agency.[79]

Now when the signatory signs her message by attaching their private encryption to a portion of the message they also include a copy of the certificate. This shows who issued the certificate, when it was issued, and whether or not it is still valid. If the contractual counterparty is at all suspicious, they can contact the certification agency and ask for the identity of the signatory to be confirmed. Through the joint use of a secret, and in theory incorruptible, private key and the certificate of identity, all of Reed's functions of a signature may be fulfilled, including the two subsidiary functions. In fact, in some ways a digitally signed document is preferable to a physical document. A digital signature can be used not only to authenticate a document but also to guarantee the document has not been altered. In the real world we use forensics to determine whether a document has been altered post-signature but the risk remains that a page may be removed and replaced by a different page or gaps filled with additional words or numbers. With an electronically signed document we can reduce the risk of such fraud. All electronic documents have an in-built integrity check known as a 'checksum' or a 'hash sum'. This is a numerical value of all the data held in the file and is used by computers to check for accidental damage (corruption) or transmission errors in the file. In any complex file that number is uniquely created by the value of the contents of the file and will record any change, no matter how minor in the document, even the addition or removal of a single space. To protect the integrity of a signed document it is commonplace to encrypt the hash value of the document when signing. This both creates the electronic signature and protects the integrity of the document.

18.7 **Conclusions**

Contract formation is probably the most commonplace legally regulated activity in the online environment. It is at once also the simplest and yet most complex online activity from a legal perspective. As we have seen, informal contracts are easily concluded, yet raise a number of issues. Where is the contract domiciled, what are the terms of the contract, and when is the contract concluded? These three Ws are the WWW of contract lawyers. Traditional rules on contract formation, as seen in cases like *Thornton v Shoe Lane Parking* and *Entores Ltd v Miles Far East Corporation*, assist greatly in the domestic interpretation of these issues. But in the online environment a consumer is just as likely to conclude a contract with an American or French trader as a UK-based trader. Here, provisions such as the UNCITRAL model law and the Electronic Commerce Directive

[79] Art. 13(1).

assist. Additionally, consumer protection laws assist a consumer should they find themselves disputing the position with their counterparty.

This is only part of the story though. Formal contracts have rules as to form and often require a signature; something impossible in the traditional sense when dealing with a digital document. Complex rules have been developed as to the form of both documents and signatures, with heavy reliance being placed on highly technical solutions such as PKE encryption technology. Yet despite all these challenges, we find in reviewing this chapter an almost complete absence of case law dealing with these subjects. Why is this? It is because, on the whole, we make it work without the need for legal interventions. Online retailers have extremely detailed terms and conditions and generally those who do not act reasonably and fairly do not last long in the cut-throat online business environment. Although an essential body of law, the rules on electronic contract formation and interpretation will, in all likelihood, continue to be little relied upon in court.

TEST QUESTIONS

Question 1

Liam is a student living in London. He has recently bought a new laptop computer from 'Student Supplies Ltd' (SSL) an online retailer based in Bolton. The laptop was sold under SSL's standard terms and conditions which state that the contract is concluded when the goods are shipped and that goods may only be returned for a refund if they are faulty under the Consumer Protection Act 2015. They further state that refunds will only be given if goods are returned in their original packaging within five days of receipt and that the buyer must bear the cost of both the return and the original shipping costs. The SSL website makes no reference to any right to cancel under distance-selling provisions and indeed gives few details about SSL. There is no business address, company registration, or phone number, and the returns address is simply a PO Box.

Liam has had the laptop for six weeks but now his sister Leona has given him her old laptop which she no longer needs. He has asked you if he can return the laptop and get his money back from SSL. Advise Liam.

Question 2

The requirements needed to obtain a qualified electronic signature are far too onerous and mean there is no comparison between a simple manuscript signature and the qualified electronic signature which is designed to replace it. Until a simpler method of replicating the manuscript signature is found for the digital environment, the use of electronic signatures will remain uncommon.

Discuss.

FURTHER READING

Books

A Davidson, *The Law of Electronic Commerce* (2009)

S Mason, *Electronic Signatures in Law* (2012)

F Wang, *Law of Electronic Commercial Transactions: Contemporary Issues in the EU, US and China* (2014)

Chapters and articles

Z Akhtar, 'Distant Selling, E Commerce and Company Liability', *European Competition Law Review* 497 (2012)

J Dumortier and N Vandezande, 'Critical Observations on the Proposed Regulation for Electronic Identification and Trust Services for Electronic Transactions in the Internal Market', *ICRI Research Paper* 9 (2012)

J Luzak, 'To Withdraw Or Not To Withdraw? Evaluation of the Mandatory Right of Withdrawal in Consumer Distance Selling Contracts Taking Into Account Its Behavioural Effects on Consumers', 37 *Journal of Consumer Policy* 91 (2014)

O Orifowomo and J Agbana, 'Manual Signature and Electronic Signature: Significance of Forging a Functional Equivalence in Electronic Transactions', 24 *International Company and Commercial Law Review* 357 (2013)

C Reed, 'What Is a Signature?', 3 *JILT* (2000)

19 Electronic payments

Like contracting, payment is one of these complex legal relationships we tend not to think of on a day-to-day basis. When we buy something we hand over some banknotes, or more likely today place our credit or debit card into a chip and PIN device, or simply wave our smartphone over a contactless payment reader. Behind this though is a complex banking system which allows all this to function: the ability to make payment allows services to be supplied immediately and orders for products to be processed without delay. Online, the issue of secure payment at a distance (i.e. without both parties being present at the same place at the same time), sometimes over borders, is a more complex problem and as we shall see the solution used to date has been relatively inelegant, while alternatives have proven difficult to develop and establish.

19.1 Payments

19.1.1 Token payments

The most familiar payment system is the token system. Tokens are the method used in physical currency where a token (a banknote or coin) is exchanged for the supply of goods and services. The token system has a number of benefits which led to it becoming the dominant form of real-world currency for over 3,000 years.

First, tokens have, over the years, become easily portable and easily stored with banknotes replacing old-fashioned coin-based currency from the eighteenth century onwards. Second, tokens such as banknotes and coins are both fungible and divisible. This means that they are interchangeable (one £10 note is as good as the next) and are capable of subdivision into smaller units (a £10 note can be divided into two £5 notes or ten £1 coins). These functions are essential to liquidity, the function of money that allows it to be traded at a fixed value, including for other currency. This allows for change to be given allowing goods of a lesser value to be traded for a banknote of a higher value with change (tokens of a lower value) being used as the makeweight in the transaction. Third, tokens are a physical store of value. This is vital to retain confidence in a currency and leads to most tokens being secured or guaranteed by the central bank or treasury.[1] Collectively tokens are an extremely efficient way of fulfilling the three key functions of money:

[1] In the UK Bank of England notes are issued by the central bank while coins are issued by the Royal Mint, an executive agency of the Treasury.

Highlight The key functions of money

The three key functions of money are to act as:

1. a means of exchange
2. a unit of measurement
3. a comparator of the value of goods and service.

Tokens also fulfil the secondary function of liquidity:

Highlight The qualities that assist liquidity

The three key qualities of money that assist liquidity are:

1. portability and storability
2. fungibility
3. divisibility.

If any new form of monetory exchange is to replace cash tokens, it must at least fulfil these functions.

19.1.2 **Alternative payment systems**

Several alternatives have developed over the years, mostly based upon substitution of a debt, novation, and funds transfer. The most common alternative to the token system of currency until recent years was debt substitution. This is where a debt owed to one party is 'paid off' by substituting a debt owed by another. This is the design of the cheque payment system wherein a debt owed by the bank to its customer is used to make payment to a third party. Thus a customer has money on deposit with her bank; the bank is her debtor to the value of the money she has on deposit. The customer then buys goods and pays by cheque. In doing so, she pays her debt for the goods she has bought by transferring part of the debt the bank owes her. The bank pays her debt and reduces its indebtedness to her by the same amount.

Debt substitution is a way of reducing the risks associated with carrying money, but it has few of the benefits of cash tokens. It cannot be used as a unit of measurement or as a comparator of the value of goods or services. It is not fungible, is not divisible, and vitally is not as easily transferable as cash tokens. In other words, forms of debt substitution are strictly not money but are a money substitute. The cheque was initially popular for higher-value transactions where the allied risks of carrying large amounts of money could be negated. Recently a new phenomenon has seen debt substitution become the dominant form of debt settlement in the UK, due to the replacement of the cheque with the chip and PIN (and contactless) debit card. The general and widespread use of the debit card even for low-value transactions, thanks to the convenience it offers, has seen debt substitution become increasingly popular and now the value and number of debit card transactions eclipses cash token transactions in the UK high street.[2] Many people refer to chip and PIN or contactless debit card transactions as electronic payments, although as we shall see below this is not strictly true; rather, they are electronically enabled payments, meaning that the payment technology uses digital tools to make the system more reliable and secure, but they are in form debt substitution payments, not true electronic payments.

Another popular payment system, which has proven in particular to be extremely popular with internet transactions, is payment by credit card. Although to the user a credit card transaction may appear to be functionally the same as a debit card transaction—a piece of plastic is handed over and a PIN is used to authorize the transaction—they are in fact very different in function. Whereas a debit card relies upon money the customer has placed with the bank (or perhaps an agreed overdraft), a credit card works by having the credit card company assume the customer's debt for them and then provide the customer with credit to the same value. This uses a principle known as novation: the replacing of one contract or obligation with another. When a customer pays by credit card, the credit card company agrees to take on the debt the customer owes to the supplier and makes payment as if it were the customer. It simultaneously issues credit to the customer to the same value as the debt incurred, creating or extending contractual relationships between the credit card company and the supplier, and the credit card company and the customer. In function a credit card payment, like a debit card payment, is a money substitute not a form of money. Like a debit card it offers none of the functions of money. Also in common with a debit card payment, although people often think of credit card payments as electronic payments they are not—they are electronically enabled payments only.

Finally there is payment by fund transfer. This is not an option for traditional high-street transactions as it involves a direct transfer from one bank account to another. It tends to be used for commercial transactions and for property transactions, as well as for regular payments, such as bills and subscriptions, and for payments using internet banking services. There are a number of names for different types of fund transfer: a standing order is an order to pay a predetermined amount at the instigation of the account holder on a certain date or at a certain frequency; a direct debit allows the payee to debit varying amounts from the payer's account at the payee's request while a Clearing House Automated Payment System (CHAPS) transfer is a same-day inter-account transfer. These types of transfers are often collectively known as 'electronic fund transfers' (EFTs) along with internet account transfers and direct credits. This terminology has also extended to cover credit and debit card purchases with these often being referred to as 'electronic funds transfers at the point of sale' (EFTPoS). Again the common message is that none of these alternative payment systems are money in the true sense of the word. Money remains only cash tokens, this being the only form of payment which possesses the functions of money. This raises the obvious question: if more and more trade occurs in a purely digital environment where cash tokens cannot

[2] L Dodds, 'The end of cash as we know it?' *The Telegraph* (London, 11 March 2015) <http://www.telegraph.co.uk/news/shopping-and-consumer-news/11456380/The-end-of-cash-as-we-know-it.html>; L Eccles, 'For the first time we're buying more with cards than with cash' *Daily Mail* (London, 21 May 2015) <http://www.dailymail.co.uk/news/article-3090292/For-time-buying-cards-cash-Payments-coins-notes-48.html>.

be exchanged and over distances where it is impractical to send cash tokens by traditional means, how do we develop a functional currency for the information society?

19.1.3 Early e-money

To date the answer to that question has been rather disappointing. The predominant methods of online payment are forms of funds transfer, being a mixture of debit card payments, credit card payments, and funds transfer payments (often via PayPal). There are obvious reasons for the uptake of funds transfer systems such as credit and debit cards. First, there is a history of using such payment systems for distance selling transactions through 'card not present' systems used previously for telephone or mail order purchases. Second, sellers can rely upon guarantees from the card issuer that payment will be made, thus reducing the risk of fraud. Third, buyers (when using credit cards) have guarantees in the event that the goods or services either are not delivered or are of unsatisfactory quality.[3] Also payment by debit or credit card is extremely convenient for consumers as most already have such cards and therefore do not need to take any further action to allow them to make online payments. Thus, until recently, electronic money has tended in reality to mean EFTPoS payments using credit or debit cards. But, as we have already seen, such systems are not forms of money, only alternative payment methods.

In the 1990s a number of private organizations did try to develop viable digital cash, or e-cash systems. These came in a variety of forms that tried to copy the functions of money to a greater or lesser extent.

Probably the first system to achieve widespread coverage in the UK was Mondex. This was a smartcard payment system first introduced in 1994. To use Mondex, one needed a Mondex card: a smartcard which used an embedded chip as an electronic wallet. One would 'charge up' the card by visiting specially enabled ATM machines and then one could spend amounts from the card by visiting retailers who accepted Mondex. Mondex was a version of electronic cash. It had many of the features of cash tokens: it was easily portable, fungible, and divisible and, like cash tokens, the Mondex user was anonymous. Mondex-style technology is now being used in current near field communication (NFC) smartcard systems including the London Transport Oyster Card and Apple Pay/Android Pay. The problem with Mondex was that it was inconvenient. Only Mondex-registered businesses which had installed Mondex readers would accept it for payment. In addition, if your Mondex card was lost or stolen, then, like real cash, you lost whatever was charged on to it. Consumers continued to prefer debit cards over Mondex and soon it was removed from the market.

Around the same time, other e-cash systems were being developed to function purely in the online environment. Digicash was a software-based solution which installed an 'electronic wallet' on your hard drive: a protected space which, using encryption technology, was secure. The customer could buy Digicash tokens which were simple encrypted files containing some tracking data to prevent forgery (a digital serial number) which was stored in the wallet. When the customer wanted to pay a retailer she

[3] Under s. 75 of the Consumer Credit Act 1974, if the customer has a claim against the supplier of goods or services which have a value of between £100 and £30,000 and she has paid for these goods or services by credit card, she has an equivalent claim against the credit issuer (her credit card company).

could transfer tokens to the value of the goods bought, just like real cash. It functioned like Mondex for online transactions. It fulfilled most of the functions of cash. It was fungible, divisible, and anonymous. However, it was not easily portable (it was tied to the wallet, which was tied to the hard drive) but as it was designed as an online currency this did not matter. For the first time it offered the opportunity to develop a true digital cash system which fulfilled the three key functions of money. It was possible to use Digicash as a means of exchange, a unit of measurement, and as a comparator of the value of goods and service. Digicash spawned a number of imitators including Cyphermint and later Peppercoin; a system designed to make so-called micropayments. Today, the nearest modern equivalent is Bitcoin which will be discussed below.

In the 1990s there was a great deal of hope that systems such as Mondex, Digicash, and Cyphermint would soon render traditional cash tokens obsolete.[4] They seemed to offer all the functionality of cash with fewer of the drawbacks. In particular, as e-cash was merely a series of data encoded either on a smartcard or in a secure wallet on a hard drive, there were none of the associated costs absorbed by banks and other financial institutions in transporting cash from site to site. Also stolen 'cash' could, in some circumstances, be remotely deactivated rendering theft of less value while it may even be possible to refund the customer for any loss suffered if it were established that the cash had not been spent or redeemed. With these obvious benefits, why today do we still use debit cards and banknotes in place of Mondex? Why do we pay for goods online with credit or debit cards instead of Digicash or Cyphermint (or even Bitcoin which retains a niche role in online payments)? The answers to all these questions demonstrate the complexity of redesigning the centuries-old concept of physical cash tokens.

First, consumers are extremely conservative with cash and payment methods. Given the perceived risks of financial loss, consumers tend to trust established names with their money: high-street banks such as Barclays, Lloyds, and NatWest are trusted, even after the recent financial crisis. Companies with no track record such as Digicash and Cyphermint do not have the same position of trust. Second, consumers were happy to use their credit and debit cards both online and offline. The perceived advantage of anonymity offered by e-cash systems was outweighed by the advantage that the card issuer would assume most of the risks of fraud associated with online transactions.[5] It appeared that consumers would even use their credit cards to purchase pornography with little embarrassment, leaving few market opportunities for the new entrants.[6] Third, the technology was unreliable and untested. Who provided the best system? Which was most secure? There was no way for consumers to know. Fourth, and most important, all these electronic cash providers were private companies. Nearly all of them were recent start-ups with no record of financial stability. With the exception of a few specialist cases, such as the Scottish and Ulster banks, cash tokens are almost exclusively issued by, and guaranteed by, the state. US dollars are only issued by the US Treasury and the US Mint; euros are only issued by the European Central Bank or by national mints of Euro states; pound sterling is unusual in allowing private clearing banks to issue notes alongside the Bank of England, but even then this may only be

[4] See e.g. S Levy, 'E-Money (That's What I Want)' (*Wired 2.12* December 1994) <http://www.wired.com/1994/12/emoney/>.

[5] I Grigg, 'How DigiCash Blew Everything' <http://cryptome.org/jya/digicrash.htm>.

[6] See S Lubove, 'Visa's Porn Crackdown' *Forbes* (New York, 1 May 2003) <http://www.forbes.com/2003/05/01/cz_sl_0501porn.html>.

done with a financial guarantee from the Bank of England in the shape of the Bank of England Giant and Titan notes held by the issuers of these banknotes.[7] In short, consumers only have confidence in cash tokens issued by, and/or guaranteed by, either the central bank or government of the issuing state. This was the problem with cyberspace. There was no government, no central bank, and no pre-existing financial framework, only private organizations and competing technologies. If electronic cash was ever to take off it needed something to boost consumer confidence in e-cash issuers.

19.2 **The Electronic Money Directive 2000 (now repealed)**

As part of its information society programme the European Commission had been working on the text of the Electronic Money Directive for some time. It was eventually passed on 18 September 2000 and its aim was to give public confidence in electronic money issuers by implementing strict standards of financial probity. The Directive added a new phrase to our lexicon; an 'electronic money institution' (EMI):

Highlight Electronic money institutions (EMIs)

An undertaking or any other legal person, other than a credit institution, which issues means of payment in the form of electronic money.

[Art. 1(3)(a)]

EMIs were subject to stringent regulation: by Art. 1(5) the business of EMIs was tightly restricted.

Highlight The business of electronic money institutions

1. the issuing of electronic money
2. the provision of closely related financial and non-financial services such as the administering of electronic money by the performance of operational and other ancillary functions related to its issuance, and the issuing and administering of other means of payment but excluding the granting of any form of credit
3. the storing of data on the electronic device on behalf of other undertakings or public institutions.

In effect, this was that EMIs, unless they were also credit institutions as defined in the Banking Directive,[8] could not undertake any form of business, financial or otherwise, unrelated to their operations as EMIs. This prevented third-party businesses

[7] See 'Giants and Titans: Secrecy surrounding £1m banknotes' (*BBC News*, London 25 January 2013) <http://www.bbc.co.uk/news/uk-21185646>.

[8] Now the Recast Banking Directive, Dir. 2006/48/EC.

such as Microsoft or Cisco from becoming EMIs, leaving the way clear for banks and other credit institutions to occupy the role with only specialist niche companies such as Digicash for competition.

To bolster public confidence, EMIs were given strict financial requirements. By Art. 4(1) they were required to hold initial capital funds of €1m and were required to retain a funding level of at least that amount for as long as they remained an EMI. Further, by Art. 4(2) they were required to retain operating funds which were at least equal to the higher of the current value of all electronic money they have in circulation or the average value of their money in circulation in the preceding six months. Further, financial controls were to be found in Art. 5. EMIs must have investments which equal their outstanding liabilities (including all electronic money in circulation) and these investments must be in a list of pre-approved low-risk, high-liquidity form of investment vehicles. This is a double-edged sword. It made EMIs highly secure and highly liquid, meaning that an issuer should never find themselves unable to make payment on any call against money tokens they had issued, but it meant that they could not invest in higher-return investment vehicles, which carry higher risk but offer better rewards, and vitally they could not lend money received from customers who buy electronic money tokens unless they were approved credit institutions (banks), meaning there was little financial incentive to set up an EMI. The Commission believed these stringent new rules would engender public confidence in electronic money institutions leading to a rapid take-up of e-cash systems and a move away from the reliance placed on credit and debit card payments for online transactions, as well as the possibility of new forms of offline payments technologies. Critics argued that the Directive was too restrictive and that potential EMIs would be put off by the strict requirements of Arts. 4 and 5.[9]

It quickly became clear that the critics were right. By 2006 there were only nine active EMIs in the EU, while a further two were licensed but not operating.[10] In addition, a further 72 bodies were operating under the waiver scheme permitted by Art. 8. This could be applied where certain narrow exemptions were met. These are either that (a) the total liabilities of the EMI never normally exceeds €5m and never actually exceeds €6m and the maximum credit per person is €150;[11] or (b) the electronic money issued by the issuer is not of a value of more than €10m, the maximum credit per person is €150, and the electronic money is only accepted by the issuer or any subsidiaries of the issuer which perform ancillary functions related to electronic money issued or distributed by the issuer;[12] or (c) the electronic money issued by the issuer is not of a value of more than €10m, the maximum credit per person is €150 and is accepted as payment only by a limited number of undertakings, which can be clearly distinguished by their location in the same premises or other limited local area; or their close financial or business relationship with the issuing institution, such as a common marketing or distribution

[9] See e.g. M Kohlbach, 'Making Sense of Electronic Money' (2004) 1 *JILT* <http://www2.warwick.ac.uk/fac/soc/law/elj/jilt/2004_1/kohlbach/>.

[10] European Commission, DG Internal Market, 'Evaluation of the E-Money Directive (2000/46/EC) Final Report', 17 February 2006, 2.2.1 <http://ec.europa.eu/internal_market/payments/docs/emoney/evaluation_en.pdf>.

[11] Dir. 2000/46/EC, Art. 8(1); The Financial Services and Markets Act 2000 (Regulated Activities) (Amendment) Order 2002, SI 2002/682, reg. 9C(4).

[12] Dir. 2000/46/EC, Art. 8(2); SI 2002/682, reg. 9C(5).

scheme.[13] These schemes tend to be for smartcard payment schemes used in gyms, university campuses, or in offices.[14] Wider electronic money schemes tended to be limited to pre-pay schemes which were exempt from the Directive,[15] the best-known such schemes being pre-pay mobile phones and transport schemes such as Transport for London's pre-pay Oyster Card. These figures made it clear that by 2006 the Directive had failed. Worse, it became apparent that it may be holding back the development of functional electronic money schemes.

In the seven years since the Directive had been promulgated, the focus of electronic money had changed radically. When the Directive was designed the focus had been on online payment systems such as Digicash or Cyphermint, but now electronic cash meant convenient real-world payment systems including travel card payment systems such as the Oyster Card, payment by mobile phone, and second-generation Mondex technology such as pre-pay debit cards. A number of schemes were being planned to make use of the convenience of these technologies. For example, Transport for London had plans to allow the Oyster Card to become a digital wallet which could be used for small-value purchases such as newspapers, coffees, or tobacco.[16] The problem for them was that to implement the scheme they would require an electronic money institution licence from the FSA as they would no longer be exempted and would be unlikely to qualify for a small e-money licence as they would almost certainly exceed the €10m maximum. To try to achieve this they sought partnership with established technology providers such as Barclays, but in 2006 it was announced the scheme would be scrapped. Instead, Transport for London licensed Barclaycard to use their Oyster payment technology in the Barclaycard OnePulse credit card.

Another developing scheme was the use of mobile phones to make small payments, usually by SMS payment systems. This is used by Transport for London to allow for payment of the Central London Congestion Charge by SMS message; many local councils also used the system to allow payment of parking charges. The problem with systems which allow SMS payment is that technically it turned a pay-as-you-go mobile phone into a digital wallet for the purposes of the Electronic Money Directive. This is because pay-as-you-go phones store value on them, unlike contract phones in which liabilities are paid at the end of the contract period. This created a potential problem. If mobile phone operators were issuing electronic money, which it seemed they were if they allowed pre-pay customers to pay for third-party goods or services using their phone credit, then they would need (a) a licence from the FSA, and (b) to comply with Art. 1(5) of the Directive, they would have to give up all operations other than those relating to their business as an EMI (including operating a mobile phone network). This outcome was clearly absurd and so the Commission undertook a review of the Directive

[13] Dir. 2000/46/EC, Art. 8(3); SI 2002/682, reg. 9C(6).

[14] For instance the FSA issued a small e-money issuer certificate to the *London Evening Standard* for its (now defunct) Eros pre-pay scheme.

[15] Art. 1(3)(b) stated that '"electronic money" shall mean monetary value as represented by a claim on the issuer which is: (i) stored on an electronic device; (ii) issued on receipt of funds of an amount not less in value than the monetary value issued; and (iii) *accepted as means of payment by undertakings other than the issuer*'. This is replicated at SI 2002/682, reg. 2. The key phrase (highlighted) makes it clear the closed pre-pay schemes are not regulated by electronic money regulations.

[16] A McCue, 'London Transport Targets Oyster "e-money" Trials in 2005' (*ZDNet.com*, 21 July 2005) <http://www.zdnet.com/article/london-transport-targets-oyster-e-money-trials-in-2005/>.

in the hope that changes could be made to make it more relevant to electronic money as it was developing in the real world.

19.3 Review of the Electronic Money Directive and the 2009 Electronic Money Directive

The review took place between 2004 and 2006. It opened with a review of the application of the Directive to mobile phone operators, which began with a consultation paper in May 2004[17] and led to the publication of the report 'Application of the E-Money Directive 2000/46/EC to Mobile Operators' in January 2005.[18] The report concluded that 'legal uncertainty is damaging the sector, because it prevents investments in new technologies, undermines the consolidation and competitiveness of innovative services as well as the launch of supplementary digital services'.[19] It noted that expert commentators questioned whether it was correct to capture mobile operators within the definition of electronic money institutions, mainly because of a very restrictive interpretation of the conditions listed in Art. 1 of the Electronic Money Directive,[20] and recommended that mobile phone operators should benefit from a separate 'risk-based' regulatory structure rather than the strict structural rules which apply to electronic money issuers under the Directive. This, the Commission believed, was possible due to the already strict regulatory structure which surrounds the mobile phone industry and which contains a number of provisions designed to protect the consumer.[21]

These recommendations were taken forward in the subsequent review of the Directive which opened with a consultation paper in July 2005 which asked, among other things, 'Should a special EU regime be introduced for institutions issuing E-Money as a non-core part of their business (e.g. mobile operators and other "hybrid" prepaid instrument providers)?'; 'Have the harmonised provisions of the E-Money Directive eliminated legal uncertainty in the field of E-Money?'; and vitally, 'Has the Directive encouraged new market entrants?'[22]

This consultation concluded in February 2006 with the publication of a 168-page report, 'Evaluation of the E-Money Directive (2000/46/EC) Final Report'.[23] This found that in general the uptake of electronic money in the EU had been disappointing, noting that 'e-money market has developed more slowly than expected, and is far from reaching its full potential', and that 'the take-up of card-based e-money has remained low

[17] European Commission, DG Internal Market, 'A Consultation Paper on the Treatment of Mobile Operators under the E-money Directive 2000/46/EC' 10 May 2004 <http://ec.europa.eu/internal_market/payments/docs/emoney/2004–05-consultation_en.pdf>.

[18] European Commission, DG Internal Market, 'Application of the E-money Directive 2000/46/EC to Mobile Operators', 18 January 2005 <http://ec.europa.eu/internal_market/payments/docs/emoney/summary_en.pdf>.

[19] Ibid. 2.

[20] Ibid.

[21] Ibid. 16–17.

[22] European Commission, DG Internal Market, 'Questionnaire on the Electronic Money Directive (2000/46/EC)' 14 July 2005 <http://ec.europa.eu/internal_market/payments/docs/emoney/questionnaire_en.pdf>.

[23] European Commission, DG Internal Market, 'Evaluation of the E-Money Directive (2000/46/EC) Final Report' 14 July 2005 <http://ec.europa.eu/internal_market/payments/docs/emoney/evaluation_en.pdf>.

in most EU Member States. Card-based e-purses in many countries have been discontinued, and for most of those that remain, usage remains very limited . . . [as] e-money cards are still used almost exclusively at unmanned stations (public telephones, car parks, vending machines).'[24] The report does see light at the end of the tunnel noting:

> the recent emergence of contactless cards may provide a new impulse to card-based e-money. Such cards are currently issued almost exclusively by public transport providers, and can at present only be used to pay for transport services. However, this may change relatively soon, and there seem to also be significant potential benefits in the use of contactless e-money cards for other types of entities such as financial service providers, retailers, telecoms, utilities, sports stadiums and local councils.[25]

The report recognized that these schemes are being held back by the strict rules of the Directive and, although it was not within the scope of the report to make recommendations formally, a number of proposals are made to free-up the marketplace and to allow for systems such as contactless payment smartcards or payment by mobile phone to develop. These proposals are to be found in two key recommendations: the first, that mobile phone operators are either given a blanket waiver or that the waiver provisions in Art. 8 be extended to 'closely related third parties (such as third parties delivering mobile content services to customers of the mobile operators)';[26] and the second, that the Commission consider 'creating an exemption whereby smartcards that are used exclusively to pay for public transport, but are accepted as payment by more than one transport provider, would not be considered e-money'.[27]

These amendments would have assisted slightly in freeing up the regulation of electronic money issuers in the EU, but these still would fail to address the key critique of the Directive, that the restrictive systemic regulation of electronic money issuers means that they cannot compete with credit institutions (banks and credit card issuers) in the electronic money marketplace. On the vital questions of liquidity and security the report found that:

> there is a considerable degree of support for the idea that certain elements of the regulatory framework are disproportionate to the risks posed by the activities of e-money issuers, and that a less restrictive regime may have been sufficient to ensure the stability and soundness. Many industry stakeholders find the overall set of rules 'too blunt', and argue that there is room for adopting a more risk-based approach without endangering the stability of issuers or the adequate protection of consumers.[28]

To this end, the report suggested that a separate study be undertaken, looking at the financial and non-financial risks involved in the issuance of e-money.

In many ways the report was underwhelming and somewhat disappointing. Its aim had never been to propose widespread changes to the Directive, but with Europe clearly lagging behind the rest of the world in the development of electronic cash tokens it was clear that a Directive which had in mind payment systems in the online world was

[24] Ibid. 2.2.1.
[25] Ibid.
[26] Ibid. 5.4.1.1.
[27] Ibid. 5.4.1.2. Note this allows for an integrated 'travelcard' system but still does not allow travel payment cards like the Oyster card to be used to pay for goods or services other than transport.
[28] Ibid. 5.4.4.2.

now holding back the development of electronic cash alternatives in the real world. The report seemed to suggest the Directive was, on the whole, working well and only needed a few minor adjustments.

Following the report, the Commission continued to review the scope and role of the Directive. Finally in October 2009 after a further three years of development and review, the new Electronic Money Directive was passed.[29] It codifies the (now) extremely complex laws applicable to EMIs. In the period since the original Electronic Money Directive was passed three subsequent directives had been passed which affect EMIs. These directives—the Payment Services Directive[30] and the Capital Requirements Directives (of which there are two)[31]—made major changes to the framework of banking and credit services in the EU.

The Payment Services Directive introduced new liquidity and security regulations for all payment service providers, including EMIs, but also introduced a new form of financial institution—the payment institution.[32] Payment institutions are permitted to make and remit payments on behalf of customers but are not allowed to issue credit (that being the preserve of credit institutions) or issue electronic money (that being the preserve of credit institutions and EMIs). Thus the Payment Services Directive creates a three-tier system; with banks and similar institutions (known as credit institutions) at the apex, EMIs in the middle, and payment institutions at the base. The problem with the Payment Services Directive was the very different rules on probity which are now applied to payment institutions when compared to electronic money institutions.

As discussed earlier, an EMI was required to hold initial capital of €1m and to retain that level of capital for as long as they remained an electronic money institution. In addition, they were required to retain operating funds at least equal to the higher of the value of all electronic money they have in current circulation or the average value of their money in circulation in the preceding six months, these funds to be held in approved low-risk, high-liquidity form of investment vehicles.[33] As we have discussed in relation to mobile phone operators, electronic money institutions may not carry out operations not linked to their role as electronic money institutions. By comparison, a payment institution under the Payment Services Directive need only provide initial capital of between €20,000 and €125,000, depending upon the type of operation they intend to offer, and they may carry out business operations unrelated to their role as payment institutions. The Commission recognized that these changes made the provisions of the Electronic Money Directive appear punitive by comparison:

> [The law provides an] inconsistent legal framework with a disproportionate prudential regime, inconsistent waivers and passporting procedures as well as the application of anti-money laundering rules to electronic money services. This overall legal inconsistency will increase once the

[29] Dir. 2009/110/EC, OJ L267/7. Given effect in the UK via the Electronic Money Regulations 2011, SI 2011/99.

[30] 2007/64/EC.

[31] Dir. 2006/48/EC relating to the taking up and pursuit of the business of credit institutions and Dir. 2006/49/EC on the capital adequacy of investment firms and credit institutions.

[32] The Payment Services Directive is outside the scope of this analysis. Anyone interested in the detail of the Directive may read D Mavromati, *The Law of Payment Services in the EU: The EC Directive on Payment Services in the Internal Market* (Kluwer Law International 2008).

[33] See 19.2 'The Electronic Money Directive'.

Payment Services Directive provisions have been implemented (by November 2009), since some of the requirements for the prudential regime of payment institutions differ widely from those applicable today to electronic money institutions.[34]

To this end the new Electronic Money Directive brings major changes. The initial capital requirement is reduced and the rules on liquidity are changed to bring them more in line with the Payment Services Directive,[35] while vitally the rule restricting electronic money issuers to carry on business as only an electronic money issuer are swept away by Art. 6(1).

Highlight Article 6(1)

Institutions shall be entitled to engage in any of the following activities:

(a) the provision of payment services listed in the Annex to Directive 2007/64/EC;

(b) the granting of credit related to payment services referred to in points 4, 5 or 7 of the Annex to Directive 2007/64/EC, where the conditions laid down in Article 16(3) and (5) of that Directive are met;

(c) the provision of operational services and closely related ancillary services in respect of the issuing of electronic money or to the provision of payment services referred to in point (a);

(d) the operation of payment systems as defined in point 6 of Article 4 of Directive 2007/64/EC and without prejudice to Article 28 of that Directive;

(e) business activities other than issuance of electronic money, having regard to the applicable Community and national law.

This finally allows mobile phone operators and others such as Apple to be licensed as electronic money institutions without fear of this affecting their ability to carry on their core business.

There is little doubt that this was a long-overdue development: by relaxing the key provisions on liquidity and allowing electronic money institutions to carry on unrelated business the millstones around the old Directive were swept away. What is interesting is what electronic money became in the nine years between the original Directive and the new one. In 2000 it was envisaged that the problem was with online payments. Customers were relying on credit and debit cards to make payment; this was extremely inefficient with high transaction costs and with no means for consumer-to-consumer-payments. It seemed that what was missing was an internet currency—money rather than payment methods. The Commission believed there was a demand for electronic money to facilitate online electronic commerce and believed that the Electronic Money Directive would provide the framework for this to grow. We now know there is little

[34] Proposal for a Directive of the European Parliament and of the Council on the taking up, pursuit and prudential supervision of the business of electronic money institutions, amending Directives 2005/60/EC and 2006/48/EC and repealing Directive 2000/46/EC, 3.

[35] Art. 5 has a complex set of principles to be employed in calculating the liquidity principle.

demand for electronic money in the online environment.[36] Customers like the security and convenience offered by card payments. Even the problem of consumer-to-consumer cash payments has been solved by a variety of online clearing systems which allow individuals or small businesses to accept credit card payments, or bank transfer payments without the need to enter into partnership with the major card payment clearing services. The success of Google Checkout, and more spectacularly PayPal, seems to suggest we do not need money in the true sense online; payment methods are sufficient.

Instead, electronic money has begun, surprisingly, to flourish in the real world. People carry less cash than they used to as they rely more on payment methods. This means it is more likely that people will not have change for small-value transactions such as paying for parking, for transport, or for low-value items such as coffee or a newspaper. Additionally, for banks and for vendors coins are very inefficient. They cost a lot to transport and need constant security. Conversely, at low values, payment methods are also inefficient due to the transaction costs involved. Electronic money, although it does still come with transactions costs, is a cheaper and simpler method of real-world payment and, with the widespread adoption of near field communication technology (used for contactless payments including Apple Pay and Android Pay), it is now clear that the high street, not the internet, is the natural home for the next stage of electronic money development. And with the relaxation of the strict rules found in the first Electronic Money Directive the EU is finally in the right place to reap the rewards of such technologies, as we are seeing in a variety of exciting applications such as Apple Pay (which can be installed on your phone or your Apple Watch),[37] Android Pay,[38] Barclays Pingit,[39] and a national travel card system, like Oyster, known as ITSO to be effective across England and Wales in the next few years.[40]

19.4 **Bitcoin and cryptocurrencies**

One area, which has developed quite independently of the legal framework, is cryptocurrency, of which the best-known example is Bitcoin. Bitcoin works on similar principles to PKE signatures which were discussed in chapter 18. It is built around the same Public Key Encryption technology, but this time, instead of verifying the identity of a signatory, it verifies the transfer of value from one user to another.

Bitcoin is a peer-to-peer currency. It does away with the idea of a trusted party who verifies the value of the currency (such as a central bank or financial institution). Instead, in the words of its creator, Satoshi Nakamoto,[41] 'an electronic payment system based on cryptographic proof instead of trust, allowing any two willing parties to

[36] One exception to this is of course in game cash for online gaming, such as 'Gold' in *World of Warcraft*, 'Platinum Pieces' in *Everquest*, and 'Points' in *Xbox Live*. Another exception is Bitcoin, discussed below.

[37] <http://www.apple.com/uk/apple-pay/>.

[38] <http://www.android.com/pay/>.

[39] <https://pingit.com/>.

[40] <http://www.itso.org.uk/>.

[41] Satoshi Nakamoto is a pseudonym of either an individual or a group. Several attempts have been made to 'unmask' Nakamoto but to date none have been convincing.

transact directly with each other without the need for a trusted third party.'[42] The system works through two vital underpinnings. The first is a chain of electronic signatures, and the second a distributed database of these transactions known as the blockchain database. To use a cryptocurrency such as Bitcoin the end user first needs to install a wallet, much as with Digicash, but hereafter the similarities end. You then get your bitcoins in one of three ways: you can buy them from an exchange, receive them as payment for goods or services, or you can mine for them (more below). For most initial users this means buying bitcoins from an exchange or dealer, of which there are many. Once you have your bitcoins you can begin to spend them. This is where the value of bitcoins can be seen for they operate like token payments. While exchanges quote the market price for one Bitcoin (on November 5 2015 this was £262.95) you are rarely going to spend a whole Bitcoin. In fact, the Bitcoin protocol does not really work with whole Bitcoin, but with a smaller unit, called a Satoshi (after Satoshi Nakamoto). Since 1 Bitcoin equals 100,000,000 Satoshi, the smallest amount you can spend is 1 Satoshi or around 0.0000026p on 5 November 2015. Thus to buy a coffee at £2.40 you would spend 923,077 sat.

How do you do this in practice? When you buy or receive Bitcoin you load them into your wallet. Each Satoshi represents an address (similar to a serial number on a banknote). When you spend your Satoshi you transfer these addresses to the recipient. How, though, are you prevented from then spending them again, this is called double spending, or merely fraudulently creating more Bitcoin? This is prevented by the operation of the electronic signature chain and the blockchain database. When you transfer Bitcoin (or Satoshi) you digitally sign a hash of the previous transaction and the public key of the next owner and add these to the end of the coin. This creates a chain of ownership (which is anonymous as no one is certifying identity of any of the owners of the key pairs), showing each transaction and the identity of the new owner. Also, as the whole process is cryptographically secure it cannot be altered. The recipient of the payment can verify the signatures to verify the chain of ownership, thus preventing theft and embezzlement. This, however, does not in of itself prevent double spending; this is where the blockchain comes in. The blockchain is a distributed database of all the transactions for every Bitcoin. It records the chain of transactions and the hash of each previous block. This is all-time stamped so that the chain of transactions for any Bitcoin address (or Satoshi) is completely recorded. This prevents double spending as an attempt to re-transact an already transacted address will be apparent from the chain for that address. The blockchain is distributed through all the nodes using the Bitcoin protocol but one thing anticipated by Satoshi Nakamoto was that this would use up a lot of processing power and electricity. To encourage people to be good citizens and to offer up capacity he suggested an incentive scheme. The first transaction in any block, the 'minting' of the coin creates a new coin owner by that person. However, there is no central mint to create the coins so Nakamoto drew an analogy to gold mining: 'the steady addition of a constant of amount of new coins is analogous to gold miners expending resources to add gold to circulation. In our case, it is CPU time and electricity that is expended. The incentive can also be funded with transaction fees.'[43] This is

[42] S Nakamoto, *Bitcoin: A Peer-to-Peer Electronic Cash System*: <https://bitcoin.org/bitcoin.pdf>.

[43] Ibid.

a process known as Bitcoin mining. Bitcoin users can buy specially adapted 'mining equipment' which processes hash data and over time earns the user Bitcoin. This is the third way of earning Bitcoin.

What is the legal position of Bitcoin in the UK? It is not issued by an EMI and therefore is not legal under the Electronic Money Directive 2009. Equally, it is not issued by a central bank, and in England and Wales it does not qualify as legal tender under s. 1 of the Currency and Bank Notes Act 1954 or s. 2 of the Coinage Act 1971. It doesn't even qualify for the same status as Scottish or Northern Irish banknotes as authorized and approved currency under Part 6 of the Banking Act 2009. Essentially the Bitcoin has no legal status in the UK, but despite this many UK-based websites and even high-street shops, cafes, and pubs accept Bitcoin. Indeed, the widespread acceptance of Bitcoin into the mainstream is causing the government slowly to interact with and acknowledge Bitcoin. On 3 March 2014 HMRC published its policy paper 'Bitcoin and Other Cryptocurrencies'.[44] In this HMRC reviewed the tax implications of payment in cryptocurrency, in particular, whether or not Value Added Tax (VAT) was due on cryptocurrency operations and payments. The advice was that income received from Bitcoin mining was not subject to VAT, and that when Bitcoin is exchanged for sterling or other currencies, no VAT is due on the value of the bitcoins themselves. However, 'VAT is due in the normal way from suppliers of any goods or services sold in exchange for Bitcoin or other similar cryptocurrency. The value of the supply of goods or services on which VAT is due will be the sterling value of the cryptocurrency at the point the transaction takes place.' This essentially treats cryptocurrency like cash payments. Meanwhile, the Bank of England has issued several bulletins on cryptocurrency; among other things, focus on the potential uses of the blockchain ledger for traditional currencies.[45] Recently, Andrew Haldane, the Chief Economist of the Bank even suggested the Bank could issue its own cryptocurrency, maybe even to replace paper currency.[46] Also, recently Bitcoin has begun to be acknowledged in legislative measures. The explanatory note to s. 44 (5) of the Consumer Rights Act 2015 (right to a refund for digital content) records that:

> subsection (5) does not mean that a trader can refund the consumer by giving them back the virtual currency. Rather, to satisfy this requirement a trader must give the consumer back the money originally paid for the in-game currency, using the means of payment that the consumer used to buy that in-game currency (unless the consumer expressly agrees otherwise). However, digital currencies (or cryptocurrencies) that can be used in a variety of transactions with a number of traders, and exchanged for real money, are much more akin to real money (e.g. bitcoins). Where the consumer uses these types of digital currency to pay for digital content, the trader can (and must, unless the consumer agrees) repay the consumer in the digital currency.

[44] <http://www.gov.uk/government/publications/revenue-and-customs-brief-9–2014-bitcoin-and-other-cryptocurrencies>.

[45] R Ali, 'Innovations in Payment Technologies and the Emergence of Digital currencies' *Bank of England Quarterly Bulletin* Q3 2014 <http://www.bankofengland.co.uk/publications/Documents/quarterlybulletin/2014/qb14q3digitalcurrenciesbitcoin1.pdf>; R Ali, 'The Economics of Digital Currencies' *Bank of England Quarterly Bulletin* Q3 2014 <http://www.bankofengland.co.uk/publications/Documents/quarterlybulletin/2014/qb14q3digitalcurrenciesbitcoin2.pdf>.

[46] A Haldane, *How low can you go?* 18 September 2015 <http://www.bankofengland.co.uk/publications/Pages/speeches/2015/840.aspx>.

Also the explanatory note to s. 14 (3) of the Serious Crime Act 2015 (seized money etc.) records that:

> subsection (3) inserts new subsections (7A) and (7B) into section 67 which confer a power on the Secretary of State to amend, by order, section 67 [of the Proceeds of Crime Act 2002] so as to apply the money seizure power to money held by other financial institutions or other realisable cash or cash-like instruments or products, for example share accounts, pension accounts or 'bitcoins'.

Thus, although not yet of any specific legal standing in the UK, cryptocurrencies, and in particular Bitcoin, are attracting the attention of the central bank, the tax authorities, and the legislature. It is surely only a matter of time until they are formally regulated as a form of currency.

19.5 **Conclusions**

According to the song, 'money makes the world go round'. While, hopefully, we are not as avaricious a society as to be dominated by our desire for money, there is no doubt that e-commerce needs to be able to service the basic financial requirements of any commercial sector if it is to continue to grow. Initially, there were concerns that the development of e-commerce would be negatively affected by an inability to pay for goods and services online by any means except card payment systems. Card payments lacked many of the functions of money—in particular, they lacked anonymity and they were expensive to operate. It was feared that the lack of anonymity meant that users would worry about identity fraud and they would not buy goods or services online which may cause embarrassment. For suppliers there was a concern that the transaction fees meant that they could not be used economically for small-value transactions as the fees payable would outweigh the payment received.

All these predictions have proven to be false. Customers have embraced payment by card. They do fear identity fraud, but know their card issuer will reimburse them for any losses they incur. They have no embarrassment about using their cards to make payment because the feeling of anonymity a computer screen gives means they would rather buy Viagra online than in a pharmacy, and in any event goods bought online have to be shipped to their home anyway so why worry about giving your credit card details. Industry, realizing that cards were to become the dominant online payment system, developed alternatives to cash payments for low-value transactions—using a mixture of subscription services and advertising supported services.

Some things, initially not predicted, have also come to pass. Electronic money has found a new lease of life in the real world—the convenience of payment by mobile phone being the driving force behind one arm of the technology, while the familiarity of smartcard systems as a means of payment for public transport is driving another. For all involved in the money supply chain, the benefits offered by electronic money are clear. The risks of forgery are reduced, the costs of production are removed and, most importantly, there are no cash deposits in banks, stores, or in armoured cars to steal. It seems that the rise of cryptocurrencies may herald the next movement in money as a form of token. Token-based payment systems (cash money in old language) will, like music, film, and photographs, become a series of ones and zeros. Although new risks will arise, and there will be a need to ensure that the exchanges and blockchain are secure,[47] there seems little doubt that a wholesale migration to electronic money could reduce traditional forms of criminal activity.

TEST QUESTIONS

Question 1

Is it too late to develop an effective online e-money sector in Europe? Did the first Electronic Money Directive kill off any chance of such a business sector developing, due to its draconian rules on liquidity?

Question 2

Is it now time to bring cryptocurrency systems formally within the framework of the Electronic Money Directive? Advise the European Commission on what you see as being the key provisions of a model Cryptocurrency Directive.

FURTHER READING

Books

S Hoegner (ed.), The *Law of Bitcoin* (2015)

D Mavromati, *The Law of Payment Services in the EU: The EC Directive on Payment Services in the Internal Market* (2008)

P Vigna and M Casey, *Cryptocurrency: How Bitcoin and Digital Money are Challenging the Global Economic Order* (2015)

Chapters and articles

M Kohlbach, 'Making Sense of Electronic Money', 1 *JILT* (2004)

B Regnard-Weinrabe et al., 'Mobile Payments and the New E-money Directive', *Computer and Telecommunications Law Review* 117 (2011)

N Vandezande, 'Between Bitcoins and Mobile Payments: Will the European Commission's New Proposal Provide More Legal Certainty?, 22 *IJLIT* 295 (2014)

[47] One key setback for Bitcoin was the Mt Gox scandal, see J Elgot, 'Ex-boss of MtGox bitcoin exchange arrested in Japan over lost $390m' *The Guardian* (London, 1 August 2015) <http://www.theguardian.com/technology/2015/aug/01/ex-boss-of-mtgox-bitcoin-exchange-arrested-in-japan-over-lost-480m>.

PART VI

Privacy in the information society and future developments

The financial value of data is such that individual privacy is often set aside in the pursuit of commercial advantage. The information society makes it easy for individuals to be monitored and tracked: how much data are we willing to trade for convenience? How does the law strike a balance between data privacy and data brokering? How will the law in this area develop?

Data protection

As has been alluded to at several points in the previous chapters, one of the effects of the information society is a divorce of identity from the person. Basically this means that with more of our everyday lives being ordered or even accessed via an internet connection we increasingly use proxy data to identify who we are. These include true proxies such as passwords and user IDs, bank or credit card information, email addresses; and personal data such as date of birth, place of birth, mother's maiden name, first school attended, or nowadays biometric data such as a digital record of a fingerprint or facial scan data taken from a digital image. This places our identity at unique risk in the modern society as a large proportion of our transactions are validated by reference to proxies rather than to direct identification. This leads to at least two distinct threats to our data, and therefore to our identity. The first is identity theft or identity fraud. This is a malicious assault on our identity proxies carried out with criminal intent. This particular aspect of data harm has been discussed already in chapter 15. The second is the misapplication, mishandling, or misprocessing of data. This is (usually) innocent and benign in intent, although the impact may not be. This may be something as simple as failing to secure data, a charge laid before the UK Government at several points during 2007 as they in quick succession lost data relating to 25 million child benefit recipients,[1] 3 million candidates for the driving theory test,[2] 168,000 NHS patient records,[3] and 40,000 housing benefit claimants;[4] or it may be that the data is inaccurate or out of date leading to an unfair outcome in a computerized decision-making process,[5] or it may be that against the wishes of the data subject the data is sold or transferred to a third party for purposes such as marketing.[6] It is the latter risks that will form the focus of this chapter.

[1] For a full discussion of the affair. see K Poynter, *Review of information security at HM Revenue and Customs: Final Report* (London, 2008) <https://ntouk.files.wordpress.com/2015/06/poynter_review250608.pdf>.

[2] H Mulholland, 'Details of 3m learner drivers lost, government admits' *The Guardian* (London, 17 December 2007) <http://www.guardian.co.uk/uk/2007/dec/17/politics.helenemulholland>.

[3] D Rose, 'More personal data lost as nine NHS trusts admit security breaches' *The Times* (London, 24 December 2007).

[4] J Ungoed-Thomas, 'More financial data discs lost' *The Times* (London, 2 December 2007).

[5] Famously lampooned in the 'Little Britain sketch' 'computer says no'. For those on the receiving end of a computerized decision-making process though there is little to laugh about. See J Bing 'Code, Access and Control' in M Klang and A Murray (eds.), *Human Rights in the Digital Age* (Routledge-Cavendish 2005).

[6] See D Garrie and R Wong, 'The Future of Consumer Web Data: A European/US Perspective' [2007] *International Journal of Law and Information Technology* 129; P Bernal, 'Web 2.5: The Symbiotic Web' [2010] 24 *International Review of Law, Computers & Technology* 25.

20.1 **Digitization, data, and the regulation of data industries**

In chapter 3 we discussed how digitization created the information society. Among the issues discussed there was the inherent value of digitized information.[7] As we discovered, digital information is commercially more valuable than analogue information. As a result, a multibillion pound industry had grown up around this new product. Some companies gather data to act as an adviser to others. An example of such a company would be Experian. Experian are the world's largest credit reference and scoring agency. They ingather data from a variety of sources such as lenders, the electoral roll, and lists of County Court judgments, and score the risk of lending to individuals. Their services are used by all forms of credit agencies including mortgage lenders and credit card issuers to determine whether to make loans to individuals.

Other companies gather data to improve their service to their customers. Examples of such schemes include customer loyalty cards such as the Tesco Clubcard and the Nectar Card. These gather data on customers' buying habits and allow the retailer to tailor their stock and staffing levels accordingly, as well as offering customers rewards such as discount vouchers and promoting to customers related goods and services.

A third type of company carries out market research using gathered data with a view to selling their insights, or tailored advertising products, to clients. These include traditional market research companies like Brand Institute and Neilsen, but more and more includes internet companies, with Google being a leading provider in this area. Google gathers vast amounts of search data and then sells specialist online advertising (Google Ads) which are much more focused on the target market than traditional media advertising. By offering this service Google has become the largest media advertising company globally, including from 2007 surpassing ITV1, to become the UK's largest media advertiser.[8]

Fourth, there are companies which act as information brokers for others. These companies gather information and sell it on as packaged data for the purposes of product development, advertising, and promotion, or other purposes. This may include social networking sites such as Facebook, or mobile phone operators, or it may be specialist information gatherers such as so-called 'adware' companies, like Gator or When U, who gather data on internet habits and then sell that information on to third parties.

Finally, there are the organizations on the fringes of what is legal. These are groups that gather data to create massive databases of customer details including mailing lists, email lists, and phone lists. These are then used for direct mailing or cold calling to try to sell goods and services. Some organizations involved in this industry are responsible and act completely legally, such as The Database Manager, Electric Marketing, or even BT. Others, though, are less responsible and exist at the fringes of what is required under the Data Protection Act.

All these companies want personal data. It is the lifeblood of their operations but it is costly to gather and process. As a result, a number of digital processes have been developed to make it easier and cheaper to ingather and store such data, but such automation of data gathering risks our data privacy since computers have no ability to evaluate the nature of data or its sensitivity. Thus, a strict legal regime is required to regulate the

[7] See ch. 3.

[8] See D Sabbagh, 'Google shows ITV a vision of the future' *The Times* (London, 30 October 2007).

industry as a whole. This regime needs to ensure that when data is gathered, individuals are aware of what data is being gathered, why it is being gathered, and how it will be stored. It needs to ensure that there are standards within the industry to ensure data is accurate, up to date, secure, and fairly processed. Further, it needs to ensure that, if sold or transferred, data remains protected and cannot be sold or transferred for reasons unconnected with its original gathering. Finally, there needs to be an enforcement procedure to ensure that all these things are done and that there is oversight of the industry as a whole.

20.1.1 **The changing face of data protection laws in Europe**

The current oversight and enforcement regime, as applicable in the UK, is to be found in the Data Protection Act 1998. This gives effect in the UK to the Data Protection Directive 1995[9] and the bulk of this chapter will discuss the current regulatory regime. However, readers should be aware that a new regime will come into place at some point in 2018 when the General Data Protection Regulation (GDPR) comes into force. When the Charter of Fundamental Rights of the European Union[10] was agreed in 2000, EU citizens gained a new fundamental right; the right to the protection of their individual personal data.[11] The EU Charter became law in December 2009[12]—the view within the European Commission had been that the current state of data protection law did not meet this fundamental right standard. In their citizen factsheet explaining why reform was necessary the Commission stated that:

> the current rules also need to be modernised—they were introduced when the Internet was still in its infancy. Rapid technological developments and globalisation have brought new challenges for data protection. With social networking sites, cloud computing, location-based services and smart cards, we leave digital traces with every move we make. In this 'brave new data world' we need a robust set of rules. The EU's data protection reform will make sure our rules are future-proof and fit for the digital age.'[13]

They proposed a new General Data Protection Regulation to harmonize and extend our data protection rights into a number of areas which will be discussed below in detail at 20.6.[14] However, the particular strength of the new law is the way it is drafted. As it is a Regulation rather than a Directive it creates a binding regime for all EU member states, removing the fragmentation of approach seen in the application of the Data Protection Directive, where some countries, such as Germany, have developed a strict interpretation of the Directive, whereas others, such as the UK, have developed a more laissez-faire approach. The problem is that in the 21 years since the Directive was promulgated the business of data gathering and processing has changed beyond recognition. The arrival of e-commerce and social network platforms, along with online tracking and

[9] Dir. 95/46/EC.

[10] 2000/C 364/01.

[11] At Art. 8(1).

[12] Although agreed in 2000 the Charter did not become legally binding until the entry into force of the Treaty of Lisbon, in December 2009. See 2012/C 326/02.

[13] <http://ec.europa.eu/justice/data-protection/document/review2012/factsheets/1_en.pdf>.

[14] COM(2012) 11. Finalized as Regulation (EU) No. XXX/2016 of the European Parliament and Council on the protection of individuals with regard to the processing of personal data and on the free movement of such data (General Data Protection Regulation). Text available online at <https://external.neilzone.co.uk/GDPR_compromise_text_indexed.pdf>.

data-gathering technologies, means that an online business, or indeed any business with an online presence is likely to be found to be gathering data in all EU member states simultaneously and thereby likely to be subject to the controls of 28 national data protection regimes and authorities. The driving force behind the Regulation is twofold:

(1) to ensure non-EU companies, such as Tumblr for example, become subject to EU data protection regulation when they target EU citizens; and
(2) to ensure companies established in the EU such as Google (whose European Headquarters are in Dublin) and Facebook (also Dublin) can submit themselves to the supervision of one local supervisory authority and know they are in compliance with EU data protection law across the Union.

The General Data Protection Regulation will become the new law for data protection in the EU in 2018. But as this book is published in 2016, and as a new edition will be due in 2019 it would not be prudent to write this chapter as if the new law were already in place. As a result, discussion of the General Data Protection Regulation will be limited to section 20.6 below where the key provisions of the Regulation will be identified and discussed.

20.2 The Data Protection Act 1998: data and data processing

The Act begins by defining data and personal data. First, we define what data is covered by the Act, then further define if that data is personal data or sensitive personal data and therefore covered by relevant regulatory provisions of the Act.

Highlight Data (Data Protection Act 1998, s. 1(1))

'data' means information which:

(a) is being processed by means of equipment operating automatically in response to instructions given for that purpose,
(b) is recorded with the intention that it should be processed by means of such equipment,
(c) is recorded as part of a relevant filing system or with the intention that it should form part of a relevant filing system,
(d) does not fall within paragraph (a), (b) or (c) but forms part of an accessible record as defined by section 68,
(e) is recorded information held by a public authority and does not fall within any of paragraphs (a) to (d).

The definition in s. 1(1) is derived from the Directive's definition of a 'personal data filing system' as 'any structured set of personal data which are accessible according to specific criteria, whether centralized, decentralized or dispersed on a functional or geographical basis'.[15] The 1998 Act therefore covers data held in manual filing systems as well as digital data. To be covered by the provisions of the Act data has simply to have one of two characteristics: (1) it must be either digital data which is intended to be computer processed; or (2) it is manual data which forms part of a relevant filing system. This means it must be indexed or stored in a fashion which indicates it forms part of an indexed collection of material.[16] If the material held is 'data' for the purposes of the Act, there then follow two further subdivisions.

Personal data is data which:

> relates to a living individual who can be identified (a) from those data, or (b) from those data and other information which is in the possession of, or is likely to come into the possession of, the data controller, and includes any expression of opinion about the individual and any indication of the intentions of the data controller or any other person in respect of the individual.[17]

Understanding personal data is the key to understanding the DPA for it is only the processing of personal data which is regulated. Thus by s. 17 'personal data must not be processed unless an entry in respect of the data controller is included in the register maintained by the Commissioner under section 19', while all the rights awarded to the data subject under Part II (and discussed below) also only apply to personal data. Thus the distinction between data and personal data is key. Only the storage, processing, and transfer of personal data is controlled and regulated.

In addition to personal data the 1998 Act provides additional protection for data known as 'sensitive personal data'. This is defined in s. 2.

Highlight Sensitive personal data

Sensitive personal data is personal data consisting of information as to:

(a) the racial or ethnic origin of the data subject,

(b) his political opinions,

(c) his religious beliefs or other beliefs of a similar nature,

(d) whether he is a member of a trade union,

(e) his physical or mental health or condition,

(f) his sexual life,

(g) the commission or alleged commission by him of any offence, or

(h) any proceedings for any offence committed or alleged to have been committed by him, the disposal of such proceedings or the sentence of any court in such proceedings.

[15] Dir. 95/46/EC, Art. 2(c).

[16] To be precise, s. 1(1) defines a 'relevant filing system' as 'any set of information relating to individuals to the extent that, although the information is not processed by means of equipment operating automatically in response to instructions given for that purpose, the set is structured, either by reference to individuals or by reference to criteria relating to individuals, in such a way that specific information relating to a particular individual is readily accessible'.

[17] DPA 1998, s. 1(1).

The common theme of sensitive personal data is that it is data which may be used to discriminate against an individual. As such, there is a special regime for such data both in the Directive,[18] and the Data Protection Act. The Act applies special conditions to the processing of data of this nature in Sch. 3. These conditions will be discussed below.

As is clear from s. 1(1) a key concept of the Act is data processing. It is referred to in both s. 1(1)(a) and 1(1)(b). Processing is a key term as it is the act of working with the data, and it is this act which usually triggers relevant regulatory provisions of the Act.

Highlight Processing data

Processing, in relation to information or data, means obtaining, recording, or holding the information or data or carrying out any operation or set of operations on the information or data, including:

(a) organisation, adaptation or alteration of the information or data,

(b) retrieval, consultation or use of the information or data,

(c) disclosure of the information or data by transmission, dissemination or otherwise making available, or

(d) alignment, combination, blocking, erasure or destruction of the information or data.

This definition makes it clear that mere consultation of data is a data process. The Act, though, goes further and also defines several other key terms applied throughout the Act. 'Use' is defined alongside 'disclosing' as 'including using or disclosing the information contained in the data'[19] while 'obtaining or recording' are defined as 'including obtaining or recording the information to be contained in the data'.[20] Although these definitions may be criticized as being underdeveloped and somewhat circular, they do assist greatly, in particular with the offence of unlawfully obtaining personal data under s. 55.

The remainder of the structural provisions of the 1998 Act define the personnel of the data protection environment. There are three key persons identified by the Act. Data subjects are defined as 'an individual who is the subject of personal data'; a data controller is 'a person who (either alone or jointly or in common with other persons) determines the purposes for which and the manner in which any personal data are, or are to be, processed'; and a data processor is 'any person (other than an employee of the data controller) who processes the data on behalf of the data controller'.[21] Since data processing is often outsourced to specialist companies, the data controller/data processor distinction allows the Act to control both aspects of data management and processing.

At the heart of the Data Protection Act are the Data Protection Principles. By s. 4(4) 'it shall be the duty of a data controller to comply with the data protection principles

[18] Art. 8 deals with 'special categories of data'. This provides that 'Member States shall prohibit the processing of personal data revealing racial or ethnic origin, political opinions, religious or philosophical beliefs, trade-union membership, and the processing of data concerning health or sex life' except where special provisions as laid out in Art. 8 apply.

[19] DPA 1998, s. 1(2)(b).

[20] DPA 1998, s. 1(2)(a).

[21] All definitions taken from s. 1(1) of the Data Protection Act 1998.

in relation to all personal data with respect to which he is the data controller'. Perhaps somewhat unusually for a set of principles so central to the operation of the Act they are found in Sch. 1.

Highlight The Data Protection Principles

(1) Personal data shall be processed fairly and lawfully and, in particular, shall not be processed unless:

(a) at least one of the conditions in Schedule 2 is met, and

(b) in the case of sensitive personal data, at least one of the conditions in Schedule 3 is also met.

(2) Personal data shall be obtained only for one or more specified and lawful purposes, and shall not be further processed in any manner incompatible with that purpose or those purposes.

(3) Personal data shall be adequate, relevant and not excessive in relation to the purpose or purposes for which they are processed.

(4) Personal data shall be accurate and, where necessary, kept up to date.

(5) Personal data processed for any purpose or purposes shall not be kept for longer than is necessary for that purpose or those purposes.

(6) Personal data shall be processed in accordance with the rights of data subjects under this Act.

(7) Appropriate technical and organisational measures shall be taken against unauthorised or unlawful processing of personal data and against accidental loss or destruction of, or damage to, personal data.

(8) Personal data shall not be transferred to a country or territory outside the European Economic Area unless that country or territory ensures an adequate level of protection for the rights and freedoms of data subjects in relation to the processing of personal data.

Although all of the principles are of equal weight, in many ways the key principle is the first principle. This is the general principle that data processing shall be carried out in a fair and reasonable manner. This is an extremely vague term, which, despite being supported by conditions for the fair processing of data in Schs. 2 and 3 (discussed below), has caused problems for courts in the UK and further afield.

20.2.1 **Processing data**

The first issue is the rather vague term 'processing'. This is defined by the Directive as 'any operation or set of operations which is performed upon personal data, whether or not by automatic means',[22] while the Data Protection Act defines it as 'obtaining, recording, or holding the information or data or carrying out any operation or set of operations on the information or data'.[23] This is potentially a very expansive set which

[22] Dir. 95/46/EC, Art. 2(b).
[23] DPA 1998, s. 1(1).

could cover anything from hardcore data mining of gathered personal data by commercial organizations to individuals mentioning friends and family on personal web pages without permission, or otherwise in accordance with the Directive and Act. Was it really the intent of the Directive to be so widely applied?

The leading case to date on the question of 'processing' in accordance with the Directive is the Swedish case of *Bodil Lindqvist*.[24] Mrs Lindqvist, in addition to her day job as a maintenance worker, worked as a catechist in the parish of Alseda in Sweden. She took a data processing course to allow her to develop an online presence for her church. At the end of 1998, Mrs Lindqvist set up internet pages using her personal computer in order to allow parishioners preparing for their confirmation to obtain information they might need. At her request, the administrator of the Swedish Church's website set up a link between those pages and that site.

The pages in question contained information about Mrs Lindqvist and 18 colleagues in the parish, sometimes including their full names and in other cases only their first names. Mrs Lindqvist also described, in a mildly humorous manner, the jobs held by her colleagues and their hobbies. In many cases family circumstances and telephone numbers and other matters were mentioned. She also stated that one colleague had injured her foot and was on half-time on medical grounds. It was established that Mrs Lindqvist had not informed her colleagues of the existence of those pages or obtained their consent, nor did she notify the Datainspektionen (Swedish supervisory authority for the protection of electronically transmitted data) of her activity. She removed the pages in question as soon as she became aware that they were not appreciated by some of her colleagues.

Mrs Lindqvist was charged by Swedish authorities with breach of the Swedish Data Protection Act on the grounds that she had: (a) processed personal data by automatic means without giving prior written notification to the Datainspektionen; (b) processed sensitive personal data (injured foot and half-time on medical grounds) without authorization; and (c) transferred processed personal data to a third country without authorization. Mrs Lindqvist accepted the facts of the case but challenged that her activities (placing material on a website) did not qualify as 'processing' data under the Directive and thereby the relevant Swedish law. The Swedish Court of Appeal referred the case to the European Court of Justice for their interpretation of the Data Protection Directive.

In a wide-ranging opinion the ECJ found that:

Highlight The Decision of the ECJ in *Bodil Lindqvist*

(1) The act of referring, on an internet page, to various persons and identifying them by name or other means constituted the processing of personal data within the meaning of Art. 3(1).

(2) The processing of personal data such as that described in answer to the first question was not covered by any of the exceptions given in Art. 3(2).

(3) Reference to the fact that a colleague had injured her foot and was on half time on medical grounds constituted personal data concerning health within the meaning of Art. 8(1).

→

[24] [2004] QB 1014 (ECJ).

(4) Personal data which came from a person who had loaded them onto an internet site which then appeared on the computer of a person in a third country were not directly transferred between those two people but through the computer infrastructure of the hosting provider where the page was stored. Thus, operations such as those carried out by Lindqvist did not constitute a transfer of data to a third country within the meaning of Art. 25.

(5) The provisions of the Directive did not, in themselves, bring about restrictions which conflicted with the right to freedom of expression. It was for the national courts responsible for applying implementing legislation to ensure a fair balance between the rights and interests in question.

(6) Nothing prevented Member States from extending the scope of national legislation implementing the Directive to areas not included in the scope thereof provided that no other provision of Community law precluded it.

This clearly gives an extremely expansive interpretation of 'processing'. Even the simplest act of placing information on a personal website qualifies. This makes the interpretation of 'fairness' of paramount importance, as only when data is processed 'fairly and lawfully' is the first data protection principle met.

More recently the CJEU has returned to this issue in the case of *Ryneš v Úřad pro ochranu osobních údajů*.[25] Mr Ryneš had installed a CCTV camera on the exterior of his house, which recorded movements not only on his private property, but also the public footpath outside. He said he installed the camera to protect his family and his property, as there had been previous vandalism to his property. After the installation of the CCTV, his house windows were broken once more. The CCTV footage was used to identify two individuals, one of whom questioned whether the use of the CCTV system was permissible under the Czech data protection law. Mr Ryneš argued that the 'domestic processing exception' found in Art. 3(2) of the Directive applied.

The Czech court referred this question to the CJEU, asking: 'Can the operation of a camera system installed on a family home for the purposes of the protection of the property, health and life of the owners of the home be classified as the processing of personal data "by a natural person in the course of a purely personal or household activity" within the meaning of Article 3(2) of Directive 95/46/EC, even though such a system monitors also a public space?'[26] The court first clarified that the capture of an identifiable image of a person on a CCTV system is personal data within the definition of the Directive.[27] It then clarified that 'surveillance in the form of a video recording of persons, as in the case before the referring court, which is stored on a continuous recording device—the hard disk drive—constitutes, pursuant to Article 3(1) of Directive 95/46, the automatic processing of personal data.'[28] This just left the question of whether Mr Ryneš was covered by the domestic processing exception. The court noted that the decision

[25] C-212/13 11 December 2014 <http://curia.europa.eu/juris/liste.jsf?num=C-212/13>.
[26] Ibid. [18].
[27] Ibid. [22].
[28] Ibid. [25].

in *Google Spain SL and Google Inc. v AEPD*,[29] provided that 'the protection of the fundamental right to private life guaranteed under Article 7 of the Charter of Fundamental Rights of the European Union (the Charter) requires that derogations and limitations in relation to the protection of personal data must apply only in so far as is strictly necessary.'[30] As a result the court found:

> The processing of personal data comes within the exception provided for in the second indent of Article 3(2) of Directive 95/46 only where it is carried out in the purely personal or household setting of the person processing the data. Accordingly, so far as natural persons are concerned, correspondence and the keeping of address books constitute, in the light of recital 12 to Directive 95/46, a 'purely personal or household activity' even if they incidentally concern or may concern the private life of other persons. To the extent that video surveillance such as that at issue in the main proceedings covers, even partially, a public space and is accordingly directed outwards from the private setting of the person processing the data in that manner, it cannot be regarded as an activity which is a purely 'personal or household' activity for the purposes of the second indent of Article 3(2) of Directive 95/46.[31]

The court, as in *Bodil Lindqvist*, ultimately applied an extremely strict interpretation of the domestic processing exemption. This is possibly because Art. 3(2) says it only applies to 'a *purely* personal or household activity'. One other thing to note is that the court did find that the domestic court was correct not to fine Mr Ryneš as 'the application of Directive 95/46 makes it possible, where appropriate, to take into account—in accordance, in particular, with Articles 7(f), 11(2), and 13(1)(d) and (g) of that directive—legitimate interests pursued by the controller, such as the protection of the property, health and life of his family and himself, as in the case in the main proceedings.'[32]

The leading UK case on fairness is *Johnson v Medical Defence Union Ltd.*[33] The claimant, Mr Johnson, was a consultant orthopaedic surgeon with over 20 years' clinical experience. He was, from 1980, a member of the Medical Defence Union (MDU), a mutual society which provides advice and professional liability insurance cover to its members. He was reported as having 'never been the subject of a claim for alleged professional negligence'.[34] However, it was reported that 'over the years he [had] sought advice and assistance from the MDU in relation to professional questions and problems that concerned him, including complaints made against him. His contact with the MDU, and that from others about him, gave rise to the opening at least since 1991 of 17 MDU files.'[35]

As a result of a review of their files the MDU wrote to Mr Johnson in January 2002 informing him they would not renew his membership at the end of his current subscription. The letter gave no reasons. Mr Johnson sought the reasons, but none were provided. He claims he suffered damage to his professional reputation and financial loss because of the MDU's actions. He made a claim under s. 13 of the Data Protection Act 1998 seeking compensation for unfair processing of his personal data.

[29] Case C-131/12 13 May 2014. Discussed in depth below at 20.5.4.
[30] *Ryneš*, see (n. 25) [28].
[31] Ibid. [31]–[33].
[32] Ibid. [34].
[33] [2007] EWCA Civ 262.
[34] Ibid. [2].
[35] Ibid.

At an initial hearing before Rimer J in 2006 all of Mr Johnson's claims were dismissed.[36] In particular he found that:

> [The MDU's risk policy] was formulated against the background of a contractual relationship between the MDU and its members under which the MDU had and has an absolute discretion to terminate a member's membership and in which it was in the interests of all members that it should have a sound risk assessment policy. There might be legitimate scope for disagreement between those competent to judge these things as to whether the MDU risk assessment policy was sound or otherwise, or as to whether it could be improved. But I have no reason to believe that it was arrived at other than after proper consideration and that it was regarded as other than the most appropriate policy for the needs of the MDU . . . The MDU could process his data in the circumstances in which it did perfectly fairly without his [Mr Johnson's] input, and the evidence from the MDU witnesses satisfied me that his input would be unlikely to have made any difference to the assessment of his case: because, put shortly, the policy regards a member's input as essentially irrelevant.[37]

Therefore, according to Rimer J, Mr Johnson's suggestion that he 'was entitled to have his data processed and case considered by reference to his own inexpert assertions as to the risk assessment policy that the MDU should apply' should be rejected.[38]

Mr Johnson appealed. His appeal was based on the foundation that the MDU's policy was flawed. In particular, he believed two flaws led to his personal data held by the MDU being processed unfairly. The first was that the MDU's policy of assessing members according to number of incidents or complaints rather than according to their outcome meant he was penalized, and second, because of that policy, the risk assessment review process used by the MDU did not allow any explanation by the member of the various incidents reported to it.

On 28 March 2007 the Court of Appeal dismissed Mr Johnson's claim. They held that the MDU's processing of Mr Johnson's personal data for the purpose of conducting a risk assessment review was, in relation to all but two of the files in question, fair and lawful under the Act, and dismissed Mr Johnson's claim for compensation. Arden LJ noted that 'Mr Johnson gave his consent to the processing of personal data for a number of purposes, including risk management. The directive requires consent to be unambiguous (Article 7). However, in my judgment, Mr Johnson did not have to know the nature of the MDU's risk assessment policy to give a valid consent for this purpose.'[39] She went on to note:

> the judge [Rimer J] did not accept Mr Johnson's submission, either in relation to the lead files or the non-lead files, that the MDU had an obligation to consult Mr Johnson about the processing exercise or to invite his representations upon it. In my judgment the judge was right to hold that the fairness principle did not require this. As a general proposition a party to a contract cannot in my judgment use the fairness principle as a means of upsetting any contractually permitted use of information where, as here, processing was foreseeable. I see no basis for displacing this general proposition in this case.[40]

The unfair processing of the remaining two files was held not to have caused damage to Mr Johnson. The court paid particular regard to the fact that Mr Johnson had signed up

[36] *Johnson v The Medical Defence Union Ltd* [2006] EWHC 321 (Ch).
[37] Ibid. [110].
[38] Ibid. [202].
[39] [2007] EWCA Civ 262 [145].
[40] Ibid. [148]–[149].

to the MDU's risk assessment policy and agreed to the processing of his personal data for this purpose, and the court held that the review was carried out within the terms of this policy. In terms of compensation, the court held that even if Mr Johnson had shown there to be a breach of the Data Protection Act, there is nothing within the Act that would give him the right to compensation for a general loss of reputation. The court noted that a defamation claim would be a more appropriate course of action for this, and that, had the MDU breached the Data Protection Act in processing Mr Johnson's personal data, he would have been able to claim for losses and distress 'by reason of a data controller's contravention of the Data Protection Act'.[41]

More recently, the Court of Appeal has revisited this question in the case of *Google Inc. v Vidal-Hall*.[42] The case concerned the operation by Google of what has become known as the 'Safari workaround'. The Safari browser has default privacy settings which block third-party cookies, including the Google's DoubleClick ID Cookie. However, it was alleged that Google took advantage of exceptions in the Safari settings to install a cookie on the users' computer without their permission. This cookie allowed Google to identify Miss Vidal-Hall (and others) via her/their browser which allowed Google to profile them for DoubleClick advertising. As was reported by the court 'the tracking and collation of the claimants' browser generated information was contrary to the defendant's publicly stated position that such activity could not be conducted for Safari users unless they had expressly allowed it to happen.'[43] Miss Vidal-Hall and two others brought claims for misuse of private information, breach of confidence, and breach of the Data Protection Act.

As the claimants are based in England and as Google is a Delaware corporation with its head office in California, permission had to be sought to serve proceedings outside the jurisdiction of England and Wales. In the High Court Tugendhat J allowed permission finding that 'in respect of the claims for misuse of private information and under the Data Protection Act the court had jurisdiction to try both claims. He concluded that the claimants had clearly established that this jurisdiction was the appropriate one in which to try both claims.'[44] Google appealed and raised four issues: (1) that misuse of private information is not a tort; (2) that under s. 13 of the Data Protection Act there cannot be a claim for compensation without pecuniary loss; (3) that it was not a triable issue whether browser generated information was personal data; and (4) in relation to the claims for misuse of private information and under the Data Protection Act there was no real and substantial cause of action.

In many ways the first of these is the most important but it is not a specifically data protection issue so we will not dwell upon it except to say that the court found:

> We cannot find any satisfactory or principled answer to the question why misuse of private information should not be categorised as a tort for the purposes of service out of the jurisdiction. Misuse of private information is a civil wrong without any equitable characteristics. We do not need to attempt to define a tort here. But if one puts aside the circumstances of its 'birth', there is nothing in the nature of the claim itself to suggest that the more natural classification of it as a tort is wrong . . . in the absence of any sound reasons of policy or principle

[41] Ibid. [72].
[42] [2015] EWCA Civ 311.
[43] Ibid. [3].
[44] Ibid. [12].

> to suggest otherwise, we have concluded in agreement with the judge that misuse of private information should now be recognised as a tort for the purposes of service out the jurisdiction. This does not create a new cause of action. In our view, it simply gives the correct legal label to one that already exists. We are conscious of the fact that there may be broader implications from our conclusions, for example as to remedies, limitation and vicarious liability, but these were not the subject of submissions, and such points will need to be considered as and when they arise.[45]

This is a very important decision in itself. It indicates that where an abuse of personal data occurs one need not rely upon data protection principles and the Data Protection Directive/Act. There is a separate head of claim for the tort of misuse of private data. Next came the vital decision, could a s. 13 claim be brought where there was no claim for pecuniary loss? In *Johnson* the Court of Appeal had stated that as the claimant had not proved pecuniary loss he could not claim to have suffered damage within the meaning of s. 13(1). However, the court noted that 'it is plain that his (Buxton LJ's) conclusion on the compensation issue was not necessary for his determination of the appeal'.[46] It therefore concludes that 'what was said in *Johnson v MDU* as to the proper interpretation of section 13 of the DPA was obiter dicta and not binding on this court'.[47] With *Johnson* safely distinguished the court turned its attention to the question of s. 13, allowed claims for a non-pecuniary loss. The court noted that 'since what the Directive purports to protect is privacy rather than economic rights, it would be strange if the Directive could not compensate those individuals whose data privacy had been invaded by a data controller so as to cause them emotional distress (but not pecuniary damage)'[48] and found support for this proposition from the decision of the ECJ in *Leitner v TUI Deutschland GmbhH & Co. KG*[49] which found that: 'in the construction of a different directive, namely Directive 90/314/EEC on package travel. The ECJ held that article 5 of that directive, which referred to compensation for "damage" resulting from a failure to perform or the improper performance of a package holiday contract, conferred a right to compensation for non-material damage.'[50] However, the court went on to hold that:

> on a literal interpretation of section 13(2), an individual who suffers distress by reason of a contravention by a data controller of any of the requirements of the DPA is entitled to compensation only if (i) he also suffers pecuniary or material loss by reason of the contravention or (ii) the contravention relates to the processing of personal data for the 'special purposes' (journalism, artistic or literary purposes). It is common ground that none of the claimants in the present proceedings can satisfy the conditions of section 13(2). They are not even able to establish an entitlement to nominal damages which would be sufficient to satisfy section 13(2)(a); and the alleged contraventions in their cases do not relate to the processing of personal data for any of the special purposes.[51]

This means, in the view of the court, that s. 13(2) is incompatible with its construction of Art. 23 of the Directive. However, the court was not in a position to interpret s. 13(2)

[45] Ibid. [43], [51].
[46] Ibid. [67].
[47] Ibid. [68].
[48] Ibid. [7].
[49] [2002] ECR 1-1631.
[50] [2015] EWCA Civ 311 [73].
[51] Ibid. [83].

as compatible with Art. 23 under the *Marleasing* principle[52] as 'the court cannot invoke the Marleasing principle to adopt a meaning which is "inconsistent with a fundamental feature of the legislation"'.[53] The court expressed what can best be described as confusion surrounding why s. 13(2) was clearly narrower than Art. 23:

> In view of the importance to the DPA scheme as a whole of the provisions for compensation in the event of any contravention by a data controller, the limits set by Parliament to the right to compensation are a fundamental feature of the legislation. If we knew why Parliament had decided to restrict the right to compensation for distress in the way that it did, it would be impossible for the court, under the guise of interpretation, to subvert Parliament's clear intention. The court would, in effect, be legislating against the clearly expressed intention of Parliament on an issue that was central to the scheme as whole. We do not consider that it can make any difference that we do not know why Parliament decided to restrict the right to compensation in this way. It is sufficient that, for whatever reason, Parliament decided not to permit compensation for distress in all cases. Instead, it produced a carefully calibrated scheme which permits compensation for distress but only in certain tightly defined circumstances.[54]

As a result the only option open to the claimants would be for them to sue the state for failure to apply the Directive correctly.

This, however, was not the end of this issue. The court then considered whether s. 13(2) should be disapplied in so far as it is incompatible with Art. 23 of the Directive. This is possible according to the principles articulated by the Court of Appeal in *Benkharbouche and Janah v Embassy of Sudan & Ors*.[55] The court noted that:

> as this court stated in *Benkharbouche* (i) where there is a breach of a right afforded under EU law, article 47 of the Charter is engaged; (ii) the right to an effective remedy for breach of EU law rights provided for by article 47 embodies a general principle of EU law; (iii) (subject to exceptions which have no application in the present case) that general principle has horizontal effect; (iv) in so far as a provision of national law conflicts with the requirement for an effective remedy in article 47, the domestic courts can and must disapply the conflicting provision; and (v) the only exception to (iv) is that the court may be required to apply a conflicting domestic provision where the court would otherwise have to redesign the fabric of the legislative scheme.[56]

Counsel for the respondents argued that 'the court cannot devise a legislative scheme which differs from that enacted by Parliament. That is a matter for Parliament'.[57] However, the court found that they would not be 'devising a legislative scheme'; rather, just disapplying an incompatible provision of domestic law. 'What is required in order to make section 13(2) compatible with EU law is the disapplication of section 13(2), no more and no less. The consequence of this would be that compensation would be recoverable under section 13(1) for any damage suffered as a result of a contravention by a data controller of any of the requirements of the DPA. No legislative choices have

[52] The principle that the courts of member states should interpret national law enacted for the purpose of transposing an EU Directive into its law, so far as possible, in the light of the wording and the purpose of the Directive in order to achieve the result sought by the Directive. From *Marleasing SA v La Comercial Internacional de Alimentacion SA* [1990] ECR I-04135.

[53] [2015] EWCA Civ 311 [88] citing Lord Nicholls in *Ghaidan v Godin-Mendoza* [2004] 2 AC 557.

[54] Ibid. [93].

[55] [2015] EWCA Civ 33.

[56] [2015] EWCA Civ 311 [98].

[57] Ibid. [102].

to be made by the court.'[58] As a result the court was willing to hold that s. 13(2) could be disappplied in this fashion under the *Benkharbouche* principle.

Having made these decisions, the court quickly disposed of the remaining two questions. By following the advice from the Art. 29 Working Party that 'In general terms, a natural person can be considered as "identified" when, within a group of persons, he or she is "distinguished" from all other members of the group. Accordingly, the natural person is "identifiable" when, although the person has not been identified yet, it is possible to do it',[59] the court found that 'we think the case that the [browser generated information] constitutes personal data under section 1(1)(a) of the DPA is clearly arguable: it is supported by the terms of the Directive, as explained in the Working Party's Opinion, and the decision of the ECJ in Lindqvist.'[60] Finally, the court found that the claimants had a real and substantial cause of action: 'compensatory damages may be relatively modest (as they often are in claims for misuse of private information and for breaches of the DPA) albeit that there is also a claim for aggravated damages in the present case . . . But that is not the beginning or end of the matter. As Mr Tomlinson says, the damages may be small, but the issues of principle are large.'[61]

The substantive issues in this case remain to be tried. This is only a procedural hearing to determine whether it was possible to serve an order of proceedings out of jurisdiction and whether there is a prima facie claim. The High Court and the Court of Appeal have both said yes. At the time of writing the latest development in the case is that the Supreme Court has agreed to hear an appeal on two grounds. The appellant (Google) had raised three claims: (1) Whether the Court of Appeal was right to hold the claimant's claims for misuse of private information are claims made in tort for the purposes of the rules relating to service out of the jurisdiction; (2) Whether the Court of Appeal was right to hold that s. 13(2) of the Data Protection Act 1998 was incompatible with Art. 23 of the Directive; and (3) Whether the Court of Appeal was right to disapply s. 13(2) of the Data Protection Act 1998 on the grounds that it conflicts with the rights guaranteed by Arts. 7 and 8 of the EU Charter of Fundamental Rights. The Supreme Court ruled that 'permission to appeal be refused on ground one (the issue whether the claim is in tort) because this ground does not raise an arguable point of law'. However, it allowed appeals to be taken on the other two grounds.[62] The appeal will no doubt be heard in 2016 at which point a reference to the CJEU is likely. This means it is likely to be late 2017 before we get the final word on these procedural issues before a substantive hearing can even begin. *Vidal-Hall* is unlikely to be disposed of completely before the current law it is disputing is replaced with the new legal framework of the General Data Protection Regulation.

What is apparent from all these cases is the complexity of processing in accordance with the regulatory provisions. Mrs Lindqvist appeared to be engaged in an innocent activity, which she no doubt felt was a private matter. Likewise, Mr Ryneš believed he was processing for a private purpose and for the protection of his property. Both, however, fell foul of the law as their actions went further than their domestic purposes

[58] Ibid. [105].
[59] Opinion 4/2007.
[60] [2015] EWCA Civ 311 [115].
[61] Ibid. [139].
[62] <https://www.supremecourt.uk/news/permission-to-appeal-decisions-28-july-2015.html>.

and had potential to impact on the data privacy of others. By comparison, The Medical Defence Union was involved in high-level data processing with the potential to affect adversely the professional career of Mr Johnson and others who were subject to its risk assessment review, while Google appear to be aware that their 'Safari workaround' was leading them into uncharted legal waters. Ultimately, though, we know that Mrs Lindqvist's actions were in breach of the Swedish Data Protection law (and the Directive) while Mr Ryneš' actions were similarly in breach of Czech data protection law (and the Directive). At the same time, the actions of the MDU were fair, while Google's remain mired in the mists of the detail of EU and UK data protection law. How can a data controller process data with confidence given the complexity of the first data protection principle?

20.3 **Conditions for the processing of personal data**

To assist data controllers in fulfilling the First Principle Schs. 2 and 3 list conditions in which the principle is met. Schedule 2 states that personal data processing should only take place when:

Highlight Conditions which allow the processing of data

1. The data subject has given his consent to the processing.
2. The processing is necessary:
   (a) for the performance of a contract to which the data subject is a party, or
   (b) for the taking of steps at the request of the data subject with a view to entering into a contract.
3. The processing is necessary for compliance with any legal obligation to which the data controller is subject, other than an obligation imposed by contract.
4. The processing is necessary in order to protect the vital interests of the data subject.
5. The processing is necessary:
   (a) for the administration of justice,
   (aa) for the exercise of any functions of either House of Parliament,
   (b) for the exercise of any functions conferred on any person by or under any enactment,
   (c) for the exercise of any functions of the Crown, a Minister of the Crown or a government department, or
   (d) for the exercise of any other functions of a public nature exercised in the public interest by any person.
6. The processing is necessary for the purposes of legitimate interests pursued by the data controller or by the third party or parties to whom the data are disclosed, except where the processing is unwarranted in any particular case by reason of prejudice to the rights and freedoms or legitimate interests of the data subject.

In cases of sensitive personal data Sch. 3 is applied instead. This states that the processing of sensitive personal data should only take place on one or more of the following occasions:

Highlight Conditions which allow the processing of sensitive personal data

1. The data subject has given his explicit consent to the processing of the personal data.
2. The processing is necessary for the purposes of exercising or performing any right or obligation which is conferred or imposed by law on the data controller in connection with employment.
3. The processing is necessary:
   (a) in order to protect the vital interests of the data subject or another person, in a case where:
      (i) consent cannot be given by or on behalf of the data subject, or
      (ii) the data controller cannot reasonably be expected to obtain the consent of the data subject, or
   (b) in order to protect the vital interests of another person, in a case where consent by or on behalf of the data subject has been unreasonably withheld.
4. The processing:
   (a) is carried out in the course of its legitimate activities by any body or association which:
      (i) is not established or conducted for profit, and
      (ii) exists for political, philosophical, religious or trade-union purposes,
   (b) is carried out with appropriate safeguards for the rights and freedoms of data subjects,
   (c) relates only to individuals who either are members of the body or association or have regular contact with it in connection with its purposes, and
   (d) does not involve disclosure of the personal data to a third party without the consent of the data subject.
5. The information contained in the personal data has been made public as a result of steps deliberately taken by the data subject.
6. The processing:
   (a) is necessary for the purpose of, or in connection with, any legal proceedings (including prospective legal proceedings),
   (b) is necessary for the purpose of obtaining legal advice, or
   (c) is otherwise necessary for the purposes of establishing, exercising or defending legal rights.
7. The processing is necessary:
   (a) for the administration of justice,
   (aa) for the exercise of any functions of either House of Parliament

→

→

(b) for the exercise of any functions conferred on any person by or under an enactment, or

(c) for the exercise of any functions of the Crown, a Minister of the Crown or a government department.

8. The processing is necessary for medical purposes and is undertaken by:

   (a) a health professional, or

   (b) a person who in the circumstances owes a duty of confidentiality which is equivalent to that which would arise if that person were a health professional. In this paragraph 'medical purposes' includes the purposes of preventative medicine, medical diagnosis, medical research, the provision of care and treatment and the management of healthcare services.

9. The processing:

   (a) is of sensitive personal data consisting of information as to racial or ethnic origin,

   (b) is necessary for the purpose of identifying or keeping under review the existence or absence of equality of opportunity or treatment between persons of different racial or ethnic origins, with a view to enabling such equality to be promoted or maintained, and

   (c) is carried out with appropriate safeguards for the rights and freedoms of data subjects.

10. The personal data are processed in circumstances specified in an order made by the [Secretary of State] for the purposes of this paragraph.

20.3.1 **Consent**

Most commonly, data is processed according to the first condition of processing data. That is, 'The data subject has given his consent to the processing' or for sensitive personal data; 'The data subject has given his *explicit* consent to the processing of the personal data.' What in practice does this mean?

We are all familiar with the opt-in and opt-out boxes frequently used by data controllers at the point where they gather the data. Is the provision of an opt-out box sufficient to qualify as consent? What about explicit consent for sensitive personal data? Such boxes are commonplace; often with both being used in quick succession such as tick to opt in to receive data from us and tick to opt out to our passing data on to third parties. The extensive use of such boxes is enough to tell us that broadly they comply with the first condition (at least for personal data), but there are some limits to their use.

The first thing to note is that neither 'consent' nor 'explicit consent' are defined by the Act. This means in applying these terms courts will as usual refer to the ordinary usage of the terms and, as the Data Protection Act is derivative of the Directive, to the Directive where appropriate. The term consent is defined in the *OED* as to 'give permission, express willingness or agree' while 'explicit' is defined as 'leaving nothing merely implied'. Applying these definitions, it appears that consent may be given by means of an opt-out box remaining unchecked since, by not recording dissent, permission, willingness, or agreement may be applied. Explicit consent though would appear to require some form of positive indication of consent so as to avoid any implication being required to be drawn.

This suggests opt-in boxes are okay but opt-out boxes are not when dealing with sensitive personal data. This interpretation is supported by Art. 2(h) of the Directive which states 'the data subject's consent shall mean any freely given specific and informed indication of his wishes by which the data subject signifies his agreement to personal data relating to him being processed'. The only potential difficulty is the question of the use of the term 'informed' in Art. 2(h). Informed consent is slightly different to consent and suggests the data subject is given rather more information than is found in a standard opt-out or opt-in box. It is noticeable that the word 'informed' did not make it into either Sch. 2 or Sch. 3. This position is further clouded by an opinion issued by the Article 29 Working Party (an independent review body set up under Art. 29 of the Directive). In an opinion issued in 2004 on 'unsolicited communications for marketing purposes' (spam) and the application of the Privacy and Electronic Communications Directive,[63] the Working Party found that:

> Consent given on the occasion of the general acceptance of the terms and conditions governing the possible main contract (e.g., a subscription contract, in which consent is also sought to send communications for direct marketing purposes) must respect the requirements in Directive 95/46/EC, that is, be informed, specific and freely given. Provided that these latter conditions are met, consent might be given by the data subject for instance, through the ticking of a box.
>
> Implied consent to receive such mails is not compatible with the definition of consent of Directive 95/46/EC and in particular with the requirement of consent being the indication of someone's wishes, including where this would be done 'unless opposition is made' (opt-out). Similarly, pre-ticked boxes, e.g., on websites are not compatible with the definition of the Directive either.

This suggests opt-out boxes are not compatible with the Directive at any level, but as this decision relates to a reference under the Privacy and Electronic Communications Directive and as Working Party opinions are advisory not adjudicatory this opinion is of no direct effect on the continued use of opt-out boxes. The opinion of the Working Party has recently been upheld by the County Court in the unreported spam case of *Mansfield v John Lewis Partnership*.[64] The court held that for the purposes of Art. 13(1) of the Directive on Privacy and Electronic Communications an opt-out box was not sufficient to give *prior explicit* consent. Again, although this is not directly applicable to the Data Protection Act, it suggests the continued use of opt-out boxes is inadvisable. At the very least, if an opt-out box is used, it must be sufficiently prominent and must explain to what use your data will be put in order to be effective. Even then, the decision in *Mansfield*, while not binding as a County Court decision, sows doubt on the practice.

Once your consent is given, the data controller may fairly process the data in accordance with the first condition of data processing, but it should be noted that consent is not permanent. The data subject may withdraw consent at any time. Curiously, despite the face that this is not directly specified in the Directive or the Act, ss. 10 and 11 allow the data subject to prevent processing for the purpose of direct marketing or where the processing may cause damage or distress and Art. 9 of the Directive on Privacy and

[63] Dir. 2002/58/EC.

[64] Discussed in ch. 6 at 6.6.4.

Electronic Communications allows consent to be withdrawn at any time in relation to the processing of location data. However, consent is only one of a number of 'fair processing' conditions. Both Schs. 2 and 3 list a number of such conditions which may allow processing without the consent of the data subject.

Most of the conditions set out in Sch. 2 are to allow for the usual functioning of pre-existing legal obligations, such as the right to process to conclude or perform a contract, or the right to process to comply with a legal obligation, or in the administration of justice. Two interesting conditions are condition 4: processing in the vital interests of the data subject, and condition 6: processing necessary for the purposes of legitimate interests pursued by the data controller. It is difficult to explain with any certainty when either of these conditions is fulfilled given the rather generic nature of these conditions. One can imagine that condition 4 may be fulfilled by a financial institution or employer who is taking steps to protect the data subject from fraud or identity theft. Thus, credit and debit card companies routinely monitor card transactions for evidence that a card has been cloned or stolen. This may qualify under condition 4. Condition 6 is more difficult to pin down. While the Act states that 'The Secretary of State may by order specify particular circumstances in which this condition is, or is not, to be taken to be satisfied',[65] to date no such order has been made. It is hard to imagine what form of processing may be *necessary* for the purposes of legitimate interests pursued by the data controller rather than merely convenient or expedient. As Professor Lloyd observes '[a] lthough many situations may be identified in which it will be useful for the data controller to hold information, the restrictions associated with the adjective "necessary" must constantly be borne in mind.'[66]

20.3.2 **Processing sensitive personal data**

The conditions found in Sch. 3, are by comparison more focused upon the type of data which is classified as sensitive personal data. Thus, we find processing in relation to employment, processing carried out by trade unions and religious organizations, processing for medical purposes, and processing for the purposes of racial or ethnic monitoring are permitted alongside the usual conditions in favour of processing in the administration of justice and for carrying on the duties of the Crown.

The most interesting conditions in Sch. 3 are condition 3: 'The processing is necessary in order to protect the vital interests of the data subject or another person, in a case where consent cannot be given by or on behalf of the data subject, or the data controller cannot reasonably be expected to obtain the consent of the data subject, or in order to protect the vital interests of another person, in a case where consent by or on behalf of the data subject has been unreasonably withheld'; and condition 10: 'The personal data are processed in circumstances specified in an order made by the Secretary of State.'

Condition 3 will probably be applied in emergency medical situations such as where the data subject is unconscious and medical personnel need to consult their medical records or take a medical history from relatives. It would also extend to consulting the data subjects records where that was necessary to treat a third party,

[65] Sch. 6, para. 6(2).

[66] I Lloyd, *Information Technology Law* (7th edn, OUP 2014) 97.

perhaps where the third party appears to have contacted a transmittable disease from the data subject and the data subject is unreasonably refusing to allow them access to his records.

Condition 10 allows for further conditions which allow sensitive personal data to be processed without the consent of the data subject. It has been used to pass no fewer than five orders which extend the conditions in which sensitive personal data may be processed. The most extensive of the five is the Data Protection (Processing of Sensitive Personal Data) Order 2000.[67] This Order adds no fewer than eight additional conditions which allow for the processing of sensitive personal data:

(1) for the prevention and detection of an unlawful act;

(2) to protect against malpractice or misfeasance;

(3) to allow for counselling advice and support;

(4) for the carrying on of insurance and pensions business;

(5) for equal opportunities monitoring including monitoring of religious discrimination and discrimination on health grounds;

(6) for monitoring of political opinion by political parties;

(7) for research purposes; and

(8) 'where processing is necessary for the exercise of any functions conferred on a constable by any rule of law'.

A further extension was provided by the Data Protection (Processing of Sensitive Personal Data) (Elected Representatives) Order 2002.[68] This provides that elected representatives[69] may process sensitive personal data in order to fulfil their function as elected representatives, while the Data Protection (Processing of Sensitive Personal Data) Order 2006[70] extends the grounds still further to allow processing of data relating to payment cards for the purposes of 'administering or cancelling' that card when it has been used in the commission of an offence involving indecent photographs or pseudo-photographs of children. The idea behind this provision is to allow law enforcement authorities to be able to inform card issuers that the card has been used in the commission of an offence, thereby allowing the card issuer to cancel the data subject's account. The intent is to make it more difficult for the data subject to be able to use a payment card to obtain harmful materials in future.[71] More recently, two further orders have extended greater processing rights. The Data Protection (Processing of Sensitive Personal Data) Order 2009[72] allows for processing of information about a prisoner, including information relating to the prisoner's release from prison, for the purpose of informing a Member of Parliament about the prisoner and arrangements for the prisoner's release. This allows the Ministry of Justice to inform MPs, subject to conditions

[67] SI 2000/417.

[68] SI 2002/2905.

[69] Being MPs, MSPs, UK MEPs, Members of the Welsh and Northern Irish Assemblies, Local Authority Councillors, Elected Mayors, and Members of the London Assembly and Common Council of the City of London.

[70] SI 2006/2068.

[71] See Explanatory Memorandum to the Data Protection (Processing of Sensitive Personal Data) Order 2006: <http://www.opsi.gov.uk/si/em2006/uksiem_20062068_en.pdf>.

[72] SI 2009/1811.

of confidentiality, about details of high-risk offenders who have been released into their constituency. The most recent order, to date, is the Data Protection (Processing of Sensitive Personal Data) Order 2012.[73] This is a specialist Order allowing for disclosure data relating to the Hillsborough Stadium disaster to allow the Hillsborough Independent Panel to carry out their inquiry.

What is clear is that the protections afforded by the data protection principles are limited. Processing may take place for any number of conditions listed in Schs. 2 and 3 without the consent of the data subject, and the government may at any time extend these conditions by Statutory Instrument. Although the data protection principles provide a framework that says processing is fair and reasonable, and although they require data to be kept secure and up to date, the true means of scrutiny and supervision of data controllers are to be found elsewhere in the Data Protection Act.

20.3.3 **Exporting personal data**

One issue not often considered by lawyers, but often by data controllers, was the effect of Art. 25 of the Data Protection Directive: 'Member States shall provide that the transfer to a third country of personal data which are undergoing processing or are intended for processing after transfer may take place only if, without prejudice to compliance with the national provisions adopted pursuant to the other provisions of this Directive, the third country in question ensures an adequate level of protection', as given effect by data protection principle 8: 'Personal data shall not be transferred to a country or territory outside the European Economic Area unless that country or territory ensures an adequate level of protection for the rights and freedoms of data subjects in relation to the processing of personal data.' The reasoning behind the Article and Principle are clear; without some form of transfer limitation, unscrupulous data controllers could simply export data to a state which offers a lower level of protection to data subjects for processing, and then transfer the results back into the EU for action. This is particularly easily done online where the whole process may appear to the end user to be instantaneous.

In order to comply with Art. 25, and to be able to continue to trade in an unhindered fashion with EU states, a number of countries have adopted data protection laws and principles which meet with Art. 25.[74] One particular sticking point over the years has been data exportation to the United States. The United States takes a philosophically different view to the EU on how data protection should be effected. Whereas the EU supports a holistic, rights-based approach which protects all data of the data subject, the United States favours a sectoral and self-regulatory approach.[75] To allow for the free flow of data from the EU to the United States a legal fiction was created. The fiction created was called the safe harbour agreement and was a negotiated trade settlement between the EU Commission and the US Department of Commerce. In essence, the safe harbour

[73] SI 2012/1978.

[74] See e.g. Article 29 Working Party, Opinion 6/2009 on the level of protection of personal data in Israel or Article 29 Working Party, Opinion 11/2011 on the level of protection of personal data in New Zealand.

[75] G Steinke, 'Data Privacy Approaches from US and EU Perspectives' (2002) 19 *Telematics and Informatics* 193; LB Movius and N Krup, 'US and EU Privacy Policy: Comparison of Regulatory Approaches' (2009) 3 *International Journal of Communication* 169.

decision[76] allowed US-based companies to self-certify that their data processing practices met EU standards. They then have to register this self-certification in a recognized safe harbour scheme which is monitored or regulated by an independent statutory body which can protect personal privacy effectively and has jurisdiction to investigate complaints. The Department of Commerce and the Federal Trade Commission regulate the primary scheme, although there are smaller specialist ones such as an air carrier scheme operated by the Department of Transportation. This scheme is actually a legal fiction since the United States does not meet EU data protection principles. However, it was an effective fiction which allowed for the massive volumes of international transfers of data between the EU and the US; transfers which are the lifeblood of technology companies such as Apple, Facebook, Google, and Microsoft.

However, in summer 2013 the Snowden revelations threatened to undermine the safe harbour agreement. Among the many revelations in the Snowden documents, discussed in full in chapter 21, was the exposure of a programme known as Prism. Prism is a large-scale state data-gathering programme in which the US National Security Agency gathers and stores large volumes of internet communications data from technology and telecommunications companies based in the United States, such as Google, Microsoft, Facebook, and Apple. The data is requested under a warrant obtained under the FISA Amendments Act of 2008.[77] The disclosure of the Prism programme suggested the safe harbour agreement was unable to provide the level of protection needed to meet the requirements of Art. 25 because, although other EU states, including the UK, have parallel data-gathering programmes at state level, the EU member states are bound by the principles of the EU Charter, whereas the United States Federal Government is not.

One man who took this view was Maximilian Schrems, an Austrian privacy activist and founder of civil society group Europe v Facebook.[78] He had been campaigning against Facebook's data-gathering programme before the Snowden revelations. He first became interested in Facebook's data privacy programme when studying law during a semester abroad at Santa Clara University in Silicon Valley. It is reported that Schrems decided to write a paper on Facebook's lack of awareness of European privacy law, after being surprised by what the company's privacy lawyer, Ed Palmieri, said to his class on the subject.[79] He later made a request under Art. 12 to receive what information Facebook held on him and received a CD containing over 1,200 pages of data, which he published at Europe v Facebook with personal information redacted. In summer 2013 he filed a complaint with the Irish Data Protection Commissioner alleging that Facebook's policy of exporting data to the United States was unlawful under Art. 25 due to its role in and compliance with the Prism programme.[80] When the Data Protection Commissioner ruled that Facebook had no case to answer Schrems filed an application

[76] Commission Decision of 26 July 2000 pursuant to Directive 95/46/EC of the European Parliament and of the Council on the adequacy of the protection provided by the safe harbour privacy principles and related frequently asked questions issued by the US Department of Commerce, 2000/520/EC.

[77] See 21.1.2.

[78] <http://europe-v-facebook.org/EN/en.html>.

[79] K Hill, 'Max Schrems: The Austrian Thorn In Facebook's Side' *Forbes* (New York, 7 February 2012) <http://www.forbes.com/sites/kashmirhill/2012/02/07/the-austrian-thorn-in-facebooks-side/#2715e4857a0b6411de406b30>.

[80] Facebook's European Headquarters are in Ireland, hence the complaint to the Irish DPC.

for judicial review in the Irish High Court. When the case was heard in June 2014 the court immediately referred the case to the CJEU.

The High Court sent two questions to the CJEU: (1) Whether in the course of determining a complaint which has been made to an independent office holder who has been vested by statute with the functions of administering and enforcing data protection legislation that personal data is being transferred to another third country (in this case, the United States of America) the laws and practices of which, it is claimed, do not contain adequate protections for the data subject, that office holder is absolutely bound by the Community finding to the contrary contained in [Decision 2000/520] having regard to Article 7, Article 8 and Article 47 of [the Charter], the provisions of Article 25(6) of Directive [95/46] notwithstanding? (2) Or, alternatively, may and/or must the office holder conduct his or her own investigation of the matter in the light of factual developments in the meantime since that Commission decision was first published? The first question essentially asks whether the Irish Data Protection Commissioner is bound by the safe harbour agreement and must find data transfers which comply with it to be lawful, notwithstanding the rights to privacy, data privacy, and an effective remedy found in the EU Charter. The second asks whether the Commissioner may by his own investigation find that the export does not comply with the Directive, notwithstanding the safe harbour agreement.

The court gave its decision on 6 October 2015 and in so doing perhaps went further than the High Court had envisaged when it referred the case.[81] The court first answered the questions referred. It noted that the very act of transferring data was a data process in of itself[82] and that by Art. 8(3) of the Charter and Art. 28 of the Directive:

> national supervisory authorities are responsible for monitoring compliance with the EU rules concerning the protection of individuals with regard to the processing of personal data, each of them is therefore vested with the power to check whether a transfer of personal data from its own Member State to a third country complies with the requirements laid down by Directive 95/46.[83]

This means that national supervisory authorities such as the Irish Data Protection Commissioner have a general supervisory authority which they can use to block data transfers. However, as Art. 25(6) allows the Commission to adopt a decision finding that a third country ensures an adequate level of protection, as is the case with the safe harbour, in these cases:

> until such time as the Commission decision is declared invalid by the Court, the Member States and their organs, which include their independent supervisory authorities, admittedly cannot adopt measures contrary to that decision, such as acts intended to determine with binding effect that the third country covered by it does not ensure an adequate level of protection. Measures of the EU institutions are in principle presumed to be lawful and accordingly produce legal effects until such time as they are withdrawn, annulled in an action for annulment or declared invalid following a reference for a preliminary ruling or a plea of illegality.[84]

As such, the answer to the first question is that the Irish Data Protection Commissioner is bound by Decision 2000/520 (the safe harbour decision) until it is declared invalid.

[81] *Maximillian Schrems v Data Protection Commissioner* (C-362/14) EU:C:2015:650.
[82] Ibid. [45].
[83] Ibid. [47].
[84] Ibid. [52].

Even so, what happened next was a powerful message from the court. It found that it would be:

> contrary to the system set up by the Directive and to the objective of Articles 25 and 28 for a Commission decision adopted pursuant to Article 25(6) to have the effect of preventing a national supervisory authority from examining a person's claim concerning the protection of his rights and freedoms in regard to the processing of his personal data which has been or could be transferred from a Member State to the third country covered by that decision.[85]

As a result the court found that state supervisory bodies such as the Irish Data Protection Commissioner do have the right to review the transfer of data under a decision such as the safe harbour decision, notwithstanding the normal principle.[86]

This was only the appetizer though; the main course was to come. The court noted that:

> as is apparent from the referring court's explanations relating to the questions submitted, Mr Schrems contends in the main proceedings that United States law and practice do not ensure an adequate level of protection within the meaning of Article 25 of the Directive. As the Advocate General has observed in points 123 and 124 of his Opinion, Mr Schrems expresses doubts, which the referring court indeed seems essentially to share, concerning the validity of Decision 2000/520.

As a result, the court declared that 'in such circumstances, having regard to what has been held in paragraphs 60 to 63 of the present judgment and in order to give the referring court a full answer, it should be examined whether that decision complies with the requirements stemming from Directive 95/46 read in the light of the Charter.'[87] This was what Mr Schrems had hoped for but was strictly beyond what the referring court had asked. The court was now going to examine the legality of the safe harbour agreement itself. Remember at this point, that the safe harbour agreement was the only thing which permitted the safe transfer of personal data from the EU to the US under Art. 25. Should the court find the agreement to be unlawful it had a direct impact upon a multibillion dollar industry.

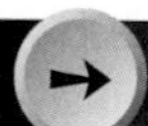

Highlight The decision of the CJEU in *Schrems*

(1) Decision 2000/520 does not contain any finding regarding the existence, in the United States, of rules adopted by the State intended to limit any interference with the fundamental rights of the persons whose data is transferred from the European Union to the United States, interference which the State entities of that country would be authorised to engage in when they pursue legitimate objectives, such as national security.

(2) Nor does Decision 2000/520 refer to the existence of effective legal protection against interference of that kind.

→

[85] Ibid. [56].
[86] Ibid. [66].
[87] Ibid. [67].

→

(3) The Commission's own analysis of Decision 2000/520 shows that the United States authorities were able to access the personal data transferred from the Member States to the United States and process it in a way incompatible, in particular, with the purposes for which it was transferred, beyond what was strictly necessary and proportionate to the protection of national security.

(4) Data subjects had no administrative or judicial means of redress enabling, in particular, the data relating to them to be accessed and, as the case may be, rectified or erased.

(5) Legislation permitting the public authorities to have access on a generalised basis to the content of electronic communications must be regarded as compromising the essence of the fundamental right to respect for private life, as guaranteed by Article 7 of the Charter.

(6) Legislation not providing for any possibility for an individual to pursue legal remedies in order to have access to personal data relating to him, or to obtain the rectification or erasure of such data, does not respect the essence of the fundamental right to effective judicial protection, as enshrined in Article 47 of the Charter.

(7) Consequently, without there being any need to examine the content of the safe harbour principles, it is to be concluded that Article 1 of Decision 2000/520 fails to comply with the requirements laid down in Article 25(6) of Directive 95/46, read in the light of the Charter, and that it is accordingly invalid.

As may be expected the fallout from the *Schrems* decision was great. On the European side of the Atlantic the decision was greeted as a strong vindication of the fundamental right of privacy. The European Commission[88] and the Article 29 Working Party[89] made bullish statements about how this protected fundamental rights. Meanwhile US regulators were understandably less enthusiastic. Federal Trade Commissioner, Julie Brill admitted that 'although I and other close observers of the European privacy scene have been discussing the potential implications of the Schrems case for some time, the decision clearly came as a shock to many policy makers and companies in the United States', and that 'during a discussion held just last week in the heart of Silicon Valley, a Member of the US House of Representatives who hails from that area of California stated that the *Schrems* decision measured 7.8 on the Richter scale. For those of you not as familiar with earthquakes as they are in California, that is an enormous shock that would seriously test most bridges. It also makes the need for building stronger and more durable bridges that much clearer.'[90]

[88] European Commission Statement: First Vice-President Timmermans and Commissioner Jourová's press conference on Safe Harbour following the Court ruling in case C-362/14 (Schrems) (6 October 2015) <http://europa.eu/rapid/press-release_STATEMENT-15-5782_en.htm>.

[89] Article 29 Data Protection Working Party, Statement on the Implementation of the Judgment of the Court of Justice of the European Union in *Schrems v Data Protection Commissioner* (Brussels, 16 October 2015) <http://ec.europa.eu/justice/data-protection/article-29/press-material/pressrelease/art29_press_material/2015/20151016_wp29_statement_on_schrems_judgement.pdf>.

[90] J Brill, 'Transatlantic Privacy After Schrems: Time for An Honest Conversation' Keynote Address at the Amsterdam Privacy Conference, 23 October 2015 <https://www.ftc.gov/system/files/documents/public_statements/836443/151023amsterdamprivacy1.pdf>.

Unsurprisingly both sides have been quick to mobilize to try and find a replacement for the safe harbour agreement. A communication from the Commission committed it to developing a 'renewed and sound framework for transfers of personal data to the United States'.[91] Negotiations are currently under way to provide a new safe harbour agreement now called privacy shield, and reports from the media suggest that such an agreement should be reached by March 2016 so should be in place by the time you read this book.

20.4 Supervision of data controllers: data subject rights

Data controllers are supervised using a variety of means, including public scrutiny, oversight by the Information Commissioner, and where necessary the application of the criminal law. As already discussed, the first level of control is that data controllers are required to notify the Information Commissioner *before* they begin to process personal data.[92] This information is then entered onto the publicly accessible Register of Data Controllers, yet this is of limited value in a society where nearly almost every commercial organization will be a data controller. It can, though, provide a starting point for data subjects who are seeking to ensure that data held on them is accurate, up to date, and is being stored and processed fairly. This is essential because the primary control mechanism for day-to-day enforcement of data protection principles is through the actions of data subjects.

20.4.1 Subject access: *Durant v the Financial Services Authority*

Self-policing of personal data is a key aspect of the Act and to assist with this data subjects are given an assortment of low-level enforcement powers. The first is that they may under s. 7 make a subject access request. This requires data controllers to reveal to the data subject if they hold data on them and what use they make of that data. This includes detailing what data the data controller holds, to whom, if anyone, they disclose that data, and any information, if available, as to the source of the data. This information should be given to the data subject within 40 days of the application being received by the data controller.[93]

The aim of s. 7 is to allow data subjects to check what data is held on them and how that data is being processed and/or transmitted on. This investigatory right then arms data subjects with the necessary information to allow them to take further action such as applying for data to be deleted or corrected, or if necessary to report the actions of the data controller to the Information Commissioner for investigation.

That is not to say this procedure is without risk. It would obviously be a breach of the data protection principles, in particular principle 7, if data were revealed under a s. 7 application to the wrong person.[94] To prevent this, there are a number of measures which are designed to protect the data subject. By s. 7(3) the data controller may require

[91] Communication from the Commission to the European Parliament and the Council on the Transfer of Personal Data from the EU to the United States of America under Directive 95/46/EC following the Judgment by the Court of Justice in Case C-362/14 (Schrems) COM(2015) 566 final.

[92] DPA 1998, ss. 16 and 17.

[93] See s. 7(8).

[94] Imagine, if you will, an investigative journalist obtaining medical details of a well-known political or business figure by means of a false application under s. 7.

the data subject to provide further information to prove his identity and may refuse to comply with a subject access request until this information is supplied. This information may take the form of personal identifiers such as passwords or identification numbers or it may take the form of physical identifiers such as a passport or driving licence. Further to this, s. 7(4) deals with conjoined or commixed data. These are forms of data in which the information held on the data subject is linked to data held on other persons.

Conjoined data is data which is held in a single file or folder about two or more data subjects, but which as far as possible treats data subjects separately. An example may be a personnel review file on a sales and marketing team which evaluates each member of the team in comparison with each other, rating their relative strengths and weaknesses and evaluating their teamwork. Commixed data is data relating to two or more persons which has come together to form a single file or entry. An example may be a joint mortgage application of two persons which forms a single mortgage file with the lender.

By s. 7(4):

> Where a data controller cannot comply with the request without disclosing information relating to another individual who can be identified from that information, he is not obliged to comply with the request unless:
>
> (a) the other individual has consented to the disclosure of the information to the person making the request, or
>
> (b) it is reasonable in all the circumstances to comply with the request without the consent of the other individual.

The questions of what qualifies as 'data relating to another individual who can be identified' and when it is reasonable to comply with a request absent the other data subject's permission, have been considered by the Court of Appeal in *Durant v Financial Services Authority*.[95]

The appellant was an erstwhile customer of Barclays Bank, against whom he had brought proceedings which ended unsuccessfully for the appellant in 1993. Since then he had sought, without success, disclosure of various records in connection with the dispute giving rise to the litigation because he believed that the records might assist him to reopen his claims or to secure an investigation into the conduct of the bank. In September and October 2001 he made two requests to the FSA in its role as the regulator for the financial services sector, seeking disclosure of personal data held by it, both electronically and in manual files. The FSA in response provided Mr Durant with copies of documents it held in computerized form, some of which had been redacted so as not to disclose the names of others. It refused his request for access to the unredacted documents. It also refused the whole of his request for information held on manual files on the ground that the information sought was not 'personal' within the definition of 'personal data' in s. 1 of the Data Protection Act 1998 and that, even if it was, it did not constitute 'data' within the separate definition of that word in s. 1(1)(c) in the sense of forming part of a 'relevant filing system'.

The court was faced with several questions: (1) What is a 'relevant filing system'? (2) Which data is 'personal' data under that Act? (3) Does a data subject have an entitlement to have access to unredacted data under s. 7? and (4) What limits may be placed on access to conjoined and commixed data?

[95] [2004] FSR 28.

In answering the first two questions the court first divided all the files Mr Durant sought access to into four categories. These were:

(i) a file relating to the systems and controls Barclays Bank was required to maintain and which was subject to control by the FSA. This file was in date order and also contained a few documents relating to part of the appellant's complaint against the bank, which concerned such systems and controls;

(ii) a file relating to complaints by customers of Barclays Bank to the FSA. The file was subdivided alphabetically by reference to the complainant's name and contained, behind a divider marked 'Mr Durant', a number of documents relating to his complaint filed in date order;

(iii) a Bank Investigations Group file, relating and organized by reference to issues or cases concerning Barclays Bank, but not necessarily identified by reference to an individual complainant. It contained a sub-file marked 'Mr Durant', which contained documents relating to his complaint. Neither the file nor the sub-file was indexed in any way save by reference to the name of the appellant on the sub-file itself; and

(iv) Company Secretariat papers comprising a sheaf of papers in an unmarked transparent plastic folder held by the FSA's Company Secretariat, relating to Mr Durant's complaint about the FSA's refusal to disclose to him details and the outcome of its investigation of his complaints against Barclays Bank. This file was not organized by date or any other criterion.

The court found:[96]

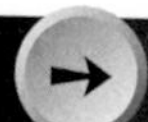

Highlight Relevant filing systems (from *Durant v FSA*)

A relevant filing system for the purpose of the Act, is limited to a system:

(1) in which the files forming part of it are structured or referenced in such a way as clearly to indicate at the outset of the search whether specific information capable of amounting to personal data of an individual requesting it under s. 7 is held within the system and, if so, in which file or files it is held; and

(2) which has, as part of its own structure or referencing mechanism, a sufficiently sophisticated and detailed means of readily indicating whether and where in an individual file or files specific criteria or information about the applicant can be readily located.

On this basis it was found that none of the further types of files were 'relevant filing systems' as 'none of the files in question is so structured or indexed as to provide ready access to it . . . an ability of staff readily to identify and locate whole files, even those organised chronologically and/or by reference to his and others' names, is not enough'.[97]

[96] Per Auld LJ at [50].
[97] Ibid. [51].

This was a rather surprising outcome as it had been thought data held in organized files were covered and, as in particular file (ii), the Barclay's complaints file, was organized by reference to the complainants' names, this seemed to fit the definition of 'relevant filing system' in s. 1 of the Act. However, what Auld LJ pointed out was that the Act requires the information to be structured in such a way that 'specific information relating to a particular individual is readily accessible'. In the FSA file Mr Durant's complaint recorded in file (ii) was not so structured. The data was indexed first by reference to Barclays Bank, then by complainant: in effect this was a file about Barclays Bank which mentioned Mr Durant, rather than a file about Mr Durant. Thus, with respect to Mr Durant, it was not 'relevant' to him. This, though, did not dispense with the question of how to deal with conjoined and commixed data. Although it may be that the files were not 'relevant', they may still contain personal data.

To this end Auld LJ began his analysis of what constitutes personal data with a warning.[98]

Highlight Auld LJ's warning

[The subject access right] is not an automatic key to any information, readily accessible or not, of matters in which he may be named or involved. Nor is to assist him, for example, to obtain discovery of documents that may assist him in litigation or complaints against third parties. As a matter of practicality and given the focus of the Act on ready accessibility of the information—whether from a computerised or comparably sophisticated non-computerised system—it is likely in most cases that only information that names or directly refers to him will qualify.

With this said, Auld LJ then went on to analyse what qualifies as 'personal data':[99]

Highlight Personal Data (from *Durant v FSA*)

Mere mention of the data subject in a document held by a data controller does not necessarily amount to his personal data . . . It seems to me that there are two notions that may be of assistance. The first is whether the information is biographical in a significant sense, that is, going beyond the recording of the putative data subject's involvement in a matter or an event that has no personal connotations, a life event in respect of which his privacy could not be said to be compromised. The second is one of focus. The information should have the putative data subject as its focus rather than some other person with whom he may have been involved or some transaction or event in which he may have figured or have had an interest, for example, as in this case, an investigation into some other person's or body's conduct that he may have instigated. In short, it is information that affects his privacy, whether in his personal or family life, business or professional capacity.

[98] Ibid. [27].
[99] Ibid. [28].

This is a vital distinction that may be best thought of in terms of a stage play. There are characters who are central to a stage play, for instance Hamlet in the eponymous Shakespeare tragedy. Then there are characters who support the telling of the story: for instance, Ophelia and Laertes. No one would claim the play is about Ophelia or Laertes, but they are essential for the story of Hamlet. So is the case of personal data. Personal data is, in Auld LJ's words, information which has 'the putative data subject as its focus': it is about the lead character not the supporting cast. In the instant case none of the data Mr Durant requested access to was 'personal data'. In each case, although he was mentioned and details about him and his complaints were recorded, he was not the central character of the files in question.

How then does one know if they are a central character or merely supporting cast in any given file? According to Auld LJ it is a question of 'a continuum of relevance or proximity to the data subject as distinct, say, from transactions or matters in which he may have been involved to a greater or lesser degree'.[100] This means data controllers and perhaps later the Information Commissioner or judges will have to evaluate the degree to which the data subject is the focus of the data in question based upon the biographical focus of the data. Data which is clearly focused on the data subject will be personal data, even if others are mentioned; data which is clearly focused on a third party is not, even if it mentions the data subject. Data in between remains somewhat in a grey area to be decided on the facts in a case-by-case analysis.

The answers to these questions led to the dismissal of Mr Durant's claim to access the further information which had been withheld from him, but what about his claim to have unredacted versions of data already supplied to him? Auld LJ suggested a two-stage approach be taken when considering redaction of data. The first is to ask whether the data redacted 'is necessarily part of the personal data that the data subject has requested'.[101] He defines 'necessarily' as 'Where a data controller cannot comply with the request without disclosing information about another individual who can be identified from the information.' If such information about another is not 'necessarily' part of personal data sought, then 'the data controller, whose primary obligation is to provide information, not documents, can, if he chooses to provide that information in the form of a copy document, simply redact such third-party information because it is not a necessary part of the data subject's personal data'.[102] If the data is 'necessarily' part of the data subject's personal data then the second stage is applied. This requires the data controller to balance the interests of the data subjects in question. Should the revealing of personal data about other data subjects appear to be a greater intrusion of privacy, or carry greater risk of harm than the process of redacting does to the original data subject's access request, then the data may be redacted. Should there be little risk to other data subjects, then the interests of the data subject who made the access request should be protected and unredacted data should be supplied. In Auld LJ's words:

> In short, it all depends on the circumstances whether it would be reasonable to disclose to a data subject the name of another person figuring in his personal data, whether that person is a source, or a recipient or likely recipient of that information, or has a part in the matter the

[100] Ibid.
[101] Ibid. [65].
[102] Ibid.

subject of the personal data. Beyond the basic presumption or starting point, I believe that the courts should be wary of attempting to devise any principles of general application one way or the other.[103]

This left one final question for the court: what discretion do the courts and data controllers have when dealing with subject access requests which may involve conjoined or commixed data? Mr Durant had asked the court to compel the FSA to release to him the data they had retained and redacted under s. 7(9). Although this became a moot point during the analysis applied in answering the prior questions, Auld LJ did question when it may be appropriate for a court to so do. His answer was not terribly clear but he did make two points strongly. The first was that the court's discretion under s. 7(9) is general and untrammelled, the second that when dealing with the disclosure of data relating to a third party it may be difficult for a court to order the data be retained if it found it to be reasonable for the data subject to have access to the data. This seems to be a weak support for the view that if the data relating to a third party forms a necessary part of the data relating to the data subject's access request, the court should order the data to be released to the data subject, notwithstanding the effect this may have on the third party.

In sum, *Durant* is a simple case dealing with complex issues. The case is simple because, as noted by another of the judges in the case, Buxton LJ, 'the information sought by Mr Durant was by no stretch of the imagination a borderline case'.[104] Mr Durant was seeking to use the subject access right found in the Data Protection Act to effect pre-trial discovery in the hope of finding evidence to allow him to raise a further claim against either Barclays Bank or the FSA. This was a clear abuse of the s. 7 procedure. In future there will be more borderline cases which will be much more difficult for judges. The complexity of the case was in the type of data in question: most data is not 'clean' data about a single data subject. Data is processed and reordered regularly. It is commixed and conjoined to create new data and identifying 'a' data subject or 'the' data subject is increasingly difficult. It is less often about Hamlet: a central character surrounded by a supporting cast. More often we are dealing with a complex ensemble piece with no clear central role. This will prove continually more complex for both data controllers and the courts.

20.4.2 Revising subject access: *Edem v IC & Financial Services Authority*

The Court of Appeal has more recently reviewed the decision in *Durant* in the case of *Edem v IC & Financial Services Authority*.[105] Mr Edem had made an earlier complaint to the FSA about a UK bank. He clearly felt that complaint had been mishandled as he requested 'a copy of all information that the Authority held about him and "my complaint that the FSA had failed to correctly regulate Egg PLC"' under the Freedom

[103] Ibid. [66]. In the instant case the court found Mr Durant had no right to unredacted copies of the data supplied to him as in most cases it was not 'necessarily part of the personal data that he had requested'. On the two occasions the data redacted did pass the first hurdle of the test it fell down at the second hurdle as 'they were of the name of an FSA employee which, in itself, can have been of little or no legitimate value to Mr Durant and who had understandably withheld his or her consent because Mr Durant had abused him or her over the telephone' (at [67]).

[104] Ibid. [80].

[105] [2014] EWCA Civ 92.

of Information Act 2000. The FSA refused to release certain information which they believed could identify three employees, on the basis that there is an exemption under s. 40(2) for data which falls within the definition of personal data under the Data Protection Act. Mr Edem challenged this on the basis that it defeated his Freedom of Information Act request, which had been made for legitimate reasons, and on the basis that individuals could not be identified just by their names as attached to emails. By the time the case arrived at the Court of Appeal a single issue remained live; whether information amounting to the names of these three individuals who had worked on the complaints constituted 'personal data' under s. 1(1) of the Data Protection Act. The individuals in question were all junior employees who did not have public-facing roles. In giving the decision of the court Moses LJ began by reviewing the guidance of Auld LJ in *Durant*. In that case of course Auld LJ had famously stated 'mere mention of the data subject in a document held by a data controller does not necessarily amount to his personal data',[106] suggesting that the data in this case may not qualify as personal data under s. 1(1). To determine whether it did one would usually apply the *Durant* test (as we have just seen) to determine whether or not data is personal data which is: (1) biographical, or (2) focused on the data subject. This is exactly what the first-tier tribunal had done in *Edem*,[107] but Moses LJ believed this was incorrect:

> The First-Tier Tribunal were wrong to apply Auld LJ's 'notions' in this case. There is no reason to do so. The information in this case was plainly concerned with those three individuals. Neither of Auld LJ's notions had any application and to seek to apply them runs contrary to the Statute, the Directive, and the jurisprudence of the Court of Justice, to which I have already referred. It is important not to misunderstand the context in which Auld LJ referred to those 'notions'.[108]

What did Moses LJ mean by this? After a short discussion of the circumstances which led Mr Durant to bring his claim, Moses LJ concludes that the 'notions' were Auld LJ's way of 'explaining why information and documents in which Mr Durant's name appeared were not personal data relating to him'.[109] In the current case the question was whether disclosure of a person's name is disclosure of personal data. As Moses LJ notes: 'a name is personal data unless it is so common that without further information, such as its use in a work context, a person would remain unidentifiable despite its disclosure.'[110]

The *Edem* case adds to our understanding of the meaning of personal data in s. 1 of the Act. To date the only authoritative definition of what did and did not constitute personal data was the *Durant* decision. Too often data controllers would refer to *Durant* as an unbendable authority on the question. To many observers this seemed rather inflexible and the new interpretation found post-*Edem* deals with these concerns and also gives greater guidance to data controllers. *Durant* may now be seen as an internal test. It applies when data subjects are seeking information about themselves in records and files; it is about defining the character or role of the data subject, is he Hamlet or Laertes? The *Edem* interpretation is an external test. It applies when individuals are seeking to obtain data about others. This is a very different scenario as this is a potential

106 [2004] FSR 28 [28].
107 [2014] EWCA Civ 92 [16].
108 Ibid. [17].
109 Ibid. [20].
110 Ibid.

infringement of one's right to data protection as found in Art. 8 of the EU Charter of Fundamental Rights.[111] As a result the test is different; it is simply to apply s. 1(1) of the Data Protection Act 1998: personal data means data which relates to a living individual who can be identified.

20.4.3 Correcting and managing data

Following a subject access request the data subject may, should they find data which is inaccurate or out of date, make a number of applications to have the data corrected or if necessary destroyed. By s. 10 the data subject may object to processing likely to cause damage or distress. The damage or distress must be 'substantial' and the harm 'unwarranted'. This is achieved by making an application in writing to the data controller. The data controller then must within 21 days either reply to the data subject stating that they have stopped processing the data in question or that they intend to do so, or must state reasons why they believe the data subject's request is unjustified either in whole or in part.[112] In the event the data controller refuses to comply with the data subject's request, the data subject may apply to the court under s. 10(4) for an order forcing compliance. This, like the s. 7(9) order discussed in *Durant,* is at the discretion of the court. Often s. 10 applications are made by the families of recently deceased relatives to have their names removed from automated lists such as marketing lists. Since, strictly speaking, in such cases the application does not come from the data subject, data controllers usually accede to such requests. By s. 11, the data subject may specifically apply to prevent processing for direct marketing purposes. Such an application must be in writing and the data controller must comply with the application within a reasonable period. Direct marketing is defined as 'communication (by whatever means) of any advertising or marketing material which is directed to particular individuals'.[113] This wide definition includes direct mail, marketing calls, spam email, and spam texts. To assist with the management of s. 11 many direct marketers work with an industry association to allow for blanket opt-out applications. Thus the Telephone Preference Service allows individuals to opt out of marketing calls while the Mail Preference Service performs the same function for direct mail.

Section 12 allows data subjects to object to systems of automated decision-making. This is similar in form to the rights awarded under ss. 10 and 11. The data subject may write to the data controller requiring that the data controller takes no decision, or allows no decision to be taken on his behalf, purely on the processing by automatic means of personal data. The data controller must, within 21 days of receipt of such a notice, inform the data subject whether any such decisions were made, and if necessary make arrangements to make a new decision, detailing the steps that will be taken to do that. Again, if the data controller unreasonably refuses to comply with the data subject's application, the court may at its discretion require the data controller to comply.[114] Requests under s. 12 are also commonly made by data subjects in relation to automated 'credit-scoring' systems which may, due to their closed set of algorithms, produce a result which is unfairly prejudicial to the data subject, such as, for instance, in cases of

[111] 2000/C 364/01.
[112] DPA 1998, s. 10(3).
[113] DPA 1998, s. 11(3).
[114] DPA 1998, s. 12(8).

military personnel who frequently move address; a factor which impacts negatively on creditworthiness.

Finally, under s. 14 the data subject is given a strong and wide-ranging right to correct or destroy data relating to them. To enforce the right under s. 14 the data subject must apply to the court. The court may then 'order the data controller to rectify, block, erase or destroy those data and any other personal data in respect of which he is the data controller and which contain an expression of opinion which appears to the court to be based on the inaccurate data'. In truth, application to the court under s. 14 is very much a last resort which both data subjects and data controllers wish to avoid. Thus, it is in the interests of data controllers to have accurate and up-to-date information: data is only valuable if it is accurate. A simple request to a data controller to delete inaccurate data, or to update details is usually well received and, if the data controller does not comply, the data subject may enroll the assistance of the Office of the Information Commissioner who may be able to broker a deal. Section 14 is therefore a long-stop provision designed to be used where parties cannot broker a reasonable settlement.

20.4.4 The right to be forgotten

Case study *Mario Costeja González*[115]

In the late 1990s a Spanish citizen by the name of Mario Costeja González was the subject of a debt recovery action by the Spanish state. It appears that he owed the Ministry of Labour and Social Affairs debts by way of social security payments. At the time it is certain neither he nor the Spanish state could imagine the impact his debt and the recovery of it would have. As part of the process of recovering the debt, the Ministry ordered a sale of items of Real Estate by way of a public auction and to maximise the return at auction they placed an announcement of the auction in the newspaper *La Vanguardia*. The auction proceeded and in the normal run of affairs that would have been the end of the matter.

Unfortunately *La Vanguardia* later digitized that copy of the newspaper and now it can be accessed online.[116] This of itself would not be a problem for Sr González except this data (like much internet data) was then indexed by Google which meant that when you searched for his name the most prominent data returned was this information relating to a long-extinguished debt. Obviously, Sr González felt this affected his standing in business and generally reflected data which should be deleted under the principles of Art. 6(1)(c) of the 1995 Data Protection Directive; that data must be 'adequate, *relevant* and not excessive' and Art. 8 of the Charter of Fundamental Rights of the European Union that one has a right to data privacy. Therefore, in March 2010 Sr González lodged a complaint with the Agencia Española de Protección de Datos (AEPD), the Spanish data protection agency, claiming that *La Vanguardia* must delete or amend the irrelevant data in a way to prevent his identification and that Google must stop linking to it in search returns.

[115] *Google Spain SL and Google Inc. v AEPD*, Case C-131/12 13 May 2014 <http://curia.europa.eu/juris/liste.jsf?num=C-131/12> [14].

[116] <http://hemeroteca.lavanguardia.com/preview/1998/01/19/pagina-23/33842001/pdf.html>.

In July 2010 AEPD issued their findings. They found that *La Vanguardia* needed to take no action as they simply recorded information which had legally been published and which was correct.[117] However, they found that Google in producing search returns were processing data and were subject to data protection provisions. This suggested Google's actions were in breach of Spanish data protection law.[118] Google challenged this decision before the Spanish High Court and they referred it to the CJEU. The long-awaited decision of the CJEU was published in May 2014 and it has had wide-reaching implications for operators of websites and search engines. The court found that search engine operators were date controllers for the purpose of Art. 2(d) of the Data Protection Directive as they 'determine the purposes and means of that activity (search) and thus of the processing of personal data that it itself carries out within the framework of that activity'[119] and that they processed data in accordance with Art. 2(b).[120] This meant the Directive covered the activities of search engine operators such as Google and the defence that Google had argued that they merely indexed data held by others was not made out.

The next question was whether the provisions of the Directive only applied to Google Spain (as established in the EU) or whether they also applied to Google Inc. when dealing with an EU citizen. The court found that the operations carried out by Google Inc. outside the EU but for the purpose of providing a service through their establishment in the EU, and through which profit was generated by advertising and promotion, were within the geographical scope of the Directive.[121] On this basis the court found that 'it follows that Article 4(1)(a) is to be interpreted as meaning that processing of personal data is carried out in the context of the activities of an establishment of the controller on the territory of a Member State, within the meaning of that provision, when the operator of a search engine sets up in a Member State a branch or subsidiary which is intended to promote and sell advertising space offered by that engine and which orientates its activity towards the inhabitants of that Member State.'[122]

This merely left the question of whether Google had a duty to remove links to out-of-date information upon request of the data subject. The court began by noting that under Art. 12(b) data subjects have the right to request erasure or rectification of data which does not comply with the provisions of the Directive,[123] while under Art. 14(a) data subjects have the right to object to processing of personal data where they have not given permission for its processing and the processing is not in compliance with a legal or contractual obligation.[124] Starting from this base, the court noted that processing was likely to significantly impact the data subject's right to both privacy and data protection and that, as a result, 'it is clear that it cannot be justified by merely the economic interest which the operator of such an engine has in that processing'. The court did, however, note that others may have a legitimate interest in being able to access this information for it is not the intent of data protection law to allow private censorship of data. To counterbalance this risk, the court noted that:

[117] Ibid. [16].
[118] Ibid. [17].
[119] Ibid. [33].
[120] Ibid. [25]–[32].
[121] Ibid. [55].
[122] Ibid. [60].
[123] Ibid. [70].
[124] Ibid. [76].

> a fair balance should be sought in particular between that interest and the data subject's fundamental rights under Articles 7 and 8 of the Charter [with those of others interested in the data]. Whilst it is true that the data subject's rights protected by those articles also override, as a general rule, that interest of internet users, that balance may however depend, in specific cases, on the nature of the information in question and its sensitivity for the data subject's private life and on the interest of the public in having that information, an interest which may vary, in particular, according to the role played by the data subject in public life.[125]

Having done this balancing exercise the court found that Sr González was justified in his application:

> in order to comply with the rights laid down in those provisions (Arts. 12(b) and 14(a)) the operator of a search engine is obliged to remove from the list of results displayed following a search made on the basis of a person's name links to web pages, published by third parties and containing information relating to that person, also in a case where that name or information is not erased beforehand or simultaneously from those web pages, and even, as the case may be, when its publication in itself on those pages is lawful.[126]

The fallout from this decision has been extensive and wide-reaching. The European Commission has published a fact sheet for citizens and for operators of web pages and other intermediary services.[127] Many newspapers and journals have attacked the judgment as being a form of private censorship (despite the balancing provision set out in the judgment),[128] Google have been criticized for the way they are handling right to be forgotten requests with the high level of publicity they are bringing to the complexity of complying;[129] and have sought clarification on the ruling.[130] The UK House of Lords has produced a highly critical report on the judgment, finding that 'neither the 1995 Directive, nor the Court's interpretation of the Directive, reflects the current state of communications service provision, where global access to detailed personal information has become part of the way of life' and 'it is no longer reasonable or even possible for the right to privacy to allow data subjects a right to remove links to data which are accurate and lawfully available.'[131] Despite these criticisms, EU data protection

[125] Ibid. [81].

[126] Ibid. [88].

[127] <http://ec.europa.eu/justice/data-protection/files/factsheets/factsheet_data_protection_en.pdf>.

[128] O Solon, 'EU "right to be forgotten" ruling paves way for censorship' *Wired UK* (London, 13 May 2014) <http://www.wired.co.uk/news/archive/2014–05/13/right-to-be-forgotten-blog>; A Hern, 'Wikipedia swears to fight "censorship" of "right to be forgotten" ruling' *The Guardian* (London, 6 August 2014) <http://www.theguardian.com/technology/2014/aug/06/wikipedia-censorship-right-to-be-forgotten-ruling>; J Ball, 'EU's right to be forgotten: Guardian articles have been hidden by Google' *The Guardian* (London, 2 July 2014) <http://www.theguardian.com/commentisfree/2014/jul/02/eu-right-to-be-forgotten-guardian-google>; R Williams, 'Telegraph stories affected by EU "right to be forgotten"' *Daily Telegraph* (London, 3 September 2015) <http://www.telegraph.co.uk/technology/google/11036257/Telegraph-stories-affected-by-EU-right-to-be-forgotten.html>; N McIntosh, 'List of BBC web pages which have been removed from Google's search results' (*BBC Blog*, 25 June 2015) <http://www.bbc.co.uk/blogs/internet/entries/1d765aa8–600b-4f32-b110-d02fbf7fd379>.

[129] S Gibbs, 'Google hauled in by Europe over "right to be forgotten" reaction', *The Guardian* (London, 24 July 2014) <http://www.theguardian.com/technology/2014/jul/24/google-hauled-in-by-europe-over-right-to-be-forgotten-reaction>.

[130] A White, 'Google Seeks Feedback on EU Right to Be Forgotten' *Bloomberg News* (New York, 28 August 2014) <http://www.bloomberg.com/news/2014–08–28/google-seeks-feedback-on-eu-right-to-be-forgotten.html>.

[131] House of Lords, European Union Committee: *EU Data Protection law: A 'right to be forgotten'?* HL Paper 40, (TSO London, 30 July 2014), 22 <http://www.publications.parliament.uk/pa/ld201415/ldselect/ldeucom/40/40.pdf>.

regulators are pushing forward with a more ambitious plan: to require Google to remove links to pages under the right to be forgotten programme, not only on Google's identified 'European' search sites such as google.co.uk or google.fr but also on the main google.com search portal. This is being pressed on the basis that 'the various geographic extensions are simple means of access to the processing. Therefore, if the search engine agrees to delist a result, it must do it on all the extensions, in compliance with the ECJ's decision.'[132] The main action pressing this is a claim in France where the regulator the Commission Nationale de L'informatique et des Libertés (CNIL) is pressing Google under a delisting order to remove data from the main google.com site. On May 21 2015, CNIL ordered Google to de-index certain data across all extensions of the search engine:

> the service provided by the company via its search engine 'Google search' constitutes a single processing. Indeed, the different domain names that the company chose to implement to facilitate the local use of its service are only means of access to this processing. Thus, when [Google Inc.] launched its service in 1997, it was accessible only from the website 'www.google.com' and it has been extended to different domain names only over time.[133]

Google appealed this decision but on September 21 2015 this appeal was rejected by CNIL. In its decision it noted that 'if the right to be forgotten were limited to certain extensions, it could be easily circumvented. Indeed, it would be possible to retrieve a delisted result by simply using another extension (i.e., another means of access), such as .com, thereby depriving the right to be forgotten of its effectiveness'.[134] The decision means that Google will now be fined for failing to comply with the order. It has been reported that 'CNIL will likely begin to apply sanctions including the possibility of a fine in the region of €300,000 against Google, should the company refuse to comply with the order.'[135] Google will then be able to appeal the decision and the fine with the Conseil d'Etat who are likely to refer it to the CJEU.

Clearly the debate surrounding the right to be forgotten and the right to erasure as proposed in Art. 17 of the General Data Protection Regulation (discussed below) will remain subject to debate and scrutiny for the immediate future.

20.5 State supervision of data controllers

If the data controller acts unreasonably, either in response to data subject requests or by processing data in breach of the data protection principles, it is the responsibility of the Office of the Information Commissioner in the first instance to take action.

[132] C Umhoefer and C Chancé, 'Right To Be Forgotten: The CNIL Rejects Google Inc.'s Appeal against Cease and Desist Order' *DLA Piper Privacy Matters* (London, 22 September 2015) <http://blogs.dlapiper.com/privacymatters/right-to-be-forgotten-the-cnil-rejects-google-inc-s-appeal-against-cease-and-desist-order/>.

[133] Decision No. 2015–047 of May 21, 2015 putting Google Inc. on formal notice. Discussed in C Umhoefer and C Chancé, 'Right To Be Forgotten: New Enforcement Trends and Perspectives' *DLA Piper Privacy Matters* (London, 4 August 2015) <http://blogs.dlapiper.com/privacymatters/right-to-be-forgotten-new-enforcement-trends-and-perspectives-2/>.

[134] C Umhoefer and C Chancé, Ibid.

[135] S Gibbs, 'French data regulator rejects Google's right-to-be-forgotten appeal' *The Guardian* (London, 21 September 2015) <http://www.theguardian.com/technology/2015/sep/21/french-google-right-to-be-forgotten-appeal>.

The Information Commissioner's first line of control is of course the notification procedure. By ss. 17 and 21 it is an offence to process personal data without first notifying the Information Commissioner. Obviously there have to be exemptions to this rule in the information society or everyone would be required to submit for notification as even the simple everyday task of storing a friend's mobile phone number, email, or address in your phone would constitute processing personal data. This is why s. 36 states: 'Personal data processed by an individual only for the purposes of that individual's personal, family or household affairs (including recreational purposes) are exempt from the data protection principles and the provisions of Parts II and III.' In addition to this, there are numerous further exceptions which assist in the management of the notification procedure and exempt a number of public interest and public policy procedures. Thus we find in s. 33 an exemption for processing for the purpose of research, history, and statistics, while s. 32 provides an exemption for processing for journalistic, artistic, and literary purposes including 'the special importance of the public interest in freedom of expression [and] publication in the public interest'. Most exemptions though are for processing carried out by public bodies in the discharge of their duties. Thus s. 28 exempts processing for reasons of national security, while s. 29 exempts processing carried out for the detection and prosecution of crime and for the collection of taxation revenues, and s. 31 exempts the activities of a number of regulators such as the Financial Services Authority and the Charities Commission. The number and width of exceptions found in Part IV of the Act mean that an extensive proportion of processing may be carried out without notification. This, along with the fact that notification provides little practical information as to how data is being processed, means that the enforcement and educational provisions found in Parts V and VI of the Act remain crucial.

20.5.1 The Information Commissioner as regulator

The lower level regulatory functions of the Information Commissioner are to be found in Part VI. By s. 52 the Information Commissioner may make codes of practice. These are non-binding guidelines designed to form a template for good practice within an industry sector. The Commissioner has issued a number of such guidelines in industry sectors such as CCTV, health, education, and marketing. In addition, a number of general codes cover subjects such as data security, information sharing, and dealing with enquiries. This educational function provides basic guidelines for data controllers, but beyond this the Commissioner retains an important role in the direct investigation and prosecution of breaches of the Act. The regulatory framework is little changed from that seen in the 1984 Act. The Information Commissioner may begin an assessment at any time, but in particular under s. 42 a data subject may request the Commissioner to begin an assessment. Should the Commissioner deem an assessment to be necessary then the primary investigative weapon of the Commissioner is the Information Notice which may be served under s. 43. This requires the data controller to furnish the Commissioner with the information set out in the Information Notice within a time specified in the notice. Failure to comply with the notice is an offence under s. 47. The notice carries a right to appeal to the Information Tribunal under s. 48.[136] In addition to

[136] On appeal the Tribunal may uphold or overturn the notice. Under s. 49(6) there is a further right of appeal to the High Court/Court of Session on a point of law.

the standard Information Notice, there is a Special Information Notice which may be served under s. 44. This is used where the data controller claims an exemption under s. 32 for data processed in the pursuit of literary, journalistic, or artistic purposes. In effect, the rights and responsibilities, including the right to appeal, are the same as for an Information Notice but such notices are used expressly to discover whether the processing being carried out by the data controller qualifies for the exemption given. In exceptional circumstances where either speed is of the essence, or where the Information Commissioner believes that serious abuses of the data protection principles are ongoing, the Commissioner may elect to request a search warrant under Sch. 9. This allows him, and his staff, with the prior agreement of a circuit judge, to enter the premises of the data controller and to inspect any documents, materials, or equipment found therein. There are extensive protections surrounding search warrants under the Act and in general they may only be issued if the data controller has previously unreasonably refused entry to the Information Commissioner's staff. In addition to the usual search powers, there is also the power under Sch. 9(3) to 'seize any documents or other material found there which may be such evidence'. This may be particularly useful in later issuing an enforcement notice or in bringing a prosecution.

Once the Commissioner obtains the necessary information under the Information, or Special Information, Notice, or following an on-site investigation, he will then decide whether further action is necessary. If he decides to press on he may take a number of further actions. If, following the implementation of a Special Information Notice he finds that the processing in question is not exempted, by s. 32 he may issue a Determination under s. 45 which details why he believes the processing is not exempt. Following a Determination he may issue an enforcement notice under s. 46 which restricts the processing of data until such time as the data controller complies with the requirements of the Act including notification. Alternatively, where the Commissioner is satisfied that 'a data controller has contravened or is contravening any of the data protection principles', he may serve an enforcement notice under s. 40. This is similar to an Information Notice in that it carries a right of appeal under s. 48 and failure to comply is an offence under s. 47, but it is much more wide-ranging in effect. The Commissioner may use an enforcement notice to restrict or even prevent processing of some or all data held by the data controller, or he may require the rectification or even destruction of inaccurate or out-of-date data. In effect, an enforcement notice may make any requirements of a data controller to ensure compliance with the Act and the data protection principles. The issue of enforcement notices is worryingly common. The Commissioner keeps a record of enforcement notices issued and agreed formal undertakings[137] on the Information Commissioner's Office (ICO) website.[138] This data reveals that in calendar years 2014/15 86 undertakings and 20 enforcement notices were agreed/issued.

Previously the Commissioner's direct powers of enforcement were exhausted by the issuing of an enforcement notice, but this changed in April 2010 when the ICO was awarded the power to make monetary notices (fines by any other name) of up to a prescribed amount,

[137] A formal undertaking is where the data controller voluntarily agrees to make changes to their data processes without the need to issue a formal notice following an assessment. If the data controller fails to implement the undertaking a formal notice will then be issued.

[138] <https://ico.org.uk/action-weve-taken/>.

currently £500,000.[139] In 2014/15, 30 monetary penalty notices were issued with the largest penalty being a notice of £200,000 issued on three occasions: to the Crown Prosecution Service after laptops containing videos of police interviews with 43 victims and witnesses were stolen from a private film studio;[140] to Help Direct UK Ltd, a lead generation company for sending out tens of thousands of unsolicited marketing text messages offering services including the reclaim of PPI payments, bank refunds, and loans;[141] and Home Energy & Lifestyle Management Ltd, a green energy company that it made over 6 million calls as part of a massive automated call-marketing campaign offering 'free' solar panels.[142]

20.6 The General Data Protection Regulation

In January 2012 EU Vice-President, Commissioner Viviane Reding, published proposals to reform European data protection rules, including a draft revised Data Protection Regulation.[143] At this time it was their intention to have a new legal framework in place by 2015 but, as we shall see, delays mean it will not take effect until sometime in 2018. The need for a new framework is apparent: the current law was passed in 1995[144] and had been drafted and negotiated in the period 1992–1995. This was a time before the modern internet, smartphones, social media platforms, and major data corporations such as Google and Facebook. The CJEU has sometimes been forced to take expansive and creative interpretations of the current law to make it fit for the modern world.[145] In addition, the 1995 Directive had been passed before the EU Charter which created a fundamental right in data privacy[146] and, as a Directive, had been subject to divergent interpretation, both in implementing legislation and by domestic courts, meaning that it was no longer the unified regime it was intended to be. The General Data Protection Regulation (GDPR) was to correct this but was subject to extensive delay and renegotiation. An almost final version of the text was finally agreed in December 2016 with the successful conclusion of six months of trialogue negotiations between the European Commission, the European Parliament, and the Council of the European Union.[147] It seems likely, though, that the Regulation will not be adopted by Parliament until late spring/early summer 2016, meaning that the Regulation will enter into force in late

[139] See s. 55A DPA 1998; Reg. 2 The Data Protection (Monetary Penalties) (Maximum Penalty and Notices) Regulations 2010, SI 2010/31.

[140] <https://ico.org.uk/media/action-weve-taken/mpns/1560074/crown-prosecution-service-monetary-penalty-notice.pdf>.

[141] <https://ico.org.uk/media/action-weve-taken/mpns/1560036/help-direct-uk-ltd.pdf>.

[142] <https://ico.org.uk/action-weve-taken/enforcement/home-energy-and-lifestyle-management-ltd/>.

[143] COM(2012) 11 final (Brussels, 25 January 2012) <http://ec.europa.eu/justice/data-protection/document/review2012/com_2012_11_en.pdf>.

[144] Dir. 95/46/EC of the European Parliament and of the Council of 24 October 1995 on the protection of individuals with regard to the processing of personal data and on the free movement of such data <http://eur-lex.europa.eu/LexUriServ/LexUriServ.do?uri=CELEX:31995L0046:en:HTML>.

[145] As for example in *Google Spain*, see (n. 115).

[146] Art. 8.

[147] COM(2012) 11. Finalized as Regulation (EU) No XXX/2016 of the European Parliament and Council on the protection of individuals with regard to the processing of personal data and on the free movement of such data (General Data Protection Regulation). Text available online at <https://external.neilzone.co.uk/GDPR_compromise_text_indexed.pdf>.

spring/early summer 2018. Until that date the law remains as discussed in this chapter. In this final section we will look at the major changes the Regulation will bring into effect during 2018.

The first substantial change in the GDPR is the scope of the Regulation. Following guidance in a number of cases, including *Google Spain*, the Regulation extends the scope of EU data protection law not only to data controllers, processors, or subjects based in the EU, but also to:

> the processing of personal data of data subjects who are in the Union by a controller or processor not established in the Union, where the processing activities are related to: (a) the offering of goods or services, irrespective of whether a payment of the data subject is required, to such data subjects in the Union; or (b) the monitoring of their behaviour as far as their behaviour takes place within the European Union.[148]

This will cover the activities of non-EU data controllers/processors who target EU citizens through online activity. Companies covered by this could include the likes of SnapChat or Craigslist, who offer a targeted service at EU customers but (in January 2016) did not have a presence in the EU. The scope of protected data remains the same as under the current law: personal data meaning:

> any information relating to an identified or identifiable natural person; an identifiable person is one who can be identified, directly or indirectly, in particular by reference to an identifier such as a name, an identification number, location data, online identifier or to one or more factors specific to the physical, physiological, genetic, mental, economic, cultural or social identity of that person.[149]

As with the current law there is a set of data protection principles. In the December 2015 draft there are 6 principles.

Highlight Data Protection Principles[150]

Personal data must be:

(a) processed lawfully, fairly and in a transparent manner in relation to the data subject (lawfulness, fairness and transparency);

(b) collected for specified, explicit and legitimate purposes and not further processed in a way incompatible with those purposes; further processing of personal data for archiving purposes in the public interest, or scientific and historical research purposes or statistical purposes shall, in accordance with Article 83(1), not be considered incompatible with the initial purposes; (purpose limitation);

(c) adequate, relevant and limited to what is necessary in relation to the purposes for which they are processed (data minimisation);

→

[148] Art. 3(2).
[149] Art. 4(1).
[150] Art. 5(1).

(d) accurate and, where necessary, kept up to date; every reasonable step must be taken to ensure that personal data that are inaccurate, having regard to the purposes for which they are processed, are erased or rectified without delay (accuracy);

(e) kept in a form which permits identification of data subjects for no longer than is necessary for the purposes for which the personal data are processed; personal data may be stored for longer periods insofar as the data will be processed solely for archiving purposes in the public interest, or scientific and historical research purposes or statistical purposes in accordance with Article 83(1) subject to implementation of the appropriate technical and organisational measures required by the Regulation in order to safeguard the rights and freedoms of the data subject (storage limitation);

(f) processed in a way that ensures appropriate security of the personal data, including protection against unauthorised or unlawful processing and against accidental loss, destruction or damage, using appropriate technical or organisational measures (integrity and confidentiality).

The Regulation also retains the conditions for the processing of data and sensitive personal data (here renamed special categories of personal data).

Highlight Lawful processing of data

Processing of personal data shall be lawful only if and to the extent that at least one of the following applies:[151]

(a) the data subject has given consent to the processing of their personal data for one or more specific purposes;

(b) processing is necessary for the performance of a contract to which the data subject is party or in order to take steps at the request of the data subject prior to entering into a contract;

(c) processing is necessary for compliance with a legal obligation to which the controller is subject;

(d) processing is necessary in order to protect the vital interests of the data subject or of another natural person;

(e) processing is necessary for the performance of a task carried out in the public interest or in the exercise of official authority vested in the controller;

(f) processing is necessary for the purposes of the legitimate interests pursued by the controller or by a third party, except where such interests are overridden by the interests or fundamental rights and freedoms of the data subject which require protection of personal data, in particular where the data subject is a child. This shall not apply to processing carried out by public authorities in the performance of their tasks.

151 Art. 6.

Highlight Processing of special categories of personal data

(1) The processing of personal data, revealing racial or ethnic origin, political opinions, religious or philosophical beliefs, trade-union membership, and the processing of genetic data, biometric data in order to uniquely identify a person or data concerning health or sex life and sexual orientation shall be prohibited.

(2) Paragraph 1 shall not apply if one of the following applies:

(a) the data subject has given explicit consent to the processing of those personal data for one or more specified purposes, except where Union law or Member State law provide that the prohibition referred to in paragraph 1 may not be lifted by the data subject; or

(b) processing is necessary for the purposes of carrying out the obligations and exercising specific rights of the controller or of the data subject in the field of employment and social security and social protection law in so far as it is authorised by Union law or Member State law or a collective agreement pursuant to Member State law providing for adequate safeguards for the fundamental rights and the interests of the data subject; or

(c) processing is necessary to protect the vital interests of the data subject or of another person where the data subject is physically or legally incapable of giving consent; or

(d) processing is carried out in the course of its legitimate activities with appropriate safeguards by a foundation, association or any other non-profit-seeking body with a political, philosophical, religious or trade-union aim and on condition that the processing relates solely to the members or to former members of the body or to persons who have regular contact with it in connection with its purposes and that the data are not disclosed outside that body without the consent of the data subjects; or

(e) the processing relates to personal data which are manifestly made public by the data subject; or

(f) processing is necessary for the establishment, exercise or defence of legal claims or whenever courts are acting in their judicial capacity; or

(g) processing is necessary for reasons of substantial public interest, on the basis of Union or Member State law which shall be proportionate to the aim pursued, respect the essence of the right to data protection and provide for suitable and specific measures to safeguard the fundamental rights and the interests of the data subject; or

(h) processing is necessary for the purposes of preventive or occupational medicine, for the assessment of the working capacity of the employee, medical diagnosis, the provision of health or social care or treatment or the management of health or social care systems and services on the basis of Union law or Member State law or pursuant to contract with a health professional and subject to the conditions and safeguards referred to in paragraph 4; or

(hb) processing is necessary for reasons of public interest in the area of public health, such as protecting against serious cross-border threats to health or ensuring high standards of quality and safety of health care and of medicinal products or medical devices, on the basis of Union law or Member State law which provides for suitable and specific

→

→

measures to safeguard the rights and freedoms of the data subject, in particular professional secrecy; or

(i) processing is necessary for archiving purposes in the public interest, or scientific and historical research purposes or statistical purposes in accordance with Article 83(1) based on Union or Member State law which shall be proportionate to the aim pursued, respect the essence of the right to data protection and provide for suitable and specific measures to safeguard the fundamental rights and the interests of the data subject.[152]

Despite this large list of exceptions, the primary methodology for meeting the lawful processing requirement remains the consent of the data subject. The conditions for consent are found in Art. 7 and they are not dissimilar to the conditions in the current Data Protection Directive. The primary requirement is that the data controller must be able to demonstrate that 'consent was given by the data subject to the processing of their personal data'.[153] In obtaining consent, the controller must have been clear in their communications with the data subject and must have presented the request for consent 'in a manner which is clearly distinguishable from the other matters, in an intelligible and easily accessible form, using clear and plain language'.[154] The Regulation makes a specific point of addressing what may be called conditional consent: the requirement that consent to data processing is given as part of the conditions of use of a product or service. By Art. 7(4) 'when assessing whether consent is freely given, utmost account shall be taken of the fact whether, among others, the performance of a contract, including the provision of a service, is made conditional on the consent to the processing of data that is not necessary for the performance of this contract.' Consent in relation to children must be given by their parent or guardian and must be verifiable.[155] Finally, the data subject is given the right to withdraw their consent at any time.[156]

A new supervisory regime is created. There is no longer a requirement to notify or register with the relevant data protection authorities. Instead data controllers/processors need to 'implement appropriate technical and organisational measures to ensure and be able to demonstrate that the processing of personal data is performed in compliance with this Regulation'.[157] This includes explicit recognition of the concept of privacy by design, designing processes, systems, and technology in a way that is likely to protect the data privacy of the data subject,[158] and the appointment of a data protection officer who is given a substantial regulatory responsibility and authority within their workplace. Where the processing is carried out by a public authority, except for courts or independent judicial authorities when acting in their judicial capacity, or where, in the private sector, processing is carried out by a controller whose core activities consist of

[152] Art. 9.
[153] Art. 7(1).
[154] Art. 7(2).
[155] A child is any person under 16, although Member States may by law substitute a lower age which shall not be below 13 years. Art. 8(1).
[156] Art. 7(3).
[157] Art. 22(1).
[158] Art. 23.

processing operations that require regular and systematic monitoring of the data subjects, a person with expert knowledge of data protection law and practices should assist the controller or processor to monitor internal compliance with the Regulation.[159] The data protection officer is to be 'in a timely manner involved in all issues which relate to the protection of personal data' and is protected by their employer: 'he or she shall not be dismissed or penalized by the controller or the processor for performing his tasks. The data protection officer shall directly report to the highest management level of the controller or the processor.'[160] In creating this role the Regulation brings in-house much of the regulatory responsibility of the Information Commissioner.

Of course there remains both the need for state supervision and the role of the independent supervisory authority.[161] The independent supervisory authority is given substantial powers under Art. 53 including powers to issue warnings and reprimands and most potently issue administrative fines under Art. 79 of 'up to €20,000,000, or in case of an undertaking, up to 4 per cent of the total worldwide annual turnover of the preceding financial year, whichever is higher'.[162] The supervisory system is at the same time streamlined for data controllers/processors. In the case of businesses that operate across the EU, there will no longer be a requirement that they register with and subject themselves to the supervisory authority of 28 regulators. By Art. 51a 'the supervisory authority of the main establishment or of the single establishment of the controller or processor shall be competent to act as lead supervisory authority for the cross-border processing of this controller or processor.' This means that businesses will only need to work closely with one independent supervisory authority: this is achieved because the new law, being in the form of a Regulation rather than Directive, will be the same across the EU with no domestic implementation requirements.

There are a few new substantive provisions in the Regulation. In the initial discussions of the Regulation in early 2012, the most actively discussed new subject right was the proposal for a 'right to be forgotten'. Over time this has become watered down to a narrower 'right to erasure' under Art. 17. This allows a data subject to 'obtain from the controller the erasure of personal data concerning him or her without undue delay' where that data is:

(a) no longer necessary in relation to the purposes for which they were collected or otherwise processed;

(b) the data subject has withdrawn their consent;

(c) the data subject has objected to automated decision-making;

(d) the data has been unlawfully processed;

(e) the data should be erased in compliance with a legal obligation; or

(f) the data was collected by an information society provider and relates to a child.

Events though have arguably overtaken this provision with the decision in the *Google Spain* case.[163]

[159] Art. 35.
[160] Art. 36.
[161] Chapter VI, Arts. 46–54.
[162] Art. 79(3a), Art. 79(3aa).
[163] *Google Spain SL and Google Inc. v AEPD*, see (n. 115).

In fact it may be argued that, when implemented, the right to erasure will actually narrow the rights currently enjoyed by EU citizens and residents. Second, data subjects are given a new right to be informed of data breaches which may affect them. By Art. 31

> In the case of a personal data breach, the controller shall without undue delay and, where feasible, not later than 72 hours after having become aware of it, notify the personal data breach to the supervisory authority competent in accordance with Article 51, unless the personal data breach is unlikely to result in a risk for the rights and freedoms of individuals.

This is to allow data subjects to take steps to secure personal data, such as passwords, which may have been compromised in the breach. Finally, by Art. 18 the data subject is given the right to data portability, this is the right to 'receive the personal data concerning him or her, which he or she has provided to a controller, in a structured and commonly used and machine-readable format and have the right to transmit those data to another controller without hindrance from the controller to which the data have been provided'.[164]

As noted, this will become law at some point in 2018, at which time updates will be made to this text via the Online Resource Centre.

20.7 **Conclusions**

Data management and data processing are ubiquitous activities in the information society. As Cate demonstrated, the unique properties of digital data make it more valuable and therefore more commercialized than analogue data ever was. But with so many decisions automated and so much personal information now held in the form of proxy data the risk of harm to the individual is great. The Data Protection Act is our first line of defence against invasions of data privacy and against unfair and unreasonable data processing.

The Act is, as we have seen, less directive; more a series of guidelines for data controllers and data processors. The heart of the Act is in the data protection principles found in Sch. 1 and in the interpretative provisions seen in Schs. 2 and 3. The application of the Act, due to its framework approach can sometimes seem counterintuitive. To find Mrs Lindqvist responsible for processing data in an unfair fashion for placing some humorous anecdotes on a web page, or Mr Ryneš for operating a camera for the protection of his private dwelling, while holding that the Medical Defence Union acted within the terms of the Act in processing Mr Johnson's data to determine whether to continue to offer cover to a client who had never made a claim on his insurance, seems perverse; yet when one thinks of the Directive and Act as frameworks or guides for fair processing these decisions make sense. The MDU had a clear policy which was fair and reasonable; Mrs Lindqvist and Mr Ryneš acted without thought, policy, or permission.

There remains, though, the concern that this framework approach does little to protect the data privacy of individuals. The Act, the Directive, and even the forthcoming Regulation instead focus on data integrity and data security. This may be seen in the concerns of the Article 29 Working Party with regard to opt-in/opt-out boxes or in the decision of *Durant* where Mr Durant was denied access to data about himself (albeit in that case reasonably). The concern is that data protection laws, originally designed

[164] Art. 18(2).

in the 1990s for an environment where most data was gathered in a traditional form and was merely stored and processed on computer, are out of date in an environment where data is gathered from a multiplicity of sources and is processed and transferred automatically and instantly. This is the data environment we find ourselves in now, and this is the focus of the next chapter.

TEST QUESTIONS

Question 1

Mariella lives in London. She is a keen, if unsuccessful, blogger (with a very limited following). Her most recent blog wants to dispel the myth (held by many of her friends overseas) that Londoners are addicted to online gambling. She describes a number of her London friends—a reputable dentist living in the Kensington area, a journalist who has recently been nominated for a prestigious award, and a teacher in a primary school close to Mariella's home, and outlines how they use online gambling sites for multiple purposes, including simply keeping up with friends in online poker rooms while gambling very limited amounts. Although Mariella does not name these individuals, she is contacted by one of them and asked to edit her blog post to remove some of this information. She refuses and her friend complains to the Information Commissioner's Office (ICO). When investigating, the ICO also realizes that Mariella is an avid Go-Pro user and posts her Go-Pro footage, filmed all over London, on her blog.

Mariella has come to you for advice. She wants to know whether she is in fact processing personal data within the meaning of data protection law and, if so, whether there are any exemptions that she could invoke to avoid ICO regulation.

Question 2

Do you agree with how the Court of Justice reconciles data protection and freedom of expression in the *Google Spain* judgment? How will the judgment affect the future development of search services? In particular, what are its jurisdictional implications?

FURTHER READING

Books

P Bernal, *Internet Privacy Rights: Rights to Protect Autonomy* (2014)

P Carey, *Data Protection: A Practical Guide to UK and EU Law* (4th edn, 2015)

C Kuner, *Transborder Data Flows and Data Privacy Law* (2013)

O Lynskey, *The Foundations of EU Data Protection Law* (2015)

V Mayer-Schönberger, *Delete: The Virtue of Forgetting in the Digital Age* (2009)

Chapters and articles

P Bernal, 'Web 2.5: The Symbiotic Web' 24 *International Review of Law, Computers & Technology* 25 [2010]

F Ferretti, 'Data Protection and the Legitimate Interest of Data Controllers: Much Ado about Nothing or the Winter of Rights?' 51(3) *Common Market Law Review* 843 (2014)

B Koops, 'The Trouble with European Data Protection Law' 4 *International Data Privacy Law* 250 (2014)

C Kuner, 'The European Commission's Proposed Data Protection Regulation: A Copernican Revolution in European Data Protection Law' *Privacy and Security Law Report* 1 (2012)

O Lynskey, 'Deconstructing Data Protection: The "Added-value" of a Right to Data Protection in the EU Legal Order' 63 *International and Comparative Law Quarterly* 569 (2014)

B van der Sloot, 'Do Data Protection Rules Protect the Individual and Should They? An Assessment of the Proposed General Data Protection Regulation' *International Data Privacy Law* 307 (2014)

State surveillance and data retention

The digitization of data affects not only digital information held on a computer or in a relevant filing system. It is also affecting how information is gathered, processed, and interpreted in the real world by states. Digital surveillance is now the cornerstone of signals intelligence (SIGINT) and computer network exploitation (CNE) in all states, with vast sums being expended on SIGINT and CNE programs.[1] These can take a number of forms from basic digital interception, storage, and transmission facilities, to device tracking, biometric tracking, and threat assessment. It can also use a variety of tools from remote video surveillance tools such as CCTV and drone surveillance, to tracking tools such as GSM and GPS tracking, and data and identity authentication tools such as biometrics. By choosing a selection of tools it is possible for governments, or private citizens, to track an individual, to monitor his behaviour, and to monitor his communications network, which data may be used for a variety of purposes.[2] This chapter will examine some of the technologies involved, discuss the challenge they pose to the current legal settlement and ask what, if anything, needs to be done to protect the rights of the individual against the forever developing technologies for digital surveillance.

21.1 State surveillance

We have always understood that governments have had the ability to intercept communications, to monitor and track movements, and to obtain data from third parties under warrants, but, until the revelations of National Security Agency (NSA) contractor Edward Snowden in May 2013, we were unaware of the truly massive scale of state surveillance programmes. New terms entered the lexicon based upon Snowden's considerable data release. We now use terms such as Prism (a clandestine surveillance program under which the NSA collects internet communications from at least nine major US internet companies), Upstream (interception and collection by the NSA of telephone and internet traffic from the internet backbone), Tempora (the UK equivalent

[1] Computer Network Exploitation is essentially the hacking by state intelligence services of computer networks. It already accounts of 30 per cent of the raw intelligence that Government Communications Headquarters (GCHQ) collects, and will no doubt continue to increase.

[2] NSA General Counsel Stewart Baker has said, 'metadata absolutely tells you everything about somebody's life. If you have enough metadata, you don't really need content.' While General Michael Hayden, former director of the NSA and the CIA, recently upped the stakes saying 'We kill people based on metadata.' See D Cole 'We Kill People Based on Metadata' *The New York Review of Books* (New York, 10 May 2014) <http://www.nybooks.com/daily/2014/05/10/we-kill-people-based-metadata/>.

of Upstream, a data-gathering system that is used by Government Communications Headquarters (GCHQ) to buffer internet communications extracted from fibre-optic cables, so that these can be processed and searched at a later time), XKeyscore (a computer system first used by the NSA for searching and analysing global internet data), and Bullrun/Edgehill (a highly classified project aimed at defeating, or undermining, or influencing, encryption standards and implementations operated by NSA/GCHQ) in day-to-day communications. Prior to late 2013, though, we were unaware of the existence of all of these programmes (and many more).[3] Some have called Edward Snowden a hero,[4] others a traitor.[5] Whatever your view is of Edward Snowden it is clear that the so-called 'Snowden Files' have realigned the privacy/surveillance discourse in the UK and further afield as changes, or proposed changes, to surveillance laws have been seen in the United States, the European Union, the United Kingdom, France, Germany, the Netherlands, Switzerland, and many more places as governments seek to place their state surveillance policies on a sound legal footing.

21.1.1 **The current UK legal framework for interception**

We, as citizens, understand that part of our contract with the state allows the state to carry out surveillance programmes for the purposes listed in Art. 8(2) ECHR: 'in the interests of national security, public safety or the economic wellbeing of the country, for the prevention of disorder or crime, for the protection of health or morals, or for the protection of the rights and freedoms of others'. As a result, we accept that law enforcement agencies and the security and intelligence services will carry out surveillance operations in our collective interests. We rely on the principle of proportionality to ensure that these operations do not become a form of state control over the populace as happened in former East Germany. As their powers of surveillance and data gathering are so extensive, legislative controls are necessary to prevent abuse or unwarranted intrusion. This is why we have a strict legal framework to control the powers and ability of the state to monitor its own citizens and those external to the state.

The first control is the ECHR itself and Art. 8. As already noted, state surveillance is only compliant with Art. 8 where it fits within the Art. 8(2) exceptions which require that the interference with privacy be necessary in a democratic society, in accordance with law, and proportionate. The ECtHR has given guidance in all three of these. In *Klass & Ors v Germany*,[6] the court started from the premise that democratic societies were under threat from highly sophisticated forms of espionage and terrorism with the

[3] An overview of the Snowden Files can be obtained via <http://www.theguardian.com/us-news/the-nsa-files>.

[4] S Chakrabarti, 'Let me be clear—Edward Snowden is a hero' *The Guardian* (London, 14 June 2015) <http://www.theguardian.com/commentisfree/2015/jun/14/edward-snowden-hero-government-scare-tactics>; T Huddleston Jr., 'Steve Wozniak: Edward Snowden is "a hero to me"' *Fortune Magazine* (New York, 26 May 2015) <http://fortune.com/2015/05/26/steve-wozniak-edward-snowden/>.

[5] M Hastings, 'Snowden's clearly an anarchist and traitor. Those who endorse him are just as dangerous' *Daily Mail* (London, 8 April 2015) <http://www.dailymail.co.uk/debate/article-3029612/MAX-HASTINGS-Snowden-s-clearly-anarchist-traitor-endorse-just-dangerous.html>; C Moore, 'Edward Snowden is a traitor, just as surely as George Blake was' *Daily Telegraph* (London, 5 July 2013) <http://www.telegraph.co.uk/technology/internet-security/10162351/Edward-Snowden-is-a-traitor-just-as-surely-as-George-Blake-was.html>.

[6] (1978) 2 EHRR 214.

result that the state had to be able, in order effectively to counter such threats, to undertake the secret surveillance of subversive elements operating within its jurisdiction. The court therefore accepted that the existence of some legislation granting powers of secret surveillance over the mail, post, and telecommunications was, under exceptional conditions, necessary in a democratic society in the interests of national security and/or for the prevention of disorder or crime. In fixing the conditions under which the system of surveillance is to be operated, the court noted that the domestic legislature enjoys a certain discretion, and that it is certainly not for the court to substitute for the assessment of the national authorities of what might be the best policy in this field. However, although domestic legislatures have a wide discretion, this is not unlimited. Because of the danger that such a law poses to democracy, the court emphasized that states do not have unlimited discretion to subject persons within their jurisdiction to secret surveillance measures in the name of the struggle against espionage and terrorism. As powers of secret surveillance of citizens characterize a police state, they are tolerable only in so far as the means provided for by the legislation to achieve such aims remain within the bounds of what is necessary in a democratic society. The interest of the respondent state in protecting its national security must be balanced against the seriousness of the interference with the applicant's right to respect for his private life.[7]

This raises the question of whether the activity of the state is in accordance with law. In a line of case law, the court has established that this requirement will only be met when three conditions are satisfied:[8]

Highlight In accordance with the law according to the ECtHR

(1) the impugned measure must have some basis in domestic law and, with regard to the quality of the law at issue,

(2) it must be accessible to the person concerned, and

(3) it must have foreseeable consequences.

This was reviewed in *Malone v UK*.[9] Mr Malone had been charged with an offence based in part upon information received through a telephone tap placed on his phone line under a warrant from the Secretary of State. Mr Malone argued there was no law permitting this; the only relevant provision being s. 80 of the Post Office Act 1969 which said:

> A requirement to do what is necessary to inform designated persons holding office under the Crown concerning matters and things transmitted or in course of transmission by means of postal or telecommunication services provided by the Post Office may be laid on the Post Office for the like purposes and in the like manner as, at the passing of this Act, a requirement may be laid on the Postmaster General to do what is necessary to inform such persons concerning matters and things transmitted or in course of transmission by means of such services provided by him.

[7] Ibid. See also *Leander v Sweden* (1987) 9 EHRR 433.

[8] *Kennedy v United Kingdom* [2011] 52 EHRR 4; *Rotaru v Romania* [2000] ECHR 192; *Kruslin v France* (1990) 12 EHRR 547; *Huvig v France* (1990) 12 EHRR 528; *Amann v Switzerland* (2000) 30 EHRR 843.

[9] (1984) 7 EHRR 14.

The court accepted that the requirements of the Convention, notably in regard to foreseeability, could not be exactly the same in the special context of interception of communications for the purposes of police investigations. In particular, the requirement of foreseeability could not mean that an individual should be enabled to foresee if and when the authorities were likely to intercept his communications so that he could adapt his conduct accordingly. Nevertheless, the law should be sufficiently clear in its terms to give citizens an adequate indication as to the circumstances in which, and the conditions on which, public authorities were empowered to resort to this secret and potentially dangerous interference with the right to respect for private life and correspondence. Since the implementation, in practice, of measures of secret surveillance of communications was not open to scrutiny by the individuals concerned or the public generally, it would be contrary to the rule of law for the legal discretion granted to the executive to be expressed in terms of an unfettered power. Consequently, the law should indicate the scope of any such discretion conferred on the competent authorities and the manner of its exercise with sufficient clarity, having regard to the legitimate aim of the measure in question, to give the individual adequate protection against arbitrary interference.[10]

In the joined cases of *Kruslin v France* and *Huvig v France*, the court reflected that tapping and other forms of interception of telephone conversations represented a serious interference with private life and correspondence and had accordingly to be based on a law that was particularly precise. It was essential to have clear, detailed rules on the subject, especially as the technology available for use was continually becoming more sophisticated.[11]

Finally, the interference with liberty must be proportionate. This was considered in *S & Marper v UK*.[12] The case concerned two individuals who had fingerprint and DNA evidence taken from them during criminal investigations. In one case the individual was acquitted at trial, in the other charges were not pressed. The individuals then applied to have their collected information destroyed but the police refused. In the House of Lords Lord Steyn referred specifically to the value of the fingerprint and DNA databases built up by the police under s. 64(1A) of the Police and Criminal Evidence Act 1984:

> almost 6,000 DNA profiles had been linked with crime-scene stain profiles which would have been destroyed under the former provisions. The offences involved included 53 murders, 33 attempted murders, 94 rapes, 38 sexual offences, 63 aggravated burglaries, and 56 cases involving the supply of controlled drugs. On the basis of the existing records, the Home Office statistics estimated that there was a 40 per cent chance that a crime-scene sample would be matched immediately with an individual's profile on the database. This showed that the fingerprints and samples which could now be retained had in the previous three years played a major role in the detection and prosecution of serious crime.[13]

On this basis, he found the law to be proportionate:

> Lord Steyn saw five factors which led to the conclusion that the interference was proportionate to the aim: (i) the fingerprints and samples were kept only for the limited purpose of the

[10] This judgment led directly to the passing of the Interception of Communications Act 1985.
[11] *Kruslin v France*; *Huvig v France*, see (n. 8).
[12] (2009) 48 EHRR 50.
[13] Ibid. [17].

detection, investigation and prosecution of crime; (ii) the fingerprints and samples were not of any use without a comparator fingerprint or sample from the crime scene; (iii) the fingerprints would not be made public; (iv) a person was not identifiable from the retained material to the untutored eye; and (v) the resultant expansion of the database by the retention conferred enormous advantages in the fight against serious crime.[14]

The ECtHR, however, felt otherwise: it found the actions of the UK authorities to be disproportionate on four grounds.

Highlight Marper's grounds of disproportionality

(1) The gathering of blanket biometric data from all those suspected of offences whatever their age or the seriousness of the offence, and without a time limit for storage was disproportionate.

(2) There was no independent review of decisions as to whether data should be retained.

(3) Some data is particularly sensitive, the retention of cellular samples is particularly intrusive given the wealth of genetic and health information contained therein.

(4) The mere retention of data could impact an individual through stigmatization or disturbance of the presumption of innocence.

Any UK law which allows for the interception, storage, and examination of digital data must therefore comply with these principles. The current primary provisions are to be found in the Regulation of Investigatory Powers Act (RIPA) 2000. It begins by repeating the *Malone* principle that interception must be carried out in accordance with law. By s. 1 it is an offence for any person (either a person involved in an investigation of a law enforcement body or a private person) to intercept any communication in the course of its transmission by means of a public telecommunication system. This covers not only telephone calls but also emails, SMS/MMS messages, IM messages (including WhatsApp and similar), and all other forms of communication (such as Facebook updates, tweets, or search terms). It was s. 1 which brought the *News of the World* royal affairs editor to justice after he was found guilty of 'hacking' the voicemail messages of members of the Prince of Wales' staff in 2006 and which led eventually to Operation Weeting, the police operation which led to the arrests of, among others, Neville Thurlbeck, *News of the World* chief reporter; Ian Edmondson, former *News of the World* news editor; and James Weatherup, *News of the World* assistant news editor, for breaches of the Act, and ultimately Rebekah Brooks, News International chief executive and former *News of the World* editor who was arrested (although cleared at trial) on suspicion of conspiring to intercept communications, contrary to s. 1(1) of the Criminal Law Act 1977. An exception is given in s. 3 where all persons have agreed to the recording of the communication otherwise a warrant will normally be required. Warrants may be issued under s. 7 or s. 8 and may take the form of a targeted or bulk warrant. The first thing to note about RIPA warrants is that under s. 7(1) they are issued by the Secretary of State, in practice either the Foreign Secretary or the Home Secretary, or by an appropriate member of the

[14] Ibid. [21].

Scottish Executive where devolved powers are involved. There is currently no role for judicial warrants in RIPA as are frequently found elsewhere in the world (as we shall see below when we discuss § 702 of the US Foreign Intelligence Surveillance Act 1978). The process is an executive process and RIPA warrants are more like executive orders than warrants in the normal legal sense. Most warrants issued by the Home Secretary will take the form of an internal interception warrant which is one targeted on a resident or citizen of the British Isles. By s. 7(3) such a warrant must be addressed to the person falling within s. 6(2) by whom, or on whose behalf, the application for the warrant was made. This is a list of senior law enforcement and intelligence officials and is intended to prevent such warrants being used disproportionately. An internal communications intercept warrant must be targeted. This means that the warrant must comply with s. 8(1) and (2).

Highlight Regulation of Investigatory Powers Act 2000, s. 8(1) and (2)

Contents of warrants

(1) An interception warrant must name or describe either—

(a) one person as the interception subject; or

(b) a single set of premises as the premises in relation to which the interception to which the warrant relates is to take place.

(2) The provisions of an interception warrant describing communications the interception of which is authorised or required by the warrant must comprise one or more schedules setting out the addresses, numbers, apparatus or other factors, or combination of factors, that are to be used for identifying the communications that may be or are to be intercepted.

This prevents mass or bulk surveillance from being carried out on residents or citizens of the UK since legally a warrant must be targeted on a person or a location. In addition to this, though, there is s. 8(4) which deals with warrants for external communications. This is a quite different kind of warrant, usually issued by the Foreign Secretary to GCHQ or the Secret Intelligence Service (SIS). It is a normal s. 7(1) warrant but with an added s. 8(4) certificate and it is governed by s. 8(4) and (5).

Highlight Regulation of Investigatory Powers Act 2000, s. 8(4) and (5)

Contents of warrants.

(4) Subsections (1) and (2) shall not apply to an interception warrant if–

(a) the description of communications to which the warrant relates confines the conduct authorised or required by the warrant to conduct falling within subsection (5); and

(b) at the time of the issue of the warrant, a certificate applicable to the warrant has been issued by the Secretary of State certifying–

→

→

(i) the descriptions of intercepted material the examination of which he considers necessary; and

(ii) that he considers the examination of material of those descriptions necessary as mentioned in section 5(3)(a), (b) or (c).

(5) Conduct falls within this subsection if it consists in–

(a) the interception of external communications in the course of their transmission by means of a telecommunication system; and

(b) any conduct authorised in relation to any such interception by section 5(6).

A s. 8(4) warrant with certificate can therefore only be used for external communications, these are communications which originate or terminate outside the British Isles. As these do not need to be targeted, they can be used to develop a bulk interception capability within the legal framework of RIPA.[15] This much was known; what was not known was the size and scale of this operation.

21.1.2 State surveillance programmes: Five Eyes, Upstream, and Tempora

The focus of this text is on the laws of the UK's jurisdictions but before we get to the current, and proposed, UK law in this arena it is worth first discussing some of the capabilities of the states involved by looking at some of the most invasive digital surveillance programmes in place. I have already mentioned in outline some of the better-known programmes operated mostly through the NSA and GCHQ. The first thing to be aware of is the data-sharing agreements in place between friendly states. Both the US and the UK are members of a group known as 'Five Eyes'. This is an intelligence alliance between the US, the UK, Canada, Australia, and New Zealand. It is based on a series of multilateral agreements known collectively as the UKUSA Signals Intelligence Agreement which began in 1940 and which co-opted the last Five Eyes members (Australia and New Zealand) in 1956.[16] The network grew in importance and scope throughout the cold war and several foreign security services were co-opted to share data within the Five Eyes network. This has led to speculation about the existence of shadow intelligence sharing networks such as Nine Eyes, which adds Denmark, France, the Netherlands, and Norway; Signal Seniors Europe (sometimes called Fourteen Eyes) which includes Germany, Belgium, Italy, Spain, and Sweden; and even Forty-one Eyes adding in all others in the allied coalition in Afghanistan.[17] In fact in 2013 *The Guardian* reported that 'the exclusivity of the various coalitions grates with some, such as Germany, which

[15] It should be noted that the entire GCHQ external surveillance programme was on 12 December 2014 authorized by only 18 s. 8(4) warrants. Parliamentary Intelligence and Security Committee, *Privacy and Security: A modern and transparent legal framework* (HMSO 2015) [98]. These warrants allowed GCHQ to intercept in the region of 50 billion communications daily.

[16] Agreements from 1940 to 1956 were declassified in 2010 and may be found at the National Archive site at <http://discovery.nationalarchives.gov.uk/results/r/?_q=ukusa>.

[17] E MacAskill and J Ball, 'Portrait of the NSA: no detail too small in quest for total surveillance' *The Guardian* (London, 2 November 2013) <http://www.theguardian.com/world/2013/nov/02/nsa-portrait-total-surveillance>.

is using the present controversy to seek an upgrade. Germany has long protested at its exclusion, not just from the elite Five Eyes but even from Nine Eyes. Minutes from the UK intelligence agency GCHQ note: "The NSA's relationship with the French was not as advanced as GCHQ's . . . the Germans were a little grumpy at not being invited to join the 9-Eyes group."[18]

It is clear therefore that considerable intelligence sharing goes on between states, with the UK at the heart of the highest-level intelligence sharing networks. In fact, it is likely to be the case that the relationship between the NSA and GCHQ is the heart of all intelligence sharing activities across the North Atlantic.[19] Against this backdrop Edward Snowden has revealed details of some of the key programmes operated by Five Eyes partners. Primary programmes include Upstream a programme operated by the NSA. This is a large-scale data-gathering programme in which the NSA gathers the content and metadata of communications as they pass through fibre-optic cables. The data is gathered under Executive Order 12333[20] which grants wide authority to the agencies within the US Intelligence Community 'to collect, retain or disseminate information concerning United States persons only in accordance with procedures established by the head of the agency concerned and approved by the Attorney General'.[21] Where there are gaps in the Upstream data, such as where that data is encrypted, this can be filled in by the Prism programme; another NSA programme.[22] This is a large-scale data-gathering programme in which the NSA gathers stored internet communications data from technology and telecommunications companies based in the United States such as Google, Microsoft, Facebook, and Apple. The data is requested under a § 702 warrant obtained under the FISA Amendments Act of 2008. This allows the Foreign Intelligence Surveillance Court, which meets in secret, to authorize the NSA (or other national security or law enforcement body) to carry out surveillance 'for a period of up to 1 year from the effective date of the authorization, the targeting of persons reasonably believed to be located outside the United States to acquire foreign intelligence information'.[23] These warrants are then served on the relevant technology or telecommunications company and may require the handing over of metadata, call records, details of contents of calls, emails, or web searches, or any number of other types of data. It is reported that much of the data is handed over in unencrypted format or with a backdoor through any encryption.[24] This means the NSA can use Prism requests to target communications that were encrypted when they travelled across the internet backbone.

[18] Ibid.

[19] N Hopkins and J Borger, 'Exclusive: NSA pays £100m in secret funding for GCHQ' *The Guardian* (London, 1 August 2013) <http://www.theguardian.com/uk-news/2013/aug/01/nsa-paid-gchq-spying-edward-snowden>.

[20] <http://www.archives.gov/federal-register/codification/executive-order/12333.html>.

[21] Ibid. [2.3].

[22] An overview of the NSA programmes and how they fit together may be found at BM Kaufman, 'A Guide to What We Now Know About the NSA's Dragnet Searches of Your Communications' ACLU Blog (New York, 9 August 2013) <https://www.aclu.org/blog/guide-what-we-now-know-about-nsas-dragnet-searches-your-communications>.

[23] HR 6304. <https://www.gpo.gov/fdsys/pkg/BILLS-110hr6304enr/pdf/BILLS-110hr6304enr.pdf>.

[24] G Greenwald et al., 'Microsoft handed the NSA access to encrypted messages' *The Guardian* (London, 12 July 2013) <http://www.theguardian.com/world/2013/jul/11/microsoft-nsa-collaboration-user-data>.

There are limitations to the Prism programme. As warrants are awarded under § 702 it cannot legally target those resident in the United States. Often this is misreported as US citizens but it is clear that §702 is a residence qualification, not one of naturalization, and US citizens may often be surveilled using the Prism system when outside the US. Also, as we shall see below, with Tempora there is a problem with restrictions based upon geographical location when it comes to using internet data. While in the days of analogue communications it was easy to identify if a telephone was based in the US or in Vietnam, it can be very difficult to determine the difference between domestic and external communications using internet technology. As we saw in chapter 2 the network uses packet switching technology and will send packets by the most efficient route in terms of network capacity, not in terms of network geography. Thus, there is no reason to assume that if files are transmitted from a computer in New York to one in Chicago that all will follow the most direct route. If the network between New York and Chicago is extremely congested one packet may go via Toronto, another via Tijuana, and another possibly even via Tel Aviv. As a result, it has been reported by the *Washington Post* that when intelligence analysts search collected and stored data 'analysts key in "selectors", or search terms, that are designed to produce at least 51 percent confidence in a target's "foreignness".'[25] The authors of the report note that this 'is not a very stringent test'. Additionally, there are few protections for UK citizens or residents[26] and none at all for non-UK EU citizens or residents. This was the foundation of the legal challenge against the legality in EU law of the process of data exportation from the EU to the US under the so-called safe harbour agreement in the case of *Schrems v Data Protection Commissioner*,[27] discussed in chapter 20.[28]

In the UK, GCHQ operates an equally invasive data gathering and retention programme. The main component of this is a programme known as Tempora, which operates with arguably less legal oversight than Upstream/Prism. Tempora is in essence a locally stored buffered version of internet communications carried via the undersea fibre-optic cables that form the backbone of the internet. In June 2013 the *Guardian* newspaper reported documents discovered in the Snowden files which showed that GCHQ had installed taps on 'more than 200 fibre-optic cables and was able to process data from at least 46 of them at a time. Each of the cables carries data at a rate of 10 gigabits per second, so the tapped cables had the capacity, in theory, to deliver more than 21 petabytes a day—equivalent to sending all the information in all the books in the British Library 192 times every 24 hours. And the scale of the programme is constantly increasing as more cables are tapped and GCHQ data storage facilities in the UK and abroad are expanded with the aim of processing terabits (thousands of gigabits) of data at a time.'[29] As the authors noted: 'For the 2 billion users of the world wide web,

[25] Ibid.

[26] There is an informal protection for UK citizens between the Five Eyes partners. A pact between partners agrees that Five Eyes partners, including the United States, must treat UK citizens as if they were their own. See GCHQ and Second Parties in GCHQ, 'Operational Legalities' *The Intercept* (New York, 22 June 2015) <https://theintercept.com/document/2015/06/22/operational-legalities-gchq-powerpoint-presentation/>.

[27] (C-362/14) EU:C:2015:650.

[28] See 20.3.3.

[29] MacAskill et al., 'GCHQ taps fibre-optic cables for secret access to world's communications' *The Guardian* (London, 21 June 2013) <http://www.theguardian.com/uk/2013/jun/21/gchq-cables-secret-world-communications-nsa>.

Tempora represents a window on to their everyday lives, sucking up every form of communication from the fibre-optic cables that ring the world.'[30] As the documents went on to explain, the buffer could store these massive amounts of data for a considerable period, 'Tempora allowed the agency to set up internet buffers so it could not simply watch the data live but also store it—for 3 days in the case of content and 30 days for metadata.'[31] In essence GCHQ had the capacity to buffer 21 petabytes of data per day, both content and metadata, and to store all that data for 3 days and the metadata for 30 days in 2013. That data being, like Upstream data, drawn directly from the fibre-optic cables that make up the internet backbone.[32] How was all this legal? Well according to GCHQ it is because they hold a relevant s. 8(4) warrant with certificate as described above.

The role played by s. 8(4) warrants is therefore similar to that of § 702 FISA warrants in the US. They are intended to allow for mass surveillance of external communications (that is, communications external to the state) while protecting the communications of those resident within the state from mass state surveillance. The idea behind both § 702 and s. 8(4) is that the state must be free to spy on external threats through programmes of mass surveillance and data gathering but that it must not turn those same powers onto its own citizens. Two things are, though, immediately apparent when one compares the § 702 legal authorization scheme used in Prism with the s. 8(4) scheme. The first is that § 702 warrants are issued by a judge, albeit one in a secret court which approves 99.97 per cent of all applications,[33] whereas s. 8(4) warrants are issued by the Secretary of State.[34] This means there is no separation of the executive and the judiciary in the s. 8(4) process. The second is that § 702 warrants are targeted on persons whereas s. 8(4) warrants are targeted on communications. This is an important but subtle distinction. It means that to comply with § 702 an analyst carrying out a Prism inquiry has to be able to demonstrate (even if it is only to 51 per cent as reported) that the inquiry does not 'intentionally target any person known at the time of acquisition to be located in the United States' and does not 'intentionally target a person reasonably believed to be located outside the United States if the purpose of such acquisition is to target a particular, known person reasonably believed to be in the United States'. In addition, the inquiry must be carried out in a manner consistent with the Fourth Amendment to the Constitution of the United States. This means that if an NSA analyst knows a communication has been sent between someone in Syria and someone in Syracuse, New York, and the intent of the inquiry is to carry out an investigation into the individual living in Syracuse, then a § 702 warrant does not cover this. However, as s. 8(4) is concerned with communications rather than persons, an equivalent GCHQ analyst examining a communication buffered by Tempora that

[30] Ibid.

[31] Ibid.

[32] We must assume the intercept and storage capacities have both increased since then. In evidence to the Joint Parliamentary Committee on the Draft Investigatory Powers Bill Eric King, Director of Don't Spy on Us suggested that GCHQ could have the capacity to actively intercept up to 25 per cent of global internet traffic. <http://data.parliament.uk/writtenevidence/committeeevidence.svc/evidencedocument/draft-investigatory-powers-bill-committee/draft-investigatory-powers-bill/written/26357.html>.

[33] C Clarke, 'Is the Foreign Intelligence Surveillance Court Really a Rubber Stamp? *Ex Parte* Proceedings and the FISC Win Rate' (2014) 66 *Stan. L. Rev. Online* 125.

[34] Regulation of Investigatory Powers Act 2000, s. 7(1).

originated in Iran and terminated in Irby, Merseyside, it would be legal under the terms of a bulk intercept warrant issued by the Secretary of State for that message to be read as part of an inquiry into the UK resident recipient of the message. Because of this, there are specific safeguards in ss. 15–16 of RIPA which seek to provide UK residents with the same form of protection as seen in § 702. The key provision, or second 'narrow section', is s. 16(2) which requires that in order to be examined, material gathered under a s. 8(4) warrant must fall within the Secretary of State's certificate and it must not be selected according to a factor that is 'referable to an individual who is known for the time being to be in the British Islands' and the purpose of which is to identify his communications. This seems to provide the same safeguards as § 702. However, there are a number of limitations to this and as noted by David Anderson QC, the Independent Reviewer of Terrorism Legislation:

> Sections 16(3)-(5) provide for two exceptions to that position:
>
> (a) The external communications of a person known to be in the British Islands may be selected for examination if the Secretary of State certifies that that is necessary for the purposes of national security, the prevention or detection of serious crime or protecting the economic wellbeing of the UK [by] s. 16(3). In practice the Foreign Secretary approves one or more lists of such targets every six months, though he can add names at any time.
>
> (b) If the person to whom the warrant is addressed concludes that there has been a relevant change of circumstances, in essence that the individual has now entered the British Islands, the material may still be selected for a brief period of time. The short window of five days that is allowed for the selection of material under RIPA s. 16 provides the opportunity to obtain a certificate from the Secretary of State that the examination of that material is necessary (ss. 16(4)-(6)) or to obtain a s. 8(1) warrant to intercept all of their communications.[35]

The second of these is not dissimilar to the provisions in § 702 which allow the NSA to monitor the communications of US citizens outside the US for a limited period. The first, however, drives a coach and horses through any concept of a safeguard. While it may be the case that as Anderson noted: 'most UK-based individuals who are subjects of interest to the security and intelligence agencies or law enforcement are however targets of s. 8(1) warrants issued by the relevant Secretary of State, which will authorise the interception of all their communications, where necessary with the assistance of GCHQ'.[36] The use of the term 'most' rather than 'all' suggests this safeguard is lacking.

21.1.3 *Liberty & Privacy International v GCHQ*

The question of safeguards was at the heart of a recent legal challenge to GCHQ's role in the Prism programme, and to the operation of the Tempora programme.[37] Challenges against operations carried out by GCHQ cannot be taken to the normal courts. Challenges to the operations of any of the intelligence services must be taken

[35] D Anderson, 'A Question of Trust: Report of the Investigatory Powers Review' (HMSO 2015) [6.55]–[6.56].

[36] Ibid.

[37] *Liberty & Ors v GCHQ & Ors* [2014] UKIPTrib 13_77-H.

to a secret court, the Investigatory Powers Tribunal.[38] Such a challenge was brought by a group of civil liberties groups led by Liberty and Privacy International. The groups essentially brought two challenges. The first was that on the alleged factual basis[39] that:

> the US Government's 'Prism' system collects foreign intelligence information from electronic communication service providers under US court supervision . . . the Claimants' communications and/or communications data might in principle have been obtained by the US Government via Prism and might in principle have thereafter been obtained by the Intelligence Services from the US Government. Thereafter, the Claimants' communications and/or communications data might in principle have been retained, used or disclosed by the (British) Intelligence Services (a) pursuant to a specific request from the intelligence services and/or (b) not pursuant to a specific request from the intelligence services.

In such a case the question for the tribunal was, does this satisfy the Art. 8(2) [of the ECHR] 'in accordance with the law requirement?'[40] The second challenge was based on the alleged facts that:

> (a) the Intelligence Services operate a programme, described as Tempora, under which fibre-optic cables are intercepted. This involves making available the contents of all the communications and communications data being transmitted through the fibre optic cables;
>
> (b) the intercepted communications and communications data may be retained for an indefinite period and automatically searched through the use of a large number of search terms, including search terms supplied by the United States National Security Agency; and
>
> (c) the intercepted communications and communications data may then be further retained, analysed and shared with other public authorities.

On this basis the question was, 'does the alleged Tempora programme and/or the s. 8(4) regime give rise to unlawful discrimination contrary to (i) Art. 14 of the ECHR (as read with Art. 8 and/or Art. 10)?'[41]

In some ways the challenge was most interesting for what it unearthed in terms of operational parameters in use at GCHQ. In a witness statement, provided by Charles Farr, then Director-General of the Office for Security and Counter Terrorism,[42] the nature of an external communication for the purposes of s. 8(4) was discussed.[43]

[38] Regulation of Investigatory Powers Act 2000, s. 65.

[39] The Tribunal will not examine the factual basis of any claim as to do so would require an inquiry into operational matters. Instead, inquiries before the tribunal proceed on the basis of assumed or alleged facts—form of moot analysis if you will.

[40] See (n. 37) [14].

[41] Ibid. [78]–[79].

[42] Now Chairman of the Joint Intelligence Committee and Head of the Joint Intelligence Organisation at the Cabinet Office.

[43] Witness statement of Charles Farr in *Liberty & Ors v GCHQ & Ors* Case No. IPT/13/92/CH, [129]–[134] <https://www.liberty-human-rights.org.uk/sites/default/files/Witness%20statement%20of%20Charles%20Farr%20on%20behalf%20of%20the%20Intelligence%20Services%2016th%20May%202014.pdf>. The Code referred to is the *Code of practice for the interception of communications* <http://www.gov.uk/government/uploads/system/uploads/attachment_data/file/97956/interception-comms-code-practice.pdf>.

Highlight Charles Farr explains 'external communications'

The distinction in paragraph 5.1 of the Code between (i) the routing of a communication and (ii) the location from which it is sent/where it is received is intended to address these different factual scenarios, and to indicate that the route that a message takes is immaterial. A 'communication' for these purposes, both in RIPA and the Code, has both a particular sender and a particular recipient. Under Paragraph 5.1 of the Code, the relevant question to ask is not via whom (or what) a message has been transmitted, but for whom (or what), objectively speaking, the message is intended. Thus, an email from a person in London to a person in Birmingham will be an internal, not external communication for the purposes of RIPA and the Code, whether or not it is routed via IP addresses outside the British Islands, because the intended recipient is within the British Islands.

A person conducting a Google search for a particular search term in effect sends a message to Google asking Google to search its index of web pages. The message is a communication between the searcher's computer and a Google web server (as the intended recipient). The Google web server will search Google's index of pages for search results and in turn send a second communication—containing those results—back to the searcher's computer (as intended recipient). Google's data centres, containing its servers, are located around the world; but its largest centres are in the United States, and its largest European centres are outside the British Islands . . . In such a case, the search would correspondingly involve two 'external communications' for the purposes of section 20 of RIPA and paragraph 5.1 of the Code.

Mr Farr goes on to confirm that a YouTube search and video delivery, the sending of a tweet or the posting of a status update, message, or any other file on Facebook would all involve external communications.[44] This is factually correct in terms of recording the form of communication in place. The servers are outside the British Isles and as a result the communication is an external communication if one takes what Orin Kerr calls an 'external perspective', that is, 'the viewpoint of an outsider concerned with the functioning of the network in the physical world rather than the perceptions of a user'.[45] However, the issue is confused by Mr Farr following what Kerr calls an internal perspective when dealing with emails between London and Birmingham routed outside the British Islands. The internal perspective is 'the point of view of a user who is logged on to the Internet and chooses to accept the virtual world of cyberspace as a legitimate construct'.[46] What we see therefore is what often occurs with law enforcement bodies and security services, an inconsistent approach applying both the internal perspective 'cyberspace is a place' and the external perspective 'cyberspace is a communications medium' simultaneously. Why should a UK resident or citizen assume that an email sent from London to Birmingham was legally different from an internet search conducted (in their view) in the privacy of their own home or a tweet or Facebook message intended to be read by friends in Manchester? This is a major problem with the current application of s. 8(4). Although there is a logical explanation for the difference in

[44] Ibid. [135]–[138].
[45] O Kerr, 'The Problem of Perspective in Internet Law' (2003) 91 *Georgetown Law Journal* 357, 360.
[46] Ibid. 359.

approaches the inconsistency in applying the internal and external perspectives makes it very difficult for the average individual to understand.

In his review of the distinction between internal and external communications the Independent Reviewer of Terrorism Legislation noted that 'This was not clear prior to the publication of Mr Farr's statement. Some have considered those distinctions counter-intuitive: for example, many people might not consider a Google search to be a communication at all, let alone an external communication.'[47] He goes on to note that: 'Further potential confusion follows from the fact that internal communications are collected under external warrants . . . As explained in the Charles Farr Statement, it is inevitable that there is "by-catch" of internal communications because s. 8(4) bulk interception takes place at the level of communications cables. It is generally accepted that the collection of such material cannot be avoided.'[48] This is the same side effect we noted with respect to Prism and § 702 warrants: there is no way to extract purely internal communications from the data feed at the point of collection, they can only be identified when examined. Thus, as technically a s. 8(4) warrant is an interception warrant, all internal communications gathered under the warrant are illegally intercepted. This is remedied by s. 5(6) which allows for collateral data to be collected if it is necessary in order to collect the information that is specified in the warrant. Yet again, we are left with the feeling that although the letter of the law is being met the spirit of it is not.

The eventual outcome of the *Liberty v GCHQ* case was an unusual yet ultimately pyrrhic victory for the claimants. The tribunal found that the activities of GCHQ were lawful and in compliance with the ECHR on the basis that the disclosures made to the tribunal in the course of its hearings (and which were published in the judgment at paras 47–48 and 126) revealed 'the existence of a safeguard rendering it less, rather than more, likely that there will be objectionable interference with privacy or arbitrary conduct by the Respondents.'[49] However, in a later order published in February 2015 the Tribunal found that: '"prior to the disclosures made and referred to in the Tribunal's Judgment of 5 December 2014 and this judgment" the Prism and/or Upstream arrangements contravened Articles 8 or 10 ECHR, but now comply.'[50] In other words, in a rare victory for the claimants, the tribunal found that GCHQ had been acting illegally in processing Prism/Upstream data before 5 December 2014 when the safeguards were publicized in the tribunal's own judgment. Nonetheless, the very act of the judgment being published corrected that illegality, rendering the programme complaint with the ECHR.

The position of the tribunal on this particular point is, though, subject to challenge in the case of *Big Brother Watch & Ors v United Kingdom*[51] which makes essentially the same claims as the *Liberty v GCHQ* case before the ECtHR. This case was adjourned in

[47] See (n. 35) [6.52].

[48] Ibid. [6.53].

[49] *Liberty & Ors v GCHQ & Ors*, see (n. 37) [154].

[50] *Liberty & Ors v GCHQ & Ors* [2015] UKIPTrib 13_77-H, [32].

[51] This challenge claims that both GCQH involvement in Prism and Upstream and operation of Tempora are in breach of the *Kennedy v UK* principles. App. No. 58170/13. <http://www.privacynotprism.org.uk/assets/files/privacynotprism/496577_app_No_58170-13_BBW_ORG_EP_CK_v_UK_Grounds.pdf>.

April 2014 to await the outcome of *Liberty v GCHQ*. The adjournment was lifted in November 2015 allowing the case to proceed. The UK government has to 21 March 2016 to respond to the case. However, while the case was adjourned developments may have overtaken the case. In December 2015 the ECtHR in *Roman Zakharov v Russia*[52] found that, although interception of communications could be pursued for the legitimate aims of protection of national security and public safety, prevention of crime and protection of the economic well-being of the country, systems of mass, secret surveillance 'may undermine or even destroy democracy under the cloak of defending it'; for that reason 'the Court must be satisfied that there are adequate and effective guarantees against abuse.'[53] In looking at the specifics of the Russian scheme for surveillance, the court concluded that there were insufficient safeguards against mismanagements in the use of the system, such as arbitrariness or abuse. They noted that this risk is particularly high in a system, such as the one in Russia, where the secret services and the police had direct access, by technical means, to all mobile telephone communications.

More recently in *Szabó & Vissy v Hungary*[54] the ECtHR noted that:

> it is a natural consequence of the forms taken by present-day terrorism that governments resort to cutting-edge technologies in pre-empting such attacks, including the massive monitoring of communications susceptible to containing indications of impending incidents. The techniques applied in such monitoring operations have demonstrated a remarkable progress in recent years and reached a level of sophistication which is hardly conceivable for the average citizen, especially when automated and systemic data collection is technically possible and becomes widespread. In the face of this progress the Court must scrutinise the question as to whether the development of surveillance methods resulting in masses of data collected has been accompanied by a simultaneous development of legal safeguards securing respect for citizens' Convention rights.[55]

In examining the Hungarian provisions, the court found that:

> given that the scope of the measures could include virtually anyone, that the ordering is taking place entirely within the realm of the executive and without an assessment of strict necessity, that new technologies enable the Government to intercept masses of data easily concerning even persons outside the original range of operation, and given the absence of any effective remedial measures, let alone judicial ones, the Court concludes that there has been a violation of Article 8 of the Convention.[56]

These two decisions, when taken alongside developments such as Resolution 68/167 of the UN General Assembly on the Right to Privacy in the Digital Age,[57] suggest a strong direction of travel from international organizations, and in particular the ECtHR. Anyone who has read the *Zakharov*, and *Szabó and Vissy* decisions will find it difficult to imagine how the ECtHR in *Big Brother Watch* can do anything other than find the actions of GCHQ, and thereby the UK government, to be in breach of Art. 8.

[52] Application No. 47143/06, 4 December 2015 <http://hudoc.echr.coe.int/eng?i=001-159324>.
[53] Ibid. [232].
[54] Application No. 37138/14, 12 January 2016 <http://hudoc.echr.coe.int/eng?i=001-160020>.
[55] Ibid. [68].
[56] Ibid. [89].
[57] 18 December 2013, <http://www.un.org/ga/search/view_doc.asp?symbol=A/RES/68/167>.

21.1.4 The Anderson/RUSI reviews

The Snowden revelations were shocking to the general public and, with challenges to the legality of a number of programmes under way including the *Liberty v UK* case before the Investigatory Powers Tribunal, and, perhaps of more concern for the government, a pending challenge before the ECtHR in *Big Brother Watch*, the government and Parliament ordered and produced a number of reviews into the operations of the Regulation of Investigatory Powers Act, the Data Retention and Investigatory Powers Act 2014 (discussed below), and other intelligence and security legislative provisions, including the Intelligence Services Act 1994. In total three reviews were published in 2015.

The first was the report of the Parliamentary Intelligence and Security Committee, 'Privacy and Security: A modern and transparent legal framework', which reported on 12 March 2015.[58] It found that current framework did provide the form of safeguards needed to meet the requirements of the ECHR but recommended that a need for greater transparency of the law, in particular in relation to data sharing and data retention (discussed below) meant a new law should be introduced to codify all the existing law in one place, or as put by the Committee 'the Government should introduce a new Intelligence Services Bill setting out, in one Act of Parliament, the functions of the three UK intelligence and security Agencies. This should consolidate the intelligence and security related provisions [of current Acts].'[59] One issue looked at, in particular, was whether judges should replace ministers as the source for interception warrants. The strong view held by the Home Secretary and by Sir David Omand, who was a former Director of GCHQ, was that minsters must retain this role, given their accountability to Parliament and the people. As the Home Secretary noted: 'I think it is important that that decision is taken by somebody who is democratically accountable to the public.' Sir David agreed: 'I think it is entirely right that a Minister takes the responsibility on herself or himself to sign the warrant and then answers for the consequences if something terrible happens.'[60] The Committee noted that alternative views had been put. This from *Liberty* for example: 'It is the proper constitutional function of the independent judiciary to act as a check on the use of State power. Judges are best suited to applying necessary legal tests to ensure that surveillance is necessary and proportionate and their involvement will improve public trust and confidence in the system of surveillance.'[61] Whereas Eric Metcalfe, barrister and former director of human rights policy at JUSTICE noted the seemingly pointless distinction between search warrants to search premises and interception warrants to intercept communications. 'There is something extraordinary about a situation in which a Secretary of State can authorise intrusion into my private communications and my phone calls, but a judge is needed to get a search warrant for a person's house.'[62] Despite these views the Committee came down strongly in favour of retaining ministerial warrants:

> While judges will provide an objective assessment of the law, what has become apparent during the course of this Inquiry is that there is a distinct advantage to authorisation by

[58] HC 1075 (HMSO 2015).
[59] Ibid. Recommendation XX.
[60] Ibid. [195].
[61] Ibid. [196].
[62] Ibid. [197].

Ministers. Ministers are well informed about the current nature of the threat and are therefore best placed to assess national security considerations. However, what is more significant is that they can apply a further test, on top of the legal tests, by taking into account the wider context of the warrant application. Given the nature of the Agencies' work, there will be circumstances where it would be lawful to use intrusive powers but there may be political or diplomatic risks involved. . . Therefore, while a judge could only assess a warrant application based on compliance with the law (and we note that judges are not immune to criticism when they make controversial decisions), Ministers can apply an additional test which judges cannot. Judges might therefore approve more warrant applications on the basis of pure legal compliance, whereas a Minister may refuse more applications based on these broader considerations.[63]

The second review was the already mentioned review of the Independent Reviewer of Terrorism Legislation, 'A Question of Trust: Report of the Investigatory Powers Review'.[64] Like the Parliamentary Intelligence and Security Committee review this is a much wider review than just interception and it also includes a review of data retention which will be discussed below. The reviewer, David Anderson QC, as we have already seen, was concerned that the divide between internal and external communications, and therefore between s. 8(1) and s. 8(4) warrants, was not clear prior to the publication of Charles Farr's witness statement.[65] In general the Independent Reviewer was concerned about transparency in the current legal settlement.

At a general level, concerns with the RIPA regime are far from new. However, they have taken on a new and renewed intensity following the leaks in the Snowden Documents. The allegations in those papers took many by surprise, as have subsequent disclosures by the Government regarding the extent of the investigatory powers used by public authorities. A number of submissions made the point that the alleged conduct should have been clear on the face of the law, or should have been highlighted by the various oversight regimes set up under RIPA and related investigatory powers legislation. The fact that significant public information is only available due to these leaks, of which a significant majority remain NCND (Neither Confirm Nor Deny), is seen as unsatisfactory. This reflects a fundamental imbalance. Those involved in investigatory powers have (naturally) far more information regarding the use of those powers than those in civil society. Yet, as explained by Dr. Paul Bernal: '[i]t is not enough for the authorities just to say "trust us": the public needs to know that they can trust the authorities'. For many, that trust has eroded, and greater transparency is needed to get it back. Indeed, following the judgment of 6 February 2015 in the Liberty IPT case, which held that the failure to make certain procedures public rendered the data-sharing regime unlawful, many saw the need to make more information available to the public. This need for further transparency is a fundamental concern of many of those with whom I discussed these issues.[66]

On this basis he also recommended new legislation:

RIPA Part I, DRIPA 2014 and Part 3 of CTSA (Counter Terrorism and Security Act) 2015 should be replaced by a comprehensive new law, drafted from scratch, which: (a) affirms the privacy of communications; (b) prohibits interference with them by public authorities, save on terms

63 Ibid. [202]–[203].
64 See (n. 35).
65 Ibid. [6.52]–[6.59].
66 Ibid. [12.5]–[12.6].

> specified; and (c) provides judicial, regulatory and parliamentary mechanisms for authorisation, audit and oversight of such interferences.[67]

He also gave clear guidance as to how this new law should be written:

> The new law should be written so far as possible in non-technical language, should be structured and expressed so as to enable its essentials to be understood by intelligent readers across the world, and should cover all essential features, leaving details of implementation and technical application to codes of practice to be laid before Parliament and to guidance which should be unpublished only to the extent necessary for reasons of national security.[68]

Further, as should be clear from the phrase 'provides judicial, regulatory and parliamentary mechanisms for authorisation', the Independent Reviewer saw a vital role for judges in this new regime. He found it remarkable that the Home Secretary could be signing as many as 2,345 interception and property warrants and renewals as she did in 2014 and asks whether this 'is the best use of the Secretary of State's valuable time'.[69] He was also concerned that even though there was no evidence of bias or impropriety, the perception of the public could be difficult to shift: 'neither the British public nor the global public can be counted on to take the probity of the Secretary of State on trust, a point pressed on me not only in the many civil society submissions on this point but by a very senior police officer.'[70] He also noted the current system may run into legal problems:

> As to the legal position, the ECHR considers that 'it is in principle desirable to entrust supervisory control to a judge' but does not require judicial authorisation, at least where individual warrants are concerned. It is possible however that a more independent authorisation mechanism may be required in the future, whether in relation to bulk warrants (where the need for robust safeguards is at its highest), or as a consequence of the CJEU's apparent insistence, in Digital Rights Ireland, on 'prior review carried out by a court or by an independent administrative authority' even in respect of (less intrusive) access to retained communications data.[71]

The system recommended by the Independent Reviewer is a judicial authorization system with the possibility for a ministerial certificate in applications with national security implications.

Highlight The proposed judicial authorisation system

When a specific interception warrant is sought for the purpose specified in Recommendation 28(b) (national security) and that purpose relates to the defence of the UK and/or the foreign policy of the Government, the Secretary of State should have the power to certify that the warrant is required in the interests of the defence and/or foreign policy of the →

[67] Ibid. Recommendation 1.
[68] Ibid. Recommendations 3–5.
[69] Ibid. [14.49].
[70] Ibid. [14.50].
[71] Ibid. [14.53].

→

UK. In such cases, the Judicial Commissioner in determining whether to issue the warrant should be able to depart from that certificate only on the basis of the principles applicable in judicial review.

A specific interception warrant should be issued only if it is established to the satisfaction of a Judicial Commissioner that:

(a) the warrant is necessary for one or both of the permitted statutory purposes (preventing or detecting serious crime or in the interests of national security);

(b) the conduct authorised by the warrant is proportionate to what is sought to be achieved by that conduct; and

(c) the assurances regarding the handling, retention, use and destruction of the intercepted material, including in relation to privileged or confidential material, are satisfactory.[72]

The certification process would leave most applications wholly in the hands of a judicial commissioner with only these few applications certified as being for the purpose of defence of the UK and/or the foreign policy of the government, subject to what has since become known as a 'double-lock procedure'. This is a procedure where the minister issues the warrant, as is the case under RIPA, but subject to a judicial review procedure by a judicial commissioner.

These are two reports with two very different views. Although both the Independent Reviewer and the Parliamentary Committee agreed on the big picture that the UK law was legal and that abuses were not taking place, they both had very different views on who should be issuing warrants and how the law should be future-proofed. Into this came the third report, the report of the Royal United Services Institute (RUSI) which had been commissioned by the then Deputy Prime Minister Nick Clegg, 'A Democratic Licence to Operate'.[73] Taking a slightly different approach this report also recommended that a new law be made, and agreed with the Independent Reviewer that 'RIPA 2000 Part I, DRIPA 2014 and Part 3 of the CTSA 2015 should be replaced by a comprehensive new law.'[74] They recommended that interception warrants should remain substantially as they are, with specific interception warrants for domestic purposes and bulk interception warrants for external interception of bulk content and communications data. On authorization, though, the RUSI report treads a middle ground between the Independent Reviewer and the Parliamentary Committee. Whereas the Parliamentary Committee felt that the current system was sufficient and the Independent Reviewer felt that a system of judicial authorization was required, the RUSI report recommended a middle ground of sorts; a system called double-lock.[75]

It may be said that there is little distinction between this and the Independent Reviewer's judicial authorization system but it is different in two vital ways. The first

[72] Ibid. Recommendations 30 and 31.

[73] RUSI (London, 2015) <https://rusi.org/sites/default/files/20150714_whr_2-15_a_democratic_licence_to_operate.pdf>.

[74] Ibid. Recommendation 1.

[75] Ibid. Recommendation 10.

Highlight The double-lock system

We recommend that the government adopts a composite approach to the authorisation of warrants, dependent on the purpose for which the warrant is sought and subsequent degree of ministerial input required. Our approach does not discriminate between whether it is law enforcement or an intelligence agency submitting the warrant.

1. Where a warrant is sought for a purpose relating to the detection or prevention of serious and organized crime, the warrant should always be authorised by a judicial commissioner. Most police and other law-enforcement warrants would fall into this category. A copy of each warrant should be provided to the home secretary (so that the home secretary and officials can periodically examine trends in serious and organized crime, for example).
2. Where a warrant is sought for purposes relating to national security (including counter-terrorism, support to military operations, diplomacy and foreign policy) and economic well-being, the warrant should be authorised by the secretary of state subject to judicial review by a judicial commissioner. The review should take place before implementation of the warrant. If there is a case of urgency the secretary of state should be able to direct that a warrant comes into force immediately, and the judicial commissioner should be notified straight away and the judicial review conducted within fourteen days.

is that the RUSI double-lock re-sites the authorization of warrants in the second category (national security) to the Secretary of State. Under the Independent Reviewer's proposals the decision would always rest with the judicial commissioner (albeit one with very restricted scope in cases where a certificate is issued). The second is that the Independent Commissioner envisaged that certificates would only be used in narrow circumstances, when the purpose of the warrant 'relates to the defence of the UK and/or the foreign policy of the Government'. By comparison RUSI's second category is much wider 'purposes relating to national security (including counter-terrorism, support to military operations, diplomacy and foreign policy) and economic well-being'.

The government now had three reports to act upon. They also knew they had a tight timetable to act for any new legislation would need to be in place by December 2016, that being the sunset date on the Data Retention and Investigatory Powers Act 2014 (discussed below). After some time working on it, it was announced in the Queen's Speech 27 May 2015 that there would be a new Investigatory Powers Bill in the 2015–16 session.

21.1.5 The draft Investigatory Powers Bill (Interception)

One of the problems for any author working in the field of information technology law is that the law never stands still. We are as I write this in the very middle of one of the biggest upheavals of UK surveillance and security law in the last 16 years. The following section is written on the published draft of the Investigatory Powers Bill which is currently undergoing pre-legislative parliamentary scrutiny with a view to a Bill being introduced before Parliament in May 2016. By the time this book is published the law may look exactly as is predicted in this section or it may have changed considerably due to pre-legislative and legislative scrutiny. The reader is therefore forewarned to check the current status and text of the Investigatory Powers Act 2016 (as it no doubt now is) before proceeding.

The draft Bill brings together all the interception powers of RIPA (and DRIPA) as well as those under the Wireless Telegraphy Act 2006. The Bill if enacted will ensure that, as recommended by the Independent Reviewer, interception powers are limited to the current nine 'intercepting authorities'.[76] It splits the form of interception warrants into targeted and bulk. Targeted warrants are regulated by Part 2, Chapter 1 (ss. 12–31). This provides that there will now be three types of targeted warrant:

(1) a targeted interception warrant (a warrant which authorizes the interception of a communication or the obtaining of communications data, or the disclosure of such data);[77]

(2) a targeted examination warrant (a warrant which authorizes the examination of intercepted material obtained under a bulk interception warrant);[78] and

(3) a mutual assistance warrant (which allows communications to be intercepted or communications data to be examined as part of a mutual assistance request under EU or other Treaty requirements).[79]

One of the most eagerly awaited questions about the draft Bill was whether these warrants would be issued by ministerial or judicial authority. The draft Bill does set up a new oversight role, the Investigatory Powers Commissioner, assisted by a number of judicial commissioners.[80] These look very much like the judicial commissioners proposed by the Independent Reviewer, indeed cl. 167(2) states: 'A person is not to be appointed as the Investigatory Powers Commissioner or another Judicial Commissioner unless the person holds or has held a high judicial office.' However, their role is, it seems, to be rather in the double-lock form proposed by RUSI. The power to issue targeted warrants remains solely with the Secretary of State (or relevant Scottish minister).[81] The role of the judicial commissioner is relegated to 'approval' under cl. 19(1). This states that their role is merely to decide 'whether to approve a person's decision to issue a warrant under this Chapter'; to do so the judicial commissioner 'must review the person's conclusions as to the following matters—(a) whether the warrant is necessary on relevant grounds, and (b) whether the conduct that would be authorised by the warrant is proportionate to what is sought to be achieved by that conduct.' This sounds like a substantial power: it seems the judicial commissioner has the authority to overrule the Secretary of State on substantive grounds although their check comes after the issuance of the warrant.[82] It is a real check on ministerial power. However, the next subsection of the Bill undermines this: 'In doing so, the Judicial Commissioner must apply the same principles as would be applied by a court on an application for judicial review.'[83] The role of the judicial commissioner is therefore

[76] The nine are: (1) GCHQ, (2) SIS, (3) MI5, (4) The Ministry of Defence, (5) HMRC, (6) The National Crime Agency, (7) The Police Service Northern Ireland, (8) Police Scotland, and (9) The Metropolitan Police. See cl., 15(1) of the draft Investigatory Powers Bill.

[77] Cl. 12(2).

[78] Cl. 12(3).

[79] Cl. 12(4).

[80] Cl. 167.

[81] Cl. 14.

[82] The approval by the Judicial Commissioner should precede the warrant coming into effect. In urgent cases it can follow up to five working days after the issuance of the warrant—see cl. 20(3).

[83] Cl. 19(2).

clearly as an administrative review not a substantive one. This is arguably an even weaker check on ministerial power than the RUSI double-lock proposal.[84]

The provisions relating to the regulation of bulk warrants (old s. 8(4) warrants) are found in Part 6, Chapter 1 (ss. 106–121). These remain focused upon external communications, now called 'overseas-related' communications.[85] The definition of 'overseas-related' communications is interesting. It is defined in cl. 106(3) as (a) communications sent by individuals who are outside the British Islands, or (b) communications received by individuals who are outside the British Islands. In the explanatory notes there is no definition of 'individuals' but rephrases this to say 'overseas-related communications' [are] communications that are sent or received by persons outside of the British Islands. This suggests a slight relaxation on the current s. 8(4) regime in that if you send a communication to a server overseas with the server replying (that is, an internet search or inquiry) this is not an 'overseas-related' communication as there is no communication to an individual or person.[86] Clearly still covered, though, would be tweets, Facebook updates, and such like, which are readable overseas. The authorization process remains the same as with targeted warrants. The Secretary of State issues warrants (in this case there is no devolved power to Scottish ministers)[87] which are then subject to review, on judicial review principles, by the judicial commissioners.[88]

Few people are pleased with the proposed settlement. Many see this as a missed opportunity to give real power to judicial officers in the warrant application and issuing process, and a missed opportunity to create a true system of judicial accountability for executive action. The Shadow Home Secretary, in a letter to the Home Secretary made some strong objections:[89]

Highlight Andy Burnham's letter to Theresa May

[You] created the impression that both the Home Secretary and a senior judge would review the evidence. Indeed, you may recall that I asked you in the House about what would happen if there was a difference of opinion between the two. On closer inspection of the wording of the Bill, it would seem that it does not deliver the strong safeguard that you appeared to

[84] This lower-level review was admitted by the Home Office in their supplementary written evidence to the Joint Committee on the draft Investigatory Powers Bill where it was stated: 'As the Committee will know, in general terms, judicial review proceedings are concerned with the lawfulness of a decision and not the substance of that decision or its merits. In line with the long established principles of judicial review, the role of the Judicial Commissioners will be to conduct a review in order to assess whether that decision was flawed, and not to re-make the decision.' Home Office—Further supplementary written evidence (IPB0147) 7 January 2016 <http://data.parliament.uk/writtenevidence/committeeevidence.svc/evidencedocument/draft-investigatory-powers-bill-committee/draft-investigatory-powers-bill/written/26437.html>.

[85] Cl. 106(2)(a).

[86] It should be noted that this may be because search data may be captured in internet connection records (see 21.2).

[87] Cl. 107.

[88] Cl. 109.

[89] Letter from the Shadow Home Secretary to the Home Secretary, 6 November 2015 <http://www.scribd.com/doc/289007039/Andy-Burnham-letter-to-Theresa-May-on-draft-investigatory-powers-bill>.

→

be accepting. The current wording of the draft Bill requires the judge to review the 'process' undertaken by the Home Secretary in the same way applied to a judicial review: 'apply the same principles as would be applied by a court on an application for judicial review.' Legal advice we have sought confirms that the current wording does not deliver what we believed was being proposed in terms of the Home Secretary and Judicial Commissioner double-lock for warrant authorisation.

If our understanding is correct, then I wanted to give you notice that we will be looking to amend the wording of the Bill in Committee to ensure it delivers what we thought was being offered—ie a judge to review the evidence and authorise, or not, the approval of a warrant, as well as the Home Secretary. This will provide the proper 'double-lock' that you referred to.

The Shadow Home Secretary is not the only person to express concerns about the form of the authorization system found in the draft Bill. The leader of the Liberal Democrats has made the same point,[90] as has former Shadow Home Secretary David Davis.[91] It may be that by the time you are reading this all of this has changed, for as Andy Burnham MP promised pressure was brought to bear in committee. Again this is the risk of writing on a moving target.

21.2 **Data retention**

There is enough content in the draft Investigatory Powers Bill to write a book, or indeed several books, and no doubt many will be written in due course. Books will be written on equipment interference (state-sanctioned computer hacking), bulk personal datasets, communications data, and internet connection records (in more depth than will be done so here), but this is not the place for all these discussions. This is a book on information technology law, not surveillance law and powers. There is, though, one area we must discuss before we can treat this chapter as complete and that is data retention powers.

As the war on terror continues, security forces find themselves constantly stretched. The risk is that at some point their stretched resources mean vital information is being lost. This was illustrated in the immediate aftermath of the 7 July 2005 attacks in London. The attacks were committed by a small group of UK nationals who had obviously been in contact with supporters of terrorism but who had not been under surveillance. What security forces feared was that there were other cells ready to commit further attacks; a fear raised further after the abortive attacks of 21 July 2005. The security forces' attempts to piece together the events preceding 7 July were hampered by their lack of available data. They wanted to know to whom bombers were talking, whom

[90] T Farron MP, 'Liberal Democrats can and must oppose a snoopers' charter' *Liberal Democrat Voice* (London, 10 November 2015) <http://www.libdemvoice.org/tim-farron-writes-liberal-democrats-can-and-must-oppose-a-snoopers-charter-48200.html>.

[91] S Moss, 'Tory rebel David Davis: "We haven't had a Stasi or a Gestapo in Britain, so are intellectually lazy about surveillance"' *The Guardian* (London, 8 November 2015) <http://www.theguardian.com/politics/2015/nov/08/david-davis-stasi-gestapo-surveillance-tory-civil-liberties>.

they were emailing, and what information they were accessing online. To assist with future investigations the UK government, as chair of the Council of Europe, suggested new measures be taken to retain private communications data in case it were needed in future by security services or law enforcement bodies. The end result was the Data Retention Directive (now repealed).[92]

This provided that member states could require telecommunications and internet service providers to retain certain forms of data for a period of not less than six months and not more than two years.[93] The types of data affected were all set out in Art. 5 and are usually known as communications data or metadata. They were

(1) data necessary to trace and identify the source of a communication;
(2) data necessary to identify the destination of a communication;
(3) data necessary to identify the date, time, and duration of a communication;
(4) data necessary to identify the type of communication;[94] and
(5) data necessary to identify users' communication equipment or what purports to be their equipment.[95]

This data was required to be retained by the telecommunications or internet service provider for the prescribed time and had to be made available to the relevant authorities upon a formal request. The UK implemented the Data Retention Directive in two stages: first, the Data Retention (EC Directive) Regulations 2007,[96] and then subsequently the Data Retention (EC Directive) Regulations 2009.[97] The 2007 Regulations covered only telecommunications data—that is, data relating to telephone calls made from fixed-line and mobile telephones. They required that telecommunications providers retain session data for voice calls (that is, the telephone numbers of both the caller and the recipient of the call, the date and duration of the call, the telephone service used, the IMSI and the IMEI of both of the telephones and, for cell phones, the cell location in which the call was made and received) for a period of 12 months.[98] The 2009 Regulations extended and revoked the 2007 Regulations to cover internet communications as well. After repeating the requirements of the 2007 Regulations with respect to fixed-line and mobile telecommunications, they then went on to require internet service providers and internet access providers to retain: (1) the name and address of the subscriber or registered user to whom an internet protocol (IP) address, user ID or telephone number was allocated at the time of the communication; (2) the DSL or dial-up number of the

[92] Dir. 2006/24/EC of the European Parliament and of the Council of 15 March 2006 on the retention of data generated or processed in connection with the provision of publicly available electronic communications services or of public communications networks (repealed).

[93] Art. 6.

[94] Such data as the telephone or internet service used.

[95] This is data such as the calling and called telephone numbers; the international mobile subscriber identity (IMSI), or the international mobile equipment identity (IMEI) of the called or calling party, or the digital subscriber line (DSL) or other end point of the originator of an internet communication.

[96] SI 2007/2199.

[97] SI 2009/859.

[98] SI 2007/2199, regs. 4 and 5. In addition, reg. 5 requires that where a call is made from an anonymous pre-paid phone, the service provider must retain a record of the date and time of the initial activation of the service and the cell ID from which the service was activated.

subscriber; (3) the date and time the subscriber logged on and off from the service; (4) email user ID details; and (5) the internet service used. Again this was required to be retained for 12 months.[99] These provisions are discussed in the past tense as they have all been ruled illegal and have been repealed by the decision of the CJEU in *Digital Rights Ireland and Seitlinger & Ors*.[100]

21.2.1 *Digital Rights Ireland and Seitlinger & Ors*

As may be deduced from the first claimant this is a challenge to the Data Retention Directive that originated in Ireland, and then was joined by a similar challenge from Austria. Both sets of claimants raised similar objections to the legality of the Directive. The High Court of Ireland sent a series of questions to the CJEU asking, among other things, whether the Directive was compatible with the right to privacy laid down in Art. 7 of the Charter of Fundamental Rights of the European Union (the Charter) and Art. 8 ECHR; whether it was compatible with the right to the protection of personal data as laid down in Art. 8 of the Charter; and whether it was compatible with the right to freedom of expression as laid down in Art. 11 of the Charter and Art. 10 ECHR.[101] The Austrian court asked rather more succinctly 'Are Articles 3 to 9 of Directive 2006/24 compatible with Articles 7, 8 and 11 of the Charter?'[102] In a concise judgment of 73 paragraphs the court answered emphatically, no. In first addressing the question of Arts. 7 and 8, the court made a few strong points that 'the obligation imposed by Articles 3 and 6 of Directive 2006/24 on providers of publicly available electronic communications services or of public communications networks to retain, for a certain period, data relating to a person's private life and to his communications, such as those referred to in Article 5 of the directive, constitutes in itself an interference with the rights guaranteed by Article 7 of the Charter', and that 'the access of the competent national authorities to the data constitutes a further interference with that fundamental right.[103] Accordingly, Articles 4 and 8 of Directive 2006/24 laying down rules relating to the access of the competent national authorities to the data also constitute an interference with the rights guaranteed by Article 7 of the Charter.'[104] With interference established, the question was whether it was proportionate. The court acknowledged that the Directive satisfies an objective of general interest (the prevention of offences and the fight against crime, in particular organized crime and international terrorism),[105] but in examining whether the data retention principles of the Directive were proportionate, found that the 'Directive covers, in a generalised manner, all persons and all means of electronic communication as well as all traffic data without any differentiation, limitation or exception being made in the light of the objective of fighting against serious crime'[106] and that it 'does not require any relationship between the data

[99] SI 2009/859, reg. 5, Sch. Part III.
[100] [2014] All ER (EC) 775.
[101] Ibid. [18.2].
[102] Ibid. [21.1].
[103] Citing *Leander v Sweden*, see (n. 7), *Rotaru v Romania*, see (n. 8), and *Weber and Saravia v Germany* [2006] ECHR 1173.
[104] [2014] All ER (EC) 775 [34]–[35].
[105] Ibid. [41]–[44].
[106] Ibid. [57].

whose retention is provided for and a threat to public security and, in particular, it is not restricted to a retention in relation (i) to data pertaining to a particular time period and/or a particular geographical zone and/or to a circle of particular persons likely to be involved, in one way or another, in a serious crime, or (ii) to persons who could, for other reasons, contribute, by the retention of their data, to the prevention, detection or prosecution of serious offences.'[107] As a result the Directive was found not to comply proportionately with Arts. 7 and 8 of the Charter.[108] Having made this finding, the court first declined to deal with the Art. 11 question, it now being moot, and then vitally struck down the Directive.

21.2.2 The Data Retention and Investigatory Powers Act 2014 (DRIPA)

The impact of the *Digital Rights Ireland* decision was that all domestic legislation passed to give local effect to the Directive was now rendered illegal under EU law, including the Data Retention (EC Directive) Regulations 2009. For a short period after the judgment, which was given on 8 April 2014, the UK government was silent as to the impact of this. Then suddenly it seemed as if a panic button had been pressed in Downing Street. On the morning of 10 July 2014 the Prime Minister and Deputy Prime Minister together announced the need for 'emergency legislation' to replace the now defunct Regulations. A Bill, entitled the Data Retention and Investigatory Powers (DRIP) Bill was published the same morning with the support of the Leader of the Opposition. The Bill cleared the Commons at 10 p.m. on 15 July 2014 and was passed into law, having had a single day of debate in the Lords, on 17 July. At the time a large number of Parliamentarians expressed barely disguised fury about the way Parliament had been sidelined. Prominent Conservative backbencher David Davis MP stated:

> My understanding is there was an argument inside government between the two halves of the coalition and that argument has gone on for three months. So what the coalition cannot decide in three months this House has to decide in one day. This seems to me entirely improper because of the role of Parliament—we have three roles. One is to scrutinise legislation, one is to prevent unintended consequences, and one is to defend the freedom and liberty of our constituents. This undermines all three and we should oppose this motion.[109]

Prominent Labour backbencher (at the time) Tom Watson MP made the highly unparliamentary statement that the Bill was 'democratic banditry, resonant of a rogue state. The people who put this shady deal together should be ashamed',[110] while another Labour backbencher David Winnick MP stated baldly: 'I consider this to be an outright abuse of parliamentary procedure. I will certainly vote against the motion, and I hope that a number of hon. Members will do so as well.'[111] Of course the Bill did pass and became the Data Retention and Investigatory Powers Act 2015 (DRIPA). The Act is a very short eight sections and seeks essentially to replace the data retention powers lost in the *Digital Rights Ireland* outcome.

[107] Ibid. [59].
[108] Ibid. [69].
[109] HC Deb vol. 584, col. 690 (15 July 2014).
[110] Ibid. col. 691 (15 July 2014).
[111] Ibid. col. 689 (15 July 2014).

The first thing to note is that, no doubt due to the behind-closed-doors discussions between the Prime Minister and Deputy Prime Minister, it has a sunset provision. By s. 8(3) 'Sections 1 to 7 (and the provisions inserted into the Regulation of Investigatory Powers Act 2000 by sections 3 to 6) are repealed on 31 December 2016.' This was to ensure a full debate would take place in the next (now current) Parliament on a proper replacement for the Data Retention Regulations. The key provision is s. 1 which replicates the data retention provisions of reg. 4 of the Regulations with one essential difference. Whereas reg. 4 stated it was 'the duty of a public communications provider to retain the communications data specified', s. 1 states that 'the Secretary of State may by notice require a public telecommunications operator to retain relevant communications data if the Secretary of State considers that the requirement is necessary and proportionate for one or more of the purposes falling within paragraphs (a) to (h) of section 22(2) of the Regulation of Investigatory Powers Act 2000.' This is the government's attempt to ensure that DRIPA is proportionate where the Directive was not. Whereas the Directive was a blanket order to retain all data for the specified period, or as noted by the court in *Digital Rights Ireland*, covered 'in a generalised manner, all persons and all means of electronic communication as well as all traffic data without any differentiation',[112] s. 1 requires the issuance of a notice which must comply with s. 22 of RIPA. The government believed, and believes, this distinguishes DRIPA from the Directive and ensures DRIPA is proportionate where the Directive was not. In addition, the government put in further safeguards, a change in reporting procedures for the Interception of Communications Commissioner (change from annual to biannual reports)[113] and the requirement that there would be a review by the Independent Reviewer of Terrorism Legislation into the framework of UK surveillance and data retention laws.[114]

Despite the amendment to the retention procedure found in s. 1, many believed DRIPA would also be found to be incompatible with Arts. 7 and 8 of the EU Charter as the Directive had been. A legal challenge was brought by two of the MPs who spoke out against DRIPA, supported by Liberty. MPs David Davis and Tom Watson brought a judicial review of the decision of the Parliament of which they are members. Bean LJ and Collins J heard the case and with incredible symmetry they gave their judgment on 17 July 2015, exactly one year after the DRIPA came into force. The Divisional Court found that s. 1 of DRIPA was unlawful.[115]

Highlight DRIPA s. 1 unlawful

The Claimants are entitled to a declaration that section 1 of the Data Retention and Investigatory Powers Act 2014 is inconsistent with European Union law in so far as:

(a) it does not lay down clear and precise rules providing for access to and use of communications data retained pursuant to a retention notice to be strictly restricted to the purpose of preventing and detecting precisely defined serious offences or of conducting criminal prosecutions relating to such offences; and

→

[112] See (n. 100).
[113] DRIPA s. 6.
[114] Ibid. s. 7. The report is discussed above at 21.1.4.
[115] *Davis & Ors v Secretary of State for the Home Department* [2015] EWHC 2092 (Admin), [114].

(b) access to the data is not made dependent on a prior review by a court or an independent administrative body whose decision limits access to and use of the data to what is strictly necessary for the purpose of attaining the objective pursued.

Careful readers will note that sub-paragraph (b) suggests that arguably the simplified 'double-lock' system found in the draft Investigatory Powers Bill (discussed above at 21.1.5) is also not compliant with Arts. 7 and 8 of the EU Charter. This part of the judgment is drawn from paragraph 62 of *Digital Rights Ireland.*

Highlight *Digital Rights Ireland* at [62]

In particular, Directive 2006/24 does not lay down any objective criterion by which the number of persons authorised to access and subsequently use the data retained is limited to what is strictly necessary in the light of the objective pursued. Above all, *the access by the competent national authorities to the data retained is not made dependent on a prior review carried out by a court or by an independent administrative body whose decision seeks to limit access to the data and their use to what is strictly necessary for the purpose of attaining the objective pursued and which intervenes following a reasoned request of those authorities submitted within the framework of procedures of prevention, detection or criminal prosecutions.* Nor does it lay down a specific obligation on Member States designed to establish such limits. [Emphasis added]

The problem for the Government with this part of the judgment in *Digital Rights Ireland*, as applied in *Davis & Ors*, is that it suggests the authorization process behind the future scheme for retention notices found in cl. 71 of the draft Investigatory Powers Bill is illegal, for, as we shall see, retention notices do not even benefit from the simplified 'double-lock' procedure, with the authorization for such notices being purely within the power of the Secretary of State, as they currently are under s. 1 of DRIPA. As a result, the government appealed this decision and on 20 November 2015 the Court of Appeal gave its judgment in *Secretary of State for the Home Department v David Davis MP & Ors.*[116]

The Court of Appeal took a different interpretation of the *Digital Rights Ireland* decision. The court did not believe it was the intent of the CJEU to lay down a mandatory requirement automatically applicable to national legislation. In fact the court thought this was highly unlikely: 'we consider that it would be surprising if the CJEU were here seeking to lay down a mandatory minimum standard of universal application without referring to any of the relevant case law and without any consideration of the competing considerations.'[117] Finding it impossible to say with certainty what the intent of paragraph 62 was, the court took the only sensible decision it could. It referred two questions to the CJEU. They are:

[116] [2015] EWCA Civ 1185.

[117] Ibid. [87].

(1) Did the CJEU in Digital Rights Ireland intend to lay down mandatory requirements of EU law with which the national legislation of Member States must comply? And

(2) Did the CJEU in Digital Rights Ireland intend to expand the effect of Articles 7 and/or 8, EU Charter beyond the effect of Article 8 as established in the jurisprudence of the ECtHR?[118]

The second question loads the issue somewhat and gives a clear guidance from the Court of Appeal as to where they stand on this. We will not know the outcome until the CJEU gives its judgment but it is clear that the Court of Appeal believes that it cannot be, nor should it be, the role of the CJEU to set minimum standards for domestic legislation. It seems likely that the CJEU will clarify its intent in para. 62 to mean something less than it was understood to mean by the Divisional Court. The outcome of the reference to the CJEU, and a related reference from Sweden on similar domestic data retention provisions there,[119] is extremely important for the potential legality (or illegality) of the data retention provisions of the draft Investigatory Powers Bill.

21.2.3 **The draft Investigatory Powers Bill (Data Retention)**

The draft Investigatory Powers Bill is, as has already been acknowledged, wide in its scope. It is intended to bring together in one place the body of the UK's interception, data retention, and equipment interference laws. We have already looked in some depth at the interception provisions of the draft Bill and here we look at the data retention provisions. The draft Bill essentially restates the provisions of DRIPA with a few extensions and additions. This is why the outcome of the reference to the CJEU in *Secretary of State for the Home Department v David Davis MP & Ors* is so important. First, by cl. 71 'The Secretary of State may by notice require a telecommunications operator to retain relevant communications data if the Secretary of State considers that the requirement is necessary and proportionate for one or more of the purposes falling within paragraphs (a) to (j) of section 46(7).' The only difference in wording between s. 1 of DRIPA and cl. 71 is the removal of the word public before telecommunications (this is due to the draft Bill introducing the concept of the private telecommunications service in addition to public telecommunications services)[120] and the replacement of s. 22(2)(a)–(h) of RIPA with cl./s. 46(7)(a)–(j) of the draft Bill which essentially repeat all the key provisions of s. 22(2) of RIPA but vitally perhaps for the legality of cl. 71 remove the previous catch-all provision of s. 22(2)(h) 'for any purpose (not falling within paragraphs (a) to (g)) which is specified for the purposes of this subsection by an order made by the Secretary of State'. By removing the power of the Secretary of State to add to the categories this arguably makes the proposed provision less likely to be struck out by either the UK or European courts. In addition, the draft Bill adds a checklist for the Secretary of State

[118] Ibid. [118].

[119] *Tele2 Sverige AB v Post-och Telestyrelsen* (Case C-203/15). <http://curia.europa.eu/juris/liste.jsf?language=en&num=C-203/15>.

[120] This is defined in the notes: 'A private telecommunications system is one that is separate from, but connected to a public telecommunications system; this will include computer networks in the home or workplace.'

which should also provide transparency to her decision-making process and so head off the issue set out in para. 61 of *Digital Rights Ireland* that 'Directive 2006/24 does not contain substantive and procedural conditions relating to the access of the competent national authorities to the data and to their subsequent use.' The checklist is in cl. 72.

Highlight Matters to be taken into account before giving retention notices (cl. 72)

(1) Before giving a retention notice, the Secretary of State must, among other matters, take into account—

(a) the likely benefits of the notice,

(b) the likely number of users (if known) of any telecommunications,

(c) service to which the notice relates,

(d) the technical feasibility of complying with the notice,

(e) the likely cost of complying with the notice, and

(f) any other effect of the notice on the telecommunications operator (or description of operators) to whom it relates.

(2) Before giving such a notice, the Secretary of State must take reasonable steps to consult any operator to whom it relates.

In addition to this check, cl. 73 allows telecommunication operators to refer notices back to the Secretary of State for review. The government clearly hope these provisions and safeguards together will allow them to escape the effects of *Digital Rights Ireland*. Much, though, will depend upon the outcome of the reference in *Secretary of State for the Home Department v David Davis MP & Ors*.

There is one final sting in the tail of the draft Investigatory Powers Bill. By cl. 71(9)(f) the definition of relevant communications data is to be extended to cover 'the internet protocol address, or other identifier, of any apparatus to which a communication is transmitted for the purpose of obtaining access to, or running, a computer file or computer program. In this subsection "identifier" means an identifier used to facilitate the transmission of a communication.' This is so-called 'internet connection records'. The explanatory note to the draft Bill describes them as 'a record of the internet services that a specific device connects to—such as a website or instant messaging application—captured by the company providing access to the internet. They could be used, for example, to demonstrate a certain device had accessed an online communications service but they would not be able to be used to identify what the individual did on that service.' These have been a highly controversial proposed addition to the data retention powers of the state. In her oral statement to Parliament the Home Secretary played down the impact of these:[121]

[121] Home Secretary: Oral Statement to the House of Commons on the Publication of draft Investigatory Powers Bill HC Deb vol. 601, col. 970 (4 November 2015).

Highlight The Home Secretary on internet connection records

It cannot be right that today the police could find an abducted child if the suspects were using mobile phones to coordinate their crime, but if they were using social media or communications apps then they would be out of reach. Such an approach defies all logic and ignores the realities of today's digital age. So this Bill will also allow the police to identify which communications services a person or device has connected to—so called Internet Connection Records.

Mr Speaker, some have characterised this power as law enforcement having access to people's full web browsing histories. Let me be clear—this is simply wrong. An Internet Connection Record is a record of the communications service that a person has used, not a record of every web page they have accessed. So, if someone has visited a social media website, an Internet Connection Record will only show that they accessed that site, not the particular pages they looked at, who they communicated with, or what they said. *It is simply the modern equivalent of an itemised phone bill.* [Emphasis added]

Many see this is much more invasive than that.

Highlight Paul Bernal on internet connection records

This means, essentially, that a rolling record of a year of everyone's browsing history will be stored. Not, it seems, beyond the top level of website (so that you've visited 'www.bbc.co.uk' but not each individual page within that website, nor what you have 'done' on that website). The significance of this data is very much underplayed, suggesting it is just a way of checking that so-and-so accessed Facebook at a particular time, in a similar way to saying 'so-and-so called the following number' on the phone, and thus the supposed 'restoring of capabilities' referred to. That, however, both misunderstands the significance of the data and of the way that we use the technology.

Our 'online life' isn't just about what is traditionally called 'communications', and isn't the equivalent of what we used to do with our old, landline phones. For most people, it is almost impossible to find an aspect of their life that does not have an online element. We don't just talk to our friends online, or just do our professional work online, we do almost everything online. We bank online. We shop online. We research online. We find relationships online. We listen to music and watch TV and movies online. We plan our holidays online. Monitoring the websites we visit isn't like having an itemised telephone bill (an analogy that more than one person used yesterday) it's like following a person around as they visit the shops (both window shopping and the real thing), go the pub, go to the cinema, turn on their radio, go to the park, visit the travel agent, look at books in the library and so forth.[122]

[122] P Bernal, 'A Few Words on Internet Connection Records' (5 November 2015) <https://paulbernal.wordpress.com/2015/11/05/a-few-words-on-internet-connection-records/>.

Elsewhere I have written that these records 'would [contain] data such as which banking services we use, which rail company or airline we tend to favour and which may reveal much about us including gender, ethnicity, religious beliefs, medical conditions, and much more'.[123] A final footnote on internet connection records at the time of writing is that *The Independent* newspaper made a Freedom of Information Act request to the Home Office for the Home Secretary's work browsing history for the last week of October 2015. In refusing the request, the Home Office stated 'we have decided that your request is vexatious because it places an unreasonable burden on the department, because it has adopted a scattergun approach and seems solely designed for the purpose of "fishing" for information without any idea of what might be revealed.'[124] Rather ironically, these are almost exactly the concerns privacy advocates are raising about cl. 71(9)(f) (with unreasonable burden on telecoms providers substituted for unreasonable burden on the department).[125]

21.3 **Conclusions**

The power of the information society is that it sets us free. We no longer need to travel to the local shops to buy goods or obtain services. We can have a tailored, personalized service based upon our previous actions and decisions and we can communicate more freely and more easily than ever before. There is, though, a price to be paid for this freedom. As the previous chapter and this one have shown, the warning of Wendell Phillips that 'Eternal vigilance is the price of liberty' is probably of greater truth today than at any point in the last 200 years. The very digital technology which sets us free also allows for perfect control and observation. Everywhere we travel online our movements are tracked and recorded. These movements may be stored for extended periods, intercepted, and interrogated by highly sophisticated computer programmes. Data from one person's movements online may be combined with movements of another to create new datasets, our conversations may be remotely monitored, tagged, and then traced.

The problem is that digital technology may not in fact be making us freer. As made clear throughout this chapter and by the efforts of Edward Snowden, the technology affords the state the opportunity to perfectly monitor and control us much more tightly than even George Orwell imagined in his dystopian classic, *1984*.

[123] A Murray, 'Finding Proportionality in Surveillance Laws' (18 December 2015) <http://theitlawyer.blogspot.co.uk/2015/12/finding-proportionality-in-surveillance.html>.

[124] J Stone, 'Theresa May wants to see your internet history, so we thought it was only fair to ask for hers' *The Independent* (London, 24 December 2015) <http://www.independent.co.uk/news/uk/politics/theresa-may-wants-to-see-your-internet-history-so-we-thought-it-was-only-fair-to-ask-for-hers-a6785591.html>.

[125] See Bernal, (n. 122); Out-Law, 'New equipment needed to capture internet connection records, say communication providers' (London, 11 December 2015) <http://www.out-law.com/en/articles/2015/december/new-equipment-needed-to-capture-internet-connection-records-say-communication-providers/>; Evidence of Andrews & Arnold Ltd. to Joint Committee on the draft Investigatory Powers Bill (London, 1 December 2015) <http://data.parliament.uk/writtenevidence/committeeevidence.svc/evidencedocument/draft-investigatory-powers-bill-committee/draft-investigatory-powers-bill/written/25372.pdf>; Supplementary written evidence of Andrews & Arnold Ltd, to Joint Committee on the draft Investigatory Powers Bill (London, 17 December 2015) <http://data.parliament.uk/writtenevidence/committeeevidence.svc/evidencedocument/draft-investigatory-powers-bill-committee/draft-investigatory-powers-bill/written/26130.pdf>.

TEST QUESTIONS

Question 1

YourSpace is an online social media and messaging platform. It is expanding its operations across the EU and wants particularly to provide its services in the UK. The YourSpace board have been advised they may need to comply with s. 71 (including s. 71(9)(f)) of the Investigatory Powers Act 2016. YourSpace is concerned about the costs that such a retention requirement will entail for it and seeks your legal advice on the potential viability of a successful legal challenge against any retention issued on it under s. 71.

Advise YourSpace.

Question 2

'Privacy is a fundamental human right, meaning that it is granted on all individuals and can only be removed or reduced under a limited set of circumstances.' Can this balance between security and privacy still be identified in the modern digital surveillance state?

FURTHER READING

Books

P Bernal, *Internet Privacy Rights: Rights to Protect Autonomy* (2014)

G Greenwald, *No Place to Hide: Edward Snowden, the NSA and the Surveillance State* (2014)

K Laidler, *Surveillance Unlimited: How We've Become the Most Watched People on Earth* (2008)

H Nissenbaum, *Privacy in Context: Technology, Policy, and the Integrity of Social Life* (2009)

K O'Hara and N Shadbolt, *The Spy in the Coffee Machine: The End of Privacy as We Know It* (2008)

Chapters and articles

D Anderson, 'The Investigatory Powers Review: A Question of Trust' 4 *European Human Rights Law Review* 331 (2015)

I Brown, 'Government Access to Private-Sector Data in the United Kingdom' *International Data Privacy Law* 230 [2012]

N Richards, 'The Dangers of Surveillance' 126 *Harvard Law Review* 1934 (2013)

C Walker, 'Data Retention in the UK: Pragmatic and Proportionate, or a Step Too Far?', 25 (4) *Computer Law & Security Review* 325 (2009)

PART VII

Future challenges for information law

Society continues to change apace. New technologies offer new opportunities and new challenges. Is the law ready for them?

The future for IT law

To draw together the many themes discussed in this book is challenging. This book has attempted to contextualize the interface between law and technology as we move from the physical society to a digital society. This has involved discussion of digital and virtual property, even virtual societies and virtual identity. It has led us to examine the value of information, including free expression, data privacy, and data protection. It has also led us into the dark side of digital technology with examination of harmful content, digital crime, and even cyberterrorism; yet this chapter is the most difficult of all to write for almost as each chapter in this book was being written it was already on the way to being out of date.

This is because of the pace of change driven by technological advances in the information society. We have gone from computers that filled rooms to computers held in the palm of your hand within 40 years. Information stored on reams of punch cards can now fit on a single memory card the size of a fingernail, and processing power increases exponentially so that a computer that costs under £300 today has more processing power than the famous Cray 1 super-computer of the 1970s which cost at least \$5m. The speed of development in computer and information technology is driven by a rule known as Moore's Law, named in honour of Intel co-founder Gordon Moore who first set out his principle of computing processing power in his 1965 paper 'Cramming More Components onto Integrated Circuits'.[1] Moore's Law, which states: 'the number of transistors that can be placed inexpensively on an integrated circuit has increased exponentially, doubling approximately every two years' has remained true since its introduction and is often credited with advances in data storage, data processing, and speed of data access.

Although there is no doubting the veracity of Moore's Law, which is driven by intense competition in the micro-circuit sector, it doesn't fully explain why so many technologies, and services, are driven forward with the same speed in the information society, so that everything, from storage capacity on HDD and memory cards to internet access speeds, to the number of pixels in a digital camera, is being driven forward at the same pace. Why is this? It is my belief that it is because Moore's Law is not the driver of change and development but the means of measuring it. The driver of change in the information society was and remains the discovery of the bit.

Much as the discovery of subatomic particles revitalized physics throughout the twentieth century with the new discipline of quantum physics making the most incredible

[1] GE Moore, 'Cramming More Components onto Integrated Circuits' (1965) 38 *Electronics* No. 8, 114.

breakthroughs,[2] the discovery of the common building block for storing, transmitting, and processing information has driven the information society forward on all fronts. This common driver of change allows designers of hardware and software, telecommunications engineers, designers of consumer digital goods, and service providers such as telecommunications companies and data processing companies to build a 'virtuous circle' where each feeds off the developments and breakthroughs of the others to allow products and services to develop with lightening speed.[3] This means that information technology, and the information society, is moving forward more quickly than the law, and textbooks, can keep up with. The ambitious aim of this chapter is to gaze into the crystal ball: an exercise in futurology which may assist the reader in staying one step ahead of developments in technology and the challenges these will surely bring to lawyers and lawmakers.

22.1 **Future developments**

22.1.1 **Greater connectivity, greater control**

Exercises in futurology are often exercises in futility. That accepted, if we are to glance into the future of information technology law we need to identify what may prove to be the key characteristics of future technology design. Commentators seem to be split as to how future technologies will affect our society.

Some suggest that as technologies get more complicated and carry out many more functions we will seek refuge in tied devices that specialize in carrying out the tasks we ask of them.[4] For them the future is centred upon consumer devices such as smartphones, PVRs, tablets, and gaming devices. These devices are so-called 'closed boxes', meaning the software supplied with them is usually proprietary—the obvious exception being the Android operating system of which more below—and cannot be studied or copied except within the very strict limits allowed by ss. 50A–50C of the Copyright, Designs and Patents Act 1988. For these commentators the natural progression of devices is that each successive generation of consumer devices becomes more powerful and contains more functions but at a cost of freedom.

[2] It took only 36 years for physics to progress from Ernest Rutherford's discovery of the atomic nucleus in 1909 to J Robert Oppenheimer's successful testing of the first atomic bomb, 'Trinity' in Los Alamos, New Mexico.

[3] An example of a virtuous circle would be in the delivery of entertainment products. First, a software development, data compression, allowed for the development of compressed sound files (MP3s). This led to an ability to trade MP3s across the improved network speeds of 56.6Kbps. This led hardware manufacturers to design an MP3 player. In turn, one manufacturer (Apple) developed an 'online shop'. Increased demand for downloads from the shop led to faster network connection speeds being required (Broadband), and this allowed for video to be downloaded. Apple (and others) then designed higher-capacity multimedia players. This allowed TV and movies to be sold via the online shop. This called for more capacity in storage and a better interface. Consumers started to demand access wherever they went and wireless capability was added. Eventually the MP3 player converged with the mobile phone as the smartphone. And demand for streaming led initially by YouTube, then services like iPlayer and Netflix, have led to LTE (4G) and Fibre.

[4] See e.g. J Zittrain, *The Future of the Internet and How to Stop It* (Yale UP 2008); J Lanier, *Who Owns the Future?* (Simon & Schuster 2013).

Case study Home video recording

- The first generation of home video recording devices was the VCR which had no copy controls and allowed for transfer from TV to video and from video to video.
- The second generation was the VCR with macrovision. This prevented copying from pre-recorded videos with macrovision protection.
- The third generation was DVD-R. This allowed not only for macrovision but also for digital TPMs to be used to prevent copying.
- The fourth generation is PVRs (HDD recorders such as Sky +). These have a variety of controls; some designed for consumer benefits, others for the benefit of the manufacturer or TV broadcaster. Sky + has a comprehensive parental control system which prevents playback of programmes rated '15' or '18' before the watershed times. Also parents can set controls for all content or varieties of content. There is also an advanced copy control mechanism called CGMS-A (copy generation management system–A) which allows Sky to encode all broadcasts with a copy activation code of either '00' copying allowed; '10' one-time only copy; or '11' no copying allowed.
- The fifth generation is remote storage and streaming delivery (NetFlix and Amazon Prime). Here the end user never possesses a full copy of the content; instead a copy is streamed on demand. This means the available library of content changes daily as content is added and removed and the end user has no way to retain a copy of the content.

The effects of Sky's CGMS–A system were keenly felt by Sky + subscribers in late 2008 when a glitch with Sky's broadcast signal caused all material stored to the HDD to be encoded '11' for a period, meaning users could not archive programmes by copying them to DVD.[5] Although in this case it was a technical glitch that had caused the problem, it served to demonstrate how fourth-generation PVRs gave control over recordings not to the user in the way a VCR, or even a third-generation DVD did, but retained an element of control to the provider. This is magnified in the fifth generation where content remains always in the possession of the streaming service. This leads Jonathan Zittrain to title closed boxes which retain a connection to their supplier 'tethered appliances'. Tethered appliances are devices, such as Sky + but also include everyday devices such as the Mp3/Mp4 players, smartphones, games systems, tablets, satnavs, and e-book readers, which 'offer a more consistent and focused user experience at the expense of flexibility and innovation'.[6] Zittrain, and others, believe that the driving force for social change in the coming years will be technologically driven unless consumers mobilize against the technology industry.[7]

Strong indications that Zittrain's vision of technologically driven black boxes will come to dominate the user experience in the coming years can be seen in the greater

[5] G Cole, 'Sky + Glitch Sparks Fears over TV Archiving' *The Guardian* (London, 4 December 2008) <http://www.guardian.co.uk/technology/2008/dec/04/television-sky-programme-backups>.

[6] Zittrain (n. 4) 59.

[7] See L Lessig, *Code Version 2.0* (Basic Books 2006) 323–4; L Lessig, *Free Culture: How Big Media Uses Technology and the Law to Lock Down Culture and Control Creativity* (Penguin 2005) 139–61; J Cannataci, 'Lex Personalitatis and Technology-driven Law' (2008) 5(1) *SCRIPTed* 1 <http://www.law.ed.ac.uk/ahrc/script-ed/vol5-1/editorial.asp>.

deployment of closed environments driven by the use of applications or apps. The king of such content delivery is of course Apple which has developed a number of stable, consumer-friendly products which remain (relatively) virus free; provide a central and easily accessible series of content stores, for music, audiovisual content, and apps; but in which environment Apple controls everything that is on your system through a closed operating system and a closed sales environment.[8] As Zittrain predicted, the security this environment gives to the user allows them to forgive Apple many indiscretions. The App Store will not for example list apps which recreate the native functions of the store, which meant that for a period after the disastrous Apple Maps launch Google was blocked from providing a Google Maps app, and even now that such an app is available and is clearly superior to the Apple offering,[9] third-party apps on Apple devices which use mapping functions must integrate with Apple Maps since integration with Google Maps (or any other non-native mapping application) is not allowed.

This is a modern version of an old-fashioned concept: the walled garden. Walled gardens were common in information and communication technologies in the 1990s. Walled gardens are proprietary and controlled areas of technology access. In the 1990s famous walled gardens were operated by leading ISPs such as America On Line (AOL) and CompuServe. These were areas of dedicated content only for subscribers of their service and which were designed to keep subscribers within the controlled area rather than in the wider web environment. These were sensible for ISPs at a time when dial-up was 28.8 or 56.6 Kbps. With connection and download speeds slow, walled gardens were locally hosted, optimized content allowing for quicker content delivery. These were sold to subscribers as safer parts of the web where the ISP could act as a gatekeeper to keep out undesirable content. A good example of such a walled garden was AOL's 'Kid Channel' which established a walled garden to prevent children from accessing inappropriate websites.[10] Of course ISPs were not doing this purely for the convenience factor or out of a sense of social responsibility; they also controlled content within this closed environment, meaning that they could sell advertising and third-party content. Around the millennium ISP-driven walled gardens started to die out. People no longer wanted controlled internet access: they wanted to experience the whole of the web. Walled gardens did not disappear though—they moved from home internet access to mobile access provided though fledgling 2G mobile networks. Like ISPs, mobile phone operators found that 2G download speeds of about 25Kbps (dependent upon infrastructure) were not fast enough and in any event phone handsets could not handle complex data like images very well. A new generation of walled gardens sprung up like Vodafone Live which replicated the model of the ISPs. By the late 2000s they had all gone; the arrival of 3G and later smartphones negated the need for walled gardens again and consumers wanted wider access.

[8] Of course you can sideload music and AV content onto your device from a computer and you can jailbreak your device to install unauthorized apps. However, if you do jailbreak your device Apple iOS updates will attempt to lock out any jailbroken content and Apple warn that you make yourself susceptible to viruses and worms.

[9] As admitted by Apple CEO Tim Cook <http://www.apple.com/uk/letter-from-tim-cook-on-maps/>.

[10] Dick Thornburgh et al., *Youth, Pornography, and the Internet* (National Academies Press 2002) 276.

However, we find ourselves now in the midst of a third generation of walled gardens. As well as Apple's lock-in system of iOS/iTunes/App Store, we have the Amazon Kindle ecosystem, and Facebook's closed and managed social network platform. These walled gardens offer arguably a more controlled experience than either the ISP or mobile walled gardens, and here the commercial imperative is clearly the driver over technical limitations. Yet consumers flock to these platforms, suggesting Zittrain is right: we will sacrifice freedom of choice in return for a functional secure environment and user experience. Sensing the threat to the open standards we have become used to, Professor Sir Tim Berners-Lee wrote a spirited defence of open web standards in the December 2010 issue of *Scientific American*.[11] In this he pointed out all that is lost in terms of creativity and wider risks to society through the construction of walled gardens:

> Many companies spend money to develop extraordinary applications precisely because they are confident the applications will work for anyone, regardless of the computer hardware, operating system or Internet service provider (ISP) they are using—all made possible by the Web's open standards. The same confidence encourages scientists to spend thousands of hours devising incredible databases that can share information about proteins, say, in hopes of curing disease. The confidence encourages governments such as those of the US and the UK to put more and more data online so citizens can inspect them, making government increasingly transparent. Open standards also foster serendipitous creation: someone may use them in ways no one imagined. We discover that on the Web every day.
>
> In contrast, not using open standards creates closed worlds. Apple's iTunes system, for example, identifies songs and videos using URIs that are open. But instead of 'http:' the addresses begin with 'itunes:,' which is proprietary. You can access an 'itunes:' link only using Apple's proprietary iTunes program. You can't make a link to any information in the iTunes world—a song or information about a band. You can't send that link to someone else to see. You are no longer on the Web. The iTunes world is centralized and walled off. You are trapped in a single store, rather than being on the open marketplace. For all the store's wonderful features, its evolution is limited to what one company thinks up.[12]

He then describes the true cost of the convenience of a walled garden.

> Some people may think that closed worlds are just fine. The worlds are easy to use and may seem to give those people what they want. But as we saw in the 1990s with the America Online dial-up information system that gave you a restricted subset of the Web, these closed, 'walled gardens,' no matter how pleasing, can never compete in diversity, richness and innovation with the mad, throbbing Web market outside their gates. If a walled garden has too tight a hold on a market, however, it can delay that outside growth.[13]

We find ourselves therefore at something of a crossroads. Walled gardens have always been part of the environment of web content but there is something different, arguably, about the current generation as opposed to the earlier generations. Whereas both first- and second-generation walled gardens were operated by service providers, and other service providers were available, third-generation walled gardens are operated by hardware suppliers (Facebook excepted). Once you have invested in your Kindle Fire or iPad you are locked in to the ecosystem supplied by Amazon or Apple. Indeed, in many ways

[11] T Berners-Lee, 'Long Live the Web' (2010) 303.6 *Scientific American* 80.
[12] Ibid. 83.
[13] Ibid.

it is incredible that these ecosystems are permitted, given the decision in the Microsoft Windows Media bundling case.[14]

If this view is correct, then the future direction of IT law will be moved further towards protecting individual rights as tethered technology intervenes more into our private actions. This view of the future of the information society thus envisages greater concentration of control in the hands of the hardware, software, and telecommunications companies, with law as the tool of the consumer. In this design, rather disappointingly, law is reactive and passive.

22.1.2 **Greater connectivity, greater freedom**

Of course one part of the walled garden discourse has been conspicuous by its absence. While we have discussed Apple and Amazon we have failed to acknowledge that the market-leading operating system for smartphones and tablets is Android.[15] Android is of course owned by Google and, in accordance with much of their free data policy, it is an open-source platform. This allows it to be freely modified and distributed by device manufacturers (such as Samsung), wireless carriers (like Verizon), and enthusiast developers. It is the antithesis of the iOS system. Yes, there are still some restrictions on what can be listed in the Google Play store but these are not as restrictive as seen on iTunes/App Store and, as the software is open source, individuals can distribute apps without going via the Google Play store.[16] The success of the open-source Android platform suggests that perhaps the techno-deterministic view demonstrated by Zittrain, Lessig, and others is wrong.[17]

This opens up a different model of the future. This sees the empowering nature of technological developments as the main driver of social change.[18] For this school of thought, although it may be true that Apple rules the iOS environment, the opportunities offered by smartphones and similar technological developments set users free, rather than controlling their actions. Yes, it is true that if you buy an iPhone you accept the rule of Apple, but this is a conscious trade-off by the consumer. They choose to buy an iPhone. If they do not like Apple's fine-grained control over the after-market for their product, they may choose to migrate to an alternative open ecosystem, as provided for by any number of Android devices, such as the Samsung Galaxy.

The point is that the end user has a choice. She may choose to buy the tied Apple device with all the controls this brings or she may choose an Android device which brings her more freedom. This is therefore a market decision: the buyer trades the

[14] Commission Decision of 24 May 2004 relating to a proceeding pursuant to Art. 82 of the EC Treaty and Art. 54 of the EEA Agreement against Microsoft Corporation (Case COMP/C-3/37.792—Microsoft).

[15] Data from Q2 2015 gives Android 82.8 per cent of the smartphone market as opposed to iOS's 13.9 per cent, while data from 2014 figures shows that in that year 67.3 per cent of new tablets were shipped with Android installed against 27.6 per cent with iOS.

[16] There are in fact a large number of alternative Android apps stores including SlideMe, GetJar, and Amazon Appstore.

[17] V Mayer-Schönberger, 'Demystifying Lessig' (2008) *Wisconsin Law Review* Issue 4, 714.

[18] See e.g. R Heilbroner, 'Do Machines Make History?' in M Smith and L Marx (eds.), *Does Technology Drive History?: The Dilemma of Technological Determinism* (MIT Press 1994); G Ropohl, 'A Critique of Technological Determinism' in P Durbin and F Rapp (eds.), *Philosophy and Technology* (Reidel 1983); L Winner, 'Do Artefacts Have Politics?, in L Winner, *The Whale and the Reactor: a Search for Limits in an Age of High Technology* (University of Chicago Press 1986).

competing values of the iOS and Android handsets, or tablets. The key for commentators who believe that technological advances offer greater freedom is that, without the advances in technology afforded by devices such as the original iPhone, the consumer does not have this choice. Advances in technology offer greater choice to the consumer: this allows the consumer to decide how much control they are willing to cede to device manufacturers in return for greater functionality.

This approach assumes that society drives technological advances rather than technological advances driving changes in society. Some new technologies make massive breakthroughs despite their design and marketing being undertaken by niche suppliers. Think of the breakthrough success of the Blackberry handset manufactured by unfashionable Canadian company Research in Motion or the dual-cyclone vacuum cleaner manufactured in the first instance by start-up company Dyson. These products broke through because people wanted what they offered: for one, email on the move, and for the other, the end to constantly buying new vacuum bags and losing power while vacuuming. Now, think of technology designed at massive cost by leading corporations which have failed because there was no market for them. Sony has probably the most unenviable history of failed platforms with Betamax, Minidisc, Laserdisc, and Universal Media Disk (UMD) all failing to find success in the market. Sony must be relieved that Blu-ray eventually won the format war with HD-DVD (although it could be said it is ultimately losing out to streaming services such as NetFlix). Why, though, so many failures from such a successful company? At each turn, their technology was the best or most convenient but Sony's desire to retain proprietary control of the format led to competitors producing cheaper and more convenient alternatives. The reason Blu-ray broke the mould is that Sony, learning from their previous mistakes, agreed to share Blu-ray technology with competitors. Sony is not the only leading company who has invested heavily in technology which has failed to find a market. Failures such as Motorola's Iridium satellite communications system and Apple's Newton hand-held PDA demonstrate that the largest and most successful of electronics companies can misjudge the market.

If it is the case that society determines whether or not a new technology succeeds in the marketplace, then this changes our assumptions for modelling legal responses to technological developments. This suggests new technologies will not, as of themselves, restrict or control the rights and choices of individuals. The law does not need therefore to react to threats posed by new technologies; instead the law must ensure that consumers have the market information they need in order to assess whether or not to invest in a new product or service. This means that the role of the law switches from being reactive to proactive. The role of the law is to ensure the market functions by allowing customers to exchange information and to allow them access to new products and services whosoever markets them.[19]

22.1.3 Developing technologies and legal responses

Whichever approach is correct, it is predicted that we will see major upheaval in the information society as developments drive us towards the next evolution of the World Wide Web, the arrival of the Internet of Things and intelligent processing (IoT/IP). These will impact hugely on all corners of society, with changes being driven by the

[19] A Murray, *The Regulation of Cyberspace: Control in the Online Environment* (Routledge 2007) ch. 6.

promise of what the new technology can offer and by the desire of users to make use of that potential. The web is in many ways the ultimate 'killer application': everyone wants access to it and in a variety of formats (home computer, smartphone, tablet, games system, etc.); it is free (excepting access charges) and is of limitless potential.

IoT/IP will change our interaction with information in all forms, and in particular will change how we locate and access data. If you are of the techno-deterministic school you will believe that the law will be called upon to respond to changes in the way data is gathered, stored, and accessed, with the major challenges being data privacy, data security, and freedom of expression. If you are a follower of the socially mediated school, then you will believe the major challenges will be in ensuring quality of access to data, data security, and data privacy.

Whichever approach you favour, the outcome is the same, IoT/IP unsettles the established legal settlement in the same way that web 2.0 unsettled copyright law, defamation, and freedom of expression. The law must evolve to reflect how *both* society and technology evolve, for the truth is that neither the techno-deterministic school nor the socially mediated school is completely correct. The information society is rooted in connections between people enabled by, and mediated by, digital technology. The area of law which deals with this is similarly rooted in both technology and society. To predict the future of information technology law we must therefore begin by predicting how technology will enable social changes in the next five to ten years.

22.2 The Internet of Things and intelligent processing

The first issue that lawyers will have to deal with is the technology of IoT/IP. This is because it is a rather more radical departure than the change from web 1.0 to web 2.0. While the development of web 2.0 was evolutionary—a democratizing process that gave more power to the user—IoT/IP has the potential to be revolutionary. A new intelligent network is emerging; a network of devices and processing power. The devices form the internet of things and include such things as personal health-monitoring wearables such as fitbit and the Apple Watch, smart home devices such as the Nest thermostat and LIFX-connected light bulbs, devices fitted to cars such as the Telematics insurance 'black box', and near field communication-enabled smartphones. The processing power comes from what the creator of web 1.0, Sir Tim Berners-Lee calls the semantic web. It is 'a Web [in which computers] become capable of analyzing all the data on the Web—the content, links, and transactions between people and computers. [Although] yet to emerge, when it does, the day-to-day mechanisms of trade, bureaucracy and our daily lives will be handled by machines talking to machines. The "intelligent agents" people have touted for ages will finally materialize.'[20]

Berners-Lee wrote this in 2000. Today the semantic web is very nearly upon us. Intelligent agents are such as Apple's Siri assistant. Siri, at a basic level, manages the day-to-day data of the user. It can schedule reminders, give you the weather forecast, send emails (via the native email software), recommend restaurants or hotels, and show locations via maps. Siri in essence is ver.1.0 of what will eventually become the semantic

[20] T Berners-Lee and M Fischetti, *Weaving the Web: The Original Design and Ultimate Destiny of the World Wide Web by its Inventor* (Harper Business 2000).

web. More sophisticated software is already in development and has been trialled as part of the Google Glass system. Google are continuing to develop this technology, both through new releases to their Google Now app[21] as well as the developments in the second edition of the Google Glass product currently ongoing. Let's imagine a near-future scenario with an advanced version of the Google Now system.

Example Semantic Google Now 2.0

Sarah is going out for the night. She wants to go to see a movie and then for some dinner afterwards at a restaurant near to the movie theatre. She takes out her Android device and says to her Google Now app 'I want to see a funny movie and then eat at a good restaurant. What are my options?' Unlike web 2.0 search engines, an intelligent or semantic assistant can understand a complex request such as this and produce complex results.

Sarah will get a limited number of personalized recommendations with a selection of movies showing in her local cinema and suitable restaurants nearby. These will be displayed as single pages of data via her device, showing the name of the movie recommended, where it is showing, when it is showing, the opportunity to link to reviews, the trailer, and the option to view the map of the cinema location. Alongside this information will be an option to open similar information for the restaurant: reviews, menus, location, opening times etc. Sarah's intelligent search assistant can even remember preferences such as 'I don't like Mexican food' and filter out inappropriate restaurants.

Then, with a command, Sarah can both book tickets for the movie and reserve a table at the restaurant; another command will allow her to invite her friend Jacob, sending him all the data including a map of where to meet and when. The system can then send an e-ticket to her smartphone so Sarah does not have to queue on her arrival and can even inform the restaurant if Sarah is likely to be late if she is caught in traffic (though the mapping function should ensure she misses any traffic problems).

We are very close to this world today. Essentially what I have described is a convergent device with the next-generation Siri/Google Now assistant and the already existing communication capabilities. In time your intelligent search assistant will have sufficient artificial intelligence to allow it to learn your preferences and then deliver to you what you want or need. It will be able to prepare a personalized newspaper, Negroponte's *Daily Me* become real,[22] drawn from stories reported worldwide and

[21] In May 2015 Google revealed an extension of Now that allows it to watch, and offer assistance in response to, your activity in any app on a device powered by its Android operating system. The feature, called Now on Tap, is activated when a user holds down the device's home button. For example, if someone suggested a particular movie during a text conversation, Now would offer up an information card summarizing reviews of that movie and presenting links to read more or view the trailer. In a conversation in which someone asked you to pick up the dry cleaning, Now would offer to remind you about this later.

[22] An idea first advanced by Nicholas Negroponte in *Being Digital* (Hodder & Stoughton 1995) 152–4, and developed extensively by C Sunstein, *Republic.com* (Princeton UP 2001).

collated on a personalized news service. Your assistant will be able to learn from your reading habits if you are interested in banking regulation, tennis, or celebrity gossip and deliver to you news specifically of interest to you. In addition, all your devices and accounts will work in harmony so if you book flights and a hotel to attend a conference in Rome, your calendar will automatically block this time out, your email account will set up an out-of-office reply, your bank account will be informed of your travel plans, thus avoiding the embarrassment of your card being refused overseas, and your calls will be automatically forwarded to your mobile (assuming these are all things you want).

It is clear from these examples that there are three defining features of IoT/IP. Two are user-experience features while the third is a technical feature.

Highlight Semantic web features

1. User immersion in the digital environment via augmented reality and the 'Internet of Things'. The human-machine interface changes from being via a screen to natural interaction.
2. Personalized services via your intelligent assistant. The idea of old-fashioned 'static' web pages is replaced with dynamic information services tailored to the user.
3. Artificial intelligence allows your devices and accounts to learn your preferences and to 'mix and mash' available data to provide tailored results.

From the lawyer's point of view the key attribute of IoT/IP is the last of these three features. Its creation involves intelligent agents which will make decisions on our behalf.[23] This changes the nature of the interaction between human and machine: we need to ask, is the machine now an actor in any transaction or does it remain simply a carrier of information?[24] This is likely to be the key issue for information technology lawyers in the next ten years.

22.3 **Law 2.0**

It is my belief that the role of the cyber lawyer and the design of the network he is seeking to control are symbiotically linked. We can trace developments in cyberlaw theory as being in parallel with technological developments. The internet has a long history which may be traced back as far as 1969 but the discipline of cyberlaw remained undeveloped until the 1990s. This is because there was no need for the separate discipline of cyberlaw before the release of web 1.0 as the internet was mainly used by a select group of researchers and was self-regulated. Research into information technology law in the 1970s and 1980s was focused on the computer itself, with books on databanks and data

[23] In truth this is not new. Intelligent agents already filter content. Cleanfeed, discussed in chs. 4 and 14, filters for obscene content, while Google Safesearch routinely filters Google search returns to remove obscene and offensive content. The difference with the semantic web is both the scale of such systems and their ability to learn; a key cornerstone of intelligence.

[24] See B Latour, *Reassembling the Social: An Introduction to Actor-Network-Theory* (OUP 2005); G Teubner, 'Rights of Non-humans? Electronic Agents and Animals as New Actors in Politics and Law' (2006) 33 *Journal of Law and Society* 497.

processing being the expected output of the researcher into law and computers, as the subject was then known.[25]

The release of web 1.0 was heralded as the beginning of serious research in, and the practice of, cyberlaw. As discussed in chapter 4, the first stage of this process was the development of the cyberlibertarian movement which responded to the apparent freedom of cyberspace with claims of an unregulable space, freed from the constraints of real-world regulation by its lack of internal borders and its virtual border with 'real space'. This corresponds to the early network environment which was seen as lawless, a digital equivalent of the old 'wild west' where individuals made claims for valuable land (cybersquatting) and regulation came from within the community only (Town Hall Democracy).[26]

The cyberpaternalist movement quickly appeared in opposition to this idealized view of self-regulation and local democracy.[27] The rise of cyberpaternalism may be mapped onto the rise of regulatory intervention in cyberspace. New initiatives such as the UNCITRAL Model Law on Electronic Commerce,[28] the intervention of the courts in early cybersquatting cases, and early attempts at legislative intervention, such as the Communications Decency Act of 1996,[29] had demonstrated that legal initiatives could affect actions in 'sovereign cyberspace'. Thus, as with cyberlibertarianism, cyberpaternalism's roots may be found in the environment it is seeking to study. Even cyberpaternalism's technocentric approach to law and the information society may be traced to the current preponderant use of technological solutions. Thus the Digital Millennium Copyright Act focuses legal protection on technical protection measures, while the Telecommunications Act of 1996 required for the installation of the so-called V-chip (a chip used to control minor access to violent or explicit content) in all TV sets sold in the US. Cyberpaternalism and cyberlibertarianism may, therefore, be seen as reflecting two stages of regulatory development seen in web 1.0. They cannot, unfortunately, claim to be at the forefront of developments as a study of the timelines shows that they formed as explanations of pre-existing structures of control within the larger environment of cyberspace.

The arrival of web 2.0 obviously changed this settlement and, as a result, one would expect a change in the views of commentators on cyberlaw and regulation. As has been extensively discussed throughout this book, web 2.0 was an evolutionary development which saw interactivity brought to the fore of the user experience with democratization of the internet being seen as the key social contribution of web 2.0. Consequently, we should have seen the development of a new parallel theory of cyberlaw: law 2.0, if you will. This was not the case. Instead we saw a further incremental development of

[25] See e.g. A Westin and M Baker, *Databanks in a Free Society: Computers, Record Keeping and Privacy* (Times Books 1972).

[26] See HH Perritt Jr, 'Cyberspace Self-Government: Town-Hall Democracy or Rediscovered Royalism?' (1997) 12 *Berkeley Technology Law Journal* 413; JP Barlow, *A Declaration of Independence for Cyberspace* 8 February 1996 <https://www.eff.org/cyberspace-independence>; D Johnson and D Post, 'Law and Borders—The Rise of Law in Cyberspace' (1996) 48 *Stanford Law Review* 1367.

[27] J Reidenberg, 'Lex Informatica: The Formation of Information Policy Rules Through Technology' (1998) 76 *Texas Law Review* 553; L Lessig, *Code and Other Laws of Cyberspace* (Basic Books 1999).

[28] Discussed in ch. 18.

[29] Discussed in ch. 14.

cyberlaw theory: law 1.5, rather than law 2.0. Law 1.5 manifested itself in the development of network communitarianism. Here commentators focused on the power of the network to connect individuals and their ability as a community to influence and to accept or reject regulatory interventions.[30] Again, the school of thought follows the environmental developments. Now, instead of the direct delivery of content seen in web 1.0 and reflected by Lawrence Lessig's model of external modalities pressing down on a pathetic dot, network communitarianism reflects the divergent network of user-generated content and social networking found in web 2.0 by focusing on concepts such as my active dot matrix.

It is clear there that since the development of the web in late 1990 at each stage of development in the environment of cyberspace there has been a corresponding development in cyberlaw theory. With this in mind, we can finally predict what is likely to be the next development in cyberlaw theory. With the development of the IoT/IP or semantic network, the focus switches from users to intelligent network agents. The semantic network in some ways sees a retreat to the values of web 1.0 with users seeking assistance from the network designers to make sense of the massive amounts of information now available online. But to retain the values of web 2.0 we seek not to return to delivered content but to extend the feeling of personalization and control that web 2.0 brings. For lawyers and lawmakers, though, the key aspect of the semantic network is the intelligent agents designed to manage the information flow. A malevolent programmer could use these to censor content, to gather personal information, to observe patterns of behaviour, or even, due to the interaction between the virtual and the physical environments, to track the physical whereabouts of individuals.

The legal issues raised by the semantic network are therefore substantially the same as those seen in both web 1.0 and web 2.0: privacy, freedom of expression, censorship, democratic discourse, property rights, and commercial interests. The difference is where the locus of power is to be found. Whereas web 1.0 was about passive consumerism and web 2.0 was about user democracy, the semantic network is about personalization and user selectivity, *but* that personalization will be done by the user in concert with their device settings: in other words our semantic search assistant has the power to tailor our informational experience.

The next school of cyberlaw is, therefore, likely to focus on the role that machines will play as intelligent agents in the network. Law 2.0 will, like the semantic network, be an evolutionary development on what we conceive of as cyberlaw today. The early building blocks of law 2.0 may already be seen in the work of Günther Teubner[31] and Mirelle Hildebrandt.[32] It is likely to ask questions, such as how may electronic agents control individuals? Who is responsible for the actions of electronic agents? Is it ethical to use electronic agents to control certain forms of expression? How may users protect their rights to personal and data privacy when they rely heavily on electronic agents?

[30] See discussion in ch. 4 and A Murray, *The Regulation of Cyberspace: Control in the Online Environment* ch. 8.

[31] See (n. 24).

[32] M Hildebrandt and B Koops. 'The Challenges of Ambient Law and Legal Protection in the Profiling Era' (2010) 73 *Modern Law Review* 428; M Hildebrandt and A Rouvroy (eds.), *The Philosophy of Law Meets the Philosophy of Technology: Autonomic Computing and Transformations of Human Agency* (Routledge 2011); M Hildebrandt, *Smart Technologies and the End of Law: Novel Entanglements of Law and Technology* (Edward Elgar 2015).

And how do we prevent abuse (including criminal abuse) of the network of electronic agents that form the backbone of the semantic web?

A central question for both philosophers and lawyers will be: does an over-reliance on technology potentially lead to injustice? Too often today individuals suffer unjustly because of poorly programmed computer systems which can make all forms of unjust decisions, from denying them access to housing or to financial benefits through to denying them access to an overseas state.[33] It is this social injustice that forms the basis of the *Little Britain* comedy sketch 'computer says no' and it brings with it the spectre of a Kafkaesque situation where someone is denied access to a just decision for reasons beyond their comprehension and which they cannot challenge because, perversely, the computer is entrusted as the arbiter in such decisions. This is likely to be a major focus of law 2.0. When intelligent agents begin making decisions based upon learned behaviour they exceed just the programmed parameters: they are likely to make errors and these errors are likely to cause harm. Thus, law 2.0 is going to be the most philosophical enquiry into law. It is going to require us to discuss identity, decision-making, fairness, and justice against a backdrop of computer-aided decision-making.

There is no reason to suspect the semantic web will be anything less than a positive revolution in the way we interact with technology. We all already benefit from some of the early fruits of the network of things through such tools as contactless payment systems, health tracking technology (and apps), GPS mapping and car tracking, and remote disabling systems used to prevent theft of high-value vehicles, smart thermostats, and smart home security cameras. Unfortunately, no one turns to lawyers when everything is going well. Lawyers tend to become involved when systems fail, when individuals suffer injustice, or when harm has occurred. Much of law 2.0 will be about anticipating these potential harms and about identifying and delineating lines of responsibility, in particular with regard to non-human actors—which, aside from animals in tort cases, are a whole new category of actors on the legal stage. My advice for anyone hoping to practise law 2.0 is therefore to read Franz Kafka's *The Trial* and Arthur C Clarke's *2001: A Space Odyssey*. Neither, I hope, are a vision of our future, but both raise questions of control, morality, and justice which will be at the centre of both the semantic network and law 2.0.

TEST QUESTIONS

Question 1

Are walled garden technologies such as the iOS ecosystem likely to affect individual liberty and freedom of choice adversely? If so, is this a legal issue or simply a consumer issue?

Question 2

Does the development of the semantic network relocate decision-making in vital areas such as privacy and freedom of expression away from the individual to data suppliers like Google? If so, what legal challenges does this raise and what should lawyers do about them?

[33] See J Bing, 'Code, Access and Control' in M Klang and A Murray (eds.), *Human Rights in the Digital Age* (Routledge-Cavendish 2005).

FURTHER READING

Books

M Hildebrandt and A Rouvroy (eds.), *The Philosophy of Law Meets the Philosophy of Technology: Autonomic Computing and Transformations of Human Agency* (2011)

M Hildebrandt, *Smart Technologies and the End of Law: Novel Entanglements of Law and Technology* (2015).

J Lanier, *You Are Not a Gadget: A Manifesto* (2011)

E Morozov, *The Net Delusion: How Not to Liberate The World* (2012)

E Pariser, *The Filter Bubble: What The Internet Is Hiding from You* (2012)

J Zittrain, *The Future of the Internet: And How to Stop it* (2008)

Chapters and articles

J Bing, 'Code, Access and Control', in M Klang and A Murray (eds.), *Human Rights in the Digital Age* (2005)

M Hildebrandt and B Koops, 'The Challenges of Ambient Law and Legal Protection in the Profiling Era', 73 *Modern Law Review* 428 (2010)

G Teubner, 'Rights of Non-humans? Electronic Agents and Animals as New Actors in Politics and Law', 33 *Journal of Law and Society* 497 (2006)

INDEX

A

B

C

D

E

H

I

K

L

Q

R

S

T

U